# THE WORLD IS A TEXT

# THE WORLD IS A TEXT

## Writing, Reading, and Thinking about Culture and Its Contexts

**Jonathan Silverman**
*Virginia Commonwealth University*
**Dean Rader**
*University of San Francisco*

Upper Saddle River, NJ 07458

**Library of Congress Cataloging-in-Publication Data**

Silverman, Jonathan.
The world is a text : writing, reading, and thinking about culture and its contexts / Jonathan Silverman, Dean Rader.
p. cm.
Includes index.
ISBN 0-13-094984-1
1. English language—Rhetoric. 2. Culture—Problems, exercises, etc. 3. Readers—Culture. 4. Critical thinking. 5. College readers. 6. Report writing. 7. Semiotics. I. Rader, Dean. II. Title.
PE1408 .S48785 2003
808'.0427—dc21

2002015200

VP, Editor-in-Chief: Leah Jewell
Sr. Acquisition Editor: Corey Good
Sr. Marketing Manager: Brandy Dawson
Editorial Assistant: John Ragozzine
Exec. Managing Editor: Ann Marie McCarthy
Production Liaison: Fran Russello
Project Manager: Karen Berry/Pine Tree Composition
Prepress and Manufacturing Buyer: Mary Ann Gloriande
Cover Designer: Robert Farar–Wagner
Cover Art: Rigo 1995, Indian Water, acrylic on wood and cement 80′ x 7′. Courtesy of artist and Gallery Paule Anglim, San Francisco, CA; Rigo 1995, Innercity Home. Courtesy of artist and Gallery Paule Anglim, San Francisco, CA; Rigo 1998, Sky/Ground (detail), acrylic on cement, 60′ x 120′. Courtesy of artist and Gallery Paule Anglim, San Francisco, CA; Rigo 1995, One Tree, acrylic on metal and living tree, 40′ x 100′. Courtesy of artist and Gallery Paule Anglim, San Francisco, CA.
Permission Specialist: Lisa Black/Kathleen Karcher
Director, Image Resource Center: Melinda Reo
Manager, Rights and Permissions: Zina Arabia
Interior Image Specialist: Beth Boyd-Brenzel
Cover Image Specialist: Karen Sanatar
Image Permission Coordinator: Fran Toepfer
Photo Researcher: Beaura K. Ringrose

This book was set in 10/12 Palatino by Pine Tree Composition, Inc., and was printed and bound by Courier Companies, Inc. The cover was printed by Coral Graphics.

Upper Saddle River, New Jersey 07458



Printed in the United States of America
10 9 8 7 6 5 4 3

ISBN: 0-13-094984-1

Pearson Education Ltd.
Pearson Education Australia PTY, Ltd.
Pearson Education Singapore, Pte. Ltd.
Pearson Education North Asia Ltd.
Pearson Education Canada, Ltd.
Pearson Educación de Mexico, S.A. de C.V.
Pearson Education—Japan
Pearson Education Malaysia, Pte. Ltd.
Pearson Education, Upper Saddle River, New Jersey

# Contents

*Alternative Table of Contents* *xv*

*Preface* *xxv*

*Acknowledgments* *xxix*

**INTRODUCTION** **1**

Semiotics: The Study of Signs (and Texts) 3
Systems of Reading: Making Sense of Cultural Texts 4
The "Semiotic Situation" (or the "Moving Text") 6
Texts, the World, You, and Your Papers 7
Learning to Read the World as a Text: Three Case Studies 10
*Reading Public Space: Starbucks* 10
*Reading a Poem: "The Red Wheelbarrow"* 11
*Reading an Advertisement* 13
Reading This Text as a Text 16
*The World Is a Text: Writing* 16
*The World Is a Text: Reading* 17
So, the World Is a Text: What Can You Do with It? 19

**The World Is a Text: Writing** **21**

How Do I Write a Text for College? Making the Transition from High School Writing, by Patty Strong 21
How Do I Make an Argument about a Building? Strategies for Constructing a Thesis and Building a Good Paper 23
*Constructing a Good Thesis* 23
*Building a Good Paper* 25
*Some Final Tips* 26

How Do I Write about Movies? A Tour Through the Writing Process 27
*Understanding the Assignment* 27
*Freewriting and Brainstorming* 28
*Deciding on a Thesis* 29
*Outlining* 29
*Writing the First Draft* 30
*Editing and Revising, Editing and Revising, Editing and Revising* 30
*Turning in the Finished Product* 31
How Am I a Text? On Writing Personal Essays 31
How Do I Know What a Good Paper Looks Like? An Annotated Student Essay 33
How Do I Get Info on Songs? Researching Popular Culture Texts 40
*Nuts and Bolts Research* 42
*Guerilla Research* 43

**The World Is a Text: Reading** **45**

**1. Reading Literature** **45**

*Worksheet* 50

JEAN TOOMER, "Blood-Burning Moon" 52
JAMES TATE, "Goodtime Jesus" 59
PABLO NERUDA, "Ode to My Socks" 60
CAROLYN FORCHÉ, "The Colonel" 62
NATHANIEL HAWTHORNE, "Young Goodman Brown" 64
WILLIAM SHAKESPEARE, "My Mistress' Eyes are Nothing Like the Sun (Sonnet 130)" 74
EMILY DICKINSON, "My Life had stood – a Loaded Gun" 75
WISLAWA SZYMBORSKA, "Slapstick" 77
KATE CHOPIN, "The Story of an Hour" 79

**The Literature Suite—Social and Economic Class 82**

LANGSTON HUGHES, "Harlem" 82
SUSAN STEINBERG, "Isla" 83
CHRIS HAVEN, "Assisted Living" 89
ADRIAN LOUIS, "Dust World" 99
THEODORE ROETHKE, "My Papa's Waltz" 101

*Reading Outside the Lines: Classroom Activities* 103
*Reading Outside the Lines: Essay Ideas* 104

2. **Reading Television** **105**

*Worksheet* *111*

SALLIE TISDALE, "Citizens of the World, Turn on Your Televisions!" 112
ARIEL GORE, "TV Can Be a Good Parent" 115
HARRY F. WATERS, "Life According to TV" 119
MICHELLE COTTLE, "How Soaps Are Integrating America: Color TV" 126
KATHERINE GANTZ, "'Not That There's Anything Wrong with That': Reading the Queer in *Seinfeld*" 130
**Student Essay:** ARCHANA MEHTA, "Society's Need for a *Queer* Solution: The Media's Reinforcement of Homophobia through Traditional Gender Roles" 152

***The Simpsons* Suite** **169**

LES SILLARS, "The Last Christian TV Family in America" 169
JAIME J. WEINMAN, "Worst Episode Ever" 171
ANNE WALDRON NEUMANN, "The Simpsons" 175
PETER PARISI, "'Black Bart' Simpson: Appropriation and Revitalization in Commodity Culture" 182

*Reading Outside the Lines: Classroom Activities* *199*
*Reading Outside the Lines: Essay Ideas* *200*

**Student Essay:** HILLARY WEST, "Media Journal: *The Rosie O'Donnell Show*" 202

3. **Reading Public Space** **206**

*Worksheet* *210*

DAPHNE SPAIN, "Spatial Segregation and Gender Stratification in the Workplace" 211
KENNETH MEEKS, "Shopping in a Mall While Black: A Coach's Story" 218
ROBERT BEDNAR, "Caught Looking: Problems with Taking Pictures of People Taking Pictures at an Exhibition" 224
KATHERINE F. BENZEL, "Room for Learning with Latest Technology" 229

**Public Space—The Suburban Suite** **233**

WILLIAM L. HAMILTON, "How Suburban Design Is Failing Teen-Agers" 233
WILLIAM BOOTH, "A White Migration North from Miami" 237

SARAH BOXER, "A Remedy for the Rootlessness of Modern Suburban Life?" 243
WHITNEY GOULD, "New Urbanism Needs to Keep Racial Issues in Mind" 247

*Reading Outside the Lines: Classroom Activities* *249*
*Reading Outside the Lines: Essay Ideas* *250*

**4. Reading Race and Ethnicity** **252**

*Worksheet* *258*

TAMAR LEWIN, "Growing Up, Growing Apart" 259
KWAME J. MCKENZIE and N.S. CROWCROFT, "Describing Race, Ethnicity, and Culture in Medical Research: Describing the Groups Studied Is Better Than Trying to Find a Catchall Name" 274
MICHAEL OMI, "In Living Color: Race and American Culture" 277
HANDSOME LAKE, "How America Was Discovered" 289
AMY TAN, "Mother Tongue" 291
JIM MAHFOOD, "True Tales of Amerikkkan History Part II: The True Thanksgiving" 296
BEVERLY DANIEL TATUM, "Why Are All the Black Kids Sitting Together in the Cafeteria?" 298
MALCOLM GLADWELL, "The Sports Taboo" 301

**Race and Ethnicity—The Multiracial Suite 311**

JEFFRY SCOTT, "Race, Labels and Identity; Millions Live in an America Bent on—and at Odds about—Categorizing Them" 311
LEONARD PITTS, JR., "Is There Room in This Sweet Land of Liberty for Such a Thing as a 'Cablinasian'? Face It, Tiger: If They Say You're Black, Then You're Black" 313
GEORGE F. WILL, "Melding in America" 315
ELLIS COSE, "Census and the Complex Issue of Race" 317
TEJA ARBOLEDA, "Race Is a Four-Letter Word" 324

*Reading Outside the Lines: Classroom Activities* *329*
*Reading Outside the Lines: Essay Ideas* *330*

**5. Reading Movies** **331**

*Worksheet* *335*

DAVID DENBY, "High-School Confidential: Notes on Teen Movies" 337

MICHAEL PARENTI, "Class and Virtue" 343
bell hooks, "Mock Feminism: *Waiting to Exhale*" 346
FREYA JOHNSON, "Holy Homosexuality Batman!: Camp and Corporate Capitalism in *Batman Forever*" 353
Four Reviews of *Moulin Rouge*: Roger Ebert, Stanley Kaufmann, Elvis Mitchell, Owen Glieberman 359

**The Movie Violence Suite 370**

LINDA WILLIAMS, "Film Bodies: Gender, Genre, and Excess" 370
Violence, Film, and Native America: LOUISE ERDRICH, "Dear John Wayne" and Sherman Alexie, "Texas Chainsaw Massacre" 385
ANDREA SACHS and SUSANNE WASHBURN, "*Time* Forum: Tough Talk on Entertainment" 388

*Reading Outside the Lines: Classroom Activities 396*
*Reading Outside the Lines: Essay Ideas 397*

**INTERCHAPTER: READING IMAGES 399**

*Worksheet 402*

America, Cowboys, the West, and Race 403
The Images of Gender 405
The Semiotics of Architecture 407
Laundry 408
Two Flags 410

**6. READING GENDER 412**

*Worksheet 418*

DEBORAH TANNEN, "Marked Women, Unmarked Men" 419
HOLLY DEVOR, "Gender Role Behaviors and Attitudes" 424
PAUL THEROUX, "Being a Man" 429
ALFONSINA STORNI, "You Would Have Me White" 433
**Student Essay:** WHITNEY BLACK, "*The Woman Warrior:* The Problem of Using Culture to Liberate Identity" 435

**The Myths of Gender Suite 440**

JILL BIRNIE HENKE, DIANE ZIMMERMAN UMBLE, and NANCY J. SMITH, "Construction of the Female Self: Feminist Readings of the Disney Heroine" 440
JANE YOLEN, "America's Cinderella" 452
MAXINE HONG KINGSTON, "No Name Woman" 460

*Reading Outside the Lines: Classroom Activities* *470*
*Reading Outside the Lines: Essay Ideas* *471*

7. **Reading the Visual Arts** **473**

*Worksheet* *479*

ALAN PRATT, "Andy Warhol: The Most Controversial Artist of the Twentieth Century?" 480
SUSAN SONTAG, "America Seen Through a Lens Darkly" 485
"Which Art Will Top The Chartes?: Four Curators Share Their Top 10 Picks and Reasoning behind the Most Influential Visual Artworks of the Past 1,000 Years" 496
E. G. CHRICHTON, "Is the NAMES Quilt Art?" 503
DEAN RADER, "(Re)Versing Vision: Reading Sculpture in Poetry and Prose" 512
SCOTT MCCLOUD, "Sequential Art: 'Closure' and 'Art'" 516
**Student Essay:** ANNE DARBY, "#27: Reading Cindy Sherman and Gender" 530

**The *Sensation* Suite 534**

DANA MACK, "It Isn't Pretty . . . But Is It Art?" 534
PETER SCHJELDAHL, "Those Nasty Brits: How Sensational Is *Sensation*?" 536
WILLIAM F. BUCKLEY JR., "Giuliani's Own Exhibit" 540
BENJAMIN IVRY, "'Modern Art Is a Load of Bullshit': Why Can't the Art World Accept Social Satire from a Black Artist?" 542

*Reading Outside the Lines: Classroom Activities* *545*
*Reading Outside the Lines: Essay Ideas* *545*

8. **Reading Advertising and the Media** **547**

*Worksheet* *554*

*Advertising* *555*

DAVE BARRY, "Some Hated Commercials Inspire Violent Fantasies" 555
MALCOLM GLADWELL, "The Coolhunt" 557
CLINT C. WILSON and FELIX GUTIERREZ, "Advertising and People of Color" 572
ROB WALKER, "Diet Coke's Underwear Strategy" 581
**Student Essay:** BRITTANY GRAY, "Hanes Her Way" 582

*News/Media* *586*

JEFF COHEN and NORMAN SOLOMAN, "15 Questions about the 'Liberal Media'" 586

KEVIN WILLIAMS and DAVID MILLER, "AIDS News and News Cultures" 588
DAVID MCGOWAN, "The America the Media Don't Want You to See" 598

**The Media Manipulation Suite 605**

STUART AND ELIZABETH EWEN, "In the Shadow of the Image" 606
WILLIAM LUTZ, "Weasel Words" 611
TRUDY LIEBERMAN, "Slanting the Story" 624

*Reading Outside the Lines: Classroom Activities* *632*
*Reading Outside the Lines: Essay Ideas* *633*

**9. READING MUSIC 635**

*Worksheet* *639*

KEVIN J.H. DETTMAR and WILLIAM RICHEY, "Musical Cheese: The Appropriation of Seventies Music in Nineties Movies" 641
**Student Essay:** FOUZIA BABER, "Is Tupac Really Dead?" 654
**Student Essay:** SARAH HAWKINS, "Right on Target: Revisiting Elvis Costello's *My Aim Is True*" 660

**Reading Music—The Song Suite 664**

DAVE MARSH, "Johnny B. Goode" 664
IAN MACDONALD, "I Am the Walrus" 666
ROBERT SHELTON, "Like a Rolling Stone" 669
MICHAEL AZERRAD, "Smells Like Teen Spirit" 671
MATT COMPTON, "Smells Like Teen Spirit" 673
CHRISTOPHER SIEVING, "Cop Out? The Media, 'Cop Killer,' and the Deracialization of Black Rage (Constructing [Mis]Representations)" 678

*Reading Outside the Lines: Classroom Activities* *698*
*Reading Outside the Lines: Essay Ideas* *699*

**10. READING TECHNOLOGY 701**

*Worksheet* *704*

DONALD A. NORMAN, "Infuriating by Design: Everyday Things Need Not Wreak Havoc on Our Lives" 705
ELIZABETH WEIL, "The Girl-Game Jinx" 710
LISA NAKAMURA, "Where Do You Want to Go Today? Cybernetic Tourism, the Internet, and Transnationality" 718

**Student Essay:** VIRGINIA COLWELL, "Mail-Order Brides: The Content of Internet Courtship" 727

**The Internet and Identity Suite 733**

FREDERICK C. MCKISSACK JR., "Cyberghetto: Blacks Are Falling Through the Net" 733
GLEN MARTIN, "Internet Indian Wars: Native Americans Are Fighting to Connect the 550 Nations—in Cyberspace" 736
BRENDA DANET, "Text as Mask: Gender and Identity on the Internet" 744
ANDREW SULLIVAN, "The InnerNet" 761

*Reading Outside the Lines: Classroom Activities* 764
*Reading Outside the Lines: Essay Ideas* 765

**APPENDIX: HOW DO I CITE THIS CAR?: GUIDELINES FOR CITING POPULAR CULTURE TEXTS 767**

Using Parenthetical References 768
Building the Works Cited Page 768
Plagiarism 769
Works Cited Examples 769
*Citing Books* 770
*Citing Articles* 771
*Electronic Sources* 772
*Other Sources* 773

*Index* 777

# Alternative Table of Contents

Below are the readings in *The World Is a Text* grouped according to subject matter, genre, or style of writing. They offer cross-chapter ways of reading individual works.

## Analytical


Michael Azerrad, "Smells Like Teen Spirit" 671
Robert Bednar, "Caught Looking: Problems with Taking Pictures of People Taking Pictures at an Exhibition" 224
Ellis Cose, "Census and the Complex Issue of Race" 317
Matt Compton, "Smells Like Teen Spirit" 673
David Denby, "High-School Confidential: Notes on Teen Movies" 337
Holly Devor, "Gender Role Behaviors and Attitudes" 424
Stuart and Elizabeth Ewen, "In the Shadow of the Image" 606
Four Reviews of *Moulin Rouge:* Roger Ebert, Stanley Kaufmann, Elvis Mitchell, Owen Glieberman 359
Handsome Lake, "How America Was Discovered" 289
Freya Johnson, "Holy Homosexuality Batman!: Camp and Corporate Capitalism in *Batman Forever*" 353
Tamar Lewin, "Growing Up, Growing Apart" 259
Ian MacDonald, "I Am the Walrus" 666
Dean Rader, "(Re)Versing Vision: Reading Sculpture in Poetry and Prose" 512
Robert Shelton, "Like a Rolling Stone" 669
Christopher Sieving, "Cop Out? The Media, 'Cop Killer,' and the Deracialization of Black Rage (Constructing [Mis]Representations) 678
Susan Sontag, "America Seen Through a Lens Darkly" 485
Beverly Daniel Tatum, "Why Are All the Black Kids Sitting Together in the Cafeteria?" 298

Paul Theroux, "Being a Man" 429
Harry F. Waters, "Life According to TV" 119
Elizabeth Weil, "The Girl-Game Jinx" 710
Jaime J. Weinman, "Worst Episode Ever" 171
Kevin Williams and David Miller, "AIDS News and News Cultures" 588

### African America

Michelle Cottle, "How Soaps Are Integrating America: Color TV" 126
Malcolm Gladwell, "The Sports Taboo" 301
bell hooks, "Mock Feminism: *Waiting to Exhale*" 346
Langston Hughes, "Harlem" 82
Benjamin Ivry, "'Modern Art is a Load of Bullshit': Why Can't the Art World Accept Social Satire from a Black Artist?" 542
Frederick C. McKissack Jr., "Cyberghetto: Blacks are Falling Through the Net" 733
Kenneth Meeks, "Shopping in a Mall While Black: A Coach's Story" 218
Peter Parisi, "'Black Bart' Simpson: Appropriation and Revitalization in Commodity Culture" 182
Leonard Pitts Jr., "Is There Room in This Sweet Land of Liberty for Such a Thing as a 'Cablinasian'? Face it, Tiger: If They Say You're Black, Then You're Black" 313
Beverly Daniel Tatum, "Why Are All the Black Kids Sitting Together in the Cafeteria?" 298
Jean Toomer, "Blood-Burning Moon" 52
Clint C. Wilson and Felix Gutierrez, "Advertising and People of Color" 572

### Asian America

America, Cowboys, The West, and Race 403
Whitney Black, "*The Woman Warrior:* The Problem of Using Culture to Liberate Identity" 435
Virginia Colwell, "Mail-Order Brides: The Content of Internet Courtship" 727
Amy Tan, "Mother Tongue" 291
Clint C. Wilson and Felix Gutierrez, "Advertising and People of Color" 572

### Argumentative/Persuasive

E. G. Chrichton, "Is the NAMES Quilt Art?" 503
bell hooks, "Mock Feminism: *Waiting to Exhale*" 346
Holly Devor, "Gender Role Behaviors and Attitudes" 424
Ariel Gore, "TV Can Be a Good Parent" 115

Whitney Gould, "New Urbanism Needs to Keep Racial Issues in Mind" 247
William L. Hamilton, "How Suburban Design Is Failing Teen-Agers" 233
Trudy Lieberman, "Slanting the Story" 624
William Lutz, "Weasel Words" 611
Donald A. Norman, "Infuriating by Design: Everyday Things Need Not Wreak Havoc on Our Lives" 705
Michael Parenti, "Class and Virtue" 343
Leonard Pitts Jr., "Is There Room in This Sweet Land of Liberty for Such a Thing as a 'Cablinasian'? Face it, Tiger: If They Say You're Black, Then You're Black" 313
Alan Pratt, "Andy Warhol: The Most Controversial Artist of the Twentieth Century?" 480
Andrew Sullivan, "The InnerNet" 761
Sallie Tisdale, "Citizens of the World, Turn on Your Televisions!" 112
Jaime J. Weinman, "Worst Episode Ever" 171
Jane Yolen, "America's Cinderella" 452

## Comparison/Contrast

Dave Barry, "Some Hated Commercials Inspire Violent Fantasies" 555
Michelle Cottle, "How Soaps Are Integrating America: Color TV" 126
David Denby, "High-School Confidential: Notes on Teen Movies" 337
Malcolm Gladwell, "The Sports Taboo" 301
Jill Birnie Henke, Diane Zimmerman Umble, and Nancy J. Smith, "Construction of the Female Self: Feminist Readings of the Disney Heroine" 440
bell hooks, "Mock Feminism: *Waiting to Exhale*" 346
Daphne Spain, "Spatial Segregation and Gender Stratification in the Workplace" 211
Deborah Tannen, "Marked Women, Unmarked Men" 419

## Definitional

E. G. Chrichton, "Is the NAMES Quilt Art?" 503
bell hooks, "Mock Feminism: *Waiting to Exhale*" 346
Ariel Gore, "TV Can Be a Good Parent" 115
William Lutz, "Weasel Words" 611
Dana Mack, "It Isn't Pretty . . . But Is It Art?" 534
Alan Pratt, "Andy Warhol: The Most Controversial Artist of the Twentieth Century?" 480
Paul Theroux, "Being a Man" 429
Jaime J. Weinman, "Worst Episode Ever" 171

## Fun

Michael Azerrad, "Smells Like Teen Spirit" 671
Fouzia Baber, "Is Tupac Really Dead?" 654
Dave Barry, "Some Hated Commercials Inspire Violent Fantasies" 555
Robert Bednar, "Caught Looking: Problems with Taking Pictures of People Taking Pictures at an Exhibition" 224
Matt Compton, "Smells Like Teen Spirit" 673
David Denby, "High-School Confidential: Notes on Teen Movies" 337
Kevin J.H. Dettmar and William Richey, "Musical Cheese: The Appropriation of Seventies Music in Nineties Movies" 641
Four Reviews of *Moulin Rouge:* Roger Ebert, Stanley Kaufmann, Elvis Mitchell, Owen Glieberman 359
Katherine Gantz, "'Not That There's Anything Wrong with That': Reading the Queer in *Seinfeld*" 130
Malcolm Gladwell, "The Coolhunt" 557
Sarah Hawkins, "Right on Target: Revisiting Elvis Costello's *My Aim Is True*" 660
Freya Johnson, "Holy Homosexuality Batman!: Camp and Corporate Capitalism in *Batman Forever*" 353
Ian MacDonald, "I Am the Walrus" 666
Dave Marsh, "Johnny B. Goode" 664
Scott McCloud, "Sequential Art: 'Closure' and 'Art'" 516
Donald A. Norman, "Infuriating by Design: Everyday Things Need Not Wreak Havoc on Our Lives" 705
William Shakespeare, "My Mistress' Eyes Are Nothing Like the Sun (Sonnet 130)" 74
Robert Shelton, "Like a Rolling Stone" 669
Christopher Sieving, "Cop Out? The Media, 'Cop Killer,' and the Deracialization of Black Rage (Constructing [Mis]Representations)" 678
Andrew Sullivan, "The InnerNet" 761
James Tate, "Goodtime Jesus" 59
Sallie Tisdale, "Citizens of the World, Turn on Your Televisions!" 112
Rob Walker, "Diet Coke's Underwear Strategy" 581
Jaime J. Weinman, "Worst Episode Ever" 171
"Which Art Will Top the Chartes?: Four Curators Share Their Top 10 Picks and Reasoning behind the Most Influential Visual Artworks of the Past 1,000 Years" 496

## Games (Sports and other)

Malcolm Gladwell, "The Sports Taboo" 301
Kenneth Meeks, "Shopping in a Mall While Black: A Coach's Story" 218
Leonard Pitts Jr., "Is There Room in This Sweet Land of Liberty for Such a Thing as a 'Cablinasian'? Face it, Tiger: If They Say You're Black, Then You're Black" 313

Elizabeth Weil, "The Girl-Game Jinx" 710
George F. Will, "Melding in America" 315

## Gender/Sexuality

Kate Chopin, "The Story of an Hour" 79
Brenda Danet, "Text as Mask: Gender and Identity on the Internet" 744
Anne Darby, "#27: Reading Cindy Sherman and Gender" 530
Holly Devor, "Gender Role Behaviors and Attitudes" 424
Emily Dickinson, "My Life had stood – a Loaded Gun" 75
Carolyn Forché, "The Colonel" 62
Katherine Gantz, "'Not That There's Anything Wrong with That': Reading the Queer in *Seinfeld*" 130
Jill Birnie Henke, Diane Zimmerman Umble, and Nancy J. Smith, "Construction of the Female Self: Feminist Readings of the Disney Heroine" 440
bell hooks, "Mock Feminism: *Waiting to Exhale*" 346
Freya Johnson, "Holy Homosexuality Batman!: Camp and Corporate Capitalism in *Batman Forever*" 353
Maxine Hong Kingston, "No Name Woman" 460
Archana Mehta, "Society's Need for a *Queer* Solution: The Media's Reinforcement of Homophobia Through Traditional Gender Roles" 152
Daphne Spain, "Spatial Segregation and Gender Stratification in the Workplace" 211
Susan Steinberg, "Isla" 83
Alfonsina Storni, "You Would Have Me White" 433
Andrew Sullivan, "The InnerNet" 761
Wislawa Szymborska, "Slapstick" 77
Deborah Tannen, "Marked Women, Unmarked Men" 419
Paul Theroux, "Being a Man" 429
Elizabeth Weil, "The Girl-Game Jinx" 710
Hillary West, "Media Journal: *The Rosie O'Donnell Show*" 202
Linda Williams, "Film Bodies: Gender, Genre, and Excess" 370
Jane Yolen, "America's Cinderella" 452

## Mexican/Hispanic America

Ellis Cose, "Census and the Complex Issue of Race" 317
Clint C. Wilson and Felix Gutierrez, "Advertising and People of Color" 572

## Informational/Expository

Dave Barry, "Some Hated Commercials Inspire Violent Fantasies" 555
Michelle Cottle, "How Soaps Are Integrating America: Color TV" 126

Kevin J.H. Dettmar and William Richey, "Musical Cheese: The Appropriation of Seventies Music in Nineties Movies" 641
Holly Devor, "Gender Role Behaviors and Attitudes" 424
Kwame J. McKenzie and N.S. Crowcroft, "Describing Race, Ethnicity, and Culture in Medical Research: Describing the Groups Studied Is Better Than Trying to Find a Catchall Name" 274
Deborah Tannen, "Marked Women, Unmarked Men" 419
George F. Will, "Melding in America" 315
Clint C. Wilson and Felix Gutierrez, "Advertising and People of Color" 572

## International/Global

Ian MacDonald, "I Am the Walrus" 666
Virginia Colwell, "Mail-Order Brides: The Content of Internet Courtship" 727
Four Reviews of *Moulin Rouge:* Roger Ebert, Stanley Kaufmann, Elvis Mitchell, Owen Glieberman 359
Carolyn Forché, "The Colonel" 62
Benjamin Ivry, "'Modern Art is a Load of Bullshit': Why Can't the Art World Accept Social Satire from a Black Artist?" 542
Kwame J. McKenzie and N.S. Crowcroft, "Describing Race, Ethnicity, and Culture in Medical Research: Describing the Groups Studied Is Better Than Trying to Find a Catchall Name" 274
Lisa Nakamura, "Where Do You Want to Go Today? Cybernetic Tourism, the Internet, and Transnationality" 718
Pablo Neruda, "Ode to My Socks" 60
Anne Waldron Neumann, *"The Simpsons"* 175
Peter Schjeldahl, "Those Nasty Brits: How Sensational is *Sensation*?" 536
William Shakespeare, "My Mistress' Eyes Are Nothing Like the Sun (Sonnet 130)" 74
Wislawa Szymborska, "Slapstick" 77
Paul Theroux, "Being a Man" 429

## Literature (Fiction, Literary Non-Fiction, and Poetry)

Sherman Alexie, "Texas Chainsaw Massacre" 386
Kate Chopin, "The Story of an Hour" 79
Emily Dickinson, "My Life had stood – a Loaded Gun" 75
Louise Erdrich, "Dear John Wayne" 385
Stuart and Elizabeth Ewen, "In the Shadow of the Image" 606
Carolyn Forché, "The Colonel" 62
Chris Haven, "Assisted Living" 89
Nathaniel Hawthorne, "Young Goodman Brown" 64

Langston Hughes, "Harlem" 82
Handsome Lake, "How America Was Discovered" 289
Adrian Louis, "Dust World" 99
Pablo Neruda, "Ode to My Socks" 60
Dean Rader, "(Re)Versing Vision: Reading Sculpture in Poetry and Prose" 512
Theodore Roethke, "My Papa's Waltz" 101
William Shakespeare, "My Mistress' Eyes Are Nothing Like the Sun (Sonnet 130)" 74
Susan Steinberg, "Isla" 83
Wislawa Szymborska, "Slapstick" 77
Amy Tan, "Mother Tongue" 291
James Tate, "Goodtime Jesus" 59
Jean Toomer, "Blood-Burning Moon" 52

## Native America

Sherman Alexie, "Texas Chainsaw Massacre" 386
Louise Erdrich, "Dear John Wayne" 385
Handsome Lake, "How America Was Discovered" 289
Adrian Louis, "Dust World" 99
Jim Mahfood, "True Tales of Amerikkkan History Part II: The True Thanksgiving" 296
America, Cowboys, the West, and Race 403
Glen Martin, "Internet Indian Wars: Native Americans Are Fighting to Connect the 550 Nations—in Cyberspace" 736

## Personal Essay (uses first person)

Teja Arboleda, "Race Is a Four-Letter Word" 324
Robert Bednar, "Caught Looking: The Problem with Taking Pictures of People Taking Pictures at an Exhibition" 224
Matt Compton, "Smells Like Teen Spirit" 673
Malcolm Gladwell, "The Coolhunt" 557
Malcolm Gladwell, "The Sports Taboo" 301
Ariel Gore, "TV Can Be a Good Parent" 115
Whitney Gould, "New Urbanism Needs to Keep Racial Issues in Mind" 243
Archana Mehta, "Society's Need for a *Queer* Solution: The Media's Reinforcement of Homophobia Through Traditional Gender Roles" 152
Anne Waldron Neumann, "*The Simpsons*" 175
Donald A. Norman, "Infuriating by Design: Everyday Things Need Not Wreak Havoc on Our Lives" 705

Leonard Pitts Jr., "Is There Room in This Sweet Land of Liberty for Such a Thing as a 'Cablinasian'? Face it, Tiger: If They Say You're Black, Then You're Black" 313
Amy Tan, "Mother Tongue" 291
Deborah Tannen, "Marked Women, Unmarked Men" 419
Beverly Daniel Tatum, "Why Are All the Black Kids Sitting Together in the Cafeteria?" 298
Sallie Tisdale, "Citizens of the World, Turn on Your Televisions!" 112
Hillary West, "Media Journal: *The Rosie O'Donnell Show*" 202

## Race/Ethnicity

Teja Arboleda, "Race Is a Four-Letter Word" 330
Fouzia Baber, "Is Tupac Really Dead?" 654
Dave Marsh, "Johnny B. Goode" 664
William Booth, "A White Migration North from Miami" 237
William F. Buckley, "Giuliani's Own Exhibit" 540
Ellis Cose, "Census and the Complex Issue of Race" 317
Michelle Cottle, "How Soaps Are Integrating America: Color TV" 126
Violence, Film, and Native America: Louise Erdrich, "Dear John Wayne" and Sherman Alexie, "Texas Chainsaw Massacre" 385
Malcolm Gladwell, "The Sports Taboo" 301
Whitney Gould, "New Urbanism Needs to Keep Racial Issues in Mind" 247
Langston Hughes, "Harlem" 82
Benjamin Ivry, "'Modern Art Is a Load of Bullshit': Why Can't the Art World Accept Social Satire from a Black Artist?" 542
Handsome Lake, "How America Was Discovered" 289
Tamar Lewin, "Growing Up, Growing Apart" 259
Kwame J. McKenzie and N.S. Crowcroft, "Describing Race, Ethnicity, and Culture in Medical Research: Describing the Groups Studied Is Better Than Trying to Find a Catchall Name" 274
Frederick C. McKissack Jr., "Cyberghetto: Blacks are Falling Through the Net" 733
Dana Mack, "It Isn't Pretty . . . But Is It Art?" 534
Jim Mahfood, "True Tales of Amerikkkan History Part II: The True Thanksgiving" 296
Glen Martin, "Internet Indian Wars: Native Americans Are Fighting to Connect the 550 Nations—in Cyberspace" 736
Kenneth Meeks, "Shopping in a Mall While Black: A Coach's Story" 218
Lisa Nakamura, "Where Do You Want to Go Today? Cybernetic Tourism, the Internet, and Transnationality" 718
Michael Omi, "In Living Color: Race and American Culture" 277

Peter Parisi, "'Black Bart' Simpson: Appropriation and Revitalization in Commodity Culture" 182
Leonard Pitts Jr., "Is There Room in This Sweet Land of Liberty for Such a Thing as a 'Cablinasian'? Face it, Tiger: If They Say You're Black, Then You're Black" 313
Peter Schjeldahl, "Those Nasty Brits: How Sensational is *Sensation*?" 536
Susan Steinberg, "Isla" 83
Alfonsina Storni, "You Would Have Me White" 433
Amy Tan, "Mother Tongue" 291
Beverly Daniel Tatum, "Why Are All the Black Kids Sitting Together in the Cafeteria?" 298
Jean Toomer, "Blood-Burning Moon" 52
Harry F. Waters, "Life According to TV" 119
George F. Will, "Melding in America" 315
Clint C. Wilson and Felix Gutierrez, "Advertising and People of Color" 572

**Researched Essays (works with citations)**

Fouzia Baber, "Is Tupac Really Dead?" 654
Katherine F. Benzel, "Room for Learning with Latest Technology" 229
Virginia Colwell, "Mail-Order Brides: The Content of Internet Courtship" 727
Matt Compton, "Smells Like Teen Spirit" 673
Brenda Danet, "Text as Mask: Gender and Identity on the Internet" 744
Kevin J.H. Dettmar and William Richey, "Musical Cheese: The Appropriation of Seventies Music in Nineties Movies" 641
Holly Devor, "Gender Role Behaviors and Attitudes" 424
Katherine Gantz, "'Not That There's Anything Wrong with That': Reading the Queer in *Seinfeld*" 130
Jill Birnie Henke, Diane Zimmerman Umble, and Nancy J. Smith, "Construction of the Female Self: Feminist Readings of the Disney Heroine" 440
Christopher Sieving, "Cop Out? The Media, 'Cop Killer,' and the Deracialization of Black Rage (Constructing [Mis]Representations)" 678
Freya Johnson, "Holy Homosexuality Batman!: Camp and Corporate Capitalism in *Batman Forever*" 353
Kwame J. McKenzie and N.S. Crowcroft, "Describing Race, Ethnicity, and Culture in Medical Research: Describing the Groups Studied Is Better Than Trying to Find a Catchall Name" 274
Archana Mehta, "Society's Need for a *Queer* Solution: The Media's Reinforcement of Homophobia Through Traditional Gender Roles" 152

Lisa Nakamura, "Where Do You Want to Go Today? Cybernetic Tourism, the Internet, and Transnationality" 718
Donald A. Norman, "Infuriating by Design: Everyday Things Need Not Wreak Havoc on Our Lives" 705
Michael Omi, "In Living Color: Race and American Culture" 277
Peter Parisi, "'Black Bart' Simpson: Appropriation and Revitalization in Commodity Culture" 182
Daphne Spain, "Spatial Segregation and Gender Stratification in the Workplace" 211
Beverly Daniel Tatum, "Why Are All the Black Kids Sitting Together in the Cafeteria?" 298
Clint C. Wilson and Felix Gutierrez, "Advertising and People of Color" 572
Jane Yolen, "America's Cinderella" 452

## Social and Economic Class

William Booth, "A White Migration North from Miami" 237
Sarah Boxer, "A Remedy for the Rootlessness of Modern Suburban Life?" 243
Whitney Gould, "New Urbanism Needs to Keep Racial Issues in Mind" 247
William L. Hamilton, "How Suburban Design Is Failing Teen-Agers" 233
Chris Haven, "Assisted Living" 89
Langston Hughes, "Harlem" 82
Tamar Lewin, "Growing Up, Growing Apart" 259
Adrian Louis, "Dust World" 99
David McGowan, "The America the Media Don't Want You to See" 598
Michael Parenti, "Class and Virtue" 343
Theodore Roethke, "My Papa's Waltz" 101
Susan Steinberg, "Isla" 83
Harry F. Waters, "Life According to TV" 119

## Young Adults/Teenagers/Children

Fouzia Baber, "Is Tupac Really Dead?" 654
Matt Compton, "Smells Like Teen Spirit" 673
David Denby, "High-School Confidential: Notes on Teen Movies" 337
Malcolm Gladwell, "The Coolhunt" 557
Ariel Gore, "TV Can Be a Good Parent" 115
William L. Hamilton, "How Suburban Design Is Failing Teen-Agers" 233
Nathaniel Hawthorne, "Young Goodman Brown" 64
Jill Birnie Henke, Diane Zimmerman Umble, and Nancy J. Smith, "Construction of the Female Self: Feminist Readings of the Disney Heroine" 440

Tamar Lewin, "Growing Up, Growing Apart" 259
Jim Mahfood, "True Tales of Amerikkkan History Part II: The True Thanksgiving" 296
Kenneth Meeks, "Shopping in a Mall While Black: A Coach's Story" 218
Beverly Daniel Tatum, "Why Are All the Black Kids Sitting Together in the Cafeteria?" 298
Elizabeth Weil, "The Girl-Game Jinx" 710

# Preface

From an early age, we are readers, both of so-called traditional texts—fiction, poetry, and drama—and nontraditional texts—movies, television, and especially people. While the schooling process focuses on the former, our everyday living focuses on the latter.

As a human being, this type of reading is crucial for being an active participant in the world. But too often this "informal" reading is given short shrift in the classroom. While we agree that training in reading traditional texts such as novels, short stories, poetry, and plays is a crucial aspect of an education, perhaps *the* crucial aspect, we also believe that the methods used in learning to read traditional texts can be applied to nontraditional ones as well—with the overall goal of understanding the world around us and reducing the distance between the classroom and the "real world."

Our book comes out of these ideas. While there are many popular culture readers out there, good ones in fact, we never quite found the book we wanted; one that focused on the classroom experience and the writing situation. We think the classroom should be a dynamic place, and we think writing and discussion is crucial to learning how to think. *The World Is a Text* is as much a book for teachers as it is for students in that regard. We hope that our questions, introductions, and exercises give teachers the tools they need to teach students how to write with clarity and intelligence, to read more actively and astutely, and finally to engage the world more actively. While all three missions are crucial, the first two are clearly more aimed at academic achievement. The last we think is critical in our missions as teachers. We believe students who read their worlds more actively are not only better students, but better citizens of the world.

For its pedagogy, *The World Is a Text* relies on a modified semiotic approach; it is based on the assumption that reading occurs at all times and places. It also relies on traditional critical skills employed by literary scholars and the generally contextual approach employed by cultural studies scholars. The book also features a sophisticated way of thinking about texts, writing, and the rhetorical moment. Taking as its major theoretical framework I.A. Richards' claim that rhetoric is a philosophic inquiry into how words work in discourse, *The World Is a Text* considers how various texts enact rhetorical strategies and how students might begin not only to recognize these strategies but write their own. Textual analysis (reading) and textual formation (writing) jointly contribute to the larger process of knowledge making. Thus, *The World Is a Text* is interested in helping students to ask not simply *what* something means but *how* something means.

And because knowledge making requires knowledge of how we make arguments and sentences and theses and assertions, this book goes one step further than similar readers in that, in our experience, writing remains a secondary concern for most anthologies. One of our goals is to make the writing experience a vital part of the entire book from the introduction, to the section on writing, to each individual reading. For instance, Section I, "The World Is a Text: Writing" takes a comprehensive approach to the various stages of the writing process. We walk students through selecting a topic, brainstorming, outlining, developing a thesis, and revising. We offer help with research and citation. We even provide a unique chapter on making the transition from high school to college writing. One of our goals is to help students make these connections between reading and writing, thinking and writing, revising and revisioning.

*The World Is a Text* also has its focus in encountering media and texts in general; each chapter has questions that encourage students not only to respond to readings but the texts and media themselves. Every chapter has an introduction that focuses on reading media and individual "texts" (not the readings themselves). In the readings that follow, each piece features questions geared toward both reading and writing. And its general apparatus in the form of worksheets and classroom exercises encourages students to use the readings as a starting point for their own explorations of television, race, movies, art, and the other media and texts we include here.

On a more theoretical level, we show how language in text and context functions to produce meaning. And we talk about how writing is fundamentally linked to other aspects of critical inquiry like reading, listening, thinking, and speaking. Ultimately, part of our approach comes from Kenneth Burke. Just as he argues that all literature is a piece of rhetoric, we suggest that all texts are rhetoric and that every moment is a potential moment for reading and therefore for writing.

What we envision this book will do for students is help them bridge culture and text. However, we present material in a way that provides context, direction and structure. In that sense, the book is traditional; however, the expanded nature of what a text is makes our approach innovative. We hope that, in turn, this will allow students to expand their idea of reading and therefore expand their critical relationship to the world. In an academic setting, where accountability and practicality are watchwords, giving students a more interpretative way of looking at and writing about the world seems especially appropriate.

# Acknowledgments

The authors need to acknowledge more people than can comfortably fit, but here's a start.

First of all, we want to express our gratitude to everyone at Prentice Hall, especially our editor, Corey Good, and his helpful assistant, John Ragozzine. We also want to thank Leah Jewell, Brandy Dawson, Lisa Black, and Carrie Brandon. We thank Karen Berry and everyone at Pine Tree Composition.

We are also grateful for the advice, critiques, and suggestions from the people who graciously agreed to review and comment on *The World Is a Text* in manuscript form: Eileen Murray (Norwich University), Wendy K. Bruce (Ball State University), Angela B. Fulk (John Brown University), Rolf Samuels (Viterbo University), Laura Gray-Rosendale (Northern Arizona University), Felicia Carr (George Mason University), Gary Thompson (Saginaw Valley State University), Craig Kleinman (SUNY–Ulster), Lloyd E. Rohler (University of North Carolina–Wilmington), Kenneth Womack (Penn State–Altoona), Susan Nash (University of Oklahoma), and David Susman (Salt Lake Community College). We are also appreciative of the many other people who read and commented on the manuscript but who are not mentioned here.

For their valuable assistance in preparing the manuscript, we want to thank Kimberly Garrett, Bexie Towle, Mary Abler, Ninni Gebauer, Tara Sablan, Ray Rimas, and Colleen Stevens. For their help with the reading gender chapter, we'd like to thank Rachel Crawford and Nicole Raeburn, for the reading race and ethnicity chapter, Katherine Clay Bassard, for reading the technology chapter, Michael Heller, and for the introduction, Patty Strong. We also want to thank Miles McCrimmon for reading an early version of the proposal. We also thank the Paule Anglim Gallery of San Francisco and Rigo for allowing us to use the wonderful murals on the cover of this book.

In areas of institutional and collegial support, the following were of especial help: Catherine Ingrassia, Marcel Cornis-Pope, Richard Fine, Margret Vopel Schluer, Sharon Call Laslie, Ginny Schmitz, Bill Tester, Tom De Haven, Laura Browder, David Latanae, Nick Sharp, Elizabeth Savage, Randy Lewis, Emily Roderer, Pat Perry, Elizabeth Cooper, Elizabeth Hodges, Bill Griffin, James Kinney, Margaurette Harkness, Michael Keller, Leslie Shiel, Nick Frankel, Faye Pritchard, Angier Brock Caudle, Traci Wood, Katie Henninger, Kathie Tovo, Frank Goodyear, Anne Collins, Jan Lisiak, Teresa Genaro, Suzanne Forgarty, Michael Tanner, Dan Marano, Elisabeth Piedmont-Marton, Jeffrey Meikle, Mark Smith, Greg Barnhisel, Fouzia Baber, Anne Darby, Matt Compton, Matt King, Carlease Briggs, Virginia Colwell, Rita Botts, Sarah Hawkins, Whitney Black, Tracy Seeley, Eileen Chia-Ching Fung, Alan Heinemann, Patricia Hill, Carolyn Brown, Carolyn Webber, Sean Michaelson, John Pinelli, Robert Bednar, Wendy McCredie, Leonard Schulze, Jean-Pierre Metereau, Steven Vrooman, Beth Barry, Amy Randolph, T. Paul Hernandez, Chris Haven, Brian Clements, George McCoy, Michael Strysick, Brian Brennan, Mike Henry, LeAnne Howe, Cary Cordova, Monica Chiu, Andrew Macalister, Aranzazu Borrachero, Cecilia Santos, Vamsee Juluri, Jeff Paris, Christopher Kamrath, Susan Steinberg, Susan Paik, Peter Novak, and Heather Barkley.

Additionally, we thank the English Department at Virginia Commonwealth University, the VCU James Branch Cabell Library, the Andover Summer Session, the Department of English and Communication Studies at Texas Lutheran University, and the Department of English and the Dean's Office of the University of San Francisco, particularly Associate Dean of Arts Jennifer Turpin and her excellent staff.

Finally, we thank Melvin Silverman, Beverly Silverman, Jason Silverman, Christian Leahy, Joel Silverman, Alba Estanoz, Gary and Ginger Rader, Barbara Glenn, and Amy and Adam Kice.

We are most grateful to all of you who have adopted this book for your classes and a particularly hearty thank you to all of the students who have made, for better or worse, this text a part of your world.

Jonathan Silverman
*Virginia Commonwealth University*

Dean Rader
*University of San Francisco*

# INTRODUCTION

We are born readers. From an early age, we make sense of everything by drawing conclusions based on our experiences—similar to the process we undertake when we now read a book for school or pleasure. We read from the first time when we as babies express recognition of our parents. This continues throughout childhood, adolescence, and adulthood. We become better at reading traditional texts such as short stories, novels, and poems (formal reading) through our schooling and nontraditional texts such as television, architecture, and people through our experience (informal reading), often a parallel and intersecting process. In both forms of reading, we learn how to understand what symbols mean and figure out what the author is "saying" as we try to understand our complicated relationships with other people and places; we learn what a "nice" neighborhood looks like or how to determine when a potential mate "likes" us. Over the course of our lives, we determine, question, and revise thousands of different beliefs based on our own readings. We perform acts of informal reading when encountering popular culture and the media. When we attempt to make sense of a movie or television or news report, to put it in perspective with our experiences, we are reading and interpreting. Of course, this kind of reading may not be exactly the same type of interpretation we do with the short stories and poems we receive in English classes, but making sense of people, images, ideas, and places remains a significant form of interpretation nonetheless. Because this reading is so important, and because we do so much of it, we should think of our entire world as something that can and should be read. In short, we can think of the world as a text.

How and what we read in this text that is our world is important—we make decisions about whom we spend time with, where we live, and other important considerations based on informal reading. We construct a worldview based on our informal readings and the readings of other people. We influence other people's readings, and they influence ours. A comment or even a physical reaction from a parent, teacher, or friend can guide our responses to a text. Sometimes these influences are harmless—not liking a particular band or television show because a friend does not is no big deal. But often these influences can have consequences that go beyond simple dislike or like; we can learn to read the world in limiting, prejudicial ways that affect not only our lives but the lives of our fellow citizens. If we imitate our parents' (or friend's or neighbor's or teacher's) negative reaction to people of particular ethnicities or accept abusive behavior by friends or family toward a certain gender, we have incorporated someone else's negative reading into our own worldview, much like we might accept a *Cliff's Notes* view of *The Great Gatsby* as our own. But for better or worse, our readings are not permanent. As we grow older and become more adept at reading our world, we constantly rewrite our worldview. That's where this book comes in.

Our goal is to help you take texts (movies, pieces of art, experiences, people, places, ideas, traditions, advertisements) both familiar and unfamiliar to you and *read* them. Many of these texts will be visual or have visual elements, and you "see" them rather than "read" them. Instead of looking through them by not actively interpreting, we will ask you to look *at* them—to slow down and look at them in ways you may not have previously. Additionally, we want you to try formalizing this reading process. What we mean by formal here is the process we undertake when analyzing literature (or depending on your training, art, music, or movies). One of the primary elements of formal reading is the breaking down of a text into smaller elements and interpreting them. Analyzing a short story for themes, character development, and figurative language (symbols, metaphors, etc.) is formal reading, as is explicating a poem. Looking at a poem's rhyme, meter, symbolism, tone, structure, and design is a formal process that involves posing questions about what the poem is trying to do and how it does it. While it may feel natural to think of reading or "decoding" poems in this way, approaching an advertisement or a television show or a gender may feel a bit foreign at first. Over the course of reading this book, we hope that this process will cease to feel alien and begin to seem natural, especially as you become more familiar with analyzing the elements associated with these texts.

In other words, the traditional analytical "work" you have done in English classes is something we want to imitate here. We believe that texts, including those that are nontraditional such as public spaces, songs, and advertisements, have meanings that can be uncovered through the exploration of their elements. You may know a public space seems ugly—but we want you to understand why. You may already sense that advertisements use sex to sell products, but we want you to understand how. The idea is not only to slow the interpretive process down but to make more conscious your meaning-making, a process you undertake all the time—whether you intend to or not.

## SEMIOTICS: THE STUDY OF SIGNS (AND TEXTS)

All reading we do, perhaps anything we do, is backed up by various ideas or theories—from the simple idea that the acts we undertake have consequences both good and bad to the more complex theories about relativity and gravity. In this book, we rely on a theory that the world itself is open to interpretation, that we can make meaning out of just about anything. The idea that the world is a text open to interpretation is itself a theory, which has a strong connection to semiotics, the study of signs. In this part of the introduction, we are going to elaborate on the idea of semiotics as a way of having you understand some of the assumptions we've made when writing this textbook. You can use the rest of the book without focusing too much on the theory.

In semiotics, the main idea is that everything is a sign of sorts. You already know what signs are, as you encounter them everywhere. There are traffic signs, signs telling whether something is open or closed, signs in your classroom telling you not to smoke, or cheat, or where the exit is. You do very little work in trying to understand these signs, which seemingly need no interpretation. Once you understand what "stop" means, or that red in fact means "stop," or that green means "go," or that yellow means "slow down" or "caution," there is little need to actively interpret these signs each time you see them. Of course, you did not always know what these signs meant; at some point in your childhood, you picked up the ideas behind these signs and now take them for granted.

We have a broader idea of signs (or texts) in this book. A sign is an object or idea or combination of the two that refers to something besides itself, and it depends on others to recognize that it's a sign. The red octagon, plus the letters "S" "T" "O" "P," mean "stop" to most of us through the combination of the shape, color, and letters; a blue diamond with "HALT" on it would catch our attention, but we would not treat it in the same way, though halt and stop are synonyms, and a blue diamond is a perfectly fine combination of color and shape. The stop sign as we now know it carries a meaning beyond a simple combination of word, color, and shape.

Another example: we know an "open" sign at a store means the store is transacting business. But "open" itself is an arbitrary sign, unique to English-speaking cultures. In Spanish, for example, "abierto" means "open." And in some places, a sign will contain both abierto and open to indicate that it's signifying to two different sets of clientele. "Open" and "abierto" can both be signs, but so can their presence together be a sign. If we saw an abierto and an open sign in one place, we might draw conclusions about where we were (a neighborhood where English and Spanish are spoken), who owned the restaurant or store (bilingual owners?), and who their audience was (primarily speakers of Spanish and English). In other

words, the presence of both signs is itself a sign—taken together they create meaning.

Semioticians ("sign-studiers") have a more formal way of referring to signs. Ferdinand de Saussure, a Swiss linguist working in the nineteenth and twentieth centuries, believed that signs contained two elements: the *signifier* and the *signified*, which, taken together, often create meaning. The signifier is the object that exists and the signified is what it means. In other words, the letters o-p-e-n are the signifier, and the message that a place is open for business is the signified, and the external reality is that the store or restaurant is open for business. Similarly, using our stop sign example, the actual red sign with the STOP written in white letters is the signifier. The signified is the message that you must bring your car to a complete halt when you approach this sign.

## SYSTEMS OF READING: MAKING SENSE OF CULTURAL TEXTS

Sometimes the same signifiers (physical signs) can have different signifieds (meanings). For instance, what do you think of when you see the word "pan"? Most of you probably imagine an item for cooking. Or, you might think of a critic "panning" or critiquing a bad movie. However, a Spanish speaker who saw the word pan in our bilingual store would most likely imagine bread. The signifier "pan" in Spanish cultures refers not to an item for cooking but to what English speakers think of when they see the signifier "bread." Thus, people from both cultures would experience the same signifier, but what is signified would be entirely different.

However, we don't even need other languages for there to be various signified meanings for the same signifier. Photographers may think of a pan or wide-angle shot. Scholars of Greek mythology may think of the Greek god who is half goat and half man. The letters "p," "a," and "n" remain the same, but the meanings change; the sign—the word—"pan" has different meanings. On the other hand, we have the same signified but with different signifiers. For example, "soda," "pop," or "Coke" are all different signifiers that different people from different parts of the country use to refer to a flavored carbonated drink.

So when we talk about signs, we are not only talking about physical signs but a system of reading. In this system, we can interpret images, words whose letters are arbitrarily assigned meaning, and experiences really just about anything. Sometimes we make these interpretations with little or no effort and sometimes with a lot of work. Many semioticians believe that everything is a sign, including the way we are writing this introduction. The words are signs, and so is the way you are reading them (it's simply a more complex way of saying that everything is a text).

And more complex signs of course do not reveal themselves so easily. For example, let's consider a very famous sign (or text)—the *Mona Lisa.* Its power in some part comes from its simplicity and its *unreadability*. We don't know why she is smiling, we only have a vague idea of who she is, and we will likely never know. That smile, or half-smile, has become so famous that its life as a sign has transcended even its power as an image. The painting is a signifier, but its signified is ambiguous and difficult to determine. If we look at the various images of the *Mona Lisa* on shirts, mousepads, posters,

even variations of the original (we like the version where Mona Lisa has a big black moustache) we can agree that the *Mona Lisa* has become a symbol of something 1) traditional, 2) artistic, 3) commercial, and yet 4) universal, and perhaps 5) modern. We can agree that something about its power has not diminished despite or because of its age. But our signified—our mental concept of what "Mona Lisa-ness" is—depends on what perspective we bring to the reality of this artwork. Does it signify our definition of a masterpiece? A commodity? A self-portrait by the artist?

We don't know exactly (but people guess all the time). And that's why sometimes sign reading is so frustrating. Some signs are easier to read and understand, so easy that we don't even know that we are reading. Others, like paintings—and more importantly, human relationships—are more difficult. One of the most complex components of reading texts is suspending judgments about a text's values. In your initial semiotic analysis—your initial reading of a text—try to consider all aspects of a text before applying a label like "good" or "bad" (or interesting or boring). Such labels can only come after a thorough reading of the text under question. Later, if you want to argue if a text has problems, then you would use the details, the information you gleaned from your reading, to support these assertions in your papers. In attacking the *Mona Lisa*, for example, it would be acceptable to most professors for you to guess about what you thought da Vinci meant in painting her if you can defend your guess. Reading visually, in fact, often means such guessing is a natural part of doing any sort of paper.

Overall, the basic idea behind semiotics should not be foreign to you—on a fundamental level, it simply means reading and interpreting nontraditional objects like you would a short story or a poem.

## THE "SEMIOTIC SITUATION" (OR THE "MOVING TEXT")

As you may have guessed, you do this type of work all the time. You read human relationships all the time, having developed this skill over your years of reading your world. For instance, let's say you are walking down Wall Street in New York City. You see a man dressed in a suit, talking on a cell phone, carrying a copy of the *Wall Street Journal*, and yelling "Sell Microsoft at 42! Sell! Sell! Sell!" What would you assume his profession is? He could be a lawyer. He could be a banker. But given the context (where you are, which is Wall Street), what he's talking about (stocks) and how he's dressed (a suit), the best interpretation of this text might be that he is a stockbroker. You could be wrong, but based on the clues of the text, that's a pretty good reading.

We perform this work constantly. For example, on first dates we try to read the other person for cues of attraction and enjoyment; quarterbacks read a defense before every play and every pass; we read a classroom when we enter it; we read a friend's house and especially his or her room. These moments are what we call "semiotic situations." They are moments in which we try to make sense of our surroundings or interpret one aspect of our surroundings based on the signs or texts of our situation. The copy of the *Wall Street Journal*, the cell phone, the man's comments—all are signs which represent a text that can be read. But when we read these signs together they help us make sense of the larger text (the man) and the larger text than that (Wall Street) and an even larger text than that (America). As you may have guessed by now, this act of reading can even help you make sense of the largest text of all—the world—in both literal and mythical ways.

Because we are always trying to make sense of the world, because we are always reading, we often find ourselves in semiotic situations. This book builds on your own methods of reading and tries to sharpen them so that you will become more critical and thoughtful readers of the complex text that is our world. We keep returning to the reading metaphor because it aptly describes the process of making sense of our surroundings. When we read a poem or a short story, we pay attention to detail: we look for symbols, metaphors, and hidden themes. We "read between the lines." To read between the lines means to read not only what's there, but what's *not* there. We do this frequently as well; we "read into things." Beer commercials never come right out and suggest that attractive, straight, single women will immediately become attracted to straight men if the men drink a certain kind of beer, but that is implied in almost every ad. People we are interested in dating may not tell us what kind of people they are, where they come from, what kind of music they like or what their political leanings are, but by paying attention to the clothes they wear or the comments they make, we may be able to begin to piece together a better interpretation of the text that is this person. In other words, we already know how to read books and poems, but we also know how to read the world itself. This book will help you bring together your ideas from formal and informal, conscious and unconscious reading.

## TEXTS, THE WORLD, YOU, AND YOUR PAPERS

Hopefully, by now you understand what we mean by reading the world as a text, and this approach seems both comfortable and interesting to you. However, you are probably wondering how any of this figures into your freshman writing course. As you have probably figured out by this time in your academic career, writing is fundamentally connected to reading and to thinking. In fact, the great British novelist E.M. Forster (*A Room with a View* and *Howard's End*) once wrote, "How can I tell what I think till I see what I've said?" To our knowledge, there has never been a great writer who was not also a great thinker. What's more, to be a great thinker and a great writer, we must also be great readers. Writing is so intimately tied to thinking and thinking so intimately tied to the act of *reading* the world and one's surroundings, that the three form a kind of trinity of articulation and expression:

Of course, by "reading" we mean not only reading books and newspapers and magazines but the semiotic situation or the nontraditional text, the practice of reading the world. Writing, thinking, and reading are a symbiotic process, a cycle in which they feed off and influence each other. Thus, if we are reading and thinking, then the chances are we will be better prepared to do good writing.

Good writing is also grounded on solid rhetorical principles, as is good reading (as we have broadly defined it so far). Rhetoric comes from the Greek word *rhetorik*, which means to turn or to swerve. Today, when we think of something as being rhetorical, we think of argumentation or persuasion. This definition hasn't changed much from Aristotle's original assertion that rhetoric is "the faculty of observing in any given case the available means of persuasion." We hope this book improves your faculty for observing how texts use persuasion, just as your writing course will help you write persuasive essays. We like I.A. Richards' claim that rhetoric is a philosophic inquiry into how words work in discourse or public discussion. That means that as a reader and a writer, you are figuring out the relationship between words, signs, and culture. Our goal is to help you learn to see the rhetorical strategies of various texts and also to get you started writing your own. We are firm believers that textual analysis (reading) and textual formation (writing) jointly contribute to the larger process of knowledge making. Thus, we are interested in helping you to ask not simply *what* something means but *how* something means. This is why reading will help your writing: it teaches you how to be savvy consumers and producers of texts. You'll get to know texts from the inside out.

Part of that process will necessarily include writing. Writers and thinkers have long seen writing as a means of helping us think. When we think abstractly, we tend to gloss over ideas so fast that we don't slow down and articulate them. They are more sensations than thought. To put them down on paper, to compose them into sentences, ideas, reasons, is harder than thinking. Indeed, if you have done freewriting exercises, you may have had no idea what you thought about something until you wrote it down. It's no surprise that journaling or keeping a diary is vitally important to writers. The act of writing can often be an act of unlocking: the door opens and ideas, reactions, fears, and hopes walk right out of your head and on to the page and say "Here I am!" Sometimes, we wish they had stayed inside, but this is where the interesting work happens, and here is where learning to read the world as a text can help you as you learn to write on a college level. Learning to write well allows us to move outside of the box and out into the world of ideas, interaction, and exchange. And learning to read outside our traditional ideas of what it means to read will expand your mind even further.

Writing about the world as a text may not only facilitate writing and thinking but writing and feeling. While we certainly do not want to diminish the logical aspect of writing, we want to pay attention to a component of writing that is often overlooked, and that is the emotional component. Franz Kafka, Emily Dickinson, Pablo Neruda and dozens of other writers turned and continue to turn to writing because it simply made and makes them feel good. Writing is or can be rewarding, refreshing, rejuvenating. In part, writing means sharing, participating in a community of language and ideas. We learn about others and ourselves through writing because writing is simultaneously self-exploration and self-examination. We see ourselves in a larger context. Of course, we may not always like what we discover (perhaps traces of sexism or racism or classism), but uncovering those elements of our personality and understanding them is an extremely rewarding experience. Writing that is honest, candid, and reflective attracts us because those are traits we value.

At the same time, we do not want to neglect the idea that writing is a difficult process to master. Between them, the authors have written thousands of papers, articles, handouts, tests, reports, and now this book. In almost every case, they went through multiple drafts, stared at the computer screen, cursed whatever picture was on the wall for its interference, and struggled at various points along the way. In fact, this very introduction went through between fifteen and twenty drafts. In some ways, writing is very much like exercising: it doesn't always feel great when you are doing it, but when you are finished it is both rewarding and good for you. Both the authors are *drafters* by nature—we believe that while writing is a form of thinking, several drafts are often needed to make that thinking into something worth showing the public.

By now, you should be beginning to see some direct connections between writing and reading. Only by reading well can you write well. A good essay is an essay that makes sense of a topic using detail, insight and purpose—the same traits one uses to read. We believe that the readings and questions in this book will be a good springboard for that writing process. Some of the essays may anger you, but that's okay. Some will make you laugh, some will confuse you, and some will make you see a movie or a place or a gender in ways you never have before. We hope that these essays not only will show you what writing can do but that the readings in this book will spark your imagination, that these readings will push you toward the writing process so that your own work will be as vigorous and as provocative as the essays presented here.

## LEARNING TO READ THE WORLD AS A TEXT: THREE CASE STUDIES

In this section, we want to walk you through the act of interpretation, of reading semiotically; that is, we want to help you read certain texts in ways that you may find unfamiliar. However, as articulated earlier, we feel that living critically in the world means living as an informed, questioning, engaged person. Learning to read the world as a text is a good way to begin.

### Reading Public Space: Starbucks

One of the most familiar places in our modern world is the coffee shop, and in particular, Starbucks. As a ubiquitous presence, it could make for an interesting "read"—many ideas about the world could come from reading a Starbucks. With this in mind, we sat down one morning in a Starbucks and did a reading.

We began with note taking, just writing down what we saw and thought. This is a transcribed version.

> **Note taking:** brown, green, red, brown patterned carpet.
> Green
> Lighting non-fluorescent
> Curves
> Wood—metal
> Tables different types
> Products art—decoration
> Logo "coffee-related art" photos
> Baby chairs, modern garbage cans
> Advertisements, baskets, games, "Cranium" wood
> Handicapped bathrooms—*The New York Times*, windows, mahogany, metal door handles, pull to get in, push
> Music: "cool," varied

With this information we can begin to construct a series of observations that could develop into ideas:

> Starbucks relies on moderate earth tones for decoration.
> Their seating places are made of durable materials.
> Their artwork is a mix of coffee photographs and advertisements.
> There is lots of light. The lighting they use is bright but not harsh, avoiding fluorescent light.
> Their advertisements are prominent within the store. Their products are geared to the middle and upper classes both by design and content. (Oops—an argument slipped in!)

As you can see by the last statement, in the process of writing down observations, arguments about the text itself may slip in, which is what we were hoping for. In this case, the idea that Starbucks is geared toward a particular target audience is an argument and potentially one that you might pursue in a paper. How could you make this a paper? You could expand the idea of a target audience into multiple paragraphs: one about products, another about décor, maybe one about music, and perhaps another about the location of the particular Starbucks you are in.

If we were going to construct a thesis statement, it might sound like this: Starbucks appeals to the middle and upper classes through a combination of its décor, music, products and location.

Well, that thesis statement is okay and would work to organize a paper, but it is still pretty vague. We could ask why Starbucks wants to sell its wares to a particular demographic through its design—well, we know this already, they are a commercial venture. But the question of "how" still raises itself—we can see the target audience and the tools, but how they are using them is a different story. Maybe another question is this: What is Starbucks trying to sell *besides* coffee? What experience can someone hope to get by entering Starbucks? We would argue that Starbucks is trying to sell an idea of "cool" or "hip" to its customers. And for its target audience of middle and upper class people—cool is something these people may feel they need to buy. So a new thesis could be: "Starbucks tries to sell its idea of cool to the middle and upper classes through its hip music, sturdy, smooth décor, its sleek and streamlined products."

This could still improve, but notice that this thesis gives you an automatic organization of paragraphs about décor, music, merchandise, and location.

## Reading a Poem: "The Red Wheelbarrow"

It's likely that your professor will ask you to write a paper on one of the literary texts in this book. While you may have had some practice writing basic literary papers in high school, you may not have much experience thinking and writing about poetry on a sophisticated level. Let's say your instructor wants you to write an analytical paper on a poem. We know that many of you become very nervous, very anxious in the presence of poetry, but we want to calm your fears a bit. Poems are nothing more than words placed strategically to create an enhanced reading experience. To make sense of a poem, all you need to do is slow down and look at the individual components. Much of poetry is instinctual, so trust your reactions, and trust your observations. Write things down. We would encourage you to make notes in the margins of your book or handout.

To help you in learning how better to read a poem, we will walk you through a reading process for a short but puzzling poem. We've chosen William Carlos Williams' famous (or infamous) poem "The Red Wheelbarrow":

**The Red Wheelbarrow**

so much depends
upon

the red wheel
barrow

glazed with rain
water

beside the white
chickens.

Before we try to figure out what this poem might "mean," let's take a couple of steps back and look *at* the poem before looking *through* it. If, as we suggest, the world is a constructed text that can be read semiotically, then so can a poem. If you look at the poem's design, its shape, what do you see? First of all, the poem is very short and has extremely compact lines. In fact, the second line of each stanza only has one word. You may also see that the poem is very symmetrical. As you noticed, the second line of each stanza has one word, while the first line of every stanza has three words. So there are four words per stanza and four stanzas in the poem. Also, as students have noted, each of the four stanzas look like little square wheelbarrows. Additionally, you may have seized on the kinds of words Williams places in the second lines—"upon," "barrow," "water," and "chickens." All have two syllables and, except for "upon," all are concrete nouns. Very interesting, you may be thinking, but how can reading the poem this way help me understand what the poem *means*?

In poetry, form usually contributes to content, which is to say that how a poem looks and sounds and feels probably has a lot to do with the message it's trying to send. In any poem, look at what words are stressed, where lines end and the next line (or stanza) begins. Like a cinematographer, the poet controls where your eye goes both as a reader and as a viewer. As one of our students jotted in her reading journal, "the sound stops on the nouns and so does your eye." Indeed, it is as though Williams is creating visually what he accomplishes through language. So, if we transfer this observation over to what he might be trying to do thematically, we see that the form of the poem (how it looks and sounds) resembles its theme (what it says or means). It seems as though the meaning of the poem lies in these concrete words "barrow," "water," and "chickens." What kind of words are these? One student noted that "all three words are basic things—

a tool, an animal, and a mineral." That is an excellent observation, and it tells us a great deal. But the poem is not simply a picture of chickens, water, and wheelbarrows. There is something more: namely, the first stanza. The first line of every novel, short story, and poem is often profoundly important, as it sets the stage for the entire text. Here, the first line does a great deal of work. How would the text be different if the poem began without the "So much depends / upon"?

We are left to wonder *what* depends upon these things. What does depend upon chickens, water, and a wheelbarrow? A lawyer? A textbook author? A student? A farmer? Perhaps one reading of the poem is that for a farmer or a rancher, his or her entire life depends upon rain, animals, and equipment. But would Williams construct such a visual text merely to make a comment about what a farmer needs? Remember, the poem is also a visual text, and as such, demands to be looked at in a certain way. As we have already noted, you may find that each of the four stanzas looks like a little wheelbarrow, effectively creating a picture of four square wheelbarrows. Perhaps a literal reading only gives us partial understanding of the poem. A larger meaning might come from the visuals of the poem—how we *see* the poem and the world. If we can look at a poem and see wheelbarrows, perhaps we can look at wheelbarrows and see poetry. A fuller reading of the poem would take the form and the content into account and suggest that so much depends upon how we see the everyday objects of the world. Of course, this is but one reading of the poem, but we think it's a good one given the connections we made between how the poem looked and the words in it.

This leads to a larger point. When reading a poem or a short story, it's very important to pay close attention to the details of the text. Instead of making the poem bigger than it is (thinking a poem is about God or death or the devil or birth), try to see the poem as something *smaller* than you think it is. Look at its individual components. See how they come together.

## Reading an Advertisement

Though you may only read poetry now and again, you probably read advertisements on a daily basis. On television, on the radio, in magazines, on the Web and now even at the movies, we confront advertisements in almost every aspect of our lives. Researchers suggest we see between 100 and 300 advertisements per day, whereas it would probably be unusual if you were to read 100 poems in an entire year. What's more, most experts agree that the American public believes or is open to at least one advertisement out of every eight that it sees. That may not sound like much, but if you see 100 ads per day for 365 days, that's 36,500 ads per year. If researchers are correct, then you probably believe or consider at least 4,562 per year. Think that's a lot? Consider this. The average 19-year-old has probably been paying attention to advertisements for about thirteen years. So, if these estimates are correct, most 19-year-old Americans have taken into their consciousness and devoted some aspect of their reasoning ability to over 59,000 ads over the course of their lifetime. If you are 19, then you have likely seen over 450,000 ads. By the time you are thirty, it's probable that over one million ads will have made their way into your brain.

By now, it is a cliché to claim that ads sell an image but . . . ads sell an image. They not only sell images of us and their products but also of a culture. In advertiser's lingo, this is called the "promise." Ads make promises to people all the time, but these tend to be implied or suggested promises. When you read an advertisement, ask yourself what kind of promise the ad is making to you. But ads also work to cultivate another image—their own. This is why so many companies are very protective of their names, trademarks, and product usage. For instance, you may be familiar with the recent court case in which Mattel toys sued the rock band Aqua over a critical song about "Barbie." And, in an example closer to home, we were denied permission from Tommy Hilfiger to reprint the advertisement we describe below. So, keep in mind that while ads may be funny and informative and persuasive, they help promote the company's image.

Thus, reading the image that a company tries to cultivate is all part of the larger experience of reading an advertising text. And now that you've had some background on advertising and some practice reading public space and poetry, we're going to walk you through the process of reading an ad. We have chosen a popular Tommy Hilfiger ad that features six young, handsome/beautiful, smiley people (two white men, two black men, a white woman, and a black woman) lounging around in red, white, and blue Hilfiger clothes on the expansive front lawn of a country home. The large house stands in the right corner of the photo, and in the upper left-hand corner of the photo, a big American flag waves just over the left shoulder of one of the models. Advertising Tommy cologne, the ad's tag line reads in large white letters along the bottom, "tommy: the real american fragrance."

When we began to read this ad so that we could write about it (the same process you will engage in), we asked ourselves, what textual cues are in the ad? Here is what we saw: In this ad for Tommy Hilfiger cologne, all the people in the photograph are young, well scrubbed, and attractive. And they are happy! Now, what about the setting of the photograph? Where does it take place? It appears to be a rural area, perhaps a country club or a farmhouse in New England. What other textual cues or signs do you see? In this ad, we see a large American flag waving in the upper-left hand corner of the ad. The text, "tommy: the real american fragrance," runs along the bottom fourth of the image, while a picture of the featured cologne balances the flag in the bottom right-hand corner. Smaller than the American flag but similar to it, the Tommy Hilfiger logo hovers above the writing, but seems to be affixed to the white woman's body.

Then we asked ourselves, how do we describe the appearance of the people in the ad? How are they dressed? Well, for one thing, they are all wearing Tommy Hilfiger clothes. This tells us a lot. What is the demographic for Tommy Hilfiger clothes? Who buys them? Who hangs out in large, well-kept farmhouses in New England, who spends time at a country club? The answer to all of these questions seems to be middle-class or upper-middle-class white Americans, though the ad suggests that Tommy Hilfiger clothes and cologne appeal to a plurality of people—perhaps even that Tommy clothes and cologne promise racial harmony, an upper-middle-class lifestyle, *and* a good time.

But is this so? We decided to make a list of who or what is missing—what is *not* in this picture. Off the top of our heads, we came up with quite a list: people who look poor, anyone over 30, any sign of work (a briefcase, a shovel, a computer, a uniform), anyone who is even remotely overweight, a Mexican flag, a tenement building, any sign of anger, Native Americans, anything having to do with a city, any reference to a blue collar or working class situation, clothes other than Tommy Hilfiger clothes, people who are unattractive, reading material such as books or a newspaper, and finally, any clue as to what these people are doing dressed in Tommy Hilfiger clothes out in the country. What message does the absence of these things send? Is this ad suggesting something about the role of these things in the "real America"? We don't know exactly, but by asking these questions we might come closer to understanding not only the ad, but the culture from which it comes and the culture it tries to sell.

Advertisers use various techniques to get us to respond to their ads, most of which involve making the viewer feel desired, accepted, important, or exclusive. What individual techniques does this ad use to make us feel these things? The flag? The pretty, happy people sitting close together? The sense of affluence suggested by the large house out in the country? The sense of racial harmony evoked by the people of various ethnicities laughing together? Now, when you combine all of these cues, what is the overall argument or promise of the ad? Take this one step further: what does this text suggest about how Tommy Hilfiger, the company, sees itself? And, what does this text suggest about how Tommy Hilfiger, the company, sees America? Does this version of America mesh with your own? Does this version of America reflect mainstream American values?

Though we ended up with more questions than answers here, finding what questions to ask helps us understand the text we're looking at. In more general terms, learning how to read advertisements will not only make you more aware about companies and how they market their products and themselves but also how mainstream advertising and media outlets create a vision or even a myth of our culture. What's more (and perhaps at this moment, most important to you), learning how to read advertisements, poems, and public spaces will help you write better papers, as the reading process is fundamentally linked to the writing process.

## READING THIS TEXT AS A TEXT

As you can see, the process of writing a paper involves posing a number of questions about the text you are writing, looking closely at your paper, and trying to organize and arrange an argument. Of course, this process is the same for *reading* a text; both involve thinking and in particular, explorative thinking. We hope that you see the necessary connections between reading and writing, writing and reading and that you understand how the processes of both facilitate the other. Learning to read with care, insight, knowledge, and openness will help you write with those same qualities.

We hope that our book is written with insight, knowledge, and openness, just as we hope that you will read it with such. To augment this, we are going to give you a brief overview of the rest of the book, so that you can become a particularly good reader of the text that is *The World Is a Text*. To that end, we have arranged the book to help you with the writing and the reading processes. We'll begin with an overview of the writing section.

### The World Is a Text: Writing

Let us be clear at the outset that we have designed our section on writing as an *introduction* to the writing process. By no means should you consider this section a comprehensive guide to constructing papers. Our section here is merely an overture to the symphony that is your paper. Virtually no other books of this kind discuss the difficult process of transitioning from high school writing to college writing. *The World Is a Text* is unique in this regard, as we begin our section on writing with a short explanation of how college essays differ from high school essays. The segment entitled "How Do I Write a Text for College? Making the Transition from High School Writing" is not so much a nuts and bolts essay as it is a description of how your thinking (and therefore your writing) process will need to change to do college level writing. We think you'll find this segment very helpful, and we recommend that you read it first.

One of the most difficult challenges facing beginning college writers is figuring out what they want to say in their papers. Actually settling on a thesis can be frustrating. Sadly, there is no guaranteed remedy for the malady of the elusive thesis; however, we have provided some steps that should make the thesis process slightly less anxiety provoking in the next segment. "How Do I Make an Argument about a Building? Strategies for Constructing a Thesis and Building a Good Paper" walks you through the process of moving from a topic to a thesis by helping you hone in on what it is you are trying to argue. Sometimes, we make assertions and don't even know it. This section should help you arrive at a tenable thesis.

Next, we offer a brief but useful overview of how you might go about writing a paper on a popular culture text in "How Do I Write about Movies?

A Tour Through the Writing Process." Even if you are writing a descriptive paper or an analytical essay, generally, you will need to have some kind of thesis. This segment will walk you through the entire writing process, beginning with brainstorming and ending with the glorious act of turning in the paper. Naturally, you should follow the guidelines your instructor provides for you; however, if she or he does not give you specific guidelines to follow, we believe that you will find it most helpful to follow the process outlined in this portion of the text when writing your own papers.

It is quite common for instructors to assign a personal essay as the first major assignment in a first-year writing class. To help you with this assignment, we have provided an overview of the personal essay. "How Am I a Text? On Writing Personal Essays" suggests the ways in which you are a text, worthy and ready to be read. You have a wealth of experiences and a mind full of ideas. This segment offers some very solid advice that should facilitate the move from private topic to public writing.

Finally, we end this segment with some information on researching popular culture texts. If you have to write a research paper in your course, pay very close attention to this segment. The simple act of going to the library and figuring out how and where to look can be intimidating, but we have broken it down into a manageable process.

Even though we think this section will provide a good entree into the book as a whole, there is a wealth of information out there. Online writing labs like those at Purdue University and the University of Texas are accessible on the World Wide Web and have more detailed information than we can provide here. For more complete descriptions of writing, rhetoric and the construction of papers, consult our sister publication *Strategies for Successful Writing: A Rhetoric, Research Guide, Reader, and Handbook*, edited by James A. Reinking, Andrew W. Hart, and Robert von der Osten (also published by Prentice Hall).

## The World Is a Text: Reading

Of course, this is the most important section of the book—the section where you will spend most of your time. To make navigation of these chapters easy for you, we have designed each chapter the same way, so you should have no trouble navigating the readings, the worksheets, or the questions. You will find the following in each chapter:

I. Introduction
II. Worksheet
III. Readings
    General essays
    a. questions (This Text: Reading/Your Text: Writing)
    Suite of readings
    b. questions (This Text Reading/Your Text: Writing)

IV. Reading Outside the Lines
  a. Classroom exercises
  b. Essay ideas

In the book, we have several goals. We want to help you become a better reader of the world generally and a better reader of texts like television and movies specifically. We also want to make you a better reader of essays about those topics. We remain confident that your increased abilities as a reader will translate into better writing.

To help with these missions, the book focuses both on the texts like public space and art, and readings about these texts. Our introductions orient you to the text being read and to some basic questions and issues surrounding these areas of study. Following the introduction in each chapter is a worksheet which focuses on both the readings in the chapter and interpretation of the general text (like gender or public space). Read these worksheets closely *before* you read the rest of the chapter.

Each chapter contains essays that focus on different aspects of texts like television and race and then a group of texts about a particular topic—called "suites"—such as *The Simpsons* (television) or the controversial *Sensation* exhibition (visual arts). These grouped essays are to show the different ways you might approach a topic with the hope that you can use some of these ideas in approaching your own interpretation of television shows or paintings. In analyzing these essays, your will develop a better sense of how writers write.

As you read, your primary objective will be to identify the author's main points, the argument or arguments she or he tries to make. This is called the author's "rhetorical strategy," and deciphering a rhetorical strategy is just like reading any other kind of text. You will want to pay attention to the evidence that the author uses to make his or her point. Does she use statistics, personal experience, research, rumor, or the experiences of others? Read each entry at least twice. On the first reading, make notes. If there is a word you don't recognize or an idea that puzzles you, underline or highlight it. Try to find the author's thesis, and mark that. Underline other important points throughout the piece. On your second read, take your level of analysis one step further by asking questions about the passages you underlined. This process will help your transition into writing.

After each entry, you will find two sets of questions. The first set, called "This Text: Reading," is designed to help you understand the text you have just read. The second set, entitled "Your Text: Writing," will help get you started writing about the text (public space, music, race, etc.) or the article itself.

Following the texts are some supplemental items that should help with class discussion and will assist you in thinking about a paper topic. In many of the chapters, we've also included a sample student paper. These are papers actually written by our students on the same topics and texts as you, so that you can see how someone in a similar semiotic situation might turn a text to read into a text to be written. We are not suggesting that you mimic these papers: we want to give you an idea of how such a paper might look. Not all are examples of stellar writing, but if you and your instructors go over them in class, they will help you visualize your own papers.

Finally, since you have worked your way through this rather long introduction to *reading* texts, we thought it might be useful for you if we read our own text. We like this book a lot; in fact, we feel very strongly about its premise: that you can become a better writer, a better student, that you can *be* in the world more fully if you are a critical, thoughtful, insightful reader of the world around you.

Our book relies on the premise that we are always reading and interpreting consciously or not. *The World Is a Text*'s goals are to 1) help you understand the relationship between reading traditional texts such as novels, short stories, and poems and other less traditional texts such as movies, the Internet, art works, and television. Equally important, 2) we want you to discover that perhaps the most valuable way of learning about the world is through writing about it. Last, and perhaps most important, 3) we want you to learn to read your surroundings actively. The first two premises are geared more toward academic achievement; the third is oriented toward helping you become a better citizen of the world, a more active participant in the world in which you live.

Some of you may take exception to specific aspects of this book. Particular images, individual essays, or even parts of our introductions may make you mad, they may upset you, and they may challenge some of your most secure assumptions. We think that is good. We believe critical inquiry is part of the college experience. Another kind of problem that you or your instructor may have with our book is what is *not* in it. We understand that there are many texts we could have included in these chapters. It pains us to think of all the great stories, essays, poems, and art works that we had to leave out. But such is the nature of textbooks. There are also many different texts we could have read, such as sports, video games, cars, business, relationships, and families. But we wanted to leave some things out there for you to explore on your own.

## SO, THE WORLD IS A TEXT: WHAT CAN YOU DO WITH IT?

Though digesting the book's contents is a lifetime project, a project the authors still regularly undertake and refine, our hope is that after reading this book and writing your papers that you will engage the world more actively. Doing so will make you more of an actor in your own show and enable you to understand your role in the world.

We are not saying the book will have immediate measurable effects, but the more you engage the world as a text, the more you will see subtleties as well as potential forms of manipulation. You may notice the beauty of a public courtyard or the ugliness of a building. You may find yourself arguing with film directors, questioning the structure of a sitcom, and raising objections about a political ad. But engaging the world need not be a grim, political task. You may also find that you are able to see the subtle beauty in a house in your neighborhood or the amusing effectiveness of an ad or the cleverness of a lyric. Developing higher critical faculties also allows you more control of them. Students sometimes complain that English teachers "read too much" into things or that "we're taking the fun out of watching television." If we do these things, it has to do with our ability to turn our critical abilities on and off; thinking almost becomes a new toy once you realize you can understand the world better and in different ways. Don't get us wrong—we watch dumb movies just as you do. However, if we want to engage that dumb movie—to better examine its particular dumbness—we can do that too.

We want you to have the same abilities; more than the particular skill of watching movies, we want you to engage the world more actively. In doing so, you may enhance, in all sorts of ways, the text that is your life.

*Note on format:* This book is formatted in Modern Language Association style, known by most scholars and teachers as "MLA style." Throughout the book, however, you will see several other styles of formatting including American Psychological Association (APA), Chicago or Turabian, and AP style. Each discipline such as English or history or psychology has its own preferred form. Because the book covers so many different types of texts and crosses disciplines, and our readers will come from many disciplines, we have decided to keep to the original style of the article or book portion we are reprinting whenever possible.

# The World Is a Text
# WRITING

## HOW DO I WRITE A TEXT FOR COLLEGE? MAKING THE TRANSITION FROM HIGH SCHOOL WRITING

*by Patty Strong*

Writing is thinking. This is what we teachers of college writing believe. Hidden inside that tiny suitcase of a phrase is my whole response to the topic assigned me by my colleague, Jonathan Silverman, one of the authors of the textbook you are currently reading. Knowing my background as a former teacher of high school English, Dr. Silverman asked me to write a piece for students on the differences between writing in high school and writing in college. I have had some time to ponder my answer, and it is this: Writing is thinking. Now that's not very satisfactory, is it? I must unpack that suitcase of a phrase. I will open it up for you, pull out a few well traveled and wearable ideas, ideas that you may want to try on yourself as you journey through your college writing assignments.

Writing is thinking. I suggest that this idea encompasses the differences between high school writing and the writing expected from students on a college level, not because high school teachers don't expect their students to think, but rather that most students themselves do not approach the writing as an *opportunity to think*. Students might construct many other kinds of sentences with writing as subject: Writing is hard. Writing is a duty. Writing is something I do to prove that I know something.

When I taught high school English, I certainly assigned writing in order to find out what my students knew. Did they, for example, know what I had taught them about the light and dark symbolism in chapter 18 of *The Scarlet Letter*? Did they know precisely what Huck Finn said after he reconsidered his letter to Miss Watson ("All right, then, I'll *go* to hell!") and did they know what I, their teacher, had told them those words meant in terms of Huck's moral development? Could my students spit this information back at me in neat, tidy sentences? That's not to say I didn't encourage originality and creativity in my students' writing, but those were a sort of bonus to the bottom line knowledge I was expecting them to be able to reproduce.

College writing is different precisely because it moves beyond the limited conception that writing is writing what we already know. In college, students write to discover what they don't know, to uncover what they didn't know they knew. Students in college should not worry about not having anything to write, because it is the physical and intellectual act of writing, of moving that pen across the page (or tapping the keyboard) that produces the thoughts that become what you have to write. The act of writing will produce the thinking. This thinking need not produce ideas you already know to be true, but should explore meanings and attitude and questions, which are the things that we all wonder and care about.

My discussion of these matters has so far been fairly abstract, caught up in the wind of ideas. Practical matters are of importance here, too, so I will address some points that as a college student you should know. First, your professors are not responsible for your education—you are. While your teachers may in fact care very much that you learn and do well in your coursework, it is not their responsibility to see that you are successful. Your college teacher may not do things you took for granted like reminding you of assignments and tests and paper deadlines. They probably won't accept your illness or the illness of a loved one or a fight with a girlfriend as legitimate excuses for late work. Sloppy work, late work, thoughtless work, tardiness, absences from class—these things are the student's problems. Successful college students accept responsibility for their problems. They expect that consequences will be meted out. Successful students do not offer excuses, lame or otherwise, although they may offer appropriate resolutions. Successful students understand that their education is something they are privileged to own, and as with a dear possession, they must be responsible for managing it. If you wrecked your beloved car, would you find fault with the person who taught you how to drive?

On to the writing task at hand. You will want to write well in college. You probably want to write better and more maturely than you have in the past. To do this, you must be willing to take thinking risks, which are writing risks. I read an interesting quote the other day that I shared with my writing students because I believed it to be true and pretty profound. The American writer Alvin Toffler wrote that "The illiterate of the twenty-first century will not be those who cannot read and write, but those who cannot learn, unlearn, and relearn." And so it's true that when you come to the university for your "higher education" you must be willing to unlearn some old things and relearn them in new ways. That's probably true for just about every academic subject you will explore during your university career, and it is certainly true about the writing courses you will take.

Writing is thinking. Writing will lead you toward thought. Your college writing teachers will expect more of your thinking, thinking you have come to through the process of writing and rewriting. In order to get where you need to be, you must relearn what writing is. You must see that writing is not duty, obligation, and regurgitation, but opportunity, exploration, and discovery. The realization that writing is thinking and that thinking *leads* to writing is the main idea behind this book—the simple notion that the world is a text to be thought and written about. The successful college writer understands that he or she writes not just for the teacher, not just to prove something to the teacher in order to get a grade, but to uncover unarticulated pathways to knowledge and understanding.

## HOW DO I MAKE AN ARGUMENT ABOUT A BUILDING? STRATEGIES FOR CONSTRUCTING A THESIS AND BUILDING A GOOD PAPER

We will preface this section with a disclaimer. While we believe the information we provide here is universally useful and pertinent, you should always adhere to the directions your instructor gives you. You can, and probably should, use the material here to augment your professor's directions, but it should not supplant what your professor gives you.

### Constructing a Good Thesis

That being said, we'll move on to helping you construct a thesis and build a paper. The most important first step is to distinguish among a topic, a thesis, and a thesis statement. Let's say you are writing a paper about Affirmative Action. The topic is what you are writing about, which is Affirmative Action. Your thesis is the argument you are making about Affirmative Action. Your thesis statement is the actual articulation, the statement in which you unpack or explain your thesis. Now, a thesis statement does not have to be (nor should it be) one simplified sentence; in fact, it could and probably should be two or three sentences, or even a full paragraph. So, we might break down these three components as follows:

*Topic:* what you are writing about (Affirmative Action)

*Thesis:* what you argue *about* your topic (Affirmative Action is a necessary law)

*Thesis statement:* the reason or explanation of your overall thesis—this usually appears in one or two paragraphs (Affirmative Action is a necessary law because it prevents discriminatory hiring practices. Minorities, women, people with disabilities and gay and lesbian workers have suffered discrimination for decades. Affirmative Action not only redresses past wrongs but sets a level playing field for all job applicants. In short, it ensures democracy.)

The topic is generally the least of your concerns. Your instructor will help you with your topic and may even provide one for you. The real task of writing a paper is figuring out your thesis. You should note that while we will use the word "thesis" throughout, we remain mindful that it is an imperfect term. Your instructor may prefer "focus," "controlling idea," or "argument," all of which are good terms. However, "thesis," as you will see in a minute, is preferable to us because of its etymology (what the roots of the word mean together).

Many students worry that they do not have a thesis when they begin their paper. That's normal, and in a way preferable in the quest to find a thesis that is truly an argument. Sometimes it's enough to have what we might refer to as a "thesis question"—a question that when answered through writing and perhaps research will give you your thesis. Often you will have to write a first draft of your essay before a thesis finally emerges. Remember that writing is exploration, is discovery. So it may take some freewriting, brainstorming, outlining, and drafting before you really land on a thesis. But stay with it. You'll find it.

Perhaps the most confusing aspect of the thesis for students is the realization that a good thesis means you might be wrong! In fact, you will know you are on the right track to a good thesis, if you think someone might be able to argue *against* your point. Writing is grounded in rhetoric, a Greek term for argument or persuasion. Your goal in your papers is not to sway your audience but to get them to consider your ideas. Thus your thesis needs to be something that you can argue about. The most effective strategy we've found with our students is to use the example of the hypo*thesis*. As most of you know, a hypothesis is an educated guess. A thesis is the same thing. In the Greek, thesis means a proposition, an idea. Hypo is Greek for "under" or "beneath." So, literally, a hypothesis is a "proposition laid down." Your thesis is the same thing. It is not a fact; it is not a statement. It is an idea, a proposition that you lay down on paper and then set out to support. You are not absolutely sure that Affirmative Action is a necessary law, but you believe it is. You are pretty sure it is, but you also know that someone could write an essay arguing why it should be abolished. This disagreement is how you know you have a good thesis, because you will have to provide good reasons and convincing examples to support your assertion about the necessity for Affirmative Action.

Why does a thesis need to be an educated guess? Because if a thesis is a statement of fact, you have nothing to argue. If your thesis is "Affirmative Action is a law that was designed to prevent discrimination," you have nothing to argue. There is nothing at stake, nothing to debate. Even a thesis like "Affirmative Action is an important law" is rather weak. Virtually no one would suggest that Affirmative Action is not important. It has been extraordinarily important in American culture. So, again, that is not the best thesis you could come up with, though it remains better than our first example. However, arguing that it is a *necessary* law makes your thesis more provocative, more risky. Therefore, it is likely to draw interest, to get people excited. They will want to see your reasons and think about the examples you provide.

So, to recap. Let's say you are writing on the essays in Chapter 7 in this book. Your topic is censorship and the *Sensation* exhibit.

> *Weak thesis:* The *Sensation* exhibit in New York raised a lot of questions about censorship and public money.

This is a weak thesis because it is a statement of fact. No one would debate this point.

> *Better thesis:* The *Sensation* exhibit in New York deserved to run its course despite public opinion.

This is a better thesis because it proposes something a bit controversial. Many people, including the mayor of New York at the time, would argue against this thesis. That tells you that you are on the right track.

> *Even better thesis:* It was important that the *Sensation* exhibit in New York was not cancelled, despite public opposition, because freedom of speech and freedom of expression are critical parts of American ideas of liberty.

This thesis is even better because it provides a bit more precision and it gives a reason. It will be easier, then, for this writer to prove the thesis because the reason is already articulated.

## Building a Good Paper

Building a good paper is relatively simple, once you understand the formula. By formula, we do not mean a standard five-paragraph essay. Instead of thinking of your paper in terms of numbers of paragraphs, think of your paper in terms of numbers of reasons. If you are arguing about Affirmative Action, how many reasons do you want to include in your paper to support your point? Do you want seven? No, that's too many. One? That's too few. Generally, we suggest two to four reasons for a standard three to six page paper. If you are writing a longer paper, like a research paper, then you may want four or five reasons to drive home your point. But the danger of including too many reasons in your paper is that they wind up having the opposite of the intended effect. Rather than bolstering your argument by the sheer number of reasons, you tend to weaken it because you dilute it. Instead of writing one paragraph on six reasons, write three paragraphs on three reasons. That way, you can go in depth and prove your points with insight, clarity and thoroughness.

The key to this approach is the paragraph. Paragraphs are the building blocks for your essay. Every paragraph is like a mini-essay. Just as your essay has a thesis statement, so does your paragraph have a topic sentence—a sentence in which you lay out the main idea for that paragraph. Once you write your topic sentence, set out to provide examples to support your claims. For instance, let's say your topic sentence is: "The *Sensation* exhibit was an important test for American culture because First Amendment rights were at stake." What might be your next move? You should probably quote the First Amendment, or at least part of it. Then, explain how the *Sensation* exhibit was protected by the First Amendment. Give examples of specific pieces from the show that are pertinent to this discussion. This is also the right time to bring in quotes from other people that support your assertions. If you quote from another source, or if you quote from a primary text, be sure you explain how the passage you've quoted supports your thesis. The quote can't do that itself—you have to tell your audience why that quote is important. Finally, and this is very important, end your paragraphs well. The most common mistake students make when writing paragraphs is that they tend to trail off. Make that last sentence a kind of connector—make it tie everything in the paragraph back to the topic sentence.

Start on your next paragraph with the same model. Keep doing this until you have yourself a paper. Then go back and revise and edit, revise and edit, revise and edit.

## Some Final Tips

- Distinguish between a topic and a thesis.
- Your thesis doesn't have to be one concise sentence; it can be several sentences, perhaps even an entire paragraph. It might even be helpful to think of your thesis as your focus, your idea that you are trying to support.
- "Thesis" comes from "hypothesis." A hypothesis is an educated guess. So is your thesis. It's an educated guess, an idea that you are trying to support. You don't have to develop an over-the-top airtight argument, you simply want your reader to consider your point of view.
- Writing is conversation; it is dialogue. Keep asking questions of yourself, your writing and your topic. Ask yourself, "Why is this so?" Make sure you answer. *Be specific; be thorough.*
- Consider your audience. You should never assume they have read the text you are writing about, so don't toss around names or scenes without explaining them a little. It's called giving context. There is a big difference between giving context (valuable information) and summarizing the plot (regurgitation).
- *Five Steps to Writing a Good Paper*

  **1.** Formulate a good, supportable thesis.

2. Then, set out to explain or prove your thesis in well constructed paragraphs using your own interpretation and details from the text to support your points.
3. Quote from other sources or provide details from the primary text.
4. Explain *why* the passage you've quoted is important to your overall thesis.
5. Keep working through your paper in the same way.

## HOW DO I WRITE ABOUT MOVIES? A TOUR THROUGH THE WRITING PROCESS

We'd like to begin by underscoring how important the reading process is for the writing process. Both the reading process and the writing process are about discovery, insight, ordering, and argument. We don't want to spend too much time on this section because your instructor may have very specific directions for you about how she or he wants you to construct your paper, but we would like to offer a brief overview not so much of the process of completing or constructing a paper but the process of writing a paper. That is, in this section, we are less concerned with the product and more interested in the process.

The process of writing differs from the product of writing. When we say product, we are referring to the produced or finished version—the completed paper that you will submit to your instructor. The writing process is the always complex, sometimes arduous, often frustrating, and frequently rushed series of events that eventually lead you to the finished product. There are as many theories on and diagrams of the writing process as there are writers, so we will not bore you with an overview of all of them. Chances are, your instructor or your institution's writing center has a series of handouts or guidelines that will help you along the way, but we thought we would take you on a quick tour of what we see as the most important highlights of the writing process: getting the assignment, freewriting and brainstorming, deciding on a thesis, outlining, writing the first draft, editing and revising, editing and revising, editing and revising, turning in the finished product.

### Understanding the Assignment

This is usually the easiest part of the writing process, but it is also one of the most important. And because you are learning how to be savvy readers of various texts, this task should be easy for you. First of all, you should read the assignment for the paper as you would read a poem or an advertisement. Look for textual clues that seem particularly important. In fact, we recommend making a list of questions about the assignment itself:

- What questions do I have to answer in order to complete or answer the assignment? Do I have a research or writing question that my paper must answer?
- Does my assignment contain any code words, such as "compare," "analyze," "research," "unpack," or "explore"? If so, what do these terms mean?
- What text or texts am I supposed to write about? Do I understand these texts?
- What is my audience? Whom am I writing for?
- What are the parameters of the assignment? What can I do? What can I not do? Is there anything I don't understand before beginning?

One of the biggest mistakes students make is paying too little attention to the assignment. Like any text, it will contain textual cues to help you understand it.

## Freewriting and Brainstorming

Freewriting and brainstorming are crucial to the writing process because they generally produce your topic. While both freewriting and brainstorming are similar, there are some differences. Though there are no hard and fast rules here, we tend to think of freewriting as helping you land on a topic and brainstorming as helping you discover what you want to say about that topic. Freewriting involves the random and uncensored act of writing down anything that comes into your mind on a particular topic. Some of our students set a stopwatch at two minutes, and within that two minutes, write down anything and everything that pops into their heads. When the two minutes are up, they review the list to see if any pattern or ideas emerge. From this list of random and often wacky stuff, you can generally narrow down a topic. Let's say your assignment is to analyze the film *Moulin Rouge*, and you see that you jotted down several things that have to do with the way the movie looks. From that, you could decide that you want to write on the innovative "look" of the movie.

At this point, you can move on to brainstorming. Here, you take a blank piece of paper, or sit down in front of a blank computer screen, and write the topic of your paper across the top: The "look" of *Moulin Rouge*. Now, write down everything that pops into your head about the look of *Moulin Rouge*. See if you can come up with 10 to 20 ideas, observations or questions. When you are done, look closely at your list. Does a pattern emerge? Are there certain questions or ideas that seem to fit together? Let's say you've written "freaky colors," "looks like a painting," "seems fake," "colors probably symbolize something," "what things in the movie are red?" "what is red a symbol for?" "the camera angles were very unique," "the scenes didn't look real—I think on purpose," "it felt like fantasy." Based on these observations, it looks like you could write a paper in which you argue that "fake" sets and backdrops, outlandish colors, and the film's resemblance to paintings give the movie an intentional feeling of fantasy and make-believe.

The goal here is to try to hone in on your topic but also to hone in on what you want to say about that topic—that's called your thesis.

## Deciding on a Thesis

We should say that we are a bit uncomfortable using the word thesis here. Some instructors prefer focus, others controlling idea, others like argument. All work, yet none quite explain exactly what's expected of a thesis. Writing a thesis is perhaps the most important part of your paper, so if you find you are having trouble coming up with one, we suggest you consult more detailed information on arriving at a thesis and writing a paper in, "How Do I Make an Argument about a Building? Strategies for Constructing a Thesis and Building a Good Paper." But, for now, we will offer some basic tips on formulating a thesis.

First of all, you should be able to distinguish among a topic, a thesis, and a thesis statement. Your topic is what you are writing about (the "look" of *Moulin Rouge*). Your thesis is what you want to argue or posit (that the look of the film is designed to create and enhance the feeling of fantasy and make-believe in the movie). The thesis statement is where you actually articulate your thesis in the paper itself. The thesis statement does *not* have to be (in fact it should not be) one single sentence at the end of your first paragraph, as many people are taught in high school. Rather, it may take two or three sentences, perhaps a whole paragraph, to state your thesis. Regardless, it should be clear, it should be defensible, and it should be a kind of argument. A thesis statement should answer for your readers "What is this paper about? What does the writer believe?"

## Outlining

Once you have your topic, you need to organize your paper. Outlines are helpful because they provide a visual map of your paper so that you can see where you're going and where you've been. An outline is also useful in enabling you to see if your ideas fit together, if the paper coheres, and if the paper is equally distributed among your various points. If you find yourself getting stuck or suffering from writer's block, an outline might help push you along. Additionally, an outline presents your ideas in a logical format, and it shows the relationship among the various components of your paper. Traditionally, a paper will have one or two paragraphs of introduction, and the thesis will appear somewhere in those first two paragraphs. Be sure you write out your thesis statement when you do your outline.

Next, you will outline the body paragraphs, which make up the majority of the paper and are the most important. You should probably not include more than three or four main points in your paper—we advocate two or three, but your instructor may differ—so you'll need to decide how many paragraphs you want to devote to each topic. If, in your paper on *Moulin Rouge*, you decide your three main points are going to be "fake sets and backdrops," "outlandish colors," and "the resemblance to painting," then you will need to explain each of these ideas, give specific examples from the movie and then explain how they support your thesis. This process may take two paragraphs per topic or it may take as many as five or six. Of course, the conclusion closes the paper; it can be anywhere from one to three paragraphs and should restate your thesis in a new but conclusive way.

Most of you had to make an outline in high school, so you should be familiar with the process. If not, your instructor will have specific ideas about how to help you develop one, and there are many good resources on the World Wide Web.

## Writing the First Draft

Now you are ready to begin writing. You may find it easiest to skip the introduction altogether and start writing the first body paragraph. The building block of every good paper is the paragraph; in fact, the paragraph is a kind of microcosm of the entire paper. Just as you need a good thesis statement for your paper, so do you need a good topic sentence for every paragraph. Try to make every paragraph a thorough exploration of a single topic. One of the most important aspects of a good paragraph is the final sentence of the paragraph. The final sentence is crucial because it should connect what you've been writing about in your paragraph back to the topic sentence, which should implicitly help support your thesis.

Sentence by sentence, paragraph by paragraph, you should start building your paper. Remember to give as much detail as possible. Include examples from the text you are writing about, and try to avoid plot summary or unnecessary description. Remember: *Analyze, don't summarize.* In other words, do not only provide information—make sense of it for us.

Once you've finished your first draft, you may discover that buried somewhere in your closing paragraph is the very good articulation of the thesis you've been trying to prove for several pages. This happens because, as we've said, writing is a discovery process. So by working through your ideas, your arguments, your textual examples, you finally hit upon what you've been trying to say all along. Now that you have a better idea of what you want to say, it's time for the real work—editing and revising.

## Editing and Revising, Editing and Revising, Editing and Revising

The single biggest mistake student writers make is turning in their first draft. The first draft is little more than a blueprint—it's merely a process. In the editing and revising stage, you convert the process of writing into the written product. Here, you turn a bad paper into a decent one or a good paper into a great one. You can clear up confusing sentences, focus your argument, correct bad grammar, and, most importantly, make your paper clearer and more thorough.

There are a number of strategies for editing and revising, so we'll give you a couple of our favorites. First of all, when you are ready to edit and revise, read your paper through *backwards*. That's right. Start at the very end, and read it backwards, one sentence at a time. This forces you to slow down and see the sentence as its own entity. It's probably the most useful strategy for correcting your own writing. Even more helpful is getting a peer to read your paper. Another person can point out errors or inconsistencies or vague statements that you may miss because you are too close to the process. Last, we recommend that while you may write hot, you should edit cold. What we mean by this is that you need to step back from your paper when you edit. Look at it objectively. Try not to get caught up in your prose or in your argument. Work on being succinct and clear.

It may take several drafts (in fact it should) before you feel comfortable with your paper. So, we recommend at least *three* different processes of editing and revising before turning in your paper. We advocate going back over and looking at your language one last time. Don't use words that are not part of your vocabulary; try to avoid stating the obvious. Be original, be honest, be engaged. We urge you above all else to think complexly but write simply.

### Turning in the Finished Product

The most enjoyable part of the process! Double check spelling and grammatical issues. Check your citations if you did a research paper, and go over your bibliography.

Turn in the paper and go celebrate!

## HOW AM I A TEXT? ON WRITING PERSONAL ESSAYS

We think the best papers come from one's own viewpoint—after all, writing is thinking, and for the most part, the thinking you do is your own. The texts you have been writing about, however, were texts you could read with a more general perspective.

But say your professor wants a personal essay, as many freshman composition instructors do. Is it possible to write one using the ideas and techniques of reading texts? Of course. You are a text, and so are your experiences, feelings, ideas, friends, and relatives. What's more, your experiences and emotions are not culture-neutral—they have in some ways been influenced by the expectations living in our culture has generated. Take for example one of four ideas often used as personal essay topics in freshmen classes: the prom, the class trip to the beach, the loss of a loved one, or coming to college.

Just so you know, these are the topics we instructors often brace ourselves for, because students often have so little new to say about them. The essays are often laden with description of familiar landscapes, emotions, and events at the expense of any real reflection—they do not tell us anything new about the prom or grief.

Yet, in some way, even going to the beach should be a rich textual experience. Here's why: not only are you going to the beach, but going to the beach with ideas of the beach in mind, with cultural expectations of what beaches are like, what people do at beaches, etc. For example, how do we know to wear bathing suits, wear sunscreen, and play volleyball at the beach? Not only because we have done it before, but because we have seen others do it before and have incorporated their ideas about beachgoing into our beachgoing.

So if you write about the prom or a loved one getting ill or dying, try to focus not only on the emotions attached to such an event but your emotional expectations. Did you "not know how to feel"? Why? Was it because you had expected to feel a certain way? How did you know how to act? Were there cultural clues? Did you see a movie about a prom or about death? Proms are a particularly American phenomenon, and have been featured in any number of movies, usually teen romances (see David Denby's piece in Chapter 5 about that). Use that knowledge about the prom (or any other subject) in your own writing.

Take another common example. Dying in America has any number of traditions attached to it, depending on what American subculture you belong to. Foreign cultures have very different ways of looking at death. How you view death or illness also may have to do with religious beliefs, the closeness of your family, etc. But even these ideas about illness and death come from somewhere, and you owe your reader your best guess at how you came to them. So do ideas about what brothers, mothers, fathers, and grandmothers should be if you choose to write about them.

What we are talking about here is what personal essayists often call reflection—the idea that we are not only describing our lives but contemplating them. Entering college is a particularly ripe time for contemplation; at a minimum, you will have a new learning environment, but for most of you, there will be a change in friendships and social environments as well. For some of you, it will be time for even more upheaval—you may change your career path, or your worldview. You probably won't know all this if you decide to write about entering college, but you will have some ideas about what your expectations for college are and where you received them. The university setting is a rich cultural text; reading it may provide you additional insight into your own experiences there.

There are more subjects that are worthy of personal reflection than we can count here (the ones we have already named are some of the hardest). The idea is to take an experience or event, put it in your own perspective, and reflect on how your perspective may fit in with others. Anything from a trip to the grocery store to a road trip to a phone call to a visit can be the subject of a reflective essay; so can relationships with other people. But what you have to do in these essays is to make sure they matter not only to you but to others as well—that's why focusing on putting your experiences in a cultural perspective can make your writing worth reading (not just worth writing).

Some of you might object to this sort of self-analysis, and wonder why you can't just simply describe your experiences in a paper. For some papers and some teachers, that might be acceptable. But if writing is thinking and writing about oneself is thinking and self-discovery, you owe your reader—and yourself—your best shot at unearthing cultural expectations.

One last note about personal essays. Students often misunderstand their purpose. Though the topic of the personal essay might be your experience, the personal essay is not written for you but for your audience. The story that you tell about the beach or the prom or the death of a loved one is not as important as what you learned from the event. Simply recounting your trip to the beach is not nearly as interesting as what you saw, observed, and learned from your trip to the beach. Even more important is to consider what your audience can learn from what you learned. How can your experiences help the reader? The two great advantages you have as a personal essayist are recognition and discovery. In the best personal essay about a prom, the reader will recognize something familiar (an awkward moment, a romantic dance, the smell of hairspray), but will also discover something new about the text that is a prom because of your essay. So, as you sit down to draft a personal essay, think about how you might use this opportunity to help your reader learn something new about a topic they think they already know.

## HOW DO I KNOW WHAT A GOOD PAPER LOOKS LIKE? AN ANNOTATED STUDENT ESSAY

Sometimes, students have the ability to write good papers; they just can't visualize them. They simply don't know what a good paper *looks* like, what its components are.

Below is an annotated student paper. You will see that we have highlighted the positive aspects of the essay and also some elements that need work. One thing we like about this piece is a good move from general information to specific. The best papers are those with a clear, narrow focus. This student's thesis is also clear and well developed.

An unannotated version of this essay appears later in Chapter 9 if you want to consult it again. Sample student papers appear throughout *The World Is a Text.*

## "Smells Like Teen Spirit"

*Matt Compton*

In 1991 a song burst forth onto the music scene that articulated so perfectly the emotions of America's youth that the song's writer was later labeled the voice of a generation (Moon). That song was Nirvana's "Smells Like Teen Spirit," and the writer was Kurt Cobain; one of the most common complaints of the song's critics was that the lyrics were unintelligible (Rawlins). But while some considered the song to be unintelligible, to many youth in the early 90s, it was exactly what they needed to hear. Had the song been presented differently, then the raw emotions that it presented would have been tamed. If the lyrics had been perfectly articulated, then the feelings that the lyrics express would have been less articulate, because the feelings that he was getting across were not clear in themselves. One would know exactly what Kurt Cobain was saying, but not exactly what he was feeling. The perfect articulation of those raw emotions, shared by so many of America's youth, was conveyed with perfect inarticulation.

Good beginning—the "burst forth" is passive but here it seems to work.

Good clarification, although he almost moves too quickly into unintelligibility.

This is a strong explanation, although it probably could have been condensed a bit.

The thesis is great—it's argumentative and clever. We know here what the rest of the paper is about. However, the passive "was conveyed" could be turned into the active "Cobain conveyed."

1991 was a year when the music scene had become a dilute, lukewarm concoction being spoon-fed to the masses by corporations (Cohen). The charts and the radio were being dominated by "hair bands" and pop ballads; popular music at the time was making a lot of noise without saying anything (Cohen). Behind the scenes "underground" music had been thriving since the early eighties. Much of this underground music was making a meaningful statement, but these musicians shied away from the public eye. The general public knew little about them, because they had adopted the ideology that going public was selling out (Dettmar). Nirvana was a part of this "underground" music scene.

The writer gives a good background of the atmosphere before the song. Those more familiar with the era might raise objections to the definitiveness of the conclusion—but he uses a source to back up his opinion. We may not agree but have to respect this research.

In 1991 Nirvana broke the credo, signing with a major label, DGC, under which they released the chart-smashing *Nevermind.* "Smells Like Teen Spirit" was the first single from the record, and it became a huge hit quickly (Cohen). Nirvana stepped up and spoke for the twenty something generation, which wasn't exactly sure what it wanted to say (Azerrad 223–233). A huge part of America's youth felt exactly what Cobain was able to convey through not just "Smells Like Teen

The topic sentence is weak here—there's a lot going on in this paragraph and the first sentence and even the second don't adequately prepare the reader for the information.

Spirit" but all of his music. Nirvana shot into superstar status and paved the way for an entire "grunge" movement (Moon). No one complained that they could not hear Cobain, but many did complain that they could not understand what he was saying.

The information itself is good—he's revisiting the ideas he talked about in his thesis, which in some ways makes up for the lack of organization in this paragraph.

Kurt Cobain did not want his music to just be heard and appreciated; he wanted it to be "felt" (Moon). His music often showed a contrast of emotions; it would change from a soft lull, to a screaming rage suddenly. And few could scream with rage as could Cobain (Cohen). There is a Gaelic word, "yarrrrragh," which "... refers to that rare quality that some voices have, an edge, an ability to say something about the human condition that goes far beyond merely singing the right lyrics and hitting the right notes." This word was once used to describe Cobain's voice by Ralph J. Gleason, *Rolling Stone* critic (Azerrad 231). It was that voice, that uncanny ability to show emotions that Cobain demonstrated in "Smells Like Teen Spirit."

Good move to the songwriter, Kurt Cobain, though the transition might have been stronger. Good topic sentence.

Cool Gaelic reference. Excellent research (though he could have cited a little more elegantly).

Cobain's raging performance spoke to young Americans in a way that no one had in a long while (Moon). Michael Azerrad wrote in his 1993 book, *Come as You Are: The Story of Nirvana*, "Ultimately it wasn't so much that Nirvana was saying anything new about growing up in America; it was the way they said it" (Azerrad 226). Cobain's music was conveying a feeling through the way that he performed. It was a feeling shared by many of America's youth, but it was also a feeling that could not have been articulated any other way than the way that Cobain did it (Cohen).

Another good topic sentence.

Again a good use of research, though the repetition of Azerrad is unnecessary in parenthesis.

The strong final sentence not only supports the topic sentence of the paragraph but the thesis of the paper.

"Smells Like Teen Spirit" starts out with one of the most well-known guitar riffs of the 90s. The four chord progression was certainly nothing new, nothing uncommon. The chords are played with a single guitar with no distortion, and then suddenly the bass and drums come in. When the drums and bass come in the guitar is suddenly distorted, and the pace and sound of the song changes. The song's introduction, with its sudden change, forms a rhythmic "poppy" chord progression to a raging, thrashing of the band's instruments (Moon), sets the pace for the rest of the song.

This topic sentence is a bit on the narrative side and does not connect well with the previous paragraph.

The description does an excellent job of describing how the song sounds. It's a very difficult task to do this well.

The chaos from the introduction fades, and it leads in to the first verse, which gives the listener a confused feeling (Azerrad 213). In the first verse the tune of the song is carried by the drums and bass alone, and a seemingly lonely two-note guitar part that fades in and out of the song. The bass, drums and eerie guitar give the listener a "hazy" feeling. Here Cobain's lack of articulation aids in the confused feeling, because as he sings, one can catch articulate phrases here and there. The words that

This is a very good topic sentence—it not only leads us from the last paragraph but sums up the current one.

the listener can discern allow them to draw their own connections. Cobain's lyrics do in fact carry a confused message, "It's fun to lose, and to pretend" (Azerrad 213).

The pre-chorus offers up clear articulation of a single word, but this articulation is the perfect precursor to the coming chorus. As the first verse ends, the pre-chorus comes in; Cobain repeats the word "Hello" fifteen times. The repetition of the word Hello draws the confusion that he implicates in the first verse to a close, and in a way reflects on it. As the tone and inflection of his voice changes each time he quotes "Hello," one is not sure whether he is asking a question or making a statement, or both. It is like he is saying, "Hello? Is anybody at home?" while at the same time he exclaims, "Wake up and answer the door!"

The reflection that he implicates in the pre-chorus builds to the raw raging emotions that he expresses in the chorus, as the guitar suddenly becomes distorted, and he begins to scream (Azerrad 214, 226). In the chorus he screams, but somehow the words in the chorus are actually more articulate than those in the verse. As Cobain sings, "I feel stupid, and contagious," anyone who has ever felt like a social outcast understands exactly what Cobain is saying (Cohen), and they understand exactly why he must scream it.

I remember the first time that I heard that line and thinking about it; I was about thirteen, and I thought that there was no better word than "contagious" to describe the way it feels being in a social situation and not being accepted. Because no one wants to be around that person, they will look at the person with disgust, as if they have some highly *contagious* disease. There is certainly a lot of anger and confusion surrounding those feelings. People needed to hear Cobain scream; they knew how he felt, because they knew how they felt.

People who were experiencing what Cobain was expressing understood what he was saying, because they understood how he felt. In much the same way when someone hits their hand with a hammer that person does not lay down the hammer and calmly say, "Ouch, man that really hurt." They throw the hammer down, and simultaneously yell an obscenity, or make an inarticulate roar, and one knows that they are going to lose a fingernail. Anyone who has smashed their finger with a hammer understands why that person is yelling; in the same way anyone who has felt "contagious" or confused about society knows why Cobain is screaming about feeling "stupid and contagious." Cobain is not examining society. He is experiencing the same things as his audience (Moon); he is "going to lose

Good quote from the song. (He might have cited the song itself, but wanted Azerrad's ideas.)

Another good topic sentence. And here the transition is much better implied than those earlier mentioned.

An insightful analysis of what seems to be a pretty simple lyric. This is excellent work—complicating the simple is a staple of good work in reading culture. The writer also makes a good analogy here.

Omit unnecessary "actually."

Again good reading of the song. So far the writer has done a lot of strong work in 1) contextualizing the song 2) analyzing its music and 3) its lyrics. It's almost a formula for doing this type of work.

This personal aside adds to the paper in our opinion—but you should check with your teacher before including it.

Another analogy—comparison, done in reasonable doses is an effective technique in doing analysis—particularly if one does it thoughtfully.

a fingernail." As the chorus draws to a close, the music still rages, but it changes tempo and rhythm slightly.

The move back to narrative is jarring.

The chorus is the most moving part of the song; it is a display of pure emotion. In the chorus Cobain demonstrates what it was that connected with so many; his lyrics said what he meant (Moon). But what he said had been said before, and whether he was articulate or not, people felt what he meant. It was the articulation of that feeling that gained the song such high praise (Moon).

Good topic sentence, though it could be condensed into one sentence.

The chorus ends with the phrase, "A mulatto, an albino, a mosquito, my libido"; this line is a reference to social conformity. Cobain is referring to things, or the ideas associated with them that are "outside" of social conformity, and then relating those things back to himself with the phrase "my libido" (Azerrad 210–215). This end to the chorus again goes back to reflect on the feelings expressed in the chorus, and ties them together with a return to the confusion expressed in the verses.

See above—the topic sentence is doing excellent work but not doing it as "writerly" as it could be done.

The articulation of the lyrics in the second verse gives the confusion more focus than in the first verse. He begins the second verse with the lyric, "I'm worse at what I do best, and for this gift I feel blessed." Although the lyrics are more articulate in the second verse, the feelings of confusion are still there, due to the tempo and rhythm of the music. After Cobain has sung the second verse he returns to the pre-chorus, the repetition of the word Hello. The cycle begins anew.

We like the way the writer connects ideas, music, and lyrics together again.

"Smells Like Teen Spirit" in its entirety gives the listener a complete feeling after listening to it, especially if that listener is feeling confused and frustrated. The song carries one through an entire cycle of emotions, from confusion, to reflection, to frustration. Tom Moon, a Knight-Ridder Newspaper writer, described Nirvana's music as having moments of "tension and release." Being carried through those emotions allows the listener to "vent" their own feelings of confusion and frustration, and at the same time know that someone else feels the same way (Azerrad 226–227). Despite the connection that Cobain made with many there were still many who did not "get" the song; these people often complained about the inarticulation of the lyrics (Azerrad 210).

Good summary of the song's meaning/content. The writer does a good job of making sure the reader is following his argument.

Weird Al Yankovic utilized the common criticism of the song in his parody "Smells Like Nirvana"; Yankovic parodied "Smells Like Teen Spirit," based entirely on Cobain's obscure articulation. Yankovic is known for parodying popular music, and with lines such as, "And I'm yellin' and I'm screamin', but I don't know what I'm saying," Yankovic stated exactly what

Now, he switches to other voices. Because the choice is both surprising and apt, the use of Weird Al is a good choice for a source/comparison.

so many of the song's critiques had, though he did it with a genuine respect for the song, and its impact (Rawlins).

Weird Al Yankovic's version struck a note with many who liked Cobain's music but could not understand his lyrics (Rawlins). There were many people who did not understand the feelings of confusion, frustration, and apathy that Cobain was getting across. In 1991 when "Smells Like Teen Spirit" first came out I was only 9, and I did not like that kind of music at all. I remember my brother, who is nine years older than me, and who listened to a lot of "heavy metal," bought Yankovic's *Off the Deep End*, with his parody "Smells Like Nirvana" on it. He thought it was funny because he did not like Nirvana. He never really connected with Cobain's message; even though he did not get what Cobain was saying, he could still enjoy the music. When I became older I did connect with Cobain's music, and Nirvana was one of my favorite bands. My brother never did understand, like many people who never did understand what it was that Cobain was saying (Azerrad 210).

Again, we like the personal reference. It's not as relevant as the other one, but it somehow gives the argument more weight if we know where the writer is "coming from."

Nirvana made the generation gap clear. It was Nirvana that spoke for a large part of that generation (Moon), where no one else had ever really addressed the confusion and frustration about growing up in America at that time, or at least no one had expressed it in the same way that Nirvana did. They were not the first to vocalize a problem with corporate America, but they were the first *popular* band to convey the feelings that many were feeling *because* of growing up in corporate America, in the way that they did. Cobain did not just show that he has experienced those feelings, but that he was still *experiencing* them, and many young people connected with that (Moon).

The transition isn't strong here, but the topic sentence is good... it again summarizes—this time the band, not the song.

The corporate America reference is not clear here. As readers, we vaguely know what he is talking about, but he doesn't use sources in the same way he has when making similar points.

In 1992 singer-songwriter Tori Amos illustrated why Cobain's "Smells Like Teen Spirit" had connected with so many by making a cover of the song that was a clear contrast to the original. She rendered the song with a piano, and a clear articulate voice. Her cover of the song became fairly popular, because it was different, and because many people could now understand the lyrics that Cobain had already popularized (Rawlins). The cover was interesting, to say the least; however, it would have been impossible for her version ever to have had the same impact as Cobain's (Rawlins). The lyrics to the song have meaning, and depth, but the emotions that the song conveyed were in and of themselves abstract.

Again—the writer puts comparison to good use. Some writers make the mistake of doing multiple comparisons which all make the same point. Here the writer uses Tori Amos, whose work is very different from both Nirvana and Weird Al to useful effect—reinforcing his argument.

Amos's version of the song articulated each word clearly, her clear voice hit each note on key; her song was comparable to a ballad. Cobain's "Smells Like Teen Spirit" could be described as "sloppy," his guitar distorted through much of the song; he either screamed or mumbled most of the song (Azerrad 214). The two versions of the song illustrate a clear contrast: it is as if Cobain is "angry about being confused" (Azerrad 213), while Amos sings the song to lament Cobain's feelings.

Amos's version of the song became popular for the same reason that it could never have paved the way as Cobain's version did. It was like a ballad, and after everyone heard what Cobain was saying, about society, about America, about growing up, there is one clear emotion that follows the confusion and frustration: sadness. Her "ballad-like" cover of "Smells Like Teen Spirit" exemplified that sadness. But at the same time, people had written ballads about being confused or frustrated, and performed them as Amos performed "Smells Like Teen Spirit"; that was nothing new. However, no one had yet *demonstrated* such clear and yet abstract confused, frustrated emotions as Cobain did, and at that moment in time that was exactly what America needed to hear (Azerrad 224–225).

The writer does a good job of extending the comparison as a way of bringing his own argument to a close.

Cobain had written and performed a song about his own confusion, and in the process he had connected with young people all over the United States (Moon). He had helped those people to understand their own confusion better. The problem with "Smells Like Teen Spirit" was not that Cobain was not articulate; he could not have articulated his point more clearly than he did. The problem was that not everyone knew what he was talking about, just like not everyone knows what it is like to strike their finger with a hammer. And in the same way, if someone doesn't know what it is like they might say something foolish like, "That couldn't hurt *that* bad," or "What's *his* problem?" when someone else hits their finger with a hammer, and they make an inarticulate roar. That roar expresses exactly what that person is feeling, but only those who know that feeling, can really understand it. As Michael Azerrad, author of *Come as You Are: The Story of Nirvana* put it, "you either get it, or you don't" (Azerrad 227). Thus was the case with Cobain's music. "Smells Like Teen Spirit" was his inarticulate roar; it was articulate in that it expressed exactly what he was trying to point out; however, not everyone could grasp what that was.

The conclusion approaches, with the writer putting the work into final context.

The conclusion could be a little stronger—the writer might have taken this argument beyond Nirvana or put it in a little greater context. He chose instead to close the work by restating the thesis, which is an acceptable way to end the paper.

Overall, the work this paper does is outstanding—it approaches a "cultural text"—a famous song and brings the reader multiple perspectives on it, using comparison, literary and sound analysis, and analogy. It's a good model for doing this type of work.

## Works Cited

Azerrad, Michael. *Come as You Are.* New York: Doubleday, 1993.

Cohen, Howard and Leonard Pitts. "Kurt Cobain Made Rock for Everyone but Kurt Cobain." *Knight Ridder/Tribune* 8 April 1994: Infotrac.

Dettmar, Kevin. "Uneasy Listening, Uneasy Commerce." *The Chronicle of Higher Education*. 14 Sept. 2001: 18. Lexis-Nexis.

Moon, Tom. "Reluctant Spokesman for Generation Became the Rock Star He Abhorred." *Knight-Ridder/Tribune* 9 April 1994. Infotrac.

Nirvana. *Nevermind*. David Geffen Company, 1991.

Rawlins, Melissa. "From Bad to Verse." *Entertainment Weekly*. 5 June 1992: 57. Infotrac.

## HOW DO I GET INFO ON SONGS? RESEARCHING POPULAR CULTURE TEXTS

Researching a nontraditional text may seem daunting. You may ask yourself who could have possibly written about Barbie dolls or *The Matrix*. Or you may not have written a paper that engages popular culture as a research topic. After all, isn't research about "serious" topics? Traditionally, you have probably written research papers about historical events or movements, or about the author of a literary work, or perhaps literary movements. But despite seeming more difficult, students writing research papers about popular culture have a lot of resources at their disposal. There is a large and ever-increasing amount of work written on popular culture such as music, the movies, technology, art, found objects, television, etc. There's even more work done on the more political elements of this textbook, such as gender and media.

Because researching popular culture topics seems daunting, you might be tempted to amass as much information as possible before beginning your writing. However, we believe that one of the best ways of researching a paper about popular culture is to make sure you have a take on whatever text you are analyzing before researching. That way, you have your ideas to use as a sounding board for others that might come your way. Finding out what you think about the text will also allow you to research more effectively and probably more efficiently.

Generally, the trick to researching papers about popular culture is not only to find work that engages your specific topic but something general or *contextual* about your topic as well. In the case of *The Matrix*, a widely popular and critically well received movie from 2000, science fiction movies would be a good general subject to look up, but so would "computers and culture." Broadly defined, *The Matrix* is a science fiction movie, but it's also a movie "about" the roles of computers in society. One of the movie's primary arguments is that our culture is quickly moving toward one that is run by computers with decreasing human control. It's the subject of more than a few movies, including *2001: A Space Odyssey*, but its message is even more crucial given the remarkable growth of the Internet over the last decade. One could research the philosophical argument the movie is making, that man and computers are somewhat at odds. One could research how other movies or books have treated this subject both within the science fiction genre and outside it. The movie also has a political bent, about the nature of not only computers but corporations, who seem to run Neo's life before he realizes what the Matrix is. It's also about the culture of computers, which Neo is immersed in before his transformation. It's also about the future as well as the present, a temporal argument (about time). All these contexts—philosophical, genre-based, cultural, political, temporal—have strong research possibilities; the papers you would end up with would be very different from each other. You can also see why understanding what you are arguing would affect how you research a topic.

Another possibility for research is music CDs. Instead of thinking of particular contexts right away, you might begin by asking some questions of the text. For example, take as a text Johnny Cash's album *Solitary Man: American Recordings III*, which came out in 1999. Johnny Cash is a musician who has been recording music for almost 50 years; he received his start about the same time and in the same place as Elvis Presley but now has the same record producer as the Beastie Boys, a popular rap group. Such biographical constructions may shape your paper's direction, or they may not. In either case, in writing this paper, you might listen to the album, note some of the themes, signs and symbols, and ideas. You might ask yourself: Is Johnny Cash writing about issues he has written about before? You could find this out by listening to other albums or seeking research materials about his recording career. You could also ask: What is it about the life of Cash that makes him write songs like this? Material contained either in biographies of Cash himself or general histories of country music would help this paper. Another question: Is Johnny Cash part of the recognizable genre of country music or a different genre altogether? Again, a general work about country music would help you answer this question. Any of these questions would be the beginning of a good research paper. If you wanted to focus only on the album, you could also read other reviews, and after you have staked out your own position, argue against other readings of this album.

Movies and music are good choices for research because they are texts which in some ways mirror traditional texts—movies have narratives like novels, and songs have lyrics that resemble poetry. But even found objects have strong possibilities for research. Things like cars or dolls are not only easily described but have long traditions of scholarship, especially within cultural contexts. In the case of dolls, histories of dolls in American culture or toys would provide historical context; the same would be true for cars. As you get closer to the present time, your methods of research may change. In the case of cars, current writers may not be writing about the context of a new car model, but they certainly review them, and examining the criteria of car reviews may give you insight into the cultural context of a car. So might advertisements. Researching popular culture can include placing different primary sources (the source itself like *Solitary Man* or *The Matrix* or advertisements for either of these texts) in context with one another, or using secondary sources—sources about the primary text, such as reviews, or scholarly articles, ones that are peer reviewed, reviewed by experts, and often have footnotes.

The most difficult thing about doing this research is its flexibility. The authors have long encountered students who do enjoy this type of work but are also overwhelmed by the possibilities in approaching popular culture texts. Most of the students eventually come away with not only a better understanding of their particular text but of researching generally.

## Nuts and Bolts Research

Clearly, your university library is the place to start. Books have a much more comprehensive perspective on any possible text. Think broadly when approaching what books you might look at; think about what category the books you are looking for might fall into. One of the best ways of doing this is through a keyword search involving "the perfect book." For a book about Johnny Cash, a simple keyword search on Johnny Cash might provide some books. If not, a keyword search with history, country, and music might provide some results. If it does, write down a call number, the physical address of the book in the library, and head for the stacks; most libraries have separate floors or sections for their collection of books. When you get there, find the book you have written down, but also be careful to look around on the shelves for other possibilities. Both authors have found that some of their best sources have come from browsing on the shelves.

Then it's on to periodicals. The *Reader's Guide to Periodicals* is a complete nonelectronic guide to periodicals such as newspapers and major magazines. You may be tempted to skip anything not on line, but electronic sources only generally go back a decade, so for any type of historical research, you should probably hit the *Reader's Guide.*

When you do hit the computer, try to use an electronic database your university subscribes to; search engines like Google or Yahoo! are limited in what they will come up with and may get sources which are not reliable. The overall difference between InfoTrac and Lexis-Nexis and Internet searching is that InfoTrac and Lexis-Nexis for the most part have articles that appear in print form, generally, though not always, making them more reliable sources. The authors both like electronic databases like InfoTrac and Lexis-Nexis, which many universities subscribe to. InfoTrac is an index to periodicals which tend to be scholarly, with footnotes, though some more popular magazines are there as well. Some of the articles on InfoTrac are full text articles, which means the full version will appear on the screen; some you will have to head to the library to find. Lexis-Nexis contains full-text articles from most large American and European newspapers as well as many magazines. It has a database which is geared toward general news and opinion and other databases geared toward sports, arts, science, and law. If you are working with popular culture sources, the arts index, which contains reviews, may be helpful. Speaking of computers, you may also find the Library of Congress Web site, *http://www.loc.gov,* helpful. Overall, in doing research, be creative.

## Guerilla Research

Okay, you've hit your limited library, and you can't find what you need. Try a bookstore like Borders or Barnes & Noble, bring some index cards and a notebook, and take notes on the books you want. Try an interlibrary loan if you know the book you need and can't find it—in most places, it's free. And if you want an alternative, look at Amazon.com, where you can research books, movies, and albums.

# The World Is a Text
# READING

# 1

## READING LITERATURE

Of all the texts in this book, undoubtedly you have had the most training reading literary ones. Whether you realized it or not, those days in high school of slogging through some nineteenth century novel or puzzling over a poem by Emily Dickinson were excellent training not only for reading other literary texts but for reading the world. For, as we explained in the introduction, the tools you have been taught to employ to read literature—paying attention to detail, reading between the lines, looking at formal elements of the poem or story, thinking about the author's background—will help you "read" or make sense of the text that is the world around you. This chapter provides some provocative literary texts to help hone and improve your reading skills. In fact the introduction you are reading at this very moment will help prepare you for reading literary texts in a more sophisticated and comprehensive way.

Before we begin a discussion about how to read literature, we'd like to linger a moment at the word "literature;" in fact, we use the term "literary" above with some trepidation. As you may have noticed, many bookstores distinguish between "literature" and "fiction," and we are fairly confident that most of your high school teachers would do the same. You may be wondering why *The World Is a Text* does not include a Stephen King short story or a Shel Silverstein poem. But, more likely, you did not expect a college-level textbook to reprint something as "popular" as a Stephen King story or a passage from Tom Clancy or John Grisham or Danielle Steele. Perhaps you think of William Faulkner as literature and John Grisham as entertainment. One is toiled over; the other is enjoyed. For centuries, but in particular in the last 20 years, writers, teachers, and scholars have argued about so-called "high" and "low" art. One of the goals of *The World Is a Text* is to question these assumptions, and in every other chapter, particularly in Chapter 7, we provide readings that explore preconceived notions about art, value, and entertainment.

In this opening chapter, we have decided to take a slightly different approach in two notable ways. First of all, unlike the rest of the book, this section is comprised of primary source material—that is, instead of reprinting essays about literature, we have reprinted literature itself. The reasoning behind this decision is to foreground the vocabulary and the process of "reading" in its broadest terms. You already know that to "read" a poem means to look at it closely—but you may not know how to "read" gender or television or public space with the same care and attention to detail. So, we want to begin the book with something familiar. Second, popular literature does not enjoy the same universal experience as movies, television shows, songs, videos, or fashion. You would be hard pressed to name a short story or poem written in the last 10 years that everyone in your class has read. But you could name any number of songs, TV programs, commercials, and movies that everyone knows. Simply put, we come to stories and poems in different ways than we come to other forms of popular media. What is important to know, though, is that we are not trying to claim that these stories and poems are any more valuable than any other kind of text. Our goal in printing them first is to kind of ease you into the process of reading the world as a text by asking you to read texts from a familiar world, that of literature.

While television and movies often dominate the public's attention, reading and production of literature remains one of the most enduring human endeavors because of its ability to inspire us (and this may be why we come to literature less frequently—it tends to overwhelm us). For a variety of reasons, reading allows a form of engagement and escape that is different from watching a movie or television show. Though some of you may prefer television or movies to reading, a large percentage of Americans cite reading as among their favorite hobbies or avocations.

However, where we might disagree is about what type of reading and literature constitutes a good experience. While most of us would agree that few experiences compare to reading a good book or a good poem, we may disagree on that term "good." We all have different ideas of what "good" or "important" or "rewarding" reading might be, and in most cases, we can defend these definitions. Accordingly, you might have put together a very different reader than we have. Certainly, you would have chosen different stories or poems to reprint. In this section, we have given you a very small sampling of what we think is interesting literature. We think these selections are worth your effort to read and think about them not simply because they are "deep" or "complex"—which is how some define what literature is—but because they raise important questions about what it means to be alive on this planet. Literature is not life, but it is about what it means to be alive and about the living of life.

For us, literature is the discourse that most resembles life itself because, like life, literature can always be reread, re-examined, and reconsidered in a new light. Many of us will puzzle over an event that happened to us until we can understand it. We can and should do the same with literature, both in finding the same type of understanding we seek in interpreting our own life events, as well as breaking down a piece of literature into more managable parts for interpretation. We love comic strips, but rarely do we reread *Garfield* or *Blondie*. We also like crime novels and novels of suspense, but your typical Patricia Cornwell or John Grisham novel does not always fare well on a second read because we often do not see the complexity in the work that mirrors our own complex lives. Most comics and most popular fiction are plot based, and our lives are more than plot. When you tell someone a story about a first date or a wonderful trip, you don't just relay events in chronological order, you imbue your tale with emotions and ideas, both of which often change over time. Our point is that we want you to read literature closely and with care because good literature stands up to numerous readings and can, over time and immediately, unfold in illuminating ways—just like life. Thus, we've chosen these particular stories and poems for *The World Is a Text* because these texts create meaning on a number of different levels, just as your life means and makes meaning on a variety of levels. Our hope is that by being sophisticated readers of literary texts, you will become sophisticated readers of the text that is this big, complex world. Below we offer a number of things you might consider in reading literary texts.

## Literature demands active reading.

We have all had the frustrating experience of skimming over a few pages of a chemistry textbook only to find that we remember next to nothing. Worse is the realization that, after reading a couple of pages of some book, you have absolutely no memory of what your eyes have been scanning for the past several minutes. Too often we read but we don't really *read*. This introduction, and this book as a whole, will try to help you become an active as opposed to a passive reader. To read passively is to read a text solely for the information it provides. This kind of reading is fine for, say, a recipe or the sports page or a set of instructions, but literature is not written merely to inform. Literature is a complex text, perhaps the most complex of texts; thus, you must read actively. To read actively is to read critically. Reading critically means paying attention to more than the words in bold. Reading critically means being a willing and active participant in the reading process.

On a more practical level, this type of reading requires rereading (just like formal writing requires rewriting [revising]). Accordingly, we recommend reading each text twice. Read it the first time for plot; read it the second time to explore issues of theme, setting, character, dialogue, social or political overtones, technique, symbol or metaphor, conflicts, and tone. Read with a pencil or pen in hand. Circle words that annoy you or that you don't know. Write yourself questions in the margins. Make notes in your book—make your book an interactive space.

## Literature is made up of genres.

Reading poetry and literary prose is much different than reading a recipe, a biology text, or a fashion magazine. Most of the time, those texts are written solely to convey information, while, as we've noted, literature delivers more than information. To help do that, writers find appropriate genres or styles for their work. A genre is a kind of classification. In literature, there are many genres and subgenres, though the major ones are poetry, fiction, drama, and nonfiction prose. In this chapter, we will concentrate on poetry and prose.

Both poems and fiction explore difficult issues and ideas, pose troubling questions, create microcosms of human existence, bring conflicts to the forefront, and reveal to us the magic and beauty of life. For most authors, a story or a poem is vastly different from a diary or a memo because it is something made, something artful, something written to provoke us intellectually, emotionally, and aesthetically. As we have said in the introduction, one can read anything and determine meaning, but writers of literature often intend for us to read their works in a deep, meditative manner.

Prose fiction relies on characters, plot, conflict and dialogue for these effects. Often, these aspects of a novel or story will be particularly rich and complex because people are complex, and regardless of everything else we may talk about in conjunction with it, fiction is ultimately about people. You have all encountered memorable characters in novels and stories, and, no doubt, you have discussed their psychology, their decisions, their hopes, and their dreams. One advantage literature has over films, television and music is that writers have more time and space and the tool of language to help flesh out a character's nuances. Additionally, as you are probably aware, authors often use characters as symbols for types or for specific ideas. For instance, in Nathaniel Hawthorne's "Young Goodman Brown," Faith is not merely named that; she is a symbol for faith itself. Likewise, in "Blood-Burning Moon," Jean Toomer creates the character of Bob Stone as a symbol or metaphor for a certain kind of white Southerner. Thus, characters tend to embody or manifest the values they represent. Finally, we turn to fiction for entertainment and edification because our lives are themselves one big story that we are always trying to make sense of.

It may be shorter, but don't think you will get off the hook with poetry. Poetry requires even more care than fiction. We read poetry for its many rewards: its sounds, meanings, images, the pleasures of language, emotion, and ideas. Many poems challenge our intellect—the poet's word play, or how puns trigger powerful, emotional responses. Some poems please us because they illuminate feelings or emotions that perhaps we were not aware of or sensed only vaguely. In the best poetry, as in the best fiction, there is very little distinction between ideas and emotion, between intellect and intuition. They work together. In a Shakespearean sonnet, we are moved not only by the beautiful language or the romantic sentiment but by its profound ideas. In the best instances, the combination of sounds, images, theme, and ideas in a poem causes us to see the magic of the world and our place in it in an entirely different light.

## Literature is a product not only of the author but of the society and culture of the author.

This may seem obvious, but you may not be aware of the degree to which cultural forces influence literary texts. For instance, it is likely that very different issues were on Susan Steinberg's mind when she wrote "Isla" than were on Nathaniel Hawthorne's mind when he wrote "Young Goodman Brown." He was male; she is female. He is dead; she is alive. He is white; she is Jewish. She is from Baltimore and lives in California; he lived his entire life in New England. She was raised in a Jewish culture; he was Protestant. Naturally, the work of these authors will carry variant cultural codes and will make unique arguments about their respective cultures.

But literary composition extends beyond theme. You will notice that Emily Dickinson's poem looks and sounds different than James Tate's poem, which looks and sounds much different than Carolyn Forché's poem. The expectations of what a poem should look and sound like have changed over time: We have moved from valuing ordered, complex exercises to valuing poems that explode traditional rules governing literature. There is no way that James Tate's poem could have been written in 1880. Similar subject matter for Carolyn Forché's poem could not have been found in the United States in 1979. In these two instances, we see how the theme and the form of the poem arise out of the "writing situation" of the authors.

We urge you to keep not only the culture of the writers in mind as you read but your culture as well. How does your own cultural background affect how you read literature?

### Literature is interactive.

The great Argentine writer Jorge Luis Borges claimed that the ultimate author of any piece of literature is the *reader*. As reader, you have the freedom (and the responsibility) to create how characters look, how they speak, what the landscape looks like, or even how a poet's voice sounds. You also have the luxury of controlling the speed of reading: you can stop, reread, put the book down and come back later. You can take your time, mull over an idea or a metaphor. You don't have to wonder, as in watching television, if you'll miss the romantic kiss if you go to the bathroom. A writer may have written the book, but *you* bring the book to life. The book needs you to animate it, to invent voices, landscapes, facial expressions. The great Mexican poet Octavio Paz wrote that the poem is not a literary form but the meeting place between poetry and humanity. Perhaps literature needs us because that is one of the places where we find ourselves and others. Here is where being an active reader remains profoundly important. You must enter the world of the text.

Remember, the text needs you. Don't let the text down! Read it with care. Make it a part of who you are. Make literature a part of the complex text that is you.

## Worksheet

Because this is the first chapter and because we want you to transfer how you think about literary texts to other kinds of texts, we are going to provide you with a slightly more detailed worksheet here than you will find in the rest of the book. So, if you find yourself stuck in a chapter, feel free to turn back to this worksheet and ask yourself these very questions, paying attention to these same concepts throughout the book.

### THIS TEXT

- What are the major themes of the work? What is the author trying to suggest?
- What techniques does the author use to get his or her point across? Why *these* techniques?
- What are we to make of the characters or personas in the text? What is their function? What is their race? Their social class? Are they like you? How?
- Where does the text take place? When is it set?
- What are the main conflicts of the text? What issues are at stake?

- What kinds of issues of identity is the author working on in the text?
- Is there tension between the self and society in the text? How? Why?
- What is the agenda of the author? Why does she or he want me to think a certain way?
- How is the text put together? How does it make meaning? What techniques is the author using?
- Did I like this? Why, or why not?

## A SHORT GLOSSARY OF TERMS

### Fiction

**Plot:** The story that is being told. The arc of the narrative; its beginning, middle, and end.

**Character:** What kinds of people appear in stories? What values do they represent? Are they realistic; are they stereotypes?

**Setting:** When and where does the story take place?

**Conflict:** In high school, you thought of conflict as man vs. nature or man vs. himself. Now, think in more complex terms. What are the sources of tension in the story? What cultural norms and values are driving these tensions?

**Theme:** What is the moral of the story? What is the story trying to do? What message does the story send?

**Dialogue:** The conversations that take place in a story. How does what a character says reveal who that person is?

**Symbol and metaphor:** Try to resist thinking in very specific terms about symbol. For instance, it's not very useful to claim that the gun in the Emily Dickinson poem stands for God or that the moon in "Blood-Burning Moon" symbolizes death. Rather, think of the associations or connotations of a gun; what emotions, behaviors or myths might a big moon evoke? Limiting literary devices to hard and fast symbolism tends to straitjacket literature. Even a character like Faith in "Young Goodman Brown" doesn't stand for one kind of faith.

### Poetry

**Structure:** What is the architecture of the poem? Does it rhyme? Does it have a consistent meter or rhythm? Is it a sonnet, haiku, or a villanelle? Does it have fixed stanzas? In almost every case, a poem's structure will support or enhance the poem's theme.

**Tone:** What is the tone or feeling of the poem? Often, poems rely on evocation; that is, they evoke or elicit reactions or emotions through their tone.

**Sound:** Read poems aloud. Several times. Pay attention to alliteration, assonance, and rhyme. How does a poem become art through its sound?

**Theme:** Like prose, poems have themes, though often they are more open-ended. Still, a poem will suggest something. Avoid asking what a poem *means*; instead, ask what it *does* and what it *suggests*.

### Outside This Text

**Cultural work:** The literary critic Jane Tompkins argues that we should value literature not so much for its structure or tone or plot but for how it affects and reflects culture—the cultural work it performs. Think about what kind of cultural work your text does.

**Emotional and intellectual impact:** Literature affects us on a number of levels. How does a text make us feel and think? How are the two linked?

## BLOOD-BURNING MOON (1923)

Jean Toomer

Published as part of Toomer's groundbreaking collection of poems and short stories entitled *Cane*, "Blood-Burning Moon" presents a reading of three different people linked by one troubling reality. Toomer claimed to be a product of seven different ethnicities, and his story explores both internal realities and external racial realities of characters in the deep South.

### *1*

UP FROM THE SKELETON STONE WALLS, up from the rotting floor boards and the solid hand-hewn beams of oak of the pre-war cotton factory, dusk came. Up from the dusk the full moon came. Glowing like a fired pine-knot, it illumined the great door and soft showered the Negro shanties aligned along the single street of factory town. The full moon in the great door was an omen. Negro women improvised songs against its spell.

Louisa sang as she came over the crest of the hill from the white folks' kitchen. Her skin was the color of oak leaves on young trees in fall. Her breasts, firm and up-pointed like ripe acorns. And her singing had the low murmur of winds in fig trees. Bob Stone, younger son of the people she worked for, loved her. By the way the world reckons things, he had won her. By measure of that warm glow which came into her mind at thought of him, he had won her. Tom Burwell, whom the whole town called Big Boy, also loved her. But working in the fields all day, and far away from her, gave him no chance to show it. Though often enough of evenings he had tried to. Somehow, he never got along. Strong as he was with hands upon the ax or plow, he found it difficult to hold her. Or so he thought. But the fact was that he held her to factory town more firmly than he thought for. His black balanced, and pulled against, the white of Stone, when she thought of them. And her mind was vaguely upon them as she came over the crest of the hill, coming from the white folks' kitchen. As she sang softly at the evil face of the full moon.

A strange stir was in her. Indolently, she tried to fix upon Bob or Tom as the cause of it. To meet Bob in the canebrake, as she was going to do an hour or so later, was nothing new. And Tom's proposal which she felt on its way to her could be indefinitely put off. Separately, there was no unusual significance to either one. But for some reason, they jumbled when her eyes gazed vacantly at the rising moon. And from the jumble came the stir that was strangely within her. Her lips trembled. The slow rhythm of her song grew agitant and restless. Rusty black and tan spotted hounds, lying in the dark corners of porches or prowling around back yards, put their noses in the air and caught its tremor. They began plaintively to yelp and howl. Chickens woke up and cackled. Intermittently, all over the countryside dogs barked and roosters crowed as if heralding a weird dawn or some ungodly awakening. The women sang lustily. Their songs were cotton-wads to stop their ears. Louisa came down into factory town and sank wearily upon the step before her home. The moon was rising towards a thick cloud-bank which soon would hide it.

> Red nigger moon. Sinner!
> Blood-burning moon. Sinner!
> Come out that fact'ry door.

## 2

Up from the deep dusk of a cleared spot on the edge of the forest a mellow glow arose and spread fan-wise into the low-hanging heavens. And all around the air was heavy with the scent of boiling cane. A large pile of cane-stalks lay like ribboned shadows upon the ground. A mule, harnessed to a pole, trudged lazily round and round the pivot of the grinder. Beneath a swaying oil lamp, a Negro alternately whipped out at the mule, and fed cane-stalks to the grinder. A fat boy waddled pails of fresh ground juice between the grinder and the boiling stove. Steam came from the copper boiling pan. The scent of cane came from the copper pan and drenched the forest and the hill that sloped to factory town, beneath its fragrance. It drenched the men in circle seated around the stove. Some of them chewed at the white pulp of stalks, but there was no need for them to, if all they wanted was to taste the cane. One tasted it in factory town. And from factory town one could see the soft haze thrown by the glowing stove upon the low-hanging heavens.

Old David Georgia stirred the thickening syrup with a long ladle, and ever so often drew it off. Old David Georgia tended his stove and told tales about the white folks, about moon-shining and cotton picking, and about sweet nigger gals, to the men who sat there about his stove to listen to him. Tom Burwell chewed cane-stalk and laughed with the others till someone mentioned Louisa. Till some one said something about Louisa and Bob Stone, about the silk stockings she must have gotten from him. Blood ran up Tom's neck hotter than the glow that flooded from the stove. He sprang up. Glared at the men and said, "She's my gal." Will Manning laughed. Tom strode over to him. Yanked him up and knocked him to the ground. Several of Manning's friends got up to fight for him. Tom whipped out a long knife and would have cut them to shreds if they hadnt ducked into the woods. Tom had had enough. He nodded to Old David Georgia and swung down the path to factory town. Just then, the dogs started barking and the roosters began to crow. Tom felt funny. Away from the fight, away from the stove, chill got to him. He shivered. He shuddered when he saw the full moon rising towards the cloud-bank. He who didnt give a godam for the fears of old women. He forced his mind to fasten on Louisa. Bob Stone. Better not be. He turned into the street and saw Louisa sitting before her home. He went towards her, ambling, touched the brim of a marvelously shaped, spotted, felt hat, said he wanted to say something to her, and then found that he didnt know what he had to say, or if he did, that he couldnt say it. He shoved his big fists in his overalls, grinned, and started to move off.

"Youall want me, Tom?"

"Thats what us wants, sho, Louisa."

"Well, here I am—"

"An here I is, but that aint ahelpin none, all th same."

"You wanted to say something? . ."

"I did that, sho. But words is like th spots on dice: no matter how y fumbles em, there's times when they jes wont come. I dunno why. Seems like th love I feels fo yo done stole m tongue. I got it now. Whee! Louisa, honey, I oughtnt tell y, I feel I oughtnt cause yo is young an goes t church an I has had other gals, but Louisa I sho do love y. Lil gal, Ise watched y from them first days when youall sat right here befo yo door befo th well an sang sometimes in a way that like t broke m heart. Ise carried y with me into th fields, day after day, an after that, an I sho can plow when yo is there, an I can pick cotton. Yassur! Come near beatin Barlo yesterday. I sho did. Yassur! An next year if ole Stone'll trust me, I'll have a farm. My own. My bales will buy yo what y gets from white folks now. Silk stockings an purple dresses—course I dont believe what some folks been whisperin as t how y gets them things now. White folks always did do for niggers what they likes. An they jes cant help alikin yo, Louisa. Bob Stone likes y. Course he does. But not th way folks is awhisperin. Does he, hon?"

"I dont know what you mean, Tom."

"Course y dont. Ise already cut two niggers. Had t hon, t tell em so. Niggers always tryin t make somethin out a nothin. An then besides, white folks aint up t them tricks so much nowadays. Godam better not be. Leastawise not with yo. Cause I wouldnt stand f it. Nassur."

"What would you do, Tom?"

"Cut him jes like I cut a nigger."

"No, Tom—"

"I said I would an there aint no mo to it. But that aint th talk f now. Sing, honey Louisa, an while I'm listenin t y I'll be makin love."

Tom took her hand in his. Against the tough thickness of his own, hers felt soft and small. His huge body slipped down to the step beside her. The full moon sank upward into the deep purple of the cloud-bank. An old woman brought a lighted lamp and hung it on the common well whose bulky shadow squatted in the middle of the road, opposite Tom and Louisa. The old woman lifted the well-lid, took hold the chain, and began drawing up the heavy bucket. As she did so, she sang. Figures shifted, restless-like, between lamp and window in the front rooms of the shanties. Shadows of the figures fought each other on the gray dust of the road. Figures raised the windows and joined the old woman in song. Louisa and Tom, the whole street, singing:

Red nigger moon. Sinner!
Blood-burning moon. Sinner!
Come out that fact'ry door.

## 3

Bob Stone sauntered from his veranda out into the gloom of fir trees and magnolias. The clear white of his skin paled, and the flush of his cheeks turned purple. As if to balance this outer change, his mind became consciously a white man's. He passed the house with its huge open hearth which, in the days of slavery, was the plantation cookery. He saw Louisa bent over that hearth. He went in as a master should and took her. Direct, honest, bold. None of this sneaking that he had to go through now. The contrast was repulsive to him. His family had lost ground. Hell no, his family still owned the niggers, practically. Damned if they did, or he wouldnt have to duck around so. What would they think if they knew? His mother? His sister? He shouldnt mention them, shouldnt think of them in this connection. There in the dusk he blushed at doing so. Fellows about town were all right, but how about his friends up North? He could see them incredible, repulsed. They didnt know. The thought first made him laugh. Then, with their eyes still upon him, he began to feel embarrassed. He felt the need of explaining things to them. Explain hell. They wouldnt understand, and moreover, who ever heard of a Southerner getting on his knees to any Yankee, or anyone. No sir. He was going to see Louisa to-night, and love her. She was lovely—in her way. Nigger way. What way was that? Damned if he knew. Must know. He'd known her long enough to know. Was there something about niggers that you couldnt know? Listening to them at church didnt tell you anything. Looking at them didnt tell you anything. Talking to them didnt tell you anything—unless it was gossip, unless they wanted to talk. Of course, about farming, and licker, and craps—but those werent nigger. Nigger was something more. How much more? Something to be afraid of, more? Hell no. Who ever heard of being afraid of a nigger? Tom Burwell. Cartwell had told him that Tom went with Louisa after she reached home. No sir. No nigger had ever been with his girl. He'd like to see one try. Some position for him to be in. Him, Bob Stone, of the old Stone family, in a scrap with a nigger over a nigger girl. In the good old days . . . Ha! Those were the days. His family had lost ground. Not so much, though. Enough for him to have to cut through old Lemon's canefield by way of the woods, that he might meet her. She was worth it. Beautiful nigger gal. Why nigger? Why not, just gal? No, it was because she was nigger that he went to her. Sweet . . . The scent of boiling cane came to him. Then he saw the rich glow of the stove. He heard the voices of the men circled around it. He was about to skirt the clearing when he heard his own name mentioned. He stopped. Quivering. Leaning against a tree, he listened.

"Bad nigger. Yassur, he sho is one bad nigger when he gets started."

"Tom Burwell's been on th gang three times fo cuttin men."

"What y think he's agwine t do t Bob Stone?"

"Dunno yet. He aint found out. When he does—Baby!"

"Aint no tellin."

"Young Stone aint no quitter an I ken tell y that. Blood of th old uns in his veins."

"Thats right. He'll scrap, sho."

"Be gettin too hot f niggers round this away."

"Shut up, nigger. Y dont know what y talkin bout."

Bob Stone's ears burned as though he had been holding them over the stove. Sizzling heat welled up within him. His feet felt as if they rested on red-hot coals. They stung him to quick movement. He circled the fringe of the glowing. Not a twig cracked beneath his feet. He reached the path that led to factory town. Plunged furiously down it. Halfway along, a blindness within him veered him aside. He crashed into the bordering canebrake. Cane leaves cut his face and lips. He tasted blood. He threw himself down and dug his fingers in the ground. The earth was cool. Cane-roots took the fever from his hands. After a long while, or so it seemed to him, the thought came to him that it must be time to see Louisa. He got to his feet and walked calmly to their meeting place. No Louisa. Tom Burwell had her. Veins in his forehead bulged and distended. Saliva moistened the dried blood on his lips. He bit down on his lips. He tasted blood. Not his own blood; Tom Burwell's blood. Bob drove through the cane and out again upon the road. A hound swung down the path before him towards factory town. Bob couldnt see it. The dog loped aside to let him pass. Bob's blind rushing made him stumble over it. He fell with a thud that dazed him. The hound yelped. Answering yelps came from all over the countryside. Chickens cackled. Roosters crowed, heralding the bloodshot eyes of southern awakening. Singers in the town were silenced. They shut their windows down. Palpitant between the rooster crows, a chill hush settled upon the huddled forms of Tom and Louisa. A figure rushed from the shadow and stood before them. Tom popped to his feet.

"Whats y want?"

"I'm Bob Stone."

"Yassur—an I'm Tom Burwell. Whats y want?"

Bob lunged at him. Tom side-stepped, caught him by the shoulder, and flung him to the ground. Straddled him.

"Let me up."

"Yassur—but watch yo doins, Bob Stone."

A few dark figures, drawn by the sound of scuffle, stood about them. Bob sprang to his feet.

"Fight like a man, Tom Burwell, an I'll lick y."

Again he lunged. Tom side-stepped and flung him to the ground. Straddled him.

"Get off me, you godam nigger you."

"Yo sho has started somethin now. Get up."

Tom yanked him up and began hammering at him. Each blow sounded as if it smashed into a precious, irreplaceable soft something. Beneath them, Bob staggered back. He reached in his pocket and whipped out a knife.

"Thats my game, sho."

Blue flash, a steel blade slashed across Bob Stone's throat. He had a sweetish sick feeling. Blood began to flow. Then he felt a sharp twitch of pain. He let his knife drop. He slapped one hand against his neck. He pressed the other on top of his head as if to hold it down. He groaned. He turned, and staggered towards the crest of the hill in the direction of white town. Negroes who had seen the fight slunk into their homes and blew the lamps out. Louisa, dazed, hysterical, refused to go indoors. She slipped, crumbled, her body loosely propped against the woodwork of the well. Tom Burwell leaned against it. He seemed rooted there.

Bob reached Broad Street. White men rushed up to him. He collapsed in their arms.

"Tom Burwell. . . ."

White men like ants upon a forage rushed about. Except for the taut hum of their moving, all was silent. Shotguns, revolvers, rope, kerosene, torches. Two high-powered cars with glaring search-lights. They came together. The taut hum rose to a low roar. Then nothing could be heard but the flop of their feet in the thick dust of the road. The moving body of their silence preceded them over the crest of the hill into factory town. It flattened the Negroes beneath it. It rolled to the wall of the factory, where it stopped. Tom knew that they were coming. He couldnt move. And then he saw the search-lights of the two cars glaring down on him. A quick shock went through him. He stiffened. He started to run. A yell went up from the mob. Tom wheeled about and faced them. They poured down on him. They swarmed. A large man with dead-white face and flabby cheeks came to him and almost jabbed a gun-barrel through his guts.

"Hands behind y, nigger."

Tom's wrists were bound. The big man shoved him to the well. Burn him over it, and when the woodwork caved in, his body would drop to the bottom. Two deaths for a godam nigger. Louisa was driven back. The mob pushed in. Its pressure, its momentum was too great. Drag him to the factory. Wood and stakes already there. Tom moved in the direction indicated. But they had to drag him. They reached the great door. Too many to get in there. The mob divided and flowed around the walls to either side. The big man shoved him through the door. The mob pressed in from the sides. Taut humming. No words. A stake was sunk into the ground. Rotting floor boards piled around it. Kerosene poured on the rotting floor boards. Tom bound to the stake. His breast was bare. Nails scratches let little lines of blood trickle down and mat into the hair. His face, his eyes were set and stony. Except for irregular breathing, one would have thought him already dead. Torches were flung onto the pile. A great flare muffled in black smoke shot upward. The mob yelled. The mob was silent. Now Tom could be seen within the flames. Only his head, erect, lean, like a blackened stone. Stench of burning flesh soaked the air. Tom's eyes popped. His head settled downward. The mob yelled. Its yell echoed against the skeleton stone walls and sounded like a hundred yells. Like a hundred mobs yelling. Its yell thudded against the thick front wall and fell back. Ghost of a yell slipped through the flames and out the great door of the factory. It fluttered like a dying thing down the single street of factory town. Louisa, upon the step before her home, did not hear it, but her eyes opened slowly. They saw the full moon glowing in the great door. The full moon, an evil thing, an omen, soft showering the homes of folks she knew. Where were they, these people? She'd sing, and perhaps they'd come out and join her. Perhaps Tom Burwell would come. At any rate, the full moon in the great door was an omen which she must sing to:

Red nigger moon. Sinner!
Blood-burning moon. Sinner!
Come out that fact'ry door.

---

## This Text: Reading

1. In a book devoted to trying to get students to read various kinds of texts closely so that they might better understand the ideas and values the text embodies, why do you think we chose this short story as our first text? What does a close reading of this story reveal about America? About race? About class? About gender? About power? About sexuality?
2. Bob lingers over the word "nigger." Why can't he think of Louisa in any other terms? Why must that word always precede her name?

3. Given the ending of the story, is Toomer prophesizing about race relations in America?

### YOUR TEXT: WRITING

1. Write a short story from the perspective of three different characters. Is this difficult? The stream of consciousness of Bob Stone is both captivating and potentially confusing. What is the purpose of showing us how Stone thinks?
2. Write a comparative paper in which you explore "Blood-Burning Moon" and "Why Are All the Black Kids Sitting Together in the Cafeteria?" from Chapter 4. How do these two pieces compare in terms of their readings of the "otherness" of black and white cultures?
3. Write a personal essay exploring your own views on the intersection of race, gender, and class.

## GOODTIME JESUS (1979)

James Tate

Perhaps the funniest American poem of the last thirty years, "Goodtime Jesus" continues to surprise, anger, and please students twenty years after its original publication. Tate's reading of the text that is Jesus offers a humorous but human perspective on a figure not often portrayed as an actual human. Do you find Tate's reading of Jesus sympathetic?

JESUS GOT UP ONE DAY a little later than usual. He had been dreaming
so deep there was nothing left in his head. What was it?
A nightmare, dead bodies walking all around him, eyes rolled
back, skin falling off. But he wasn't afraid of that. It was a beautiful
day. How 'bout some coffee? Don't mind if I do. Take a little
ride on my donkey, I love that donkey. Hell, I love everybody.

### THIS TEXT: READING

1. If you are a Christian, you may find Tate's representation of Jesus offensive. Yet, you may also find it liberating, funny, and humanizing. How do you account for such contradictions?
2. Like "The Colonel," "Goodtime Jesus" does not look like a typical poem. What makes this text a poem?
3. Read Gerard Manley Hopkins' stunning poem "The Windhover" and compare his vision of Jesus to Tate's. Which is more accurate? Which text is more innovative?

### YOUR TEXT: WRITING

1. Write a paper comparing "Goodtime Jesus" with Gerard Manley Hopkins' poem "The Windhover." Both are poems about Jesus and both "see" Jesus through a culturally appropriate lens. Does one reveal a different Jesus than the other? How? Why?
2. Write a paper comparing "Goodtime Jesus" and "Slapstick." What do these poems suggest about the matrix between heaven and earth?
3. Based on Tate's representation of Jesus, write a character sketch of Jesus. What is this Jesus like? What does he do for fun? How does this view of Jesus differ from views in the Gospels?

## ODE TO MY SOCKS (1954)

Pablo Neruda

We love this poem. Like William Carlos Williams (author of "The Red Wheelbarrow," which is in your introduction), Chilean poet Pablo Neruda is famous for finding the poetic in the everyday. In this poem, he locates magic and poetry in a pair of socks. In what way are the socks a text?

MARU MORI BROUGHT ME
a pair
of socks
which she knitted herself
with her sheepherder's hands,
two socks as soft
as rabbits.
I slipped my feet into them
as though into
two cases
knitted
with threads of
twilight
and goatskin.
Violent socks,
my feet were two fish made
of wool,
two long sharks
sea-blue, shot
through by one golden thread,
two immense blackbirds,
two cannons

my feet
were honored
in this way
by these
heavenly
socks.
They were
so handsome
for the first time
my feet seemed to me
unacceptable
like two decrepit
firemen, firemen
unworthy
of that woven
fire,
of those glowing
socks.
Nevertheless
I resisted
the sharp temptation
to save them somewhere
as schoolboys
keep
fireflies,
as learned men
collect
sacred texts,
I resisted
the mad impulse
to put them
into a golden
cage and each day give them
birdseed
and pieces of melon.
Like explorers
in the jungle who hand
over the very rare
green deer
to the spit
and eat it
with remorse,
I stretched out
my feet
and pulled on the magnificent

socks
and than my shoes.
The moral
of my Ode is this:
beauty is twice
beauty
and what is good is doubly
good
when it is a matter of two
socks
made of wool
in Winter.

---

### This Text: Reading

1. This poem is one of Neruda's "Odas Elementales" (Elemental Odes), in which he praises basic, everyday things. Why do good socks deserve such praise?
2. How does the form of Neruda's poem augment its theme and its tone? Would reading the poem be different if it were rhymed and were written in long, horizontal lines?
3. In celebrating something as mundane as socks, what else is Neruda celebrating?

### Your Text: Writing

1. Write a paper comparing Neruda's ode with the famous "Ode on a Grecian Urn" by John Keats. How are the poems similar? How do they differ? What is the purpose of an ode?
2. Write a comparison/contrast paper in which you explore "Ode to My Socks" and another of Neruda's many odes, like "Ode to Salt." What does Neruda want his odes to do here?
3. Write a paper comparing "Ode to My Socks" with "The Red Wheelbarrow." Thematically and formally, they share a great deal. What? Why?

## THE COLONEL (1978)

Carolyn Forché

---

Originally published as part of a small section of poems called "The El Salvador Poems" that appeared in her book *The Country Between Us*, "The Colonel" has emerged as perhaps the most famous contemporary American poem. Its journalistic language and disturbing subject matter raise questions about what we consider "poetic." Do you think this text is, in fact, a poem?

WHAT YOU HAVE HEARD IS TRUE. I was in his house. His wife carried a tray of coffee and sugar. His daughter filed her nails, his son went out for the night. There were daily papers, pet dogs, a pistol on the cushion beside him. The moon swung bare on its black cord over the house. On the television was a cop show. It was in English. Broken bottles were embedded in the walls around the house to scoop the kneecaps from a man's legs or cut his hands to lace. On the windows there were gratings like those in liquor stores. We had dinner, rack of lamb, good wine, a gold bell was on the table for calling the maid. The maid brought green mangoes, salt, a type of bread. I was asked how I enjoyed the country. There was a brief commercial in Spanish. His wife took everything away. There was some talk of how difficult it had become to govern. The parrot said hello on the terrace. The colonel told it to shut up, and pushed himself from the table. My friend said to me with his eyes: say nothing. The colonel returned with a sack used to bring groceries home. He spilled many human ears on the table. They were like dried peach halves. There is no other way to say this. He took one of them in his hands, shook it in our faces, dropped it into a water glass. It came alive there. I am tired of fooling around he said. As for the rights of anyone, tell your people they can go fuck themselves. He swept the ears to the floor with his arm and held the last of his wine in the air. Something for your poetry, no? he said. Some of the ears on the floor caught this scrap of his voice. Some of the ears on the floor were pressed to the ground.

---

## This Text: Reading

1. Is this text a poem? Why or why not?
2. "The Colonel" is an excellent example of form and content mirroring each other. How would you describe the tone of this poem? What kind of language and vocabulary does the poet employ? How and why does this poem remind students of journalism?
3. Students generally love this poem because it seems utterly unpoetic. What are your expectations of poetry? How does this poem explode those expectations?

## Your Text: Writing

1. Write a comparison/contrast paper on "The Colonel" and "Goodtime Jesus." How are they similar? Different? How do their forms contribute to the meaning of the poems?
2. Write an essay on the relationship between art and politics. Look at other texts that are artistic representations of terrible events—movies like

*Schindler's List*, *Life Is Beautiful*, and *Boys Don't Cry*; literary texts like Walt Whitman's "When Lilacs Last in the Dooryard Bloom'd." Can art accurately represent horrible events?

3. Find a copy of Forche's book *The Country Between Us*, and write a paper on the El Salvador poems, from which "The Colonel" comes. What are some similarities among the poems?

## YOUNG GOODMAN BROWN (1835)

Nathaniel Hawthorne

One of the classic texts of 19th-century literature, Hawthorne's story seems as relevant today as it was in the 1860s. His critique of Puritan America may remind you of his famous novel *The Scarlet Letter*. Famous for its symbolism, "Young Goodman Brown" remains an insightful reading of early American values.

YOUNG GOODMAN BROWN came forth at sunset, into the street of Salem village, but put his head back, after crossing the threshold, to exchange a parting kiss with his young wife. And Faith, as the wife was aptly named, thrust her own pretty head into the street, letting the wind play with the pink ribbons of her cap, while she called to Goodman Brown.

"Dearest heart," whispered she, softly and rather sadly, when her lips were close to his ear, "pr'ythee, put off your journey until sunrise, and sleep in your own bed tonight. A lone woman is troubled with such dreams and such thoughts, that she's afeard of herself, sometimes. Pray, tarry with me this night, dear husband, of all nights in the year!"

"My love and my Faith," replied young Goodman Brown, "of all nights in the year, this one night must I tarry away from thee. My journey, as thou callest it, forth and back again, must needs be done 'twixt now and sunrise. What, my sweet, pretty wife, dost thou doubt me already, and we but three months married!"

"Then God bless you!" said Faith, with the pink ribbons, "and may you find all well, when you come back."

"Amen!" cried Goodman Brown. "Say thy prayers, dear Faith, and go to bed at dusk, and no harm will come to thee."

So they parted; and the young man pursued his way, until, being about to turn the corner by the meeting-house, he looked back and saw the head of Faith still peeping after him, with a melancholy air, in spite of her pink ribbons.

"Poor little Faith!" thought he, for his heart smote him. "What a wretch am I, to leave her on such an errand! She talks of dreams, too.

Methought, as she spoke, there was trouble in her face, as if a dream had warned her what work is to be done tonight. But, no, no! 'twould kill her to think it. Well; she's a blessed angel on earth; and after this one night, I'll cling to her skirts and follow her to Heaven."

With this excellent resolve for the future, Goodman Brown felt himself justified in making more haste on his present evil purpose. He had taken a dreary road, darkened by all the gloomiest trees of the forest, which barely stood aside to let the narrow path creep through, and closed immediately behind. It was all as lonely as could be; and there is this peculiarity in such a solitude, that the traveller knows not who may be concealed by the innumerable trunks and the thick boughs overhead; so that, with lonely footsteps, he may yet be passing through an unseen multitude.

"There may be a devilish Indian behind every tree," said Goodman Brown to himself; and he glanced fearfully behind him, as he added, "What if the devil himself should be at my very elbow!"

His head being turned back, he passed a crook of the road, and looking forward again, beheld the figure of a man, in grave and decent attire, seated at the foot of an old tree. He arose, at Goodman Brown's approach, and walked onward; side by side with him.

"You are late, Goodman Brown," said he. "The clock of the Old South was striking, as I came through Boston; and that is full fifteen minutes agone."

"Faith kept me back awhile," replied the young man, with a tremor in his voice, caused by the sudden appearance of his companion, though not wholly unexpected.

It was now deep dusk in the forest, and deepest in that part of it where these two were journeying. As nearly as could be discerned, the second traveller was about fifty years old, apparently in the same rank of life as Goodman Brown, and bearing a considerable resemblance to him, though perhaps more in expression than features. Still, they might have been taken for father and son. And yet, though the elder person was as simply clad as the younger, and as simple in manner too, he had an indescribable air of one who knew the world, and would not have felt abashed at the governor's dinner-table, or in King William's court, were it possible that his affairs should call him thither. But the only thing about him, that could be fixed upon as remarkable, was his staff, which bore the likeness of a great black snake, so curiously wrought, that it might almost be seen to twist and wriggle itself like a living serpent. This, of course, must have been an ocular deception, assisted by the uncertain light.

"Come, Goodman Brown!" cried his fellow-traveller, "this is a dull pace for the beginning of a journey. Take my staff, if you are so soon weary."

"Friend," said the other, exchanging his slow pace for a full stop, "having kept covenant by meeting thee here, it is my purpose now to return whence I came. I have scruples, touching the matter thou wot'st of."

"Sayest thou so?" replied he of the serpent, smiling apart. "Let us walk on, nevertheless, reasoning as we go, and if I convince thee not, thou shalt turn back. We are but a little way in the forest, yet."

"Too far, too far!" exclaimed the goodman, unconsciously resuming his walk. "My father never went into the woods on such an errand, nor his father before him. We have been a race of honest men and good Christians, since the days of the martyrs. And shall I be the first of the name of Brown, that ever took this path and kept"—

"Such company, thou wouldst say," observed the elder person, interrupting his pause. "Well said, Goodman Brown! I have been as well acquainted with your family as with ever a one among the Puritans; and that's no trifle to say. I helped your grandfather, the constable, when he lashed the Quaker woman so smartly through the streets of Salem. And it was I that brought your father a pitch-pine knot, kindled at my own hearth, to set fire to an Indian village, in King Philip's War. They were my good friends, both; and many a pleasant walk have we had along this path, and returned merrily after midnight. I would fain be friends with you, for their sake."

"If it be as thou sayest," replied Goodman Brown, "I marvel they never spoke of these matters. Or, verily, I marvel not, seeing that the least rumor of the sort would have driven them from New England. We are a people of prayer, and good works to boot, and abide no such wickedness."

"Wickedness or not," said the traveller with the twisted staff, "I have a very general acquaintance here in New England. The deacons of many a church have drunk the communion wine with me; the selectmen, of divers towns, make me their chairman; and a majority of the Great and General Court are firm supporters of my interest. The governor and I, too—but these are state-secrets."

"Can this be so!" cried Goodman Brown, with a stare of amazement at his undisturbed companion. "Howbeit, I have nothing to do with the governor and council; they have their own ways, and are no rule for a simple husbandman like me. But, were I to go on with thee, how should I meet the eye of that good old man, our minister, at Salem village? Oh, his voice would make me tremble, both Sabbath-day and lecture-day!"

Thus far, the elder traveller had listened with due gravity, but now burst into a fit of irrepressible mirth, shaking himself so violently that his snake-like staff actually seemed to wriggle in sympathy.

"Ha! ha! ha!" shouted he, again and again; then composing himself, "Well, go on, Goodman Brown, go on; but, prithee, don't kill me with laughing!"

"Well, then, to end the matter at once," said Goodman Brown, considerably nettled, "there is my wife, Faith. It would break her dear little heart; and I'd rather break my own!"

"Nay, if that be the case," answered the other, "e'en go thy ways, Goodman Brown. I would not, for twenty old women like the one hobbling before us, that Faith should come to any harm."

As he spoke, he pointed his staff at a female figure on the path, in whom Goodman Brown recognized a very pious and exemplary dame, who had taught him his catechism in youth, and was still his moral and spiritual adviser, jointly with the minister and Deacon Gookin.

"A marvel, truly, that Goody Cloyse should be so far in the wilderness, at night-fall!" said he. "But, with your leave, friend, I shall take a cut through the woods, until we have left this Christian woman behind. Being a stranger to you, she might ask whom I was consorting with, and whither I was going."

"Be it so," said his fellow-traveller. "Betake you to the woods, and let me keep the path."

Accordingly, the young man turned aside, but took care to watch his companion, who advanced softly along the road, until he had come within a staff's length of the old dame. She, meanwhile, was making the best of her way, with singular speed for so aged a woman, and mumbling some indistinct words, a prayer, doubtless, as she went. The traveller put forth his staff, and touched her withered neck with what seemed the serpent's tail.

"The devil!" screamed the pious old lady.

"Then Goody Cloyse knows her old friend?" observed the traveller, confronting her, and leaning on his writhing stick.

"Ah, forsooth, and is it your worship, indeed?" cried the good dame. "Yea, truly is it, and in the very image of my old gossip, Goodman Brown, the grandfather of the silly fellow that now is. But, would your worship believe it? my broomstick hath strangely disappeared, stolen, as I suspect, by that unhanged witch, Goody Cory, and that, too, when I was all anointed with the juice of smallage and cinque-foil and wolf's-bane"—

"Mingled with fine wheat and the fat of a new-born babe," said the shape of old Goodman Brown.

"Ah, your worship knows the recipe," cried the old lady, cackling aloud. "So, as I was saying, being all ready for the meeting, and no horse to ride on, I made up my mind to foot it; for they tell me, there is a nice young man to be taken into communion tonight. But now your good worship will lend me your arm, and we shall be there in a twinkling."

"That can hardly be," answered her friend. "I may not spare you my arm, Goody Cloyse, but here is my staff, if you will."

So saying, he threw it down at her feet, where, perhaps, it assumed life, being one of the rods which its owner had formerly lent to Egyptian Magi. Of this fact, however, Goodman Brown could not take cognizance. He had cast up his eyes in astonishment, and looking down again, beheld neither Goody Cloyse nor the serpentine staff, but his fellow-traveller alone, who waited for him as calmly as if nothing had happened.

"That old woman taught me my catechism!" said the young man; and there was a world of meaning in this simple comment.

They continued to walk onward, while the elder traveller exhorted his companion to make good speed and persevere in the path, discoursing so aptly, that his arguments seemed rather to spring up in the bosom of his auditor, than to be suggested by himself. As they went, he plucked a branch of maple, to serve for a walking-stick, and began to strip it of the twigs and little boughs, which were wet with evening dew. The moment his fingers touched them, they became strangely withered and dried up, as with a week's sunshine. Thus the pair proceeded, at a good free pace, until suddenly, in a gloomy hollow of the road, Goodman Brown sat himself down on the stump of a tree, and refused to go any farther.

"Friend," said he, stubbornly, "my mind is made up. Not another step will I budge on this errand. What if a wretched old woman do choose to go to the devil, when I thought she was going to Heaven! Is that any reason why I should quit my dear Faith, and go after her?"

"You will think better of this by-and-by," said his acquaintance, composedly. "Sit here and rest yourself awhile; and when you feel like moving again, there is my staff to help you along."

Without more words, he threw his companion the maple stick, and was as speedily out of sight as if he had vanished into the deepening gloom. The young man sat a few moments by the road-side, applauding himself greatly, and thinking with how clear a conscience he should meet the minister, in his morning-walk, nor shrink from the eye of good old Deacon Gookin. And what calm sleep would be his, that very night, which was to have been spent so wickedly, but purely and sweetly now, in the arms of Faith! Amidst these pleasant and praiseworthy meditations, Goodman Brown heard the tramp of horses along the road, and deemed it advisable to conceal himself within the verge of the forest, conscious of the guilty purpose that had brought him thither, though now so happily turned from it.

On came the hoof-tramps and the voices of the riders, two grave old voices, conversing soberly as they drew near. These mingled sounds appeared to pass along the road, within a few yards of the young man's hiding-place; but owing, doubtless, to the depth of the gloom, at that particular spot, neither the travellers nor their steeds were visible. Though their figures brushed the small boughs by the way-side, it could not be seen that they intercepted, even for a moment, the faint gleam from the strip of bright sky, athwart which they must have passed. Goodman Brown alternately crouched and stood on tip-toe, pulling aside the branches, and thrusting forth his head as far as he durst, without discerning so much as a shadow. It vexed him the more, because he could have sworn, were such a thing possible, that he recognized the voices of the minister and Deacon Gookin, jogging along quietly, as they were wont to do, when bound to some ordination or ecclesiastical council. While yet within hearing, one of the riders stopped to pluck a switch.

"Of the two, reverend Sir," said the voice like the deacon's, "I had rather miss an ordination-dinner than tonight's meeting. They tell me that some of our community are to be here from Falmouth and beyond, and others from Connecticut and Rhode Island; besides several of the Indian powows, who, after their fashion, know almost as much deviltry as the best of us. Moreover, there is a goodly young woman to be taken into communion."

"Mighty well, Deacon Gookin!" replied the solemn old tones of the minister. "Spur up, or we shall be late. Nothing can be done, you know, until I get on the ground."

The hoofs clattered again, and the voices, talking so strangely in the empty air, passed on through the forest, where no church had ever been gathered, nor solitary Christian prayed. Whither, then, could these holy men be journeying, so deep into the heathen wilderness? Young Goodman Brown caught hold of a tree, for support, being ready to sink down on the ground, faint and overburthened with the heavy sickness of his heart. He looked up to the sky, doubting whether there really was a Heaven above him. Yet, there was the blue arch, and the stars brightening in it.

"With Heaven above, and Faith below, I will yet stand firm against the devil!" cried Goodman Brown.

While he still gazed upward, into the deep arch of the firmament, and had lifted his hands to pray, a cloud, though no wind was stirring, hurried across the zenith, and hid the brightening stars. The blue sky was still visible, except directly overhead, where this black mass of cloud was sweeping swiftly northward. Aloft in the air, as if from the depths of the cloud, came a confused and doubtful sound of voices. Once, the listener fancied that he could distinguish the accent of townspeople of his own, men and women, both pious and ungodly, many of whom he had met at the communion-table, and had seen others rioting at the tavern. The next moment, so indistinct were the sounds, he doubted whether he had heard aught but the murmur of the old forest, whispering without a wind. Then came a stronger swell of those familiar tones, heard daily in the sunshine, at Salem village, but never, until now, from a cloud of night. There was one voice, of a young woman, uttering lamentations, yet with an uncertain sorrow, and entreating for some favor, which, perhaps, it would grieve her to obtain. And all the unseen multitude, both saints and sinners, seemed to encourage her onward.

"Faith!" shouted Goodman Brown, in a voice of agony and desperation; and the echoes of the forest mocked him, crying—"Faith! Faith!" as if bewildered wretches were seeking her, all through the wilderness.

The cry of grief, rage, and terror, was yet piercing the night, when the unhappy husband held his breath for a response. There was a scream, drowned immediately in a louder murmur of voices, fading into far-off laughter, as the dark cloud swept away, leaving the clear and silent sky above Goodman Brown. But something fluttered lightly down through the air, and caught on the branch of a tree. The young man seized it, and beheld a pink ribbon.

"My Faith is gone!" cried he, after one stupefied moment. "There is no good on earth; and sin is but a name. Come, devil! for to thee is this world given."

And maddened with despair, so that he laughed loud and long, did Goodman Brown grasp his staff and set forth again, at such a rate, that he seemed to fly along the forest-path, rather than to walk or run. The road grew wilder and drearier, and more faintly traced, and vanished at length, leaving him in the heart of the dark wilderness, still rushing onward, with the instinct that guides mortal man to evil. The whole forest was peopled with frightful sounds; the creaking of the trees, the howling of wild beasts, and the yell of Indians; while, sometimes the wind tolled like a distant church-bell, and sometimes gave a broad roar around the traveller, as if all Nature were laughing him to scorn. But he was himself the chief horror of the scene, and shrank not from its other horrors.

"Ha! ha! ha!" roared Goodman Brown, when the wind laughed at him. "Let us hear which will laugh loudest! Think not to frighten me with your deviltry! Come witch, come wizard, come Indian powow, come devil himself! and here comes Goodman Brown. You may as well fear him as he fear you!"

In truth, all through the haunted forest, there could be nothing more frightful than the figure of Goodman Brown. On he flew, among the black pines, brandishing his staff with frenzied gestures, now giving vent to an inspiration of horrid blasphemy, and now shouting forth such laughter, as set all the echoes of the forest laughing like demons around him. The fiend in his own shape is less hideous, than when he rages in the breast of man. Thus sped the demoniac on his course, until, quivering among the trees, he saw a red light before him, as when the felled trunks and branches of a clearing have been set on fire, and throw up their lurid blaze against the sky, at the hour of midnight. He paused, in a lull of the tempest that had driven him onward, and heard the swell of what seemed a hymn, rolling solemnly from a distance, with the weight of many voices. He knew the tune; it was a familiar one in the choir of the village meetinghouse. The verse died heavily away, and was lengthened by a chorus, not of human voices, but of all the sounds of the benighted wilderness, pealing in awful harmony together. Goodman Brown cried out; and his cry was lost to his own ear, by its unison with the cry of the desert.

In the interval of silence, he stole forward, until the light glared full upon his eyes. At one extremity of an open space, hemmed in by the dark wall of the forest, arose a rock, bearing some rude, natural resemblance either to an altar or a pulpit, and surrounded by four blazing pines, their tops aflame, their stems untouched, like candles at an evening meeting. The mass of foliage, that had overgrown the summit of the rock, was all on fire, blazing high into the night, and fitfully illuminating the whole field. Each pendant twig and leafy festoon was in a blaze. As the red light arose and fell, a numerous congregation alternately shone forth, then disappeared in shadow, and again grew, as it were, out of the darkness, peopling the heart of the solitary woods at once.

"A grave and dark-clad company!" quoth Goodman Brown.

In truth, they were such. Among them, quivering to and fro, between gloom and splendor, appeared faces that would be seen, next day, at the council-board of the province, and others which, Sabbath after Sabbath, looked devoutly heavenward, and benignantly over the crowded pews, from the holiest pulpits in the land. Some affirm, that the lady of the governor was there. At least, there were high dames well known to her, and wives of honored husbands, and widows, a great multitude, and ancient maidens, all of excellent repute, and fair young girls, who trembled lest their mothers should espy them. Either the sudden gleams of light, flashing over the obscure field, bedazzled Goodman Brown, or he recognized a score of the church-members of Salem village, famous for their especial sanctity. Good old Deacon Gookin had arrived, and waited at the skirts of that venerable saint, his reverend pastor. But, irreverently consorting with these grave, reputable, and pious people, these elders of the church, these chaste dames and dewy virgins, there were men of dissolute lives and women of spotted fame, wretches given over to all mean and filthy vice, and suspected even of horrid crimes. It was strange to see, that the good shrank not from the wicked, nor were the sinners abashed by the saints. Scattered, also, among their palefaced enemies, were the Indian priests, or powows, who had often scared their native forest with more hideous incantations than any known to English witchcraft.

"But, where is Faith?" thought Goodman Brown; and, as hope came into his heart, he trembled.

Another verse of the hymn arose, a slow and mournful strain, such as the pious love, but joined to words which expressed all that our nature can conceive of sin, and darkly hinted at far more. Unfathomable to mere mortals is the lore of fiends. Verse after verse was sung, and still the chorus of the desert swelled between, like the deepest tone of a mighty organ. And, with the final peal of that dreadful anthem, there came a sound, as if the roaring wind, the rushing streams, the howling beasts, and every other voice of the unconverted wilderness, were mingling and according with the voice of guilty man, in homage to the prince of all. The four blazing pines threw up a loftier flame, and obscurely discovered shapes and visages of horror on the smoke-wreaths, above the impious assembly. At the same moment, the fire on the rock shot redly forth, and formed a glowing arch above its base, where now appeared a figure. With reverence be it spoken, the apparition bore no slight similitude, both in garb and manner, to some grave divine of the New England churches.

"Bring forth the converts!" cried a voice, that echoed through the field and rolled into the forest.

At the word, Goodman Brown stepped forth from the shadow of the trees, and approached the congregation, with whom he felt a loathful brotherhood, by the sympathy of all that was wicked in his heart. He could have well nigh sworn, that the shape of his own dead father beckoned him to advance, looking downward from a smoke-wreath, while a woman, with dim features of despair, threw out her hand to warn him back. Was it his mother? But he had no power to retreat one step, nor to resist, even in thought, when the minister and good old Deacon Gookin seized his arms, and led him to the blazing rock. Thither came also the slender form of a veiled female, led between Goody Cloyse, that pious teacher of the catechism, and Martha Carrier, who had received the devil's promise to be queen of hell. A rampant hag was she! And there stood the proselytes, beneath the canopy of fire.

"Welcome, my children," said the dark figure, "to the communion of your race! Ye have found, thus young, your nature and your destiny. My children, look behind you!"

They turned; and flashing forth, as it were, in a sheet of flame, the fiend-worshippers were seen; the smile of welcome gleamed darkly on every visage.

"There," resumed the sable form, "are all whom ye have reverenced from youth. Ye deemed them holier than yourselves, and shrank from your own sin, contrasting it with their lives of righteousness, and prayerful aspirations heavenward. Yet, here are they all, in my worshipping assembly! This night it shall be granted you to know their secret deeds; how hoary-bearded elders of the church have whispered wanton words to the young maids of their households; how many a woman, eager for widow's weeds, has given her husband a drink at bed-time, and let him sleep his last sleep in her bosom; how beardless youth have made haste to inherit their father's wealth; and how fair damsels—blush not, sweet ones—have dug little graves in the garden, and bidden me, the sole guest, to an infant's funeral. By the sympathy of your human hearts for sin, ye shall scent out all the places—whether in church, bed-chamber, street, field, or forest—where crime has been committed, and shall exult to behold the whole earth one stain of guilt, one mighty blood-spot. Far more than this! It shall be yours to penetrate, in every bosom, the deep mystery of sin, the fountain of all wicked arts, and which inexhaustibly supplies more evil impulses than human power—than my power at its utmost—can make manifest in deeds. And now, my children, look upon each other."

They did so; and, by the blaze of the hell-kindled torches, the wretched man beheld his Faith, and the wife her husband, trembling before that unhallowed altar.

"Lo! there ye stand, my children," said the figure, in a deep and solemn tone, almost sad, with its despairing awfulness, as if his once angelic nature could yet mourn for our miserable race. "Depending upon one another's hearts, ye had still hoped that virtue were not all a dream! Now are ye undeceived! Evil is the nature of mankind. Evil must be your only happiness. Welcome, again, my children, to the communion of your race!"

"Welcome!" repeated the fiend-worshippers, in one cry of despair and triumph.

And there they stood, the only pair, as it seemed, who were yet hesitating on the verge of wickedness, in this dark world. A basin was hollowed, naturally, in the rock. Did it contain water, reddened by the lurid light? or was it blood? or, perchance, a liquid flame? Herein did the Shape of Evil dip his hand, and prepare to lay the mark of baptism upon their foreheads, that they might be partakers of the mystery of sin, more conscious of the secret guilt of others, both in deed and thought, than they could now be of their own. The husband cast one look at his pale wife, and Faith at him. What polluted wretches would the next glance show them to each other, shuddering alike at what they disclosed and what they saw!

"Faith! Faith!" cried the husband. "Look up to Heaven, and resist the Wicked One!"

Whether Faith obeyed, he knew not. Hardly had he spoken, when he found himself amid calm night and solitude, listening to a roar of the wind, which died heavily away through the forest. He staggered against the rock, and felt it chill and damp, while a hanging twig, that had been all on fire, besprinkled his cheek with the coldest dew.

The next morning, young Goodman Brown came slowly into the street of Salem village, staring around him like a bewildered man. The good old minister was taking a walk along the graveyard, to get an appetite for breakfast and meditate his sermon, and bestowed a blessing, as he passed, on Goodman Brown. He shrank from the venerable saint, as if to avoid an anathema. Old Deacon Gookin was at domestic worship, and the holy words of his prayer were heard through the open window. "What God doth the wizard pray to?" quoth Goodman Brown. Goody Cloyse, that excellent old Christian, stood in the early sunshine, at her own lattice, catechising a little girl, who had brought her a pint of morning's milk. Goodman Brown snatched away the child, as from the grasp of the fiend himself. Turning the corner by the meeting-house, he spied the head of Faith, with the pink ribbons, gazing anxiously forth, and bursting into such joy at sight of him, that she skipt along the street, and almost kissed her husband before the whole village. But Goodman Brown looked sternly and sadly into her face, and passed on without a greeting.

Had Goodman Brown fallen asleep in the forest, and only dreamed a wild dream of a witch-meeting?

Be it so, if you will. But, alas! it was a dream of evil omen for young Goodman Brown. A stern, a sad, a darkly meditative, a distrustful, if not a desperate man, did he become, from the night of that fearful dream. On the Sabbath-day, when the congregation were singing a holy psalm, he could not listen, because an anthem of sin rushed loudly upon his ear, and drowned all the blessed strain. When the minister spoke from the pulpit, with power and fervid eloquence, and with his hand on the open Bible, of the sacred truths of our religion, and of saint-like lives and triumphant deaths, and of future bliss or misery unutterable, then did Goodman Brown turn pale, dreading lest the roof should thunder down upon the gray blasphemer and his hearers. Often, awaking suddenly at midnight, he shrank from the bosom of Faith, and at morning or eventide, when the family knelt down at prayer, he scowled, and muttered to himself, and gazed sternly at his wife, and turned away. And when he had lived long, and was borne to his grave, a hoary corpse, followed by Faith, an aged woman, and children and grandchildren, a goodly procession, besides neighbors, not a few, they carved no hopeful verse upon his tombstone; for his dying hour was gloom.

---

### THIS TEXT: READING

1. "Young Goodman Brown" is loaded with symbolism: the names, the pink ribbons, the journey, the boundary between civilization and wilderness. Taking all of these into consideration, what is Hawthorne's main theme?
2. Hawthorne is perhaps best known for his novel *The Scarlet Letter*, that, like "Young Goodman Brown," is also set during the Puritan era. Why might Hawthorne believe that events that took place in the 1600s might affect events or values in the 1800s? Or the 2000s?
3. We think "Young Goodman Brown" may be the most representative American short story. Why?

### YOUR TEXT: WRITING

1. Write an essay in which you explore the symbolism of wilderness and civilization. Why doesn't Goodman Brown want to venture very deep into the wilderness? What does the wilderness represent to him and to the Puritans?
2. Do a character sketch of Goodman Brown. How would you characterize his personality? What kind of man is he?
3. Compare "Young Goodman Brown" and "Isla." How are both stories about religion?

## MY MISTRESS' EYES ARE NOTHING LIKE THE SUN (SONNET 130) (1609)

William Shakespeare

---

We have gone against the grain and decided to publish a poem by a little known author named William Shakespeare. You may have heard of him. Renowned for plays like *Romeo and Juliet* and *Hamlet*, he is also a pretty good poet. Here, Shakespeare offers a unique perspective on Renaissance notions of beauty.

MY MISTRESS' EYES ARE NOTHING like the sun,
Coral is far more red, than her lips red,
If snow be white, why then her breasts are dun:

If hairs be wires, black wires grow on her head:
I have seen roses damasked, red and white,
But no such roses see I in her cheeks,
And in some perfumes is there more delight,
Than in the breath that from my mistress reeks.
I love to hear her speak, yet well I know,
That music hath a far more pleasing sound:
I grant I never saw a goddess go,
My mistress when she walks treads on the ground.
And yet by heaven I think my love as rare,
As any she belied with false compare.

---

### This Text: Reading

1. This is a funny and often imitated poem. What is the source of the poem's humor?
2. As you know, the poem is a sonnet, a particular form of poetry. How does the poem work within the sonnet form?
3. In what way is the poem both an insult and a compliment?

### Your Text: Writing

1. Write an analytical paper focusing on the language of flattery. Of course, you can compare this poem to other Renaissance love poems. How does this poem fit into the tradition of love poetry?
2. Write a comparison/contrast paper on this sonnet and Neruda's "Ode to My Socks." How are they similar? In what ways, other than the obvious, do they differ?
3. Write a personal essay on your experience of reading this poem. What was your reaction? How did it make you feel? Is it a good poem? Why? What is your favorite line? Would you like to have such a poem written about you?

## MY LIFE HAD STOOD – A LOADED GUN (POEM 759) (1863)

Emily Dickinson

---

One of the most enigmatic and intriguing poems from nineteenth-century America, Dickinson's text remains open to any number of interpretations. Whether you see the poem as a religious awakening, a sexual awakening, a feminist realization, a poetic epiphany or some other moment of insight, we are certain you will find it thematically compelling and rhythmically pleasing.

My Life had stood – a Loaded Gun –
In Corners – till a Day
The Owner passed – identified –
And carried Me away –

And now We roam in Sovereign Woods –
And now We hunt the Doe –
And every time I speak for Him –
The Mountains straight reply –

And do I smile, such cordial light
Upon the Valley glow –
It is as a Vesuvian face
Had let its pleasure through –

And when at Night – Our good Day done –
I guard My Master's Head –
'Tis better than the Eider-Duck's
Deep Pillow – to have shared –

To foe of His – I'm deadly foe –
None stir the second time –
On whom I lay a Yellow Eye –
Or an emphatic Thumb –

Though I than He – may longer live
He longer must – than I –
For I have but the power to kill,
Without—the power to die—

---

## This Text: Reading

1. In what way could this poem be a kind of confession about finding God and Christianity?
2. In what way could this poem be a kind of confession about falling in love and the poet's first sexual experience?
3. In what way could this poem be a kind of confession about coming to consciousness regarding gender equality and women's rights?

## Your Text: Writing

1. Write a persuasive paper in which you argue one of the readings in the questions above. Be sure to support your assertions with specific examples from the poem itself.

2. Write a paper exploring and explaining the gun and weaponry symbolism in the poem.
3. Compare this poem to another Dickinson poem, perhaps "After great pain, a formal feeling comes." How are these poems about a kind of awakening or awareness?

## SLAPSTICK (1993)

### Wislawa Szymborska

Winner of the Nobel Prize for Literature, Polish author Szymborska reads both angels and humans in an unusual but engaging way. Her reference to "slapstick," a kind of farcical physical comedy made popular by vaudeville performances and early funny movies, makes an argument about how nonearthly beings may perceive us.

IF THERE ARE ANGELS,
I doubt they read
our novels concerning thwarted hopes.

I'm afraid, alas,
they never touch the poems
that bear our grudges against the world.

The rantings and railings
of our plays
must drive them, I suspect,
to distraction.

Off-duty, between angelic—
i.e., inhuman—occupations,
our slapstick
from the age of silent film.

To our dirge wailers,
garment renders,
and teeth gnashers,
they prefer, I suppose,
that poor devil

who grabs the drowning man by his toupee
or, starving, devours his own shoelaces
with gusto.

From the waist up, starch and aspirations;
below, a startled mouse
runs down his trousers.
I'm sure
that's what they call real entertainment.

A crazy chase in circles
ends up pursuing the pursuer.
The light at the end of the tunnel
turns out to be tiger's eye.
A hundred disasters
mean a hundred comic somersaults
turned over a hundred abysses.

If there are angels,
they must, I hope,
find this convincing,
this merriment dangling from terror,
not even crying Save me Save me
since all of this takes place in silence.

I can even imagine
that they clap their wings
and tears run from their eyes
from laughter, if nothing else.

---

## This Text: Reading

1. Like Tate in "Goodtime Jesus," Szymborska offers a secular twist on a sacred subject; yet, like Tate, she also clearly loves the subject at hand. What are some similarities between her angels and Tate's Jesus?
2. The title of Szymborska's poem evokes early silent films starring people like Buster Keaton and Charlie Chaplin. In what way is her poem cinematic?
3. How does Szymborska's vision of angels shed light on our lives as humans? How does she put human life into perspective?

## Your Text: Writing

1. Write a paper comparing "Slapstick" with an old Buster Keaton movie. In what way are human endeavors like a slapstick movie?
2. Explicate this poem (to explicate means to "unpack"). Traditionally, an explication is a line-by-line explanation of the poem. So, take your time and work through the poem, explaining symbol, metaphor, tone, style, and rhythm. How are these things connected?

3. Write a paper comparing "Slapstick" with "Goodtime Jesus." Explore how both authors read the human and the holy.

## THE STORY OF AN HOUR (1894)

Kate Chopin

Chopin's famous short story will not take you any where near an hour to read, but you will probably be thinking about it for hours after you finish it. It is a study in economy. We know so much about the main character in so little space. The ending, one of the best in literature, holds many layers of meaning.

KNOWING THAT MRS. MALLARD was afflicted with a heart trouble, great care was taken to break to her as gently as possible the news of her husband's death.

It was her sister Josephine who told her, in broken sentences; veiled hints that revealed in half concealing. Her husband's friend Richards was there, too, near her. It was he who had been in the newspaper office when intelligence of the railroad disaster was received, with Brently Mallard's name leading the list of "killed." He had only taken the time to assure himself of its truth by a second telegram, and had hastened to forestall any less careful, less tender friend in bearing the sad message.

She did not hear the story as many women have heard the same, with a paralyzed inability to accept its significance. She wept at once, with sudden, wild abandonment, in her sister's arms. When the storm of grief had spent itself she went away to her room alone. She would have no one follow.

There stood, facing the open window, a comfortable, roomy armchair. Into this she sank, pressed down by a physical exhaustion that haunted her body and seemed to reach into her soul.

She could see in the open square before her house the tops of trees that were all aquiver with the new spring life. The delicious breath of rain was in the air. In the street below a peddler was crying his wares. The notes of a distant song which some one was singing reached her faintly, and countless sparrows were twittering in the eaves.

There were patches of blue sky showing here and there through the clouds that had met and piled one above the other in the west facing her window.

She sat with her head thrown back upon the cushion of the chair, quite motionless, except when a sob came up into her throat and shook her, as a child who has cried itself to sleep continues to sob in its dreams.

She was young, with a fair, calm face, whose lines bespoke repression and even a certain strength. But now there was a dull stare in her eyes, whose gaze was fixed away off yonder on one of those patches of blue sky. It was not a glance of reflection, but rather indicated a suspension of intelligent thought.

There was something coming to her and she was waiting for it, fearfully. What was it? She did not know; it was too subtle and elusive to name. But she felt it, creeping out of the sky, reaching toward her through the sounds, the scents, the color that filled the air.

Now her bosom rose and fell tumultuously. She was beginning to recognize this thing that was approaching to possess her, and she was striving to beat it back with her will—as powerless as her two white slender hands would have been.

When she abandoned herself a little whispered word escaped her slightly parted lips. She said it over and over under her breath: "free, free, free!" The vacant stare and the look of terror that had followed it went from her eyes. They stayed keen and bright. Her pulses beat fast, and the coursing blood warmed and relaxed every inch of her body.

She did not stop to ask if it were or were not a monstrous joy that held her. A clear and exalted perception enabled her to dismiss the suggestion as trivial.

She knew that she would weep again when she saw the kind, tender hands folded in death; the face that had never looked save with love upon her, fixed and gray and dead. But she saw beyond that bitter moment a long procession of years to come that would belong to her absolutely. And she opened and spread her arms out to them in welcome.

There would be no one to live for her during those coming years; she would live for herself. There would be no powerful will bending hers in that blind persistence with which men and women believe they have a right to impose a private will upon a fellow-creature. A kind intention or a cruel intention made the act seem no less a crime as she looked upon it in that brief moment of illumination.

And yet she had loved him—sometimes. Often she had not. What did it matter! What could love, the unsolved mystery, count for in face of this possession of self-assertion which she suddenly recognized as the strongest impulse of her being!

"Free! Body and soul free!" she kept whispering.

Josephine was kneeling before the closed door with her lips to the keyhole, imploring for admission. "Louise, open the door! I beg; open the door—you will make yourself ill. What are you doing, Louise? For heaven's sake open the door."

"Go away. I am not making myself ill." No; she was drinking in a very elixir of life though that open window.

Her fancy was running riot along those days ahead of her. Spring days, and summer days, and all sorts of days that would be her own. She breathed a quick prayer that life might be long. It was only yesterday she had thought with a shudder that life might be long.

She arose at length and opened the door to her sister's importunities. There was a feverish triumph in her eyes, and she carried herself unwittingly like a goddess of Victory. She clasped her sister's waist, and together they descended the stairs. Richards stood waiting for them at the bottom.

Some one was opening the front door with a latchkey. It was Brently Mallard who entered, a little travel-stained, composedly carrying his grip-sack and umbrella. He had been far from the scene of accident, and did not even know that there had been one. He stood amazed at Josephine's piercing cry; at Richards' quick motion to screen himself from the view of his wife.

But Richards was too late.

When the doctors came they said she had died of heart disease—of joy that kills.

---

## This Text: Reading

1. Time is very important in this story. A lot happens in an hour, yet it only took you about 10 minutes (or less) to read the story. Explain how so much can happen in such a short time.
2. The ending of this story is dramatic, shocking, and deservedly famous. What kind of cultural complexities and expectations is Chopin working with here?
3. How might this story fit in the chapter on gender? How is it a feminist text?

## Your Text: Writing

1. Write a paper comparing "The Story of an Hour" and Holly Devor's piece on gender roles (in Chapter 6). How does the main character "do" gender? Why does it "kill" her?
2. Compare this story with "No Name Woman" (also in Chapter 6). How are both stories about escape and gender?
3. Do you see any similarities between this story and "Young Goodman Brown"? Write a paper arguing how both stories are critiques of American values.

# The Literature Suite—Social and Economic Class

Before the printing press was invented and books were published the act of reading was privileged. The invention of the printing press alleviated that to some degree, but to this day, there remain hundreds of privileged activities in America that only people with a certain income can have access to. There are obvious things like country club memberships, a house in the Hamptons, and a Mercedes convertible. However, in a country that is supposed to be casteless and classless, we are reminded of social and economic class all the time. Homeless men and women walk the streets of our cities; thousands of Americans cannot afford health insurance; college tuition is increasingly prohibitive; even phone service assumes a stable residence and a steady income.

The following five texts explore issues of social and economic class in different but complementary ways. On one hand, Adrian Louis' poem about the third-world conditions of most American Indian reservations slaps the reader in the face with a starkness commensurate with the poem's subject matter. On the other, Chris Haven's "Assisted Living" is a much more subtle look at a middle-class man's obsession with social climbing. The poems by Roethke and Hughes, although written about the same time and with similar attention to rhyme and meter, reflect diverse perspectives on class—perspectives that may be attributable to distinctions in race. Another important aspect of class is the issue of form—how something looks, what it appears to be. Susan Steinberg's text "Isla" raises issues of class not simply in terms of its theme but also its form. And, like the other authors in this section, Steinberg links issues of race and class. As a whole, this suite poses questions about the often-ignored role of class in today's society and literature's relation to "high" art and upper-class values.

## HARLEM (1951)

### Langston Hughes

WHAT HAPPENS to a dream deferred?

Does it dry up
like a raisin in the sun?
Or fester like a sore——
And then run?
Does it stink like rotten meat?
Or crust and sugar over——
like a syrupy sweet?

Maybe it just sags
like a heavy load.

*Or does it explode?*

## ISLA (2000)

### Susan Steinberg

1. NEVER TUCK the napkin.
2. Four stars means tops. One two three four. Meaning the top. Número uno.
3. Spread the napkin like this. A flick and drop. Do it. These are real cloth. A flick. Drop in the lap.
4. Tell the waitress your drink. Tea please por favor and bread.
5. Always ask for by the window. For the sunset.
6. Sugar is the enemy. It gets in the blood and spreads. We all get it from the sugar. Our one enemy number one is sweets.
7. Trust me. They aren't Jews. There by the kitchen. Don't look.
8. White sand is all you need. Setting sun. What more could you need.
9. Salt slows the blood. It poisons. Take a glass of water. Pour in a shaker of salt. Now two. The blood from salt.
10. Never buy German made.
11. Seabirds are dirty and beggars.
12. An aperitif. Rouge. A twist.
13. They work the native girls hard. These girls are close to your age. They make a nickel an hour. Just nickels in a four star. How would you survive. This is why we tip. We're known for good tipping.
14. Hard liquor is the enemy. It poisons the bloodstream. Hard liquor is for the crass. The whiskies and gins. They can have it.
15. There are things your old pop knows.
16. Never gamble.
17. Never smoke.
18. Sometimes we cheat.
19. Red sunsets are all you need. See the sailboats. A picture postcard. When have you seen a red sunset. Think. Never. I like the blue boat there but sailboats tip. One tilt and splash.
20. New Yorkers are crass. Look at that fellow eating. By the kitchen. What a piece of meat. Look. Showy. An animal from New York you know it. That slob. Napkin tucked. He's hard from the city living don't I know it.
21. Aperitifs come rouge and blonde. Some ice and a twist of lemon and you sip. Aperitifs come first before dinner. With a twist. Sip slow. After dinner drinks come after.

22. When you want more tea. Cuando quieres más tea. Say more tea. Dices más tea por favor.
23. The waitress thinks you're my girlfriend.
24. Blonde. Ice and a twist.
25. They make nickels an hour. They have children at home. They live in shanties in ghettoes. How would you survive. They start when they're thirteen. No car no trips. No Sunday school. Some start at twelve.
26. Never bring home a New Yorker. You'll kill me. Never bring home a non Jew.
27. A trip for my girl and we deserve it don't we Sweetie.
28. Never feed the seabirds. They carry sickness. They eat garbage from the ghettoes. Let the slobs bring them bread.
29. You can tell non Jews. Even dark haired ones. The small handbags. Plastic beads. Fake stones.
30. I can still get a young girl.
31. Four stars means tops. Not three but four. Straighten. Look proud. Four stars Sweetie. Wait until your mother hears. Her head will go through the roof.
32. Never sit by the kitchen. You don't want to hear it. The clatter. Or see it.
33. Never go to the ghetto.
34. We'll start with this. Soup. Then this. Ensalada. How old are you. I guess seventeen. Am I right. Seventeen. Sweetie what do you think. How old is she. Wipe your face. She must be seventeen. This here's my girlfriend. You laugh. This is my lucky lady. Say hello Sweetie. Say hola to the waitress. Hola Sweetie. I want this here and my lucky girlfriend will have this and done well cooked. And bring me a clean knife.
35. First blow on the spoon.
36. If it's too hot add ice.
37. New Yorkers are showy. They drive German cars. You know this.
38. Playing slots is not gambling. Five dollars big deal. Nickels.
39. Place the knife on the plate. All the way top and bottom against the rim. Not like this but like this. It shouldn't touch the table.
40. Never ride a sailboat. One tip then splash and you drown. Would you like to drown. Would you. You don't want to find out. Trust me.
41. Leave a bite on your plate.
42. We can fool the waitress. She's staring. Look. I'll put my arm around you. Sit still. Don't look she's looking. We're so bad.
43. Jews don't drink beer with dinner. They don't drink milk. They don't drink hard liquor. We don't have the stomachs. Besides.
44. No one drinks the native coffee. It will put you under the table. You could stand a knife up in their coffee.
45. Taste before salting. Always. Why presume. Your mother the way she shakes the salt. She salts meat. Soup. Foods salted. Am I right. She

would salt a cake if you didn't take the shaker. Her blood will screech to a halt. I always told her. Watch it.

46. You're the tops.
47. Jews don't call dinner supper.
48. If you laugh then laugh quiet.
49. New Yorkers are slobs. Look tugging on his meat. Crass. A zoo animal.
50. Cut three squares of meat. Then eat them one two three. Then cut three more. Then eat one two three.
51. Your eyes are bigger than your stomach.
52. You need fat on the skeleton. Why don't you eat up. You would never survive a roundup. Do you know what a roundup is. What do they teach in that slob Sunday school. You need some fat.
53. If it turned cold send it back.
54. Blondes are lookers. The New Yorker's date. Mean looking but a blonde. That my Sweetie is a looker. By the kitchen. Your mother was a looker a long way back.
55. You don't eat the garnish.
56. Cut smaller pieces. Do you want to choke.
57. We can't go into the ghetto. We can drive around the edge. I can show you how the other half survives. Would you like that Sweetie. They carry pistols and knives. They sell their trinkets. We don't need that garbage. And the poor children. We'll keep our doors locked.
58. Un vaso de vino. For my young lady. White or red. Wait don't tell me. Blanco o rojo. Am I right. Blanco or rojo Sweetie. How about it. She's shy and always has been. She can sip some blanco. Her mother's head will shoot to the stars. Her first glass.
59. Solamente cuando su madre no está aquí. Comprendes.
60. Your pop takes care. This ring will be yours. Solid fourteen. This is fashion. Not a trinket. Your mother chose the stone and one day my sweets. All for you. But what's the hurry am I right.
61. The world is unfair. A looker and a slob. Turn slowly and tell me. The blonde with the. Tell me is she a looker. Mean looking with the cigarette. The lipstick. Now look. Am I right. Don't look.
62. If you can't pay you wash dishes.
63. The middle of the island is a zoo. Pistol shooting. Stray goats. They shoot dogs and live in shanties. They live in ghettoes. Such litter. They race cars.
64. I'll never let you starve.
65. There are things we do when no one's looking. Everyone does. Your old pop isn't so bad. There are just things that happen. You understand this Sweetie. Things. Comprendes for me por favor.
66. We all used to struggle. We ate soup from cans. Before you Sweetie. Before we left the zoo. But we danced. We went dancing. But soups from cans imagine can you.

67. Let's be extravagant.
68. Tap the water glass for attention. Ting ting. Or raise one finger like this.
69. American coffee por favor black no sugar. Más tea for my lady.
70. Eat up. You're a skeleton. Skin on a skeleton. Don't you like dinner. This isn't a joke. Eat up. Let's see you eat. Is it any good. Chew first then swallow. Slow. This isn't a race.
71. German cars are the enemy. Do you know this. Do you know why. What do they teach you on Sundays. Peace and love. The happy world. To hell. Ask me about the car seats. Come on Sweetie. Ask me about the ghettoes.
72. There are things your old pop knows.
73. Dessert is for slobs. The sugar is what kills. The sugar got all your grandparents. All your aunts and uncles. That and the smoking. The drinking. All of them. Ask your mother and still she eats desserts. She pours the salt. She smokes and drinks. Did you know this. She keeps it quiet. You didn't know.
74. The waitress thinks I'm twenty years younger.
75. The waitress never went to school. Imagine no school Sweetie.
76. There is always someone better smarter funnier. Always someone richer happier better. Always someone nipping at your seat. Shoving you the way out. Tell your poor mother. She never listened. You have to watch it or you'll fall. I warned her. She was in fashion. I got a fat wallet. They colored her hair. Fatter and they painted her nails. Magic. How she looked on our honeymoon. But now. Shape up I told her. Someone will push you out. Did she listen. Eat Sweetie. Watch it I told her. Does she listen.
77. The waitress is no older than seventeen. She's closer to your age. You're close to seventeen hard to believe. You're fourteen hard to believe.
78. Your pop's a strong man. Look at the size of this fist. Let's see your little hand Sweetie. Make a fist. I could crush that little thing.
79. I'll never let you get hurt.
80. They grow up quick here. They know how to make a man happy. They cook can they ever. Rice and beans and meat from their farms. Imagine a farm of stupid skinny goats Sweetie. Would you eat goat. They eat the meat and boy can they clean a house. They treat men as men. The boss of the house. They work as maids. Waitresses. They know when enough's enough. They know how to give. How to listen. How to milk a goat. And they keep quiet.
81. Chew then swallow. There's no race.
82. You can always send it back.
83. Watch your old pop in action. Come here honey. Ting. Ting. An after dinner por favor. Surprise me.

84. I'm the boss. Do you hear me. I can always disown you.
85. You never can win.
86. Sometimes we lie.
87. Obesity is a crime that poor slob. He should be dragged out and shot. I'll hold a pistol. You grab the steak knife. Cut off his fingers. He'll still eat poor slob. We can take his date and drive and drive until they find us.
88. Never drive German made.
89. I was an expert dancer way back. Ask your mother.
90. Breathe the air. It's the real thing. Salt air. Sun. You can taste it in the air.
91. You're my lucky lady. My Sweetie. Say hola to the waitress. My girl here's a good girl. She goes to school. Not a brain though. You know what a brain is. She's not the brainy type. Cómo se dice. Who knows right. But she'll make me proud. I have plans for this one. I have a business. I'm el presidente. She'll learn the ropes. Just a joke. She's not good with business. Easy. Where's your humor. A joke Sweetie. Joking.
92. You're number one.
93. Say dónde está el cuarto de baño.
94. No dessert. I'm watching it. How about you Sweetie. Do you dare. Some cake. Pie. Look at those eyes. Her eyes are bigger than her stomach. Look at her looking but I think she knows better.
95. I love you Sweetie.
96. Picture the ghettoes. Shanties. Little shack houses. Hardly a window. Goats chewing the dried up grass. Thin dirt roads. Cars racing past. They race into children. We're so lucky. Guess what else. They toss children from roofs. The accidents.
97. The only good German is a what Sweetie. The only good German is a what German. Come on Sweetie.
98. You're a lucky thing.
99. You're Jewish first. American second. German last.
100. The slots age is eighteen. I'll give you five dollars. All those nickels. Your mother's head will hit the ceiling. We won't tell her. She used to be different way back. She was some looker. You don't remember. This was in New York. She could dance. We danced like a couple of kids.
101. American coffee. You can always tell American.
102. The salt air clears the head. Don't worry about your mother. She'll snap back. I did nothing wrong. We'll send a postcard. I did nothing at all. She can't say I did. What has she said. She can't say anything. I warned her. You can't listen to her.
103. You wave away musicians like this. A flick of the wrist. They're a pain in the seat. They play for tips. Beggars.

104. Never bring home a musician.
105. We can make you eighteen. Some lipstick. Magic. Four years older. You'll be my girlfriend. We'll dance.
106. I should never have married your mother.
107. The sky's the limit. How about that Sweetie. How about we get you in fashion. New shoes Sweetie. The ones they wear now. The ones they wear here. Tops. Lipsticks. You'll come back a new you. Your mother will die from shock. We'll get you a hairdo. New nails. The sun's the limit.
108. The Germans are the enemy. They got your great grandparents.
109. You die you rot.
110. I always told her no children. She was too young. And why did I need children. She should have never. She wasn't ready. Accidents happen. But did she listen. Does she ever.
111. It's good to get away. You leave everything behind. But it catches you Sweetie. I hate to say it. But it nips you in the seat.
112. Never ask me why.
113. You pour a dot of cream. Wait. Another dot. Wait. See how it lightens. If you pour too much you mess the whole cup. I mean do you want coffee or a glass of milk. Ask yourself.
114. I deserve the best don't I. She couldn't give the best. She gave half that. A quarter that. This fat wallet and she gave nothing. Don't I deserve the most.
115. Guess the check. Hurry Sweetie. Guess it. A hint. Think high. Higher. Higher. You'll never guess. Never.
116. Don't stare. Look at them stumbling out. Poor slobs.
117. A nice Jew is all you need. A nice home. I'll fill your wallet. You don't need your mother. You don't need school. Finish junior high if you like. Find a nice Jew. A nice house. Take an island honeymoon.
118. Don't listen to your mother.
119. You're Jewish first. American second. German last.
120. Your mother never loved her child.
121. You're my número uno.
122. Wipe your face.
123. Take the check. You're paying. You're my lucky girlfriend right. Dinner's on you. Come on Sweetie. Where's your wallet. Show the waitress your fat wallet. Who's going to pay if not you. There are dishes waiting. Come on Sweetie. We're waiting for you. Come on. Waiting.
124. A joke. Just a joke. Where's your humor. Both of you.
125. Put the napkin on your plate.
126. You are your own worst enemy.
127. A five dollar tip can buy a new goat.
128. A trip just you and me. It's been fun hasn't it. We'll get you in fashion. Then we can see some of that white sand and look for shells. We can lie around the sand like a couple of kids. How about it Sweetie. We'll

race past the ghetto. I have friends in there. Would you eat goat. We can race through the ghetto and see what's what.

129. How about it Sweetie. Let's do this again sometime. While we still can.
130. I love you Sweetie. How about that.
131. Wipe here Sweetie. Wipe your eyes.
132. Give me the napkin. Let me help.
133. How can I help.
134. How can I help Sweetie.

## ASSISTED LIVING (2000)

Chris Haven

AT AN INTERSECTION Jules passed every day, an old man was leaning against the post of a sign that said "Left Turn Only," with not one but two arrows pointing decisively left, into thin air. Jules tapped the steering wheel of his two-year-old Infiniti, leased with the hope that it would lend his buyers confidence to see their real estate agent in a luxury car, presumably not desperate to make a sale. "Come on," he said to the light, stubbornly red on all sides, letting no traffic through. Another glance at the man caught him staring into Jules's tinted window, with an unmistakable jutted thumb directed solely at Jules.

*Don't pick up hitchhikers,* thought Jules. He tried to lock his eyes forward, but could still feel the eyes of the man boring through his window. *Don't sleep with your sister, don't eat human flesh, and don't pick up hitchhikers.* "Rules to live by," he said aloud, but immediately regretted it because the man seemed to bend his head forward, as if Jules were speaking to him.

It wasn't unusual for Jules to see someone standing by the road in Houston, even in heat like this: every day on two separate corners he passed what looked like homeless people selling the newspaper; twice a year blue-shirted firemen from the nearby station held out their boots for donations so they could trot out that oversized check on the telethon; another man up north sat on a plastic cooler selling roses; Jules had even seen junior high cheerleaders with their pompons, panhandling for money to go to camp. But this old guy didn't seem to be begging. He wore a lime-green collared sport shirt and brown Sansabelt pants, freshly laundered. His skin looked clean, ruddy—not the earthy tan of the Caucasian homeless. The only reason for concern: a patchwork of gauzy, illogical bandages scattered along his left arm.

Jules's hesitation about picking up strangers along the road ran deep. He'd grown up in a prison town, where signs warned: "Hitchhikers May Be Escaping Inmates." It caused him even now to look with suspicion on anyone without access to a car. Still, if the light had not turned, Jules felt he would have been forced to at least acknowledge the man, whose gaze had turned into the most penetrating of questions. Relieved, Jules followed the momentum of traffic. But in checking his rearview mirror, Jules thought he saw the man swoon forward and almost fall.

What if this guy really needed help? Jules had an appointment to show a house to a young couple; he knew they couldn't afford it, but still he had to keep up his contacts. He checked the dashboard clock—if he drove straight there, he'd still have half an hour to kill before the couple arrived. He turned onto the access road of the highway, but he couldn't stop thinking about the old man, faltering in the ninety-degree heat. The temperature indicator inside the Infiniti read a comfortable *72 deg F*. The draft from the vents had blown one patch on each of his forearms frigid—too much air for one man, really. It was excessive, almost shameful. "What the hell," Jules said, and circled into the U-turn lane.

Any thoughts of the man being dangerous were erased when Jules pulled alongside. Up close, the stare that Jules had thought penetrating seemed merely blank. The man still clutched the signpost, but he no longer held out his thumb. Jules flicked on his hazards and stepped out of the car. The man's round, beaverish face seemed not to register Jules's presence at all. "Excuse me," Jules said, not quite knowing what to say. The man's mouth hung open, as if a message were stuck in his throat. Jules put his hand on the man's back, thinking if he could get the man to straighten from his stoop the message might dislodge, like water through an unkinked garden hose.

"Can I help?"

The man's eyes cleared, as if Jules had spoken magic words. "Yes. I think you can." Jules half expected some fairy tale plot twist, to be granted a reward, but instead the man retreated again into his eyes. No golden eggs from this goose.

In the street, the light had turned green, and the inert Infiniti had caused a minor traffic jam. "Come on," Jules said, rushing to close the deal. "We can talk in the car." The man made no response, but allowed Jules to unbend his fingers from the post and lead him by the elbow to the passenger side of the car. They had to move carefully to dodge the traffic—the other cars nudged boldly by as if the two men were merely traffic cones. Jules slammed the door on the man's pants leg once before finally settling him in.

So there it was, Jules thought. He'd picked up his first hitchhiker—had maybe even forced the guy into it. Sitting in the car, Jules looked the man over. He still did not seem like a vagrant, but it occurred to Jules that he was no expert on the matter. Even if the man did ask for a handout, he probably wasn't going to pull out a knife. The real danger resided in the responsibility Jules had committed himself to.

Since Jules had no wife waiting at home, he figured whatever problems this action might present would at most affect only himself. Jules began to feel good about picking this guy up, that he was willing to risk the unknown in order to help this stranger. In the car, the man seemed much larger than he had on the street. Jules sniffed the air—the body odor was noticeable, but not overpowering. Jules had a sudden fear that the man might be incontinent and ruin the upholstery. But what if he did? Wasn't the value of the good deed in direct proportion to the grief it caused? Still, Jules could easily let the man out, deposit him back on the corner. He could make his appointment, carry on with life as usual. But another wave of traffic had gathered behind them, urging him on, and as if obeying the will of momentum, Jules put the car in gear and made the choice to move forward.

Jules was hoping that the man might volunteer some information, a question, point him in a direction. Instead the man gazed out the side window, seemingly content with the ride.

"Gotta be hot standing out there." Jules took quick inventory of the man's appearance. The bandages did not betray a serious injury, and were too high for an IV. He wore no hospital bracelet. "Were you waiting for someone?"

"My son," the man said to the window.

"I see." Jules panicked, afraid he'd made a terrible mistake. "So he was picking you up on that corner?"

The man crossed his hands in his lap in the posture of someone who'd been handcuffed. "He lives in California."

"Is he here visiting?" Jules was nearing the intersection where he would need to make the U-turn if he had indeed interfered by removing the man from a prearranged meeting place.

"The hound goes to California."

"Right," Jules said, deciding yes, the man was crazy. "A riddle." The messages of the demented that Jules had heard on city streets before usually had a religious theme, with plenty of references to prophecy and apocalypse. Inevitably, the messenger believed himself to be, or closely linked to, Jesus Christ.

"The *grey* hound," the man said, impatiently.

"You mean a *bus stop*? You're nowhere near a bus stop, I'm afraid." Jules checked the clock. He still had twenty minutes to make his appointment.

"Sometimes I get confused," the man said. Then he turned to Jules, held his gaze and said, "But I have moments of total clarity."

"Great," Jules said. *But how am I supposed to tell the difference*?

The man looked away.

Jules felt bad about being short with the guy. "Let me start over. My name is Jules Henry." After waiting what he felt was a polite amount of time for a response, Jules asked, "So what is your name?"

"Otto," he said. "But I don't think that's right."

Jules couldn't help being amused. "Can I *call* you Otto?"

The man seemed to hold this question in front of him, as if considering the freshness of a carton of milk. "If you don't mind being mistaken."

"Otto," Jules said. "Close enough for me."

Jules asked Otto a series of leading questions, with little success. He could not determine where the man lived (he said "inside"), although he mentioned Katy and Linda, two streets miles apart, and parallel to one another. Otto had settled comfortably in his seat and did not betray the slightest inclination towards leaving. Jules himself felt strangely comfortable with Otto, finding it refreshing to finally entertain a passenger in his car who was unsuspicious of him and his motives. More often his clients would keep some distance, which he attributed to their fears of salesmen. Jules thought that some of them even held their purses tighter, or leaned more heavily on their wallets.

Time had come—Jules had to leave now to make his appointment. It shouldn't take long, Jules figured, and afterwards he could decide what to do with Otto. Besides, where else did the old man have to go?

"How about checking out a house, Otto?"

"Seven," Otto said decisively.

"I'll take that as a yes."

His clients were already at the house, Tammy waiting in the car while Tony knelt in his chinos inspecting the foundation for cracks. Jules knew that Tony didn't know the first thing about foundations, but it gave him something important to do that helped show his young wife that he was capable. Jules had learned a lot about the two over the past few weeks. Tony's background was a little poorer than Tammy's, and she was just a little too pretty for him. Looking at these larger houses was part of a ruse that infected their whole marriage, Jules surmised, a ruse that would eventually crumble around Tony's ankles. The life Jules had imagined for Tony and Tammy was just one example of a marriage in which Jules wanted no part, more evidence in favor of living alone.

When Tammy saw Jules's car, she walked over and waited for Jules to open his door. "Tony's distracted as usual," she said, leaning towards the Infiniti. Jules was uncomfortable with the tension he felt around Tammy. Her right cheekbone raised slightly higher than the other when she smiled, suggesting a wink. He felt she was flirting, but was reasonably sure her object was his car and not himself.

Before Jules could open the passenger door, Otto had done it himself, suddenly becoming purposeful, as if he had arrived at his own home.

"Oh—" Tammy said, cut short. "Guess there's a big demand today," she said, a note of competition in her voice.

"No, no. He's not a buyer. This is . . ."

"My son," Otto said, grabbing Tammy's hand from her side, shaking it vigorously.

Tony joined them, circles of grass stains on the knees of his chinos. He must have heard Otto because Tony took his hand eagerly and said, "It's nice to meet you, Mr. Henry. Your son has been quite a help to us."

"Otto isn't my father," Jules said, and in response to the confusion he saw on their faces added, "He's my grandfather."

Why Jules decided to promote Otto from slightly demented stranger to grandfather he didn't know. But as soon as Jules said it, he liked the idea of adopting this man. Jules felt Otto needed him. Not like Tony and Tammy or any of his clients thought they needed him, but in a more basic, vital way. Who knows what might have happened to him on that busy intersection? Jules began to think he had saved Otto's life.

Jules unlocked the door to the five-bedroom Cape Cod. Normally he would have walked Tony and Tammy through the house, highlighting the recent maintenance, age of the appliances, condition of the roof. But this time he let them find their own way, instead focusing his attention on Otto.

"Ever been in a house like this, Otto?"

Otto studied the vaulted ceiling. "Yes," he said. "I've been in this one."

Jules started. Was this one of Otto's moments of clarity? Had he found the man's home? "No kidding? When?"

"Today," he said and smiled.

"Good one," Jules said. Maybe Otto was understanding more than Jules had thought. "This deal will run about a quarter mil," Jules said. Then behind his hand he whispered, "Tony will get approved at 180 max."

Otto nodded. "Everybody needs approval."

Tony and Tammy clambered down the stairs, beaming. "Oh Jules," Tammy said. "You've outdone yourself." From Tammy, this could have meant anything. She "loved" every house she saw. Hers was an indecipherable ranking system that ran from "cute" to "darling." But Tony, usually full of energy, looked strangely concerned, ruffled. He asked Jules about deed restrictions, as usual.

"In your packet," Jules said. "Homeowner's dues are forty, surveillance another fifty."

He left the couple whispering to each other, rifling through papers, paying no attention to the house at all. Papers—the separation between the house and the dream. Some people had a fear of the dotted line. Even to the sweetest deal some people couldn't sign their name, almost like they didn't believe they deserved happiness.

"Come on Otto, let's check out the upstairs." Inadvertently, Jules slapped his leg, as if calling a dog. He felt immediately ashamed.

Upstairs, Jules stepped onto a balcony that overlooked the backyard. He leaned against the railing and imagined what Tony and Tammy must be thinking. Otto joined him, warily peeking over the balcony.

"They've probably got this place all outfitted: barbecue, swingset, happy kids. The works," Jules said. "But they don't get it. A house is a structure, you know what I mean?"

"Don't dwell in the future," Otto said, backing away from the railing.

"Exactly," Jules said. "I don't mind showing dream houses. No sales, but I figure everybody needs a dream house, a place to go. I've seen people actually get their dream house. But it's never the same. Lot of times they end up selling it right back. The only place for a dream house is in your imagination. Because a dream can't fit into a structure. That, my friend, is why I rent."

Jules turned, but Otto was not on the balcony. "What about you, Otto? How about if you buy this house? I could cut you a killer deal. Otto?"

Jules found him inside the bedroom, pants at his thighs, peeing in a corner.

"Holy—" Jules lunged toward Otto, but held back. The pouch of Otto's shorts hung limp from the waistband, which clung tightly across the loose flesh of his rear end. "Otto!"

Otto finished, pulled up his pants. When he saw Jules, Otto's face screwed up like an infant's, tears squirting nickel stains onto his shirt.

The puddle was surprisingly small, disappearing quickly into a dark stain. Jules jerked his head around the empty room, finding nothing to clean the mess. Another couple of minutes and it would soak into the pad. Almost as soon as he realized his helplessness, Jules decided he didn't care. What was one little corner of carpet?

"Jules?" Tony called from the bottom of the stairs, hesitantly climbing the steps.

"Yes," Jules said, then loudly called, "No—you stay there. I'll come down." Jules left the balcony doors open to dissipate the smell. Holding Otto's arm to his body like a football, Jules led him down the stairs.

"We really appreciate your time today," Tony said. "I know we've been a bother . . ."

"No bother," Jules said.

"Don't bother," Otto said, yanking his arm back.

Tony and Tammy both smiled politely as Otto opened the front door. "Will you be around later?" Tony asked Jules.

"Voice mail," Jules said, leading them out the door as quickly as possible, before the smell could hit them. "Always voice mail."

Tammy smiled her goodbye to Jules with that chin-down, winking smile that Jules figured had worked on a line of men from her father to her teachers, boyfriends, mechanics, clerks, straight through to her husband. Yes, Jules admitted, probably it even worked on him.

Otto, who had stopped crying, arrested Tony before he got to his car. He held him by the shoulders as if explaining a rule to a child. "Make it work."

Tony smiled nervously before Otto released him. Jules thought Tony probably thought Otto was giving him a message. About buying a house. About his marriage, maybe. When Otto turned away Jules noticed Otto's shirttail peeking out of his fly. Jules laughed silently. Make it work—the old man could've just meant his zipper. *Tony*, thought Jules. *Poor bastard*.

In the car, Otto sniffled. "It's okay. Don't worry," Jules said. "Carpet cleaners—it'll be like new." After a showing Jules would usually check his messages, do the follow-ups. But he felt guilty for putting Otto in a position where he could embarrass himself. Jules decided he would make it up to Otto.

"You ever have a dream house, Otto? Let me show you the ones I have." Jules drove by his area listings, reciting the floor plans from memory. What size family should occupy, potential for appreciation, resale value.

Outside the first house—a two-bedroom split-level—Otto said, "Too close to the highway."

"Come on Otto, what would it take for me to put you in this house? I've gotta make you a sale."

Jules drove by about twenty of the homes on his list, and pitched the rest from his listings book. Otto always countered, sometimes dead-on, other times nonsensical: "Too much house," or "Not enough yard," or "The easement's too wide."

"You're smart to be careful. When you buy a house, you don't buy bricks and wood. You buy a concept," Jules said, tapping his temple. "A house isn't a financial investment, but the beginning of a relationship."

Otto fidgeted, adjusted the air conditioning vent.

"You buy that?" Otto didn't respond, and Jules thought he looked skeptical. "Me, either," Jules said. "Hard to see having a relationship with a house. I guess people are the only ones who can have relationships."

"Your ship has come in," Otto said.

"So what'll it be, Otto? At least pick a favorite. Which one did you like best?"

Otto paused, as if considering the question. "This one," he said, stroking the leather interior.

"Which? The car?" Jules nodded. "I should have guessed—you're a mobile kind of guy."

Then, from a remote place in the car, a grumbling danced into Jules's ears. Jules clicked off the air conditioner to listen, afraid something might be wrong with the car. When the grumbling sounded a second time, Jules pinpointed its origin: Otto's belly.

"Feed the kitty," Otto said.

Jules had meant to drive to a nice, sit-down restaurant, but when Otto recognized a Wendy's sign he could not be talked out of it. At the drive-through Otto waited for the voice in the speaker, then leaned over Jules's lap and ordered: "Spicy Chicken Sandwich, Biggie Fries, and a Biggie Drink." With all the holes in Otto's memory, Jules was amazed how these fast-food terms had taken hold.

When it came time to pay, Otto calmly passed his wallet to Jules. The sight of such a common object as a wallet took Jules by surprise. It was like finding a collar buried beneath the fur of a dog you'd thought was a stray. The wallet was a sign that Otto had a tangible identity, even if to Otto himself that identity remained elusive. Jules unfolded the wallet, found a driver's license. Otto Kightling. In the photo, he was wearing the same green shirt, as if the picture had been taken that day. Jules shook his head. "Damn thing's current."

"Pass the fries," Otto said.

Jules paid with his own money and used his cell phone to call information. This was the first time he'd used the phone for anything resembling an emergency. When the salesman had sold Jules the phone he'd pitched a list of imagined dangers—blowouts, carjackings, overturned semis—conjuring doom that awaited you when you were away from home. Mobility came with a price, apparently, but at no time did the salesman mention disoriented old men eating chicken sandwiches in your car. Jules dialed. "What do you know, Otto? You're in the book." The woman who answered identified herself as Linda, Otto's daughter. Mystery solved. "Linda. 701 Katy. Got it."

Otto munched on his fries, having already dispatched the sandwich. "We've got to get you home now, old boy," Jules said. "You're finally going home."

Otto made no response, but stopped eating. His face seemed to tighten, and his color went gray. Why wouldn't he want to go home? Maybe Linda didn't treat Otto very well. He didn't seem to be abused, not physically anyway, but who could tell? Jules started to panic. He stopped the car. Jules knew he couldn't just take Otto home to live with him, but maybe he could let him sleep on the couch, until they figured something out. Just as Jules was about to ask Otto what he thought of the idea, Otto burped.

"Spicy," he said, exhaling. Otto sipped his drink, and the color returned to his face. Then Otto looked around, as if noticing something for the first time.

"We're not moving," he said.

"Are you ready to go home?" Jules asked.

"We should be moving."

Jules started the car, headed toward Otto's house. *Just as well,* Jules thought, feeling foolish. *Can't even recognize a little gas attack.*

Otto's house looked solid enough—A-frame, all wood. In an older neighborhood, but well-kept. Still, it lay outside the desirable center loop of the city. "Convert that carport into a garage, and plop this house down six miles from here, you'd add thirty-five K to the bottom line."

"Houses don't plop," Otto said.

"Hard to argue with that," Jules said, stopping the car. "So this is it?" Jules hoped Otto would show some recognition of the house, but all he said was, "I have a son in California."

"California?" For a moment, Jules thought it might be possible—to drive away and try to find that son. California sounded nice. Jules had heard the ocean breezes made it cool, even in the summer.

Otto leaned over, whispered, "As soon as I remember his name, I'm going out to see him."

"If this were a movie," Jules said, "You and I would go to California. Be a great buddy picture."

"I don't think this is a movie," Otto said. "Is it?"

What else could Jules do? He walked Otto to the door.

Linda looked to be nearly as old as Otto, deep, honest lines marking her face. Jules noticed a faint smell of cigarette smoke mixed with bath powder. The deep earth tones of the carpet and dark wood paneling—twenty years out of style—made the house seem close, like heavy hands of air squeezed him on all sides. Though it was late in the evening, Linda was still dressed, her walking shoes on, purse on the table. Ready to act, if asked. When she saw Jules and Otto, she seemed interested, but not overly concerned. "How far did he make it?"

"Picked him up just off 290, close to the loop."

Linda shook her head. "He's never made it that far before," she said. "But he always finds his way back home."

She regarded Otto as if he were her own child, a toddler who, even though mischievous, managed to be lovable in spite of his misbehavior. Otto retrieved an empty coffee cup from the kitchen shelf and sat expectantly at the table. Linda poured his coffee, completing what Jules thought must serve as Otto's returning-home ritual. The cup read *World's #1 Dad.*

"He mentioned something about a son in California," Jules said.

"Did he?" she said. "News to me. He's always wanted a son, though. No telling what kind of life he lives in his head. Maybe it's better . . ."

But Jules wasn't ready to dismiss Otto so easily. Maybe he did have a son, one she didn't know about. Jules wanted Linda to know that he was still on Otto's side. "Seems risky," Jules said, trying to put a note of disapproval in his voice. "Counting on this city to bring him back."

"I know," she said, apparently unoffended. "I've made arrangements. It's not a home—they call it assisted living."

"I've heard of it," Jules said. Before, he'd always thought of places like that as a boost to business, recycling people's homes back into the market. But today he wanted to tell Linda that she shouldn't abandon her father like that. Otto deserved better.

"What about those bandages on his arm?" Jules asked suspiciously.

"He likes to play in the medicine cabinet," she shrugged. "I've had to take out everything that might hurt him." Linda watched Otto sip his coffee. "I hope he wasn't a problem. Can I pay you?"

"Absolutely not," Jules said, indignant, then felt Otto's wallet bulging in his pocket. "Here," Jules offered, red-faced. "I, uh, needed it for his ID. Go ahead and check it."

Linda took the wallet, but before she could open it Otto poured the contents of his coffee cup onto the kitchen table. The steaming liquid inched its way towards the edge of the table. Linda ran for a towel and mopped up the spill before it hit the floor.

"Cleaning up," Otto said, delighted.

"I suppose I should go," Jules said, seeing there was nothing he could do here. He patted Otto on the back. "If I can help . . ." he said, and gave Linda his card.

She put the towel down. "Real estate?" Linda said. "Daddy was an agent, you know."

"No kidding?" Jules looked at Otto, who flashed a conspiratorial look.

"Forty years," she said. "No retirement, of course."

"I hear you," Jules said. "Health insurance?"

"No, no. That makes it hard . . ." Her voice trailed off a little, then she said, "I figure he sold nearly a thousand homes."

Otto looked up from the table. "I've been in his home," he said secretively.

Linda smiled at her father. "That's nice."

In the ensuing silence, Jules realized that he had to leave right then. No matter what he'd thought earlier, he knew now that he couldn't be the one to rescue this man. "Otto, it's been a pleasure," Jules said. "Sorry we couldn't make a deal."

"I've been in your home," Otto said.

"Yes," Jules said, his foot in the door, ready to escape. "And you're welcome there anytime."

On his way home Jules received a page from Tony. Their pre-approval had come through, and they were ready to make an offer of 220. Jules couldn't believe it—the offer was low, but he was sure it would fly. Tony had done it. He'd put Tammy in her dream home. *Poor bastard,* Jules thought again, imagining the avalanche of new promises Tony would always be struggling to fulfill.

As Jules gathered the fast food trash from the passenger seat of his car and walked to his apartment, he experienced the familiar pull of home, the weariness in the body that came from letting down the defenses of the day. When he closed the door behind him the plate on the knob, loose for months now, rattled comfortably against his hand. He flipped the light switch, but only the ceiling fan came on—he must have turned off the bulb at the cord that morning. Even though the room was pitch dark, Jules decided not to turn on the light. His apartment stretched before him, hidden. The fan churned the air, steamy from the day's heat. Jules tried to walk the wide middle path from his living room to the kitchen. How hard could it be? He took a few tentative steps forward, and the corner of something sharp dug into his shoulder. Unable to place what he had bumped into, Jules grabbed his shoulder and backed away, his heart pounding, for a second wondering if he was even in the right apartment. Even after he recognized the object as his television stand, and even though he knew it was ridiculous, Jules had the unmistakable feeling that he was being watched. Tested. He put his hands out and groped his way along the wall. In the dark, his apartment seemed larger than he remembered, and he could not gauge his steps correctly. Jules staggered to the kitchen, stumbling once over a dining room chair, and, with the help of the blue glow from the numbers 3:24 on the microwave clock—not even close to the right time—he finally put Otto's trash in the wastebasket. On his way out of the kitchen, Jules brushed his hand on the bottom frame of a small mirror. He felt it topple and tried to catch it, but it fell to the floor, shattering. He knew he should just turn the light on, clean up the mess. What a stupid way to hurt yourself. But Jules decided it was worth the risk. He had to keep trying. I can do this, he thought. I can find my way. This was his home, these were his things. There was an order here—he just had to uncover it. Glass crunched under his feet as he moved forward. This is a test, he thought, and he knew then that all anyone could hope to do in the world was respond somehow, even if the response made no sense.

## DUST WORLD (1992)

Adrian Louis

for Sherman Alexie

### *I.*

WHIRLWINDS OF HOT AUTUMN DUST
paint every foolish hope dirty.
I stand in the impudent ranks of the poor
and scream for the wind to abate.
Prayers to Jesus might be quicker
than these words from blistered hands
and liquor, but the death wind
breaks the lines to God.
I have no sylvan glades of dreams,
just dust words
for my people dying.

### *II.*

With pupil-dilated *putti* in arms
three teenaged mothers
on the hood of a '70 Chevy
wave at me like they know me.
Inside the video rental
a small fan ripples sweat
and scatters ashes upon two young attendants
practicing karate kicks and ignoring me

because they're aware I could dust
their wise asses individually or collectively.
They're products of Pine Ridge High
which means they would have had two strikes
against them even if they did graduate
and these two clowns never did.
I guess they're almost courting me,
in a weird macho way almost flirting,
because I'm fatherly, half buzzed-up,
and have biceps as thick as their thighs.
Heyyyy . . . ever so softly,
this is the whiskey talking now.

## *III.*

With pupils dilated and beer in hand
three teenaged mothers court frication
more serious than their sweet Sioux butts
buffing the hood of their hideous car.
When I glide my new T-bird
out of the video store parking lot
they wave like they really know me.
One of the girls, beautiful enough
to die for except for rotten teeth
smiles and I suck in my gut
and lay some rubber.
I cruise through a small whirlwind
of lascivious regrets
and float happily through the dark streets
of this sad, welfare world.

This is the land that time forgot.
Here is the Hell the white God gave us.
The wind from the Badlands brings
a chorus of chaos and makes everything dirty.
I meander past my house and stop briefly
before driving back to where
the young girls are.
I park my car and re-enter the store.
The two young boys are still dancing
like two cats in mid-air, snarling, clawless
and spitting. No harm done.
I stare them down and place two cassettes,

both rated X, on the counter.
It's Friday night and I'm forty years old
and the wild-night redskin
parade is beginning.

## MY PAPA'S WALTZ (1942)

### Theodore Roethke

THE WHISKEY ON YOUR BREATH
Could make a small boy dizzy;
But I hung on like death:
Such waltzing was not easy.

We romped until the pans
Slid from the kitchen shelf;
My mother's countenance
Could not unfrown itself.

The hand that held my wrist
Was battered on one knuckle;
At every step you missed
My right ear scraped a buckle.

You beat time on my head
With a palm caked hard by dirt,
Then waltzed me off to bed
Still clinging to your shirt.

## THIS TEXT: READING

1. Hughes' poem is a scathing indictment of mainstream American culture. Why is the speaker so upset? Is his/her anger justified?
2. Who is the speaker of the poem? Hughes? Someone else?
3. In what way is Steinberg's "Isla" about social class? Does the form of the text affect its theme?
4. How would you describe the narrator of "Isla"? Is the narrator the same person as the main character? Is the main charater rich? Poor? Middle class? How would the character define "upper class"?
5. How are the main character from "Isla" and Jules from "Assisted Living" similar? Both are male and probably about the same age. Would they define class similarly?

6. Explain how Louis reconciles the classist tradition of reading and writing poetry with the troubling theme of class in this particular poem. How might the act of writing or saying a poem be tied to his Indian ancestry and culture?
7. Consider the ways in which Louis' "Dust World" and Hughes' "Harlem" overlap. How are the poems similar? Is theirs a shared project?
8. Does the form of "My Papa's Waltz" contribute to its explorations of economic class? What might waltz be a metaphor for?
9. "Assisted Living" provides a good example of how Americans read for class. In other words, we look for things that might reveal someone's class or display our own. Where are some instances of this in the story?

## Your Text: Writing

1. Adrian Louis ("Dust World") is only one of a few Native writers whose aim is to expose the appalling economic conditions on many of America's Indian reservations. Write a paper demonstrating how his poem does this important but disturbing cultural work.
2. In an interview with the authors, Haven claimed that the main character's name, Jules, is a coincidence. Write a paper in which you explain the significance of his name to his character and the theme of the story.
3. Students often have very different readings of "My Papa's Waltz." For some, it's a poem about abuse, but for others, it's a poem about a blue collar family celebrating the way they work and live—hard. Which reading corresponds to your own? Write an analytical essay in which you analyze what codes about class the poem transmits.
4. What force does a poem about this subject have that an essay on the same topic would lack? That is, does this poem have an affect on you that an essay might not? Why? Write a paper comparing a poem and an essay that deal with issues of class (Parenti's piece "Class and Virtue" in Chapter 5, for instance).
5. Do you think Americans tend to associate blue collar families with violence and dysfunction? Why? Is Roethke playing with this cultural assumption? Is Steinberg?
6. Write an essay comparing "Harlem" and "My Papa's Waltz." How do they do similar cultural work? How does race play into the themes of the poems?
7. Write an essay in which you write about both form and content. How does the tone, style, and form of "Dust World" raise questions about issues of class? What about "Isla"? You might try a comparison/contrast essay in which you look at the formal aspects of "Dust World" and "Isla."

# READING OUTSIDE THE LINES

## Classroom Activities

1. On the blackboard, write out "The Red Wheelbarrow" (from the Introduction) as one sentence. How does that alter how you see the poem? Now take a sentence from a newspaper article and write it in poetic form. How does that change your view of the sentence? How much is a poem's visible structure a part of the way we understand it?
2. Read "My Papa's Waltz" out loud in class two or three times. How does the sound of the poem mimic the rhythm of a dance or waltz? Can you think of other examples of this phenomenon?
3. Form a small group of four to six people. One person begins by writing a four-line stanza about class. Pass the poem around, each person writing his or her own four-line stanza about class, until everyone has completed a stanza. Read your poem to the class. What does it suggest about class? How does it differ from the version that you would have written if you got to finish it yourself?
4. Talk about the word class. Why is your college class called a class? What is the connection between this somewhat random group of people and social or economic class?
5. In class, talk about the race, gender, and background of each of the authors in this chapter. How might their background influence their texts?
6. Compare "Blood-Burning Moon" to the Williams essay on gender or the Sherman Alexie poem, both of which appear in the Movie Suite in Chapter 5. What role should literature take in exposing societal violence?
7. Select one of the texts from this chapter that you like the best. Identify what you think is the most important passage or line or stanza and write a paper in which you argue why the poem or story turns on this individual portion of text.
8. Traditionally, critics and philosophers argued that art should celebrate the beautiful, what Matthew Arnold called "sweetness and light." But, in the last 100 years, literature has taken a turn toward realism. Does literature have a responsibility to expose or reveal societal ills? Write an essay in which you explore this idea, using two texts from this chapter to illustrate.
9. The great American poet Wallace Stevens writes in his poem "An Ordinary Evening in New Haven" that "the theory of poetry is the theory of life." Write an essay in which you analyze two poems from this chapter

using Stevens' claim as your starting point. Be sure to explain what you think Stevens means by this statement.

## Essay Ideas

1. Write a comparison/contrast essay on Neruda's "Ode to My Socks" and another more traditional ode, like John Keats' "Ode on a Grecian Urn." What do they have in common? Other good comparison/contrast papers include gender issues in Dickinson's "My Life had stood" and Chopin's "The Story of an Hour"; Louis' "Dust World" and Hughes' "Harlem."
2. Compare differing but overlapping perspectives on the South in "Blood-Burning Moon" and "Assisted Living."
3. Write an argumentative paper in which you demonstrate how and why Williams' "The Red Wheelbarrow" is a poem. Be sure to articulate the criteria by which you define a poem. Or do a paper that argues the opposite, but be sure to define the criteria as well.
4. Explore how both "The Story of an Hour" and "Blood-Burning Moon" depict the limited options for women in the South in the late 1800s and early 1900s. Have things changed? If so, how much?
5. William Carlos Williams writes in his poem "Asphodel That Greeny Flower" that "it is difficult to get the news from poems, though men die everyday for lack of what is found there." Write an essay in which you explain what Williams means and demonstrate what, exactly, one does get from poems. What does "The Red Wheelbarrow" give us that the news does not?
6. Write an essay in which you consider "The Colonel" and "Dust World" not as literary documents but as political documents. What kind of political statement do they make?
7. On the blackboard, list, as a class, various characteristics of individual characters within a particular story. How does a story make meaning through its characters? How do characters carry and evoke values that they never actually talk about within the story itself?
8. Pass out song lyrics to the class. In what ways do songs resemble poems? Is there any appreciable difference besides the addition of music?

# 2

# READING TELEVISION

You may be surprised by how much you already know about *reading* television as opposed to *watching* television. For example, you undoubtedly know the structure of sitcoms, talk shows, and sporting events. You know about the probable audiences of these particular shows, and you probably know something about plot devices, laugh tracks, and the way television networks spread out and time commercials.

The fact that you are familiar with television shows is more help than hindrance in writing about them. But watching television is different than reading television. Watching is passive; reading is active. Take, for example, the act of reading a traditional text such as a poem or a short story. When reading these texts, they force us to confront and unlock their meanings. We read passages over and over and think about the way writers arrange words as well as more general concerns such as theme and plot. And we are taught to think about what short stories mean. Yet when we watch television, we rarely attend to these concerns. We have been watching television since we were small children, with little guidance on how to watch; our parents, our friends, and newspapers and magazines may tell us what we can and should watch, but once we get in front of the television we tend to let the show dictate our response without our interaction. To understand television, we have to learn to question the structure and content of television shows as well as the presence and absence of ideas, people, and places. And so when watching television, we should consider a number of things.

### The structure of television makes us watch passively.

When we read a book or magazine or newspaper, the text is in our hands. We can start and stop reading whenever we want to; we can re-read at our convenience. We can underline these texts and make notes on them. We can, of course, take this particular text with us on the bus, to the bathroom, to the coffee shop. However, when we watch television, we are already physically disconnected from the text. Unless we have a Watchman or some small, portable television, we cannot pick it up, and worse, we cannot mark it up. Only recently have we been able to control its flow with a remote control. But even when we watch with the remote control, there is a laugh track telling us not only when but how to laugh, commercial interruptions telling us to wait, and familiar plot conventions telling us to respond in certain predictable ways.

Furthermore, various aspects of modern life contribute to consumption of television that is not particularly critical. For instance, it's likely that your home lends itself to passive television watching. Most people arrange their dens so that the TV is the center of the room and focal point when we sit down. And, after a long day of work, there is something strangely comforting about settling down in front of the television for an episode of *Friends*, a baseball game, or a movie. Our architecture, our work, and our home lives facilitate thinking of the act of watching television as an act of disengagement.

Are networks and television producers conspiring to have us watch this way? Some of television's harsher critics, like Neil Postman, would say yes, but others would not be so bold. It is important to remember that the way television has evolved has led to seeing television as a kind of remedy, and we have to work around this perception by watching a show with critical engagement, taking notes, and if possible, replaying the show before sitting down to write about it.

## Unlike literature, with television, there is not a recognizable author.

When we pick up a book, we know who has written it—the name of the author is usually displayed as prominently as the title. Once we know who has written a book, we can choose to use this information accordingly. Traditionally, when scholars study written texts, they have focused on the words on the page, the symbols, the themes, and the plot contained within, but many have also used the life of the author, and the author's other texts, to gain a deeper understanding of a particular text. Though modern scholars have diminished the power of authorial reputation, the author, even if less important to scholars, still exists and may exist most profoundly for readers.

Who authors less traditional texts is not always as clear. In movies, for example, we have two, and sometimes three people, to whom to attach authorship: the screenwriter, the director, and sometimes either the producer or cinematographer; in architecture, sometimes an entire firm serves as an author.

In television, even more so than movies, there is no discernable author. We might consider the show's writers the authors, but as you well know, writing is only a small part of a visual text. There are the various settings, the clothing the actors wear, and the angles cameras use. In addition, we never know quite who has composed a particular show. There are writers listed, but we also hear stories about actors writing their own lines, as well as the presence of ad-libbed material. In addition, unlike authors of their own works who are responsible for virtually all of the production of the text (except of course for the book itself), the producers of a television show do not have the same direct connection to the texts they construct. They often play defining roles in shaping elements of the text that we can also make use of—the casting, the setting, the themes, even who technically writes the show—but do not do the writing, the set construction or the casting themselves.

So the question is how do we or can we refer to a show's author? One way is to refer to the show's *authors*, and use as a possibility for discussion what the presence of group authorship means to a particular text as opposed to discussing a single author. In any case, the question of authorship is one large difference between television and more traditional texts.

## Television shows are character driven, genre based, and plot oriented.

Television shows are much more genre driven than the traditional texts we read. Where we tend to gravitate toward literary texts that "transcend" genre, television shows operate almost exclusively within genres. A genre is a type of a medium with established and expected formulas and devices. Romances and Westerns are prime examples of novel genres. Most works of fiction that critics consider as literary do not fit into a particular category of novel such as romances, Westerns, and science fiction; it's rare that a literature class will discuss works from these categories. Literary critics often consider them to be formulaic, with easily predicted plots. In recent years, critics have begun to study these works more carefully, but their interest in these texts has probably not often made it into your classroom.

Television, on the other hand, is all about genre. Dramas, comedies, and action shows, or various hybrids like "dramedies," all have recognizable components. So do traditional texts, but often in television shows, they are omnipresent. We know what to expect from sitcoms, gritty police dramas, and shows about families. The fact that shows about hospitals, lawyers, and the police comprise almost 80 percent of the hour-long dramas on prime-time network television speaks to the ubiquity of genre. In fact, innovative programs like *The Days and Nights of Molly Dodd, Northern Exposure, Twin Peaks,* and *Freaks and Geeks* had short lives on television because they could not be placed in any particular genre. Viewers didn't know how to watch them because they didn't know what to expect from them. One of the reasons television shows are neglected as a field of study in the college classroom is because they are genre oriented; if television shows were novels, we never would study them.

So in writing about television, we have to understand that in large part shows fall into a particular category and ask whether an individual show "transcends" the normal fare of that genre, as well as what conventions of that genre a particular show follows. Once we start thinking about genre we might also think about how this might affect the audience's viewing experience.

## The audience pays for its free television.

On its surface, network television would appear to be free; however, upon closer scrutiny, it turns out that we do pay for TV in a number of ways. First of all, we buy (and keep buying) more and more expensive television sets. Secondly, most Americans get their programming through monthly cable or satellite subscriptions that add up to between $300 and $600 per year. Contrast the price of a TV set and cable with the fee of a library card, which is free, and TV may not seem like such a bargain.

These are direct costs that we remain aware of for the most part. What we may not consider, though, are the indirect ways we pay for television. Instead of charging viewers to watch, television networks present commercials, paid for by advertisers. Advertisers, in turn, choose shows in which to advertise. Then, the price for those ads likely gets passed onto you in the purchase price of the items you buy.

But we pay for television in another way as well, and that is with our time and attention. If you watch a commercial, then you are essentially paying for that program with your time. Advertisers know this and plan accordingly. You can often tell what audience an advertiser thinks it is getting by watching its commercials. Because they in part are responsible for paying for a show, advertisers do play a role in what makes it to television, although the networks play a much larger role. If a show's content is considered controversial, advertisers may shy away, with the idea that it may lose potential customers who attach the advertisers to the show's content. If advertisers do not want to advertise with a show, the show may not survive.

The size of an audience may also play a factor in how we view the show. We might think about how a show geared toward appealing to millions differs from a novel, which often has (and can have) a more limited appeal. Television is entertainment for the masses, and its direct connection to commerce is another factor we have to look at when writing about it.

## What is not there is often as important as what is.

What is not in a show is often as important as what is in it. For example, as Oprah Winfrey pointed out when the cast of *Friends* came on her show, there is no black "friend." Winfrey's observation raises another: what does the absence of minorities of any kind in a city of incredible diversity say about the creators of a show? (We can make the same comments about any number of sitcoms: see *Everyone Loves Raymond, Dharma and Greg, Frasier, Drew Carey*, and *Seinfeld* [at least *Seinfeld* is smart enough to talk about its relative whiteness].) The ethnicity of the casts may send a message about the target audience for the show but also what kind of family, relationship or group is considered "normal" or "cool." Unlike 30 years ago, there are now a number of programs that feature people of color that are, in fact, written and perhaps even directed by people of color, which was usually *not* the case even 20 years ago. Despite this notable improvement, many American groups get little or no representation on TV. For instance, as this book goes to press, there is no show that looks at Asian American, Arab American, Hispanic American or Native American families, relationships, or culture on prime-time television. Whether it is people of a certain age, particular areas of the country or world, or specific jobs, many aspects of modern life do not appear on television.

When looking at sitcoms or other television shows, also note the presence or absence of traditional gender roles, realistic dialogue, and typical, real-time events. Looking for absence rather than presence is difficult but rewarding.

## Visual media have specific concerns.

Television is a visual medium compared to traditional texts such as short stories and poems. Thus, we have to take into account how a show looks as well as sounds. The visual presence comes most obviously in its setting. In some shows, the setting is crucial. In *Seinfeld*, for example, New York City drives a great deal of the plot. In *The Simpsons*, the Midwestern averageness of Springfield often determines the issues the show addresses, sometimes explaining a character's actions. *Friends* is set in New York, but how much really is New York a "character" in the show (as opposed to in *Seinfeld* for example)? We also might look at three other settings—the coffee shop, Rachel and Monica's apartment, and Joey and Chandler's apartment. Are they appropriate for people of their age and wealth? Are they particularly male or female? What does the coffee shop represent to these characters and the audience?

You might also ask how the clothing of each cast member contributes to the audience member's idea of who and what the character is supposed to represent. On shows like *Drew Carey, Seinfeld, Friends, NYPD Blue,* and even *Oprah,* clothing plays a crucial role in what the audience is supposed to understand about the show's characters, or in the case of *Oprah,* the host. Finally, you might ask how cameras are used and the colors that dominate the broadcast. A show like *NYPD Blue* uses hand-held cameras, ostensibly for a more realistic look. A soap opera uses close-ups held for a number of seconds before cutting away to another scene or commercial. What do these techniques say about the shows in which they used? Overall, the visual elements are crucial to understanding some of the show's intended and unintended messages, and its distinction from more traditional texts.

## Finding themes is easy, but finding meaningful ones is difficult.

Themes are the intended meanings that authors give their works. For example, a theme of Harper Lee's *To Kill a Mockingbird* would be that racism can interfere with justice, and this interference is highly destructive to a society's fabric. Every text has a theme, and whether we know it or not, we pick up on a text's thematics.

Of all the elements involved with watching television, the theme is the most easily discerned and often the least interesting. Most often, any television theme revolves around tolerance and patience and above all, the problematic nature of jumping to conclusions. Although many critics sometimes justifiably complain about the violence of television shows, most shows favor right over wrong, happiness over sadness, lessons learned over lessons forgotten. So looking for theme is often the easiest task a television reader has.

What's more difficult is trying to understand whether the television author(s) handled these lessons too simplistically or offensively, or at the expense of the quality of the show. In other words, does the theme take away from the show's other elements? In watching sitcoms, finding the theme is easy, but one must be careful. *The Simpsons,* for example, has a traditional television sitcom theme in many of its shows but often brutally satirizes American culture. So which message is more important? Clearly, what happens during the show matters more than what happens at its end, which the authors of *The Simpsons* often use to criticize the conventions of television itself.

Overall, the medium of television has a number of general concerns that play into our enjoyment as well as our critical stance. As a writer, you do not have to take into account all of the above, but thinking about them is a good way of breaking free of your traditional relationship to television. There are also more specific ways of analyzing a television show. Following this introduction we give a list of questions you can ask of a television show.

# Worksheet

## THIS TEXT

1. How does the background of the authors influence their ideas about television?
2. Do the authors have different ideas about class, race, and gender and their place in television? In what ways?
3. While it will be impossible for you to know this fully, try to figure out the writing situation of each author. Who is the audience? What does the author have at stake?
4. What is his or her agenda? *Why* is she or he writing this piece?
5. What social, political, and cultural forces affect the author's text? What is going on in the world as he or she is writing?
6. What are the main points of the essay? Can you find a thesis statement anywhere?
7. How does the author support his argument? What evidence does he use to back up any claims he might make?
8. Is the author's argument valid and/or reasonable?
9. Do you find yourself in agreement with the author? Why or why not?
10. Does the author help you *read* television better than you did before reading the essay? If so, why?
11. How is the reading process different if you are reading an essay as opposed to a short story or poem?
12. What is the agenda of the author? Why does she or he want us to think a certain way?
13. Did you like this? Why or why not?
14. Do you think the author likes television?

## BEYOND THIS TEXT: READING TELEVISION

**Genre:** What genre are we watching? How do the writers let us know this? (Visually, orally, etc.)

**Characters:** Who are the characters? Do they represent something beyond actors in a plot? How do the writers want us to perceive them, and why? How would changing the characters change the show?

**Setting:** What are the settings? What do they say about the show? What do the writers want us to think about the setting? Could the show take place somewhere else and remain the same?

**Plot:** What happens? Is the plot important to understanding/enjoying the show?

**Themes:** What do the show's writers think about the issues/ideas/subjects they present? (Themes are what writers believe about issues, ideas, and subjects, *not* the ideas and issues themselves.)
**Figurative language:** What symbols, metaphors, motifs present themselves in the show? What effect does their repetition have?
**Visual constructions:** How do the writers make us see (or hear) the show?
**Absences:** What is missing? What real-world notions are not represented in the show?
**Conventional/nonconventional:** In what ways is the show typical of its genre? Atypical?
**Race/ethnicity/gender/class:** How do the writers talk (or not talk about) these issues?

---

# CITIZENS OF THE WORLD, TURN ON YOUR TELEVISIONS!

Sallie Tisdale

In this piece written for *Salon* (1998), Sallie Tisdale takes a personal approach to watching television, celebrating an aspect of television that most people criticize: channel surfing.

SUNDAY AFTERNOON. There's a special on the history of guns on the History Channel. "How was the dream of rapid-fire ever to be realized?" the commentator asks over a scene of Civil War soldiers desperately stuffing musket balls into their barrels. The cheesy Spanish-language soap opera "Salud, Dinero y Amor" is on. I learn to count to 12 in Japanese, but promptly forget. Today, I am reminded, is Sukkoth, the Jewish celebration of the harvest and the wandering of the tribes. I watch a few minutes of "Baywatch," long enough to see a beautiful, blonde oddly sculptured female lifeguard revived from drowning with no apparent spiritual improvement. The Weather Channel lists airport delays around the country. George Bush is on "Booknotes," and he is fascinatingly boring, describing world-shaking events in a dull nasal monotone. I pass through a documentary on postwar Germany, a Christian eulogy for dead scuba divers, a local broadcast of the city council, duller than Bush.

QVC. Call 1-800-555-1515 to buy the Diamonique Graduated Tennis Earrings in 14K gold with a retail value of $100 at an introductory price of $63.24 in three easy payments of only $21.08 a month.

Today I am soothed by the remote control, by the low demand and the steady change of television, its endless evolution and willingness to admit anything, anything at all. Once upon a time, I didn't own a television. Then I moved into a hippie household guiltily addicted to the NCAA season—but everyone tuning into "The Rockford Files" on Saturday night, too. And then there was "Dallas." And then color.

And then color begat ESPN.

There's a First Amendment debate on one of the cable-access channels. A nice old western a few channels up, one of those white people fantasies where all the pioneers are clean and smell nice. MTV is running a marathon of "Daria" cartoons. Daria is a smart, nerdy teenage girl. "They say high school is supposed to be the happiest time of your life," a boy tells Daria, and she answers, "Only if your life is incredibly short." In between episodes are brief snatches of the "Virtual Bill Declassified Grand Jury Testimony" and an ad for "Bride of Chucky" ("Chucky Gets Lucky").

TLC has a documentary on South Florida.

It's football on ESPN. Click. The real sport is on the networks. San Diego is ahead of Houston by one run in the third inning. Randy Johnson has a batting average of .091, worse than mine and good God, I can't believe he swung at that. "Randy Johnson has shown he's not particularly enamored of hitting," says the color commentator, just before Johnson strikes out.

ESPN at night. "Sesame Street" in the morning. Big Bird was begat by "Mister Rogers' Neighborhood." My son wrote Mister Rogers a letter once, complimenting him on his sweaters and informing him that his—my son's—name was now Frisky. Mister Rogers promptly wrote back and told Frisky he liked him just the way he was.

Then Mister Rogers begat "Hill Street Blues," and "Hill Street Blues" begat "St. Elsewhere" and "St. Elsewhere" begat the VCR.

QVC. Call 1-800-555-1515 for a Diamonique seven-inch Simulated Ruby Tennis Bracelet in 14K gold, retail price of $490, on sale at the introductory price of $299.95 in five easy payments of only $59.99 a month.

"This is October," says the talking head on the Weather Channel, "a transitional and turbulent month."

Two teenage girls show the viewer how to win a video game on one of the cable-access channels, the camera switching from their earnest, clear faces to the computer screen and back. It's like a movie of a film about a video game in a play on television, and the girls are completely at home there.

The History Channel is discussing how the Springfield rifle led to the Gatling gun.

There were movies to rent, and exercise videos. And a few years ago, "The X-Files." Xena. And now, Buffy.

I love television. I love the ad for a Samsung cellular telephone with voice recognition, so you can say "Frank," and it dials Frank's number. I love the "Virtual Bill Declassified Grand Jury Testimony" jokes. I love the arm-lifting evangelical testimony, the untranslated programs with low production values in Farsi and Korean and Chinese, meant for anyone but me. I love the weird local talk shows where conspiracy theorists and drag queens discuss areas of mutual interest. I love these windows on a world much larger than what I come across in my little daily commutes to store and post office, much larger and more varied than I could possibly experience in one city, one country, one life.

I love the great equalization of a world beamed to all of us—a world where, if you skim gently up and down the channels, you are exposed to enough contradictory Weltanschauungs to fill a galaxy and none of them seem more correct or powerful than the next.

But only George Bush could talk about war and put me to sleep.

There's a good slide show on the city's cable access, the Police Chief's Forum on "Less Lethal Use of Force," with pictures of blunt trauma injuries from bean-bag shot and rubber bullets. "This is not just a way to hurt someone," he tells the solemn audience, who nod carefully.

Back to Daria. Back to Virtual Bill. Back in time for an ad for tonight's "Celebrity Death Match," a violent clay animation show where Elvis punches out a stoned Jerry Garcia, and Janeane Garofalo gives Cindy Crawford a bloody compound fracture. Back to Stone Phillips smilingly describing a harrowing fishing boat accident, followed by an ad for a show promising a look "inside the head of a serial killer."

I love this great heterogeneous culture of tastes, where everything goes, where almost nothing is forbidden because someone, somewhere, is interested. I love the way it forces me to see how much I define what is good and bad in the world, what is right and wrong, how strongly I hold my opinions about what people should think and do and want. Television demands that I reconsider the centrality of my point of view. Television tells me, without apology, that these are only my opinions and have nothing to do with the lives of other people, who feel just as strongly as I do in completely different ways.

ESPN. The Seahawks and Kansas City in pouring rain and dark. That looks like a good time, but I pass—click—another football game—click—Ken Olin weeping on the witness stand. "She had a mind like quicksilver," he moans. "She could be funny, generous and very feminine." Click.

"Mossy Oak's Hunting the Country" is going to talk about rattlin' for game on TNN. But down in the low numbers, on the increasingly ineffectual networks, Houston and San Diego are tied in the fifth. A few channels up, the Rev. Josie C. Holmes of the Spoken Word Ministry sings R&B gospel with organ accompaniment.

I like television a lot better than the Internet. I am still taken aback by the claims people make about the Internet, about its "interactivity," its variety. The Internet, the Web, all of computerland, is still a tiny paradigm, still dominated by a small portion of people of a certain education and class, still mostly male, still a king's ransom available only to the very few. The Internet responds to my opinions, searches for what I want to see, gives me only what I'm willing to wait for, pay for, know. The Internet shrinks my world. Television expands it.

Television is truly the common denominator, the commonest. It is the world's middle. Watching television is the third most time-consuming activity in the world, behind only working and sleeping. (Is that wrong? Is that bad? Is your opinion more correct than that of the billion people watching right now?) I take all these frames and passing words together and throw them in a pot and I find something of everyone. Television is and must be and cannot be anything but average and at the same time it can't be anything but endless variety and change. I can't be a citizen of a world and not pay attention.

QVC. Call 1-800-555-1515 to get the Diamonique Triple Row Channel Set Band Ring in 14K gold, which retails at $270 and is "new today" for only $218.75.

"We're giving you," says the announcer, "what you have asked for!"

---

### THIS TEXT: READING

1. What ideas about television is Tisdale writing against?
2. How is her approach to television different from most critics?
3. What is her general "reading" of television? Do you share it?
4. How would you classify her approach? Is it effective? Appropriate for a magazine? How about a paper?
5. What might a critic of television generally argue against her position? Do you consider Tisdale a critic?

### YOUR TEXT: WRITING

1. Write a paper on your television watching habits or the habits of someone close to you. What might an anthropologist or observer of culture say about the way you watch television?
2. Write a similar paper on the idea of scanning for music or surfing on the Web. What can you say positively about sampling bits of culture at one time? Negatively? Do you think this reflects some trend in our culture?
3. Write a paper that celebrates other overlooked aspects of television watching or some other less desirable act in participating in public or private life (such as waiting in line). What are some ways you could approach a topic like this?

## TV CAN BE A GOOD PARENT

Ariel Gore

---

In this 1998 piece, Ariel Gore, the author of *The Hip Mama Survival Guide,* takes to task a report that decries the influence of television on children in this persuasive paper.

LET ME GET this straight.

The corporations have shipped all the living-wage jobs off to the developing world, the federal government has "ended welfare" and sent poor women into sub-minimum wage "training programs" while offering virtually no child-care assistance, the rent on my one-bedroom apartment just went up to $850 a month, the newspapers have convinced us that our kids can't play outside by themselves until they're 21 and now the American Academy of Pediatrics wants my television?

I don't think so.

Earlier this month, the AAP released new guidelines for parents recommending that kids under the age of 2 not watch TV. They say the box is bad for babies' brains and not much better for older kids. Well, no duh.

When I was a young mom on welfare, sometimes I needed a break. I needed time to myself. I needed to mellow out to avoid killing my daughter for pouring bleach on the Salvation Army couch. And when I was at my wits' end, Barney the Dinosaur and Big Bird were better parents than I was. My daughter knows that I went to college when she was a baby and preschooler. She knows that I work. And, truth be told, our television set has been a helpful co-parent on rainy days when I've been on deadline. Because I'm the mother of a fourth-grader, Nickelodeon is my trusted friend.

There was no TV in our house when I was a kid. My mother called them "boob tubes." But that was in the 1970s. My mother and all of her friends were poor—they were artists—but the rent she paid for our house on the Monterey (Calif.) Peninsula was $175 a month and my mother and her friends helped each other with the kids. The child care was communal. So they could afford to be poor, to stay home, to kill their televisions. I, on the other hand, cannot.

Now the AAP is saying I'm doing my daughter an injustice every time I let her watch TV. The official policy states that "Although certain television programs may be promoted [to young children], research on early brain development shows that babies and toddlers have a critical need for direct interactions with parents and other significant caregivers for healthy brain growth and the development of appropriate social, emotional, and cognitive skills. Therefore, exposing such young children to television programs should be discouraged."

Maybe my brain has been warped by all my post-childhood TV watching, but I'm having a little trouble getting from point A to point B here. Babies and toddlers have a critical need for direct interactions with actual people. I'm with them on this. "Therefore, exposing such young children to television programs should be discouraged." This is where they lose me. I can see "Therefore, sticking them in front of the TV all day and all night should be discouraged." But the assumption that TV-watching kids don't interact with their parents or caregivers is silly. Watching TV and having one-on-one interactions with our kids aren't mutually exclusive.

I've been careful to teach my daughter critical thinking in my one-woman "mind over media" campaign. It started with fairytales: "What's make-believe?" and "How would you like to stay home and cook for all those dwarves?" Later we moved on to the news: "Why was it presented in this way?" and "What's a stereotype?" But if you think I was reading "Winnie the Pooh" to my toddler when I thought up these questions, think again. I was relaxing with a cup of coffee and a book on feminist theory while Maia was riveted to PBS.

I read to my daughter when she was little. We still read together. But even a thoughtful mama needs an electronic baby sitter every now and again. Maybe especially a thoughtful mama.

Not surprisingly, the television executives feel there's plenty of innocuous programming on television to entertain young kids without frying their brains. "It's a bunch of malarkey," said Kenn Viselman, president of the itsy bitsy Entertainment Co., about the new policy. Itsy bitsy distributes the British show "Teletubbies," which is broadcast on PBS. While I prefer Big Bird to Tinky Winky, I have to agree with him when he says, "Instead of attacking shows that try to help children, the pediatricians should warn parents that they shouldn't watch the Jerry Springer show when kids are in the room."

The AAP's policy refers to all television, of course, but it's hard not to feel like they're picking on PBS. "Teletubbies" is the only program currently shown on non-cable television marketed toward babies and toddlers. Just two weeks ago, the station announced a $40 million investment to develop six animated programs for preschoolers. The timing of the AAP's report is unfortunate.

Cable stations offer a wider variety of kid programming. Take for example Nick Jr., an offshoot of the popular Nickelodeon channel. On weekdays from 9 a.m. to 2 p.m., the programming is geared specifically toward the preschool set. "Our slogan for Nick Jr. is 'Play to Learn'," Nickelodeon's New York publicity manager, Karen Reynolds, told me. "A child is using cognitive skills in a fun setting. It's interactive. With something like 'Blues Clues,' kids are talking back to the TV. They are not just sitting there."

Still, the station has no beef with the new AAP policy on toddlers. "Nick Jr. programs to preschool children ages 2 to 5, but we are aware that children younger than 2 may be watching television," said Brown Johnson, senior vice president of Nick Jr. "We welcome a study of this kind because it encourages parents to spend more time bonding and playing with their children."

In addition to telling parents that young children shouldn't watch television at all and that older kids shouldn't have sets in their bedrooms, the AAP is recommending that pediatricians ask questions about media consumption at annual checkups. The difference between recommending less TV-watching and actually mandating that it be monitored by the medical community is where this could become a game of hardball with parents. What would this "media file" compiled by our doctors be used for? Maybe television placement in the home will become grounds for deciding child custody. ("I'm sorry, your honor, I'll move the set into the bathroom immediately.") Or maybe two decades from now Harvard will add TV abstention to their ideal candidate profile. ("'Teletubbies' viewers need not apply.") Better yet, Kaiser could just imprint "Poor White Trash" directly onto my family's medical ID cards. Not that those cards work at the moment. I'm a little behind on my bill.

I called around, but I was hard-pressed to find a pediatrician who disagreed with the academy's new policy. Instead, doctors seemed to want their kids to watch less TV, and they're glad to have the AAP's perhaps over-the-top guidelines behind them. "If all your kids did was an hour of Barney and 'Sesame Street' a day, I don't think that the academy would have come out with that statement," said a pediatrician at La Clinica de la Raza in Oakland, Calif., who asked not to be named. "It's not the best learning tool." And he scoffs at the notion of "interactive" TV. "It's not a real human interaction. When you're dealing with babies and toddlers, this screen is an integral part of their reality. You want kids to be able to understand interaction as an interaction. It's like the Internet. We're getting to a place where all of your relationships are virtual relationships."

Fair enough.

I'm not going to say that TV is the greatest thing in the world for little kids—or for anyone. I'm not especially proud of the hours I spend watching "Xena: Warrior Princess," "The Awful Truth" and "Ally McBeal." Mostly I think American television is a string of insipid shows aired for the sole purpose of rounding up an audience to buy tennis shoes made in Indonesian sweatshops.

But it seems that there is a heavy middle-class assumption at work in the AAP's new policy—that all of us can be stay-at-home moms, or at least that we all have partners or other supportive people who will come in and nurture our kids when we can't.

I say that before we need a policy like this one, we need more—and better—educational programming on TV. We need to end the culture of war and the media's glorification of violence. We need living-wage jobs. We need government salaries for stay-at-home moms so that all women have a real career choice. We do not need "media files" in our pediatricians' offices or more guilt about being bad parents. Give me a $175 a month house on the Monterey Peninsula and a commune of artists to share parenting responsibilities, and I'll kill my TV without any provocation from the AAP at all. Until then, long live Big Bird, "The Brady Bunch" and all their very special friends!

---

## THIS TEXT: READING

1. What are Gore's main arguments against the American Academy of Pediatrics recommendation? In what ways does she agree with the report?

2. How does Gore suggest parents and children watch television?
3. What do you think about the relationship between children and television?

### Your Text: Writing

1. Write about your own experience watching television growing up. Do you find your own experiences match Gore's?
2. Find the report that Gore is talking about either on-line or in the library. Does she read the report accurately? Write your own reaction to the report.
3. Watch a television show aimed for kids. Notice what values the show embraces. Now notice the advertising. Is it age appropriate? Are the values at odds with the television show? Write a short paper about your viewing experience.
4. If you have a younger sister or brother or know a child, watch a kid's show with them. Ask them questions as they watch, and after. Write a short paper about your experience.

## LIFE ACCORDING TO TV

Harry F. Waters

Harry Waters wrote this piece about television demographics for *Newsweek* in 1982. Though the article is mostly reportage, it does relay some of the assumptions about the world television viewers are exposed to.

> You people sit there, night after night. You're beginning to believe this illusion we're spinning here. You're beginning to think the tube is reality and your own lives are unreal. This is mass madness!
>
> —*Anchorman Howard Beale in the film* Network

> If you can write a nation's stories, you needn't worry about who makes its laws. Today television tells most of the stories to most of the people most of the time.
>
> —*George Gerbner, Ph.D.*

THE LATE PADDY CHAYEFSKY, who created Howard Beale, would have loved George Gerbner. In *Network*, Chayefsky marshaled a scathing, fictional assault on the values and methods of the people who control the world's most potent communications instrument. In real life, Gerbner, perhaps the nation's foremost authority on the social impact of television, is quietly using the disciplines of behavioral research to construct an equally devastating indictment of the medium's images and messages. More than any spokesman for a pressure group, Gerbner has become the man that television watches. From his cramped, book-lined office at the University of Pennsylvania springs a steady flow of studies that are raising executive blood pressures at the networks' sleek Manhattan command posts. George Gerbner's work is uniquely important because it transports the scientific examination of television far beyond familiar children-and-violence arguments. Rather than simply studying the link between violence on the tube and crime in the streets, Gerbner is exploring wider and deeper terrain. He has turned his lens on TV's hidden victims—women, the elderly, blacks, blue-collar workers and other groups—to document the ways in which video-entertainment portrayals subliminally condition how we perceive ourselves and how we view those around us. Gerbner's subjects are not merely the impressionable young; they include all the rest of us. And it is his ominous conclusion that heavy watchers of the prime-time mirror are receiving a grossly distorted picture of the real world that they tend to accept more readily than reality itself.

The 63-year-old Gerbner, who is dean of Penn's Annenberg School of Communications, employs a methodology that meshes scholarly observation with mundane legwork. Over the past 15 years, he and a tireless trio of assistants (Larry Gross, Nancy Signorielli and Michael Morgan) videotaped and exhaustively analyzed 1,600 prime-time programs involving more than 15,000 characters. They then drew up multiple-choice questionnaries that offered correct answers about the world at large along with answers that reflected what Gerbner perceived to be the misrepresentations and biases of the world according to TV. Finally, these questions were posed to large samples of citizens from all socio-economic strata. In every survey, the Annenberg team discovered that heavy viewers of television (those watching more than four hours a day), who account for more than 30 percent of the population, almost invariably chose the TV-influenced answers, while light viewers (less than two hours a day), selected the answers corresponding more closely to actual life. Some of the dimensions of television's reality warp:

- *Sex:* Male prime-time characters outnumber females by 3 to 1 and, with a few star-turn exceptions, women are portrayed as weak, passive satellites to powerful, effective men. TV's male population also plays a vast variety of roles, while females generally get typecast as either lovers or mothers. Less than 20 percent of TV's married women with children work outside the home—as compared with more than 50 percent in real life. The tube's distorted depictions of women, concludes Gerbner, reinforce stereotypical attitudes and increase sexism. In one Annenberg survey, heavy viewers were far more likely than light ones to agree with the proposition: "Women should take care of running their homes and leave running the country to men."
- *Age:* People over 65, too, are grossly underrepresented on television. Correspondingly, heavy-viewing Annenberg respondents believe that

the elderly are a vanishing breed, that they make up a smaller proportion of the population today than they did 20 years ago. In fact, they form the nation's most rapidly expanding age group. Heavy viewers also believe that old people are less healthy today than they were two decades ago, when quite the opposite is true. As with women, the portrayals of old people transmit negative impressions. In general, they are cast as silly, stubborn, sexually inactive and eccentric. "They're often shown as feeble grandparents bearing cookies," says Gerbner. "You never see the power that real old people often have. The best and possibly only time to learn about growing old with decency and grace is in youth. And young people are the most susceptible to TV's messages."

- *Race:* The problem with the medium's treatment of blacks is more one of image than of visibility. Though a tiny percentage of black characters come across as "unrealistically romanticized," reports Gerbner, the overwhelming majority of them are employed in subservient, supporting roles—such as the white hero's comic sidekick. "When a black child looks at prime time," he says, "most of the people he sees doing interesting and important things are white." That imbalance, he goes on, tends to teach young blacks to accept minority status as naturally inevitable and even deserved. To assess the impact of such portrayals on the general audience, the Annenberg survey forms included questions like "Should white people have the right to keep blacks out of their neighborhoods?" and "Should there be laws against marriages between blacks and whites?" The more that viewers watched, the more they answered "Yes" to each question.
- *Work:* Heavy viewers greatly overestimated the proportion of Americans employed as physicians, lawyers, athletes and entertainers, all of whom inhabit prime-time in hordes. A mere 6 to 10 percent of television characters hold blue-collar or service jobs vs. about 60 percent in the real work force. Gerbner sees two dangers in TV's skewed division of labor. On the one hand, the tube so overrepresents and glamorizes the elite occupations that it sets up unrealistic expectations among those who must deal with them in actuality. At the same time, TV largely neglects portraying the occupations that most youngsters will have to enter. "You almost never see the farmer, the factory worker or the small businessman," he notes. "Thus not only do lawyers and other professionals find they cannot measure up to the image TV projects of them, but children's occupational aspirations are channeled in unrealistic directions." The Gerbner team feels this emphasis on high-powered jobs poses problems for adolescent girls, who are also presented with views of women as homebodies. The two conflicting views, Gerbner says, add to the frustration over choices they have to make as adults.
- *Health:* Although video characters exist almost entirely on junk food and quaff alcohol 15 times more often than water, they manage to

remain slim, healthy and beautiful. Frequent TV watchers, the Annenberg investigators found, eat more, drink more, exercise less and possess an almost mystical faith in the curative powers of medical science. Concludes Gerbner: "Television may well be the single most pervasive source of health information. And its overidealized images of medical people, coupled with its complacency about unhealthy life-styles, leaves both patients and doctors vulnerable to disappointment, frustration and even litigation."

- *Crime:* On the small screen, crime rages about 10 times more often than in real life. But while other researchers concentrate on the propensity of TV mayhem to incite aggression, the Annenberg team has studied the hidden side of its imprint: fear of victimization. On television, 55 percent of prime-time characters are involved in violent confrontations once a week; in reality, the figure is less than 1 percent. In all demographic groups in every class of neighborhood, heavy viewers overestimated the statistical chance of violence in their own lives and harbored an exaggerated mistrust of strangers—creating what Gerbner calls a "mean-world syndrome." Forty-six percent of heavy viewers who live in cities rated their fear of crime "very serious" as opposed to 26 percent for light viewers. Such paranoia is especially acute among TV entertainment's most common victims: women, the elderly, non-whites, foreigners and lower-class citizens.

  Video violence, proposes Gerbner, is primarily responsible for imparting lessons in social power: it demonstrates who can *do* what to whom and get away with it. "Television is saying that those at the bottom of the power scale cannot get away with the same things that a white, middle-class American male can," he says. "It potentially conditions people to think of themselves as victims."

At a quick glance, Gerbner's findings seem to contain a cause-and-effect, chicken-or-the-egg question. Does television make heavy viewers view the world the way they do or do heavy viewers come from the poorer, less experienced segment of the populace that regards the world that way to begin with? In other words, does the tube create or simply confirm the unenlightened attitudes of its most loyal audience? Gerbner, however, was savvy enough to construct a methodology largely immune to such criticism. His samples of heavy viewers cut across all ages, incomes, education levels and ethnic backgrounds—and every category displayed the same tube-induced misconceptions of the world outside.

Needless to say, the networks accept all this as enthusiastically as they would a list of news-coverage complaints from the Ayatollah Khomeini. Even so, their responses tend to be tinged with a singular respect for Gerbner's personal and professional credentials. The man is no ivory-tower recluse. During World War II, the Budapest-born Gerbner parachuted into the mountains of Yugoslavia to join the partisans fighting the Germans.

After the war, he hunted down and personally arrested scores of high Nazi officials. Nor is Gerbner some videophobic vigilante. A Ph.D. in communications, he readily acknowledges TV's beneficial effects, noting that it has abolished parochialism, reduced isolation and loneliness and provided the poorest members of society with cheap, plug-in exposure to experiences they otherwise would not have. Funding for his research is supplied by such prestigious bodies as the National Institute of Mental Health, the surgeon general's office and the American Medical Association, and he is called to testify before congressional committees nearly as often as David Stockman.

## *Mass Entertainment*

When challenging Gerbner, network officials focus less on his findings and methods than on what they regard as his own misconceptions of their industry's function. "He's looking at television from the perspective of a social scientist rather than considering what is mass entertainment," says Alfred Schneider, vice president of standards and practices at ABC. "We strive to balance TV's social effects with what will capture an audience's interests. If you showed strong men being victimized as much as women or the elderly, what would comprise the dramatic conflict? If you did a show truly representative of society's total reality, and nobody watched because it wasn't interesting, what have you achieved?"

CBS senior vice president Gene Mater also believes that Gerbner is implicitly asking for the theoretically impossible. "TV is unique in its problems," says Mater. "Everyone wants a piece of the action. Everyone feels that their racial or ethnic group is underrepresented or should be portrayed as they would like the world to perceive them. No popular entertainment form, including this one, can or should be an accurate reflection of society." On that point, at least, Gerbner is first to agree; he hardly expects television entertainment to serve as a mirror image of absolute truth. But what fascinates him about this communications medium is its marked difference from all others. In other media, customers carefully choose what they want to hear or read: a movie, a magazine, a best seller. In television, notes Gerbner, viewers rarely tune in for a particular program. Instead, most just habitually turn on the set—and watch by the clock rather than for a specific show. "Television viewing fulfills the criteria of a ritual," he says. "It is the only medium that can bring to people things they otherwise would not select." With such unique power, believes Gerbner, comes unique responsibility: "No other medium reaches into every home or has a comparable, cradle-to-grave influence over what a society learns about itself."

## *Match*

In Gerbner's view, virtually all of TV's distortions of reality can be attributed to its obsession with demographics. The viewers that prime-time sponsors most want to reach are white, middle-class, female and between 18 and

49—in short, the audience that purchases most of the consumer products advertised on the tube. Accordingly, notes Gerbner, the demographic portrait of TV's fictional characters largely matches that of its prime commercial targets and largely ignores everyone else. "Television," he concludes, "reproduces a world for its own best customers."

Among TV's more candid executives, that theory draws considerable support. Yet by pointing a finger at the power of demographics, Gerbner appears to contradict one of his major findings. If female viewers are so dear to the hearts of sponsors, why are female characters cast in such unflattering light? "In a basically male-oriented power structure," replies Gerbner, "you can't alienate the male viewer. But you can get away with offending women because most women are pretty well brainwashed to accept it." The Annenberg dean has an equally tidy explanation for another curious fact. Since the corporate world provides network television with all of its financial support, one would expect businessmen on TV to be portrayed primarily as good guys. Quite the contrary. As any fan of "Dallas," "Dynasty" or "Falcon Crest" well knows, the image of the company man is usually that of a mendacious, dirty-dealing rapscallion. Why would TV snap at the hand that feeds it? "Credibility is the way to ratings," proposes Gerbner. "This country has a populist tradition of bias against anything big, including big business. So to retain credibility, TV entertainment shows businessmen in relatively derogatory ways."

In the medium's Hollywood-based creative community, the gospel of Gerbner finds some passionate adherents. Rarely have TV's best and brightest talents viewed their industry with so much frustration and anger. The most sweeping indictment emanates from David Rintels, a two-time Emmy-winning writer and former president of the Writers Guild of America, West. "Gerbner is absolutely correct and it is the people who run the networks who are to blame," says Rintels. "The networks get bombarded with thoughtful, reality-oriented scripts. They simply won't do them. They slam the door on them. They believe that the only way to get ratings is to feed viewers what conforms to their biases or what has limited resemblance to reality. From 8 to 11 o'clock each night, television is one long lie."

Innovative thinkers such as Norman Lear, whose work has been practically driven off the tube, don't fault the networks so much as the climate in which they operate. Says Lear: "All of this country's institutions have become totally fixated on short-term bottom-line thinking. Everyone grabs for what might succeed today and the hell with tomorrow. Television just catches more of the heat because it's more visible." Perhaps the most perceptive assessment of Gerbner's conclusions is offered by one who has worked both sides of the industry street. Deanne Barkley, a former NBC vice president who now helps run an independent production house, reports that the negative depictions of women on TV have made it "nerve-racking" to function as a woman within TV. "No one takes responsibility for the social impact of their shows," says Barkley. "But then how do you decide where it all begins? Do the networks give viewers what they want? Or are the networks conditioning them to think that way?"

Gerbner himself has no simple answer to that conundrum. Neither a McLuhanesque shaman nor a Naderesque crusader, he hesitates to suggest solutions until pressed. Then out pops a pair of provocative notions. Commercial television will never democratize its treatments of daily life, he believes, until it finds a way to broaden its financial base. Coincidentally, Federal Communications Commission chairman Mark Fowler seems to have arrived at much the same conclusion. In exchange for lifting such government restrictions on TV as the fairness doctrine and the equal-time rule, Fowler would impose a modest levy on station owners called a spectrum-use fee. Funds from the fees would be set aside to finance programs aimed at specialized tastes rather than the mass appetite. Gerbner enthusiastically endorses that proposal: "Let the ratings system dominate most of prime time but not every hour of every day. Let some programs carry advisories that warn: 'This is not for all of you. This is for nonwhites, or for religious people or for the aged and the handicapped. Turn it off unless you'd like to eavesdrop.' That would be a very refreshing thing."

## *Role*

In addition, Gerbner would like to see viewers given an active role in steering the overall direction of television instead of being obliged to passively accept whatever the networks offer. In Britain, he points out, political candidates debate the problems of TV as routinely as the issue of crime. In this country, proposes Gerbner, "every political campaign should put television on the public agenda. Candidates talk about schools, they talk about jobs, they talk about social welfare. They're going to have to start discussing this all-pervasive force."

There are no outright villains in this docudrama. Even Gerbner recognizes that network potentates don't set out to proselytize a point of view; they are simply businessmen selling a mass-market product. At the same time, their 90 million nightly customers deserve to know the side effects of the ingredients. By the time the typical American child reaches the age of reason, calculates Gerbner, he or she will have absorbed more than 30,000 electronic "stories." These stories, he suggests, have replaced the socializing role of the preindustrial church: they create a "cultural mythology" that establishes the norms of approved behavior and belief. And all Gerbner's research indicates that this new mythological world, with its warped picture of a sizable portion of society, may soon become the one most of us think we live in.

Who else is telling us that? Howard Beale and his eloquent alarms have faded into off-network reruns. At the very least, it is comforting to know that a real-life Beale is very much with us . . . and *really* watching.

### THIS TEXT: READING

1. What is Waters's point in describing the world according to television? Do you agree or disagree—why or why not?
2. What is Waters assuming about television's audience when describing this "world"? Do you think these assumptions are appropriate? Do they apply to you?
3. This piece is now twenty years old—what do you think has changed since he wrote it? Are the ideas Gerbner wrote still valid today?

### YOUR TEXT: WRITING

1. Pick a night of television and a network and do your own demographic study. Who makes up the casts of the shows? What values do the shows display? Imply?
2. One of the techniques for watching popular culture the authors employ is to follow the implications of character action. For example, if a character is portrayed as strong or weak, smart or dumb, greedy or kind, what happens to them can be an indication of how the authors feel about that general type of character.
3. Imagine yourself in "television world"—what would it look like? How would people act in it? How would it sound? How would this world be different from the world you live in now? Write a short essay on your experiences in television world.

## HOW SOAPS ARE INTEGRATING AMERICA: COLOR TV

Michelle Cottle

Michelle Cottle writes about how the mixing of cultures is changing the way soap operas are produced—and watched. Though the piece (2001) is mostly reportage, pay attention to the argument Cottle is making.

LOVEBIRDS MIGUEL AND CHARITY (who happens to be a witch) watch in horror as the smoke from a burning boat begins to suffocate Tabitha (also a witch) and Timmy (her enchanted doll), trapped inside. In the shadows nearby, the deranged arsonist, Norma, babbles to herself about her triumph but frets that someone will try to save the imperiled duo. Meanwhile, at a posh resort in Bermuda, the filthy-rich and utterly wicked Julian Crane is attempting to seduce the beautiful, naive, and thoroughly inebriated Theresa, unbeknownst to Theresa's older brother Luis, who, as fate would have it, is in the adjacent suite sharing a romantic evening with his true love, Sheridan, who is also Julian's sister (and whom Julian and his father, Alistair, are plotting to kill in order to end her relationship with Luis). Julian is supposed to be using his Bermuda trip to divorce Ivy, who at that very moment is back in (the fictional New England town of) Harmony, eavesdropping on Sam (the object of her affections), Grace (Sam's wife), and David, who claims that Grace has long been his wife.

Viewers got all this—and much, much more—in last Thursday's episode of "Passions," NBC's newest, hippest, weirdest daytime drama. Just over two years old and geared toward younger viewers, "Passions" is a bit more campy than its elder brethren but still delivers pretty much what you'd expect from a soap opera: poor production values, absurd plotlines, gorgeous cast members, and wretched acting. With all the scheming, screwing, and attempted killing that go on, soaps could be Exhibit A in Bill Bennett's case that television is turning America into a modern-day Sodom.

Except that when it comes to race, the soaps are a shining model of what America claims it wants to be: diverse, integrated, and more or less equal. While activists continue to grumble about the bland whiteness of prime-time television, the big-three networks—in a bid to pump up sagging ratings—have begun a major push to lure minority viewers, particularly Latinos, to their daytime dramas. The result is Spanish simulcasts and subtitles, story lines that deal with Hispanic culture, and more Latino faces onscreen. Moreover, unlike prime time, when blacks and Latinos tend to appear in segregated shows (think Damon Wayans) or stereotypical roles (think Latina maids), the minorities in soaps are folded into integrated, middle-class (not to mention upper-class) story lines. On "daytime," African Americans, Hispanics, Caucasians, and enchanted dolls all live, love, lie, and forgive together in a melodramatic melting pot. It's enough to make you put down your vacuum cleaner, buy a box of Kleenex, and stand up and cheer.

Make no mistake: The integration of daytime television is primarily about the pursuit of green. Over the past decade, with more women working outside the home, soap operas have suffered a ratings slump. (Industry execs also blame the O.J. trial for preempting the soaps and breaking fans' viewing habits.) Even the most popular show, "The Young and the Restless," has suffered a 28 percent ratings slide since 1994. To make matters worse, the average age of soap viewers is on the rise, up nine years since 1991, which bodes ill for ad revenues. (Younger viewers tend to be freer with their spending.) All of which has sent daytime TV execs scrambling.

For a variety of reasons, Latinos are a prime target. For starters, the raw numbers are mouthwatering: According to the 2000 census, there are some 35 million Hispanics living in the United States—and market research shows that young Latinos tend to spend more of their disposable income than their non-Latino counterparts. Best of all, many Latinos (or, more often, Latinas) already have a taste for the genre. Telenovelas, Spanish-language soap operas, are a staple of Spanish-language television and are extraordinarily popular among Hispanics in the United States. Soap producers are praying that, with a little strategic tweaking, they can get telenovela fans hooked.

Most basically, much daytime programming now offers Spanish subtitles or optional Spanish audio. In addition, many soaps' websites include show summaries and star bios en español. More significantly, some shows are mimicking the format of telenovelas, which feature faster-paced story lines that wrap up after several weeks or months, instead of dragging on for years like traditional soaps. CBS executives hold regular meetings on how to use elements from the telenovelas to draw Latino audiences to "The Bold and the Beautiful," says publicist Kevin McDonald. ABC has already adopted the telenovela format on "Port Charles" and, earlier this summer, brought in a Latino consulting company to help develop plotlines and characters that appeal to Hispanic viewers. An added bonus, notes Felicia Behr, the network's senior vice president for daytime programming, is that the telenovela's faster pace appeals to young people, who like to "get conclusions" after a few weeks. Over the past few weeks, says Behr, numbers for "Port Charles" among women in the key 18-to-49 age range rose 36 percent, while its numbers among teens tripled.

The most obvious change, however, is in front of the camera: more Latino faces, particularly in central roles. Behr reports that ABC recently introduced another Hispanic character on "All My Children" and expanded the Hispanic family on "One Life to Live," keeping them "at the forefront of the story for a long time." In May, CBS added an Argentinean and a Colombian cast member to star, respectively, as a fashion model and a fashion designer—no blue-collar laborers here—on "The Bold and the Beautiful" (or, if you prefer, "Belleza y Poder"). But leading the multicultural charge is NBC's "Passions": Of its four core families, two are white, one is black, and one is Hispanic. (Hispanic-Irish, to be more precise. Intermarriage—while still rare on prime time—is becoming de rigueur in soap land.) The yummy Lopez-Fitzgerald brothers have developed quite a fan club, with young Miguel (Jesse Metcalfe) named AOL's Teen Celebrity of the Month in August. And when two older members of the Lopez-Fitzgerald clan were planning for a double wedding in July, the writers recruited the hottest talk-show host on Spanish-language television to guest star as a visiting aunt; her husband was played by a veteran telenovela actor.

A few Latino faces here and there may not sound like much, until you consider their stark absence during prime time. Although the census shows that Hispanics now make up 12.5 percent of the U.S. population, they represent only 2 percent of characters in prime time, according to the California-based advocacy group Children Now. African Americans fare somewhat better, in part because of a high-profile boycott threat last year by the NAACP. Nonetheless, of the 22 shows premiering this season, only two had minority leads.

Worse, unlike the assimilationist soaps, prime-time programming frequently pursues segregation as a marketing strategy. The vast majority of sitcoms boast either all-white or all-black casts—and leave Latinos completely out of the picture. (Weekly dramas do a better job—think Detective Ed Green on "Law and Order" or Dr. Peter Benton on "ER"—but mainly after ten o'clock in the evening. As Children Now points out, during the earlier hours, when most kids are watching, the world looks like a very segregated place.) Soaps, by contrast, try not to ghettoize minority characters in marginal or stereotypical roles. For the most part, they manage to acknowledge their characters' Latino heritage without treating them differently from other characters, says Felix Sanchez, CEO of the P.R. firm TerraCom and a founder of the National Hispanic Foundation for the Arts. "Daytime at least identifies characters as Latinos and allows them to fall into the same classic soap opera character traps."

It's true, of course, that the TV culture into which Latinos are being assimilated is a culture of schlock. But soap opera role models are better than no televised role models at all. Moreover, the soaps—which have long served as a farm system for prime time—also give young Latino actors, writers, and directors a foot in the network door. The list of soap actors turned megastars is long and distinguished, including Meg Ryan, Demi Moore, Tommy Lee Jones, Alec Baldwin, Dustin Hoffman, Christopher Reeve, and Puerto Rican pop-music phenom Ricky Martin. Seven years ago, Martin was hamming it up on "General Hospital" as singing bartender Miguel Morez. Today, he's living la . . . Well, you get the picture. Viva la revolucion.

---

## This Text: Reading

1. What effect do you think seeing integration on television has on changing people's attitudes?
2. If you answered that you thought it had positive effects, what does that say about the impact of television in our lives? If you answered no effects or negative ones, what elements do you think can change the way we look at race and ethnicity?
3. Along the same lines, television commercials rarely feature actors of only one race. Do you think integrating commercials could have positive effects? Why or why not?
4. Why might soap operas be good vehicles for social change? Why might they not be effective for social change?

## Your Text: Writing

1. Watch a soap opera and watch how the show handles race and ethnicity. Now watch a nighttime drama and watch how it handles these ideas. Do they address them directly or indirectly? Write a short paper comparing the two types of show.
2. Write a short paper about the effect you think television shows have on the way we view a particular social issue.

3. Write a short paper about what is realistic in a soap opera and why that realism is important.

# "NOT THAT THERE'S ANYTHING WRONG WITH THAT": READING THE QUEER IN *SEINFELD*

Katherine Gantz

Katherine Gantz uses the lens of "queer theory" in her 2000 discussion of *Seinfeld*. Notice how Gantz strictly defines not only the term "queer" but the particular questions she intends to ask of her text using "queer."

THE WORLD OF MASS CULTURE, especially that which includes American television, remains overwhelmingly homophobic. Queer theory offers a useful perspective from which to examine the heterosexism at the core of contemporary television and also provides a powerful tool of subversion. The aim of this article is twofold: first, it will outline and explain the notion of a queer reading; second, it will apply a queer reading to the narrative texts that comprise the situation comedy *Seinfeld*. The concept of the queer reading, currently en vogue in literary analysis, has evolved from a handful of distinct but connected sources, beginning with the popularization of the term "queer." In 1989, the AIDS activist group ACT UP created Queer Nation, an offshoot organization comprised of lesbians and gays dedicated to the political reclaiming of gay identity under the positively recoded term "queer."[1] The group was initially formed as a New York City street patrol organized to help counteract escalating hate crimes against gays. As Queer Nation gained visibility in the public eye, the use of "queer," historically a derogatory slur for homosexuals, entered into standard parlance in the gay and lesbian press.[2] Eve Kosofsky Sedgwick's *Epistemology of the Closet*[3] appropriated the term with a broadened interpretation of "queer," suggesting not that literature be read with the author's possible homosexuality in mind but instead with an openness to the queer (homoerotic and/or homosexual) contexts, nuances, connections, and potential already available within the text. The concept of "queerness" was elaborated once more in 1991, with the publication of *Inside/Out: Lesbian Theories, Gay Theories*;[4] within this assemblage of political, pedagogical, and literary essays, the term was collectively applied to a larger category of sexual non-straightness, as will be further explained.

As the political construction of "queer" became increasingly disciplinized in academia, the emerging body of "queer theory" lost its specifically homosexual connotation and was replaced by a diffuse set of diverse sexual identities. Like the path of feminism, the concept of queerness had been largely stripped of its political roots and transformed into a methodological approach accessible to manipulation by the world of predominantly heterosexual, white, middle-class intellectuals. It is with this problematic universalization of queer theory in mind that I undertake an application of queer reading.

In what could be deemed a reinsertion of the subversive into a "straightened" discipline, Alexander Doty's book *Making Things Perfectly Queer: Reading Mass Culture*[5] has taken the queer reading out of the realm of the purely literary and applied it to analyses of film and television texts. From this ever-transforming history of the queer reading, the popular situation comedy *Seinfeld* lends itself well to a contemporary application.

In the summer of 1989, NBC debuted a tepidly received pilot entitled *The Seinfeld Chronicles*, a situation comedy revolving around the mundane, urbane Manhattan existence of stand-up comic Jerry Seinfeld. Despite its initially unimpressive ratings, the show evolved into the five-episode series *Seinfeld* and established its regular cast of Jerry's three fictional friends: George Costanza (Jason Alexander), ex-girlfriend Elaine Benes (Julia Louis-Dreyfus), and the enigmatic neighbor Kramer (Michael Richards). By its return in January 1991, *Seinfeld* had established a following among Wednesday-night television viewers; over the next two years, the show became a cultural phenomenon, claiming both a faithful viewership and a confident position in the Nielsen ratings' top ten. The premise was to write a show about the details, minor disturbances, and nonevents of Jerry's life as they occurred before becoming fodder for the stand-up monologues that bookend each episode. From the start, *Seinfeld*'s audience has been comprised of a devoted group of "TV-literate, demographically desirable urbanites, for the most part—who look forward to each weekly episode in the Life of Jerry with a baby-boomer generation's self-involved eagerness," notes Bruce Fretts, author of *The "Entertainment Weekly" "Seinfeld" Companion*.[6] Such obsessive identification and self-reflexive fascination seems to be thematic in both the inter- and extradiegetic worlds of *Seinfeld*. The show's characters are modeled on real-life acquaintances: George is based on Seinfeld's best friend (and series cocreator) Larry David; Elaine is an exaggeration of Seinfeld's ex-girlfriend, writer Carol Leifer; Kramer's prototype lived across the hall from one of David's first Manhattan apartments.[7] To further complicate this narcissistic mirroring, in the 1993 season premiere entitled "The Pilot" (see videography for episodic citations), Jerry and George finally launch their new NBC sitcom *Jerry* by casting four actors to portray themselves, Kramer, and Elaine. This multilayered Möbius strip of person/actor/character relationships seems to be part of the show's complex appeal. Whereas situation comedies often dilute their cast, adding and removing characters in search of new plot possibilities, *Seinfeld* instead interiorizes; the narrative creates new configurations of the same limited cast to keep the viewer and the characters intimately linked. In fact, it is precisely this concentration on the nuclear set of four personalities that creates the *Seinfeld* community.

If it seems hyperbolic to suggest that the participants in the *Seinfeld* phenomenon (both spectators and characters included) have entered into a certain delineated "lifestyle," consider the significant lexicon of Seinfeldian code words and recurring phrases that go unnoticed and unappreciated by the infrequent or "unknowing" viewer. Catch phrases such as Snapple, the Bubble Boy, Cuban cigars, Master of My Domain, Junior Mints, Mulva, Crazy Joe Davola, Pez, and Vandelay Industries all serve as parts of the group-specific language that a family shares; these are the kinds of self-referential in-jokes that help one *Seinfeld* watcher identify another.[8] This sort of tightly conscribed universe of meaning is reflected not only by the decidedly small cast but also by the narrative's consistent efforts to maintain its intimacy. As this article will discuss, much of *Seinfeld*'s plot and humor (and, consequently, the viewer's pleasure) hinge on outside personalities threatening—and ultimately failing—to invade the foursome. Especially where Jerry and George are concerned, episodes are mostly resolved by expelling the intruder and restoring the exclusive nature of their relationship. The show's camera work, which at times takes awkward measures to ensure that Jerry and George remain grouped together within a scene, reinforces the privileged dynamic of their relationship within the narrative.

Superficially speaking, *Seinfeld* appears to be a testament to heterosexuality: in its nine-year run, Jerry sported a new girlfriend in almost every episode; his friendship with Elaine is predicated on their previous sexual relationship; and all four characters share in the discussion and navigation of the (straight) dating scene. However, with a viewership united by a common coded discourse and an interest in the cohesive (and indeed almost claustrophobic) exclusivity of its predominantly male cast, clearly *Seinfeld* is rife with possibilities for homoerotic interpretation. As will be demonstrated, the construction, the coding, and the framing of the show readily conform to a queer reading of the *Seinfeld* text.

Here I wish to develop and define my meanings of the word "queer" as a set of signifying practices and a category distinct from that of gay literature. Inspired by Doty's work, I will use "queer"—as its current literary usages suggest—as relating to a wide-ranging spectrum of "nonnormative" sexual notions, including not only constructions of gayness and lesbianism but also of transsexualism, transvestism, same-sex affinity, and other ambisexual behaviors and sensibilities. Queerness at times may act merely as a space in which heterosexual personalities interact, in the same ways that a queer personality may operate within an otherwise heterosexual sphere. In this system, "queer" does not stand in opposition to "heterosexual" but instead to "straight," a term that by contrast, suggests all that is restrictive about "normative" sexuality, a category that excludes what is deemed undesirable, deviant, dangerous, unnatural, unproductive. "Queer," then, should be understood not so much as an intrinsic property but more as the outcome of both productive and receptive behaviors—a pluralized, inclusive term that may be employed by and applied to both gay and nongay characters and spectators.[9]

The second point I wish to clarify about the use of the term "queer" as it relates to my own textual analysis of a mass culture text is the indirect, nonexplicit nature of the queer relationships represented in *Seinfeld*. Explicit references to homosexuality subvert the possibility of a queer reading; by identifying a character as "gay," such overt difference serves to mark the other characters as "not gay." Sexual perimeters become limited, fixed, rooted in traditional definitions and connotations that work contrary to the fluidity and subtle ambiguity of a queer interpretation. It is precisely the unspokenness ("the love that dare not speak its name") of homoeroticism between seemingly straight men that allows the insinuation of a queer reading. As Doty rightly notes, queer positionings are generated more often through the same-sex tensions evident in "straight films" than in gay ones:

> Traditional narrative films [such as *Gentlemen Prefer Blondes* and *Thelma and Louise*], which are ostensibly addressed to straight audiences, often have greater potential for encouraging a wider range of queer responses than [such] clearly lesbian- and gay-addressed films [as *Women I Love* and *Scorpio Rising*]. The intense tensions and pleasures generated by the woman-woman and man-man aspects within the narratives of the former group of films create a space of sexual instability that already queerly positioned viewers can connect in various ways, and within which straights might be likely to recognize and express their queer impulses. (8)

Of course, there is a multitude of possibilities for the perception and reception of queer pleasures, but, to generalize from Doty's argument, the implications in the case of the *Seinfeld* phenomenon suggest that while queer-identified viewers may recognize the domesticity between Jerry and George as that of a gay couple, straight viewers may simply take pleasure in the characters' intimate bond left unbroken by outside (heterosexual) romantic interruptions.

This is not to say that *Seinfeld* ignores the explicit category of homosexuality; on the contrary, the show is laden with references and plot twists involving gay characters and themes. In separate episodes, Elaine is selected as the "best man" in a lesbian wedding ("The Subway"); George accidentally causes the exposure of his girlfriend Susan's father's affair with novelist John Cheever ("The Cheever Letters"); and, after their breakup, George runs into Susan with her new lesbian lover ("The Smelly Car"). At its most playful, *Seinfeld* smugly calls attention to its own homosexual undercurrents in an episode in which Jerry and George are falsely identified as a gay couple by a female journalist ("The Outing").[10] Due to the direct nature of such references to homosexuality, these are episodes that slyly deflect queer reading, serving as a sort of lightning rod by displacing homoerotic undercurrents onto a more obvious target.

Such smoke-screen tactics seem to be in conflict with the multitude of queer-identified semiotics and gay icons and symbols at play within the *Seinfeld* text. Most notably, no "queer-receptive" viewer can look at the *Seinfeld* graphic logo (at the episode's beginning and before commercials) without noticing the inverted triangle—hot pink during the earliest seasons—dotting the "i" in "Seinfeld."[11] Although the symbol dates back to the Holocaust (used to mark homosexuals for persecution), the pink triangle has recently been recuperated by gay activists during ACT UP's widely publicized AIDS education campaign, "Silence Equals Death," and has consequently become a broadly recognized symbol of gayness.

Even if the pink triangle's proactive gay recoding remains obscure to the "unknowing" viewership (i.e., unfamiliar with or resistant to queerness), *Seinfeld* also offers a multitude of discursive referents chosen from a popular lexicon of more common gay signifiers that are often slurs in use by a homophobic public. In an episode revolving around Jerry and Kramer's discussion of where to find *fruit*—longstanding slang for a gay men—Jerry makes a very rare break from his standard wardrobe of well-froned button-up oxfords, instead sporting a T-shirt with the word "QUEENS" across it. Although outwardly in reference to Queens College, the word's semiotic juxtaposition with the theme of fruit evokes its slang connotation for effeminate gay men.

Narrative space is also queerly coded. Positioned as Jerry and George's "place" (or "male space"), the restaurant where they most often meet is "Monk's," a name that conjures up images of an exclusively male religious society, a "brotherhood" predicated on the maintenance of masculine presence/feminine absence, in both spiritual and physical terms.

Recurring plot twists also reveal a persistent interest in the theme of hidden or falsified identities. As early as *Seinfeld*'s second episode ("The Stakeout"), George insists on creating an imaginary biography for himself as a successful architect before meeting Jerry's new girlfriend. Throughout the *Seinfeld* texts, the foursome adopts a number of different names and careers in hopes of persuading outsiders (most often potential romantic interests) that they lead a more interesting, more superficially acceptable, or more immediately favorable existence than what their real lives have to offer: George has assumed the identity of neo-Nazi organizer Colin O'Brian ("The Limo"); Elaine has recruited both Jerry and Kramer as substitute boyfriends to dissuade unwanted suitors ("The Junior Mint" and "The Watch"); Kramer has posed as a policeman ("The Statue") and has even auditioned under a pseudonym to play himself in the pilot of *Jerry* ("The Pilot"). Pretense and fabrication often occur among the foursome as well. In "The Apartment," Jerry is troubled by Elaine's imminent move into the apartment above him. Worried that her presence will "cramp his style," he schemes to convince her that she will be financially unable to take the apartment. In private, Jerry warns George that he will be witness to some "heavy acting" to persuade Elaine that he is genuinely sympathetic. Unshaken, George answers: "Are you kidding? I lie every second of the day; my whole life is a sham." This deliberate "closeting" of one's lifestyle has obvious connections to the gay theme of "passing,"[12] the politically discouraged practice of hiding one's homosexuality behind a façade of straight respectability. One might argue that *Seinfeld* is simply a text about passing—socially as well as sexually—in a repressive and judgmental society. It must be noted, however, that George and Jerry are the only two characters who do not lie to each other; they are in fact engaged in maintaining each other's secrets and duplicities by "covering" for one another, thus distancing themselves somewhat from Kramer and Elaine from within an even more exclusive rapport.[13]

Another thematic site of queerness is the mystification of and resulting detachment from female culture and discourse. While Jerry glorifies such male-identified personalities as Superman, the Three Stooges, and Mickey Mantle, he prides himself in never having seen a single episode of *I Love Lucy* ("The Phone Message"). Even Elaine is often presented as incomprehensible to her familiar male counterparts. In "The Shoes," Jerry and George have no problem creating a story line for their situation comedy, *Jerry*, around male characters; however, when they try to "write in" Elaine's character, they find themselves stumped:

**Jerry:** [In the process of writing the script.] "Elaine enters." . . . What does she say . . . ?

**George:** [Pause.] What *do* they [women] say?

**Jerry:** [Mystified.] I *don't know.*

After a brief deliberation, they opt to omit the female character completely. As Jerry explains with a queerly loaded rationale: "You, me, Kramer, the butler. . . . Elaine is too much." Later, at Monk's, Elaine complains about her exclusion from the pilot. Jerry confesses: "We couldn't write for a woman." "You have *no idea*?" asks Elaine, disgusted. Jerry looks at George for substantiation and replies: "None." Clearly, the privileged bond between men excludes room for an understanding of and an interest in women; like Elaine in the pilot, the feminine presence is often simply deleted for the sake of maintaining a stronger, more coherent male narrative.

Jerry seems especially ill at ease with notions of female sexuality, perhaps suggesting that they impinge on his own. In "The Red Dot," Jerry convinces the resistant George that he should buy Elaine a thank-you gift after she procures him a job at her office. Despite George's tightfisted unwillingness to invest money in such social graces as gift giving, he acquiesces. The duo go to a department store in search of an appropriate gift for Elaine. Jerry confesses: "I never feel comfortable in the women's department; I feel like I'm just a *little* too close to trying on a dress." While browsing through the women's clothing, George describes his erotic attraction to the cleaning woman in his new office:

**George:** . . . she was swaying back and forth, back and forth, her hips swiveling and her breasts—uh . . .

**Jerry:** . . . convulsing?

George reacts with disdain at the odd word choice, recognizing that Jerry's depiction of female physicality and eroticism is both inappropriate and unappealing. (It should be noted that the ensuing sexual encounter between George and the cleaning woman ultimately results in the loss of both their jobs; true to the pattern, George's foray into heterosex creates chaos.)

Although sites of queerness occur extensively throughout the *Seinfeld* oeuvre, the most useful elucidation of its queer potential comes from a closer, more methodical textual analysis. To provide a contextualized view of the many overlapping sites of queerness—symbolic, discursive, thematic, and visual—the following is a critique of three episodes especially conducive to a queer reading of *Seinfeld*'s male homoerotic relationships.

"The Boyfriend" explores the ambiguous valences of male friendships. Celebrated baseball player Keith Hernandez stars as himself (as does Jerry Seinfeld among the cast of otherwise fictional characters), becoming the focal point of both Jerry's and, later, Elaine's attentions. Despite Elaine's brief romantic involvement with Keith, the central narrative concerns Jerry's interactions with the baseball player. Although never explicitly discussed, Jerry's attachment to Keith is represented as romantic in nature.

The episode begins in a men's locker room, prefiguring the homoerotic overtones of the coming plot. The locker room is clearly delineated as "male space"; its connection to the athletic field posits it as a locale of physicality, where men gather to prepare for or to disengage from the privileged (and predominantly homophobic) world of male sports. The locker room, as a site of potential heterosexual vulnerability as men expose their bodies to other men, is socially safe only when established as sexually neutral—or, better still, heterosexually charged with the machismo of athleticism. This "safe" coding occurs almost immediately in this setting, accomplished through a postgame comparison of Jerry's, George's, and Kramer's basketball prowess. As they finish dressing together after their game, it is the voracious, ambisexual Kramer who immediately upsets the precarious sexual neutrality, violating the unspoken code of locker-room decorum:

**Kramer:** Hey, you know this is the first time we've ever seen each other naked?

**Jerry:** Believe me, *I* didn't see anything.

**Kramer:** [With disbelief.] Oh, you didn't sneak a peek?

**Jerry:** No—did you?

**Kramer:** Yeah, I snuck a peek.

**Jerry:** Why?

**Kramer:** Why not? What about you, George?

**George**: [Hesitating] Yeah, I—snuck a peek. But it was so fast that I didn't see anything; it was just a blur.

**Jerry:** I made a conscious effort *not* to look; there's certain information I just don't want to have.

Jerry displays his usual disdain for all things corporeal or carnal. Such unwillingness to participate in Kramer's curiosity about men's bodies also secures Jerry firmly on heterosexual ground, a necessary pretext to make his intense feelings for Keith "safe." The humor of these building circumstances depends on the assumption that Jerry is straight; although this episode showcases *Seinfeld*'s characteristic playfulness with queer subject matter, great pains are taken to prevent the viewer from ever believing (or realizing) that Jerry is gay.

After Kramer leaves, Jerry and George spot Hernandez stretching out in the locker room. With Kramer no longer threatening to introduce direct discussion of overtly homoerotic matters, the queer is permitted to enter into the narrative space between Jerry and George. Both baseball aficionados, they are bordering on giddy, immediately starstruck by Hernandez. Possessing prior knowledge of Keith's personal life, Jerry remarks that Hernandez is not only a talented athlete but intelligent as well, being an American Civil War buff. "I wish *I* were a Civil War buff," George replies longingly. Chronically socially inept, George is left to appropriate the interests of a man he admires without being able to relate to him more directly.[14]

Keith introduces himself to Jerry as a big fan of his comedy; Jerry is instantly flattered and returns the compliment. As the jealous and excluded George looks on (one of the rare times that Jerry and George break rank and appear distinctly physically separated within a scene), Keith and Jerry exchange phone numbers and plan to meet for coffee in the future. Thus, in the strictly homosocial, theoretically nonromantic masculine world of the locker room, two men have initiated an interaction that becomes transformed into a relationship, consistently mirroring traditional television representations of heterosexual dating rituals. The homoerotic stage is set.

Later, at Monk's, Jerry complains to Elaine that three days have passed without a call from Keith. When Elaine asks why Jerry doesn't initiate the first call, he responds that he doesn't want to seem overanxious: "If he wants to see me, he has my number; he should call. I can't stand these guys—you give your number to them, and then they don't call."

Here, in his attempts not to seem overly aggressive, Jerry identifies with the traditionally receptive and passive role posited as appropriate female behavior. By employing such categorization as "these guys," Jerry brackets himself off from the rest of the heterosexual, male dating population, reinforcing his identification with Elaine not as Same (i.e., straight male) but as Other (Elaine as Not Male, Jerry as Not Straight). Elaine responds sympathetically:

**Elaine:** I'm sorry, honey.

**Jerry:** I mean, I thought he liked me, I really thought he liked me—we were getting along. He came over to *me*, I didn't go over to *him*.

**Elaine:** [Commiserating.] I know.

**Jerry:** Here I meet this guy, this *great* guy, ballplayer, best guy I ever met in my life . . . well, that's it. I'm *never* giving my number out to another guy again.

Jerry is clearly expressing romantic disillusionment in reaction to Keith's withdrawal from their social economy. Elaine further links her identity—as sexually experienced with men—to Jerry's own situation:

**Elaine:** Sometimes I give my number out to a guy, and it takes him a *month* to call me.

**Jerry:** [Outraged.] A *month?* Ha! Have him call *me* after a month—let's see if *he* has a prayer!

Thus, Jerry's construction of his relationship with Keith is one bound by the rules of heterosexual dating protocol and appropriate exchange; the intensity of his feelings and expectations for his relationship with Keith have long surpassed normative (that is, conventional, expected, tolerable), straight male friendship. By stating that Keith's violation of protocol will result in Jerry's withdrawal, it is clear that Jerry is only willing to consider any interactions with Keith in terms of a romantic model—one that, as suggested by Keith's relative indifference, is based in fantasy.

Elaine suggests that he simply put an end to the waiting and call Keith to arrange an evening out. Jerry ponders the possibility of dinner but then has doubts:

**Jerry:** But don't you think that dinner might be coming on too strong? Kind of a turnoff?

**Elaine:** [Incredulous.] Jerry, it's a *guy*.

**Jerry:** [Covering his eyes.] It's all very confusing.

Throughout the episode, Jerry is content to succumb to the excitement of his newfound relationship, until the moment when someone inevitably refers to its homoerotic nature (terms such as "gay" and "homosexual" are certainly implied but never explicitly invoked). Elaine's reminder that Jerry's fears about a "turnoff" are addressed to a man quickly ends his swooning; he covers his eyes as if to suggest a groggy return from a dream-like state.

To interrupt and divert the narrative attention away from Jerry's increasingly queer leanings, the scene abruptly changes to George at the unemployment office, where he is hoping to maneuver a thirteen-week extension on his unemployment benefits.[15] There, George evades the questions of his no-nonsense interviewer Mrs. Sokol until she forces him to provide one name of a company with which he had recently sought employment. Having in truth interviewed nowhere, he quickly concocts "Vandelay Industries," a company, he assures her, he had thoroughly pursued to no avail. Further pressed, he tells Mrs. Sokol that they are "makers of latex products." His blurting-out of the word "latex" must not be overlooked here as a queer signifier directly associated with the gay safe-sex campaigns throughout the last decade. Whereas "condoms" as a signifier would have perhaps been a more mainstream (straight) sexual symbol, latex evokes a larger category of products—condoms, gloves, dental dams—linked closely with the eroticization of gay safe-sex practices. When Mrs. Sokol insists on information to verify his claim, it is telling that George provides Jerry's address and phone number as the home of Vandelay latex. George's lie necessitates a race back to Jerry's to warn him of the impending phone call; once again, he will depend on Jerry's willingness to maintain a duplicity and to adopt a false identity as the head of Vandelay Industries.

As if to await the panicked arrival of George, the scene changes to Jerry's apartment, where he is himself anxiety ridden over his impending night out with Keith. In a noticeable departure from his usual range of conservative color and style, he steps out of his bedroom, modeling a bright orange and red shirt, colors so shocking that they might best be described as "flaming." Pivoting slightly with arms outstretched in a style suggesting a fashion model, he asks Elaine's opinion. Again, she reminds him: "Jerry, he's a guy." Agitated (but never denying her implication of homoerotic attraction), he drops his arms, attempting to hide his nervous discomfort.

Jerry's actual evening out with Keith remains unseen (closeted) until the end of the "date"; the men sit alone in the front seat of Keith's car outside of Jerry's apartment. In the setup that prefigures the close of Elaine's date with Keith later in the episode, Jerry sits in the passenger seat next to him; a familiar heterosexual power dynamic is at play. Keith, as both the car owner and driver, acts and reacts in his appropriate masculine role. Jerry, within the increasingly queer context of an intimate social interaction with another man, is left to identify with what we recognize as the woman's position in the car. As the passenger and not the driver, he has relinquished both the mechanical and social control that defines the dominance of the male role. In a symbolic interpretation of power relations, Jerry's jump into the feminized gender role is characterized by the absence of the steering wheel:

**Jerry:** [Aloud to Keith.] Well, thanks a lot, that was really fun. [Thinking to himself.] Should I shake his hand?

This anxiety and expectation over appropriate and mutually appealing physical contact expresses the same kind of desire—that is, sexual—that

Keith will express with Elaine later on; whereas Keith will long for a kiss, Jerry's desires have been translated into a more acceptable form of physical contact between men. It would seem that part of Jerry's frustration in this situation comes from the multiplicity of gender roles that he plays. Whereas in his interactions with George, Jerry occupies the dominant role (controlling the discourse and the action), he is suddenly relegated to a more passive (feminine) position in his relationship with the hypermasculine Keith Hernandez. Part of the tension that comprises the handshake scene stems not only from Jerry's desire to interact physically *and* appropriately but also from wanting to initiate such an action from the disadvantaged, less powerful position of the (feminine) passenger's seat. I would suggest that the confusion arising out of his relationship with Keith is not strictly due to its potentially homosexual valences but is also the result of the unclear position (passive/dominant, feminine/masculine, nelly/butch) that Jerry holds within the homoerotic/homosexual coupling.

Once again, the humor of this scene is based on the presupposition that Jerry is straight and that this very familiar scene is not a homosexual recreation of heterosexual dating etiquette but simply a parody of it. Nonetheless, Jerry's discomfort over initiating a handshake betrays the nature of his desire for Keith. From behind the steering wheel (the seat of masculine power), Keith invites Jerry to a movie over the coming weekend. Jerry is elated, and they shake hands: a consummation of their successful social interaction. However, Keith follows up by telling Jerry that he would like to call Elaine for a date; the spell broken, Jerry responds with reluctance and thinly veiled disappointment.

Back in Jerry's apartment, George jealously asks for a recounting of Jerry's evening with Keith. Again, the handshake is reinforced as the symbol of a successful male-to-male social encounter:

**George:** Did you shake his hand?

**Jerry:** Yeah.

**George:** What kind of a handshake does he have?

**Jerry:** Good shake, perfect shake. Single pump, not too hard. He didn't have to prove anything, but firm enough to know he's there.

George and Jerry share a discourse, laden with masturbatory overtones, in which quantifying and qualifying the description of a handshake expresses information about the nature of men's relationships. This implicit connection between male intimacy and the presence and quality of physical contact clearly transcends the interpretation of the handshake in a heterosexual context. Upon hearing that Jerry had in fact shaken hands with Keith, George follows with the highly charged question: "You gonna see him again?" Here, the use of the verb "to see," implying organized social interaction between two people, is typically in reference to romantic situations; George has thus come to accept Jerry in a dating relationship with Keith.

Elaine enters and immediately teases Jerry: "So, how was your date?" Not only has she invaded Jerry and George's male habitat, but she has once again made explicit the romantic nature of Jerry's connection to Keith that he can only enjoy when unspoken. Jerry is forced to respond (with obvious agitation): "He's a guy." Elaine quickly reveals that she and Keith have made a date for the coming Friday, perhaps expressing an implicit understanding of a rivalry with Jerry. Realizing that such plans will interfere with his own "date" with Keith, Jerry protests with disappointment and resentment. Elaine mistakes his anger as being in response to some lingering romantic attachment to her:

**Elaine:** I've never seen you jealous.

**Jerry:** You weren't even *at* Game Six—you're not even a fan!

**Elaine:** Wait a second . . . are you jealous of *him* or are you jealous of *me*?

Flustered and confused, Jerry walks away without responding, allowing the insinuation of a queer interpretation to be implied by his silence.

Jerry steps outside of the apartment just as Kramer enters; he sits alone with Elaine as George disappears into the bathroom. Predictably, it is just as Kramer finds himself next to the phone that the call from the unemployment bureau arrives; Kramer, the only one uninformed about George's scheme, answers the phone and responds with confusion, assuring the caller that she has reached a residential number, not Vandelay Industries. Having overheard, George bursts from the bathroom in a panic, his pants around his ankles. Despite his frantic pleading with Kramer to pass him the phone, Kramer is already hanging up; the defeated George collapses on the floor. Precisely at this moment, Jerry reenters the apartment. In a highly unusual aerial shot, the camera shows us Jerry's perspective of George, face down, boxer shorts exposed, and prone, lying before him on the floor in an obvious position of sexual receptivity. Jerry quips: "And you want to be my latex salesman." Once again, Jerry's reinvocation of latex has powerful queer connotations in response to seeing George seminude before him.

The next scenes juxtapose Elaine and Keith's date with Jerry's alternate Friday night activity, a visit to see his friends' new baby. Elaine, the focal point of a crowded sports bar discussing Game Six of the World Series with Keith, has occupied the very place (physically and romantically) that Jerry had longed for. In the accompanying parallel scene of Jerry, he seems both out of place and uncomfortable amid the domestic and overwhelmingly heterosexual atmosphere of the baby's nursery. The misery over losing his night on the town to Elaine is amplified by his obvious distaste for the nuclear family, the ultimate signifier of "straightness."

The scene again changes to Keith and Elaine alone in his car, this time with Elaine in the passenger seat that Jerry had previously occupied. Elaine, comfortable in her familiar and appropriate role as passive/feminine, waits patiently as Keith (in the privileged masculine driver's seat) silently wonders whether or not he should kiss her, mirroring Jerry's earlier internal debate over suitable intimate physical contact. Although they kiss, Elaine is unimpressed. Later, just as George had done, Jerry pumps Elaine for information about her date. When Elaine admits that she and Keith had kissed, Jerry pushes further: "What *kind* of kiss was it?" Incredulous at Jerry's tactlessness, Elaine does not respond. Jerry at last answers her standing question: "I'm jealous of everybody."

Keith calls, interrupting one of the few moments in the episode when Jerry and George share the scene alone. After hanging up, he explains with discomfort that he has agreed to help Keith in his move to a new apartment. George seems to recognize and identify with Jerry's apprehension over this sudden escalation in their rapport. "This is a big step in the male relationship," Jerry observes, "the biggest. That's like going all the way." Never has Jerry made such a direct reference to the potential for sexual contact with Keith. Of course, Keith has by no means propositioned Jerry, which makes the queer desire on Jerry's part all the more obvious in contrast with the seemingly asexual nature of Keith's request. However, Jerry has made clear his own willingness to homoeroticize his friendship with another man. By likening "going all the way" to moving furniture, Jerry is able to fantasize that Keith shares Jerry's homosexual desire. Ingeniously, he has crafted an imaginary set of circumstances that allow him to ignore Keith's preference for Elaine as a sexual object while tidily completing his fantasy: Keith has expressed desire for Jerry, but now Jerry has the luxury of refusing his advance on the moral ground that he will not rush sexual intimacy. Once Keith arrives, Jerry tells him that he cannot help him move, explaining that it is still too soon in their relationship. Again, by positing Keith in the masculine role of sexual aggressor, Jerry in turn occupies the stereotypically feminine role of sexual regulator/withholder.

Kramer and Newman arrive just as Jerry declines Keith's request; not surprisingly, Kramer jumps at the opportunity to take Jerry's place. As he and Newman disappear out the door to help Keith move his furniture, Jerry commiserates with Elaine over the phone: "You broke up with him? Me too!" Even as Jerry's homoerotic adventure has drawn to a close, Kramer's last-minute appearance lends an air of sexual unpredictability to end the episode on a resoundingly queer note.

In contrast to "The Boyfriend," in which the queer subtext is exploited as the source of the humor, "The Virgin" and its companion episode "The Contest" present an equally queer narrative expressed in subtler and more indirect ways. Within these interwoven episodes, the "knowing" spectator—one familiar with gay culture and receptive to potentially homoerotic situations—is essentially bombarded by queer catchphrases and code words, gay themes, and gay male behavior, while the "unknowing" spectator would most likely only recognize a traditionally "straight" plot about heterosexual dating frustrations. "The Virgin" drops its first "hair-pins" almost immediately;[16] Jerry and George are drinking together in a bar when Jerry spots Marla, a beautiful woman whom he recognizes across the room. "She's in the closet business—reorganizes your closet and shows you how to maximize your closet space. She's looked into my closet." In the same instant that we are introduced to a potential female love object for Jerry, she is immediately identified with the closet, a widely recognized metaphor referring to a gay person's secret sexual identity. Queerly read, Marla could be interpreted as (and will in fact become) a nonthreatening, nonsexual female object. Having "looked into his closet," Marla functions as a woman who is aware of Jerry's homosexuality and will be willing to interact with him in ways that will permit him to pass while still maintaining the homoerotic connections to the men around him. By allowing him this duplicity, she will indeed maximize Jerry's "closet space."

While at the bar, George bemoans the fact that he is miserable in his relationship with television executive Susan, his first girlfriend in some time. He is instead more interested in the new partnership that he has developed with Jerry, writing his new situation comedy pilot for NBC. The ostensibly platonic nature of such privileged male–male relations becomes further queered by Jerry's insistence that George "maintain appearances" with Susan until she has persuaded the network to pick up their pilot. The Seinfeldian recurring theme of hidden identities and guarded appearances puts into place the knowing viewer's suspicions about the homosexual potential between George and Jerry.

In the following scene, the spectator is given a rare view of Jerry's bedroom, made even more rare by the presence of a woman with him. Although the scene employs the standard formula for a possible sexual encounter (a man and woman alone in his bedroom), the couple remains perpetually framed inside Jerry's open closet; Jerry's coded homosexuality, symbolically surrounding the couple as they speak, prevents the sex scene from occurring.

To further complicate Jerry's interaction with Marla, his friends start to invade the apartment, interrupting the potential for intimacy. First, Kramer intrudes, taking over the television in the living room. (He is desperate to see *The Bold and the Beautiful*, a show whose soap opera genre is largely identified with a female viewership.) Jerry kicks Kramer out only to have Elaine buzz over the intercom a moment later. In the few private moments left, Marla confesses that the reason for her breakup with her exboyfriend was his impatience with her virginity. Elaine arrives before they can discuss it.

Marla and Elaine, Jerry's current and past romantic interests, stand in stark contrast to one another. The timid, traditional, and virginal Marla is further desexualized in the presence of the heterosexually active Elaine; this contrast is intensified by Elaine's crass description of her embarrassment at a recent party when she accidentally let her diaphragm slip out of her purse. As she laughs knowingly, Jerry winces, sensing Marla's shock at Elaine's casual remark: "You never know when you might need it." This exaggerated reference to female sexuality makes Marla's virginity even more pronounced; she is unable to hide her discomfort any longer and excuses herself in haste. It seems that Jerry, socially and romantically attached to a woman horrified by even the discussion of sex, could himself not be further from heterosexual activity.

Upon hearing that her indiscretion has lost Jerry a potential girlfriend, Elaine chases after Marla in hopes of repairing the damage. Over coffee at Monk's (clearly a female invasion of Jerry and George's male space), Elaine tries to dissuade Marla from her horror of sex with men. However, her lecture quickly dissolves into a listing of male failings: their thoughtlessness, manipulations, and fear of emotional attachment after sex. Despite Elaine's outward intentions to reunite Jerry and Marla, she has instead instilled an intensified mistrust of men. Once again, Jerry's friends have been the cause of his distancing from women; he remains insulated in the homoerotic network of his male friends and is ushered through acceptable straight society by his platonic female friend.

In a strange reversal of roles, George is still engaged in a romantic relationship with a woman (even if he is unwillingly "maintaining appearances" with Susan). At the crucial meeting with the NBC executives, George greets Susan with a kiss, an appropriate and public gesture of straightness. However, by exposing Susan as his girlfriend, George compromises her professional standing with the network. Not only is she fired, but she also breaks off her relationship with George (and consequently later "becomes" a lesbian).[17] Despite George's delight at having inadvertently rid himself of Susan, the overall message is clear: straying out of his queer context sparks destructive results in the straight world.

Juxtaposed with George's ultimately disastrous straight kiss is one of Jerry's own; he and Marla, back in his bedroom, are finally embracing passionately. The (hetero)sexual potential suggested in this scene is diffused, however, by the viewer's instant recognition that the couple is not only framed by Jerry's closet but in fact that they are embracing inside of it. Marla, as a nonsexualized female object with knowledge and access to Jerry's closet(edness), poses no threat of engaging in "real" sexual intimacy with Jerry. Their embrace is made comically awkward by the clutter of Jerry's hanging clothes around them; the encounter is again cut short as Marla recalls Elaine's unflattering depiction of typical male behavior after sex. Even in absentia, Jerry's friends precipitate the woman's departure and his own separation from the possibility of (hetero)sex.

"The Contest" follows up on this storyline; Jerry is still patiently dating the virginal Marla while, as usual, spending the bulk of his social time with George, Kramer, and Elaine. As George arrives to join them for lunch at

Monk's, he announces sheepishly (yet voluntarily) that he had been "caught" by his mother. Although never explicitly mentioned, George is clearly making reference to masturbation. Believing himself to be alone in his mother's house, he was using her copy of *Glamour* magazine[18] as erotic material when his mother entered and discovered him masturbating. In her shock, Mrs. Costanza had fainted, hurt herself in the fall, and ultimately wound up in traction. It is essential to note the homosexual underpinnings of masturbation as a sexual act; the fetishization of one's (and in this case, George's) own genitalia is often closely linked in psychoanalytic theory to the narcissism and reflexive fixation associated with same-sex desire. Mrs. Costanza was not reacting so much to her recognition of her son as sexual but instead to his inappropriate sexual object choice, the (his) penis. George has paid dearly for being exposed to straight eyes while practicing queer pleasure.

Traumatized by his experience, George announces that he is swearing off such activity for good. Jerry and Kramer are skeptical of the claim, and the three men find themselves in a contest—regulated by the "honor system"—to see which of them can abstain the longest from masturbating. The wager is steeped in homoerotic potential; in fact, the three *Seinfeld* men have entered into a kind of sanitized "circle jerk" in which they monitor (and consequently augment) each other's sexual tension, voyeuristically waiting to see who will be the first to "relieve" himself. When Elaine, who has been listening to their conversation from the periphery of their queer circle, wants to enter the contest as well, the men protest that she would have an unfair advantage. As Kramer explains: "It's easier for women—it's part of *our lifestyle*." By creating a stiff binary opposition between women and "our lifestyle," he not only employs a phrase closely associated with the "alternative lifestyle" of homosexuality, but he also demonstrates an obvious ignorance and detachment from female sexuality, perpetuating myths about the limited appetite and imagination of the female sexual drive. Despite her protests, Elaine is forced to stake fifty dollars extra to even the odds before entering into the contest.

In the next scene, the foursome returns to Jerry's apartment, where Kramer immediately spots a naked woman in the window across the street.[19] The sexually ravenous Kramer is unable to control himself; he excuses himself immediately and returns to announce what we had been led to predict: "I'm out." Of the three male characters, Kramer takes on the most ambisexual valence, moving freely from the homoerotic circle shared with Jerry and George to the distinctly heterosexual desire he expressed for the naked woman. While highly sexualized, neither Kramer's intimate and often seductive relationship with Jerry and George nor his frequent erotic encounters with women serve to posit him in clear homo- or heterosexual territory. Functioning as a sort of sexual fulcrum depending on the social context, Kramer may well be acting as *Seinfeld*'s embodiment of queerness.

The three remaining contestants are left to their own frustrations. In her aerobics class, Elaine finds herself positioned behind John F. Kennedy

Jr., the popular object of white, privileged heterosexual female desire. George is disturbed and aroused by his discovery that the privacy curtain separating his mother's hospital bed from her beautiful roommate's creates an erotic silhouette of the stranger's nightly sponge bath.[20] Locked in a passionate embrace in the front seat of Jerry's car, Marla pulls back and asks Jerry to "slow down"; he politely acquiesces, assuring Marla that her virginity is not hindering his enjoyment of their relationship.

On the surface, Marla's virginity is posited as an intensifying factor of her attractiveness; the withholding of not only sex but also of her sexuality seems to make the possibility of physical intimacy even more inaccessible—and thus desirable. In fact, Marla's virginity is a crucial element to balance (and perhaps camouflage) the more important discussions and representations of masturbation. Marla's introduction to the periphery of Jerry's bet with Kramer, George, and Elaine serves a twofold purpose. First, her virginity becomes both a presence and an obstacle between Jerry and Marla, impeding any progress toward a heterosexual encounter. Second, without Marla as Jerry's ostensible love object, the "masturbation episode" would take on a glaringly homosexual tone. Marla's presence serves to divert attention away from what is more or less a circle jerk among homosexualized men: a collective and voyeuristic study of each other's (auto)erotic activity, focusing—if we may momentarily exclude Elaine's participation—on the male orgasm brought on reflexively by the male participants. As a virgin, Marla serves to deflect the queerness of the contest away from Jerry while never threatening the homoerotic trinity of Jerry, George, and Kramer.

Elaine, by comparison, is indeed a heterosexually active female. Why is Elaine allowed to participate in the otherwise queerly coded masturbatory abstinence contest? In effect, she never truly is cast as an equal participant. Throughout the episode, she is consistently figured as the "odd man out"; at the restaurant table where the triangulated male bodies of Jerry, George, and Kramer construct the terms of the bet, Elaine is seated in the corner of the booth. Within the frames, she appears either alone or with her back partially turned to the camera, surrounded by the men who look toward her, clearly separated from the intimate boy talk of the others who share the booth with her. As mentioned before, the men's misconception that women are naturally predisposed to such masturbatory abstinence works to further distance female sexuality—and thus females—from their own collective experience of (same-sex) desire. Perhaps most importantly, Elaine's strongest connection to the trio is through her relationship with Jerry, a friendship that is predicated on their previous failure as (hetero)sexual partners. Her potentially menacing role as Straight Female is mitigated by her position as Not Love Object. Elaine may participate in the contest from the sidelines without truly interrupting its homosexual valence.

Despite the remaining contestants' boasts of being "queen of the castle" and "master of my domain," their sexual frustrations are evident in the four juxtaposed scenes of their private bedrooms: Jerry appears restless in his bed of white linens; George thrashes beneath his sheets printed with cartoon dinosaurs;[21] Elaine is sleepless in her darkened room; Kramer, however, long having satisfied his desire, snores peacefully.

Grumpy from his sleepless night, Jerry tells Kramer that he can no longer tolerate the view of the naked neighbor across the street. As he prepares to go over and ask the woman to draw her shades, the infuriated Kramer tries to stop him, doubting Jerry's sanity for wanting to block their view of a beautiful nude woman. Kramer has called into question Jerry's priorities, which seem to be clear: Jerry privileges his participation in the queerly coded contest over the visual pleasure Kramer experiences from the nude woman.

In the next series of juxtaposed bedroom shots, the viewer discovers from Elaine's restful sleep that she has given in. The next morning, as she sheepishly relinquishes her money, she explains that rumors of JFK Jr.'s interest in her had prompted her moment of weakness. Jerry marvels that "the queen is dead," thereby leaving only himself and George to compete for the pot.

In the following scene, two embracing figures are stretched out on the couch in Jerry's dark apartment. In the close-up shot, we see that Marla is on top of Jerry; not only does this physicality suggest a heightened potential for sexual intimacy between the ordinarily distant couple, but Jerry's positioning on the bottom of the embrace casts him in the stereotypically feminine, passive role of a woman in a straight couple (a role evocative of the one he occupied in his relationship with Keith Hernandez). In keeping with the episode's (and indeed the show's) pattern, such menacing circumstances should surely create chaotic results.

Taking her cue from Jerry's receptive position, the previously hesitant Marla becomes the aggressor, initiating a (masculine) invitation to have sex: "Let's go in the bedroom." From beneath her, Jerry's somewhat timid voice sounds unsure: "*Really?*" Now too close for comfort, Jerry must find a way to disengage from the heterosexual situation in which he is now entangled; Marla's virginity is no longer a sufficient buffer. When Marla asks why he looks so tense, he thoughtlessly (or so it would appear) recounts the details of the contest to explain his (ostensible) relief at the chance to have sex with her. Marla reacts with horror and disgust and quickly exits, leaving Jerry alone.

On the street, Marla bumps into Elaine, who is eagerly awaiting the arrival of JFK Jr. for their first arranged meeting. Marla pulls away from Elaine in revulsion: "I don't want to have anything to do with you or your perverted friends. Get away from me, you're horrible!" Having clearly identified Jerry, George, and Kramer as sexually deviant (i.e., not "straight"), Marla leaves, removing the safe, female heterosexual anchor that her presence provided to the otherwise transparently queer contest.

Believing that JFK Jr. stood her up, Elaine complains to Jerry only to hear from George that Kennedy had just driven away with Marla. As they look out the window, Jerry spots Kramer in the arms of the beautiful woman across the street.

In the final series of four bedroom shots, Jerry and George are at last also enjoying a restful sleep; Kramer snores next to his new lover, and Marla compliments "John" on his sexual prowess. Whereas the two latter scenes depict the postorgasmic satisfaction of the two heterosexual partners that share it, the two former scenes are ambiguous by contrast: no explanation is provided for how or why Jerry and George relieved their pent-up sexual energies at the same time. With no female love object available (no recent viewings of the erotic sponge bath for George, and Jerry's potential lover has left him) to dehomosexualize Jerry and George's two-member circle jerk, the viewer is left with the suggestion that they have satisfied their sexual frustrations together. Intensified by the "success" of the hypervirile JFK Jr. in the face of Jerry's sexual failure with Marla, the narrative closes with individual shots of George and Jerry—alone and yet paired off. Quite apart from the strong homoerotic sensibility of "The Contest"'s construction, the simple and familiar plot resolution—the duo's inability to sustain a romantic relationship with a woman leaves them again alone with each other—marks the episode as incontrovertibly queer.

*Seinfeld*'s narrative design would, at first glance, seem to lack the depth necessary in character and plot to facilitate a discussion of the complexities of homoerotic male relationships. The sort of nonspecific, scattered quality of the *Seinfeld* text, however, makes it well suited to the fluid nature of a queer reading, whose project is more concerned with context than fixity, more with potential than evidence. Nonetheless, *Seinfeld* is full of both context and evidence that lead the text's critics toward a well-developed queer reading. *Seinfeld* enjoys a kind of subculture defined by a discursive code that unites its members in a common lexicon of meaning. The narrative restricts its focus to the foursome, containing and maintaining the intimate bonds between the show's three men and its one woman (the latter being clearly positioned as sexually incompatible and socially separate from the others). Directly related to this intense interconnection, the foursome often causes each member's inability to foster outside heterosexual romantic interests.

Jerry and George share the most intimate relationship of them all; they aid each other in perpetuating duplicities while remaining truthful only with one another. They are the two characters who most frequently share a frame and who create and occupy male-coded narrative spaces, whether in the domestic sphere of Jerry's apartment or in the public sphere at Monk's.

All of these relationships are in motion amid a steady stream of other discursive and iconic gay referents. Their visibility admits the "knowing" viewer into a queerly constructed *Seinfeld* universe while never being so explicit as to cause the "unknowing" viewer to suspect the outwardly "normal" appearance of the show.

Reading the queer in *Seinfeld* sheds a revealing light on the show's "not that there's anything wrong with that" approach to representations of male homoeroticism. While sustaining a steadfast denial of its gay undercurrents, the text playfully takes advantage of provocative semiotic juxtapositions that not only allow but also encourage the "knowing" spectator to ignore the show's heterosexual exterior and instead to explore the queerness of *Seinfeld*.

### Selected *Seinfeld* Videography

(*Seinfeld*. Created by Jerry Seinfeld and Larry David. NBC-TV, 1989–98.)

"The Apartment." Writ. Peter Mehlman. 4 Apr. 1991.
"The Boyfriend." Writ. Larry David and Larry Levin. 12 Feb. 1992.
"The Café." Writ. Tom Leopold. 6 Nov. 1991.
"The Cheever Letters." Writ. Larry David. 28 Oct. 1992.
"The Contest." Writ. Larry David. 13 Nov. 1992.
"The Dog." Writ. Larry David. 9 Oct. 1991.
"The Junior Mint." Writ. Andy Robin. 18 Mar. 1993.
"The Limo." Writ. Larry Charles. 26 Feb. 1992.
"The Outing." Writ. Larry Charles. 11 Feb. 1993.
"The Phone Message." Writ. Larry David and Jerry Seinfeld. 13 Feb. 1991.
"The Pllot." Writ. Larry David. 20 May 1993.
"The Red Dot." Writ. Larry David. 11 Dec. 1991.
"The Shoes." Writ. Larry David and Jerry Seinfeld. 4 Feb. 1993.
"The Smelly Car." Writ. Larry David and Peter Mehlman. 15 Apr. 1993.
"The Stakeout." Writ. Larry David and Jerry Seinfeld. 31 May 1990.
"The Statue." Writ. Larry Charles. 11 Apr. 1991.
"The Subway." Writ. Larry Charles. 8 Jan. 1992.
"The Virgin." Writ. Larry David. 11 Nov. 1992.
"The Watch." Writ. Larry David. 30 Sept. 1992.

## Notes

All dialogue quoted in this essay, unless otherwise indicated, comes from my own transcriptions of the television programs in question.

1. Dave Walter, "Does Civil Disobedience Still Work?" *Advocate*, 20 Nov. 1990, 34–38.
2. For further discussion of the political and semiotic history of the word "queer," see Ernesto Laclau, *New Reflections on the Revolution of Our Time* (London: Verso, 1990); Teresa de Lauretis, "Queer Theory: Lesbian and Gay Sexualities," *differences* 3:2 (1991): iii–xviii; Michelangelo Signorile, "Absolutely Queer: Reading, Writing, and Rioting," *Advocate*, 6 Oct. 1992, 17.
3. Eve Kosofsky Sedgwick, *Epistemology of the Closet* (Berkeley: University of California Press, 1990).
4. Diana Fuss, ed. *Inside/Out: Lesbian Theories, Gay Theories* (New York: Routledge, 1991).

5. Alexander Doty, *Making Things Perfectly Queer: Reading Mass Culture* (Minnesota: University of Minnesota Press, 1993).
6. Bruce Fretts, *The Entertainment Weekly "Seinfeld" Companian* (New York: Warner Books, 1993), 12.
7. Bill Zehme, "Jerry and George and Kramer and Elaine: Exposing the Secrets of *Seinfeld*'s Success," *Rolling Stone* 660–61 (6–22 July 1993): 40–45, 130–31.
8. As evidence of this Seinfeldian shared vocabulary, I offer one of my primary resources for this paper, *The Entertainment Weekly "Seinfeld" Companion.* Author Bruce Fretts creates a partial glossary of these terms, situating them in their episodic contexts, cross-referencing them with the episodes in which the term recurs, and finally providing a chronological plot synopsis of episodes 1–61, ending with the 1993 season premiere, "The Pilot."
9. Doty outlines the political and semiotic complexities of the term "queer" in his insightful introduction to *Making Things Perfectly Queer.*
10. My essay takes its title from this episode; while combating the rumor of their homosexuality, the phrase "not that there's anything wrong with that" serves as Jerry and George's knee-jerk addendum to their denials. The catchphrase becomes a running joke through the episode, being echoed in turn by Jerry's and George's mothers and, later, by Kramer as well.
11. During the 1994 season, the *Seinfeld* triangle suddenly switched to blue. Might this suggest that the show's creators wished to distance themselves from an overly gay-identified icon, or does a queer interpretation suggest that Jerry is simply attempting to be more butch during that period? The 1995 season was marked with an ambiguous green triangle; the icon continued to change in each following season. One can only speculate that the shift away from the pink triangle is meant to mirror the shift away from the queerness of the early seasons—as evidenced by Susan's abrupt renunciation of lesbianism and subsequent return to George (my thanks to colleagues Melinda Kanner and Steve Bishop for their insightful ideas on this subject).
12. A particularly useful example of this theme occurs in "The Café," in which George, terrified of his girlfriend Monica's request that he take an IQ test, fears that he will not be able to pass. Out of desperation, he arranges for the more intelligent Elaine to take the test for him by passing it out to her through an open window. Jerry too has approved their secret plan to pass George off as an intelligent, appropriate partner for Monica: "Hey, I love a good caper!" Despite their best efforts to dupe Monica by presenting George in a false light, she discovers their duplicity and breaks up with him.
13. When questioned, Jerry makes no secret about the intensity of his "friendship" with George; in "The Dog," he confesses that they talk on the phone six times a day—coincidentally, the same number of times a day that he gargles.
14. A queer reading of the social differences between Jerry and George reveals a substratum of conflict: within the homoerotic dynamic that groups them together as a couple, George is constantly portrayed as crude, unrefined, and in need of direction. When George is paired with Jerry in the intimate, caretaking relationship they share, their connection suggests a domestic partnership in which Jerry, the more successful and refined of the duo, acts as their public voice, correcting George's social missteps, allowing them to "pass" less noticeably through acceptable, urban, upper-middle-class society.

15. It should be noted that George's presentation as both unemployed and desperate accentuate the clear class differences between him and Jerry, the successful stand-up comic being courted by a celebrity athlete.
16. In *Gay Talk* (New York: Paragon Books, 1972), Bruce Rodgers defines the expression "drop hairpins" (also "drop beads" or "drop pearls") as "to let out broad hints of one's sexuality" (69). Historically rooted in gay male culture, this expression is useful here to express the texts' many links to gay icons and lexicon. It should be noted, however, that the intentionality suggested by the phrase "drop hairpins" is problematic in the context of this paper, as I am not entering into an analysis of whether or not the creators of *Seinfeld* have knowingly or inadvertently produced a heavily queer text.
17. In "The Smelly Car," George runs into Susan for the first time since their breakup and is shocked to see her with Mona, her new lover. Although Susan alludes to her longstanding attraction to women, George makes multiple references to how he "drove her" to lesbianism. After Mona is inexplicably seduced by Kramer's mystique, Susan makes a new romantic contact in Allison, another of George's ex-girlfriends. The implication is not only that George is a failure as a heterosexual but also that, even in his attempts to connect romantically with women, he is attracted to inappropriate (or equally conflicted) female object choices.
18. George's use of *Glamour*, a women's fashion magazine, is a notably odd choice for visual sexual stimulation. In contrast to such heterosexual pornography as *Playboy*, in which nude women are presented in ways to elicit sexual responses from men, George has instead found sexual pleasure from a magazine whose focus is women's beauty culture—fashion, health, cosmetics—and not women themselves. It is essential to recognize that George's masturbatory activity was not in response to heterosexual desire for women's bodies but instead connected to something only indirectly related to their appearances.
19. In contrast to George's interest in *Glamour*, Kramer provides us with a more familiar example of an "appropriate" erotic stimulus for the heterosexual male; the sight of a nude woman directly and immediately enacts Kramer's sexual response.
20. This visual joke is revived in "The Outing": having been falsely identified in the newspaper as Jerry's lover, George attempts to set his shocked and still-hospitalized mother "straight." However, the tempting silhouette of the beautiful patient and her nurse has been replaced by the erotic shapes of a muscular male attendant sponge-bathing a brawny male patient.
21. Again, the spectator is privy to a subtle material reference to the class distinctions apparent within the coupling of Jerry and George; the contrast in their choices of bed linens—Jerry's tasteful white and George's childish, colorful pattern—provide a point of reference from which to understand the power dynamic between them as middle- to upper-middle-class (Jerry) and lower-middle- to working-class (George) gay men.

---

## This Text: Reading

1. Gantz indicates to an extent her writing situation when she labels American television as "homophobic." How does this play out in her essay?

2. Gantz focuses on "queer theory" in this essay, which she essentially uses as a lens to view her text. Are there other lenses we might use in discussing popular culture? Using another lens such as gender, race, or class, examine *Seinfeld* or some other popular text.
3. What other works might yield the same type of results with examination by queer theory?
4. Why might *Seinfeld* be a particularly good show to examine? Does Gantz indicate this in her essay?
5. In what ways might queer theory apply in your daily experiences of reading?

### YOUR TEXT: WRITING

1. Using the same lens of queer theory as Gantz, examine another popular television show.
2. Using another lens (such as race, gender, class), examine *Seinfeld* or another popular show. How does reading through a particular theory affect the writing process?
3. Write a short response paper to the essay itself. What did you like about it? What if anything disturbed you about it?

## SOCIETY'S NEED FOR A *QUEER* SOLUTION: THE MEDIA'S REINFORCEMENT OF HOMOPHOBIA THROUGH TRADITIONAL GENDER ROLES

Archana Mehta

Archana Mehta wrote this paper in a sophomore level writing and research class at Virginia Commonwealth University in spring 2001. The class was asked to find a "cultural text"—a text with cultural implications or importance—and research the connections it makes to academic and personal contexts. Here Mehta writes about the popular television show *Will and Grace* and comes up with some surprising conclusions about the place of gays and lesbians on the show.

"HEY, DO YOU have a minute? I need to tell you something really important and I do not know who else to turn to."

"Sure," I replied, oblivious to what my friend was going to tell me. By the seriousness of his tone and the lifeless expression on his face, I could tell that the next couple of sentences that would pass through his mouth would be serious, but I could not determine or predict the magnitude of what he was going to discuss with me.

"Okay, I don't know exactly how to tell you this, but . . ." his voice faded out and his eyes looked down to the floor as if he was terribly embarrassed and withdrawn from any emotion. Slowly he handed me his leather journal with the page to be read already open. Dead silence followed. I began to read the writing silently to myself.

> . . . And I now gradually began to realize, on an intellectual level, what I was. Why did that take so long? I think because when one grows up and hears words like "gay" or "homosexual," one thinks of rather horrid people, who are disgusting, ugly, and immoral. Many times I would think of some of the many images that people have about gay men and would try to convince myself that their actions were revolting. I thought: I cannot be one of them! And yet, deep down, I knew I was. What I began to understand was that the term "homosexual" really did not denote anything but a description of a male person who is emotionally and sexually attracted to another male. It did not represent anything, in itself, regarding the looks, behavior or values of anyone. I know that gay people are like everyone else—some are nice, some are rude, some are beautiful, some are ugly, some are young, some are old, etc.—this is how I convince myself that the person I am and the actions that I carry out are okay . . .

To this day, I still do not remember clearly how I initially reacted because homosexuality was a foreign concept to me. Now that I know someone who is indeed gay, my perceptions have changed a great deal. For the first time I realize how hard it is to deal with homosexuality in our society. I see the struggles that my friend encounters and the identity crises he faces, such as where he stands in his group of friends, how he is expected to behave, whether he should be open about it or not, etc. Why should anyone have to deal with these emotions because of who he is and what he believes? Why did his sexuality have to determine his identity and how his family, friends and society perceive him? Why does something so private as one's sexuality have to be discriminated against and looked down upon?

Before that day, I admit that I joked about the subject, participated in the typical gay comments and believed in many of the stereotypes that existed about homosexuals. I differentiated homosexuality and considered it a different form of identification just like a great deal of people do in our society. I ask myself why we, as a society, encourage differentiating individuals who do not follow heterosexuality and why they are deemed abnormal. My conclusion to this question was plain and simple: homosexuals act differently than what is expected in society. They do not follow the "normal" behavior that traditional gender roles outline for individuals. Some clear examples are that homosexuals lead promiscuous lifestyles, carry the AIDS virus, attend lavish parties and lead disorderly lives, enjoy shopping, and speak and walk a certain way and most obviously, they have sex with individuals of the same sex. In other words, they appear not to carry out the specific roles that are molded and expected for people in society.

Learning about my friend's homosexuality for the first time gave me an opportunity to analyze the existence of homosexuality in our culture as a form of identity. The emergence of a distinct homosexual population, the formation of their culture and their quest for acceptance and assimilation of their identity within mainstream culture is one of the most interesting and dynamic social transformations in American history. Homosexuality has gone from being an unspoken subject to a common topic of debate that appears in universities, politics and especially in mass media such as television. In fact, television conveys the traditional ideas, beliefs and generalizations that already exist about homosexuality in society. It is an excellent tool that is used to understand the status of homosexuality in our culture because, like a mirror, it reflects some very important beliefs and values permeating our society. When analyzing different sitcoms, cartoons and news broadcasts shown on television, one can say a great deal about the social and societal organization in the public, and it is especially apparent with the topic of homosexuality. Even though homosexuality is increasingly shown on television still does not imply that it is accepted. In fact, these television shows are "denormalizing" homosexuality even more by incorporating the idea of traditional gender roles even further.

Briefly observing the wide array of television shows that involve homosexuality, a great deal can be said about the status of homosexuality and how society perceives this form of sexual orientation. In the show *Ellen*, which was a very popular show for several years, the main character, played by Ellen Degeneres, decided to take a positive turn in her show by "coming out" to the public that she was gay in 1997. After her announcement, she incorporated the lifestyle of a gay person in her show very realistically, and to no surprise, the ratings plummeted. Furthermore, she was mocked on other shows such as *The Late Night Show, The Conan O'Brien Show* and even *Saturday Night* because of her sexual orientation and disparaged for her decision to go public.

On the other hand, when the NBC show *Friends* decided to show two lesbian women, Carol and Susan, raising a child together, the ratings did not alter at all because the portrayal was not realistic and was in fact very comedic. For example, the two women buy a shirt for their child that says, "I love my mommies" and both of them are mocked by the other characters because they breastfeed their child together. Not once does the show actually give a positive view on homosexual parenting. Susan and Carol are depicted as incapable of raising a child due to the lack of male influence in the child's life. Furthermore, the jokes made against Susan and Carol revolve around their "sexual practices" rather than making any positive comments about their personalities. Since Susan and Carol are not following the traditional gender roles, they are laughed at and looked down upon by other heterosexual characters on the show. Consequently, the lesbian couple on *Friends* is portrayed on television through a heterosexual view, as opposed to Ellen's realistic homosexual view, and this form of entertainment indicates the status of homosexuality in society. Why is the comedic version of homosexuality more popular than the realistic version of homosexuality on television? It shows us that homosexuality is not taken seriously. This indicates that the shows shown on primetime television are heterosexualized, meaning they are made to satisfy a heterosexual audience. In the cases of *Ellen* and *Friends*, the homosexual characters do not follow traditional gender roles and more importantly in *Friends*, the show's divergence from traditional gender roles is designed specifically to entertain rather than educate. What does this suggest about the audience? The audience, or society, does not really care to learn or understand the realistic homosexual subculture; rather they prefer it as a form of entertainment. Not wanting to understand and learn about true homosexuality suggests that there is a homophobia in our society that results from the traditional gender roles that we are taught and raised with.

Perhaps the epitome of all television shows that openly and comically portrays the lifestyles and the interactions between homosexuals and heterosexuals, and distinctly differentiates these two groups of people on primetime television, is *Will and Grace*. In fact this television show conveys a great deal about society's expectations. The show includes three main characters, Will, Grace, and Jack, who are very fascinating because they each have contrasting personalities and they demonstrate different sexual orientations. The portrayal of homosexuality on this show is represented in stark contrast to the heterosexual characters, suggesting that homosexuality is a deviant form of sexuality due to its straying from traditional gender roles. Consequently, it is apparent that the television is one of the many tools used in society to promote and preserve traditional gender roles, which generates a homophobia in the majority heterosexual population.

Grace, as a preserver of the traditional female gender role, represents the "straight heterosexual." Working for a decorating firm, Grace is perky, loud, vivacious, and fashionable. She plays the role of the typical woman, chasing after love and trying to find the "perfect" man thus ensuring her happiness. Grace also lives with her roommate/best friend Will, an extremely educated, intellectual lawyer. Additionally, Will is known for his subtle gayness. Occasionally, he shops with Grace and together they gossip about cute men. In fact, together they discuss how there is a "drought of good looking men in their lives." Interestingly, Will is the "tolerated" homosexual. Since he gives the impression that he is straight based on his looks and behavior, he seems to be more socially accepted. Outwardly, to an objective onlooker, Will appears to preserve the traditional male gender role. Thus, it is not easy to discriminate his sexual orientation, as it is apparent in the third major character Jack who is spunky, well dressed, clumsy, emotional and very overtly gay. He is the complete antithesis of Will and Grace, demonstrating the typical images that are tagged onto gay men. Whenever he speaks, he moves his hands in grandiose ways, acts overly expressive when discussing his emotions, speaks with a slight lisp and wears tight pants and collared shirts from expensive stores like Banana Republic. In addition to dressing well, he is loud, energetic, and very vocal about being gay. He openly flirts with other men at malls and clubs as well as loves to dance to "girly" songs by Brittany Spears and Ricky Martin. Jack appears to follow the non-traditional male gender role. He is "girly" and an embarrassing person to be seen with because of his idiosyncrasies, from which the show derives much of its humor. Most importantly, both Will and Jack, although to different degrees, represent the stereotypical homosexual, and Grace represents the typical heterosexual.

Even though the sitcom is very comical, the portrayal of the characters on *Will and Grace* definitely represents how television serves as a mirror reflecting reality by showing the contents, values and beliefs of homosexuality in our society. In addition, the show exemplifies how television reinforces reality for viewing audiences by shaping their attitudes and strengthening traditional gender roles and how any deviation is considered abnormal. Moreover, the broadcasting of this show definitely expresses a great deal about how society has progressed from keeping certain issues taboo to becoming more open. However, the mere presentation of this sitcom to the entire population of the United States does not necessarily indicate that homosexuality is accepted. Hence, an interpretation of several theories on the topic of homosexuality may help one to understand the status of homosexuals in society as well as what the cultural implications of a show such as *Will and Grace* mean to the common person.

Before understanding the perceptions and status of homosexuality in our society, it is important to interpret the different theories explaining the evolution of the term homosexual and how it eventually relates to traditional gender roles. (Due to the broadness of homosexuality, which can include bisexuals, transsexuals and lesbians, the topic of this paper will discuss homosexuality among men only.) The essentialists are a group of people who believe that identity is natural and fixed. They therefore strongly ascertain that people who are homosexual are this way due to biological reasons (McCormick 450). Consequently, they hold that there are two distinct types of people: people who are homosexual and people who are heterosexual. Leading essentialist scientists in the area of psychoneuroendocrinology believe that erotic/romantic attraction and desire for same-sex in both men and women are due to biological variables, such as genes, hormones, and brain neuroanatomy (McCormick 459). Similarly, Paul Robinson, in his essay "Freud and Homosexuality" discusses how Sigmund Freud held an important essentialist view because he believed that the essence of homosexuality was in the mind and recognized its causes to be a result of the variation of a child's upbringing (92). According to Freud, the child is homosexual because he/she fixates at an early stage of development or psychological growth (Robinson 92). Robinson also brings to attention that Freud "repeatedly, almost compulsively, refers to heterosexuality as the 'normal' result . . . of psychological maturity" (92). Since essentialists view homosexuality as a scientific anomaly, they strongly reason that this form of sexual orientation is a sickness like Parkinson's disease. Hence, essentialists try to cure homosexuality. It is evident from the essentialist view that as science advanced, social scientists explicated variation in populations. Hence, homosexual people, who were the observed minority in society, became a sort of experimental group. Consequently, they became even more differentiated in society and were considered anti-normative.

Contrary to this, the constructionist position, which opposes the essentialist, believes that identity is changeable and culture-dependent. Michel Foucault, a prominent French historian and constructionist, provides an interesting argument in his book *The History of Sexuality* that the term "homosexual" never existed before the year 1870 (43). According to him, same-sex sex acts have existed since the beginning of time, and even though religious and political leaders condemned them, everyone knew that they could "fall" to such temptations (43). Since anyone could submit to this sin, the population as a whole is susceptible to such activity. No one is born to behave in this manner. According to Foucault, it was not until after 1870 that the concept of the "homosexual" came into an identifiable type of person (43). The homosexual began to be identified in terms of his sexual activities. Rather than existing as only a behavior, it became solidified into a label. Foucault states, "The sodomite had been a temporary aberration; the homosexual was now a species" (43).

In fact, Annamarie Jagose, a senior lecturer at Melbourne University supports the idea that homosexuality became differentiated due to society's expectations. She states that "homosexuality [became] a social role" (13). This invention of the term homosexuality parallels the ideas of Foucault, who feels that sexuality became an identity due to society as well. Foucault theorizes the reason for sexuality becoming an identity. He strongly believes that Western society during the 1800s preoccupied themselves with discussing the nature of sex for two reasons. One reason was the necessity to confess all sexual practices in the Christian culture to pastors in order to monitor each person's sexual encounters, behaviors and desires in order to trace for sin (Foucault 17–35). In general, sex was a sin of flesh; hence it was important to incorporate all details. Foucault states further that there was a "task of telling...oneself...as often as possible, everything that might concern the interplay of innumerable pleasures, sensations, and thoughts which, through the body and the soul, had some affinity with sex" (20). The second reason was that society fixated on discovering the truth about sex and regulating it (17–35). Hence, sexuality became an even more reinforced and essential aspect in society. People believed that sex could be controlled through massive discussions or public "discourse" (Foucault 15). This need to converse became an obsession in order to research, analyze and understand the nature of sexuality. However, during the nineteenth century, the need to discuss sexuality in order to monitor the population gradually transformed into a need to understand sexuality in a scientific manner in order to satisfy the desire to understand such behaviors (Foucault 53–73). These scientific doctrines began to identify and postulate several unnatural sexual behaviors. Before, discourse regulated behaviors, but now it was observed and explained by logical reason; hence, homosexuality and other forms of sexual behaviors were distinguished into their own groups (Foucault 55). Homosexual relations had been seen as a sin that could be committed from time to time, but now a group of "homosexuals" emerged (Foucault 43). The idea of sexuality became fundamental part of the person. Most importantly, Foucault continues his claim that sexuality was not instinctive; on the contrary, it was a social construction that can exist in one society, but not in other societies (Foucault 53–73).

Now that the emergence of the term homosexual as a societal construction is well understood, the term can be further linked to the theories of gender. Annamarie Jagose, author of *Introduction to Queer Theory*, states, "there is a crucial distinction between homosexual behavior which is ubiquitous and homosexual identity, which evolves under specific...conditions" (15). This statement supports that homosexual behavior is considered deviant because those who actively and openly participate in same-sex activities are categorized and ostracized due to societal conditions and restraints such as gender. Moreover, Judith Lorber, a current writer of feminist theory discusses the meaning of gender in our culture in her essay "The Social Construction of Gender." Lorber writes, "Gender is so much the routine ground of everyday activities that questioning it is taken for granted" (20). Many people do not even recognize that many of the activities, thoughts and behaviors that we possess are shaped by gender. Hence, Lorber creates a very important point in that much of the generalizations that people have about homosexuality are the result of gender. The information regarding the concept of gender is vast as in how the formation of the word affects and sculpts our society. However, in this research paper, the effects of gender on homosexuality and heterosexuality will be the main focus.

The idea of gender, originally created on the basis of genitalia, also involves the "assignment of sex" to each individual, mainly the perceptions of masculine and feminine characteristics (Lorber 20). Essentially, gender generates roles for the masculine and feminine identity such as the female as the child bearer whereas the male is the provider of the family. Gender is habitual and limits what females and males can do (Lorber 21). In fact, gender binds and forces us to be what others want us to be. For example, from my observations, when a child is born, depending on the sex, the child is raised completely differently. If the child is a girl, then she wears pink clothes and plays with dolls, teddy bears and kitchen sets. However, if a child is a boy, he is given athletic equipment, trucks and cars to play with and is taught to be strong both physically and emotionally. Thus, society molds children into behaving and thinking in certain ways from the very beginning, especially in the way they are expected to participate in activities. More importantly, a girl is taught to express her feelings, whereas the boy is guided into being a tough and aggressive person, not showing his feelings as much. Maasik and Solomon, two leading gender theorists, articulately define that gender is "a culturally constructed belief system that dictates the appropriate roles and behavior for men and women in society" (438).

These observations on gender in society are summarized further by Chrys Ingraham, author of the essay "The Heterosexual Imaginary," who believes that "femininity and masculinity are achieved characteristics... [and that] maleness and femaleness are 'ascribed traits'" (185). It is important to realize that from this statement that maleness and femaleness can have variations in the extent of how masculine or feminine a person can be; however, a distinction in society between the two sexes and how they should behave exists. Consequently, society does not maintain the flexibility to carry out behaviors from the two sexes. Instead, Ingraham writes that gender is a form of "organizing relations between the [two] sexes" (186). According to Judith Lorber, a professor of women's studies, as a result of gender, society began to perceive heterosexuality as the way relationships should be solidified (Lorber 23). It is assumed that attraction for the opposite sex is the natural way. In the essay "Heterosexuality and Social Policy," Jean Carabine theorizes about existence of heterosexuality. She maintains that society continues to make heterosexuality the natural form of sexual relationship, creating a general perception that to be a homosexual is unnatural (61). It became the norm to have sex between the male and the female, since the function of sex was for reproduction (Lorber 23). The existence of gender molds such specific roles for partners in sexual relationships that any sort of deviance from the dominant culture signifies a rejection of culture itself. Thus, individuals in society who are "rejecting culture" by not following gender-created heterosexuality are punished and looked down upon. Consequently, gender not only creates such distinctions in sexuality such as determining what is normal and what is not, but it also creates a homophobia for those who do not follow the norm. Holly Devor validates this assumption by saying, "society demands [specific] gender performances [and relationships] from us and rewards, tolerates, or punishes us differently for conformity to, or digression from, social norms" (414).

Since gender creates distinctions between male and female and organizes the "normal" sexual relations between these two groups, it is evident that the presence of homosexuality creates a homophobia in our culture. Several examples can be seen in a single episode of *Will and Grace*. The actions of each of the characters reproduce, reaffirm and reflect the dominant ideologies of traditional gender roles and how homosexuality is deviant from these roles in our culture. For example, as previously established, Will, Grace and Jack all depict the stereotypical roles of homosexuals and heterosexuals. When a cute male tenant moves into an apartment on Will and Grace's floor, both Will and Grace attempt to get the newcomer's attention and they do so by demonstrating typical methods of approach to get a date with this guy. Grace, dressed in a tight mini-skirt and a flamboyant shirt, draws attention to her breasts and legs in order to grab his attention; however, Will, who is also wearing tight jeans, converses with him and reveals his gayness with hints of gay remarks. Both characters are reaffirming and reflecting society's homosexual and heterosexual roles as well as their assigned gender roles. Grace behaves as a typical woman by wearing showy clothes and using her body to seduce men. Will remains confused between the "normal" male and female roles; wearing tight jeans and tight shirts, he tries to be flirtatious in a masculine, but "gay" way. Yet, when does an individual choose to conform to a specific type of gender role? It is the mass media that subconsciously reinforce such ways of thinking in the American public.

Similarly, both Will and Grace exemplify the roles expected of their gender when they shop with Grace's heterosexual boyfriend, Nathan, at Barney's in New York City. The juxtaposition of the three characters is very interesting. Will and Grace eagerly shop and look for the sexiest and most fashionable clothes and Nathan sits on the ledge complaining about how shopping is boring and can "drive people crazy." While Nathan talks about how he is missing the World Series on television, Will is trying on tight jeans from Paris and staring at himself in the mirror. Grace comments on how the jeans are too "girly," but despite her comment, Will still tries them on and buys them. The interesting part of this scene is that all the humorous parts have to do with Will trying on the jeans and having the same enthusiasm to shop as Grace. Furthermore, when all three return to the apartment, Nathan heads straight to the television set while Will and Grace go through piles of clothes and agree that they make great "shopping buddies." This scene says a great deal about how society perceives homosexuals and stereotypes them as having feminine characteristics such as loving to shop. In addition, the fact that Nathan, the heterosexual man, goes straight to the television to watch a baseball game again shows the expected male gender role.

Similarly, Jack's role in the show also sparks a lively debate about homosexuality. In the beginning of the show, Jack wakes up wearing a short, tight pink bathrobe and talks about how he needs to get one of Brittany Spears's souvenirs from E-bay. When Jack takes off his bathrobe, he is wearing a fitted short t-shirt that has a picture of the Eiffel Tower. The focus is on Nathan laughing at and mocking Jack, while Jack frolics around the room trying to get his tea ready. In addition, Nathan is wearing sweatpants and a sports jersey. In one aspect, the television show implies homosexuals are not taken seriously, and it also reflects and reinforces the general belief that they tend to have feminine characteristics. Once again, the "normal" structure for gender is emphasized: that males are supposed to have masculine characteristics and females are supposed to have feminine characteristics and any person who shows a mixture is considered abnormal, which can be seen through Jack and Will.

It is apparent from the juxtaposition between heterosexual and homosexual characters that a very conservative, underlying theme continues to permeate the show's storyline: traditional gender roles are preserved. The heterosexual male watches his sports, dresses casually, acting tough while the heterosexual female shops, puts on make-up and uses her body as a means to gain male attention. This contrasts with the two homosexual characters who do not fit into the conventional gender roles at all and appear to be "deviants" according to society's standards. Inevitably, people continue to think that homosexuals are abnormal and find humor in such portrayals. This representation of nontraditional gender roles contributes to a great deal of homophobia in our society.

At first, when watching a show such as *Will and Grace,* one thinks that television openly discusses controversial issues. In fact, it was initially believed that addressing such issues was a jump forward for American society. Looking back several years ago, television shows avoided homosexual issues or, at best, alluded to jokes pertaining to homosexuality. Even *Beverly Hills 90210,* a popular prime-time drama known to be a pioneer dealing with teenage issues, rarely touched upon the topic of homosexuality. One could almost conclude that the American society is in the midst of a sexual revolution; perhaps society is finally accepting this form of sexual identity. However, watching shows such as *Dawson's Creek, Road Rules, Friends* and *The Real World* in addition to *Will and Grace* in detail reveal that television is not as liberal as many believe. In fact, it carries out society's preconceived notions about homosexuality. Television persists to please the major, dominating heterosexual audience by reiterating their belief that homosexuals are confused and do not follow the traditional gender roles, and so are labeled "abnormal." Television can be described as having a pendulum effect, shifting between society shaping television and vice versa. The dominating, heterosexual audience's beliefs and myths shape the portrayal of homosexuality on television. As a result, these labels for homosexuals mold the way people act and think toward homosexuals even further.

More importantly, deviating from socially normal gender roles, *Will and Grace* presents a negative image of homosexuals by exaggerating Will and Jack's behavior. Although they represent different extremes on the spectrum of homosexuality with Will being the "straighter" gay and Jack being the very overt and vocal gay, their characters are embellished to such a degree that encourages generalizations that they do not adhere to gender roles. Not only do viewers mock both characters, but even Will, the "straighter" gay, mocks his friend Jack just for being more gay than himself. This post-modern form of portrayal is a type of camp which undermines the category of homosexuality through parody and mimicry. Camp weakens the model of identity because homosexuality is unnecessarily exaggerated for the sake of comedy and hence, forms an inaccurate truth. *Will and Grace* supports an oppressive homosexual identity, which the public inherits, and exercises the belief that homosexuals are the subordinate and the inferior form of identity due to nontraditional gender roles they seem to exhibit. Hence, the portrayal of Will and Jack is indeed a form of entertainment for the heteronormative population.

The preservation of gender roles and heterosexuality through this subtle form of entertainment shows that the larger population still remains homophobic in both behavior and thought. The term "coming out" is an excellent example of vocabulary that is used by the typical homophobe. The idea implies that to tell one of his sexual preference requires an announcement. Even a person "coming out of the closet" still remains equally oppressed because this visible form of identity only leads to discrimination and stereotypes. In fact this can be seen in *Will and Grace* when Jack decides to go to his mother's home to tell her about his homosexuality. At first he is apprehensive, but when he finally gets the courage to tell her, his mother's immediate reaction is that "there were many clues when [he was] a child." She mentions that as child he loved the nursery rhyme "rub-a-dub-dub, three men in a tub" (which by the way, was a very funny remark because everyone watching the show began to laugh) and caught him wearing her high-heeled shoes, dressing in her clothes and trying on lipstick a few times. Jack's mother mentions his past in such a humorous manner that once again he feels restrained. Whether Jack did or did not "come out of the closet," he still feels the pressure of society's standards. Furthermore, Jack's mother continually mentions his confused gender when he was a child, once again showing how he was viewed as abnormal because he did not play with a football or with video games. In short, he did not display the expected male gender role. Society excels at eliminating and discriminating against deviances from heterosexuality by maintaining the limited cultural gender roles. Any person varying from this becomes an outcast, separated from society and looked down upon. Both Will and Jack go to gay bars and clubs during their free time. Therefore, they only feel normal meeting other homosexuals in an environment that eliminates ideas of restricted gender roles. By creating shows such as *Will and Grace* for a largely heterosexual population, the ideology of homophobia works to reinforce the power of heterosexism in our society.

The magnitude of homophobia is subtle, but it is apparent because a distinct and separated culture of homosexuality exists as a result of discrimination and ostracism by the majority heterosexual population. Rachel Kranz, a firm supporter of gay rights, defines homophobia as "the irrational fear of homosexuals and...the hatred for gay men...and the view that they are somehow inferior to heterosexuals" (Kranz 155). This fear of homosexuality brought about by gender roles has created a distinct homosexual culture. For example, Alan Bray, author of *Homosexuality in Renaissance England*, expresses that after the emergence of the term homosexual in the mid 1800s there came the formation of a very well established community for homosexuals called Molly houses (84). Bray states that the Molly houses were a place where men could gather and "sex was the root of the matter...

it was as likely to be expressed in drinking together, in flirting and gossip and in a circle of friends as in actual liaisons" (84). In addition, Bray comments that the formation of a distinct culture was evident in the "ways of dressing, of talking, distinctive gestures and distinctive acts with an understood meaning, its own jargon" (86). The Molly houses were very important to the history of homosexuality because the definition of homosexuality as a distinct and different culture was put into use in society. There was a separate community with its own identity within the larger community.

In fact, Nancy Achilles addresses the two concerns of how and why a separate culture of homosexuality occurred and ties it in with the idea of homophobia. She states, in her essay "The Development of the Homosexual Bar as an Institution," that "an institution must arise from a particular social situation.... When an individual experiences strain in the social system, he may become motivated toward deviance... the choice [being]... to alienate himself from his environment altogether and attempt to chart his own life course" (3). Achilles justifies such actions because she believes that it is important for the "deviant form" to find a support group who may understand his social wants and needs (4). Not only does it allow for homosexuals to meet and socialize, but the individual remains comfortable within his own "type." Achilles states that the most important function of the bar is "to permit... the formation of sexual relationships. Sexual contacts may be made on the street, in the park, or on the bench, [but] the bar is the only place where these contacts... can be made with a reasonable degree of safety and respectability" (5). This statement reveals that the larger society disparages the formation of a same-sex intimate relationship, and that it must be done in a location where the "normal" heterosexual is not around. Furthermore, the existence of institutions such as gay bars and gay clubs are not only for homosexuals, but for all types of "sexual deviants" such as transvestites and lesbians. This form of gathering caused by separation of heterosexuality and homosexuality implies that in a bar, interaction between "deviants" is easier and appropriate because there are no traditional gender roles present. Achilles' observation underscores that homophobia exists in our society.

The raiding of the Stonewall Inn, a private club in New York City consisting of a predominantly gay clientele, on June 28th, 1969, is the most notorious symbol of the extreme homophobia that exists in the American culture. In the early morning hours, several police raided the bar, claiming that the charge was for illegal sale of alcohol (Kranz 23). Police raids on bars in New York City were not uncommon (Kranz 23). However, the existing trend of the raids that summer was very obvious in that they were geared toward bars consisting of homosexual, transsexual and lesbian individuals (Kranz 24). It was the second time in a week that the police targeted the bar; fourteen other gay bars had also been raided that week (Kranz 36). During the raid, police officers checked the identifications of all the patrons, but most were free to leave, with the exception of the staff and a few homosexuals (Kranz 37). Later on that day, crowds of people, especially young, gay men, gathered in front of the bar, and they did so by handholding, kissing, and forming a chorus line, overtly defying traditional gender roles, for three days (Kranz 24). The Stonewall riot represented not only a fight against police, but a fight against the American heterosexist society. In fact, the Stonewall Riot can be considered a turning point for homosexuals because it gave birth to the Gay Liberation movement for homosexuals and other "sexual deviants." It was from this riot that Americans realized the growing need and desire for homosexuals to have a rightful position in society. In fact, many commentators have described Stonewall as the "shot heard round the homosexual world" (Jagose 30). Consequently, during this Gay Liberation movement numerous organizations emerged around the country in order to bring about change for homosexuals (Kranz 25).

The events of Stonewall indicate the obvious segregation between the two forms of sexuality, and because heterosexuality is considered the "natural" and stable construction due to gender, homosexuality appears to be the inferior form, always being compared to the natural heterosexual form. Annamarie Jagose validates this when she states "heterosexuality is equally the construction whose meaning is dependent on the changing cultural models" (35). This means that heterosexuality is a derivation from the gender roles made by society, just as much as homosexuality. So the important question is why should homosexuality gain the reputation that it has? This is a major concern for a group of people called Queer Theorists, a prominent group who gained popularity during the Gay Liberation movement (Jagose 73).

Queer Theorists believe that the reason why the American society is homophobic and gives homosexuality an inferior and negative reputation is because of traditional gender roles. Consequently, they believe that in order to eliminate the existence of homophobia, the only solution is to eradicate traditional gender roles. In order to eliminate traditional gender roles, they have introduced the very abstract term "queer." Queer Theorists believe that the term homosexual was invented by a group of people who did not understand the difference between heterosexual and homosexual (Jagose 95). According to queer theorists, homosexuality and heterosexuality is not as black and white as it appears. There is a mix of gray in this form of identification, and so the term queer was invented. Queer destroys and eliminates the traditional meaning of "gay" and "lesbian," and "homosexual." According to Jagose, these are "homophobic normative definitions" (88).

The goal of queer theorists is to "denaturalize" the categories into a broader definition (Jagose 72–100). Hence, the definition of queer is non-specificity. The term is meant to include all types of sexual practices and eradicate the distinction between homosexual and heterosexual, because theoretically speaking, queer encompasses those terms and includes all individuals. This invention of the term "queer" basically intends to remove traditional gender roles. The fact that traditional gender roles are not included indicates that the ideas of femininity and masculinity do not have to be so clear cut as gender roles create. Instead, an individual can exercise any form of attitude, behavior and thought, which includes sexual practice. For example, a male can behave, dress and act as feminine as he wants and vice versa.

Thus, one of the most important functions of the advent of the word queer is that it includes all forms of "sexual deviants" such as homosexuals, bisexuals and transvestites into the same category as heterosexuals (Jagose 72–100). Together they are grouped under the same heading, essentially eliminating distinctions such as gender labels, generalizations and stereotypes, which creates heterosexual normativity (Jagose 96). This goal of eliminating all forms of differences is a major theme of Gay Liberation, so that all people can gain equal rights and representation in society. Unlike *Will and Grace,* which purposefully differentiates the homosexuals, Will and Jack, from the heterosexual characters, Grace and Nathan, Queer Theorists hope to eliminate such distinctions. For example, in one episode Jack and Will are at the studios of the NBC *Today Show* and in order to gain Al Roker's attention, Will leans over and French-kisses Jack. The people surrounding Will and Jack all gasp and in the background of the show, you can hear the audience laughing hysterically. However, when Grace and Nathan kiss on the show, no big deal is made. Queer Theorists would see the different reactions from the audience to the kisses on *Will and Grace* as a form distinction between homosexuality and heterosexuality in our society that should not exist. Jagose brilliantly points out that since queer is "suggestive of a whole range of sexual possibilities . . . normal and pathological, straight, and gay, masculine men and feminine women," all sexual behaviors grouped under one broad category are considered normal (98).

Since Queer Theorists believe that "queer" encompasses all individuals in one category, Calvin Thomas, in his essay "Straight with a Twist," states that "there is . . . a straight affiliation with the term 'queer'" (84). In fact, Thomas takes the word queer to a whole new level by describing how any individual can be called queer. He believes that every individual exhibits queer tendencies in their gender roles and sexual behaviors. He states, ". . . straights, who would be barred definitionally from the terms 'gay,' 'lesbian,' or 'bisexual,' could not be excluded from the domain of the queer" (Thomas 86). Thus, Queer Theory expands the scope of its analysis to all kinds of behaviors, including those who are gender-conforming, gender-bending and those who practice "non-normative" forms of sexuality. A person's sexuality is molded by a complex array of social codes and forces, constantly pressured by individual beliefs and institutional powers. At all times, an individual tries to conform to the ideas of what is normal and to avoid what is deviant. Consequently, the invention of the term "queer" ideally hopes to eliminate the complexity of social construction on sexuality caused by gender so that every individual is no longer ostracized, discriminated against and even laughed at because of his/her sexuality.

Imagine the ideals of Queer Theorists actually succeeding in eliminating traditional gender roles and creating the term "queer" to encompass all existent categories of sexuality under one umbrella. How would society respond to such changes? How would people act and behave? Since television acts like a mirror and reflects the social organization in our society, perhaps observing an episode of *Will and Grace* through the eyes of a Queer Theorist would guide us. First of all, the four characters—Will, Grace, Jack and Nathan—would not be referred to as the "homosexual characters and the heterosexual characters" because they would no longer be identified through such words. In fact, each of the four characters are all queer in their own unique way. Will and Jack will no longer be mocked for being "too feminine" because gender roles do not exist. Consequently, when Will is frightened by an old, high-school bully who works with him and feels threatened and cannot defend himself, or when he decides to go shopping with Grace in order to look for tight jeans, Will will not be mocked because he is acting too "girly." He will be admired for his individuality. In addition, Jack frolicking around in a pink-bathrobe and singing and dancing to Ricky Martin will not be seen as abnormal. Grace chasing after her men will be seen in the same light as Will chasing after men. Nathan watching his sports on television and dressed in a sports jersey will no longer be compared to Jack dressed in tight Banana Republic clothes because traditional gender roles would no longer be followed. Will and Jack French kissing will be at an equal level to Grace and Nathan kissing. In other words, everyone is equal. Everyone is different. Everyone is individual. No one is being laughed at because of their sexual identity, rather everyone is being laughed at because of their queerness. In addition, since queer includes all sexualities, why not include bisexuals, transvestites, lesbians and drag queens as well, in order to get a larger representation of the population? After all, this is a *queer* show. Moreover, rather than having all Caucasian queers, the addition of Asian, Hispanic, African American, European, Native American and Eskimo queers would be included as well since the mainstream American audience that network TV tries so hard to reach is composed of many persons from different backgrounds, different sexualities, and different queerness.

A portrayal as the one described accurately and realistically represents the queer life in America. Consequently, all people exhibiting sexual deviance will eventually be accepted and no longer be subjected to the bigotry and intolerance of the larger homophobic population. The invention of the term queer in a whole new light may actually succeed in eliminating conventional beliefs on sexuality in which society can eliminate the idea of sexuality as an identity. In fact, the innovation of Queer Theory in society will not only eliminate differences, but would offer a wider range of comedy so that instead of laughing at a certain type of people, everyone can just laugh together. Consequently, by eliminating sexual distinctions, Queer Theorists hope to "open [a] mesh of possibilities, gaps, overlaps, dissonances and resonances, lapses and excesses of meaning [so that] the constituent elements of anyone's gender, of anyone's sexuality aren't made or can't be made" (Thomas 86). The idea of queer is a term that potentially can eliminate all forms of contradictions and bigotry in our nation's social structure. Perhaps the utilization of this word will finally bring to end a history of heterosexuality in our society and triumph in creating equality for all.

### Works Cited


Achilles, Nancy. "The Development of the Homosexual Bar as an Institution." *Sociology of Homosexuality*. Eds. Wayne R. Dynes and Stephen Donaldson. New York: Garland Publishing, Inc., 1992. 2–18.

Bray, Alan. *Homosexuality in Renaissance England*. London: Gay Men's Press, 1982.

Carabine, Jean. "Heterosexuality and Social Policy." *Theorising Heterosexuality*. Ed. Diane Richardson. Philadelphia: Open University Press, 1996. 55–74.

Devor, Holly. "Becoming Members of Society: Learning the Social Meanings of Gender." *Gender Blending: Confronting the Limits of Duality*. English 200 packet.

Foucault, Michel. *The History of Sexuality*. Trans. Robert Hurley. New York: Pantheon Books, 1978.

Ingraham, Chrys. "The Heterosexual Imaginary: Feminist Sociology and Theories of Gender." *Queer Theory/Sociology*. Ed. Steven Seidman. Massachusetts: Blackwell Publishers Ltd., 1996. 168–193.

Jagose, Annamarie. *An Introduction to Queer Theory*. New York: New York University Press, 1996.

Kranz, Rachel and Tim Cusick. *Gay Rights*. New York: Facts on File Inc., 2000.

Lorber, Judith. "The Social Construction of Gender." *Women's Lives: Multicultural Perspectives*. Eds. Gwyn Kirk and Margo Okazawa-Rey. California: Mayfield Publishing Company, 2001. 20–24.

Maasik, Sonia, and Jack Solomon. "We've Come a Long Way, Maybe." *Signs of Life in the U.S.A.: Readings on Popular Culture for Writers*. 3rd ed. Boston: Bedford/St. Martin's, 2000. 437–446.

McCormick, C.M. and Witelson, S.F. "A Cognitive Profile of Homosexual Men Compared to Heterosexual Men and Women." *Psychoneuroendocrinology*. Chicago: University of Chicago Press, 1991. 459–473.

Robinson, Paul. "Freud and Homosexuality." *Homosexuality and Psychology*. Eds. Tim Dean and Christopher Lane. Chicago: University of Chicago Press, 2001. 91–97.

Thomas, Calvin. "Straight with a Twist: Queer Theory and the Subject of Heterosexuality." *The Gay 90s: Disciplinary and Interdisciplinary Formations in Queer Studies*. Eds. Thomas Foster, Carol Siegel, and Ellen E. Berry. New York: New York University Press, 1997.


---

## This Text: Reading

1. Notice the way Mehta mixes the personal with the observational with the analytical while researching. What about this approach makes this a successful paper? Is it an approach you think you can imitate in your own work?

2. Compare this article to Katherine Gantz's piece on *Seinfeld*. What differences do you notice between the two works? How does each work discuss what it means to be gay or lesbian? What differences in the piece have to with the authors of the pieces or the shows themselves?
3. What other shows might benefit from the approach that Mehta takes? What "lenses" (queer theory, race theory, gender theory, etc.) might you put on in order to write about television or other popular culture media?
4. Why does this piece in itself make a case for television's importance as a text to be studied?

## YOUR TEXT: WRITING

1. Find a television show that you feel has social issues attached to it—even if those issues are not immediately apparent. Watch the show, take notes, and then do an analysis of the work.
2. Do a compare and contrast of two shows that engage similar issues (examples could be *NYPD Blue* and *Law and Order* or *Third Watch* or *Seinfeld* and *Will and Grace* or *Friends*).
3. Write a paper which ties your own experience to a show you are fond of.

# *The Simpsons* Suite

Now on television for more than a decade, and its permanence assured by a prominent place in syndication, *The Simpsons* is like no other show on television. It's a cartoon that's both a sitcom and very much a cartoon. It satirizes everything in its sight, including itself, in a way few shows have ever done—especially in prime time. And yet it is exactly like other shows on television—it stars a family in a small town, whose problems are ultimately resolved in the sitcom manner week after week. Some argue that it's this tension between fantasy and reality, dark humor and family resolution that gives the show its edge and its appeal.

Because it takes on so many targets and takes liberty with a number of television conventions, *The Simpsons* has drawn a lot of critical attention. In this suite, writers examine the show from a number of different contexts. Les Sillars writes about the show's relationship to modern Christianity (1991), Jaime Weinman writes about the relationship between fans and *The Simpsons* over the very viewer-friendly Internet (2000), Anne Waldron Neumann talks about the relationship between kids and *The Simpsons* from an Australian viewpoint (1996), while Peter Parisi analyzes the phenomenon of the "Black Bart" T-shirt (1993).

## THE LAST CHRISTIAN TV FAMILY IN AMERICA

Les Sillars

IN AN OLDER EPISODE of the animated television series *The Simpsons*, Marge, the mother, is trying to tell her deplorable husband Homer that she is pregnant with their third child. "Can't talk now—praying," he interrupts. "Dear Lord, the gods have been good to me and I am thankful. For the first time in my life everything is absolutely perfect the way it is. So here's the deal: you freeze everything as it is and I won't ask for anything more. If that is OK, please give me absolutely no sign. [pause] OK, deal. In gratitude, I present to you this offering of cookies and milk. If you want me to eat them for you, please give me no sign. [pause] Thy will be done."

It may be hard to believe, but *The Simpsons* is the most religious show on prime-time television, according to Gerry Bowler, a philosophy professor at Canadian Nazarene College in Calgary and the chairman of the Centre for the Study of Christianity and Contemporary Culture. In a symposium entitled "The Media and Family Values" two weeks ago, Prof. Bowler contended that the show "takes religion's place in society seriously enough to do it the honour of making fun of it." Despite its legitimate criticisms the show is trashed among the faithful, he contended, because they don't get its satirical humour.

Prof. Bowler says that he forbade his daughters to watch the show, until one time he caught them at it and they insisted that he watch a couple of episodes. He discovered that practically all the characters are religious and most attend the First Church of Springfield. The Bible is referred to frequently. Typical example: the Simpsons argue over whether they should allow Otto, the emotionally-retarded, metalhead school bus driver, to stay in their house. Marge says, "Doesn't the Bible say, 'Whatsoever you do to the least of my brothers, that you do unto me'?" Stuck for a reply, Homer stammers, "Yes, but doesn't the Bible also say, 'Thou shalt not take... moochers into thy... hut'?"

"Prayer of all kinds abounds on *The Simpsons*," continued Prof. Bowler. Take, for example, the famous mealtime offering by Bart Simpson, the glib but basically good-hearted 10-year-old anarchist and vandal: "Dear God, we paid for all this stuff ourselves, so thanks for nothing." When Bart sells his soul to a friend for $5, thinking he was taking advantage of a chump, he becomes uneasy and wants it back only to discover his friend has already traded it for Pogs. "Are you there, God?" he prays in desperation. "I'm afraid some weirdo's got my soul."

More strikingly, however, honest prayer almost always works. God knocks down a pin for the all-Christian bowling team, the Holy Rollers. When Homer pleads, "God, if you really are a God, you'll get me tickets to that football game," the doorbell rings immediately and there is Ned Flanders, the goody-two-shoes evangelical next-door neighbour, offering tickets.

People pray on *The Simpsons* because the characters understand that God, the Devil, Heaven, Hell and angels are real, observed Prof. Bowler. After a traffic accident, Bart is denied entrance to Heaven for not hanging onto the escalator handrail and for spitting over the edge on the way up. When Bart gets to Hell, the Devil has to confess there's been a mistake. "Boy, is my face red," says Satan. In another episode, Homer sells his soul to the Devil for a doughnut. In a parody of *The Devil and Daniel Webster*, Marge wins it back at a trial by showing Homer had already romantically pledged his soul to her.

*The Simpsons* has perfectly legitimate barbs to launch about Christian judgmentalism and hypocrisy, continued Prof. Bowler. When Ned enters church after being arrested for a traffic offense, he is greeted with whispering voices: "There he is, Ned Flanders, the fallen one," and "The evil one," and "Bet he's the one who wrote 'Homer' all over the bathroom." Although Reverend Lovejoy preaches against "Gambling: the Eighth Deadly Sin," his church holds Bingo, Reno and Monte Carlo Nights.

The Simpsons writers also cast a satirical eye on the too-good-to-be-true Christian family life, represented by the Flanders, without glorifying or excusing the unexemplary lives of the Simpsons. The Flanders children play "Clothe the Leper" and "Build the Mission." Ned and Maude go to a marriage counselor because, as Ned explains, "Sometimes Maude, God bless her, she underlines passages in my Bible when she can't find hers." When one of the children swears, Ned sends him off to bed without a Bible story, causing him to cry. Maude asks if he isn't being a bit harsh and Ned replies, "You knew I had a temper when you married me."

In fact Ned Flanders, according to Prof. Bowler, is "television's most effective [non-angelic] exponent of a Christian life well-lived." Moreover, Bart and Homer always lose, good triumphs, family values are affirmed and the best character in the show is an evangelical.

So why don't Christians like it? For one thing, said Prof. Bowler, alluding to the long-standing belief among some that Jesus never laughed, there is often a tension between religion and humour. Besides, "the ideologically-charged believer on any side of a question finds humour difficult to deal with."

That is why many atheists don't much care for *The Simpsons* either. On one Internet chat group Dr. Bowler visited last year, an atheist wrote that the show is "more of a Sunday School program than ever. The central message of the show, I've noticed, is that the only good people are religious and that those who are not are immoral. I stopped watching it in disgust a long time ago." Another atheist, quoting a character on the show, complained that it "puts the fun back in fundamentalism."

Moreover, "*The Simpsons* is unquestionably the most culturally literate show on television, except for perhaps *Jeopardy*," said Prof. Bowler. Many Christians are not informed enough to catch the allusions to film, rock and roll, literature, politics, history, philosophy and television, he said. They don't get the jokes, leaving behind only "images of a drunken father trying to strangle his rude little boy. Who, indeed, would want to watch that?"

Not everyone agrees the show is particularly sympathetic to religion. "They deal with spiritual issues from time to time in the same irreverent fashion they deal with everything else," says Thomas Johnson, senior writer at the Media Research Center in Virginia. He pegs *Touched by an Angel* as the program most supportive of faith. As for whether the show draws animosity because people don't get the jokes, "I would think that's fair to say about any sort of satire, even more so with *The Simpsons* because it is a cartoon."

Even Prof. Bowler admits that the show is popular in many circles because Bart "is a character that says, 'Eat my shorts' and so [fans] get to wear a T-shirt that says, 'Eat my shorts'." Despite this, he contends the show is not particularly harmful, even for children. "I don't think *The Simpsons* is healthy, either," he adds. "It's a case of where if you're a mature Christian and you get all the jokes, you could watch it."

## WORST EPISODE EVER

Jaime J. Weinman

**Milhouse:** We gotta spread this stuff around. Let's put it on the Internet!
**Bart:** No! We have to reach people whose opinions actually matter!

—*From* The Simpsons *episode "Wild Barts Can't Be Broken," 1998*

AFTER 10 YEARS, *The Simpsons* remains one of the most critically acclaimed shows on TV. You'll find it on the "best" list of almost every TV critic, along with words of praise for staying irreverent and funny after all these years.

But if you turn to alt.tv.simpsons, the show's Internet discussion group, it's as if a different show is being talked about. New episodes are routinely panned and held up as evidence that *The Simpsons* has been vulgarized and cheapened. For example, the reviews for this season's opening episode (the one with Mel Gibson) include phrases like "a weak offering of recycled themes," "not many laughs" and, best of all, "I think Homer was hired as a script consultant for this episode."

The most interesting and articulate contributors to the group—the ones who can actually spell and punctuate—are the ones who argue most passionately that the show has, in the words of fan Ondre Lombard, "turned into a cold, cynical, anything-for-a-joke series with one-dimensional characters." The harshest critics regularly open their missives with the tagline "Worst episode ever."

Of course, all long-running shows get accused of having lost it, and nowhere more so than on Internet newsgroups. TV writers who read the newsgroups—and many of them do for the immediate feedback it provides—sometimes become frustrated with these dedicated but hypercritical fans. For example, Larry David once said that he stopped reading *Seinfeld*-related posts when every new episode started being pointed to as a sign of the show's decline.

The difference with *The Simpsons* is that the writers of the show have sometimes struck back—in interviews, and even on the show itself. The most obvious dig at the fans came in a scene in the episode that first aired Feb. 9, 1997. It began with the still-unnamed Comic Book Guy saying: "Last night's 'Itchy & Scratchy' was, without a doubt, the worst episode ever. Rest assured that I was on the Internet within minutes, registering my disgust throughout the world. As a loyal viewer," he added, "I feel they owe me."

"What?" said Bart. "They've given you thousands of hours of entertainment for free. What could they possibly owe you? If anything, you owe them."

The Comic Book Guy's answer: "Worst episode ever."

The scene was a hilarious, slightly cruel kiss-off from the writers to the Internet fans, one that pretty much ended any rapport that might have existed between one group and the other.

Back in 1993, writer Bill Oakley was sending friendly e-mail messages to selected *Simpsons* enthusiasts; by 1997, Oakley was telling *Time Out* magazine about Internet fans who "take [the show] too seriously to the point of absurdity." And in 1998, producer Ian Maxtone-Graham, interviewed by the London Independent, referred to "the beetle-browed people on the Internet," adding: "They see everything as part of a vast plan.... That's why they're on the Internet and we're writing the show." (Some of the more bitter alt.tv.simpsons regulars have taken to calling him "Ian Haxtone-Graham" in retaliation.)

It's hard not to be a little sympathetic to the writers on this. "The producers [of a show] need to pay attention to feedback from the viewers," says TV programming consultant Marc Berman. "But they can't agree with all of it." Also, most of the feedback the *Simpsons* writers have been getting has, in fact, been positive: The ratings and the TV critics are both telling them that they're doing a fine job. But for some of the Net fans, this success and acclaim is one of the problems with the show as it now stands; they feel it's made the show's creative team lazy and self-satisfied.

As alt.tv.simpsons regular Ben Collins wrote: "The staff believes its own hype. When *TV Guide* says 'The Simpsons' is better than ever... the producers run with it, and drag the show through the same rut it's been in for two seasons."

But why are these Internet reviewers so much tougher on the show than the professional critics? Well, what *critics* usually praise about *The Simpsons* is its irreverence toward everything crass and crazy in American culture, its harsh satire. The die-hard fans tend to be more interested in the characters as people than as vehicles for social criticism. While they enjoy the satire, above all they see *The Simpsons* as a character comedy, at its best when most compassionate toward the flawed-but-lovable Simpson family. Many of these fans cite the early "Lisa's Substitute"—the Dustin Hoffman episode, and the most serious and poignant *Simpsons* episode of all—as a favorite.

It's this element of compassion that fans find lacking in the recent flood of "wacky" episodes; to quote Lombard, in the last few seasons "the satire tends to forsake character realism. Stories these days don't tend to deal with the... feelings of the characters." Emotionally affecting episodes have been rare of late, as *The Simpsons* has placed more emphasis on cartoony action.

Almost every episode now seems to end with some sort of violent action climax. Already this season, Homer survived an assassination attempt by a horde of evil restaurant owners, the kids torched a pile of evil robot toys and the whole family was attacked by rampaging farm animals. Some fans point to these outlandish plots as evidence that creator Matt Groening's original rule for the show—that *The Simpsons* would never do anything a real, non-cartoon family wouldn't do—has been violated.

To the TV critics, what matters most is that the show is still taking on the big cultural targets; the fans are quicker to object when a joke, however nervy, gets in the way of the characterization—or worse, when characterization is violated for the sake of an easy joke. In the ninth-season episode "Bart Star," Lisa showed up at football tryouts, expecting to stir up controversy and fight discrimination against women in sports. When she discovered that the team already had three female members, she lost interest and left; she didn't care about football, just about taking up a new cause. It was a nice bit of self-parody, but many fans saw it as a betrayal of the character, an indication that the writers had misread Lisa's personality, turning her from a sweet girl with a social conscience into a self-righteous, preachy troublemaker.

You could say that this kind of attitude is presumptuous for supposing that fans know more about the characters than the writers do. Certainly some of the writers have seen it that way; in one of the episode capsules, a longtime fan recalls getting a private e-mail from a *Simpsons* writer saying "that he cares more about Lisa than any 'abject admirer of Lisa Simpson.'"

The fans could counter by pointing out that just because someone writes for a show doesn't mean he's necessarily in a position to understand what the show was originally like. In that notorious interview, Maxtone-Graham admitted that he had hardly ever watched *The Simpsons* before he was hired. The current executive producer, Mike Scully, didn't join the show until the fifth season, when, in the opinion of some fans, its humor had already started to shift toward simple cartooniness, and Homer had started to dominate the show.

Which brings us to one of the most often-used phrases on alt.tv.simpsons, "Jerkass Homer." This refers to a new characterization of Homer that has supposedly become prevalent in recent seasons, a Homer who is not simply dumb but disgusting and semi-sociopathic. This is the Homer who, in the season opener, showed Mel Gibson his wife's wedding ring and said, "It's a symbol of our marriage, signifying that I own her." Fan Dale G. Abersold wrote, "This new Homer displays only three characteristics: lust, greed, and stupidity. Yes, [the] old Homer was lustful, he was greedy, he was dumb...but he was so much more. Can you imagine the current Homer thrust into the classic episodes of the first two seasons?"

Well, maybe you can, at that; despite the implication that Homer has become more boorish over the years, it's hard to imagine a bigger jerkass than the Homer of the show's first couple of seasons, the Homer who told Bart, "Always make fun of those different from you." The difference, perhaps, is that the early Homer usually had to apologize for his behavior, learning how to be a better husband and father. (Even if he usually forgot these lessons by the time the next episode started.) As Homer began to replace Bart as the show's great cultural icon, the writers seemed to become more indulgent toward his antics; follies he would once have learned a lesson from are now seen as kind of cute, by the writers and by the wider public that made Homer a TV hero of the '90s.

You could argue, then, that the characters haven't changed so much as the attitudes that inform the way the characters are written—that *The Simpsons* is different because the producers and the public expect different things of it. Or you could argue that nothing has changed at all, as Scully did in a recent interview: "You can sit down and watch an episode we did 10 years ago or one we did last year and the characters are still the same."

But whatever you think, and whatever *The Simpsons* might become in the next couple of seasons, the alt.tv.simpsons regulars will keep writing, disappointed with what the show has become—still devoted to what it used to be.

## THE SIMPSONS

Anne Waldron Neumann

A FRONT-PAGE ARTICLE in the Melbourne *Age* (13th September 1996) reported that the American cartoon program *The Simpsons* is still, nearly seven years after its debut, among Australia's most-watched children's television shows, receiving "unconditional approval from an overwhelming majority of children surveyed." These children know that *The Simpsons* is "not primarily aimed at a child audience," but its "more adult themes" increase their enjoyment because they are "presented in a way that children thought could be easily understood." The same *Age* article reported the results of another survey, however: *The Simpsons* is the show most Australian parents forbid their children. What is going on here? Why is one of children's most loved shows most hated by their parents?

Love and hate may well focus on Bart Simpson, the cartoon's ten-year-old hell-raising anti-hero. In every title sequence, Bart stays after school to write twenty times on the blackboard: "I will not expose the ignorance of the faculty," "'Bart Bucks' are not legal tender," "I will not belch the national anthem." But what do these sentences mean to older if not younger viewers? Since *The Simpsons* is an American show, Australian parents may have cross-cultural reasons for their dislike: perhaps *The Simpsons* portrays a crudeness and a materialism Australians associate with what they least admire in American culture. Or perhaps Australian parents have more global misgivings: *The Simpsons* encourages immorality, aggression, and disrespect for authority, whether these qualities are peculiarly American or not. One thing *is* clear, however: Australian parents think fictions matter. Fictions—made-up stories—matter because, while some fictional television shows may be beneficial, others—perhaps including *The Simpsons*—are not.

Now when academics like me, who specialize in the political and moral uses of fiction, hear that fiction is important, our ears prick up. Fiction is important? Oh wow, I knew it! I always knew it. Fiction has social consequences after all! If some fictions harm, then others may heal.

How do we define harm, however? What complicates such discussions is that our definitions of harm vary. Today most of us would define inciting aggression and violence as harm. But some of us also feel uneasy about fictions that encourage disrespect for socially accepted or politically legitimated authority. Others think some social authorities *should* be delegitimised rather than blindly accepted—that Bart *should* expose the faculty's ignorance—and that fiction can do this important cultural work.

Once we have defined harm for ourselves, moreover, a still harder question arises: How can we *know* that fictional narratives actually do the harm they seem to threaten? Are they sufficient to change social behaviour in themselves, or do they depend on the larger social context to reinforce them? Do violent television shows really incite violence, for example? The jury seems to be out on this one. Though many viewers watch violence without becoming violent, current evidence suggests that for some violent people, some of the time, some violent shows are associated with violent behaviour.

Perhaps the hardest question of all, finally, is whether any given show falls within this or some other harmful category. Does whatever violence *The Simpsons* depicts increase the violence of its viewers, for example? In fact, *The Simpsons* addresses this question directly. Every afternoon after school, Bart, Lisa and their friends gather before their respective televisions to watch *The Itchy and Scratchy Show*, a cartoon-within-a-cartoon. As its theme song promises, the perpetually warring cat and mouse who are the show's central characters "Fight, fight, fight, scratch, scratch, scratch" their way through every episode. And, after seeing Itchy hit Scratchy with a mallet, Bart and Lisa's baby sister brains her father Homer with his own hammer. Appalled, the children's mother Marge lobbies to tone down Itchy and Scratchy's violence. Reduced to offering each other lemonade instead of lignite, Itchy and Scratchy lose their audience. All up and down Bart and Lisa's street, children simultaneously open their front doors on an idyllic world of golden afternoon sunshine, the songs of nesting birds, and the allure of forgotten playground equipment. For one brief moment, they enjoy the childhood of communal outdoor play we grownups remember (except that I personally—I don't know about you—spent many of *my* afternoons listening to children's programs on the radio). Inevitably, of course, Itchy and Scratchy set down the sweet pitcher tinkling with ice and amity to resume their blowtorches and chainsaws. (Marge learns that local wowsers have banned Michelangelo's David from Springfield's museum because it has a you-know-what and decides her campaign against Itchy and Scratchy was really censorship.)

But that *The Itchy and Scratchy Show* is a cartoon-within-a-cartoon suggests something important about how *The Simpsons* works. It constantly reflects—and thus reflects on—popular culture. Bart and Lisa watch Itchy and Scratchy, really a show-within-a-show-within-a-show, on *The Krusty the Klown Show*, just as I watched *Our Gang* comedies on *The Howdy Doody Show* as a child in the American fifties. Australian children may recognise Sylvester and Tweety Bird or Road Runner and Wile E. Coyote in Itchy and Scratchy. And adults may see, in the brouhaha about Michelangelo's David, the American controversy over exhibiting Robert Mapplethorpe's photographs. Thus *The Simpsons* allows children to *own* their media consumption. It allows them to reflect on whether shows like *The Simpsons* influence their behaviour, just as Itchy and Scratchy may or may not influence Bart and Lisa as well as their baby sister Maggie.

In fact, children own their media consumption on *The Simpsons* so thoroughly that, in one episode, Bart and Lisa write successful episodes for *The Itchy and Scratchy Show*. In their first script, Itchy, a barber, smears Scratchy's head with honey and releases fire ants: Scratchy is not just shorn or scalped; he is flensed—reduced to a clacking skeleton. Children, it seems, have even more violent imaginations than *Itchy and Scratchy*'s adult scriptwriters. There is nothing scriptwriters can devise, this episode suggests, that children haven't imagined before them.

Is this invitation to reflect on their media consumption partly why children like *The Simpsons*? Certainly my ten-year-old daughter, encouraged by this invitation, has developed, among her other drawing styles, the ability to imagine new situations within *The Simpsons'* cartoon world. Inspired too by Archie Andrews comics about American teenagers (my own favorite reading at a similar age), Hannah depicts various pre-teen members of the "I Hate Bart Club" giving their reasons for hating Bart. One of Hannah's pictures not only recalls how many Australian parents are members of the "I Hate Bart Club" but also suggests that children like my daughter, though devoted fans, can understand and acknowledge such ambivalence.

Though a parent myself, I admire Bart's inner-child in-your-face sass more than Archie Andrews' 1950s acquiescence. Wouldn't we rather our children said, "Eat my shorts!"—one of Bart's famous tag lines—than swallow their discontent or voice it with the cruder alternatives we can all imagine? Mightn't allowing children to vent their disrespect relatively mildly actually promote respect? I fault Archie Andrews comics, moreover, because they misled me about the real life of high school. I expected dates, dances, hamburgers, new outfits, and no homework. On the positive side, however, I approached high school with real enthusiasm. And I remember my one year at a large government high school no better than I remember Archie's spinster-teacher Miss Grundy, his principal Mr. Weatherby, and afternoons with Jughead and Moose down at Pop's soda shop. To me, in other words, Archie Andrews inhabited something like a real world. Today's children identify less and judge more. They seem to decide more easily where *The Simpsons* reflects real life, and where it does not.

In other words, *The Simpsons* encourages children to be postmodern about their television viewing, nearly as postmodern as academics discussing fictional constructedness, intertextuality, and metafiction or self-reflexivity, some buzz words of postmodernity. For intertextuality (a text's relationship to other texts) and self-reflexivity, see *Itchy and Scratchy*. And for acknowledging fictional constructedness, what can beat my daughter constructing her own fictions based on *The Simpsons*?

These traits, intertextuality and conscious fictionality, characterize much older literature and thus cannot be exclusively postmodern, of course.

But that today's children are more self-reflective and post-modern about their media consumption than their non-academic parents was confirmed for me by the children who reviewed Disney's *Hunchback of Notre Dame* for Melbourne's *Age* (September 12th). Their responses were most sophisticated. Michael Masters, eleven, did not say the movie was sad, for example. He said he sometimes "felt like crying because the writers made it so sad." Katherine Russell, twelve, agreed—not that the film was funny or sad but that it "really *drags you into* the humour, the sadness, the excitement, and the joy." Several children praised the computer graphics. Others saw that the film was intended to teach how gypsies have been persecuted but that it presented Esmeralda as a powerful female role model, "a really good moral" according to Ruth Malloy, twelve. Humphrey Hughes, eight, missed this latter point, proving that fictions don't always have their intended moral effect but confirming that children realize fictions are *constructed*. Humphrey found Esmeralda much stronger than the king's guards and thus not "very much like a girl": Disney's *Hunchback* was poor fiction, Humphrey concluded—poor in the sense of unbelievable—because Esmeralda was "a bit too clever for a girl."

These youthful critics' awareness of fiction's constructedness, their postmodern distance, their less willing suspension of disbelief, may explain why many children today find movies less scary or disturbing than we adults did at their age. When my younger brother and I were six and seven, our mother took us to see the original *Hunchback of Notre Dame* in a small country town in New Mexico. The movie was already in progress, and Gordie and I walked down the aisle together while our mother bought the tickets. We were halfway down, as I remember it, when Charles Laughton turned to face the camera. Gordie and I got a good look at his hump, at one eye scrunched up under the bony ridge of his brow, and the other pushed down to his cheekbone. With one accord, we wheeled around and marched back up the aisle and out into the sunshine, leaving our mother to argue with the woman in the ticket booth about why she should be given her money back. No fictional constructedness for me and Gordie. No ability to tell ourselves that Charles Laughton's dreadful eyes were make-up, that a leather brace and prosthesis produced his painfully contorted posture, that *writers* made the movie scary or sad. If we adults find *The Simpsons* disturbing, we should remember that our children may not.

We adults were not totally backward as children, of course, not totally unworthy of comparison with Bart: though my brother, now a graduate of Harvard and Chicago Law School and for many years an idealistic poverty lawyer, never belched our national anthem, I was enraptured by his tunefully burped Taps, the melancholy bugle call that announces sundown on American military bases. But, for better or worse, today's children are forwarder than we were. Does the postmodern awareness of the *Age*'s youthful critics suggest that, if children are less scared by scary movies, they may also be more immune to fiction's moral messages? Walt Disney said he would rather entertain and thereby perhaps teach than teach and maybe entertain. But if children see, as twelve-year-old Ruth Malloy did, that *The Hunchback*'s moral message is a moral message, will they still swallow it, sugar-coated or not? Their refusal would be a loss indeed to anyone interested in the positive political and moral power of fiction. But it might also influence how some cartoons today deliver their messages.

Disney's *Hunchback* contains some satire, but many of its moral messages are presented to youthful viewers using positive examples: *do* show the strength of an Esmeralda, the selflessness of a Quasimodo. *The Simpsons* is more exclusively satiric. Many more of its moral and social messages are presented in reverse: *don't* imitate Itchy and Scratchy; hesitate, at least, before whole-heartedly admiring Bart's smart-ass disrespect. Maybe such satirical messages-in-reverse work better with our postmodern children. Like Bart writing on the blackboard, "I will not belch the national anthem," this late-twentieth-century descendant of eighteenth-century realist satire shows youthful viewers follies and vices to avoid. How could you make so many points about environmental contamination in a children's comedy, for example, than by featuring, as *The Simpsons* does in Homer, an insensitive, doughnut-loving oaf who is also safety inspector in a nuclear power plant?

*The Simpsons* not only identifies follies and vices to avoid clearly enough for most children today. It may dismay adult viewers because it acknowledges follies and imperfections in even apparently ideal families. For example, *The Simpsons* offers Homer's oafish perspective on his nearly-perfect, determinedly-cheerful next-door-neighbour Ned Flanders—he of the "okely-dokely" and "Heidey-ho, neighbor!" Ned Flanders is a Christian in the current American sense: his sons *never* watch *Itchy and Scratchy* and play no game racier than "Name that Bible Passage." *The Simpsons* is thus the only American show to make fun of the Christian right and get away with it. I find Ned both very sympathetic *and* very sympathetically treated, as the *Age*'s youthful critics might express it. But I can see why Homer detests a neighbor who shows up his all-too-human meanness. And I certainly understand why even Ned's pastor is peeved when Ned phones in the wee hours to discuss his endless moral scruples.

*The Simpsons* acknowledges, in short, that Ned's monocultural fundamentalism won't work for everyone. And it is determinedly multicultural, which I find a plus. Yet it manages to poke fun at some sacred cows of political correctness. Take the show's African-American doctor, for example. When Bart is born (we see in a flashback) Dr. Julius Hibberd sports an Afro and dashiki and, because Homer is temporarily absent, gives Marge a congratulatory pamphlet, "So You've Decided to Ruin Your Life!" (a neat comment on the single parenthood that troubles poor communities especially and a chance for *all* watching parents to vent their ambivalence). Dr. Hibberd's career has prospered, however. In the show's "now," he wears three-piece gray suits and has become socialized as the typical hurried and uncaring American doctor. That is, a member of the ethnic group lowest in the American pecking order is shown to have achieved both professional upper-middle-class status and the same damned insensitivity as everyone else.

Despite such satire, *The Simpsons* is not *just* satire, however. At this point in my essay, *a propos* the fun made of Ned Flanders and Dr. Hibberd, I ask my danghter whether *The Simpsons* has any positive moral messages. "Definitely," Hannah assures me, "it has about a million moral messages." Her immediate example: Homer thinks the grass is always greener on the other side of the fence (Ned Flanders' infuriatingly manicured lawn is on the other side of Homer's fence), but all people are different and must be respected as such.

Alas, Homer himself represents a group recently "different" and less respected: embattled white male blue-collar Americans who may suddenly lose their factory jobs and health-care benefits, leaving their wives to work minimum-wage jobs without benefits in fast-food outlets or convenience stores. These other-people's-grass-is-always-greener Homers of America and Australia—the poor working stiffs, the worryingly disaffected white males—seem most susceptible to the racist, nationalist and anti-government paranoias I discussed in a recent essay on "*The X Files* and the Longing for Belief" (*Quadrant*, September). (*The Simpsons* even flirts with the post-colonial issue of formerly colonised peoples re-invading the imperial center: when Marge convinces Homer he has neglected Lisa for Bart, Homer himself applies for that second job in a convenience store so he can buy Lisa a pony. "Yes!" cries Apu, the Kwik-E-Mart's Indian owner, "I always wanted to have one of Them working for Me!")

Nevertheless, Homer largely avoids racist, nationalist and anti-government paranoias. How is this possible? Partly Homer avoids these paranoias because *The Simpsons*' writers *want* him to. Their hearts are in the politically-correct, multicultural place. But how do they imagine he *can* avoid them? Could *The Simpsons* teach moral lessons not just to watching children but to the wider culture?

Homer is saved from overwhelming fear and envy by the nearly constant affection and support of his wife Marge. (Homer and Marge even have an enthusiastic sex life, disabusing our children of the notion that we adults "did it" as many times as we have children and then stopped.) Marge is not perfect: she holds her family together but is sometimes pushed to the edge. Marge is thus what psychiatry calls the "good-enough mother," nearly always available to her children, teaching them they can indeed influence the world around them, but not so totally available that she unfits them for real life whose slings and arrows our children cannot always deflect.

Marge is not only an affectionate and supportive wife and mother, however. She is also much closer than Homer to America's middle class. She is a social activist, for example (witness her campaign to subdue Itchy and Scratchy), and she brings her family the new tidings of feminism and positive parenting (see her advocacy for bright but neglected Lisa). The biggest problem I find in *The Simpsons* as a middle-class American wife myself is why Marge stays with Homer. The biggest problem I find as a would-be-politically-correct commentator is why blue-collar Homer is depicted as so nearly irredeemable, a lovable slob but still a slob. But I still admire Marge for staying with him. By her loyalty, Marge stands in *The Simpsons* for the support women can offer men, and for solidarity between the middle and working classes. Her affection assures Homer that she will help him adjust to today's changing gender roles. And her faith that they will always manage financially assures Homer of her support during economic downturn.

Marge thus models a more cohesive society. If women, without conceding their feminist demands, could help men understand and accept them, if the middle class could assure workers of support while adjusting to changing labor conditions (for example, by supporting tax incentives to companies who do not downsize), our world would be closer to the golden sunshine, birdsong and communal endeavor the show's children experience when Itchy and Scratchy drop their animosity. If what parents dislike about *The Simpsons* is its acknowledgment of social imperfections, we can learn from our children that acknowledging imperfection need not stop us striving for perfection. In fact, we will stop striving unless we acknowledge imperfections.

I started this essay by discussing the harm fiction like *The Simpsons* might do. But I end by agreeing with my daughter. *The Simpsons* offers a million moral messages, enough to instruct any child or even any adult attracted by the show's entertainment value. How does *The Simpsons* score on discussing specific adult themes like the pleasures of wine, women and song, or—let us say—the dangers of booze, babes and blackjack? Wine is hardly a problem for any major *Simpsons* character: Marge gets tiddly only occasionally; Homer sticks to a few beers at Mo's Tavern after work and a few more in the fridge at home; and *The Simpsons'* resident lush Barney could never entice children to follow his example (*he* belches *everything*, not just the national anthem). As for sexual temptations, both Marge and Homer contemplate adultery in separate episodes; both resist. And I defy Victorian politicians to demonstrate more clearly the evils of gambling (a working-class curse especially) than *The Simpsons'* ruthless industrialist who, in one episode, re-invests his nuclear power plant's profits in a casino: "I have discovered the perfect business," Montgomery Burns gloats. "People rush in, empty their pockets, and scurry out!"

Mr. Burns thus forgets that workers like Homer must be accepted and supported rather than exploited. In fact, Homer resembles a cartoon Archie Bunker minus the racism. Like Homer, Archie, an American television icon of the 1970s, was a blue-collar working stiff with an unfailingly supportive wife (Edith) and a socially aware younger family member like Lisa: the only character in Archie's life with advanced ideas was the son-in-law he persisted in calling "Meathead." But Archie was never persuaded by Meathead's arguments, as Homer is by Marge's affection. "You catch more flies with honey than with vinegar," we know, and Meathead was too vinegary. But Edith, in most episodes, was too much honey. Unlike Marge, she seldom countered her husband, and brought to her marriage less new social awareness. During the show's tide sequence, she and Archie harmonised at the piano in praise of the good old days. As I remember the words:

> People knew where they were then.
> Girls were girls, and men were men.
> Mister, we could use a man
> Like Herbert Hoover again.
> Didn't need no welfare state.
> Folks like us, they had it made.
> Gee, our old La Salle ran great.
> Those were the days!

Today we provide social welfare—if not a welfare *state*—for those *not* "like us" who don't have it made. And Archie Bunkers and Homer Simpsons are no longer like "us." Yet the title of the Archie Bunker show, *All in the Family*, insists that Archies and Homers are part of the American or Australian family and must be accepted and assimilated. Marge's love for Homer not only models solidarity across genders and classes. Because she recognises Homer's imperfections, her love will last longer. *The Simpsons* not only acknowledges imperfections in our own, or even in the larger human family. It teaches us that slight *perfections* can be found—as they can in Homer—even in those we believe most imperfect. I can't think of a better recipe for social cohesion.

## "BLACK BART" SIMPSON: APPROPRIATION AND REVITALIZATION IN COMMODITY CULTURE[1]

Peter Parisi

DURING THE SUMMER OF 1990, the streets of cities across the country witnessed a striking and unusual gesture in popular culture: the appropriation and re-interpretation of a mass media figure by minority group members. That summer, *The Simpsons*, a crudely drawn television cartoon that itself portrayed the cultural impact of mass media upon ideals of family and small-town life, had completed a hit season. A merchandising blitz followed up on the success, flooding stores and streets with T-shirts depicting Matt Groening's highly publicized characters: the militant under-achiever Bart Simpson; his feckless and juvenile father Homer; patient, long-suffering mother Marge; and two sisters, bright, sensitive Lisa and, wide-eyed baby Maggie who perpetually and noisily sucks a pacifier.

The summer was not far advanced, however, before innumerable blacks, men and women, young and middle-aged, appeared in cities nationwide, wearing T-shirts adorned with the bootlegged image of Bart but now dark-skinned and posed in a variety of black identities.[2] Fusing Air Jordan and MC Hammer, "Air Bart" slam dunks a basketball and says, "you can't touch this." Home Boy Bart inquires pugnaciously, "Yo, homeboy, what the hell are you looking at?" "Rastabert, Master of Respect" sprouts dreadlocks, sports a red, green and gold headband and growls, "Watch it, Mon. 'Irie'," or, in a variation on the Rastafarian theme, becomes "Rasta-Dude Bart Marley" or "RastaBart." On other shirts, Black Bart and white Bart shake hands; Black Bart appears alongside Nelson Mandela, saying "Apartheid. No!" or "My Hero!" and Black Bart insists, "I didn't do it." "Asiatic Bart" wears the robes and skull cap of a Black Muslim and, borrowing the group's rhetoric, declares himself "Cream of the Planet Earth, Dude!" Bedecked with gold chain and snazzy sneakers, Black Bart glares from another shirt that reads, "You should understand," playing on another Afrocentric T-shirt motto: "It's a Black thing. You wouldn't understand." Still another shirt mixes a pacific message with a glaring Bart, joined by sister Lisa and a graphic of the African continent. The message read, "It's cool being black" and in a box beneath, "We are all brothers and sisters so live in unity, love and peace" (118).

One striking, scatological variant suggests how pungently these graphic figures could embody and play with social meanings. Across its top, the shirt carries the legend, "Crack Kills" and across the bottom "Black Power." Pictured between is a discomfited "white" Bart clenched between the buttocks of a sizable black woman with wavy hair and purple toenails. The shirt was striking in its irreverent treatment of phrases and terms—Crack Kills, Black Power—usually regarded as too solemn for parody.

Prices for the bootlegs in the summer of 1990 ranged from six to ten dollars, and dropped to five the following summer as the craze faded and authorities clamped down on copyright violations in the fashion industry. The total number of shirts sold is virtually impossible to determine. Obviously, no industry figures were kept. Nor would it be easy to enumerate all the designs. Unlicensed as they were, the bootleggers could freely crib, modify or invent ideas. At least two versions of the "Air Bart/'You Can't Touch This'" shirt circulated and another variant featured "BartHammer." There were apparent local variations. In Washington, Mills described shirts in which Bart utters lines from rap songs, a form that was uncommon in New York City.

Black Bart was not the first popular icon appropriated and modified to reflect African-American culture. *The New York Times* article about Black Bart noted that "there have been occasional blackened Betty Boops and a few attempts last year to recast Bat Man as 'Black Man'..." (Marriot C1).

Also in 1988, New York street vendors sold sweatshirts depicting Mickey Mouse in a warm-up suit and gold chains, saying, "Yo Baby, Yo Baby, Yo! Let's get busy!" (i.e., let's make love). And a cartoonist and graphic artist, J.T. Liehr, who worked in a Philadelphia screen printing shop used by T-shirt designers, said his shop produced not only black versions of Bart Simpson, but also of Charlie Brown and Budweiser mascot Spuds Mackenzie, who was transmuted to a spliff-smoking Rastafarian, "Buds MacSensie" (a reference to high-grade, "sinsemilla" marijuana). "Whatever was popular at the time was modified to be black," Lichr said.

If not the first, the Black Bart T-shirt was yet the most popular Afrocentric appropriation of mass culture iconography. As illicit or anarchic as it may have been, the underground fashion industry that spawned the shirts managed to distribute them "coast to coast" ("When Life Imitates Bart" 61). The *Washington Past* (Mills), *New York Times* (Marriot) and *Newsweek* ("When Life Imitates Bart") found the phenomenon worthy of notice, with *The New York Times* calling Black Bart "one of the most enduring T-shirt images of the summer" (Marriot C1).

## *African-Americans and the Active Audience*

The consumption and display of Black Bart T-shirts represents a noteworthy case study within the growing scholarly interest in the creative activity of the mass audience, or, as Janice A. Radway puts it consumers' "power as individuals to resist or alter the ways in which... objects mean or can be used" (221). In *Reading the Popular*, John Fiske says popular culture "is always a culture of conflict,... involv[ing] the struggle to make social meanings that are in the interest of the subordinate and that are not those preferred by the dominant ideology" (2). "In the practices of consumption," he adds, "the commodity system is exposed to the power of the consumer, for the power of the system is not just top-down, or center-outward, but always two-way, always a flux of conflicting powers and resistances" (31).

Recent work on audience activity—see, for instance, David Eason and Fred Fogo's review (3–5)—has not much reflected on the contemporary culture-making activity of African-Americans. This is unfortunate not only because the influence of African-American culture on American popular culture is pervasive and under-estimated, but because "audience activity," in the sense of reaction to and upon dominant cultural products, has necessarily been essential to culture-making within the African diaspora. Both the frequently opposed views of E. Franklin Frazier—that African heritage was virtually erased during slavery—or of Melville Herskovits—that African-American culture takes shape around specific survivals of African civilization—imply vigorous interaction with Euro-American culture (see Holloway ix and Philips 225–226). Moreover, an essential feature of African-American culture is precisely the responsiveness of audience—consider the "call and response" pattern (Levine 218), the "second line" of musicians in jazz, or the dialectical interaction between improvising performer and inspired-and-inspiring audience that Charies Keil finds central to "the dialectics or mechanics of soul" (174–175).

Lawrence Levine in *Black Culture and Black Consciousness* and Charles Keil in *Urban Blues* have usefully studied both aspects of African-American popular culture. Keil describes a relationship of "appropriation and revitalization" (43) between African-American and Euro-American culture. This conception, developed in a discussion of LeRoi Jones' *Blues People*, envisions an essentially compensatory relationship in which dominant culture appropriates, largely through mass media "covers" of African-American work, and African-Americans respond by "reexpressing American Negro identity and attitudes in a new revitalized way" (45). However, if we focus too deeply on black culture as expropriated victim and reactor, we risk undervaluing its vitality and effectiveness. In culture-making it is often difficult to distinguish action from reaction, defense from offense. As Albert Murray has said:

> Much is forever being made of the deleterious effects of slavery on the generations of Black Americans that followed. But for some curious reason, nothing at all is ever made of the possibility that the legacy left by the enslaved ancestors of blues-oriented contemporary U.S. Negroes includes a disposition to confront the most unpromising circumstances and make the most of what little there is to go on, regardless of the odds—and not without finding delight in the process...(69–70)

Consequently, Levine's description of the appropriation–revitalization process proves somewhat more helpful in assessing the ongoing vitality of African-American popular culture. He describes the cultural interplay between African- and Euro-American culture as a "complex and multidimensional" relationship, "a pattern of *simultaneous* acculturation and revitalization" (italics added, 444). "Cultural diffusion between whites and blacks was by no means a one-way street with blacks the invariable beneficiaries," he writes. "Afro-American impact upon wide areas of American expressive culture has become increasingly obvious, though it has not yet been adequately assessed."

And in fact examples employed by Keil, Levine and others describe many instances in which black culture clearly acts upon dominant culture, not defensively or reactively, but actively, perspicaciously, and with satirical penetration. For instance, Keil acutely observes how "a distinctively Negro style" animates "established white American entertainment forms," such as sports. He points to "the nothing ball and sucker ball as pitched by Satchel Paige, the base as stolen by Maury Wills, the basket catches of Willie Mays, the antics of the Harlem Globetrotters, the beautiful ritualization of an ugly sport by Sonny Liston and Muhammed Ali" (15). Similarly, George Nelson in *Elevating the Game* has described the growth in recent years of

(Harlem) Wearing Black Bart Simpson shirt, 125 St., NY, NY. *Photo credit Beryl Goldberg, © 1991.*

air-borne, slam-dunking basketball technique. These "symbolic transformations," as Keil calls them, represent not a return to roots, but a genuine invigoration of the possibilities of popular cultural forms.

African-American culture by definition and necessity works in relation to dominant culture products. But the result is often distinct cultural invention. Speaking of black music, for instance, Schafer and Riedel note "a basic force behind all genres and modes of black music" in "the ability to absorb, rework, and develop every musical material and influence, to be protean, taking on any shape yet remaining substantially the same in feeling or spirit" (22). Maultsby describes how the black spiritual developed as "slaves...frequently fashioned Protestant psalms, hymns, and spiritual songs into new compositions by altering the structure, text, melody, and rhythm." They thus created an essentially autonomous art form, a "body of religious music created or adapted by slaves and performed in a distinctly African style" (198).

Nor does African-American culture's ability to actively "absorb, rework and develop" operate solely in melodic spheres. As John W. Roberts says in *From Trickster to Badman*, the lyrics of the spiritual were not simple adoptions of Biblical texts but careful selections of figures and episodes significant to black historical and social experience. Roberts quotes Sterling Brown:

> Paul...is generally bound in jail with Silas, to the exclusion of the rest of his busy career. Favored heroes are Noah, chosen of God to ride down the flood; Joshua, who caused the wall of Jericho to fall...; Jonah, symbol of hard luck changed at last; and Job, the man of tribulation who still would not curse his God. (110)

Roberts continues, quoting Levine, in "the world of the spirituals, it was not the masters or the mistresses but God and Jesus and the entire pantheon of Old Testament figures who set the standards, established the precedents, and defined the values...." It was a black world in which no reference was ever made to any white contemporary (110). A similar creative adaptation occurs in the Rastafarian re-interpretation of the Bible as a critique of dominant society ("Babylon") and manifesto of revolution and apocalypse, as Hebdige has described (33–35). A similar perspicacious and satiric adaptation is evident in dance: the cakewalk, John Storm Roberts notes in *Black Music of Two Worlds*, "began as a slaves' parody of white 'society' ways" (199).

The point of this survey is not simply and comfortably to assimilate the Black Bart T-shirt to this honorable tradition. But if, as Frederick Perls, Ralph Hefferline and Paul Goodman have permasively argued (227–235), the process of creative adjustment is fundamental in all human conduct, we might expect it to persist even in the purchase and display of mass-produced commodities. The point is not that buying and wearing a T-shirt is as creative as singing the blues, or even dancing to them. But the deployment of such a commodity can constitute a cultural maneuver parallel to those we have just surveyed in the tradition of appropriation and revitalization as enacted in culture-making that employs the purchase of commodities. And the maneuver may engender group affirmations of some cultural significance.

Still, a variety of curiosities enter the picture when creative adjustment or appropriation and revitalization operate within the culture of mass media and commodities. As we shall see, the creators of Black Bart T-shirts may not be black, and some may question the cultural value of images of a self-declared dropout and mischief maker. Yet in the end, I will argue, the Black Bart T-shirt makes a significant comment upon the culture of mass media and enhances African-American identity. It also makes us aware of other instances of potential cultural power through the deployment of commodities.

## *Complications of Commodity Culture*

T-shirts, however ephemeral or "commodified," are not entirely unlikely means of social communication. Since the mid-1970s when they emerged as outerwear embellished with product images and slogans, they have functioned as literal "fashion statements," a kind of personalized advertising. The commodities displayed on them are heavy with "lifestyle" connotations—not a jar of mayonnaise, say, but a brand of beer, a soft drink, a travel destination, a rock group—entities that presumably evoke occasions and emotions significant of the wearer's personality, taste and allegiances. Correspondingly, Behling's classification of T-shirt types for an empirical study (1988)—cynical, advertising, environmental, health and exercise, political, feminism, prestige, and off-color humor—suggests the association between the T-shirt and causes, issues and activities close to the wearer's central values. The affirmation involved can have tangible social significance. When stutterers, in a study by Silverman, wore a T-shirt saying, "I stutter. So what?" store clerks were found to perceive them more positively. The apparent personal transformations negotiated by the shirt occur on a more informal level too. A mother overhearing a discussion of Black Bart T-shirts, said, "Oh yes, my son wanted one of those, but I wouldn't get him one. He has enough attitude already." Merely to don the shirt is to be taken over by an "attitude."

The Black Bart T-shirt arguably furthers group identification and cohesion and makes as well a lively implicit commentary on contemporary media. The fact that the shirt appropriates figures from an ongoing television show carries a special impact. Although television, as separate studies by Richard Allen, Fred Bales, and Carolyn Stroman ("Mass Media Effects and Black Americans") have found, is a medium highly popular and credible with African-Americans, its origins and production are largely impervious to popular modification. To be sure, in the last 20 years African-

Americans have been portrayed more frequently and more positively on television, as Stroman notes ("Twenty Years Later"). But other scholars have pointed out that this gain brings a reduction of significant dimensions of black culture. Sherry Bryant-Johnson remarks on the loss of significant expressive features of black ethnic background; Ilona Holland notes that the non-standard dialect employed by blacks on television is not true to black English as actually spoken, and Todd Gitlin and Martin Bayles contend that televised representations of African-Americans back away from the presentation of realistic characters in realistic backgrounds. Without overestimating the cultural impact of a mere T-shirt, we may yet suggest that sporting the blazonry of Black Bart "broadcasts" an unsanctioned commentary on *The Simpsons* show that reverses this tendency. As we will discuss in more detail below, the Black Bart T-shirt extends the social rules portrayed on the show to include raffish, urban personae—Rastafarians, "homeboys," rappers, and Black Muslims—all of whom may seem vaguely threatening and who find scant representation in the mass media.

But at the same time, an environment of commodities and postmodern "intertextuality" complicate this affirmative culture-making picture. Appropriation and revitalization in commodity culture turn and return upon each other. Matt Groening, creator of *The Simpsons,* has recognized both the economic expropriation and artistic creativity of the Black Bart phenomenon. "You have to have mixed feelings when you're getting ripped off," he said (qtd. in Mills). But his ambivalence did not prevent him from making the "rip-off" into material for further cartooning. In "Life in Hell," another of his strips, Groening depicts Akbar and Jeff, identical figures who inexplicably wear fezs and may be brothers or lovers, and who bootleg themselves. Working from "Akbar & Jeff's Bootleg Akbar & Jeff T-shirt Hut," they vend "Blakbar and Jeff" T-shirts, including "Air Akbar" and "Akbar and Jeff go funky reggae." Dreadlocks sprouting from under his fez, one says, "Irie, Mon." The other responds, "What?" Groening thus plays with the very cultural gaps that engender the Black Bart T-shirt. A warning label on the cartoon intones: "we will prosecute bootleggers of our bootlegs and don't you forget it."

Fox Television itself briefly adapted the possible connection between a white Bart and a black Bart to its own purposes. A black-oriented show, *True Colors,* was for a time programmed to follow *The Simpsons* presumably to compete more successfully with the top-10 *Bill Cosby Show.* Advertisements for the new pairing played upon the identity of Bart and the young black hero of *True Colors,* placing their images side by side, comparing the two dancing, and having Bart say of the young black star, "He's my idol!"

More fundamental matters arise when we ask, who are the creators of Black Bart Simpson T-shirts? It is not easy to offer a definitive answer. One might ask vendors and producers of the T-shirts, but given the illegality of their operations, they could easily suspect that a scholar's interest was but a clever ruse to hunt copyright violators. Nonetheless, in T-shirt screen printing shops some aspects of the production process comes into public view. And according to some testimony from this source, the designers and producers of Black Bart and other black-oriented T-shirts emerge from a group hardly associated with empathy for African-American culture—the "middleman minority" of immigrant Korean business people in the United States.

Korean merchants in general display a strong presence in "low-end retailing" of inexpensive items such as wigs, handbags, martial arts supplies, jewelry and casual apparel, including T-shirts, much of which makes an appeal to the cultural interests of low-income groups. J.T. Liehr, the graphic artist and cartoonist quoted earlier, said that about half a dozen Korean merchants regularly used his shop to order silk screens for black-oriented shirts that were vended in Center City and west Philadelphia. "Of all the shirts aimed at blacks, I rarely saw black people involved in making them," Liehr said. (White "progressives," he added, typically produced anti-apartheid and Nelson Mandela T-shirts.) Nor did the Korean producers of Afrocentric material with their shoestring budgets seem likely to employ much help of any sort, to say nothing of black artists or collaborators, Liehr said.

Origins exert a powerful conceptual spell. The cultural and economic conflicts between Koreans and African-Americans have received so much publicity that many observers are likely to aver that if Koreans designed Black Bart T-shirts, their cultural value cannot be high. Korean–black antipathies figure prominently in such recent African-American films as Spike Lee's *Do the Right Thing* and Frederick Singleton's *Boyz in the 'Hood*. Blacks cite such grievances as the failure of Korean merchants to live in the communities where they work, firing black workers, refusing credit to black customers, treating them as potential shoplifters, and failing to contribute to black charities.[3] The possible Korean production of Black Bart T-shirts can echo too closely the old story of the financial exploitation of black cultural interests and creations for the profit of other groups. Certainly too, the likely Korean origins of the Black Bart products sit oddly in the tradition of African-American cultural creativity sketched above. And in fact it might be suspected that the casual relation to value terms that we noted in the "Crack Kills/Black Power" T-shirt implies the detached and distant perspective of a culture alien to African-American concerns.[4]

Disapproval of the possible Korean production of the shirts links with a more general disapproval of the Bart figure, black or white, by authority figures of both races. A *People Weekly* article called "Eat My Shirts!" described how principals in California and Ohio banned Bart Simpson T-shirts bearing the label "Underachiever" or Bart's rude query, "Who the hell are you?" Bart's underachieving can be viewed as particularly dangerous when the school dropout rate among many young people, including African-Americans, stands at worrisome rates. T-shirt vendor Id-Deen said she had heard a Black Muslim imam criticize Bart's disrespect for his parents. In a

*Jet* magazine article headlined "Black Bart T-shirt raises concern among blacks," a black man chastises wearers at a black fraternity picnic: "With all the Black heroes in the world—Mandela and Malcolm and Martin—and that's what you are showing our children?" (In fairness, Black Bart on one shirt himself declares Mandela his "hero.") But the very effort to dismiss the Black Bart T-shirt in the name of more "positive" African-American values can contradict itself. The *Jet* article approvingly quotes an African-American vendor from Baltimore who invokes the very negative stereotypes the article seems to protest: "We are the only people in the world that let somebody take a White cartoon character, paint it Black and then sell it to us for 10 bucks."

Condemning Black Bart on the basis of his possible origins may offer a comfortable sense of superiority to the buyers' presumed foolishness but it does nothing to explain his popularity. Thousands of urban blacks proudly donned and displayed the image of Black Bart Simpson. Many even sported the "Crack Kills" variant. They did not do it to make Koreans rich or increase school dropout rates. The financial economy of popular culture wherein Korean entrepreneurs produce Black Bart T-shirts and the cultural economy wherein African-Americans eagerly buy and display them are "parallel" and "semi-autonomous," as Fiske notes in *Understanding Popular Culture* (26). "Every act of consumption is an act of cultural production, for consumption is always the production of meaning," he says (35).

For its wearers, the Black Bart T-shirt must possess an active, affirmative meaning. And as we examine this popularity the idea reasserts itself that the phenomenon, for all the curiosities surrounding it, stands in discernible continuity with more traditional, creative acts of African-American adaptation of materials from dominant culture: Koreans and African-Americans do, after all, share minority status. Spike Lee acknowledges as much in *Do the Right Thing* when the film's hero Mookie, recognizing the bond, sees to it that a family of Korean greengrocers are spared the racial conflagration that closes the film. Furthermore, there is, as Simon Bronner has pointed out, ample procedent in American culture for a group apparently detached from the African-American community to nonetheless take a central role in circulating African-American culture more widely. Although these cultural brokers may be viewed with hostility by African-Americans (witness Spike Lee's treatment of Jewish nightclub owners in *Mo' Better Blues*), in many cases the broker evinces genuine aesthetic appreciation—consider, Alan Freed's promotion of rock 'n' roll music or John Hammond's of jazz and blues. If an anonymous Korean entrepreneur understands how a black Betty Boop or Bart Simpson will appeal to African-American cultural interests, so be it. Cross-cultural understanding is not beyond the capacities of any ethnic or racial group.

Moreover, it is not as if the Black Bart figure is without its own positive vitality. Bart Simpson and Black Bart may hate school but they are at least "street smart." Black Bart's bold social assertiveness and multiplication of social roles is more imaginative than mindless. If Bart Simpson infuriates principals by calling himself an "underachiever—and proud of it," he must at least comprehend the schoolmaster's jargon. On the show Bart is certainly no scholar but is not without intellectual interest. He shows a near Jesuitical expertise with questions that torture his Sunday school teacher, like whether heaven will admit "a robot with a human brain." In other words, those concerned about the "model" set by the Bart figures might give more weight to the intelligence and penetration implicit in ironic play.

## *How Does a T-Shirt Mean?*

What then is the social meaning of Black Bart and how is it engendered? Young wearers of Black Bart T-shirts formulate the pleasure and meaning of this imagery with full understanding of the cultural dissonance that circulates around the Bart figure. In interviews, 11 Black and Hispanic public school students at first vigorously condemned the show, charging that Bart uses bad language, even the "S-word" and "the F-word" (which of course are not heard on television). They acknowledged solemnly that Bart does not do his homework. A seven-year-old Hispanic boy showed best how the condemnation was "in the air." He could provide no specifics about the show, but nonetheless opined heatedly that it was unnecessarily obscene and violent. "You can't learn anything from that! You don't learn your A-B-C's!" he said. It is hardly likely that on their own children gather at recess to murmur this sort of disapproval of *The Simpsons.* This lad's opinions were adapted from the children's precocious presumptions about adult views of cartoons. A six-year-old boy described the essence of the process: "The parents, they don't like Bart Simpson because they don't want us to turn out cussing when we grow up because they don't want us turning out in jail."[5]

If they piously intoned the "dangers" of Bart, the children nonetheless all but universally could produce details about the show, and in many cases said they owned Simpsons T-shirts or other products. And their more active pleasure in its meanings soon surfaced. A nine-year-old girl, who solemnly called the show "a bad influence," also vividly described an incident in which Lisa comforted baby Maggie, her tone clearly indicating she found it touching. Two girls, aged 10 and 11, who were also best friends, spontaneously said of a "Bart Marley" T-shirt, "It's nice...It's colorful and stuff." With her friend's agreement, one stated explicitly that she recognized the show's "bad examples" to serve a larger function:

> I don't think Bart Simpson was made to offend anyone but to show how the kids act. And some kids...do act like that. But Bart Simpson, I don't think he was made to do bad things. Bart Simpson...is taking the children's offense

> and Homer and Maggie [Marge] are taking the parents' offense and it's showing how we all act together."

Allowing for a fourth-grader's vocabulary, this is the perceptive observation that the show portrays family dynamics rather than glorifying bad behavior. Of Black Bart, one of the pair said, "what's nice is that there is a black person in here, his name is Bart too and they have colorful colors too." Her friend seconded the political aspect:

> On the commercials they don't show that many black people and in the magazines they hardly show any black people. All you see is white. And I don't understand why white people are scared of us because there's nothing wrong with our color.

Youngsters construct the figure of Black Bart from an active, perceptive re-interpretation of materials on the show. They select particular features of Bart Simpson's style that resonate with African-American culture, particularly his hair and dress. Krebs quoted a 14-year-old boy holding that Bart Simpson himself seemed black: "You never see white people with spiked hair like that—that's the way blacks look." Another commented, "I think Bart acts more like a black kid than a white one, especially the way he wears clothing and styles his hair." Larger elements of Bart's Simpson's character undergird Black Bart's appeal. Bart Simpson offends authority figures in part because he focuses on his own goals and pleasures, responding with singular detachment to the lures and values of adult society. One boy approved the way Bart "doesn't give a damn about anything" (qtd. in "When Life Imitates Bart"). Bart's "rowdiness" and "unvarnished chutzpah ...speak particularly well to many black youngsters who are growing up in a society that often alienates them," said Russell Adams, chair of the Afro-American Studies Department at Howard University (qtd. in Marriott C3).

As noted earlier, the Black Bart T-shirts mobilize an implicit critique of the range of black roles on the show. The show's characterizations commendably include more than a token number of people of color. The show also plays with the sociology of racial and ethnic identity. For instance, the local convenience store is owned and operated by a regular character, Apu, who is Indian or Pakistani. African-Americans are numerous and presented in positive roles. Several of Bart's friends and schoolmates and Clarence, the mayor of Springfield City, along with the Simpson's family physician, are black. The physician, Dr. Hibbert, is an "intertextual" reference, the show's Bill Cosby. Hibbert relaxes at home in the multi-colored sweaters favored by Cosby as Dr. Cliff Huxtable (*The Cosby Show* aired at the same time as *The Simpsons*). Bart knows plenty about alternative identities. He avidly collects "Radioactive Man" comics and pretends variously he is "Bart-Man," "The Caped Avenger," a ninja, and other characters. The Black Bart T-shirt builds on Bart's mischief and imagination along with the show's sociological realism to expand its spectrum of roles.

The T-shirts further domesticate these identities by steeping them in the show's acceptance and popularity. Correspondingly, many of the shirts feature a double gesture of pugnacious self-assertion and openness. "Rastabart" warns, "Watch it, Mon" but adds "Irie" ("everything's fine"). Black Bart glares and says, "It's cool being black," but a box on the T-shirt notes, "We are all brothers and sisters so live in unity, love and peace." Another changes the saying, "It's a black thing. You wouldn't understand" to "It's a black thing. You should understand"—a statement that at least opens the possibility that someone not black *could* potentially "understand." Even the "Crack Kills/Black Power" design considered from a wearer's perspective embodies a raw humor, assimilating "black power" to a carnivalesque, scatological tradition of "funky butt" humor.

Though he lives in and as a commodity, Black Bart's energetic transformations and evocations of multiple identities arguably connect with longer traditions from folk culture, recalling for instance the African-American trickster figure, whose transformations *From Trickster to Badman* Roberts has described. He also appears to draw upon the dynamic surrounding the figure of the entertainer in black culture. As Keil has described him, the African-American entertainer is not simply a charming personality skilled in some single area of public amusement. He is rather an "identity expert," whose mastery of stances and poses possesses ritual power to construct identity and social cohesion, in the process defining "a special domain of Negro culture wherein black men have proved and preserved their humanity" (15). Without effacing the difference between a T-shirt cartoon and actual, personal performance, it would nonetheless seem that Black Bart's tricky signifying evokes cultural identity and cohesion. Worn in the streets, the Black Bart figure makes a cultural assertion, a species of enacted rhetoric, commenting upon the arena of television and making it a forum for African-American values and images. As T-shirt vendor Deborah Id-Deen said, the Black Bart T-shirt "gives black people a sense that they're famous."

## *Conclusion*

The possible political value of this sense of "fame" is easy to underestimate. As Levine points out,

> There has been an unfortunate if understandable tendency in our political age to conceive of protest in almost exclusively political and institutional terms. Thus group consciousness and a firm sense of the self have been confused with political consciousness and organization, "manhood" has been equated with armed rebellion, and resistance with the building of a revolutionary tradition.

Levine further explains how black song serves a constructive social function that may be extended even to the public display and deployment of commodities such as the Black Bart T-shirt:

> To state that black song constituted a form of black protest and resistance does not mean that it necessarily led to or even called for any tangible and specific actions, but rather that it served as a mechanism by which Negroes could be relatively candid in a society that rarely accorded them that privilege, could communicate this candor to others whom they would in no other way be able to reach, and, in the face of the sanctions of the white majority, could assert their own individuality, aspirations, and sense of being. (240)

The Black Bart T-shirt too arguably mediates a communicative candor and assertion of self and group identification.

The Black Bart T-shirt is not alone as an expressive use of a commodity to support personal and social identity and convey resistant social messages. Consider, for instance, the insouciant rejection of school deportment expressed in the gracefully untied laces of urban high tops and super sneakers. The gesture rejects that fundamental school rule—"tie your shoelaces!"—yet the shoes stay on and in fact imply spirited, gymnastic agility. "Boom boxes" or "ghetto blasters" and cars fitted with elaborate sound systems blaring rap or salsa create mobile, auditory cultural environments that are expansive—and instantly collapsible. Dance party DJs, MCs and rappers enact an even more creative relation to the commodity. They treat the completed tape or record as itself artistic material. The DJs select, reorder, "sample" and "scratch" these existing commodities into a new composition or "mix," which "priest-like" they offer up for the dancing communion of "everybody in the house."

But as the appropriation–revitalization process works in the post-modernist era with pastiche and quotation of completed, existing texts, the cultural conflict Fiske describes also manifests itself in palpable cultural and legal controversy. The racial apocalypse that concludes Spike Lee's *Do the Right Thing* begins over the use of a boom box. Sound control ordinances are passed to quell the sound-system cars (but allow exceptions for political sound trucks). Poaching on the territory of copyrighted mass media commodities, whether by T-shirt manufacturers or DJ samplers, meets prosecution for copyright violation.

But however contentiously or even illegally they go about it, these practices accomplish something significant for group life in commodity culture. They serve a social-psychological function akin to the "soul strategy" of the blues as Keil describes it: to "increase feelings of solidarity, boost morale, strengthen the consensus" (164–5). The Black Bart T-shirt and similar appropriated and revitalized commodities suggest the significant creative precisely, in the midst of commodity culture and post-modernism.

## Notes

1. This paper was originally delivered at the 1991 annual meeting of the Popular Culture Association. For their helpful comments on versions of this essay, the author wishes to thank Simon Bronner, Gary Daily, Clemmie Gilpin, Charles Keil, Suren Lalvani and William Mahar. Craig Smith provided valuable information on T-shirt production.
2. This paper will not concern itself with the many other appropriations of the ubiquitous Bart Simpson. Suffice it to say that his mischievous image was used for a variety of causes and by no means did they all represent marginalized groups. Bart was swiftly enlisted in the Gulf War: Windbreakers in Tijuana cast him as Rambo, strangling Saddam Hussein and saying, "I am your worst nightmare." On a T-shirt he urinated on a map of Iraq. Editors of the conservative *Campus Review* at the University of Iowa put a slingshot in Bart's hands and had him threaten, "Back off Faggot!" sparking a lawsuit and complaints to local human rights organizations (see "Suits and debate follow display of cartoon poster"). In California, Republican campaign strategists used Bart's visage to accuse gubernatorial candidate Dianne Feinstein of "cheating" in a debate ("The Rehabilitation of Bart Simpson"). A cartoon circulated within Xerox culture incorporated Bart as well. With obscene logic it fused two key traits in characters of the show—Bart's physicality and Baby Maggie's perpetual plying of her pacifier. The photocopied drawing, circulated in south central Pennsylvania and reported printed on a T-shirt in New Orleans, finds Bart, his pants about his knees, with baby Maggie, and Mother Marge screaming in the background. Bart says, "But Mom, she lost her pacifier!" We leave to the reader's imagination what means Bart found to replace it.
3. See Light and Bonacich 322. Kim in "The Big Apple Goes Bananas Over Korean Fruit Stands" and *New Urban Immigrants: The Korean Community in New York* and McKinley describe the relations of Blacks and Koreans in New York City. In general, as Light and Bonacich note, Korean merchants in low-end retailing gain valuable entry to the American market and in the process provide American corporate interests with a variety of indirect benefits. Koreans pioneer in and distribute corporate goods in low-productivity sectors of the market, help keep labor cheap and unorganized, and, promote the idea that the United States is a land where hard work is rewarded (though most entrepreneurs in fact will spend generations working long hours for low pay) (354–400). The increased economic connections between Korea and the United States is also reflected in the fact that, as Basler reports, "The Simpsons" animation is produced at Akom Studio in Seoul.
4. In fact the shirt was more offensive than other Black Bart T-shirts. T-shirt vendor Deborah Id-Deen described it *sotto voce*, asserting solemnly that she may have sold Black Bart T-shirts but she would never sell the "Crack Kills" T-shirt. Yet it was also worn and distributed at least from New York City to Washington D.C. where Mills described it.
5. The students were members of a "student activities committee" representing grades from kindergarten through fifth at the Benjamin Franklin Academic Prep School, Harrisburg, PA. They spoke to me on the understanding they would not be identified. The author wishes to thank the children for their help, Norma Gotwalt, director of the Harrisburg Division of Elementary Education, and Joann Griffin, principal of the Benjamin Franklin Academic Prep School.

## Works Cited

Allen, Richard L. "Communication Research on Black Americans." Paper presented at the Symposium on Minority Audiences and Programming Research. Lenox, MA, Oct. 1980. ERIC ED.

Bales, Fred. "Television Use and Confidence in Television by Blacks and Whites in Four Selected Years." *Journal of Black Studies* 16.3 (1986).

Basler, Barbara. "Peter Pan, Garfield and Bart—all Have Asian Roots." *The New York Times* 2 Dec. 1990.

Bayles, Martha. "Blacks on TV: Adjusting the Image." *New Perspectives* 17.3 (1985).

Behling, Dorothy U. "T-Shirts as Communicators of Attitudes." *Perceptual and Motor Skills* 66 (1988).

"Black Bart Simpson T-shirt Raises Concern Among Blacks." *Jet* 27 Aug. 1990, 37.

Bronner, Simon. Personal Communication. 18 Sept. 1991.

Bryant-Johnson, Sherry. "Blacks on TV Soaps: Visible but Neutralized." *Perspectives: The Civil Rights Quarterly* 15.3 (1983).

de Certeau, Michel. *The Practice of Everyday Life*. Trans. Steven F. Rendall. Berkeley: U of California P, 1984.

Eason, David, and Fred Fogo. "The Cultural Turn in Media Studies." *Mass Comm Review* 15.1 (1988).

"Eat My Shirts! Pesky Bart Simpson Tees Off a California Principal—and Gets Kicked Out of School for Swearing." *People Weekly* 21 May 1990: 130.

Fiske, John. *Reading the Popular*. Boston: Unwin, 1989.

———. *Understanding Popular Culture*. Boston: Unwin, 1989.

Frazier, E. Franklin. *The Negro Church in America*. Boston, 1963.

Gitlin, Todd. "Prime-Time Whitewash." *American Film* 9.2 (Nov. 1983).

Groening, Matt. "Life in Hell." Cartoon. *Village Voice*, 7 Aug. 1990: 8.

Hebdige, Dick. *Subculture: The Meaning of Style*. London: Methuen, 1979.

Herskovits, Melville J. *The Myth of the Negro Past*. 1941. Boston: Beacon, 1958.

Holland, Ilona E. "Nonstandard English on Television: A Content Analysis." Paper presented at the Annual Meeting of the International Communication Association. Chicago, 22–26 May 1986. ERIC ED.

Id-Deen, Deborah. Personal Interview. 10 Nov. 1990.

Keil, Charles. *Urban Blues*. Chicago: The U of Chicago P, 1966.

Kim, Illsoo. "The Big Apple Goes Bananas Over Korean Fruit Stands." Asia 4 (1981).

———. *New Urban Immigrants: The Korean Community in New York*. Princeton: Princeton UP, 1981.

Krebs, Jeanette. "Black Bart: T-shirts Depict TV Kid with Dark Skin." *Patriot-News* [Harrisburg, PA] 29 July 1990.

Levine, Lawrence W. *Black Culture and Black Consciousness: Afro-American Folk Thought from Slavery to Freedom*. New York: Oxford UP, 1977.

Liehr, J.T. Telephone Interview. 20 Dec. 1990.

Light, Ivan, and Edna Bonacich. *Immigrant Entrepreneurs: Koreans in Los Angeles, 1965–1982*. Berkeley: U of California P, 1988.

Marriott, Michel. "I'm Bart, I'm Black and What About It?" *New York Times* 19 Sept. 1990.

Maultsby, Portia K. "Africanisms in African-American Music." *Africanisms in American Culture*. Ed. Joseph E. Holloway. Bloomington: Indiana UP, 1990.

Mills, David. "Bootleg Black Bart Simpson, the Hip-Hop T-Shirt Star." *Washington Post*. 28 June 1990: D1.
Murray, Albert. *Stomping the Blues*. New York: McGraw Hill, 1976.
Nelson, George. *Elevating the Game: Black Men and Basketball*. New York: Harper Collins, 1992.
Perls, Frederick, Ralph F. Hefferline and Paul Goodman. *Gestalt Therapy: Excitement and Growth in the Human Personality*. New York: Dell, 1951.
Philips, John Edward. "The African Heritage of White America." Ed. Joseph E. Holloway. *Africanisms in American Culture*. Bloomington: Indiana UP, 1990.
Radway, Janice A. *Reading the Romance: Women, Patriarchy, and Popular Literature*. Chapel Hill: U of North Carolina P, 1984.
"The Rehabilitation of Bart Simpson." *Mother Jones* Jan.-Feb. 1991.
Roberts, John Storm. *Black Music of Two Worlds*. New York: Praeger, 1972.
Roberts, John W. *From Trickster to Badman: The Black Folk Hero in Slavery and Freedom*. Philadelphia: U of Pennsylvania P, 1989.
Schafer, William J. & Johannes Riedel. *The Art of Ragtime*. Baton Rouge: Louisiana State University, 1973.
Silverman, Franklin H., Michele Gazzolo, & Yvonne Peterson. "Impact of a T-shirt Message on Stutterer Stereotypes: A Systematic Replication." *Journal of Fluency Disorders* 15.1 (1990).
Stroman, Carolyn A. "Mass Media Effects and Black Americans." *Urban Research Review* 9.4 (1984).
——— et al. "Twenty Years Later: The Portrayal of Blacks on Prime-Time Television." Paper presented at the Annual Meeting of the Association for Education in Journalism and Mass Communication. Portland, OR, 2–5 July 1988.
"Suits and Debate Follow Display of Cartoon Poster." *New York Times* 25 Nov. 1990.
"When Life Imitates Bart." *Newsweek* 23 July 1990.
Yoo, Woong Nyol. "Business Owners in New York's Harlem Struggle Against Anti-Korean Prejudice." *Koreatown* 19 Oct. 1981.

## This Text: Reading

1. Which approach to *The Simpsons* do you like the best? Why? The least?
2. In many ways, sitcoms are more about the journey and not about the destination. In other words, what happens in the sitcom—making us laugh—instead of its resolution—giving us a moral—is more important. Do you think this applies to *The Simpsons*? Which writers would agree with this assessment?
3. Is *The Simpsons* a parody (mocking an existing form) or a satire (humor criticizing existing institutions with the hope of improvement), or both? If so, what is it parodying and/or satirizing? Are these effective forms of parody/satire?
4. Who does *The Simpsons* appeal to? Do you think that's the aim of its creators?

5. How does making *The Simpsons* a cartoon affect its ability to make us laugh and perhaps deliver a message? What would change about the television show if it had live actors?

### YOUR TEXT: WRITING

1. Watch *The Simpsons* closely (ideally, with a remote control in hand). Note the targets of satire in the first ten minutes of the show. Now think about a number of questions: What do these targets have in common? Who would benefit if these targets were to be reformed? Write a paper about the targets of satire in *The Simpsons*.
2. Notice the settings of the various locations. What do you think the creators/writers had in mind when "constructing" them? How do they comment on television settings; American settings? Write a short paper about the settings in *The Simpsons*.
3. Think about the characters. Who are they supposed to represent? Are they "accurate" portrayals of a certain type? In what ways do the characters seem "real" to you? Do they seem more real than other television characters? Write a short paper about the symbolic/metaphoric nature of the characters in *The Simpsons*.

---

## READING OUTSIDE THE LINES

## Classroom Activities

### Realistic?

Watch a show in class taking notes on what is realistic about the show. Do you find its setting realistic? Its dialogue? The characters—both in the way they act and their gender, ethnic, and class make-up? In what ways do the show's creators try to be realistic? In what ways are they admitting that television shows are not realistic? Do you think whether a show is realistic an important consideration in whether you watch it? What are the differences between television shows and "real life"?

### Advertising

Watch the commercials in a particular television show. Can you tell from them who its target audience is? Do you think advertisers are reaching their intended audience?

### Is this a good show?

What are your criteria for saying a show is "good"? Are they similar or different than the ones you might use for literature and/or movies?

### Casting

Who would play you in a sitcom about your life? Why would you make this choice?

### Genre

What is your favorite type of television show? Why? Do you feel you have something in common with others who like these types of shows?

### Show loss

Talk about a show that went off the air that you miss. What emotions did you feel when this show ended its run? Do you think the run ended too early? What do you think makes a successful television show?

## Essay Ideas

### The General Television Assignment

In this paper, you will read an episode of a television show and write a paper analyzing some aspect of it. What do we mean by "read" and "analyze"? You might start by describing the text at hand, performing an inventory of sorts. Then think about what these elements say about the text; what conclusions can you draw about the work from the observations you have made? A television show has traditional elements of texts such as a narrative and symbolic language of one sort or another, as well as visual elements which contribute to the show's meaning.

#### Look at the Fashion

For this paper, notice the way the characters dress on a particular television show. From what you know about fashion, what are the creators of the show trying to convey with their choices of fashion for their characters? Are they hoping to tie into prevailing opinions about the way certain groups (those of color, class, gender, and age) dress in providing clues on how we're supposed to understand these characters? Taken together, what conclusions can we draw from the fashion choices of the creators?

#### Analyze the Theme

In most sitcoms and many dramas, there is an explicit "moral of the story" that those who script the episode attach to the ending. Taking one such show, a night of shows on a particular network, or an accumulation of the same shows, what sorts of morals are presented to the audience? Do you think the creators think these morals are important? If so, do they present an honest attempt to educate the audience, or are they a vehicle for laughs? Do you know any shows that do not have "a moral of the story"? How would you compare them to the shows that do have morals?

### The Unintended vs. the Intended

Sometimes television shows are explicit about what they are trying to convey. Sometimes, however, what is not present in a show says as much about the show as what is there. Taking for a cue a comment Oprah Winfrey made to the cast of *Friends* on her show "Why isn't there a black 'friend' on their show?", look at a popular sitcom and try to determine what may or may not be missing on a show. You might focus on the racial make-up of the characters or their gender, class, and/or age.

### Real vs. Unreal

Many people would say that they watch television "to escape reality." In what ways do the producers of shows try to be "real"? In what ways do they ignore reality? You may have already noticed that we tend to watch characters in action with other characters, and that basic human functions like bathing, eating, sleeping, and going to the bathroom are ignored. On a more philosophical level, you may also notice that the problems these characters face are resolved relatively quickly, and the communication between characters is highly evolved. For this paper, you might discuss what overall effect the inclusion of "reality" might have on the audience.

### Understand the Audience

Creators of television shows often target their shows to particular audiences—or their advertisers do, in order to see a greater return on their investment. Watch a television show, or several, and see if you can determine what demographic they are appealing to or what show their advertisers feel they are. Are the two audiences different? Is one more broad than the next? What do you think are some of the problems inherent in targeting a particular demographic?

### Race and Ethnicity

For the longest time, race and ethnicity has been an issue on television. Watch a show and see what they say and do not say about questions of race and ethnicity. Do members of a particular race play a particular role on the show? Do these roles embrace or reject previous stereotypes?

### Honor the Show

Write an essay on why you feel a show is "good." Your first step, of course, is defining what you mean by "good." Does good mean writing that is

funny, realistic, philosophical, or a combination of these factors or others? Is defined by the quality of the actors? Can you define what a good television show is without constructing the criteria from the show you like? What other shows fit into the definition you constructed?
—or—

**Disparage the Show**

Write an essay on why you feel a show is "bad," going through the same process as you did when you defined what "good" meant. A useful exercise is to write both positive and negative reviews.

**Follow the Character**

What single character on a television show do you most identify with? Why? Does this identification make you at all uncomfortable? What this identification say about you and the television character?

## Media Journal

Using the worksheet at the front of the book as a guide, we want you to follow a phenomenon for the length of the course. It could be a television show, a continuing story in the newspaper (make sure you choose one that will continue), or a continuing event (such as a sport). Each journal entry should provide some sort of commentary on the phenomena, moving beyond general plot concerns. A brief (two or three sentence) summary is fine but should not dominate the entry. See "Media Journal, *The Rosie O'Donnell Show*," by Hillary West, for an example.

# MEDIA JOURNAL: *THE ROSIE O'DONNELL SHOW*

Hillary West

### *Week of February 14, 1999*

Rosie just might be a control freak. She controls her audience. She controls her guests and she controls her production.

The very young Olympic gold medalist, Tara Lapinski appeared as Rosie's first guest on Wednesday February 17. Rosie fired questions and comments at her left and right. Tara seemed to be ok with it. What else was she to do? She was trying to plug her special that was to air that night. Maybe Rosie knew ahead that Tara would need a lot of prodding. After the interview I noticed that I was standing in the middle of my kitchen staring at the television. There was nothing relaxing or restful about watching that bit. Now that I think about it I am always standing up when I watch the show. Rosie is quick witted and clever. It is part of her charm. But, maybe it is a little intense as well.

Rosie's next guest was fellow talk show host, Matt Lauer. Her demeanor was dramatically different. She immediately opens with the statement, "Matt, you threatened me." Evidently, earlier that morning Matt was hosting "Good Morning America" and two young ladies appeared at his outside gate where the crowds gather for the show and on the air expressed their concern that they could not get on the Rosie show for that afternoon. Matt, on live TV, gave Rosie an ultimatum, put the girls on the show or he would not come on as a guest that afternoon. That afternoon Rosie accused Matt of threatening her. He agreed. Perhaps he realized he had stepped over a line. He had stepped over Rosie's line. It is Rosie's show and she is definitely in control. But, we should never underestimate the innate goodness of Rosie. Not only did the girls get into the Rosie show, they were invited on stage to sit with Matt Lauer during his interview. Rosie played it very cool. Was she kidding or was she genuinely irritated that she had been pushed into an awkward position? Throughout the interview with Matt, Rosie was very subdued, so unlike her encounter with Tara. But, by inviting the girls to come on stage, it certainly made Rosie look like the hero, even though she may not have appreciated having been manipulated. Or, the entire episode could have been a joke.

Rosie may feel a great need to control all that she can because she extends herself so much to others. We are always learning of how she is helping someone, family, friends, neighbors, or just fans who want to meet her or one of her guests. She is very friendly with her audience. It is as if they have all come over for a drink and she is the hostess. But, she has control over the audience. She is in the limelight and they are under the darker lights. She decides if members of the audience will be mentioned or not. It can be very spontaneous and at random. This Wednesday, while in the middle of a conversation with her band leader, John, she calls out, "Oh, I just realized it is Ash Wednesday!" Several people in the audience still had their ashes on their foreheads and she was trying to make out what it was that made them look so different from the others. She was friendly, amusing and made everyone feel at ease. But, Rosie was the one in charge. The cameras then shot to those in the audience to whom Rosie was referring.

Maybe this brief encounter with Matt Lauer has revealed a different Rosie. Or, it could be that she has a weakness: the need to control. She can control whether or not she wants to be overweight, funny, successful, or a good mom. It is interesting that there is no man in her life to share with the raising of her children. Maybe she doesn't want to share the opportunity because she will have to relinquish some of her control. To be as successful as Rosie has become, she must have some drive that pushes her along. If it is the need to control all that surrounds her, then fine. As long as she doesn't hurt anyone.

### *Week of March 15, 1999*

It might be fake, but I don't think it is. Rosie is an honest, real life role model. She probably has some idea of the impact she makes, but maybe not. Everyone loves her and she seems to appear to be genuinely grateful when people are kind to her. As a role model she is generous, sincere, sensitive and moral.

Barbara Walters was a guest this week on Rosie. Rosie has mentioned many times that she would not and did not watch the Monica Lewinsky interview. Yet, Rosie is all too happy to have Barbara on her show and they are obviously very close. Rosie speaks her mind, though. She immediately reminds Barbara that she did not watch the interview and she doesn't want to talk about it because it upsets her so. Then Rosie launches into a two to three minute discourse about the fate of Hillary Clinton. Seldom does Rosie give a candid opinion about an issue. Perhaps it is because she is so adamant about things. Whatever the reason, the world listened and Rosie's opinion was duly noted. Tens of thousands of middle class moms heard her and have been influenced by what she had to say.

Rosie is believable because she is one of them. She cheats on her exercise and diet regime because she has had "a stressful week." What woman, what person could not relate to that? We crave her words, her thoughts, her opinions because she makes a difference and she is like us so maybe we could make a difference too even with all our faults. Rosie's stressful week began at an event, in her honor, whereby a celebrity friend was singing a song as a tribute to her and fell off the slage. The friend was alright but Rosie was not. She cried uncontrollably and all week she couldn't stop thinking about her friend. Each time she would mention the incident tears would well up in her eyes. Rosie was definitely not herself this week.

Her sensitivity makes her an emotional wreck and by some that may be perceived as a weakness. But her general audience relates to her sympathetic nature because they see themselves in the same light. For Rosie it means another session in therapy. For her viewers it probably means three more donuts and more exercise in the famous Rosie Chub Club.

What you don't want to do with Rosie is get on her list! Once the word is down, this stubborn Irish woman is not budging. If she doesn't like you, she doesn't like you. She has been very vocal about how she feels about Monica Lewinsky and consequently Bill Clinton. Although she loves the actors on *Party of Five*, her favorite TV show, she is very critical of their moral behavior. She is the last of the do gooders and does not allow R rated language on the show as she once again reminded Barbara Walters. Barbara, in mentioning the film *When Harry Met Sally* refrained, at Rosie's request from using the word orgasm. It's not even a swear word! Her strict Catholic upbringing must be the basis for her high moral fiber.

Every day members of the audience receive gifts. They are sponsor promotional pieces and the audience loves them. But Rosie's generosity stems far beyond that. She always pumps her celebrity guests for donations to E-bay to be auctioned off so that the proceeds will help needy children. And because she interacts so much with her audience, she learns quickly of a need. One visiting family lost their home and pets to a devasting fire. Rosie, sympathetic to the sorrow of the children, made arrangements for the family to receive a new cat and dog. Another elderly woman had not seen her sister in nine years and Rosie gifted her with a plane trip, car and driver and hotel room to visit her sister. Rosie confesses that giving things away makes her feel better and after all, she has had a "stressful week."

She isn't perfect, we all know that. But she is a positive role model for a sea of viewers who probably don't feel very good about themselves and spend too much time watching television and yelling at their kids. Rosie helps viewers see the good in themselves despite their faults because she is open about her own weaknesses. It is easy to look up to someone who is honest about who she is. I hope I don't discover one day that Rosie is a total hoax and I have been tricked into thinking she is a decent human being.

# 3

# Reading Public Space

To a large degree, we exist in relation to our surroundings. Whether we are in our bedrooms, bathrooms, coffeehouses, classrooms, a stadium or a record store, we are always someplace, and understanding our relationship to these places and spaces gives us a better understanding of the world. How? By providing us tools to understand the way the physical world influences our inner world, the way those constructing spaces influence us—or attempt to.

In this introduction, we will talk about public and private space, architecture, and design. What we mean by space is the environment created by human-made activities, built areas, such as classrooms, stadiums, shopping malls, and dorm rooms. Architecture and design are forces that help construct these places and spaces.

In a sense, architects and designers are the authors of buildings and public spaces; they construct architecture and public space through a series of decisions. And if you look around you, not only will you see a series of decisions made by architects and designers but also by the people who pay the designers, and the people who use or live in that particular space.

For example, architects may have had some leeway in designing your classroom, but their decisions about certain aspects of design or comfort might have been affected by their cost. The kind of institution you attend, whether it's a private or public university or college, probably had some impact on these decisions. The designers or architects were limited by function—putting in a fireplace or a wet bar in a classroom would be inappropriate. And the designers were undoubtedly influenced by the period in which they lived; if you think about it, you can pinpoint the date within 20 years of construction based on colors, materials, and lighting. For instance, square or rectangular buildings built with brick or cinder blocks reflect the architectural style of the 60s and 70s, whereas a wooden Victorian house was probably built as much as 100 years earlier.

Such decisions also exist in corporate or retail venues. If you walk into a Starbucks, for example, you will see the results of a series of carefully made judgments: the color scheme, the décor and the lighting, the font type of the signs which describe coffee products, where all of this is placed. It's not hard to gather from these aspects of design that Starbucks is going for both "cool" and familiar in its space. They want customers to feel they are not only purchasing coffee, but that they are having some unexpressed secondary experience as well.

Is it one element that gives us this idea? No—it's a series of details taken together. Drawing conclusions from architectural decisions and public space is not much different than making these conclusions from reading literature; each has its own "grammar," symbols, and themes that we interpret to get a picture of the work as a whole. Here are some other things to think about when considering public space and architecture.

## Colors and shapes often have symbolic value.

Part of the grammar we wrote about in the last paragraph, color and shape help architects and designers speak to the public in a language they understand, either consciously or subconsciously. While there is no formula, psychologists have shown that particular shapes and colors have psychological effects on their viewers. There are also traditional uses of color and shape that designers and architects draw upon, again, as a sort of grammar of construction. Of course, homeowners may think they choose colors and shapes because they look "pretty," or "nice," but what they mean by pretty is of course arbitrary as well.

Combinations of these colors and shapes often form recognizable designs that are imitated repeatedly. For example, arches, columns, and white picket fences often symbolize ideas that often go beyond their simple presence—arches and columns have often stood for power and tradition, and the white picket fence stands for tradition as well, but perhaps a different kind of tradition. Thus elements of design, both in public space and on human-made constructions, are texts that ask to be read in a certain way. A house with a white picket fence around it is a much different text than a house with a high metal security gate enclosing it.

## Cost and community often contribute to the design of a public or private space.

While most designers seek to make buildings and space both beautiful and useful, there are other factors that often interfere with these stated goals. Cost is always a factor—people can only build what they can afford, and some materials are prohibitively expensive for a given function. Design help can also cost money.

The surrounding community also plays a role in design. Community standards, often in the form of zoning laws, will have an effect on what something looks like. Zoning regulations determine the use of a particular piece of property and, depending on the locale, can also determine the size and function of what's built on a piece of property. Even politics can help determine how something is designed. For example, at the University of Texas at Austin in the 1970s, a prominent student meeting-place was significantly altered when the administration built large planters to restrict student gatherings protesting administration policies. Similarly, at the State University of New York at Binghamton, a beloved and locally famous open space in the center of campus called the "Peace Quad," where students gathered to read, protest, talk, eat, and listen to music, was recently paved over so that a large new building could be erected in its place. Regrettably, issues of class and race can also affect public and private spaces. For example, there are very few upper class communities near industrial plants, nor does one often find a poor neighborhood that has easy access to the attractive elements of a city.

### Space can be manipulative and comforting.

Designers have conscious ideas about the world they construct. Designers often think about how and where they want people involved with their work. In a poorly designed building, perhaps designers do not think enough about these concerns. In your life, how do these elements work? Think about sidewalks. Do they always take you where you want to go? What about doorways? Are they always at the most convenient place? In your own room, think about where you put your desk, your chairs, and your bed: what is your main concern in placing them—your convenience or someone else's? All of those decisions influence those who enter your room. Think too about most classrooms at your institution. What do they resemble? Do they create a certain mood? Is talking about a movie or a story different in a large classroom than in a café? Why? Sometimes places are "user-friendly"; others are less so, either through oversight by designers, or more deliberately as in the case of the Peace Quad or student protest space at the universities mentioned before.

### Users have ways of altering landscapes that can have personal and political implications.

One of these ways is through decoration. Think about your own experience. Posters lining a room, particularly in the dorm rooms and bedrooms of your contemporaries, are almost always there to send a message—that the inhabitant is a man or a woman, someone concerned with music, art, beer, and/or cars. Some rooms scream that the inhabitants are trying to be cool, while others ooze sophistication.

When one gets older, it is usually time to say goodbye to the rock posters, M.C. Escher prints, and the beer ads, but what to replace them with becomes a question all of us grapple with for the rest of our lives. Some people decide they have a style they feel comfortable with and make their decisions based on that; others feel their way through the process; still others delegate their design choices to someone else. But there are effects from these decisions, whether they are intended or unintended. It's important to understand that the space you live in—how you decorate it, your traces within it—is a kind of text that people can and do read to understand something about you.

## Other elements can change the landscape in ways not imagined by designers.

Graffiti alters the public landscape, and so does public art. Neglect can change public space, as well as new construction surrounding a previous design. How we use and design space gives some indication of our personality, among other things. Walking into someone's dorm room, office, or living room gives some indication of who they are (and who they think they are). When you walk into a business, you also receive some indication of how they view themselves. For example, compare the interior at McDonalds to a fancy restaurant, to a TGIFridays or Applebee's or Chili's; the interiors and exteriors are littered with clues about what these places think they are about. Similarly, how do Mexican restaurants tell us that they are Mexican? How do Chinese restaurants create a Chinese setting? Think too about the way movies and television shows set scenes; often the settings of movies give us an indication of how we're supposed to view the characters. In *Frasier* or *Friends*, for example, we see the presence of couches, the bright lighting, the expensive, clean apartments (in the case of *Friends*, far too expensive for New Yorkers their age) as clues in how we're supposed to relate to them.

Ultimately, the space that surrounds us says a number of things about that particular location—who inhabits that space, what the space is used for, and how we are to read that space. Additionally, we can discern a great deal about what kinds of spaces or buildings are important given the amount and kind of space devoted to them. As you read this chapter, think about how certain spaces force you to interpret the world in a certain way.

# Worksheet

## THIS TEXT

1. How does the background of the authors influence their ideas about public space?
2. Do they define public space differently? In what ways?
3. Do the authors have different ideas about class, race, and gender? In what ways?
4. Try to figure out the writing situation of each author. Who is the audience? What does the author have at stake? What is the agenda of the author? Why does she or he want me to think a certain way?
5. What is his or her agenda? Why is she or he writing this piece?
6. What social, political, and cultural forces affect the author's text? What is going on in the world as he or she is writing?
7. What are the main points of the essay? Is there a specific thesis statement? Remember that it doesn't have to be one sentence—it could be several sentences or a whole paragraph.
8. What type of evidence does the author use to back up any claims she might make?
9. Is the author's argument reasonable?
10. Do you find yourself in agreement with the author? Why or why not?
11. Does the author help you *read* public space better than you did before reading the essay? If so, how?
12. How is the reading process different if you are reading an essay as opposed to a short story or poem?
13. Did I like this? Why or why not?

## BEYOND THIS TEXT: READING PUBLIC SPACE

**Shapes:** What are some of the dominant shapes you see in a public space or building? Do they symbolize anything to you? Are they supposed to? Do they remind you of other shapes in other spaces? How do the shapes relate to the space's use?

**Colors:** What are the dominant colors? What emotions do they evoke? Why? How would the space or architecture change if the color changed? How does the color relate to the space's use?

**Size:** How big is this place? How does this affect the way you view it, and the feelings it inspires? Is there a way to change the size to evoke different feelings? In what ways do the space's or architecture's size relate to its use?

**Use:** What is the use of this particular space or architecture? How do we know from the elements you see? Do you see unintended uses that might result from this construction? Do you see an emphasis on practicality or ornament in this space?

**Interaction between architecture and space:** How do the two work together? What elements in the architecture affect the way the space is constructed? Are there ways of changing this interaction?

**Overall beauty:** What is your general view of the place's beauty? What standards or criteria do you find yourself relying on?

**Emotional response:** What is your overall emotional response to this place? Why? What elements contribute to this response? What elements could you change that might provoke a different response?

**Overall statement:** What do you think this space or architecture says? What is it trying to say? How might this gap between what it says and is trying to say be changed?

# SPATIAL SEGREGATION AND GENDER STRATIFICATION IN THE WORKPLACE

Daphne Spain

Daphne Spain wrote this essay as part of a larger work, *Gendered Spaces* (1992). In this work, she writes about the way a specific type of public space—the workplace—and gender interact, an argument that you might find has implications beyond the workplace.

TO WHAT EXTENT do women and men who work in different occupations also work in different spaces? Baran and Teegarden (1987, 206) propose that occupational segregation in the insurance industry is "tantamount to spatial segregation by gender" since managers are overwhelmingly male and clerical staff are predominantly female. This essay examines the spatial conditions of women's work and men's work and proposes that working women and men come into daily contact with one another very infrequently. Further, women's jobs can be classified as "open floor," but men's jobs are more likely to be "closed door." That is, women work in a more public environment with less control of their space than men. This lack of spatial control both reflects and contributes to women's lower occupational status by limiting opportunities for the transfer of knowledge from men to women.

It bears repeating that my argument concerning space and status deals with structural workplace arrangements of women as a group and men as a group, *not* with occupational mobility for individual men and women. Extraordinary people always escape the statistical norm and experience upward mobility under a variety of circumstances. The emphasis here is on the ways in which workplaces are structured to provide different spatial arrangements for the typical working woman and the typical working man and how those arrangements contribute to gender stratification....

## *Typical Women's Work: "Open-Floor Jobs"*

A significant proportion of women are employed in just three occupations: teaching, nursing, and secretarial work. In 1990 these three categories alone accounted for 16.5 million women, or 31 percent of all women in the labor force (U.S. Department of Labor 1991, 163, 183). Aside from being concentrated in occupations that bring them primarily into contact with other women, women are also concentrated spatially in jobs that limit their access to knowledge. The work of elementary schoolteachers, for example, brings them into daily contact with children, but with few other adults. When not dealing with patients, nurses spend their time in a lounge separate from the doctors' lounge. Nursing and teaching share common spatial characteristics with the third major "women's job"—that of secretary.

Secretarial/clerical work is the single largest job category for American women. In 1990, 14.9 million women, or more than one of every four employed women, were classified as "administrative support, including clerical"; 98 percent of all secretaries are female (U.S. Department of Labor 1991, 163, 183). Secretarial and clerical occupations account for over three-quarters of this category and epitomize the typical "woman's job." It is similar to teaching and nursing in terms of the spatial context in which it occurs.

Two spatial aspects of secretarial work operate to reduce women's status. One is the concentration of many women together in one place (the secretarial "pool") that removes them from observation of and/or input into the decision-making processes of the organization. Those decisions occur behind the "closed doors" of the managers' offices. Second, paradoxically, is the very public nature of the space in which secretaries work. The lack of privacy, repeated interruptions, and potential for surveillance contribute to an inability to turn valuable knowledge into human capital that might advance careers or improve women's salaries relative to men's.

Like teachers and nurses, secretaries process knowledge, but seldom in a way beneficial to their own status. In fact, secretaries may wield considerable informal power in an organization, because they control the information flow. Management, however, has very clear expectations about how secretaries are to handle office information. Drawing from their successful experience with grid theory, business consultants Robert Blake, Jane Mouton, and Artie Stockton have outlined the ideal boss-secretary relationship for effective office teamwork. In the first chapter of *The Secretary Grid*, an American Management Association publication, the following advice is offered:

> The secretary's position at the center of the information network raises the issue of privileged communications and how best to handle it. Privileged communication is information the secretary is not free to divulge, no matter how helpful it might be to others. And the key to handling it is the answer to the question. "Who owns the information"? The answer is, "The boss does."... The secretary's position with regard to this information is that of the hotel desk clerk to the contents of the safety deposit box that stores the guest's valuables. She doesn't own it, but she knows what it is and what is in it. The root of the word *secretary* is, after all, *secret:* something kept from the knowledge of others. (Blake, Mouton, and Stockton 1983, 4–5; emphasis in original)

In other words, secretaries are paid *not* to use their knowledge for personal gain, but only for their employers' gain. The workplace arrangements that separate secretaries from managers within the same office reinforce status differences by exposing the secretary mainly to other secretaries bound by the same rules of confidentiality. Lack of access to and interaction with managers inherently limits the status women can achieve within the organization.

The executive secretary is an exception to the rule of gendered spatial segregation in the workplace. The executive secretary may have her own office, and she has access to more aspects of the managerial process than other secretaries. According to another American Management Association publication titled *The Successful Secretary:* "Probably no person gets to observe and see management principles in operation on a more practical basis than an executive secretary. She is privy to nearly every decision the executive makes. She has the opportunity to witness the gathering of information and the elements that are considered before major decisions are made and implemented" (Belker 1981, 191).

Yet instructions to the successful executive secretary suggest that those with the closest access to power are subject to the strictest guidelines regarding confidentiality. When physical barriers are breached and secretaries spend a great deal of time with the managers, rules governing the secretary's use of information become more important. The executive secretary is cautioned to hide shorthand notes, remove partially typed letters from the typewriter, lock files, and personally deliver interoffice memos to prevent unauthorized persons from gaining confidential information from the boss's office (Belker 1981, 66).

The executive secretary has access to substantial information about the company, but the highest compliment that can be paid her is that she does not divulge it to anyone or use it for personal gain. Comparing the importance of confidentiality to the seal of the confessional, Belker counsels secretaries that "the importance of confidentiality can't be overemphasized. Your company can be involved in some delicate business matters or negotiations, and the wrong thing leaked to the wrong person could have an adverse effect on the result.... Years ago, executive secretaries were sometimes referred to as confidential secretaries. It's a shame that title fell out of popular usage, because it's an accurate description of the job" (Belker 1981, 73–74).

### *Typical Men's Work: "Closed-Door Jobs"*

The largest occupational category for men is that of manager. In 1990, 8.9 million men were classified as "executive, administrative, and managerial." This group constituted 14 percent of all employed men (U.S. Department of Labor 1991, 163, 183). Thus, more than one in ten men works in a supervisory position.

Spatial arrangements in the workplace reinforce these status distinctions, partially by providing more "closed door" potential to managers than to those they supervise. Although sales and production supervisors may circulate among their employees, their higher status within the organization is reflected by the private offices to which they can withdraw. The expectation is that privacy is required for making decisions that affect the organization. Rather than sharing this privacy, the secretary is often in charge of "gate-keeping"—protecting the boss from interruptions.

Just as there are professional manuals for the successful secretary, there are also numerous guidelines for the aspiring manager. Harry Levinson's widely read *Executive* (1981) (a revision of his 1968 *The Exceptional Executive*) stresses the importance of managerial knowledge of the entire organization. A survey of large American companies asking presidents about suitable qualities in their successors revealed the following profile: "A desirable successor is a person with a general knowledge and an understanding of the whole organization, capable of fitting specialized contributions into profitable patterns.... The person needs a wide range of liberal arts knowledge together with a fundamental knowledge of business.... A leader will be able to view the business in global historical and technical perspective. Such a perspective is itself the basis for the most important requisite, what one might call 'feel'—a certain intuitive sensitivity for the right action and for handling relationships with people" (Levinson 1981, 136).

The importance of knowledge is stressed repeatedly in this description. The successful manager needs knowledge of the organization, of liberal arts, and of business in general. But equally important is the intuitive ability to carry out actions. This "feel" is not truly intuitive, of course, but is developed through observation and emulation of successful executives. Levinson identifies managerial leadership as "an art to be cultivated and developed," which is why it cannot be learned by the book; rather, "it must be learned in a relationship, through identification with a teacher" (Levinson 1981, 145).

Because the transfer of knowledge and the ability to use it are so crucial to leadership, Levinson devotes a chapter to "The Executive as Teacher." He advises that there is no prescription an executive can follow in acting as a teacher. The best strategy is the "shine and show them" approach—the manager carries out the duties of office as effectively as possible and thereby demonstrates to subordinates how decisions are made. There are no formal conditions under which teaching takes place; it is incorporated as part of the routine of the business day. In Levinson's words, "The process of example-setting goes on all the time. Executives behave in certain ways, sizing up problems, considering the resources ... that can be utilized to meet them, and making decisions about procedure. Subordinates, likewise, watch what they are doing and how they do it" (Levinson 1981, 154).

Just as in the ceremonial men's huts of nonindustrial societies, constant contact between elders and initiates in necessary for the transmission of knowledge. Levinson implies that it should be frequent contact to transfer most effectively formal and informal knowledge. Such frequent and significant contact is missing from the interaction between managers and secretaries. Given the spatial distance between the closed doors of managers and the open floors of secretaries, it is highly unlikely that sufficient contact between the two groups could occur for secretaries to alter their positions within the organization.

In addition to giving subordinates an opportunity to learn from the boss, spatial proximity provides opportunities for subordinates to be seen by the boss. This opportunity has been labeled "visiposure" by the author of *Routes to the Executive Suite* (Jennings 1971, 113). A combination of "visibility" and "exposure," visiposure refers to the opportunity to "see and be seen by the right people" (Jennings 1971, 113). Jennings counsels the rising executive that "the abilities to see and copy those who can influence his career and to keep himself in view of those who might promote him are all-important to success." The ultimate form of visiposure is for the subordinate's manager to be seen by the right managers as well. Such "serial visiposure" is the "sine qua non of fast upward mobility" and is facilitated by face-to-face interaction among several levels of managers and subordinates (Jennings 1971, 113–14).

Both Levinson and Jennings acknowledge the importance of physical proximity to achieving power within an organization, yet neither pursues the assumptions underlying the transactions they discuss—that is, the spatial context within which such interactions occur. To the extent women are segregated from men, the transfer of knowledge—with the potential for improving women's status—is limited.

## *Office Design and Gender Stratification*

Contemporary office design clearly reflects the spatial segregation separating women and men. Secretaries (almost all of whom are women) and managers (nearly two-thirds of whom are men) have designated areas assigned within the organization....

Privacy can be a scarce resource in the modern office. Empirical studies have shown that privacy in the office involves "the ability to control access to one's self or group, particularly the ability to *limit others' access to one's workspace*" (Sundstrom 1986, 178; emphasis added). Business executives commonly define privacy as the ability to control information and space. In other words, privacy is connected in people's minds with the spatial reinforcement of secrecy. Studies of executives, managers, technicians, and clerical employees have found a high correlation between enclosure of the work space (walls and doors) and perceptions of privacy; the greater the privacy, the greater the satisfaction with work. Employees perceive spatial control as a resource in the workplace that affects their job satisfaction and performance (Sundstrom, Burt, and Kemp 1980; Sundstrom 1986).

Not surprisingly, higher status within an organization is accompanied by greater control of space. In the Sundstrom study, most secretaries (75 percent) reported sharing an office; about one-half (55 percent) of bookkeepers and accountants shared an office; and only 18 percent of managers and administrators shared space. Secretaries had the least physical separation from other workers, while executives had the most (Sundstrom 1986, 184).

Two aspects of the work environment are striking when the spatial features of the workplaces for secretaries and executives are compared: the low number of walls or partitions surrounding secretaries (an average of 2.1), compared with executives (an average of 3.5), and the greater surveillance that accompanies the public space of secretaries. Three-quarters of all secretaries were visible to their supervisors, compared with only one-tenth of executives. As one would expect given the physical description of their respective offices, executives report the greatest sense of privacy and secretaries the least (Sundstrom 1986, 185). Doors do not necessarily have to be closed or locked in order to convey the message of differential power; they merely have to be available for closing and be seen as controlled at the executive's discretion (Steele 1986, 46).

The spatial distribution of employees in an office highlights the complex ways in which spatial segregation contributes to gender stratification. Workers obviously are not assigned space on the basis of sex, but on the basis of their positions within the organization. Theoretically, managers have the most complex jobs and secretaries have the least complex, yet research on secretaries and managers with equal degrees of office enclosure suggests that women's space is still considered more public than men's space. Sundstrom found that "in the workspaces with equivalent enclosure—private offices—[respondents] showed differential ratings of privacy, with lowest ratings by secretaries. This could reflect social norms. Secretaries have low ranks, and co-workers or visitors may feel free to walk unannounced into their workspaces. However, they may knock respectfully at the entrance of the workspaces of managers.... *Perhaps a private office is more private when occupied by a manager than when occupied by a secretary*" (Sundstrom 1986, 191; emphasis added). This passage suggests that even walls and a door do not insure privacy for the typical working woman in the same way they do for the typical working man. Features that should allow control of workspace do not operate for secretaries as they do for managers.

### Works Cited

Baran, Barbara, and Suzanne Teegarden. 1987. "Women's Labor in the Office of the Future: A Case Study of the Insurance Industry." In *Women, Households, and the Economy*, edited by Lourdes Beneria and Catharine R. Stimpson, pp. 201–24. New Brunswick, N.J.: Rutgers University Press.

Belker, Loren. 1981. *The Successful Secretary*. New York: American Management Association.

Blake, Robert, Jane S. Mouton, and Artie Stockton. 1983. *The Secretary Grid*. New York: American Management Association.

Jennings, Eugene Emerson. 1971. *Routes to the Executive Suite*. New York: McGraw-Hill.

Levinson, Harry. 1981. *Executive*. Cambridge: Harvard University Press.

Steele, Fritz. 1986. "The Dynamics of Power and Influence in Workplace Design and Management." In *Behavioral Issues in Office Design*, edited by Jean D. Wineman, pp. 43–64. New York: Van Nostrand Reinhold.

Sundstrom, Eric. 1986. "Privacy in the Office." In *Behavioral Issues in Office Design*, edited by Jean Wineman, pp. 177–202. New York: Van Nostrand Reinhold.

Sundstrom, Eric, Robert Burt, and Douglas Kemp. 1980. "Privacy at Work: Architectural Correlates of Job Satisfaction and Job Performance." *Academy of Management Journal* 23 (March): 101–17.

U.S. Department of Labor. 1991. *Employment and Earnings* 38 (January). Washington, D.C.: Bureau of Labor Statistics.

---

## This Text: Reading

1. Do think such constructions of public space matter? Are symbolic values of space crucial in our world?
2. Do you think genders have different ways of looking at public space? If so, where does this difference come from? Why does it persist?
3. What do you think Spain's "writing situation" is? Is she writing from experience or observation? Can you tell by reading her essay? Why does this distinction matter?

## Your Text: Writing

1. Find another environment where gender and space interact. What about the space you describe makes it connect to the particular gender?
2. Think about other public spaces or buildings where separation of people into genders, races, or classes is built into the design (*hint:* think of places where people spend more or less money to sit in different places). Are those spaces considered problematic in the same way Spain thinks about the workplace? Write a paper that addresses this question.

3. Look at several dorm rooms or apartments of friends both male and female. Write a short paper that discusses which elements in particular define these spaces as particularly male or female.
4. Look at other things that are "gendered," such as advertisements, clothing, and cars. How do these gendered texts compare to the gendered spaces you described earlier? What elements do designers of any text use to designate gender? Write a paper that ties gendered space to another gendered text.

## SHOPPING IN A MALL WHILE BLACK: A COACH'S STORY

Kenneth Meeks

Kenneth Meeks wrote this essay as part of *Driving While Black* (2000), a book about racial profiling. This story talks about the division between public and private spaces in a powerful and immediate way.

HOWIE EVANS WAS the basketball coach for the University of Maryland at Eastern Shore in 1985. That year he and his team were on a three-game exhibition tour in South Carolina. When they arrived in Columbia on Thanksgiving Day for their second game, the team unpacked their bags, put on their warm-up uniforms, and stretched their legs. They were hungry from their travels. The National Urban League's local chapter had a planned Thanksgiving Day dinner for the basketball team, but until then they needed something to eat.

Normally, the coach wouldn't allow his players to roam around the city. It takes away the strength in their legs. But on this particular day he bent the rules. It was an exhibition game, so he let his team out. They picked a mall about a quarter of a mile from the hotel.

Evans immediately spotted trouble when the team stepped into the shopping mall. Two security guards who had been sitting nearby went into action. Evans didn't say anything to his team about the guards behind them, but he remained mindful. As the team meandered into the center of the mall, they split into little cliques. A few disappeared into clothing stores, another went into a music store, and a few more just window-shopped. Evans himself went into a Radio Shack to buy some batteries. He never expected to see the two guards placing six of his players against the wall.

"What's going on?" Evans asked as he walked up on the scene.

The taller guard, who had sergeant stripes sewn into his uniform, answered. "They stole something from one of the stores."

"What did you see them take?"

The sergeant paused to eyeball Evans. "Who are you?"

"I'm their coach," Evans answered. He pulled out his identification. "Did you see them take anything?"

"No," the sergeant answered, "but somebody told us they did."

"Show me who told you they saw my team steal something. I want to know what he saw."

"We can't do that. He's not here."

Antennas went up. "What? You're going to search these young men based on something somebody told you, and—by your own admission—he's not even here in the mall?"

"I'm doing my job."

Evans took a deep breath and chose his words carefully.

"You know, I watched you guys when we first came in here. You were sitting by the door, and when we got about fifty feet away from you, you got up and started following us. We've only been in here twenty minutes, and already you've accused us of stealing something. Why were you following us in the first place?"

The sergeant fumbled for an answer.

"I'm not going to let you search these kids out here in public," Evans continued confidently. "If you want to search them, you're going to have to take us down to the police station."

"I'll have to call them," the sergeant explained, almost as if he hoped the idea would make Evans stand down.

"So call them. If you don't, I will."

The sergeant detained the six players against the wall while Evans huddled with the rest of his team. Spectators watched from the wings.

"Look at these guys. What are they doing now?" a black woman whispered.

It broke Evans's heart that black people were walking away shaking their heads in embarrassment because they assumed that these young black men had done something wrong. The team promised him that no one had stolen anything and that it was all a setup. In fact, a black security guard was called to the scene—Evans now believes to justify that no one was being a racist—but after a few minutes of sizing up the situation, he threw his hands in the air in disgust.

"You guys are harassing them," the black guard said and walked away.

"We need you to stay here," the sergeant commanded.

"Give me a break."

But the sergeant wasn't hearing it.

While everyone waited for the police to arrive, Evans found a pay phone and called the local chapter of the NAACP. He explained his situation and asked them to send an attorney down to the scene. His second phone call was to the local black newspaper. He informed one of the editors of what was happening to his players. It was mere coincidence that a reporter for a local mainstream newspaper was in the mall at the time. Evans and the young reporter discussed everything.

In the meantime the sergeant let the six kids relax with the rest of the team, but he wanted everyone in a group.

"Don't panic," Evans told his team.

Evans suddenly saw the situation escalate into a potentially dangerous one. He had reasons to keep his team calm. Most of his players were young freshmen and sophomores who had never been on a collegiate road trip before. And for most of them this was their first time away from home on Thanksgiving.

On the other hand, the team was up against an out-and-out Southern racist with a gun. The sergeant stood about six feet and two hundred pounds, walking among the posse of the basketball players with an overbearing attitude and his hand continuously touching his gun. As Evans saw it, the sergeant was trying to impress the other guard by showing that he could take on these young black athletes, that he was someone who was used to grabbing black kids and throwing them up against the wall on a regular basis.

Evans kept a level head and remained very professional. He never raised his voice, just maintained a dignified degree of intelligence and poise. "Are you trying to intimidate us by walking around us with your hand on your gun? Don't you think that's dangerous?"

"I have the safety catch on," he answered.

"I would hope so," Evans said. "But doesn't that present a very intimidating presence, you walking around with your hand on your gun? These kids aren't going anywhere. They will move only if I tell them to move. If I told these kids to get up and run out, they would. But then you'd probably shoot one of them in the back. Right?"

A call blared over the walkie-talkie. The police were here. The sergeant met with the police and the manager of the mall, a man in his late twenties or early thirties, separately while Evans waited with his team.

Finally the manager walked over to Evans. "My guy said that they stole something."

"You know the only reason your guys stopped these kids was because they're black. Look at all these other kids in the mall; no one stopped them. These kids are college kids, and they're wearing identifying uniforms, so why would they go into a store and steal something with all this ID on? They don't even have pockets."

But the manager wasn't convinced.

"Your guy also didn't tell you that the person who told him these kids stole something isn't in the mall either. And your guy didn't see them steal anything."

The manager listened carefully, then walked away to confer with his team. "Stay here."

They took a long time.

"So what are you guys going to do?" Evans finally asked as he approached them. "You are accusing these guys of something simply based on who they are. As soon as my lawyer comes—I have an attorney on the way—we're willing to go to the police station, where you can search these kids. But if you search them here, I'm going to bring a lawsuit against you."

"You have a lawyer?" Everyone was surprised. "Just wait for us over there. We'll be there when we're done."

Evans remembers overhearing one of them calling him a wise guy and saying, "They always bring up this we-stopped-them-because-they-were-black stuff."

From a distance Evans could see that the police officers, who were also white, were concerned. "You guys had better handle this. We're leaving."

The policemen left before the NAACP attorney arrived. And as Evans filled in the details for the attorney, the sergeant's case seemed to crumble. Close to two hours after the team walked into the mall, the manager finally had little choice but to let them go.

"Perhaps you wouldn't have a problem, Coach, if you didn't have all these kids coming into the mall at the same time."

"What are you talking about? What am I supposed to do? Bring them in two at a time, go back and bring in two more? This is a team. Would you say that to anybody else? I think you owe us an apology."

"Don't get stressed, Coach," said the attorney from the NAACP. "They're always stopping our kids at this mall."

Neither Howie Evans nor his team ever received a formal apology from the city of Columbia, South Carolina, the manager of the mall, or the security agency hired to patrol it.

## *Arrest People of Color First, Then Ask Questions*

Professor Charles Ogletree remembers the story of an artist who went to shop in a department store with an American Express card. He spent a couple of thousands of dollars in a very short time. He bought suits, clothes, a whole bunch of other items, and he signed his name. After he completed his shopping, one of the clerks who accepted his purchase got nervous and phoned the police. The police jumped the young man outside the store as he got into his car. They arrested him, brought him back into the store—brutalizing him in the process—and only after a few minutes of investigation discovered that he was the person whose name was on the credit card. When the clerk was asked by newspaper reporters the next day, after consulting with her bosses, why she had called the police, she answered, "Oh, it wasn't because he was black. That had nothing to do with it. It was because he was making some bad decisions in the things he was purchasing."

Ogletree is a professor at the Harvard School of Law and directs its Criminal Justice Institute. As the author of *Beyond the Rodney King Story*, a book relating to the NAACP's vision for policing the police, Ogletree is considered a leading authority in the world of legal issues regarding the police and its relationship to the minority community. He says "driving while black" was only the tip of the iceberg. Police misconduct goes deeper than racial profiling.

"As much as we talk about the drivers, there is also a crime called 'riding while black.' And for those of you who walk through the cities of New York, Washington, D.C., Los Angeles, Chicago, and Houston, there is a crime called 'walking while black.' And we don't see the books as much, but those of you who jog through Central Park, or Lincoln Park in Washington, D.C., or any park in Anywhere, USA, there is a crime called 'jogging while black.' There is also a nondiscriminatory crime that crosses gender lines called 'shopping while black.' You get all the tension in the world in department stores, so we all really have the phenomenon called 'living while black.' It's inevitable."

The sad element of the story above is that the police grabbed the young man without first checking to see if he really was the person who was signing the American Express transactions.

## *Can Security Guards Stop People?*

One New York City police officer I spoke with concerning the power of a security guard said a security guard has the power of a peace officer; a guard isn't allowed to carry a firearm, but as a part of his duties, if he sees someone shoplifting, he can stop and hold that person until a police officer arrives. Police officers call this a 1011, where security is holding someone in a commercial place. But let's take this a step further. The clerk who works the cash register, or the salesperson who is helping a customer, or even another customer who is just browsing has the same right to detain an individual as does a security guard. In cases where other citizens witness a crime in progress, any of those citizens can make a "civilian arrest" and detain the wrongdoer until a police officer arrives on the scene. In a civilian arrest, the good citizen has the right to physically restrain the bad citizen until an officer arrives. (But don't hurt anyone; the law gets tricky when someone is physically injured.)

So yes, security guards have the right to detain individuals, and they have the right to profile. Howard Amos, Jr., a part-time security guard who works various stadium security details like the Louisville Gardens in downtown Louisville, Kentucky, explained, "If there is an opera and everyone is dressed in formal clothing and all of a sudden someone walks in wearing overalls with a lit cigarette in his mouth, as a security guard I have the right to profile him, though it's not necessarily racial. And, as a security guard, I have the right to hold him or keep him from entering the opera. It's a security guard's job to watch the door to see who is coming and going into a show or a mall or whatever is being guarded. If a guard believes a particular individual is coming into a particular guarded area to commit a crime or to do someone harm, the security guard has the right to hold a person in the name of security. That's how the police do it.

"Probable cause also applies to security guards. They are considered policemen without guns. Security guards are considered the 'judge on the scene.' However, if a guard asks someone to leave and the person challenges the guard's authority, then a police officer has to be called to the scene."

Take this hypothetical situation: Say a photographer sneaks his camera equipment into a Janet Jackson concert, and it's clearly posted that taking photographs during the show is not permitted. If a guard confronts the photographer, he might use the tone of his voice to assert his authority, but the guard cannot by law confiscate the photographer's equipment or film. If a challenge erupts, it is a wise idea for the photographer to request the presence of a police officer immediately. Again, a security guard does not have the right to confiscate personal property.

### Tidbit

*North Carolina became the first state to create a Traffic Stop Bureau in March 1999; Connecticut was second, when the governor signed into law a similar bill on June 28, 1999. Other states seriously considering passage of state laws requiring traffic-stop data-collection units include California, Florida, Illinois, Maryland, Massachusetts, Ohio, Pennsylvania, Texas, Virginia, and Wisconsin. As of winter 2000, the governor of California vetoed a bill that had passed in the General Assembly.*

---

## This Text: Reading

1. What does this particular story say about public space and race?
2. Is a mall public or private space? Is this distinction important in this case or any other?
3. What is Meeks' writing situation? Do you think he came to this situation through experience or study? Does the writing situation matter in this particular case—why or why not?
4. Are there people who are also "reverse profiled"—given special treatment in public or private space based on their looks?

## Your Text: Writing

1. Although not everyone has been a victim of racial profiling or even prejudice, we all have witnessed such acts either through our own experience or through media stories. One can certainly think of this as a public space issue—what authorities of any sort are doing when they racially profile

are essentially identifying someone's use of space as problematic. Write about the assumptions people in power make when profiling.

2. Write a short paper assessing "reverse profiling," the preferential use of public and private space.
3. Do some research on how public space has been used for prejudicial purposes in the past.

## CAUGHT LOOKING: PROBLEMS WITH TAKING PICTURES OF PEOPLE TAKING PICTURES AT AN EXHIBITION

Robert Bednar

Here Robert Bednar writes about the odd relationship we have with nature and public space, using his experience with photography and tourism as a way of talking about the national park. This piece, part of his dissertation (1997), is part of a larger manuscript about public spaces and national parks.

THE STORY BEGINS in the Black Hills of South Dakota where, as clichéd as it may sound, I had a sort of epiphany one gray August day in 1991. The epiphany occurred on day five of what would be a fourteen-day, 7,000-mile caffeine-paced reconnaissance trip through ten states in the West that started and ended in Salt Lake City, Utah. I decided to go on the trip while I was working in a fish fossil quarry in southwestern Wyoming for the summer. I thought I should take advantage of the proximity of Wyoming to many other western states I had not visited before. I also wanted to experience travelling "Out West" on the same time scale as the "typical tourists" I was beginning to become interested in academically.

For days I sped through Utah, Colorado, Wyoming, and Nebraska. I rarely stopped for anything but periodic photo opportunities and gas and food fill-ups, and rarely slowed down the pace except in my nightly searches for National Forest campsites. But as I approached the South Dakota border from the sand hills of Nebraska, I started to notice that the roads were becoming more and more crowded and the driving pace was becoming more and more frenetic. A rainstorm was also moving in, darkening the sky and giving an ominous feel to the whole experience. For the rest of the way, the rainy highways leading into the Black Hills were packed with vehicles that displayed cultural allegiance to the myth of the west. Caravans of RVs with names like "Frontiersman," "Caribou," "Wanderer II," and "Tioga" were travelling alongside automobiles called "Pathfinder," "Wrangler Renegade," "Cherokee," and "Explorer." Both were intermixed with bands of bikers in black leather chaps and shirts and jackets with images of eagles and cow skulls on them. I saw license plates from states as far away as Vermont, Florida, and California, and as near as Montana and Minnesota.

The parking lot at the National Monument was full, so I parked my truck next to the other vehicles parked in the impromptu overflow parking on the lawn beside the parking lot. I slipped on my raincoat and prepared to face the rain. As I grabbed my camera off the seat beside me and got out of the truck, I noticed that some bikers next to me were also grabbing their still cameras and video cameras out of their saddle bags. I decided that instead of going directly to the viewing deck I would wait out the rain inside the Visitor Center directly behind it. I wandered around the Visitor Center looking at the displays, books, and postcards, surrounded by other jostling bodies doing the same. After nearly a week of solitary travel, it felt good to commune with other tourists involved in a common endeavor. I joined the people crowding around a TV screen that was playing a video about the heroic feats involved in the production of the sculpture. Because I came in in the middle of the video, I stayed on to watch the first half when the last half was over. Before long, I noticed that the rain outside had turned to a fine mist, so I wandered out onto the designated scenic overlook (which in this case was actually a scenic underlook). I took several photos of the stone faces with my camera—photos framed the same way as the post cards I had seen earlier in the Visitor Center. The only difference was that in my pictures the sky was gray, not blue. I noticed that many of the other visitors were taking similar pictures.

Soon, however, huge drops began pelting those of us standing on the one hundred square foot landing just below the Monument. I fled to the Visitor Center, but I noticed that few of my companions were joining me. Despite the rain, the pilgrims were still drawn magnetically to the wall at the edge of the viewing platform where they alternately gazed at and photographed the stone faces, and took pictures of each other standing in front of the Monument. I crept outside again and found a spot next to the few other wimps standing under the building's awning, and watched what became for me something "photographable" as a dramatic spectacle that overshadowed the intended drama of the patriotic faces carved into the side of the granite outcropping. Perhaps it was because the rain obscured the distant view, or perhaps it was because I was traveling alone and thus had no one to pose with, but, either way, the foreground of the vista became much more interesting to me than the presented vista. The gray Monument off in the distance started to look like a huge unreal hologram or backdrop prop compared to the physicality of the people there at the underlook performing their elaborately choreographed (though apparently authorless) stageplay. As I started thinking about how all of these people had learned how to act their part in this cultural drama, I pulled out my camera again, and began taking pictures of the context surrounding what I was supposed to see instead of the thing itself.

As I stood there now taking pictures and thinking about the implications of what I was seeing, I noticed that a young Japanese-American boy had become bored with his family's posing ritual and had begun looking at me as I took pictures of people on the viewing deck. I guess I had been making more of a spectacle of myself than I had intended. Soon, the boy raised his little automatic camera and took my picture, drawing me into the scene I had been observing from afar and implicating me in the action. I was no longer an invisible passive observer, a detached post tourist. Now, as the result of a single momentary action, I had become—like the people having their pictures taken in front of the Monument and the Monument itself—something photographable according to a tourist aesthetic.

Even now I am surprised that in the rush of the "decisive moment" I had the presence of mind to quickly snap a picture of the boy as the boy "took" my picture as I "took" his picture taking my picture taking his picture, etc. The spiraling of images was dizzying to me then and still is now as I recall it and try to construct a sentence that will do it justice. The photograph I took is not very well focused and didn't really "catch" the boy in the action of taking my picture, but I have put it here because the image continues to speak to me. The boy had already started to put his camera down when I snapped my picture, but he was still looking at me. Moreover, in the picture his parents are also looking at me, wondering perhaps why their son had wasted his film, how I felt about what he had done, and whether my photographing them was hostile. I still wonder what the boy's family did with his picture of me. Did they incorporate the picture into their own family album (do they have one?) and narrate my actions as "another roadside attraction," or did they edit the picture out as an irrelevant "kid picture"? I wonder similar things about the other pictures I have taken of people looking into my camera trying to figure out what I was doing—where did they locate me?

I have told so many people this story that it has started off its own set of new meanings as my friends and students have incorporated it into their

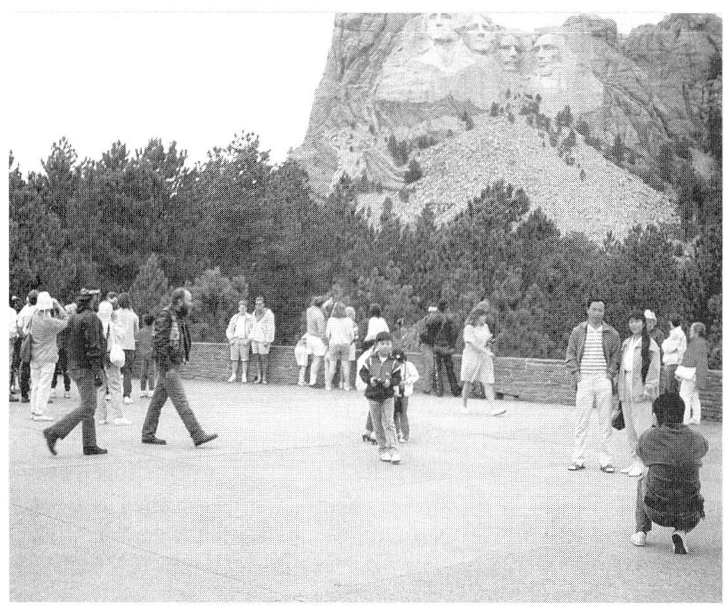

own sets of representations of touristic encounters with Mount Rushmore and with touristic landscapes in general. I began to see my experience of being implicated in the field of action as a lesson I had learned from reading Mark Klett's article, "A View of the Grand Canyon in Homage to William Bell," just before I took my trip. It would be an understatement to say that Klett's article was on my mind as I traveled. Indeed, the article was so central for me that I have titled my Mount Rushmore picture "A View of Mount Rushmore in Homage to Mark Klett."

I mention this not only to acknowledge my debts to Klett, but also to further illustrate how the process of landscape tourism works in the field for me as well as the tourists I have studied. As I began to explore the phenomenon further, I found that my experience at Mount Rushmore could serve as a case study in the ways that portions of a landscape are made both visible and meaningful for the people encountering them. Every place I visited I carried with me a set of complex legacies that I had inherited from my particular upbringing and my academic training. Learning how this worked for me as well as my "subjects" helped me understand that whether we consciously apprehend it at the site or not, all photographs of place pay homage to previous acts of inhabitation and image-making.

As I argued in the Snapshot Semiotics Overview, when we visit a landscape that has been designated a tourist landscape, we inhabit not only a landscape but also an imagescape. Just as William Bell's photographs were part of the imagescape Klett inhabited as he photographed Taroweap Point, Klett's words and images were part of the imagescape I temporarily inhabited at Mount Rushmore. They helped me notice the context that foregrounded the site, and they helped me think about ways of representing it. They helped me see my own reflection in the people I was studying as well. They did not "cause" or "determine" my epiphany in any simplistic sense, but they did highlight things that I had not yet learned to articulate. My role in doing the present study is to further that process of highlighting. I hope to add my modest input to the imagescape that my readers will inhabit if they visit one of the sites under discussion after temporarily inhabiting my text, or even if they do not.

But, more important, my picture of the boy at Mount Rushmore has served as a constant reminder to me that while I was "studying" this phenomenon as an academic, I was also thoroughly implicated in it. I started this project bewitched by Baudrillardian explanations for the role of images in postmodern culture. As a self-consciously ironic post-tourist, I reveled in the idea that the landscapes tourists were visiting had been rendered hyperreal by their long history of representations. Like DeLillo's Murray, I gained power from that knowledge, and congratulated myself for being detached enough from those unfortunates who were mistaking a presented nature for nature itself. The obverse of the satisfaction I felt when I "understood" tourism this way was the solace I took in knowing of and seeking out places off the beaten trail where I could find authentic nature in its raw unmediated form. When I went to tourist sites I thought of myself as a disembodied tourist of tourism, but when I went camping, backpacking, or hiking off the beaten trail I thought of my self as an entirely embodied wilderness adventurer. The longer I inhabited this discourse and the more time I spent at tourist sites, however, the more I began to understand the limitations of nihilistic postmodernism as a strategy for both being-in-the-world and for studying the ways that others do the same. And as I started looking around me I found more people like myself who were trying to teach themselves and others the same lessons I was trying to teach myself every time I looked at that Mount Rushmore picture hanging on my wall.

---

## This Text: Reading

1. What is your experience with tourist places? What had you noticed about them before reading this essay?
2. What type of relationship do you have with public or private spaces generally? Do you notice or have you noticed when those who have constructed a space try to guide your actions?
3. What type of tourist places do you prefer—amusement parks, national parks, museums, etc.? Why? If you go to a national park do you prefer to follow well marked trails or your own? Why?

### YOUR TEXT: WRITING

1. Document your own experience in trying to navigate public space either familiar or unfamiliar to you. In what ways does your environment control your actions? Is this a necessity?
2. Write a short paper talking about your experience in a national park. Think back about the way you were guided—or not guided—in your experience. What effect does reading Bednar's piece and reflection have on your memories?

## ROOM FOR LEARNING WITH LATEST TECHNOLOGY

Katherine F. Benzel

We are all familiar with the problems of classrooms—they are often sterile places which, depending on your location, suffer from a lack of windows, poor ventilation, and uncomfortable seating. If we've sat in these types of rooms all our lives, it may never occur to us that there might be better classrooms. Here Katherine Benzel writes (1998) about one ideal classroom.

AN EXAMPLE OF A ROOM whose effective performance is not communicated visually on a floor plan is the class-lab recently installed in the Meyer Memorial Library at Stanford University. About two years ago Stanford set out to design a prototypical room for learning with the latest technology.[1] At that time the design decision makers sought the participation of the users to identify how they wanted the classroom to perform. From a collaboration of students and teachers, the idea of what a classroom should be became very clear:

> A classroom is a space that supports learning relationships through flexibility, small groups, eye contact, greater interaction, and a sense of community (this is hard to communicate in a floor plan).
>
> Everyone wants technology, but nobody wants it to dominate the setting as it so often does when bulky, noisy computer stations are rigged up (permanent computer stations are easy to show in a floor plan).

Here is the solution that was provided:

> *Laptop computers* (like pencils, these would not appear on a floor plan)
> *Floor sockets* (they would appear on an electrical plan)
> *Beanbag chairs* (they almost defy being frozen in a plan)
> *Lightweight tables* (they are drawn in a plan in one configuration)

*Carpet squares* to conveniently conceal and reveal the floor sockets (they usually appear on a materials board)

Everything technological is there—the Internet, laser printers, and video—but it is not so evident.

The genius of the solution is that it reduces a complex set of requirements to a simple framing of action. The solution has the potential to

1. Make the technology, like any other common tool, almost invisible
2. Create relationships between people within a social context where they may adjust more directly to others
3. Allow people to control their environment with a sense of autonomy and participation
4. Fulfill the promise the room bears to integrate the social and spatial systems to which it belongs
5. Form one unified and superior comprehensive image called community out of a multitude of elements and people

In the Meyer Memorial Library scheme, the computer stations that shut in users and shut out all the others, creating barriers among students and between student and teacher, are gone. Laptop computers can be picked up from a library cart, and tables and chairs can be rearranged at a moment's notice. The final solution includes another important requirement: windows. At first the classroom was in a basement, a location no one liked. Once it was shifted to a second floor corner location, large windows opened up the classroom to the sun above and the main quadrangle below. With brightly backlit computer screens, the windows can be left unshuttered, letting the sun and view become part of the space. The context of community, the connection to the larger world, and an open exchange of ideas are reinforced as the room overlooks the university quadrangle. The "quad" defines a center and paths where different people come together into a shared form of life.

Emerging from a collaboration of students and teachers rather than from a weighty abstract design theory or objective, the solution for the class-lab is in agreement with the users—students and teachers—and the shapes of their particular lessons and instincts. The design of the room is about people and communication, not technology and PCs; it helps the participants interact with the space and with each other. Through simple eye contact and face-to-face dialogue, students can be made aware of the different opinions held by each yet have a shared sense of themselves as one class in one place. Referring to Goethe's quote, the class has the opportunity to see "itself united into a noble body" rather than separated into quasi-secretive screen viewers and therefore is more likely to be "induced into oneness" and "enlivened by one spirit." This gathering environment becomes an important social learning tool from which all schools and grades can benefit. There is no doubt that this solution is expensive; however, taking into account our urgent need for building community and maintaining effective teaching at all levels, a cost–benefit analysis has to come down in favor of the benefit:

> The making of places—our homes, our neighborhoods, our places of work and play—not only changes and maintains the physical world of living; it also is a way we make our communities and connect with other people.[2]

Inasmuch as this classroom adjusts itself to the shape of each teacher's lesson, it may not look "designed" in a drawing. After all, in expressing learning relationships within a sense of community, the beanbag chairs are not squarely and uniformly lined up but are spontaneous, ordinary, and fluid clusters of face-to-face talking and listening. The beauty of the room resides not only in how good it looks but in how well it establishes human and spatial relationships, how well it performs in terms of learning. This room, like every room, is a process of seeing and doing, thought-provoking, in agreement with our instincts, attractive and popular by nature.

## *Room as Community*

Along with a view inward toward its special function, the classroom must have a view outward toward society and nature in order to serve functional as well as socially moral ends. To reiterate, life and room belong together. A classroom is synonymous with participating in the world because as a real place with real people it is part of a larger whole in both a local and a worldly, temporary, and permanent sense. Students can gain character and values in addition to knowledge through face-to-face interaction with teachers who mold those qualities. In this way, the classroom embodies human and spatial togetherness because it is a place where individuals can acquire an identity and a society. In agreement with Alberti, a classroom can be compared to a city square. As an urban meeting place, the square is designed as an enclosure (room concept) to bring together an assortment of individuals arriving from different directions into a community. According to Christian Norberg-Schulz, to open up a world of possibilities for meeting and choice, the square must have three general properties: *density* (there is no city or urban interior space where buildings are scattered), *variety* (the idea of meeting implies both variety and unity), and *continuity* (the experience of a totality is basically a continuous process)[3]:

> As our choice forms part of a totality, however, it does not isolate us, but rather allows for participation. Again we recognize the profound meaning of using the place as our primary self-identification. It implies respect for the totality in which we take part, and the realization that our part is meaningful because it belongs to a world.[4]

The ideal room offers a universal outlook, a wider dimension of time and place, and an interconnection between people and their inner and outer space. The ideal room helps individuals acquire knowledge, skill, and responsibility by enticing them to see more, question more, imagine more, know more, do more, and control more. The ideal room fully engages the senses, keeps the intellect and imagination alert, provides physical comfort, and can put dignity back into ordinary life. The room as a meeting place for individual choice within a community provides for the natural process of change and brings potential into being. If history is a guide, the rituals associated with inhabiting the room help us become totally present within ourselves and our world.

### Notes

1. "At Stanford, a Class-Lab Friendly to Computers," *New York Times*, April 3, 1996, p. B8.
2. Lynda H. Schneekloth and Robert G. Shibley, *Placemaking: The Art and Practice of Building Communities* (New York: Wiley, 1995), p. 1.
3. Christian Norberg-Schulz, *The Concept of Dwelling* (New York: Rizzoli, 1985), pp. 51–55.
4. Norberg-Schulz, *The Concept of Dwelling*, p. 51.

---

## This Text: Reading

1. Why do you think there are not more rooms like the one described in the article? Is it only a matter of cost?
2. Do you think this class would function better in the room described in the article?
3. Talk about an ideal room—or almost ideal room—you are familiar with. What makes this particular room ideal? Is it form meeting function (the idea matching the reality of the room) or just a particular comfort you have with the room?
4. In what ways might technology make a classroom less receptive to learning? Are there types of learning that could suffer in the type of classroom Benzel describes?

## Your Text: Writing

1. Invent your own ideal classroom. What elements would it have in it? How would it be shaped? How would you balance comfort with the need to pay attention?
2. Write a paper where you describe your experiences in a classroom, both satisfying and less so. How might a better classroom have helped you learn better?

# Public Space—The Suburban Suite

Suburbia has dominated the American living landscape for almost half a century, and although it's not an American invention, the suburb and all that's attached to it has become a prototypically American living arrangement. But the suburbs have never been without their critics, who have criticized the reliance on cars, the social and often racial and ethnic isolation, and conformity attached to the suburbs. Here William Hamilton (1999) writes about the impact of suburbs on teenagers, while William Booth (1998) examines the reverse migration of whites from cities to the suburbs in South Florida.

In response to the continued sprawl of suburbs, architects and town planners have proposed the idea of making newer suburbs more like small towns of old. New Urbanism, most prominently displayed in *The Truman Show*'s (1998) real-life setting of Seaside, Florida, has become increasingly popular in the last decade. The architectural and public space movement encourages a return to small-town living, which revolves around common spaces and a layout that encourages walking and more social interaction. Here Sarah Boxer (1998) and Whitney Gould (1999) examine the idea of New Urbanism.

## HOW SUBURBAN DESIGN IS FAILING TEEN-AGERS

William L. Hamilton

AS QUICKLY AS THE WORD "alienation" can be attached to the idea of youth, the image of isolation can be attached to a picture of the suburbs. Is there an unexplored relationship between them? It is a question parents and urban planners alike are raising in the aftermath of the Columbine High School shootings in Littleton, Colo.

At a time when the renegade sprawl of suburbs themselves is being intensely scrutinized, the troubling vision of a nation re-pioneered in vast tracts of disconnected communities has produced uneasy discussion about the psychological disorientation they might house. Created as safe havens from the sociological ills of cities, suburbs now stand accused of creating their own environmental diseases: lack of character and the grounding principles of identity, lack of diversity or the tolerance it engenders, lack of attachment to shared, civic ideals. Increasingly, the newest, largest suburbs are being criticized as landscapes scorched by unthoughtful, repetitious building, where, it has been suggested, the isolations of larger lots and a car-based culture may lead to disassociation from the reality of contact with other people.

Designers of the newest American suburbs say they have largely ignored or avoided one volatile segment of the population—teen-agers. In recent conversations, three dozen urban planners, architects, environmental psychologists and sociologists, and experts on adolescent development agreed that specific community planning and places for teen-agers to make their own are missing.

"They're basically an unseen population until they pierce their noses," said William Morrish, a professor of architecture and the director of the Design Center for American Urban Landscape at the University of Minnesota. "They have access to computers and weaponry. The sense of alienation that might come from isolation or neglect will have a much larger impact than it might have before. And there are no questions coming from the design community about what we can be doing about this. We don't invite them in."

Virtually every other special interest has been addressed by enlightened suburban designers—the elderly, the disabled, families with young children. But, said Andres Duany, a planner who is a leading proponent of the "new urbanism," a model of suburban design based on principles of traditional towns, "it's the teen-agers I always bring up as a question mark." Mr. Duany said that he had only once or twice included teen-agers in the public process of planning a suburban development.

"It's a good point," he said, as though it were an unlikely idea. "I should talk to the kids."

Though teen-agers tend to resist advice and choose their own turf as a territorial issue of establishing self-identity, most experts interviewed say that design could constructively anticipate and accommodate anxieties of adolescence. They agreed that teen-agers need a place to congregate in and to call their own; it is a critical aspect of relieving the awkward loneliness of adolescence. Between home and school—spheres compromised by the presence of parents or the pressure of performance—places for teen-agers in the suburbs are as uncommon as sidewalks.

"It's a paradoxical situation," said Ray Suarez, host of "Talk of the Nation" on National Public Radio and author of *The Old Neighborhood* (The Free Press, 1999), a study of suburban migration. "Parents move there for their children; their children are dying to get out." Like much of the Western United States, Denver is experiencing vertiginous suburban growth. From 1990 to 1996, the metropolitan area expanded by two-thirds, to its current size of 535 square miles.

"Typical of the Denver metro area are the new suburbs, where 'downtown' is a four-way intersection with three shopping centers and a condo development," said Charles Blosten, community services director for Littleton's city planning division. Highlands Ranch, Denver's largest suburban development, has its own ZIP code, "nothing but rooftops and miles and miles of nothing," he said of the numbing vista of houses. "It's got to affect people."

The idea that place has an impact on adolescent development and socialization is accepted by most experts on the suburbs but is only now beginning to be studied. "A culture of impersonality has developed in the suburbs by the way they're laid out," said Jonathan Barnett, a professor of regional planning at the University of Pennsylvania and author of *The Fractured Metropolis* (HarperCollins, 1996). In the newer suburbs, "the standard of houses is high, but the standard of community isn't," he continued, adding, "It's most people's impression of modern life."

And the people it stands to impress the most are children. "They are the most vulnerable people growing up there," said Dr. Jose Szapocznik, a professor of psychiatry and behavioral sciences and director of the Center for Family Studies at the University of Miami. "As a child you're disabled by not being able to walk anywhere. Nothing is nearby."

Mr. Morrish said he thought that public transportation to metropolitan downtowns was crucial for high school students. He said that the ability to access "the system"—the world adults create—was a vital form of empowerment.

"What to do after school, how to get to the city, to see other people and how to negotiate this without parents," he said, posing the issues. "Teen-agers have to have better access to the public realm and public activity." He recalled a conversation with a group of high school students who met with the Design Center, which invites teen-agers to group meetings when it is commissioned to study neighborhoods.

"One girl said, 'All I've got is the Pizza Hut,'" Mr. Morrish said. "'You go there a lot or you go to somebody's house—we're tired of both.'"

Between home and school, in a landscape drawn by cars and the adults who drive them, is there even a particular place that teen-agers can call their own? Peter Lang, a professor of architecture at the New Jersey Institute of Technology and an editor of *Suburban Discipline* (Princeton Architectural Press, 1997), a collection of essays, said: "In most suburbs, there's not even a decent park, because everyone has a backyard. But older kids never play in the backyard. They'll find even the crummiest piece of park."

Typically, the students at Columbine High School went to Southwest Plaza, a two-level mall that has video arcades, food courts and stores, supervised by security guards and closed by 9 P.M. "Like any suburban community, there's not a lot of places to go and hang out," Mr. Blosten said of Littleton. "I tell you this because that's where my daughter goes—the mall."

Mr. Lang said he thought that places like malls were not adequate gathering spaces for teen-agers, calling them, like many public suburban venues, commercially and environmentally "controlled space." He added, "They are not places for free expression or hanging out."

Disagreeing that suburbs create greater alienation is Dr. Laurence Steinberg, a professor of psychology at Temple University and director of the MacArthur Foundation Research Network on Adolescent Development and Juvenile Justice. But he said that he thought recent tragedies like the incident in Littleton do "wake people up to the notion that there is parental disengagement in affluent suburbs." He added: "We did a study on latchkey kids. The kids most likely to be left unattended for long periods were middle class, in sprawling professional suburbs. Isolated for long periods of time, there's no counterbalancing force to fantasy."

The desire for more and cheaper land that has pushed suburbs to rural exurbia may result in teen-agers who are alone for large parts of the day. Mr. Morrish pointed out that in communities like Modesto, in the San Joaquin Valley in central California, people commute to jobs in the San Francisco area, where they enroll their children in schools.

"Some people in California are taking their kids with them," he said, "making the kids commute."

The planners who have been most vocally and visibly at work on restructuring the suburban model have been "new urbanists" like Mr. Duany. Their solutions to the wheeling nebulae of tract development are based on tighter concentrations of houses, businesses and public spaces connected by townlike elements—porches, sidewalks and parks—that have largely disappeared from the new residential landscape.

If teen-agers find their place there, in new towns like Columbia and Kentlands in Maryland or Celebration, the Disney-built town in Florida, it is not because of any bravery on the planners' part. They often foster nostalgic views of families with young children. But like conventional suburbs, they overlook the inevitability of teen-agers in their design.

Peter Katz, who with Vincent Scully wrote *The New Urbanism: Toward an Architecture of Community* (McGraw-Hill, 1993), spoke of the importance to teen-agers of a place that existed only for them, neither hidden and ignored nor exposed and supervised—in effect, a secret place in full view.

On a visit, Mr. Katz discovered that for Celebration's teen-agers, it was a narrow bridge, "with low railings, that goes from downtown to the health club." He continued: "They find each other. They sit on the railing. It's on the route to daily life—not a back alley, but not the town square." Mr. Katz suggested that such a structure could become a conscious part of a community design for teen-agers.

For Diane Dorney, a mother with two teen-age children who lives in Kentlands, Md., a 10-year-old "new urban" suburb of some 1,800 people, the hallmarks of town life work well for both parents and children. Ms. Dorney and her husband, Mark, moved their family from a typical townhouse development.

"We wanted to raise our kids in a place that provided more than just a house," she said. "It's a diverse community, of age and income," with older people, young couples, families. Ms. Dorney said that she thought the gaze of the town created a sense of extended family and moral weight that were its most important success.

"Someone sneaking down the street to have a cigarette—they don't get away with it," she said. "I don't think teen-agers should be left on their own until they're caught at the small things." She continued, "When they go into the big things, they know how big they are." She added: "And we have another way of knowing these kids, other than the bad things. They're your neighbors, too. You're always seeing them. You give them another chance."

## A WHITE MIGRATION NORTH FROM MIAMI

William Booth

EVERYTHING HERE IS NICE AND NEAT, just the way Joanne Smith likes it. The developers call their new city on the edge of the Everglades "Our Home Town," and Smith agrees. "It's more like America," she says.

Like thousands of others, Smith moved to this planned community 40 miles north of Miami just a few years ago, searching for a safe and secure neighborhood like this one, where both modest homes and rambling mansions sit against the manicured landscape of palm and hibiscus, and gated streets called Wagon Way and Windmill Ranch gently curve around the shallow lagoons and golf links.

Weston is a boomtown filling with refugees. But the migrants pouring into this part of Broward County are rarely those from the Caribbean, Central and South America—the immigrants to the south who have transformed Miami and surrounding Dade County into a metropolis proudly called by its business and political leaders "The Gateway to Latin America." Instead, the refugees here are mostly native-born and white, young and old, and they have been streaming up from Miami for years now, creating a new version of the traditional "white flight" in reaction not to black inner cities, but to immigration.

While Miami is unique in many respects, because of both geography and politics, the out-migration of whites is occurring in other high-immigration cities. New York and Los Angeles, for example, each lost a million U.S.-born residents in the last decade, as they gained a million immigrants.

According to an analysis of the most recent census data, for almost every immigrant who came to Miami-Dade County in recent years, a white non-Hispanic left.

"I loved Miami, but it's a mad scene down there now," said Smith, who is semi-retired and asked that her occupation not be given. Before her move to Weston, Smith lived in Miami for two decades, "in a nice neighborhood gone bad. People say things, 'Oh that's change and that's progress,' but I like it clean and green—and everybody speaking English," Smith says.

In discussions about the historic demographic transformations occurring in the United States, which is absorbing almost 1 million immigrants a year, most of the attention focuses quite naturally on the newcomers: Who are they and where are they from and how do they make their way in America?

But immigration is a two-way street—and the welcome the immigrants receive from the native-born is crucial for the continued idea of America as a fabled "melting pot." Of course, there are many whites—and blacks, too—who have remained in Miami-Dade County, to either continue their lives as before or accept, even embrace the Latin tempo of Miami, who have learned how to pronounce masas de puerco at lunchtime and to fake a respectable merengue dance step, who enjoy the culture, the business opportunities and caffeinated hustle of a metropolis dominated by immigrants. No one could call Miami dull.

But it is almost as if there are two kinds of native whites—those who can deal with multiculturalism that has transformed Miami over the past several decades and those who choose not to. Either way, if the country is to successfully transform itself into a completely multicultural industrialized nation, what these internal migrants say—and there are millions of them around the country—needs to be heard and understood.

Those transplants interviewed by *The Washington Post*, including those who asked that their names not be used, take pains to explain that, for the most part, the people like them who are moving out of Miami-Dade to Broward are not anti-immigrant xenophobes.

In several dozen interviews with a cross-section of these "domestic migrants," a picture emerges of a segment of the non-Hispanic white population in Miami-Dade County that feels marginalized, exasperated and sometimes bitter, and who move from Dade to Broward with a mix of emotions.

Migrants to Broward give many reasons for the move north: Their money buys a bigger, newer house in Broward; they are tired of the traffic and congestion; they worry about crime; they complain about the overcrowded schools; those with young families often say they are looking for a place where their children can play ball in the front yard and ride their bikes down the block.

But all these things, the good and bad, can also be found in booming Broward County. Sooner or later, many of the refugees moving north mention immigration and the sense that they are no longer, as many transplants describe it, "comfortable."

Phil Phillips was born and raised near what is today downtown Miami, where his father worked for the Immigration and Naturalization Service during the postwar years, at a time when the immigrants to Florida were mostly from Europe. Phillips served in the Navy, taught vocational classes at Miami High School, and made a living running a small air conditioning and refrigeration business.

Until the rise of Fidel Castro in Cuba, Phillips described the Miami of yesteryear as a more sleepy, more southern town. It had its glitz in the fanciful playground of Jackie Gleason's city of Miami Beach, but the county was still filled with open land and farms.

"Miami was a very happy place," Phillips remembers with nostalgia. "We had our demarcations, don't get me wrong. But we didn't have the animosity." When pressed, Phillips does remember that the beaches, restaurants and nightclubs were often segregated, not only for African Americans. Jews had their own country clubs.

The Miami of black-and-white all began to change with the arrival of the Cubans in the early 1960s. "The vast majority of the Cubans came here and worked two and three jobs," said Phillips, who is retired and living in Weston. A man who worked with his hands all his life, Phillips respects that. "I saw them do it. And in time, they took over, and some people resent that. But that's the way it is."

"There's this myth out there that a Cuban will screw an American in a deal," Phillips says. "I don't think that is so, but that's the feeling the whites have, and it's because the two sides don't communicate, sometimes they can't communicate, and so they don't understand the other guy."

Phillips has seen decades of change, as the demographics of his home town kept skewing toward Hispanics, in fits and starts. After the first big influx of Cubans in the 1960s, there was Cuba's Mariel boatlift in 1980. Then all through the proxy wars and upheavals in Central America and the Caribbean through the 1980s and 1990s, refugees from Nicaragua, Honduras, El Salvador and Haiti kept coming to Miami.

"We're great in America at blaming somebody else for our problems," Phillips said. "But I will tell that for a lot of the people who leave Miami, they might not tell you, but they're leaving because of the ethnics."

Phillips offered his opinions as he sat sipping soup at the counter of a new restaurant here in Weston opened by Tim Robbie, whose family owned the Miami Dolphins for years, before they sold out to Wayne Huizenga, who is "The Man" in Broward County, as much as Jorge Mas Canosa, the power behind the Cuban American National Foundation, was "The Man" in Miami before his death last year.

Robbie was raised in Miami. His family, lead by his father Joe, was a civic institution. But Robbie himself recently moved to Weston, too.

"I know a lot of our friends down in Miami were disappointed with us," Robbie said. "They asked: How can you do this to us?"

Robbie agreed that something akin to "the tipping point" phenomenon might be at work, whereby one or two families in a social or business network can leave a community and nothing much changes. But at some point, if enough people leave, the balance suddenly tips, and large groups start selling their homes, and over a period of several years, they create mass demographic shifts.

Robbie himself said he was comfortable down south in Miami, but concedes that many are not. "Anglos are accustomed to being in the majority, and down in Dade, they're not. And that puts some people outside of their comfort zone. People tend to like to stick together."

Robbie's business partner is Bob Green, who also moved from Miami to Broward. A longtime denizen of funky and fun Coconut Grove, Green describes himself as one of those who never would have thought about moving north to Broward.

But then he saw the new business opportunities, and also found himself liking a place like Weston. "It has this midwestern feeling," Green said. "More downhome and friendly."

This mass internal migration is the latest version of a classic "push–pull" model of residential segregation, whereby many whites in Miami feel lured north by the offerings of a development like Weston, but also feel pushed out of Miami—not only by their fatigue with crime or congestion, but the cultural and demographic upheavals caused by three decades of immigration.

Peter Schott is a tourism official who is changing jobs and, reluctantly, moving with his wife, who works for a cruise ship line, to Broward. The couple, both in their thirties and expecting their first child, are looking for a bigger home. Schott says he will miss the exotic, foreign feel of Miami. Miami, Schott says, is a media noche, the name for a Cuban sandwich, while Broward he fears is "white bread and baloney." While he will miss Miami, Schott knows that many of those moving north to Broward may not.

"Some people are real frank," he said. "They say they want to be with more people more like us. If they're white Americans, they want white Americans around them."

For non-Hispanic, non-Spanish-speaking whites to survive in Miami, there is no choice but to move, or to adapt. "It is our city now," many Cuban Americans say, and the numbers tell part of the story.

In the 1990s, some 95,000 white non-Hispanics left Miami-Dade County, decreasing that group's presence by 16 percent, to around 492,000, or about one-fifth of the county population.

They either moved away or, in the case of elderly residents, particularly in the Jewish community, died. (The Jewish population in Miami-Dade County has decreased from about 250,000 to 100,000 in the last two decades. The new destination for Jewish retirees and younger migrants is Broward and Palm Beach counties.)

As whites left Miami, they poured into Broward. Between 1990 and 1997, the white non-Hispanic population here increased by about 82,000, or 8 percent, to more than a million residents.

These dramatic numbers follow an equally large out-migration of whites during the 1980s. So many non-Hispanic whites left Miami-Dade in the previous decade that Marvin Dunn, a sociologist at Florida International University, who has followed the trend, said in 1991, "You get down to the point below which those who are going to leave have left and the others are committed to stay. I think we're close to that with whites."

But Dunn was wrong. The whites keep leaving.

"White migration to Miami-Dade has essentially stopped," said William Frey, a demographer at the University of Michigan, who coined the phrase "demographic balkanization" to describe the ongoing trend of ethnic and racial groups to self-segregate—not only within a city, but from city to city, and from state to state.

"The two appear almost like mirror images of each other," Frey said of Broward and Miami-Dade counties. "There is definitely something going on here and we can only guess what it is. But this 'One America' that Clinton talks about is clearly not in the numbers. Segregation and non-assimilation continue."

Many times, native whites on the move explain that Miami now feels to them like "a foreign country," that they feel "overwhelmed" by the presence not just of some Spanish-speakers, but so many.

"You order a Coke without ice," said an executive and mother of three who moved to Broward from Miami in 1996 and asked that her name not be used. "And you get ice. You say no starch and you get starch. You call government offices, and they can't take a decent message in English. You spell your name letter by letter and they get it wrong. They keep saying 'Que? Que? Que?' (Spanish for 'What?') You go to the mall, and you watch as the clerks wait on the Spanish speakers before you. It's like reverse racism. You realize, my God, this is what it is like to be the minority."

"The white population feels increasingly beleaguered," said George Wilson, a sociologist at the University of Miami who is studying the phenomenon.

"Their whole domain is changing at the micro-level," Wilson continued. "At the malls, in the schools. A lot of the whites I talk to say they feel challenged by the rapid ethnic and cultural change. A whole population of whites has gone from a clear majority to a clear minority in a very short time ... and a lot of them simply say, 'To hell with this,' and move up the road."

This feeling of being the beleaguered minority is creating among some a new consciousness of "white ethnicity," and for those who see America's future as a relatively harmonious multicultural state based on shared ideas of capitalism and freedom, this may not bode well.

For if whites do not want to share power and place, or if they feel increasingly shoved aside or overwhelmed in the cities and states with high immigration, they will continue to vote with their feet, by moving away, creating not a rainbow of citizens, but a more balkanized nation, with jobs, university enrollments, public spending, schools all seen through ethnic or racial prisms, including among whites.

Several of those interviewed complain that the politics of Miami-Dade are dominated by the issues of the newcomers, particularly the Cuban Americans, who wait for the fall of Fidel Castro; they see in the city hall, where a number of officials were recently indicted and convicted of taking kickbacks after it was discovered that the city was broke, a "banana republic" of ethnic cronyism; they dislike being referred to in Spanish media as "the Americans" by Miami's Hispanic residents and politicians, as if they were the foreigners.

And many balk at the dominance of Spanish—on television, in official news conferences, on the radio, in schools and meetings and in their day-to-day lives. The movement of so many whites from Miami-Dade to Broward is viewed by many Hispanics as understandable, even natural, though hardly something to be encouraged.

"We had a tremendous exodus of Anglos, especially Anglos who did not feel comfortable with the new demographics of Miami, who were intimidated by the Spanish language and the influx of different people," said Eduardo Padron, a Cuban American and president of the Miami-Dade Community College. "It is a natural trend for them to move out. Many of them kept working in Miami, but they found refuge in Broward."

Padron believes the rapidity of demographic changes, and the creation of a Hispanic majority, was "intimidating" for many whites, particularly those who did not speak any Spanish.

Some whites interviewed say they know they may seem like "whiners," as one woman put it, but they feel they are not being met halfway by the newcomers, and this is an especially acute feeling in Miami, where Cuban Americans and other immigrants from Latin America now dominate the political landscape, serving as city and county mayors and council members. Both of Miami's representatives to Congress are Cuban Americans.

Recent elections reveal that voters in Miami-Dade select candidates along stark racial and ethnic lines in classic bloc voting. The 1995 county mayor's race, pitting Cuban American Alex Penelas against African American Arthur Teele, Jr., turned almost entirely on demographic lines, with exit polls showing that the overwhelming majority of Cuban Americans voted for Penelas, as most blacks voted for Teele. What did whites do? A lot of them did not vote at all.

Over the years, there has been sporadic, organized resistance by whites in Miami to hold back the changes. One group, calling itself Citizens of Dade United, was successful in passing a referendum in 1980 that declared English the "official language" of county government. But it was overturned in 1993. Enos Schera, who is a co-founder of the group and who is now 71, is still filled with vinegar, and says he refuses to move from Miami—though he says he and his group have received death threats.

"I'm staying to fight this crazy thing," Schera said. "I'm not a bad guy, but I don't want to be overrun. They come here and get all the advantages of being in America and then they insult you right on top of it." He is writing a book about the changes. "That will tell all," he promises.

But it seems as if Schera is fighting in retreat. He, and his group, have largely been relegated to the role of stubborn whites whose time is over.

Many of the others, like Weston resident Joanne Smith, have already left. "There's no room for us in the discussion," said Smith. "It's like we were the oppressors."

Smith says she likes to eat at Cuban restaurants, has Hispanic neighbors in Weston and admires the strength and striving of the newcomers. She herself is the granddaughter of immigrants, from Europe. But Smith feels the immigrants should try harder to understand the feelings of native Americans. "If they can survive coming here on a raft," she says, "they can learn to speak English."

Here at Weston, almost all of the communities are closed with security gates, requiring a visitor to punch a code or be cleared by a guard before entering the enclaves. In addition to the gates, a private security firm patrols the neighborhoods.

One researcher on the topic, Edward Blakely of the University of Southern California in Los Angeles, says that gated communities like Weston's are the fastest growing new developments around the country. Blakely deplores the trend, claiming it creates "fortress neighborhoods," dividing citizens, creating walls between "us" and "them."

But obviously, many home buyers like the concept, and many of the residents of Weston say one of the things they like most about the neighborhood is its sense of community, of safety and the ability of their children to ride their bicycles on the streets.

Yet the gates cannot keep demographic change at bay. Though two of every three residents in Weston is white, most of them in their thirties, about one in four are Hispanic. But these are the most assimilated, often second-generation, solidly middle-class Cuban Americans who come north for the same new schools and golf courses as the white migrants, allowing almost everyone to continue to live within their comfort zone.

But not all. As one three-year resident, who declined to give her name, observed, "I keep hearing more and more Spanish in the grocery store. I don't know if they live here or are just working here. But I started to see some Spanish magazines for sale. Maybe I didn't move far enough north."

## A REMEDY FOR THE ROOTLESSNESS OF MODERN SUBURBAN LIFE?

Sarah Boxer

ATTACKS ON SUBURBIA are as old as cul-de-sacs. Suburbs have always been derided as bourgeois, consumerist and conformist. But now they have become the enemy of family values, too. That's right. Karl Zinsmeister, the editor of the conservative magazine *The American Enterprise*, has written that "suburbia is actually a fairly radical social experiment," one that can be linked to "the disappearance of family time, the weakening of generational links... the anonymity of community life, the rise of radical feminism, the decline of civic action, the tyrannical dominance of TV and pop culture over leisure time."

What is to be done? A group of architects and planners who have named themselves the Congress for the New Urbanism have vowed to halt the spread of faceless, car-centered suburbs by promoting friendly, people-centered towns with corner stores and public greens.

They call for some old-fashioned things: walkable neighborhoods with a mix of residences, businesses and public places; straight and narrow streets; wide sidewalks, and no cul de sacs. They believe houses should be built close enough together and close enough to the sidewalks to define streets and public squares. Above all, they want strong town centers and clear town boundaries. No one, they believe, should live more than a five-minute walk from most of their errands. (Otherwise, what's to stop people from getting in their cars and driving?) And like their British counterpart, the Urban Villages Group, the architects favored by the Prince of Wales, they want to preserve old towns and cities through "infill," building on unused urban lots.

"No one can be opposed to those principles," said Alex Krieger, a professor of urban design at Harvard University. They are like "mom and apple pie," he said. Yet many new-urban towns have been scorned as cutesy, regressive and un-urban. The new urbanists—or neo-traditionalists—should instead be called the "new suburbanists," some say, because they are less interested in planning principles than in porches, picket fences and gabled roofs.

Seaside, designed in the early 1980's by Elizabeth Plater-Zyberk and Andres Duany, two of the founders of new urbanism, is the oldest new-urban town. Built on a stretch of the Florida panhandle, Seaside was meant to foster community life and beach access. The houses, a pastiche of historical styles in pastel colors, are set close to one another and connected by straight brick streets and a network of sand walkways cutting through the middle of each block. When the town is finished, it is supposed to have 350 houses and 300 apartments, a school, an open-air market, a town hall, a tennis club, an amphitheater, a post office, and a number of shops, offices and beach pavillions.

If you're having trouble picturing it, think of the idyllic town in the movie *The Truman Show*. That was no movie set. That was Seaside.

Since Seaside was built, new urbanism has won a lot of fans and building contracts. There are dozens of new-urban towns and projects built or under construction, including Celebration in Florida, Laguna West in California and Kentlands in Maryland. The Department of Housing and Urban Development is renovating some of its public housing according to new urbanist principles: more porches, more fences, lower buildings, narrower streets. Jane Jacobs, the author of *The Death and Life of Great American Cities*, has praised the movement as "sound" and "promising." And publications from *The Sierra Club Yodeler* to *The American Enterprise* have smiled on the new urbanists.

"But is their particular vision of urbanization an innovative model appropriate to the 21st century," Michelle Thompson-Fawcett asked in the journal *Urban Design International*, "or is it regressive nostalgia?"

New urbanism is, by definition, nostalgic. Towns built on a human scale, with strong centers and clear edges, have been around for 5,000 years, said Robert Davis, the developer of Seaside and the chairman of the new-urban Congress. It is only in the last 50 years, with the rise of modernism, he said, that Americans have forgotten how to build them.

The new urbanists want to induce neighborliness with architecture. In this sense they are utopian. Like the modernist master planners of the 1930's, they believe social change can be brought about through architecture and planning. The difference is that most of them hate modernism.

While the modernists "tried to get to the future by destroying the past," Robert Fishman, the author of *Bourgeois Utopias*, said, the new urbanists "are reviving the past in order to change" the present. That, the new urbanists think, is why many architecture schools view them with contempt.

Most schools of architecture are "so in the grips of the modernist ideology and so defensive of the avant-garde that they see the Congress for the New Urbanism as fundamentally conservative," said Daniel Solomon, a founder of the movement. Peter Katz, the author of *The New Urbanism: Toward an Architecture of Community*, said that the nation's most powerful architects, particularly those in New York, "laugh at the poor souls who live in suburbia."

Kenneth Frampton, an architecture professor at Columbia University, agrees that many architecture schools (though he excludes Columbia) have ignored some questions about land settlement. But what bothers most professors about the new urbanists, he said, is not their critique of suburbia or land settlement. It is their design ideas.

The new-urbanist charter says nothing explicit about what styles are acceptable. Yet because many new urbanists believe that modernism ruined American cities, nearly all of their designs rely heavily on building styles from the past. Kentlands in Maryland is full of Georgian houses. Celebration, Disney's village in Florida, is full of brand new Victorians and Colonials.

"What's upsetting" about new urbanism, said Mr. Frampton, "is that the imagery is so retrograde." It is based on a "sentimental iconography" as if there were something inherently good about Victorians, Georgians and Colonials and something inherently bad about modernism. To be fair, there were a lot of modernists in the 1930's who advocated low-rise, high density housing, he said. Besides, the kind of modernism that the new urbanists see as their enemy is a straw man. No one is advocating tearing down whole cities to make way for skyscrapers.

"If you want to look for the demon that destroyed Main Street in America," Mr. Frampton said, "it is not the modern movement but the American bureaucracy that opened the way for freeways and suburbanization."

The railroads were deliberately undermined by the automobile industry, he said, adding, "That was an economic, a capitalist, operation," not an architectural one.

New urbanism has not attacked the root of the problem sufficiently, suggested Alex Marshall, who has often written about new urbanism for *Metropolis* magazine. "What new urbanism tries to do is imitate older communities that existed before the automobile" without getting rid of the automobile. But if you want to return to these older forms of life, he said, you "have to bring back the transportation system." If you simply change the way houses are built, "it's like changing hemlines."

New urbanists like to see themselves as radicals, said Mr. Krieger, who was once a supporter of the movement and is now a critic. But, he added, they are "no longer the radical fringe but conventional wisdom." Developers have begun using the term new urbanism to sell their projects.

That's not to say the movement hasn't had a good effect, Mr. Krieger said. The Department of Housing and Urban Development has dedicated $2.6 billion to "Hope Six," a nationwide plan to rebuild mid-century public housing according to new urbanist principles. From Boston to Cleveland to Helena, Mont., high-rise projects are being replaced by town houses with porches and fences. "That is the part of the movement that most impresses me," said Mr. Krieger.

The problem, Mr. Marshall noted, is that most new-urban developments are not urban at all. They are rich developments on the town's edge. "They are sprawl under another name," he said, and they are as restrictive as any suburban development. Most are privately run by homeowners' associations that give developers extraordinary control.

For example, in Celebration, Disney's new-urban town, the deed restrictions specify what kind of drapery, roofing tiles and political signs are allowed. "Disney has a history of making warm and fuzzy dog movies," said Evan McKenzie, the author of *Privatopia*, a book on housing associations, but "they can take your dog if it makes too much noise."

"It's as if the people are saying: 'Who needs democracy? It's utopia already!'" said Mr. McKenzie.

People are looking for homeyness and safety, and they don't mind giving up some freedoms for it. In Kentlands, there is a gate in front of each entry into the development, Mr. Krieger said. "It's a decorative gate but it evokes the same associations as a real gate. It's a subtle form of 'Keep Out.'"

If decorative gates can evoke the same response as real gates, then maybe the look of neighborliness—porches, wide sidewalks and village greens—can evoke real neighborliness. Or can it?

The one big criticism about new-urban towns is that they are fake towns. Given that, it's curious that the developer of Seaside agreed to let *The Truman Show*, a movie about a real man in a false world, be filmed in Seaside. The movie all but said, "This is not really a town but the shell of a town, an image of a town," Mr. Krieger said.

After the filming was over, the painted plywood storefronts that had been put up for the movie stayed up for months because the developer liked the way they looked, Mr. Krieger said. After all, looking like a real town is the next best thing to being one.

## NEW URBANISM NEEDS TO KEEP RACIAL ISSUES IN MIND

Whitney Gould

IN THE STRUGGLE TO BUILD new towns and rebuild old ones, there's one issue no one wants to talk about much: race. And when it does come up, people tend to dance around it or dress it in euphemisms.

At a recent meeting here of the Congress for the New Urbanism, though, race had just about everyone buzzing—and the guy who started the buzz, writer James Howard Kunstler, wasn't even on the program. Kunstler, author of an anti-sprawl polemic titled *The Geography of Nowhere,* popped up from the mostly white audience at a panel on gentrification issues and said blacks should stop blaming their problems on whites. The real challenge? "Tell your kids to be nicer to white people," he exhorted. "Turn your baseball hats around, get interested in reading and quit trying to scare everyone."

A shouting match ensued. And no wonder. Could Kunstler, a middle-aged white guy and well-known provocateur, not have known how offensive his racial stereotyping would be? Did he really think that if every black person in America behaved like a well-read ambassador from *Gentleman's Quarterly* or *Vogue,* lily-white enclaves would suddenly become rainbow communities? And, as my colleague Eugene Kane observed [on these pages last week], weren't those shooters at Columbine High in Colorado a couple of white kids?

In fairness to the New Urbanists, Kunstler was not representative of the four-day gathering, which was earnest and thoughtful. But whatever his intentions, the bull-in-a-china-shop author in a very crude way did do one useful thing: He brought race front and center among a group of city-builders who have preferred to keep the spotlight more on the physical aspects of urban revitalization than on the social and economic integration that is crucial to the enduring health of communities.

The physical stuff is important, to be sure. Street-friendly architecture, slower streets and a mix of housing, businesses and public spaces all within walking distance: These are the sensible underpinnings of New Urbanism (and Old Urbanism, as well). That approach to development can make communities more neighborly, more humanly scaled and less dependent on the car. Milwaukee's new master plan for the downtown grows out of those principles. Two fledgling New Urbanist communities that I profiled recently, Middleton Hills west of Madison and CityHomes in Milwaukee, show how attractive such subdivisions can be.

But Middleton Hills is virtually all white, and CityHomes is overwhelmingly black. And there's little evidence that other New Urbanist communities are appreciably more integrated. In turn, most of the new housing being built in downtown Milwaukee is upscale, leaving working-class folks and/or minorities pretty much out of the picture. Indeed, census statistics show that 98% of the African-American population in the entire metro area lives in the City of Milwaukee, making this the most segregated of 50 large urban areas in the country.

You can argue, I suppose, that some of this segregation is voluntary: people choosing to live among folks like themselves. (Never mind that there are whites and people of color who prefer diversity.) You can argue, too, that this is just the market talking: developers going where the money is. (Never mind, too, that there is plenty of money to be made in mixed-use development.)

In fact, as experts at a University of Wisconsin–Milwaukee conference noted recently, federal highway and housing subsidies for years promoted sprawl, with all of its inevitable racial isolation and social inequity.

And today, as builders' and realtors' groups push to build smaller, more affordable houses in the suburbs, they run up against zoning rules that mandate huge minimum lot sizes and large houses. Even if the intent is not racist, the effect of such rules is both racially and economically discriminatory, shutting out working-class minorities and whites alike—and this at a time when retail and service jobs in the suburbs are going begging.

To wrap such exclusionary zoning in the mantle of environmentalism and the fight against sprawl strains credulity. After all, developers who can't build in one place will just move farther into the hinterlands. How does that promote smarter land use?

We could change all of this if we had the political will to do so. Reforming those onerous zoning rules would be a good place to start. Improving transit links to the suburbs would also help. And we could create new incentives for builders to include more modestly priced homes within new developments, whether in the city or the suburbs. Let's be clear: This doesn't mean concentrations of prison-like public housing, just some attractive single-family homes and townhouses that ordinary folks—black and white, young and old—could afford.

None of this would come easily. Such changes inevitably bring up the issue that no one wants to talk about: race. While it may be too much to expect planners and developers to solve the problems of social inequity, can we not at least hope they won't make those problems worse? How sad if New Urbanism, the most progressive planning tool in decades, were to become merely an excuse for creating beautifully designed communities as racially alienated as the old ones.

## This Text: Reading

1. What is your opinion of suburbs? Is this based on your own experience or what you have seen displayed in popular culture?
2. What are the advantages and disadvantages of living in the suburbs?
3. Are there ways of changing the suburbs to eliminate some of the disadvantages?
4. Do you think the behavior of teenagers is affected by the construction of public space?
5. What assumptions about suburbs are the practitioners of the New Urbanism making? Are those assumptions accurate?
6. Why is the idea of Main Street so attractive to us? Is it built on false assumptions?

## Your Text: Writing

1. Write a short piece about your experience in the suburbs.
2. What would you say the philosophy of suburban life is? Write a paper articulating what you think this philosophy is.
3. What are the defining architectural ideas behind living in the suburbs? How do these ideas affect the way people live?
4. Drive through a suburban community—both old and new. What do you notice about the public spaces and the way houses look? What do those aspects of the suburbs suggest about life there?
5. Write a short piece about the positive nature of the suburbs. Are there any cultural texts that would aid in your examination?
6. If you have grown up in the suburbs, think about your relationship to the suburbs at different times in your life. Is there a point at which you remember changing your ideas about where you live?
7. If you do not live in the suburbs, think about when you realized that there were places different from where you lived. Think about what you thought about these places growing up and what you think about them now.

---

# READING OUTSIDE THE LINES

## Classroom Activities

1. Look around your classroom. How do you know it's a classroom? Of course, there are the chalkboard and the desks, but what other qualities does this room have that makes it a classroom? How is it designed? Does it facilitate learning, alertness, and discussion?

2. Walk outside the classroom. What elements identify the walk as a college campus? What emotions does the walk evoke? Could it be improved?
3. What does the public space outside the classroom building say? Does it identify the campus as any particular type of school—private, public, urban, rural, suburban? What would a potential student read into this particular space? Would they be inclined to come to school or not because of this reading? Why or why not?
4. What particular place makes you feel the most comfortable? Least? Frightened? What is it about the spaces themselves that evoke these emotions? Are they human driven or architecturally or design driven? Can you think of a space that has bad or good memories driven mostly by the space itself?
5. Design the perfect classroom. What would it look like? What would it have in it? Where would everyone sit? What tools would everyone have? How would being in this classroom change your learning experience?
6. Design the perfect building at college. What would it look like? What would it have in it?

## Essay Ideas

### Building as analogy

Find a building you want to write about. Does it remind you of something besides a building in 1) its physical construction; 2) the emotional response it encourages; 3) its purpose; or 4) its structure? In what way are these disparate elements alike? Different? What does the analogy in general say about commonalties of texts generally?

### Emotional response

Walk around a building or a public area such as a mall or your school's common area. What do you "feel"? What about the place makes you feel such an emotion? Are these effects intended or unintended?

### Commercial versus artistic

What dominates this particular building or space—its artistic aspects or commercial ones? Or do the two work together?

### My favorite place

If possible, analyze a place you feel close to and figure out why you feel that way. Is there a theme attached to this place? How would you describe the décor? The architecture? Do you feel your attachment to this place—or places like it—is unique?

**Does this building or space "work"?**

Find a place—do you think it succeeds on its own terms? What are its "terms"—what criteria is it trying to fulfill? Does is succeed? Why or why not?

**The person from the space**

Go to an office or a dorm room or car, or some place that "belongs" to someone. What can you tell about this person from the space? How did you arrive at your judgments? Are there other ways to interpret the information?

**The common element**

Compare similar spaces. What makes them similar? What are their differences? What do their differences or similarities say about this type of space?

# 4

# Reading Race and Ethnicity

Of all the introductions we have written, this one made us feel the most uncomfortable. Writing about people, the way they appear, and the relationship between their appearance and attributed behavior is a minefield for any prospective author. We wanted to put our anxiety on the table right away because we believe that this anxiety mirrors the way you might feel when you are talking about race and ethnicity whether you are Hispanic, African-American, Asian-American, American Indian, white, or some combination of ethnicities.

As you will notice in reading this introduction, we are constantly hedging—saying "to a degree" or "to some extent." And there's a reason for this hesitation. When it comes to race or ethnicity, there are few if any absolutes. For one, individuals don't have group experiences—and yet they do. Group experiences happen to individuals when a series of individuals have similar experiences. For example, if several people from a particular ethnic group have a similar but discrete experience because of how someone perceives them, they have had a group experience of prejudice. Anyone who has had racial epitaphs uttered at them has had this experience; those words are directed at someone not because of who they are inside, but because of how they look.

When these experiences occur because of perceived common characteristics—both people are of the same race, ethnicity, or gender—an individual experience becomes a group one. At the same time, individuals themselves have experiences imposed on them because they are perceived to be a member of a group. Prejudice, then, projects perceived or assumed group characteristics on a single person or groups of people. Again, saying a group of people is not qualified to do particular work because of how they look or the ethnicity they belong to is a clear example of prejudice.

To an overwhelming degree, these experiences are socially constructed. Indeed, most scientists believe that race is a social, not a biological, construction. In other words, race as it was commonly perceived in the past—as a way of attributing characteristics (usually negative, if they were not white) to individuals of a common group—is not scientifically or biologically defensible. Scientists believe that perceived traits of races are a product of social experiences, despite the way we often visually identify someone of a particular race. In other words, one's skin color does *not* determine race; factors contributing one's race are far more complex.

We are *not* saying that biology does not determine the color of one's skin; clearly biology determines the color of our skin, as it does the color of our eyes. What we are saying (and what most scientists also argue) is that the idea that biological traits are associated with a particular skin color is false. As humans of different shades of color, we are much more alike biologically than we are different. Even if some groups do have higher incidents of disease (African Americans with Sickle Cell Anemia, Jews with Tay-Sachs disease), environmental factors largely shape their existence. For example, Americans are much more likely to have heart conditions compared to the French; the characteristics of Americans are more alike than characteristics of different groups, which is to say that our biology and our cultural community connect us in more ways than our perceptions of race might suggest.

Self-perception is even more of a factor in racial or ethnic identity, as people often "switch" ethnicities or at least change how they see themselves as belonging to a certain group. For instance, a study cited in one of our readings shows that over one-third of respondents in a census identified themselves as a different ethnicity than when they had taken the same census only two years later. This is not to say that race isn't important—it is. Race and ethnicity, even if socially constructed, guide so much of our public life. By putting the burden on social constructions of race, we have to think about the way we construct race more completely rather than accept that race and ethnicity are the way things are.

In the past, people from various groups had a tendency to consciously impose a set of values onto certain groups of people based simply on skin color, a tendency certainly diminished in the last 50 years (though we would be the last people to claim that this type of behavior is gone, and the first to acknowledge that prejudice is still very much a part of too many people's lives). Our goal in this chapter is to help you become more sensitive readers of race and ethnicity by becoming more aware of the social forces that construct the text of race and racism.

## The determination that race, ethnicity, and class are socially constructed has led to new ways of thinking about our identity that have political and social implications.

Not too long ago, and for most of the history of the Western world, people made assumptions about other people based on their appearance, most notably their skin color. White people assumed blacks were less intelligent or that American Indians were savages. For centuries, groups have enslaved people from other groups based on that group's race or ethnicity. In the last few decades, we have gone from the biological construction of race, one based on parentage, to one based more on social groups and associations. Hispanic means less than it did twenty years ago, as does Native American; we tend to view Native Americans by tribe or nation, and those from Central and South America, the Caribbean, and Mexico by country of origin, by nationality, rather than the catchall of ethnicity. These linguistic markers more accurately get at a more true measure of someone's identity, as anyone familiar with Native American, Latin American or Asian or African history can tell you.

## To a degree, race and ethnicity are visually constructed, but those visual constructions are hardly a clean read.

We tend to categorize people by their appearance, not by their biological background, for the most obvious reason: we have no other way of reading people. We do construct race, ethnicity, and gender, and its multiplicity of meanings and ideas visually, not only through a person's skin, but what they wear, how they walk, how tall or short they are. We are not trying to demonize this process as much as we are trying to draw attention to it. Like other visual constructions, it has to be slowed down and digested more actively. Thus, every time we see someone and register that person's skin color, we are doing a reading of his or her ethnicity. We pick up on external codes that we think cue us into that person's racial background, but what, really do those cues tell us? For one, even if we can determine if someone is Chinese or Russian or Kenyan or Navajo, that tells us very little about who she is as a person, what he likes to eat, what she is good at, how smart he is, what sports she plays, or what his values are.

## To some extent, reading the "otherness" in someone's appearance makes us uncomfortable because of reasons both political and personal.

We want to be—and are explicitly trained—to be democratic in the way we view others, by the way they act toward us, not the way they look. "Don't judge a book by its cover," we say, but we are always judging books by their covers and people by their appearance, and this makes many of us feel uncomfortable. This discomfort is magnified when it comes to race and ethnicity and gender and class because we know our constructions have political, cultural, social and personal consequences for us and for the people we're trying to understand. Our democratic nature wants us to read neutrally and our other less controllable side does not because we have been conditioned through decades and even centuries of reading values into otherness. Perhaps you have noticed or even commented on someone's ethnicity, then felt strange about it. This is because we want things that may seem to be mutually exclusive—to acknowledge someone's difference, but not be affected by it. Yet how can we *not* be affected by something we notice and then think about?

## Definitions of race are always changing.

In the late nineteenth and early twentieth centuries and to some extent afterwards, groups we now think of us ethnic groups were considered racial groups. For instance, at the turn of the century, Jews and Italians were considered racial groups (not ethnic groups). Similarly, fewer than fifty years ago, many places in the South considered anyone to be African-American if they had an African-American ancestor; this was called the "one-drop" rule. Because the vast majority of Americans do not think this way now, it may seem difficult to believe that this past existed, but understanding it is crucial in understanding the way things are now.

## Although we claim to be nondiscriminatory now, discriminatory practices in the past have influenced the present social, political, economic, and cultural structure of our country.

This may seem like a highly political statement, and it is. But the authors believe that discrimination in the past gave the white male majority a head start in this generation; race theorists call this phenomenon "white privilege." As you know, blacks, Asians, Hispanics and Native Americans were frequently, if not regularly, denied admission to colleges, job interviews, loans, access to restaurants and hotels and even basic medial service. Affirmative action, the idea that employers and schools should actively seek historically underrepresented individuals to fill their slots, is a response to this phenomenon by ensuring that minorities get fair consideration by employers and admission offices (for the most part, affirmative action does *not* involve a quota system despite misconceptions popularly articulated). But the theory behind affirmative action, looking for ways to engage the past while living in the future in making decisions about schools and employment, is not only a government program but a factor in admitting legacies to colleges, incorporating one's progeny into a family business, etc. While preferential treatment may be decried as un-American in some quarters—after all, the Bill of Rights says all men are created equal—the fact is the past has always shaped how people are treated in the present.

What's more, generations of broken promises, abuses of power, and institutional discrimination and oppression have left some members of minority communities bitter toward institutions of power and law. People are smart. They know that history repeats itself; they know that the past is always present in some form or another. Thus, the reality of slavery, the history of American Indian genocide and removal, the memory of Asian internment, is a legacy that still affects how members of these groups see America and its institutions, and it's a legacy that contemporary America must take seriously.

## Race, ethnicity, and gender are political constructions as well as social ones.

We now think of members of so-called races as political groups as well as social ones. If you read about politics, you will notice commentators talking about how a candidate was trying to "appeal to African Americans" or "appeal to women." The recognition that these groups have political power in one sense has empowered members of these groups and given them political power in ways they may not have had. But of course, some people within these groups do not want to be identified as group members; it too easily reminds them of the way society constructs their identity negatively. For example, Toni Morrison, the Nobel Prize winning author, has said that she does not want to be thought of as an African-American writer but merely as a writer. The tendency, the need, in America to preface any such statement with the racial descriptor, goes to show how completely we see race and, perhaps, how often we cannot see past it.

Even more important, the goals of an ethnicity as a whole may not be those of the individual. In fact, it may be impossible to state, with any certainty, what the goals of any one ethnicity may be, as all people are complex and in the process of change. Supreme Court Judge Clarence Thomas will have very different ideas about what African Americans need than will the Reverend Jesse Jackson or Minister Louis Farrakhan, even though all are intelligent, upper class African-American men. Which of the three best represents black Americans? That may depend on what group of black Americans you poll.

## Stereotyping occurs as a result of our perceived view of racial or ethnic characteristics.

Unless you are the rare completely neutral human being, someone the authors feel does not exist, you attach stereotypes to groups—even if they seem like stereotypes that are positive, such as all professors are smart, nuns are nice, etc. You may also have beliefs that are negative. The problem, of course, with all stereotypes is their propensity to attribute group characteristics to individuals. Believing all Jews are smart or all African Americans are athletic can have subsequent negative effects that balance out any positives.

How do we acquire our stereotypes? Some believe stereotypes are based on a grain of truth. That sort of thought makes the authors and others nervous, because the next logical step is thinking they are inherent or natural. Researchers believe we pick up stereotypes in a variety of ways, including through popular culture and our upbringing. That's why we have stressed throughout this book the importance of looking for treatments of race and ethnicity as they appear—or don't appear—in texts.

## Your view of these issues probably depends on your personal relationships as well as political affiliation.

When surveying the landscape of these issues, we are likely to take our personal experiences and make them universal. If we are white and have African-American friends or relatives, not only are we more likely to be more sympathetic to black causes, we are probably going to take the part of the whole for better or worse. If we have no friends of color, and our only exposure is through popular culture and our political affiliations, that too will shape the way we look at race and ethnicity. It's an overgeneralization to be sure, but the authors believe that proximity brings understanding in ways that reading about race and ethnicity can never bring. So does, we believe, actively thinking about the ways we construct race and ethnicity.

## Class is a more crucial element in American life than many people think.

Class also has similar connections to both self-identity and outside reality. Studies show most Americans believe they are middle class. And because there is no set way of determining what someone's class is, someone who is making $100,000 a year can call themselves middle class; so can someone who is making $20,000 a year. Are their lives different? Absolutely. But they may not see that. Of course, class issues run through issues of race and ethnicity, in ways both simple and complex. Some researchers believe that race and ethnicity are mostly a class problem; with the members of ethnic groups disproportionately represented among the nation's poor, there probably is some validity to this claim. But since the nation has had a long bloody history of clashes between ethnicities of the same class, it's hard to see class as the primary issue in racial or ethnic discrimination.

On the other hand, perceptions of reality can be as strong or stronger than reality itself, and in a capitalist country that tends to link economic prosperity with personal worth, the prevailing perceptions of what groups have more can shape how we see certain people. Thus, while class may not be the primary factor in racial discrimination, it is difficult when talking about race to separate it from issues of class.

The complicated nature of race and ethnicity is reflected here in the selections, which include a variety of perspectives and methodologies to consider.

## Worksheet

### THIS TEXT

1. While it will be impossible for you to know this fully, try to figure out the writing situation of each author. Who is the audience? What does the author have at stake? What is his or her agenda? *Why* is she or he writing this piece?
2. What social, political, and cultural forces affect the author's text? What is going on in the world as he or she is writing?
3. How does the author define race and ethnicity? Is the definition stated or unstated?
4. When taken as a whole, what do these texts tell you about how we construct race and ethnicity?
5. How do stories and essays differ in their arguments about race and ethnicity?
6. Is the author's argument valid and reasonable?
7. Ideas and beliefs about race and ethnicity tend to be very sensitive, deeply held convictions. Do you find yourself in agreement with the author? Why or why not? Do you agree with the editors' introduction?
8. Does the author help you *read* race and ethnicity better than you did before reading the essay? If so, why? How do we learn to read race and ethnicity?
9. Did you like this? Why or why not?
10. What role does science play in the essay?

### BEYOND THIS TEXT: READING RACE AND ETHNICITY

**Media:** How are different ethnicities portrayed in the news or magazine article? Is the author taking the "part for the whole" (talking to one member of a group as representative of all members of the group)?

**Advertising:** How are different ethnicities portrayed in the print or broadcast ad? Is there anything that "signals" their ethnicity—is clothing used as a "sign" of their color or identity? Is the advertiser using a "rainbow effect" in the ad, appearing to be inclusive by including multiple ethnicities? Does this effect seemed forced or genuine?

**Television:** How are different ethnicities portrayed in a particular television show? Do they conform to predictable stereotypes? Are the people of color more than merely representative? Is there a lone African American or Hispanic American on a mostly white show? One white person on an African-American dominated show? Are the members of different races allowed to date? Does their dating engage the idea of intergroup dating or ignore it?

**Movies:** How are different ethnicities portrayed in the movie? Do they conform to predictable stereotypes? Are the people of color the first to be targeted for death (if it's an action movie)? Are the people of color more than merely representative? Is there a lone African American or Hispanic American in a mostly white movie? One white person in an African-American dominated movie? Are the members of different races allowed to date? Does their dating engage the idea of intergroup dating or ignore it?

# GROWING UP, GROWING APART

Tamar Lewin

Tamar Lewin wrote this story as part of *The New York Times* 2000 series on "How Race Is Lived in America." It focuses on the experiences of a group of friends of different backgrounds who are facing social pressure to split apart now that they are teenagers.

BACK IN EIGHTH GRADE, Kelly Regan, Aqeelah Mateen and Johanna Perez-Fox spent New Year's Eve at Johanna's house, swing-dancing until they fell down laughing, banging pots and pans, watching the midnight fireworks beyond the trees in the park at the center of town.

They had been a tight threesome all through Maplewood Middle School—Kelly, a tall, coltish Irish-Catholic girl; Aqeelah, a small, earnest African-American Muslim girl; and Johanna, a light-coffee-colored girl who is half Jewish and half Puerto Rican and famous for knowing just about everyone. It had been a great night, they agreed, a whole lot simpler than Johanna's birthday party three nights before. Johanna had invited all their friends, white and black. But the mixing did not go as she had wished.

"The black kids stayed down in the basement and danced, and the white kids went outside on the stoop and talked," Johanna said. "I went out and said, 'Why don't you guys come downstairs?' and they said they didn't want to, that they just wanted to talk out there. It was just split up, like two parties."

The same thing happened at Kelly's back-to-school party a few months earlier.

"It was so stressful," Kelly said. "There I was, the hostess, and I couldn't get everybody together."

"Oh, man, I was, like, trying to help her," Aqeelah said. "I went up and down and up and down. But it was boring outside, so finally I just gave up and went down and danced."

This year the girls started high school, and what with the difficulty of mixing their black and white friends, none took on the challenge of a birthday party.

It happens everywhere, in the confusions of adolescence and the yearning for identity, when the most important thing in life is choosing a group and fitting in: Black children and white children come apart. They move into separate worlds. Friendships ebb and end.

It happens everywhere, but what is striking is that it happens even here. In a nation of increasingly segregated schools, the South Orange–Maplewood district is extraordinarily mixed. Not only is the student body about half black and half white, but in the last census, blacks had an economic edge. This is the kind of place where people—black and white—talk a lot about the virtues of diversity and worry about white flight, where hundreds will turn out to discuss the book *Why Are All the Black Kids Sitting Together in the Cafeteria?* People here care about race.

But even here, as if pulled by internal magnets, black and white children begin to separate at sixth grade. These are children who walked to school together, learned to read together, slept over at each other's houses. But despite all the personal history, all the community good will, race divides them as they grow up. As racial consciousness develops—and the practice of grouping students by perceived ability sends them on diverging academic paths—race becomes as much a fault line in their world as in the one their parents hoped to move beyond.

As they began high school, Kelly, Johanna and Aqeelah had so far managed to be exceptions. While the world around them had increasingly divided along racial lines, they had stuck together. But where their friendship would go was hard to say. And like a Greek chorus, the voices of other young people warned of tricky currents ahead.

### *Different but Inseparable*

On her first day at Columbia High School, Kelly Regan took a seat in homeroom and introduced herself to the black boy at the next desk.

"I was trying to be friendly," she explained. "But he answered in like one word, and looked away. I think he just thought I was a normal white person, and that's all he saw."

She certainly looks like a normal white person, with her pale skin and straight brown hair. But in middle school, she trooped with Aqeelah and Johanna to Martin Luther King Association meetings; there were only a handful of white girls, but Kelly says she never felt out of place. "Some people say I'm ghetto," she said, shrugging. "I don't care."

She had always had a mixed group of friends, and since the middle of eighth grade had been dating a mixed-race classmate, Jared Watts. Even so, she expected that it would be harder to make black friends in the ninth grade. "It's not because of the person I am," she said, "it's just how it is."

Kelly's mother, Kathy, is fascinated by her daughter's multiracial world.

"It's so different from how I grew up," said Ms. Regan, a nurse who met Kelly's father, from whom she is divorced, at a virtually all-white Catholic school. "Sometimes, in front of the high school, I feel a little intimidated when I see all the black kids. But then so many of them know me, from my oldest daughter or now from Kelly, and they say such a nice, 'Hi, Mrs. Regan,' that the feeling goes away."

Johanna Perez-Fox is intensely sociable; her mane of long black curls can often be sighted at the center of a rushed gossip session in the last seconds before class. As she sees it, her mixed background gives her a choice of racial identity and access to everybody. "I like that I can go both ways," said Johanna, whose mother is a special-education teacher and whose father owns a car service.

Johanna has a certain otherness among her black friends. "If they say something about white people, they'll always say, 'Oh, sorry, Johanna,'" she said. "I think it's good. It makes them more aware of their stereotypes."

Still, she was put off when a new black friend asked what race she was.

"People are always asking, 'What are you?' and I don't really like it," she said. "I told him I'm half white and half Puerto Rican, and he said, 'But you act black.' I told him you can't act like a race. I hate that idea. He defended it, though. He said I would have a point if he'd said African-American, because that's a race, but black is a way of acting. I've thought about it, and I think he's right."

Aqeelah Mateen's parents are divorced, and she lives in a mostly black section of Maplewood with her mother, who works for AT&T. She also sees a lot of her father, a skycap at Newark Airport, and often goes with him to the Newark mosque, where he is an imam.

Aqeelah is a girl of multiple enthusiasms, and in middle school, her gutsy good cheer kept her close to black and white friends alike. But in high school, the issue of "acting black" was starting to become a persistent irritant.

After school one day, Aqeelah and two other black girls were running down the hall when one of them accidentally knocked a corkboard off the wall. Aqeelah told her to pick it up, but the girl kept going.

"What's the matter with you?" Aqeelah asked. "You knocked it over, you pick it up."

"Why do you have to be like a white person?" her friend retorted. "Just leave it there."

But Aqeelah picked it up.

"There's stuff like that all the time, and it gets on my nerves," she said later. "Like at track, in the locker room, there's people telling a Caucasian girl she has a big butt for a white person, and I'm like, 'Who cares, shut up.'"

### *On an Even Playground*

Johanna and Aqeelah met in kindergarten and have been friends from Day 1; Kelly joined the group in fifth grade.

"Nobody cared about race when we were little," Johanna said. "No one thought about it."

On a winter afternoon at South Mountain Elementary School, that still seemed to be the case. There were white and black pockets, but mostly the playground was a picture postcard of racial harmony, white girls and black girls playing clapping games, black boys and white boys shooting space aliens. And when they were asked about race and friendships, there was no self-consciousness. They just said what they had to say.

"Making friends, it just depends on what you like to do, and who likes to do those things," said Carolyn Goldstein, a white third grader.

"I've known Carolyn G. since kindergarten," said a black girl named Carolyn Morton. "She lives on my block. She's in my class. We even have the same name. We have so many things the same!"

As for how they might be different, Carolyn Goldstein groped for an answer: "Well, she has a mom at home and my mom works, and she has a sister, and I don't."

They know race matters in the world, they said, but not here.

"Some people in some places still feel prejudiced, so I guess it's still a kind of an issue, because Martin Luther King was trying to save the world from slaves and bad people and there still are bad people in jail," Carolyn Morton said, finishing up grandly. "I hope by the year 3000, the world will have peace, and the guys who watch the prisoners can finally go home and spend some time with their families."

### *A Shifting Sandbox*

All through middle school, Johanna, Kelly and Aqeelah ate lunch together in a corner of the cafeteria where they could see everyone. The main axis of their friendship was changeable: In seventh grade, Johanna and Kelly were the closest. In eighth grade, as Kelly spent more time with Jared, Johanna and Aqeelah were the tightest.

But at the end of middle school, the three were nominated as class "best friends." And while they saw their classmates dividing along racial lines, they tried to ignore it. "In middle school, I didn't want to be aware of the separation," Kelly said. "I didn't see why it had to happen."

Most young people here seem to accept the racial split as inevitable. It's just how it is, they say. Or, it just happens. Or, it's just easier to be with your own kind.

When Sierre Monk, who is black, graduated from South Mountain, she had friends of all races. But since then, she has moved away from the whites and closer to the blacks. Now, in eighth grade, she referred to the shift, sometimes, as "my drift," as in, "After my drift, I began to notice more how the black kids talk differently from the white kids."

Sierre said her drift began after a sixth-grade argument.

"They said, 'You don't even act like you're black,'" she remembered. "I hadn't thought much about it until then, because I was too young. And I guess it was mean what they said, but it helped me. I found I wanted to behave differently after that."

Sierre (pronounced see-AIR-ah) had come from a mostly white private school in Brooklyn. She is the granddaughter of Thelonius Monk, the great jazz pianist, and more than most families, her parents—Thelonius, a drummer, and Gale, who manages her husband's career and father-in-law's estate—have an integrated social life.

For Gale Monk, it has come as something of a surprise to hear Sierre talk about her new distance from her white friends.

What about the bat mitzvah this weekend? Ms. Monk asked.

Well, that's just because we used to be friends, Sierre said.

"What do you mean? She's in and out of this house all the time. I can't remember how many times she's slept over or been in my kitchen."

"That was last year, Mom. This year's different. Things have changed."

And Sierre's mother allows that some separation may be healthy.

"I don't have any problem with the black kids hanging together," she said. "I think you need to know your own group to feel proud of yourself."

There is a consensus that the split is mostly, though hardly exclusively, a matter of blacks' pulling away.

Marian Flaxman, a white girl in Sierre's homeroom, puts it this way: "You know, you come to a new school and you're all little and scared, and everybody's looking for a way to fit in, for people to like them. At that point, I think we were just white kids, blah, and they were just black kids, blah, and we were all just kids. And then a few black kids began thinking, 'Hey, we're black kids.' I think the black kids feel like they're black and the white kids feel like they're white because the black kids feel like they're black."

And Sierre does not really disagree: "Everybody gets along, but I think the white kids are more friendly toward black or interracial kids, and the black kids aren't as interested back, just because of stupid stereotypical stuff like music and style."

What they cannot quite articulate, though, is how much the divide owes to their growing awareness of the larger society, to negative messages about race and about things like violence and academic success. They may not connect the dots, but that sensitivity makes them intensely alert to slights from friends of another race, likely to pull away at even a hint of rejection.

Sometimes it is simply a misread cue, as when a black girl, sitting with other black girls, holds up a hand to greet a white friend, and the white girl thinks her greeting means, "I see you, but don't join us." Sometimes it is an obvious, if oblivious, offense: A black boy drops a white friend after discovering that the friend has told another white boy that the black family's food is weird.

And occasionally, the breach is startlingly painful: A white seventh grader considers changing schools after her best friend tells her she can no longer afford white friends. Months later, the white girl talked uncomfortably about how unreachable her former friend seemed.

"I'm not going to go sit with her at the 'homey' table," she said, then flushed in intense embarrassment: "I'm not sure I'm supposed to say 'homey.' I'm not sure that's what they call themselves; maybe it sounds racist."

And indeed, the black girl believed that some of the things her former friend had said did fall between insensitive and racist.

For their part, both mothers, in identical tones, expressed anger and hurt about how badly their daughters had been treated. Each, again in identical tones, said her daughter had been blameless. But the mothers had never been friends, and like their daughters, never talked about what happened, never heard the other side.

Marian Flaxman went to a mostly black preschool, and several black friends from those days remain classmates. But, she said, it has been years since she visited a black friend's home.

"Sometimes I feel like I'm the only one who remembers that we used to be friends," she said. "Now we don't say hello in the halls, and the most we'd say in class is something like, 'Can I borrow your eraser?'"

Asked if she knew of any close and lasting cross-race friendships, she was stumped, paging through her yearbook and offering up a few tight friendships between white and mixed-race classmates.

Diane Hughes, a New York University psychology professor who lives in South Orange, has studied the changing friendships of children here. In the first year of middle school, she found, black children were only half as likely as they had been two years before to name a white child as a best friend. Whites had fewer black friends to start with, but their friendships changed less. But blacks and whites, on reaching middle school, were only half as likely as third graders to say they had invited a friend of a different race home recently.

By the end of middle school, the separation is profound.

At 10 p.m. on a Friday in October, 153 revved-up 13-year-olds squealed and hugged their way into the South Orange Middle School cafeteria for the Eighth Grade Sleepover. At 11 they were grouped by birthday month, each group to write what they loved about school.

They loved Skittles at lunch ... the Eighth Grade Sleepover ... Ms. Wright, the health teacher/basketball coach/Martin Luther King Club adviser. And at the March table, a white boy wrote "interracial friendships."

But the moment the organized activities ended, the black and white eighth graders separated. And at 2 a.m., when the girls' sleeping bags covered the library floor and the boys' the gym, they formed a map of racial boundaries. The borders were peaceful, but there was little commerce across territorial lines. After lights out, some black girls stood and started a clapping chant.

"I can't," one girl called.

"Why not?" the group called back.

"I can't."

"Why not?"

"My back's hurting and my bra's too tight."

It grew louder as other black girls threaded their way through the darkness to join in.

"I can't."

"Why not?"

"I shake my booty from left to right."

Marian, in her green parrot slippers, was in a group of white girls up front, enjoying, listening, but quiet.

"It's cool, when they start stuff like that, or in the lunchroom when they start rumbling on the table and we all pick it up," she said. "It's just louder. One time in class this year, someone was acting up, and when the teacher said sit down, the boy said, 'It's because I'm black, isn't it?' I thought, no, it's not because you're black; that's stupid. It's because you're being really noisy and obnoxious. And it made me feel really white. And then I began thinking, well, maybe it is because he's black, because being noisy may be part of that culture, and then I didn't know what to think."

## *Jostling for Position*

Aqeelah, Kelly and Johanna refuse to characterize behavior as black or white; they just hate it, they insist, when anyone categorizes them in racial terms.

"I think what makes Kelly and Johanna and me different is that we're what people don't expect," Aqeelah said. "I'm the only Muslim most people know, and one of two African-Americans on my softball team. There's Kelly, a white girl playing basketball, and Johanna, when people ask if she's white or Puerto Rican, saying, 'Both.'"

Most students are acutely aware of the signposts of Columbia High's coexisting cultures. The popular wisdom has it that the black kids dominate football and basketball, the white kids soccer, softball and lacrosse. Black kids throw big dancing parties in rented spaces; white parties are more often in people's homes, with a lot of drinking. Everyone wears jeans, but the white kids are more preppy, the black kids more hip-hop. Black kids listen to Hot 97, a hip-hop station, or WBLS, which plays rhythm and blues; white kids favor rock stations like Z100 or K-Rock.

"I know a lot of Caucasians listen to Hot 97, too," Aqeelah said, "but even if I had a list of 200 Caucasians who listen to it, everyone still thinks it's an African-American thing."

Even though the two cultures are in constant, casual contact—and a few students cross back and forth easily—in the end, they are quite separate.

Jason Coleman, a black graduate who just finished his freshman year at Howard University, remembers how the cultures diverged, separating him from the white boy with whom he once walked to school.

"The summer before high school, we just went different ways," he said. "We listened to different music, we played different sports, we got interested in different girls. And we didn't have much to say to each other anymore. That's the time you begin to develop your own style, and mine was a different style that his."

Jason's style included heavy gold chains, a diamond ear stud, baggy pants and hair in short twists. Asked to define that style, he hesitated, then said, "I guess what bothers me least is if you say that I follow hip-hop fashion."

At the start of high school, much of Jason's energy went toward straddling the divide between hip-hop kid and honors student. He was in frequent physical fights, though never with white students; that doesn't seem to happen. Although blacks are now a slight majority at the school, he, like many of the black students, felt an underlying jostling about who really owns the school. And he felt dismissed, intellectually and socially, by some teachers and classmates.

"African-Americans may be the majority, but I don't think they feel like the majority because they don't feel they get treated fairly," he said. "You see who gets suspended, and it's the African-American kids. I had one friend suspended for eating a bagel in homeroom because his teacher said he had an attitude. That just wouldn't happen to a Caucasian boy. It doesn't have to be a big thing to make you feel like it's not really your school. We can all hold hands and talk about how united we are, but if the next day you run into a girl from your classes at the mall with her mother and she doesn't say hello, what's that?"

To avoid these issues, Jason chose a predominantly black college, Howard, and he seemed relaxed there this year. The gold chains and diamond were gone, and he was studying hard to go to medical school, as his father and brother had.

White students at Columbia High have their own issues. Many feel intimidated by the awareness that they are becoming a minority at the school, that they tend not to share academic classes, or culturally much else, with a lot of the black students. It is striking that while there are usually a few black or multiracial children in the school's white groups, whites rarely enter the black groups. Many white students are reluctant to be quoted about the racial climate, lest they seem racist. But some recent graduates are more forthcoming.

"A lot of the black kids, it was like they had a really big chip on their shoulder, and they were mad at the world and mad at whites for running the world," said Jenn Caviness, a white graduate who attends Columbia University. "One time, in 10th grade, in the hall, this black kid shoved me and said, 'Get out of the way, white crack bitch.' I moved, because he was big, but I was thinking how if I said something racial back, I would have been attacked. It was very polarized sometimes."

She and others, however, say the cultural jockeying has an upside—a freedom from the rigid social hierarchy that plagues many affluent suburban high schools.

"If you're different here, it doesn't matter, because there's so many kinds of differences already," Johanna explained when asked to identify the cool kids, the in crowd. "There's no one best way to be."

In Johanna's commercial art class one day, there was a table of black boys, a table of white girls and a mixed table, where two black girls were humming as they worked. A white girl asked what the song was.

They told her, and she said, "It's really wack."

Yeah, one answered, "You don't know music like we know music."

"Yeah, and you don't know music like I know music."

"I know," the black girl said, smiling. "It's like two completely different tastes."

## *Acting Black, Acting White*

Aqeelah, Kelly and Johanna did not have many classes together this year, but they had grown up in a shared academic world. While they are not superstars, they do their work and are mostly in honors classes. But if that common ground has so far helped keep them together, the system of academic tracking more often helps pull black and white children apart.

Whenever people talk about race and school, the elephant in the room—rarely mentioned, impossible to ignore—is the racial imbalance that appears when so-called ability grouping begins. Almost all American school districts begin tracking sometime before high school. And when they do, white students are far more likely than blacks to be placed in higher-level classes, based on test scores and teacher recommendations.

Nationwide, by any measure of academic performance, be it grades, tests or graduation rates, whites on average do better than blacks. To some extent, it is a matter of differences in parents' income and education. But the gap remains even when such things are factored out, even in places like this. Experts have no simple explanation, citing a tangle of parents' attitudes, low expectations of mostly white teaching staffs and some white classmates, and negative pressure from black students who believe that doing well isn't cool, that smart is white and street is black.

It can be a vicious circle—and a powerful influence on friendships.

Inevitably, as students notice that honors classes are mostly white and lower-level ones mostly black, they develop a corrosive sense that behaving like honors students is "acting white," while "acting black" demands they emulate lower-level students. Little wonder that sixth grade, when ability grouping starts here, is also when many interracial friendships begin to come apart.

"It sometimes bothers me to see how many of my African-American friends aren't in the higher-level classes, and how they try to be cool around their friends by acting up and trying to be silly and getting in fights," said Sierre, who this year moved up to honors in everything but math. "A lot of them just aren't trying. They're my friends, but I look at them and think, 'Why can't you just be cool and do your work?'"

The district does not release racial breakdowns of its classes. But at Columbia High, which is 45 percent white, ninth-grade honors classes usually seem to be about two-thirds white, middle-level classes more than two-thirds black, and the lowest level—"basic skills"—almost entirely black. The imbalance is at least as great at Marian and Sierre's middle school.

Honors is where students mix most.

"You really see the difference when you're not in honors," said Kelly, who was in middle-level English this year. "In middle level, there aren't so many white kids, and whenever you break into groups, people stick with their own race."

The contrasts are stark. In Aqeelah's mostly white honors history class, the students argued passionately about the nature of man as they compared Hobbes, Locke, Voltaire and Rousseau. But the next period, when the all-black basic-skills class arrived, the students headed to the library to learn how to look up facts for a report on a foreign country.

"I'm still taken aback, shocked, each time I walk into a class and see the complexion," said LuElla Peniston, a black guidance counselor at the school. "It should be more balanced."

The issue has become especially delicate as the district has become progressively blacker, as more students have moved in from poorer neighboring towns with troubled schools, and as the ranking on state tests has slipped. Five years ago, a quarter of the district's children were black; now, with blacks a slight majority, many people worry that the district could tip too far. (Of course, black and white parents tend to have different ideas about how far is too far.)

The schools are still impressive. Columbia High always sends dozens of graduates, black and white, to top colleges. It produced Carla Peterman, a black Rhodes scholar, and Lauryn Hill, the hip-hop star, who still lives in town. This year Columbia had more National Achievement Scholarship semifinalists—an honor for top-scoring black seniors in the National Merit Scholarship Program—than any school in the state. And last year it had an 88 percent passing rate on the state high school proficiency test, three points above average.

Still, in a society that often associates racial minorities with stereotypes of poverty, the district has an image problem. Many parents—whites, but also some blacks—talk nervously about "those kids with the boomboxes out in front of school," and wonder if they should start checking out private schools or another district.

The district's administrators have been grappling with questions of racial balance and ability grouping for years. In middle school, for example, students can temporarily move up a level, to try more challenging work. But the program is used mostly by white families—to push a child or remove him or her from a mostly black classroom—so it has only increased the skew.

Many white parents, Ms. Peniston says, are adamant about not letting their children be anywhere below honors. "They either push very hard to get their children into the level where they want them, or they leave," she said.

It is not an issue only for whites. Many black parents worry that the schools somehow associate darker-skinned children with lower-level classes.

When Kelly's boyfriend, Jared Watts, transferred from South Orange Middle School to Maplewood Middle, he was placed in lower-level classes, something his parents discovered only on parents' night.

"There were all these African-American families, asking all these basic questions," said Jared's mother, Debby Watts. "I looked around and realized they'd put him in the wrong group. I was so upset I made my husband do the calling the next day. They moved him up right away. But you can't help but wonder if it would have happened if he'd been white."

Sierre Monk's parents are watching her grades, and thinking that unless she is put in honors classes in high school next year, they will move her to private school.

Sierre says she is comfortable with her white honors classmates, even if her best friends now are black.

"I feel friendly to a lot of the white kids, and still e-mail some of them," she said. As she sees it, she can be a good student without compromising her African-American credentials. Not everyone, she observes, has been so culturally dextrous.

"A lot of people think of the black kids in the top classes, the ones who don't hang out with a lot of African-Americans, as the 'white' black kids," she said. "I'd never say it to them, but in my head I call them the white black kids, too."

Still, she said, she was happiest in her middle-level math class, where every student but one was black.

"It's my favorite, because I can do well there without struggling," she said. "And I feel closest to that class, because I have so many friends there. Once I was waiting outside, alone, when I heard a group of white kids talking about, 'Oh, those kids in Level 3, they must be stupid.' I don't want to associate with people who think like that."

### *Fissures, Chasms, Islands*

It was hard for Aqeelah, Kelly and Johanna to get together this year. They had different lunch periods, different study halls. Only Johanna and Kelly had any classes together. Johanna was on the varsity swim team, Kelly was on the ninth-grade basketball team and Aqeelah ran indoor track. The three could go weeks without getting together.

But they were still close. In the fall, when Johanna had big news to share about a boy she liked, she was on two phone lines simultaneously, telling Kelly and Aqeelah the latest.

When they finally met for dinner at Arturo's Pizza in November, their pleasure in being together was visible.

Aqeelah was a little late, so Kelly chose an orange soda for her. When she arrived, they were their usual frisky selves, waving to everyone who walked by and talking about the old friends they didn't see anymore and the new people they felt friendly with but would not yet ask to the movies.

They were still in giggle mode when Aqeelah said, "I get made fun of by everybody," and Johanna broke in, "Why, because you're short?" and they collapsed into laughter.

But a second later, Aqeelah was not laughing. She had her head down and her eyes covered, and when she looked up, a tear was leaking down her cheek.

"No, it's really confusing this year," she said. "I'm too white to be black, and I'm too black to be white. If I'm talking to a white boy, a black kid walks by and says, 'Oh, there's Aqeelah, she likes white boys.' And in class, these Caucasian boys I've been friends with for years say hi, and then the next thing they say is, 'Yo, Aqeelah, what up?' as if I won't understand them unless they use that kind of slang. Or they'll tell me they really like 'Back That Thing Up' by Juvenile. I don't care if they like a rapper, but it seems like they think that's the only connection they have with me.

"Last year this stuff didn't bother me, but now it does bother me, because some of the African-American kids, joking around, say I'm an Oreo."

Johanna and Kelly were surprised by her pain; they had not heard this before. But they did sense her increasing distance from them.

"It's like she got lost or something," Kelly said. "I never see her."

Aqeelah had always been the strongest student of the three, the only one in a special math class, one rung above honors. But by winter, she was getting disappointing grades, especially in history, and beginning to worry about being moved down a level. Math was not going so well either, and so she dropped track to focus on homework. She was hoping to make the softball team, and disappointed that neither of her friends was trying out. "I'll never see you," she complained.

All three, of course, have always had other friends, and they still did.

Much of Kelly's social life was with her racially mixed lunch group. She felt herself moving further from some of her white friends, the ones who hang out only with whites. "It seems like they have their whole clique," she said, and she was not terribly interested in them. Against the grain, she was still working to make friends with blacks, particularly with a basketball teammate.

Johanna found herself hanging out more with blacks, much as her older sister had—though not her brother, a college freshman whose high school friends were mostly white.

"In middle school, there were black and white tables in the cafeteria and everything, but people talked together in the hallways," Johanna said. "Now there's so many people, you don't even say hi to everybody, and sometimes it seems like the black and white people live in such different worlds that they wouldn't know how to have fun together anymore."

The three girls celebrated separately this New Year's Eve—Kelly with Jared, Johanna at a party with her family, Aqeelah at her father's mosque for Ramadan.

Kelly still tried to bring them together. One Friday night, she called Johanna and Aqeelah on the spur of the moment, and they came over in their pajamas. And at Kelly's last basketball game, in late February, Johanna and Aqeelah sat and joked with Jared, Kelly's mother, her grandmother and little brother.

The next day Kelly and Jared broke up. Kelly said she was sad and working hard to keep up her friendship with Jared, but that's about all she was saying.

And as spring arrived, Kelly, Johanna and Aqeelah acknowledged that, at least for now, their threesome had pretty much become a twosome.

Johanna and Kelly were still very tight, and did something together almost every weekend. But these days Aqeelah talked most to a black girl, a longtime family friend. It was partly logistics: Aqeelah would run into her daily at sixth period and after school, at her locker.

"I don't know why I don't call Johanna or Kelly," she said. "They'll always have the place in my heart, but not so much physically in my life these days. It seems like I have no real friends this year. You know how you can have a lot of friends, but you have no one? Everyone seems to be settled in their cliques and I'm just searching. And the more I get to know some people, the more I want to withdraw. I'm spending a lot more time with my family this year."

It's not that Aqeelah was falling apart. She was still her solid self, with all her enthusiasms—for *Dawson's Creek*, movies, and the Friday noon service at the mosque. But increasingly, the gibes about being too white were getting to her. One day, walking to class with a black boy who is an old friend, she blew up when he told her she had "white people's hair."

"I just began screaming, 'What's wrong with these people in this school?' and everyone stared at me like I was crazy," she said. "Everyone, every single person, gets on my nerves."

## *Lessons and Legacies*

The story of Aqeelah, Kelly and Johanna is still unfolding. But those who have gone before know something about where they may be headed.

Aqeelah's struggle is deeply familiar to Malika Oglesby, who arrived from a mostly white school in Virginia in fifth grade and quickly found white friends. Several black boys began to follow her around, taunting her. Lowering her eyes, she recited the chant that plagued her middle-school years: "Cotton candy, sweet as gold, Malika is an Oreo."

"I don't think I knew what it meant the first time, but I figured it out pretty fast," she said.

Jenn Caviness, one of her white friends from that time, clearly remembers Malika's pain.

"Malika was in tears every other day, they just tormented her," she said. "We all felt very protective, but we didn't know how to stop it."

Malika felt powerless, too.

"I didn't tell my parents about it, I didn't tell my sister, but it was a hard time," she said. "If you'd asked me about it at the time, I would have said that there was absolutely no issue at all about my having chosen all those white friends. But that's not true. By the end of seventh grade, I was starting to be uncomfortable. Everybody was having little crushes on everybody among my friends, but of course nobody was having a crush on me. I began to feel like I was falling behind, I was just the standby."

The summer before high school, she eased into a black social group.

"I found a black boyfriend, and I kind of lost contact with everyone else," said Malika, who now attends Howard.

And yet, when Malika finished talking about her Oreo problem, when Jason recalled his fighting days, when others finished describing difficult racial experiences, a strange thing happened. They looked up, unprompted, and said how much they loved the racial mix here and the window it opened onto a different culture.

"Columbia High School was so important and useful to me," said Jenn, immediately after recounting how she had been pushed in the hall by a black boy. "It shaped a lot of parts of my personality."

She and the others remembered a newfound ease as high school was ending, when the racial divide began to fade.

"Senior year was wonderful, when the black kids and the white kids got to be friends again, and the graduation parties where everyone mixed," said Malika. "It was so much better."

Many parents say that is a common pattern.

"It is an ebb and flow," said Carol Barry-Austin, the biracial mother of three African-American children. "Middle-school kids need time to separate and feel comfortable in their racial identity, and then they can come back together. I remember when I wanted to give my oldest daughter a sweet-16 party, she said no, because she couldn't mix her black and white friends. But by the time she got to a graduation party, she could."

This year, among the seniors, there was a striking friendship between Jordan BarAm, the white student council president, and Ari Onugha, the black homecoming king.

They met in ninth grade when Jordan was running for class president and knew he needed the black vote. Ari, he had heard, was the coolest kid in school, and he went to him in such a low-key and humorous way that Ari was happy to help out. From that unlikely start, a genuine friendship began when both were in Advanced Placement physics the next year.

This year they had several Advanced Placement classes together, and they talked on the phone most nights, Jordan said, "about everything"—homework, girls, college. Ari was admitted to the University of Pennsylvania's Wharton School and Jordan to Harvard.

"No one looking at me would ever think I'm in Advanced Placement," said Ari, who wears baggy Girbaud pants, a pyramid ring and a big metal watch. "Most of the black kids in the honors classes identify with white culture. I'm more comfortable in black culture, with kids who dress like me and talk like me and listen to the same music I do."

Ari and Jordan have a real friendship, but one with limits. On weekends, Ari mostly hangs out with black friends from lower-level classes, Jordan with a mostly white group of top students. When Ari and his friends performed a wildly successful hip-hop dance routine at the Martin Luther King Association fashion show, Jordan, like most white students, did not go. And when Jordan and his friends put together a fund-raising dance for a classmate with multiple sclerosis, Ari did not show up.

"We've tried to get him to white parties, everyone wants him there, but he either doesn't come or doesn't stay long," Jordan said.

Jordan thinks a lot about race and has been active in school groups to promote better racial understanding—something he has tried unsuccessfully to draw Ari into.

And while Ari often visits Jordan's home, Jordan has only rarely, and briefly, been to Ari's.

Ari laughed. "Hey, dude, you could come."

### This Text: Reading

1. How do others treat these students? From your own experience, where do you think their attitude toward their friendship comes?
2. What is the semiotic situation here? In what ways are outsiders "reading" this group of friends, individually and as a group? In what way are the insiders doing this reading? What signs do the friends display? How do others assign readings to these groups?
3. How would you describe the writing approach Lewin takes? Is there another way she could have told this story? Is this approach effective in approaching questions of identity? Why or why not?
4. This article is part of a series by *The New York Times* on "How Race is Lived in America." Why do you think the *Times* devoted time and energy to this question at this point in American history?

### Your Text: Writing

1. Writing from your own experience, was there a time when you let others decide who your friends were? Was this decision based on a particular reading of this person?
2. Do you remember when you first realized that others were different from you in appearance? Who had influence in helping you determining this?
3. Do you think this essay represents a particular reality in American today? What encourages us to be close to others who may not look like us? What discourages us?

## DESCRIBING RACE, ETHNICITY, AND CULTURE IN MEDICAL RESEARCH: DESCRIBING THE GROUPS STUDIED IS BETTER THAN TRYING TO FIND A CATCHALL NAME

Kwame J. McKenzie and N.S. Crowcroft

> Kwame J. McKenzie and N.S. Crowcroft wrote this piece for the *British Medical Journal* (1994), one of England's most prominent medical periodicals. In it, they take a scientific approach to the question of racial identity. (Note: This work is formatted according to APA guidelines.)

THE TERMINOLOGY OF RACE, ethnicity, and culture is a source of continuing debate and will change because of fashion and politics (1). Given our diversity, the fact that ethnicity is now most often self classified, and that both ethnicity and culture are dynamic it seems unlikely that an agreed taxonomy can be achieved. But if researchers want to be able to compare results of studies now and in the future a framework is needed for the classification of ethnic or cultural groups.

The nearest we have to an agreed classification in the United Kingdom are the categories used by the Office of Population Censuses and Surveys in the 1991 census (2). This is a pragmatic classification that balances ease of collection against a need to produce data on the population. It is of limited use as a measure of sociocultural differences (3).

This leaves a void in which there are many different terms used for groups. For instance, a black Baptist born in the U.K. but whose parents were born in Jamaica might be called Afro-Caribbean, black British, of Caribbean origin U.K. born, West Indian, and, of course, Jamaican. It also leaves those who wish to research ethnic differences in health with studies that are difficult to compare and in the position of having to decide on an ad hoc basis what to call their ethnic groupings.

Terminology should reflect the hypothesis under consideration (1). For example, the OPCS classification may be adequate for assessing access to services (3). If cultural differences are thought to be the predominant influence on patterns of disease, however, those cultural differences should be measured and govern the categorisation used. For instance, if it were thought that religion and being born in the U.K. were important determinants of the risk of committing suicide, then groups for comparison could logically be: U.K. born practising Muslim, non-U.K. born practising Muslims, U.K. born practising Sikh, U.K. born non-practising Sikh, U.K. born practising Baptist, and so on. If researchers believe that race underlies differences in disease patterns then the onus is on them to prove that race has a biological correlate relevant to the disease in question, since race is a poor predictor of biological difference or risk (4),(5).

When it comes to reporting research the aim is to produce results that are easily compared, now and in the future, by following the basic principle taught to medical students: if you do not know the right name for something then describe it. Names should be as descriptive as possible and should reflect how these groups were demarcated. Authors should describe fully in their methods section the logic behind their ethnic groupings and how these were assigned. In their discussion authors should be careful not to draw conclusions which go beyond their data. For instance, it would be difficult for researchers who had demarcated people on racial grounds to proffer a cultural explanation for their findings.

The BMJ's new guidelines on this subject do not try directly to answer the vexed question "What should we call them?" but gives advice on how to go about making such a decision. The terms used should be those which most accurately reflect how people have been assigned to groups.

In the real world many researchers find it difficult to know whether ethnicity, culture, or race are important and so cannot produce hypothesis-led classifications at the start of their research. The simplest solution is to collect a range of information that will help describe the groups being researched. This can be collected by using the OPCS categories and then adding extra information, driven by the hypothesis, such as country of birth, parents' country of birth, mother tongue, special diets, religion practised, and years in the U.K. Information on socioeconomic status should also be collected, since it is a confounder that is often neglected in comparisons between ethnic groups (6). The relative contributions of each factor can then be estimated, and when the research is reported the terminology should reflect the nature of the factors that have been evaluated.

Discussion about research into cultural or ethnic grouping is often reduced to arguments about terminology. In our experience doctors often try to use names that will offend as few people as possible rather than those that impart as much information as possible. They worry not only about the groups they are researching but also about editors and readers. "U.K. Afro-Caribbean" is easier to read than "black people of Caribbean origin born and living in the U.K.," but less informative.

Nevertheless, some readers will probably be disappointed that this editorial does not contain a simple list of politically correct terms to use. Apart from the fact that fashions in terminology change, the more important objection is that such a list would not curtail the growing number of reports describing work that cannot be interpreted or compared. Until we agree on how culturally or ethnically to demarcate the people of the world—and people stop mixing—the best advice for researchers remains to collect as much information as possible and describe what they have done.

## Notes

1. McKenzie, K.J., and Crowcroft, N.S. Race, ethnicity, culture, and science. *BMJ* 1994; 309:286–7.
2. White, P. A question on ethnic group for the census: findings from the 1989 census test post-enumeration survey. *Population Trends* 1990; 59:11–20.
3. Silltoe, K. *Asking about race*. London: Office of Population Censuses and Surveys, 1987.
4. Hill, A.V.S. *Molecular markers of ethnic groups*. In: Cruickshank, J.K., Beevers, D.G., eds. *Ethnic factors in health and disease*. London: Wright, 1989:25–31.
5. Sheldon, T.A., and Parker, H. Race and ethnicity in health research. *J Public Health Med* 1992; 14:104–10.
6. Senior, P.A., and Bhopal, R. Ethnicity as a variable in epidemiological research. *BMJ* 1994; 309:327–30.

---

## THIS TEXT: READING

1. Although this appears in a medical journal, how relevant are the ideas to the "average" reader? How does its appearance in a medical journal affect your opinion about its objectivity and truthfulness?

2. Notice the way McKenzie and Crowcroft approach using outside sources. Is this an approach you might take in your own work? Why or why not?
3. Do you agree with their definitions of race and ethnicity? In what ways do these definitions work against the ones you have?
4. This particular article is from the United Kingdom, yet encompasses both European and American experience. How does its nation or origin affect your opinion about its effectiveness as an argument?
5. What do you think is motivating McKenzie and Crowcroft's article? What about their subject, time, or both do you think has led to this article?
6. What are some of the signs McKenzie and Crowcroft name in their article? What problems do they see with using them?

### YOUR TEXT: WRITING

1. Find a social phenomenon which you would like to research. What type of studies would be helpful in researching this topic?
2. McKenzie and Crowcroft's paper is argumentative, though it's heavily researched. Is there an argument you have with others that could stand some research?

## IN LIVING COLOR: RACE AND AMERICAN CULTURE

Michael Omi

Michael Omi is a scholar who often writes about race and ethnicity. In this argumentative essay (1989), he takes on the stereotypes television "speaks" in when they talk about race and ethnicity.

IN FEBRUARY 1987, Assistant Attorney General William Bradford Reynolds, the nation's chief civil rights enforcer, declared that the recent death of a black man in Howard Beach, New York and the Ku Klux Klan attack on civil rights marchers in Forsyth County, Georgia were "isolated" racial incidences. He emphasized that the places where racial conflict could potentially flare up were "far fewer now than ever before in our history," and concluded that such a diminishment of racism stood as "a powerful testament to how far we have come in the civil rights struggle."[1]

Events in the months following his remarks raise the question as to whether we have come quite so far. They suggest that dramatic instances of racial tension and violence merely constitute the surface manifestations of a

[1]Reynolds's remarks were made at a conference on equal opportunity held by the bar association in Orlando, Florida. *The San Francisco Chronicle* (7 February 1987).

deeper racial organization of American society—a system of inequality which has shaped, and in turn been shaped by, our popular culture.

In March, the NAACP released a report on blacks in the record industry entitled "The Discordant Sound of Music." It found that despite the revenues generated by black performers, blacks remain "grossly underrepresented" in the business, marketing, and A&R (Artists and Repertoire) departments of major record labels. In addition, few blacks are employed as managers, agents, concert promoters, distributors, and retailers. The report concluded that:

> The record industry is overwhelmingly segregated and discrimination is rampant. No other industry in America so openly classifies its operations on a racial basis. At every level of the industry, beginning with the separation of black artists into a special category, barriers exist that severely limit opportunities for blacks.[2]

Decades after the passage of civil rights legislation and the affirmation of the principle of "equal opportunity," patterns of racial segregation and exclusion, it seems, continue to characterize the production of popular music.

The enduring logic of Jim Crow is also present in professional sports. In April, Al Campanis, vice president of player personnel for the Los Angeles Dodgers, explained to Ted Koppel on ABC's *Nightline* about the paucity of blacks in baseball front offices and as managers. "I truly believe," Campanis said, "that [blacks] may not have some of the necessities to be, let's say, a field manager or perhaps a general manager." When pressed for a reason, Campanis offered an explanation which had little to do with the structure of opportunity of institutional discrimination within professional sports:

> [W]hy are black men or black people not good swimmers? Because they don't have the buoyancy.... They are gifted with great musculature and various other things. They're fleet of foot. And this is why there are a lot of black major league ballplayers. Now as far as having the background to become club presidents, or presidents of a bank, I don't know.[3]

Black exclusion from the front office, therefore, was justified on the basis of biological "difference."

The issue of race, of course, is not confined to the institutional arrangements of popular culture production. Since popular culture deals with the symbolic realm of social life, the images which it creates, represents, and disseminates contribute to the overall racial climate. They become the

---

[2]Economic Development Department of the NAACP, "The Discordant Sound of Music (A Report on the Record Industry)," (Baltimore, Maryland: The NAACP, 1987), pp. 16–17.

[3]Campanis's remarks on *Nightline* were reprinted in *The San Francisco Chronicle* (April 9, 1987).

subject of analysis and political scrutiny. In August, the National Ethnic Coalition of Organizations bestowed the "Golden Pit Awards" on television programs, commercials, and movies that were deemed offensive to racial and ethnic groups: *Saturday Night Live,* regarded by many media critics as a politically "progressive" show, was singled out for the "Platinum Pit Award" for its comedy skit "Ching Chang" which depicted a Chinese storeowner and his family in a derogatory manner.[4]

These examples highlight the *overt* manifestations of racism in popular culture—institutional forms of discrimination which keep racial minorities out of the production and organization of popular culture, and the crude racial caricatures by which these groups are portrayed. Yet racism in popular culture is often conveyed in a variety of implicit, and at times invisible, ways. Political theorist Stuart Hall makes an important distinction between *overt* racism, the elaboration of an explicitly racist argument, policy, or view, and *inferential* racism which refers to "those apparently naturalized representations of events and situations relating to race, whether 'factual' or 'fictional,' which have racist premises and propositions inscribed in them as a set of *unquestioned assumptions.*" He argues that inferential racism is more widespread, common, and indeed insidious since "it is largely *invisible* even to those who formulate the world in its terms."[5]

Race itself is a slippery social concept which is paradoxically both "obvious" and "invisible." In our society, one of the first things we notice about people when we encounter them (along with their sex/gender) is their *race.* We utilize race to provide clues about *who* a person is and *how* we should relate to her/him. Our perception of race determines our "presentation of *self,*" distinctions in status, and appropriate modes of conduct in daily and institutional life. This process is often unconscious; we tend to operate off of an unexamined set of *racial beliefs.*

Racial beliefs account for and explain variations in "human nature." Differences in skin color and other obvious physical characteristics supposedly provide visible clues to more substantive differences lurking underneath. Among other qualities, temperament, sexuality, intelligence, and artistic and athletic ability are presumed to be fixed and discernible from the palpable mark of race. Such diverse questions as our confidence and trust in others (as salespeople, neighbors, media figures); our sexual preferences and romantic images; our tastes in music, film, dance, or sports; indeed our very ways of walking and talking are ineluctably shaped by notions of race.

---

[4]Ellen Wulfhorst, "TV Stereotyping: It's the 'Pits,'" *The San Francisco Chronicle* (August 24, 1987).

[5]Stuart Hall, "The Whites of Their Eyes: Racist Ideologies and the Media," in George Bridges and Rosalind Brunt, eds., *Silver Linings* (London: Lawrence and Wishart, 1981), pp. 36–37.

Ideas about race, therefore, have become "common sense"—a way of comprehending, explaining, and acting in the world. This is made painfully obvious when someone disrupts our common sense understandings. An encounter with someone who is, for example, racially "mixed" or of a racial/ethnic group we are unfamiliar with becomes a source of discomfort for us, and momentarily creates a crisis of racial meaning. We also become disoriented when people do not act "black," "Latino," or indeed "white." The content of such stereotypes reveals a series of unsubstantiated beliefs about who these groups are, what they are like, and how they behave.

The existence of such racial consciousness should hardly be surprising. Even prior to the inception of the republic, the United States was a society shaped by racial conflict. The establishment of the Southern plantation economy, Western expansion, and the emergence of the labor movement, among other significant historical developments, have all involved conflicts over the definition and nature of the *color line*. The historical results have been distinct and different groups have encountered unique forms of racial oppression—Native Americans faced genocide, blacks were subjected to slavery, Mexicans were invaded and colonized, and Asians faced exclusion. What is common to the experiences of these groups is that their particular "fate" was linked to historically specific ideas about the significance and meaning of race.[6] Whites defined them as separate "species," ones inferior to Northern European cultural stocks, and thereby rationalized the conditions of their subordination in the economy, in political life, and in the realm of culture.

A crucial dimension of racial oppression in the United States is the elaboration of an ideology of difference or "otherness." This involves defining "us" (i.e., white Americans) in opposition to "them," an important task when distinct racial groups are first encountered, or in historically specific periods where preexisting racial boundaries are threatened or crumbling.

Political struggles over the very definition of who an "American" is illustrates this process. The Naturalization Law of 1790 declared that only free *white* immigrants could qualify, reflecting the initial desire among Congress to create and maintain a racially homogeneous society. The extension of eligibility to all racial groups has been a long and protracted process. Japanese, for example, were finally eligible to become naturalized citizens after the passage of the Walter-McCarran Act of 1952. The ideological residue of these restrictions in naturalization and citizenship laws is the equation within popular parlance of the term "American" with "white," while other "Americans" are described as black, Mexican, "Oriental," etc.

Popular culture has been an important realm within which racial ideologies have been created, reproduced, and sustained. Such ideologies

---

[6]For an excellent survey of racial beliefs see Thomas F. Gossett, *Race: The History of an Idea in America* (New York: Shocken Books, 1965).

provide a framework of symbols, concepts, and images through which we understand, interpret, and represent aspects of our "racial" existence.

Race has often formed the central themes of American popular culture. Historian W. L. Rose notes that it is "curious coincidence" that four of the "most popular reading-viewing events in all American history" have in some manner dealt with race, specifically black/white relations in the south.[7] Harriet Beecher Stowe's *Uncle Tom's Cabin*, Thomas Ryan Dixon's *The Clansman* (the inspiration for D. W. Griffith's *The Birth of a Nation*), Margaret Mitchell's *Gone with the Wind* (as a book and film), and Alex Haley's *Roots* (as a book and television miniseries), each appeared at a critical juncture in American race relations and helped to shape new understandings of race.

Emerging social definitions of race and the "real American" were reflected in American popular culture of the nineteenth century. Racial and ethnic stereotypes were shaped and reinforced in the newspapers, magazines, and pulp fiction of the period. But the evolution and ever-increasing sophistication of visual mass communications throughout the twentieth century provided, and continue to provide, the most dramatic means by which racial images are generated and reproduced.

Film and television have been notorious in disseminating images of racial minorities which establish for audiences what these groups look like, how they behave, and, in essence, "who they are." The power of the media lies not only in their ability to reflect the dominant racial ideology, but in their capacity to shape that ideology in the first place. D. W. Griffith's aforementioned epic *Birth of a Nation*, a sympathetic treatment of the rise of the Ku Klux Klan during Reconstruction, helped to generate, consolidate, and "nationalize" images of blacks which had been more disparate (more regionally specific, for example) prior to the film's appearance.[8]

In television and film, the necessity to define characters in the briefest and most condensed manner has led to the perpetuation of racial caricatures, as racial stereotypes serve as shorthand for scriptwriters, directors, and actors. Television's tendency to address the "lowest common denominator" in order to render programs "familiar" to an enormous and diverse audience leads it regularly to assign and reassign racial characteristics to particular groups, both minority and majority.

Many of the earliest American films deal with racial and ethnic "difference." The large influx of "new immigrants" at the turn of the century led to a proliferation of negative images of Jews, Italians, and Irish which were assimilated and adapted by such films as Thomas Edison's *Cohen's*

---

[7]W.L. Rose, *Race and Region in American Historical Fiction: Four Episodes in Popular Culture* (Oxford: Clarendon Press, 1979).

[8]Melanie Martindale-Sikes, "Nationalizing 'Nigger' Imagery Through *Birth of a Nation*," paper prepared for the 73rd Annual Meeting of the American Sociological Association (September 4–8, 1978) in San Francisco.

*Advertising Scheme* (1904). Based on an old vaudeville routine, the film featured a scheming Jewish merchant, aggressively hawking his wares. Though stereotypes of these groups persist to this day,[9] by the 1940s many of the earlier ethnic stereotypes had disappeared from Hollywood. But, as historian Michael Winston observes, the "outsiders" of the 1890s remained: "the ever-popular Indian of the Westerns; the inscrutable or sinister Oriental; the sly, but colorful Mexican; and the clowning or submissive Negro."[10]

In many respects the "Western" as a genre has been paradigmatic in establishing images of racial minorities in film and television. The classic scenario involves the encircled wagon train or surrounded fort from which whites bravely fight off fierce bands of Native American Indians. The point of reference and viewer identification lies with those huddled within the circle—the representatives of "civilization" who valiantly attempt to ward off the forces of barbarism. In the classic Western, as writer Tom Engelhardt observes, "the viewer is forced behind the barrel of a repeating rifle and it is from that position, through its gun sights, that he receives a picture history of Western colonialism and imperialism."[11]

Westerns have indeed become the prototype for European and American excursions throughout the Third World. The cast of characters may change, but the story remains the same. The "humanity" of whites is contrasted with the brutality and treachery of nonwhites; brave (i.e., white) souls are pitted against the merciless hordes in conflicts ranging from Indians against the British Lancers to Zulus against the Boers. What Stuart Hall refers to as the imperializing "white eye" provides the framework for these films, lurking outside the frame and yet seeing and positioning everything within; it is "the unmarked position from which ... 'observations' are made and from which, alone, they make sense."[12]

Our "common sense" assumptions about race and racial minorities in the United States are both generated and reflected in the stereotypes presented by the visual media. In the crudest sense, it could be said that such stereotypes underscore white "superiority" by reinforcing the traits, habits, and predispositions of nonwhites which demonstrate their "inferiority." Yet a more careful assessment of racial stereotypes reveals intriguing trends and seemingly contradictory themes.

While all racial minorities have been portrayed as "less than human," there are significant differences in the images of different groups. Specific

---

[9]For a discussion of Italian, Irish, Jewish, Slavic, and German stereotypes in film, see Randall M. Miller, ed., *The Kaleidoscopic Lens: How Hollywood Views Ethnic Groups* (Englewood, N.J.: Jerome S. Ozer, 1980).

[10]Michael R. Winston, "Racial Consciousness and the Evolution of Mass Communications in the United States," *Daedalus*, vol. III, No. 4 (Fall 1982).

[11]Tom Engelhardt, "Ambush at Kamikaze Pass," in Emma Gee, ed., *Counterpoint: Perspectives on Asian America* (Los Angeles: Asian American Studies Center, UCLA, 1976), p. 270.

[12]Hall, "Whites of Their Eyes," p. 38.

racial minority groups, in spite of their often interchangeable presence in films steeped in the "Western" paradigm, have distinct and often unique qualities assigned to them. Latinos are portrayed as being prone toward violent outbursts of anger; blacks as physically strong, but dim-witted; while Asians are seen as sneaky and cunningly evil. Such differences are crucial to observe and analyze. Race in the United States is not reducible to black/white relations. These differences are significant for a broader understanding of the patterns of race in America, and the unique experience of specific racial minority groups.

It is somewhat ironic that *real* differences which exist within a racially defined minority group are minimized, distorted, or obliterated by the media. "All Asians look alike," the saying goes, and indeed there has been little or no attention given to the vast differences which exist between, say, the Chinese and Japanese with respect to food, dress, language, and culture. This blurring within popular culture has given us supposedly Chinese characters who wear kimonos; it is also the reason why the fast-food restaurant McDonald's can offer "Shanghai McNuggets" with teriyaki sauce. Other groups suffer a similar fate. Professor Gretchen Bataille and Charles Silet find the cinematic Native American of the Northeast wearing the clothing of the Plains Indians, while living in the dwellings of Southwestern tribes:

> The movie men did what thousands of years of social evolution could not do, even what the threat of the encroaching white man could not do; Hollywood produced the homogenized Native American, devoid of tribal characteristics or regional differences.[13]

The need to paint in broad racial strokes has thus rendered "internal" differences invisible. This has been exacerbated by the tendency for screenwriters to "invent" mythical Asian, Latin American, and African countries. Ostensibly done to avoid offending particular nations and peoples, such a subterfuge reinforces the notion that all the countries and cultures of a specific region are the same. European countries retain their distinctiveness, while the Third World is presented as one homogeneous mass riddled with poverty and governed by ruthless and corrupt regimes.

While rendering specific groups in a monolithic fashion, the popular cultural imagination simultaneously reveals a compelling need to distinguish and articulate "bad" and "good" variants of particular racial groups and individuals. Thus each stereotypic image is filled with contradictions: The bloodthirsty Indian is tempered with the image of the noble savage; the *bandido* exists along with the loyal sidekick; and Fu Manchu is offset by Charlie Chan. The existence of such contradictions, however, does not negate the one-dimensionality of these images, nor does it challenge the

---

[13]Gretchen Bataille and Charles Silet, "The Entertaining Anachronism: Indians in American Film," in Randall M. Miller, ed., *Kaleidoscopic Lens*, p. 40.

explicit subservient role of racial minorities. Even the "good" person of color usually exists as a foil in novels and films to underscore the intelligence, courage, and virility of the white male hero.

Another important, perhaps central, dimension of racial minority stereotypes is sex/gender differentiation. The connection between race and sex has traditionally been an explosive and controversial one. For most of American history, sexual and marital relations between whites and nonwhites were forbidden by social custom and by legal restrictions. It was not until 1967, for example, that the U.S. Supreme Court ruled that antimiscegenation laws were unconstitutional. Beginning in the 1920s, the notorious Hays Office, Hollywood's attempt at self-censorship, prohibited scenes and subjects which dealt with miscegenation. The prohibition, however, was not evenly applied in practice. White men could seduce racial minority women, but white women were not to be romantically or sexually linked to racial minority men.

Women of color were sometimes treated as exotic sex objects. The sultry Latin temptress—such as Dolores Del Rio and Lupe Velez—invariably had boyfriends who were white North Americans; their Latino suitors were portrayed as being unable to keep up with the Anglo–American competition. From Mary Pickford as Cho-Cho San in *Madame Butterfly* (1915) to Nancy Kwan in *The World of Suzie Wong* (1961), Asian women have often been seen as the gracious "geisha girl" or the prostitute with a "heart of gold," willing to do anything to please her man.

By contrast, Asian men, whether cast in the role of villain, servant, sidekick, or kung fu master, are seen as asexual or, at least, romantically undesirable. As Asian American studies professor Elaine Kim notes, even a hero such as Bruce Lee played characters whose "single-minded focus on perfecting his fighting skills precludes all other interests, including an interest in women, friendship, or a social life."[14]

The shifting trajectory of black images over time reveals an interesting dynamic with respect to sex and gender. The black male characters in *The Birth of a Nation* were clearly presented as sexual threats to "white womanhood." For decades afterwards, however, Hollywood consciously avoided portraying black men as assertive or sexually aggressive in order to minimize controversy. Black men were instead cast as comic, harmless, and nonthreatening figures exemplified by such stars as Bill "Bojangles" Robinson, Stepin Fetchit, and Eddie "Rochester" Anderson. Black women, by contrast, were divided into two broad character types based on color categories. Dark black women such as Hattie McDaniel and Louise Beavers were cast as "dowdy, frumpy, dumpy, overweight mammy figures"; while those "close to the white ideal," such as Lena Horne and Dorothy Dandridge, became

[14]Elaine Kim, "Asian Americans and American Popular Culture" in Hyung-Chan Kim, ed., *Dictionary of Asian American History* (New York: Greenwood Press, 1986), p. 107.

"Hollywood's treasured mulattoes" in roles emphasizing the tragedy of being of mixed blood.[15]

It was not until the early 1970s that tough, aggressive, sexually assertive black characters, both male and female, appeared. The "blaxploitation" films of the period provided new heroes (e.g., *Shaft*, *Superfly*, *Coffy*, and *Cleopatra Jones*) in sharp contrast to the submissive and subservient images of the past. Unfortunately, most of these films were shoddy productions which did little to create more enduring "positive" images of blacks, either male or female.

In contemporary television and film, there is a tendency to present and equate racial minority groups and individuals with specific social problems. Blacks are associated with drugs and urban crime, Latinos with "illegal" immigration, while Native Americans cope with alcoholism and tribal conflicts. Rarely do we see racial minorities "out of character," in situations removed from the stereotypic arenas in which scriptwriters have traditionally embedded them. Nearly the only time we see young Asians and Latinos of either sex, for example, is when they are members of youth gangs, as *Boulevard Nights* (1979), *Year of the Dragon* (1985), and countless TV cop shows can attest to.

Racial minority actors have continually bemoaned the fact that the roles assigned them on stage and screen are often one-dimensional and imbued with stereotypic assumptions. In theater, the movement toward "blind casting" (i.e., casting actors for roles without regard to race) is a progressive step, but it remains to be seen whether large numbers of audiences can suspend their "beliefs" and deal with a Latino King Lear or an Asian Stanley Kowalski. By contrast, white actors are allowed to play anybody. Though the use of white actors to play blacks in "black face" is clearly unacceptable in the contemporary period, white actors continue to portray Asian, Latino, and Native American characters on stage and screen.

Scores of Charlie Chan films, for example, have been made with white leads (the last one was the 1981 *Charlie Chan and the Curse of the Dragon Queen*). Roland Winters, who played Chan in six features, was once asked to explain the logic of casting a white man in the role of Charlie Chan: "The only thing I can think of is, if you want to cast a homosexual in a show, and you get a homosexual, it'll be awful. It won't be funny... and maybe there's something there."[16]

Such a comment reveals an interesting aspect about myth and reality in popular culture. Michael Winston argues that stereotypic images in the visual media were not originally conceived as representations of reality, nor were they initially understood to be "real" by audiences. They were, he suggests, ways of "coding and rationalizing" the racial hierarchy and

---

[15]Donald Bogle, "A Familiar Plot (A Look at the History of Blacks in American Movies)," *The Crisis*, Vol. 90, No. 1 (January 1983), p. 15.

[16]Frank Chin, "Confessions of the Chinatown Cowboy," *Bulletin of Concerned Asian Scholars*, Vol. 4, No. 3 (Fall 1972).

interracial behavior. Over time, however, "a complex interactive relationship between myth and reality developed, so that images originally understood to be unreal, through constant repetition began to *seem* real."[17]

Such a process consolidated, among other things, our "common sense" understandings of what we think various groups should look like. Such presumptions have led to tragicomical results. Latinos auditioning for a role in a television soap opera, for example, did not fit the Hollywood image of "real Mexicans" and had their faces bronzed with powder before filming because they looked too white. Model Aurora Garza said, "I'm a real Mexican and very dark anyway. I'm even darker right now because I have a tan. But they kept wanting to make my face darker and darker."[18]

Historically in Hollywood, the fact of having "dark skin" made an actor or actress potentially adaptable for numerous "racial" roles. Actress Lupe Velez once commented that she had portrayed "Chinese, Eskimos, Japs, squaws, Hindus, Swedes, Malays, and Japanese."[19] Dorothy Dandridge, who was the first black woman teamed romantically with white actors, presented a quandary for studio executives who weren't sure what race and nationality to make her. They debated whether she should be a "foreigner," an island girl, or a West Indian.[20] Ironically, what they refused to entertain as a possibility was to present her as what she really was, a black American woman.

The importance of race in popular culture is not restricted to the visual media. In popular music, race and race consciousness has defined, and continues to define, formats, musical communities, and tastes. In the mid-1950s, the secretary of the North Alabama White Citizens Council declared that "Rock and roll is a means of pulling the white man down to the level of the Negro."[21] While rock may no longer be popularly regarded as a racially subversive musical form, the very genres of contemporary popular music remain, in essence, thinly veiled racial categories. "R & B" (Rhythm and Blues) and "soul" music are clearly references to *black* music, while Country & Western or heavy metal music are viewed, in the popular imagination, as *white* music. Black performers who want to break out of this artistic ghettoization must "cross over," a contemporary form of "passing" in which their music is seen as acceptable to white audiences.

The airwaves themselves are segregated. The designation "urban contemporary" is merely radio lingo for a "black" musical format. Such

---

[17]Winston, "Racial Consciousness," p. 176.

[18]*The San Francisco Chronicle*, September 21, 1984.

[19]Quoted in Allen L. Woll, "Bandits and Lovers: Hispanic Images in American Film," in Miller, ed., *Kaleidoscopic Lens*, p. 60.

[20]Bogle, "Familiar Plot," p. 17.

[21]Dave Marsh and Kevin Stein, *The Book of Rock Lists* (New York: Dell Publishing Co., 1981), p. 8.

categorization affects playlists, advertising accounts, and shares of the listening market. On cable television, black music videos rarely receive airplay on MTV, but are confined instead to the more marginal BET (Black Entertainment Television) network.

In spite of such segregation, many performing artists have been able to garner a racially diverse group of fans. And yet, racially integrated concert audiences are extremely rare. Curiously, this "perverse phenomenon" of racially homogeneous crowds takes place despite the color of the performer. Lionel Richie's concert audiences, for example, are virtually all-white, while Teena Marie's are all-black.[22]

Racial symbols and images are omnipresent in popular culture. Commonplace household objects such as cookie jars, salt and pepper shakers, and ashtrays have frequently been designed and fashioned in the form of racial caricatures. Sociologist Steve Dublin in an analysis of these objects found that former tasks of domestic service were symbolically transferred onto these commodities.[23] An Aunt Jemima-type character, for example, is used to hold a roll of paper towels, her outstretched hands supporting the item to be dispensed. "Sprinkle Plenty," a sprinkle bottle in the shape of an Asian man, was used to wet clothes in preparation for ironing. Simple commodities, the household implements which help us perform everyday tasks, may reveal, therefore, a deep structure of racial meaning.

A crucial dimension for discerning the meaning of particular stereotypes and images is the *situation context* for the creation and consumption of popular culture. For example, the setting in which "racist" jokes are told determines the function of humor. Jokes about blacks where the teller and audience are black constitute a form of self-awareness; they allow blacks to cope and "take the edge off" of oppressive aspects of the social order which they commonly confront. The meaning of these same jokes, however, is dramatically transformed when told across the "color line." If a white, or even black, person tells these jokes to a white audience, it will, despite its "purely" humorous intent, serve to reinforce stereotypes and rationalize the existing relations of racial inequality.

Concepts of race and racial images are both overt and implicit within popular culture—the organization of cultural production, the products themselves, and the manner in which they are consumed are deeply structured by race. Particular racial meanings, stereotypes, and myths can change, but the presence of a *system* of racial meanings and stereotypes, of racial ideology, seems to be an enduring aspect of American popular culture.

The era of Reaganism and the overall rightward drift of American politics and culture has added a new twist to the question of racial images and

---

[22]*Rock & Roll Confidential*, No. 44 (February 1987), p. 2.

[23]Steven C. Dublin, "Symbolic Slavery: Black Representations in Popular Culture," *Social Problems*, Vol. 34, No. 2 (April 1987).

meanings. Increasingly, the problem for racial minorities is not that of misportrayal, but of "invisibility." Instead of celebrating racial and cultural diversity, we are witnessing an attempt by the right to define, once again, who the "real" American is, and what "correct" American values, mores, and political beliefs are. In such a context, racial minorities are no longer the focus of sustained media attention; when they do appear, they are cast as colored versions of essentially "white" characters.

The possibilities for change—for transforming racial stereotypes and challenging institutional inequities—nonetheless exist. Historically, strategies have involved the mobilization of political pressure against an offending institution(s). In the late 1950s, for instance, "Nigger Hair" tobacco changed its name to "Bigger Hare" due to concerted NAACP pressure on the manufacturer. In the early 1970s, Asian American community groups successfully fought NBC's attempt to resurrect Charlie Chan as a television series with white actor Ross Martin. Amidst the furor generated by Al Campanis's remarks cited at the beginning of this essay, Jesse Jackson suggested that a boycott of major league games be initiated in order to push for a restructuring of hiring and promotion practices.

Partially in response to such action, Baseball Commissioner Peter Ueberroth announced plans in June 1987 to help put more racial minorities in management roles. "The challenge we have," Ueberroth said, "is to manage change without losing tradition."[24] The problem with respect to the issue of race and popular culture, however, is that the *tradition* itself may need to be thoroughly examined, its "common sense" assumptions unearthed and challenged, and its racial images contested and transformed.

---

[24]*The San Francisco Chronicle* (June 13, 1987).

---

## THIS TEXT: READING

1. Omi's work engages popular culture actively and takes it seriously. Why do you think Omi thinks television is important to write about?
2. From what perspective is Omi writing? Do you think the problems he identifies in 1987 are still around today?
3. Who do you think is Omi's intended audience? Do you think they watch television?

## YOUR TEXT: WRITING

1. Watch an evening of television and note the presence of race and ethnicity. Do the same issues come up? Do you think things have changed since 1987? Why or why not? Write a paper assessing the status of race and ethnicity in American television, focusing either on a particular show or evening of television.

2. What stereotypes generally remain present in American television? Are the same stereotypes present in American movies? If stereotypes in movies and television are different, what differences between the two media do you think account for the difference in portrayals?
3. Take a television show you like and note how it treats those of different ethnicities. Do these portrayals show an understanding of members of these groups or rely on previously-held ideas about them?

## HOW AMERICA WAS DISCOVERED

Handsome Lake

Handsome Lake is a Seneca tribesman who wrote this piece in the nineteenth century to protest the treatment of American Indians at the hands of whites.

ACCORDING TO CHIEF CORNPLANTER, Handsome Lake taught that America was discovered in the manner here related.

A great queen had among her servants a young minister. Upon a certain occasion she requested him to dust some books that she had hidden in an old chest. Now when the young man reached the bottom of the chest he found a wonderful book which he opened and read. It told that the white men had killed the son of the Creator and it said, moreover, that he had promised to return in three days and then again forty but that he never did. All his followers then began to despair but some said, "He surely will come again some time." When the young preacher read this book he was worried because he had discovered that he had been deceived and that his Lord was not on earth and had not returned when he promised. So he went to some of the chief preachers and asked them about the matter and they answered that he had better seek the Lord himself and find if he were not on the earth now. So he prepared to find the Lord and the next day when he looked out into the river he saw a beautiful island and marveled that he had never noticed it before. As he continued to look he saw a castle built of gold in the midst of the island and he marveled that he had not seen the castle before. Then he thought that so beautiful a palace on so beautiful an isle must surely be the abode of the son of the Creator. Immediately he went to the wise men and told them what he had seen and they wondered greatly and answered that it must indeed be the house of the Lord. So together they went to the river and when they came to it they found that it was spanned by a bridge of gold. Then one of the preachers fell down and prayed a long time and arising to cross the bridge turned back because he was afraid to meet his Lord. Then the other crossed the bridge and knelt down upon the grass and prayed but he became afraid to go near the house. So the young man went boldly over to attend to the business at hand and walking up to the door knocked. A handsome man welcomed him into a room and bade him be of ease. "I wanted you," he said. "You are bright young man; those old fools will not suit me for they would be afraid to listen to me. Listen to me, young man, and you will be rich. Across the ocean there is a great country of which you have never heard. The people there are virtuous, they have no evil habits or appetites but are honest and single-minded. A great reward is yours if you enter into my plans and carry them out. Here are five things. Carry them over to the people across the ocean and never shall you want for wealth, position or power. Take these cards, this money, this fiddle, this whiskey and this blood corruption and give them all to the people across the water. The cards will make them gamble away their goods and idle away their time, the money will make them dishonest and covetous, the fiddle will make them dance with women and their lower natures will command them, the whiskey will excite their minds to evil doing and turn their minds, and the blood corruption will eat their strength and rot their bones."

The young man thought this a good bargain and promised to do as the man had commanded him. He left the palace and when he had stepped over the bridge it was gone, likewise the golden palace and also the island. Now he wondered if he had seen the Lord but he did not tell the great ministers of his bargain because they might try to forestall him. So he looked about and at length found Columbus, to whom he told the whole story. So Columbus fitted out some boats and sailed out into the ocean to find the land on the other side. When he had sailed for many days on the water the sailors said that unless Columbus turned about and went home they would behead him but he asked for another day and on that day land was seen and that land was America. Then they turned around and going back reported what they had discovered. Soon a great flock of ships came over the ocean and white men came swarming into the country bringing with them cards, money, fiddles, whiskey and blood corruption.

Now the man who had appeared in the gold palace was the devil and when afterward he saw what his words had done he said that he had made a great mistake and even he lamented that his evil had been so enormous.

---

## This Text: Reading

1. What are some of the signs in Handsome Lake's story? Why are they so important?
2. "How America Was Discovered" is an allegory, a story that contains a clear lesson in it. What is the moral to this story? What story is this story both directly and indirectly commenting on?
3. In what way is this an accurate portrayal of how America was discovered? In what ways is it inaccurate? Are the inaccuracies deliberate? Why?
4. Handsome Lake's tale is highly political and some would say, confrontational. Does it surprise you? Why or why not?

### YOUR TEXT: WRITING

1. Write a story similar to Handsome Lake's about an event you feel has been sanitized in American history.
2. Do you think this is an effective story in explaining many American Indians' point of view about exploration? What other American allegories or myths can you recall? Write a short essay that describes the power of myth to tell a story.

## MOTHER TONGUE

Amy Tan

Amy Tan is the well known author of *The Joy Luck Club* and other novels. In this 1991 piece, she writes about her experiences with her mother and her mother's use of language.

I AM NOT A SCHOLAR of English or literature. I cannot give you much more than personal opinions on the English language and its variations in this country or others.

I am a writer. And by that definition, I am someone who has always loved language. I am fascinated by language in daily life. I spend a great deal of my time thinking about the power of language—the way it can evoke an emotion, a visual image, a complex idea, or a simple truth. Language is the tool of my trade. And I use them all—all the Englishes I grew up with.

Recently, I was made keenly aware of the different Englishes I do use. I was giving a talk to a large group of people, the same talk I had already given to half a dozen other groups. The nature of the talk was about my writing, my life, and my book, *The Joy Luck Club*. The talk was going along well enough, until I remembered one major difference that made the whole talk sound wrong. My mother was in the room. And it was perhaps the first time she had heard me give a lengthy speech, using the kind of English I have never used with her. I was saying things like, "The intersection of memory upon imagination" and "There is an aspect of my fiction that relates to thus-and-thus"—a speech filled with carefully wrought grammatical phrases, burdened, it suddenly seemed to me, with nominalized forms, past perfect tenses, conditional phrases, all the forms of standard English that I had learned in school and through books, the forms of English I did not use at home with my mother.

Just last week, I was walking down the street with my mother, and I again found myself conscious of the English I was using, the English I do use with her. We were talking about the price of new and used furniture and I heard myself saying this: "Not waste money that way." My husband was with us as well, and he didn't notice any switch in my English. And then I realized why. It's because over the twenty years we've been together I've often used that same kind of English with him, and sometimes he even uses it with me. It has become our language of intimacy, a different sort of English that relates to family talk, the language I grew up with.

So you'll have some idea of what this family talk I heard sounds like, I'll quote what my mother said during a recent conversation which I videotaped and then transcribed. During this conversation, my mother was talking about a political gangster in Shanghai who had the same last name as her family's, Du, and how the gangster in his early years wanted to be adopted by her family, which was rich by comparison. Later, the gangster became more powerful, far richer than my mother's family, and one day showed up at my mother's wedding to pay his respects. Here's what she said in part: "Du Yusong having business like fruit stand. Like off the street kind. He is Du like Du Zong—but not Tsung-ming Island people. The local people call putong, the river east side, he belong to that side local people. That man want to ask Du Zong father take him in like become own family. Du Zong father wasn't look down on him, but didn't take seriously, until that man big like become a mafia. Now important person, very hard to inviting him. Chinese way, came only to show respect, don't stay for dinner. Respect for making big celebration, he shows up. Mean gives lots of respect. Chinese custom. Chinese social life that way. If too important won't have to stay too long. He come to my wedding. I didn't see, I heard it. I gone to boy's side, they have YMCA dinner. Chinese age I was nineteen."

You should know that my mother's expressive command of English belies how much she actually understands. She reads the Forbes report, listens to Wall Street Week, converses daily with her stockbroker, reads all of Shirley MacLaine's books with ease—all kinds of things I can't begin to understand. Yet some of my friends tell me they understand 50 percent of what my mother says. Some say they understand 80 to 90 percent. Some say they understand none of it, as if she were speaking pure Chinese. But to me, my mother's English is perfectly clear, perfectly natural. It's my mother tongue. Her language, as I hear it, is vivid, direct, full of observation and imagery. That was the language that helped shape the way I saw things, expressed things, made sense of the world.

Lately, I've been giving more thought to the kind of English my mother speaks. Like others, I have described it to people as "broken" or "fractured" English. But I wince when I say that. It has always bothered me that I can think of no way to describe it other than "broken," as if it were damaged and needed to be fixed, as if it lacked a certain wholeness and soundness. I've heard other terms used, "limited English," for example. But they seem just as bad, as if everything is limited, including people's perceptions of the limited English speaker.

I know this for a fact, because when I was growing up, my mother's "limited" English limited my perception of her. I was ashamed of her

English. I believed that her English reflected the quality of what she had to say. That is, because she expressed them imperfectly her thoughts were imperfect. And I had plenty of empirical evidence to support me: the fact that people in department stores, at banks, and at restaurants did not take her seriously, did not give her good service, pretended not to understand her, or even acted as if they did not hear her.

My mother has long realized the limitations of her English as well. When I was fifteen, she used to have me call people on the phone to pretend I was she. In this guise, I was forced to ask for information or even to complain and yell at people who had been rude to her. One time it was a call to her stockbroker in New York. She had cashed out her small portfolio and it just so happened we were going to go to New York the next week, our very first trip outside California. I had to get on the phone and say in an adolescent voice that was not very convincing, "This is Mrs. Tan."

And my mother was standing in the back whispering loudly, "Why he don't send me check, already two weeks late. So mad he lie to me, losing me money."

And then I said in perfect English, "Yes, I'm getting rather concerned. You had agreed to send the check two weeks ago, but it hasn't arrived."

Then she began to talk more loudly. "What he want, I come to New York tell him front of his boss, you cheating me?" And I was trying to calm her down, make her be quiet, while telling the stockbroker, "I can't tolerate any more excuses. If I don't receive the check immediately, I am going to have to speak to your manager when I'm in New York next week." And sure enough, the following week there we were in front of this astonished stockbroker, and I was sitting there red-faced and quiet, and my mother, the real Mrs. Tan, was shouting at his boss in her impeccable broken English.

We used a similar routine just five days ago, for a situation that was far less humorous. My mother had gone to the hospital for an appointment, to find out about a benign brain tumor a CAT scan had revealed a month ago. She said she had spoken very good English, her best English, no mistakes. Still, she said, the hospital did not apologize when they said they had lost the CAT scan and she had come for nothing. She said they did not seem to have any sympathy when she told them she was anxious to know the exact diagnosis, since her husband and son had both died of brain tumors. She said they would not give her any more information until the next time and she would have to make another appointment for that. So she said she would not leave until the doctor called her daughter. She wouldn't budge. And when the doctor finally called her daughter, me, who spoke in perfect English—lo and behold—we had assurances the CAT scan would be found, promises that a conference call on Monday would be held, and apologies for any suffering my mother had gone through for a most regrettable mistake.

I think my mother's English almost had an effect on limiting my possibilities in life as well. Sociologists and linguists probably will tell you that a person's developing language skills are more influenced by peers. But I do think that the language spoken in the family, especially in immigrant families which are more insular, plays a large role in shaping the language of the child. And I believe that it affected my results on achievement tests, IQ tests, and the SAT. While my English skills were never judged as poor, compared to math, English could not be considered my strong suit. In grade school I did moderately well, getting perhaps B's, sometimes B-pluses, in English and scoring perhaps in the sixtieth or seventieth percentile on achievement tests. But those scores were not good enough to override the opinion that my true abilities lay in math and science, because in those areas I achieved A's and scored in the ninetieth percentile or higher.

This was understandable. Math is precise; there is only one correct answer. Whereas, for me at least, the answers on English tests were always a judgment call, a matter of opinion and personal experience. Those tests were constructed around items like fill-in-the-blank sentence completion, such as, "Even though Tom was _____, Mary thought he was _____." And the correct answer always seemed to be the most bland combinations of thoughts, for example, "Even though Tom was shy, Mary thought he was charming," with the grammatical structure "even though" limiting the correct answer to some sort of semantic opposites, so you wouldn't get answers like, "Even though Tom was foolish, Mary thought he was ridiculous." Well, according to my mother, there were very few limitations as to what Tom could have been and what Mary might have thought of him. So I never did well on tests like that.

The same was true with word analogies, pairs of words in which you were supposed to find some sort of logical, semantic relationship—for example, "Sunset is to nightfall as _____ is to _____." And here you would be presented with a list of four possible pairs, one of which showed the same kind of relationship: red is to stoplight, bus is to arrival, chills is to fever, yawn is to boring. Well, I could never think that way. I knew what the tests were asking, but I could not block out of my mind the images already created by the first pair, "sunset is to nightfall"—and I would see a burst of colors against a darkening sky, the moon rising, the lowering of a curtain of stars. And all the other pairs of words—red, bus, stoplight, boring—just threw up a mass of confusing images, making it impossible for me to sort out something as logical as saying: "A sunset precedes nightfall" is the same as "a chill precedes a fever." The only way I would have gotten that answer right would have been to imagine an associative situation, for example, my being disobedient and staying out past sunset, catching a chill at night, which turns into feverish pneumonia as punishment, which indeed did happen to me.

I have been thinking about all this lately, about my mother's English, about achievement tests. Because lately I've been asked, as a writer, why there are not more Asian Americans represented in American literature. Why are there few Asian Americans enrolled in creative writing programs? Why do so many Chinese students go into engineering? Well, these are broad sociological questions I can't begin to answer. But I have noticed in surveys—in fact, just last week—that Asian students, as a whole, always do significantly better on math achievement tests than in English. And this makes me think that there are other Asian-American students whose English spoken in the home might also be described as "broken" or "limited." And perhaps they also have teachers who are steering them away from writing and into math and science, which is what happened to me.

Fortunately, I happen to be rebellious in nature and enjoy the challenge of disproving assumptions made about me. I became an English major my first year in college, after being enrolled as pre-med. I started writing nonfiction as a freelancer the week after I was told by my former boss that writing was my worst skill and I should hone my talents toward account management.

But it wasn't until 1985 that I finally began to write fiction. And at first I wrote using what I thought to be wittily crafted sentences, sentences that would finally prove I had mastery over the English language. Here's an example from the first draft of a story that later made its way into *The Joy Luck Club*, but without this line: "That was my mental quandary in its nascent state." A terrible line, which I can barely pronounce.

Fortunately, for reasons I won't get into today, I later decided I should envision a reader for the stories I would write. And the reader I decided upon was my mother, because these were stories about mothers. So with this reader in mind—and in fact she did read my early drafts—I began to write stories using all the Englishes I grew up with: the English I spoke to my mother, which for lack of a better term might be described as "simple"; the English she used with me, which for lack of a better term might be described as "broken"; my translation of her Chinese, which could certainly be described as "watered down"; and what I imagined to be her translation of her Chinese if she could speak in perfect English, her internal language, and for that I sought to preserve the essence, but neither an English nor a Chinese structure. I wanted to capture what language ability tests can never reveal: her intent, her passion, her imagery, the rhythms of her speech and the nature of her thoughts.

Apart from what any critic had to say about my writing, I knew I had succeeded where it counted when my mother finished reading my book and gave me her verdict: "So easy to read."

---

## This Text: Reading

1. Tan points out that language is a sign for others trying to read her mother. What other non-visual elements might be signs? How do we normally read them?
2. Talk about the way we discuss or react to people with accents. Why do accents mark, or set off as different, people? Is there any established non-marked way of speaking? Who speaks this way?

3. How do you think Tan feels about the situation in which she is placed by having to serve as her mother's "agent"? Is there a way around it?

### YOUR TEXT: WRITING

1. Write an essay talking about ways we mark people as different through non-visual means though popular culture. What forms of popular culture are especially guilty of this?
2. One of the things that Tan's essay brings up is the idea of Americanness. How should we define such a concept? Are there degrees of Americanness? Research and see what others say about this.
3. In what way is this an argument? What is Tan arguing? In your own work, use a story to argue a particular point.

## TRUE TALES OF AMERIKKKAN HISTORY PART II: THE TRUE THANKSGIVING

Jim Mahfood

Jim Mahfood is a comic artist who often takes on stereotypes and race in his work. On the next page is his 1998 response to popular ideas about Thanksgiving.

### THIS TEXT: READING

1. If you have read Scott McCloud's piece, what do you think he would say about this cartoon? In what ways does the reader participate in making meaning here?
2. Compare Mahfood's approach to Handsome Lake's, another piece concerned with Native American issues.
3. What other subtext does Mahfood address with the boy's tee shirt? With the girl's Native American garb? Are these relevant to the main storyline? Why or why not?
4. What perspective do you think Mahfood is writing/drawing from? What do you think is motivating his writing?
5. Who do you think is Mahfood's audience? Does your answer depend on consideration of the medium he's using?

### YOUR TEXT: WRITING

1. Find a political cartoon and analyze it in terms of signs.
2. Write a short essay discussing why visual texts can communicate ideas effectively. You might compare a visual text and written text that have similar ideas but present them differently.

true tales of AMERIKKKAN HISTORY PART II: the true Thanksgiving

HIYA MICAH!! WHAT DID YOU AND YOUR FAMILY DO FOR THANKSGIVING LAST WEEK?
MY FAMILY DOESN'T CELEBRATE THANKSGIVING, BILLY.
NINTENDO

WHAT??!! WHY NOT???
MY DADDY SAYS THANKSGIVING IS A HORRIBLE LIE, AND A SLAP IN THE FACE TO OUR PEOPLE AND OUR CULTURE.

BUT- BUT I DON'T UNDERSTAND...
MY DADDY SAYS THANKSGIVING NEVER REALLY HAPPENED. HE SAYS THE PILGRIMS WERE EVIL, SELFISH MEN SENT BY THE DEVIL TO DESTROY OUR PEOPLE, STEAL OUR LAND, RAPE OUR WOMEN, AND POISON US WITH HIS LIQUOR AND GUNS...
intel inside

HUH?? BUT- BUT THAT CAN'T BE TRUE!! WE LEARNED ABOUT THANKSGIVING IN SCHOOL! MY MOMMY + DADDY TOLD ME ABOUT IT. THEY SAID THE PILGRIMS WERE NICE PEOPLE!
YOUR PARENTS HAVE BEEN BRAINWASHED BY THE SAME PEOPLE THAT LIED TO YOU, BILLY...
COCA COLA

ZUH??
MY DADDY SAYS THE SAME WHITE MEN THAT DESTROYED MY PEOPLE WROTE THE HISTORY BOOKS YOU READ IN SCHOOL. HE SAYS THEY JUST SORTA MADE STUFF UP, YAKNOW, TO MAKE THEMSELVES LOOK GOOD...
TOMMY

BUT- BUT WHAT ABOUT TV AND THE MOVIES?? EVERYONE KNOWS THAT COWBOYS ARE THE GOOD GUYS AND INDIANS ARE THE BAD GUYS. 'MEMBER the LONE RANGER AND TONTO?
TONTO ACTUALLY MEANS "FOOL".
IT'S ALL A SICK JOKE, BILLY...
KANSAS CITY CHIEFS

MY GOD.... WH- WHY HAS THIS HAPPENED, THEN???
BASICALLY, MY DADDY SAYS THE WHITE MAN IS THE ONLY CREATURE ON EARTH THAT WOULD KILL HIS OWN BROTHER FOR POWER. HE SAYS THAT OUR PEOPLE ARE JUST ONE OF THE MANY CASUALTIES IN THE DEVIL'S QUEST FOR CONTROL. DADDY SAYS THE WHITE MAN IS PRETTY GOOD AT FUCKING OVER MINORITIES.
Marlboro

USA

WELL...
I BET MY DADDY COULD STILL BEAT UP YOUR DADDY.
I BET HE COULD, BILLY.
I BET HE COULD.
CALVIN KLEIN

A 40 oz. COMICS PRODUCTION

3. How does your previous experience with comics affect your ability to take political cartoons seriously? Write a short essay making the case for teaching visual culture at an early age.

## WHY ARE ALL THE BLACK KIDS SITTING TOGETHER IN THE CAFETERIA?

Beverly Daniel Tatum

Beverly Tatum is a psychologist who writes about race and race relations in America. This essay is taken in part from her book, *Why Are All the Black Kids Sitting Together in the Cafeteria? And Other Conversations About Race* (1999). Here she argues that both teachers and students need to talk actively about race, especially in the teen-age years when identity is being formed.

WALK INTO ANY RACIALLY MIXED high school cafeteria at lunch time and you will instantly notice an identifiable group of black students sitting together. Conversely, there are many white students sitting together, though we rarely comment about that. The question is "Why are the black kids sitting together?"

It doesn't start out that way. In racially mixed elementary schools, you often see children of diverse racial boundaries playing with one another, sitting at the snack table together, crossing racial boundaries with an ease uncommon in adolescence.

Moving from elementary school to middle school means interacting with new children from different neighborhoods than before, and a certain degree of clustering by race might therefore be expected, presuming that children who are familiar with one another would form groups. But even in schools where the same children stay together from kindergarten through eighth grade, racial grouping begins by the sixth or seventh grade. What happens?

One thing that happens is puberty. As children enter adolescence, they begin to explore the question of identity, asking "Who am I? Who can I be?" in ways they have not done before. For black youths, asking "Who am I?" includes thinking about "Who I am ethnically? What does it mean to be black?"

Why do black youths, in particular, think about themselves in terms of race? Because that is how the rest of the world thinks of them. Our self-perceptions are shaped by the messages we receive from those around us, and when young black men and women reach adolescence, the racial content of those messages intensifies.

Here is a case in point. If you were to ask my 10-year-old son, David, to describe himself, he would tell you many things: that he is smart, that he likes to play computer games, that he has an older brother. Near the top of his list, he would likely mention that he is tall for his age. He would probably not mention that he is black, though he certainly knows that he is. Why would he mention his height and not his racial group membership?

When David meets new adults, one of the first questions they ask is "How old are you?" When David states his age, the inevitable reply is, "Gee, you're tall for your age!"

It happens so frequently that I once overheard David say to someone, "Don't say it, I know. I'm tall for my age." Height is salient for David because it's salient for others.

When David meets new adults, they don't say, "Gee, you're black for your age!" Or do they?

Imagine David at 15, six-foot-two, wearing the adolescent attire of the day, passing adults he doesn't know on the sidewalk. Do the women hold their purses a little tighter, maybe even cross the street to avoid him? Does he hear the sound of automatic door locks on cars as he passes by? Is he being followed around by the security guards at the local mall? Do strangers assume he plays basketball? Each of these experiences conveys a racial message.

At 10, race is not yet salient for David, because it's not yet salient for society. But it will be.

### Understanding Racial Identity Development

Psychologist William Cross, author of *Shades of Black: Diversity in African American Identity*, has offered a theory of racial identity development that I have found to be a very useful framework for understanding what is happening with those black students in the cafeteria. In the first stage of Cross's five-stage model, the black child absorbs many of the beliefs and values of the dominant white culture, including the idea that it's better to be white.

Simply as a function of being socialized in a Eurocentric culture, some black children may begin to value the role models, lifestyles and images of beauty represented by the dominant group more highly than those of their own cultural group. But the personal and social significance of one's racial group membership has not yet been realized, and racial identity is not yet under examination.

### The Encounter Stage

Transition to the next stage, the encounter stage, is typically precipitated by an event—or series of events—that forces the young person to acknowledge the personal impact of racism.

For example, in racially mixed schools, black children are much more likely to be in a lower track than in an honors track. Such apparent sorting along racial lines sends a message about what it means to be black. One young honors student said, "It was really a very paradoxical existence, here I am in a school that's 35 percent black, you know, and I'm the only black in my class. That always struck me as odd. I guess I felt that I was different from the other blacks because of that."

There are also changes in the social dynamics outside the school. In racially mixed communities, you begin to see what I call the "birthday party effect." The parties of elementary school children may be segregated by gender, but not by race. At puberty, when the parties become sleepovers or boy–girl events, they become less and less racially diverse.

Black girls who live in predominantly white neighborhoods see their white friends start to date before they do. One young woman from a Philadelphia suburb described herself as "pursuing white guys throughout high school" to no avail. Because there were no black boys in her class, she had little choice. She would feel "really pissed off" that those same white boys would date her white friends.

Another young black woman attending a desegregated school to which she was bussed was encouraged by a teacher to attend the upcoming school dance. Most of the black students did not live in the neighborhood and seldom attended the extracurricular activities. The young woman indicated that she wasn't planning to come. Finally the well-intentioned teacher said, "Oh come on, I know you people love to dance." This young woman got the message.

### *Coping with Encounter*

What do these encounters have to do with the cafeteria? Do experiences with racism inevitably result in so-called self-segregation?

While a desire to protect oneself from further offense is understandable, it's not the only factor at work. Imagine the young eighth-grade girl who experienced the teacher's use of "you people" and the dancing stereotype as a racial affront. Upset and struggling with adolescent embarrassment, she bumps into a white friend who can see that something is wrong. She explains. Her white friend responds—perhaps in an effort to make her feel better—and says, "Oh, Mr. Smith is such a nice guy, I'm sure he didn't mean it like that. Don't be so sensitive."

Perhaps the white friend is right, but imagine your own response when you are upset, and your partner brushes off your complaint, attributing it to your being oversensitive. What happens to your emotional thermostat? It escalates. When feelings, rational or irrational, are invalidated, most people disengage. They not only choose to discontinue the conversation but are more likely to turn to someone who will understand their perspective.

In much the same way that the eighth-grade girl's white friend doesn't get it, the girls at the "black table" do. Not only are black adolescents encountering racism and reflecting on their identity, but their white peers—even if not racist—are unprepared to respond in supportive ways.

The black students turn to each other for the much needed support they are not likely to find anywhere else.

We need to understand that in racially mixed settings, racial grouping is a developmental process in response to an environmental stressor, racism. Joining with one's peers for support in the face of stress is a positive coping strategy. The problem is that our young people are operating with a very limited definition of what it means to be black, based largely on cultural stereotypes.

---

### This Text: Reading

1. Do you find yourself personally involved (or implicated) in Tatum's analysis? How do you think she would respond to your response?
2. Tatum raises some interesting ideas about race in her discussion. In what ways is she performing a semiotic analysis of the idea of race? In what ways have race and ethnicity contributed to "semiotic situations" in your own life?
3. Where does her analysis fit into what we traditionally think of as the American Dream?
4. Why is the cafeteria such an important location for a discussion like this? What happens in a cafeteria that might not happen in a classroom?

### Your Text: Writing

1. Using your own experiences, write an essay about the role race and ethnicity have played—or didn't play—in your experiences growing up.
2. Tatum's essay balances personal experience with research; do you think this method of writing is effective? Why or why not? Do you think this is important for this type of topic? Why or why not?
3. Can you think of a personal topic that would benefit from a combined research/personal approach?

## THE SPORTS TABOO

Malcolm Gladwell

---

Malcolm Gladwell is a writer for *The New Yorker* who often writes about social issues. In this essay (1997) he uses an analogy to describe the relationship between perceived race and sports achievement.

### *1.*

THE EDUCATION OF ANY ATHLETE BEGINS, in part, with an education in the racial taxonomy of his chosen sport—in the subtle, unwritten rules about what whites are supposed to be good at and what blacks are supposed to be good at. In football, whites play quarterback and blacks play running back; in baseball whites pitch and blacks play the outfield. I grew up in Canada, where my brother Geoffrey and I ran high-school track, and in Canada the rule of running was that anything under the quarter-mile belonged to the West Indians. This didn't mean that white people didn't run the sprints. But the expectation was that they would never win, and, sure enough, they rarely did. There was just a handful of West Indian immigrants in Ontario at that point—clustered in and around Toronto—but they owned Canadian sprinting, setting up under the stands at every major championship, cranking up the reggae on their boom boxes, and then humiliating everyone else on the track. My brother and I weren't from Toronto, so we weren't part of that scene. But our West Indian heritage meant that we got to share in the swagger. Geoffrey was a magnificent runner, with powerful legs and a barrel chest, and when he was warming up he used to do that exaggerated, slow-motion jog that the white guys would try to do and never quite pull off. I was a miler, which was a little outside the West Indian range. But, the way I figured it, the rules meant that no one should ever outkick me over the final two hundred metres of any race. And in the golden summer of my fourteenth year, when my running career prematurely peaked, no one ever did.

When I started running, there was a quarter-miler just a few years older than I was by the name of Arnold Stotz. He was a bulldog of a runner, hugely talented, and each year that he moved through the sprinting ranks he invariably broke the existing four-hundred-metre record in his age class. Stotz was white, though, and every time I saw the results of a big track meet I'd keep an eye out for his name, because I was convinced that he could not keep winning. It was as if I saw his whiteness as a degenerative disease, which would eventually claim and cripple him. I never asked him whether he felt the same anxiety, but I can't imagine that he didn't. There was only so long that anyone could defy the rules. One day, at the provincial championships, I looked up at the results board and Stotz was gone.

Talking openly about the racial dimension of sports in this way, of course, is considered unseemly. It's all right to say that blacks dominate sports because they lack opportunities elsewhere. That's the "Hoop Dreams" line, which says whites are allowed to acknowledge black athletic success as long as they feel guilty about it. What you're not supposed to say is what we were saying in my track days—that we were better because we were black, because of something intrinsic to being black. Nobody said anything like that publicly last month when Tiger Woods won the Masters or when, a week later, African men claimed thirteen out of the top twenty places in the Boston Marathon. Nor is it likely to come up this month, when African-Americans will make up eighty per cent of the players on the floor for the N.B.A. playoffs. When the popular television sports commentator Jimmy (the Greek) Snyder did break this taboo, in 1988—infamously ruminating on the size and significance of black thighs—one prominent

N.A.A.C.P. official said that his remarks "could set race relations back a hundred years." The assumption is that the whole project of trying to get us to treat each other the same will be undermined if we don't all agree that under the skin we actually are the same.

The point of this, presumably, is to put our discussion of sports on a par with legal notions of racial equality, which would be a fine idea except that civil-rights law governs matters like housing and employment and the sports taboo covers matters like what can be said about someone's jump shot. In his much heralded new book *Darwin's Athletes*, the University of Texas scholar John Hoberman tries to argue that these two things are the same, that it's impossible to speak of black physical superiority without implying intellectual inferiority. But it isn't long before the argument starts to get ridiculous. "The spectacle of black athleticism," he writes, inevitably turns into "a highly public image of black retardation." Oh, really? What, exactly, about Tiger Woods's victory in the Masters resembled "a highly public image of black retardation"? Today's black athletes are multimillion-dollar corporate pitchmen, with talk shows and sneaker deals and publicity machines and almost daily media opportunities to share their thoughts with the world, and it's very hard to see how all this contrives to make them look stupid. Hoberman spends a lot of time trying to inflate the significance of sports, arguing that how we talk about events on the baseball diamond or the track has grave consequences for how we talk about race in general. Here he is, for example, on Jackie Robinson:

> The sheer volume of sentimental and intellectual energy that has been invested in the mythic saga of Jackie Robinson has discouraged further thinking about what his career did and did not accomplish.... Black America has paid a high and largely unacknowledged price for the extraordinary prominence given the black athlete rather than other black men of action (such as military pilots and astronauts), who represent modern aptitudes in ways that athletes cannot.

Please. Black America has paid a high and largely unacknowledged price for a long list of things, and having great athletes is far from the top of the list. Sometimes a baseball player is just a baseball player, and sometimes an observation about racial difference is just an observation about racial difference. Few object when medical scientists talk about the significant epidemiological differences between blacks and whites—the fact that blacks have a higher incidence of hypertension than whites and twice as many black males die of diabetes and prostate cancer as white males, that breast tumors appear to grow faster in black women than in white women, that black girls show signs of puberty sooner than white girls. So why aren't we allowed to say that there might be athletically significant differences between blacks and whites?

According to the medical evidence, African-Americans seem to have, on the average, greater bone mass than do white Americans—a difference that suggests greater muscle mass. Black men have slightly higher circulating levels of testosterone and human-growth hormone than their white counterparts, and blacks overall tend to have proportionally slimmer hips, wider shoulders, and longer legs. In one study, the Swedish physiologist Bengt Saltin compared a group of Kenyan distance runners with a group of Swedish distance runners and found interesting differences in muscle composition: Saltin reported that the Africans appeared to have more blood-carrying capillaries and more mitochondria (the body's cellular power plant) in the fibres of their quadriceps. Another study found that, while black South African distance runners ran at the same speed as white South African runners, they were able to use more oxygen—eighty-nine per cent versus eighty-one per cent—over extended periods: somehow, they were able to exert themselves more. Such evidence suggested that there were physical differences in black athletes which have a bearing on activities like running and jumping, which should hardly come as a surprise to anyone who follows competitive sports.

To use track as an example—since track is probably the purest measure of athletic ability—Africans recorded fifteen out of the twenty fastest times last year in the men's ten-thousand-metre event. In the five thousand metres, eighteen out of the twenty fastest times were recorded by Africans. In the fifteen hundred metres, thirteen out of the twenty fastest times were African, and in the sprints, in the men's hundred metres, you have to go all the way down to the twenty-third place in the world rankings—to Geir Moen, of Norway—before you find a white face. There is a point at which it becomes foolish to deny the fact of black athletic prowess, and even more foolish to banish speculation on the topic. Clearly, something is going on. The question is what.

## 2.

If we are to decide what to make of the differences between blacks and whites, we first have to decide what to make of the word "difference," which can mean any number of things. A useful case study is to compare the ability of men and women in math. If you give a large, representative sample of male and female students a standardized math test, their mean scores will come out pretty much the same. But if you look at the margins, at the very best and the very worst students, sharp differences emerge. In the math portion of an achievement test conducted by Project Talent—a nationwide survey of fifteen-year-olds—there were 1.3 boys for every girl in the top ten per cent, 1.5 boys for every girl in the top five per cent, and seven boys for every girl in the top one per cent. In the fifty-six-year history of the Putnam Mathematical Competition, which has been described as the Olympics of college math, all but one of the winners have been male. Conversely, if you look at people with the very lowest math ability, you'll find more boys than girls there, too. In other words, although the average math ability of boys and girls is the same, the distribution isn't: there are more males than females at the bottom of the pile, more males than females at the top of the pile, and fewer males than females in the middle. Statisticians refer to this as a difference in variability.

This pattern, as it turns out, is repeated in almost every conceivable area of gender difference. Boys are more variable than girls on the College Board entrance exam and in routine elementary-school spelling tests. Male mortality patterns are more variable than female patterns; that is, many more men die in early and middle age than women, who tend to die in more of a concentrated clump toward the end of life. The problem is that variability differences are regularly confused with average differences. If men had higher average math scores than women, you could say they were better at the subject. But because they are only more variable the word "better" seems inappropriate.

The same holds true for differences between the races. A racist stereotype is the assertion of average difference—it's the claim that the typical white is superior to the typical black. It allows a white man to assume that the black man he passes on the street is stupider than he is. By contrast, if what racists believed was that black intelligence was simply more variable than white intelligence, then it would be impossible for them to construct a stereotype about black intelligence at all. They wouldn't be able to generalize. If they wanted to believe that there were a lot of blacks dumber than whites, they would also have to believe that there were a lot of blacks smarter than they were. This distinction is critical to understanding the relation between race and athletic performance. What are we seeing when we remark black domination of elite sporting events—an average difference between the races or merely a difference in variability?

This question has been explored by geneticists and physical anthropologists, and some of the most notable work has been conducted over the past few years by Kenneth Kidd, at Yale. Kidd and his colleagues have been taking DNA samples from two African Pygmy tribes in Zaire and the Central African Republic and comparing them with DNA samples taken from populations all over the world. What they have been looking for is variants—subtle differences between the DNA of one person and another—and what they have found is fascinating. "I would say, without a doubt, that in almost any single African population—a tribe or however you want to define it—there is more genetic variation than in all the rest of the world put together," Kidd told me. In a sample of fifty Pygmies, for example, you might find nine variants in one stretch of DNA. In a sample of hundreds of people from around the rest of the world, you might find only a total of six variants in that same stretch of DNA—and probably every one of those six variants would also be found in the Pygmies. If everyone in the world was wiped out except Africans, in other words, almost all the human genetic diversity would be preserved.

The likelihood is that these results reflect Africa's status as the homeland of Homo sapiens: since every human population outside Africa is essentially a subset of the original African population, it makes sense that everyone in such a population would be a genetic subset of Africans, too. So you can expect groups of Africans to be more variable in respect to almost anything that has a genetic component. If, for example, your genes control how you react to aspirin, you'd expect to see more Africans than whites for whom one aspirin stops a bad headache, more for whom no amount of aspirin works, more who are allergic to aspirin, and more who need to take, say, four aspirin at a time to get any benefit—but far fewer Africans for whom the standard two-aspirin dose would work well. And to the extent that running is influenced by genetic factors you would expect to see more really fast blacks—and more really slow blacks—than whites but far fewer Africans of merely average speed. Blacks are like boys. Whites are like girls.

There is nothing particularly scary about this fact, and certainly nothing to warrant the kind of gag order on talk of racial differences which is now in place. What it means is that comparing elite athletes of different races tells you very little about the races themselves. A few years ago, for example, a prominent scientist argued for black athletic supremacy by pointing out that there had never been a white Michael Jordan. True. But, as the Yale anthropologist Jonathan Marks has noted, until recently there was no black Michael Jordan, either. Michael Jordan, like Tiger Woods or Wayne Gretzky or Cal Ripken, is one of the best players in his sport not because he's like the other members of his own ethnic group but precisely because he's not like them—or like anyone else, for that matter. Elite athletes are elite athletes because, in some sense, they are on the fringes of genetic variability. As it happens, African populations seem to create more of these genetic outliers than white populations do, and this is what underpins the claim that blacks are better athletes than whites. But that's all the claim amounts to. It doesn't say anything at all about the rest of us, of all races, muddling around in the genetic middle.

## 3.

There is a second consideration to keep in mind when we compare blacks and whites. Take the men's hundred-metre final at the Atlanta Olympics. Every runner in that race was of either Western African or Southern African descent, as you would expect if Africans had some genetic affinity for sprinting. But suppose we forget about skin color and look just at country of origin. The eight-man final was made up of two African-Americans, two Africans (one from Namibia and one from Nigeria), a Trinidadian, a Canadian of Jamaican descent, an Englishman of Jamaican descent, and a Jamaican. The race was won by the Jamaican-Canadian, in world-record time, with the Namibian coming in second and the Trinidadian third. The sprint relay—the 4 × 100—was won by a team from Canada, consisting of the Jamaican-Canadian from the final, a Haitian-Canadian, a Trinidadian-Canadian, and another Jamaican-Canadian. Now it appears that African heritage is important as an initial determinant of sprinting ability, but also that the most important advantage of all is some kind of cultural or environmental factor associated with the Caribbean.

Or consider, in a completely different realm, the problem of hypertension. Black Americans have a higher incidence of hypertension than white Americans, even after you control for every conceivable variable, including income, diet, and weight, so it's tempting to conclude that there is something about being of African descent that makes blacks prone to hypertension. But it turns out that although some Caribbean countries have a problem with hypertension, others—Jamaica, St. Kitts, and the Bahamas—don't. It also turns out that people in Liberia and Nigeria—two countries where many New World slaves came from—have similar and perhaps even lower blood-pressure rates than white North Americans, while studies of Zulus, Indians, and whites in Durban, South Africa, showed that urban white males had the highest hypertension rates and urban white females had the lowest. So it's likely that the disease has nothing at all to do with Africanness.

The same is true for the distinctive muscle characteristic observed when Kenyans were compared with Swedes. Saltin, the Swedish physiologist, subsequently found many of the same characteristics in Nordic skiers who train at high altitudes and Nordic runners who train in very hilly regions—conditions, in other words, that resemble the mountainous regions of Kenya's Rift Valley, where so many of the country's distance runners come from. The key factor seems to be Kenya, not genes.

Lots of things that seem to be genetic in origin, then, actually aren't. Similarly, lots of things that we wouldn't normally think might affect athletic ability actually do. Once again, the social-science literature on male and female math achievement is instructive. Psychologists argue that when it comes to subjects like math, boys tend to engage in what's known as ability attribution. A boy who is doing well will attribute his success to the fact that he's good at math, and if he's doing badly he'll blame his teacher or his own lack of motivation—anything but his ability. That makes it easy for him to bounce back from failure or disappointment, and gives him a lot of confidence in the face of a tough new challenge. After all, if you think you do well in math because you're good at math, what's stopping you from being good at, say, algebra, or advanced calculus? On the other hand, if you ask a girl why she is doing well in math she will say, more often than not, that she succeeds because she works hard. If she's doing poorly, she'll say she isn't smart enough. This, as should be obvious, is a self-defeating attitude. Psychologists call it "learned helplessness"—the state in which failure is perceived as insurmountable. Girls who engage in effort attribution learn helplessness because in the face of a more difficult task like algebra or advanced calculus they can conceive of no solution. They're convinced that they can't work harder, because they think they're working as hard as they can, and that they can't rely on their intelligence, because they never thought they were that smart to begin with. In fact, one of the fascinating findings of attribution research is that the smarter girls are, the more likely they are to fall into this trap. High achievers are sometimes the most helpless. Here, surely, is part of the explanation for greater math variability among males. The female math whizzes, the ones who should be competing in the top one and two per cent with their male counterparts, are the ones most often paralyzed by a lack of confidence in their own aptitude. They think they belong only in the intellectual middle.

The striking thing about these descriptions of male and female stereotyping in math, though, is how similar they are to black and white stereotyping in athletics—to the unwritten rules holding that blacks achieve through natural ability and whites through effort. Here's how *Sports Illustrated* described, in a recent article, the white basketball player Steve Kerr, who plays alongside Michael Jordan for the Chicago Bulls. According to the magazine, Kerr is a "hard-working overachiever," distinguished by his "work ethic and heady play" and by a shooting style "born of a million practice shots." Bear in mind that Kerr is one of the best shooters in basketball today, and a key player on what is arguably one of the finest basketball teams in history. Bear in mind, too, that there is no evidence that Kerr works any harder than his teammates, least of all Jordan himself, whose work habits are legendary. But you'd never guess that from the article. It concludes, "All over America, whenever quicker, stronger gym rats see Kerr in action, they must wonder, How can that guy be out there instead of me?"

There are real consequences to this stereotyping. As the psychologists Carol Dweck and Barbara Licht write of high-achieving schoolgirls, "[They] may view themselves as so motivated and well disciplined that they cannot entertain the possibility that they did poorly on an academic task because of insufficient effort. Since blaming the teacher would also be out of character, blaming their abilities when they confront difficulty may seem like the most reasonable option." If you substitute the words "white athletes" for "girls" and "coach" for "teacher," I think you have part of the reason that so many white athletes are underrepresented at the highest levels of professional sports. Whites have been saddled with the athletic equivalent of learned helplessness—the idea that it is all but fruitless to try and compete at the highest levels, because they have only effort on their side. The causes of athletic and gender discrimination may be diverse, but its effects are not. Once again, blacks are like boys, and whites are like girls.

## 4.

When I was in college, I once met an old acquaintance from my high-school running days. Both of us had long since quit track, and we talked about a recurrent fantasy we found we'd both had for getting back into shape. It was that we would go away somewhere remote for a year and do nothing but train, so that when the year was up we might finally know how good we were. Neither of us had any intention of doing this, though, which is why it was a fantasy. In adolescence, athletic excess has a certain appeal—during high school, I happily spent Sunday afternoons running up and down snow-covered sandhills—but with most of us that obsessiveness soon begins to fade. Athletic success depends on having the right genes and on a self-reinforcing belief in one's own ability. But it also depends on a rare form of tunnel vision. To be a great athlete, you have to care, and what was obvious to us both was that neither of us cared anymore. This is the last piece of the puzzle about what we mean when we say one group is better at something than another: sometimes different groups care about different things. Of the seven hundred men who play major-league baseball, for example, eighty-six come from either the Dominican Republic or Puerto Rico, even though those two islands have a combined population of only eleven million. But then baseball is something that Dominicans and Puerto Ricans care about—and you can say the same thing about African-Americans and basketball, West Indians and sprinting, Canadians and hockey, and Russians and chess. Desire is the great intangible in performance, and unlike genes or psychological affect we can't measure it and trace its implications. This is the problem, in the end, with the question of whether blacks are better at sports than whites. It's not that it's offensive, or that it leads to discrimination. It's that, in some sense, it's not a terribly interesting question; "better" promises a tidier explanation than can ever be provided.

I quit competitive running when I was sixteen—just after the summer I had qualified for the Ontario track team in my age class. Late that August, we had travelled to St. John's, Newfoundland, for the Canadian championships. In those days, I was whippet-thin, as milers often are, five feet six and not much more than a hundred pounds, and I could skim along the ground so lightly that I barely needed to catch my breath. I had two white friends on that team, both distance runners, too, and both, improbably, even smaller and lighter than I was. Every morning, the three of us would run through the streets of St. John's, charging up the hills and flying down the other side. One of these friends went on to have a distinguished college running career, the other became a world-class miler; that summer, I myself was the Canadian record holder in the fifteen hundred metres for my age class. We were almost terrifyingly competitive, without a shred of doubt in our ability, and as we raced along we never stopped talking and joking, just to prove how absurdly easy we found running to be. I thought of us all as equals. Then, on the last day of our stay in St. John's, we ran to the bottom of Signal Hill, which is the town's principal geographical landmark—an abrupt outcrop as steep as anything in San Francisco. We stopped at the base, and the two of them turned to me and announced that we were all going to run straight up Signal Hill backward. I don't know whether I had more running ability than those two or whether my Africanness gave me any genetic advantage over their whiteness. What I do know is that such questions were irrelevant, because, as I realized, they were willing to go to far greater lengths to develop their talent. They ran up the hill backward. I ran home.

---

## This Text: Reading

1. What do you think of the analogy that Gladwell raises? What are some objections you have or do you think others have had? How would Gladwell answer those?
2. Why is the sports question in regard to race such an important and generally sensitive one?
3. What role does Gladwell attribute to sociology in achieving sports success?
4. What are some of the signs of sports—some elements of sports that can be read as signs, items to interpret? Are there semiotic situations you can think of?
5. Who is Gladwell's audience? Why do you think he's writing about this topic?

## Your Text: Writing

1. Gladwell uses the personal voice in the essay, but the essay's content is mostly about what research has been done on this topic. What do you think of this approach? Is this one you can imitate? Think of a social issue that you have a stake in and try your hand at this approach, using this article as a model.
2. What are some other issues that are "taboo"? Write an essay exploring another subject that is generally off limits for discussion.

# Race and Ethnicity—The Multiracial Suite

The idea of bi- or multiracial identity has become one of the most visible issues when discussing the nature of race. The issue is clearly a semiotic issue as well as a social one. When someone like Tiger Woods identifies himself as multiracial, the very question of whether race is a visual construction, a self-identified characteristic, or a combination of both comes up for question. The idea of being multiracial was also a prominent one in the last census, where for the first time, citizens could choose their race and ethnicity or a combination.

In these selections, Tiger Woods' idea that he is "Cablinasian"—Caucasian, African American, and Asian—is explored by a variety of observers who address these questions of racial identity in a number of different ways and from different perspectives of involvement; for example, Leonard Pitts (1997) is a prominent African-American columnist, George Will (1997) a prominent white conservative one. Other perspectives are more journalistic; Jeffry Scott (1997) interviews experts on the multiracial context of Woods' declaration. Ellis Cose (1997) writes on the 2000 census, while Teja Arborleda (1998) writes about his experiences as someone with multiple ethnicities.

## RACE, LABELS AND IDENTITY; MILLIONS LIVE IN AN AMERICA BENT ON—AND AT ODDS ABOUT—CATEGORIZING THEM

Jeffry Scott

WHEN 21-YEAR-OLD GOLFER Tiger Woods won the Masters and was hastily embraced as emblematic of African-Americans' achievement, he did, for some, the unthinkable: He declared that he's not black.

Suddenly Woods had put the face on a long-simmering debate that now burns hot in newspapers, magazines (*Time, Newsweek*), and on TV talk shows from "The Oprah Winfrey Show" to "Talkback Live" to "Meet the Press" (where Colin Powell was asked about his bloodline).

Woods—who explained on "Oprah" that he used to call himself "Cablinasian" as a self-coined acronym for his one-eighth Caucasian, one-fourth African-American, one-eighth American Indian, one-fourth Thai, and one-fourth Chinese heritage—wittingly or not, had become the champion of an estimated 2 million Americans of mixed parentage seeking sociopolitical acceptance.

"Tiger Woods could not have come at a better time," says Susan R. Graham, head of the Roswell-based Project Race. "The public can now see a face of what it means to be multiracial." Graham is among those who will appear this month at hearings in Washington to argue that a "mixed race" category should be included in the next U.S. census. Government officials' preliminary recommendation is expected in July.

The debate cuts to the core of how Americans identify themselves. Says Duke University professor of cultural anthropology, Lee D. Baker: "Race is an American obsession. People have to be categorized one way or the other, and if they aren't, then people become very uneasy."

And it has divided minority communities. Both the NAACP and the Latino activist group, National Council of La Raza, oppose inclusion of the "mixed race" category, fearing it will shrink their numbers and political clout, imperil government minority programs, and perhaps throw open to question what exactly constitutes a race and a minority.

"The government has no business segregating the population by race," says Candy Mills, editor of *Interrace*, an Atlanta-based magazine for parents of mixed heritage children. "There is no scientific definition of race. It doesn't help the problem. It creates division instead of a shared sense of community."

The 1990 U.S. census offered five choices of who we are: black; white; American Indian or Alaskan Native; Asian or Pacific Islander; and other.

No matter what one checks, it doesn't matter in this country, argues Jon Michael Spencer, a professor of American Studies at the University of Virginia, and author of the just-published *The New Colored People: The Mixed-Race Movement in America*.

"If you look black, you are black," he says.

Spencer says being "black" in America is a misnomer: "We all know people in our family who are white or Native American. About 70 percent of African-Americans could claim to be multiracial."

While Graham maintains that Americans who check "mixed race" in the next census will almost entirely come from the group that checked "other" in 1990, Spencer says many blacks may check "multiracial" to "avoid the stigma of being black."

For Craig and Diane Morancie of Tucker, who are among the estimated 3 million married couples of different races in the United States (he is black; she is white), multiracial isn't an issue. It's a reality they've begun in earnest to grapple with since the birth nine months ago of fraternal twin boys, Allan and Stephen.

Diane is making connections with the Interracial Family Alliance in Atlanta. "I want them to realize there are other children like them, and families like ours," she says.

The couple plans to "raise the boys in the black culture because they look black, and that's the way the world will see them," she says. The Morancies will celebrate Christmas and Kwanzaa; and Allan and Stephen will be taught "their black heritage," which includes the Caribbean influences of the island of Trinidad, where Craig's parents were born.

Diane says she is sympathetic to the "multiracial" cause. Still, when the boys were born, the couple marked "black" as their race. If some see a stigma in being black, Diane does not.

"I know one of the issues about multiracial is you don't want your kids to be a minority," she says. "But we see being a minority as no problem. If we did, Craig and I wouldn't have married in the first place."

## IS THERE ROOM IN THIS SWEET LAND OF LIBERTY FOR SUCH A THING AS A "CABLINASIAN"? FACE IT, TIGER: IF THEY SAY YOU'RE BLACK, THEN YOU'RE BLACK

Leonard Pitts Jr.

MIAMI—THREE STORIES. One you may already know: Tiger Woods, the young golf champion, who looks black, told Oprah Winfrey last week that he is not. Or at least, not just. Mr. Woods, whose ancestry is Caucasian, black, American Indian and Asian, told the talk-show host that he considers himself a "Cablinasian."

If you want to know why that makes me wince, listen to the second and third stories. One deals with Homer Plessy, who looked white. In 1892, Plessy, who described himself as "one-eighth" black, was ejected from a Whites Only train car. He took his grievance all the way to the Supreme Court—and lost. The other is about Gregory H. Williams, now Ohio State law school dean, who also looks white. But back in 1954, when he was a boy, he learned that his father was "half black." Williams' life of middle-class comforts promptly crumbled into an abyss of poverty and humiliation for a time.

So we have a black guy who isn't black, but two white guys who were.

Not ironic enough for you? Then try this: White golfer Fuzzy Zoeller is catching hell for racially disparaging remarks he made about Mr. Woods, the black man who isn't.

By tradition, as the winner of this year's Masters Tournament, Mr. Woods will be responsible for deciding the menu for next year's Champion's Dinner. Mr. Zoeller fretted that the "little boy" might "serve fried chicken next year.... Or collard greens or whatever the hell they serve."

Good eatin', Fuzz.

Let me begin by advising Mr. Zoeller that you can do a lot worse for a Sunday dinner than fried chicken and collard greens. Top it off with some rice and gravy, and you got yourself some good eatin' there, Fuzz.

Next, let me respectfully point out to Mr. Woods that it wasn't his Asian ancestry, his Indian roots or, Lord knows, his Caucasian-ness that drew Mr. Zoeller's nasty humor. Rather it was the fact of being black.

It's at times like these that I really wonder about the nation's nascent "biracial" movement. Meaning those half-blacks, quarter-blacks and others who push for new census categories and phraseology to reflect the fact that they are other than just black. It's a splendidly logical argument that unfortunately flies smack in the face of everything 221 years of American history has taught us about race.

Which is that black matters. Indeed, matters more than almost anything else you are. Ask Homer Plessy. Ask Gregory Williams.

I'm not without empathy for those who insist on acknowledging a multitiered racial heritage. Recently I met a black woman with a white husband who argued that to call her children black instead of biracial is to accept an old racist conceit: that white is a thing of such pristine purity that it becomes tainted and changed by even a drop of black blood.

Good point. But I'm still not ready to jump on the biracial bandwagon.

## *Black Japtalians*

In the first place, despite all the recent hype, that bandwagon is not exactly new; many black people can shake from the family tree someone who isn't black. So what does "biracial" mean? You think Cablinasian is funny? We had a silly phrase of our own when we were kids: "black Japtalians."

In the second place, in some instances, the desire to be biracial seems more than anything else a desire to escape being black. To escape the onus attached to that word. Given black people's long and torturous history of self-loathing, I'm always suspicious of anyone with brown skin who says he is something else.

In my experience, that suspicion is typical of us people in marginalized groups. They need numbers in order to impress politicians and social scientists with their strength and clout. More, they need heroes in order to put an appealing face on that which has been labeled defective and poor. And so, the group is eager—anxious—to claim its own. And, ultimately, wary of individual members who opt out.

Why do you think gay groups are so eager to "out" high-profile gays? Why do you think advocates for the disabled were so desperate to see the new memorial to Franklin Roosevelt portray his paralysis from polio?

Why do I care?

And why do you think Tiger Woods means a thing to me, a guy who cares less than a little about golf?

It's simple. I want to claim him. I want him for my side.

No, I'm not unmindful of how silly that sounds, how childish is all this talk of one-eighths and half-black. I know anthropologists will tell you that "race" as we define it is meaningless—carries no scientific weight. African-American, white, Irish, Polish, Chinese...at some level, just empty labels.

My only reply is even sillier and more childish: I didn't start this. I'm just trying to survive it.

Race may carry no weight in the world of science, but it has plenty in the world of American women and men. Let the black anthropologist who doubts it try hailing a cab in New York City.

Yes, it's a cliché, but no less real for that. In fact, I decided on a whim to test the cliche the last time I was in Manhattan. Walked through midtown in a driving rain and couldn't get a cabbie to stop. Could not.

Can you guess how that feels? What a humiliation that is?

After half an hour, drenched and burning with a fire you don't want to know, I gave up and did what I usually do in New York. Went to a hotel doorman and asked him to flag a cab, thanked him and tipped him for a service I should never have needed.

It strikes me as evidence of God's absurdist sense of humor that Tiger Woods' excellent adventure—his victory at the Masters, his appearance on Oprah, his run-in with Zoeller—all came as the nation celebrated the half-century anniversary of Jackie Robinson's integration of Major League Baseball. It's a confluence of events not unlike the Hale-Bopp comet and lunar eclipse that thrilled sky-watchers a few weeks back, a rich juxtaposition of race and sports, past and present, that tells us a great deal about how much progress we have made in this country. And how much we have not.

Because for all the confusion and debate about fractions of color, who is black and who is not, one thing remains clear and telling to me: Jackie Robinson would not have been able to get a cab in New York that day. And I suspect even a "Cablinasian" would have wound up standing wet and angry in the rain.

# MELDING IN AMERICA

George F. Will

AN ENORMOUS NUMBER OF PEOPLE—perhaps you—are descended, albeit very indirectly, from Charlemagne. And an enormous number are descended from Charlemagne's groom. Trace your pedigree back far enough, you may find that you are an omelet of surprising ingredients.

Booker T. Washington, Frederick Douglass, Jesse Owens and Roy Campanella each had a white parent. Martin Luther King Jr. (who had an Irish grandmother, and some Indian ancestry), W.E.B. Du Bois and Malcolm X had some Caucasian ancestry. The NAACP estimates that 70 percent of those who identify themselves as African American are of mixed racial heritage. And then there is Tiger Woods, who calls himself "Cablinasian"—Caucasian, black, Indian, Asian. Bear such things in mind as the Office of Management and Budget decides whether to make a small but consequential change in the census form. The 1790 census classified Americans in three categories—free white male, free white female, slave. In 1850 "free colored" was added. Then came mulatto, octoroon and quadroon (one-eighth and one-quarter black). In 1890 Chinese and Japanese were included as distinct races. Today there are five categories—white, black, Asian/Pacific Islander, American Indian/Native Alaskan and other.

Now there is a rapidly spreading belief that the "other" category is unsatisfactory, because it does not contribute to an accurate snapshot of the population, and it offends sensibilities: Why should a child of a white-black marriage be required to identify with one parent, or as an "other"? So OMB is considering adding a sixth category—"multiracial."

This would serve the accuracy of the census in a nation experiencing a rapid surge in interracial marriages, which increased about 550 percent between 1960 and 1990. The number of children in interracial families rose from 500,000 in 1970 to 2 million in 1990. Between 1960 and 1990 the percentage of African American marriages involving a white spouse more than tripled, from 1.7 percent to 6 percent. Sixty-five percent of Japanese-Americans marry someone of another race.

The multiracial category would serve civic health by undermining the obsession with race and ethnicity that fuels identity politics. Such politics proceed on the assumption that individuals are defined by their membership in this or that racial or ethnic group, often a group that cultivates its sense of solidarity by nurturing its grievances. The multiracial category is opposed by many who have a stake in today's racial spoils system, and thus favor maintaining the categories that help Balkanize America.

It is estimated—probably too conservatively—that 10 percent of blacks would check a "multiracial" box on the census form. As more and more people accurately identify themselves as "multiracial," the artificial clarity of identity politics will blur. The more blurring the better, because it will impede application of the principle of categorical representation—the principle that people of a particular group can only be understood, empathized with and represented by members of that group.

Today some native Hawaiians want out of the Asian/Pacific Islander category, and some Indian and native Alaskans do not want the native Hawaiians included in their category. Some Creoles, Americans of Middle Eastern descent (there are 2 million of them), and others want their own categories. Such elbow-throwing prickliness is one consequence of government making membership in distinct grievance-groups advantageous.

Race and ethnicity are not fixed, easily definable scientific categories. The law once regarded the Irish "race" as nonwhite. Today, ethnicity and race can be, to some degree, matters of choice. Many Hispanics regard "Hispanicity" as an attribute of race, others are more inclined to identify themselves as Hispanic when it is not presented as a racial category.

OMB's decision will follow last week's report from the Commission on Immigration Reform, which recommends a "new Americanization movement" emphasizing the melding of individuals rather than the accommodation of groups. It argues that national unity should be built upon a shared belief in constitutional values, and that the nation "admits immigrants as individuals" and must "emphasize the rights of individuals over those of groups."

Today the government concocts "race-conscious remedies" such as racial preferences for conditions it disapproves. This encourages Americans to aggregate into groups jockeying for social space. Perhaps it would be best to promote the desegregation of Americans by abolishing the existing five census categories, rather than adding a sixth.

However, the "multiracial" category could speed the dilution of racial consciousness. One criticism of this category is that "multiracial" does not denote a protected class under the law and therefore gathering data about those who think of themselves as "multiracial" serves no statutory purpose. To which the sensible response is: good.

Take this writer. English by culture, British by passport; and beneath that in my veins courses a dollop of Irish, a drop of Jewish, a pinch of German, combined with a heap of Anglo-Saxon. Scratch the skin, and we're all multiracial.

## CENSUS AND THE COMPLEX ISSUE OF RACE

Ellis Cose

RACIAL CLASSIFICATION HAS ALWAYS BEEN a serious—if maddeningly imprecise—business, determining who gets access to which wing of the American dream. Slave or freeman, citizen or alien. "Tell me your color," America proclaimed, "and I'll tell you your place."

The nation has long outgrown the days when slavery was a color-coded calling and naturalization was restricted to "aliens being free white persons," but the legacy of color consciousness remains. Too often our culture embraces the notion—even as our laws reject it—that all races are not equal. Nowhere is that assumption more apparent than in our accepted definition of race. For whereas one drop of "black blood" is generally considered sufficient to render one black, whiteness is not so easily bestowed.

Many people are now suggesting that the time has come to reject racial definitions rooted in slavery (and in the drive to re-create a sharp black-white divide that miscegenation had, in some respects, erased). Isn't it time, some critics ask, to rethink, and perhaps dismantle, a racial categorization system whose primary function is to separate and divide? What's the point, they ask, in forcing people into black, white, yellow, or red boxes that cannot possibly accommodate America's growing racial diversity, particularly when the black box is fundamentally different from the others, carries the full baggage of slavery, and defies all common sense? Why, they ask in effect, must a person with any degree of black African ancestry be forced to pretend that no other racial heritage counts?

The questions come most insistently and most urgently from those who make up what has been dubbed the "multiracial movement" and who resent being asked to deny a major part of who they are. Though the issue of racial classification is important to multiracial persons of all conceivable backgrounds, it has assumed a particular importance for those whose heritage is, to some degree, black. For unlike Americans of other races, blacks have largely been defined by the so-called one-drop rule: the presumption that a small percentage of black ancestry effectively cancels out any other racial claim.

Sorting out the matter of racial identification is not the only, or even the most important, task facing the U.S. Bureau of the Census as the decennial census approaches. Correcting the chronic undercounting of certain groups is, in some sense, a larger problem. But the issue of racial categorization may well be the most explosive issue on the table. People have strong feelings about how they are grouped, particularly when it comes to race; and often people's sense of where they belong is very different from the place where others tend to put them.

Race is such a subjective and squishy concept that there is no objective way of determining who is right. Moreover, as philosopher and artist Adrian Piper has observed: "The racial categories that purport to designate any of us are too rigid and oversimplified to fit anyone accurately." At a time when the very idea of racial categories is under assault, the Census Bureau is charged with carrying out what may well be an impossible task.

Piper's own sense of the absurdity of America's concepts of distinct racial groups arises from being a "black" person whom many people assume to be "white." She seemed so white to her third-grade private school teacher that the woman wondered whether Piper knew that she was black. Piper, of course, is only one of a long line of people who have found their appearance to be at odds with what America insisted that they were.

In 1983, for instance, an appeals court ruled that a Louisiana woman must accept a legal designation of black, though by all outward appearances she was white. The woman, Susie Guillory Phipps, who was then forty-nine, had lived her entire life as a white person. Upon hearing the court's decision, she told a *Washington Post* reporter: "My children are white. My grandchildren are white. Mother and Daddy were buried white. My Social Security card says I'm white. My driver's license says I'm white. There are no blacks out where I live, except the hired hands." Phipps had discovered that the state considered her black on obtaining a copy of her birth certificate in order to get a passport. Her attempt to change the designation eventually led her to court. A genealogist who testified for the state uncovered ancestors Phipps knew nothing about and calculated that she was 3/32 black. That was sufficient to make her black under a Louisiana law decreeing that a person who was as little as 1/32 black could not be considered white.

That Louisiana law was unique in this modern era in writing racial classifications into law, but the acceptance of the notion that "black" encompasses virtually everyone with black African ancestry is widespread. It is embodied not only in census data but in civil rights law. Consequently, many people who care about such laws find the matter of re-examining racial categories (especially of who belongs in the "black" category) to be unsettling.

Not that anyone believes that the current categories—spelled out in Office of Management and Budget Directive No. 15—reflect the true diversity of who Americans are. The population of the United States, as even defenders of the present system will acknowledge, consists of much more than four racial clusters (American Indian or Alaskan native, Asian or Pacific islander, black, white) and one relevant ethnic group (Hispanic). An array of spokespersons for an assortment of ethnically or racially interested organizations have proposed that the current categories be changed, or at least expanded. They have made arguments for Middle Easterners to be seen as something other than white, for Hawaiians to be grouped with Native Americans, and for Hispanics to be made into a separate racial (as opposed to ethnic) group. The most intriguing argument, however, comes from those who insist that the Census Bureau should sanction a multiracial category that would, at a minimum, encompass the children of those who come from different racial groups.

Susan Graham, a white woman married to a black man in Roswell, Georgia, told the U.S. House Subcommittee on Census, Statistics, and Postal Personnel that she was not at all happy with census bureaucrats who had told her that biracial children should be assigned the mother's race because "in cases like these, we always know who the mother is and not always the father." She apparently was not so much angered at the suggestion of uncertain paternity as at the fact that no present category reflected her biracial children's full heritage. Instead of making her choose between black and white boxes, she said, the Census Bureau ought to have a category called "multiracial."

As Lawrence Wright reported in the July 25, 1994, *New Yorker* magazine, the proposal "alarmed representatives of the other racial groups for a number of reasons, not the least of which was that multiracialism threatened to undermine the concept of racial classification altogether."

Without question, the current categories are, in many respects, arbitrary. They reflect the conventions of a slave-holding past and serve the needs of various political agendas, but they have nothing to do with the science of genealogy, or for that matter, with science at all. Nor is their meaning always clear. Directive No. 15 instructs that "the category which most closely reflects the individual's recognition in his community should be used for purposes of reporting on persons who are of mixed racial and/or ethnic origin." But what about those people who, like Susan Graham, believe multiracial is the only label that fits? As the incidence of interracial marriage increases, more and more people will no doubt find themselves in Susan Graham's shoes.

In 1992, in Bethesda, Maryland, several hundred such people came together for the "first national gathering of the multiracial community," as described by Bijan Gilanshah, in the December 1993 *Law and Inequality* journal. Gilanshah saw the meeting as an important development in the evolution of a growing social movement. Multiracial individuals, he wrote, existed in a "state of flux." The gathering was only one sign of many that they were "demanding clarification of their nebulous social and legal status and seeking official recognition as a distinct, powerful social unit with idiosyncratic cultural, social and legal interests."

Gilanshah pointed to several bits of evidence in support of his conclusion. Nearly 10 million people had elected to place themselves in the "other" category in the 1990 census, he noted, and interracial unions had sharply increased, seemingly tripling between 1970 and 1990, even as a host of self-described multiracial organizations were springing up around the country. Many of the multiracial activists, he noted, had intense feelings on the subject. "For the multiracial movement, failure of the government to include a multiracial category would result in cultural genocide," argued Gilanshah.

Julie C. Lythcott-Haims, writing in the Harvard *Civil Rights Civil Liberties Law Review* for the summer 1994, made a similar argument. Her primary concern was with adoption policies aimed at ensuring that children are placed with adoptive parents of their own race. She objected to such policies, pointing out that race matching cannot always work "because millions of children are born not merely of one race." Lythcott-Haims went on to make a broader argument whose implications stretched beyond her immediate concern of adopted children. The Census Bureau, she said, should accept a multiracial category "based on the logic that if people must be categorized according to race, these categories should be more accurate."

Lythcott-Haims was especially emphatic in her rejection of the so-called one-drop rule. The assumptions underlying it, she wrote, are "blatantly racist because the central premise is that 'Black blood' is a contaminant while 'White blood' is pure." Moreover, she noted, some multiracial people are uncomfortable declaring one of their racial lines to be better or more worthy of acknowledgment than the other: "The Multiracial person can hardly advocate the superiority or inferiority of one race without touching off a potentially damaging identity struggle within herself."

For Lythcott-Haims, the quest of multiracial individuals for their own racial designation was anything but a trivial pursuit. "If you identify as Black or Asian and our society officially classified you as White, how would you feel? If you identify as White and society required you to call yourself Latino, how would you feel?...If we send in our forms but the Census chooses not to recognize us for what we are, it is as if we do not officially exist," she wrote.

Without question, Lythcott-Haims and Gilanshah are correct in noting the absurdity of the current classification scheme. It is folly to force people to try to fit into narrow boxes that do not reflect their real complexity or their true sense of identity. But that does not necessarily mean that a multiracial box would make racial categories any less absurd or render them any more accurate.

For one thing, a multiracial designation does not really categorize a person racially. It simply indicates that a person fits into more than one category. Consequently, it could end up being even less precise than the groupings we have now. If the rubric applies to anyone of racially diverse ancestry, it could conceivably apply to most Americans now considered "blacks" as well as to a substantial portion of those who belong to other recognized racial groups.

Even if it is taken (as many proponents would like) to apply only to those with two parents of recognizably different racial stock, it is not a very accurate descriptor. A multiracial box (unless it spelled out what racial heritages were subsumed by the designation) would put the offspring of a white person and a Native American in the same pigeonhole as the offspring of a black person and a Chinese American. While the offspring of both unions would certainly be multiracial, not many Americans would consider them to be of the same race. In all likelihood, society would still consider the black-Asian child to be black (or perhaps mixed) and the white-Native American child to be white. They would probably, in any number of circumstances, be treated quite differently.

A *New York Times* poll of 1991, for instance, found that 66 percent of whites were opposed to a relative marrying a black person, whereas 45 percent were opposed to a relative marrying a Hispanic or Asian person. Clearly, in the eyes of many of those respondents, all multiracial families are not created equal. If part of the purpose of census classifications is to permit the government to determine how various groups are treated, aggregating groups whose only common denominator is that their parents are racially different would not do much to advance that purpose.

But even assuming one could agree that all people with parents of different racial stock should be considered members of a new race called "multiracial," what about those people who do not really care for that designation? What about the numerous offspring of black and white unions, for instance, who insist on calling themselves black? Providing them with a multiracial box would not guarantee that they would check it. And what about the children of "multiracial" parents? If the designation only applied to the first generation, would children of multiracial people become (like many light-skinned "blacks" who are clearly of mixed ancestry) monoracial by the second generation? Or would those children twenty years from now be fighting for yet another redefinition of race?

And what about Hispanics? Obviously many Latinos find the current categories lacking. They are uncomfortable with a system that insists that they define themselves either as black or white. In the 1990 census, roughly half of the Latinos in California described themselves as neither white, black, American Indian, nor Asian. They were "other." But that does not mean that a "multiracial" grouping is the solution.

Certain Latino leadership organizations, after all, prefer a designation that would set Hispanics apart from other groups racially, not one that would throw them into one huge category that combines all people of mixed racial heritage. Moreover, many Latin American cultures recognize an array of racial delineations much more complex than those acknowledged in the United States. Brazil, for instance, once had more than forty different racial categories. And Latin societies have come up with an array of terms to note the differences in those who are light-skinned and "European looking" and those who are not.

In an essay "Empowering Hispanic Families: A Critical Issue for the '90s," Frank F. Montalvo observed: "At the heart of the Hispanic experience in the United States is a form of racism that both binds light and dark Latinos to each other and divides them into separate groups. Race may prove to be a more pernicious element in their lives than are linguistic, cultural and socioeconomic differences." It is not at all clear that allowing Latinos the option of describing themselves as multiracial would resolve the problems many have with the current categories or would allow Latinos to express the true racial complexity of their cultures.

In an article in *Transition* entitled "Passing for White, Passing for Black," Adrian Piper tried to explain the phenomenon of people whom the United States had designated as "black" deciding to live their lives as "white": "Once you realize what is denied you as an African-American simply because of your race," wrote Piper, "your sense of the unfairness of it may be so overwhelming that you may simply be incapable of accepting it. And if you are not inclined toward any form of overt political advocacy, passing in order to get the benefits you know you deserve may seem the only way to defy the system."

The suspicion in some quarters is that the new emphasis on a multiracial category may be motivated by a desire to escape into a more socially congenial category, at least for those who face the alternative of being forced into the black box. The multiracial category, after all, is not really new. The rise of the mulatto category during Colonial times was an acknowledgment that the offspring of black-white unions were not necessarily either black or white. But after emancipation the in-between status of mulattoes "threatened the color line," as Gilanshah, among others, has noted. So the mulattoes were pushed into the black category.

Gilanshah obviously does not equate the new multiracial group with the privileged mulattoes of yesteryear. But in many respects, the language of the multiracial lobby invites such a comparison. Many advocates of the new designation see multiracial individuals as ambassadors between groups. Gilanshah, for instance, argues that society would benefit from having multiracial people who are uniquely positioned to be "sensitive, objective negotiators of inter-group racial conflict." But to assume that only designated multiracial people can be a bridge between races is to assume that others cannot be. It is also to reawaken recollections about the middleman role of American mulattoes and Latin American mestizos, groups who were assigned a status lower than that of whites but higher than that of the groups with whom the whites had mixed. Their purpose, at least in part, was to reduce ethnic tensions and to keep people in their assigned places.

The Reverend Jesse Jackson has looked not to American history but to South Africa and its "colored" class to find an analogue to the multiracial category. Sociologist and anthropologist Pierre L. Van Den Berghe makes the same comparison: "It boggles my mind that the United States, in the late 20th Century, is [considering] reinventing the nonsense that South Africa invented 300 years ago," Van Den Berghe told a reporter for the *Los Angeles Times*. A separate multiracial category, he argued, would further "the inanity of race classification." Moreover, he saw the category as redundant. African Americans, he asserted, are in fact already "mixed-race."

None of this is to say that there is anything wrong with people defining themselves as multiracial. In many respects, it is certainly a better descriptor than black, white, American Indian, or Asian. And indeed, during the next year, as the Census Bureau tests its various racial indicators, the multiracial category should be given its due. The bureau should evaluate whether a new multiracial category would increase the census's clarity or simply heighten confusion. Certainly, if multiracial persons are allowed to describe themselves as multiracial and then forced to specify how, the quality of the information gathered should not diminish and would perhaps be enhanced.

Still, adoption by the census of a multiracial box is not likely to accomplish much of what its proponents seem to seek. It would not prevent Americans from assuming that people who "look black" are black, whatever their other heritage. It would not provide a reliable anchor in racial identity, since multiracial is not so much an identity as an acknowledgment of multiple heritages. And it would not change current thinking that divides people into often opposing racial and ethnic groups.

It would not, for instance, persuade the members of the National Association of Black Social Workers, who have been outspoken for more than twenty years in advocating that "black" children go only to "black" families, to shift their position suddenly. Nor is it likely to mean a change in the practice of discrimination in employment or elsewhere. It certainly would not help, and might well hurt, enforcement of laws dealing with housing discrimination, employment discrimination, and voting rights.

In the *New Yorker* magazine, Lawrence Wright observed: "Those who are charged with enforcing civil rights laws see the multiracial box as a wrecking ball aimed at affirmative action, and they hold those in the mixed-race movement responsible." Wright wonders about the practical effect: "Suppose a court orders a city to hire additional black police officers to make up for past discrimination. Will mixed-race officers count? Will they count wholly or partly?"

Proponents of the multiracial classification obviously do not tend to see themselves in such a light. They are not so much making a political protest as a personal statement about identity. And the question they raise is clearly an important one and, in some sense, an inevitable one.

Certainly it is possible to envision a "multiracial" box, perhaps in addition to an "other" box, that would not undermine civil rights laws or launch demands for special status for a multiracial "race." The option would simply allow people to describe themselves as what they perceive themselves to be. And if that box also forced people to designate in what ways they were mixed, the information could eventually be aggregated in whatever way would be useful. In short, the purposes of the data collection process could be served, while people were allowed to make a statement about their personal identity. No census box, however, will solve the larger problems of race in this country. Nor will a census box resolve anyone's sense of racial alienation or provide a secure racial identity.

Ideally, one day we will get beyond the need to categorize. Certainly, geneticists and other scientists are concluding that racial categories make little sense. But the tendency to categorize is strong and will clearly be with us for a while. For the time being those who are struggling with such issues might be well advised to heed the words of Adrian Piper, who declared, "No matter what I do or do not do about my racial identity, someone is bound to feel uncomfortable. But I have resolved that it is no longer going to be me."

## RACE IS A FOUR-LETTER WORD

Teja Arboleda

I'VE BEEN CALLED *nigger* and a neighbor set the dogs on us in Queens, New York.

I've been called *spic* and was frisked in a plush neighborhood of Los Angeles.

I've been called *Jap* and was blamed for America's weaknesses.

I've been called *Nazi* and the neighborhood G.I. Joes had me every time.

I've been called *Turk* and was sneered at in Germany.

I've been called *Stupid Yankee* and was threatened in Japan.

I've been called *Afghanistani* and was spit on by a Boston cab driver.

I've been called *Iraqi* and Desert Storm was America's pride.

I've been called *mulatto, criollo, mestizo, simarron, Hapahaoli, masala, exotic, alternative, mixed-up, messed-up, half-breed,* and *in between.* I've been mistaken for Moroccan, Algerian, Egyptian, Lebanese, Iranian, Turkish, Brazilian, Argentinean, Puerto Rican, Cuban, Mexican, Indonesian, Nepalese, Greek, Italian, Pakistani, Indian, Black, White, Hispanic, Asian, and being a Brooklynite. I've been mistaken for Michael Jackson and Billy Crystal on the same day.

I've been ordered to get glasses of water for neighboring restaurant patrons. I've been told to be careful mopping the floors at the television station where I was directing a show. Even with my U.S. passport, I've been escorted to the "aliens only" line at Kennedy International Airport. I've been told I'm not dark enough. I've been told I'm not White enough. I've been told I talk American real good. I've been told, "Take your humus and your pita bread and go back to Mexico!" I've been ordered to "Go back to where you belong, we don't like *your* kind here!"

I spent too much time and energy as a budding adult abbreviating my identity and rehearsing its explanation. I would practice quietly by myself, reciting what my father always told me: "Filipino-German." He never smiled when he said this.

My father's dark skin told many stories that his stern face and anger-filled tension couldn't translate. My mother's light skin could never spell empathy—even suntanning only made her turn bright red. My brother Miguel and I became curiosity factors when we appeared in public with her. During the past 34 years, my skin has lightened, somewhat, but then in the summers (even in New England where summers happen suddenly, and disappear just as quickly), I can darken several degrees in a matter of hours. This phenomenon seems a peculiar paradigm to which people's perceptions of my culture or race alter with the waning and waxing of my skin tone. I can almost design others' perceptions by counting my minutes in the sun. My years in Japan, the United States, Germany, and the numerous countries, cities, and towns through which I've traveled, have proven that my flesh is irrelevant to the language I speak, to the way I walk and talk, or the way I jog or mow my lawn or to the fact that I often use chopsticks to eat. It is irrelevant to *who* or *what* I married, my political viewpoints, my career, my hopes, desires and fears.

I don't remember being taught by my parents never to *question* skin color, yet when I compare the back of my hand to these pages, I cannot help myself—I must know. Like a sickness coursing through my veins with the very blood that makes me who I am, I ask: What color am I? And, what color was I yesterday? Tomorrow? There is also that pesky, familiar feeling I get when, in the corner of my eye, I catch passing strangers with judgments written on their brows. Maybe paranoia, maybe vanity, but the experiences and memories of too often being "different" or "undefinable" have left me with a weary sense of instant verdict on my part. And sometimes I study their thousands of faces, hoping somehow to connect. I know that they ask themselves the same questions, as they are plagued by the same epidemic, asking and reasking themselves, ourselves, "Who and what are we?"

Overadapting to new environments has become second nature to me, as my father and my mother eagerly fed me culture. As a child I felt like I was being dragged to different corners of the planet with my parents, filling their need for exploration and contact, and teaching us the value and beauty of difference. Between packing suitcases and wandering through unfamiliar territory, all I had ever wanted was to be "the same."

They were successful in some respects—I do believe I am liberal in my thinking—but inevitably there was a price to pay. With each step, each move, each landing through the thick and tenuous atmosphere of a new culture, my feet searched for solid ground, for something familiar. The concept of home, identity, and place become ethereal, like a swirl of gases circling in orbit, waiting for gravity to define their position.

In a sense, I have been relegated to ethnic benchwarmer, on a hunt for simplicity in a world of confusing words that deeply divide us all. In response, I learned to overcompensate. New places and new faces have rarely threatened me, but I have a desperate need to belong to whatever group I'm with at any particular moment. I soak in the surrounding elements to cope with what my instincts oblige, and deliver a new temporary self. I am out of bounds, transcending people and places. I carry within my blood the memories of my heritage connected in the web of my mind, the marriage of history and biology. I breathe the air of my ancestors as if it were fresh from the sunrises of their past. I am illogical, providing argument to traditional categories of race, culture, and ethnicity. I am a cultural chameleon, adapting out of necessity only to discover, yet again, a new Darwinism at the frontiers of identity.

"What are you, anyway?" sometimes demandingly curious Americans like to ask. "I'm Filipino-German," I used to say. I have never been satisfied with abbreviating my identity to the exclusion of all the other puzzle pieces that would then be lost forever in shadowy corners where no one ever looks.

Do I throw a nod at a Black brother who passes me on the street? And if I did so, would he understand why I did? Do I even call him "brother?" Does *he* call *me* "brother?" If not, should he call me a "half-brother," or throw me a half nod? In the United States do I nod or bow to Japanese nationals in a Japanese restaurant? Would they know to bow with me? In Jamaica Plain, Massachusetts, if a Hispanic male gestures hello to me, is it a simple greeting, or a gesture of camaraderie because I might be Hispanic? Do I dress up to go to a country club because, in the eyes of its rich White men, I would otherwise live up to their idea of the stercotypical minority? Should I dance well, shaking and driving my body like Papa's family afforded me, or should I remain appropriately conservative to preserve the integrity of a long-gone Puritan New England? Do I shave for the silver hallways of white-collar high-rises so as not to look too "ethnic?" Do I agree to an audition for a commercial when I know the reason I'm there is just to fill in with some skin color for an industry quota?

"I know you're *something*," someone once said. "You have some Black in you," another offered. "He must be ethnic or something," I've overheard. "I've got such a boring family compared to yours," another confided. "You're messed-up," an elementary school girl decided. "Do you love your race?" her classmate wondered. "*What* did you marry?" I've been asked. "*Who* did you marry?" I've been asked. "Is she just like you?" I've been asked. "You are the quintessential American," someone decided.

* * *

America continues to struggle through its identity crisis, and the simple, lazy, bureaucratic checklist we use only serves to satisfy an outdated four-letter word—*race*. Like the basic food groups, it is overconsumed and digested, forming a hemorrhoid in the backside of the same old power struggle. I am only one of many millions of Americans, from this "League of Outsiders," demanding a change in the way we are designated, routed, cattle-called, herded, and shackled into these simplified classifications.

The United States is going through growing pains. The immigrants coming to the United States and becoming citizens are no longer primarily of European origin. But let's not fool ourselves into thinking that America is only now becoming multicultural.

In 1992, *Time* magazine produced a special issue entitled, "The New Face of America" with the subtitle, "How immigrants are shaping the world's first multicultural society." The cover featured a picture of a woman's face. Next to the face was a paragraph that suggested her image was the result of a computerized average of faces of people of several different races.

The operative words on the cover are "races," "culture," and "first." Race and culture are very different words. Race in America is predominantly determined by skin color. Culture is determined by our experiences and our interactions within a society, large or small.

Then there is this idea of being "first." Are we to say that this continent was never populated by a mix of people? Are we to say that the Lacota and Iroquois were of exactly the same culture? What about the different Europeans who settled here later on? Of course, African slaves were not all from the same tribe, and they certainly were not of the same culture as the slave traders.

In the middle of the magazine, there was a compilation, more like a chart of photographs of people from all over the world. The editor and computer artist scanned all the pictures into a computer. Then, by having the computer average the faces together, they produced a variety of facial combinations. Remember, however, they said on the cover, "People from different *races* ... to form the world's first *multicultural* society." But in the body of the article and its accompanying pictures, many people were not identified by their *race*, but rather by their *nationalities*—such as Italian and Chinese—in other words *citizenship*, a very different word.

Through it all, *Time* was trying to educate us, but at the same time, we're miseducated. The world—not just this country—has always been and always will be a multicultural environment. So what is it about the words *multicultural* or *diversity* that is confusing or overwhelming?

In the next 20 years, the average American will no longer be technically White. This will have to be reflected in the media, in the workplace, and in the schools, not out of charitable interest, but out of necessity. More people are designating themselves as multiracial or multicultural. People continue to marry across religious, cultural, and ethnic barriers. A definition for "mainstream society" is harder to find.

* * *

My mother's father, Opa, died a year after Oma passed away. The day after the funeral in Germany, my mother's relatives told her, for the first time, that her father was not really her father (i.e., biologically). All the people who knew the true identity of her father have long since passed away. So, if my mother's biological father was, let's say, Italian or Russian, does that make her German-Italian or German-Russian? She says no. German, only German, because that's how she was raised.

My brother, Miguel, married a Brazilian. (*Pause.*) Do you have an image in your head of what she looks like? I did when he first told me about her over the phone. Well, she is Brazilian by culture and citizenship, but her parents are Japanese nationals who moved to Brazil in their early 20s to escape poverty in Japan after World War II. So she *looks stereotypically* Japanese. But she speaks Portuguese and doesn't interact socially like most Japanese do.

* * *

I offer myself as a case study in transcending the complex maze of barriers, pedestals, doors, and traps that form the boundaries that confine human beings to dominant and minority groups.

I am tired. I am exhausted. I am always looking for new and improved definitions for my identity. My very-mixed heritage, culture, and international experiences seem like a blur sometimes, and I long for a resting place. A place where I can breathe like I did in my mother's womb: without having to open my mouth.

## THIS TEXT: READING

1. Whose take on this issue did you like the best? Why?
2. Did all the authors take a similar approach to the idea of Woods' Cablinasian? If not, how did their approaches differ? What was the most effective?
3. Why do you think Woods' declaration touched so many nerves? What do people have at stake when it comes to race and ethnicity?

4. Are all the writers appealing to the same audience? How would you determine this? What situations are they writing from?
5. What are some of the political implications of being or declaring yourself multiracial?
6. What might be some of the personal implications of being or declaring yourself multiracial?

### YOUR TEXT: WRITING

1. Can you think of any popular culture texts that deal with the question of multiracial issues? How do they treat it? Write a short paper examining this question.
2. Write about the stability or instability of racial identity in this country. What are some of the ways we demonstrate these ideas in American culture? Write a short paper exploring this idea.
3. Ultimately, do you think identity should be self-determined rather than determined from without? What are the barriers to this idea? Write a short paper explaining your position.
4. Do some research on the past idea of being multiracial. What have Americans thought of this idea in the past?

---

## READING OUTSIDE THE LINES

### Classroom Activities

1. Although most scientists believe that race is socially constructed, that still leaves open the question of how we construct our ideas of race. In class, discuss some of the ways you see this process working in culture attributed to particular ethnic groups, and in white America as well.
2. In his essay, "In Living Color: Race and American Culture," Michael Omi discusses the way race and ethnicity are portrayed on television. Using your own observations, discuss how popular culture treats race and ethnicity.
3. Discuss clothing and what pieces of clothing signify in general. Do you tend to characterize different groups by what clothes they wear?
4. After reading Beverly Tatum's piece, talk about the presence of race and ethnicity on campus. Do you notice patterns that can be inferred? Do you feel your campus is enlightened about race and ethnicity?
5. Some people still believe races and ethnicities have particular cultures, or cultures which are generated from groups from particular ethnicities.

Discuss the phenomenon of people from different cultures participating in each other's culture.

6. Watch *Do the Right Thing* in class. What ideas about race does Spike Lee explore? What about his narrative makes you uncomfortable? What do you think his ideas about race are?
7. Watch *Mississippi Burning* with *Rosewood*. Compare how the two treat the idea of African-American participation in remedying racism. What problems do you see in the narratives? What have the filmmakers emphasized in their narratives? Is it at the expense of more "real" or important issues?
8. Watch two television shows, one with an all white or largely white cast, and one with an all African-American or largely African-American cast. How does each treat the idea of race and ethnicity?
9. Using the same shows, notice the commercials playing—how do these construct a view of race and/or ethnicity?

## Essay Ideas

1. Trace the evolution of the portrayal of race and/or ethnicity in a particular medium—television, movies, art, public space. Has it changed in your lifetime? Why or why not?
2. Go to the library or the computer and do a keyword search on a particular ethnicity and a politician's name (example: "Cheney" and "African-American"). What comes up when you do this? Is there a trend worth writing about?
3. Do some research on the nature of prejudice. What do researchers say about its nature?
4. Get stories or novels from 75 years ago; look and see how different authors, African-American, white, Italian, Jewish, etc., portrayed people of different skin color and ethnicity. How would you characterize the treatment as a whole?
5. What are the signs that are encoded in race and ethnicity? How are they portrayed in popular culture and the media? Do a sign analysis of a particular show or media phenomenon.
6. Watch two television shows, one with a largely white cast, one with a largely African-American cast. Compare how each deals with the idea of race or ethnicity.
7. Using the same shows, notice the commercials playing—how do these construct a view of race and/or ethnicity?
8. Look at a film or films made by African-American, Hispanic, or other ethnic directors. How do these directors deal with the idea of race and ethnicity, compared to white directors dealing with similar ideas?

# 5

# Reading Movies

The contemporary American poet Louis Simpson writes in one of his poems "Every American is a film critic." He is probably right. Just about everyone we know loves movies, and as much as we love movies, we love talking about them. And when we watch movies, along with television for that matter, we often feel qualified as critics; we freely disagree with movie reviewers and each other. As Oscar Wilde once claimed, in literature as in love, we are shocked by what others choose. That may be doubly so for movies.

Despite our familiarity with movies and our apparent willingness to serve as movie critics, we sometimes resist taking a more analytical approach to them. For many of us, movies are an "escape" from school or analytical thinking. After a long day at school or at work, most of us want to sit in front of a big screen and veg out with *Armageddon* or *Mission Impossible* for a couple of hours. Your authors confess that we have been known to veg out too, so we aren't knocking the idea of losing oneself in front of a seemingly mindless action flick. However, we do want you to be aware of the fact that movies are never *just* mindless action flicks. They are always some kind of cultural text, loaded with ideas about a particular culture, either consciously or unintentionally expressed. For instance, some film and cultural critics have argued that the *Star Wars* movies create a sense of nostalgia for the value systems of the 1950s; values that by today's standards may seem racist, sexist, and blindly patriotic. To others, *Fatal Attraction* is more than a suspenseful movie about a crazed psycho-killer boiling a bunny. Some see the film as an allegory on AIDS, in that the film reinforces the central fear of AIDS—if you sleep around, you risk death. Still others see the film as a document that confirms the backlash against women during the conservatism of the Reagan years. In a much different vein, cultural critics and film historians have argued that genre movies like comedies, family melodramas, and gangster flicks tell stories about and reinforce mainstream American values. For instance, many have argued that Westerns like *The Searchers, Red River*, and *Broken Arrow* reflect an era's views on race, justice, and the frontier. You may disagree with these particular readings, but they show how movies can be a rich source for cultural exploration and debate.

However, there are obstacles when mining movies for cultural interpretation. In some ways, our familiarity with movies becomes a liability when trying to analyze them. Because you have seen so many movies, you may believe that you already know how to read them. In some ways you do. As informal movie critics, you are already geared toward analyzing the plot of a movie or determining whether the movie is realistic or funny or appropriately sad. And if asked about the music, fashion, setting, and dialogue in a movie, you would likely be able to analyze these aspects. But you probably do not undertake the same process of close "reading" you do in literature when you read movies; you probably have not been taught to look *through* the plot and dialogue of movies to see the film as a cultural text. Though at times difficult, the process is often rewarding. Some things we look for in the movies from recent years may make a good start for your own explorations: Pay attention to how many Asian or American Indians you see in contemporary movies; watch for roles for strong, confident women; look for movies in which poor or blue collar people are treated not as a culture but as interesting individuals; see how many films are directed by women or minorities; pay attention to product placements (that is, brand products such as soda cans, cereal, kinds of cars, or computers) in movies. Work on seeing cinematic texts as products, documents, and pieces of evidence from a culture.

## Like literature and music, movies are comprised of genres.

Movies, perhaps even more than literature and music, are comprised of genres, such as Westerns, science fiction, comedy, drama, adventure, horror, documentaries, and romance. You may not think about film genres that often, but you probably prepare yourself for certain movies depending on the genre of that particular film. You come to comedies prepared to laugh; you arrive at horror movies prepared to be scared; you go to "chick flicks" expecting romance, passion, and a happy ending. If you don't get these things in your movie experience, you will likely feel disappointed, as though the film didn't hold up its end of the bargain. Notice, in reading both the selections here and in movie reviews generally, how critics do or do not pay attention to genre. Though they should be familiar with genre, many critics insist on reviewing all movies as if they are supposed to be as earnest and dramatic as *Casablanca* or *Titanic*, when movies like *Happy Gilmore* or *Dumb and Dumber* clearly try to do different things.

The idea of genre in movies is as old as Hollywood itself. In the early days of Hollywood, the studio system thrived on genre movies, and in fact, genre films were pretty much all that came out of Hollywood for several decades. Even today, blockbuster movies are most often genre pieces that adhere to the criteria of that particular genre. *Titanic* is not *There's Something About Mary*. Different genres evoke different emotions, and they comment on different values.

Being aware of genres and their conventions. When you "read" a film, think about how it fits into a particular genre. Taking into account formal, thematic, and cultural forces (the Cold War, civil rights, Vietnam, feminism, the Great Depression) will allow you to see movie production as a dynamic process of exchange between the movie industry and its audience. You should be mindful of why we like certain genres and what these genres tell us about ourselves and our culture. The fact that some writers and critics distinguish between "movies" (cinema for popular consumption) and "films" (cinema that tries to transcend or explode popular genre formulations) suggests the degree to which genres influence how we read movie texts.

## Movies are a powerful cultural tool.

A hundred years ago, people satisfied their cravings for action, suspense, and character development by reading books and serials; today, we go to the movies, or, more and more frequently, avoid the communal experience of the theater for the private experience of renting videos and DVDs. We are living in a visual age. In America, video and visual cultures have become the dominant modes of expression and communication, and learning to "read" these media with the same care, creativity, and critical acumen with which we read written texts is crucial. To better understand the phenomenon of movies, we need to contextualize the movie experience within American culture, asking in particular how thoroughly American movies affect American culture.

And movies are not just indicators for American culture—they determine culture itself. Fashion, songs, modes of behavior, social and political views and gender and racial values are all underscored by movies. For instance, *Wayne's World* made certain songs and phrases part of everyday American life. On a more complex level, many critics claim the movie *Guess Who's Coming to Dinner*, in which a wealthy white woman brings home her black fiancée, went a long way toward softening racial tensions in the 1960s. We even define eras, movements, and emotions by movies—the 1960s is often symbolized by *Easy Rider*; the 1970s by *Saturday Night Fever* and *Star Wars*; the 1980s by movies like *Fast Times at Ridgemont High* and *Do the Right Thing*; and the 1990s by *Titanic* and *You've Got Mail*. Because more people see movies than read books, one could argue that the best documents of American popular culture are movies. Thus, we tend to link the values and trends of certain eras with movies from those eras. Movies both reflect culture and help us understand culture.

Movies also guide our behavior. In contemporary society, we often learn how to dress, how to talk, and even how to court and kiss someone, from the cinema. In fact, for many young people, their model for a date, a spouse, and a romantic moment all come from what they have seen in movies. In other words, influential models for people, aspects of their hopes and dreams, come not from life but from movies. So, as you read the following pieces and as you watch movies, ask yourself if the things you desire, you desire because movies have planted those seeds.

## The advertising and marketing of a movie affect how we view the movie and how the studio views itself and us.

Next time you watch previews in a theatre or on a video or DVD you have rented, pay attention to how the film being advertised is presented to you. Be aware of how movies are packaged, how they are marketed, how actors talk about them in interviews. Whether you know it or not, you are being prepped for viewing the movie by all of these texts. Even independent films have become mainstream by marketing themselves as similar to other (popular) independent movies. Marketing is selling, and studios fund, market, and release movies not so much to make the world a better place but primarily to make money (though directors and actors may have different motivations). Also, unlike a book publisher, a studio has likely paid tens of millions of dollars to make a movie, so it needs a lot of us to go see it. We might ask ourselves how these considerations affect not only the advertising but the movie itself.

Additionally, Hollywood studios rarely have your best interest at heart. This is not to say that studios want to make you an evil person, but movie-makers have only rarely seen themselves as educators. For instance, few studios fund documentaries. Few studios seem eager to make movies about poets, painters, composers, or philosophers because they know that not many people will go to see them. It is important to realize that movie studios began as a financial enterprise; studios and the film industry grew as America and American capitalist ideals grew. Nowadays, the topics and subjects of movies have been largely market-tested just like any other consumer product such as toys, soft drinks, and shoes.

## Movies use various techniques to manipulate audiences.

Manipulation is not necessarily a pejorative or negative term. Here, we mean it in all of its contexts. Film is such a wonderful media because it is so easily manipulated. Directors use music, lighting, special effects, and clever editing to help make their movies more powerful. Music reinforces feelings of excitement (*Raiders of the Lost Ark*), fear (*Jaws*), romance (*Titanic*), or anger (*Do the Right Thing*). Lighting and filters make people, especially women, appear more delicate or fragile. The famous film star from the 1930s and 1940s, Marlene Dietrich, would only be shot from one side and insisted on being lit with overhead lights. The first several minutes of *Citizen Kane* (1941), widely considered the best American film ever made, are shot largely in the dark to help drive home the sense that the reporters are "in the dark" about media mogul Charles Foster Kane. In movies like *Independence Day, Titanic, Pearl Harbor* and *Planet of the Apes*, special effects make the story we are watching feel less like light and shadow and more like reality. Even how a filmmaker places a camera affects how we view the film. The close-up, spookily lit shots of Anthony Hopkins' face in *Silence of the Lambs* make us feel like Hannibal Lector might eat *our* liver with "some fava beans and a nice Chianti." Similarly, in many Westerns, the camera is placed at knee level, so that we are always looking up at the cowboy, reinforcing his stature as a hero. Director Orson Welles does similar things in *Citizen Kane*. Alfred Hitchcock was a master of placing the camera in manipulative places. From *Psycho* to *Rear Window* to *Rope*, we see exactly what he wants us to see and how he wants us to see it. We see nothing more than what the camera shows us.

There are other forms of manipulation as well. Many people feel Steven Spielberg's movies end with overly manipulative scenes that pluck at the heartstrings of the audience, forcing over-determined emotions because of over-the-top melodrama. Such accusations are often leveled at teen romance flicks and so-called bio-pics because they make a person's life seem more maudlin, more heart-wrenching than it could possibly be.

Costumes, colors, sounds and sound effects, editing, and set design all contribute to how the movie comes to us. Sound and music are particularly effective. In *Star Wars*, for instance, each character has a specific musical profile—a kind of theme song—whose tone mirrors how you are supposed to feel about that character. You probably all remember the dark, deep foreboding music that always accompanies Darth Vader. Like music, the clothes a character wears tell us how to feel about that person. The costumes of Ben Affleck and Will Smith probably reinforce gender expectations, as do the clothes of Julia Roberts or Jennifer Lopez. How a space ship or a dark, scary warehouse looks puts us in the mood so that the plot and action can move us. Savvy viewers of movies will be aware of the ways in which films try to manipulate them because in so doing, they will be better able to read other forms of manipulation in their lives.

# Worksheet

## THIS TEXT

1. While it will be impossible for you to know this fully, try to figure out the writing situation of each author. Who is the audience? What does the author have at stake? What is his or her agenda? Why is she or he

writing this piece? For instance, would David Denby, a white male, give the same reading of *Waiting to Exhale* as bell hooks?
2. What are the main points of the essay? Can you find a thesis statement anywhere?
3. Do you think the authors "read into" movies too much? If so, why do you say this?
4. As you read the essays, pay attention to the language the critics use to read movies.
5. If you have not seen the movies the authors mention, rent the movies and watch them—preferably with a group of people from your class.
6. Try to distinguish between a review and an argumentative or persuasive essay. Additionally, you should be aware of a distinction between a short capsule review, which is more of a summary, and a longer analytical review (like the ones printed here).

## BEYOND THIS TEXT

### Film Technique

**Camera angles and positioning:** How is the camera placed? Is it high, low, to the side? And how does it move? Is it a hand-held camera, or is it stationary? How does it determine how you *see* the movie?

**Lighting:** Light and shading are very important to movies. Are there shadows? Is the film shot during the day or mostly at night? How do shadows and light affect the movie and your experience of it?

**Color and framing:** Often, directors try to give certain scenes an artistic feel. Is the shot framed similar to a painting or photograph? Does the movie use color to elicit emotions? How does the movie frame or represent nature?

### Content

**Theme:** What are the themes of the movie? What point is the director or writer trying to get across?

**Ideology:** What ideas or political leanings does the movie convey? Are there particular philosophies or concepts that influence the message the movie sends?

### The Whole Package

**Celebrities:** What movie stars appear (or don't appear) in the movie? How do certain stars determine what kind of movie a film is? Do the actors ever look ugly or dirty or tired or sloppy?

**Technology:** What kind of technology is at work in the film? How do special effects or stunts or pyrotechnics affect the film viewing experience?

**Genre:** What genre does a particular movie fit into? Why? What are the expectations of that genre?
**Culture:** As a cultural document, a cultural text, what does this movie say about its culture? How does it transmit values? What kinds of ideas and values does it hold up or condemn?
**Effectiveness:** Does the movie "work" as a movie? Why? Why not? What cultural forces might be influencing your criteria of effectiveness?

# HIGH-SCHOOL CONFIDENTIAL: NOTES ON TEEN MOVIES

David Denby

Denby, a film critic for *The New Yorker*, offers an insightful reading of the best and worst from one of the most popular (and popular to criticize) movie genres—the teen movie. Written in 1999, this essay is a good example of a definitional argument. Notice how Denby is very clear about establishing the criteria by which he judges teen movies.

THE MOST HATED YOUNG WOMAN in America is a blonde—well, sometimes a redhead or a brunette, but usually a blonde. She has big hair flipped into a swirl of gold at one side of her face or arrayed in a sultry mane, like the magnificent pile of a forties movie star. She's tall and slender, with a waist as supple as a willow, but she's dressed in awful, spangled taste: her outfits could have been put together by warring catalogues. And she has a mouth on her, a low, slatternly tongue that devastates other kids with such insults as "You're vapor, you're Spam!" and "Do I look like Mother Teresa? If I did, I probably wouldn't mind talking to the geek squad." She has two or three friends exactly like her, and together they dominate their realm—the American high school as it appears in recent teen movies. They are like wicked princesses, who enjoy the misery of their subjects. Her coronation, of course, is the senior prom, when she expects to be voted "most popular" by her class. But, though she may be popular, she is certainly not liked, so her power is something of a mystery. She is beautiful and rich, yet in the end she is preëminent because … she is preëminent, a position she works to maintain with Joan Crawford-like tenacity. Everyone is afraid of her; that's why she's popular.

She has a male counterpart. He's usually a football player, muscular but dumb, with a face like a beer mug and only two ways of speaking—in a conspiratorial whisper, to a friend; or in a drill sergeant's sudden bellow. If her weapon is the snub, his is the lame but infuriating prank—the can of Sprite emptied into a knapsack, or something sticky, creamy, or adhesive deposited in a locker. Sprawling and dull in class, he comes alive in the halls and in the cafeteria. He hurls people against lockers; he spits, pours, and sprays; he has a projectile relationship with food. As the crown prince, he claims the best-looking girl for himself, though in a perverse display of power he may invite an outsider or an awkward girl—a "dog"—to the prom, setting her up for some special humiliation. When we first see him, he is riding high, and virtually the entire school colludes in his tyranny. No authority figure—no teacher or administrator—dares correct him.

Thus the villains of the recent high-school movies. Not every American teen movie has these two characters, and not every social queen or jock shares all the attributes I've mentioned. (Occasionally, a handsome, dark-haired athlete can be converted to sweetness and light.) But as genre figures these two types are hugely familiar; that is, they are a common memory, a collective trauma, or at least a social and erotic fantasy. Such movies of the past year as "Disturbing Behavior," "She's All That," "Ten Things I Hate About You," and "Never Been Kissed" depend on them as stock figures. And they may have been figures in the minds of the Littleton shooters, Eric Harris and Dylan Klebold, who imagined they were living in a school like the one in so many of these movies—a poisonous system of status, snobbery, and exclusion.

Do genre films reflect reality? Or are they merely a set of conventions that refer to other films? Obviously, they wouldn't survive if they didn't provide emotional satisfaction to the people who make them and to the audiences who watch them. A half century ago, we didn't need to see ten Westerns a year in order to learn that the West got settled. We needed to see it settled ten times a year in order to provide ourselves with the emotional gratifications of righteous violence. By drawing his gun only when he was provoked, and in the service of the good, the classic Western hero transformed the gross tangibles of the expansionist drive (land, cattle, gold) into a principle of moral order. The gangster, by contrast, is a figure of chaos, a modern, urban person, and in the critic Robert Warshow's formulation he functions as a discordant element in an American society devoted to a compulsively "positive" outlook. When the gangster dies, he cleanses viewers of their own negative feelings.

High-school movies are also full of unease and odd, mixed-up emotions. They may be flimsy in conception; they may be shot in lollipop colors, garlanded with mediocre pop scores, and cast with goofy young actors trying to make an impression. Yet this most commercial and frivolous of genres harbors a grievance against the world. It's a very specific grievance, quite different from the restless anger of such fifties adolescent-rebellion movies as "The Wild One," in which someone asks Marlon Brando's biker "What are you rebelling against?" and the biker replies "What have you got?" The fifties teen outlaw was against anything that adults considered sacred. But no movie teenager now revolts against adult authority, for the simple reason that adults have no authority. Teachers are rarely more than a minimal, exasperated presence, administrators get turned into a joke, and parents are either absent or distantly benevolent. It's a teen world, bounded by school, mall, and car, with occasional moments set in the fast-food outlets where the kids work, or in the kids' upstairs bedrooms, with their pin-ups and rack stereo systems. The enemy is not authority; the enemy is other teens and the social system that they impose on one another.

The bad feeling in these movies may strike grownups as peculiar. After all, from a distance American kids appear to be having it easy these days. The teen audience is facing a healthy job market; at home, their parents are stuffing the den with computers and the garage with a bulky S.U.V. But most teens aren't thinking about the future job market. Lost in the eternal swoon of late adolescence, they're thinking about their identity, their friends, and their clothes. Adolescence is the present-tense moment in American life. Identity and status are fluid: abrupt, devastating reversals are always possible. (In a teen movie, a guy who swallows a bucket of cafeteria coleslaw can make himself a hero in an instant.) In these movies, accordingly, the senior prom is the equivalent of the shoot-out at the O.K. Corral; it's the moment when one's worth as a human being is settled at last. In the rather pedestrian new comedy "Never Been Kissed," Drew Barrymore, as a twenty-five-year-old newspaper reporter, goes back to high school pretending to be a student, and immediately falls into her old, humiliating pattern of trying to impress the good-looking rich kids. Helplessly, she pushes for approval, and even gets herself chosen prom queen before finally coming to her senses. She finds it nearly impossible to let go.

Genre films dramatize not what happens but how things feel—the emotional coloring of memory. They fix subjectivity into fable. At actual schools, there is no unitary system of status; there are many groups to be a part of, many places to excel (or fail to excel), many avenues of escape and self-definition. And often the movies, too, revel in the arcana of high-school cliques. In last summer's "Disturbing Behavior," a veteran student lays out the cafeteria ethnography for a newcomer: Motorheads, Blue Ribbons, Skaters, Microgeeks ("drug of choice: Stephen Hawking's 'A Brief History of Time' and a cup of jasmine tea on Saturday night"). Subjectively, though, the social system in "Disturbing Behavior" (a high-school version of "The Stepford Wives") and in the other movies still feels coercive and claustrophobic: humiliation is the most vivid emotion of youth, so in memory it becomes the norm.

The movies try to turn the tables. The kids who cannot be the beautiful ones, or make out with them, or avoid being insulted by them—these are the heroes of the teen movies, the third in the trio of character types. The female outsider is usually an intellectual or an artist. (She scribbles in a diary, she draws or paints.) Physically awkward, she walks like a seal crossing a beach, and is prone to drop her books and dither in terror when she stands before a handsome boy. Her clothes, which ignore mall fashion, scandalize the social queens. Like them, she has a tongue, but she's tart and grammatical, tending toward feminist pungency and precise diction. She may mask her sense of vulnerability with sarcasm or with Plathian rue (she's stuck in the bell jar), but even when she lashes out she can't hide her craving for acceptance.

The male outsider, her friend, is usually a mass of stuttering or giggling sexual gloom: he wears shapeless clothes; he has an undeveloped body, either stringy or shrimpy; he's sometimes a Jew (in these movies, still the generic outsider). He's also brilliant, but in a morose, preoccupied way that suggests masturbatory absorption in some arcane system of knowledge. In a few special cases, the outsider is not a loser but a disengaged hipster, either saintly or satanic. (Christian Slater has played this role a couple of times.) This outsider wears black and keeps his hair long, and he knows how to please women. He sees through everything, so he's ironic by temperament and genuinely indifferent to the opinion of others—a natural aristocrat, who transcends the school's contemptible status system. There are whimsical variations on the outsider figure, too. In the recent "Rushmore," an obnoxious teen hero, Max Fischer (Jason Schwartzman), runs the entire school: he can't pass his courses but he's a dynamo at extracurricular activities, with a knack for staging extraordinary events. He's a con man, a fundraiser, an entrepreneur—in other words, a contemporary artist.

In fact, the entire genre, which combines self-pity and ultimate vindication, might be called "Portrait of the Filmmaker as a Young Nerd." Who can doubt where Hollywood's twitchy, nearsighted writers and directors ranked—or feared they ranked—on the high-school totem pole? They are still angry, though occasionally the target of their resentment goes beyond the jocks and cheerleaders of their youth. Consider this anomaly: the young actors and models on the covers of half the magazines published in this country, the shirtless men with chests like burnished shields, the girls smiling, glowing, tweezed, full-lipped, full-breasted (but not too full), and with skin so honeyed that it seems lacquered—these are the physical ideals embodied by the villains of the teen movies. The social queens and jocks, using their looks to dominate others, represent an American barbarism of beauty. Isn't it possible that the detestation of them in teen movies is a veiled strike at the entire abs-hair advertising culture, with its unobtainable glories of perfection? A critic of consumerism might even see a spark of revolt in these movies. But only a spark.

My guess is that these films arise from remembered hurts which then get recast in symbolic form. For instance, a surprising number of the outsider heroes have no mother. Mom has died or run off with another man; her child, only half loved, is ill equipped for the emotional pressures of school. The motherless child, of course, is a shrewd commercial ploy that makes a direct appeal to the members of the audience, many of whom may feel like outsiders, too, and unloved, or not loved enough, or victims of some prejudice or exclusion. But the motherless child also has powers, and will someday be a success, an artist, a screenwriter. It's the wound and the bow all over again, in cargo pants.

As the female nerd attracts the attention of the handsomest boy in the senior class, the teen movie turns into a myth of social reversal—a Cinderella fantasy. Initially, his interest in her may be part of a stunt or a trick: he is leading her on, perhaps at the urging of his queenly girlfriend. But his gaze lights her up, and we see how attractive she really is. Will she fulfill the eternal American fantasy that you can vault up the class system by removing your specs? She wants her prince, and by degrees she wins him over, not just with her looks but with her superior nature, her essential goodness. In the male version of the Cinderella trip, a few years go by, and a pale little nerd (we see him at a reunion) has become rich. All that poking around with chemicals paid off. Max Fischer, of "Rushmore," can't miss being richer than Warhol.

So the teen movie is wildly ambivalent. It may attack the consumerist ethos that produces winners and losers, but in the end it confirms what it is attacking. The girls need the seal of approval conferred by the converted jocks; the nerds need money and a girl. Perhaps it's no surprise that the outsiders can be validated only by the people who ostracized them. But let's not be too schematic: the outsider who joins the system also modifies it, opens it up to the creative power of social mobility, makes it bend and laugh, and perhaps this turn of events is not so different from the way things work in the real world, where merit and achievement stand a good chance of trumping appearance. The irony of the Littleton shootings is that Klebold and Harris, who were both proficient computer heads, seemed to have forgotten how the plot turns out. If they had held on for a few years they might have been working at a hip software company, or have started their own business, while the jocks who oppressed them would probably have wound up selling insurance or used cars. That's the one unquestionable social truth the teen movies reflect: geeks rule.

There is, of course, a menacing subgenre, in which the desire for revenge turns bloody. Thirty-one years ago, Lindsay Anderson's semi-surrealistic "If ..." was set in an oppressive, class-ridden English boarding school, where a group of rebellious students drive the school population out into a courtyard and open fire on them with machine guns. In Brian De Palma's 1976 masterpiece "Carrie," the pale, repressed heroine, played by Sissy Spacek, is courted at last by a handsome boy but gets violated—doused with pig's blood—just as she is named prom queen. Stunned but far from powerless, Carrie uses her telekinetic powers to set the room afire and burn down the school. "Carrie" is the primal school movie, so wildly lurid and funny that it exploded the clichés of the genre before the genre was quite set: the heroine may be a wrathful avenger, but the movie, based on a Stephen King book, was clearly a grinning-gargoyle fantasy. So, at first, was "Heathers," in which Christian Slater's satanic outsider turns out to be a true devil. He and his girlfriend (played by a very young Winona Ryder) begin gleefully knocking off the rich, nasty girls and the jocks, in ways so patently absurd that their revenge seems a mere wicked dream. I think it's unlikely that these movies had a direct effect on the actions of the Littleton shooters, but the two boys would surely have recognized the emotional world of "Heathers" and "Disturbing Behavior" as their own. It's a place where feelings of victimization join fantasy, and you experience the social élites as so powerful that you must either become them or kill them.

But enough. It's possible to make teen movies that go beyond these fixed polarities—insider and outsider, blond-bitch queen and hunch-shouldered nerd. In Amy Heckerling's 1995 comedy "Clueless," the big blonde played by Alicia Silverstone is a Rodeo Drive clotheshorse who is nonetheless possessed of extraordinary virtue. Freely dispensing advice and help, she's almost ironically good—a designing goddess with a cell phone. The movie offers a sunshiny satire of Beverly Hills affluence, which it sees as both absurdly swollen and generous in spirit. The most original of the teen comedies, "Clueless" casts away self-pity. So does "Romy and Michele's High School Reunion" (1997), in which two gabby, lovable friends, played by Mira Sorvino and Lisa Kudrow, review the banalities of their high-school experience so knowingly that they might be criticizing the teen-movie genre itself. And easily the best American film of the year so far is Alexander Payne's "Election," a high-school movie that inhabits a different aesthetic and moral world altogether from the rest of these pictures. "Election" shreds everyone's fantasies and illusions in a vision of high school that is bleak but supremely just. The movie's villain, an overachieving girl (Reese Witherspoon) who runs for class president, turns out to be its covert heroine, or, at least, its most poignant character. A cross between Pat and Dick Nixon, she's a lower-middle-class striver who works like crazy and never wins anyone's love. Even when she's on top, she feels excluded. Her loneliness is produced not by malicious cliques but by her own implacable will, a condition of the spirit that may be as comical and tragic as it is mysterious. "Election" escapes all the clichés; it graduates into art.

---

## This Text: Reading

1. David Denby is a middle-aged man who writes for *The New Yorker*, which is to say, he may not be as intimately familiar with the teen experience as you. Is his reading of teen life in the late 1990s accurate?
2. Why does Denby like *Election* better than the other films he mentions? What does it do that the others do not? Would a 16-year-old girl from the suburbs agree with Denby? Why or why not? What about an Hispanic or American Indian male—are they likely to appreciate the same movies as Denby?
3. What about recent movies like *Save the Last Dance* or *Crazy Beautiful*? How would they fit into Denby's schema?

### YOUR TEXT: WRITING

1. Write an essay in which you argue that a certain movie is the "best teen film." What criteria would you use? (Don't use more than three.)
2. Write an essay on a recent teen movie like *Save the Last Dance, Crazy Beautiful,* or *American Pie*. How do these movies reflect American values? Would a real teenager make a different movie?
3. Write a compare/contrast essay in which you look at a recent teen movie and one from the '50s. How are they similar? Different?

## CLASS AND VIRTUE

Michael Parenti

A long-time critic of contemporary media, Parenti suggests how and why Hollywood movies reinforce class distinctions in American society. Drawing from several types of movies, Parenti's argumentative essay (1992) claims that American movies support the virtues of the upper class.

THE ENTERTAINMENT MEDIA present working people not only as unlettered and uncouth but also as less desirable and less moral than other people. Conversely, virtue is more likely to be ascribed to those characters whose speech and appearance are soundly middle- or upper-middle class.

Even a simple adventure story like *Treasure Island* (1934, 1950, 1972) manifests this implicit class perspective. There are two groups of acquisitive persons searching for a lost treasure. One, headed by a squire, has money enough to hire a ship and crew. The other, led by the rascal Long John Silver, has no money—so they sign up as part of the crew. The narrative implicitly assumes from the beginning that the squire has a moral claim to the treasure, while Long John Silver's gang does not. After all, it is the squire who puts up the venture capital for the ship. Having no investment in the undertaking other than their labor, Long John and his men, by definition, will be "stealing" the treasure, while the squire will be "discovering" it.

To be sure, there are other differences. Long John's men are cutthroats. The squire is not. Yet, one wonders if the difference between a bad pirate and a good squire is itself not preeminently a matter of having the right amount of disposable income. The squire is no less acquisitive than the conspirators. He just does with money what they must achieve with cutlasses. The squire and his associates dress in fine clothes, speak an educated diction, and drink brandy. Long John and his men dress slovenly, speak in guttural accents, and drink rum. From these indications alone, the viewer knows who are the good guys and who are the bad. Virtue is visually measured by one's approximation to proper class appearances.

Sometimes class contrasts are juxtaposed within one person, as in *The Three Faces of Eve* (1957), a movie about a woman who suffers from multiple personalities. When we first meet Eve (Joanne Woodward), she is a disturbed, strongly repressed, puritanically religious person, who speaks with a rural, poor-Southern accent. Her second personality is that of a wild, flirtatious woman who also speaks with a rural, poor-Southern accent. After much treatment by her psychiatrist, she is cured of these schizoid personalities and emerges with a healthy third one, the real Eve, a poised, self-possessed, pleasant woman. What is intriguing is that she now speaks with a cultivated, affluent, Smith College accent, free of any low-income regionalism or ruralism, much like Joanne Woodward herself. This transformation in class style and speech is used to indicate mental health without any awareness of the class bias thusly expressed.

Mental health is also the question in *A Woman Under the Influence* (1974), the story of a disturbed woman who is married to a hard-hat husband. He cannot handle—and inadvertently contributes to—her emotional deterioration. She is victimized by a spouse who is nothing more than an insensitive, working-class bull in a china shop. One comes away convinced that every unstable woman needs a kinder, gentler, and above all, more middle-class hubby if she wishes to avoid a mental crack-up.

Class prototypes abound in the 1980s television series *The A-Team*. In each episode, a Vietnam-era commando unit helps an underdog, be it a Latino immigrant or a disabled veteran, by vanquishing some menacing force such as organized crime, a business competitor, or corrupt government officials. As always with the make-believe media, the A-Team does good work on an individualized rather than collectively organized basis, helping particular victims by thwarting particular villains. The A-Team's leaders are two white males of privileged background. The lowest ranking members of the team, who do none of the thinking or the leading, are working-class palookas. They show they are good with their hands, both by punching out the bad guys and by doing the maintenance work on the team's flying vehicles and cars. One of them, "B.A." (bad ass), played by the African-American Mr. T., is visceral, tough, and purposely bad-mannered toward those he doesn't like. He projects an image of crudeness and ignorance and is associated with the physical side of things. In sum, the team has a brain (the intelligent white leaders) and a body with its simpler physical functions (the working-class characters), a hierarchy that corresponds to the social structure itself.[1]

Sometimes class bigotry is interwoven with gender bigotry, as in *Pretty Woman* (1990). A dreamboat millionaire corporate raider finds himself all alone for an extended stay in Hollywood (his girlfriend is unwilling to join him), so he quickly recruits a beautiful prostitute as his playmate of the month. She is paid three thousand dollars a week to wait around his superposh hotel penthouse ready to perform the usual services and accompany him to business dinners at top restaurants. As prostitution goes, it is a dream gig. But there is one cloud on the horizon. She is low-class. She doesn't know which fork to use at those CEO power feasts, and she's bothersomely fidgety, wears tacky clothes, chews gum, and, y'know, doesn't talk so good. But with some tips from the hotel manager, she proves to be a veritable Eliza Doolittle in her class metamorphosis. She dresses in proper attire, sticks the gum away forever, and starts picking the right utensils at dinner. She also figures out how to speak a little more like Joanne Woodward without the benefit of a multiple personality syndrome, and she develops the capacity to sit in a poised, wordless, empty-headed fashion, every inch the expensive female ornament.

She is still a prostitute but a classy one. It is enough of a distinction for the handsome young corporate raider. Having liked her because she was charmingly cheap, he now loves her all the more because she has real polish and is a more suitable companion. So suitable that he decides to do the right thing by her: set her up in an apartment so he can make regular visits at regular prices. But now she wants the better things in life, like marriage, a nice house, and, above all, a different occupation, one that would allow her to use less of herself. She is furious at him for treating her like, well, a prostitute. She decides to give up her profession and get a high-school diploma so that she might make a better life for herself—perhaps as a filing clerk or receptionist or some other of the entry-level jobs awaiting young women with high school diplomas.[2]

After the usual girl-breaks-off-with-boy scenes, the millionaire prince returns. It seems he can't concentrate on making money without her. He even abandons his cutthroat schemes and enters into a less lucrative but supposedly more productive, canny business venture with a struggling old-time entrepreneur. The bad capitalist is transformed into a good capitalist. He then carries off his ex-prostitute for a lifetime of bliss. The moral is a familiar one, updated for post-Reagan yuppiedom: A woman can escape from economic and gender exploitation by winning the love and career advantages offered by a rich male. Sexual allure goes only so far unless it develops a material base and becomes a class act.[3]

## Notes

1. Gina Marchetti, "Class, Ideology and Commercial Television: An Analysis of *The A-Team*," *Journal of Film and Video*, 39, Spring 1987, pp. 19–28.
2. See the excellent review by Lydia Sargent, *Z Magazine*, April 1990, pp. 43–45.
3. *Ibid.*

---

## This Text: Reading

1. Parenti's examples may seem a bit dated to you, though you have probably seen *Pretty Woman*. Can you think of more recent examples of classist and sexist films?

2. Find Parenti's thesis statement. *Hint:* He hits you with it right off the bat. Do you agree with his contention about Hollywood?
3. How do Parenti's claims resemble some of the issues raised by the Literature Suite on class in Chapter 1?

### YOUR TEXT: WRITING

1. *Sling Blade* is a fairly popular movie that deals with issues of class. Write an essay on *Sling Blade, The Full Monty, Titanic* or some other movie that foregrounds class tensions. How does Hollywood deal with class? Is that different than the way an independent film might approach class?
2. *Pretty Woman* bears a strong resemblance to *Cinderella,* which is also about class. Write an essay in which you explore the links between gender and class. Are issues of power involved?
3. Write a comparative essay in which you compare a film and a short story or poem in terms of what each has to say about social and economic class.

## MOCK FEMINISM: *WAITING TO EXHALE*

bell hooks

Taken from her provocative book *Reel to Reel: Race, Sex, and Class at the Movies*, bell hooks' essay (1996) offers a reading of the popular movie *Waiting to Exhale*. Unlike most reviews that praised the film for its depiction of black women, hooks' review charges the film merely masks harmful stereotypes.

IN THE PAST A BLACK FILM was usually seen as a film by a black filmmaker focusing on some aspect of black life. More recently the "idea" of a "black film" has been appropriated as a way to market films that are basically written and produced by white people as though they in act represent and offer us—"authentic" blackness. It does not matter that progressive black filmmakers and critics challenge essentialist notions of black authenticity, even going so far as to rethink and interrogate the notion of black film. These groups do not have access to the levels of marketing and publicity that can repackage authentic blackness commodified and sell it as the "real" thing. This was certainly the case with the marketing and publicity for the film *Waiting to Exhale.*

When Kevin Costner produced and starred in the film *The Bodyguard* with Whitney Houston as co-star, the film focused on a black family. No one ever thought to market it as a black film. Indeed, many black people refused to see the film because they were so disgusted by this portrayal of interracial love. No one showed much curiosity about the racial identity of the screenwriters or for that matter, anybody behind the scenes of this film. It was not seen as having any importance, for black women by the white-dominated mass media. Yet *Waiting to Exhale*'s claim to blackness, and black authenticity, is almost as dubious as any such claim being made about *The Bodyguard*. However, that claim could be easily made because a black woman writer wrote the book on which the movie was based. The hiring of a fledgling black director received no critical comment. Everyone behaved as though it was just normal Hollywood practice to offer the directorship of a major big-budget Hollywood film to someone who might not know what they are doing.

The screenplay was written by a white man, but if we are to believe everything we read in newspapers and popular magazines, Terry McMillan assisted with the writing. Of course, having her name tacked onto the writing process was a great way to protect the film from the critique that its "authentic blackness" was somehow undermined by white-male interpretation. Alice Walker had no such luck when her book *The Color Purple* was made into a movie by Steven Spielberg. No one thought this was a black film. And very few viewers were surprised that what we saw on the screen had little relationship to Alice Walker's novel.

Careful publicity and marketing ensured that *Waiting to Exhale* would not be subjected to these critiques; all acts of appropriation were carefully hidden behind the labeling of this film as authentically a black woman's story. Before anyone could become upset that a black woman was not hired to direct the film, McMillan told the world in *Movieland* magazine that those experienced black women directors in Hollywood just were not capable of doing the job. She made the same critique of the black woman writer who was initially hired to write the screenplay. From all accounts (most of them given by the diva herself) it appears that Terry McMillan is the only competent black woman on the Hollywood scene and she just recently arrived.

It's difficult to know what is more disturbing: McMillan's complicity with the various acts of white supremacist capitalist patriarchal cultural appropriation that resulted in a film as lightweight and basically bad as *Waiting to Exhale*, or the public's passive celebratory consumption of this trash as giving the real scoop about black women's lives. Some bad films are at least entertaining. This was just an utterly boring show. That masses of black women could be cajoled by mass media coverage and successful seductive marketing (the primary ploy being that this is the first film ever that four black women have been the major stars of a Hollywood film) to embrace this cultural product was a primary indication that this is not a society where moviegoers are encouraged to think critically about what they see on the screen.

When a film that's basically about the trials and tribulations of four professional heterosexual black women who are willing to do anything to get and keep a man is offered as a "feminist" narrative, it's truly a testament to the power of the mainstream to co-opt progressive social movements and strip them of all political meaning through a series of contemptuous ridiculous representations. Terry McMillan's novel *Waiting to Exhale* was not a feminist book and it was not transformed into a feminist film. It did not even become a film that made use of any of the progressive politics around race and gender that was evoked however casually in the novel itself.

The film *Waiting to Exhale* took the novelistic images of professional black women concerned with issues of racial uplift and gender equality and turned them into a progression of racist, sexist stereotypes that features happy darkies who are all singing, dancing, fucking, and having a merry old time even in the midst of sad times and tragic moments. What we saw on the screen was not black women talking about love or the meaning of partnership and marriage in their lives. We saw four incredibly glamorous women obsessed with getting a man, with status, material success and petty competition with other women (especially white women). In the book one of the women, Gloria, owns a beauty parlor; she is always, always working, which is what happens when you run a small business. In the movie, girlfriend hardly ever works because she is too busy cooking tantalizing meals for the neighbor next door. In this movie food is on her mind and she forgets all about work, except for an occasional phone call to see how everything is going. Let's not forget the truly fictive utopian moment in this film that occurs when Bernie goes to court divorcing her husband and wins tons of money. This is so in the book as well. Funny though, the novel ends with her giving the money away, highlighting her generosity and her politics. McMillan writes: "She also wouldn't have to worry about selling the house now. But Bernadine wasn't taking that fucker off the market. She'd drop the price. And she'd send a nice check to the United Negro College Fund, something she'd always wanted to do. She'd help feed some of those kids in Africa she'd seen on TV at night ... Maybe she'd send some change to the Urban League and the NAACP and she'd definitely help out some of those programs that BWOTM [Black Women on the MOVE] had been trying to get off the ground for the last hundred years. At the rate she was going, Bernadine had already given away over a million dollars." Definitely not a "material girl." It would have taken only one less scene of pleasure fucking for audiences to have witnessed Bernie writing these checks with a nice voice-over. But, alas, such an image might have ruined the racist, sexist stereotype of black women being hard, angry, and just plain greedy. No doubt the writers of the screenplay felt these "familiar" stereotypes would guarantee the movie its crossover appeal.

Concurrently, no doubt it helps that crossover appeal to set up stereotypically racist, sexist conflicts between white women and black women (where if we are to believe the logic of the film, the white woman gets "her" black man in the end). Let's remember. In the novel the movie is based on, only one black man declares his love for a white woman. The man Bernie meets, the lawyer James, is thinking of divorcing his white wife, who is dying of cancer, but he loyally stays with her until her death, even though he makes it very clear that the love has long since left their marriage.

Declaring his undying love for Bernie, James moves across the country to join her, sets up a law practice, and gets involved with "a coalition to stop the liquor board from allowing so many liquor stores in the black community." Well, not in this movie! The screen character James declares undying love for his sick white wife. Check out the difference between the letter he writes in the novel. Here is an excerpt: "I know you probably thought that night was just something frivolous but like I told you before I left, it meant more to me than that. Much more. I buried my wife back in August, and for her sake, I'm glad she's not suffering anymore ... I want to see you again, Bernadine, and not for another one-nighter, either. If there's any truth to what's known as a 'soul mate,' then you're as close to it as I've ever come ... I'm not interested in playing games, or starting something I can't finish. I play for keeps, and I'm not some dude just out to have a good time ... I knew I was in love with you long before we ever turned the key to that hotel room." The image of black masculinity that comes through in this letter is that of a man of integrity who is compassionate, in touch with his feelings, and able to take responsibility for his actions.

In the movie version of *Waiting to Exhale*, no black man involved with a black woman possesses these qualities. In contrast to what happens in the book, in the film, James does not have a one-nighter with Bernie, because he is depicted as utterly devoted to his white wife. Here are relevant passages from the letter he writes to Bernie that audiences hear at the movie: "What I feel for you has never undercut the love I have for my wife. How is that possible? I watch her everyday. So beautiful and brave. I just want to give her everything I've got in me. Every moment. She's hanging on, fighting to be here for me. And when she sleeps, I cry. Over how amazing she is, and how lucky I've been to have her in my life." There may not have been any white women as central characters in this film, but this letter certainly places the dying white wife at the center of things. Completely rewriting the letter that appears in the novel, which only concerns James's love and devotion to Bernie, so that the white wife (dead in the book but brought back to life onscreen) is the recipient of James's love was no doubt another ploy to reach the crossover audience: the masses of white women consumers that might not have been interested in this film if it had really been about black women.

Ultimately, only white women have committed relationships with black men in the film. Not only do these screen images reinforce stereotypes, the screenplay was written in such a way as to actively perpetuate them. Catfights between women, both real and symbolic, were clearly seen by the screenwriters as likely to be more entertaining to moviegoing audiences than the portrayal of a divorced black woman unexpectedly meeting her true love—an honest, caring, responsible, mature, tender, and loving black man who delivers the goods. Black women are portrayed as so shrewish in this film that Lionel's betrayal of Bernie appears to be no more than an act of self-defense. The film suggests that Lionel is merely trying to get away from the black bitch who barges in on him at work and physically attacks his meek and loving white wife. To think that Terry McMillan was one of the screenwriters makes it all the more disheartening. Did she forget that she had written a far more emotionally complex and progressive vision of black female-male relationships in her novel?

While we may all know some over-thirty black women who are desperate to get a man by any means necessary and plenty of young black females who fear that they may never find a man and are willing to be downright foolish in their pursuit of one, the film was so simplistic and denigrating in its characterization of black womanhood that everyone should be outraged to be told that it is "for us." Or worse yet, as a reporter wrote in *Newsweek*, "This is our million man march." Whether you supported the march or not (and I did not, for many of the same reasons I find this film appalling), let's get this straight: We are being told, and are telling ourselves that black men need a political march and black women need a movie. Mind you—not a political film but one where the black female "stars" spend most of their time chainsmoking themselves to death (let's not forget that Gloria did not have enough breath to blow out her birthday candle) and drowning their sorrows in alcohol. No doubt McMillan's knowledge of how many black people die from lung cancer and alcoholism influenced her decision to write useful, unpreachy critiques of these addictions in her novel. In the novel the characters who smoke are trying to stop and Black Women on the Move are fighting to close down liquor stores. None of these actions fulfill racist fantasies. It's no accident that just the opposite images appear on the screen. Smoking is so omnipresent in every scene that many of us were waiting to see a promotional credit for the tobacco industry.

Perhaps the most twisted and perverse aspect of this film is the way it was marketed as being about girlfriend bonding. How about that scene where Robin shares her real-life trauma with Savannah, who is busy looking the other way and simply does not respond. Meaningful girlfriend bonding is not about the codependency that is imaged in this film. At its best *Waiting to Exhale* is a film about black women helping each other to stay stuck. Do we really believe that moment when Savannah rudely disses Kenneth (even though the film has in no way constructed him as a lying cheating dog) to be a moment of profound "feminist" awakening. Suddenly audiences are encouraged to believe that she realizes the dilemmas of being involved with a married man, even one who has filed for a divorce. Why not depict a little mature communication between a black man and a black woman. No doubt that too would not have been entertaining to crossover audiences. Better to give them what they are used to, stereotypical representations of black males as always and only lying, cheating dogs (that is, when they are involved with black women) and professional black women as wild, irrational, castrating bitch goddesses.

Nothing was more depressing than hearing individual black women offering personal testimony that these shallow screen images are "realistic portrayals" of their experience. If this is the world of black gender relations as they know it, no wonder black men and women are in serious crisis. Obviously, it is difficult for many straight black women to find black male partners and/or husbands. Though it is hard to believe that black women as conventionally feminine, beautiful, glamorous, and just plain dumb as the girlfriends in this film can't get men (Bernie has an MBA, helped start the business, but is clueless about everything that concerns money; Robin is willing to have unsafe sex and celebrate an unplanned pregnancy with a partner who may be a drug addict; Gloria, who would rather cook food for her man any day than go to work; Savannah has sex at the drop of a hat, even when she does not want to get involved). In the real world these are the women who have men standing in line.

However, if they and other black women internalize the messages in *Waiting to Exhale* they will come to their senses and see that, according to the film, black men are really undesirable mates for black women. Actually, lots of younger black women, and their over-thirty counterparts, go to see *Waiting to Exhale* to have their worst fears affirmed: that black men are irresponsible and uncaring; that black women, no matter how attractive, will still be hurt and abandoned, and that ultimately they will probably be alone and unloved. Perhaps it feels less like cultural genocide to have these messages of self-loathing and disempowerment brought to them by four beautiful black female "stars."

Black women seeking to learn anything about gender relationships from this film will be more empowered if we identify with the one black female character who rarely speaks. She is the graceful, attractive, brown-skinned lawyer with naturally braided hair who is a professional who knows her job and is also able to bond emotionally with her clients. Not only does she stand for gender justice (the one glimpse of empowering feminist womanhood we see in this film), she achieves that end without ever putting men down or competing with any woman. While we never see her with a male partner, she acts with confident self-esteem and shows fulfillment in a job well done.

The monetary success of a trashy film like *Waiting to Exhale*, with its heavy sentimentality and predicable melodrama shows that Hollywood recognizes that blackness as a commodity can be exploited to bring in the bucks. Dangerously, it also shows that the same old racist/sexist stereotypes can be appropriated and served up to the public in a new and more fashionable disguise. While it serves the financial interests of Hollywood and McMillan's own bank account for her to deflect away from critiques that examine the politics underlying these representations and their behind-the-scenes modes of production by ways of witty assertions that the novel and the film are "forms of entertainment, not anthropological studies," in actuality the creators of this film are as accountable for their work as their predecessors. Significantly, contemporary critiques of racial essentialism completely disrupt the notion that anything a black artist creates is inherently radical, progressive, or more likely to reflect a break with white supremacist representations. It has become most evident that as black artists seek a "crossover" success, the representations they create usually mirror dominant stereotypes. After a barrage of publicity and marketing that encouraged black people, and black women in particular, to see *Waiting to Exhale* as fictive ethnography, McMillan is being more than a bit disingenuous when she suggests that the film should not be seen this way. In her essay, "Who's Doin' the Twist: Notes Toward a Politics of Appropriation," cultural critic Coco Fusco reminds us that we must continually critique this genre in both its pure and impure forms. "Ethnographic cinema, in light of its historical connection to colonialist adventurism, and decades of debate about the ethics of representing documentary subjects, is a genre that demands a special degree of scrutiny." Just because writers and directors are black does not exempt them from scrutiny. The black female who wrote a letter to the *New York Times* calling attention to the way this film impedes the struggle to create new images of blackness on the screen was surely right when she insisted that had everyone involved in the production of this film been white and male, its blatantly racist and sexist standpoints would not have gone unchallenged.

---

## THIS TEXT: READING

1. At first, you might find hooks overly critical of *Waiting to Exhale*. But are her contentions reasonable? Does she make sense? Why? Why not?
2. What political and cultural forces are influencing her review of the film? Or, what can you glean about her political leanings from her review? What is hooks' writing situation?
3. Do you agree with hooks that a seemingly harmless film like *Waiting to Exhale* is culturally dangerous?

## YOUR TEXT: WRITING

1. Write your own review of *Waiting to Exhale*. Do you focus on the representations of gender, or are you more interested in plot and character development?
2. Compare *Waiting to Exhale* with *How Stella Got Her Groove Back*. Both movies are adaptations of Terry McMillan novels. How are the films similar? How are they different? How does the film version depart from the novel?
3. Write a personal essay in which you analyze Hollywood representations of *your* gender and ethnicity. For instance, if you are a Hispanic male, write an essay in which you analyze how Hispanic males are represented in movies. What do you notice?
4. Write a comparative paper analyzing what hooks has to say about women in *Waiting to Exhale* with the Suite in Chapter 6. How do women define representations of women?

# HOLY HOMOSEXUALITY BATMAN!: CAMP AND CORPORATE CAPITALISM IN *BATMAN FOREVER*

Freya Johnson

Both intellectually challenging and humorously insightful, Johnson's surprisingly candid essay (1995) sheds light on the semiotics of gayness in the popular movie *Batman Forever*. Is Johnson reading too much into the film, or are American audiences not reading enough into it? Johnson's essay and our own reaction to it and the movie may allow an interesting reading of sexual orientation and American culture.

> Only someone ignorant of the fundamentals of psychiatry and the psychopathology of sex can fail to realize a subtle atmosphere of homoeroticism which pervades the adventure of the mature "Batman" and his young friend "Robin."
>
> —*Frederic Wertham,* Seduction of the Innocent

SO PSYCHIATRIST FREDERIC WERTHAM warned parents and lawmakers in 1953, as he detailed the "factually proven" method by which comic books turned innocent children into homosexually and pederastically inclined "deviants and perverts." In this hilariously paranoiac document of homophobic panic, he unwittingly anticipates queer theoretical practice as he ransacks the comics for "clues" (nowadays we call them "signifiers") revealing the homoeroticism leaking from the pages of the books into impressionable pre-pubescent brains. Sure enough, his spot-the-homo routine reveals Bruce Wayne and "Dick" Grayson (Wertham supplies the snide quotation marks) enacting "the wish dream of two homosexuals living together" as Wertham presents this condemning evidence:

> Sometimes Batman ends up in bed injured and young Robin is shown sitting next to him. At home they lead an idyllic life. They are Bruce Wayne and "Dick" Grayson. Bruce is described as a "socialite" and the official relationship is that Dick is Bruce's ward. They live in sumptuous quarters, with beautiful flowers in large vases, and have a butler, Alfred. Batman is sometimes shown in a dressing gown ...

Obviously, they *must* be fags: otherwise they'd have a butler named "Butch," live in cramped quarters littered with beer-cans, wouldn't show concern for one another's injuries or be caught dead in a dressing gown and cultivate only (what?) cactuses in small ugly metal pots?

More damning than the flowers and dressing gowns, however, is that the "muscular male supertype whose primary sex characteristics are usually well emphasized, is in the setting of certain stories the object of homoerotic sexual curiosity and stimulation." In that case, one can easily imagine a now-decrepit Wertham feverishly taking notes in the back of the theater when Dick dons his Robin costume in *Batman Forever* and the camera lovingly focuses on what looks like a glowing violet dildo showing through the codpiece of his uniform. "We're not just friends," says Dick, "we're partners"; the next shot is the dynamic duo's clasped hands. Indeed, queer signification so saturates *Batman Forever* that it would be inaccurate to call it a subtext. With his earring, haircut and leather jacket Chris O'Donnell looks like he's just come straight from an ACT UP meeting, while Val Kilmer's body is exposed and eroticized only in the scenes with O'Donnell (as he wanders out of the shower bare-chested in towel, is treated for injuries, or puts on the new bat-suit while the image of his butt-cleavage fills the screen). During the sterile "love-scenes" with Nicole Kidman he remains fully clothed as the camera coyly pans down only as far as the top of his chest at most: her body entirely escapes the emblematic "male gaze" of cinema and her breasts or legs never once fill the screen.

How did director Joel Schumacher get away with turning loose so many queer signifiers to float freely about in Warner Brothers' biggest asset? By turning the queer *sub*text hidden beneath the surface of many Batman representations into an overtly queer *supra*text that goes right over the head of the mainstream viewing audience. Although Batman and Robin are shrieking "queer," Jim Carrey's Riddler (who even the willfully obtuse *National Review* managed to describe as "campy") is much much queerer. Yet because he's a villain, his prancing around in a diamond tiara and skin-tight green unitard exclaiming "Spank me!" doesn't offend the sensibilities of the homophobic mainstream McAudience: in fact, it draws their attention away from the homoerotic electricity between the heroes and invites the misreading "if the bad guy's gay, the good guys must be straight," while Two-Face's troops of thugs tricked out in now universally recognizable (thanks to *Pulp Fiction*) queer S&M gear help keep queerness and villainy aligned. And significantly, it's Ed Nygma's extreme reaction to his rejection by Bruce Wayne, a rejection that mimics a straight man's rejection of homosexual advances ("We're two of kind"; "You were supposed to understand," laments Ed), that drives him to criminality.

In fact the villains mirror and exaggerate the heroes in more than just homoerotics: their *raison d'être* also originates in some traumatic event that has irrevocably altered their lives—a correlation which is certainly no accident. Schumacher reports ignoring the previous Bat-films and looking instead to the original 1939–40's DC Batman comics to inspire *Batman Forever*, comics in which it's the villains' traumas that drive them to madness, crime and a quest for world domination. As Bill Botchel points out in *The Many Lives of the Batman* (1991), these villains, who share Bruce Wayne's status as respected members of society, enact the contemporaneous anxieties about fascism suffusing the culture during Batman's early years. They are similar to Bruce Wayne, perhaps, in the same way that American society is similar to a European fascist state (similar origins), yet the differences are oh-so-crucial as Wayne turns his trauma-forged obsessions toward upholding goodness and the democratic ideal while his opponents strive to become nightmarish versions of the Nazi *Übermensch*. This Democracy vs. Fascism conflict is retooled for *Batman Forever* and played out as Good Corporate Capitalism vs. Bad Corporate Capitalism.

We first hear of Bruce Wayne as the camera pans over the sunlit commercial district of Gotham City while a newscaster reports "Billionaire Bruce Wayne has extended his trend-setting profit-sharing program to the employees of the highly successful electronics division of Wayne Enterprises." Swooping inside Wayne's skyscraper (which is crowned with a massive statue of muscle-bound Atlas holding up the globe), we find him in the midst of a corporate walk-through, African-American woman exec by his side, benignly smiling on his employees who are working, we are told, on such projects as "fire remediation" and "alternative fuels." After listening politely to E. Nygma's psychotically enthusiastic presentation of his "brain-wave" device, he turns down the project on ethical grounds ("it just raises too many questions"), thanks the crew of employees, tells them the factory "looks great," and departs.

This benevolent democratic corporate capitalism (Wayne even extends "full benefits" to the widow of Nygma's first victim, despite the official verdict of suicide as cause-of-death) where workers share in the profits from projects which benefit society and ethical concerns are placed above marketing potential, is in direct contrast to Nygma's version of unbridled capitalist exploitation. Literalizing predatory capitalism (with start-up capital obtained by robbery, no less) his product actually *feeds* off the consumer, invading their minds and channeling their brain waves to the Riddler. His blissed-out expression and shuddering body as he absorbs these waves leaves no doubt that the thrill is sexual as well as intellectual. That the Riddler's corporate headquarters is topped with a giant Nygma-Box (in contrast to Wayne's Atlas) underscores the masturbatory self-consumption of "Bad Capitalism," and lest we miss this elision of malignant consumption with sexual perversion the Riddler lasciviously gloats to Batman during the film's penultimate scene that his new improved mind-reading version of the device will soon spread throughout the world, feeding him "credit card numbers, bank codes and sexual fantasies." (Also echoing, perhaps, the homophobic panic surrounding queer discourse "contaminating" mainstream culture and penetrating the sanctity of the home, which has many an irate PTA member screeching about the Internet's capacity to bring queer newsgroups and chatrooms into their child's bedroom.)

Since the Riddler aligns "Bad Capitalism" with "Bad Sexuality," it's hardly surprising to find that the film's proforma heteronormative narrative manifests when Wayne is performing his role of "Good Capitalist." His ethical rejection of Nygma's design is coded as sexual rejection, while his first meeting with Dr. Meridian for a "consultation" (wherein he refers to the riddle as a "love letter" and the sender as a "he") results in her being his date to the Circus opening-night extravaganza for Gotham's wealthy elite—his public performance of the ultra-successful business tycoon bound up with his performance of heterosexuality.

She again performs the date-function for Wayne at the capitalist debutante ball where the mind-reading version of the Nygma-Box is unveiled and Nygma usurps Wayne's media-appellation of "Gotham's most eligible bachelor," while also coopting his public manifestation and sporting identical glasses, suit, and haircut—mimicking Wayne right down to the mole on his cheek and the token woman on his arm. On loan from Two-Face and overtly ogling Wayne, Nygma's date is clearly for appearances sake only as is his dance with Dr. Meridian during which he openly camps it up, saucily flirting with Wayne and making it abundantly clear that the women are entirely ancillary to the coded transactions between the men. Although Wayne's "romance" with Dr. Meridian satisfies the plot-level demand for heteronormativity, its credibility is perpetually undermined by both its stock formulaicity and by the similarity of Wayne's supposed genuineness to Nygma's obvious self-conscious falsity.

But what is the pay-off of marketing this safely contained and topically sanitized Camp suitable for mass-consumption—"Bat-Camp" if you will—to the mainstream audience? In fact, Bat-Camp appears to be central to Warner Bros.'s carefully designed campaign to woo back its wavering corporate sponsors who were disconcerted by the darkness and violence of *Batman Returns*. Following the film's release angry parents' groups lashed out at the studio, licensees and promotional partners, prompting McDonald's Corp. (the largest and most desirable promo-partner) to change its film promotional strategy; retailers howled as Batman products languished on store shelves; and the film took in a disappointing $90 million less domestically than its predecessor. Clearly the studio needed to lighten up the film in order to entice wary licensees back to the table for a third course, and began by replacing director Tim Burton with Joel Schumacher (who's come a long way since his days as a window display designer). When Warner Bros.'s marketing mavens unveiled the new Batman characters to about 200 potential corporate sponsors thereby "setting the mood for *Batman Forever*," Schumacher was charged with convincingly presenting the transformation of the old Dark Knight into the new Bat Lite. Remarked one attendee, "It was lighthearted, particularly with Schumacher joking around. He said—and we could tell because he's very flamboyant—that it was going to be a more adventurous, entertaining Batman." Apparently this "flamboyance" paid off: Warner Bros. lined up a reported $45–$50 million worth of media money commitments from McDonald's, Kellogg's, Kenner Toys and others. Following in the tradition of the first comic books which debuted in 1933 not as commodities-in-themselves but as marketing devices—promotional giveaways and premiums for such companies as Proctor and Gamble,

Milk-O-Malt, and Kinney Shoe Stores—*Batman Forever* was conceived as much as a promotional vehicle for its corporate sponsors as a product in its own right.

Given the importance of the sub-teen market to the film's heavy-weight promo-partners and Schumacher's determination "not to have kids terrified" but instead to create a movie "light enough to be a living comic book," the deployment of Bat-Camp makes perfect marketing sense—theorists have long noted camp's appeal to children's sense of play, their love of exaggeration, and their consciousness of the gap between who they are and who they would like to pretend to be. And according to some, its irreverence toward gender difference and mockery of the extremes of femininity and masculinity titillates kids because it implicitly undermines the authority of parents who are seen to embody these constructions.

But Bat-Camp even goes one step further in converting what Susan Sontag once termed "a secret sensibility" into mass market symbolic currency. As well as being consciously about capitalism and consumption, *Batman Forever* self-consciously draws attention to its own status as a marketing vehicle and commodity, highlighting its own artificiality with playful irony and making reference to its position within the matrix of production and promotion surrounding the movie. With today's media-savvy audience who take the homoeconomic synergy among mega-corporations as a given, there is no need to disguise promotional relationships; instead, the film affectionately mocks these connections and flatters the audience by letting them in on the joke.

By the time the movie was released mid-June, everyone had seen the Batman McDonald's commercial (airing since May) in which Batman turns down his butler's offer of a sandwich with the line "No thanks—I'll get drive-through" before zooshing away in the Batmobile. But this was not just the standard commercial-inspired-by-feature-film: it was the actual first scene of the film, a revelation that had the audience giggling immediately. Just as camp highlights and mocks gender by exaggeration and reversal of gender-norms, "Campy Capitalism" does the same thing to its own constructions. That the movie opens with a commercial rather than the commercial spinning off from the movie draws attention to usually veiled marketing mechanisms by this reversal of the standard form in which commercial relationships are publicly represented, thereby reminding us of the film's artificiality at the moment when the viewer is traditionally called upon to exercise a willing suspension of disbelief. After this postmodern version of the invocation of the muse, even the "serious" moments in the film are given a possibly ironic valance. In other words, this nod to the viewer's knowledge of the film's status as a promotional vehicle invites the audience to participate in the movie's light-hearted irreverence toward itself.

When Nygma upbraids Two-Face for ostentatiously crashing his party without prior warning, his complaint that "We could have pre-sold the movie rights!" is as much the film's campy reference to its own well documented marketing strategies as it is Nygma's campy awareness of his strategy for marketing himself. Both the Wayne Enterprises logo that looks like Warner Bros.'s minus the "B," and the "GNN" news which replaces the generic newscasts of the previous movies, remind us of the fictional nature of the world inside the film by meta-commercial references to the world outside. Meanwhile, Dr. Meridian's sarcastic question to Batman "or do you prefer black leather and a whip?" does double discursive duty as an extra-textual reference to *Batman Returns* (and the heavily hyped Michelle Pfeiffer as Catwoman) as well as an internal reference to the fictive world of the three films for the sake of some nominal consistency.

But perhaps the most telling example of this commercial performativity is what *has* to be a corporate tie-in for The Club (because when a product fills the screen for several precious seconds in a big budget film it is *never* an accident—e.g., E.T.'s Reese's Pieces) in which Batman—who has just deployed some of his emblematic Batgadgets to penetrate concrete, scale a skyscraper, secure a plummeting multi-ton metal canister and harness a helicopter—is foiled when Two-Face snaps The Club onto the helicopter's steering wheel, thereby forcing him to evacuate. Whether this is a serious commercial suggestion that The Club is unassailable, or a parody of commercials suggesting The Club is unassailable, seems impossible to determine, and is ultimately unimportant. To the marketing-conscious consumer this spot may be taken as a refusal to patronize, a sharing of an in-joke, a kind of "Outing" of itself; with the unaware viewer it does the same work as a traditional irony-free commercial.

The movie's climactic scene, then, where Batman triumphantly tells the Riddler he had to save both Dr. Meridian and Robin because he is both Bruce Wayne and Batman, while allowing for a wistfully optimistic bisexual reading, can be taken as a metaphor for the film's campy marketing and marketing of camp—replacing polymorphous perversity with poly-commodified performativity, one might say. Although *Batman Forever* highlights its own commercial artifice, it carefully maintains its promotional earnestness beneath the veneer of irreverence: without the metatext we still have product tie-ins, commercial spin-offs, and a film custom designed for its corporate sponsors. The irony about promotion is, after all, for promotional purposes. And the film may be replete with queer signification, but the heteronormative narrative and over-the-top Riddler provide the homophobic viewer with just enough plausible deniability for the rumors that the Caped Crusaders are queers. So provided the queen is put safely back in his box in the end, the McAudience can tolerate him as a viable means of producing an appealing yet suitable kid's film without resorting to nauseating Care Bears variety sweetness; meanwhile their offspring clamor for a Batman Super Value Meal and limited-time-only (Collect all six!) McDonald's commemorative *Batman Forever* mug.

### THIS TEXT: READING

1. This is a complex essay on a very popular text. Can you locate Johnson's thesis? What she is trying to argue? Also, how does she support her thesis with details from the text?
2. Johnson uses some complex terms like "heteronormative," "camp," and "performativity." Look these words up in a good dictionary. Are their definitions helpful? Ask your instructor to define "camp."
3. What is Johnson's justification for linking capitalism and homosexuality in the movie?

### YOUR TEXT: WRITING

1. Write a paper in which you look at gay/lesbian issues in a movie that does not *appear* to be about gay and lesbian issues.
2. Write a response to Johnson. Do you agree with her thesis?
3. Do you see a link between capitalism and Hollywood? Write an analytical paper in which you scrutinize the values of Hollywood and American capitalism.

## FOUR REVIEWS OF *MOULIN ROUGE:* ROGER EBERT, STANLEY KAUFMANN, ELVIS MITCHELL, OWEN GLIEBERMAN

One of the most talked about movies of the new millennium, *Moulin Rouge* (2001), directed by Australian Baz Luhrmann, divided critics and audiences alike. Here, we have provided four reviews by four of the most respected American film critics, each with a different reading of the film. Our purpose in asking you to read four different reviews of the same text is to demonstrate how and why people can interpret one text many different ways. Notice how each reviewer focuses on alternate aspects of the movie and how the reviews are arguments for reading the movie a certain way.

## *Moulin Rouge*

Roger Ebert

LIKE ALMOST EVERY AMERICAN college boy who ever took a cut-rate flight to Paris, I went to the Moulin Rouge on my first night in town. I had a cheap standing-room ticket way in the back, and over the heads of the crowd, through a haze of smoke, I could vaguely see the dancing girls. The tragedy of the Moulin Rouge is that by the time you can afford a better seat, you've outgrown the show.

*Moulin Rouge* the movie is more like the Moulin Rouge of my adolescent fantasies than the real Moulin Rouge ever could be. It isn't about tired, decadent people, but about glorious romantics, who believe in the glitz and the tinsel—who see the nightclub not as a shabby tourist trap but as a stage for their dreams. Even its villain is a love-struck duke who gnashes his way into the fantasy, content to play a starring role however venal.

The film is constructed like the fevered snapshots created by your imagination before an anticipated erotic encounter. It doesn't depend on dialogue or situation but on the way you imagine a fantasy object first from one angle and then another. Satine, the heroine, is seen not so much in dramatic situations as in poses—in postcards for the yearning mind. The movie is about how we imagine its world. It is perfectly appropriate that it was filmed on sound stages in Australia; Paris has always existed best in the minds of its admirers.

The film stars Nicole Kidman as Satine, a star dancer who has a deadly secret; she is dying of tuberculosis. This is not a secret from the audience, which learns it early on, but from Christian (Ewan McGregor), the would-be writer who loves her. Toulouse-Lautrec (John Leguizarno), the dwarf artist, lives above Christian, and one day comes crashing through the ceiling of their flimsy tenement, sparking a friendship and collaboration: They will write a show to spotlight Satine's brilliance, as well as "truth, beauty, freedom and love." (I was reminded of Gene Kelly and Donald O'Connor's motto in *Singin' in the Rain:* "Dignity. Always dignity.") The show must be financed; enter the venal Duke of Worcester (Richard Roxburgh), who wants to pay for the show and for Satine's favors. The ringmaster is Zidler (Jim Broadbent), impresario of the Moulin Rouge.

Each of these characters is seen in terms of their own fantasies about themselves. Toulouse-Lautrec, for example, is flamboyant and romantic; Christian is lonely and lovelorn; Satine has a good heart and only seems to be a bad girl; Zidler pretends to be all business but is a softy, and the Duke can be so easily duped because being duped is the essence of his role in life. Those who think they can buy affection are suckers; a wise man is content to rent it.

The movie was directed by Baz Luhrmann, an Australian with a background in opera, whose two previous films were also experiments in exuberant excess. *Strictly Ballroom* made a ballroom competition into a flamboyant theatrical exercise, and his *William Shakespeare's Romeo + Juliet* updated the play into a contempo teenage rumble. He constructs *Moulin Rouge* with the melodrama of a 19th century opera, the Technicolor brashness of a 1950s Hollywood musical and the quick-cutting frenzy of a music video. Nothing is really "period" about the movie—it's like a costume revue taking place right now, with hit songs from the 1970s and 1980s (you will get the idea if I mention that Jim Broadbent sings "Like a Virgin").

I am often impatient with directors who use so many cuts their films seem to have been fed through electric fans. For Luhrmann and this material, it is the right approach. He uses so many different setups and camera angles that some of the songs seem to be cut not on every word of the lyrics, but on every syllable. There's no breathing room. The whole movie is on the same manic pitch as O'Connor's "Make 'em Laugh" number in *Singin' in the Rain.* Everything is screwed up to a breakneck pitch, as if the characters have died and their lives are flashing before our eyes.

This means the actors do not create their characters but embody them. Who is Satine? A leggy redhead who can look like a million in a nightclub costume, and then melt into a guy's arms. Who is Christian? A man who embodies longing with his eyes and sighs—whose very essence, whose entire being, is composed of need for Satine. With the Duke, one is reminded of silent films in which the titles said "The Duke," and then he sneered at you.

The movie is all color and music, sound and motion, kinetic energy, broad strokes, operatic excess. While it might be most convenient to see it from the beginning, it hardly makes any difference; walk in at any moment and you'll quickly know who is good and bad, who is in love and why—and then all the rest is song, dance, spectacular production numbers, protestations of love, exhalations of regret, vows of revenge and grand destructive gestures. It's like being trapped on an elevator with the circus.

## Seeing Is Disbelieving

Stanley Kauffmann

IN 1996 A BRASH YOUNG AUSTRALIAN DIRECTOR named Baz Luhrmann, with one film and some hit songs to his credit, made a modernized version of *Romeo and Juliet*. The first thing we saw was a television set with a newscaster speaking the opening chorus. The setting was "Verona Beach" in the 1990s; the balcony scene took place in a swimming pool; the characters were racially diversified, drove large convertibles, and carried pistols. I can't say that I enjoyed the film, but I admired its—odd word though it is—sincerity. More than most "concept" theater productions of Shakespeare that I have seen, this film showed conviction rather than blatant bravado, an attempt to convey the idea that Shakespearean truth persists through the ages. Its very wildness evoked some of the passion of the original.

Now Luhrmann has made *Moulin Rouge* (20th Century Fox), which has a very different agenda. Those who remember John Huston's film of that name (1952) may expect another biography of Toulouse-Lautrec, with giant sufferings in a pygmy body. Toulouse is in the new film, but only as one of the attendant gargoyles. The focus, we think at the start, is on a young English writer in Paris at the start of the last century and his rocky love affair with the star of the Moulin Rouge, the famous cabaret, which he can see from his window.

If that focus were maintained, this film might have some *vie Parisienne* glamour and some *La Bohème* pathos. But the focus soon shifts to Luhrmann. He seems much less interested in his story than he is in Luhrmann virtuosity. Intense close-ups of lovers' faces, kissing or just breathing in each other's breath; intense close-ups of almost everyone; grotesque makeup on all the actors except the lovers and the cabaret dancers; a cascade of kaleidoscopic cuts and juxtapositions—these are what the director really wants us to admire, it seems.

But that second focus, too, dissolves into another. The virtuosity is being used to an almost savage end. For the first fifteen minutes or so, we are stunned by the incessant flow of splendiferous settings and images, spectacular cabaret shows. The production design by Catherine Martin, who costumed *Romeo and Juliet* and who also collaborated on the costumes here with Angus Strathie, is lush. The cinematography of Donald M. McAlpine, who did *My Brilliant Career, Breaker Morant*, and of course *Romeo and Juliet*, not only exploits the bizarre luxury of the boudoirs and the cabaret shows, it gives the whole art nouveau ambience a garish decadence.

But there is more. Luhrmann is out to subvert the very ambience that he and his collaborators have created. The first hint is in the score. We soon begin to hear anachronistic music—from *The Sound of Music* to a Madonna number. Sometimes we hear familiar pop lyrics spoken as dialogue. (The screenplay, by the way, is by Luhrmann and Craig Pearce, and it certainly is by the way.) This musical incongruity leads to easy laughs, as the audience recognizes the latter-day music in this fin-de-siècle story, but, more importantly, it helps Luhrmann's ultimate basic purpose. He wants to make us aware of the means by which he is manipulating us. With this mix of period and mod music, with the Punchinello quality of most of his people, he wants to flay the period open. Not, it seems, because he particularly hates the *Belle Epoque*, but because he hates the process of romantic manipulation. With the musical ridicule and with much else that follows, he mocks the manufacture of sentimental reverence.

The framework of the screenplay is the book that the writer-hero, Christian, is whacking out on a typewriter in a Parisian garret a year after his love affair began. We move from huge close-ups of his typing to the cabaret across the way and to Christian's encounter, a year earlier, with Satine, the star. He is quickly in love, she is in whatever she prefers to be in at the moment. ("I choose my emotions," she says at one point.) A fabulously rich duke is also smitten with her, and so far as any drama is ignited, which is not very far, it is in the suitors' rivalry for Satine, poor but fervent love versus gilded whim. But the only real interest stirred by the plot is in recognition—picking out the occasional lifts from Dumas's play *La Dame aux Camélias* and Piave's libretto for *La Traviata*. Christian actually does throw money in Satine's face after she has left him for the duke; she actually is dying of consumption. These "lifts" are there for the same reason as the anachronistic music: mockery. "Oh, you're moved by Dumas and Verdi, are you?" Luhrmann seems to say. "Well, take a look at the mechanics."

The net result of all this cinematic whirling, of the "wrong" music and of the parodic plot, is that nothing at all in the film moves us. (How could we be moved by a film that has hot scenes played on top of an immense dummy elephant?) Characters are only programmed composites; anguishes are flooded across the screen as part of the décor. And this, too, is part of Luhrmann's craftiness. He wants us to be unmoved. He wants us to see the emotional climaxes as trickeries, disclosed here by a caustic postmodernist. With near-Brechtian brutality, swathed though it is in silks and frills, he is scoffing at the fabrications of romance.

This procedure makes rough demands on his actors. They are compelled to plunge into torrents of feeling though they have no real beings. Satine's line about choosing emotions seems to apply to the whole cast and is part of the "exposure." Satine is played by Nicole Kidman, insofar as she is recognizable. She is aggressively made up, with a mouth that is meant to suggest more than a mouth; she is furiously costumed; and she is thrust at us, on beds and trapezes, as the summa of sex. Because she has no reality, it is a tough job; and in any case Kidman is no Dietrich.

Christian is played by the Scottish actor Ewan McGregor, who does everything he is asked to do as heatedly as possible; but he, too, has to contend with the deliberately pseudo-emotional script and style. Besides, Luhrmann and McAlpine apparently noticed that McGregor has a slight resemblance to Laurence Olivier, so we get a number of Heathcliff shots, even to the lock of hair on the forehead—another subtle mockery of romance.

Jim Broadbent, the affable Englishman who was W.S. Gilbert in *Topsy-Turvy*, plays the manager and compère of the cabaret, as egregiously made-up as most of the actors. Broadbent is miscast; guile and show-biz warmth do not come easily to him. (Remember an antecedent in this sort of role, Peter Ustinov in *Lola Montes*.) The gifted John Leguizamo, who was Luhrmann's Tybalt in 1996, is here Toulouse, hobbling and grimacing away, but with no person. Richard Roxburgh, as the duke, is insufficiently ducal, even in this charade.

We are left, then, with a work that is spheres away from Luhrmann's *Romeo and Juliet*, which was ultimately an attempt to be true. This film intricately disguises the fact that it is a disguise. Underneath its swirls and swoonings, we see at the last a hatred of what it is lavishly doing.

# *Moulin Rouge:* An Eyeful, an Earful, Anachronism

Elvis Mitchell

THE OPERATIVE WORD in Baz Luhrmann's *Moulin Rouge,* the story of a doomed love between a writer (Ewan McGregor) and a dancer (Nicole Kidman), is rouge. In this movie there are more volatile or seductive shades of red than even Toulouse-Lautrec might have dreamed of.

Few films since the gorgeous dreamscapes of the old Technicolor process, in which the dye was printed right on the stock, have cajoled as much out of a single color as Mr. Luhrmann has out of red in *Moulin Rouge.* His visual daring has produced the modern-day equivalent of vintage films like *The Garden of Allah* that were so gaga over the advent of color that they never pounded out a coherent narrative. And neither does *Moulin Rouge.*

The reds show more emotional range than anyone in the movie, partially because Mr. Luhrmann has the eye of an artist; he sees this manic musical playing in his head and is driven to put it onto the screen. The character with whom he probably has the most in common is Lautrec, who is given the least characterization. That is not to say anyone else gets a whole lot more.

What Mr. Luhrmann has done is take the most thrilling moments in a movie musical—the seconds before the actors are about to burst into song and dance, when every breath they take is heightened—and made an entire picture of such pinnacles. As a result every moment in the film feels italicized rather than tumescent; *Moulin Rouge* has a frenetic innocence that seems almost asexual. It will speak to the young people who roll DVD's back and forth to their favorite scenes and think in narrative shorthand. That is the way Mr. Luhrmann's mind works. This movie is simultaneously stirring and dispiriting.

*Moulin Rouge* is set in Paris in "1899, the summer of love," says the writer, Christian (Mr. McGregor). He meets Lautrec (John Leguizamo), who here is a performance artist, as he rehearses a stage production he is calling a "spectacular spectacular." He and his fellow performers literally crash into Christian's flat, which is just below Lautrec's. Pulled into helping out, the hapless Christian meets Satine (Ms. Kidman), the dancer who causes him, as they used to say in such pictures, much joy and much pain. When he first beholds Satine, who is called "the Sparkling Diamond," his lips part, and his eyes gleam like jewels; they're glazed with love light.

Mr. Luhrmann's directing style is almost a brand of obsessive-compulsive disorder. He has too much to say and grows faint over the prospect of getting all of the thoughts and ideas and words and production numbers out of his head.

The movie musical was moribund long before the MTV D.J. Matthew Pinfield ever got in front of a camera. Mr. Luhrmann has made the first musical that trumps the achievement of MTV, producing whirlwind excitement on a steady schedule. Every scene in *Moulin Rouge* is a trove of jump cuts and flamboyant camera moves; we can only hope that the gifted cinematographer Donald M. McAlpine is paid by the mile.

There are a number of elegant touches, starting with the opening credits; Mr. Luhrmann reminds us that the stage was the home of the musical, and the first shot of *Moulin Rouge* is framed with a proscenium arch as a conductor leads an orchestra through a playing of the 20th Century Fox fanfare. This kind of antic bravura is a lovely, overripe moment, a rare instance in which Mr. Luhrmann slows his picture's heartbeat down to that of, say, a hummingbird's.

He starts the film in black and white, evoking the wonderful French films of the 1930's and 40's in which the cramped streets felt like sets, and moves into Christian's full-color world.

Heartsick and lost, Christian narrates the story of his unfortunate contact with Satine, who is supposedly wasting away from consumption. Since Ms. Kidman is such a strapping specimen that she could fling Mr. McGregor into the next arrondissement, her imperiled state is hard to swallow, despite the ladylike coughs of blood into her handkerchief. When she straddles him, you wait for a referee to give a 10-count and fear for his rib cage, which is probably not the intended effect.

Christian pines for Satine, but he's not enough for her. The Duke of Worcester (Richard Roxburgh) wants her, too. This vulgar impresario can do something that Christian cannot: deprive Satine of her livelihood. He threatens to shut down the Moulin Rouge, the nasty-gals dance hall where she works, unless he gets his way, and her. Harold Zidler (Jim Broadbent), who runs the place, talks the duke into financing a show starring Satine, and Christian is sneaked in as the writer.

In telling the story, Mr. Luhrmann pilfers music and movies like a fearless home invader; he kicks the door down and takes what he wants right off the table. The movie vaults from *La Bohème* to *La Traviata* to *Camille* to *Cabaret.*

It's not a novel idea to use anachronism as an anchor for musical numbers; *A Knight's Tale,* which opened last week, employs the same tactic. But it has never been done as unremittingly as it is here. In one number, Patti LaBelle's sweaty "Lady Marmalade" morphs into the snarling grunge melancholy of Nirvana's "Smells Like Teen Spirit," a combination that would be lost on even D.J. Qbert and the Columbia Record Club.

When the number works, as when Mr. Broadbent gives a new snap of the suspenders to Madonna's "Like a Virgin," it can be invigorating. But these songs became part of the cultural canvas because they distilled a single gesture, which is undeniably the true essence of pop. The lines "Oh, well, whatever, never mind" (from "Smells Like Teen Spirit") or "Voulez-vous coucher avec moi ce soir?" (from "Lady Marmalade") are given air in those original songs. Hijacked from their moorings, they float aimlessly.

Christian recites a litany of songs using the word love—his rap includes "Silly Love Songs," "All You Need Is Love," "Up Where We Belong," "Don't Leave Me This Way" and the ubiquitous "Heroes"—to Satine as a come-on. When he arrives at "In the Name of Love," which U2 dedicated to the Rev. Dr. Martin Luther King Jr., it's unseemly. Yet the scene goes by so fast that there's nothing to savor. Mr. Luhrmann shovels in so much so often that he never gives the movie a moment to exhale.

The film is undeniably rousing, but there is not a single moment of organic excitement because Mr. Luhrmann is so busy splicing bits from other films. Is he capable of gracefulness? It's hard to tell. He is interested in his actors, but he is perpetually dashing around them and Catherine Martin's startling production design. (The movie is filled with wall-to-wall dancing, but you're barely aware of it.)

The actors who know how to present themselves come off best. Mr. Broadbent, who has both a savvy naturalism and an outsize presence, can find a way to fit into the busy tapestry. Mr. Leguizamo, who is best at responding to other actors, is stranded. Mr. Luhrmann used his wiliness much more effectively in *William Shakespeare's "Romeo and Juliet"* than he does here. But "*Romeo*" had the humidity of a musical, and Mr. Luhrmann knew how to frame his stars' dewy-pink skins and aw-shucks dimples.

Mr. McGregor is capable of a conspiratorial warmth, as if he were letting the audience in on a secret the rest of the cast will never know. But here he is consigned to staring at Ms. Kidman, which emasculates him. He is even stripped of his soft Scottish brogue; he's a plush-toy puppy without a tail. Ms. Kidman is incredibly game; you get the feeling she would set herself aflame if Mr. Luhrmann asked her. She is not quite up to the lush sexpot thing asked of her; she is more like a big, friendly tomboy. Yet when Mr. Luhrmann photographs her as if she were starring in a Helmut Newton version of *All That Jazz,* you can see why she's a movie star.

*Moulin Rouge* will be accused of having no heart. But the truth is just the opposite. The movie has so much heart that the poor overworked organ explodes in every scene. You'll have to admit that there's nothing else like it, and young audiences, especially girls, will feel as if they had found a movie that was calling them by name.

## Ballroom Blitz

Owen Gleiberman

OUT OF THE ETHEREAL GASSES of pop culture, a revolution is coalescing. You could hear it when Björk, in the middle of all that Dogmafied early-'60s drabness, broke into her soaring rhapsodies of sacrificial selfhood in *Dancer in the Dark*. You could hear it, more recently, in MTV's "hip hopera" *Carmen* or even in *A Knight's Tale,* where Heath Ledger brandishes his medieval weapon to the schlock-funky strains of "Takin' Care of Business." Is this irony, postmodern collage, or pure next-millennium passion? All of the above. Love it or not, the rock musical is back—not just revived but genetically reconstituted, its central nervous system newly wired by the transformative aesthetic of music video.

In Baz Luhrmann's *Moulin Rouge,* a whirling fantasia of rococo kitsch set in the legendary Paris nightclub circa 1900, the characters are ladies, gentlemen, dandies, courtesans, and bohemians—a remembrance, in other words, of things very much past—but we experience them in frenzied jump-cut flashes, as if the director had staged the movie during an absinthe hallucination. When they open their mouths to express their inner selves, out come some of the most cherished pop songs of the late 20th century ("Roxanne," "Like a Virgin," "Smells Like Teen Spirit"), as well as snippets of "The Sound of Music" and other pre-counterculture standards. Christian (Ewan McGregor), an idealistic young writer devoted to the pursuit of "truth, beauty, and love," is ushered into the baroque sanctum of Satine (Nicole Kidman), the star of the Moulin Rouge's naughty stocking-flash stage show and the most coveted courtesan in Paris. After a few stabs at conversation, he lapses into a woozy-warm rendition of Elton John's "Your Song," and damned if the movie doesn't caress our eardrums with romance. Moments later, the black sky has gone twirly-psychedelic.

The rock opera, of course, is nothing new, but in *Moulin Rouge,* the spectacle of rock employed in a period setting, funny and absurd as it often appears, speaks to us in a new and galvanizing way. It slashes through the distance that so many of us feel toward musicals, not just because the songs here really are *our* songs, but because the very incongruity evokes that casual, private dream world in which rock has become the daily libretto of our lives. As someone who considers himself a happy child of *A Hard Day's Night* and *Tommy, Scorpio Rising* and *Saturday Night Fever* and MTV, I was more than willing to meet Luhrmann's flaky, bedazzled experiment halfway. Visually, the movie, with its sumptuous digitized landscapes that turn Paris into a nocturnal urban layer cake, is a mirage of fin de siècle decadence: the gloriously cluttered slope of Montmartre, the red-light windmill that sits atop the Moulin Rouge, advertising sin as a kind of mock-historical prerogative.

But *Moulin Rouge,* seductive as it can be, is also an extravaganza of shrill camp. What's wrong with the picture has nothing to do with its audacious soundtrack; it's that the film seems to have been directed by a madman with a palm buzzer. Luhrmann, who made *Strictly Ballroom* and the revved-into-incoherence *William Shakespeare's Romeo + Juliet,* shoves pinched and overly made-up faces at us, and he smashes all sense of space and time, so that the floor of the Moulin Rouge comes off as a bad-trip version of Studio 54 crossed with the *Star Wars* cantina. The place is decorated with grotesque caricatures like Toulouse-Lautrec, played by John

Leguizamo with a lisp that redefines tongue-tied, and the rouged impresario Zidler (Jim Broadbent), a nightmare of unctuousness who makes the *Cabaret* emcee look demure. Luhrmann, it's clear, wants to be *accused* of going too far, but the result is a musical that substitutes irony for pop passion, misanthropic disjointedness for lyrical flow. Even the leads are beautiful robo-archetypes, tragic in outline only.

Christian is in love with Satine, but she has been promised to the Duke of Worcester (Richard Roxburgh), a supercilious fop who has agreed to finance the Moulin Rouge's new theatrical stage. The duke has been made into such a stylized aristo-idiot that there's virtually no tension to the triangle. Nicole Kidman has an ivory beauty and an accomplished whiplash-dominatrix style but not, perhaps, the eccentric dynamism of a true star. As Satine, she's introduced singing "Diamonds Are a Girl's Best Friend" (with a brief segue into "Material Girl"), and Luhrmann is so busy piling on the overripe Marilyn/Madonna symbolism that we're not allowed to figure out who, exactly, this woman is. She becomes lovers with Christian, but Kidman never quite connects with McGregor, who strikes the only notes of genuine emotion in the movie.

Luhrmann may turn out to be the Gen-Y Ken Russell—a put-on libertine who bends the world around his gaudy hysterical rhythms. In *Moulin Rouge*, for all of his glitzoid artifice, he's rarely successful at using songs to gratify the musical junkie's primal desire to merge with the characters' hearts. By the second half, most of the rock spirit has leaked out of the movie, replaced by lugubrious neo-studio-system clichés. One has to wonder: Can the new rock musical survive, even thrive? You better believe it will, even if it has to go further than *Moulin Rouge* does, refining and cultivating its own excess, to attain something like innocence.

---

## THIS TEXT: READING

1. Taken as a whole, what do these four reviews suggest about *Moulin Rouge*? Is the film a success? Does the aggregate of the reviews paint an accurate portrait of what the film tries to do?
2. Which of the reviews do you agree with most? Why?
3. All four of the reviewers are males, yet, as Elvis Mitchell argues, the film is probably aimed largely at young women. Would a female reviewer have a different take on the film? Also, do the four reviews reflect a "typical" male perspective?

## YOUR TEXT: WRITING

1. Write your own review of *Moulin Rouge*, taking into account each of the reviews in this book. How do the reviews change how you see the movie?
2. Give a formal reading of the movie. By "formal," we mean focus on the form or style or technique of the movie. Explain the use of color, music,

camera angles, tracking shots, pans, and special effects. How is the movie less of a story and more of an "experience"?

3. Track down some reviews of *Moulin Rouge* written by women. How do men and women see the movie differently? How do you account for these variances?

# The Movie Violence Suite

The content of movies remains a hot-button issue in contemporary American society. Parents, theologians, teachers, politicians, and entertainers from all media have been quick to sound off regarding the issue of violence in movies. With the rise in popularity of seemingly violent movies like *Pulp Fiction, Natural Born Killers, Hannibal, Reservoir Dogs, From Dusk 'til Dawn,* and the Oscar-winning *Unforgiven,* we have witnessed an equally prevalent rise in concern over what kind of violence is acceptable on the big screen. Some people believe that repeated viewings of violent scenes prompts people to engage in violent behavior; yet studies of crime statistics in Canada (which gets all major American movies) and Japan (where movies are even more violent) reveal significantly lower violent criminal activity than the U.S. While no one is sure exactly what to make of such statistics or, for that matter, the claims of those who say that certain violent movies actually *have* affected their behavior in an adverse way, we do know that this issue is not going away any time soon.

In this section, we want to offer some alternative perspectives on "movie violence." Rather than thinking of movie violence simply in terms of how many actors pretend to be shot or stabbed or blown up, we would like to consider movie violence more broadly. Beginning with Linda Williams' now famous essay on gender in horror films, we would like to suggest that some kinds of violence against women remain profoundly subtle and unquestioned. Her chart of genre and violence raises provocative questions about how we define "violence." Similarly, when people talk about movie violence, virtually no one mentions the long history of violence against American Indians in Westerns. These two poems by Louise Erdrich (Ojibwe) and Sherman Alexie (Spokane/Coeur d'Alene) make some direct connections between film violence, American culture, and Manifest Destiny. We close this suite with a suite of responses by writers, politicians, and public figures to a special forum on media violence that appeared in *Time* magazine in 1995. This plurality of voices may comfort or annoy you, but regardless of your reaction, we suspect that after this suite, you will read movie violence more comprehensively.

## FILM BODIES: GENDER, GENRE, AND EXCESS

Linda Williams

WHEN MY SEVEN-YEAR-OLD SON and I go to the movies, we often select from among categories of films that promise to be sensational to give our bodies an actual physical jolt. He calls these movies that seem to grab and wrench our bodies "gross." My son and I agree that the fun of "gross" movies is in their display of sensations that are on the edge of respectable. Where we disagree—and where we as a culture often disagree, along lines of gender, age, or sexual orientation—is in which movies are over the edge, too "gross."

To my son, the good "gross" movies are those with scary monsters like Freddy Krueger (of the *Nightmare on Elm Street* series) who rip apart teenagers, especially teenage girls. These movies both fascinate and scare him. I have noticed that he is actually more interested in talking about than seeing them. A second category, one that I like and my son doesn't, is that of sad movies that make you cry. These are gross in their focus on unseemly emotions—emotions that may remind him too acutely of his own powerlessness as a child but that I admit to enjoying in a guilty, perverse sort of way. A third category, of both intense interest and disgust to my son (he makes the puke sign when speaking of it), he can only describe euphemistically as "the *K* word." *K* is for kissing. To a seven-year-old boy, nothing is more obscene than kissing.

There is no accounting for taste, especially in the realm of the "gross." As a culture, we most often invoke the term to designate excesses that we wish to exclude; to say, for example, which of the Robert Mapplethorpe photos we draw the line at but not to say what form and structure and function operate within the representations deemed excessive. Because so much attention goes to determining where to draw the line, discussions of the gross are often a highly confused hodgepodge of different categories of excess. For example, pornography is today more often deemed excessive for its violence than for its sex, while horror films are excessive in their displacements of sex into violence. In contrast, melodramas are deemed excessive for their gender and sex-linked pathos, for their naked displays of emotion. Ann Douglas once referred to the genre of romance fiction as "soft-core emotional porn for women."[1]

Alone or in combination, heavy doses of sex, violence, and emotion are dismissed by one faction or another as having no logic or reason for existence beyond their power to excite. Gratuitous sex, gratuitous violence and terror, gratuitous emotion are frequent epithets hurled at the phenomenon of the "sensational" in pornography, horror, and melodrama. This essay explores the notion that there may be some value in thinking about the form, function, and system of seemingly gratuitous excesses in these three genres. For if, as it seems, sex, violence, and emotion are fundamental elements of the sensational effects of these three types of films, the designation "gratuitous" is itself gratuitous. My hope, therefore, is that by thinking comparatively about all three "gross" and sensational film body genres, we might be able to get beyond the mere fact of sensation to explore its system and structure as well as their effects on the bodies of spectators.

## *Body Genres*

The repetitive formulas and spectacles of film genres are often defined by their differences from the classical realist style of narrative cinema. These classical films have been characterized as efficient, action-centered, goal-oriented linear narratives driven by the desire of a single protagonist, involving one or two lines of action, and leading to definitive closure. In their influential study of the classical Hollywood cinema, Bordwell, Thompson, and Staiger call this the Classical Hollywood style.[2]

As Rick Altman has noted in a recent article, both genre study and the study of the somewhat more nebulous category of melodrama have long been hampered by assumptions about the classical nature of the dominant narrative to which melodrama and some individual genres have been opposed.[3] Altman argues that Bordwell, Thompson, and Staiger, who locate the Classical Hollywood style in the linear, progressive form of the Hollywood narrative, cannot accommodate "melodramatic" attributes like spectacle, episodic presentation, or dependence on coincidence except as limited exceptions, or "play," within the dominant linear causality of the classical.

Altman writes, "Unmotivated events, rhythmic montage, highlighted parallelism, overlong spectacles—these are the excesses in the classical narrative system that alert us to the existence of a competing logic, a second voice."[4] Altman, whose own work on the movie musical has necessarily relied upon analyses of seemingly "excessive" spectacles and parallel constructions, thus makes a strong case for the need to recognize the possibility that excess may itself be organized as a system. Yet analyses of systems of excess have been much slower to emerge in the genres whose nonlinear spectacles have centered more directly upon the gross display of the human body. Pornography and horror films are two such systems of excess. Pornography is the lowest in cultural esteem, gross-out horror is next to lowest.

Melodrama, however, refers to a much broader category of films and a much larger system of excess. It would not be unreasonable, in fact, to consider all three of these genres under the extended rubric of melodrama, considered as a filmic mode of stylistic and emotional excess that stands in contrast to more "dominant" modes of realistic, goal-oriented narrative. In this extended sense, melodrama can encompass a broad range of films marked by "lapses" in realism, by "excesses" of spectacle and displays of primal, even infantile, emotions, and by narratives that seem circular and repetitive. Much of the interest of melodrama to film scholars over the last fifteen years originates in the sense that the form exceeds the normative system of much narrative cinema. I shall limit my focus here, however, to a narrower sense of melodrama, leaving the broader category of the sensational to encompass the three genres I wish to consider. Thus, partly for purposes of contrast with pornography, the melodrama I will consider here will consist of the form that has most interested feminist critics—that of "the woman's film," or "weepie." These are films addressed to women in their traditional status under patriarchy—as wives, mothers, abandoned lovers—or in their traditional status as bodily hysteria or excess, as in the frequent case of the woman "afflicted" with a deadly or debilitating disease.[5]

What are the pertinent features of bodily excess shared by these three "gross" genres? First, there is the spectacle of a body caught in the grips of intense sensation or emotion. Carol J. Clover, speaking primarily of horror films and pornography, has called films that privilege the sensational "body genres."[6] I am expanding Clover's notion of low body genres to include the sensation of overwhelming pathos in the "weepie." The body spectacle is featured most sensationally in pornography's portrayal of orgasm, in horror's portrayal of violence and terror, and in melodrama's portrayal of weeping. I propose that an investigation of the visual and narrative pleasures found in the portrayal of these three types of excess could be important to a new direction in genre criticism that would take as its point of departure—rather than as an unexamined assumption—questions of gender construction as well as gender address in relation to basic sexual fantasies.

Another pertinent feature shared by these body genres is the focus on what could probably best be called a form of ecstasy. While the classical meaning of the original Greek word is insanity and bewilderment, more contemporary meanings suggest components of direct or indirect sexual excitement and rapture, a rapture that informs even the pathos of melodrama.

Visually, each of these ecstatic excesses could be said to share a quality of uncontrollable convulsion or spasm—of the body "beside itself" in the grips of sexual pleasure, fear and terror, and overpowering sadness. Aurally, excess is marked by recourse not to the coded articulations of language but to inarticulate cries—of pleasure in porn, screams of fear in horror, sobs of anguish in melodrama.

Looking, and listening, to these bodily ecstasies, we can also notice something else that these genres seem to share: though quite differently gendered with respect to their targeted audiences—with pornography aimed, presumably, at active men and melodramatic weepies aimed, presumably, at passive women, and with contemporary gross-out horror aimed at adolescents careening wildly between the two masculine and feminine poles—in each of these genres the bodies of women figured on the screen have functioned traditionally as the primary *embodiments* of pleasure, fear, and pain.

In other words, even when the pleasure of viewing has traditionally been constructed for masculine spectators, as in most traditional, heterosexual pornography, it is the female body in the grips of an out-of-control ecstasy that has offered the most sensational sight. So the bodies of women have tended to function, ever since the eighteenth-century origins of these genres in the Marquis de Sade, Gothic fiction, and the novels of Richardson, as both the *moved* and the *moving*. It is thus through what Foucault has called the sexual saturation of the female body that audiences of all sorts have received some of their most powerful sensations.[7]

There are, of course, other film genres that both portray and affect the sensational body—e.g., thrillers, musicals, comedies. I suggest, however, that the film genres with especially low cultural status—which have seemed to exist as excesses to the system of even the popular genres—are not simply those that sensationally display bodies on the screen and register effects in the bodies of spectators. Rather, what may especially mark these body genres as low is the perception that the body of the spectator is caught up in an almost involuntary mimicry of the emotion or sensation of the body on the screen, along with the fact that the body displayed is female. An example of another "body genre" that, despite its concern with all manner of gross activities and body functions, has not been deemed gratuitously excessive is physical clown comedy—probably because the reaction of the audience does not mimic the sensations experienced by the central clown. Indeed, it is almost a rule that the audience's physical reaction of laughter does not coincide with the often deadpan reactions of the clown.

In the body genres I am isolating here, however, the success of these genres often seems to be measured by the degree to which the audience sensation mimics what is seen on the screen. Whether this mimicry is exact—e.g., whether the spectator at the porn film actually experiences orgasm, whether the spectator at the horror film actually shudders in fear, whether the spectator of the melodrama actually dissolves in tears—the success of these genres seems a self-evident matter of measuring bodily response. Examples of such measurement can be readily observed: in the "peter meter" capsule reviews in *Hustler* magazine, which measure the power of a porn film in degrees of erection of little cartoon penises; in horror films that are measured in terms of screams, fainting, and heart attacks in the audience (consider the career of horror-producer William Castle and such films as his 1959 *The Tingler*); and in the longstanding tradition of measuring women's films in terms of one-, two-, or three-handkerchief movies.

What seems to bracket these particular genres from others is an apparent lack of proper aesthetic distance, a sense of overinvolvement in sensation and emotion. We feel manipulated by these texts, an impression that the very colloquialisms "tearjerker" and "fearjerker" express—and to which we could add pornography's even cruder sense as texts to which some people might be inclined to "jerk off." The rhetoric of violence of the jerk suggests the extent to which viewers feel too directly, too viscerally, manipulated by the text in specifically gendered ways. Mary Ann Doane, for example, writing about the most genteel of these jerkers—the maternal melodrama—equates the violence of this emotion to a kind of "textual rape" of the targeted female viewer, who is "feminized through pathos."[8]

Feminist critics of pornography often evoke similar figures of sexual/textual violence when describing the operation of this genre. Robin Morgan's famous slogan "Pornography is the theory, and rape is the practice" is well known.[9] Implicit in this slogan is the notion that women are the objectified victims of pornographic representations, that the image of the sexually ecstatic woman so important to the genre is a celebration of female victimization and a prelude to female victimization in real life.

Less well known, but related, is the observation of the critic of horror films, James Twitchell, who notices that the Latin *horrere* means "to bristle."

He describes the way the nape hair stands on end during moments of shivering excitement. The aptly named Twitchell thus describes a kind of erection of the hair founded in the conflicting desires of "fight and flight."[10] While male victims in horror films may shudder and scream as well, it has long been a dictum of the genre that women make the best victims. "Torture the women!" was the famous advice given by Alfred Hitchcock.[11]

In the classic horror film the terror of the female victim shares the spectacle along with the monster. Fay Wray and the mechanized monster that made her scream in *King Kong* (Merian C. Cooper and Ernest B. Schoedsack, 1933) is a familiar example of the classic form. Janet Leigh in the shower in *Psycho* (Alfred Hitchcock, 1960) is a familiar example of a transition to a more sexually explicit form of the tortured and terrorized woman. And her daughter, Jamie Lee Curtis in *Halloween* (John Carpenter, 1978), can serve as the more contemporary version of the terrorized woman victim. In both of these later films the spectacle of the monster seems to take second billing to the increasingly numerous victims slashed by the sexually disturbed but entirely human monsters.

In the woman's film a well-known classic is the long-suffering mother of the two early versions of *Stella Dallas* (King Vidor, 1937) who sacrifices herself for her daughter's upward mobility. Contemporary filmgoers could recently see Bette Midler going through the same sacrifice and loss in the film *Stella* (John Erman, 1990). Debra Winger in *Terms of Endearment* (James L. Brooks, 1983) is another familiar example of this maternal pathos.

With these genre stereotypes in mind we should now ask about the status of bodily excess in each of these genres. Is it simply the unseemly, "gratuitous" presence of the sexually ecstatic woman, the tortured woman, the weeping woman—and the accompanying presence of the sexual fluids, the blood and the tears that flow from her body and that are presumably mimicked by spectators—that marks the excess of each type of film? How shall we think of these bodily displays in relation to one another as a system of excess in the popular film? And, finally, how excessive are they really?

The psychoanalytic system of analysis that has been so influential to film study in general and to feminist film theory and criticism in particular has been remarkably ambivalent about the status of excess in its major tools of analysis. The categories of fetishism, voyeurism, and sadism and masochism frequently invoked to describe the pleasures of film spectatorship are, by definition, perversions. Perversions are usually defined as gratuitous sexual excesses, specifically as excesses that result when "proper" end goals are deflected onto substitute goals or objects—fetishes instead of genitals, looking instead of touching, and so forth. Yet the perverse pleasures of film viewing are hardly gratuitous. They have been considered so basic that they have often been presented as norms. What is a film, after all, without voyeurism? Yet, at the same time, feminist critics have asked, what is the position of women within this pleasure geared to a presumably sadistic "male gaze"?[12] To what extent is she its victim? Is the orgasmic woman of pornography and the tortured woman of horror merely in the service of the sadistic male gaze? And is the weeping woman of melodrama appealing to the abnormal perversions of masochism in female viewers?

These questions point to the ambiguity of the terms of perversion used to describe the normal pleasures of film viewing. Without attempting to go into any of the complexities of this discussion here—a discussion that must ultimately relate to the status of the term "perversion" in theories of sexuality themselves—let me simply suggest the value of not invoking the perversions as terms of condemnation. As even the most cursory reading of Freud shows, sexuality is, by definition, perverse. The "aims" and "objects" of sexual desire are often obscure and inherently substitutive. Unless we are willing to see reproduction as the common goal of the sexual drive, then we have to admit, as Jonathan Dollimore has put it, that we are all perverts. Dollimore's goal of retrieving the "concept of perversion as a category of cultural analysis," as a structure intrinsic to all sexuality rather than extrinsic to it, is crucial to any attempt to understand cultural forms—such as our three body genres—in which fantasy predominates.[13]

## *Structures of Perversion in the "Female Body Genres"*

Each of the three body genres I have isolated hinges on the spectacle of a "sexually saturated" female body, and each offers what many feminist critics would agree to be spectacles of feminine victimization. But this victimization is very different in each type of film and cannot be accounted for simply by pointing to the sadistic power and pleasure of masculine subjects punishing or dominating feminine objects.

Many feminists have pointed to the victimization of the woman performers of pornography who must actually do the acts depicted in the film as well as to the victimization of characters within the films.[14] Pornography, in this view, is fundamentally sadistic. In weepies, on the other hand, feminists have pointed to the spectacles of intense suffering and loss as masochistic.

While feminists have often pointed to the women victims in horror films who suffer simulated torture and mutilation as victims of sadism,[15] more recent feminist work has suggested that the horror film may present an interesting, and perhaps instructive, case of oscillation between masochistic and sadistic poles. This argument, advanced by Clover, has suggested that pleasure, for a masculine-identified viewer, oscillates between identifying with the initial passive powerlessness of the abject and terrorized girl-victim of horror and her later, active empowerment.

This argument holds that when the girl-victim of a film like *Halloween* finally grabs the phallic knife, or ax, or chain saw to turn the tables on the monster-killer, viewer identification shifts from an "abject terror gendered feminine" to an active power with bisexual components. A gender-confused monster is foiled, often symbolically castrated by an "androgynous final girl."[16] In slasher films, identification with victimization is a roller-coaster ride of sadomasochistic thrills.

We could thus initially schematize the perverse pleasures of these genres in the following way: pornography's appeal to its presumed male viewers would be characterized as sadistic, horror films' appeal to the emerging sexual identities of its (frequently adolescent) spectators would be sadomasochistic, and women's films' appeal to presumed female viewers would be masochistic.

The masochistic component of viewing pleasure for women has been the most problematic term of perversion for feminist critics. It is interesting, for example, that most of our important studies of masochism—for example, those by Gilles Deleuze, Kaja Silverman, and Gaylyn Studlar—have all focused on the exoticism of masculine masochism rather than the familiarity of female masochism. Masochistic pleasure for women has paradoxically seemed either too normal—too much the normal yet intolerable condition of women—or too perverse to be taken seriously as pleasure.[17]

There is thus a real need to be clearer than we have been about what is in masochism for women—how power and pleasure operate in fantasies of domination that appeal to women. There is an equal need to be clearer than we have been about what is in sadism for men. Here the initial opposition between these two most gendered genres—women's weepies and male heterosexual pornography—needs to be complicated. I have argued elsewhere, for example, that pornography has been allied too simplistically with a purely sadistic fantasy structure. Indeed, those troubling films and videos that deploy instruments of torture on the bodies of women have been allied so completely with masculine viewing pleasures that we have not paid enough attention to their appeal to women, except to condemn such appeal as false consciousness.[18]

One important complication of the initial schema I have outlined would thus be to take a lesson from Clover's more bisexual model of viewer identification in horror film and stress the sadomasochistic component of each of these body genres through their various appropriations of melodramatic fantasies that are, in fact, basic to each. All of these genres could, for example, be said to offer highly melodramatic enactments of sexually charged, if not sexually explicit, relations. The subgenre of sadomasochistic pornography, with its suspension of pleasure over the course of prolonged sessions of dramatic suffering, offers a particularly intense, almost parodic, enactment of the classic melodramatic scenario of the passive and innocent female victim suffering at the hands of a leering villain. We can also see in horror films of tortured women a similar melodramatization of the innocent victim. An important difference, of course, lies in the component of the victim's overt sexual pleasure in the scenario of domination.

But even in the most extreme displays of feminine masochistic suffering, there is always a component of either power or pleasure for the woman victim. We have seen how identification in slasher horror films seems to oscillate between powerlessness and power. In sadomasochistic pornography and in melodramatic weepies, feminine subject positions appear to be constructed in ways that achieve a modicum of power and pleasure within the given limits of patriarchal constraints on women. It is worth noting as well that *non*sadomasochistic pornography has historically been one of the few types of popular film that has not punished women for actively pursuing their sexual pleasure.

In the subgenre of sadomasochistic pornography, however, the female masochist in the scenario must be devious in her pursuit of pleasure. She plays the part of passive sufferer in order to obtain pleasure. Under a patriarchal double standard that has rigorously separated the sexually passive "good girl" from the sexually active "bad girl," masochistic role play offers a way out of this dichotomy by combining the good girl with the bad: the passive "good girl" can prove to her witnesses (the superego who is her torturer) that she does not will the pleasure that she receives. Yet the sexually active "bad girl" enjoys this pleasure and has knowingly arranged to endure the pain that earns it. The cultural law that decides some girls are good and others are bad is not defeated, but within its terms pleasure has been negotiated and "paid for" with a pain that conditions it. The "bad girl" is punished, but in return she receives pleasure.[19]

In contrast, the sadomasochistic teen horror film kills off the sexually active "bad girls," allowing only the nonsexual "good girls" to survive. But these good girls are, as if in compensation, remarkably active, to the point of appropriating phallic power to themselves. It is as if this phallic power is granted so long as it is rigorously separated from phallic or any other sort of pleasure. For these pleasures spell sure death in this genre.

In the melodramatic woman's film we might think to encounter a purer form of masochism on the part of female viewers. Yet even here the female viewer does not seem to be invited to identify wholly with the sacrificing good woman, but rather with a variety of different subject positions, including those which empathically look on at her own suffering. While I would not argue that there is a very strong sadistic component to these films, I do argue that there is a strong mixture of passivity and activity—and a bisexual oscillation between the poles of each—in even this genre.

For example, the woman viewer of a maternal melodrama such as *Terms of Endearment* or *Steel Magnolias* (Herbert Ross, 1989) does not simply identify with the suffering and dying heroines of each. She may equally identify with the powerful matriarchs, the surviving mothers who preside over the deaths of their daughters, experiencing the exhilaration and triumph of survival. The point is simply that identification is neither fixed nor entirely passive.

While there are certainly masculine and feminine, active and passive, poles to the left and right of the positions that we might assign to these three genres (see accompanying table), the subject positions that appear to be constructed by each of the genres are not as gender-linked and as

An Anatomy of Film Bodies

| Genre | Pornography | Horror | Melodrama |
|---|---|---|---|
| Bodily excess | Sex | Violence | Emotion |
| Ecstasy —shown by | Ecstatic sex<br>Orgasm<br>Ejaculation | Ecstatic violence<br>Shudders<br>Blood | Ecstatic woe<br>Sobs<br>Tears |
| Presumed audience | Men (active) | Adolescent boys (active/passive) | Girls, women (passive) |
| Perversion | Sadism | Sadomasochism | Masochism |
| Originary fantasy | Seduction | Castration | Origin |
| Temporality of fantasy | On time! | Too early! | Too late! |
| Genre cycles "Classic" | Stag films (1920s–1940s): *The Casting Couch* | "Classic" horror: *Dracula*<br>*Frankenstein*<br>*Dr. Jekyll and Mr. Hyde*<br>*King Kong* | "Classic" women's films<br>Maternal melodrama: *Stella Dallas*<br>*Mildred Pierce*<br>Romance: *Back Street*<br>*Letter from an Unknown Woman* |
| Contemporary | Feature-length hard-core porn: *Deep Throat*<br>*The Punishment of Anne*<br>Femme Productions<br>Bisexual<br>Trisexual | Post-*Psycho:* *The Texas Chainsaw Massacre*<br>*Halloweer*<br>*Dressed to Kill*<br>*Videodrome* | Male and female "weepies": *Steel Magnolias*<br>*Stella*<br>*Dad* |

gender-fixed as has often been supposed. This is especially true today as hard-core pornography gains appeal with women viewers. Perhaps the most recent proof in this genre of the breakdown of rigid dichotomies of masculine and feminine, active and passive, is the creation of an alternative, oscillating category of address to viewers. In addition to the well-known heterosexual hard core, which once addressed itself exclusively to heterosexual men and now has begun to address itself to heterosexual couples and women as well, and in addition to homosexual hard core, which has addressed itself to gay and (to a lesser extent) lesbian viewers, there is now a new category of video called bisexual. In these videos men do it with women, women do it with women, men do it with men, and then all do it with one another—in the process breaking down a fundamental taboo against male-to-male sex.[20]

A related interpenetration of the formerly more separate categories of masculine and feminine is seen in what has come to be known in some quarters as the "male weepie." These are mainstream melodramas engaged in the activation of the previously repressed emotions of men and in breaking the taboos against male-to-male hugs and embraces. The father-son embrace that concludes *Ordinary People* (Robert Redford, 1980) is exemplary. More recently, paternal weepies have begun to compete with the maternal—such as the conventional *Dad* (David Goldberg, 1989) or the less conventional *Twin Peaks* (David Lynch, 1990–1991), with its wild paternal displays.

The point is certainly not to admire the "sexual freedom" of this new fluidity and oscillation—the new femininity of men who hug and the new masculinity of women who leer—as if it represented any ultimate defeat of phallic power. Rather, the more useful lesson might be to see what this new fluidity and oscillation permits in the construction of feminine viewing pleasures once thought not to exist at all. (It is instructive, for example, that women characters in the new bisexual pornography are shown verbally articulating their visual pleasure as they watch men perform sex with men.)

The deployment of sex, violence, and emotion would thus seem to have very precise functions in these body genres. Like all popular genres, they address persistent problems in our culture, in our sexualities, in our very identities. The deployment of sex, violence, and emotion is thus in no way gratuitous and in no way strictly limited to each of these genres. Each deployment of sex, violence, and emotion is a cultural form of problem solving; each draws upon related sensations to address its problems. As I have argued in *Hard Core*, pornographic films now tend to present sex as a problem, and the performance of more, different, or better sex is posed as the solution.[21] In horror films a violence related to sexual difference is the problem; more violence related to sexual difference is also the solution. In women's films the pathos of loss is the problem; repetitions and variations of this loss are the generic solution.

## *Structures of Fantasy*

All of these problems are linked to gender identity and might be usefully explored as genres of gender fantasy. It is appropriate to ask, then, not only about the structures of perversion but also about the structures of fantasy in each of these genres. In doing so, we need to be clear about the nature of fantasy itself. For fantasies are not, as is sometimes thought, wish-fulfilling linear narratives of mastery and control leading to closure and the attainment of desire. They are marked, rather, by the prolongation of desire and by the lack of fixed position with respect to the objects and events fantasized.

In their classic essay "Fantasy and the Origins of Sexuality," Jean Laplanche and J. B. Pontalis argue that fantasy is not so much a narrative that enacts the quest for an object of desire as it is a setting for desire, a place where conscious and unconscious, self and other, part and whole meet. Fantasy is the place where "desubjectified" subjectivities oscillate between self and other, occupying no fixed place in the scenario.[22]

In the three body genres discussed here, this fantasy component has probably been better understood in horror film, a genre often understood as belonging to the "fantastic." However, it has been less well understood in pornography and melodrama. Because these genres display fewer fantastic special effects and because they rely on certain conventions of realism—e.g., the activation of social problems in melodrama; the representation of real sexual acts in pornography—they seem less obviously fantastic. Yet the usual criticisms—that these forms are improbable, that they lack psychological complexity and narrative closure, and that they are repetitious—become moot as evaluation if they are considered intrinsic to their engagement with fantasy.

There is a link, in other words, between the appeal of these forms and their ability to address, if never really to "solve," basic problems related to sexual identity. Here I would like to forge a connection between Laplanche and Pontalis's structural understanding of fantasies as myths of origin that try to cover the discrepancy between two moments in time and the distinctive temporal structure of these particular genres. Laplanche and Pontalis argue that fantasies which are myths of origin address the insoluble problem of the discrepancy between an irrecoverable original experience presumed to have actually taken place—as in the case of the historical primal scene—and the uncertainty of its hallucinatory revival. The discrepancy exists, in other words, between the actual existence of the lost object and the sign that evokes both this existence and its absence.

Laplanche and Pontalis maintain that the most basic fantasies are located at the juncture of an irrecoverable real event that took place somewhere in the past and a totally imaginary event that never took place. The "event" whose temporal and spatial existence can never be fixed is thus ultimately that of "the origin of the subject"—an origin that psychoanalysts tell us cannot be separated from the discovery of sexual difference.[23]

It is this contradictory temporal structure of being situated somewhere between the "too early" and the "too late" of the knowledge of difference that generates desire that is most characteristic of fantasy. Freud introduced the concept of "original fantasy" to explain the mythic function of fantasies that seem to offer repetitions of and "solutions" to major enigmas confronting the child.[24] These enigmas are located in three areas: the enigma of the origin of sexual desire, an enigma that is "solved," so to speak, by the fantasy of seduction; the enigma of sexual difference, "solved" by the fantasy of castration; and, finally, the enigma of the origin of self, "solved" by the fantasy of family romance or return to one's origin.[25]

Each of the three body genres I have been describing could be seen to correspond in important ways to one of these original fantasies. Pornography, for example, is the genre that has seemed to endlessly repeat the fantasies of primal seduction, of meeting the other, seducing or being seduced by the other in an ideal "pornotopia" where, as Steven Marcus has noted, it is always bedtime.[26] Horror is the genre that seems to endlessly repeat the trauma of castration, as if to "explain," by repetitious mastery, the original problem of sexual difference. And melodramatic weepie is the genre that seems to endlessly repeat our melancholic sense of the loss of origin, the impossible hope of returning to an earlier state that is perhaps most fundamentally represented by the body of the mother.

Of course, each of these genres has a history and does not simply "endlessly repeat." The fantasies activated by these genres are repetitious, but not fixed and eternal. If traced back to origin, each could probably be shown to have emerged with the formation of the bourgeois subject and the intensifying importance to this subject of specified sexualities.

But the importance of repetition in each genre should not blind us to the very different temporal structure of repetition in each fantasy. It could be, in fact, that these different temporal structures constitute the different utopian component of problem solving in each form. Thus the typical (nonsadomasochistic) pornographic fantasies of seduction operate to "solve" the problem of the origin of desire. Attempting to answer the insoluble question of whether desire is imposed from without through the seduction of the parent or whether it originates within the self, pornography answers this question by typically positing a fantasy of desire coming from within the subject *and* from without. Nonsadomasochistic pornography attempts to posit the utopian fantasy of perfect temporal coincidence: a subject and object (or seducer and seduced) who meet one another "on time!" and "now!" in shared moments of mutual pleasure that it is the special challenge of the genre to portray.

In contrast to pornography, the fantasy of recent teen horror corresponds to a temporal structure that suggests the anxiety of not being ready, the problem, in effect, of "too early!" Some of the most violent and terrifying moments of the horror film occur when the female victim meets the psycho-killer-monster unexpectedly, before she is ready. The female victims who are not ready for the attack die. This surprise encounter, too early, often takes place at a moment of sexual anticipation when the female victim thinks she is about to meet her boyfriend or lover. The monster's violent attack on the female victims vividly enacts a symbolic castration that often functions as a kind of punishment for an ill-timed exhibition of sexual desire. These victims are taken by surprise in the violent attacks that are then deeply felt by spectators (especially the adolescent male spectators drawn to the slasher subgenre) as linked to the knowledge of sexual difference. Again the key to the fantasy is timing—the way the knowledge of sexual difference too suddenly overtakes both characters and viewers, offering a knowledge for which we are never prepared.

Finally, in contrast to pornography's meeting "on time!" and horror's unexpected meeting "too early!" we can identify melodrama's pathos of the "too late!" In these fantasies the quest to return to and discover the origin of the self is manifest in the form of the child's fantasy of possessing ideal parents in the Freudian family romance, in the parental fantasy of possessing the child in maternal or paternal melodrama, and even in the lovers' fantasy of possessing one another in romantic weepies. In these fantasies the quest for connection is always tinged with the melancholy of loss. Origins are already lost; the encounters always take place too late, on deathbeds or over coffins.[27]

Italian critic Franco Moretti has argued, for example, that literature that makes us cry operates via a special manipulation of temporality: what triggers our crying is not just the sadness or suffering of the character in the story but a very precise moment when characters in the story catch up with and realize what the audience already knows. We cry, Moretti argues, not just because the characters do, but at the precise moment when desire is finally recognized as futile. The release of tension produces tears—which become a kind of homage to a happiness that is kissed goodbye. Pathos is thus a surrender to reality, but it is a surrender that pays homage to the ideal that tried to wage war on it.[28] Moretti thus stresses a subversive, utopian component in what has often been considered a form of passive powerlessness. The fantasy of the meeting with the other that is always too late can thus be seen as a reflection of the utopian desire that it not be too late to merge again with the other who was once part of the self.

Obviously there is a great deal of work to be done to understand the form and function of these three body genres in relation to one another and in relation to their fundamental appeal as "original fantasies." And obviously the most difficult work of understanding this relation between gender, genre, fantasy, and structures of perversion will come in the attempt to relate original fantasies to historical context and specific generic history. However, one thing already seems clear: these "gross" body genres, which may seem so violent and inimical to women, cannot be dismissed as evidence of a monolithic and unchanging misogyny, as either pure sadism for male viewers or as masochism for females. Their very existence and popularity hinges upon rapid changes taking place in relations between the sexes and by rapidly changing notions of gender—what it means to be a man or a woman. To dismiss them as bad excess—whether of explicit sex, violence, or emotion, or as bad perversions, whether of masochism or sadism—is not to address their function as cultural problem solving. Genres thrive, after all, on the persistence of the problems they address; but genres thrive also in their ability to recast the nature of these problems.

Finally, as I hope this analysis of the melodrama of tears suggests, we may be wrong in our assumption that the bodies of spectators simply reproduce the sensations exhibited by bodies on the screen. Even those masochistic pleasures associated with the powerlessness of the "too late!" are not absolutely abject. Even tearjerkers do not operate to force a simple mimicry of the sensation exhibited on the screen. Powerful as the sensations of the jerk might be, we may only be beginning to understand how they are deployed in generic and gendered cultural forms.

## Notes

I owe thanks to Rhona Berenstein, Leo Braudy, Chick Callenbach, Paul Fitzgerald, Mandy Harris, Brian Henderson, Jane Gaines, Marsha Kinder, Eric Rentschler, and Pauline Yu for generous advice on drafts of this essay.

1. Ann Douglas, "Soft-Porn Culture," *New Republic* 30 (August 1980): 25.
2. David Bordwell, Kristin Thompson, and Janet Staiger, *The Classical Hollywood Cinema: Film Style and Mode of Production to 1960* (New York: Columbia University Press, 1985).
3. Rick Altman, "Dickens, Griffith, and Film Theory Today," *South Atlantic Quarterly* 88, no. 2 (Spring 1989): 321–359.
4. Ibid., pp. 345–346.
5. For an excellent summary of many of the issues involved with both film melodrama and the "woman's film," see Christine Gledhill's introduction to the anthology *Home Is Where the Heart Is: Studies in Melodrama and the Woman's Film* (London: British Film Institute, 1987). For a more general inquiry into the theatrical origins of melodrama, see Peter Brooks, *The Melodramatic Imagination* (New Haven: Yale University Press, 1976). And for an extended theoretical inquiry and analysis of a body of melodramatic women's films, see Mary Ann Doane, *The Desire to Desire* (Bloomington: Indiana University Press, 1987).
6. Carol J. Clover, "Her Body, Himself: Gender in the Slasher Film," *Representations* 20 (Fall 1987): 187–228.
7. Michel Foucault, *The History of Sexuality*, vol. 1, *An Introduction*, translated by Robert Hurley (New York: Pantheon Books, 1978).
8. Doane, *The Desire to Desire*, p. 95.
9. Robin Morgan, "Theory and Practice: Pornography and Rape," in *Take Back the Night: Women on Pornography*, edited by Laura Lederer (New York: Morrow, 1980), p. 139.
10. James Twitchell, *Dreadful Pleasures: An Anatomy of Modern Horror* (New York: Oxford, 1985), p. 10.
11. Clover, "Her Body, Himself," discusses the meanings of this famous quote.
12. Laura Mulvey, "Visual Pleasure and Narrative Cinema," *Screen* 16, no. 3 (1975): 6–18.
13. Dollimore's project, along with Teresa de Lauretis's more detailed examination of the term "perversion" in Freudian psychoanalysis (in progress), will be central to any detailed attempts to understand the perverse pleasures of these gross body genres. See Jonathan Dollimore, "The Cultural Politics of Perversion: Augustine, Shakespeare, Freud, Foucault," *Genders* 8 (July 1990): 2–16.
14. See, for example, Andrea Dworkin, *Pornography: Men Possessing Women* (New York: Perigee Books, 1979), and Catherine MacKinnon, *Feminism Unmodified: Discourses on Life and Law* (Cambridge: Harvard University Press, 1987).
15. Linda Williams, "When the Woman Looks," in *Re-Vision: Essays in Feminist Film Criticism*, American Film Institute Monograph Series, edited by Mary Ann Doane, Patricia Mellencamp, and Linda Williams (Frederick, Md.: University Publications of America, 1984), pp. 83–97.
16. Clover, "Her Body, Himself," pp. 206–209.
17. Gilles Deleuze, *Masochism: An Interpretation of Coldness and Cruelty*, translated by Jean McNeil (New York: Braziller, 1971); Kaja Silverman, "Masochism and Subjectivity,"

*Framework* 12 (1980): 2–9, and "Masochism and Male Subjectivity," *Camera Obscura* 17 (1988): 31–66; and Gaylyn Studlar, *In the Realm of Pleasure: Von Sternberg, Dietrich, and the Masochistic Aesthetic* (Urbana: University of Illinois Press, 1985).

18. See my *Hard Core: Power, Pleasure, and the 'Frenzy of the Visible'* (Berkeley: University of California Press, 1989), pp. 184–228.
19. I discuss these issues at length in ibid.
20. Titles of these relatively new (post-1986) hard-core videos include *Bisexual Fantasies: Bi-Mistake; Karen's Bi-Line; Bi-Dacious: Bi-Night; Bi and Beyond: The Ultimate Fantasy; Bi and Beyond II; Bi and Beyond III; Hermaphrodites.*
21. Williams, *Hard Core*, pp. 120–152.
22. Jean Laplanche and J. B. Pontalis, "Fantasy and the Origins of Sexuality," *International Journal of Psychoanalysis* 49, no. 1 (1968): 16.
23. Ibid., p. 11.
24. Sigmund Freud, "Instincts and Their Vicissitudes," in *The Standard Edition of the Complete Psychological Works of Sigmund Freud* (London: Hogarth Press, 1957), 14: 117–140.
25. Laplanche and Pontalis, "Fantasy," p. 11.
26. Steven Marcus, *The Other Victorians: A Study of Sexuality and Pornography in Mid-Nineteenth-Century England*, rev. ed. (New York: New American Library, 1974), p. 269.
27. Steve Neale, "Melodrama and Tears," *Screen* 27, no. 6 (November–December 1986): 6–22.
28. Franco Moretti, "Kindergarten," in *Signs Taken for Wonders* (London: Verso, 1983), p. 179.

# DEAR JOHN WAYNE

Louise Erdrich

August and the drive-in picture is packed.
We lounge on the hood of the Pontiac
surrounded by the slow-burning spirals they sell
at the window, to vanquish the hordes of mosquitoes.
Nothing works. They break through the smoke screen for blood.

Always the lookout spots the Indians first,
spread north to south, barring progress.
The Sioux or some other Plains bunch
in spectacular columns, ICBM missiles,
feathers bristling in the meaningful sunset.

The drum breaks. There will be no parlance.
Only the arrows whining, a death-cloud of nerves
swarming down on the settlers
who die beautifully, tumbling like dust weeds

into the history that brought us all here
together: this wide screen beneath the sign of the bear.

The sky fills, acres of blue squint and eye
that the crowd cheers. His face moves over us,
a thick cloud of vengeance, pitted
like the land that was once flesh. Each rut,
each scar makes a promise: *It is*
*not over, this fight, not as long as you resist.*

*Everything we see belongs to us.*

A few laughing Indians fall over the hood
slipping in the hot spilled butter.
*The eye sees a lot, John, but the heart is so blind.*
*Death makes us owners of nothing.*
He smiles, a horizon of teeth
the credits reel over, and then the white fields

again blowing in the true-to-life dark
The dark films over everything.
We get into the car
scratching our mosquito bites, speechless and small
as people are when the movie is done.
We are back in our skins.

How can we help but keep hearing his voice,
the flip side of the sound track, still playing:
*Come on boys, we got them*
*where we want them, drunk, running.*
*They'll give us what we want, what we need.*
Even his disease was the idea of taking everything.
Those cells, burning, doubling, splitting out of their skins.

## TEXAS CHAINSAW MASSACRE

Sherman Alexie

What can you say about a movie so horrific even its title scares people away?
—*Stephen King*

I
have seen it
and like it: The blood,
the way like *Sand Creek*

even its name brings fear,
because I am an American
Indian and have learned
words are another kind of violence.

This vocabulary is genetic.

When Leatherface crushes the white boy's skull
with a sledgehammer, brings it down again and again
while the boy's arms and legs spasm and kick wildly
against real and imagined enemies, I remember

another killing floor

in the slaughter yard from earlier in the film,
all the cows with their stunned eyes and mouths
waiting for the sledgehammer with fear so strong
it becomes a smell that won't allow escape. I remember

the killing grounds

of Sand Creek
where 105 Southern Cheyenne and Arapaho women and children
and 28 men were slaughtered by 700 heavily armed soldiers,
led by Colonel Chivington and his Volunteers. *Volunteers.*

Violence has no metaphors; it does have reveille.

Believe me, there is nothing surprising
about a dead body. This late in the 20th century
tears come easily and without sense:
taste and touch have been replaced
by the fear of reprisal. I have seen it

and like it: The butchery, its dark humor
that thin line "between art and exploitation,"
because I recognize the need to prove blood
against blood. I have been in places
where I understood *Tear his heart out
and eat it whole.* I have tasted rage
and bitterness like skin between my teeth.

I have been in love.

I first saw it in the reservation drive-in
and witnessed the collected history
of America roll and roll across the screen,
voices and dreams distorted by tin speakers.

"Since then, I have been hungry
for all those things I haven't seen."

This country demands that particular sort of weakness:
we must devour everything on our plates
and ask for more. Our mouths hinge open.
Our teeth grow long and we gnaw them down
to prevent their growth into the brain. I have

seen it and like it: The blood,
the way like music
it makes us all larger
and more responsible
for our sins,
because I am an American
Indian and have learned

hunger becomes madness easily.

## *TIME* FORUM: TOUGH TALK ON ENTERTAINMENT

Compiled by Andrea Sachs and Susanne Washburn

Everybody agrees it's vulgar and violent. The question is why, and what should be done about it

DE GUSTIBUS NON EST DISPUTANDUM was the way the ancient Romans put it: there is no point arguing about matters of taste. But that was easy for the Romans to say; they—and their children—weren't awash in a tide of explicit films, TV programs and recorded music. We are. And the consequences of this condition—even the question whether there are any consequences—have spurred arguments that grow more intense as mass entertainment becomes more pervasive. In the aftermath of Bob Dole's latest attack on Hollywood, *TIME* asked some prominent people who produce or comment on the arts for their reactions.

LYNNE CHENEY, *Fellow, American Enterprise Institute*

In one scene of Oliver Stone's film *Natural Born Killers* the hero drowns his girlfriend's father in a fish tank and kills her mother by tying her down on her bed, pouring gasoline on her and burning her alive. Meanwhile, a raucous, laugh-filled sound track tells the audience to regard this slaughter as the funniest thing in the world. Is it any wonder that millions of Americans are concerned about kids growing up in a culture that sends such messages—or that someone who wants to be our President would talk about it?

A lot of the commentary about Bob Dole's remarks on Hollywood has focused on whether he has gained political advantage from them, and I think there is no question but that he has. Not so much because he has positioned himself better with the cultural right, but because, as Americans across the political spectrum realize, he is right—just as President Clinton was right a few years ago when he castigated rap singer Sister Souljah for saying that blacks have killed one another long enough and that it was time for them to start killing whites. When you glamorize murder, as *Natural Born Killers* does; or glorify violence against women, as does 2 Live Crew; when lyrics are anti-Semitic, as Public Enemy's are, or advocate hatred of gays and immigrants, as those of Guns 'N Roses do, it's not just conservatives who know something has gone wrong; any thinking liberal does too.

Those producing this garbage tell us we're naive. *Natural Born Killers* isn't an attempt to profit from murder and mayhem, says Oliver Stone. It's a send-up of the way the tabloid press exploits violence—a claim that would be a lot more convincing if Stone would contribute to charity the multimillion dollar profits the movie earned last year. Time Warner CEO Gerald Levin, whose company produced *Natural Born Killers* and has put out much of the most offensive music, says that rappers like Ice-T are misunderstood: when Ice-T chants "Die, die, die, pig, die," he is not really advocating cop killing, but trying to put us in touch with the "anguished" mind of someone who feels this way.

This is nonsense—rationalization of the most obvious sort. What we need to do, each of us as individuals, is let those who are polluting the culture know that we are going to embarrass them and shame them until they stop, until they use their vast talents and resources to put us in touch with our best selves—instead of with the worst parts of our nature.

### JOHN EDGAR WIDEMAN, *Author and professor*

Which is more threatening to America—the violence, obscenity, sexism and racism of movies and records, or the stark reality these movies and music reflect? If a messenger, even one who happens to be black and a rapper, arrives bearing news of a terrible disaster, what do we accomplish by killing the messenger?

I wasn't around when black people were barred from playing drums. But I know the objections to African drumming weren't aesthetic; Southern legislators feared the drums' power to signal a general slave revolt. I was around when finding black music on the radio was a problem. Growing up in Pittsburgh, Pennsylvania, the only way to hear the latest rhythm-and-blues sounds after dark was searching the scratchy hyperspace for Randy's Record Shack beaming up from Nashville, Tennessee.

Banning, ignoring, exploiting, damning black art has a long history. Protecting black freedom of expression and participation at all levels of society began just yesterday. So it's not accidental that politicians reaffirm the doublespeak and hypocrisy of America's pretensions to democracy. Let's deregulate everything; let the marketplace rule. Except when rap music captures a lion's share of the multi-billion dollar music market. Then, in the name of decency and family values, we're duty bound to regulate it. On the other hand, in areas of the economy where black people are appallingly underrepresented—the good jobs, for instance, that enable folks to maintain families—we should abhor intervention because it's not fair.

The best art interrogates and explodes consensus. Recall how traditional African-American gospel music, transformed in the 1960s to freedom songs, the oratory of Martin Luther King and the essays of James Baldwin inspired and guided us. But we can't have the best art unless we are willing to risk living with the rest, the second rate and 15th rate, the stuff that eventually Xs itself because its worthlessness teaches us not to buy or listen.

We must not lose patience and stop paying attention. We must not mistake jingoism or propaganda or sensationalism for art. We must not fear change, fear the shock and disruption true art inflicts. We must not smother what we don't want to hear with the drone of morally bankrupt, politically self-serving Muzak.

## DONNA BRITT, *Syndicated columnist*

As a columnist who often writes about how American parents of every color, income and political stripe feel they're engaged in a losing war with cultural swill, I was glad to hear Bob Dole lambaste the entertainment industry. Every parent I know feels bombardment; who cares who thrusts it under the microscope?

Sure, it's hypocritical. Dole, who long ignored the issue, is playing politics by reducing a complex and unwieldy problem to too-easy sound bites. But who isn't? People who excoriate Dole for hypocrisy in blasting movies in which fictional characters use the same assault weapons he supports in real life ignore that his most passionate attackers make fortunes off the depravity they're protecting. Free speech invokers who say only parents are responsible for policing what their children hear and see overlook that even good parents—who've never been busier or had a more pervasive pop culture to contend with—are sometimes too overwhelmed to fight. Bad parents—and there are millions—aren't even trying. But we all must share the planet with the kids they're raising badly.

## PAUL SCHRADER, *Screenwriter and director*

I don't know which is more appalling—the conservatives' hypocrisy or the entertainment industry's sanctimony.

There are solid arguments here, both Dole's and the libertarian response. You'll never know it from what you hear or read. That's because the debate, as framed by Dole and the entertainment industry, is not about values or freedom. It's about popularity. Hollywood calls popularity money; politicians call it votes.

The entertainment conglomerates are fond of invoking the First Amendment. That's because there's precious little excuse for what they've been up to the past 20 years. We've worked so long and hard at making audiences dumber, they have actually become dumber.

Is Dole up to anything different? Several years ago, I was involved in a public debate over a film I adapted from Nikos Kazantzakis' *The Last Temptation of Christ*. It was assailed as blasphemous by religious conservatives, most of whom had not seen the film. I realized at the time it didn't matter whether they had seen it. This was not a debate about the spiritual values of *Last Temptation*; this was a fight about who controls the culture. *Last Temptation*, like other cultural totems—flag burning, Robert Mapplethorpe, gun control, NEA, abortion—had become a symbol of cultural hegemony.

Yes, the entertainment industry is an empty, soulless empire. I can't bring myself to defend many of the films now made; I can't even defend those Dole approves of. Hollywood must examine itself. Its greed is sickening. It must judge the social impact, not just the popularity impact, of what it does. So must politicians who seek to exploit cultural values.

KATHA POLLITT, *Poet, writer and social critic*

People like pop culture—that's what makes it popular. Movies drenched in sex and gore, gangsta rap, even outright pornography are not some sort of alien interstellar dust malevolently drifting down on us, but products actively sought out and beloved by millions. When fighting to abolish the NEA and other government support for the arts, conservatives are quick to condemn "cultural elitism" and exalt the majority tastes served by the marketplace. So how can they turn around and blame entertainment corporations for following the money and giving mass audiences what they want? Talk about elitism!

I too dislike many pop-culture products, although probably not the ones that bother Senator Dole. But the fact is, no system of regulation or voluntary restraint is going to have much effect on mass entertainment. And I'd like to hear how Dole squares his antiviolence stand with his ardent support for the NRA and the overturning of the assault-weapons ban. Guns don't kill people; rap music kills people? Oliver Stone movies kill people? Please.

Ultimately, culture reflects society—for a violent nation, violent amusements. But if Senator Dole and his fellow conservatives are serious about elevating American tastes, they'd do better to encourage greater variety in culture than to seek to homogenize it even further. Let them increase the NEA budget until it at least equals that for military bands. Let them restore to the public schools the art and music and performance programs that have been cut in the name of "getting back to basics." Let them support public radio and television—or not complain when the kids watch Beavis and Butthead and their parents watch "Married ... With Children," a show whose raw humor at the expense of family values enriches not some Hollywood liberal, by the way, but Newt Gingrich's publisher, Rupert Murdoch.

That Dole and other cultural conservatives claim to speak out of concern for women is particularly galling. What have they ever done for women? These are the same people who were silent when Republican Congressmen compared poor single mothers to mules and alligators, who want to ban abortion. If these men want to do something about entertainment that insults women, why not start with Rush Limbaugh and his references to pro-choice women as "feminazis"? Oh, but I forgot. Criticizing gangsta rap for demeaning women is defending "American values." Criticizing right-wing talk radio for doing the same is "politically correct."

DANYEL SMITH, *Music editor, VIBE magazine*

Senator Bob Dole's recent attacks on hip-hop music and violent films are as ugly and transparent as some of the so-called gangsta rappers he wants to huff and puff and blow away. Like those of the worst rappers, Dole's views sound tinny and half-desperate. Like the lamest films, Dole goes for the spectacular (guns, violence, melodrama) rather than the substantive (love, sex, race, class). The main thing Dole, weak rappers and weak movies share is an ultimate goal: money. Staten Island hip-hoppers Wu-Tang Clan said it best with their 1994 hit single, "C.R.E.A.M." (Cash Rules Everything Around Me).

The mass of folks going to the movies and buying records are in their teens, 20s and early 30s. The optimism of *Forrest Gump* rang false for a lot of us. *The Lion King* offered moments of uplift that faded when the lights came up. But hip-hop songs such as KRS, "One's Build & Destroy," Gang Starr's "Just to Get a Rep" and Tupac Shakur's "Holler If Ya Hear Me" sound fierce and true, reflecting in mood and content the real world around me and many hundreds of thousands of fans.

Yes, sexism runs rampant through hip-hop. But it, like the violence in the music, runs rampant through the world, and needs to be protested and dealt with—not just silenced on the whim of an ambitious politician. The assumption that simply because the Notorious B.I.G. raps around gunfire in a song, people are going to run out and shoot stuff up is insulting and tired. We are trying to make sense of the world—just like every generation has had to do. Forgive us if our salve is your sandpaper, but we are not you—and we're not sure we want to be.

BILL BRADLEY, *Democratic Senator from New Jersey*

I applaud Senator Dole. Almost by any measure, the airwaves have become the pathways for too much trash. Violence without context and sex without attachment come into our homes too frequently in ways that we cannot control unless we are monitoring the television constantly.

Studies show that by the time a kid reaches 18, he's seen 26,000 murders on TV. That has implications. It creates a sense of unreality about the finality, pain, suffering and inhumanity of brutal violence. The question really is, What is government's role? The answer has got to be more citizenship in the boardroom, not censorship. The public has got to hold boards of directors, executives and corporations accountable for making money out of trash.

For example, if you see something that offends you, find out who the sponsor is, find out who's on its board of directors, find out where they live, who their neighbors are, their local clubs, churches and synagogues. Send a letter to the members of the board at their homes and ask whether they realize they are making huge profits from the brutal degradation of other human beings. Then send a copy of that letter to all of their neighbors and friends. You can also begin to put economic pressure on a corporation. Because the market that the economic conservative champions undermines the moral character that the social conservative desires, you have to try to introduce into the functioning of the market a moral sensibility that is usually absent.

DAVID MAMET, *Playwright*

Politics seems to me much like the practice of stage magic. The magician is rewarded for appearing to perform that which we know to be impossible. We onlookers agree to endorse his claims and applaud his accomplishments if he can complete his performance before getting caught out. Similarly, we know, in our hearts, that politicians running for office are, in the main, mountebanks. They promise us an impossible future, or in the case of Senator Dole, a return to an imaginary pristine past.

It is in our nature to credit the ridiculous for the sake of the momentary enjoyment it affords. We do so at the magic show, at the car showroom and during the electoral process. It has long been the favored trick of the Republican Party to seek support through the creation of a villain. This imaginary being, whose presence stands between us and a Perfect World, this pornographer, this purveyor of filth, this destroyer of the family is he or she who used to be known by the name of communist, fellow traveler, labor agitator. Other historical names include nigger lover, papist, Yellow Peril, faggot and Jew.

It is the pleasure of the demagogue to turn otherwise sane people one against the other by this ancient trick, in order to further his or her own personal ends.

Yes, popular culture, in the main, is garbage. Perhaps it always has been, I don't know. I know we have a legitimate human desire for leadership, and Senator Dole's demagoguery corrupts this desire into a search for a victim and a longing for revenge. Whether as entertainment or politics, I find such actions objectionable.

STANLEY CROUCH, *Critic*

Regardless of the political opportunism that may propel the rising attack on the entertainment industry, the attention is more than a good thing because our mass popular culture is the most influential in the world. But when questions are raised about that industry's irresponsible promotion of certain material, the industry's executives tell us it has no influence. Everyone has to know that is a steaming pile of shuck. At its best, popular art has been part of our ongoing redefinition of American life, moving us to question our prejudices and our political policies, our social fears and the ways in which we live our personal lives.

But what we are faced with now is the panting exploitation of all our worst inclinations. We see the cult of slut chic in which Madonna has been such an influence across all lines of race and style that video after video looks like a combination of film-school virtuosity and bimbo routines with a backbeat. We see films in which dramatic intensity is replaced by the shock of gore that takes place in a ruthless universe of amoral one-liners derived from James Bond.

Narcissism and anarchic resentment are promoted in such a calculated fashion that numskull pop stars pretend to be rebels while adhering to the most obvious trends. The executives who promote these performers say that the issue is one of "freedom of expression," while others claim that we are getting "reports from the streets." But the rapper Ice Cube told an interviewer that his work was for young people and that if his audience wanted something else he would give it to them. That is not the statement of a rebel.

These people are not about breaking taboos, they are about making money, and they know where to draw the line. A few years ago, there was an understandable controversy about the anti-Semitic statements of Professor Griff when he was a member of the rap group Public Enemy. He was soon gone from the group. That is a perfect example of how responsibly the industry can work. We will hear no "reports from the streets" that give voice to the mad ravings of Khalid Muhammad or Louis Farrakhan, regardless of the young black people who cheer them at rallies. We have no idea how often the words "nigger," "bitch" and "ho" have been recorded in gangsta rap, but we can be comfortably sure that no rap group will ever be signed and promoted if it uses the word "kike" as frequently. Nor should it be.

Why is this? Because the Third Reich proved beyond all reasonable doubt what the constant pumping of hate-filled images and inflammatory statements can do to a culture. I do not believe censorship is the answer. But I have no doubt good taste and responsibility will not limit the entertainment industry's ability to provide mature work that attacks our corruption, challenges our paranoia and pulls the covers off the shortcomings that

Balkanize us. What we need is simply the same sense of responsibility and dire consequences that we bring to the issue of anti-Semitism.

## This Text: Reading

1. What do you make of Williams' chart? Does it hold true according to your experience?
2. When people speak of media violence, they rarely mention pornography. In what way is pornography violence? Is it more harmful than say, a Western shootout?
3. For what recent movies would Williams' assertions be appropriate?
4. Erdrich's poem centers itself around the notion of violence, concentrated in the icon (and body) of John Wayne. How is Wayne a symbol for violence? How does Erdrich's poem alter the context of watching a Western movie?
5. Like Erdrich, Alexie transforms filmic violence into a symbol for violence against American Indians. Is his poem successful? What connections is he trying to make? In his poem called "My Heroes Have Never Been Cowboys," Alexie claims that Indians are "all extras" in the great Western that is American history. Explain what he means.
6. How do the poems by Alexie and Erdrich affect your notions of film violence and American history?
7. Based on their comments regarding film violence in "Tough Talk on Entertainment," can you determine each writer's political leanings? How?
8. Which of the five perspectives do you agree with most? With which one do you find yourself in the most disagreement? Is there one that seems to you exactly in the middle of the road?
9. Do any of these perspectives support the claims of Williams, Erdrich, or Alexie? Do you see any overlap between one of these five responses and the other three texts in this suite?

## Your Text: Writing

1. Write a comparative essay on "Dear John Wayne" and "Texas Chainsaw Massacre." Both are about violence, race, and movies, yet they take very different approaches. How does reading them together affect how we see them individually?
2. Write a paper in which you compare how women are represented in horror films to how women are represented in advertisements.
3. Write an analytical essay exploring representations of men in horror films. Do men come off better than women? Do you know of any horror movies written or directed by women?

4. Why do you think so few commentators in the "Tough Talk" segment talk about violence toward women and minorities? Do we have too narrow a view of movie violence? What about violence toward the environment? Toward the poor?
5. Write a research paper in which you examine the topic of media violence. Is there compelling evidence that movie violence translates into human violence?

---

# READING OUTSIDE THE LINES

## Classroom Activities

1. As a class, watch one of the movies under review in this section. Write your own review of the movie without talking to anyone else in class about the movie. Then, after a class discussion, write yet another review of the movie. How does your own reading of the movie change after class discussion?
2. Watch a movie in class and write a group review. What are the major points of disagreement? On what was it easy to agree?
3. View any of the movies that you have read about in the previous texts. Do you agree with the writers? Why or why not?
4. Is watching a movie in class different than watching one at home or in a theatre? Why? Have a class discussion on the space of watching movies.
5. Write a poem about the *experience* of watching a particular film (like Erdrich's "Dear John Wayne"). How does writing a poem about a movie differ from writing a journal entry or a formal paper? Is there a relationship between poems and film?
6. Bring advertisements or commercials about particular movies to class. Discuss the demographic the studio is targeting. Do the commercials and ads *tell* you how to read the movie?
7. As you watch a movie in class, write down every form of manipulation you notice (such as music, close-ups, special effects, camera angles, unusual editing, intense colors).
8. Watch a recent movie that was praised by critics but was seemingly ignored by the general public (*Three Kings, Red, Simple Men, Vanya on 42$^{nd}$ Street, The Straight Story, Rushmore, Secrets and Lies, You Can Count on Me, Boys Don't Cry, American Movie, The Winslow Boy, Ghost World*). Why do you think not many people saw these films? Why do you think critics loved these particular movies? Is there tension between critical and popular taste?

9. Talk about the criteria and expectations of different genres in class. What characteristics must a romantic comedy have? What is the purpose of a Western? What does an action–adventure movie need to do? What makes a good scary movie?
10. Find a copy of the American Film Institute's top 100 American movies. Talk about the list in class. Why did these movies make the list? What movies are missing? Why?

## Essay Ideas

1. What is your favorite teen movie? Would you establish different criteria than Denby? Why? What would your criteria be? Write an essay in which you argue that a specific movie is the ideal teen movie.
2. Chances are, you have seen *Moulin Rouge* or *Pearl Harbor*. Write your own analytical review of one of these films. Feel free to reference one of the reviews you have read. Perhaps you will agree or disagree with one (or many) of the reviewers. Be sure to analyze the film; don't simply write a plot summary.
3. bell hooks's review of *Waiting to Exhale* is a pretty provocative text. Track down a positive review of the film and write a comparison/contrast paper in which you not only identify but explore the variant readings of the films.
4. Write an essay on a director's body of work. People like Steven Spielberg, Woody Allen, Quentin Tarantino, Penny Marshall, Stanley Kubric, John Sayles, Spike Lee, Michael Bay, Paul Verhoven, or Howard Hawkes, who have directed a number of different movies, will make your essay more interesting. Is there an overarching theme to their movies? How have they contributed to film history? To American culture?
5. Write an essay in which you explore issues of gender in one or two recent movies. Perhaps you can pick a movie directed by a woman and one directed by a man. How are women represented? How are women's bodies presented or framed? Male bodies? Do the women have strong roles, or are they limited, stereotypical roles? Do the women date or love men their own age, or are the men much older? Do the women have good jobs and healthy lifestyles?
6. Write an essay in which you explore issues of race. As in gender, how are issues of race and power represented in the film? What kind of music runs through the film? Are minority characters filmed or framed differently than Anglo characters? There is an old joke that the one black character in a horror film is one of the first to die. Is this still the case? While there are a number of wonderful movies by people of color (*Do the Right Thing, Smoke Signals, The Joy Luck Club, Mississippi Masala, El*

*Mariachi*), you might also consider how minorities are represented in movies made by Anglos.

7. Explore notions of class in American cinema. How often are poor people in movies? While there may be women and people of color in Hollywood and in the studio system, how well does Hollywood understand low-income America? Are there realistic film portrayals of working class or low-income families? Some would say that America is more classist than racist: Is this theory proven or refuted by Hollywood?
8. Write an essay in which you offer a reading of a film based solely on the film techniques: sound, lighting, camera angles, music, framing, and editing. How can technique determine meaning?

# Interchapter: Reading Images

This is a book primarily comprised of words, but let's be honest—we like pictures. With the proliferation of television, movies, video games, computers, and advertising, we have become a culture that tends to define itself through visual images. The act of reading *these* words on *this* page remains a visual activity. As we explain in the introduction, reading is nothing more than visual decoding of images so familiar that we do not even think of them as images. We don't think of text on the page as pictures, but each word is a small picture of curved, slanted and dotted marks that we call "letters." When we put certain combinations of these letters together, they conjure up a particular idea or image in our heads. While words are images themselves and reflect other images, we're more concerned here with the way we constantly decode, often with little conscious effort, the multiple images that we encounter each day—from people's faces to television shows to book covers to signs to architecture. One of this book's main ideas, in fact, is slowing down the reading process of visual images. As you may have noticed, almost all of the chapters in this book involve visual decoding of some sort.

Our book's insistence on this type of reading stands behind our idea to simply present some images here as a way of focusing our attention on the visual. The kinds of images we offer in this chapter need little introduction, but we will provide a brief entree into our thinking behind this chapter. First of all, we present pairs of images. We remain interested in how images speak (both directly and indirectly) to each other and how details of specific images become highlighted or accentuated when placed in context with another picture. For instance, a small, older wooden house in a working class neighborhood may appear quite different depending on its context. Next to the White House, it may seem tiny and almost shabby, but next to a grass hut from a Third World country, it could appear downright spacious and luxurious. In this chapter, you will be given six combinations of images. Our hope is that you will engage a semiotic reading not only of the individual images but that you will do a semiotic analysis of the pair of images.

To this end, we've identified and reiterated a few points about reading visual images:

## Images are texts that can and should be read.

Again, as we point out in our discussion of semiotics in the Introduction to this text, we ask that you apply the vocabulary and attention you devote to reading written texts to reading visual texts. When we open a book or look at directions or scan a newspaper, we are conscious of the act of reading.

We know that our eyes move across a page and process information, and most important, we are conscious of the information that this process of looking produces. That is, we know we are reading for information, for content—we know that there is a message to most written texts.

However, the title and the thesis of this book is that the world is a text; that means that all images are texts, and as such, demand to be read as thoroughly as a poem or textbook. In fact, we would argue that visual images such as advertisements, television and movies, photographs, album covers, movie posters, and T-shirts should be read with particular care because images transmit so many values and assumptions but are transmitted quietly and subconsciously. Because images do not come in the language of analysis (words), we tend not to analyze them as closely, if at all. We urge you to analyze all images.

## Reading images is usually an informal rather than a formal process.

As we note above, reading images tends to be an informal process—that is, we are not aware of the process of reading images. We take them in and move on, giving very little thought to the thousands of visual cues we see every few seconds. To formalize the process of reading images, all we need to do is become conscious readers of images as constructed texts. For instance, this morning if you combed your hair, washed, shaved, put on make-up—if you thought about what to wear at all—then you did some work in constructing yourself as a text. You knew that today, like every other day, you were going to be read, on some level, and you wanted to send certain cues. Perhaps you wanted to suggest that you are alternative, conservative, athletic, bookish, or sophisticated. Depending on the image you wanted to project, you would don the appropriate signifiers.

When the other students look at you as you walk into class or as patrons in the coffee shop regard you as you order a latte, they do an informal reading of you—even if it is very brief and even if they don't know they are doing it at all. They might notice something has changed about you, but they would likely acquire even this information informally—virtually no one would actively ask the question, "How has X changed her appearance today? Let me take a thorough inventory of hairstyle, clothing, grooming." The same kind of quick informal reading usually goes into our appraisal of images. How often do we *really* stop to consider everything, all the details, that contribute to the overall message of the image? Here is where reading images mirrors reading visual arts—we must be aware of issues of composition, how the image is put together. As soon as you begin asking questions about what message a certain image is supposed to send, as soon as you read the image on *your own terms*—that is, when you begin to read the image not as the image wants to be read but as something to analyze—then you will formalize the reading process and begin to see the world in a more complex way.

## The reader/viewer always participates in the construction and significance of the image.

The Confederate flag, the "Stars and Bars," has become one of the most controversial American images in the last 50 years. Perhaps more than any other American icon, the Stars and Bars reveals how deeply our own backgrounds, culture, and political beliefs determine how we "read" images. For some white southerners, the flag stands as a symbol of rebellion and independence. For white northerners or those not from the South, the Stars and Bars may reinforce negative stereotypes about southern culture. For yet another population, African-Americans, the Stars and Bars stands a salient and prominent symbol of slavery and racism. Why do each of these groups have such different interpretations of a simple red rectangle, crossed by two blue bars and some white stripes? The answer is simple. We cannot "see" the flag (or any image) outside of our own ideas.

Whether the image under debate is a photo of Osama bin Laden, Bill Clinton talking with Monica Lewinsky, a topless supermodel, a multiracial couple, an electric chair, a fetus, a church, or a chemistry textbook, we each bring to the image our own set of assumptions and prejudices. This realization is important because it underscores the gap between intention and reception. By intention or intent, we mean the motivation behind producing or displaying the text, whereas reception is the reaction to the text—how the text is received. In many instances, intention and reception have nothing to do with each other. Recently, a local judge hung a copy of the Ten Commandments above his bench inside a public courtroom. Some local residents were outraged, claiming that hanging up the Ten Commandments was publicly stating that the judge would rule from a position that is sympathetic to an Old Testament Judeo-Christian perspective, thereby admitting de facto discrimination against non-Christians. Was the judge intending to send this message? Probably not. Is this message a valid *reception* of the text? Probably.

In addition, the American flag means something different in Afghanistan than it does in Ireland. The logo for the Atlanta Braves sends one message to folks in Georgia and another to folks on the Rosebud Indian reservation in South Dakota. The photograph of new first lady Hillary Rodham Clinton holding hands with outgoing first lady Barbara Bush incites very different reactions depending on your political leanings. Our point is that no reading of an image is ever value free. We are active participants in the construction and reception of an image, and by extension, the world.

# Worksheet

## THIS TEXT

1. What is the semiotic situation of the image? What are its signifiers?
2. What social, political, and cultural forces affect the image?
3. What visual cues appear in the text?
4. What kinds of details, symbols, and codes send messages in the image?
5. What is the composition of the image?
6. Do you think there might be any tension between the image's intention and reception?
7. What kind of story does the image tell? How does it tell that story?
8. Does the image rely on patriotic or sentimental associations to manipulate the viewer?
9. Can you sum up the theme of the image?

## BEYOND THIS TEXT

**Media:** How do news programs, magazines, and newspapers use images to tell stories or convey ideas?

**Advertising:** Advertising is perhaps the most notorious user of loaded images. How do magazine ads and billboards use images to help sell products? What values do we tend to see in ads? What kind of associations, people, and cultures tend to reappear over and over?

**Television:** To what degree does television rely on images? Would you sit in front of a TV if there were only words and no picture? How are characters in shows carefully constructed texts? And, what about commercials? How do commercials use images to manipulate viewers?

**Movies:** Do movies use images differently than television? If so, how?

**Icons:** The swastika. The peace symbol. The bald eagle. A cactus. A white cowboy hat. The McDonalds golden arches. The American flag. The Mexican flag. High heels. All of these are icons. How do icons rely on strong values associated with visual images? How are icons constructed texts?

**Public space:** How do public and private areas rely on images to get us to feel a certain way? More specifically, what roles do billboards and murals play in public life? What about things like posters or framed art in a dorm room, bedroom, or house?

**Music:** How does what a band looks like, or what an album looks like, influence the way we look at a band?

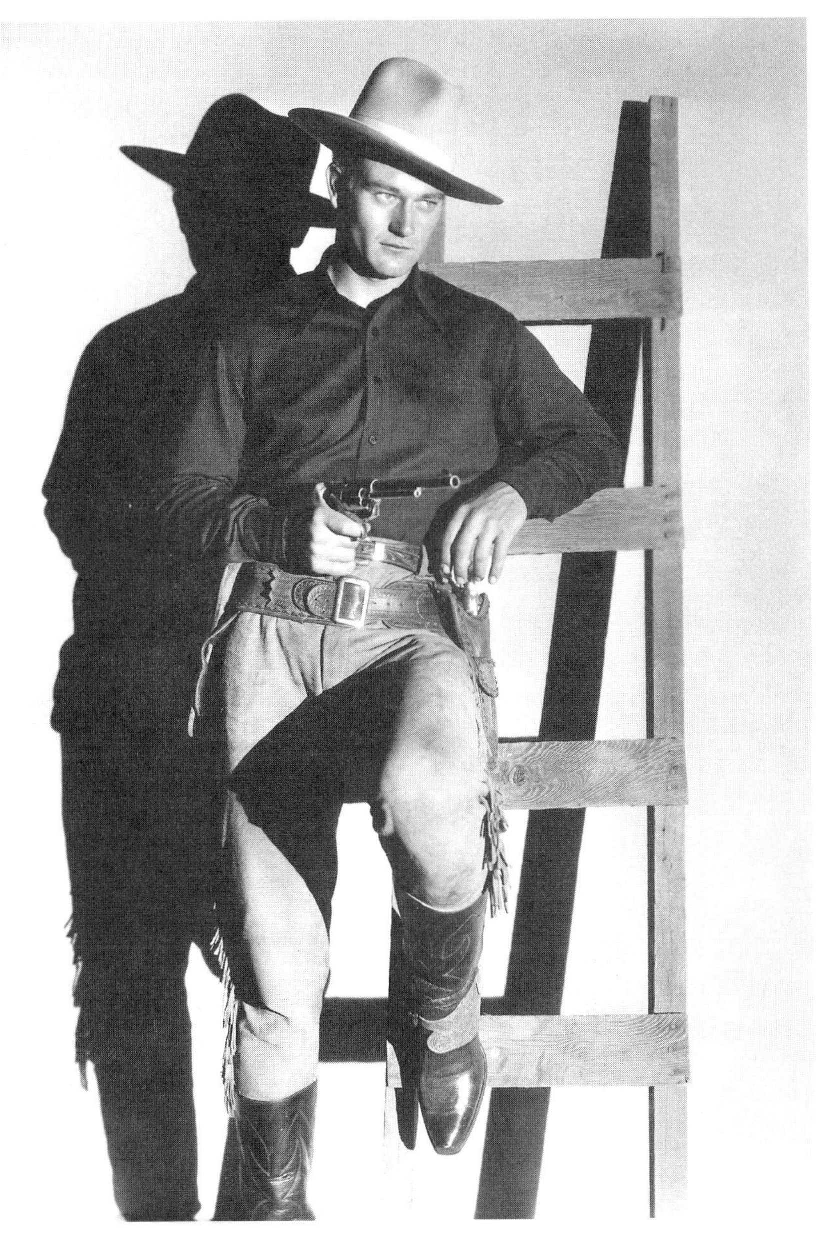

Awards

LEISURE SERVICES DEPT.
CUSTOMER RESEARCH
LOCK IT
OR

## These Texts: Reading

1. The photograph of John Wayne contains a number of signifiers. How many icons or symbols do you see in the photograph?
2. Does the photo of Jackie Chan seem out of place next to John Wayne? Why? If the shot of Chan included all of the icons in the photo of Wayne, would it seem even more odd?
3. What are the similarities between the Mona Lisa and Britney Spears?
4. How do a photograph and painting differ in terms of their signifiers? Does one allow more input from the viewer?
5. Greek Revival houses in the United States often have unsavory connotations, namely as fraternity houses and plantations. Why do you think this is the case?
6. How do the two "laundry" photographs represent different notions of what laundry does and is?
7. Can you gauge your physical reaction when looking at the American flag versus the Mexican flag? Do the colors symbolize different things for you in each flag?
8. Which flag do you find more aesthetically pleasing?

## Your Text: Writing

1. Write a comparison/contrast essay on the cowboy images. How does race figure into the myth of the American West?
2. Give a semiotic reading of the images of the Mona Lisa and Britney Spears. Identify at least three signifiers in each image.
3. Why do you think the White House and many other official buildings are modeled on the Parthenon and Greek architecture in general? What kind of message does such a structure send?
4. Write a descriptive paper on the place where you do your laundry. How is the act of doing or hanging laundry in a public place an intimate act?
5. Compare or contrast the laundry photos. How are they similar? What is missing from each?
6. Write down the first five things that pop into your head when you see the Mexican flag. Do the same for the American flag. Write an essay in which you explore the different values you assign to each.

# 6

# READING GENDER

"What do they mean 'Reading Gender?'—how can you *read* gender? Isn't it obvious?" If you are reading this introduction for the first time, we suspect this is what a lot of you are thinking right now. For many of you, details of gender are cut and dried, black and white, male and female. For that reason alone this book warrants a chapter on gender, but, as you will soon see, there are many other reasons why one might be interested in reading gender in a sophisticated way.

Without question, gender has become one of the most hotly contested subjects in American culture. What's more, it's been hotly contested and at the forefront of public debate for centuries. Ancient poets like Sappho or early Greek plays like Aristophanes' *Lysistrata* were exploring issues of inequality between the genders long before Gloria Steinem, perhaps the most public feminist of the past three decades. More recently than Sappho or Aristophanes, an amazing Mexican nun named Sor Juana de la Cruz wrote poems and letters extolling the virtues of education for women and insisting on Biblical imperatives for equality. And over 200 years before Susan Faludi's *Backlash*, a controversial book appearing in 1992 that posited a backlash against American women, Mary Wollstencraft wrote an important and influential essay entitled "Vindication on the Rights of Women" in which she called for a recognition of women as "rational creatures" capable of the same intellectual and emotional proficiency as men. So while certain aspects of this chapter may feel new to you, in truth, people have been reading gender for centuries.

Still, perhaps it would be beneficial to talk about what we mean by the term "gender." When we use "gender" we refer to socially constructed behaviors and identity tags, such as "feminine" and "masculine." Gender should not be confused with "sex," which speaks only to biological differences between males and females. "Sex" then refers to biology, "gender" to culture and society.

If you've read the chapters on movies or television, then you know that having experience reading a certain text is not the same as reading it well. Similarly, many of you have significant experience reading genders, but you may not be very probing readers of gender. This chapter in particular (and college in general) is designed to remedy that. On one hand, reading gender implies a kind of superficial determination of another person's sex. In recent times, it can be somewhat difficult to tell if a person is a man, a woman, or neither. Those of you with a soft spot for classic rock may remember a similar line from the long-haired Bob Seeger, who, in his song "On the Road Again," adopts the persona of someone who finds his long hair disturbing: "same old cliché / Is it a woman or a man?" This statement and the simple fact that we assume that we can tell if a person is male or female suggests that there are traits or cues that might tip us off. These codes or behaviors are called "doing gender," and we all do gender at some point. "Doing gender" means participating in any behavior associated with a certain gender such as painting your nails, growing a beard, and wearing high heels, earrings, make-up, neckties, and sports jerseys. In each of the previous examples, every one of you associated a certain trait with a certain gender. Did you link painting nails with men or wearing neckties with women? Probably not, but it is likely that most of you have seen a man sport painted nails or a woman wear a necktie. These people are playing with typical expectations of gender, and to some degree, we all do that a little bit. In fact, if, like us, you've lived in New York or San Francisco where gender diversity is more common and more accepted, then you've likely encountered women with facial hair and men in heels.

If there are external traits in a culture, then it's probable that there are assumed internal gender traits in a culture as well. Though these external indicators may seem minor, ultimately, as you have probably noticed by now, doing gender often translates into men doing dominance and women doing submission. For instance, in America, most people tend to associate nurturing behavior with women and aggressive behavior with men. Similarly, women are dainty while men are rough; women are refined, whereas men are brutish. But is this always the case? As you read this, you are probably thinking of some dainty guys you know and some brutish women. What's more, you should be able to identify specific moments in your own lives and in the lives of your parents, siblings and close friends when they have, even if for an instant, done something that reminded you of another gender. The point is that we carry so many assumptions, many of them dangerous, about genders that we may discover that we have already *interpreted* gender before we have read and thought deeply about gender and genders.

Our goal in this chapter is to encourage you to rethink any preconceptions about gender and expectations of gender. Why do we expect women to be "emotional"? Why do we expect men to be "responsible"? Why is there societal pressure on women to be thin? Why aren't men expected to wear make-up and shave their legs? Why is there no male equivalent for "slut"? Why aren't women taught to see marriage as the end of a certain kind of independence the same way men are? Why don't boys get dressed up and play groom? Why are all of our presidents men? Why are most kindergarten teachers women? These are puzzling phenomena that raise more questions than answers; however, what we do know is that learning to read gender as a text will help you make sense of the world as roles become less black and white, less right and wrong, less male and female.

Social scientists remind us that gender is socially constructed, and therefore, in a way, we are recruited to gender. Consequently, society tends to punish those who don't conform to its gender roles. The goal of this chapter is to help you read the various means of recruitment; we want you to become savvy readers of the texts that encourage you to *do* gender.

## While one's sex may be determined by biology, gender is constructed.

What we mean by "constructed" is that gender is built, invented, created. Of course, though some gender traits might seem to be related to one's biological make-up, gender can be thought of as constructed or "performed." We can think of these traits in both external and internal terms. For instance, our culture assigns certain behaviors or characteristics to maleness. These may include strength, rationality, virility, affluence, and stability. To send out cues that he possesses all these things, a man may bulk up, he may wear designer clothes and drive a sports car, he may watch and play a lot of sports, he may date a lot of women or men. However, what if the values our culture assigned to maleness were grace, daintiness, refinement, monogamy, and nurturing? What if *these* traits were the most male traits? Would men still bulk up, watch football, go hunting, watch *Rambo* movies, and drive pickups? Some might, but most would not. Why? Because they would be ostracized and stigmatized, not seen as "real" men, according to society's expectations of masculine behavior.

Of course, doing gender is not reserved for straight folks. Chances are, you are familiar with terms like "butch," "femme," and "queen." That these terms exist suggests how important gender constructs are to our identities, and they reveal how, even in same-sex relationships, we do gender. What's more, as many gay and lesbians will confirm, gender has nothing to do with biology. Most gays and lesbians would argue that genders are, in fact, fluid. For many, having a penis does not prohibit someone from being or living as a woman, just as having breasts and a vagina does not prohibit many people from living or passing as a man. Here, the distinction between "sex" and "gender" is critical. You may have your own assumptions about how gay men and women do gender, just as you have expectations about how straight men and women do gender.

Just as external elements connote gender, so do internal elements. For instance, what if mainstream heterosexual female behavior were characterized by aggression, dominance, sexual assertiveness and independence? Would women still wait for men to make the first move? Would women still link their sense of identity with men? Would women think of marriage in the same way? Would women feel differently about their bodies? Would women be afraid to beat their dates in bowling or fear appearing smarter than their male partners? So, without even knowing it, you are probably performing or doing gender in various aspects of your lives. There is not necessarily anything wrong with this; however, you should be aware that there can be negative implications, and we would encourage you to read your own gender and the genders of others with increased care and sensitivity.

## Our perceptions of gender can be influenced by a number of factors, including stereotypes, tradition, and popular culture.

We are all aware of stereotypes surrounding gender: Women are better communicators, men are stronger, men like power tools, women like "chick flicks." Without realizing it, you may make gendered assumptions about traits of women versus men. For instance, if you are in a grocery store, and you want to know the ingredients for a cake, who are you most likely to ask: a woman or a man? If someone tells you they have a wonderful new doctor, are you more likely to assume it's a man or a woman? If you hear that someone went on a shooting spree in a school, are you most likely to assume that person was male or female? Stereotypes are amazingly powerful, and we may not realize the degree to which our thoughts, beliefs, and actions are shaped by them.

Similarly, cultural and family traditions continue to affect how we see ourselves and other genders. We have a number of female and male friends who complain about how, after every holiday dinner, the men adjourn to the living room to watch sports, while the women clear the tables and do the dishes. At that same dinner, it's likely that the father or grandfather carves the turkey or ham and perhaps even says the prayer. One might say that these are roles that both genders silently agree to, yet others might say that these behaviors reflect and inscribe a pattern suggesting that the important duties are reserved for men, while cleaning remains "women's work." Thus, we grow up not merely ascribing values to genders but linking the importance of specific genders to the importance our society places on the kind of work and duties we think of as "female" and "male."

Perhaps most persuasive of all is popular culture. How many of our preconceptions about gender come from billboards, television shows, advertisements, movies, and commercials? Research indicates quite a bit. For instance, psychologists and advertisers suggest that the average viewer believes about one in eight commercials she or he watches. That may not seem like a great deal, but over the course of eighteen or nineteen years, you have seen (and probably internalized) a number of commercials, many of which have, no doubt, influenced your own views of gender. From rock and country music lyrics to commercials for cleaning products to NFL pregame shows to advertisements for jeans and tequila to television sitcoms to the infamous beer commercials, images of men and women doing gender flood us from all sides. Because of this, pop culture can fuse into stereotype, and tradition can meld into popular culture—at times we may not know which comes from which. So many people conform to the expectations of gender roles, that gender roles appear natural or innate. We urge you to stop and think for a moment before assuming anything about gender.

### Feminism (or feminisms) can and should be supported by both men and women.

Often we ask our students if they believe that women should be paid the same as men. They say yes. We ask them if they think men are inherently smarter than women. They say no—usually an emphatic no. We ask them if they believe that women should be afforded the same opportunities for employment as men. They all say yes. We ask them if they think that there should be equality between men and women. All claim there should. Yet, when we ask how many are feminists, virtually none raise their hands. This reality continues to be perplexing and frustrating.

There are any number of definitions of feminism, ranging from very open definitions (if you think men and women should be treated equally then you are a feminist) to more forceful definitions, such as Barbara Smith's ("Feminism is the political theory and practice that struggles to free *all* women: women of color, working class women, poor women, Jewish women, disabled women, lesbians, old women—as well as white, economically privileged, heterosexual women."). Some people think that a definition of feminism must be religiously conceived, since much discrimination has ties to religious conservatism (a feminist is a person who supports the theory that God the Mother is equal to God the Father). Though neither of the authors are women, both consider themselves feminist and lean toward a definition of feminism that is broad enough to take in all interested parties. For us, feminism is the understanding that there has been an imbalance between how men and women have been treated and that balance among genders must be restored. We also tend to believe that feminism implies more than a passing interest in bringing about this change; feminists must, on some level, act in a way that helps facilitate a more equitable balance. These actions might be as small as refraining from using sexist language or as large as protesting in front of the Capitol. Thus, we prefer the term "feminisms" because it acknowledges the fact that feminism is as individual as each individual.

For some reason, many students associate feminism with hating men, not shaving legs, not being charming, being militant, being strident and in general, being unlikable. None of these traits has ever been part of the mission of feminism. Rather, feminism as an idea, as an ideology, has always been about equality. In fact, there remains no single feminism but, as we've suggested, inclusive and intriguing "feminisms." Instead of thinking of feminisms as exclusionary, it is more helpful and more accurate to think of feminisms as inclusive.

## There is a double standard in America regarding men and women.

You really don't need a textbook to tell you this—most of you already know it. Most women would acknowledge that they feel a palpable pressure to be thin, virginal, and refined, whereas American culture not only allows but encourages males to be physically comfortable, sexually adventurous, and crass. Similarly, women who work in the corporate world have argued for decades that female behavior characterized as bitchy, cold, and calculating when enacted by women is praised and considered commanding, rational, and strategic when carried out by men. On the other hand, both men and women have suggested recently that cultural pressure on men to be in control, in charge, and emotionally cool, leaves little room for personal growth and fulfillment.

Even though America has grown immensely in terms of gender equity, there remain dozens of unwritten or even unspoken codes that both men and women feel compelled to adhere to. Thus, how people of different genders act in the world has everything to do with cultural expectations placed on their genders. Moreover, when men and women do gender properly—that is, as society dictates they should—they make gender seem invariable and inevitable, which then seems to justify structural inequalities such as the pay gap, the lack of elected female politicians, or even good roles for women in theater, film, and television.

In short, issues of gender involve more than leaving the toilet seat up; they arise out of personal, public, private, and cultural worlds. We hope that this chapter will make you a more engaged reader of how gender gets enacted in each of these worlds.

# Worksheet

## THIS TEXT

1. While it will be impossible for you to know this fully, try to figure out the writing situation of each author. Who is the audience? What does the author have at stake? What is his or her agenda? Why is she or he writing this piece?
2. What social, political, and cultural forces affect the author's text? What is going on in the world as he or she is writing?
3. This is a chapter about gender, so, obviously, you should be aware of the gender of the author.
4. How does the author define gender? Does s/he confuse "gender" and "sex"?
5. When taken as a whole, what do these texts tell you about how we construct gender?
6. How do stories and essays differ in their arguments about gender?
7. Is the author's argument valid? Is it reasonable?
8. Ideas and beliefs about gender tend to be very sensitive, deeply held convictions. Do you find yourself in agreement with the author? Why or why not? Do you agree with the editors' introduction?
9. Does the author help you read gender better than you did before reading the essay? If so, why? How do we learn to read gender?
10. If you are reading a short story or poem, then where does the text take place? When is it set?
11. What are the main conflicts in the text? What issues are at stake?
12. What kinds of issues of identity is the author working with in the text?
13. Is there tension between the self and society in the text? How? Why?
14. How do gender codes and expectations differ among cultures?
15. Did I like this? Why or why not?

## BEYOND THIS TEXT

**Media:** How are men and women portrayed in television shows, movies, video games, and music videos? Does the media try to set the criteria for what is "male" and what is "female?" How do they do this?

**Advertising:** How are women and men portrayed in magazine ads? Do advertisers tend to associate certain products or tasks with a specific gender? How do ads influence how we read gender roles?

**Television:** Is there much variance in how men are portrayed on television? What kinds of shows are geared toward men? What about women? What kinds of activities do we see women do on television? Are gender roles related to stereotypes about race, class, and geography?

**Movies:** Many actors and actresses bemoan the lack of good movie roles for women. Why is this the case? Can you think of many movies in which a younger man falls for an older woman? How often do women rescue men in movies? Why is male nudity so rare and female nudity so coveted?

**Public space:** How do we know that a place is geared toward men or women? What visual clues do we see?

# MARKED WOMEN, UNMARKED MEN

Deborah Tannen

As though she were a student who had just read *The World Is a Text*, linguist Deborah Tannen uses an academic conference as a semiotic setting to read three other women. Based on textual cues or signs of the women's hair, clothes, and mannerisms, this 1993 essay gives a reading of each of these "texts," suggesting that women, more than men, are marked by cultural expectations.

SOME YEARS AGO I was at a small working conference of four women and eight men. Instead of concentrating on the discussion I found myself looking at the three other women at the table, thinking how each had a different style and how each style was coherent.

One woman had dark brown hair in a classic style, a cross between Cleopatra and Plain Jane. The severity of her straight hair was softened by wavy bangs and ends that turned under. Because she was beautiful, the effect was more Cleopatra than plain.

The second woman was older, full of dignity and composure. Her hair was cut in a fashionable style that left her with only one eye, thanks to a side part that let a curtain of hair fall across half her face. As she looked down to read her prepared paper, the hair robbed her of bifocal vision and created a barrier between her and the listeners.

The third woman's hair was wild, a frosted blond avalanche falling over and beyond her shoulders. When she spoke she frequently tossed her head, calling attention to her hair and away from her lecture.

Then there was makeup. The first woman wore facial cover that made her skin smooth and pale, a black line under each eye and mascara that darkened already dark lashes. The second wore only a light gloss on her lips and a hint of shadow on her eyes. The third had blue bands under her eyes, dark blue shadow, mascara, bright red lipstick and rouge; her fingernails flashed red.

I considered the clothes each woman had worn during the three days of the conference: In the first case, man-tailored suits in primary colors with solid-color blouses. In the second, casual but stylish black T-shirts, a floppy collarless jacket and baggy slacks or a skirt in neutral colors. The third wore a sexy jump suit; tight sleeveless jersey and tight yellow slacks; a dress with gaping armholes and an indulged tendency to fall off one shoulder.

Shoes? No. 1 wore string sandals with medium heels; No. 2, sensible, comfortable walking shoes; No. 3, pumps with spike heels. You can fill in the jewelry, scarves, shawls, sweaters—or lack of them.

As I amused myself finding coherence in these styles, I suddenly wondered why I was scrutinizing only the women. I scanned the eight men at the table. And then I knew why I wasn't studying them. The men's styles were unmarked.

The term "marked" is a staple of linguistic theory. It refers to the way language alters the base meaning of a word by adding a linguistic particle that has no meaning on its own. The unmarked form of a word carries the meaning that goes without saying—what you think of when you're not thinking anything special.

The unmarked tense of verbs in English is the present—for example, visit. To indicate past, you mark the verb by adding ed to yield visited. For future, you add a word: will visit. Nouns are presumed to be singular until marked for plural, typically by adding s or es, so visit becomes visits and dish becomes dishes.

The unmarked forms of most English words also convey "male." Being male is the unmarked case. Endings like ess and ette mark words as "female." Unfortunately, they also tend to mark them for frivolousness. Would you feel safe entrusting your life to a doctorette? Alfre Woodard, who was an Oscar nominee for best supporting actress, says she identifies herself as an actor because "actresses worry about eyelashes and cellulite, and women who are actors worry about the characters we are playing." Gender markers pick up extra meanings that reflect common associations with the female gender: not quite serious, often sexual.

Each of the women at the conference had to make decisions about hair, clothing, makeup and accessories, and each decision carried meaning. Every style available to us was marked. The men in our group had made decisions, too, but the range from which they chose was incomparably narrower. Men can choose styles that are marked, but they don't have to, and in this group none did. Unlike the women, they had the option of being unmarked.

Take the men's hair styles. There was no marine crew cut or oily longish hair falling into eyes, no asymmetrical, two-tiered construction to swirl over a bald top. One man was unabashedly bald; the others had hair of standard length, parted on one side, in natural shades of brown or gray or graying. Their hair obstructed no views, left little to toss or push back or run fingers through and, consequently, needed and attracted no attention. A few men had beards. In a business setting, beards might be marked. In this academic gathering, they weren't.

There could have been a cowboy shirt with string tie or a three-piece suit or a necklaced hippie in jeans. But there wasn't. All eight men wore brown or blue slacks and nondescript shirts of light colors. No man wore sandals or boots; their shoes were dark, closed, comfortable and flat. In short, unmarked.

Although no man wore makeup, you couldn't say the men didn't wear makeup in the sense that you could say a woman didn't wear makeup. For men, no makeup is unmarked.

I asked myself what style we women could have adopted that would have been unmarked, like the men's. The answer was none. There is no unmarked woman.

There is no woman's hair style that can be called standard, that says nothing about her. The range of women's hair styles is staggering, but a woman whose hair has no particular style is perceived as not caring about how she looks, which can disqualify her for many positions, and will subtly diminish her as a person in the eyes of some.

Women must choose between attractive shoes and comfortable shoes. When our group made an unexpected trek, the woman who wore flat, laced shoes arrived first. Last to arrive was the woman in spike heels, shoes in hand and a handful of men around her.

If a woman's clothing is tight or revealing (in other words, sexy), it sends a message—an intended one of wanting to be attractive, but also a possibly unintended one of availability. If her clothes are not sexy, that too sends a message, lent meaning by the knowledge that they could have been. There are thousands of cosmetic products from which women can choose and myriad ways of applying them. Yet no makeup at all is anything but unmarked. Some men see it as a hostile refusal to please them.

Women can't even fill out a form without telling stories about themselves. Most forms give four titles to choose from. "Mr." carries no meaning other than that the respondent is male. But a woman who checks "Mrs." or "Miss" communicates not only whether she has been married but also whether she has conservative tastes in forms of address—and probably other conservative values as well. Checking "Ms." declines to let on about marriage (checking "Mr." declines nothing since nothing was asked), but it also marks her as either liberated or rebellious, depending on the observer's attitudes and assumptions.

I sometimes try to duck these variously marked choices by giving my title as "Dr."—and in so doing risk marking myself as either uppity (hence sarcastic responses like "Excuse me!") or an overachiever (hence reactions of congratulatory surprise like "Good for you!").

All married women's surnames are marked. If a woman takes her husband's name, she announces to the world that she is married and has traditional values. To some it will indicate that she is less herself, more identified by her husband's identity. If she does not take her husband's name, this too is marked, seen as worthy of comment: she has done something; she has "kept her own name." A man is never said to have "kept his own name" because it never occurs to anyone that he might have given it up. For him using his own name is unmarked.

A married woman who wants to have her cake and eat it too may use her surname plus his, with or without a hyphen. But this too announces her marital status and often results in a tongue-tying string. In a list (Harvey O'Donovan, Jonathan Feldman, Stephanie Woodbury McGillicutty), the woman's multiple name stands out. It is marked.

I have never been inclined toward biological explanations of gender differences in language, but I was intrigued to see Ralph Fasold bring biological phenomena to bear on the question of linguistic marking in his book *The Sociolinguistics of Language*. Fasold stresses that language and culture are particularly unfair in treating women as the marked case because biologically it is the male that is marked. While two X chromosomes make a female, two Y chromosomes make nothing. Like the linguistic markers s, es or ess, the Y chromosome doesn't "mean" anything unless it is attached to a root form—an X chromosome.

Developing this idea elsewhere, Fasold points out that girls are born with fully female bodies, while boys are born with modified female bodies. He invites men who doubt this to lift up their shirts and contemplate why they have nipples.

In his book, Fasold notes "a wide range of facts which demonstrates that female is the unmarked sex." For example, he observes that there are a few species that produce only females, like the whiptail lizard. Thanks to parthenogenesis, they have no trouble having as many daughters as they like. There are no species, however, that produce only males. This is no surprise, since any such species would become extinct in its first generation.

Fasold is also intrigued by species that produce individuals not involved in reproduction, like honeybees and leaf-cutter ants. Reproduction is handled by the queen and a relatively few males; the workers are sterile females. "Since they do not reproduce," Fasold says, "there is no reason for them to be one sex or the other, so they default, so to speak, to female."

Fasold ends his discussion of these matters by pointing out that if language reflected biology, grammar books would direct us to use "she" to include males and females and "he" only for specifically male referents. But they don't. They tell us that "he" means "he or she," and that "she" is used only if the referent is specifically female. This use of "he" as the sex-indefinite pronoun is an innovation introduced into English by grammarians in the 18th and 19th centuries, according to Peter Muhlhausler and Rom Harre in "Pronouns and People." From at least about 1500, the correct sex-indefinite pronoun was "they," as it still is in casual spoken English. In other words, the female was declared by grammarians to be the marked case.

Writing this article may mark me not as a writer, not as a linguist, not as an analyst of human behavior, but as a feminist—which will have positive or negative, but in any case powerful, connotations for readers. Yet I doubt that anyone reading Ralph Fasold's book would put that label on him.

I discovered the markedness inherent in the very topic of gender after writing a book on differences in conversational style based on geographical region, ethnicity, class, age and gender. When I was interviewed, the vast majority of journalists wanted to talk about the differences between women and men. While I thought I was simply describing what I observed—something I had learned to do as a researcher—merely mentioning women and men marked me as a feminist for some.

When I wrote a book devoted to gender differences in ways of speaking, I sent the manuscript to five male colleagues, asking them to alert me to any interpretation, phrasing or wording that might seem unfairly negative toward men. Even so, when the book came out, I encountered responses like that of the television talk show host who, after interviewing me, turned to the audience and asked if they thought I was male-bashing.

Leaping upon a poor fellow who affably nodded in agreement, she made him stand and asked, "Did what she said accurately describe you?" "Oh, yes," he answered. "That's me exactly." "And what she said about women—does that sound like your wife?" "Oh yes," he responded. "That's her exactly." "Then why do you think she's male-bashing?" He answered, with disarming honesty, "Because she's a woman and she's saying things about men."

To say anything about women and men without marking oneself as either feminist or anti-feminist, male-basher or apologist for men seems as impossible for a woman as trying to get dressed in the morning without inviting interpretations of her character. Sitting at the conference table musing on these matters, I felt sad to think that we women didn't have the freedom to be unmarked that the men sitting next to us had. Some days you just want to get dressed and go about your business. But if you're a woman, you can't, because there is no unmarked woman.

---

## This Text: Reading

1. What do you make of Tannen's claim that women are "marked"? Is that an appropriate word?
2. Would you agree with her that men are not marked?
3. What is Tannen's evidence for her claims? Is it solid evidence? Do Tannen's arguments follow a logical progression?

## Your Text: Writing

1. Go to a coffee shop or a restaurant and read a group of women sitting together. Are they marked? How? Then write an essay, similar to Tannen's,

on your reading of the women. How do contemporary cultural expectations of women influence how you read other women?
2. Write an essay on how men are marked.
3. Are there other female markings that Tannen does not mention? Write an essay in which you give a reading of other kinds of female markings.
4. Read Maxine Hong Kingston's "No Name Woman," and write an essay in which you demonstrate how the aunt was marked.

## GENDER ROLE BEHAVIORS AND ATTITUDES

Holly Devor

Taken from her 1989 book *Gender Blending: Confronting the Limits of Duality*, Holly Devor argues that terms like "masculinity" and "femininity" are problematic because they tend to signify "natural" roles of men and women. However, Devor suggests that these terms are little more than social constructions. Devor has a sophisticated argument, so, as you read, pay attention to how she makes and supports her assertions about gender roles; also, if you are writing a research paper, note how Devor works her research into her prose and into her arguments.

THE CLUSTERS OF SOCIAL DEFINITIONS used to identify persons by gender are collectively known as femininity and masculinity. Masculine characteristics are used to identify persons as males, while feminine ones are used as signifiers for femaleness. People use femininity or masculinity to claim and communicate their membership in their assigned, or chosen, sex or gender. Others recognize our sex or gender more on the basis of these characteristics than on the basis of sex characteristics, which are usually largely covered by clothing in daily life.

These two clusters of attributes are most commonly seen as mirror images of one another, with masculinity usually characterized by dominance and aggression, and femininity by passivity and submission. A more evenhanded description of the social qualities subsumed by femininity and masculinity might be to label masculinity as generally concerned with egoistic dominance and femininity as striving for cooperation or communion.[1]

---

[1]Egoistic dominance is a striving for superior rewards for oneself or a competitive striving to reduce the rewards for one's competitors even if such action will not increase one's own rewards. Persons who are motivated by desires for egoistic dominance not only wish the best for themselves but also wish to diminish the advantages of others whom they may perceive as competing with them. See Maccoby, p. 217.

Characterizing femininity and masculinity in such a way does not portray the two clusters of characteristics as being in a hierarchical relationship to one another but rather as being two different approaches to the same question, that question being centrally concerned with the goals, means, and use of power. Such an alternative conception of gender roles captures the hierarchical and competitive masculine thirst for power, which can, but need not, lead to aggression, and the feminine quest for harmony and communal well-being, which can, but need not, result in passivity and dependence.

Many activities and modes of expression are recognized by most members of society as feminine. Any of these can be, and often are, displayed by persons of either gender. In some cases, cross gender behaviors are ignored by observers, and therefore do not compromise the integrity of a person's gender display. In other cases, they are labeled as inappropriate gender role behaviors. Although these behaviors are closely linked to sexual status in the minds and experiences of most people, research shows that dominant persons of either gender tend to use influence tactics and verbal styles usually associated with men and masculinity, while subordinate persons, of either gender, tend to use those considered to be the province of women.[2] Thus it seems likely that many aspects of masculinity and femininity are the result, rather than the cause, of status inequalities.

Popular conceptions of femininity and masculinity instead revolve around hierarchical appraisals of the "natural" roles of males and females. Members of both genders are believed to share many of the same human characteristics, although in different relative proportions; both males and females are popularly thought to be able to do many of the same things, but most activities are divided into suitable and unsuitable categories for each gender class. Persons who perform the activities considered appropriate for another gender will be expected to perform them poorly; if they succeed adequately, or even well, at their endeavors, they may be rewarded with ridicule or scorn for blurring the gender dividing line.

The patriarchal gender schema currently in use in mainstream North American society reserves highly valued attributes for males and actively supports the high evaluation of any characteristics which might inadvertently become associated with maleness. The ideology which the schema grows out of postulates that the cultural superiority of males is a natural out-growth of the innate predisposition of males toward aggression and dominance, which is assumed to flow inevitably from evolutionary and

---

[2]Judith Howard, Philip Blumstein, and Pepper Schwartz, "Sex, Power, and Influence Tactics in Intimate Relationships," *Journal of Personality and Social Psychology* 51 (1986), pp. 102–09; Peter Kollock, Philip Blumstein, and Pepper Schwartz, "Sex and Power in Interaction: Conversational Privileges and Duties," *American Sociological Review* 50 (1985), pp. 34–46.

biological sources. Female attributes are likewise postulated to find their source in innate predispositions acquired in the evolution of the species. Feminine characteristics are thought to be intrinsic to the female facility for childbirth and breastfeeding. Hence, it is popularly believed that the social position of females is biologically mandated to be intertwined with the care of children and a "natural" dependency on men for the maintenance of mother-child units. Thus the goals of femininity and, by implication, of all biological females are presumed to revolve around heterosexuality and maternity.[3]

Femininity, according to this traditional formulation, "would result in warm and continued relationships with men, a sense of maternity, interest in caring for children, and the capacity to work productively and continuously in female occupations."[4] This recipe translates into a vast number of proscriptions and prescriptions. Warm and continued relations with men and an interest in maternity require that females be heterosexually oriented. A heterosexual orientation requires women to dress, move, speak, and act in ways that men will find attractive. As patriarchy has reserved active expressions of power as a masculine attribute, femininity must be expressed through modes of dress, movement, speech, and action which communicate weakness, dependency, ineffectualness, availability for sexual or emotional service, and sensitivity to the needs of others.

Some, but not all, of these modes of interrelation also serve the demands of maternity and many female job ghettos. In many cases, though, femininity is not particularly useful in maternity or employment. Both mothers and workers often need to be strong, independent, and effectual in order to do their jobs well. Thus femininity, as a role, is best suited to satisfying a masculine vision of heterosexual attractiveness.

Body postures and demeanors which communicate subordinate status and vulnerability to trespass through a message of "no threat" make people appear to be feminine. They demonstrate subordination through a minimizing of spatial use: people appear feminine when they keep their arms closer to their bodies, their legs closer together, and their torsos and heads less vertical then do masculine-looking individuals. People also look feminine when they point their toes inward and use their hands in small or childlike gestures. Other people also tend to stand closer to people they see as feminine, often invading their personal space, while people who make frequent appeasement gestures, such as smiling, also give the appearance of femininity. Perhaps as an outgrowth of a subordinate status and the need to avoid conflict with more socially powerful people, women tend to excel over men

---

[3]Chodorow, p. 134.

[4]Jon K. Meyer and John E. Hoopes, "The Gender Dysphoria Syndromes: A Position Statement on So-Called 'Transsexualism'," *Plastic and Reconstructive Surgery* 54 (Oct. 1974), pp. 444–51.

at the ability to correctly interpret, and effectively display, nonverbal communication cues.[5]

Speech characterized by inflections, intonations, and phrases that convey nonaggression and subordinate status also make a speaker appear more feminine. Subordinate speakers who use more polite expressions and ask more questions in conversation seem more feminine. Speech characterized by sounds of higher frequencies are often interpreted by listeners as feminine, childlike, and ineffectual.[6] Feminine styles of dress likewise display subordinate status through greater restriction of the free movement of the body, greater exposure of the bare skin, and an emphasis on sexual characteristics. The more gender distinct the dress, the more this is the case.

Masculinity, like femininity, can be demonstrated through a wide variety of cues. Pleck has argued that it is commonly expressed in North American society through the attainment of some level of proficiency at some, or all, of the following four main attitudes of masculinity. Persons who display success and high status in their social group, who exhibit "a manly air of toughness, confidence, and self-reliance" and "the aura of aggression, violence, and daring," and who conscientiously avoid anything associated with femininity are seen as exuding masculinity.[7] These requirements reflect the patriarchal ideology that masculinity results from an excess of testosterone, the assumption being that androgens supply a natural impetus toward aggression, which in turn impels males toward achievement and success. This vision of masculinity also reflects the ideological stance that ideal maleness (masculinity) must remain untainted by female (feminine) pollutants.

Masculinity, then, requires of its actors that they organize themselves and their society in a hierarchical manner so as to be able to explicitly quantify the achievement of success. The achievement of high status in one's social group requires competitive and aggressive behavior from those who wish to obtain it. Competition which is motivated by a goal of individual achievement, or egoistic dominance, also requires of its participants a degree of emotional insensitivity to feelings of hurt and loss in defeated others, and a measure of emotional insularity to protect oneself from becoming vulnerable to manipulation by others. Such values lead those who subscribe

---

[5]Erving Goffman, *Gender Advertisements* (New York: Harper Colophon Books, 1976); Judith A. Hall, *Non-Verbal Sex Differences: Communication Accuracy and Expressive Style* (Baltimore: Johns Hopkins University Press, 1984); Nancy M. Henley, *Body Politics: Power, Sex and Non-Verbal Communication* (Englewood Cliffs, New Jersey: Prentice Hall, 1979); Marianne Wex, *"Let's Take Back Our Space": "Female" and "Male" Body Language as a Result of Patriarchal Structures* (Berlin: Frauenliteraturverlag Hermine Fees, 1979).

[6]Karen L. Adams, "Sexism and the English Language: The Linguistic Implications of Being a Woman," in *Women: A Feminist Perspective,* 3rd edition, ed. Jo Freeman (Palo Alto, Calif.: Mayfield, 1984), pp. 478–91; Hall, pp. 37, 130–37.

[7]Elizabeth Hafkin Pleck, *Domestic Tyranny: The Making of Social Policy Against Family Violence from Colonial Times to the Present* (Cambridge: Oxford University Press, 1989), p. 139.

to them to view feminine persons as "born losers" and to strive to eliminate any similarities to feminine people from their own personalities. In patriarchally organized societies, masculine values become the ideological structure of the society as a whole. Masculinity thus becomes "innately" valuable and femininity serves a contrapuntal function to delineate and magnify the hierarchical dominance of masculinity.

Body postures, speech patterns, and styles of dress which demonstrate and support the assumption of dominance and authority convey an impression of masculinity. Typical masculine body postures tend to be expansive and aggressive. People who hold their arms and hands in positions away from their bodies, and who stand, sit, or lie with their legs apart—thus maximizing the amount of space that they physically occupy—appear most physically masculine. Persons who communicate an air of authority or a readiness for aggression by standing erect and moving forcefully also tend to appear more masculine. Movements that are abrupt and stiff, communicating force and threat rather than flexibility and cooperation, make an actor look masculine. Masculinity can also be conveyed by stern or serious facial expressions that suggest minimal receptivity to the influence of others, a characteristic which is an important element in the attainment and maintenance of egoistic dominance.[8]

Speech and dress which likewise demonstrate or claim superior status are also seen as characteristically masculine behavior patterns. Masculine speech patterns display a tendency toward expansiveness similar to that found in masculine body postures. People who attempt to control the direction of conversations seem more masculine.[9] Those who tend to speak more loudly, use less polite and more assertive forms, and tend to interrupt the conversations of others more often also communicate masculinity to others. Styles of dress which emphasize the size of upper body musculature, allow freedom of movement, and encourage an illusion of physical power and a look of easy physicality all suggest masculinity. Such appearances of strength and readiness to action serve to create or enhance an aura of aggressiveness and intimidation central to an appearance of masculinity. Expansive postures and gestures combine with these qualities to insinuate that a position of secure dominance is a masculine one.

Gender role characteristics reflect the ideological contentions underlying the dominant gender schema in North American society. That schema leads us to believe that female and male behaviors are the result of socially directed hormonal instructions which specify that females will want to have children and will therefore find themselves relatively helpless and dependent on males for support and protection. The schema claims that males are innately aggressive and competitive and therefore will dominate over

---

[8]Goffman, *Gender Advertisements;* Hall; Henley; Wex.

[9]Adams; Hall, pp. 37, 130–37.

females. The social hegemony of this ideology ensures that we are all raised to practice gender roles which will confirm this vision of the nature of the sexes. Fortunately, our training to gender roles is neither complete nor uniform. As a result, it is possible to point to multitudinous exceptions to, and variations on, these themes. Biological evidence is equivocal about the source of gender roles; psychological androgyny is a widely accepted concept. It seems most likely that gender roles are the result of systematic power imbalances based on gender discrimination.[10]

[10]Howard, Blumstein, and Schwartz; Kollock, Blumstein, and Schwartz.

---

### This Text: Reading

1. Many of Devor's claims resemble the claims in the introduction to this chapter. Make a list of "masculine" and "feminine" traits. Based on your list, what do you make of Devor's assumptions? Are any changing? What political or cultural movements or concerns might be affecting Devor's readings of gender?
2. According to Devor, how do children acquire gender roles? Do you agree? What evidence does Devor use to support her assertions that gender is constructed?

### Your Text: Writing

1. Write an essay on your own history of doing gender. What gender roles do you engage in? Which ones do you avoid?
2. Make a list of various gender roles of a different gender than yourself. What is the basis for this list? If you showed it to someone of that gender, would he or she agree with you?
3. Write a paper in which you talk about your own gender assumptions.
4. Read Susan Steinberg's "Isla" (Chapter 1). Write an essay on gender roles in this story.
5. Think of gender roles as film roles. Write an essay in which you explore how men and women are represented differently in film or on television. Use specific examples to support your points.

## BEING A MAN

Paul Theroux

---

In this 1985 essay, Theroux offers a reading of masculinity from the perspective of someone who "always disliked being a man." Much like Devor, Theroux is troubled by the expectations of masculine behavior and finds writing at variance with many of them.

THERE IS A PATHETIC SENTENCE in the chapter "Fetishism" in Dr. Norman Cameron's book *Personality Development and Psychopathology*. It goes, "Fetishists are nearly always men; and their commonest fetish is a woman's shoe." I cannot read that sentence without thinking that it is just one more awful thing about being a man—and perhaps it is an important thing to know about us.

I have always disliked being a man. The whole idea of manhood in America is pitiful, in my opinion. This version of masculinity is a little like having to wear an ill-fitting coat for one's entire life (by contrast, I imagine femininity to be an oppressive sense of nakedness). Even the expression "Be a man!" strikes me as insulting and abusive. It means: Be stupid, be unfeeling, obedient, soldierly, and stop thinking. Man means "manly"—how can one think about men without considering the terrible ambition of manliness? And yet it is part of every man's life. It is a hideous and crippling lie; it not only insists on difference and connives at superiority, it is also by its very nature destructive—emotionally damaging and socially harmful.

The youth who is subverted, as most are, into believing in the masculine ideal is effectively separated from women and he spends the rest of his life finding women a riddle and a nuisance. Of course, there is a female version of this male affliction. It begins with mothers encouraging little girls to say (to other adults) "Do you like my new dress?" In a sense, little girls are traditionally urged to please adults with a kind of coquetushness, while boys are enjoined to behave like monkeys towards each other. The nine-year-old coquette proceeds to become womanish in a subtle power game in which she learns to be sexually indispensable, socially decorative, and always alert to a man's sense of inadequacy.

Femininity—being ladylike—implies needing a man as witness and seducer; but masculinity celebrates the exclusive company of men. That is why it is so grotesque; and that is also why there is no manliness without inadequacy—because it denies men the natural friendship of women.

It is very hard to imagine any concept of manliness that does not belittle women, and it begins very early. At an age when I wanted to meet girls—let's say the treacherous years of thirteen to sixteen—I was told to take up a sport, get more fresh air, join the Boy Scouts, and I was urged not to read so much. It was the 1950s and if you asked too many questions about sex you were sent to camp—boy's camp, of course: the nightmare. Nothing is more unnatural or prisonlike than a boy's camp, but if it were not for them we would have no Elks' Lodges, no pool rooms, no boxing matches, no Marines.

And perhaps no sports as we know them. Everyone is aware of how few in number are the athletes who behave like gentlemen. Just as high school basketball teaches you how to be a poor loser, the manly attitude towards sports seems to be little more than a recipe for creating bad marriages, social misfits, moral degenerates, sadists, latent rapists, and just plain louts. I regard high school sports as a drug far worse than marijuana, and it is the reason that the average tennis champion, say, is a pathetic oaf.

Any objective study would find the quest for manliness essentially right-wing, puritanical, cowardly, neurotic, and fueled largely by a fear of women. It is also certainly philistine. There is no book-hater like a Little League coach. But indeed all the creative arts are obnoxious to the manly ideal, because at their best the arts are pursued by uncompetitive and essentially solitary people. It makes it very hard for a creative youngster, for any boy who expresses the desire to be alone seems to be saying that there is something wrong with him.

It ought to be clear by now that I have something of an objection to the way we turn boys into men. It does not surprise me that when the President of the United States has his customary weekend off he dresses like a cowboy—it is both a measure of his insecurity and his willingness to please. In many ways, American culture does little more for a man than prepare him for modeling clothes in the L.L. Bean catalogue. I take this as a personal insult because for many years I found it impossible to admit to myself that I wanted to be a writer. It was my guilty secret, because being a writer was incompatible with being a man.

There are people who might deny this, but that is because the American writer, typically, has been so at pains to prove his manliness that we have come to see literariness and manliness as mingled qualities. But first there was a fear that writing was not a manly profession—indeed, not a profession at all. (The paradox in American letters is that it has always been easier for a woman to write and for a man to be published.) Growing up, I had thought of sports as wasteful and humiliating, and the idea of manliness was a bore. My wanting to become a writer was not a flight from that oppressive role-playing, but I quickly saw that it was at odds with it. Everything in stereotyped manliness goes against the life of the mind. The Hemingway personality is too tedious to go into here, and in any case his exertions are well known, but certainly it was not until this aberrant behavior was examined by feminists in the 1960s that any male writer dared question the pugnacity in Hemingway's fiction. All the bullfighting and arm wrestling and elephant shooting diminished Hemingway as a writer, but it is consistent with a prevailing attitude in American writing: one cannot be a male writer without first proving that one is a man.

It is normal in America for a man to be dismissive or even somewhat apologetic about being a writer. Various factors make it easier. There is a heartiness about journalism that makes it acceptable—journalism is the manliest form of American writing and, therefore, the profession the most independent-minded women seek (yes, it is an illusion, but that is my point). Fiction-writing is equated with a kind of dispirited failure and is only manly when it produces wealth—money is masculinity. So is drinking. Being a drunkard is another assertion, if misplaced, of manliness. The American male writer is traditionally proud of his heavy drinking. But we are also a very literal-minded people. A man proves his manhood in America in old-fashioned ways. He kills lions, like Hemingway; or he hunts ducks, like Nathanael West, or he makes pronouncements like, "A man should carry enough knife to defend himself with," as James Jones once said to a *Life* interviewer. Or he says he can drink you under the table. But even tiny drunken William Faulkner loved to mount a horse and go fox hunting, and Jack Kerouac roistered up and down Manhattan in a lumberjack shirt (and spent every night of *The Subterraneans* with his mother in Queens). And we are familiar with the lengths to which Norman Mailer is prepared, in his endearing way, to prove that he is just as much a monster as the next man.

When the novelist John Irving was revealed as a wrestler, people took him to be a very serious writer, and even a bubble reputation like Eric (*Love Story*) Segal's was enhanced by the news that he ran the marathon in a respectable time. How surprised we would be if Joyce Carol Oates were revealed as a sumo wrestler or Joan Didion active in pumping iron. "Lives in New York City with her three children" is the typical woman writer's biographical note, for just as the male writer must prove he has achieved a sort of muscular manhood, the woman writer—or rather her publicists—must prove her motherhood.

There would be no point in saying any of this if it were not generally accepted that to be a man is somehow—even now in feminist-influenced America—a privilege. It is on the contrary an unmerciful and punishing burden. Being a man is bad enough; being manly is appalling (in this sense, women's lib has done much more for men than for women). It is the sinister silliness of men's fashions and a clubby attitude in the arts. It is the subversion of good students. It is the so-called Dress Code of the Ritz-Carlton Hotel in Boston, and it is the institutionalized cheating in college sports. It is the most primitive insecurity.

And this is also why men often object to feminism, but are afraid to explain why: of course women have a justified grievance, but most men believe—and with reason—that their lives are just as bad.

---

## This Text: Reading

1. Why does Theroux not like being a man? Are his reasons valid? Is his argument and progression well reasoned?
2. Can you think of "any concept of manliness that does not belittle women"? What do you make of the way Theroux claims we turn boys into men? Do you agree with him? Do you share his distaste?
3. Do Theroux's claims about manliness and writing still hold true? Why? Why not? His piece seems a bit dated—how can you tell it was written in a previous era?

## Your Text: Writing

1. Write an essay entitled "On Being a Woman." How will yours differ from Theroux's?

2. Write an essay about being the opposite gender. What would be good about being the other gender? What would not be so good?
3. Does Bob Stone in "Blood-Burning Moon" (Chapter 1) suffer from illusions about proper male behavior? What about certain movie characters, like James Bond? Write an essay in which you examine male behavior in various texts.
4. This is the only text in this section written by a man. Write an essay on the fact that there is only one piece by a man in a chapter about gender. Should it be evenly balanced? Is the rest of *The World Is a Text* balanced in terms of gender? Should there be a female co-author?

## YOU WOULD HAVE ME WHITE

Alfonsina Storni

One of South America's most important poets, Alfonsina Storni spent most of her life in Argentina until her death in 1938. "Tu me quieres blanca" was published in 1918 and remains her most famous poem and a significant text for North and South American women. Edgy and poetic, angry and beautiful, her poem is a strong statement on the universal stereotyping of women. As a side note, you should know that in Spanish, "white" is *blanca*. However, *blanca* also means "empty" and "blank."

| | |
|---|---|
| Tú me quieres alba,<br>me quieres de espumas,<br>me quieres de nácar.<br>Que sea azucena<br>sobre todas, casta.<br>De perfume tenue.<br>Corola cerrada. | You want me white,<br>you want me foam,<br>you want me pearl.<br>That I would be white lily,<br>above all the others, chaste.<br>Of tenuous perfume.<br>Closed corolla. |
| Ni un rayo de luna<br>filtrado me haya.<br>Ni una margarita<br>se diga mi hermana.<br>Tú me quieres nívea,<br>tú me quieres blanca,<br>tú me quieres alba. | That not even a ray of filtered<br>moonlight have me.<br>Nor a daisy<br>call itself my sister.<br>You want me snowy,<br>you want me white,<br>you want me dawn. |
| Tú que hubiste todas<br>las copas a mano,<br>de frutos y mieles | You who had all<br>the cups in hand,<br>Your lips purple |

los labios morados.
Tú que en el banquete
cubierto de pámpanos
dejaste las carnes
festejando a Baco.
Tú que en los jardines
negros del engaño
vestido de rojo
corriste al estrago.
Tú que el esqueleto
conservas intacto
no sé todavía
por cuáles milagros,
me pretendes blanca
(Dios te lo perdone),
me pretendes casta
(Dios te lo perdone),
ime pretendes alba!

Huye hacia los bosques;
vete a la montaña;
límpiate la boca;
vive en las cabañas;
toca con las manos
la tierra mojada;
alimenta el cuerpo
con raíz amarga;
bebe de las rocas;
duerme sobre escarcha;
renueva tejidos
con salitre y agua;

Habla con los pájaros
y lévate al alba.
Y cuando las carnes
te sean tornadas,
y cuando hayas puesto
en ellas el alma
que por las alcobas
se quedó enredada,
entonces, buen hombre,
preténdeme blanca,
preténdeme nívea,
preténdeme casta.

with fruits and honey.
You who at the banquet
covered with ferns
relinquished your flesh
celebrating Bacchus.
You who in black
gardens of deceit
dressed in red
ran yourself to ruin.
You whose skeleton
is still intact
by what miracles
I'll never know,
you want me to be white
(God forgive you),
you want me to be chaste
(God forgive you),
you want me to be dawn!

Go to the woods;
go to the mountains;
wash out your mouth;
live in a hut;
touch the damp earth
with your hands;
nourish your body
with bitter roots;
drink from stones;
sleep on frost;
restore your body
with saltpeter and water;

Speak with birds
and get up at dawn.
And when your flesh
is restored to you,
and when you've put the
back into the flesh
which was entrapped
in bedrooms,
then, good man,
pretend I'm white,
pretend I'm snowy,
pretend I'm chaste.

### This Text: Reading

1. How do the connotations of *blanca* in Spanish alter your reading of the poem?
2. Why does Storni want her man to "go to the mountains," "wash out his mouth" and "live in a hut"? Why must he restore his flesh? Why will returning to nature accomplish this?
3. How is Storni using the various symbolisms surrounding "white"?
4. Why does Storni think the man in question needs God's forgiveness?

### Your Text: Writing

1. Who is Storni addressing here? Write an essay in which you explore issues of male and female gender in the poem.
2. Give a feminist reading of the poem. What kind of statement is Storni making about how men see women?
3. Write an essay in which you explore the various connotations of whiteness in Storni's poem and *Snow White.*

## *THE WOMAN WARRIOR*: THE PROBLEM OF USING CULTURE TO LIBERATE IDENTITY

Whitney Black

The problem paper or issue paper is a common assignment at the University of San Francisco. In this kind of paper, students are asked to identify a problem in a particular text—an issue they disagree with, a question about a character, a problem with race, ethnicity or gender, or simply a faulty argument—and foreground that problem in a paper. Rather than trying to resolve the problem as in most assignments, a problem paper forces students not only to identify and articulate a problem but to explore that problem in depth. Students close the paper not with an answer to the problem but with more questions about it. This kind of assignment works well as preparation for a longer research paper, as the research can help eventually provide information that allows the writer to respond to the problem. Here, Whitney Black, a student at USF, raises questions about culture and gender in Maxine Hong Kingston's *The Woman Warrior* in this 2002 essay.

THE WOMAN WARRIOR is Maxine Hong Kingston's personal account of her struggle to find identity, specifically the challenge of forging an identity as a woman. Kingston's memoir depicts her journey to find her voice, advocating rebellion against the cultural governances of both China and America that function to define and constrict femininity. Kingston critiques the constructed feminine ideal of both cultures, pursuing an identity that shuns authority and cultural guidelines of supposed womanhood. *The Woman Warrior* is certainly productive in liberating women from the boundaries of cultural edict; however, in freeing identity from authority, certain problems inevitably arise from Kingston's presentation of authority. To necessitate bucking authority, Kingston must present the most confining aspects of authority; at times her novel perpetuates certain stereotypes of Chinese culture, exploiting the culture as misogynistic, patriarchal, and enslaving. As a minority author writing within America, the consequence of critiquing Chinese culture's devaluation of women exceeds her critique of American culture. Mainstreaming her work has the effect of transforming *The Woman Warrior* into an emblem of Asian culture. The biggest problem I have with Kingston's memoir is that in propagating a selfhood free from boundary, Kingston juxtaposes her struggle against a foreign culture she accuses of silencing women, reworking certain historical myths of Asian culture to drive her feminist agenda. *The Woman Warrior* appears to depend and appeal to presuppositions that exist in America about China and the subjugation of Chinese women. Kingston's plea for women to find a voice may be productive for the women's movement, but by presenting authority at its most deplorable, her work seems counter-productive for the Chinese, and American perceptions of their culture. *The Woman Warrior* emerges as overtly female, often relying on base stereotypes to prove a feminist point, instead of writing to defy stereotypes of Asian culture. Kingston wages a seemingly singular war, redefining what a woman can be, while contributing to a stereotypical American definition of what Asian culture is.

Though Kingston attacks the connotations of femininity in both China and America, disapproving of American ideals is far less controversial. American readers are much more apt to be influenced by her depictions of China than of America, because Kingston represents a "cultural insider" (Chu 91), presenting Chinese culture to an "outsider" audience. Kingston, in writing to be popularized, conforms to American notions of China, and manipulates those notions to champion a female cause. If the book was written for an Asian audience one could assess Kingston's work as a commentary on China, written to evoke a change of treatment toward Chinese women. However, the book was not intended for a Chinese audience, nor is *The Woman Warrior*'s intent to address problems, and thus fix problems, within the culture she critiques. She often exploits problems of Chinese culture to pursue her cause. As a minority author, writing both within America and for an American audience, the book carries some problematic weight. Asian American literature is largely underrepresented by the literary canon; the unfair reality of writing from the margins of society is that once the work is mainstreamed, literature of a singular voice becomes *the* work and the voice of an entire culture. Kingston's memoir tends to disregard this responsibility, exaggerating and solely focusing on the negative aspects of her culture, manipulating historical myths and truths for her own intent. While underrepresentation posits an unfair burden on minority writers, the burden is a reality I feel Kingston should have been more socially sensitive to. Her audience is clearly the American woman struggling to resolve who she is with who she is supposed to be; Kingston's work has problems because she appeals to this audience at the expense of Asian culture.

Kingston's memoir has moments of contrived bitterness, depicting Asian culture as anti-woman, anti-daughter, and anti-independence of women. Kingston claims that she is haunted by her past, by her silenced ancestors, leaving the impression that she is ultimately haunted by China and its treatment of women. The opening chapter of Kingston's memoir unfolds with the cautionary tale of the "No Name Woman," representing the antithesis of what Kingston desires for herself. Kingston distances herself from the No Name Woman not because she is nameless and without identity, but because Chinese society forced her to be all of those things. Kingston uses the aunt's tale to depict what happens to women living in China, exposing China as a culture that drives women to suicide if they neglect their role as obedient and meek. Kingston does not begrudge women appearing weak, choosing instead to attack the culture that binds them to these traits. Kingston's memoir is composed of numerous accounts of Chinese women, most of whom appear weak, silent, and imprisoned to Chinese culture that disregards them and justifies the assumption that it's "better to raise geese than daughters." According to Kingston's recollection of the No Name Woman, her aunt is a victim of a patriarchal Chinese edict that denies women identity, compels women to suicide, ultimately silencing women who defy conformity by renouncing their very existence. The aunt's life and death encompass a cautionary story; Brave Orchid tells the tale under the warning that Kingston "must never tell anyone."

The retelling of the aunt's story acts to cement the worst American held beliefs of Chinese treatment of women, silencing women in both life and in death. *The Woman Warrior* has been criticized as underestimating the power and the voice of women within China; Kingston has been accused of "losing sight of [Chinese women's] role as strong and willful [...] representing her own stereotypical characterization of Chinese women [...]" (Woo 181). Kingston's memoir is resolute in showing the misfortune of being a woman in Chinese culture, never straying from her resolve, never presenting deviations productive to readdressing race relations within the American psyche. Many of the people within Kingston's memoir who are Chinese embody the "weak" traits derivative of being a woman in China. Moon Orchid, No Name Woman and the quiet schoolmate who refuses to speak symbolize and exploit Kingston's grievances with Asian culture. Her subordinate female characters seem a bit too contrived, overly stereotypical to show the effects of being a woman confined by authority. Presenting these women to an American reader is decidedly unfortunate; Kingston achieves her goal of eliciting sympathy for silenced women, but does so by relying on a disdain for Chinese culture. She takes liberties with her aunt's story, and with the historical myth of Fa Mu Lan, writing to ignite compassion for her aunt's abusive treatment, turning Fa Mu Lan into a hyper-female warrior, reworking the story to befit her audience and intent (both female).

As I have said, Kingston is clearly writing a text about women and identity, though Kingston has license to appeal to any audience she chooses, the feminist slant of her book has overarching problems. Aside from appealing to pre-existing stereotypes Americans possess, Kingston also seems exceedingly consumed with the plight of women, barely addressing the problem of race relations within America. In writing for a female American audience, Kingston is only slightly critical of the "American-feminine" ideal, and much less forthright in attacking the racist attitude existing in America toward Asian Americans. Kingston "points out Euro-American sexism" (Chu), because sexism helps her cause, but what about Euro-American racism? It is as though Kingston separated her gender from her race and ethnicity, using her "Asian-ness" simply as a tool to showcase the struggle of women, ignoring the struggle of her race within America. *The Woman Warrior* almost leaves the conclusion that in targeting a female American audience, she is sensitive to America's treatment of women, but overly cautious in discussing race relations. If she is critical of any culture it is decidedly Chinese, citing Chinese as the "language of impossible stories," a language Kingston strove to silence in her journey to find a voice as a woman in America. In ignoring race in America, Kingston's memoir almost pits oppression against one another, the oppressed female against the oppressed Asian American.

I worry about her continuous critique of Chinese culture, because although I abhor stifling Kingston's freedoms as a writer, the problems of her writing still exist. While I applaud Kingston's memoir for articulating female empowerment, it is harder to be satisfied with how she mistreats culture to empower her intention. *The Woman Warrior* gives the impression of being excessively dependent on Western stereotypes, making her efforts seem contrived, appealing to American women by appealing to cultural preconceptions and the identity struggle most females are familiar with. Kingston's work is defiant in advocating women, but what about Asian culture? Is it possible for Kingston to address her struggle as a woman, without addressing her struggle as an Asian American? Could the memoir have been as "womanly powerful" without Kingston's appeal to negative Western ideology about Chinese culture? As a minority author, writing literature that is underrepresented by the canon, is it her responsibility to create stereotype-breaking work? Or is it the canon's responsibility to offer more Asian-American literature, alleviating this pressure because a single voice will no longer become emblematic? Or should the reader be responsible to gather a bigger picture of the culture they are reading about, shunning a book's information as the only source to understand a foreign culture? Even if her memoir is detrimental to Asian culture, shouldn't she still be allowed to sight her opinion, her experience? Is it okay that Kingston reworks her "true" experiences to push her feminist cause? The labeling of her memoir as nonfiction—obviously she intends for the book to be received as true, but clearly aspects are *not* wholly true, manipulated to serve a (feminist) point; is this ethical? In fighting a female battle that partially ignores a racial battle, can the book really be considered productive, or is *The Woman Warrior* detrimental because it relies on a hierarchy of oppression, the content of the memoir seemingly to attest that pursuing one fight is more important than pursuing another. Isn't rebellion most productive when the oppressed coalesce, come together regardless of gender, race, class, to take on the oppressor?

## Works Cited

Chu, Patricia. "Warrior Woman." *A Resource Guide to Asian American Literature*. Ed. Sau-Ling Cynthia Wong and Stephen H. Sumida. New York: Modern Language Association of America, 2001. 86–96.

Woo, Deborah. "Maxine Hong Kingston: The Ethnic Writer and the Burden of Dual Authenticity." *Amerasia Journal* 16, No. 1 (1990).

---

## This Text: Reading

1. What is the main problem the author identifies in *The Woman Warrior*?
2. What is the author's thesis? Does she support it sufficiently?
3. What "problems" do you find with the author's problem paper?

## Your Text: Writing

1. Write your own problem paper about any text you may be "reading." What kinds of problems might you identify?
2. If you have a research project, make a list of questions that you would like your research to answer. How can you make the answers to these questions part of your thesis?
3. Write a personal essay exploring your own views on the intersection of race, gender, and class.

# The Myths of Gender Suite

In her essay "Cinderella: Saturday Afternoon at the Movies," Louise Bernikow writes about how, for her, watching Cinderella was like watching a woman in peril: "The girl onscreen, as I squirm in my seat, needs to be saved. A man will come and save her. Some day my prince will come. Women will not save her. They will thwart her." Bernikow goes on to argue that *Cinderella* teaches two bad lessons: that women are each other's enemies and that women need a man to save them.

Many writers agree with Bernikow. Indeed, scholars have argued that womens' sense of men, other women, and themselves are shaped by powerful cultural myths that get replayed over and over in fairy tales and folktales. What's more, it's just as likely that men's notions of gender roles are influenced by these stories. Thus, repeated viewing of *Cinderella* and *Snow White* and reading or being read any number of similar fairytales, will probably make women feel they need to be saved and will probably also make men feel women need to be saved.

In this suite, we have selected three different texts that explore myths and gender. The first two focus on cultural myths retold by the Disney Studios. "Construction of the Female Self: Feminist Readings of the Disney Heroine" is a traditional academic paper that traces the representation of women across five different Disney films and several decades. Jane Yolen's piece examines *Cinderella* in particular because she claims that Cinderella comes to represent *the* ideal American woman, that the film links female behavior and expectations with larger American values.

Though each of these readings focuses on how myths have influenced women, we would like to urge you to think about how these myths alter how men see the world as well. This is especially the case in the piece by Maxine Hong Kingston. In her "talk story," Kingston uncovers the hidden rules governing female behavior in China. Through a mixture of literature, folklore and autobiography, Kingston tells a story about the relationship between gender and culture.

Ultimately, we are in control of how we see the world, but we should also understand that we are not always in control of the messages encoded in cultural texts. Our goal is that we all can become better readers of gender, regardless of the setting.

## CONSTRUCTION OF THE FEMALE SELF: FEMINIST READINGS OF THE DISNEY HEROINE

Jill Birnie Henke, Diane Zimmerman Umble, Nancy J. Smith

THIS ESSAY EXAMINES THE WAY in which the female self is constructed in five Disney films: *Cinderella, Sleeping Beauty, The Little Mermaid, Beauty and the Beast*, and *Pocahontas*. Standpoint feminist theory and feminist scholarship on the psychological development of the perfect girl are used to form questions about selfhood, relationships, power, and voice. Although heroines have expressed voice and selfhood in some of the later films, Disney's interpretations of children's literature and history remain those of a white, middle-class, patriarchal society.

Americans swim in a sea of Disney images and merchandise. Children can watch Disney videos before they brush their teeth with Disney character toothbrushes, go to sleep in *Beauty and the Beast* pajamas, rest their heads on *The Little Mermaid* pillow cases, check the time on *Pocahontas* watches, and drift off to sleep listening to Cinderella sing, "No matter how your heart is grieving, if you keep on believing, the dream that you wish will come true" on their tape recorders. American children and their families watch Disney stories over and over again courtesy of their home video recorders. The Disney corporation produces myriad texts that form part of the cultural experience of American children and adults. Not only does Disney create a "wonderful world" of images, but the corporation also makes money in the process.

Disney re-releases its animated features to theaters on a seven-year rotation as a marketing strategy to attract a following in each new generation (Landis, "Hibernation," p. 5D). Following theatrical showings, video cassettes are sold for a limited time. *Aladdin* earned $200 million in theaters in 1993, while its predecessor *Beauty and the Beast* grossed $20 million from the sale of videotapes alone (Landis, "Princely," p. 1D). This home video library provides families with opportunities for repeated viewing of such Disney films as *The Little Mermaid, Sleeping Beauty, Cinderella*, and *Pocahontas*.

This essay focuses on five animated features that span over fifty years of Disney storytelling and that portray a heroine as central to the story line: *Cinderella* (1950), *Sleeping Beauty* (1959), *The Little Mermaid* (1989), *Beauty and the Beast* (1991), and *Pocahontas* (1995).[1] In light of the ubiquity of Disney's images, sounds, and stories, we examine the kind of world the Disney corporation constructs through its animated feature films, specifically what it means to be young and female.

This project grew out of our own experiences as media consumers, teachers, scholars, and mothers of daughters. We began with the assumption that mass media articulates cultural values about gender by portraying women, men, and their relationships in particular ways. In addition, Julia Wood (1994) argues that the media also reproduces cultural definitions of gender by defining what is to be taken for granted. Disney stories, then, have become part of a cultural repertoire of ongoing performances and reproductions of gender roles by children and adults; moreover, these stories present powerful and sustained messages about gender and social relations. Because our analysis is shaped by conversations with our daughters and our students as they began to adopt a critical stance toward Disney texts, the analytical framework we apply to these films is based on a synthesis of two streams of feminist thought: the psychological development of females, and standpoint feminist theory. Together, the perspectives illuminate the meaning and implications of Disney's filmic portrayal of girls.

### *The Oxymoron of Power and the Perfect Girl*

Research by Carol Gilligan and her colleagues chronicles the psychological development of women's conceptualizations of the self. Gilligan (1982) argues that women learn to value connections with others and at least in part define themselves through their relationships with others. Orenstein (1994), who examines the related concern of how gender is constructed in the classroom, describes the hidden curriculum that teaches girls to view silence and compliance as virtues. Those values present a dilemma for bright girls who must simultaneously be "selfless and selfish, silent and outspoken, cooperative and competitive" (pp. 36–37). After studying white middle-class girls at all-girls schools, Brown and Gilligan (1992) suggest that the solution to this dilemma rests with females' invention of a self: the "perfect girl." The perfect girl, in white middle-class America, is "the girl who has no bad thoughts or feelings, the kind of person everyone wants to be with, the girl who, in her perfection, is worthy of praise and attention, worthy of inclusion and love.... [She is the] girl who speaks quietly, calmly, who is always nice and kind, never mean or bossy" (p. 59). Yet, these same girls know from their own experiences that people do get angry, wish to speak, and want to be heard. The consequence of these contradictory gender/social messages is that a girl is "caught between speaking what she knows from experience about relationships and increased pressure to negate this knowledge for an idealized and fraudulent view of herself and her relationships" (p. 61). Hence, Brown and Gilligan (1992) conclude that on the way to womanhood a girl experiences a loss of voice and loss of a sense of self as she silences herself.

During the process of this intellectual and emotional silencing, girls also are developing physically in new ways. According to Brown and Gilligan (1992), changes in girls' bodies "visually disconnect them from the world of childhood and identify them in the eyes of others with women" (p. 164). Girls conflate standards of beauty and standards of goodness by learning to pay attention to their "looks" and by listening to what others say about them. They learn to see themselves through the gaze of others, hear about themselves in ways that suggest they can be perfect, and believe that relationships can be free of conflict. These girls "struggle between knowing what they know through experience and what others want them to know, to feel and think" (p. 64). As a result, girls learn that speaking up can be disruptive and dangerous because it might put relationships at risk. The cruel irony is that by withholding their voices, girls also risk losing relationships that are genuine and authentic. In effect, girls struggle daily with the "seduction of the unattainable, to be all things to all people, to be perfect girls and model women" (p. 180).

Julia Wood's (1992) critique of Gilligan's line of research expands our application of Gilligan's work on the construction of the female self to Disney films. Wood explores the tension between Gilligan's apparently essentializing stance and a post-structural stance which emphasizes the structural effects of cultural life on individuals. The result is what Wood calls "standpoint epistemology."

"Standpoint theory prompts study of conditions that shape lives and the ways individuals construct those conditions and their experiences within them" (Wood, 1992, p. 15). For women, this theory helps explain how a female's position within a culture shapes her experiences. Because cultures define people by gender, race, and class, they often impose limits on women's experiences and women's ability to appreciate the experiences of others. Standpoint feminism argues that women have been and still are treated as "others" and "outsiders" in patriarchal societies. Although women's experiences are diverse to be sure, Wood (1992) argues that scholars should look for conditions among women that unify them. Oppression, for example, is one condition that seems universal among women: "Survival for those with subordinate status often depends quite literally on being able to read others, respond in ways that please others, and assume responsibility for others' comfort" (p. 16).

Yet, differences among women, as individuals and as members of identifiable categories within broadly shared social conditions, should not be overlooked. Our analysis of Disney characters responds to this call by articulating their similarities and their differences. Indeed, our analysis suggests that one value of standpoint feminist epistemology lies in unveiling which differences are conspicuously absent. For example, the heterosexist assumption underlying all five Disney films is not only the dominant social construct influencing relationships, it is the only social construct. None of the female figures questions that assumption. Standpoint theory, then, provides the means to understand how women's voices are muted and how women can regain their voices and become empowered (Wood, 1991).

Mary Parker Follett, an American intellectual whose ideas were touted by the business community in the 1940s, wrote about the construction and use of power in society in *Creative Experience* (1924). "Coercive power," Parker Follett wrote, "is the curse of the universe; coactive power, the enrichment of every human soul" (p. xii). In later works she defined two types of power—"power-over" and "power-with": "It seems to me that whereas power usually means power-over, the power of some person or group over some other person or group, it is possible to develop the conception of power-with, a jointly developed power, a co-active, not a coercive power" (1944, p. 101). While Parker Follett did not explicitly use the expression "power from within," this understanding is embedded in her discussion of the need for social constructs which preserve the integrity of the individual. She argues that a society can only progress if individuals' internal needs are met in the processes adopted by the group.

Parker Follett's conceptualization of power, in conjunction with the principles contained in standpoint feminist theory and Gilligan's perspective on the psychological development of girls, forms the foundation for a series of questions that the following analysis of Disney's animated films hopes to answer: How do the worlds of Disney films construct the heroine's sense of self? To what degree is her self-knowledge related to or in response to her relationships with others? Do Disney heroines model the "perfect girl"? On the way to womanhood, what does the Disney heroine give up? What are the ways in which the female characters experience their lives as "others" and themselves as strangers in their relationship to self and others? And what are the power dynamics of those relationships?

Until the recent publication of *From Mouse to Mermaid: The Politics of Film, Gender, and Culture* (Bell, Haas, & Sells, 1995), few scholarly analyses addressed the foregoing questions about gender constructions in the worlds of Disney animated films.[2] However, with the Bell, Haas, and Sells' edition, critical analyses of Disney discourses entered a new phase. This edited collection maps "the ideological contours of economics, politics, and pedagogy by drawing Disney films as vehicles of cultural production" (p. 7). Within this ideological map, the cultural reproduction of gender is examined by several authors.

For example, Jack Zipes (1995) argues that characterizations of Disney heroines remain one-dimensional and stereotypical, "arranged according to a credo of domestication of the imagination" (p. 40). The values imparted in Disney fairy tales are not those of original folk tellers, nor of the original writers such as Perrault or Andersen; instead, they are the values of Disney's male writers. Thus, even when the fairy tale is supposed to focus on the heroine (Snow White, Cinderella, Sleeping Beauty, Beauty, or the Little Mermaid), "these figures are pale and pathetic compared to the more active and demonic characters in the film" (p. 37). These alleged heroines are "helpless ornaments in need of protection, and when it comes to the action of the film, they are omitted" (p. 37). In contrast, while Laura Sells' (1995) Marxist feminist analysis of *The Little Mermaid* sees the story's resolution as a "dangerous message about appropriation" (p. 185), Sells remains hopeful nevertheless because "Ariel enters the white male system with her voice—a stolen, flying voice that erupted amidst patriarchal language, a voice no longer innocent because it resided for a time in the dark continent that is the Medusa's home" (p. 185).

Our analysis elaborates upon the two themes that Zipes and Sells introduce: the relative power or powerlessness of the Disney heroine, and the discovery or loss of that heroine's voice. Thus, our exploration of the construction of the female self and the interaction of that self with other film characters corroborates and extends the work of Bell, Haas, and Sells. We utilize standpoint feminist theory, Follett's theories of power, and Gilligan and Brown's theories of female psychological development to chronicle the nature and evolution of Disney's construction of the female self.

## *Construction of the Female Self*

Disney's early heroines, Cinderella and Aurora, are portrayed as helpless, passive victims who need protection. Indeed, Cinderella is the quintessential "perfect girl," always gentle, kind, and lovely. Their weaknesses are contrasted with the awesome and awful power of the evil women with whom they struggle. However, later Disney films shift from simple stories of passive, young virgins in conflict with evil, mature women to more complex narratives about rebellion, exploration, and danger. Heroines Ariel, Belle, and Pocahontas display an increasingly stronger sense of self, of choice, and of voice.

This growing empowerment of Disney heroines is reflected in shifting depictions of their intimate relationships. While early heroines fall in love at first sight and easily marry to live happily ever after, love relationships for the later heroines come at a cost. Ariel temporarily gives up her voice and ultimately relinquishes her cultural identity. Belle discovers love only through trials, sacrifice, and learning to look beneath the surface. Ultimately, though, her love releases the Beast from the bonds of his own selfishness so they, too, are "empowered" to live happily ever after together.

Of all of Disney's characters, Pocahontas seems to break new ground. The narrative begins with her as a young woman in possession of a strong, well-developed sense of self, and a conviction that her destiny only remains to be discovered. Unlike other Disney heroines, she resists losing her identity to another for the sake of a marriage relationship. Her position and value in her community, her relationships with other females, and her understanding of her interdependence with the earth provide the most holistic picture yet of a co-actively empowered character in Disney animated films.

In her classic essay, "The Solitude of Self," Elizabeth Cady Stanton (1892) advanced a feminist vision in which women experience the sovereignty of the self, and women and girls are empowered from within. Stanton indicted patriarchy for systematically denying women the skills and rights to exist as sovereign selves. Over a century later, feminists still envision a diversity of female figures acting on the world from knowledge of their own worth and dreams. Are traces of these visions contained in Disney's filmic heroines?

The five films we examine situate the central female character—who is portrayed as gentle, kind, beautiful, and virginal—in an oppressive social milieu where mothers or other sources of female guidance and wisdom are largely absent. Until *Pocahontas*, in fact, these young heroines faced the challenges of their lives without the benefit of other women's support, nurturance, or guidance.

Cinderella, Aurora, Ariel, Belle, and Pocahontas also share another quality: they all have dreams. Each differs, however, in her power to make that dream come true. The conventional Disney tale introduces the heroine near the film's beginning through a song in which she expresses these dreams. For example, viewers first meet Cinderella when she awakens from a dream and sings, "No matter how your heart is grieving, if you keep on believing, the dream that you wish will come true." Minutes later, viewers discover that her daily reality is anything but dreamy. Supported by an army of mice and barnyard animals who come to her aid, Cinderella is continuously reminded by humans in the household that she is unworthy of their "refined" company. Cinderella's stepmother and stepsisters control Cinderella, keeping her locked away from both society and opportunity. Cinderella is portrayed as powerless to act on her own behalf. Hence, she can only dream.

Perhaps Cinderella best illustrates the Disney pattern of subjugating and stifling heroines' voices and selfhood. Her gentleness and goodness are defined by her lack of resistance to abuse by her stepfamily in the film's world. She never disobeys an order, never defends her rights, and never challenges their authority over her. She rarely eats, seldom sleeps, and receives not even the simplest of courtesies, except from her animal friends. Her father's fortune is squandered for the benefit of her stepsisters. She is powerless to control her own fate in her own home. Unable to control her own time, she also is unable to control her own destiny. Cinderella does not act, she only reacts to those around her, a sure sign of both external and internalized oppression. In the face of all this abuse, she somehow remains gentle, kind and beautiful—the perfect girl.

Similarly, *Sleeping Beauty*'s Aurora is a playful teenager whose friends are forest animals, and whose dream is expressed in the song "Some day my prince will come." Aurora is on the verge of celebrating her sixteenth birthday—the day her identity will be revealed to her. At this point she has no knowledge that she really is a princess who was betrothed at birth. Her parents' choices for her define Aurora's destiny and she has no voice in shaping that destiny.

Like Cinderella, Aurora is obedient, beautiful, acquiescent to authority, and essentially powerless in matters regarding her own fate. Furthermore, there is no one Aurora can trust. Although the fairies "protect" her from the truth about her identity and the curse on her future "for her own good," Aurora can take no action on her own behalf. Passively, she is brought back to the castle where she falls under the spell of Maleficent, touches the spinning wheel, and sleeps through most of the film while others battle to decide her future. When she awakens, she finds her "dream come true," a tall, handsome prince who rescues her from an evil female's curse.

Beginning with *The Little Mermaid*, however, the female protagonist shows signs of selfhood. Near the beginning of the film, Ariel sings of her dream to explore and her feelings of being misunderstood. She also expresses frustration and resistance: "Betcha on land they understand. Bet they don't reprimand their daughters. Bright young women, sick of swimmin', ready to stand." She asks, "When's it my turn?"

In contrast to the two previous demure female protagonists, Ariel is characterized as willful and disobedient. She follows her dreams even though she knows her actions run counter to the wishes of her father, King Triton. As a result, Triton charges the crab, Sebastian, with chaperoning his daughter "to protect her from herself." One might also read his actions as patriarchy's efforts to prevent her from achieving an independent identity. However, despite Triton's efforts to control Ariel, she explores, she asks questions, she makes choices, and she acts. For example, she rescues the human, Prince Eric, from the sea. She strikes a bargain with the sea witch, Ursula, to trade her voice for legs. Additionally, she prevents Eric's marriage to Ursula and protects him from Ursula's attack in the film's final battle. Nevertheless, it is Eric who finally kills the sea witch and it is Triton whose power enables Ariel to return to the human world by transforming her permanently into a human. Thus, while Ariel chooses to leave her own people for a life with Eric, it is still not her power but her father's power which enables her dreams to come to fruition.

Articulating one's own dreams and wishes—possessing an autonomous voice—is a strong indicator of the development of selfhood. Little wonder, then, that alarms sound for feminists concerned with the psychological development of girls and women's sense of self when Ariel literally sacrifices her voice and mermaid body to win Eric's love. What is gained by females who silence themselves in a masculinist society? What are the costs to their psychic selves for not doing so? Scholars in feminist psychological development describe the seductiveness of external rewards by denying one's selfhood (Brown & Gilligan, 1992). Having a voice, a sense of selfhood, is risky because it is inconsistent with images of the "perfect girl" or the true woman. When one's loyalty is not to the "masculinist system," one can end up on the margins at best and at worst socially "dead." Ultimately, Ariel's voice is silenced and she sacrifices her curiosity to gain the love of a man.

Reality for Belle in *Beauty and the Beast* means being female and wanting to experience adventure in the "great wide somewhere." Like the earlier Disney heroines, Belle dreams of having "so much more than they've got planned." Belle is the first of the Disney heroines to read, but her reading also alienates her from others in the community. She experiences herself as an "other." Townspeople call her peculiar and say that "she doesn't quite fit in." While Belle is aware of their opinions of her, and understands that she is supposed to marry a villager, raise a family, and conform, she also knows that she *is* different and *wants* something different—something "grand." Although Belle is unsure about how to attain her dreams, she does refuse to marry Gaston, the community "hunk" and its most eligible bachelor. She reads rather than socialize with the villagers, and she accepts that she can be nothing other than different from them. Belle likes herself and trusts her own judgment. Nevertheless, Belle is marginalized by the community for her uniqueness, for her sense of self.

Unlike her counterparts in *Cinderella* and *Sleeping Beauty*, Belle is no damsel in distress. Neither is she a helpless witness to the film's action nor removed from it. Belle occupies double the screen time of any other character in the film (Thomas, 1991), and Belle acts for herself. She dreams of more than a "provincial life"; she wants adventure and, as she sings, "for once it might be grand, to have someone understand, I want so much more than they've got planned." The line might have continued, "for a girl!"

Gaston, the village brute, is attracted to Belle because of her appearance not her brain. He sings that she's "the most beautiful, so that makes her the best." He offers her a place in the community with his marriage proposal. While other women swoon for his attention, Belle rejects him: "His little wife. No, sir. Not me!" Belle's sense of self is strong enough that she refuses to settle for less than a relationship which acknowledges and values her mind, in essence, her self. However, when her father is captured by the Beast, Belle comes to his rescue and offers herself in his place. By trading her life for her father's, she seems to have relinquished her selfhood. Once a prisoner in the Beast's castle, she laments to Mrs. Potts, a kind teapot, that she has lost her father, her dreams, "everything." However, this lament suggests that she still has dreams of her own and a sense of identity apart from that of a dutiful daughter.

Belle's dilemma occurs in part because she has a caring, co-active power relationship with her father (Parker Follett, 1944). Decision making undertaken by women who attempt to maintain selfhood but also exist in a power-with relation to others becomes much more complex, as Gilligan (1977) notes. This complexity is further illustrated by the choices that Belle subsequently makes in her relationship with the Beast. Belle negotiates the conflict she feels between freedom from the Beast and her growing affection for him. She decides not to leave him in the woods after he rescues her from wolves. Although she could escape, she chooses to help him instead. Later in the film, she again chooses to return to the Beast's castle to warn him of the impending mob, even though the Beast has released her from her promise to stay in his castle.

Like Ariel, Belle has freedom to make choices and to act on her own behalf as well as on the behalf of others; and she exercises that freedom. However, whereas Ariel at least initially seems to act out of a sense of rebellion, Belle's motivation appears to come from a craving for intellectual engagement. A simple masculinist interpretation might be that Belle acts out of a sense of personal honor or duty (to sacrifice her freedom first to help her father and later to keep the Beast). A more feminist interpretation based on Gilligan's psychoanalytic developmental work and standpoint theory might be that Belle acts as a result of the tension from seeking selfhood and relationships with others simultaneously. Thus, Belle's actions can be read as a series of complex decisions about when to act, and when to care for someone, how to administer comfort, when to take matters into her own hands, when to risk her personal safety. She is concerned not only with others but with herself as well, and her actions speak to both needs.

No victim, Belle sets the terms for the bargains she makes. In this sense, she exercises more power on her own behalf than previous Disney heroines. For Cinderella, Aurora, and Ariel, someone in power established the conditions within which their dreams could be realized. For example, Cinderella's fairy godmother gave her only until midnight to make her dream come true. At Aurora's christening, the good fairy Merryweather saved Aurora from Maleficent's death curse by decreeing that Aurora would sleep until awakened by a prince's kiss. And when Ariel gave her voice to Ursula in return for the sea witch's magical ability to transform Ariel into a human, Ursula placed a three day time limit on Ariel's pursuit to win Eric's love. Unlike Belle, these females have limited and tenuous opportunities to achieve their dreams. In contrast, Belle exercises substantial control over setting the terms of her own fate. She preserves her own options—by refusing Gaston's overtures and brushing off the villagers' criticisms, and she gives others options—by freeing her father from the Beast's prison, becoming a prisoner herself, and saving the Beast from the wolves. *She* holds *their* futures in her hands. Yet, ironically, one reading of the narrative conclusion is that Belle's liberation of the Beast from his spell ends with her becoming yet another "perfect girl" who marries the prince and lives happily ever after.

Another theme introduced in *Beauty and the Beast*—heroine as teacher—is expanded in *Pocahontas*. Just as Belle teaches the Beast how to be civil, gentle, and caring, Pocahontas teaches John Smith, her tribe, and the Englishmen about nature, power, and peace. Like Belle, Pocahontas exercises power over her future. Viewers first are introduced to Pocahontas going where the wind (the spirit of her mother) leads her; as the chief's daughter, however, she knows that she must take "her place" among her people. Her father tells her, "Even the wild mountain stream must someday join the big river." She sings, "We must all pay a price. To be safe, we lose our chance of ever knowing what's around the river bend.... Why do all my dreams stand just around the river bend.... Is all my dreaming at an end?"

Like Ariel, Pocahontas defies her father in exploring her world. Like Belle, she is an active doer, not a passive victim. She also has a savage to tame in the form of an Englishman. Pocahontas introduces John Smith to the colors of the wind and to the mysteries of the world of nature. She takes political stances such as advocating alternatives to violence, and she makes choices about her life. For example, Pocahontas' decision to reject both her father's wish that she marry Kocoum, the Powhatan warrior, and John Smith's plea to go with him back to England signify that the power to control her actions is in her hands. Pocahontas' choices reflect a sense of selfhood that is a bold stroke for a Disney heroine. A feminist psychological reading might see in her decision to embrace her cultural roots an alternative to Disney's typical heterosexual narratives in which the "perfect girl's" destiny is a monogamous relationship with a (white) man. Indeed, far more than Belle, Pocahontas finds power within to express a self which is separate from that defined through relationships to a father or love interest.

Our reading of Pocahontas implies that she is clearly the most elaborate and complex character in this group of heroines. Her dreams direct her choices. She weighs the risks of choosing a smooth course versus seeking the unknown course to see what awaits her just around the river bend. With counsel from female mentors, Grandmother Willow and the spirit of the wind that symbolizes her mother, Pocahontas finds the strength to listen to her own inner voice, and to choose the less safe, uncharted course of autonomous womanhood. When confronted with the option of leaving her community in order to accompany her love interest, John Smith, she rejects his offer and instead takes her place as an unattached female leader of her people.

Pocahontas brings to the forefront the absence of diversity among Disney's previous female characters. From Cinderella through Belle, Disney's female protagonists easily could be the same characters with only slight variations in hair color. Pocahontas, too, varies only slightly in skin color, but she is the first non-Anglo heroine who is the subject of a Disney animated film. Furthermore, although some of the women may not have difficult family circumstances (e.g., Cinderella), as Caucasians, they all belong to the privileged class in their societies, as daughters of kings, Indian chiefs, and educated inventors.

As this examination of Cinderella, Aurora, Ariel, Belle, and Pocahontas demonstrates, over time Disney's female protagonists have begun to look beyond home, to practice resistance to coercion, and to find their own unique female voices. Indeed, in Pocahontas Disney offers an adventurous female who develops a sense of self in a culture other than the dominant Anglo culture, and who chooses a destiny other than that of heterosexual romantic fulfillment.

## Notes

1. When we first began our study of the Disney animated heroines, *Snow White* had not been released on video nor re-released in the theaters, so it was not included among the films we analyzed. However, the themes introduced in the two earliest films, *Cinderella* and *Sleeping Beauty*, were also present in *Snow White*. We did not include *Aladdin* because the story really centers around the boy, Aladdin, whereas Princess Jasmine is cast in a secondary role and commands little screen time. Princess Jasmine is important, however, in that she is Disney's first non-Caucasian princess.
2. Brody (1976) describes the success of Disney fairy tales from a psychoanalytic perspective. Trites (1991) contrasts Disney's version of *The Little Mermaid* with the original Hans Christian Andersen tale from a Freudian perspective. Other analysts (May, 1981; Stone, 1975) critique the way in which Disney selectively appropriates classics of children's literature. Sex role stereotyping is the focus of

work by Levinson (1975) and Holmlund (1979). They extend concerns about stereotyping using a Marxist feminist approach to the sexual politics of Disney films. Some work has celebrated the Disney tradition for its connections with the oral tradition (Allan, 1988) and its artistic accomplishments (Morrow, 1978).

## References

Allen, R. (1988). Fifty years of Snow White. *Journal of Popular Film and Television, 15,* 156–163.

Bell, E., Haas, L., & Sells, L. (Eds.). (1995). *From mouse to mermaid: The politics of film, gender, and culture.* Bloomington, IN: Indiana University Press.

Brody, M. (1976). The wonderful world of Disney—Its psychological appeal. *American Image, 33,* 350–360.

Brown, L., & Gilligan, G. (1992). *Meeting at the crossroads: Women's psychology and girl's development.* Cambridge, MA: Harvard University Press.

Collins, P. (1986). Learning from the outsider within. *Social Problems, 33,* 514–532.

Follett, M. (1924). *Creative experience.* New York: Longmans, Green.

Follett, M., Metcalf, H., & Urwick, L. (Eds.). (1944). *Dynamic administration: The collected papers of Mary Parker Follett.* New York: Harper.

Gilligan, C. (1982). *In a different voice: Psychological theory and women's development.* Cambridge, MA: Harvard University Press.

Gilligan, C. (1977). In a different voice: Women's conceptions of self and of morality. *Harvard Educational Review, 47,* 481–517.

Harding, S. (1991). *Whose science? Whose knowledge? Thinking from women's lives.* Ithaca, NY: Cornell University Press.

Holmlund, C. (Summer, 1979). Tots to tanks: Walt Disney presents feminism for the family. *Social Text,* 122–132.

Landis, D. (9 February 1993). Disney classics go into hibernation. *USA Today,* p. 5D.

Landis, D. (28 September 1993). Princely predictions for 'Aladdin' video." *USA Today,* p. 1D.

Levinson, R. (1975). From Olive Oyl to Sweet Polly Purebread: Sex role stereotypes and televised cartoons. *Journal of Popular Culture, 9,* 561–572.

May, J. (1981). Walt Disney's interpretation of children's literature. *Language Arts, 4,* 463–472.

Morrow, J. (1978). In defense of Disney. *Media and Methods, 14,* 28–34.

Murphy, P. (1995). The whole wide world was scrubbed clean: The androcentric animation of denatured Disney. In E. Bell, L. Haas, & L. Sells (Eds.), *From mouse to mermaid: The politics of film, gender, and culture* (pp. 125–136). Indianapolis, IN: Indiana University Press.

Orenstein, P. (1994). *School girls.* New York: Anchor Books, Doubleday.

Rich, A. (1986). *Of woman born: Motherhood as experience and institution.* New York: W.W. Norton & Co.

Sells, L. (1995). Where do the mermaids stand?: Voice and body in "The Little Mermaid." In E. Bell, L. Haas, & L. Sells (Eds.), *From mouse to mermaid: The politics of film, gender, and culture* (pp. 175–192). Indianapolis, IN: Indiana University Press.

Stanton, E. (1892). Solitude of self. Convention of National American Suffrage Association. Washington, D.C.

Stone, K. (1975). Things Walt Disney never told us. *Journal of American Folklore, 88,* 42–50.

Thomas, B. (1991). *Art of animation: From Mickey Mouse to Beauty and the Beast.* New York: Hyperion.

Trites, R. (1991). Disney's sub/version of Andersen's "The Little Mermaid." *Journal of Popular Film and Television, 18,* 145–152.

Wood, J. (1992). Gender and moral voice: Moving from women's nature to standpoint epistemology. *Women's Studies in Communication, 16,* 1–24.

Wood, J. (1994). *Gendered lives: Communication, gender, and culture.* Belmont, CA: Wadsworth.

Zipes, J. (1995). Breaking the Disney spell. In E. Bell, L. Haas, & L. Sells (Eds.), *From mouse to mermaid: The politics of film, gender, and culture* (pp. 21–42). Indianapolis, IN: Indiana University Press.

# AMERICA'S CINDERELLA

Jane Yolen

IT IS PART OF THE AMERICAN CREED, recited subvocally along with the pledge of allegiance in each classroom, that even a poor boy can grow up to become president. The unliberated corollary is that even a poor girl can grow up and become the president's wife. This rags-to-riches formula was immortalized in American children's fiction by the Horatio Alger stories of the 1860s and by the Pluck and Luck nickel novels of the 1920s.

It is little wonder, then, that Cinderella should be a perennial favorite in the American folktale pantheon.

Yet how ironic that this formula should be the terms on which "Cinderella" is acceptable to most Americans. "Cinderella" is *not* a story of rags to riches, but rather riches recovered; *not* poor girl into princess but rather rich girl (or princess) rescued from improper or wicked enslavement; *not* suffering Griselda enduring but shrewd and practical girl persevering and winning a share of the power. It is really a story that is about "the stripping away of the disguise that conceals the soul from the eyes of others...."[1]

We Americans have it wrong. "Rumpelstiltskin," in which a miller tells a whopping lie and his docile daughter acquiesces in it to become queen, would be more to the point.

But we have been initially seduced by the Perrault cinder-girl, who was, after all, the transfigured folk creature of a French literary courtier. Perrault's "Cendrillon" demonstrated the well-bred seventeenth-century female traits of gentility, grace, and selflessness, even to the point of graciously forgiving her wicked stepsisters and finding them noble husbands.

The American "Cinderella" is partially Perrault's. The rest is a spun-sugar caricature of her hardier European and Oriental forbears, who made their own way in the world, tricking the stepsisters with double-talk, artfully disguising themselves, or figuring out a way to win the king's son. The final bit of icing on the American Cinderella was concocted by that master candy-maker, Walt Disney, in the 1950s. Since then, America's Cinderella has been a coy, helpless dreamer, a "nice" girl who awaits her rescue with patience and a song. This Cinderella of the mass market books finds her way into a majority of American homes while the classic heroines sit unread in old volumes on library shelves.

Poor Cinderella. She has been unjustly distorted by storytellers, misunderstood by educators, and wrongly accused by feminists. Even as late as 1975, in the well-received volume *Womenfolk and Fairy Tales*, Rosemary Minard writes that Cinderella "would still be scrubbing floors if it were not for her fairy godmother." And Ms. Minard includes her in a sweeping condemnation of folk heroines as "insipid beauties waiting passively for Prince Charming."[2]

Like many dialecticians, Ms. Minard reads the fairy tales incorrectly. Believing—rightly—that the fairy tales, as all stories for children, acculturate young readers and listeners, she has nevertheless gotten her target wrong. Cinderella is not to blame. Not the real, the true Cinderella. Ms. Minard should focus her sights on the mass-market Cinderella. She does not recognize the old Ash-girl[3] for the tough, resilient heroine. The wrong Cinderella has gone to the American ball.

The story of Cinderella has endured for over a thousand years, surfacing in a literary source first in ninth-century China.[4] It has been found from the Orient to the interior of South America and over five hundred variants have been located by folklorists in Europe alone. This best-beloved tale has been brought to life over and over and no one can say for sure where the oral tradition began. The European story was included by Charles Perrault in his 1697 collection *Histories ou Contes du temps passé* as "Cendrillon." But even before that, the Italian Straparola had a similar story in a collection. Since there had been twelve editions of the Straparola book printed in French before 1694, the chances are strong that Perrault had read the tale "*Peau d'Ane*" (Donkey Skin).[5]

Joseph Jacobs, the indefatigable Victorian collector, once said of a Cinderella story he printed that it was "an English version of an Italian adaption of a Spanish translation of a Latin version of a Hebrew translation of an Arabic translation of an Indian original."[6] Perhaps it was not a totally accurate statement of that particular variant, but Jacobs was making a point about the perils of folktale-telling: each teller brings to a tale something of his/her own cultural orientation. Thus in China, where the "lotus foot," or tiny foot was such a sign of a woman's worth that the custom of foot-binding developed, the Cinderella tale lays emphasis on an impossibly small slipper as a clue to the heroine's identity. In seventeenth-century France, Perrault's creation sighs along with her stepsisters over the magnificent "gold flowered mantua" and the "diamond stomacher."[7] In the Walt Disney American version, both movie and book form, Cinderella shares with the little animals a quality of "lovableness,"[8] thus changing the intent of the tale and denying the heroine her birthright of shrewdness, inventiveness, and grace under pressure.

Notice, though, that many innovations—the Chinese slipper, the Perrault godmother with her midnight injunction and her ability to change pumpkin into coach—become incorporated in later versions. Even a slip of the English translator's tongue (*de vair*, fur, into *de verre*, glass) becomes immortalized. Such cross fertilization of folklore is phenomenal. And the staying power, across countries and centuries, of some of these inventions is notable. Yet glass slipper and godmother and pumpkin coach are not the common incidents by which a "Cinderella" tale is recognized even though they have become basic ingredients in the American story. Rather, the common incidents recognized by folklorists are these: an ill-treated though rich and worthy heroine in Cinders-disguise; the aid of a magical gift or advice by a beast/bird/mother substitute; the dance/festival/church scene where the heroine comes in radiant display; recognition through a token. So "Cinderella" and her true sister tales, "Cap o' Rushes" with its King Lear judgement and "Catskin" wherein the father unnaturally desires his daughter, are counted.

Andrew Lang's judgement that "a naked shoeless race could not have invented Cinderella,"[9] then, proves false. Variants have been found among the fur-wearing folk of Alaska and the native tribes in South Africa where shoes were not commonly worn.

"Cinderella" speaks to all of us in whatever skin we inhabit: the child mistreated, a princess or highborn lady in disguise bearing her trials with patience and fortitude. She makes intelligent decisions for she knows that wishing solves nothing without the concomitant action. We have each of us been that child.[10] It is the longing of any youngster sent supperless to bed or given less than a full share at Christmas. It is the adolescent dream.

To make Cinderella less than she is, then, is a heresy of the worst kind. It cheapens our most cherished dreams, and it makes a mockery of the true magic inside us all—the ability to change our own lives, the ability to control our own destinies.

Cinderella first came to America in the nursery tales the settlers remembered from their own homes and told their children. Versions of these tales can still be found. Folklorist Richard Chase, for example, discovered "Rush Cape,"[11] an exact parallel of "Cap o' Rushes" with an Appalachian dialect in Tennessee, Kentucky, and South Carolina among others.

But when the story reached print, developed, was made literary, things began to happen to the hardy Cinderella.[12] She suffered a sea change, a sea change aggravated by social conditions.

In the 1870s, for example, in the prestigious magazine for children *St. Nicholas*, there are a number of retellings or adaptations of "Cinderella." The retellings which merely translate European variants contain the hardy heroine. But when a new version is presented, a helpless Cinderella is born. G.B. Bartlett's "Giant Picture-Book," which was considered "a curious novelty [that] can be produced...by children for the amusement of their friends..."

presents a weepy, prostrate young blonde (the instructions here are quite specific) who must be "aroused from her sad revery" by a godmother.[13] Yet in the truer Cinderella stories, the heroine is not this catatonic. For example, in the Grimm "Cinder-Maid,"[14] though she weeps, she continues to perform the proper rites and rituals at her mother's grave, instructing the birds who roost there to:

> Make me a lady fair to see,
> Dress me as splendid as can be.

And in "The Dirty Shepherdess,"[15] a "Cap o' Rushes" variant from France, "... she dried her eyes, and made a bundle of her jewels and her best dresses and hurriedly left the castle where she was born." In the *St. Nicholas* "Giant Picture-Book" she has none of this strength of purpose. Rather, she is manipulated by the godmother until the moment she stands before the prince where she speaks "meekly" and "with downcast eyes and extended hand."

*St. Nicholas* was not meant for the mass market. It had, in Selma Lanes' words, "a patrician call to a highly literate readership."[16] But nevertheless, Bartlett's play instructions indicate how even in the more literary reaches of children's books a change was taking place.

However, to truly mark this change in the American "Cinderella," one must turn specifically to the mass-market books, merchandised products that masquerade as literature but make as little lasting literary impression as a lollipop. They, after all, serve the majority the way the storytellers of the village used to serve. They find their way into millions of homes.

Mass market books are almost as old as colonial America. The chapbooks of the eighteenth and nineteenth century, crudely printed tiny paperbacks, were the source of most children's reading in the early days of our country.[17] Originally these were books imported from Europe. But slowly American publishing grew. In the latter part of the nineteenth century one firm stood out—McLoughlin Bros. They brought bright colors to the pages of children's books. In a series selling for twenty-five cents per book, *Aunt Kate's Series*, bowdlerized folk tales emerged. "Cinderella" was there, along with "Red Riding Hood," "Puss in Boots," and others. Endings were changed, innards cleaned up, and good triumphed with very loud huzzahs. Cinderella is the weepy, sentimentalized pretty girl incapable of helping herself. In contrast, one only has to look at the girl in "Cap o' Rushes"[18] who comes to a great house and asks "Do you want a maid?" and when refused, goes on to say "... I ask no wages and do any sort of work." And she does. In the end, when the master's young son is dying of love for the mysterious lady, she uses her wits to work her way out of the kitchen. Even in Perrault's "Cinderilla,"[19] when the fairy godmother runs out of ideas for enchantment and "was at a loss for a coachman, I'll go and see, says Cinderilla, if there be never a rat in the rat-trap, we'll make a coachman of him. You are in the right, said her godmother, go and see."

Hardy, helpful, inventive, that was the Cinderella of the old tales but not of the mass market in the nineteenth century. Today's mass-market books are worse. These are the books sold in supermarket and candystore, even lining the shelves of many of the best bookstores. There are pop-up Cinderellas, coloring-book Cinderellas, scratch-and-sniff Cinderellas, all inexpensive and available. The point in these books is not the story but the *gimmick*. These are books which must "interest 300,000 children, selling their initial print order in one season and continuing strong for at least two years after that."[20] Compare that with the usual trade publishing house print order of a juvenile book—10,000 copies which an editor hopes to sell out in a lifetime of that title.

All the folk tales have been gutted. But none so changed, I believe, as "Cinderella." For the sake of Happy Ever After, the mass-market books have brought forward a good, malleable, forgiving little girl and put her in Cinderella's, slippers. However, in most of the Cinderella tales there is no forgiveness in the heroine's heart. No mercy. Just justice. In "Rushen Coatie"[21] and "The Cinder-Maid,"[22] the elder sisters hack off their toes and heels in order to fit the shoe. Cinderella never stops them, never implies that she has the matching slipper. In fact, her tattletale birds warn the prince in "Rushen Coatie":

> Hacked Heels and Pinched Toes
> Behind the young prince rides,
> But Pretty Feet and Little Feet
> Behind the cauldron bides.

Even more graphically, they call out in "Cinder-Maid"

> Turn and peep, turn and peep,
> There's blood within the shoe;
> A bit is cut from off the heel
> And a bit from off the toe.

Cinderella never says a word of comfort. And in the least bowdlerized of the German and Nordic tales, the two sisters come to the wedding "the elder was at the right side and the younger at the left, and the pigeons pecked out one eye from each of them. Afterwards, as they came back, the elder was on the left, and the younger at the right, and then the pigeons pecked out the other eye from each. And thus, for their wickedness and falsehood, they were punished with blindness all their days."[23] That's a far cry from Perrault's heroine who "gave her sisters lodgings in the palace, and married them the same day to two great lords of the court." And further still from Nola Langner's Scholastic paperback "Cinderella"[24]:

> [The sisters] began to cry.
> They begged Cinderella to forgive them for being so mean to her.
> Cinderella told them they were forgiven.
> "I am sure you will never be mean to me again," she said.
> "Oh, never," said the older sister.
> "Never, ever," said the younger sister.

Missing, too, from the mass-market books is the shrewd, even witty Cinderella. In a Wonder Book entitled "Bedtime Stories,"[25] a 1940s adaptation from Perrault, we find a Cinderella who talks to her stepsisters "in a shy little voice." Even Perrault's heroine bantered with her stepsisters, asking them leading questions about the ball while secretly and deliciously knowing the answers. In the Wonder Book, however, the true wonder is that Cinderella ever gets to be princess. Even face-to-face with the prince, she is unrecognized until she dons her magic ballgown. Only when her clothes are transformed does the Prince know his true love.

In 1949, Walt Disney's film *Cinderella* burst onto the American scene. The story in the mass market has not been the same since.

The film came out of the studio at a particularly trying time for Disney. He had been deserted by the intellectuals who had been champions of this art for some years.[26] Because of World War II, the public was more interested in war films than cartoons. But when *Cinderella*, lighter than light, was released it brought back to Disney—and his studio—all of his lost fame and fortune. The film was one of the most profitable of all time for the studio, grossing $4.247 million dollars in the first release alone. The success of the movie opened the floodgates of "Disney Cinderella" books.

Golden Press's *Walt Disney's Cinderella*[27] set the new pattern for America's Cinderella. This book's text is coy and condescending. (Sample: "And her best friends of all were—guess who—the mice!") The illustrations are poor cartoons. And Cinderella herself is a disaster. She cowers as her sisters rip her homemade ball gown to shreds. (Not even homemade by Cinderella, but by the mice and birds.) She answers her stepmother with whines and pleadings. She is a sorry excuse for a heroine, pitiable and useless. She cannot perform even a simple action to save herself, though she is warned by her friends, the mice. She does not hear them because she is "off in a world of dreams." Cinderella begs, she whimpers, and at last has to be rescued by—guess who—the mice!

There is also an easy-reading version published by Random House, *Walt Disney's Cinderella*.[28] This Cinderella commits the further heresy of cursing her luck. "How I did wish to go to the ball," she says. "But it is no use. Wishes never come true."

But in the fairy tales wishes have a habit of happening—*wishes accompanied by the proper action*, bad wishes as well as good. That is the beauty of the old stories and their wisdom as well.

Take away the proper course of action, take away Cinderella's ability to think for herself and act for herself, and you are left with a tale of wishes-come-true-regardless. But that is not the way of the fairy tale. As P.L. Travers so wisely puts it, "If that were so, wouldn't we all be married to princes?"[29]

The mass-market American "Cinderellas" have presented the majority of American children with the wrong dream. They offer the passive princess, the "insipid beauty waiting...for Prince Charming" that Rosemary Minard objects to, and thus acculturate millions of girls and boys. But it is the wrong Cinderella and the magic of the old tales has been falsified, the true meaning lost, perhaps forever.

## Notes

1. Elizabeth Cook, *The Ordinary and the Fabulous.*
2. Rosemary Minard, *Womenfolk and Fairy Tales.*
3. There are a number of stories about Ash-boys. For this study, only tales with the heroine have been considered.
4. Arthur Waley, "The Chinese Cinderella Story."
5. Marian Roalfe Cox, *Cinderella: 349 Variants.*
6. As quoted in Eileen H. Colwell, "Folk Literature: An Oral Tradition."
7. "Cinderilla: or The Little Glass Slipper," in *The Classic Fairy Tales.*
8. Frances Clarke Sayers, "Disney Accused." The word "lovableness" is Ms. Sayers' and terrifically accurate. The article is a classic.
9. Marian Roalfe Cox, *op. cit.*
10. Even boys and men share that dream. See Walter Scherf, "Family Conflicts and Emancipation in Fairy Tales."
11. Richard Chase, *American Folk Tales and Songs.*
12. There were already signs of change in the British mass-market Cinderella books. See *Aunt Louisa's Favorite Toy Book.*
13. G.B. Bartlett, "The Giant Picture Book."
14. "The Cinder-Maid."
15. "The Dirty Shepherdess."
16. Selma G. Lanes, *Down the Rabbit Hole.*
17. Virginia Haviland, *Yankee Doodle's Literary Sampler of Prose. Poetry, and Pictures.*
18. "Cap o' Rushes."
19. "Cinderilla, or The Little Glass Slipper," *op. cit.*
20. Selma Lanes, *op. cit.*
21. "Rushen Coatie."
22. "The Cinder-Maid."
23. "Cinderella," from *The Complete Grimm's Fairy Tales.*
24. Nola Langner, *Cinderella.* A fall from grace for Ms. Langner; the pictures in this are still charming.
25. Eleanor Graham, *Bedtime Stories.*
26. Richard Schickel, *The Disney Version.* The critical book on Disney. Witty and wise.
27. Retta S. Worcester and Jane Werner, *Walt Disney's Cinderella.*
28. *Walt Disney's Cinderella.*
29. P.L. Travers, "Only Connect."

## References Cited


**Perrault**

"Cinderilla, or, The Little Glass Slipper" (1889) (Robert Samber version), in Andrew Lang. *The Blue Fairy Book* (1965). New York, Dover.

"Cinderella, or, The Little Glass Slipper" (1729), translated by Robert Samber (first published in *Histories or Tales of Past Times*), in Iona and Peter Opie (1974) *The Classic Fairy Tales*, London, Oxford University Press.

**Cap o' Rushes**

"Cap o' Rushes" (Joseph Jacobs version), in Rosemary Minard (1975), *Womenfolk and Fairytales*, Boston, Houghton Mifflin.

"The Dirty Shepherdess" (French version), in Andrew Lang (1892; reprinted 1965), *The Green Fairy Book*, New York: Longmans, Green; Dover.

"Katie Woodencloak" (Norwegian version), in Stith Thompson (1945, 1973), *One Hundred Favorite Folktales*. New York: Pantheon.

"Rush Cape" (Appalachian version), in Richard Chase, (1971) *American Folk Tales and Songs*. New York: Dover.

"Rushen Coatie" (English version), in Joseph Jacobs (1894; reprinted 1968), *More English Fairy Tales*. New York: Schocken.

**Peau d'Ane**

"Donkey Skin," from *Cabinet des Fées*, in Andrew Lang (1900), *The Grey Fairy Book*. New York: Longmans, Green.

**German (*Ashenputtel*)**

"Cinderella," in Padraic Colum and Joseph Campbell (1944, 1972), *The Complete Grimm's Fairy Tales*. New York: Pantheon.

"The Cinder-Maid," in Joseph Jacobs (1916), *European Folk and Fairy Tales*, New York: Putnam.

**Russian**

"The Golden Slipper" (1945, 1973), in Afanasev, *Russian Fairy Tales*. New York: Pantheon.

**Chinese**

Waley, Arthur (1947). "The Chinese Cinderella Story," in *Folklore*, Vol. 58.

**American Mass Market**

Bartlett, G.B. (1881), "The Giant Picture Book," *St. Nicholas Magazine*. June 1881.

*Cinderella* (c. 1876), Aunt Kate's Series. New York: McLoughlin Bros.

Graham, Eleanor (1946), *Bedtime Stories*. New York: Wonder Books.

Langner, Nola (1972), *Cinderella*. New York: Scholastic.

*The New Walt Disney Treasury* (1971), New York: Golden Press.

*Walt Disney's Cinderella* (1974), New York: Random House.

Worcester, Retta S., and Werner, Jane (1950), *Walt Disney's Cinderella*. New York: Golden Press.

**Research and Critical Volumes**

Arbuthnot, May Hill, and Sutherland, Zena (1972), *Children and Books*. 4th ed. Glenview, Ill., Scott, Foresman.

*Aunt Louisa's Favorite Toy Book* (c. 1876). London: Frederick Warne.

Chase, Richard (1971), *American Folk Tales and Songs*. New York: Dover.
*Children's Literature: The Great Excluded*. Vol. 3. Philadelphia, Temple University Press.
Colwell, Eileen H. (1973), "Folk Literature: An Oral Tradition and an Oral Art," in Virginia Haviland, *Children and Literature: Views and Reviews*. Glenview, Ill.: Scott, Foresman.
Cook, Elizabeth (1969), *The Ordinary and the Fabulous*, Cambridge: Cambridge University Press.
Cox, Marian Roalfe (1893), *Cinderella: 345 Variants*. London: David Nutt.
Egoff, Sheils; Stubbs, G.T., and Ashley, L.F., eds. (1969), *Only Connect: Readings on Children's Literature*. New York: Oxford University Press.
Haviland, Virginia (1973), *Children and Literature: Views and Reviews*. Glenview, Ill.: Scott, Foresman.
Haviland, Virginia (1974), *Yankee Doodle's Literary Sampler of Prose, Poetry, and Pictures*. New York: Crowell.
Hazard, Paul (1966), *Books, Children, and Men*. Boston: Horn.
Lanes, Selma G. (1971), *Down the Rabbit Hale*. New York: Atheneum.
Leach, Maria (1972), *Funk & Wagnalls Standard Dictionary of Folklore, Mythology, and Legend*. New York: Funk & Wagnalls.
Meigs, Cornelia, et al. (1953, 1964, 1969), *A Critical History of Children's Literature*. New York: Macmillan.

# NO NAME WOMAN

## Maxine Hong Kingston

"YOU MUST NOT tell anyone," my mother said, "what I am about to tell you. In China your father had a sister who killed herself. She jumped into the family well. We say that your father has all brothers because it is as if she had never been born.

"In 1924 just a few days after our village celebrated seventeen hurry-up weddings—to make sure that every young man who went 'out on the road' would responsibly come home—your father and his brothers and your grandfather and his brothers and your aunt's new husband sailed for America, the Gold Mountain. It was your grandfather's last trip. Those lucky enough to get contracts waved goodbye from the decks. They fed and guarded the stowaways and helped them off in Cuba, New York, Bali, Hawaii. 'We'll meet in California next year,' they said. All of them sent money home.

"I remember looking at your aunt one day when she and I were dressing; I had not noticed before that she had such a protruding melon of a stomach. But I did not think, 'She's pregnant,' until she began to look like other pregnant women, her shirt pulling and the white tops of her black pants showing. She could not have been pregnant, you see, because her husband had been gone for years. No one said anything. We did not discuss it.

In early summer she was ready to have the child, long after the time when it could have been possible.

"The village had also been counting. On the night the baby was to be born the villagers raided our house. Some were crying. Like a great saw, teeth strung with lights, files of people walked zigzag across our land, tearing the rice. Their lanterns doubled in the disturbed black water, which drained away through the broken bunds. As the villagers closed in, we could see that some of them, probably men and women we knew well, wore white masks. The people with long hair hung it over their faces. Women with short hair made it stand up on end. Some had tied white bands around their foreheads, arms, and legs.

"At first they threw mud and rocks at the house. Then they threw eggs and began slaughtering our stock. We could hear the animals scream their deaths—the roosters, the pigs, a last great roar from the ox. Familiar wild heads flared in our night windows; the villagers encircled us. Some of the faces stopped to peer at us, their eyes rushing like searchlights. The hands flattened against the panes, framed heads, and left red prints.

"The villagers broke in the front and the back doors at the same time, even though we had not locked the doors against them. Their knives dripped with the blood of our animals. They smeared blood on the doors and walls. One woman swung a chicken, whose throat she had slit, splattering blood in red arcs about her. We stood together in the middle of our house, in the family hall with the pictures and tables of the ancestors around us, and looked straight ahead.

"At that time the house had only two wings. When the men came back, we would build two more to enclose our courtyard and a third one to begin a second courtyard. The villagers pushed through both wings, even your grandparents' rooms, to find your aunt's, which was also mine until the men returned. From this room a new wing for one of the younger families would grow. They ripped up her clothes and shoes and broke her combs, grinding them underfoot. They tore her work from the loom. They scattered the cooking fire and rolled the new weaving in it. We could hear them in the kitchen breaking our bowls and banging the pots. They overturned the great waist-high earthenware jugs; duck eggs, pickled fruits, vegetables burst out and mixed in acrid torrents. The old woman from the next field swept a broom through the air and loosed the spirits-of-the-broom over our heads. 'Pig.' 'Ghost.' 'Pig,' they sobbed and scolded while they ruined our house.

"When they left, they took sugar and oranges to bless themselves. They cut pieces from the dead animals. Some of them took bowls that were not broken and clothes that were not torn. Afterward we swept up the rice and sewed it back up into sacks. But the smells from the spilled preserves lasted. Your aunt gave birth in the pigsty that night. The next morning when I went for the water, I found her and the baby plugging up the family well.

"Don't let your father know that I told you. He denies her. Now that you have started to menstruate, what happened to her could happen to you. Don't humiliate us. You wouldn't like to be forgotten as if you had never been born. The villagers are watchful."

Whenever she had to warn us about life, my mother told stories that ran like this one, a story to grow up on. She tested our strength to establish realities. Those in the emigrant generations who could not reassert brute survival died young and far from home. Those of us in the first American generations have had to figure out how the invisible world the emigrants built around our childhoods fits in solid America.

The emigrants confused the gods by diverting their curses, misleading them with crooked streets and false names. They must try to confuse their offspring as well, who, I suppose, threaten them in similar ways—always trying to get things straight, always trying to name the unspeakable. The Chinese I know hide their names; sojourners take new names when their lives change and guard their real names with silence.

Chinese-Americans, when you try to understand what things in you are Chinese, how do you separate what is peculiar to childhood, to poverty, insanities, one family, your mother who marked your growing with stories, from what is Chinese? What is Chinese tradition and what is the movies?

If I want to learn what clothes my aunt wore, whether flashy or ordinary, I would have to begin, "Remember Father's drowned-in-the-well sister?" I cannot ask that. My mother has told me once and for all the useful parts. She will add nothing unless powered by Necessity, a riverbank that guides her life. She plants vegetable gardens rather than lawns; she carries the odd-shaped tomatoes home from the fields and eats food left for the gods.

Whenever we did frivolous things, we used up energy; we flew high kites. We children came up off the ground over the melting cones our parents brought home from work and the American movie on New Year's Day—*Oh, You Beautiful Doll* with Betty Grable one year, and *She Wore a Yellow Ribbon* with John Wayne another year. After the one carnival ride each, we paid in guilt; our tired father counted his change on the dark walk home.

Adultery is extravagance. Could people who hatch their own chicks and eat the embryos and the heads for delicacies and boil the feet in vinegar for party food, leaving only the gravel, eating even the gizzard lining—could such people engender a prodigal aunt? To be a woman, to have a daughter in starvation time was a waste enough. My aunt could not have been the lone romantic who gave up everything for sex. Women in the old China did not choose. Some man had commanded her to lie with him and be his secret evil. I wonder whether he masked himself when he joined the raid on her family.

Perhaps she had encountered him in the fields or on the mountain where the daughters-in-law collected fuel. Or perhaps he first noticed her in the marketplace. He was not a stranger because the village housed no strangers. She had to have dealings with him other than sex. Perhaps he worked an adjoining field, or he sold her the cloth for the dress she sewed and wore. His demand must have surprised, then terrified her. She obeyed him; she always did as she was told.

When the family found a young man in the next village to be her husband, she had stood tractably beside the best rooster, his proxy, and promised before they met that she would be his forever. She was lucky that he was her age and she would be the first wife, an advantage secure now. The night she first saw him, he had sex with her. Then he left for America. She had almost forgotten what he looked like. When she tried to envision him, she only saw the black and white face in the group photograph the men had had taken before leaving.

The other man was not, after all, much different from her husband. They both gave orders: she followed. "If you tell your family, I'll beat you. I'll kill you. Be here again next week." No one talked sex, ever. And she might have separated the rapes from the rest of living if only she did not have to buy her oil from him or gather wood in the same forest. I want her fear to have lasted just as long as rape lasted so that the fear could have been contained. No drawn-out fear. But women at sex hazarded birth and hence lifetimes. The fear did not stop but permeated everywhere. She told the man, "I think I'm pregnant." He organized the raid against her.

On nights when my mother and father talked about their life back home, sometimes they mentioned an "outcast table" whose business they still seemed to be settling, their voices tight. In a commensal tradition, where food is precious, the powerful older people made wrongdoers eat alone. Instead of letting them start separate new lives like the Japanese, who could become samurais and geishas, the Chinese family, faces averted but eyes glowering sideways, hung on to the offenders and fed them leftovers. My aunt must have lived in the same house as my parents and eaten at an outcast table. My mother spoke about the raid as if she had seen it, when she and my aunt, a daughter-in-law to a different household, should not have been living together at all. Daughters-in-law lived with their husbands' parents, not their own; a synonym for marriage in Chinese is "taking a daughter-in-law." Her husband's parents could have sold her, mortgaged her, stoned her. But they had sent her back to her own mother and father, a mysterious act hinting at disgraces not told me. Perhaps they had thrown her out to deflect the avengers.

She was the only daughter; her four brothers went with her father, husband, and uncles "out on the road" and for some years became western men. When the goods were divided among the family, three of the brothers took land, and the youngest, my father, chose an education. After my grandparents gave their daughter away to her husband's family, they had dispensed all the adventure and all the property. They expected her alone to keep the traditional ways, which her brothers, now among the barbarians, could fumble without detection. The heavy, deep-rooted women were to maintain the past against the flood, safe for returning. But the rare urge west had fixed upon our family, and so my aunt crossed boundaries not delineated in space.

The work of preservation demands that the feelings playing about in one's guts not be turned into action. Just watch their passing like cherry blossoms. But perhaps my aunt, my forerunner, caught in a slow life, let dreams grow and fade and after some months or years went toward what persisted. Fear at the enormities of the forbidden kept her desires delicate, wire and bone. She looked at a man because she liked the way the hair was tucked behind his ears, or she liked the question-mark line of a long torso curving at the shoulder and straight at the hip. For warm eyes or a soft voice or a slow walk—that's all—a few hairs, a line, a brightness, a sound, a pace, she gave up family. She offered us up for a charm that vanished with tiredness, a pigtail that didn't toss when the wind died. Why, the wrong lighting could erase the dearest thing about him.

It could very well have been, however, that my aunt did not take subtle enjoyment of her friend, but, a wild woman, kept rollicking company. Imagining her free with sex doesn't fit, though. I don't know any women like that, or men either. Unless I see her life branching into mine, she gives me no ancestral help.

To sustain her being in love, she often worked at herself in the mirror, guessing at the colors and shapes that would interest him, changing them frequently in order to hit on the right combination. She wanted him to look back.

On a farm near the sea, a woman who tended her appearance reaped a reputation for eccentricity. All the married women blunt-cut their hair in flaps about their ears or pulled it back in tight buns. No nonsense. Neither style blew easily into heart-catching tangles. And at their weddings they displayed themselves in their long hair for the last time. "It brushed the backs of my knees," my mother tells me. "It was braided, and even so, it brushed the backs of my knees."

At the mirror my aunt combed individuality into her bob. A bun could have been contrived to escape into black streamers blowing in the wind or in quiet wisps about her face, but only the older women in our picture album wear buns. She brushed her hair back from her forehead, tucking the flaps behind her ears. She looped a piece of thread, knotted into a circle between her index fingers and thumbs, and ran the double strand across her forehead. When she closed her fingers as if she were making a pair of shadow geese bite, the string twisted together catching the little hairs. Then she pulled the thread away from her skin, ripping the hairs out neatly, her eyes watering from the needles of pain. Opening her fingers, she cleaned the thread, then rolled it along her hairline and the tops of her eyebrows. My mother did the same to me and my sisters and herself. I used to believe that the expression "caught by the short hairs" meant a captive held with a depilatory string. It especially hurt at the temples, but my mother said we were lucky we didn't have to have our feet bound when we were seven. Sisters used to sit on their beds and cry together, she said, as their mothers or their slaves removed the bandages for a few minutes each night and let the blood gush back into their veins. I hope that the man my aunt loved appreciated a smooth brow, that he wasn't just a tits-and-ass man.

Once my aunt found a freckle on her chin, at a spot that the almanac said predestined her for unhappiness. She dug it out with a hot needle and washed the wound with peroxide.

More attention to her looks than these pullings of hairs and pickings at spots would have caused gossip among the villagers. They owned work clothes and good clothes, and they wore good clothes for feasting the new seasons. But since a woman combing her hair hexes beginnings, my aunt rarely found an occasion to look her best. Women looked like great sea snails—the corded wood, babies, and laundry they carried were the whorls on their backs. The Chinese did not admire a bent back; goddesses and warriors stood straight. Still there must have been a marvelous freeing of beauty when a worker laid down her burden and stretched and arched.

Such commonplace loveliness, however, was not enough for my aunt. She dreamed of a lover for the fifteen days of New Year's, the time for families to exchange visits, money, and food. She plied her secret comb. And sure enough she cursed the year, the family, the village, and herself.

Even as her hair lured her imminent lover, many other men looked at her. Uncles, cousins, nephews, brothers would have looked, too, had they been home between journeys. Perhaps they had already been restraining their curiosity, and they left, fearful that their glances, like a field of nesting birds, might be startled and caught. Poverty hurt, and that was their first reason for leaving. But another, final reason for leaving the crowded house was the never-said.

She may have been unusually beloved, the precious only daughter, spoiled and mirror gazing because of the affection the family lavished on her. When her husband left, they welcomed the chance to take her back from the in-laws; she could live like the little daughter for just a while longer. There are stories that my grandfather was different from other people, "crazy ever since the little Jap bayoneted him in the head." He used to put his naked penis on the dinner table, laughing. And one day he brought home a baby girl, wrapped up inside his brown western-style greatcoat. He had traded one of his sons, probably my father, the youngest, for her. My grandmother made him trade back. When he finally got a daughter of his own, he doted on her. They must have all loved her, except perhaps my father, the only brother who never went back to China, having once been traded for a girl.

Brothers and sisters, newly men and women, had to efface their sexual color and present plain miens. Disturbing hair and eyes, a smile like no other, threatened the ideal of five generations living under one roof. To focus blurs, people shouted face to face and yelled from room to room. The immigrants I know have loud voices, unmodulated to American tones even after years away from the village where they called their friendships out across the fields. I have not been able to stop my mother's screams in public libraries or over telephones. Walking erect (knees straight, toes pointed forward, not pigeon-toed, which is Chinese-feminine) and speaking in an inaudible voice, I have tried to turn myself American-feminine. Chinese communication was loud, public. Only sick people had to whisper. But at the dinner table, where the family members came nearest one another, no one could talk, not the outcasts nor any eaters. Every word that falls from the mouth is a coin lost. Silently they gave and accepted food with both hands. A preoccupied child who took his bowl with one hand got a sideways glare. A complete moment of total attention is due everyone alike. Children and lovers have no singularity here, but my aunt used a secret voice, a separate attentiveness.

She kept the man's name to herself throughout her labor and dying; she did not accuse him that he be punished with her. To save her inseminator's name she gave silent birth.

He may have been somebody in her own household, but intercourse with a man outside the family would have been no less abhorrent. All the village were kinsmen, and the titles shouted in loud country voices never let kinship be forgotten. Any man within visiting distance would have been neutralized as a lover—"brother," "younger brother," "older brother"—one hundred and fifteen relationship titles. Parents researched birth charts probably not so much to assure good fortune as to circumvent incest in a population that has but one hundred surnames. Everybody has eight million relatives. How useless then sexual mannerisms, how dangerous.

As if it came from an atavism deeper than fear, I used to add "brother" silently to boys' names. It hexed the boys, who would or would not ask me to dance, and made them less scary and as familiar and deserving of benevolence as girls.

But, of course, I hexed myself also—no dates. I should have stood up, both arms waving, and shouted out across libraries, "Hey, you! Love me back." I had no idea, though, how to make attraction selective, how to control its direction and magnitude. If I made myself American-pretty so that the five or six Chinese boys in the class fell in love with me, everyone else—the Caucasian, Negro, and Japanese boys—would too. Sisterliness, dignified and honorable, made much more sense.

Attraction eludes control so stubbornly that whole societies designed to organize relationships among people cannot keep order, not even when they bind people to one another from childhood and raise them together. Among the very poor and the wealthy, brothers married their adopted sisters, like doves. Our family allowed some romance, paying adult brides' prices and providing dowries so that their sons and daughters could marry strangers. Marriage promises to turn strangers into friendly relatives—a nation of siblings.

In the village structure, spirits shimmered among the live creatures, balanced and held in equilibrium by time and land. But one human being flaring up into violence could open up a black hole, a maelstrom that pulled in the sky. The frightened villagers, who depended on one another to maintain the real, went to my aunt to show her a personal, physical representation of the break she had made in the "roundness." Misallying couples snapped off the future, which was to be embodied in true offspring. The villagers punished her for acting as if she could have a private life, secret and apart from them.

If my aunt had betrayed the family at a time of large grain yields and peace, when many boys were born, and wings were being built on many houses, perhaps she might have escaped such severe punishment. But the men—hungry, greedy, tired of planting in dry soil—had been forced to leave the village in order to send food-money home. There were ghost plagues, bandit plagues, wars with the Japanese, floods. My Chinese brother and sister had died of an unknown sickness. Adultery, perhaps only a mistake during good times, became a crime when the village needed food.

The round moon cakes and round doorways, the round tables of graduated sizes that fit one roundness inside another, round windows and rice bowls—these talismans had lost their power to warn this family of the law: a family must be whole, faithfully keeping the descent line by having sons to feed the old and the dead, who in turn look after the family. The villagers came to show my aunt and her lover-in-hiding a broken house. The villagers were speeding up the circling of events because she was too shortsighted to see that her infidelity had already harmed the village, that waves of consequences would return unpredictably, sometimes in disguise, as now, to hurt her. This roundness had to be made coin-sized so that she would see its circumference: punish her at the birth of her baby. Awaken her to the inexorable. People who refused fatalism because they could invent small resources insisted on culpability. Deny accidents and wrest fault from the stars.

After the villagers left, their lanterns now scattering in various directions toward home, the family broke their silence and cursed her. "Aiaa, we're going to die. Death is coming. Death is coming. Look what you've done. You've killed us. Ghost! Dead ghost! Ghost! You've never been born." She ran out into the fields, far enough from the house so that she could no longer hear their voices, and pressed herself against the earth, her own land no more. When she felt the birth coming, she thought that she had been hurt. Her body seized together. "They've hurt me too much," she thought. "This is gall, and it will kill me." With forehead and knees against the earth, her body convulsed and then relaxed. She turned on her back, lay on the ground. The black well of sky and stars went out and out and out forever; her body and her complexity seemed to disappear. She was one of the stars, a bright dot in blackness, without home, without a companion, in eternal cold and silence. An agoraphobia rose in her, speeding higher and higher, bigger and bigger; she would not be able to contain it; there would be no end to fear.

Flayed, unprotected against space, she felt pain return, focusing her body. This pain chilled her—a cold, steady kind of surface pain. Inside, spasmodically, the other pain, the pain of the child, heated her. For hours she lay on the ground, alternately body and space. Sometimes a vision of normal comfort obliterated reality: she saw the family in the evening gambling at the dinner table, the young people massaging their elders' backs. She saw them congratulating one another, high joy on the mornings the rice shoots came up. When these pictures burst, the stars drew yet further apart. Black space opened.

She got to her feet to fight better and remembered that old-fashioned women gave birth in their pigsties to fool the jealous, pain-dealing gods, who do not snatch piglets. Before the next spasms could stop her, she ran to the pigsty, each step a rushing out into emptiness. She climbed over the fence and knelt in the dirt. It was good to have a fence enclosing her, a tribal person alone.

Laboring, this woman who had carried her child as a foreign growth that sickened her every day, expelled it at last. She reached down to touch the hot, wet, moving mass, surely smaller than anything human, and could feel that it was human after all—fingers, toes, nails, nose. She pulled it up on to her belly, and it lay curled there, butt in the air, feet precisely tucked one under the other. She opened her loose shirt and buttoned the child inside. After resting, it squirmed and thrashed and she pushed it up to her breast. It turned its head this way and that until it found her nipple. There, it made little snuffling noises. She clenched her teeth at its preciousness, lovely as a young calf, a piglet, a little dog.

She may have gone to the pigsty as a last act of responsibility: she would protect this child as she had protected its father. It would look after her soul, leaving supplies on her grave. But how would this tiny child without family find her grave when there would be no marker for her anywhere, neither in the earth nor the family hall? No one would give her a family hall name. She had taken the child with her into the wastes. At its birth the two of them had felt the same raw pain of separation, a wound that only the family pressing tight could close. A child with no descent line would not soften her life but only trail after her, ghostlike, begging her to give it purpose. At dawn the villagers on their way to the fields would stand around the fence and look.

Full of milk, the little ghost slept. When it awoke, she hardened her breasts against the milk that crying loosens. Toward morning she picked up the baby and walked to the well.

Carrying the baby to the well shows loving. Otherwise abandon it. Turn its face into the mud. Mothers who love their children take them along. It was probably a girl; there is some hope of forgiveness for boys.

"Don't tell anyone you had an aunt. Your father does not want to hear her name. She has never been born." I have believed that sex was unspeakable and words so strong and fathers so frail that "aunt" would do my father mysterious harm. I have thought that my family, having settled among immigrants who had also been their neighbors in the ancestral land, needed to clean their name, and a wrong word would incite the kinspeople even here. But there is more to this silence: they want me to participate in her punishment. And I have.

In the twenty years since I heard this story I have not asked for details nor said my aunt's name; I do not know it. People who can comfort the dead can also chase after them to hurt them further—a reverse ancestor worship. The real punishment was not the raid swiftly inflicted by the villagers, but the family's deliberately forgetting her. Her betrayal so maddened them, they saw to it that she would suffer forever, even after death. Always hungry, always needing, she would have to beg food from other ghosts, snatch and steal it from those whose living descendants give them gifts. She would have to fight the ghosts massed at crossroads for the buns a few thoughtful citizens leave to decoy her away from village and home so that the ancestral spirits could feast unharassed. At peace, they could act like gods, not ghosts, their descent lines providing them with paper suits and dresses, spirit money, paper houses, paper automobiles, chicken, meat, and rice into eternity—essences delivered up in smoke and flames, steam and incense rising from each rice bowl. In an attempt to make the Chinese care for people outside the family, Chairman Mao encourages us now to give our paper replicas to the spirits of outstanding soldiers and workers, no matter whose ancestors they may be. My aunt remains forever hungry. Goods are not distributed evenly among the dead.

My aunt haunts me—her ghost drawn to me because now, after fifty years of neglect, I alone devote pages of paper to her, though not origamied into houses and clothes. I do not think she always means me well. I am telling on her, and she was a spite suicide, drowning herself in the drinking water. The Chinese are always very frightened of the drowned one, whose weeping ghost, wet hair hanging and skin bloated, waits silently by the water to pull down a substitute.

## This Text: Reading

1. What do you make of how Henke, Umble, and Smith trace the female heroine in Disney? Is their reading fair? What cultural contexts prompted their investigation?
2. What cultural contexts may account for the transformation of Disney female heroines?
3. According to Yolen, what are the reasons for the dramatic change in how Americans *read* Cinderella? What does Cinderella symbolize for Yolen?
4. How is the Henke/Umble/Smith reading of Cinderella similar to and different from Yolen's reading of Cinderella? What accounts for the differences?
5. How is Cinderella similar to Kingston's "No Name Woman"?

6. What is the effect of transforming ethnic folktales about gender into contemporary short stories?

### YOUR TEXT: WRITING

1. Pick a myth or a folktale or a fairytale that has a female as the main character. Give a semiotic reading of the text in which you examine what messages the text sends about gender and gender roles.
2. Write a personal essay on how myths and fairy tales have shaped your ideas of gender and gender roles. What text was particularly influential in your life?
3. Based on Yolen's model, write an analytical paper in which you analyze a character from a Disney movie in terms of American values and cultures. What character seems to embody American ideals of beauty, innocence, submission, and virtue?
4. Using a myth one of the authors has mentioned, write an essay examining male gender and gender roles. What do these myths say about men? Are men as affected by myths as women? More so?
5. If women and girls tend to get their visions of female behavior from fairy tales, where do men get theirs? Write an argumentative essay in which you demonstrate which texts influence male behavior.
6. Write an essay on the links between gender and ethnicity. How do the codes and mores of a certain ethnic culture play into gender roles?

---

## READING OUTSIDE THE LINES

## Classroom Activities

1. Send all of the males to another room to discuss a specific text. Now that all the guys are absent, hold a discussion for 20 minutes on one or two texts in this section. How is your classroom experience different without males around? Why is it different?
2. In class, watch a television show from the 50s or 60s like *Leave it to Beaver* or *Father Knows Best* or *Bonanza*. Compare the gender roles to those in a show like *Will and Grace, Frasier*, or *Ally McBeal*. What has changed? What hasn't? How do cultural norms and mores affect how gender gets represented?
3. Go around the room, and ask students to identify how they are themselves "marked," or ask them to provide one example of how they "do gender."

4. As a class, identify five famous women. How do they do gender? Or, using Devor's essay, how do they adhere to feminine expectations?
5. Do the same with five famous men.
6. As a class, discuss why words like slut, whore, bitch, easy, loose, cold, frigid and manipulative are generally reserved for females. Why are similar words used to describe males, like stud, player, gigolo, pimp, shrewd and rational, so different from those used to describe women?
7. As a class, write a companion poem to Storni's "You Would Have Me White," but from a male perspective. What would the male's claim be? "You Would Have Me ______________"
8. Is America more racist or sexist? Do you think we would have a black male president first or a white woman? What's your reasoning here?
9. Have everyone in the class bring in a magazine ad that has to do with gender or gender roles. When taken together, what emerges?
10. Break up into groups and discuss the contradictions of gender we see in television, movies, music and magazines. Compare your answers.
11. Listen to some rap, country, pop and folk songs in class. How are issues of gender reinforced by song lyrics, album covers and videos?

## Essay Ideas

1. Write a paper in which you examine and debunk three stereotypes about gender.
2. Most of the essays here have dealt with gender issues and women. Write an essay in which you examine how music, sports, business, movies and even pornography determines what admirable "masculine" traits are.
3. Write a personal essay in which you examine three ways in which you do gender. What do your means of doing gender say about you?
4. Write an argumentative essay about certain texts that you think are harmful in terms of how they perpetuate gender stereotypes.
5. Read a magazine that is aimed at another gender. If you are a woman, read *Maxim, Sports Illustrated, GQ, Details, Men's Health* or *Field and Stream*; if you are a man, read *Cosmopolitan, Shape, Redbook, Ladies Home Journal, Martha Stewart Living, Ms.*, or *Working Woman*. Write a paper in which you give a semiotic analysis of the magazine.
6. Write a paper on daytime television. What messages do the commercials and the programming send to women (and men) about women (and men)?
7. As this book goes to press, there is a proliferation of pro-anorexia sites on the World Wide Web. Write a paper that is a reading of anorexia and/or bulimia. Why does this disease affect mostly middle-class white women? Why don't men suffer from these ailments?

8. Give a semiotic reading of male/female dating. What roles are men and women supposed to play early in the dating process? What behavior is okay? What is forbidden? How do we know these rules?
9. Go to the room or the apartment of a friend of yours of a different gender. Give a semiotic reading of that person's room. How is it different from yours? How does your friend's room reflect his or her gender?
10. Give a reading of the gender dynamics in your household. What gender roles do your parents or stepparents fall into? Your siblings? You?

# 7

# Reading the Visual Arts

For many of us, visual art is intimidating. When confronted with a piece of artwork, particularly if it is abstract (made more from shapes rather than recognizable figures), we do not often know how we should look at it. We want to appreciate art because we know "people" think it's important, but how to do so remains a mystery. We agree both with the fact that learning how to read art is important and that it seems a daunting task at times. That's where this chapter comes in—we hope to make it easier for you to approach what can be a rewarding and even enjoyable process. In fact, it should turn out to be one of the most rewarding skills in your repertoire as a human being.

Let's begin with a quick overview of what we mean by visual art. Though visual art has undergone transformations with the proliferation of technology, we generally mean paintings, sculptures, and photographs, though items like artistic installations (large works of art often taking up entire rooms) or collages are often considered visual arts. Traditionally, these arts are texts that make meaning through visual signs—colors, shapes, shadings, and lines—as opposed to texts that make meaning with words or music, though modern art has sought to bring both of these into its world. In this chapter, we will confine our comments to paintings, sculptures, and photographs, as these are the most common forms of visual art that you are likely to encounter in your everyday lives. Like everything else we talk about in this book, visual art is a complex text that you are encouraged and invited not simply to look at but to *read*.

One of the most important aspects to recognize about art is its universality and longevity. Long before there were written languages, there were visual ones. Since human beings could hold sticks and dab them in mud, there has been art. In caves in France, on cliffs in Utah, on tablets in the Middle East, on paper in the Orient, and on tombs in Egypt, men and women have been drawing pictures. If you have visited any of these places and seen these texts, you get a sense of the artist's overwhelming urge to represent the world—that is to re-present or remake the world. That is really all art of any kind is—an individual's way of presenting the world in a new way. Van Gogh's sunflowers, Monet's waterlillies, Picasso's musicians, El Greco's Jesus, even Jackson Pollock's splatterings are attempts to make us experience some aspect of the world in a way we had not before.

For a variety of reasons, art resonates with us in ways other media don't and perhaps can't. For one, we are visual creatures. We see millions of things every single day and in so doing rely heavily on our sight. Visual artists take our enormous practice of seeing the world and use it to make us see something new. So, in some regard, there is very little to learn. Artists use what you already use. All you have to do now is get an idea of the very few tools they use to make their art do what they want it to.

Now, on to some hints for reading and writing about the visual arts.

### Test your first reactions, both emotionally and intellectually.

Painting and photography have definite advantages over poetry and fiction in that when you look at a painting, you don't immediately ask yourself what a certain tree symbolizes or what the rain is a metaphor for. Instead of trying to figure out what the painting "means," try to pay attention to what the painting or photo "evokes." What sort of reaction or response does the piece elicit? Is there a mood or tone? Does the painting or its colors create any particular emotion? You might also ask yourself how the artist works with notions of beauty. Is the picture or sculpture conventional in its use of beauty, or does s/he challenge typical ideas of beauty? If Hieronymus Bosch's *Garden of Earthly Delights* makes you uncomfortable, then the painting has succeeded as a rhetorical and semiotic text. If Monet's paintings of waterlillies give you a sense of calmed, pastoral elegance, then Monet has probably achieved his goal. If you find Georgia O'Keeffe's paintings of flowers, pistils, and stamens strangely erotic, then you are probably experiencing the kind of reaction that she intended. A work like Picasso's *Guernica* might affect you emotionally first, then begin to move you on an intellectual level—or vice versa. Either way, artists use shapes, colors, scale, and tone to make you feel a certain way. Thus, you may be reading the text of the painting on a subconscious level and not even know it.

In many ways, poetry resembles painting more than prose, so, like poetry, paintings may take a while to work on you. But that's okay; be patient. Let yourself be drawn into the painting.

## Pay attention to the grammar or syntax of visual art.

Like written language, visual art enjoys its own set of rules and structures. You don't have to know all or many of these terms or ideas to enjoy or understand art, but it does help to decode individual artistic texts. For instance, let's look at the notion of composition. Chances are that you are in a composition course right now, and while artistic composition is slightly different, it is also quite similar. To compose is to "put together" or "assemble." It comes from two Latin words: *com* which means "together" and *poser* which means to "place or to put down." Accordingly, composition means to place together. In this way, the composition of a painting resembles the composition of your essays: Both are texts that have been assembled from various "components" (a word with the same origin). So then the composition of a work of art is the plan or placement of the various elements of the piece. Most of the time, a painting's composition is related to the principles of design, such as balance, color, rhythm, texture, emphasis and proportion.

Let's say you are looking at Leonardo da Vinci's masterpiece, *The Last Supper*. You might notice the symmetry or balance of the painting, how the table and the men are perfectly framed by the walls of the building and how Jesus is framed in the very center of the piece by the open doorway. Placing Jesus in this position, lighting him from the back, gives him a certain emphasis the disciples lack. His red robe and his blue sash add to his stature, as does his posture. He looks as though he is offering a blessing, a gesture that underscores da Vinci's interpretation of Christ as a giver and a healer. Thus how the artist places his subject (at the center) and how he depicts him (as offering both thanks and blessing) and how his subject is contrasted against the rest of the painting (in red and almost radiating light, power and glory) is a kind of argument or thesis to the painting, just as you will create an argument or thesis for your own composition.

Taken all together, then, the various components of a painting or a photograph contribute to the piece's effect.

## Recognize the role of light in art.

If you've ever studied photography, then you know that the secret to taking a picture is realizing that you are not taking a picture of the object but of light on the object. On a basic level that means without the presence of light on the object, the object couldn't be photographed. Conversely, the way light hits an object contributes to our reading. And in composing an artwork, an artist considers how to use light to articulate ideas he or she wants to get across. Contrast is an important concept in reading visual art because it is a way of combining elements to stress the differences between those elements. Thus, a painting might contrast round and square shapes, bright and muted colors, people and landscape, black and white. An artist might photograph an object in shadow or paint it black to emphasize some other aspect of the painting she or he wants to emphasize. When you look at a landscape, pay attention to how light falls on the trees, how shadows are made, how contrasts are created. It is probable that the item highlighted by light or lack of shadow is of importance to the artist. In the black and white photography of Ansel Adams, Robert Mapplethorpe, Sally Mann, and Walker Evans, light becomes a kind of protagonist, or, perhaps more useful, like a narrator in a story. The narrator helps you make sense of the importance of events in a story; so too does light illuminate what is important. It tells you how to see the photograph without letting you know it is doing so. In black and white films of the '30s and '40s, especially Film Noir movies, long shadows and darkly lit alleys create a scene and establish a tone.

Light also helps determine the perspective of a piece, the feeling that you are looking at a three-dimensional world even though you know the canvas or the photograph is only a two-dimensional surface. Think of light as a metaphor. We all use the metaphor of shading. Painters and photographers use light to represent different "shades" of reality. Art speaks to us because it is both real and unreal at the same time—we recognize objects and places and people in the paintings, but at the same time, they don't seem part of our reality. Thus, how an artist uses light will directly affect the sense of perspective of the artist, and both are very effective in taking us out of the world we know and bringing us into the world of the painting by helping us read the images in a certain way. If one part of a photograph is in shadow or a feature on a woman's face feels illuminated, then, like a closeup in a film, the artist is able to use light like a camera lens to focus your attention and, perhaps, affect your mood.

## Art reflects not only the artists themselves but also their culture.

Like music, literature, and film, the visual arts are products not only of artists but also of the culture in which the artist lives and works. It should come as no surprise that during the Middle Ages and the Renaissance, when the Catholic church dominated the religious and political landscape of Europe, that most of the paintings reflected Biblical themes. Similarly, during the Romantic period, large, dark, brooding, tumultuous paintings tended to mimic "romantic" characteristics that worked their way into both architecture and fiction. Even the earliest cave paintings and rock art focuses on themes important to the artists of the time—hunting, fishing, keeping warm, invoking the gods. The belief that art reflects the world in which it exists is called mimesis. Some people would argue that artistic movements such as Surrealism and Cubism were movements away from mimetic art because people like Marcel Duchamp, Georges Braque, Picasso, and Man Ray distorted reality in their work. However, if we consider that, at this time, most artists, writers, and thinkers found the early twentieth century to be a time of chaos, disorder, violence, alienation, and fragmentation, then one can make a compelling argument that Picasso's and Braque's fissured pictoral landscapes reflected a fissured cultural and political landscape.

It is not surprising, then, that the most important American artistic movement, Abstract Expressionism, arose when it did. Important and innovative artists working in the late 1940s and 1950s like Jackson Pollock, Mark Rothko, Robert Motherwell, Barnett Newman, Helen Frankenthaler, and Frank Stella believed that the canvas was not a place for figures, but a place for an event. Their paintings tend to be large, flat, and nonfigurative, meaning virtually no people or objects appear in their work. At this moment in American history, the Cold War was in full force, the economy was booming, people were eager to put politics behind them, and a kind of expansive, expressionistic, non-political art became attractive. Abstract Expressionism encouraged viewers to feel, rather than think. The term abstract means to draw or take away from; Abstract Expressionism was art that tried to elicit an expression or emotion that would take the viewer away from the everyday reality of people, buildings, cars, haircuts, poverty, and violence.

Currently, as our culture becomes more politically conscious, so too does our art. Andres Serrano has become famous for his photographs of guns, murdered corpses and Ku Klux Klan members; Native American artist Jaune Quick-to-See Smith assembles journalism articles about violence toward American Indians, sports mascots from teams whose mascots are Indians, and stereotypes of "natives" such as toy tomahawks and moccasins to make comments on contemporary American Indian life; photographer Cindy Sherman did a series of disturbing photographs of mutilated female mannequins as a commentary on the violence toward and objectification of women; and Michael Ray Charles, an African-American painter, has made a career out of augmenting representations of "Sambo." In each of these situations, art crosses over from the aesthetic world and into the world of ethics. Although the ties between Abstract Expressionism and the Cold War may not be as obvious as the ones tying religious art to Catholicism, they are strong nonetheless.

## Often, there is a gap between the artist and the public.

It's somewhat of a cliché by now, but what an artist finds appealing is not always what the public finds appealing. The furor over the *Sensation* exhibition, the subject of this chapter's suite, is only the most recent in a long line of controversial artistic moments. In 1989, Jesse Helms (a Republican senator from North Carolina), conservative politician and commentator Patrick Buchanan, and art critic Hilton Kramer launched an all-out attack on "The Perfect Moment," a traveling exhibit of photographs by Robert Mapplethorpe that was funded by the National Endowment for the Arts, which gets some of its money from tax dollars. Some of Mapplethorpe's photographs crossed the line of decency, according to some, because of their explicit homo-erotic themes and because two photographs were of naked children. What resulted was a long legal and cultural battle over pornography, public funding for the arts, morality, and artistic freedom. Similarly, Andres Serrano's wildly controversial photograph *Piss Christ* nearly got the NEA shut down for good. This 1987 photograph of a crucifix dropped in urine angered so many people that it brought about the most thorough scrutiny of public financial support for the arts in American history. But America is not the only battleground for art and culture. To this day, if you visit Picasso's famous painting *Guernica* in Madrid, you will likely be accosted by locals who will want to give you a revisionist reading of the painting, which still remains behind glass to protect it from vandalism.

Photography tends to draw more fire than other art forms because people do not always see photographs as texts, but as the actual world. Also, art tends to be publicly displayed. We encourage our children to go to museums to get "enlightened." If what parents find at the museum disturbs them, then the public role of art gets called into question. Even though some fringe groups have burned books and banned records, literature, music, and even painting seems to escape the level of scrutiny of film and photography. As readers of the world, be aware of the various forces that determine how we see art and how we see art's role in forging a vision of contemporary culture.

## Works of modern and contemporary art deserve your attention because they are often important texts about the contemporary world.

Chances are, if you are like most people, you are totally confused by modern art which often seems like an endless series of nonsensical images: people with square heads, splatters of paint, chaos. What's important to recognize about modern art is the audience's role in constructing the painting. While modern artists do create work that may reflect their perspective and their culture, they also rely on the viewer to bring to their work an idea about what art is and how art functions. Frequently, viewers of modern art complain that they could have done the work themselves; they focus on the craftsmanship of modern art. But the modern artist might argue that the conception of art and the discussion of what art is and what it means is what makes modern art so compelling, and being a good reader of modern and contemporary art can give you valuable insights into recent social, political, and artistic moments.

Modern art saw the rise of the most recognizable schools: cubism, expressionism, fauvism, futurism, abstract expressionism, pop art, and collage. Figures like Pablo Picasso, Paul Klee, Wassily Kandinsky, Joan Miro, Gustav Klimt, Georges Braque, Edvard Munch, Henri Rousseau, Henri

Matisse, Jackson Pollock, Robert Motherwell, Andy Warhol and a host of others ushered in an entirely new way of looking at art. Most of modern art is abstract or nonrepresentational, which means that the subjects of the paintings may not be nature or people but ideas, politics, or art itself (but they might just look like shapes). It's no coincidence that art took such a radical turn in the 20th century: The innovations in technology, literature, film, psychology, and communication found commensurate innovations in the art world. Modern artists believe that if you change the way you see the world, you change the world. So you have artists playing with reality: Paul Klee said he wanted to make the nonvisible, visible; Kandinsky claimed that form was the outer expression of inner content; Picasso once wrote that if he wanted to express the roundness of a glass, he might have to make it square. Thus the changes in the world, the growths in perspective and innovation, get reflected and chronicled in modern art.

### Reading art helps you see the world in new ways.

Again, look at the perspective of the picture or the sculpture. Has the artist made you see the world or nature or a person or an object differently? If so, how? Ask yourself how the artist has represented the world, that is, how has s/he re-presented the world? Why might an artist be interested in altering your perception of something? Perhaps because if you learn to see the world in a new way fairly often, then looking at the world will be a way of creating your own art.

# Worksheet

## THIS TEXT

1. While it will be impossible for you to know this fully, try to figure out the writing situation of each author. Who is the audience? What does the author have at stake? What is his or her agenda? Why is she or he writing this piece?
2. What are the main points of the essay? Can you find a thesis statement anywhere? Remember, it doesn't have to be one sentence—it can be several sentences or a whole paragraph.
3. What textual cues does the author use to help get his or her point across?
4. How does the author support her argument? What evidence does he use to back up any claims he might make?

5. Is the author's argument valid? Is it reasonable?
6. Do you find yourself in agreement with the author? Why or why not?
7. Does the author help you read the visual arts better than you did before reading the essay? If so, why?
8. What issues about race, ethnicity, class, and gender does the writer raise? Do you think the writer has an agenda of sorts?
9. Did you like the piece? Why or why not?

## BEYOND THIS TEXT

1. What are the major themes of the work? What is the artist trying to suggest?
2. What techniques does the artist use to get his or her message across? Why *these* techniques?
3. What are we to make of the characters in the painting or photograph? What is their function? What is their race? Their social class? Are they like you? How?
4. Where does the text take place? When is it set?
5. What are the main conflicts of the text? What issues are at stake?
6. What kinds of issues of identity is the artist working on in the text?
7. Is there tension between the self and society in the text? How? Why?
8. What is the agenda of the artist? Why does she or he want me to think a certain way?
9. How is the text put together? What is its composition? How does it make meaning?
10. What techniques is the author using? How does it adhere to issues of artistic design?
11. Did you like this artwork? Why or why not?

## ANDY WARHOL: THE MOST CONTROVERSIAL ARTIST OF THE TWENTIETH CENTURY?

Alan Pratt

In this piece, Alan Pratt gives a semiotic and a cultural reading of Andy Warhol's art and critical reception (2000). Pratt suggests that because Warhol divided critics and audience alike, he is perhaps the most controversial artist of the century. What makes Pratt's approach intriguing is that he explores the major hot button issues surrounding art and artists—their persona as artists and their "originality." Also, Pratt's essay is neither too long nor too high brow—it is very likely the kind of essay you might write.

WHEN ANDY WARHOL HIT HIS STRIDE in the early sixties by appropriating images from advertising design and serializing them with a hands-off austerity, he became a lightning rod for criticism.

Studying the public perception of the artist in 1966, critic Lucy Lippard noticed that "Warhol's films and his art mean either nothing or a great deal. The choice is the viewer's...." In retrospect, Lippard's early, tentative appraisal is revealing. While the images Warhol stumbled across have a deep resonance with the public, the problem of interpreting them is, depending one's point of view, simple or complex.

In the current polemic, Warhol's reputation still depends on the reviewer's ideological or art-historical preoccupations. If, as has been suggested, Warhol succeeded in redefining the art experience, then the critical response required redefinition as well. In retrospect, it appears that one problem that confronted critics and journalists was that established critical approaches simply didn't lend themselves to an art which they perceived as "artless, styleless, and anonymous."

While the debate still hasn't resolved itself, three interconnected issues figure prominently in the disagreements about Warhol's reputation: his persona, his originality, and his antecedents.

## *Warhol's Persona*

The problematic nature of Warhol's critical reputation is attributable, in part, to the evasive, equivocal persona he cultivated—the calculated indifference, the monosyllabic rejoinder, the flat, vacuous affect of the I-think-everybody-should-be-a-machine Warhol. And while it's true that he suffered from a debilitating shyness, he nevertheless delighted in baffling his critics.

In reviewing Warhol's life it's often impossible to distinguish the authentic Warhol from the act. As a result, a significant portion of the critical response, if only anecdotally, is to Warhol's personality. And with little that's reliable to go on, critics have wide latitude in extrapolating or inventing motives for him. Currently, psychological interpretations of Warhol's work are the fashion.

## *Warhol's Originality*

Like the problems of personality which have intrigued critics for years, the issue of Warhol's artistic legitimacy has also been the basis of ongoing debate. The subjects of some of his most famous works—the soup cans, Coke bottles, dollar bills, flowers, and cows—were apparently recommendations.

That Warhol borrowed his images from others, from photographs, advertisements, and food labels and developed a technique by which they were serially mass-produced by anonymous Factory hands remains one of the most contentious issues in the criticism.

By erasing himself from his creations, minimizing the artist's responsibility, the significance of talent, and the value of originality, Warhol challenged presumptions about what art is supposed to be and how one is to experience it. This abnegation of responsibility was deemed unethical, if not subversive, by the critical audience, further fueling the controversy about whether or not his work should even be regarded as art.

### *Warhol's Antecedents*

From the beginning, critics have addressed the connections between what Warhol was doing and what Marcel Duchamp had done. It was Duchamp who in 1914 broke the rules and outraged the art world when he began exhibiting his objets trouvés, the coat-stands, bottle racks, and bicycle wheels. Duchamp, critics suggested, had shown Warhol that appropriating common consumer items could be art.

Warhol was a particularly culpable pioneer of cultural nihilism because the silkscreened readymades—soup cans, bottles, and such—were perceived to be the apotheoses of the objets trouvés.

So why is Warhol the most controversial artist of the century? Read on:

### *Warhol's Place in Modernism*

As a study of the criticism makes clear, Warhol appalled the art establishment because he represented a complete transvaluation of the aesthetic principles that had dominated for several generations. What for years modernists had deliberately ignored or contemptuously spurned, Warhol embraced. As appropriated mass-culture images—such as his *Turquoise Marilyn* (1962)—his "art" was indistinguishable from advertising—meaning it was crass and pedestrian—and thus lampooned the modern emphasis on noble sentiment and good taste. No doubt Warhol's comments about art, that it should be effortless, that it's a business having nothing to do with transcendence, truth, or sentiment, also infuriated detractors.

Both Warhol's subject matter and his flippant attitudes toward the conventions of the art world were the antithesis of the high-seriousness of modernism. And the rub of it was that his celebrations of the inconsequential were being taken seriously. It was a nasty slap in the face for those seeped in the myths of modernism.

Warhol's aesthetic contributed to the breakdown of the hierarchial conventions of modernism, dissolving distinctions between commercial design and serious art and the boundaries between popular taste and high culture—or, as some would have it, between trash and excellence.

### *Warhol and Postmodernism*

As many observers now agree, the early 1960s mark the beginnings of a postmodern sensibility, where the modernist desire for closure and aesthetic autonomy has been rapidly replaced with indeterminacy and eclecticism.

If that's true, Warhol's art forecast and then highlighted the changes that were occurring. And it has been argued that his art anticipated many ploys of this aesthetic new world, including the emphasis on irony, appropriation, and commonism, as well as promoting intellectual engagement through negation.

### *So What's Warhol's Place in the Criticism?*

> "Criticism is so old fashioned. Why don't you just put in a lot of gossip?"
> —*Warhol to Bob Colacello, longtime editor of Warhol's magazine* Interview

In reviewing the critical record, one can conclude that Warhol's role in art history is as a transitional figure. Stylistically his work is a bellwether, and the critical issues raised about him often converge with those at the center of the modern/postmodern debate. As a "mirror of the times," Warhol criticism reflects the trepidation and enthusiasm in response to shifting paradigms. Lucy Lippard's proposition is still valid—Warhol's images are

*Andy Warhol, "Marilyn Monroe", 1962. Oil on canvas. 81" × 66¾". ™2002 Marilyn Monroe LLC by CMG Worldwide Inc. www.MarilynMonroe.com. ©2003 Andy Warhol Foundation for the Visual Arts/ARS, New York.*

*100 Soup Cans, Andy Warhol*

ambiguous. It's this ambiguity that gives his work its edge. His images function as a sort of cultural Rorschach blot allowing for the projection of personalities, theoretical orientations, and ideological biases.

Why put fifty Cambell's soup cans on canvas? So far, there are scores of explanations. And the debate rages on…

---

## This Text: Reading

1. What are the three areas that Pratt cites as being important to Warhol's success and controversy? Are these important areas?
2. What criteria does Pratt establish for being "most controversial"?
3. How does Pratt place Warhol within the context of contemporary art history?

## Your Text: Writing

1. Pick an artist and write a similar essay on that artist's work and reputation.

2. Look at some of Warhol's art. Is he an important artist? Is his art important? Is there a distinction between being an important artist and making important art?
3. What social and political events might have influenced Warhol's unique art?

## AMERICA SEEN THROUGH A LENS DARKLY

Susan Sontag

Susan Sontag's famous reading (1977) of the disturbing photographs of Diane Arbus has become a classic. Sontag places Arbus and her work within an artistic and cultural context, but she also suggests that her work stands as a kind of text of and for America. How does Arbus's (and Sontag's) vision of America mesh with your own?

IN PHOTOGRAPHY'S EARLY DECADES, photographs were expected to be idealized images. This is still the aim of most amateur photographers, for whom a beautiful photograph is a photograph of something beautiful, like a woman, a sunset. In 1915 Edward Steichen photographed a milk bottle on a tenement fire escape, an early example of a quite different idea of the beautiful photograph. And since the 1920s, ambitious professionals, those whose work gets into museums, have steadily drifted away from lyrical subjects, conscientiously exploring plain, tawdry, or even vapid material. In recent decades, photography has succeeded in somewhat revising, for everybody, the definitions of what is beautiful and ugly—along the lines that Whitman had proposed. If (in Whitman's words) "each precise object or condition or combination or process exhibits a beauty," it becomes superficial to single out some things as beautiful and others as not. If "all that a person does or thinks is of consequence," it becomes arbitrary to treat some moments in life as important and most as trivial.

To photograph is to confer importance. There is probably no subject that cannot be beautified; moreover, there is no way to suppress the tendency inherent in all photographs to accord value to their subjects. But the meaning of value itself can be altered—as it has been in the contemporary culture of the photographic image which is a parody of Whitman's evangel. In the mansions of pre-democratic culture, someone who gets photographed is a celebrity. In the open fields of American experience, as catalogued with passion by Whitman and as sized up with a shrug by Warhol, everybody is a celebrity. No moment is more important than any other moment; no person is more interesting than any other person.

* * *

The last sigh of the Whitmanesque erotic embrace of the nation, but universalized and stripped of all demands, was heard in the "Family of Man" exhibit organized in 1955 by Edward Steichen, Stieglitz's contemporary and co-founder of Photo-Secession. Five hundred and three photographs by two hundred and seventy-three photographers from sixty-eight countries were supposed to converge—to prove that humanity is "one" and that human beings, for all their flaws and villainies, are attractive creatures. The people in the photographs were of all races, ages, classes, physical types. Many of them had exceptionally beautiful bodies; some had beautiful faces. As Whitman urged the readers of his poems to identify with him and with America, Steichen set up the show to make it possible for each viewer to identify with a great many of the people depicted and, potentially, with the subject of every photograph: citizens of World Photography all.

It was not until seventeen years later that photography again attracted such crowds at the Museum of Modern Art: for the retrospective given Diane Arbus's work in 1972. In the Arbus show, a hundred and twelve photographs all taken by one person and all similar—that is, everyone in them looks (in some sense) the same—imposed a feeling exactly contrary to the reassuring warmth of Steichen's material. Instead of people whose appearance pleases, representative folk doing their human thing, the Arbus show lined up assorted monsters and borderline cases—most of them ugly; wearing grotesque or unflattering clothing; in dismal or barren surroundings—who have paused to pose and, often, to gaze frankly, confidentially at the viewer. Arbus's work does not invite viewers to identify with the pariahs and miserable-looking people she photographed. Humanity is not "one."

The Arbus photographs convey the anti-humanist message which people of good will in the 1970s are eager to be troubled by, just as they wished, in the 1950s, to be consoled and distracted by a sentimental humanism. There is not as much difference between these messages as one might suppose. The Steichen show was an up and the Arbus show was a down, but either experience serves equally well to rule out a historical understanding of reality.

Steichen's choice of photographs assumes a human condition or a human nature shared by everybody. By purporting to show that individuals are born, work, laugh, and die everywhere in the same way, "The Family of Man" denies the determining weight of history—of genuine and historically embedded differences, injustices, and conflicts. Arbus's photographs undercut politics just as decisively, by suggesting a world in which everybody is an alien, hopelessly isolated, immobilized in mechanical, crippled identities and relationships. The pious uplift of Steichen's photograph anthology and the cool dejection of the Arbus retrospective both render history and politics irrelevant. One does so by universalizing the human condition, into joy; the other by atomizing it, into horror.

The most striking aspect of Arbus's work is that she seems to have enrolled in one of art photography's most vigorous enterprises—concentrating on victims, on the unfortunate—but without the compassionate purpose that such a project is expected to serve. Her work shows people who are pathetic, pitiable, as well as repulsive, but it does not arouse any compassionate feelings. For what would be more correctly described as their dissociated point of view, the photographs have been praised for their candor and for an unsentimental empathy with their subjects. What is actually their aggressiveness toward the public has been treated as a moral accomplishment: that the photographs don't allow the viewer to be distant from the subject. More plausibly, Arbus's photographs—with their acceptance of the appalling—suggest a naïveté which is both coy and sinister, for it is based on distance, on privilege, on a feeling that what the viewer is asked to look at is really *other*. Buñuel, when asked once why he made movies, said that it was "to show that this is not the best of all possible worlds." Arbus took photographs to show something simpler—that there is another world.

The other world is to be found, as usual, inside this one. Avowedly interested only in photographing people who "looked strange," Arbus found plenty of material close to home. New York, with its drag balls and welfare hotels, was rich with freaks. There was also a carnival in Maryland, where Arbus found a human pincushion, a hermaphrodite with a dog, a tattooed man, and an albino sword-swallower; nudist camps in New Jersey and in Pennsylvania; Disneyland and a Hollywood set, for their dead or fake landscapes without people; and the unidentified mental hospital where she took some of her last, and most disturbing, photographs. And there was always daily life, with its endless supply of oddities—if one has the eye to see them. The camera has the power to catch so-called normal people in such a way as to make them look abnormal. The photographer chooses oddity, chases it, frames it, develops it, titles it.

"You see someone on the street," Arbus wrote, "and essentially what you notice about them is the flaw." The insistent sameness of Arbus's work, however far she ranges from her prototypical subjects, shows that her sensibility, armed with a camera, could insinuate anguish, kinkiness, mental illness with any subject. Two photographs are of crying babies; the babies look disturbed, crazy. Resembling or having something in common with someone else is a recurrent source of the ominous, according to the characteristic norms of Arbus's dissociated way of seeing. It may be two girls (not sisters) wearing identical raincoats whom Arbus photographed together in Central Park; or the twins and triplets who appear in several pictures. Many photographs point with oppressive wonder to the fact that two people form a couple; and every couple is an odd couple: straight or gay, black or white, in an old-age home or in a junior high. People looked eccentric because they didn't wear clothes, like nudists; or because they did, like the waitress in the nudist camp who's wearing an apron. Anybody Arbus photographed was a freak—a boy waiting to march in a pro-war parade, wearing his straw boater and his "Bomb Hanoi" button; the King and Queen of a Senior Citizens Dance; a thirtyish suburban couple sprawled in their lawn chairs; a widow sitting alone in her cluttered bedroom. In "A Jewish giant at home with his parents in the Bronx, NY, 1970," the parents look like midgets, as wrong-sized as the enormous son hunched over them under their low living-room ceiling.

The authority of Arbus's photographs derives from the contrast between their lacerating subject matter and their calm, matter-of-fact attentiveness. This quality of attention—the attention paid by the photographer, the attention paid by the subject to the act of being photographed—creates the moral theater of Arbus's straight-on, contemplative portraits. Far from spying on freaks and pariahs, catching them unawares, the photographer has gotten to know them, reassured them—so that they posed for her as calmly and stiffly as any Victorian notable sat for a studio portrait by Julia Margaret Cameron. A large part of the mystery of Arbus's photographs lies in what they suggest about how her subjects felt after consenting to be photographed. Do they see themselves, the viewer wonders, like *that?* Do they know how grotesque they are? It seems as if they don't.

The subject of Arbus's photographs is, to borrow the stately Hegelian label, "the unhappy consciousness." But most characters in Arbus's Grand Guignol appear not to know that they are ugly. Arbus photographs people in various degrees of unconscious or unaware relation to their pain, their ugliness. This necessarily limits what kinds of horrors she might have been drawn to photograph: it excludes sufferers who presumably know they are suffering, like victims of accidents, wars, famines, and political persecutions. Arbus would never have taken pictures of accidents, events that break into a life; she specialized in slow-motion private smashups, most of which had been going on since the subject's birth.

Though most viewers are ready to imagine that these people, the citizens of the sexual underworld as well as the genetic freaks, are unhappy, few of the pictures actually show emotional distress. The photographs of deviates and real freaks do not accent their pain but, rather, their detachment and autonomy. The female impersonators in their dressing rooms, the Mexican dwarf in his Manhattan hotel room, the Russian midgets in a living room on 100th Street, and their kin are mostly shown as cheerful, self-accepting, matter-of-fact. Pain is more legible in the portraits of the normals: the quarreling elderly couple on a park bench, the New Orleans lady bartender at home with a souvenir dog, the boy in Central Park clenching his toy hand grenade.

Brassaï denounced photographers who try to trap their subjects off-guard, in the erroneous belief that something special will be revealed about them.* In the world colonized by Arbus, subjects are always revealing themselves. There is no decisive moment. Arbus's view that self-revelation is a continuous, evenly distributed process is another way of maintaining the Whitmanesque imperative: treat all moments as of equal consequence. Like Brassaï, Arbus wanted her subjects to be as fully conscious as possible, aware of the act in which they were participating. Instead of trying to coax her subjects into a natural or typical position, they are encouraged to be awkward—that is, to pose. (Thereby, the revelation of self gets identified with what is strange, odd, askew.) Standing or sitting stiffly makes them seem like images of themselves.

Most Arbus pictures have the subjects looking straight into the camera. This often makes them look even odder, almost deranged. Compare the 1912 photograph by Lartigue of a woman in a plumed hat and veil ("Racecourse at Nice") with Arbus's "Woman with a Veil on Fifth Avenue, NYC, 1968." Apart from the characteristic ugliness of Arbus's subject (Lartigue's subject is, just as characteristically, beautiful), what makes the woman in Arbus's photograph strange is the bold unselfconsciousness of her pose. If the Lartigue woman looked back, she might appear almost as strange.

In the normal rhetoric of the photographic portrait, facing the camera signifies solemnity, frankness, the disclosure of the subject's essence. That is why frontality seems right for ceremonial pictures (like weddings, graduations) but less apt for photographs used on billboards to advertise political candidates. (For politicians the three-quarter gaze is more common: a gaze that soars rather than confronts, suggesting instead of the relation to the viewer, to the present, the more ennobling abstract relation to the future.) What makes Arbus's use of the frontal pose so arresting is that her subjects are often people one would not expect to surrender themselves so amiably and ingenuously to the camera. Thus, in Arbus's photographs, frontality also implies in the most vivid way the subject's cooperation. To get these people to pose, the photographer has had to gain their confidence, has had to become "friends" with them.

Perhaps the scariest scene in Tod Browning's film *Freaks* (1932) is the wedding banquet, when pinheads, bearded women, Siamese twins, and living torsos dance and sing their acceptance of the wicked normal-sized Cleopatra, who has just married the gullible midget hero. "One of us! One of us! One of us!" they chant as a loving cup is passed around the table from mouth to mouth to be finally presented to the nauseated bride by an

---

*Not an error, really. There is something on people's faces when they don't know they are being observed that never appears when they do. If we did not know how Walker Evans took his subway photographs (riding the New York subways for hundreds of hours, standing, with the lens of his camera peering between two buttons of his topcoat), it would be obvious from the pictures themselves that the seated passengers, although photographed close and frontally, didn't know they were being photographed; their expressions are private ones, not those they would offer to the camera.

exuberant dwarf. Arbus had a perhaps oversimple view of the charm and hypocrisy and discomfort of fraternizing with freaks. Following the elation of discovery, there was the thrill of having won their confidence, of not being afraid of them, of having mastered one's aversion. Photographing freaks "had a terrific excitement for me," Arbus explained. "I just used to adore them."

Diane Arbus's photographs were already famous to people who follow photography when she killed herself in 1971; but, as with Sylvia Plath, the attention her work has attracted since her death is of another order—a kind of apotheosis. The fact of her suicide seems to guarantee that her work is sincere, not voyeuristic, that it is compassionate, not cold. Her suicide also seems to make the photographs more devastating, as if it proved the photographs to have been dangerous to her.

She herself suggested the possibility. "Everything is so superb and breathtaking. I am creeping forward on my belly like they do in war movies." While photography is normally an omnipotent viewing from a distance, there is one situation in which people do get killed for taking pictures: when they photograph people killing each other. Only war photography combines voyeurism and danger. Combat photographers can't avoid participating in the lethal activity they record; they even wear military uniforms, though without rank badges. To discover (through photographing) that life is "really a melodrama," to understand the camera as a weapon of aggression, implies there will be casualties. "I'm sure there are limits," she wrote. "God knows, when the troops start advancing on you, you do approach that stricken feeling where you perfectly well can get killed." Arbus's words in retrospect describe a kind of combat death: having trespassed certain limits, she fell in a psychic ambush, a casualty of her own candor and curiosity.

In the old romance of the artist, any person who has the temerity to spend a season in hell risks not getting out alive or coming back psychically damaged. The heroic avant-gardism of French literature in the late nineteenth and early twentieth centuries furnishes a memorable pantheon of artists who fail to survive their trips to hell. Still, there is a large difference between the activity of a photographer, which is always willed, and the activity of a writer, which may not be. One has the right to, may feel compelled to, give voice to one's own pain—which is, in any case, one's own property. One volunteers to seek out the pain of others.

Thus, what is finally most troubling in Arbus's photographs is not their subject at all but the cumulative impression of the photographer's consciousness: the sense that what is presented is precisely a private vision, something voluntary. Arbus was not a poet delving into her entrails to relate her own pain but a photographer venturing out into the world to *collect* images that are painful. And for pain sought rather than just felt, there may be a less than obvious explanation. According to Reich, the masochist's taste for pain does not spring from a love of pain but from the hope of procuring, by means of pain, a strong sensation; those handicapped by emotional or sensory analgesia only prefer pain to not feeling anything at all. But there is another explanation of why people seek pain, diametrically opposed to Reich's, that also seems pertinent: that they seek it not to feel more but to feel less.

Insofar as looking at Arbus's photographs is, undeniably, an ordeal, they are typical of the kind of art popular among sophisticated urban people right now: art that is a self-willed test of hardness. Her photographs offer an occasion to demonstrate that life's horror can be faced without squeamishness. The photographer once had to say to herself, Okay, I can accept that; the viewer is invited to make the same declaration.

Arbus's work is a good instance of a leading tendency of high art in capitalist countries: to suppress, or at least reduce, moral and sensory queasiness. Much of modern art is devoted to lowering the threshold of what is terrible. By getting us used to what, formerly, we could not bear to see or hear, because it was too shocking, painful, or embarrassing, art changes morals—that body of psychic custom and public sanctions that draws a vague boundary between what is emotionally and spontaneously intolerable and what is not. The gradual suppression of queasiness does bring us closer to a rather formal truth—that of the arbitrariness of the taboos constructed by art and morals. But our ability to stomach this rising grotesqueness in images (moving and still) and in print has a stiff price. In the long run, it works out not as a liberation of but as a subtraction from the self: a pseudo-familiarity with the horrible reinforces alienation, making one less able to react in real life. What happens to people's feelings on first exposure to today's neighborhood pornographic film or to tonight's televised atrocity is not so different from what happens when they first look at Arbus's photographs.

The photographs make a compassionate response feel irrelevant. The point is not to be upset, to be able to confront the horrible with equanimity. But this look that is not (mainly) compassionate is a special, modern ethical construction: not hardhearted, certainly not cynical, but simply (or falsely) naïve. To the painful nightmarish reality out there, Arbus applied such adjectives as "terrific," "interesting," "incredible," "fantastic," "sensational"—the childlike wonder of the pop mentality. The camera—according to her deliberately naïve image of the photographer's quest—is a device that captures it all, that seduces subjects into disclosing their secrets, that broadens experience. To photograph people, according to Arbus, is necessarily "cruel," "mean." The important thing is not to blink.

"Photography was a license to go wherever I wanted and to do what I wanted to do," Arbus wrote. The camera is a kind of passport that annihilates moral boundaries and social inhibitions, freeing the photographer from any responsibility toward the people photographed. The whole point of photographing people is that you are not intervening in their lives, only visiting them. The photographer is supertourist, an extension of the anthropologist, visiting natives and bringing back news of their exotic doings and strange gear. The photographer is always trying to colonize new experiences or find new ways to look at familiar subjects—to fight against boredom. For boredom is just the reverse side of fascination: both depend on being outside rather than inside a situation, and one leads to the other. "The Chinese have a theory that you pass through boredom into fascination," Arbus noted. Photographing an appalling underworld (and a desolate, plastic overworld), she had no intention of entering into the horror experienced by the denizens of those worlds. They are to remain exotic, hence "terrific." Her view is always from the outside.

"I'm very little drawn to photographing people that are known or even subjects that are known," Arbus wrote. "They fascinate me when I've barely heard of them." However drawn she was to the maimed and the ugly, it would never have occurred to Arbus to photograph Thalidomide babies or napalm victims—public horrors, deformities with sentimental or ethical associations. Arbus was not interested in ethical journalism. She chose subjects that she could believe were found, just lying about, without any values attached to them. They are necessarily ahistorical subjects, private rather than public pathology, secret lives rather than open ones.

For Arbus, the camera photographs the unknown. But unknown to whom? Unknown to someone who is protected, who has been schooled in moralistic and in prudent responses. Like Nathanael West, another artist fascinated by the deformed and mutilated, Arbus came from a verbally skilled, compulsively health-minded, indignation-prone, well-to-do Jewish family, for whom minority sexual tastes lived way below the threshold of awareness and risk-taking was despised as another goyish craziness. "One of the things I felt I suffered from as a kid," Arbus wrote, "was that I never felt adversity. I was confined in a sense of unreality.... And the sense of being immune was, ludicrous as it seems, a painful one." Feeling much the same discontent, West in 1927 took a job as a night clerk in a seedy Manhattan hotel. Arbus's way of procuring experience, and thereby acquiring a sense of reality, was the camera. By experience was meant, if not material adversity, at least psychological adversity—the shock of immersion in experiences that cannot be beautified, the encounter with what is taboo, perverse, evil.

Arbus's interest in freaks expresses a desire to violate her own innocence, to undermine her sense of being privileged, to vent her frustration at being safe. Apart from West, the 1930s yield few examples of this kind of distress. More typically, it is the sensibility of someone educated and middle-class who came of age between 1945 and 1955—a sensibility that was to flourish precisely in the 1960s.

The decade of Arbus's serious work coincides with, and is very much of, the sixties, the decade in which freaks went public, and became a safe, approved subject of art. What in the 1930s was treated with anguish—as in *Miss Lonelyhearts* and *The Day of the Locust*—would in the 1960s be treated in a perfectly deadpan way, or with positive relish (in the films of Fellini, Arrabal, Jodorowsky, in underground comics, in rock spectacles). At the beginning of the sixties, the thriving Freak Show at Coney Island was outlawed; the pressure is on to raze the Times Square turf of drag queens and hustlers and cover it with skyscrapers. As the inhabitants of deviant underworlds are evicted from their restricted territories—banned as unseemly, a public nuisance, obscene, or just unprofitable—they increasingly come to infiltrate consciousness as the subject matter of art, acquiring a certain diffuse legitimacy and metaphoric proximity which creates all the more distance.

Who could have better appreciated the truth of freaks than someone like Arbus, who was by profession a fashion photographer—a fabricator of the cosmetic lie that masks the intractable inequalities of birth and class and physical appearance. But unlike Warhol, who spent many years as a commercial artist, Arbus did not make her serious work out of promoting and kidding the aesthetic of glamour to which she had been apprenticed, but turned her back on it entirely. Arbus's work is reactive—reactive against gentility, against what is approved. It was her way of saying fuck *Vogue*, fuck fashion, fuck what's pretty. This challenge takes two not wholly compatible forms. One is a revolt against the Jews' hyper-developed moral sensibility. The other revolt, itself hotly moralistic, turns against the success world. The moralist's subversion advances life as a failure as the antidote to life as a success. The aesthete's subversion, which the sixties was to make peculiarly its own, advances life as a horror show as the antidote to life as a bore.

Most of Arbus's work lies within the Warhol aesthetic, that is, defines itself in relation to the twin poles of boringness and freakishness; but it doesn't have the Warhol style. Arbus had neither Warhol's narcissism and genius for publicity nor the self-protective blandness with which he insulates himself from the freaky nor his sentimentality. It is unlikely that Warhol, who comes from a working-class family, ever felt any of the ambivalence toward success which afflicted the children of the Jewish upper middle classes in the 1960s. To someone raised as a Catholic, like Warhol (and virtually everyone in his gang), a fascination with evil comes much more genuinely than it does to someone from a Jewish background. Compared with Warhol, Arbus seems strikingly vulnerable, innocent—and certainly more pessimistic. Her Dantesque vision of the city (and the suburbs) has no reserves of irony. Although much of Arbus's material is the same as that depicted in, say, Warhol's *Chelsea Girls* (1966), her photographs never play with horror, milking it for laughs; they offer no opening to mockery, and no possibility of finding freaks endearing, as do the films of Warhol and Paul Morrissey. For Arbus, both freaks and Middle America were equally exotic: a boy marching in a pro-war parade and a Levittown housewife were as alien as a dwarf or a transvestite; lower-middle-class suburbia was as remote as Times Square, lunatic asylums, and gay bars. Arbus's work expressed her turn against what was public (as she experienced it), conventional, safe, reassuring—and boring—in favor of what was private, hidden, ugly, dangerous, and fascinating. These contrasts, now, seem almost quaint. What is safe no longer monopolizes public imagery. The freakish is no longer a private zone, difficult of access. People who are bizarre, in sexual disgrace, emotionally vacant are seen daily on the newsstands, on TV, in the subways. Hobbesian man roams the streets, quite visible, with glitter in his hair.

Sophisticated in the familiar modernist way—choosing awkwardness, naïveté, sincerity over the slickness and artificiality of high art and high commerce—Arbus said that the photographer she felt closest to was Weegee, whose brutal pictures of crime and accident victims were a staple of the tabloids in the 1940s. Weegee's photographs are indeed upsetting, his sensibility is urban, but the similarity between his work and Arbus's ends there. However eager she was to disavow standard elements of photographic sophistication such as composition, Arbus was not unsophisticated. And there is nothing journalistic about her motives for taking pictures. What may seem journalistic, even sensational, in Arbus's photographs places them, rather, in the main tradition of Surrealist art—their taste for the grotesque, their professed innocence with respect to their subjects, their claim that all subjects are merely *objets trouvés*.

"I would never choose a subject for what it meant to me when I think of it," Arbus wrote, a dogged exponent of the Surrealist bluff. Presumably, viewers are not supposed to judge the people she photographs. Of course, we do. And the very range of Arbus's subjects itself constitutes a judgment. Brassaï, who photographed people like those who interested Arbus—see his "La Môme Bijou" of 1932—also did tender cityscapes, portraits of famous artists. Lewis Hine's "Mental Institution, New Jersey, 1924" could be a late Arbus photograph (except that the pair of Mongoloid children posing on the lawn are photographed in profile rather than frontally); the Chicago street portraits Walker Evans took in 1946 are Arbus material, as are a number of photographs by Robert Frank. The difference is in the range of other subjects, other emotions that Hine, Brassaï, Evans, and Frank photographed. Arbus is an *auteur* in the most limiting sense, as special a case in the history of photography as is Giorgio Morandi, who spent a half century doing still lifes of bottles, in the history of modern European painting. She does not, like most ambitious photographers, play the field of subject matter—even a little. On the contrary, all her subjects are equivalent. And making equivalences between freaks, mad people, suburban couples, and nudists is a very powerful judgment, one in complicity with a recognizable political mood shared by many educated, left-liberal Americans. The subjects of Arbus's photographs are all members of the same family, inhabitants of a single village. Only, as it happens, the idiot village is America. Instead of showing identity between things which are different (Whitman's democratic vista), everybody is shown to look the same.

Succeeding the more buoyant hopes for America has come a bitter, sad embrace of experience. There is a particular melancholy in the American photographic project. But the melancholy was already latent in the heyday of Whitmanesque affirmation, as represented by Stieglitz and his Photo-Secession circle. Stieglitz, pledged to redeem the world with his camera, was still shocked by modern material civilization. He photographed New York in the 1910s in an almost quixotic spirit—camera/lance against skyscraper/windmill. Paul Rosenfeld described Stieglitz's efforts as a "perpetual affirmation." The Whitmanesque appetites have turned pious: the photographer now patronizes reality. One needs a camera to show patterns in that "dull and marvelous opacity called the United States."

Obviously, a mission as rotten with doubt about America—even at its most optimistic—was bound to get deflated fairly soon, as post–World War I America committed itself more boldly to big business and consumerism. Photographers with less ego and magnetism than Stieglitz gradually gave up the struggle. They might continue to practice the atomistic visual stenography inspired by Whitman. But, without Whitman's delirious powers of synthesis, what they documented was discontinuity, detritus, loneliness, greed, sterility. Stieglitz, using photography to challenge the materialist civilization, was, in Rosenfeld's words, "the man who believed that a spiritual America existed somewhere, that America was not the grave of the Occident." The implicit intent of Frank and Arbus, and of many of their contemporaries and juniors, is to show that America *is* the grave of the Occident.

Since photography cut loose from the Whitmanesque affirmation—since it has ceased to understand how photographs could aim at being literate, authoritative, transcendent—the best of American photography (and much else in American culture) has given itself over to the consolations of Surrealism, and America has been discovered as the quintessential Surrealist country. It is obviously too easy to say that America is just a freak show, a wasteland—the cut-rate pessimism typical of the reduction of the real to the surreal. But the American partiality to myths of redemption and damnation remains one of the most energizing, most seductive aspects of our national culture. What we have left of Whitman's discredited dream of cultural revolution are paper ghosts and a sharp-eyed witty program of despair.

---

## This Text: Reading

1. Go to your library and look at a book of Diane Arbus photographs. After doing so, does Sontag's title make more sense?
2. How does Arbus' work challenge the notion that photographs should be "idealized images"? How is this similar to Pratt's claims of Andy Warhol?
3. What does Sontag mean when she claims that Arbus "seems to have enrolled in one of art photography's most vigorous enterprises—concentrating on victims, on the unfortunate"?

## YOUR TEXT: WRITING

1. Look at an entire book of Arbus' photographs. Write an essay on this notion of the unfortunate. Why do "victims" make good subjects for art?
2. Some people accuse Arbus of exploitation. Write an essay about Arbus, photography, and exploitation.
3. Take Acton's technique of composition and apply it to some of Arbus' photographs. What kind of composition does she use? How does her composition contribute to her work's meaning?
4. Write an essay comparing an Arbus photograph(s) to those of another photographer like Robert Mapplethorpe, Andres Serrano, Walker Evans or Dorothea Lange. In each instance, these photographers did important work that arose out of specific social circumstances. How do photographs reflect and comment on society?

# WHICH ART WILL TOP THE CHARTES?: FOUR CURATORS SHARE THEIR TOP 10 PICKS AND REASONING BEHIND THE MOST INFLUENTIAL VISUAL ARTWORKS OF THE PAST 1,000 YEARS

When asked to name the most influential 10 works of art (2000), Kimberly Davenport, Director of the Rice University Art Gallery in Houston, said "This will be fun." We agree—this piece is fun. We have included it not so much as a model for your own writing but as a prompt to help you begin to think about art and influence. Notice how each of these prominent art curators differs over which works of art have been the most influential. Equally interesting is the rationale behind the choices. You may be surprised at what objects get considered "visual artworks."

## "This will be fun"

KIMBERLY DAVENPORT, *Director, Rice University Art Gallery, Houston*

When approached with the idea of coming up with a list of the 10 most influential works of the past 1,000 years, I thought, "This will be fun!" Beloved, familiar images—the Mona Lisa, a still life by Cézanne—flowed across my mind. As I sat down to write, however, the task seemed more daunting. Where in such a "Top 10" list, for instance, would fall African tribal sculpture, Indian miniatures, Amish quilts, and the sublime raked-sand gardens of Kyoto, Japan? I approached my list, finally, based on personal encounters with works that have inspired me, as well as many of the living artists with whom I have worked. Artists do not see the art of the past as frozen in time, but as a kind of living library of ideas, solutions, and inspiration. They look at works that offer insights about ways to convey space, color, light, and movement, or that redefine the nature of art itself.

1. **Giotto—Arena Chapel frescoes (1305–06).** Three narratives depicting the life of the Virgin, the life of Christ, and the Passion, Crucifixion, and Resurrection span the walls of Arena Chapel in Padua, Italy. The figures are remarkable for their humanity, not only as real bodies having bulk and weight, but for their extraordinary psychological connections to one another. Expressive, "knowing" glances between figures are zones of silent communication detached from the cacophony of events taking place.
2. **Jan Vermeer—Woman Holding a Balance (1664),** oil on canvas. Vermeer takes a simple, everyday act and through the use of light and composition transforms it into a sanctified moment of private reflection. The light flooding through the window permeates the scene and infuses it with a sense of the mystery present in the familiar.
3. **Eadweard Muybridge—Head-spring, a Flying Pigeon Interfering (1885).** Muybridge's photographic studies of motion broke down the stages of movement to reveal the components of a single action. Using the camera to demonstrate what the eye could not see, Muybridge contributed significantly to the ability of both artists and scientists to understand and portray the world around them.
4. **Marcel Duchamp—Fountain (1917),** Porcelain urinal, 23-5/8 in. tall. Duchamp changed the definition of art when he turned a detached urinal on its side, signed it with the pseudonym R. Mott, and submitted it to the exhibition of the Society of Independent Artists. By removing an everyday object from its normal context and calling it art, Duchamp empowered the artist to determine the definition of art.
5. **Kazimir Malevich—White on White (1918),** oil on canvas. Malevich was the first artist to use pure geometric abstraction as the subject of his work. "White on White" abandons any reference to the outside world in favor of the artist's depiction of pure feeling. Malevich intended this type of expression as a kind of universal language, accessible and familiar to all people.
6. **Georgia O'Keeffe—The Lawrence Tree (1929),** oil on canvas. O'Keeffe opened our eyes to the natural world in a unique way. We experience the tree not from the "superior" point of view—observing it on our own horizontal plane—but from beneath it, rooted in the earth and gazing heavenward.
7. **Pablo Picasso—Guernica (1937),** oil on canvas, 11 ft., 6 in. by 25 ft., 8 in. Picasso painted Guernica in response to the bombing of the ancient Basque city during the Spanish Civil War. The painting has become an internationally recognizable image of pacifism that testifies to

the power of art to serve as an active forum for social critique and as an instrument for change.

8. **Jackson Pollock—Alchemy (1947),** oil, aluminum paint, and string on canvas. Pollock brought physicality and intuition to the forefront of artistic consciousness. By putting the canvas on the floor and physically moving around it to fling paint onto it, Pollock created paintings significant both as objects in and of themselves and as evidence of the process of their creation.
9. **Andy Warhol—Marilyn Diptych (1962),** acrylic and silkscreen on canvas. The first work in his celebrity series exemplifies Warhol's (and our) fascination with pop culture, the creation and consequences of fame, and the influence of mass media. His deadpan approach to the world is still common in contemporary life and art.
10. **Sol LeWitt—Wall Drawing No. 652 (1990),** color ink washes superimposed. LeWitt's view of the idea as the machine that makes the art took the relationship between concept and art object to an unprecedented extreme. Drawn directly on a gallery wall, LeWitt's wall drawings are significant for their intrinsic impermanence and for their ability to be constantly renewed and re-created in different locations.

## "Difficult and frustrating"

ERICA E. HIRSHLER, *Croll Senior Curator of Paintings, Art of the Americas, Museum of Fine Arts, Boston*

I accepted this assignment thinking it would be fun, and have found instead that it has been a difficult and frustrating task. So I begin with a disclaimer: For every object I have selected, others easily could have been chosen with equally compelling arguments.

1. **Chartres Cathedral (1145–1220),** Chartres, France. For me, Chartres epitomizes spiritual power and the unity of the arts. Every aspect of its architecture, sculpture, and stained glass reflects the devotion of its makers, each individual working to create a harmonious design that expresses profound faith.
2. **Michelangelo—Sistine Ceiling (1508–1512),** frescoes, Sistine Chapel in Rome. Leonardo, Raphael, or Michelangelo? Painting or sculpture? I have changed my list countless times, and have selected the Sistine Ceiling to stand for the many accomplishments of the Italian Renaissance. A painting of compelling beauty, it celebrates both the spiritual and physical worlds.
3. **Rogier van der Weyden—The Deposition from the Cross (1435),** oil on wood. This is one of the most beautiful and moving paintings I have ever seen. Artists of the northern Renaissance are admired for

their ability to render even the smallest details of the physical world. In addition to that technical prowess, van der Weyden expressed deep psychological insight in his "Deposition," communicating great sorrow through pose, gesture, and expression.

4. **Rembrandt van Rijn—The Artist in His Studio (1627–28),** oil on panel. I have selected one image to represent Rembrandt's self portraits. In it, I see the mystery of the artist's relationship with his own work—he stands dwarfed by a canvas that only he can see, in a shadowy and obscure space. It also marks a secular, not a religious, experience; such subjects begin their steady increase in popularity during the Baroque period.
5. **Louis-Jacques-Mandé Daguerre—portrait photographs (1839 to 1840s).** The development of photographs by Daguerre and others in 1839 started a revolution in visual culture that continues today. At first regarded as mechanical representations of the physical world, and as a cheap method of creating portraits, photographs are now valued for their artistic qualities.
6. **Joseph Mallord William Turner—The Slave Ship: Slavers Throwing Overboard the Dead and Dying, Typhoon Coming On (1840),** oil on canvas. Turner devoted himself to landscape painting, which he transformed to convey not only natural effects, but also emotion and perception. In this example, his interpretation of an actual event had political impact, particularly in the United States, where it became a powerful symbol for the abolitionist movement when it entered a Boston collection.
7. **Édouard Manet—Olympia (1863),** oil on canvas. I had first thought to include on my list a nude by Titian, whose Venus of Urbino (1538) established a tradition of sensual images of women that was carried forward by many painters. Then I decided on Manet's nude, which shocked Paris by its bold representation of a naked prostitute, unembellished by the trappings of mythology, which by its very realism provoked a discussion of the nature of art.
8. **Claude Monet—Impression: Sunrise (1873),** oil on canvas. It marks the beginning of Impressionism, an artistic style that has proven to be one of the most long-lasting and popular. For Monet, the artist's perception of the visual world was paramount, and on his canvases design is as important as representation and one sees the transformation of three-dimensional worlds into two-dimensional surfaces.
9. **Pablo Picasso—Les Demoiselles d'Avignon (1907),** oil on canvas. Picasso and his colleagues believed that an artist need not be confined by a single vantage point, and invented a new method of representation that incorporated different points of view into a single image. This move toward abstraction had an enormous impact on 20th-century art.
10. **Jackson Pollock—Autumn Rhythm: Number 30, 1950,** oil on canvas. The center of the art world moved to the U.S. after World War II. Pollock's abstract, emotional celebration of the unconscious, free from

any confinement or convention, was among its most influential products, and like Manet's "Olympia," provoked new discussions about the nature of art.

## "A very humbling experience"

SUZANNE FOLDS MCCULLAGH, *Curator of Earlier Prints and Drawings, The Art Institute of Chicago*

It has been a very humbling experience trying to define the 10 greatest works of art of the past millennium. A scholar of the 18th century, I have not included a single work from that era (although Jean-Antoine Watteau's "Sign of Gersaint in Berlin" is perhaps my single favorite painting).

I have favored instead the most ambitious and successful of the vast painted decorations, architectural jewels, and sculptural schemes through the Baroque era, and masterpieces that show the depth, breadth, conceptual, and emotional power of the greatest masters of the art of painting from that point on. These are works that have shaped our civilization, and without them, we would be immeasurably spiritually bereft.

1. **Chartres Cathedral—Northwest Tower (1140);** the Rose Windows (1217–25). The only existing Gothic cathedral fully glazed with a unified program of stained glass to create a saturated, electric atmosphere. Both the tower and the stained glass make the spirit soar and serve as a landmark of architectural ensembles.
2. **Jan and Hubert Van Eyck—Ghent Altarpiece (1423–32),** oil on panel. These brothers introduced the art of oil painting at a level that it would seldom achieve. Their technical accomplishment is surpassed only by the complexity and reverence of their conception in this extraordinary altarpiece, moving in its vastness as well as its details.
3. **Masaccio—Brancacci Chapel (1427),** frescoes. The founder of Italian Renaissance painting not only introduced linear perspective but brought his figures a convincing sense of weight and volume, and a compellingly powerful, emotional tenor.
4. **Michelangelo—Sistine Chapel (1508–12 and 1535),** frescoes, Rome. Although Michelangelo considered himself a sculptor, his painted decoration of the Sistine Chapel ceiling and altar wall is simply the most comprehensive and spiritually charged ensemble of all time. Its force is so great that its impact can be read in the work of artists who have experienced it.
5. **Raphael—Vatican Stanze (1508–20),** frescoes. The papal apartments that Raphael decorated dominated the mature years of his brief life. The wide-ranging subjects of these elegant works include some of the most beautifully painted figures and the most inspirational concepts of civilization.

6. **Gianlorenzo Bernini—The Ecstasy of St. Theresa (1645–52),** marble statue, life size, Cornaro Chapel, Rome. This piece not only reveals the overwhelming emotive power of sculpture, but does so in a carefully conceived situation that takes advantage of the architectural environment. Wrapped in swirling draperies, her passionate gaze directed to heaven, Bernini's saint epitomizes the age of the Baroque, and is among the first to break traditional boundaries of media and meaning.
7. **Diego Velázquez—Las Meniñas (1656),** oil on canvas. Called by Neapolitan artist Luca Giordano the "theology of painting," this enigmatic and sublimely crafted canvas is notable for its fresh, persuasive immediacy and the seemingly disparate challenge of its mysterious psychological and political interconnections. It is a single large canvas that invites yet defies interpretation by its viewers.
8. **Rembrandt van Rijn—The Return of the Prodigal Son (1665),** oil on canvas. No Top 10 list would be complete without this giant of the Dutch school, whose humanity is expressed in Rembrandt's equally wondrous paintings, prints, and drawings. Like the late work of Titian, it is particularly in his last great paintings, especially of biblical subjects, that his narrative insight and tremendous stature as an artist is revealed.
9. **Georges Pierre Seurat—A Sunday Afternoon on the Island of La Grande Jatte (1884–86),** oil on canvas. Painting in France in the 19th century reached a height and subsequent popularity that has rarely been equaled. Few artists brought as much genius, scientific thought, theoretical insight, innovative technique, and conceptual ambition to a canvas as did Seurat in this complex masterwork.
10. **Pablo Picasso—Guernica (1937),** oil on canvas. Certainly the most talented, versatile, and productive artist of the past century, Picasso stretched his art in form and content when he created this immense and powerful diatribe against war that also eerily foretold horrors to come. Produced in an intense and volatile period, it represents the culmination of his art up to that time and speaks for modernism in general.

## "I could not resist"

STEPHAN F. F. JOST, *Director, Mills College Art Museum*

My first reaction to making a list of the 10 most influential works of the past 1,000 years was to exempt myself completely and simply say "no." In the end, I could not resist.

Are the criteria aesthetic or are influential works of art simply a product of dominant cultures? Is influence about later imitation or the number of people who seek to see the work of art today?

I tried to select objects from a broad range of cultures and media.

1. **Chartres Cathedral—the Rose Windows (1217–1225),** stained glass, Chartres, France. As part of one of the most complete medieval buildings, the Rose Windows at Chartres transform light into stunning colors and depict the teachings of the Christian faith.
2. **Huang Kung-wang—Dwelling in the Fu-ch'un Mountains (1347–1350),** handscroll, ink on paper. Huang Kung-wang was one of several great masters of the late Yüan period, and this magnum opus is one of the most influential works of the long history of Chinese landscape painting.
3. **Michelangelo—Sistine Ceiling (1508–1512),** frescoes. This work is a tour de force of painting, illusion, and design. It is also one of the most copied (and parodied) works of art.
4. **Albrecht Dürer—Melencolia I (1514),** engraving. As one of Dürer's master engravings, Melencolia I is both a stunning display of technical ability and a complex meditation on philosophy and theology.
5. **Matthias Grünewald—Isenheim Altarpiece (1510–1515),** oil on panel. Perhaps more than any other work of art, the "Isenheim Altarpiece" was the work I had the most difficult time including. While the altarpiece has inspired many artists, including Jaspar Johns, Grünewald enjoyed limited fame until the 20th century. I included this work because it inspired me to become a curator.
6. **The Koranic inscriptions on Taj Mahal (completed in 1647),** glazed tiles, Agra, India. In the Islamic world, calligraphy has long been the preeminent art form. Many of these texts begin with an invocation of the name of God and represent a particularly long, rich tradition.
7. **Benin ancestral Altarpiece of Oba Akenzua I, Brass (18th century),** Berlin, Museum für Völkerkunde. The art of Benin has been recognized as being technically and intellectually sophisticated and extraordinarily beautiful. This brass altar depicts the Oba, a Benin king, and was part of an ancestral altar.
8. **Vincent van Gogh—The Church at Auvers (1890),** oil on canvas. The vibrant colors, the humility of the subject, and the inspired handling of paint led me to select this work. Van Gogh radically represented painting as a dynamic and modern form of expression.
9. **Dorothea Lange—Migrant Mother, Nipomo, California (1936),** gelatin silver print. This photograph of a woman and her three children captures the spirit of humanity and motherhood while recognizing the harsh reality of poverty. There is also embedded in this selection the acknowledgement of the influence of American society, women artists, and photography on 20th-century culture.
10. **Various artists—AIDS Memorial Quilt (mid-1980s),** various media. I couldn't think of a more appropriate work that captures the democratic ideals of the late 20th century. With more than 41,000 panels, listing more than 80,000 names, the AIDS Memorial Quilt covers more

than 17 football fields and is a monument to the common person, expressing heartfelt emotions.

---

### THIS TEXT: READING

1. What was your experience reading these lists? Did a pattern emerge? Did the various reasonings help you arrive at a definition of art?
2. Is there a piece of art you know of that you would like to see on the list? What? Why?
3. What were some of the criteria for influential art?

### YOUR TEXT: WRITING

1. Write an essay in which you list and justify the three most influential works of visual art over the past 2000 years.
2. Write an essay in which you explain how impossible it is to make such a list. How can one narrow down *all* visual art?
3. Define visual art. Here, a church and a quilt make the list. Are these things art?
4. What do you think the authors of the article mean by "influential"? Have *you* been influenced by any of these pieces of art? Who has? How do these art objects influence us?

## IS THE NAMES QUILT ART?

E. G. Chrichton

---

E. G. Chrichton asks the same question many of you have probably asked at some point: "Is it art?" In this provocative essay (1988), Chrichton asks important questions about so-called "high art" and the role art should play in contemporary society. As you read, you might ask if Acton's ideas of composition apply to the NAMES quilt and also if Chrichton's claims about art mesh with your own. A good example of a definitional essay, note how Chrichton defines what he thinks art is, then demonstrates how the NAMES quilt meets that criteria.

IT IS BEAUTIFUL, POWERFUL, and inspirational. But is it art? The NAMES Project Quilt started in San Francisco with one cloth panel to commemorate one AIDS victim. In a little more than a year it has grown to over 5000 panels from every region in the country. For each person who has taken up needle and thread, paint, and mixed media to create a piece of the Quilt, there are many more who have walked among its connected grids, often in tears. No one with this experience would deny its force and magic as a national symbol of the AIDS tragedy. But from where does this power derive? Why has the NAMES Project Quilt captured our hearts and minds like no other project to come out of the gay community? One answer lies in the Quilt's power as art: art that lives and grows outside established art channels.

The NAMES Project organizers promote the Quilt as the "largest community arts project in the nation." They are aided by a national media that is surprisingly willing to report on events surrounding its display. The art world, however—that ivory tower that is reported to us via a handful of glossy national art magazines—has overlooked the Quilt. The art critics who write in these magazines are not rushing to interpret the Quilt's significance in the history of art.

Art is important, most people agree, but the reasons why are sometimes elusive. There is nothing elusive, though, about the NAMES Project Quilt; it is extremely concrete as visual communication. This accessibility is exactly what throws the Quilt's status as "real art" into question. Unlike much of what we find in galleries and museums, the Quilt has a connection to our daily lives that seems unrelated to the remote world of "high art," or "fine art"—art that is promoted by critics, museum curators, and art historians. To understand the source of discrepancies about how our culture defines art, it helps to look at some of the assumptions made about art and who makes them.

Art, in Western culture, is first and foremost made by the artist—that individual genius whose work and life we come to recognize through a network of museums, media, dealers, and historians. Despite the fact that a myriad of people make art, a very select few are promoted in a way that grabs our attention. This process works like any good marketing strategy: we are told which art is hot, and why, by those who seem to know best. As a result, our taste is inevitably influenced by what appears to be an objective window on aesthetics. It is very hard to regard art found outside these institutional channels as serious. We don't go to the local craft fair to find serious art. It is not the needlepoint your grandmother did, nor the sketches you do in your spare time. And it's not a project like the NAMES Quilt that thrives entirely outside the art world. "Real art" is a luxury item for sale in an elite marketplace that takes it away from the artist's hands, and any community connection we might relate to.

Critics argue a bit about art, trying to maintain the illusion of democratic options, but they essentially define "good art" around a fairly narrow set of assumptions. It is virtually impossible to understand most modern mainstream art without the translation of these intermediaries. They generally promote obscurity as a desirable feature, and cast accessibility in an untrustworthy light; art we can too easily understand is more like entertainment. And, if you want to include a social message, make it vague at best.

Given this milieu, it is no wonder that potential art fans often feel suspicious of famous artists, seeing them as con-artists instead who try to fool us into thinking their enigmatic puzzles are great art. In contrast, the Quilt seems trustworthy partly because we are the artists. Although not for sale on the art market, it generates important funding for local AIDS services networks. It is not the offspring of a famous artist, yet its scale is monumental and attention grabbing. And it isn't found where most important art is found; the "museums" where we view the Quilt are convention centers, pavilions, gymnasiums, and the Capitol Mall—hardly the retreats of high art. Yet one thing is clear: the Quilt has succeeded in creating a visual metaphor for the tragedy of AIDS that transcends individual grieving to communicate beauty and hope. What more could be expected of a great work of art?

If the establishment art world places the NAMES Quilt outside the holy realm of high art, other art traditions do not. In the early seventies, feminist artists working within the art world successfully revived an interest in the folk art of quilting and sewing bees—"low art" historically associated with women. New materials explored during this period gained acceptance as legitimate fine art ingredients: cloth, clay, and rope, for example. Many artists, both male and female, started to inject more personal and autobiographical content into their work. In general, the division between high and low art melted a little.

Several large-scale projects were also organized that introduced the idea of bringing together many people's labor into one artistic vision. Judy Chicago attracted hundreds of craftspeople to her "Dinner Party" project. The end result was a huge and complex installation illustrating the lives of specific women throughout history with china place settings around a huge table. In a very different project, the artist Christo engaged the help of hundreds of people to set up a "Running Fence" of fabric that wound for miles through northern California countryside, focusing attention on the land and its natural contours. In both cases, people skeptical about the initial vision were drawn in and became enthusiastic through participation. Chicago and Christo are the rare mainstream artists whose work and vision have crossed out of the exclusive art world to be accessible. The Vietnam War Memorial, designed by an architectural student named Maya Ying Lin, set a precedent for the simple naming of victims of a tragic war instead of merely immortalizing the warmonger leaders.

Tribal art from all ages has influenced Western artists interested in introducing ritual to their work. The holistic integration of art with the spiritual and survival needs of a community, characteristic of tribal art, appeals to many of us brought up on the doctrine of "art for art sake." Many artists have also been influenced by ancient art like the prehistoric Stonehenge. Monuments like this reveal a very different set of assumptions about art and the artist. No one knows exactly who created them—their massive scale obviously required the labor and creativity of many people, over many life spans. It seems as though the individual artistic ego was not important here, and that art had a function in society beyond visual aesthetics.

The contemporary art that is perhaps most similar to the NAMES Project Quilt are the *arpilleras* created by anonymous Chilean women resisting the fascist junta ruling their country. Pieced together from scavenged factory remnants, these patchwork pictures use decorative imagery to protest specific government policies or to commemorate "disappeared" political prisoners, often relatives of the artists. They are smuggled out of the country to communicate the conditions in Chile to the rest of the world. The *arpilleras* are also the only surviving indigenous Chilean visual art, now that murals have been destroyed and artists of all kinds murdered and imprisoned.

What the NAMES Project Quilt has in common with feminist, environmental, ancient, tribal, and Chilean art is a tradition of collaboration, a mixing of media, and an emphasis on process that makes the reason for the art just as important as the finished product. In art like this, the individual artist's identity is less important than the purpose of the art in the life of a community or people. This purpose might be the need to remember a part of history in a visual way, a means of marking time, or a tribute to the dead created not by a government, but by those who mourn. The NAMES Project Quilt started as one panel, one person's need to commemorate a dead friend. It soon expanded to a collaborative vision with a plan for how the Quilt could grow: panels approximately the size of a human body or a casket; panels to remember people who are most often cremated and leave no grave plot to visit; panels sewn together into grids—individual lost lives stitched together, woven into an enormous picture of the effect of AIDS.

This vision is dependent on the contributions of a growing number of individual artists who work alone or with others to stitch and paint a memory of someone they loved. They do this in the best tradition of quilting, using pieces from the person's life, articles of clothing, teddy bears, photographs, messages to the dead from the living who mourn them. People who have never before felt confident about making art testify about the healing nature of this participation in a larger artwork—one that also allows them to "come out" around AIDS. Instead of mourning alone, they link their grief to others both visually and organizationally. Finally, in keeping with the unifying principle of the whole Quilt, they stitch or paint the person's name who died, committing that name to an historical document that physically shows real people, not mere statistics.

Art needs an audience. The NAMES Project Quilt has an unusually large one: hundreds of thousands of us across the nation who have walked amidst the panels, stood in the sea of colorful memories, cried, found panels of people we've known, hugged strangers—in general been awed, moved, and inspired by the power of the total vision. We, the audience, have received much of the healing communicated by the artists through the ritual reading of names and physical beauty of the Quilt. It is a rare work of art that can transcend its material components to communicate this kind of collective power. A political demonstration could not have done the same. Neither could a single memorial service nor a walk through a graveyard.

* * *

There are other reasons the Quilt is effective art. The quilt form itself feels very American. It is almost apple pie in its connotations, and when used to communicate thoughts and feelings about AIDS with all the stigma, a powerful dialectic occurs. Tangible evidence of individuals who lie outside of society's favored status gets woven into a domestic metaphor. The Quilt reveals that these people had domestic lives of one kind or another—family, friends, lovers who banded together to make the panels. The quilt form historically is a feminist metaphor for integration, inclusiveness, the breaking down of barriers, the pieces of someone's life sewn together. It is not surprising that women and gay men would pick up on this traditional women's art. Sewing and weaving have been metaphors for life, death, creation, and transformation in many cultures. Just as the spider weaves from material that is pulled from inside, women have woven their ideas and emotions into cloth decorated with the symbols of their culture. The NAMES Quilt picks up on all these traditions.

The grid pattern is another important part of the Quilt's effect as art. Formed by a huge (and growing) number of individually made panels, the

The NAMES Project AIDS Memorial Quilt, October 1989. 10,848 individual (3 × 6 feet) panels. Sponsored by The NAMES Project Foundation. *(Photo: Mary Gottwald)*

Volunteers and others walk on the 21,000 panel NAMES Project AIDS Memorial Quilt in Washington.

pattern signifies inclusiveness and equality. Unlike a cemetery where class differences are obvious, this grid unites the dead regardless of who they were. It is as though the dead are woven together, visually mirroring the networks the living form to create the quilt. Within this grid pattern there is an amazing and unplanned repetition of imagery. Items of clothing dominate—remnants of someone's wardrobe, T-shirts, jeans, jewelry, glittery gowns, and sashes. Teddy bears are common, too, a kind of cuddly accompaniment to the dead, a lively symbol of rest and sleep. The dates that show up so often are shocking because of the abbreviated life spans they illustrate. Some of the most powerful panels contain messages written directly to the dead, stitched or painted: "Sweet dreams," "I miss you every day."

The NAMES Quilt bridges the gap between art and social consciousness. Art is too often peripheral to our society, seen as superfluous fluff. Political activism, on the other hand, is often perceived as uncreative and separate from culture. The Quilt is a rare successful integration of these two

AIDS quilt—overhead shot.

worlds so separate in Western culture. We should be proud of an art form that originated in the gay community and that is able to communicate beyond to other communities. What is communicated is as complex as any art would strive for, something that will have historical significance beyond all of our lives. Developed outside established art channels, shown mostly in non-art environments, the Quilt could nevertheless teach the art world a great deal about organization, collaboration on a grand scale, and the communication of an aesthetic that crosses many boundaries. Very few artists or art projects are able to reach so many people in such a way.

Parts of the art world have started to hear about the Quilt. At least two or three well-known artists have created panels. In Baltimore, the Quilt will not be hung in one of the pavilions, gymnasiums, and civic centers that house the Quilt elsewhere on its national tour—it will be hung on the walls of the Baltimore Art Museum. Organizers are excited by these developments, viewing them as evidence of the far-reaching effects of the Quilt. But what will happen to the present spirit of the Quilt? Will focus turn to "famous" panels more than others? Will museums become a more targeted locale for the Quilt, changing the vantage point from ground to wall? These are important questions because so much of the Quilt's power lies in its existence outside the official art world. It would be unfortunate if the category of "non-artist" became accentuated by more of a focus on "real" artists, and intimidated wider participation. I would hate to see the Quilt swallowed up in the land of institutional art and co-opted from its community roots.

We should be proud of the Quilt, but we should also stand back and reflect on its process as often as necessary. The NAMES Project is growing at an overwhelming pace, one that demands a look at how centralized the vision can remain. The power of the Quilt is fully communicated when people walk among the squares, physically becoming part of the vast grid, feeling tiny in scale compared to the whole. Its power also lies in its capacity to educate about AIDS in the universal language of quilting. I am concerned that continuing centralization will make the Quilt unwieldy, both in organization and in size. Will continuous expansion make it impossible to display in one location? Will people have to see it only in pictures, or only in its home resting place of San Francisco?

What about communities deeply affected by AIDS but not yet familiar with the NAMES Project Quilt? In New York City, for instance, women of color and their children form a growing percentage of victims, yet I wonder how many panels reflect this. A continued centralization of the Quilt could stand in the way of the outreach that makes the Quilt's vision so powerful. One possible solution would be regional quilts that are more accessible to people. Smaller cities have already created their own quilts and displayed them locally before sending them to join the larger work. This link to something larger is an important part of the Quilt process, and it could easily continue with local areas concentrating on new outreach before joining together regionally. Stores in areas where there are many AIDS deaths could be organized to hang quilt grids in their windows. People could get involved who would never travel to Phoenix, or Baltimore, or other places on the tour, people who would never hear about the Quilt through existing channels.

It must be hard to think about giving up control of a project that has been so successful so quickly—especially in an age of media co-optation of art and social movements. But one of the most important roles the Quilt has played is as a tool for organization: individuals networking to make panels, groups networking to form local quilt tour organizations. A central vision has been important and may be for some time to come. But AIDS is unfortunately with us for longer than that, and the vision could become stronger by branching out. The ritual unfolding of the panels and reading of names might change from region to region. New cultural influences would add new dimensions. The Northeast's Quilt might take on a very different character from the Southwest's. These differences would be exciting and would expand the Quilt's dimensions as art. It would reach more people. And the inevitable difficulties of large organizations would be strengthened by more autonomy at the local level. People could still feel part of a larger-than-life whole, yet not be subsumed by an abstraction out of reach. If four football fields of panels are overwhelming, are ten necessarily better?

These are questions and reactions I have amidst my own emotions about the power of the Quilt and its significance as art in an age when the institutions of art can be so devoid of spirit. Art and artists survive regardless of art market trends, and most art will never be seen in a museum or gallery. It is the art made by your neighbor or your lover, the art that someone is compelled to make for reasons other than money. I hope the Quilt will never be a commodity on the art market, never owned by an individual or corporation, never laid to rest in one museum. The NAMES Project Quilt is a living, breathing, changing work of art, one that was inspired by grief and grew to communicate hope. Let it continue to live in good health.

---

## This Text: Reading

1. According to Chrichton, is the NAMES quilt art?
2. How does Chrichton distinguish between "real" or "high" art and the NAMES quilt? Do you agree with this distinction?
3. What does the NAMES project share with feminist, environmental, and native art?
4. What is the audience for the NAMES quilt? How is it different than the audience for, say, the *Sensation* exhibition or a Picasso exhibit?

## Your Text: Writing

1. Write an essay in which you define art. Then look at two or three different texts and explain why they either are or are not art, according to your definition.
2. If you can see the NAMES quilt, do so. If not, try to watch a video about it or find pictures of it. Write an essay on the experience of seeing the NAMES quilt. What kind of text is it?
3. Write an essay exploring the idea of artistry and authorship. Who is the artist of the NAMES quilt? How does the quilt change how we think of art as the product of an "individual genius"? What is the role of the community in the creation of an art object?
4. Write an essay in which you explore the cultural climate in which the NAMES quilt was made. What prompted the makers of the quilt? What is the artistic situation?

# (RE)VERSING VISION: READING SCULPTURE IN POETRY AND PROSE

Dean Rader

Known neither for his poetry nor his art criticism, Dean Rader, a co-author of this book, reads a piece of sculpture through a poetic and a critical lens. Written for a 1998 symposium on storytelling, where T. Paul Hernandez's sculpture, "In the Mist of Ireland and Louisiana," was a featured piece, Rader tells two stories about one work of art. As you read both pieces, you might consider which of the two is the more "accurate" reading of the text that is Hernandez's sculpture.

## *Presence and Absence: In the Mist of Ireland and Louisiana*

To what extent can an object tell a story? T. Paul Hernandez's provocative sculpture *In the Mist of Ireland and Louisiana* tells two main stories, the first of which is a story of motion. That two heavy, seemingly immovable, cement figures offer a narrative about motion suggests that the artist is working on a number of different levels—both literally and figuratively. We are drawn immediately to the elongated necks stretching through and above the clouds. Like those of the figures in the sculpture, our eyes are pulled away from the bodies and directed toward the faces, where they and we see nothing but the other. Their desire to rise above the earthly, to transcend the confinement of the body, mirrors our own. We get tired of our bodies—we want to rise.

In a way, the figures achieve what we can only long for: a permanent state of ecstasy.

But the aura of ascending created by the figures' arched necks gives way to an equally powerful aura of descending, generated by the rain falling downward and reinforced by the fact that the figures are firmly rooted to the ground, as if they have grown into the earth. As viewers, we are more aware of the rain than the figures are—we see the rain, but the figures can see only each other. They know it is raining only by reading the air with their bodies, which, perhaps to their great disappointment (or relief) remain all-too terrestrial. Thus, the figures exist in two realms, never fully residing in either.

And then there are those necks—typical of sculptures from this phase of Hernandez's career—that keep snaking up and up through the clouds. The figures, already so vertical, are made more so by the elongated necks. I've never really known what to make of these necks. They remind me of the limbs of dolls I've seen in New Orleans. I suspect the necks are a kind of bridge between the world above the clouds and the world below them. Conduits. Symbols of transformation. Perhaps also they grow out of necessity; it's the only way the two figures can (almost) kiss without being pelleted by rain.

Slicing across the intense verticality of the piece is the outstretched arms of the man, the only horizontal movement in the sculpture. Unlike the ascending and descending motions which offer a sense of balance or symmetry, the man's gesture finds no reciprocity. She can't accept his gift! The fact that the woman has no arms does not so much balance out the man's use of his as much as it makes us aware of the link between presence and absence, which is where the technical story that the sculpture tells opens up to the more complex story of desire. To me, this is a sculpture about wanting.

And we all want.

But, to what extent can an object of desire tell a story? The man, a priest, probably St. Francis, is giving a woman a gift, a violin. The woman, who has no arms, not only cannot play the violin, she cannot even accept the gift. Hence, the man finds himself in a vulnerable position; he has extended himself. He gives something that cannot be accepted. On the other hand, the woman also finds herself in a difficult position. How can she not accept his offering? These questions lead into even more interesting questions: Why is he giving her this gift? Is the violin a token or symbol of something else? Does she want to receive this gift? Does the responsibility of accepting the gift weigh heavier than the desire that prompted him to offer her this gift? We know that the man desires, but does she?

And what about the sculpture itself—does it desire? The piece is composed of concrete yard art that has been altered and reassembled. For most people, lawn ornaments are the very antithesis of what we think of as "art." They are often cliches or stereotypes that undermine art's originality and iconoclasm, but in Hernandez's work, the everyday becomes the unique, the mundane, the magical. Like Andy Warhol and his soup cans, Hernandez appropriates images and reconstructs them and their contexts to create a new way of looking at the world and the images in it. In this way, the sculpture is itself a gift that, through looking at it, you have already received.

**The Other Gift: T. Paul Hernandez's "In the Mist of Ireland and Lousiana"**

It's true:<br>
The dead have grown weary<br>
                        of the future,<br>
An equation<br>
            for which they<br>
Have invented the formula,<br>
A landscape<br>
            already painted.

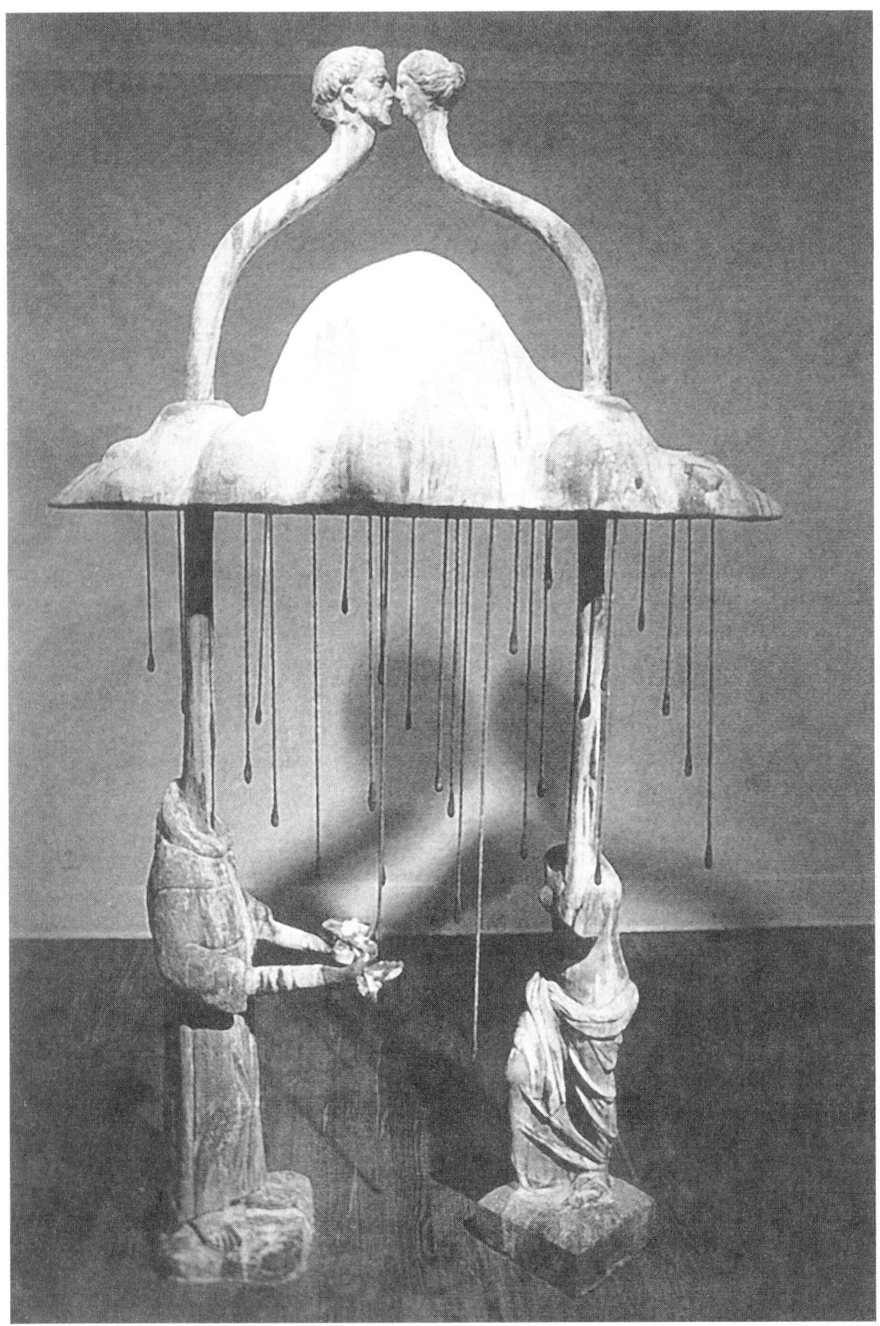

T. Paul Hernandez, *In the Mist of Ireland and Louisiana* (1997).

The dead:
　　　　they have grown tired
Of answers.

And so has she.

In the next life, though,
He will give her questions.
He will give her
Clouds
　　　　the earth
Surrenders to,
Rain
　　　the sky cannot release,

Perhaps even
The tendon of light
　　　　　　　　　　that holds their gaze.

And she:

She will give him
the memory of absence.
The place
　　　　　where the wind stops.
Waves forgetting their shapes.
Perhaps even
The half of his body
　　　　　　　　　　he had forgotten.
But the dead are tired
of lip service and empty promises:
Weary of the stories
　　　　　　　　　　　they spend eternity unwriting:

And so they gift themselves his arms,
And strap on
　　　　　　　to their dogged torsos
His limbs' bad ghosts,
　　　　　　　　　　　so that now
He might offer her
The only thing
　　　　　　　　　she's ever truly wanted.

### THIS TEXT: READING

1. Which of the two texts did you prefer—the poem, or the prose explanation?
2. How is the poem an interpretation of T. Paul Hernandez's sculpture?
3. Which reading of his sculpture do you think Hernandez likes the best?
4. Do you agree with Rader's interpretation of the sculpture in the prose segment? Why? Why not?

### YOUR TEXT: WRITING

1. Write your own poem about the sculpture. How does your version differ from Rader's? Write an essay in which you compare your poem about "In the Mist of Ireland and Louisiana" with Rader's.
2. What does the title mean? Hernandez is originally from Louisiana but has lived in Ireland. The piece refers to both Celtic and Cajun cultures. Write an essay about how Hernandez depicts these two cultures in his sculpture, or give your own semiotic reading of the sculpture.
3. Write an essay in which you explore Rader's different readings of the sculpture. How do you account for the imaginative departure of the poem? Does the sculpture warrant this interpretation?
4. Write an essay about Dean Rader publishing his own work in his own textbook. Since he is not known as a poet or an art critic, why might he subject writing outside of his comfort zone to the scrutiny of thousands of undergraduates? Is it arrogant to publish your own work in your own book? What might his co-author think of this move?

## SEQUENTIAL ART: "CLOSURE" AND "ART"

Scott McCloud

These "essays" come from Scott McCloud's *Understanding Comics* (1994), a comic about the importance—and semiotics—of comics and comic books. McCloud forces us to think about what art is and how we see it. He also raises interesting questions about the intersection of comics and art.

THIS PHENOMENON OF OBSERVING THE PARTS BUT PERCEIVING THE WHOLE HAS A NAME.
IT'S CALLED CLOSURE.

IN OUR DAILY LIVES, WE OFTEN COMMIT CLOSURE, MENTALLY COMPLETING THAT WHICH IS INCOMPLETE BASED ON PAST EXPERIENCE.
SALE
SALE

SOME FORMS OF CLOSURE ARE DELIBERATE INVENTIONS OF STORYTELLERS TO PRODUCE SUSPENSE OR TO CHALLENGE AUDIENCES.

OTHERS HAPPEN AUTOMATICALLY, WITHOUT MUCH EFFORT... PART OF BUSINESS AS USUAL.

IN RECOGNIZING AND RELATING TO OTHER PEOPLE, WE ALL DEPEND HEAVILY ON OUR LEARNED ABILITY OF CLOSURE.

IN AN INCOMPLETE WORLD, WE MUST DEPEND ON CLOSURE FOR OUR VERY SURVIVAL.

CLOSURE CAN TAKE *MANY FORMS*. SOME *SIMPLE*, SOME *COMPLEX*.
CLOSURE
CLOSURE
CL S RE

SOMETIMES, A MERE *SHAPE* OR *OUTLINE* IS ENOUGH TO TRIGGER CLOSURE.

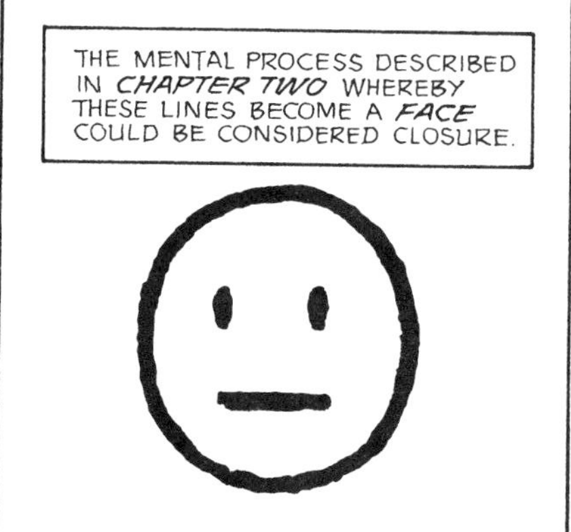
THE MENTAL PROCESS DESCRIBED IN *CHAPTER TWO* WHEREBY THESE LINES BECOME A *FACE* COULD BE CONSIDERED CLOSURE.

EVERY TIME WE SEE A *PHOTOGRAPH* REPRODUCED IN A *NEWSPAPER* OR *MAGAZINE*, WE COMMIT CLOSURE.

OUR *EYES* TAKE IN THE *FRAGMENTED*, *BLACK-AND-WHITE IMAGE* OF THE *"HALF-TONE"* PATTERNS--

--AND OUR MINDS TRANSFORM IT INTO THE *"REALITY"*--

--OF THE *PHOTOGRAPH!*

IN ELECTRONIC MEDIA, CLOSURE IS CONSTANT, EVEN OVER-POWERING!

IN FILM, CLOSURE TAKES PLACE CONTINUOUSLY-- TWENTY-FOUR TIMES PER SECOND, IN FACT-- AS OUR MINDS, AIDED BY THE PERSISTENCE OF VISION, TRANSFORM A SERIES OF STILL PICTURES INTO A STORY OF CONTINUOUS MOTION.

A MEDIUM REQUIRING EVEN MORE CLOSURE IS TELEVISION, WHICH, IN REALITY, IS JUST A SINGLE POINT OF LIGHT, RACING ACROSS THE SCREEN SO FAST THAT IT'S DESCRIBED MY FACE HUNDREDS OF TIMES BEFORE YOU CAN EVEN SWALLOW THAT CORN CHIP!!*

BETWEEN SUCH AUTOMATIC ELECTRONIC CLOSURE AND THE SIMPLER CLOSURE OF EVERYDAY LIFE--

--THERE LIES A MEDIUM OF COMMUNICATION AND EXPRESSION WHICH USES CLOSURE LIKE NO OTHER...

...A MEDIUM WHERE THE AUDIENCE IS A WILLING AND CONSCIOUS COLLABORATOR AND CLOSURE IS THE AGENT OF CHANGE, TIME AND MOTION.

* MEDIA GURU TONY SCHWARTZ DESCRIBES THIS AT LENGTH IN HIS BOOK MEDIA, THE SECOND GOD, ANCHOR BOOKS, 1983.

NOW YOU DIE!!
NO! NO!

EEYAA!!

SEE THAT SPACE BETWEEN THE PANELS? THAT'S WHAT COMICS AFICIONADOS HAVE NAMED "THE GUTTER."
AND DESPITE ITS UNCEREMONIOUS TITLE, THE GUTTER PLAYS HOST TO MUCH OF THE MAGIC AND MYSTERY THAT ARE AT THE VERY HEART OF COMICS!

HERE IN THE LIMBO OF THE GUTTER, HUMAN IMAGINATION TAKES TWO SEPARATE IMAGES AND TRANS-FORMS THEM INTO A SINGLE IDEA.

NOTHING IS SEEN BETWEEN THE TWO PANELS, BUT EXPERIENCE TELLS YOU SOMETHING MUST BE THERE!
Peek-A-Boo!
Peek-A-Boo!

COMICS PANELS FRACTURE BOTH TIME AND SPACE, OFFERING A JAGGED, STACCATO RHYTHM OF UNCONNECTED MOMENTS.

BUT CLOSURE ALLOWS US TO CONNECT THESE MOMENTS AND MENTALLY CONSTRUCT A CONTINUOUS, UNIFIED REALITY.

IF VISUAL ICONOGRAPHY IS THE VOCABULARY OF COMICS, CLOSURE IS ITS GRAMMAR.
AND SINCE OUR DEFINITION OF COMICS HINGES ON THE ARRANGEMENT OF ELEMENTS--
ABC
123
ICONOGRAPHY
CLOSURE

--THEN, IN A VERY REAL SENSE, COMICS IS CLOSURE!

I MAY HAVE DRAWN AN AXE BEING RAISED IN THIS EXAMPLE, BUT I'M NOT THE ONE WHO LET IT DROP OR DECIDED HOW HARD THE BLOW, OR WHO SCREAMED, OR WHY.

THAT, DEAR READER, WAS YOUR SPECIAL CRIME, EACH OF YOU COMMITTING IT IN YOUR OWN STYLE.

TO KILL A MAN BETWEEN PANELS IS TO CONDEMN HIM TO A THOUSAND DEATHS.

PARTICIPATION IS A POWERFUL FORCE IN ANY MEDIUM. FILMMAKERS LONG AGO REALIZED THE IMPORTANCE OF ALLOWING VIEWERS TO USE THEIR IMAGINATIONS.

BUT WHILE FILM MAKES USE OF AUDIENCES' IMAGINATIONS FOR OCCASIONAL EFFECTS, COMICS MUST USE IT FAR MORE OFTEN!

FROM THE TOSSING OF A BASEBALL TO THE DEATH OF A PLANET, THE READER'S DELIBERATE, VOLUNTARY CLOSURE IS COMICS' PRIMARY MEANS OF SIMULATING TIME AND MOTION.

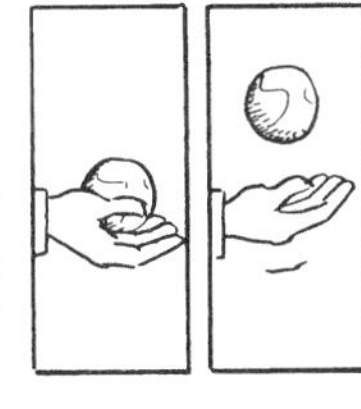

CLOSURE IN COMICS FOSTERS AN INTIMACY SURPASSED ONLY BY THE WRITTEN WORD, A SILENT, SECRET CONTRACT BETWEEN CREATOR AND AUDIENCE.
HOW THE CREATOR HONORS THAT CONTRACT IS A MATTER OF BOTH ART AND CRAFT.

LET'S TAKE A LOOK AT THE CRAFT.

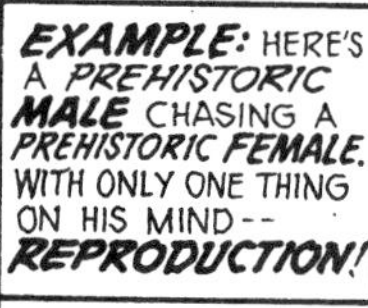

SO STRONG IS THIS INSTINCT THAT IT GOVERNS HIS EVERY MOVE! NOT ONE STEP IS WASTED IN THE PURSUIT OF HIS GOAL!

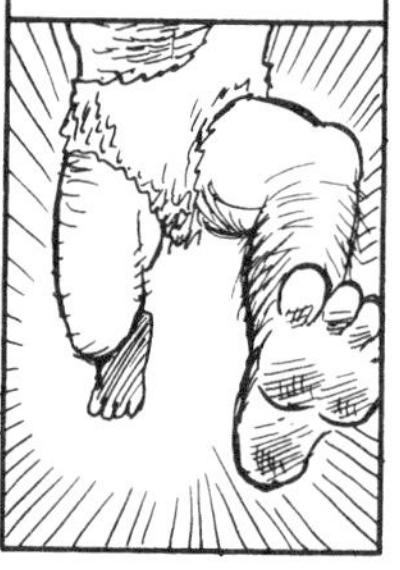

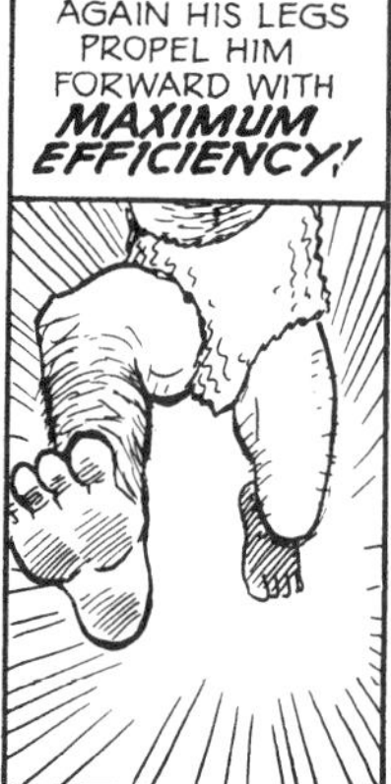

TRAPPED ON THE EDGE OF A CLIFF, HIS MIND CAN ONLY CONCEIVE OF ONE PATH TO SURVIVAL!

HE TAKES IT!

AND SURVIVES.
ROOOAARR...

HIS NEXT MOVE MIGHT BE TO LOOK FOR FOOD (SURVIVAL) OR PERHAPS ANOTHER FEMALE (REPRODUCTION).

BUT INSTEAD...
THPLPLP!!

ART.

IT'S A HAPPY FACT OF HUMAN EXISTENCE THAT WE SIMPLY CAN'T SPEND OUR EVERY WAKING HOUR EATING AND HAVING SEX! NO MATTER HOW FRANTICALLY WE PURSUE OUR GOALS, THERE WILL INEVITABLY BE TIMES WHEN WE JUST DON'T HAVE A THING TO DO!
UGH.
UGH.
HRMMM...

WHAT MAY LOOK LIKE A TRIBE OF BORED, INACTIVE CAVE-DWELLERS BELOW US IS, IN FACT, A THRIVING ART COLONY!

SEE THAT OLD WOMAN WITH THE STICK? NOTICE THE LINES SHE'S MAKING IN THE DIRT?

TODAY SHE HAS A STOMACHACHE AND HER LINES ARE TIGHT AND ANGULAR. YESTERDAY SHE FELT BETTER AND HER LINES WERE OPEN AND CURVED.

AND OVER THERE A MAN BEATS A SIMPLE RHYTHM WITH A PAIR OF STONES. HE DOESN'T KNOW WHY, BUT THE SOUND PLEASES HIM.
TAP! TAP! TAP! TAP!
TAP! TAP!

NEARBY, A BOY KICKS UP PEBBLES AND DIRT AND PUMMELS THE AIR WITH HIS FIST.

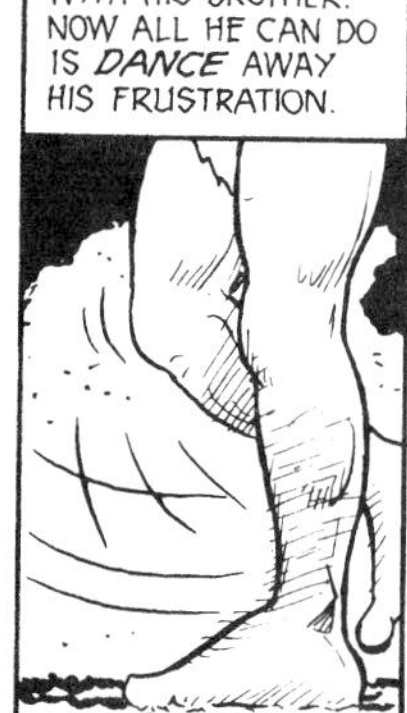
TODAY HE LOST A FIGHT WITH HIS BROTHER. NOW ALL HE CAN DO IS DANCE AWAY HIS FRUSTRATION.

WHILE OVER HERE, A LITTLE GIRL SINGS HER SONG OF YOUTH!
DOOOOOORROOOOOO YB-BIP-BIP-BIP! GREEEGAH!! WUK! WUK!

BECAUSE OF ITS INDEPENDENCE FROM OUR EVOLUTION-BRED INSTINCTS, ART IS THE WAY WE ASSERT OUR IDENTITIES AS INDIVIDUALS AND BREAK OUT OF THE NARROW ROLES NATURE CAST US IN.

OF COURSE, THE GENIUS OF "MOTHER NATURE" IS SUCH THAT EVEN THESE THINGS DO HAVE THEIR USES FROM AN EVOLUTIONARY STANDPOINT.

THREE, IN FACT.

FIRST, THEY PROVIDE EXERCISE FOR MINDS AND BODIES NOT RECEIVING OUTSIDE STIMULUS.

SECOND, THEY PROVIDE AN OUTLET FOR EMOTIONAL IMBALANCES, AIDING IN THE RACE'S MENTAL SURVIVAL.

THIRD AND PERHAPS MOST IMPORTANTLY TO OUR SURVIVAL AS A RACE, SUCH RANDOM ACTIVITIES OFTEN LEAD--

--TO USEFUL DISCOVERIES!
AAH!!
FUMF!

THIS FUNCTION WOULD ALSO BE PERFORMED IN LATER CENTURIES BY SPORTS AND GAMES.

ART AS SELF EXPRESSION, THE ARTIST AS HERO; FOR MANY, ITS HIGHEST PURPOSE.

ART AS DISCOVERY, AS THE PURSUIT OF TRUTH, AS EXPLORATION; THE SOUL OF MUCH MODERN ART AND THE FOUNDATIONS OF LANGUAGE, SCIENCE AND PHILOSOPHY.

A LOT HAS CHANGED IN HALF A MILLION YEARS, BUT SOME THINGS NEVER CHANGE.
OH NO! I'M GONNA BE LATE FOR THAT JOB INTERVIEW!

THE PROCESSES ARE MORE COMPLEX NOW, BUT THE INSTINCTS*REMAIN THE SAME. SURVIVAL AND REPRODUCTION STILL HOLD THE UPPER HAND.

*ALONG WITH THEIR MANY RELATED FEELINGS AND CUSTOMS.

YET IN ALMOST EVERYTHING WE DO THERE IS AT LEAST AN ELEMENT OF ART.

PERHAPS A LITTLE UNNECESSARY CHOREOGRAPHY ON THE ASSEMBLY LINE.
OOOH, BEHBEE!

OR THE PERSONAL STYLE OF A BICYCLE MESSENGER.
HONK! HONK!

OR JUST THE WAY WE SIGN OUR NAMES!
do herein pledg

IN SOME OCCUPATIONS, THE LATITUDE FOR SELF-EXPRESSION IS GREATER. SURVIVAL--MAKING A LIVING--GOES HAND IN HAND WITH CREATIVE DESIRE.

I THINK IT'S FAIR TO SAY THAT SOME ACTIVITIES HAVE MORE ART IN THEM THAN OTHERS.

LIFE IS A SERIES OF MINUTE DECISIONS, SOME MOTIVATED BY SURVIVAL, SOME NOT, AND PROPORTIONS DO VARY.

BUT TO PROCLAIM, AS SO MANY SO OFTEN DO, THAT--
THAT'S NOT ART!
--PRESUMES THAT ART IS AN EITHER/OR PROPOSITION. I DON'T THINK IT IS.

RARE IS THE PERSON IN ANY OCCUPATION WHO EXPRESSES NOTHING...

...AND RARE IS THE ARTIST WHO CARES NOTHING FOR SUCCESS, I.E., SURVIVAL!

BUT THE IDEAL OF THE LATTER IS ALIVE IN THE HEARTS OF MANY ARTISTS WHO MAY HOPE FOR SUCCESS, BUT WON'T ALTER THEIR WORK TO OBTAIN IT.
$$
POWER
FAME
SEX
$$$$$$

THE "FINE ARTIST"--THE PURE ARTIST-- SAYS TO THE WORLD: "I DIDN'T DO THIS FOR MONEY! I DIDN'T DO THIS TO MATCH THE COLOR OF YOUR COUCHES!
"I DIDN'T DO THIS TO GET LAID! I DIDN'T DO THIS FOR FAME OR POWER OR GREED OR ANYTHING ELSE! I DID THIS FOR ART!"

IN OTHER WORDS: "MY ART HAS NO PRACTICAL VALUE WHATSOEVER!"

"BUT IT'S IMPORTANT!"

AND SOMETIMES IT IS, THOUGH IT MIGHT TAKE A CENTURY OR TWO FOR THE REST OF THE WORLD TO FIND OUT!

"PURE" ART IS ESSENTIALLY TIED TO THE QUESTION OF PURPOSE-- OF DECIDING WHAT YOU WANT OUT OF ART.

THIS IS AS TRUE IN COMICS AS IT IS IN PAINTING, WRITING, THEATRE, FILM, SCULPTURE, OR ANY OTHER FORM...
...BECAUSE THE CREATION OF ANY WORK IN ANY MEDIUM WILL ALWAYS FOLLOW A CERTAIN PATH.

### This Text: Reading

1. What do you think McCloud's aims are in these pieces?
2. Do you agree with his idea about what art is? Why? If not, what is he leaving out?
3. Do you agree with McCloud's idea about the role of the audience in determining meaning? Do you feel you have such a role in what you watch? When do you perform such a role?
4. How does presenting this information in comic form change the way you view the information? Is it appropriate to present "serious" information in comic form? What might prevent us from receiving this information in the way the author might have intended it?
5. What is McCloud's writing situation—what is he writing against?

### Your Text: Writing

1. In a short essay, make a case for nontraditional presentation of informational material.
2. Write about the way the text itself influences the reader. Can you think of other texts whose format invokes a reaction from the reader?
3. Write your own definition of art based on your own experience as a reader.
4. Write about your own experience as a reader in participating in making meaning.
5. How would you draw your paper? Who would narrate it? What would it look like? Just for fun, draw out your paper.

## #27: READING CINDY SHERMAN AND GENDER

Anne Darby

Anne Darby wrote this examination of a Cindy Sherman photograph for Introduction to Visual Cultures, an elective class at Virginia Commonwealth University, in 2001. Here Darby weaves the personal with the critical in an effective examination of gender roles through the photograph.

AMONG THE MOST WELL KNOWN of Cindy Sherman's work are her *Untitled Film Stills* in which, using herself as a model, she creates staged scenes that could have been derived from black and white movies from the 1950s. None of these photographs were based on any specific film; they were meant to portray stereotypical female roles as created by or perpetuated by these movies in particular. To me, the most striking image in this series is *Untitled Film Still #27*, which depicts a woman dressed as if for a party with tears streaking her face. Though the aesthetic aspect of the photograph is simple, it appeals directly to the viewer, specifically women, via her own personal experience. The power of the image is in the viewer's projection and her empathy for the subject.

The woman is seated, and the photograph is cropped from the middle of her forehead to the table on which her hands are resting. In her right hand she holds a half-smoked cigarette, and her left hand is curled distractedly around some indistinguishable object. In front of her right hand are a glass of champagne and a decorative ashtray. Before her left hand lies a pack of wooden matches, and on the ring finger of that hand there is a ring with a dark stone. It is impossible to discern whether it is merely a piece of jewelry or an indication of engagement, but either way it is enough to make the viewer speculate about her future marital status and, by association, her future in general.

The table is strewn with cigarette ash, which alludes to her preoccupation. She is wearing a low cut dress with a faux leopard fur collar that spans almost the width of her shoulders. The most noticeable aspect of the photograph is the emotion displayed on her face. Her heavy eye makeup is smeared by the tears which have run down her face in dark lines. Tears have caught on her eyelashes, held there by the heavy mascara. Light glints off of the excessive liquid, distorting and accentuating her eyes. Her mouth is partially open and her collarbones protrude, which indicate that she is in mid-gasp.

We are all familiar with that moment, near the end of a heavy cry, when we begin to try to compose ourselves and regain the oxygen we have lost. It is my assumption that the moment portrayed will be more poignant and powerful to female viewers, though it is possible male viewers would be able to relate on some level. The photograph stands for me as a symbol of the struggle between a person's façade and their soul. The symbols shown can be divided into those that stand as signifiers of façade and those that portray the true self coming through.

The dress, specifically the low neckline, suggests that this woman has dressed for someone other than herself. The idea that a woman, seen as a sexual object, lets (whether passively or actively, consciously or not) other parts of her character and psyche suffer is a predominant theme in Sherman's early work. For example, her *Centerfold* series acts as commentary on pornographic images of women, and many of those images depict women in what could be sensual poses, were it not for the emotion or in some cases fear or sickness, that pervades the scene.

It has been my experience that the great majority of women to some extent project an image of who they think they are expected to be. (I know that this is also an issue with men, but that is a whole different topic, about which I am not qualified to write.) We *want* to be all of these things: beautiful, collected, intelligent, happy, witty (yet demure!) and successful. Furthermore the presence of the alcohol and the cigarette, as well as the subject's outfit, lead me to believe that she is involved in a certain lifestyle in which a woman plays a slightly different role than she does in the home or the workplace.

In a bar, at a party, or at any sort of gathering which is meant on the surface to be celebratory, most of us switch gears, and attempt to maintain a pleasant front. At a party one drinks, smokes, and talks about nothing. One is attractive and easy to get along with, never tired or moody, never undergoing stressful situations or tragedy. For a little while, that is amusing, even positive, but any length of time spent in that world causes detriment to the body and the soul. Again, this is more applicable to women than to men, and especially in the movies on which this photograph was based, but certainly not specific to those.

Alcohol and cigarettes are crutches on which one may rely to numb pain, pass time, or ignore real issues. Drinking makes one dull, and in the long term, stunts emotional growth. It causes one to lose touch with one's self. The juxtaposition of the tears with the traditional meanings associated with champagne is what makes the photograph so real. In fact, the champagne works more effectively to make this comparison than any other form of alcohol would.

The theme of a woman's misery threatening her façade has found its way many times into art and literature. I am automatically reminded of Justine, a character in Lawrence Durell's *Alexandria Quartet*. Succinctly, Justine is a beautiful woman, married to a wealthy banker, who is haunted by events of her past, most of which she is not at liberty to talk about. She had a child that was stolen from her, and she was constantly reminded of the presence of a man who had taken advantage of her in her youth, to name just a few of her woes. On the surface, she was highly visible socially, and in a position to be envied; she was untouchably beautiful, was the wealthiest woman in the city, had a husband who loved her, but inside she was ravaged by her regrets and neuroses. In a similar vein, Neil Jordan wrote a short story about a woman making idle conversation at a party while in the back of her mind wondering where it was that her soul had gone. Granted, all of the stories here have very different elements, but that particular theme ties them all together.

For me, and possibly for many other women, the smeared makeup is the most powerful single signifier of this woman's self breaking through her projected persona. When a woman prepares herself to face the world, she puts on a mask. It is a defense mechanism, as well as a beauty aid. Some women rely on this more than others, some are more conscious of it than others, but the effect is essentially the same. The activities that smear eye makeup are the activities that threaten our façade of coolness. Sleeping, crying, or a mistake in application all reveal our real human qualities. If the photograph were to be narrowed down to just the eyes and the streaks of stained tears, it would still be a loaded visual text; the rest of the photograph only elaborates on what the eyes have already said.

This photo is of Sherman herself, but because she uses herself in every image she creates, through repetition she herself is phased out of significance, giving the spotlight to each specific persona. Sherman becomes a non-element in each photograph. The significance is placed on the aspects that are different from picture to picture, which create the person, or the stereotype. Of course, if the viewer sees only one of Sherman's photographs, this is not an issue. The image is so strikingly genuine that it is difficult, even with knowledge of the subject, to imagine its staging. Also, the woman's failure to acknowledge the camera makes us believe that we really are glimpsing straight into the scene, uninvited and unnoticed.

Through staged photographs Sherman is able to solidify this nebulous concept. The success of the photograph is in the fact that it has pinpointed the perfect image to display such a moment, and such an emotion. Its delivery relies on the viewer to make it anything other than thoughtless voyeurism, but it is unlikely that an image this powerful will miss its mark.

### Works Cited

Krauss, Rosalind. *Cindy Sherman, 1975–1993*. New York: Rizzoli International. 1993.

*Photography Exhibitions*, videocassette #11. Text and Interviews by Mark Miller. Art/New York. 1982.

Sherman, Cindy. *Untitled Film Stills*. Essay by Arthur C. Danto. New York: Rizzoli. 1990.

Jordan, Neil. "Her Soul," from *The Collected Fiction of Neil Jordan*. London: Vintage. 1997.

Durrell, Lawrence. *The Alexandria Quartet*. 4 vols. New York: E.P.Dutton & Co., Inc. 1957.

---

## THIS TEXT: READING

1. What method does Darby use to examine the photograph? Do you think this method would be effective for other photographs or texts?
2. What role does gender play in our ability to understand both Darby's essay and the photograph? In what ways does Darby address these concerns within the text?

## YOUR TEXT: WRITING

1. Write a short paper that examines the role a piece of popular culture played in your life, or a way a popular culture text you think reflects your own life.
2. Find a popular culture text you think reflects a particular attitude toward gender and do a reading of it through the lens of gender.
3. Compare Darby's approach with that of Susan Sontag. Which one do you find more effective in getting at the meaning of a photograph?

# The *Sensation* Suite

In a rare moment, the world of contemporary art made national and international news in November of 1999 when an exhibit of work by cutting-edge British artists angered New York City mayor Rudy Giuliani. The exhibit is now famous for featuring a painting by Chris Ofili of the Virgin Mary that included a dollop of elephant dung on her left breast, a picture of a topless woman presiding over the Last Supper, and some installations of preserved, severed animal parts cased in water and glass by artist Damien Hirst. The mayor, incensed by what he felt was "sick stuff," threatened to cut funding for the Brooklyn Museum, which housed the controversial exhibit. The exhibit also offended then Texas governor (now President) George W. Bush. Like Giuliani, Bush argued that the exhibit was in insult to Catholicism in particular and religion in general: "I don't think we ought to be using public monies to denigrate religion." However, many artists and critics have posited that the *Sensation* show was one of the most important in recent American history.

In this suite, we present four differing readings of the same text—the *Sensation* exhibition. William Buckley, a conservative, offers a reading of the exhibit from the right, though, it should be noted, from the moderate right. Peter Schjeldahl is the art critic for *The New Yorker* and remains one of the most accessible and enjoyable readers of the contemporary art scene. While Buckley's comments come from a political perspective, Schjeldahl's come from a perspective grounded in art history and criticism. You should be able to determine both Buckley's and Schjeldahl's writing situation based on how they read the exhibit. While Benjamin Ivry talks more about Ofili than the actual exhibit, his reading of Ofili and Foil's art offers a nice perspective from others in the media. Dana Mack begins the suite with a question similar to E. G. Chrichton's about the NAMES quilt.

In this suite, we'd like you to consider how various people read not only the individual art works but the exhibit as a whole. In what way is a reading of the *Sensation* exhibit a reading of American values?

## IT ISN'T PRETTY ... BUT IS IT ART?

Dana Mack

FEW AMERICANS WAKE UP MORNINGS contemplating the question of what makes a good work of art. But surprisingly enough, three belligerent public disputes have recently centered on this very question.

New York Mayor Rudolph Giuliani made headlines last month when he vowed to withhold municipal funding if the Brooklyn Museum of Art went through with its controversial British art exhibition, *Sensation*. The major object of contention: an image of the Virgin Mary, her breast rendered in elephant dung.

Then, a few weeks later, parents in South Carolina, Georgia, and Minnesota protested the presence in public school classrooms of J.K. Rowling's bestselling Harry Potter series, one mother claiming this fantasy literature carried "a serious tone of death, hate... and... evil."

Finally, there was the public uproar in Seattle over the heavily bosomed and pregnant *Picardo Venus,* a community garden statue many find too suggestive.

In each case, those objecting to the disbursement of public funds for the display of art they find offensive insist they are not for censorship. They claim they merely want publicly funded and publicly presented artwork to reflect community standards of taste, decency, and respect for religious faith. All well and good; but who is to define those standards? Chris Ofili, painter of the *Sensation* exhibition's much maligned *Holy Virgin Mary,* claims that Mr. Giuliani falsely assigned deprecatory motives to his work. He is not out to desecrate the image of the Virgin Mary, he says.

Rather, he's a Roman Catholic earnestly coming to terms with his faith, his African heritage, and a long Western tradition of representing the Madonna.

Similarly, J.K. Rowling might claim that the Harry Potter books also stand in a long "pre-apologetic" literary tradition: Yes, they deal with magic and witchcraft. Their tone is dark. But no less a devout Christian than C.S. Lewis understood the power of pagan imagery in preparing the young imagination for the moral rigors and spiritual comforts of biblical religion. Indeed, if there is something wrong with a "tone of death" in children's literature, then we might as well jettison all our volumes of fairy tales. For these distilled popular narratives exert their charm and power precisely, as Bruno Bettelheim pointed out, because they allow children a reality-removed way to confront the "existential predicament."

And what of the *Picardo Venus*? Must she be rejected, as one citizen-critic contended, because she "glorifies fertility a little too much for kids," or because, as another said, "no normal woman looks like that"?

Do "normal" women look like Picasso painted them? Or Rubens? Did not Botticelli's immortal *The Birth of Venus* also glorify fertility? The point is that almost all the arguments we bring against public support of controversial new works are at best specious, at worst manifestly wrongheaded. Informed aesthetic judgments seem to elude us.

Faced with creative works that seem to us alien and unappealing, we are forced to fall back on that proverbial disclaimer, "I don't know much about it ... I only know what I like."

Just because an artwork doesn't make us feel warm and fuzzy doesn't mean it's worthless. The Seattle man who protests against the *Picardo Venus* on the basis that "art is supposed to evoke all these good feelings" is wrong. Good art is not necessarily pleasing. It is, however, disciplined. It is about mastery of medium, form, and style. And good art must communicate something comprehensibly worthwhile, something worthy of contemplation.

And here we get closer to the aesthetic problem facing the American public today. More and more so-called artists today call attention to themselves by shocking and agitating rather than by promoting reflection. In reaction to these salvos, the public has come to anticipate offense.

How do we move past the disturbing impasse of public contention over art and toward a healthier, more vital cultural life? One answer is to be guided in our aesthetic judgments by three important principles:

1. Art doesn't do. It says. Art is not action; it is speculation. It is looking, listening, digesting, speaking. Art can make a controversial statement; but it cannot do controversial things. If the primary effect of a so-called artwork is physical repulsion or titillation, if it acts on us rather than speaks to us, it is simply not up to the standards of art. If it makes us think, however, we should take up the challenge.
2. Art is about content, not context. Art is the schematic arrangement of forms and symbols through specific, culturally recognized mediums. If we exhibit, say, a cow's embryo in an art museum, it does not suddenly become a work of visual art simply by virtue of its surroundings.
3. Similarly, if we hung a print of Titian's *Woman on a Couch* in a biology lab, it would scarcely transform that painting into a science display. We need to be open to the possibilities of the creative process; yet, we must recognize that not everything offered up in the artistic arena is art.

The greater the knowledge, the sounder the judgment. When we venture onto the battlefield of the culture wars, we owe it to our artists and ourselves to come armed with knowledge. In a multicultural society such as America's, that means making the attempt to familiarize ourselves with the major artistic traditions of Europe, Asia, and Africa. Before we criticize, we need first to understand. Indeed, there is nothing more inspiring to good artists than a public that can be communicated with on the highest and most subtle levels of creativity and skill.

## THOSE NASTY BRITS: HOW SENSATIONAL IS *SENSATION*?

Peter Schjeldahl

I'M SORRY, BUT I THINK that this whole Brooklyn Museum deal—the Mayor, the dung, all of it—is fun. An exhibition that was hopefully and is now aptly entitled *Sensation,* of works by an assortment of sometimes strenuously naughty young British artists, was fun to start with, not to mention

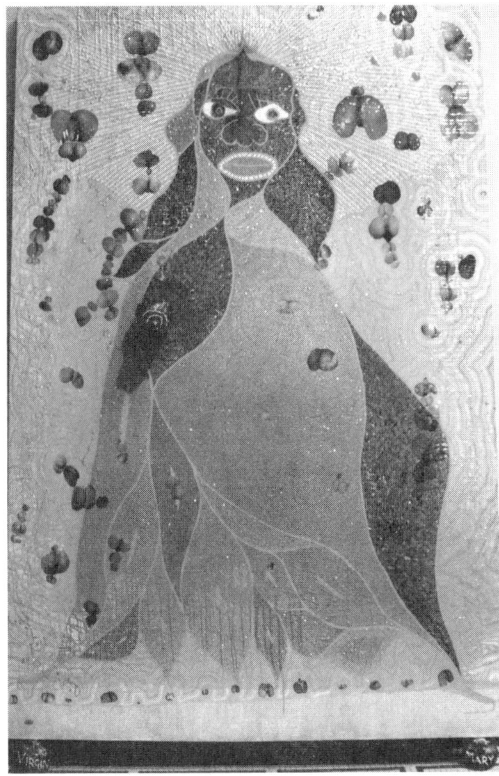

Ofili's *The Holy Virgin Mary*

good. (All the works are from the collection of the advertising mogul Charles Saatchi.) Rudolph Giuliani's P.C. intervention—politically correct in form and, I suppose, in Utica—makes it more fun. His determination to punish the grand and usually lonesome palace of culture on Eastern Parkway, where *Sensation* will run until January 9th, may assure attendance to rival that of the show's previous box-office successes, in London and Berlin. I imagine the artists shedding grateful tears, à la Sally Field: "He hates me! He really hates me!" One of them, Ron Mueck, contributed a huge self-portrait that hilariously resembles Giuliani. The museum has installed it in a gallery whose only other artwork is the object of the Mayor's wrath—*The Holy Virgin Mary,* by a thirty-one-year-old British artist of Roman Catholic faith and Nigerian ancestry named Chris Ofili.

In a show that offers plenty of other targets for indignation, the Mayor picked wrong—as might anyone who hadn't actually seen the exhibition. Ofili's lightning-rod canvas is gorgeous, sweet, and respectful of its subject, rendering her as a sternly hieratic African personage in petal-like blue robes. Much of the painting's surface shimmers ecstatically with glitter in yellow resin. Tiny collaged cutouts of bare bottoms from porn magazines evoke putti, and allude to the element of fertility in Mary's symbology, which Ofili did not invent. As for the pachyderm product, it is one smallish, attached lump, capped with what appears to be black-and-white beadwork (in reality pushpin heads) in a design of concentric circles. Elephant poop turns out to be innocuous-looking stuff, not unpleasant in color and almost decorative in texture (lots of straw). Ofili makes freer use of it in other paintings in the show. For example, turds affixed to a work entitled *Afrodizzia* are adorned with the names of black cultural heroes, including James Brown and Miles Davis. Ofili is a large-spirited artist who comes to praise, period.

Does it matter that Ofili is innocent of sacrilege? In political terms, probably not. His work's quality emerges only upon open-minded looking. It can't be summarized in a sentence, and no number of sentences will remove the lasting kick of one in which the words "the Virgin Mary" and "dung" rub shoulders. We know by now that whenever politics and art collide art loses—at least, in these United States, where anything cultural can become politicized at the drop of a grievance. In Britain, things are different. There politics gets culturized. Here we attack one another with charges of civic evil. They do it with insults, imputing personal awfulness. Now, awfulness is well within the ambit of negotiable artistic tones, while evil is not. In America, an artist can get away with many things within the art world, but he is crushed if exposed to public opinion. In England, where no one seems to get away with anything, public outrage may be hard to distinguish from cherishing. They fancy their nasties. Can we fancy them, too?

For awfulness aforethought, the cake in *Sensation* is taken by Damien Hirst's dead animals and fish, and his dying flies. In an epically disgusting sealed environment, filthy buzzers by the zillions incubate in a rotting cow's head, feed on heaps of sugar, mate, and meet death by a bug zapper as one watches or, perhaps, flees. Close behind are Sarah Lucas, the bard of East End bad-girl attitude, with her dirty-joke arrays of junk and foodstuffs, and Jake and Dinos Chapman, whose phantasmagorias of little-girl mannequins sprouting adult genitalia in odd places (faces, commonly) call for a genre coinage: pedography? I despise the Chapmans' work. I don't trust that they know half of what they are dealing with in presuming to advance themes of childhood and sex. Forget gross. I believe that the Chapmans' work is stupid—unlike that of Hirst and Lucas, with whom I feel in excellent, though unkind, hands. Hirst is some sort of great artist. His improbable balancing of brutality and finesse will thrill you if you can stand to let it.

The show's senses of "sensation" are more varied than one has been led to expect; it includes works of subtlety and even grace. Only about half of the forty-four artists go for the jugular. While we are dealing with those who do—or are reputed to—note must be taken of Marc Quinn and Sam Taylor-Wood. You have, perhaps, heard of a self-portrait bust fashioned out of nine pints of the artist's blood? That's Quinn's *Self.* It is a quiet presence in its refrigerated case, with dark, suave qualities of a lovely material that I am instantly aware of never having seen before. That the material is solid blood becomes a bit of detached information, adrift behind my eyes. Quinn's work is desperately elegant, and I like it very much. Taylor-Wood, who is a woman, makes photographic murals. *Wrecked* is a raucous burlesque of *The Last Supper,* starring pals of the artist as the disciples and—doing the Jesus thing—a bare-breasted woman. (Memo to Giuliani: sic 'em!) It will not make you forget the staggering send-up of the scene in Buñuel's "Viridiana."

Derivativeness is a major artistic issue in this show. It is sure to eclipse mere provocation as a sore spot for local art worldlings. Technical and formal imitation, often of American originals, abounds among these Brits. The sculptor Rachel Whiteread, who is the most respectably esteemed member of the crew, has made much of her career by copping an idea that Bruce Nauman nailed in the mid-sixties: taking casts of negative spaces in the real world. Nauman materialized the space under a chair. In Brooklyn, Whiteread fills a room with casts of the spaces under a hundred chairs. O.K., Nauman did his piece in dour cement. Whiteread uses tinted, light-thirsty resin, which is as appetizing as Gummy Bears. Is that difference enough? Meanwhile, Hirst's formaldehyded critters ape Jeff Koons's famous basketballs suspended in treated water, and the British artist's carnival-type spin paintings add nothing except large size and cute titles to precedents by the New Yorker Walter Robinson. Are we mad yet?

Well, the English didn't invent rock and roll, either. They just took it to peak levels. Is Whiteread Paul McCartney to Nauman's Buddy Holly? Is Hirst Mick Jagger? What, after all, is wrong with appropriating other people's high-art research to further one's own crowd-exciting development? Regarding American art, the show's message is mixed. On the one hand: sincerest flattery. On the other: a whiff of classical imperialism. You know, home country extracts raw material from colonies and sells back finished goods.

British artists have a group dialectic going, building on each other's variations. Here is a sample of critical prose from an essay in the show's catalogue by one of the artists, Martin Maloney: "Hirst, understanding [Mat] Collishaw's coup with the gunshot wound photograph, created work that brought together the joy of life and the inevitability of death, in the process transforming the secrecy of Collishaw's voyeurism into mass spectacle." Never mind what that's about. Roll the sound of it around on your brain. Maloney's confident high seriousness verges—but only verges—on Monty Python silliness. Hirst and his cohort steer happily between the sublime and the ridiculous, earning equally appropriate academic beard-stroking and tabloid frenzy. It's a matter not of "high" and "low" but of inside and outside: cooking to engage both the gourmets in the kitchen and the rabble in the soup line.

It has been said that London in the nineteen-nineties is New York in the eighties—history repeating itself as farce. By all accounts, however, the scene-makers over there are having a far better time of it than many of us did here in the viciously competitive, money-maddened, cocaine-fried eighties. This may be because the Brits have a real handle on a real conundrum—which is, roughly, how to square the special and contrarian nature of artists with the bland and complacent character of a vastly expanded audience. The two can't be squared is the British short answer. The long answer is that a high old time can be had when the situation is exacerbated as mordantly and inventively as possible. Like the honk of a foghorn in the night, the sound of an occasional exploding fatmouth indicates that these artists' course is dangerous and true.

## GIULIANI'S OWN EXHIBIT

William F. Buckley Jr.

NEW YORK SEPTEMBER 28—Mayor Rudy Giuliani of New York has given electric satisfaction, not only to many New Yorkers, but also nationwide to those who have had it with the aggressive pretensions of some artists and their impresarios. Mayor Giuliani, with his gift for barefisted formulations, focused on the Madonna exhibit (the object with porno vaginas decorating the Madonna and a clump of elephant dung on her breast), and remarked that "there is nothing in the Constitution that says that the First Amendment requires that the taxpayers fund aggressive, vicious, disgusting attacks on religion." He's got that right. He's got that almost right. What the First Amendment forbids isn't anti-religious exhibits on public property, but religious observances on public property.

The religious aspect of the dumb effrontery of the Brooklyn Museum people is the more transient question being argued. The more durable question has to do with what passes for art, and who and where responsibilities vest for passing judgment on such questions. What Giuliani has said about the *Sensation* exhibit, including the Madonna and such other features as a decomposing cow's head being munched by flies, and a sliced pig carcass . . . whatever, is that a museum partly financed by the City of New York has specifiable minimum responsibilities to the city, and that one of these is to refrain from public defecations over religious symbols.

On the matter of obscenity, the mind goes back to the last major public inquiry on the question. The sheriff of the City of Cincinnati served a grand-jury indictment in 1990 on the Contemporary Arts Center, which was featuring an exhibit of Mapplethorpe photographs which included depictions of the kind of thing men do to each other while communicating AIDS (of which Mapplethorpe died), and a bullwhip growing out of a male rectum. Well, it went to trial—and the jury exonerated the gallery on the charges of exhibiting obscenity.

An enterprising *New York Times* reporter (Isabel Wilkerson) gave the reading public a scoop by closely interviewing a juror. James Jones told the reporter exactly what had gone on in the jury room. What he said was that the jury had decided that it was simply unequipped to judge whether the exhibit was obscene under the rules set down by the Supreme Court in *Miller* v. *California* in 1973, which authorized prosecutions of matter that 1) appeals to prurient interest, 2) depicts sexual conduct in a patently offensive way, and 3) lacks serious literary, artistic, political, or scientific value.

Juror Jones reported that the panel was unanimous on the first two of the tests set down by the Court. But who were they to overrule the curator of the Cincinnati museum on whether the exhibit had serious artistic value? Mr. Jones gave an example of the problem the jurors faced. Look, he said, "it's like Picasso. Picasso, from what everybody tells me, was an artist. It's not my cup of tea. I don't understand it. But if people say it's art, then I have to go along with it."

They were troubled by it all. "Most of the eight jurors," Miss Wilkerson reported, "are working class, churchgoing family people who, even as they signed the verdict sheets, still could not believe that they were exonerating photographs that showed, in one case, a man urinating into another man's mouth. 'At one point we said to ourselves, is this really us making this decision?'"

The battery lined up against Mr. Giuliani is saying exactly what one would expect, which is that what must above all be protected is the freedom of the artist who has discovered elephant dung as his metier. Mayor Giuliani's reply is that the factor of public responsibility gets into the question, where public money is being used. His focus is on subsidized irreverence, rather than artistic independence. But he does not deny that anybody has the right to do anything with dung and Madonnas, but on their own time, under their own auspices. The effect of his ruling is rather a brake on artistic anarchy, than a call for public reverence; and it is primarily this stand of his that galvanizes public enthusiasm.

The *Sensation* show came over from London. There, sophisticated critics almost uniformly mocked it. The special hubris of artists is very much in the forefront of the dispute. "I don't understand it. But if people say it's art, then I have to go along with it." The mayor is standing up against the authority of city museum directors to rub their exhibitors' semen in the face of normal, sophisticated New Yorkers, on public premises. Mr. Giuliani is hardly a Philistine, and he has shown here at least as much courage as the depraved artist who believes that he should be protected by the United States Marines when he sorties into public museums to profane, in wild elaborations, the faith of a hundred million Americans.

# "MODERN ART IS A LOAD OF BULLSHIT": WHY CAN'T THE ART WORLD ACCEPT SOCIAL SATIRE FROM A BLACK ARTIST?

Benjamin Ivry

BRITISH ARTIST CHRIS OFILI hardly looks the type to foment revolutions: A handsome, diminutive man, the 30-year-old looks African, but he was born in Manchester and has spent his entire art career in England—except for six weeks in Africa, where he got the idea to use elephant dung as a substance in his art, for its sculptural qualities and metaphorical resonance. Not straight out of the elephant, mind you, but chemically treated to avoid putrefaction, odor and flies—unlike the gruesome work of his colleague, British artist Damien Hirst, whose cross-sectioned cows and other rotting animalia have offended gallery goers for some time now. In contrast to Hirst's putrefyingly sinister work and aggressively grubby persona, Ofili is self-confident and good-humored, given to disarming asides in interviews, such as his declaration about his sculpture *Elephantastic,* which displays a sculpted cock and hairy balls: "My balls are hairy."

Yet when Ofili recently won 20,000 pounds sterling as part of the Tate Gallery's noted Turner Prize, reaction was ill-humored indeed: The Web site ArtNet snobbily commented that Ofili is "known for garishly colored, ethnic-naive paintings with chunks of elephant dung attached to their surfaces." The assessment echoed a Brit tabloid's headline about a previous show at the Royal Academy featuring Ofili's work: "Foul Porn Invades Brit Art Gallery." An enraged British military draughtsman dumped a wheelbarrow of cow manure on the sidewalk in front of the exhibit, to prove that "modern art is a load of bullshit." It's a sentiment with which Ofili himself might agree.

It's hard to escape the conclusion that what has offended some people about Ofili is not just the elephant dung, but the combination of a black artist and dung. The military draughtsman admitted that while he was no fan of Hirst's dead animals, Ofili's dung was "the final straw." Yet Ofili is, in addition to being an imaginative artist, also a humorist and social critic of the art scene. He placed boxed ads in the tony Brit art magazine Frieze that read, simply, "Elephant Shit," amid ads announcing other art shows. He used lumps of dung to prop up some of his paintings. "Somehow it makes the painting feel more relaxed, instead of being pinned upon the wall like it's being crucified... [The painting can] stand in its own shit and watch the other paintings being crucified on the wall." He has placed dung in a paper bag for his installment *Bag of Shit,* and in 1993, held a Shit Sale in Brick Lane Market in London. He has played with the street parlance of "shit" as drugs, and the fact that some people have assumed he was selling drugs because of his dreadlocked hairstyle—hence his work *Shithead:* a piece of elephant dung, which resembles hashish, incorporating his own hair.

Ofili is all too aware of ethnic categorizing in the art world, which expects a black artist to be naive, tribal or shamanistic, and so declares about his six weeks in Zimbabwe: "It's [a] great country, but it's a foreign country for me and the idea of looking for your roots and stuff is ridiculous." He sees his success of the moment as having a token aspect, due to the fact that "maybe there aren't many good artists that coincidentally happen to be within the mainstream category of a British artist: white, heterosexual, more often than not, men." Ofili's art, despite its serious treatment of problems of culture and "sexual stereotyping," as the Turner Award citation points out, is also often amusing. The Turner Prize, despite its traditional-sounding name, has only existed since 1984 and was judged this year by a hardly academic small group that included Pet Shop Boy Neil Tennant and offbeat author Marina Warner.

Still, one of the last taboos for black artists is that of laughter: We are accustomed to somber, portentous and grandiose personalities like Nobel Prize-winner Toni Morrison. But what can prepare a gallery-goer for Ofili's works, which carefully offer a scroll with the name of the elephants from British zoos who donated the material—Liang-Liang from London Zoo, Geetza or Eza, the latter two, Ofili explains, being "the same elephant, in fact, but it's got two names"? With the celebratory gusto of Laurent de Brunhoff's Babar the elephant books, or F. Poulenc's orchestral suite they inspired, Ofili follows the elephants, not just for joy but for decorative power. He points out: "I'm interested in ideas of beauty...and elephant dung in itself is quite a beautiful object. But a different sort of beauty. And I want to bring the kind of beauty and decorativeness of the paintings together with the apparent concept of ugliness of the shit and put them together and try and make them exist."

But if some Brits seem unhappy with the idea of a droll black artist, the American art scene can be even more humorless. A recent Whitney Museum retrospective of gifted African-American artist Bob Thompson (1937–1966), an inspired combination of Nicolas Poussin, Emil Nolde and James Thurber, produced an admirable catalog published by the Whitney and the University of California Press. However, critics focused mainly on Thompson's death by drug overdose in his 20s, comparing him to Jean-Michel Basquiat, with whom he had nothing in common apart from being black. Thompson's art was given a murky, ill-focused cataloging by an unknown and unidentified Africanist scholar named Shamim Momin. But it cries out for analysis by someone as astutely entrenched in the Western art tradition as he himself was.

What brings creators like Thompson and Ofili together is more than their insistence on individuality, and the humor and beauty of their work; it's that they both refuse to be pigeonholed in any way. The brouhaha following Ofili's prize shows that his social satire is needed more than ever in the art world today. Not that he was humbled at all by the violent reaction—as he climbed the rostrum to accept his Turner Prize, he reportedly deadpanned: "Thank God. Where's my check?"

## THIS TEXT: READING

1. What was the particular sign or signs that set everyone off in this case? Why do you think that was? How are these signs normally seen in American culture?
2. What do you think the motivations of the artists were? Do you think they succeeded?
3. How would you characterize the responses to the exhibit? Are they predictable?
4. How does the idea of race enter into this discussion? Would the argument have a different tenor if the main artist were not black?
5. What do you think of Mack's definition of art? Is it your definition of art? Rudolph Giuliani's? Why do you think so many different people have different definitions of art?
6. Should government funding of art be contingent on whether the art work meets community standards of decency? Why or why not? Do artists and museums have the same right to freedom of expression even if they are taking government money?
7. Do you think the furor over the exhibit is really an argument over a semiotic situation? Why or why not?
8. The furor over the exhibit raises another question: Usually artists leave interpretation for the public. In this case, the artist defended the art work against essentially what was a misinterpretation. What do you think about the role of the artist presenting his or her work?

## YOUR TEXT: WRITING

1. Write your definition of art and give examples of how your definition works.
2. Call your local art museum and ask what their criteria for hosting an exhibit are. Ask whether their criteria include whether the work is controversial or not.
3. Compare the *Sensation* exhibit to the reception of a banned book such as J.D. Salinger's *Catcher in the Rye* or Henry Miller's *Tropic of Cancer*. Are those who banned the books using the same criteria for protesting the *Sensation* exhibit?
4. Research a paper on another argument over signs—the furor over Elvis Presley's hips rotating, or Ice T's "Cop Killer," for example.

# READING OUTSIDE THE LINES

## Classroom Activities

1. Bring in a slide or a photograph of a famous work of art. As a class, read the artistic text. How does reading it as a group change how you see it?
2. As a class, select an image from the book. Then, spend 15 minutes trying to redraw or reproduce the image. How does that change the image? How does it change how you see the image?
3. Bring a painting by Elsworth Kelley or Barnett Newman or Morris Louis to class. Or, look at a sculpture by Claes Oldenburg or Jeff Koonz. Have a discussion on whether these pieces are art. Why? Why not?
4. Look at a particularly incendiary artistic text in class, like Andres Serrano's *Piss Christ* or a Robert Mapplethorpe photograph or the Chris Ofili painting from the *Sensation* exhibit. What is the role of art, decency, and public opinion? Where and how do aesthetics and ethics meet? What cultural forces might prompt this kind of art?
5. Look at some photographs by Diane Arbus. What sort of comment is Arbus making about the world? As a class, discuss the ethics of Arbus's photos. Bring some of your own photos to class. How do your portraits of people differ from Arbus's? What do Arbus's photographs tell us about how she sees the world?
6. Look at some Warhol prints in class. Are his pieces art? Why or why not?
7. Talk about the differences between painting and photography. What can one do that the other cannot?
8. Take a field trip to look at some pieces of sculpture near or on your campus. How does sculpture adhere to the principles of artistic design?
9. Talk about the role of art in American culture. Compare how you think about art to how you think about television, film, and literature.

## Essay Ideas

1. Write a paper in which you define art, then, show why three paintings, photographs, or sculptures meet your definition of art.
2. Compare one of the images in this chapter to one of the poems in chapter one. How are painting and poetry similar? How are they different?
3. Write a poem about one of the images in this chapter, and then write an essay about the process of writing a poem about the image.
4. What is the relationship between gender and art? Many of the most famous paintings, photographs, and sculptures are of nude women. How has art altered how men and women see the female body?

5. In what way is how we see the world affected by what we believe or what we know? How does our background, our beliefs, our interests, and our personality affect how we see art? How does the political climate of our society affect how we see art?
6. Compare a Diane Arbus photograph with a classic painting. Are both art? Compare what della Francesca or da Vinci or Vermeer tries to do in his art with what Arbus tries to accomplish in hers. How might their respective cultures influence their ideas of what art should do?
7. Write an essay comparing Chrichton's questions about art and the NAMES quilt with Mack's questions about art and the *Sensation* exhibit. How do both pieces rise out of social or political unrest?
8. Look at some of the advertisements in this book. Using Acton's notion of composition, argue how advertisements adhere to notions of artistic design.
9. Write an essay in which you demonstrate and explain how a work of art makes a political statement.
10. Do you believe that public funding for the arts should be cut if the public finds the art objectionable? Can the public, if it supports an exhibit with its tax dollars, censor a work of art?
11. Write an essay on the artistic situation for one of the texts. What cultural or societal forces may influence what or how an artist creates?

# 8

# Reading Advertising and the Media

In the last 20 years, the word media has become almost an obscenity, particularly to those who are caught in its gaze. Such a sticky word demands a definition. While anything from books to magazines to news programs to radio shows to films is technically a medium—media is the plural of medium—for the purposes of this chapter, we will define the media as organizations or companies that seek to cover any kind of news in whatever form. We include advertising here as well, because although it doesn't cover anything, often it helps pay for the coverage we see. "The media" has become a symbol of a world whose happenings are broadcast 24 hours a day, where no subject seems too trivial or important to be covered. Everyone seems to think the media are too intrusive. And yet . . . we watch, and we watch, and we read, and we watch. If we didn't watch or read, the media would change because the media are not one entity, but many which change constantly. For instance, there was no cable television when the authors of this book were born, and thus no CNN. And when many of you were born, the Internet was only a military communications system, hardly the consuming force it is today. So whatever we write and think about the media now is destined to change for better or worse as our world changes.

Though the media are diverse in nature, they share a number of concerns that connect them. Almost all forms of media struggle to balance various concerns: public interest versus profit, fairness and objectivity versus bias, national coverage versus local, depth of coverage versus breadth of coverage, as well as some other more temporal concerns. The first conflict, balancing the public interest and the need to have the public watch, read, or listen, is often the one that gets the media into the most trouble; it leads to the charge that the media are shallow, intent on sensationalizing news. But all the conflicts lead to our sense that there is something "wrong" with the media, that something is not quite working right in the system. Yet, while the media are far from perfect (what is, after all?), they do perform a crucial role in American life and American culture. This introduction will begin to explain some of the difficulties and misconceptions attached to the media before going into articles that explore the media in more depth.

Separate but related elements of the media are the advertisers who have a crucial financial relationship with newspapers, magazines, web pages, television news, and television shows. In essence, advertising pays for our free television and subsidizes our purchase of magazines and newspapers—without ads, we would pay for broadcast television (it's why cable television generally and premium channels like HBO cost money) and pay a lot more for newspapers and magazines. What do advertisers get in return for their ads? The simple answer is public exposure for their products or services. The more complicated (and perhaps unintended) one is an influence in public life. Although some critics object to very existence of advertising in public life, most everyone acknowledges that advertising is the price we pay for living in a capitalist society. What is most criticized about advertising is the way advertising seeks to sell us products through manipulation and base appeals—its use of implicit and often inflated promises of various forms of happiness (sexual gratification, satiation of hunger, thinness, coolness) with the purchase of advertised items. When we consider these issues plus the sheer proximity of where and how ads and other media appear, it makes sense to think of these two entities as two sides of the same coin. While advertisers are not what people automatically think of as the media, their influence and importance in American society and their impact on various media outlets cannot be denied.

This introduction may seem one of our more political ones, but there is a reason for that: everyone, from liberals to conservatives, from the rich to the poor, from the young to the old, seems to criticize what the media do. Our purpose in asking you to "read" media and advertising in a complex way is to help you look for elements in the media worth understanding. We want to broaden and complicate your view of the media. The media are never one thing; they are complex entities made up of large and diverse elements.

## The media are a business not a public service.

While it covers the news, the media are in the business of selling newspapers or garnering ratings points. But as accepted protectors of the public interest, they also have obligations to the public—their connection to public interest is part of their business credibility. Some argue that because of the advantages given to television and radio networks by the government—exclusive use of broadcast frequencies for radio stations and various broadcast advantages to the big three television networks (NBC, CBS, and ABC)—that media outlets have further obligations to the public interest.

And yet at their hearts, the media are business organizations. As a way of trying to maintain some distance between the business side and the editorial (news) side, media organizations often try to separate the two divisions: the editorial side covers the news; the business side gets advertising and does accounting work. But these two elements often meet anyway. Special sections in magazines and in newspapers in which coverage is devoted to a particular event or phenomenon are the most obvious examples, but when we watch television some decisions seem motivated by the business component; local coverage of a business opening or prominently mentioning sponsorship of local events is an example of this interchange.

But in a media outlet with split organizations, keeping the business and editorial sides completely separate is impossible. Even the editorial side of large newspapers like *The New York Times* and *The Washington Post* may have unconscious motivations toward the business end; a newspaper is generally designed toward highlighting the most important stories, a tactic which will "sell" the newspaper to the patron. But the editorial side does not solicit ads directly, and makes little of those types of decisions. On the other hand, small town papers may make even less of a distinction between the editorial and business side. In smaller communities, the publisher, who either represents the owner or is the owner, *will* often influence editorial decisions, especially in the editorials of a paper.

So what are we to do with such information? Again, given the fact that the basic structures of media organizations are unlikely to change, the most important thing to do is to watch or read news with an active, sometimes skeptical eye, looking for links between business interests and media outlets. Even more importantly, read news widely. Look at "alternative" papers or read media criticism. Taking such steps will help you become a better reader of the media.

## The media are made up by a variety of people.

Do you think Tom Brokaw and the local weekly's columnist have similar roles in the media? Of course not—but the latter is as much a media member as the former. The large differences between members of the media (some of whom claim not to be) demonstrate what the media mean and do is complicated rather than simple. When columnists, politicians, or sport figures refer to the media, who, specifically, do they mean? Miss Manners? National Public Radio? The folks at the History Channel? The obituaries writer of your hometown newspaper? Probably they are thinking of the very few, very public media outlets like the major television networks, the overly aggressive talk radio personalities and perhaps some writers for national newspapers and magazines. But most members of "the media" are regular, virtually anonymous people who try to bring you interesting, important stories.

Although many members of the media have similar aims, their format and their audience shape their content. Radio news can only read a few paragraphs of a traditional newspaper story in its allotted time and has to rely on taped interviews to enhance it. A television news report has to focus on visual material, and national newspapers have different expectations attached to them than does the local weekly. To an extent, the format and mission of a news organization will dictate how it covers an event and sometimes even whether it will cover that event.

And different media do different things well—but the variety is what gives our media wonderful breadth and scope. Newspapers analyze long-term events better than television does, and magazines do it even better. But in covering house fires and the weather, and showing sports highlights, television is significantly better. Overall, the media have different elements that make various organizations better suited to do one job rather than another. It is important to note that there are very few absolutes when it comes to the media. Some newspapers and television stations are civic-minded organizations dedicated to upholding the public trust. Sometimes newspapers seem motivated more by financial concerns. Some ads are very entertaining. Some are offensive. Some media outlets try to present the news in the most balanced, most objective way they can. Other sources make no bones about being biased. The crucial thing is to be able to view the media generally, and advertising and the news specifically, with a critical eye.

### Despite what your favorite conservative radio or television talk show host says, the media are not particularly liberal.

You may not be familiar with the ongoing controversy of the supposed "liberal bias" of the media, but if you spend any time watching or reading columnists—both from the left (liberal) and right (conservative)—you will encounter claims of a liberal media. Actually the fact that someone points out that there is a liberal bias itself undermines the idea of one. If there is such a liberal bias, then how have we heard about it—through the conservative media.

You may think we exhibit a so-called liberal bias in taking this stance, but the business element that often shapes editorial content, especially in small communities and perhaps the networks as well, tends to be more sympathetic to conservative political ideals. And the fact that most media outlets recognize many conservative commentators probably shows how baseless this idea of a liberal media really is. Additionally, most publications do not foreground information that is of concern to liberals or liberal organizations. For instance, do you know of any major news publication with a "Labor" section? How about a section entitled "Feminism?" Or, for that matter, "Racial Equality"? Does your local radio station give an Environmental Awareness update? Probably not. However, every major paper devotes a great deal of time to its business section, and just about every radio station gives some kind of market news or stock report. Sports never get the short shrift, yet many sportswriters, owners of sports franchises, and many athletes themselves tend to be both politically and socially conservative. Lastly, simple coverage of events can reflect bias. In the September 2002 issue of *Harper's Magazine,* for example, the *Harper's* index lists the number of appearances made by corporate representatives on U.S. nightly newscasts in 2001 at 995, while the number of appearances of labor representatives was 31.

On the other hand, it may be unfair to accuse the media of leaning too far to the right. Most actors, filmmakers, and singers find affinity with left-leaning causes and, as you know, entertainment always makes the news. Both liberal and conservative groups assail the media for bias, which probably indicates that the media's bias falls somewhere in the middle. The media's political bias may or may not be of concern to you now, but it's one aspect of the media you will continually hear about as they play a larger and larger role in public discourse.

## The media are not objective, but they try to be fair.

Reporters and editors are human beings with political, social, and cultural preferences that they hope to acknowledge and put away when reporting. Reporters quickly learn they have to ask both (or many) sides questions when it comes to an issue. News stories often have this "she said, he said" quality. Does that mean the media always do a good job of being objective or fair? Definitely not, but they generally aim to do so. Those outlets with a specific political agenda are usually responsible enough to make that orientation clear in their editorial page or early in the publication or program. It's worth noting that editorial writers and columnists are absolutely under no obligation to be fair or objective; their object is to deliver their opinion for better or worse. Calls for their objectivity miss the point of what an editorial is supposed to do—deliver opinions.

Questions of objectivity and fairness are not only important when talking about the media but in your own work. As writers and researchers, we hope we are being objective when we undertake a subject, but we naturally come to any subject with a viewpoint that's shaped by our experiences and the ideas that come from them. That's why we may disagree with each other over whether we liked a movie or a book, or over which candidate we support in an election (or even who we find attractive or not).

Though reporters come with these personal likes and dislikes, they generally do understand their obligations to report the news fairly and generally serve the public interest, just as editorial writers and columnists understand their *mission* to seek to change public opinion. The bigger point here is that critics who claim a lack of objectivity from the media are uninformed about the reality of the media (sometimes deliberately so). The media often deserve the criticism they get from both liberals and conservatives, but an imperfect media is destined in any system, but in particular one whose primary focus are as business entities. Understanding these concerns will help you to understand the media in a more inclusive and a more informed way.

## Advertisers reflect consumers' desires as well as business' desire to sell to them.

There is a long-standing belief that advertising is manipulative and somehow unsavory. While we won't argue fully with those ideas, we believe it's important to think about what exactly advertising does. For one, we do think that advertising generally tries to sell us things we want (even if we "shouldn't" want them). Advertising items that consumers do not want is not a particularly effective use of advertiser's dollars. If you look at the majority of what advertisers sell, they consist of consumer items such as food, cars, clothing, electronics, and services—things that people want, though again the issue of how many of these things we should have or want is another question. Advertising can only influence a consumer so much—if a new snack food tastes like soap or broccoli, endorsements by every celebrity will still fail to sell it. Accordingly, some advertising experts believe that the greatest influence happens in choosing a brand at the point of sale, not in actually choosing to buy the product itself. Most of the marketing research that businesses do is *not* geared toward learning how to manipulate but learning what consumers will buy.

Yet the question of how far advertisers go in changing our attitudes about our world and what we should want is an open question that researchers continue to try to answer. We think that blaming advertisers for the perceived shallowness of human desire oversimplifies the roles advertisers and consumers play in deciding what they want.

In addition, both authors have been confronted in the classroom with the idea that the public is not very smart compared to the students themselves. In thinking so, students probably underestimate the intelligence of the public. If you assume the public is as savvy as yourself, you will save yourself this problem.

## Advertising and graphic design can be considered artistic.

Artistic components abound in advertising. Advertisers and directors of commercials compose their ads so that they are both aesthetically pleasing and effective at getting us to buy. Advertisers often use the same principles as artists by seeking tension, drama, comedy, and beauty in their work. And sometimes directors and artists do both commercial and more "artistic" work. For instance, film directors such as David Lynch and the Coen brothers have all done television commercials, and many artists do graphic design (including those involved in the Absolut Vodka campaign). What complicates graphic design and television commercials as art is their associations with commercial interests. Americans like to separate art from commerce; we'd rather have our artists make their money from selling their art to the community not to companies.

But what do we do when we see a funny or clever commercial or a piece of advertising that's particularly striking? Perhaps we feel at war with ourselves in trying how to place within a context what is clearly artistic expression and yet is trying to sell us something at the same time. Can we enjoy the art of advertising while decrying its influence? It's a difficult question. There are a lot of clever advertisements and interesting graphic design out there; to make a false distinction between high art and commercialism is to ignore how the texts of advertising and the texts of art actually work.

## Advertisers appeal to us through common images, whose meaning we have already learned.

Advertisers appeal to us through images that are iconic—standing directly in for something—or symbolic. Diamond manufacturers do not have to tell us that diamonds serve as an icon for sophistication and wealth—we already know that. Thus the diamond ring has become an icon for luxury, as has a spacious car with a leather interior and adjustable seats. We have learned what manicured lawns, Bermuda shorts, and gold jewelry mean by association. We know what it means to see a beach, golf clubs, a city, or any number of things or settings in a commercial. Because advertisers communicate through images as much as they do words, and these images seem to convey what they want without too much effort, looking at the visual language they use can tell us more about the role these images play in American culture.

## Researchers disagree about advertising's effects on consumers.

Many researchers, including some of the writers included here, believe there is a connection between advertisements and harmful behavior. Jean Kilbourne (not included here), for example, suggests that ads influence our children in harmful ways, particularly young women. Stuart and Elizabeth Ewen (see the Reading Media/Advertising Suite) believe in the subversiveness of the constant flow of advertising. Others are not so sure. Malcolm Gladwell's piece on "The Coolhunt" details advertisers' search for what is cool, so that can be advertised toward a sale. And Michael Schudson reports that ads influence us at the point of sale rather than on a macro level.

The authors are not convinced in one particular way, with this caveat. We believe the relationship between humans and any form of culture is complicated. We are not denying that there is a relationship between advertising and behavior—we're just not convinced about how direct it is. Similarly, we are not making any specific claims about the relationship between the media and advertising except to say that the two are increasingly intimately related and that we urge you to continue to be literate readers of both.

# Worksheet

## NEWS MEDIA

**Medium:** What form of media are you watching or reading? How does its form contribute to its coverage?

**Bias:** What point of view does the story seem to have? Are there some key words that indicate this? Do all the same stories seem to have the same viewpoint? If there is a bias, is the story still "fair"—does the reporter seek multiple perspectives?

**Signs:** When watching a newscast, how does the program communicate in image (video, photograph, graphic)? What symbols do they use? Are there any unintended meanings? How does the clothing of the reporters and anchors contribute to what we take from the newscast?

**Audience:** To what audience does the news article or news report appeal? How can you tell? Will others outside the target audience feel alienated by the report or article? What are news organizations assuming about their audience in a particular piece or the newscast, magazine, Web site, or newspaper as a whole?

**Reality:** Do the images and ideas match your idea of reality? Are they supposed to? Do they (the people reporting and presenting the news) see the world the way you do?

**Race, Ethnicity, Gender, Class:** How are images of any or all of these groups presented? Can you tell the bias of the reporter or news organization from their presentation?

## ADVERTISING

**Signs:** How does the advertisement speak to you through images? What do the images symbolize? Are there unintended meanings attached to the symbols? Can you classify the symbols into types? What do advertisers assume about the connections you will make between the signs presented and what researchers call "the point of purchase"?

**Audience:** What is the target audience of this advertisement? How do you know? What assumptions are advertisers making about their audience?

**Race, Ethnicity, Gender, Class:** How are images of any or all of these groups presented? Can you tell what advertisers think of these groups through their portrayal? Or their absence?

Advertising

# SOME HATED COMMERCIALS INSPIRE VIOLENT FANTASIES

Dave Barry

One of America's most beloved columnists, Dave Barry pokes fun at just about everything. Here, he takes on annoying commercials (1997). Barry's thesis is more implicit than explicit—can you discern an argument here?

ADVERTISERS BEWARE: MOST-HATED COMMERCIALS INSPIRE VIEWERS TO FANTASIZE ABOUT ACTS OF VIOLENCE

WHEW! DO I HAVE A HEADACHE! I think I'll take an Extra Strength Bufferin Advil Tylenol with proven cavity fighters, containing more of the lemon-freshened Borax that is recommended by doctors and plaque fighters for those days when I am feeling "not so fresh" in my personal region!

The reason I'm feeling this way is that I have just spent six straight days going through the thousands of letters you readers sent in when I asked you to tell me which advertisements you don't like.

It turns out that a lot of you really, REALLY hate certain advertisements, to the point where you fantasize about acts of violence. For example, quite a few people expressed a desire to kill the stuffed bear in the Snuggle fabric-softener commercial. "Die, Snuggle Bear! Die!" is how several put it.

Likewise, there was a great deal of hostility expressed, often by older readers, toward the relentlessly cheerful older couples depicted in the competing commercials for Ensure and Sustacal. These commercials strongly suggest that if you drink these products, you will feel "young," which, in these commercials, means "stupid." People were particularly offended by the commercial where the couple actually drinks a toast with Ensure. As Jamie Hagedorn described it: "One says, 'To your health,' and the other says, 'Uh-uh, to OUR health,' and then for some reason they laugh like ninnies. I want to hit them both over the head with a hammer."

Some other commercial personalities who aroused great hostility were Sally Struthers; the little boy who lectures you incessantly about Welch's grape juice; the young people in the Mentos commercials (as Rob Spore put it, "Don't you think those kids should all be sent to military school?"); everybody in all Calvin Klein commercials ("I am sure they are what hell is really like," observed Robert E. Waller); the little girl in the Shake 'N Bake commercial—Southerners REALLY hate this little girl—who, for what seemed like hundreds of years, said "And I helped!" but pronounced it "An ah hayulpt!" (Louise Sigmund, in a typically restrained response, wrote, "Your mother shakes chickens in hell"); Kathie Lee Gifford (Shannon Saar wrote, "First person to push Kathie Lee overboard gets an all-you-can-eat buffet!"); the smug man in the Geritol commercial who said, "My wife . . . I think I'll keep her!" (the wife smiled, but you just know that one day she will put Liquid Drano in his Ensure); the bad actor pretending to be Dean Witter in the flagrantly fake "old film" commercial that's supposed to make us want to trust them with our money; the woman in the Pantene commercial who said, "Please don't hate me because I'm beautiful" (as many readers responded, "OK, how about if we just hate you because you're obnoxious?"); and of course the Pillsbury Doughboy ("I would sacrifice my microwave to watch him inside on high for 10 hours," wrote Gene Doerfler).

Also, they are none too fond of the giant Gen X dudes stomping all over the Rocky Mountains in the Coors Light ads. (Matt Scott asks: "Will they step on us if we don't buy their beer?" Scott McCullar asks: "What happens when they get a full bladder?")

Also, many people would like Candice Bergen to just shut up about the stupid dimes.

Also, I am pleased to report that I am not the only person who cannot stand the sight of the Infiniti Snot—you know, the guy with the dark clothes and the accent, talking about Infiniti cars as though they were Renaissance art. As Kathleen Schon, speaking for many, put it: "We hate him so much we wouldn't buy one of those even if we could afford it, which we can't, but we wouldn't buy one anyway."

Speaking of car commercials, here's a bulletin for the Nissan people: Nobody likes the creepy old man, OK? Everybody is afraid when the little boy winds up alone in the barn with him. This ad campaign does not make us want to purchase a Nissan. It makes us want to notify the police. Thank you.

And listen, Chevrolet: People didn't mind the first 389 million times they heard Bob Seger wail "Like a rock!" But it's getting old. And some people wish to know what "genuine Chevrolet" means. As Don Charleston put it, "I intended to buy a genuine Chevy, but I couldn't tell the difference between the 'genuine' and all those counterfeit Chevys out there, so I bought a Ford."

But the car-related ads that people hate the most, judging from my survey, are the dealership commercials in which the announcer SHOUTS AT YOU AS THOUGH YOU ARE AN IDIOT and then, in the last three seconds of the ad reads, in very muted tones, what sounds like the entire U.S. tax code. Hundreds and hundreds of people wrote to say they hate these commercials. I should note that one person defended them: His name is George Chapogas, and he is in—of all things—the advertising business.

Perhaps by examining this actual excerpt from his letter, we can appreciate the thinking behind the shouting ads:

> I write, produce and VOICE those ads. Make a damn good living doing it, too. Maybe more than you even. And would you like to know why? Because they move metal, buddy.

Thanks, George! I understand now.

Well, I'm out of space. Tune in next week, and I'll tell you which commercial the readers hated the most; I'll also discuss repulsive bodily functions in detail. Be sure to read it! You'll lose weight without dieting, have whiter teeth in two weeks by actually growing your own hair on itching, flaking skin as your family enjoys this delicious meal in only minutes without getting soggy in milk! Although your mileage may vary. Ask a doctor! Or somebody who plays one on TV.

---

### This Text: Reading

1. What is Dave Barry's rationale for hating these commercials? What's wrong with the Snuggle Bear? Don't you think he's cute?
2. Why do we "hate" commercials? Is there a positive side, for the companies, to have the public feel so passionately about their products?
3. Are there commercials or references you don't recognize? If so, how does this affect Barry's argument?
4. What is Barry's writing situation?
5. Barry's essay is funny, and we may laugh with him, but what is he arguing? What's his thesis?

### Your Text: Writing

1. Write an essay in which you list and critique your three least favorite commercials.
2. Explore the relationship between the image an ad portrays and the actual product itself. Does hating the Snuggle Bear mean that you won't buy it to make your clothes softer?
3. Do annoying commercials turn us off products? Write an essay explaining how and why.

## THE COOLHUNT

Malcolm Gladwell

---

Malcolm Gladwell is the author of *The Tipping Point* and a frequent writer about culture for *The New Yorker*, a national magazine about the arts and politics. Here he explores the idea of cool and how advertisers try to find it (1997). In what way does Gladwell give a semiotic reading of "cool"?

Who decides what's cool? Certain kids in certain places—and only the coolhunters know who they are.

## *1.*

Baysie Wightman met DeeDee Gordon, appropriately enough, on a coolhunt. It was 1992. Baysie was a big shot for Converse, and DeeDee, who was barely twenty-one, was running a very cool boutique called Placid Planet, on Newbury Street in Boston. Baysie came in with a camera crew—one she often used when she was coolhunting—and said, "I've been watching your store, I've seen you, I've heard you know what's up," because it was Baysie's job at Converse to find people who knew what was up and she thought DeeDee was one of those people. DeeDee says that she responded with reserve—that "I was like, 'Whatever'"—but Baysie said that if DeeDee ever wanted to come and work at Converse she should just call, and nine months later DeeDee called. This was about the time the cool kids had decided they didn't want the hundred-and-twenty-five-dollar basketball sneaker with seventeen different kinds of high-technology materials and colors and air-cushioned heels anymore. They wanted simplicity and authenticity, and Baysie picked up on that. She brought back the Converse One Star, which was a vulcanized, suede, low-top classic old-school sneaker from the nineteen-seventies, and, sure enough, the One Star quickly became the signature shoe of the retro era. Remember what Kurt Cobain was wearing in the famous picture of him lying dead on the ground after committing suicide? Black Converse One Stars. DeeDee's big score was calling the sandal craze. She had been out in Los Angeles and had kept seeing the white teen-age girls dressing up like cholos, Mexican gangsters, in tight white tank tops known as "wife beaters," with a bra strap hanging out, and long shorts and tube socks and shower sandals. DeeDee recalls, "I'm like, 'I'm telling you, Baysie, this is going to hit. There are just too many people wearing it. We have to make a shower sandal.'" So Baysie, DeeDee, and a designer came up with the idea of making a retro sneaker-sandal, cutting the back off the One Star and putting a thick outsole on it. It was huge, and, amazingly, it's still huge.

Today, Baysie works for Reebok as general-merchandise manager—part of the team trying to return Reebok to the position it enjoyed in the mid-nineteen-eighties as the country's hottest sneaker company. DeeDee works for an advertising agency in Del Mar called Lambesis, where she puts out a quarterly tip sheet called the L Report on what the cool kids in major American cities are thinking and doing and buying. Baysie and DeeDee are best friends. They talk on the phone all the time.

They get together whenever Baysie is in L.A. (DeeDee: "It's, like, how many times can you drive past O.J. Simpson's house?"), and between them they can talk for hours about the art of the coolhunt. They're the Lewis and Clark of cool.

What they have is what everybody seems to want these days, which is a window on the world of the street. Once, when fashion trends were set by the big couture houses—when cool was trickle-down—that wasn't important. But sometime in the past few decades things got turned over, and fashion became trickle-up. It's now about chase and flight—designers and retailers and the mass consumer giving chase to the elusive prey of street cool—and the rise of coolhunting as a profession shows how serious the chase has become. The sneakers of Nike and Reebok used to come out yearly. Now a new style comes out every season. Apparel designers used to have an eighteen-month lead time between concept and sale. Now they're reducing that to a year, or even six months, in order to react faster to new ideas from the street. The paradox, of course, is that the better coolhunters become at bringing the mainstream close to the cutting edge, the more elusive the cutting edge becomes. This is the first rule of the cool: The quicker the chase, the quicker the flight. The act of discovering what's cool is what causes cool to move on, which explains the triumphant circularity of coolhunting: because we have coolhunters like DeeDee and Baysie, cool changes more quickly, and because cool changes more quickly, we need coolhunters like DeeDee and Baysie.

DeeDee is tall and glamorous, with short hair she has dyed so often that she claims to have forgotten her real color. She drives a yellow 1977 Trans Am with a burgundy stripe down the center and a 1973 Mercedes 450 SL, and lives in a spare, Japanese-style cabin in Laurel Canyon. She uses words like "rad" and "totally," and offers non-stop, deadpan pronouncements on pop culture, as in "It's all about Pee-wee Herman." She sounds at first like a teen, like the same teens who, at Lambesis, it is her job to follow. But teen speech—particularly girl-teen speech, with its fixation on reported speech ("so she goes," "and I'm like," "and he goes") and its stock vocabulary of accompanying grimaces and gestures—is about using language less to communicate than to fit in. DeeDee uses teen speech to set herself apart, and the result is, for lack of a better word, really cool. She doesn't do the teen thing of climbing half an octave at the end of every sentence. Instead, she drags out her vowels for emphasis, so that if she mildly disagreed with something I'd said she would say "Maalcolm" and if she strongly disagreed with what I'd said she would say "Maaalcolm."

Baysie is older, just past forty (although you would never guess that), and went to Exeter and Middlebury and had two grandfathers who went to Harvard (although you wouldn't guess that, either). She has curly brown hair and big green eyes and long legs and so much energy that it is hard to imagine her asleep, or resting, or even standing still for longer than thirty seconds. The hunt for cool is an obsession with her, and DeeDee is the same way. DeeDee used to sit on the corner of West Broadway and Prince in SoHo—back when SoHo was cool—and take pictures of everyone who walked by for an entire hour. Baysie can tell you precisely where she goes on her Reebok coolhunts to find the really cool alternative white kids ("I'd maybe go to Portland and hang out where the skateboarders hang out near that bridge") or which snowboarding mountain has cooler kids—Stratton, in Vermont, or Summit County, in Colorado. (Summit, definitely.) DeeDee can tell you on the basis of the L Report's research exactly how far Dallas is behind New York in coolness (from six to eight months). Baysie is convinced that Los Angeles is not happening right now: "In the early nineteen-nineties a lot more was coming from L.A. They had a big trend with the whole Melrose Avenue look—the stupid goatees, the shorter hair. It was cleaned-up aftergrunge. There were a lot of places you could go to buy vinyl records. It was a strong place to go for looks. Then it went back to being horrible." DeeDee is convinced that Japan is happening: "I linked onto this future-technology thing two years ago. Now look at it, it's huge. It's the whole resurgence of Nike—Nike being larger than life. I went to Japan and saw the kids just bailing the most technologically advanced Nikes with their little dresses and little outfits and I'm like, 'Whoa, this is trippy!' It's performance mixed with fashion. It's really superheavy." Baysie has a theory that Liverpool is cool right now because it's the birthplace of the whole "lad" look, which involves soccer blokes in the pubs going super-dressy and wearing Dolce & Gabbana and Polo Sport and Reebok Classics on their feet. But when I asked DeeDee about that, she just rolled her eyes: "Sometimes Baysie goes off on these tangents. Man, I love that woman!"

I used to think that if I talked to Baysie and DeeDee long enough I could write a coolhunting manual, an encyclopedia of cool. But then I realized that the manual would have so many footnotes and caveats that it would be unreadable. Coolhunting is not about the articulation of a coherent philosophy of cool. It's just a collection of spontaneous observations and predictions that differ from one moment to the next and from one coolhunter to the next. Ask a coolhunter where the baggy-jeans look came from, for example, and you might get any number of answers: urban black kids mimicking the jailhouse look, skateboarders looking for room to move, snowboarders trying not to look like skiers, or, alternatively, all three at once, in some grand concordance.

Or take the question of exactly how Tommy Hilfiger—a forty-five-year-old white guy from Greenwich, Connecticut, doing all-American preppy clothes—came to be the designer of choice for urban black America. Some say it was all about the early and visible endorsement given Hilfiger by the hip-hop auteur Grand Puba, who wore a dark-green-and-blue Tommy jacket over a white Tommy T-shirt as he leaned on his black Lamborghini on the cover of the hugely influential "Grand Puba 2000" CD, and whose love for Hilfiger soon spread to other rappers. (Who could forget the rhymes of Mobb Deep? "Tommy was my nigga / And couldn't figure / How me and

Hilfiger / used to move through with vigor.") Then I had lunch with one of Hilfiger's designers, a twenty-six-year-old named Ulrich (Ubi) Simpson, who has a Puerto Rican mother and a Dutch-Venezuelan father, plays lacrosse, snowboards, surfs the long board, goes to hip-hop concerts, listens to Jungle, Edith Piaf, opera, rap, and Metallica, and has working with him on his design team a twenty-seven-year-old black guy from Montclair with dreadlocks, a twenty-two-year-old Asian-American who lives on the Lower East Side, a twenty-five-year-old South Asian guy from Fiji, and a twenty-one-year-old white graffiti artist from Queens. That's when it occurred to me that maybe the reason Tommy Hilfiger can make white culture cool to black culture is that he has people working for him who are cool in both cultures simultaneously. Then again, maybe it was all Grand Puba. Who knows?

One day last month, Baysie took me on a coolhunt to the Bronx and Harlem, lugging a big black canvas bag with twenty-four different shoes that Reebok is about to bring out, and as we drove down Fordham Road, she had her head out the window like a little kid, checking out what everyone on the street was wearing. We went to Dr. Jay's, which is the cool place to buy sneakers in the Bronx, and Baysie crouched down on the floor and started pulling the shoes out of her bag one by one, soliciting opinions from customers who gathered around and asking one question after another, in rapid sequence. One guy she listened closely to was maybe eighteen or nineteen, with a diamond stud in his ear and a thin beard. He was wearing a Polo baseball cap, a brown leather jacket, and the big, oversized leather boots that are everywhere uptown right now. Baysie would hand him a shoe and he would hold it, look at the top, and move it up and down and flip it over. The first one he didn't like: "Oh-kay." The second one he hated: he made a growling sound in his throat even before Baysie could give it to him, as if to say, "Put it back in the bag—now!" But when she handed him a new DMX RXT—a low-cut run/walk shoe in white and blue and mesh with a translucent "ice" sole, which retails for a hundred and ten dollars—he looked at it long and hard and shook his head in pure admiration and just said two words, dragging each of them out: "No doubt."

Baysie was interested in what he was saying, because the DMX RXT she had was a girls' shoe that actually hadn't been doing all that well. Later, she explained to me that the fact that the boys loved the shoe was critical news, because it suggested that Reebok had a potential hit if it just switched the shoe to the men's section. How she managed to distill this piece of information from the crowd of teenagers around her, how she made any sense of the two dozen shoes in her bag, most of which (to my eyes, anyway) looked pretty much the same, and how she knew which of the teens to really focus on was a mystery. Baysie is a Wasp from New England, and she crouched on the floor in Dr. Jay's for almost an hour, talking and joking with the homeboys without a trace of condescension or self-consciousness.

Near the end of her visit, a young boy walked up and sat down on the bench next to her. He was wearing a black woolen cap with white stripes pulled low, a blue North Face pleated down jacket, a pair of baggy Guess jeans, and, on his feet, Nike Air Jordans. He couldn't have been more than thirteen. But when he started talking you could see Baysie's eyes light up, because somehow she knew the kid was the real thing.

"How many pairs of shoes do you buy a month?" Baysie asked.

"Two," the kid answered. "And if at the end I find one more I like I get to buy that, too."

Baysie was onto him. "Does your mother spoil you?"

The kid blushed, but a friend next to him was laughing. "Whatever he wants, he gets."

Baysie laughed, too. She had the DMX RXT in his size. He tried them on. He rocked back and forth, testing them. He looked back at Baysie. He was dead serious now: "Make sure these come out."

Baysie handed him the new "Rush" Emmitt Smith shoe due out in the fall. One of the boys had already pronounced it "phat," and another had looked through the marbleized-foam cradle in the heel and cried out in delight, "This is bug!" But this kid was the acid test, because this kid knew cool. He paused. He looked at it hard. "Reebok," he said, soberly and carefully, "is trying to get butter."

In the car on the way back to Manhattan, Baysie repeated it twice. "Not better. Butter! That kid could totally tell you what he thinks." Baysie had spent an hour coolhunting in a shoe store and found out that Reebok's efforts were winning the highest of hip-hop praise. "He was so fucking smart."

## 2.

If you want to understand how trends work, and why coolhunters like Baysie and DeeDee have become so important, a good place to start is with what's known as diffusion research, which is the study of how ideas and innovations spread. Diffusion researchers do things like spending five years studying the adoption of irrigation techniques in a Colombian mountain village, or developing complex matrices to map the spread of new math in the Pittsburgh school system. What they do may seem like a far cry from, say, how the Tommy Hilfiger thing spread from Harlem to every suburban mall in the country, but it really isn't: both are about how new ideas spread from one person to the next.

One of the most famous diffusion studies is Bruce Ryan and Neal Gross's analysis of the spread of hybrid seed corn in Greene County, Iowa, in the nineteen-thirties. The new seed corn was introduced there in about 1928, and it was superior in every respect to the seed that had been used by farmers for decades. But it wasn't adopted all at once. Of two hundred and fifty-nine farmers studied by Ryan and Gross, only a handful had started planting the new seed by 1933. In 1934, sixteen took the plunge. In 1935, twenty-one more followed; the next year, there were thirty-six, and the year after that a whopping sixty-one. The succeeding figures were then forty-six, thirty-six, fourteen, and three, until, by 1941, all but two of the two hundred and fifty-nine farmers studied were using the new seed. In the language of diffusion research, the handful of farmers who started trying hybrid seed corn at the very beginning of the thirties were the "innovators," the adventurous ones. The slightly larger group that followed them was the "early adopters." They were the opinion leaders in the community, the respected, thoughtful people who watched and analyzed what those wild innovators were doing and then did it themselves. Then came the big bulge of farmers in 1936, 1937, and 1938—the "early majority" and the "late majority," which is to say the deliberate and the skeptical masses, who would never try anything until the most respected farmers had tried it. Only after they had been converted did the "laggards," the most traditional of all, follow suit. The critical thing about this sequence is that it is almost entirely interpersonal. According to Ryan and Gross, only the innovators relied to any great extent on radio advertising and farm journals and seed salesmen in making their decision to switch to the hybrid. Everyone else made his decision overwhelmingly because of the example and the opinions of his neighbors and peers.

Isn't this just how fashion works? A few years ago, the classic brushed-suede Hush Puppies with the lightweight crepe sole—the moc-toe oxford known as the Duke and the slip-on with the golden buckle known as the Columbia—were selling barely sixty-five thousand pairs a year. The company was trying to walk away from the whole suede casual look entirely. It wanted to do "aspirational" shoes: "active casuals" in smooth leather, like the Mall Walker, with a Comfort Curve technology outsole and a heel stabilizer—the kind of shoes you see in Kinney's for $39.95. But then something strange started happening. Two Hush Puppies executives—Owen Baxter and Jeff Lewis—were doing a fashion shoot for their Mall Walkers and ran into a creative consultant from Manhattan named Jeffrey Miller, who informed them that the Dukes and the Columbias weren't dead, they were dead chic. "We were being told," Baxter recalls, "that there were areas in the Village, in SoHo, where the shoes were selling—in resale shops—and that people were wearing the old Hush Puppies. They were going to the ma-and-pa stores, the little stores that still carried them, and there was this authenticity of being able to say, 'I am wearing an original pair of Hush Puppies.'"

Baxter and Lewis—tall, solid, fair-haired Midwestern guys with thick, shiny wedding bands—are shoe men, first and foremost. Baxter was working the cash register at his father's shoe store in Mount Prospect, Illinois, at the age of thirteen. Lewis was doing inventory in his father's shoe store in Pontiac, Michigan, at the age of seven. Baxter was in the National Guard during the 1968 Democratic Convention, in Chicago, and was stationed across the street from the Conrad Hilton downtown, right in the middle of things. Today, the two men work out of Rockford, Michigan (population thirty-eight hundred), where Hush Puppies has been making the Dukes and the Columbias in an old factory down by the Rogue River for almost forty years. They took me to the plant when I was in Rockford. In a crowded, noisy, low-slung building, factory workers stand in long rows, gluing, stapling, and sewing together shoes in dozens of bright colors, and the two executives stopped at each production station and described it in detail. Lewis and Baxter know shoes. But they would be the first to admit that they don't know cool. "Miller was saying that there is something going on with the shoes—that Isaac Mizrahi was wearing the shoes for his personal use," Lewis told me. We were seated around the conference table in the Hush Puppies headquarters in Rockford, with the snow and the trees outside and a big water tower behind us. "I think it's fair to say that at the time we had no idea who Isaac Mizrahi was."

By late 1994, things had begun to happen in a rush. First, the designer John Bartlett called. He wanted to use Hush Puppies as accessories in his spring collection. Then Anna Sui called. Miller, the man from Manhattan, flew out to Michigan to give advice on a new line ("Of course, packing my own food and thinking about 'Fargo' in the corner of my mind"). A few months later, in Los Angeles, the designer Joel Fitzpatrick put a twenty-five-foot inflatable basset hound on the roof of his store on La Brea Avenue and gutted his adjoining art gallery to turn it into a Hush Puppies department, and even before he opened—while he was still painting and putting up shelves—Pee-wee Herman walked in and asked for a couple of pairs. Pee-wee Herman! "It was total word of mouth. I didn't even have a sign back then," Fitzpatrick recalls. In 1995, the company sold four hundred and thirty thousand pairs of the classic Hush Puppies. In 1996, it sold a million six hundred thousand, and that was only scratching the surface, because in Europe and the rest of the world, where Hush Puppies have a huge following—where they might outsell the American market four to one—the revival was just beginning.

The cool kids who started wearing old Dukes and Columbias from thrift shops were the innovators. Pee-wee Herman, wandering in off the street, was an early adopter. The million six hundred thousand people who bought Hush Puppies last year are the early majority, jumping in because the really cool people have already blazed the trail. Hush Puppies are moving through the country just the way hybrid seed corn moved through Greene County—all of which illustrates what coolhunters can and cannot do. If Jeffrey Miller had been wrong—if cool people hadn't been digging through the thrift shops for Hush Puppies—and he had arbitrarily decided that Baxter and Lewis should try to convince non-cool people that the shoes were cool, it wouldn't have worked. You can't convince the late majority that Hush Puppies are cool, because the late majority makes its coolness decisions on the basis of what the early majority is doing, and you can't convince the early majority, because the early majority is looking at the early adopters, and you can't convince the early adopters, because they take their cues from the innovators. The innovators do get their cool ideas from people other than their peers, but the fact is that they are the last people who can be convinced by a marketing campaign that a pair of suede shoes is cool. These are, after all, the people who spent hours sifting through thrift-store bins. And why did they do that? Because their definition of cool is doing something that nobody else is doing. A company can intervene in the cool cycle. It can put its shoes on really cool celebrities and on fashion runways and on MTV. It can accelerate the transition from the innovator to the early adopter and on to the early majority. But it can't just manufacture cool out of thin air, and that's the second rule of cool.

At the peak of the Hush Puppies craziness last year, Hush Puppies won the prize for best accessory at the Council of Fashion Designers' awards dinner, at Lincoln Center. The award was accepted by the Hush Puppies president, Louis Dubrow, who came out wearing a pair of custom-made black patent-leather Hush Puppies and stood there blinking and looking at the assembled crowd as if it were the last scene of "Close Encounters of the Third Kind." It was a strange moment. There was the president of the Hush Puppies company, of Rockford, Michigan, population thirty-eight hundred, sharing a stage with Calvin Klein and Donna Karan and Isaac Mizrahi—and all because some kids in the East Village began combing through thrift shops for old Dukes. Fashion was at the mercy of those kids, whoever they were, and it was a wonderful thing if the kids picked you, but a scary thing, too, because it meant that cool was something you could not control. You needed someone to find cool and tell you what it was.

## 3.

When Baysie Wightman went to Dr. Jay's, she was looking for customer response to the new shoes Reebok had planned for the fourth quarter of 1997 and the first quarter of 1998. This kind of customer testing is critical at Reebok, because the last decade has not been kind to the company. In 1987, it had a third of the American athletic-shoe market, well ahead of Nike. Last year, it had sixteen per cent. "The kid in the store would say, 'I'd like this shoe if your logo wasn't on it,'" E. Scott Morris, who's a senior designer for Reebok, told me. "That's kind of a punch in the mouth. But we've all seen it. You go into a shoe store. The kid picks up the shoe and says, 'Ah, man, this is nice.' He turns the shoe around and around. He looks at it underneath. He looks at the side and he goes, 'Ah, this is Reebok,' and says, 'I ain't buying this,' and puts the shoe down and walks out. And you go, 'You was just digging it a minute ago. What happened?'" Somewhere along the way, the company lost its cool, and Reebok now faces the task not only of rebuilding its image but of making the shoes so cool that the kids in the store can't put them down.

Every few months, then, the company's coolhunters go out into the field with prototypes of the upcoming shoes to find out what kids really like, and come back to recommend the necessary changes. The prototype of one recent Emmitt Smith shoe, for example, had a piece of molded rubber on the end of the tongue as a design element; it was supposed to give the shoe a certain "richness," but the kids said they thought it looked overbuilt. Then Reebok gave the shoes to the Boston College football team for wear-testing, and when they got the shoes back they found out that all the football players had cut out the rubber component with scissors. As messages go, this was hard to miss. The tongue piece wasn't cool, and on the final version of the shoe it was gone. The rule of thumb at Reebok is that if the kids in Chicago, New York, and Detroit all like a shoe, it's a guaranteed hit. More than likely, though, the coolhunt is going to turn up subtle differences from city to city, so that once the coolhunters come back the designers have to find out some way to synthesize what was heard, and pick out just those things that all the kids seemed to agree on. In New York, for example, kids in Harlem are more sophisticated and fashion-forward than kids in the Bronx, who like things a little more colorful and glitzy. Brooklyn, meanwhile, is conservative and preppy, more like Washington, D.C. For reasons no one really knows, Reeboks are coolest in Philadelphia. In Philly, in fact, the Reebok Classics are so huge they are known simply as National Anthems, as in "I'll have a pair of blue Anthems in nine and a half." Philadelphia is Reebok's innovator town. From there trends move along the East Coast, trickling all the way to Charlotte, North Carolina.

Reebok has its headquarters in Stoughton, Massachusetts, outside Boston—in a modern corporate park right off Route 24. There are basketball and tennis courts next to the building, and a health club on the ground floor that you can look directly into from the parking lot. The front lobby is adorned with shrines for all of Reebok's most prominent athletes—shrines complete with dramatic action photographs, their sports jerseys, and a pair of their signature shoes—and the halls are filled with so many young, determinedly athletic people that when I visited Reebok headquarters I suddenly wished I'd packed my gym clothes in case someone challenged me to wind sprints. At Stoughton, I met with a handful of the company's top designers and marketing executives in a long conference room on the third floor. In the course of two hours, they put one pair of shoes after another on the table in front of me, talking excitedly about each sneaker's prospects, because the feeling at Reebok is that things are finally turning around. The basketball shoe that Reebok brought out last winter for Allen Iverson, the star rookie guard for the Philadelphia 76ers, for example, is one of the hottest shoes in the country. Dr. Jay's sold out of Iversons in two days, compared with the week it took the store to sell out of Nike's new Air Jordans. Iverson himself is brash and charismatic and faster from foul line to foul line than anyone else in the league. He's the equivalent of those kids in the East Village who began wearing Hush Puppies way back when. He's an innovator, and the hope at Reebok is that if he gets big enough the whole company can ride back to coolness on his coattails, the way Nike rode to coolness on the coattails of Michael Jordan. That's why Baysie was so excited when the kid said Reebok was trying to get butter when he looked at the Rush and the DMX RXT: it was a sign, albeit a small one, that the indefinable, abstract thing called cool was coming back.

When Baysie comes back from a coolhunt, she sits down with marketing experts and sales representatives and designers, and reconnects them to the street, making sure they have the right shoes going to the right places at the right price. When she got back from the Bronx, for example, the first thing she did was tell all these people they had to get a new men's DMX RXT out, fast, because the kids on the street loved the women's version. "It's hotter than we realized," she told them. The coolhunter's job in this instance is very specific. What DeeDee does, on the other hand, is a little more ambitious. With the L Report, she tries to construct a kind of grand matrix of cool, comprising not just shoes but everything kids like, and not just kids of certain East Coast urban markets but kids all over. DeeDee and her staff put it out four times a year, in six different versions—for New York, Los Angeles, San Francisco, Austin–Dallas, Seattle, and Chicago—and then sell it to manufacturers, retailers, and ad agencies (among others) for twenty thousand dollars a year. They go to each city and find the coolest bars and clubs, and ask the coolest kids to fill out questionnaires. The information is then divided into six categories—You Saw It Here First, Entertainment and Leisure, Clothing and Accessories, Personal and Individual, Aspirations, and Food and Beverages—which are, in turn, broken up into dozens of subcategories, so that Personal and Individual, for example, includes Cool Date, Cool Evening, Free Time, Favorite Possession, and on and on. The information in those subcategories is subdivided again by sex and by age bracket (14–18, 19–24, 25–30), and then, as a control, the L Report gives you the corresponding set of preferences for "mainstream" kids.

Few coolhunters bother to analyze trends with this degree of specificity. DeeDee's biggest competitor, for example, is something called the Hot Sheet, out of Manhattan. It uses a panel of three thousand kids a year from across the country and divides up their answers by sex and age, but it doesn't distinguish between regions, or between trendsetting and mainstream respondents. So what you're really getting is what all kids think is cool—not what cool kids think is cool, which is a considerably different piece of information. Janine Misdom and Joanne DeLuca, who run the Sputnik coolhunting group out of the garment district in Manhattan, meanwhile, favor an entirely impressionistic approach, sending out coolhunters with video cameras to talk to kids on the ground that it's too difficult to get cool kids to fill out questionnaires. Once, when I was visiting the Sputnik girls—as Misdom and DeLuca are known on the street, because they look alike and their first names are so similar and both have the same awesome New York accents—they showed me a video of the girl they believe was the patient zero of the whole eighties revival going on right now. It was back in September of 1993. Joanne and Janine were on Seventh Avenue, outside the

Fashion Institute of Technology, doing random street interviews for a major jeans company, and, quite by accident, they ran into this nineteen-year-old raver. She had close-cropped hair, which was green at the top, and at the temples was shaved even closer and dyed pink. She had rings and studs all over her face, and a thick collection of silver tribal jewelry around her neck, and vintage jeans. She looked into the camera and said, "The sixties came in and then the seventies came in and I think it's ready to come back to the eighties. It's totally eighties: the eye makeup, the clothes. It's totally going back to that." Immediately, Joanne and Janine started asking around. "We talked to a few kids on the Lower East Side who said they were feeling the need to start breaking out their old Michael Jackson jackets," Joanne said. "They were joking about it. They weren't doing it yet. But they were going to, you know? They were saying, 'We're getting the urge to break out our Members Only jackets.'" That was right when Joanne and Janine were just starting up; calling the eighties revival was their first big break, and now they put out a full-blown videotaped report twice a year which is a collection of clips of interviews with extremely progressive people.

What DeeDee argues, though, is that cool is too subtle and too variegated to be captured with these kind of broad strokes. Cool is a set of dialects, not a language. The L Report can tell you, for example, that nineteen-to-twenty-four-year-old male trendsetters in Seattle would most like to meet, among others, King Solomon and Dr. Seuss, and that nineteen-to-twenty-four-year-old female trendsetters in San Francisco have turned their backs on Calvin Klein, Nintendo Gameboy, and sex. What's cool right now? Among male New York trendsetters: North Face jackets, rubber and latex, khakis, and the rock band Kiss. Among female trendsetters: ska music, old-lady clothing, and cyber tech. In Chicago, snowboarding is huge among trendsetters of both sexes and all ages. Women over nineteen are into short hair, while those in their teens have embraced mod culture, rock climbing, tag watches, and bootleg pants. In Austin–Dallas, meanwhile, twenty-five-to-thirty-year-old women trendsetters are into hats, heroin, computers, cigars, Adidas, and velvet, while men in their twenties are into video games and hemp. In all, the typical L Report runs over one hundred pages. But with that flood of data comes an obsolescence disclaimer: "The fluctuating nature of the trendsetting market makes keeping up with trends a difficult task." By the spring, in other words, everything may have changed.

The key to coolhunting, then, is to look for cool people first and cool things later, and not the other way around. Since cool things are always changing, you can't look for them, because the very fact they are cool means you have no idea what to look for. What you would be doing is thinking back on what was cool before and extrapolating, which is about as useful as presuming that because the Dow rose ten points yesterday it will rise another ten points today. Cool people, on the other hand, are a constant.

When I was in California, I met Salvador Barbier, who had been described to me by a coolhunter as "the Michael Jordan of skateboarding." He was tall and lean and languid, with a cowboy's insouciance, and we drove through the streets of Long Beach at fifteen miles an hour in a white late-model Ford Mustang, a car he had bought as a kind of ironic status gesture ("It would look good if I had a Polo jacket or maybe Nautica," he said) to go with his '62 Econoline van and his '64 T-bird. Sal told me that he and his friends, who are all in their mid-twenties, recently took to dressing up as if they were in eighth grade again and gathering together—having a "rally"—on old BMX bicycles in front of their local 7-Eleven. "I'd wear muscle shirts, like Def Leppard or Foghat or some old heavy-metal band, and tight, tight tapered Levi's, and Vans on my feet—big, like, checkered Vans or striped Vans or camouflage Vans—and then wristbands and gloves with the fingers cut off. It was total eighties fashion. You had to look like that to participate in the rally. We had those denim jackets with patches on the back and combs that hung out the back pocket. We went without I.D.s, because we'd have to have someone else buy us beers." At this point, Sal laughed. He was driving really slowly and staring straight ahead and talking in a low drawl—the coolhunter's dream. "We'd ride to this bar and I'd have to carry my bike inside, because we have really expensive bikes, and when we got inside people would freak out. They'd say, 'Omigod,' and I was asking them if they wanted to go for a ride on the handlebars. They were like, 'What is wrong with you. My boyfriend used to dress like that in the eighth grade!' And I was like, 'He was probably a lot cooler then, too.'"

This is just the kind of person DeeDee wants. "I'm looking for somebody who is an individual, who has definitely set himself apart from everybody else, who doesn't look like his peers. I've run into trendsetters who look completely Joe Regular Guy. I can see Joe Regular Guy at a club listening to some totally hardcore band playing, and I say to myself 'Omigod, what's that guy doing here?' and that totally intrigues me, and I have to walk up to him and say, 'Hey, you're really into this band. What's up?' You know what I mean? I look at everything. If I see Joe Regular Guy sitting in a coffee shop and everyone around him has blue hair, I'm going to gravitate toward him, because, hey, what's Joe Regular Guy doing in a coffee shop with people with blue hair?"

We were sitting outside the Fred Segal store in West Hollywood. I was wearing a very conservative white Brooks Brothers button-down and a pair of Levi's, and DeeDee looked first at my shirt and then my pants and dissolved into laughter: "I mean, I might even go up to you in a cool place."

Picking the right person is harder than it sounds, though. Piney Kahn, who works for DeeDee, says, "There are a lot of people in the gray area. You've got these kids who dress ultra funky and have their own style. Then you realize they're just running after their friends." The trick is not just to be able to tell who is different but to be able to tell when that difference represents something truly cool. It's a gut thing. You have to somehow just know. DeeDee hired Piney because Piney clearly knows: she is twenty-four and used to work with the Beastie Boys and has the formidable self-possession of someone who is not only cool herself but whose parents were cool. "I mean," she says, "they named me after a tree."

Piney and DeeDee said that they once tried to hire someone as a cool-hunter who was not, himself, cool, and it was a disaster.

"You can give them the boundaries," Piney explained. "You can say that if people shop at Banana Republic and listen to Alanis Morissette they're probably not trendsetters. But then they might go out and assume that everyone who does that is not a trendsetter, and not look at the other things."

"I mean, I myself might go into Banana Republic and buy a T-shirt," DeeDee chimed in.

Their non-cool coolhunter just didn't have that certain instinct, that sense that told him when it was O.K. to deviate from the manual. Because he wasn't cool, he didn't know cool, and that's the essence of the third rule of cool: you have to be one to know one. That's why Baysie is still on top of this business at forty-one. "It's easier for me to tell you what kid is cool than to tell you what things are cool," she says. But that's all she needs to know. In this sense, the third rule of cool fits perfectly into the second: the second rule says that cool cannot be manufactured, only observed, and the third says that it can only be observed by those who are themselves cool. And, of course, the first rule says that it cannot accurately be observed at all, because the act of discovering cool causes cool to take flight, so if you add all three together they describe a closed loop, the hermeneutic circle of coolhunting, a phenomenon whereby not only can the uncool not see cool but cool cannot even be adequately described to them. Baysie says that she can see a coat on one of her friends and think it's not cool but then see the same coat on DeeDee and think that it is cool. It is not possible to be cool, in other words, unless you are—in some larger sense—already cool, and so the phenomenon that the uncool cannot see and cannot have described to them is also something that they cannot ever attain, because if they did it would no longer be cool. Coolhunting represents the ascendancy, in the marketplace, of high school.

Once, I was visiting DeeDee at her house in Laurel Canyon when one of her L Report assistants, Jonas Vail, walked in. He'd just come back from Niketown on Wilshire Boulevard, where he'd bought seven hundred dollars' worth of the latest sneakers to go with the three hundred dollars' worth of skateboard shoes he'd bought earlier in the afternoon. Jonas is tall and expressionless, with a peacoat, dark jeans, and short-cropped black hair. "Jonas is good," DeeDee says. "He works with me on everything. That guy knows more pop culture. You know: What was the name of the store Mrs. Garrett owned on 'The Facts of Life'? He knows all the names of the extras from eighties sitcoms. I can't believe someone like him exists. He's fucking unbelievable. Jonas can spot a cool person a mile away."

Jonas takes the boxes of shoes and starts unpacking them on the couch next to DeeDee. He picks up a pair of the new Nike ACG hiking boots, and says, "All the Japanese in Niketown were really into these." He hands the shoes to DeeDee.

"Of *course* they were!" she says. "The Japanese are all into the tech-looking shit. Look how exaggerated it is, how bulbous." DeeDee has very ambivalent feelings about Nike, because she thinks its marketing has got out of hand. When she was in the New York Niketown with a girlfriend recently, she says, she started getting light-headed and freaked out. "It's cult, cult, cult. It was like, 'Hello, are we all drinking the Kool-Aid here?'" But this shoe she loves. It's Dr. Jay's in the Bronx all over again. DeeDee turns the shoe around and around in the air, tapping the big clear-blue plastic bubble on the side—the visible Air-Sole unit—with one finger. "It's so fucking rad. It looks like a platypus!" In front of me, there is a pair of Nike's new shoes for the basketball player Jason Kidd.

I pick it up. "This looks . . . cool," I venture uncertainly.

DeeDee is on the couch, where she's surrounded by shoeboxes and sneakers and white tissue paper, and she looks up reprovingly because, of course, I don't get it. I can't get it. "Beyooond cool, Maalcolm. Beyooond cool."

---

## This Text: Reading

1. What do you think Gladwell's opinion about advertising generally is? How about the people he writes about? What words or phrases in the essay contribute to this idea?
2. Do you know anyone who would be a good candidate for a "coolhunter"? What qualities does that person have? Are those qualities you want?
3. How do you define cool? What's the difference between the qualities advertisers and video makers think are cool and the ones you think are cool?
4. From what perspective is Gladwell writing? What audience do you think he's appealing to?
5. What do you think Gladwell's opinion of advertising is? What reveals this in the article?

## Your Text: Writing

1. Spend an afternoon in a public space and do your own cool hunt. What do you notice as being cool? What are the semiotics involved—what signs do you interpret as cool? Do you think your coolhunt would be the same as someone else's? Write a short essay on your idea of cool and how it's reflected in society.

2. Cool is a term that's been around for ages, at least since the 1930s, when it was associated with jazz music. And yet it means something different to different people in every era and is constantly undergoing change. Can you think of other words or ideas which have undergone such changes in your own life or in the culture around you? Write a short essay.
3. Do you think that once something is proclaimed as cool, it loses some or all of its "coolness"? Trace the cool factor of a particular item, like a piece of clothing or a toy.

## ADVERTISING AND PEOPLE OF COLOR

Clint C. Wilson and Felix Gutierrez

By giving semiotic readings of some disturbing advertisements, Wilson and Gutierrez demonstrate how people of color and stereotypes about ethnicities have been exploited to sell various items (1995). As you read, pay attention to how the authors blend research and their own interpretation of visual texts.

Also, as we mention in "Reading an Advertisement" in our Introduction, it is often difficult to obtain permission to reprint advertisements. As it turns out, we were denied permission to print all three ads that appear in the original version of this essay—most likely because companies have become more sensitive to the personal and legal ramifications of racial stereotyping. In one ad for Cream of Wheat, Rastus, a black servant in a chef's cap, holds a blackboard containing information about Cream of Wheat written in African American dialect. The other, an ad for Crown Royal aimed at Hispanic audiences, shows five clearly wealthy well-dressed Latinos and Latinas drinking Crown Royal at what appears to be a fancy birthday party. The text for the ad, "Comparta sus riquezas" ("Share the Wealth") is in Spanish. Finally, though AT&T did deny us permission to print the original ad, they did agree to let us run an updated one. The original shows a young Chinese girl holding a phone. Appearing in Chinese newspapers in the United States, the ad ran only in Chinese.

GIVEN THE SOCIAL AND LEGAL RESTRICTIONS on the participation of racial minorities in the society of the United States during much of this country's history, it is not hard to see how the desire to cater to the perceived views of the mass audience desired by advertisers resulted in entertainment and news content that largely ignored people of color, treated them stereotypically when they were recognized, and largely avoided grappling with such issues as segregation, discriminatory immigration laws, land rights, and other controversial issues that affected certain minority groups more than they did the White majority. Although the entertainment and editorial portrayal of non-Whites is amply analyzed in other chapters of this book, it is important to recognize that those portrayals were, to a large extent, supported by a system of advertising that required the media to cater to the perceived attitudes and prejudices of the White majority and that also reinforced such images in its own commercial messages. For years advertisers in the United States reflected the place of non-Whites in the social fabric of the nation either by ignoring them or, when they were included in advertisements for the mass audience, processing and presenting them in a way that would make them palatable salespersons for the products being advertised. These processed portrayals largely mirrored the stereotypic images of minorities in the entertainment media that, in turn, were designed to reflect the perceived values and norms of the White majority. In this way, non-White portrayals in advertising paralleled and reinforced their entertainment and journalistic images in the media.

The history of advertising in the United States is replete with characterizations that, like the Frito Bandito, responded to and reinforced the preconceived image that many White Americans apparently had of Blacks, Latinos, Asians, and Native Americans. Over the years advertisers have employed Latin spitfires like Chiquita Banana, Black mammies like Aunt Jemima, and noble savages like the Santa Fe Railroad's Super Chief to pitch their products to a predominately White mass audience of consumers. In 1984 the Balch Institute for Ethnic Studies in Philadelphia sponsored an exhibit of more than 300 examples of racial and ethnic images used by corporations in magazines, posters, trade cards, and storyboards. In an interview with the advertising trade magazine *Advertising Age,* institute director Mark Stolarik quoted the catalog for the exhibit, which capsulized the evolution of images of people of color and how they have changed.

"Some of these advertisements were based on stereotypes of various ethnic groups. In the early years, they were usually crude and condescending images that appealed to largely Anglo-American audiences who found it difficult to reconcile their own visions of beauty, order and behavior with that of non-Anglo-Americans," said Stolarik. "Later, these images were softened because of complaints from the ethnic groups involved and the growing sophistication of the advertising industry."[1]

The advertising examples in the exhibit include positive White ethnic stereotypes, such as the wholesome and pure image of Quakers in an early Quaker Oats advertisement and the cleanliness of the Dutch in a turn-of-the century advertisement for Colgate soaps. But they also featured a late 19th century advertisement showing an Irish matron threatening to hit her husband over the head with a rolling pin because he didn't smoke the right brand of tobacco. Like Quaker Oats, some products even incorporated a stereotypical image on the package or product line being advertised.

"Lawsee! Folks sho' whoops with joy over AUNT JEMIMA PANCAKES," shouted a bandanna-wearing Black mammy in a magazine advertisement for Aunt Jemima pancake mix, which featured a plump Aunt Jemima on the box. Over the years, Aunt Jemima has lost some weight, but the stereotyped face of the Black servant continues to be featured on the box. Earlier advertisements for Cream of Wheat featured Rastus, the Black servant on the box, in a series of magazine cartoons with a group of cute but ill-dressed Black children. Some of the advertisements played on stereotypes ridiculing Blacks, such as an advertisement in which a Black school teacher standing behind a makeshift lectern made out of a boldly lettered Cream of Wheat box, asks the class "How do you spell Cream of Wheat?" Others appeared to promote racial integration, such as a magazine advertisement captioned "Putting it down in Black and White," which showed Rastus serving bowls of the breakfast cereal to Black and White youngsters sitting at the same table.

Racial imagery was also integrated into the naming of trains by the Santa Fe railroad, which named one of its passenger lines the Super Chief and featured highly detailed portraits of the noble Indian in promoting its service through the Southwestern United States. In another series of advertisements, the railroad used cartoons of Native American children to show the service and sights passengers could expect when they traveled the Santa Fe line.

These and other portrayals catered to the mass audience mentality by either neutralizing or making humor of the negative perceptions that many Whites may have had of racial minorities. The advertising images, rather than showing people of color as they really were, portrayed them as filtered through Anglo eyes. This presented an out-of-focus image of racial minorities, but one that was palatable, and even persuasive, to the White majority to which it was directed. In the mid-1960s Black civil rights groups targeted the advertising industry for special attention, protesting both the lack of integrated advertisements including Blacks and the stereotyped images that the advertisers continued to use. The effort, accompanied by support from federal officials, resulted in the overnight inclusion of Blacks as models in television advertising in 1967 and a downplaying of the images that many Blacks found objectionable.

"Black America is becoming visible in America's biggest national advertising medium," reported the *New York Times* in 1968. "Not in a big way yet, but it is a beginning and men in high places give assurances that there will be a lot more visibility."[2]

But the advertising industry did not generalize the concerns of Blacks, or the concessions made in response to them, to other groups. At the same time that some Black concerns were being addressed with integrated advertising, other groups were being ignored or singled out for continued stereotyped treatment in such commercials as those featuring the Frito Bandito.

Among the Latino advertising stereotypes cited in a 1969 article[3] by sociologist Tomás Martínez were commercials for Granny Goose chips featuring fat gun-toting Mexicans, an advertisement for Arrid underarm deodorant showing a dusty Mexican bandito spraying his underarms after a hard ride as the announcer intones, "If it works for him it will work for you," and a magazine advertisement featuring a stereotypical Mexican sleeping under his sombrero as he leans against a Philco television set. Especially offensive to Martínez was a Liggett & Meyers commercial for L&M cigarettes that featured Paco, a lazy Latino who never "feenishes" anything, not even the revolution he is supposed to be fighting. In response to a letter complaining about the commercial, the director of public relations for the tobacco firm defended the commercial's use of Latino stereotypes.

"'Paco' is a warm, sympathetic and lovable character with whom most of us can identify because he has a little of all of us in him, that is, our tendency to procrastinate at times," wrote the Liggett & Meyers executive. "He seeks to escape the violence of war and to enjoy the pleasure of the moment, in this case, the good flavor of an L&M cigarette."[4] Although the company spokesman claimed that the character had been tested without negative reactions from Latinos (a similar claim was made by Frito-Lay regarding the Frito Bandito), Martínez roundly criticized the advertising images and contrasted them to what he saw as the gains Blacks were then making in the advertising field.

"Today, no major advertiser would attempt to display a black man or woman over the media in a prejudiced, stereotyped fashion," Martínez wrote.

> Complaints would be forthcoming from black associations and perhaps the FCC. Yet, these same advertisers, who dare not show "step'n fetch it" characters, uninhibitedly depict a Mexican counterpart, with additional traits of stinking and stealing. Perhaps the white hatred for blacks, which cannot find adequate expression in today's ads, is being transferred upon their brown brothers.[5]

In 1970 a Brown Position Paper prepared by Latino media activists Armando Rendón and Domingo Nick Reyes charged that the media had transferred the negative stereotypes it once reserved for Blacks to Latinos, who had become "the media's new nigger."[6] The protests of Latinos soon made the nation's advertisers more conscious of the portrayals that Latinos found offensive. But, as in the case of the Blacks, the advertising industry failed to apply the lessons learned from one group to other racial minorities.

Although national advertisers withdrew much of the advertising that negatively stereotyped Blacks and Latinos, sometimes replacing them with affluent, successful images that were as far removed from reality as the negative portrayals of the past, the advances made by those groups were not shared with Native Americans and Asians. Native Americans' names and images, no longer depicted either as the noble savage or as cute cartoon characters, have all but disappeared from broadcast commercials and print

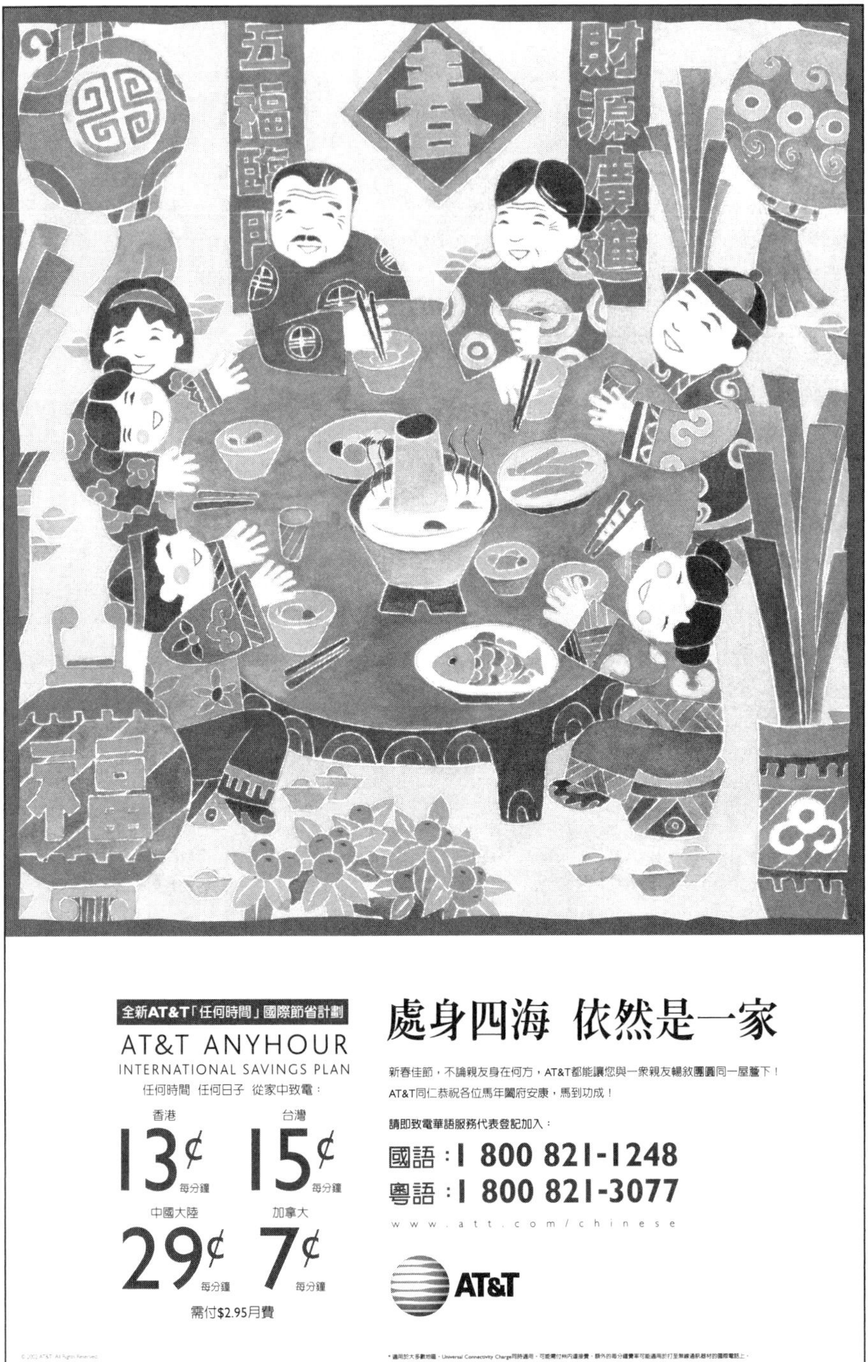

全新AT&T「任何時間」國際節省計劃

AT&T ANYHOUR

INTERNATIONAL SAVINGS PLAN

任何時間 任何日子 從家中致電：

需付$2.95月費

# 處身四海 依然是一家

新春佳節，不論親友身在何方，AT&T都能讓您與一衆親友暢敘團圓同一屋簷下！

AT&T同仁恭祝各位馬年闔府安康，馬到功成！

請即致電華語服務代表登記加入：

國語：1 800 821-1248

粵語：1 800 821-3077

w w w . a t t . c o m / c h i n e s e

U.S.-based corporations are not reluctant to put advertising in the language of their potential consumers. This advertisement for AT&T appeared in Chinese-language newspapers in the United States. *Advertisement developed for AT&T by Kang & Lee Advertising. Art reprinted by permission of AT&T and C. J. Yeh.*

advertising. The major exceptions are advertising for automobiles and trucks that bear names such as Pontiac, Dakota, and Navajo and sports teams with racial nicknames such as the Kansas City Chiefs, Washington Redskins, Florida State University Seminoles, Atlanta Braves, and Cleveland Indians. Native Americans and others have protested these racial team names and images, as well as the pseudo-Native American pageantry and souvenirs that accompany many of them but with no success in getting them changed.

Asians, particularly Japanese, continue to be dealt more than their share of commercials depicting them in stereotypes that cater to the fears and stereotypes of White America. As was the case with Blacks and Latinos, it took organized protests from Asian American groups to get the message across to the corporations and their advertising agencies. In the mid-1970s, a Southern California supermarket chain agreed to remove a television campaign in which a young Asian karate-chopped his way down the store's aisles cutting prices. Nationally, several firms whose industries have been hard-hit by Japanese imports fought back through commercials, if not in the quality or prices of their products. One automobile company featured an Asian family carefully looking over a new car and commenting on its attributes in heavily accented English. Only after they bought it did they learn it was made in the United States, not Japan. Another automobile company that markets cars manufactured in Japan under an English-language name showed a parking lot attendant opening the doors of the car, only to find the car speaking to him in Japanese. For several years Sylvania television ran a commercial boasting that its television picture had repeatedly been selected over competing brands as an off-screen voice with a Japanese accent repeatedly asked, "What about Sony?" When the announcer responded that the Sylvania picture had also been selected over Sony's, the off-screen voice ran off shouting what sounded like a string of Japanese expletives. A 1982 *Newsweek* article observed that "attacking Japan has become something of a fashion in corporate ads" because of resentment over Japanese trade policies and sales of Japanese products in the United States, but quoted Motorola's advertising manager as saying, "We've been as careful as we can be" not to be racially offensive.[7]

But many of the television and print advertisements featuring Asians featured images that were racially insensitive, if not offensive. A commercial for a laundry product featured a Chinese family that used an "ancient Chinese laundry secret" to get their customer's clothes clean. Naturally, the Chinese secret turned out to be the packaged product paying for the advertisement. Companies pitching everything from pantyhose to airlines featured Asian women coiffed and costumed as seductive China dolls or exotic Polynesian natives to pitch and promote their products, some of them cast in Asian settings and others attentively caring for the needs of the Anglo men in the advertisement. One airline boasted that those who flew with it would be under the care of the Singapore Girl.

Asian women appearing in commercials were often featured as China dolls with the small, darkened eyes, straight hair with bangs, and a narrow, slit skirt. Another common portrayal featured the exotic, tropical Pacific Islands look, complete with flowers in the hair, a sarong or grass skirt, and shell ornament. Asian women hoping to become models sometimes found that they must conform to these stereotypes or lose assignments. Leslie Kawai, the 1981 Tournament of Roses Queen, was told to cut her hair with bangs by hairstylists when she auditioned for a beer advertisement. When she refused, the beer company decided to hire another model with shorter hair cut in bangs.[8]

The lack of a sizable Asian community, or market, in the United States was earlier cited as the reason that Asians are still stereotyped in advertising and, except for children's advertising, are rarely presented in integrated settings. The growth rate and income of Asians living in the United States in the 1980s and 1990s, however, reinforced the economic potential of Asian Americans to overcome the stereotyping and lack of visibility that Blacks and Latinos challenged with some success. By the mid-1980s there were a few signs that advertising was beginning to integrate Asian Americans into crossover advertisements that, like the Tostitos campaign, were designed to have a broad appeal. In one commercial, television actor Robert Ito was featured telling how he loves to call his relatives in Japan because the calls make them think that he is rich, as well as successful, in the United States. Of course, he adds, it is only because the rates of his long distance carrier were so low that he was able to call Japan so often.

In the 1970s mass audience advertising in the United States became more racially integrated than at any time in the nation's history. Blacks, and to a much lesser extent Latinos and Asians, could be seen in television commercials spread across the broadcast week and in major magazines. In fact, the advertisements on network television often appeared to be more fully integrated than the television programs they supported. Like television, general circulation magazines also experienced an increase in the use of Blacks, although studies of both media showed that most of the percentage increase had come by the early 1970s. By the early 1970s the percentage of prime-time television commercials featuring Blacks had apparently leveled off at about 10%. Blacks were featured in between only 2% and 3% of magazine advertisements as late as 1978. That percentage, however small, was a sharp increase from the 0.06% of news magazine advertisements reported in 1960.[9]

The gains were also socially significant, because they demonstrated that Blacks could be integrated into advertisements without triggering a White backlash among potential customers in the White majority. Both sales figures and research conducted since the late 1960s have shown that the integration of Black models into television and print advertising does not adversely affect sales or the image of the product. Instead, a study by the

American Newspaper Publishers Association showed, the most important influences on sales were the merchandise and the advertisement itself. In fact, while triggering no adverse affect among the majority of Whites, integrated advertisements were found to be useful in swaying Black consumers, who responded favorably to positive Black role models in print advertisements.[10] Studies conducted in the early 1970s also showed that White consumers did not respond negatively to advertising featuring Black models, although their response was more often neutral than positive.[11] One 1972 study examining White backlash, however, did show that an advertisement prominently featuring darker-skinned Blacks was less acceptable to Whites than those featuring lighter-skinned Blacks as background models.[12] Perhaps such findings help explain why research conducted later in the 1970s revealed that, for the most part, Blacks appearing in magazine and television advertisements were often featured as part of an integrated group.[13]

Although research findings have shown that integrated advertisements do not adversely affect sales, the percentage of Blacks and other minorities in general audience advertising did not increase significantly after the numerical gains made through the mid-1970s. Those minorities who did appear in advertisements were often depicted in upscale or integrated settings, an image that the Balch Institute's Stolarik criticized as taking advertising "too far in the other direction and created stereotypes of 'successful' ethnic group members that are as unrealistic as those of the past."[14] Equally unwise, from a business sense, was the low numbers of Blacks appearing in advertisements.

> Advertisers and their ad agencies must evaluate the direct economic consequences of alternative strategies on the firm. If it is believed that the presence of Black models in advertisements decreases the effectiveness of advertising messages, only token numbers of Black models will be used,

wrote marketing professor Lawrence Soley at the conclusion of a 1983 study.

> Previous studies have found that advertisements portraying Black models do not elicit negative affective or conative responses from consumers. . . . Given the consistency of the research findings, more Blacks should be portrayed in advertisements. If Blacks continue to be under-represented in advertising portrayals, it can be said that this is an indication of prejudice on the part of the advertising industry, not consumers.[15]

## Notes

1. "Using Ethnic Images," p. 9.
2. Cited in Philip H. Dougherty, "Frequency of Blacks in TV Ads," *New York Times*, May 27, 1982, p. D19.

3. Martínez, "How Advertisers Promote," p. 10.
4. Martínez, "How Advertisers Promote," p. 11.
5. Martínez, "How Advertisers Promote," pp. 9–10.
6. Domingo Nick Reyes and Armando Rendón, *Chicanos and the Mass Media* (Washington, DC: The National Mexican American Anti-Defamation Committee, 1971).
7. Joseph Treen, "Madison Ave. vs. Japan, Inc.," *Newsweek* (April 12, 1982), p. 69.
8. Ada Kan, *Asian Models in the Media*, Unpublished term paper, Journalism 466: Minority and the Media, University of Southern California, December 14, 1983, p. 5.
9. Studies on increase of Blacks in magazine and television commercials cited in James D. Culley and Rex Bennett, "Selling Blacks, Selling Women," *Journal of Communication* (Autumn 1976, Vol. 26, No. 4), pp. 160–174; Lawrence Soley, "The Effect of Black Models on Magazine Ad Readership," *Journalism Quarterly* (Winter 1983, Vol. 60, No. 4), p. 686; and Leonard N. Reid and Bruce G. Vanden Bergh, "Blacks in Introductory Ads," *Journalism Quarterly* (Autumn 1980, Vol. 57, No. 3), pp. 485–486.
10. Cited in D. Parke Gibson, *$70 Billion in the Black* (New York: Macmillan, 1979), pp. 83–84.
11. Laboratory studies on White reactions to Blacks in advertising cited in Soley, "The Effect of Black Models," pp. 585–587.
12. Carl E. Block, "White Backlash to Negro Ads: Fact or Fantasy?" *Journalism Quarterly* (Autumn 1980, Vol. 49, No. 2), pp. 258–262.
13. James D. Culley and Rex Bennett, "Selling Blacks, Selling Women."
14. "Using Ethnic Images," p. 9.
15. Soley, *The Effect of Black Models*, p. 690.

---

## This Text: Reading

1. It's likely that you found the descriptions of some of these ads shocking. What do these advertisements tell you about how America and Americans used to see people of color?
2. This is one of the few essays that examine how all people of color have been represented. Were you surprised to read about images of Hispanics and American Indians? If so, why?
3. What is the argument of the essay?

## Your Text: Writing

1. With some research, you should be able to track down some images of a similarly disturbing nature. What is the semiotic setting of these ads? Write a paper in which you analyze the ads from today's perspective but are mindful of the ad as being a cultural document.
2. Write an essay on advertising and white people. Based on ads, what assumptions can we make about Anglos?
3. Write a comparative paper examining what Wilson and Guiterrez say about race with a similar essay from the Race chapter.

# DIET COKE'S UNDERWEAR STRATEGY

Rob Walker

# HANES HER WAY

Brittany Gray

Brittany Gray was a freshman at Virginia Commonwealth University in Richmond when she wrote this analysis of a "Hanes Her Way" ad in 2001; Rob Walker is a columnist for *Slate* magazine who writes frequently about advertising (2001). In both of these pieces, the two authors read their ads through the lens of the familiar vs. fantasy.

## Diet Coke's Underwear Strategy

DIET COKE IS CURRENTLY PROMOTING ITSELF with the tag line "That Certain Something." It's easy to understand why the pushers of any product want to associate their wares with vague but positive sentiments along these lines. It's less easy to pull it off. One new Diet Coke ad in particular offers up an example of "that certain something" that is, to put it mildly, unique. You can see this spot on Diet Coke's Web site, although I should probably warn you that you won't get anywhere on the site without Flash 5. Once it finishes loading you'll get a window with a choice for "Diet Coke Ad Clips"; click on that, then click on the third of the three ad screen shots presented to view the commercial I address here.

### *The Ad*

A man, whose face we never see, is folding laundry in his bright and airy loft. Specifically he's folding a pair of women's underwear, white with little yellow flowers. Inoffensive music plays in the background as a man's voice narrates. (This is a well-known actor who, as part of the campaign's gimmick, isn't named; I'll say who it is below.) "When we first got married, she'd wear really sexy underwear, like you see in underwear ads," the young husband muses. Here we see his blond wife, I guess in a flashback, cavorting sexily in black undergarments in the dark. A quick montage finds her looking not a day older, but in the morning light and a roomy pajama top. "After a while," the narrator continues, "she started wearing the kind of underwear that I saw in the hamper when I was a kid." Here one of the shots is of him sort of handling the underwear. "There's something oddly reassuring about thin, washed-out, cotton underwear, with little yellow flowers." Some Diet Coke cans are in evidence as the laundry-and-domesticity montage winds down and closes on an image of the blond wife and the "That Certain Something" tag line.

### *Reassuring?*

This is a strange ad. It's a really strange ad. For starters, let's just pause to note that Diet Coke apparently wants its brand to be as familiar to you as old underwear. OK? Now, let's put that aside. What's this bit about his wife's underwear being like "the kind of underwear that I saw in the hamper when I was a kid"? What does that mean? It's like his mother's underwear? Who among you entertains a wistful nostalgia for your mother's underwear? Let's see a show of hands, please. Actually, let's not.

The narrator then goes on to say that there is something "oddly reassuring about thin, washed-out cotton underwear." Well, if he finds that reassuring, I will agree with the "oddly" part. So, let's clarify what that "certain something" about Diet Coke is: Diet Coke is as "reassuring" as "thin, washed-out" underwear, reminiscent of your mother's, but worn by your wife. Run *that* by your shrink sometime.

Perhaps I'm being too literal? OK, then, forget the underwear, what's the basic theme of this little story? We have a young married couple. She used to wear sexy underwear. Although they're clearly still young, this couple has gotten over that sort of thing and settled into a less exciting, quotidian groove, in which they will presumably remain until parted by death. And the husband finds this reassuring. I have nothing against the idea of domestic bliss, but usually the sort of epiphany that this man is having (i.e., we have reached the end of a certain road here and can only hope for comfort, never again excitement) is an occasion for deep existential, how-did-I-get-here angst. But the brand managers of Diet Coke have a different take—it is as if they have chosen to say, "Here you go, pal; enjoy an ice-cold, refreshing can of *your very mortality*." Maybe that's the certain something: a resigned sense of fatalism.

Anyway, the narrator is Ben Affleck, who delivers his peculiar lines with absolute conviction—which proves, I suspect, that he does have some acting ability after all.

## Hanes Her Way

IT KNOWS WHO YOU ARE. It knows what you want. It gets into your psyche, and then—onto your television, your computer screen, your newspapers and your magazines. It is an advertisement, folks, and it's studying every little move you make, be it in the grocery store or the outlet mall. These advertisement executives know just what the consumer needs to hear to convince him or her to buy the product. Grocery stores even consult such advertisement firms on matters such as just how to set up the store in order to maximize consumer purchase. It has been watching, and it knows just what mood to set to get into the head of the consumer, and just how to set the scene.

This particular scene is a mild, relaxed morning. The sun streams in through the windows. The lighting is a tranquil yellow, and the background music is "Fade Into You" by Mazzy Star, a soft and haunting ballad which perfectly complements the temperate setting. Through a doorway a man watches a woman who is wearing a white t-shirt and white cotton underwear as she makes a bed, snapping a sheet into the air and watching it drift back down onto the bed in slow motion. Then a voiceover begins. The man talks over the music about how when they were dating, his girlfriend used to wear such tiny, sexy underwear. Then he says that now that they are married she just wears old worn cotton underwear by Hanes. He goes on to say that there is something comforting about the cotton underwear. He says he loves when he opens the laundry hamper and sees the worn out underwear in there waiting to go into the wash, because it reminds him of his mother and his childhood. The commercial then fades out on the Hanes trademark.

The ethical appeal in this commercial is particularly strong. For starters, the brand name of Hanes goes back a long way and has been trusted for years. There is nothing more comforting about buying a product than knowing that millions of people aside from oneself also trust the product. Also, the people in the ad seem to trust the product. It seems that trust and stability are the qualities that Hanes wants the customer to attribute to their underwear.

The pathos in this commercial was the strongest of all the appeals. The fact that, first of all, the couple is married, and also that the man seems to love and accept his wife so openly plays a part in the emotional appeal. It is not often that couples on television are married anymore, and when they are, their lives and marital stress are often the topic of comedy. This couple is not only happily married, but obviously has been married for a while as well, given the fact that the wife has had time to change her style of underwear *and* the fact that her Hanes Her Way cotton briefs are well worn.

Another aspect of the pathos is the setting of the scene. The tranquility of the lighting, the airy atmosphere consisting of so much white cotton and linen, and the relaxing background music all play a role in the manipulation of emotion. The way the man stands there with such a nostalgic look on his face, watching his wife and speaking about her so wistfully is meant to really touch something inside—and it does. Not only that, but the man still finds his wife beautiful, even after so many years, and even after the underwear that he initially found so attractive is gone. The entire ad evokes a sense of tranquility and comfort, seeming to say, "our product will fulfill you just the way these people are fulfilled."

The appeal to logic in this ad was for the most part absent, aside from one thing. After all, there is no real logic to a man liking his wife's underwear, nor is there any rhyme or reason behind the comfort that seeing the underwear lying in the hamper brings him, reminding him of his childhood and his mother. Hanes underwear does not make the sun come out in the morning, and it certainly won't find someone a spouse. The logic of the commercial, as well as the fact of the matter, is that Hanes underwear is comfortable—especially Hanes Her Way white cotton briefs.

The audience targeted in this commercial was without question middle-class women, probably aged 12 and up. Most men do not get misty-eyed hearing pretty music, and they are not particularly struck watching a man speak so fondly of his wife. However, women thrive on such things. Every woman loves to see a man talk about his wife as though she were the only woman on the earth, because it is such a rare occurrence.

That is not the only aspect of the ad directed at women, however. The lighting in the commercial, paired with the beautiful sunny morning, as well as the crisp white linens shown throughout the commercial, are all aimed at women in middle-class families. Women love to see that level of comfort and cleanliness within a home, as it all touches on a woman's romantic, idealistic side. Also, the fact that the couple and their home is so completely average shows that Hanes is for average, normal people. Everyone wants to feel that what they do is normal and accepted, especially women trying to run a home. It is one less thing to worry about, one less thing that can be criticized when it comes to a woman's running of her home. It also shows that the happiness of the couple is not out of reach—they are just like every other working class American couple.

These audience clinchers are not entirely in opposition to the ones used in men's underwear commercials. Many men's underwear commercials portray scenes containing rumpled beds in the morning, and fresh white linen. Underwear commercials in general seem to abound in their portrayal of morning sunrises and beautiful people making beds. In men's commercials, though, it seems that there is always that bittersweet touch of masculinity. There is constantly some muscular role model, doing the types of things that strong, ideal men should do. The man in the commercial always seems to do the same stereotyped things. He gives the dog a bath, he plays with the kids. He does the dishes with a smile, pausing to toss a handful of bubbles at his adoring wife. He goes jogging in the morning before his coffee. He shows his son how to throw a baseball just right, and of course he doesn't neglect his daughter—he tosses her into the air, and playfully dodges her blows during a pillow fight. And of course, he feels perfectly comfortable sitting around in nothing but his white cotton briefs.

Women on the other hand don't need examples of femininity. They know how to be women, and showing what the typical woman does in a day would be cheesy and clichéd. Just show a woman a good old fashioned love scene and most likely she's sold.

This commercial probably shouldn't appeal to me so strongly. It is exactly like most other commercials for women's underwear I have seen. They all have the same basic elements: white linen, sunny mornings, happy families, and beautiful, smiling people. I'm not sure if I can place my finger on exactly what made this commercial stand out for me. I think it was the combination of the music and the couple. I've never heard music like that in an underwear commercial. The music used is normally that sunny, get-up-and-go type of music, but this commercial utilized the softer sound of Mazzy Star. The voiceover and the utilization of romance really struck me too. Though the ad was not particularly original, I still felt that it was a beautifully done commercial.

The ethos of this commercial was definitely strong. The name of Hanes is one of the most trusted in underwear, and the advertisers used the stability of the marital relationship to illustrate this. However, the pathos was the most outstanding of the appeals in this ad. The fact that the underwear was made by Hanes was made known, as well as the reasons why Hanes should be trusted. However, the vivid sensory imagery in this commercial which made it so pleasing to the eye and such a joy to watch rules over the ethical appeal. A sunny morning means much more to me personally than the comfort of knowing that I'm wearing sturdy underwear, which is a comfort that is forgotten soon after putting the underwear on. A morning as beautiful as the one on TV is not commonly seen, nor is a couple more obviously in love. It is simple joys such as these that the commercial strikes at, and the joys seem to overpower the main ethical and logical appeal—that Hanes makes good underwear.

---

## This Text: Reading

1. What qualities of the advertising do Walker and Gray identify as worthy of discussion? If you have seen the ads, do you agree with their emphasis?
2. Have you purchased soda or underwear based on commercials? Where do you think your influences to purchase come from?
3. In what ways do the home generally and bedroom specifically serve as a sign? What products are most appropriate for this approach? Can you think of other places that serve similar purposes?
4. Gray's writing situation is as a student asked to do a rhetorical analysis (see Worksheet); Walker is a reporter who writes about advertising. What are the similarities between the works? Their differences? Do you feel that the differences come from their writing situations or other factors?

## Your Text: Writing

1. Perform a similar sign analysis using an advertisement that uses another familiar place (a front lawn, an office, sports field, etc.). What about the place's familiarity is part of the appeal?
2. Write a paper discussing the presence of fantasy and familiarity in a typical advertisement. What types of ads rely more on fantasy? Which on familiarity?
3. Examine the types of intimate relationships portrayed in advertisements. Write a paper examining how do advertisers use those relationships to appeal to their target audience.

News/Media

# 15 QUESTIONS ABOUT THE "LIBERAL MEDIA"

Jeff Cohen and Norman Solomon

Cohen and Solomon sling fiery arrows at what they think of as "myths" about the liberal media (1994). We print this text not to encourage you to mimic their form but as a kind of catalyst to begin thinking about how we internalize catch phrases about the media, or, for that matter, society in general.

ONE OF THE MOST ENDURING MYTHS about the mainstream news media is that they are "liberal." The myth flourishes to the extent that people don't ask pointed questions:

- If the news media are liberal, why have national dailies and newsweeklies regularly lauded those aspects of President Clinton's program that they view as "centrist" or "moderate," while questioning those viewed as liberal?
- If the news media are liberal, why is it that liberals are apt to be denigrated as ideologues, but status quo centrists or "moderates" are presented as free of ideological baggage?
- If the news media are liberal, why did most outlets praise Clinton's selection of David Gergen, who advocated Reagan policies, while pillorying civil rights lawyer Lani Guinier?
- If the news media are liberal, why did they applaud conservative White House appointees like Lloyd Bentsen and Les Aspin, while challenging liberals like Donna Shalala, Johnetta Cole and Roberta Achtenberg?

*It also helps to look back at history and ask questions:*

- If the news media are liberal, why have Clinton's meager tax hikes on the wealthy been referred to as "soaking the rich" or "class warfare," but President Reagan's giveaways to the wealthy were euphemized as "tax reform"?
- If the news media are liberal, why have national outlets been far tougher in scrutinizing Democratic presidents Carter and Clinton than Republicans Reagan and Bush?
- If the news media are liberal, why have they buried important facts, such as the shrinking of corporate income tax from 25 percent of federal expenditures in the 1960s to only about 8 percent today?

- If the news media are liberal, why have they given short shrift to reform proposals—tax-financed national health insurance, federally-supported child care, government jobs programs—that their own polls show are overwhelmingly popular with the public?

*Pundits and commentators have gained increasing prominence in the media, often eclipsing the reporters:*

- If the news media are liberal, why were the first two political pundits to appear on national TV every day of the week both conservatives: Patrick Buchanan and John McLaughlin? Was it their good looks?
- If the news media are liberal, why does the media spectrum typically extend from unabashed right-wingers to tepid centrists who go to great lengths—attacking progressive ideas and individuals—to prove they're not left-wing? Why do pundit debates on national TV have *Wall Street Journal* reporters representing "the left"?
- If the news media are liberal, why are TV pundit programs—even on "public television"—sponsored by conservative businesses like General Electric, Pepsico and Archer Daniels Midland?
- If the news media are liberal, why was Rush Limbaugh the first host in the history of American television to be allowed to use his national politics show to campaign day after day for a presidential candidate?
- If the news media are liberal, why do right-wing hosts usually dominate talk radio—even in liberal cities?
- If the news media are liberal, why are there dozens of widely syndicated columnists who champion corporate interests, but few who champion consumer or labor rights?

*In analyzing the bias of any institution, it helps to look at who owns it. Which leads to a final question:*

- If the news media are liberal, why are they owned and sponsored by big corporations that spend millions of dollars to lobby *against* liberal measures in Washington?

June 9, 1993

---

## This Text: Reading

1. What approach did Cohen and Solomon take here? Was it effective? Can you think of a subject that would benefit from simply listing material?
2. How could Cohen and Solomon taken their list and make it into a narrative? Would this have made it more effective?

3. Is Cohen and Solomon's clearly subjective viewpoint a problem—why or why not?
4. Where do you think the idea of the liberal media comes from? What do you think of the term liberal—is it a positive term or negative one? Does its meaning depend on its context?
5. What is the situation from which they are writing?

### YOUR TEXT: WRITING

1. What would the response article from conservatives contain? Write this response into a paper.
2. Think of a topic that could be covered by a list. Now turn that list into a paper.
3. Scan a newspaper. What are its obvious political leanings? Read the editorials. But what about the paper itself—what values does it appear to champion?

## AIDS NEWS AND NEWS CULTURES

Kevin Williams and David Miller

British scholars Kevin Williams and David Miller examine the reporting of AIDS and the reception of AIDS on television, both in Great Britain and the United States (1995). The public reaction to AIDS is much different today than in 1994 and 1995. As you read, pay attention to the semiotic situation of Williams and Miller. What kinds of texts are they reading?

THE FIRST REPORTED DEATH from AIDS in Britain occurred in 1982. The government, however, took very little action to prevent the spread of the disease before 1986, when, under pressure from gay activists, scientists, and clinicians involved with the disease, it launched a public health education campaign warning of the dangers of the spread of the disease to the heterosexual population. Between 1986 and 1987 there was a period of "national wartime emergency" when AIDS was a political priority at the highest level (Berridge & Strong, 1991). From 1988 onward, there was a "normalization" of the disease. AIDS treatment became a normal part of British health service provision, with information about the disease directed at specific target groups within the British population.

Television was at the heart of the government's effort to educate and inform the British public of AIDS and HIV, the virus that is believed to lead to the disease. TV advertisements were used to warn of the dangers of AIDS, and in March 1987 there was an unprecedented degree of cooperation among the BBC, ITV, and the government during "AIDS Week" on

British television. The main message of the campaign was that the disease poses a threat to everyone, heterosexuals as well as gay men and drug users. To prevent the transmission of the virus, the campaign promoted "safer sex," particularly the use of condoms. There was no overt message about sexual ethics or orientation, although "sticking to one partner" was recommended. Compulsory testing for the virus was rejected. This was the basis of the official British perspective on AIDS.

Alternative perspectives in other media, some more traditional in outlook, challenged this orthodoxy. Some groups argued that AIDS health education was nothing more than "propaganda" aimed at heterosexuals. They asserted that the threat to heterosexuals was a myth, and that measures should be taken to segregate people with AIDS from the general population. Others argued that the official response was "homophobic" and ignored the problems of "persons with AIDS" or PWAs—a term that avoids defining those with AIDS as either just medical objects ("AIDS victims") or somehow blameworthy (e.g., gay men and intravenous drug users).

The importance of information and education in the fight against AIDS has led to considerable commentary on news coverage of the disease, including media coverage in the United States, Western Europe, Australia, Zambia, and Zimbabwe, and to representations of AIDS in films, newsmagazines, and broadcasting. Despite cultural differences regarding the language and imagery used to describe and discuss sex, sexual health, and sexuality, media coverage has been characterized mostly by blame, denial, fear, and prejudice. As Lupton (1994) states, "AIDS reporting in western nations has involved imagery associated with homophobia, fear, violence, contamination, invasion, vilification, racism, sexism, deviance, heroicism and xenophobia" (p. 21). The relationship between news coverage and government policy about AIDS has also been questioned, because news coverage of AIDS has seemed to rise and fall in Britain, the United States, and France parallel with the development of government interest and concern in the disease.

Despite the fact that most people in Western countries identify television news as their main source of AIDS information, there has been a surprising lack of systematic research into the content of TV news coverage of AIDS. One recent study of U.S. network news was conducted by Cook and Colby (1992), who found that "the networks attempted to reassure at least as much as they played up the story." The attention paid to AIDS by TV network news did not correspond with the development of the severity of the epidemic or the growth of medical interest. According to Cook and Colby, the coverage had more to do with the institutional dynamics of journalism than with the nature of the AIDS epidemic. As the epidemic developed, the TV news organizations took their cue from "authoritative scientific sources and political officials to let them know when news on AIDS would happen" (Cook & Colby, 1992, p. 102). Thus the decline of AIDS coverage on U.S. TV news at different times in the 1980s can be largely attributed to government inactivity. Gay men "were shown more often as carriers than as victims," but as the story developed "gay spokespersons were identified occasionally as authoritative sources" alongside doctors, government officials, and research scientists.

## *TV News Leads the Way*

In our sample of British TV News we found that the most common type of "AIDS story" concerned the government's AIDS campaign. This constituted the largest group of news stories, ranging from items on the latest phase of the advertising campaign to announcements of policy on anonymized testing. Another significant category of news story concerned the activities of nongovernment bodies. This included the British Medical Association's training video for doctors, a Birmingham City Council scheme to involve prostitutes in AIDS education, and Football Association guidelines to players for safety.

A large number of news stories were about AIDS in other countries. Half of these stories were from the United States, and a further quarter concerned African countries. Less predictable stories, such as those about a patient being infected by HIV following a skin graft and about protests over the siting of a hospice, we assigned to a category labeled "other events and happenings." However, the most striking aspect of TV news coverage during this period was the number of stories on the situations of people living with AIDS and HIV—the second largest number of stories in our sample. These varied considerably in the ways in which they were covered, but, most important, PWAs were given the opportunity on a number of occasions to speak for themselves and their own experiences.

## *Who Got on TV News*

The range and frequency of interviews presented on television news provides one crude but important indicator of the sources used in the presentation of news events. In our sample of TV news coverage of AIDS we identified a total of 363 people who appeared in 611 interviews. The majority of these people, 70%, appeared only once and exclusively on one TV news channel. Only a small group of interviewees appeared regularly on all channels and in the contexts of a number of different stories.

The most common types of interviewees were medical and scientific experts. Other experts and professionals were also well represented: nursing staff, lawyers, counselors, caregivers, and spokespersons of organizations for people with AIDS and HIV, such as the Terrence Higgins Trust (THT), Britain's biggest AIDS charity, Body Positive, and Frontliners. However, few of these appeared more than once; the overwhelming majority (92%) appeared just once. The main exception was the leading spokesperson for the THT.

There were relatively large numbers of interviews with PWAs, but the people who appeared most regularly across the whole range of AIDS stories in our sample were government ministers. Nearly 50% of the interviews were conducted with the different ministers of health in this period. These were the central figures in the AIDS story on TV news. Most of their appearances were in news events such as press conferences. The regularity of appearance of government ministers indicates the orientation of TV news to the rhythms of political life and government activity. It is not simply a question of who gets on, however; it is also a question of how they are used in TV news stories.

## *Supporting the Official Line?*

In the period 1986–1987, the British government's response to HIV/AIDS created a sense of national emergency that was reflected in the TV news coverage. Television news programs stressed official concern about the spread of AIDS.

> The government is setting up a top-level committee to warn that there is a danger of an AIDS epidemic sweeping the country. . . . There have been warnings from health experts for some time that the deadly disease could get out of hand. It is the speed with which it can spread that is so worrying. . . . effectively the government is declaring war on AIDS. (BBC1, 9:00 p.m. newscast, November 3, 1986)

TV news bulletins closely identified themselves with the government perspective and explicitly endorsed the view of the Department of Health and Social Security. Clear and unequivocal support was given by TV news to official warnings about the spread of the disease to the heterosexual population. Although there was much debate in sections of the British print media about the threat AIDS poses to heterosexuals (Beharrell, 1993), TV news dismissed such doubts and embraced the scientific and medical consensus that was established between 1987 and 1990. Expert opinion was used to support the official line. As TV news stated in 1986: "The experts agree that everyone is at risk and it is vital to find out about AIDS and how to protect ourselves from it" (ITN, 10:00 p.m. newscast, December 1, 1986). TV news bulletins were organized around the official perspective on AIDS, and medical, scientific, and expert opinion was used in support. Standard phrases such as "doctors say" or "experts now believe" were used to legitimate statements.

The close ties between TV news and medical/scientific opinion on AIDS were apparent in the early days of news coverage of the disease. Medical and science correspondents shared their main sources' concerns about the government's initial reluctance to address the disease. The correspondents often endorsed the pressure on government to act; the BBC's science correspondent commented on the announcement of the establishment of the government's AIDS Committee in 1986:

> AIDS first appeared in Britain in 1979. Since the early 1980s specialists in the disease have been pleading for more to be done to stop it from spreading. Now it seems at last they are being listened to. (BBC1, 6:00 p.m. newscast, November 10, 1986)

TV news supported the government's campaign when it was launched and agreed with the official contention that there was the potential of an epidemic among heterosexuals. However, criticisms of the campaign centered on its lack of explicitness. As an ITN reporter stated at the outset of TV advertisements in 1986:

> The ads on television, however, will not be explicit, for example, about the use of condoms and the help some people think they will give in preventing the spread of AIDS . . . and that will, perhaps, raise questions in some people's minds about how effective the whole campaign is going to be. . . . Previous government advertising has been criticized as being too bland when compared with some private campaigns containing very explicit advice run, for example, by one of the main charities involved, the Terrence Higgins Trust. (ITN, 10:00 p.m. newscast, November 11, 1986)

TV news marginalized other kinds of criticisms of the campaign. Voluntary organizations questioned the government's information-giving approach, but little notice was paid to them. There was no coherent strand of opposition to the campaign on moral grounds in the TV news. Even when spokespersons for this perspective were interviewed, the context was usually critical of their claims. TV news coverage was firmly wedded to the medical/scientific orthodoxy, and the criticisms of the details of the government's campaign reflected concerns that the campaign failed to live up to the expectations of this group.

The TV news reporting of AIDS conformed to the ways other diseases have been covered. On health matters, doctors and scientists have a higher credibility for journalists than do other sources of information. However, within the official perspective on AIDS there were differences, and these were reflected in the TV news coverage. Thus in the TV news coverage of HIV/AIDS there were criticisms of the government campaign, but they tended to be within the bounds of the official perspective on the disease. TV news thus did report differences of opinion on the AIDS campaign, but the disagreements aired were in general within the boundaries of "appropriate and responsible" debate, always defined in practice on TV as debate between official sources.

## *Medical/Scientific Sources and TV News*

Access to TV news coverage of AIDS was dominated by medical and scientific experts. Of the 80 different scientists and doctors who appeared on TV news, 52 appeared on one occasion only. There were, however, a small number to whom the reporters returned regularly. In particular, the stories on medical and scientific research on AIDS were dominated by a small number of sources. The relationship between TV news and one of these scientific sources shows the problems inherent in such relationships.

Medical and scientific sources have a high degree of credibility in the eyes of television news personnel. Karpf (1988) points out that "being part of the scientifico-medical establishment is in itself sufficient in the media's eyes to make you a medical expert, even on an issue on which you have no specialist knowledge" (pp. 111–112). However, it is not a simple task for reporters to verify what scientific or medical sources tell them. Some journalists do not have the inclination or the knowledge to assess the quality of such information. In the absence of an objective standard by which to verify what they are told, journalists often value status and authority over other criteria in assessing the reliability of information. Eminent scientists and doctors can be excellent publicists whose opinions the media readily accept (Check, 1987). TV news has its own criteria for a source's worth. The visual and verbal requirements of the medium often outweigh concerns about the nature of what is said.

For example, the most interviewed scientist in our sample was described by the BBC's science correspondent as "one of Britain's leading experts on AIDS research" (BBC1, 6:00 p.m. newscast, September 10, 1987). In the same news story, it was reported that "a new vaccine against AIDS which is being developed in Britain may be tried out on humans within the next year." This was the same story that ITN had carried the previous February, when it reported on the work of this scientist in developing an AIDS vaccine. "Medical scientists . . . say they are hoping to start testing a vaccine on patients within 1 to 2 months" (ITN, 10:00 p.m. newscast, February 19, 1987). Yet up to the end of the 1980s this scientist had never even begun testing a vaccine, and had never published a single scientific paper on HIV or AIDS (Campbell, 1992).

## *Alternative Sources*

Despite the dominance of official sources in the form of government ministers and doctors and scientists in the TV coverage of HIV/AIDS, other nonofficial sources did gain some access to the airwaves. The best example of such source coverage was the Terrence Higgins Trust, a charity set up to represent the interests of PWAs. The main spokesperson of the THT was interviewed on 16 news broadcasts in our sample. This was second only to the minister who held the health portfolio for the longest time during our sample, Norman Fowler. The THT established itself as a source of expert information about AIDS for the media.

> The Terrence Higgins Trust, set up in memory of the first British man to die of AIDS, pioneered public awareness of the threat. (ITN, 10:00 p.m. newscast, December 4, 1986)

By 1989, TV news had accepted the expert status of the THT to the extent that it no longer introduced or described the organization on screen other than by name caption.

The ability of the THT to overcome the lack of authoritativeness of other sources outside the medical establishment came in part because of the quality of information it provided, but also because of the image it promoted. Crucial to this image was the fact that its main spokesperson conformed to the needs and perceptions of TV news organizations. As the spokesperson told us:

> I am not threatening. I am 35. I am middle class. I speak BBC-type English. I am very acceptable. I am the kind of homosexual you can take home to your mother and it is a great relief to them.

Thus through its information strategy the THT was able to influence TV news coverage of HIV/AIDS. One of the organization's achievements was the replacement of the typical two-sided TV news discussion between a doctor and an interviewer with three-way discussions that included someone affected by HIV/AIDS.

## *Covering People with AIDS*

People living with HIV or AIDS were featured prominently on TV news. Issues such as discrimination, prejudice, ignorance, and fear as well as medical and financial problems were reported. In sharp contrast to the coverage in the British print media, many of the TV news reports attempted to inform and educate about the situation of PWAs.

The largest group of TV news interviewees was made up of PWAs, whose sources of HIV transmission or sexual orientation were nowhere specified. Only 4 interviews in our sample were with PWAs who were introduced as gay, in contrast with 16 hemophiliacs, a dramatic reversal of the actual proportion of gay men and hemophiliacs with HIV or AIDS. Interviews were also broadcast with the children, partners, families, and friends of PWAs. However, in the three and a half years studied, TV news never carried an interview with the partner or lover of a gay man or with any members of a gay man's family. Such domestic settings were used only for heterosexuals, giving a quite erroneous representation that gay men do not have long-term committed relationships.

TV news did make distinctions between "guilty" and "innocent" victims. This surfaced explicitly in the coverage of HIV and hemophiliacs. One ITN headline referred to this group as the "innocent victims of AIDS" (ITN, 5:45 p.m. newscast, October 12, 1987). Meanwhile, the BBC reported on a "plea from people who got the AIDS virus by accident." The news reader explained that hemophiliacs face the threat of AIDS "through no fault of their own" (BBC1, 6:00 p.m. newscast, October 12, 1987). The obvious implication of such reporting is that gay men and drug users are to blame if they contract the virus.

Such reporting became less apparent as groups such as the THT managed to put pressure on the TV news organizations. The labeling of "innocent" and "guilty" victims was even taken up as a news story. For instance, one ITN report began with the comment that "some believe it is wrong to discriminate between different categories of victim" (ITN, 10:00 p.m. newscast, November 16, 1987). The story included an interview with a member of the THT who stated that "immaterial of how a person contracted the disease, once they've got full-blown AIDS their needs are all very much the same and they [the government] should be catering now towards those needs."

In the coverage of PWAs, television news often made comparisons between people's physical appearance before and after they contracted the disease. The image of AIDS was one of decline, decay, and wasting.

> A self-portrait on the wall constantly reminds 37-year-old Gerry of how he used to be before he was infected with AIDS. Now this talented and trained artist is living in a hospice for dying AIDS patients in Kansas City. He used to be a body builder. (ITN *Channel Four News*, 7:00 p.m., November 12, 1986)

The painfully thin, haggard young man lying alone in a hospital bed came to represent the image of AIDS in the West in the early years of the disease.

However, TV news later came to carry reports that presented a different image of PWAs. A BBC report on the activities of the London Lighthouse Hospice, an organization that cares for people with AIDS, is illustrative of the attempts made to redefine the familiar image of PWAs. The news story was structured around the perspective of those living with AIDS. As one of the interviewees said in the story, "It sets a wonderful example, to see the smiling faces here and realize that AIDS in the end is not about death, it's about life and the liveliness of people here, people who have AIDS and the people who are helping them" (BBC1, 6:00 p.m. newscast, September 22, 1988).

TV news coverage of PWAs varied, sometimes in coverage of the same event by different channels. For example, the BBC reported on a visit by the British minister of health to a San Francisco hospital that included, according to the BBC, "his first-ever meeting with a hospitalized AIDS patient" (BBC1, 9:00 p.m. newscast, January 21, 1987). The patient was described as "a homosexual and a former drug user," and the report went on to say that "many of his friends have died of the disease. He now has it himself." The patient talked of his earlier life, saying, "It was a good time and we thought nothing of having casual sex or using recreational drugs." The story concluded with the stark comment, "By statistical averages of these cases, he has about one year to live." The narrative of this news story was constructed solely around the use of a PWA to warn others, with no concern for the subject of the report.

A radically different view of the minister's visit appeared on ITN that same night. The ITN news report was structured around the indifference shown to PWAs. The TV reporter commented that the patient "is angered by people who say it is just a homosexual disease and AIDS isn't their concern" (ITN, 10:00 p.m. newscast, January 21, 1987). The patient stated: "I wish I could tell all the straight people that, look, it's a virus, it's not running around checking sexual preference or race or class or anything, you know. It is just making people sick."

These two news accounts show that once an event is defined as newsworthy it can still be covered in very different ways. A number of factors can shape the coverage, including the information available, the reporter's own views, the journalistic strategies used to gain information, the journalist's sense of news values, and the influence of sources. The TV news coverage of PWAs shows the key role that sources can play in the construction of news accounts.

## *Conclusion*

British TV news coverage of HIV/AIDS in the period discussed above was openly supportive of the government campaign and its key message about the threat of the virus to heterosexuals. Criticisms that were broadcast focused on the details of the campaign, in particular the lack of clarity and explicit language surrounding the campaign. Such criticisms reflected the view of the medical/scientific consensus established around the disease in the 1980s. Government and medical/scientific sources dominated TV news output on HIV/AIDS. Critical coverage of the government campaign reflected the concerns of the British medical/scientific orthodoxy, and the debate about HIV/AIDS on TV news primarily took place between official sources.

However, alternative sources were able to gain some access to TV news. An example is that the THT was able to establish itself as an "expert source" on problems of AIDS policy. TV news organizations, like the rest of the British media, initially went through a period of denial and victim blaming in their reporting on PWAs. In our sample there were examples of the "guilty victims" labeling that was very frequent in British print media reporting. But as the story progressed, TV news began to challenge preconceptions of PWAs and to broadcast stories that portrayed the positive struggle of PWAs, as well as to endorse efforts to combat discrimination and increase funding for care. This was the result of the activities of alternative sources such as the THT and other gay and AIDS activist groups. The other important factors in shaping coverage of AIDS over this period were (a) the medical/scientific consensus concerning the adoption of a medical rather than a moral approach to the disease—often at odds with the pronouncements of some government ministers—and (b) broadcasters' notion of "social responsibility," embodied in the noncommercial culture that historically molded the development of British broadcasting, whether public service or advertising based.

TV news coverage of AIDS in Britain has not, therefore, been neutral or objective. It has followed particular ways of understanding the disease and its consequences. Like news accounts elsewhere, these ways of understanding have been shaped by the official perspective on HIV/AIDS. However, TV news has not been uniform in the reporting of the disease, and as the AIDS story developed other sources of information were able to gain access to TV news and influence the coverage. Alternative sources of information on HIV and AIDS have been able to gain more access to TV news in Britain than in the United States. This can be explained by the ability of AIDS organizations in Britain to build alliances with other sources and to influence the news media. Only by understanding the process of negotiation that takes place between sources of information, within news media organizations, and between sources and journalists can we make sense of how issues are reported by the news media.

---

## This Text: Reading

1. According to the authors, what did television news tell us about AIDS? Have things changed? If so, how?
2. Most news is not observed by you; it is not observed by reporters. Reporters get news from other sources. How did this fact affect how AIDS was reported?
3. To what degree is America's puritanical nature affecting how AIDS gets reported?

## Your Text: Writing

1. Do some research on recent stories about AIDS. Write a paper in which you analyze AIDS coverage in the media. Is it fair? Comprehensive? Would you know if it were not?
2. Look at two or three different sources that have done stories on AIDS. Write a comparative paper in which you analyze how each source represents and covers AIDS.
3. Write a comparative paper having looked at stories on AIDS in both mainstream and gay/lesbian publications. How does the coverage differ?

# THE AMERICA THE MEDIA DON'T WANT YOU TO SEE

David McGowan

Taken from his controversial book *Derailing Democracy: The America the Media Don't Want You to See* (2000), this excerpt attempts to justify why Americans must look for news from alternative sources. You will notice that McGowan makes reference to documents the reader will encounter later—these are references to stories from his book that we have not reprinted here.

> I know of no country in which there is so little independence of mind and real freedom of discussion as in America.
>
> —*Alexis de Tocqueville (1805–1859)*

IT HAS BEEN ALMOST 40 YEARS since President Eisenhower, in his final address to the nation before leaving office in 1961, issued a rather extraordinary warning to the American people that the country "must guard against unwarranted influence, whether sought or unsought, by the military-industrial complex. The potential for the disastrous rise of misplaced power exists and will persist." Tragically, Eisenhower's warning was not heeded, and the beast has been allowed not only to grow, but to mutate into something that should more accurately be referred to as the military-industrial-media complex.

Following the same course that virtually every other major industry has in the last two decades, a relentless series of mergers and corporate takeovers has consolidated control of the media into the hands of a few corporate behemoths. The result has been that an increasingly authoritarian agenda has been sold to the American people by a massive, multi-tentacled media machine that has become, for all intents and purposes, a propaganda organ of the state.

It is precisely because most readers get their news filtered through that same organ that many will readily disagree with this assessment. The American free press is the envy of the world, they will argue, and this unprecedented ability that we as Americans have to enjoy unrestricted access to unfiltered news is one of the unique freedoms that makes America the icon of democratic ideals that we all know it to be. And it is certainly true that by all outward appearances the United States does appear to have the very epitome of a free press.

After all, do not CNN and a handful of would-be contenders broadcast a continuous stream of news to America's millions of cable subscribers? Are Tom Brokaw, Peter Jennings, Dan Rather and Ted Koppel, as well as countless lesser-knowns, not welcomed into our homes nightly, bearing the day's news—both good and bad? Would not our morning rituals seem woefully lacking without the comfort of the morning paper on the breakfast table? And don't the radio waves crackle incessantly with the political musings of Rush Limbaugh and his legions of ideological clones, while a bustling "alternative" press brings the "progressive" version of news and events to those of a slightly different political persuasion? Miss something during the week? Not to worry: *Time, Newsweek* or *U.S. News and World Report* are there with a handy weekly round-up of the big stories. Don't have time to read? No problem: *60 Minutes, 20/20, 48 Hours* and *Dateline NBC* have already read them for you—just sit back and mainline the week's events.

Yet behind this picture of plurality there are clear warning signs that an increasingly incestuous relationship exists between the media titans and the corporate military powers that Eisenhower so feared. For example, the number-one purveyor of broadcast news in this country—NBC, with both MSNBC and CNBC under its wing, as well as NBC news and a variety of "newsmagazines"—is now owned and controlled by General Electric, one of the nation's largest defense contractors. Is it not significant that as GE's various media subsidiaries predictably lined up to cheerlead the use of U.S. military force in Kosovo, it was at the same time posting substantial profits from the sale of the high tech tools of modern warfare it so shamelessly glorifies?

Would we not loudly condemn such a press arrangement were it to occur in a nation such as Russia or China? Equally alarming is that those viewers choosing to change channels to CNN, the reigning king of the cable news titans, were treated to the surreal daily spectacle of watching Christiane Amanpour, who is the wife of State Department mouthpiece James Rubin, analyze her husband's daily press briefings, as though she could objectively respond to the mounds of disinformation spewing forth from the man with whom she shares her morning coffee. Were it to occur elsewhere, would this not be denounced as symptomatic of a state-run press?

Maybe. Yet it can still be argued that corporate media ownership, despite the ominous implications, does not necessarily preclude the notion of a free press in that ownership has little to do with the day-to-day functioning of the news media. After all, one could reasonably argue, the press operates on the principle of competition to break the big story, and if one news outlet is reticent to report unfavorably on its owners or the government, surely it risks being beaten by competitors. We all know that ambitious reporters are driven by an obsessive desire to get "the scoop." Does not the mere existence of literally thousands of print and broadcast news sources, all keeping their eyes on the Pulitzer Prize, provide *ipso facto* proof of a free press? Does it not guarantee that all the news that merits reporting will arrive on our doorstep each morning in a relatively objective form?

This is a perfectly logical argument, yet there is substantial evidence that suggests that competition does not in itself overcome the interests of the corporate media. For example, while saturation coverage is given to such non-news events as the premier of a new *Star Wars* movie, there has not been a single American media source reporting the fact that the first successful human clones have been created, despite the staggering implications of such a scientific milestone. Surely a press motivated by competition to break the big story would have stumbled upon this one by now, especially considering that as of this writing, more than a year has passed since the world was blessed with the first human clone, courtesy of an American biotechnology firm.

Of course, this could be due not to media suppression, but to the simple fact that the press failed to uncover this story. However, this interpretation fails to account for the fact that this is far from being the only newsworthy event that the American media have failed to take note of, as evidenced throughout this book. It also fails to explain why the British press seem to have had little trouble unearthing this particular story, or why the U.S. news media continued to ignore the issue even after it had appeared in print in the U.K. Had this story been aired by our own press corps, it surely would have received an overwhelmingly negative response. This is, no doubt, the very reason that this story, as well as countless others, has failed to make its American debut.

Yet the illusion of a free and competitive press persists and has become ingrained to the point that it is nearly universally accepted as a truism. And with it comes the illusion that America's people are among the world's best informed. If not, then it is surely our own fault for being too lazy or otherwise preoccupied to avail ourselves of the media barrage. *Politically Incorrect*'s Bill Maher can be heard regularly haranguing guests for failing to utilize these readily-available resources to gain an informed knowledge of the issues, occasionally even offering up the opinion that anyone who has failed to do so should be stripped of the right to vote. Maher is only stating outright what is implied in the message of the media in general: the truth is right here before your eyes—you have only to partake to become an informed citizen.

But the "truth" offered by the media is a systematic and deliberate distortion of reality. In some cases, such as the previously cited example of human cloning, this distortion takes the form of outright suppression. In many other cases, it takes the form of distraction, never more prominently on display than during the O.J. Simpson media circus. The coverage afforded this case, and others such as the JonBenet Ramsey case, while creating the illusion that the press is examining the seamy underbelly of American society, does little to shed light on the very real problems facing the average American. These stories, as well as the countless tales of individual human failing that spring forth from the media fascination with the cult of celebrity, are clearly not meant to inform, but to distract and entertain.

Sometimes something far more insidious is at play than mere distraction, however. By far the most dangerous form of distortion, and one that has become increasingly prominent, involves the willful misrepresentation of issues in such a way that the "debate" on the issue then begs solutions that actually exacerbate the real problem that was being masked. In this way, problems that are themselves borne of the increasingly reactionary agenda being pursued are perceived to be solved by resorting to yet further erosion of democratic and civil rights.

One example where this phenomenon can be seen at work is in the media coverage of school shootings. Following each such incident, a pseudo debate is conducted in which the blame is variously placed on guns, rock/rap music, or video games as the cause in the rise in "youth violence." The debate is restricted to these now familiar parameters. But behind the sensational headlines, the media fail to note that youth violence has actually declined, and that these incidents are not a uniquely adolescent phenomenon, but are in fact patterned after the acts of adults, with the high school serving as the teenage equivalent of the post office or the day trading center.

The problem, viewed in a larger context, is not with the current generation of kids, but with society as a whole. The fact that Americans of all ages choose to strike out violently against society and its institutions, however infrequently, is a clear warning sign of a pronounced decay in America's social fabric. Why does the current social system, purportedly the very model of freedom and justice, breed such extreme levels of anger, frustration and despair, as well as the willingness to express these feelings in such explosive outbursts? This question is outside the media's scope.

Neither is it questioned why all of society, including our youth, is bombarded from literally all directions with the message that the use of force is an effective, and even desirable, means of achieving one's goals, and that pity and compassion for others is a sign of weakness. This message is certainly not confined to pop culture and the entertainment media.

Virtually the same message is conveyed by America's increasing reliance on brute force as an instrument of foreign policy and by the shameless glorification of U.S. military prowess. It is conveyed as well by the increasingly militarized tactics of the nation's police, most recently visible in the heavy-handed approach of the Seattle police towards the tens of thousands of overwhelmingly peaceful protestors at the December 1999 conference of the World Trade Organization. It is further reinforced by Congress each time it drafts a new round of "law and order" legislation, and by the increasingly free rein given the nation's police and correctional officers to enforce those laws.

Rather than acknowledge any of this, each school shooting will be propagandized for its fear-inducing value, with the same script being played out, leading to the same preordained solution: while repeating the mantra that "we will never be able to fully understand why these things occur" (which is certainly true if we don't ask the right questions), yet another round of reactionary sentencing legislation will be passed with additional laws designed to criminalize our children. Far from solving the underlying problems and social tensions, all such legislation will ultimately serve only to foster increased feelings of anger, resentment and hopelessness.

This is but one example of how a handful of key media players determine what the "issues" are and what the parameters of public debate on those issues will be by controlling both the flow and the shape of the news. When a problem is identified, it is defined in the narrowest of contexts so as to preempt any discussion outside of the pre-defined boundaries—any argument put forth outside of those boundaries can then be mocked or ignored. In this way, anything remotely resembling an informed public debate on the serious issues facing this country is effectively cut off.

Instead, what we have is artificially truncated debate, usually by a relentless procession of allegedly politically informed pundits clustering into various formations to populate the cable news talk shows, where the rapid fire verbiage can almost obscure the fact that nothing of relevance is actually being said. These programs, and the broadcast media in general, are not meant to enlighten; they are intended to provide a pre-packaged debate, presenting the acceptable arguments for both sides. At the same time, they are meant to entertain and distract attention away from whatever essential information is being withheld from the discussion.

An informed populace is a critical component of any truly democratic system, and a nation that has only the illusion of public debate has no more than the illusion of democracy as well. That is why it is absolutely crucial that the people of America have full access to all the information that affects their lives as citizens of this country, and of the world community. As an effort towards achieving that goal, presented here you will find some of the news that wasn't quite fit to print.

A brief discussion on sources, credibility and context is warranted here. The source material for this book falls into one of five general categories:

- U.S. government documents and statements by U.S. officials
- Documents and reports issued by Non-Governmental Organizations (NGOs), such as Amnesty International and the Justice Policy Institute
- "Mainstream" media sources, e.g. the *Los Angeles Times* and the *New York Times*
- "Alternative" media sources, including *The Nation* and *The Mojo Wire* (the electronic version of *Mother Jones*)
- The foreign press, such as the *London Times* and Australia's *The Age*

Of these five, official government documents were considered the most credible, and were therefore the most sought after. This is certainly not to suggest that the various branches of the U.S. government are noted for their honesty. On the contrary, lying is an integral element of the business of government, not only in America but around the world. However, government disinformation tends to follow a fairly steady pattern, namely casting the purveyor of the propaganda in the best possible light.

Given that the documents excerpted here tend, to the contrary, to damage America's carefully crafted public image, they were deemed to be the most credible and therefore the most difficult to refute. The other primary source of documents was from NGOs, which were considered to be somewhat less credible due to the obvious fact that all such organizations have a political agenda, leaving them open to charges of bias. It is notable, however, that the media generally finds the information released by these entities quite credible when it casts America in a positive light, carefully sidestepping the more unsavory facts, issues and trends.

The balance of the material presented here was culled from the various newsmedia sources listed above. Whenever possible, what are generally considered to be mainstream sources were consulted first, beginning with the largest and most influential of the major daily newspapers. In those cases where the mainstream media failed to yield the desired information, the alternative media was next utilized. As a last resort, the foreign press was turned to on those issues which drop completely off the American media's radar screen.

And why, given that a central argument thus far has been that the function of the media is to obscure rather than to inform, should any credence be given to these sources? For the simple reason that occasionally bits and pieces of the truth manage to filter through, and by assembling all these fragments together, it is possible to begin to construct a more accurate representation of the socio-political conditions within the United States today.

It is notable that the typical reaction when information of this sort does appear in print is to deride it as yet further proof of the supposed "liberal" bias of the press. The notion that the American media has a liberal bias has never been remotely grounded in reality, but has rather been kept alive as a myth precisely so that embarrassing press coverage could be more easily discredited. As no less a conservative than Pat Buchanan has stated with uncharacteristic candor: "For heaven sakes, we kid about the liberal media, but every Republican on Earth does that."[1]

Another area of concern on the subject of sources is that of context. It will inevitably be charged that all of the excerpts and quotations contained in this book have been taken out of context. In a literal sense, this is of course quite true. Quoting material from another source requires, by definition, removing it from its original context. To do otherwise would require reproducing all of the source materials used in this book in their entirety.

This being an obviously unworkable proposition, the real question to be asked is: has this material been excerpted in such a way as to not fundamentally change its meaning in the original context in which it appeared. I think that I can, in good conscience, state that this is indeed the case here. Of course, every writer brings his own personal bias to his work, and it is entirely possible that this writer's bias has affected this work. To claim otherwise would reek of hypocrisy.

What do all these facts, taken together as a whole, add up to? The answer, which I believe will become increasingly apparent to the reader, is an ominous trend towards a more controlled, more authoritarian form of rule in the United States, leaving increasingly more democratic rights and freedoms lying in the wake of the reactionary agenda being sold to the American people.

### Notes

1. *Los Angeles Times*, March 14, 1996.

---

## This Text: Reading

1. What is McGowan's argument here? Would you agree with his assessment of America's media? Why? Why not? How does he support his assertions?
2. McGowan employs a classic rhetorical strategy in this piece. He offers a logical rebuttal to his argument, and then rebuts the rebuttal. Is this effective? Why?
3. Based on his arguments, what are McGowan's political leanings? Does it change how you read his text? Based on the arguments of *The World Is a Text*, what are the political leanings of the authors? The publishers?

## Your Text: Writing

1. Track down a copy of *Derailing Democracy*. Write an essay on one of his chapters in the book. How do McGowan's figures and facts undermine notions of the "free press"?
2. Write an essay in which you compare this piece to Cohen and Solomon's "15 Questions about the 'Liberal Media'." How are they similar? Where do they differ?
3. What is the writing situation for McGowan? What changes are going on in the world as he writes his book? How is technology affecting how information gets dispersed?

# The Media Manipulation Suite

We all hate to be manipulated. Yet, according to the four authors featured in this suite, forces all around us are out to manipulate how we buy, how we see products, how we see the news, and how we see the world. It would appear that we hardly have any say in how the world gets interpreted, how it is presented to us. The French philosopher Jean François Lyotard claims that the world comes to us in stories; if he's right, then the tellers of those stories determine how the world arrives at our door. Without sounding like paranoid conspiracy theory buffs, we want to alert you to the reality that media can be and sometimes are manipulative. Perhaps they don't mean to be, perhaps they do—it's often impossible to tell. Regardless, both media advertising and news sources manipulate the reader and viewer in subtle and not-so-subtle ways.

For instance, there is a clear kind of manipulation that occurs in advertisements. Every time you see a print or television ad with a small, cute child and a loveable puppy, rest assured advertisers are going to work on your emotions and your values. Similarly, in recent ads for a men's hair loss remedy, the ad's text informs men that if they don't do something about their impending baldness, their wives or girlfriends will leave them for someone with a full head of hair. Both ads are different but both play on powerful aspects of our emotions—innocence and fear.

We have chosen to begin this suite with a famous essay by Stuart and Elizabeth Ewen. We like this essay because they employ the same kind of approach we advocate in *The World Is a Text*. Using allegory and symbolism, they take a literary approach, offering readings of various advertisements. In his essay on words in advertising, William Lutz points out code words that advertisers use to make false claims about their products. Though he may not realize it, he gives a semiotic reading of the language of advertisement, as we hope you will learn to do. In both essays, these writers argue that all advertising is a form of manipulation and that awareness on your part makes you better consumers and companies and businesses better producers.

Most of you are more comfortable thinking of advertising as being more consciously manipulative than the news media, but according to Trudy Lieberman, that would be a false assumption. Lieberman, who has worked in newspaper journalism for decades, chronicles how inherent conservatism in the news industry translates into an imbalance in the reporting of the news. If the world is a text, then the media is one of the major authors of that text. They tell us how to see the world, what issues are important, what to buy, how to look, what is news, what is style, what is happening. Becoming a literate reader of advertising and media texts will prove immensely helpful for you as you begin to make sense of the world as an autonomous adult.

Thus, in this suite, we'd like you to consider the writing situations of all of these authors. What might be shaping their perspectives? In addition, we'd like for you to consider your own writing situation. What is going on in the world, in advertising, and in the news that might affect how you read these texts? Finally, are these texts themselves manipulations? Are there "good" and "bad" manipulations? If so, what distinguishes the two?

## IN THE SHADOW OF THE IMAGE

Stuart and Elizabeth Ewen

MARIA AGUILAR WAS BORN twenty-seven years ago near Mayagüez, on the island of Puerto Rico. Her family had lived off the land for generations. Today she sits in a rattling IRT subway car, speeding through the iron-and-rock guts of Manhattan. She sits on the train, her ears dazed by the loud outcry of wheels against tracks. Surrounded by a galaxy of unknown fellow strangers, she looks up at a long strip of colorful signboards placed high above the bobbing heads of the others. All the posters call for her attention.

Looking down at her, a blond-haired lady cabdriver leans out of her driver's side window. Here is the famed philosopher of this strange urban world, and a woman she can talk to. The tough-wise eyes of the cabby combined with a youthful beauty, speaking to Maria Aguilar directly:

> Estoy sentada 12 horas al dia.
> Lo último que necesilo son hemorroides.
> (I sit for twelve hours a day. The last thing I need are hemorrhoids.)

Under this candid testimonial lies a package of Preparation H ointment, and the promise "Alivia dolores y picasonas. Y ayuda a reducir la hinchazón." (Relieves pain and itching. And helps reduce swelling.) As her mind's eye takes it all in, the train sweeps into Maria's stop. She gets out; climbs the stairs to the street; walks to work where she will spend her day sitting on a stool in a small garment factory, sewing hems on pretty dresses.

Every day, while Benny Doyle drives his Mustang to work along State Road Number 20, he passes a giant billboard along the shoulder. The billboard is selling whiskey and features a woman in a black velvet dress stretching across its brilliant canvas.

As Benny Doyle downshifts by, the lounging beauty looks out to him. Day after day he sees her here. The first time he wasn't sure, but now he's convinced that her eyes are following him.

The morning sun shines on the red-tan forehead of Bill O'Conner as he drinks espresso on his sun deck, alongside the ocean cliffs of La Jolla, California. Turning through the daily paper, he reads a story about Zimbabwe.

"Rhodesia," he thinks to himself.

The story argues that a large number of Africans in Zimbabwe are fearful about black majority rule, and are concerned over a white exodus. Two black hotel workers are quoted by the article. Bill puts this, as a fact, into his mind.

Later that day, over a business lunch, he repeats the story to five white business associates, sitting at the restaurant table. They share a superior laugh over the ineptitude of black African political rule. Three more tellings, children of the first, take place over the next four days. These are spoken by two of Bill O'Conner's luncheon companions; passed on to still others in the supposed voice of political wisdom.

Barbara and John Marsh get into their seven-year-old Dodge pickup and drive twenty-three miles to the nearest Sears in Cedar Rapids. After years of breakdowns and months of hesitation they've decided to buy a new washing machine. They come to Sears because it is there, and because they believe that their new Sears machine will be steady and reliable. The Marshes will pay for their purchase for the next year or so.

Barbara's great-grandfather, Elijah Simmons, had purchased a cream-separator from Sears, Roebuck in 1897 and he swore by it.

When the clock-radio sprang the morning affront upon him, Archie Bishop rolled resentfully out of his crumpled bed and trudged slowly to the john. A few moments later he was unconsciously squeezing toothpaste out of a mess of red and white Colgate packaging. A dozen scrubs of the mouth and he expectorated a white, minty glob into the basin.

Still groggy, he turned on the hot water, slapping occasional palmfuls onto his gray face.

A can of Noxzema shave cream sat on the edge of the sink, a film of crud and whiskers across its once neat label. Archie reached for the bomb and filled his left hand with a white creamy mound, then spread it over his beard. He shaved, then looked with resignation at the regular collection of cuts on his neck.

Stepping into a shower, he soaped up with a soap that promised to wake him up. Groggily, he then grabbed a bottle of Clairol Herbal Essence Shampoo. He turned the tablet-shaped bottle to its back label, carefully reading the "Directions."

"Wet hair."

He wet his hair.

"Lather."

He lathered.

"Rinse."

He rinsed.

"Repeat if necessary."

Not sure whether it was altogether necessary, he repeated the process according to directions.

Late in the evening, Maria Aguilar stepped back in the subway train, heading home to the Bronx after a long and tiring day. This time, a poster told her that "The Pain Stops Here!"

She barely noticed, but later she would swallow two New Extra Strength Bufferin tablets with a glass of water from a rusty tap.

Two cockroaches in cartoon form leer out onto the street from a wall advertisement. The man cockroach is drawn like a hipster, wearing shades and a cockroach zoot-suit. He strolls hand-in-hand with a lady cockroach, who is dressed like a floozy and blushing beet-red. Caught in the midst of their cockroach-rendezvous, they step sinfully into a Black Flag Roach Motel. Beneath them in Spanish, the words:

> Las Cucarachas entran . . . pero non pueden salir.
> (In the English version: Cockroaches check in . . . but they don't check out.)

The roaches are trapped; sin is punished. Salvation is gauged by one's ability to live roach-free. The sinners of the earth shall be inundated by roaches. Moral tales and insects encourage passersby to rid their houses of sin. In their homes, sometimes, people wonder whether God has forsaken them.

Beverly Jackson sits at a metal and tan Formica table and looks through the *New York Post*. She is bombarded by a catalog of horror. Children are mutilated . . . subway riders attacked. . . . Fanatics are marauding and noble despots lie in bloody heaps. Occasionally someone steps off the crime-infested streets to claim a million dollars in lottery winnings.

Beverly Jackson's skin crawls; she feels a knot encircling her lungs. She is beset by immobility, hopelessness, depression.

Slowly she walks over to her sixth-floor window, gazing out into the sooty afternoon. From the empty street below, Beverly Jackson imagines a crowd yelling "Jump! . . . Jump!"

Between 1957 and 1966 Frank Miller saw a dozen John Wayne movies, countless other westerns and war dramas. In 1969 he led a charge up a hill without a name in Southeast Asia. No one followed; he took a bullet in the chest.

Today he sits in a chair and doesn't get up. He feels that images betrayed him, and now he camps out across from the White House while another movie star cuts benefits for veterans. In the morning newspaper he reads of a massive weapons buildup taking place.

Gina Concepcion now comes to school wearing the Jordache look. All this has been made possible by weeks and weeks of afterschool employment at a supermarket checkout counter. Now, each morning, she tugs the decorative denim over her young legs, sucking in her lean belly to close the snaps.

These pants are expensive compared to the "no-name" brands, but they're worth it, she reasons. They fit better, and she fits better.

The theater marquee, stretching out over a crumbling, garbage-strewn sidewalk, announced "The Decline of Western Civilization." At the ticket window a smaller sign read "All seats $5.00."

It was ten in the morning and Joyce Hopkins stood before a mirror next to her bed. Her interview at General Public Utilities, Nuclear Division was only four hours away and all she could think was "What to wear?"

A half hour later Joyce stood again before the mirror, wearing a slip and stockings. On the bed, next to her, lay a two-foot-mountain of discarded options. Mocking the title of a recent bestseller, which she hadn't read, she said aloud to herself, "Dress for Success. . . . What *do* they like?"

At one o'clock she walked out the door wearing a brownish tweed jacket; a cream-colored Qiana blouse, full-cut with a tied collar; a dark beige skirt, fairly straight and hemmed (by Maria Aguilar) two inches below the knee; shear fawn stockings, and simple but elegant reddish-brown pumps on her feet. Her hair was to the shoulder, her look tawny.

When she got the job she thanked her friend Millie, a middle manager, for the tip not to wear pants.

Joe Davis stood at the endless conveyor, placing caps on a round-the-clock parade of automobile radiators. His nose and eyes burned. His ears buzzed in the din. In a furtive moment he looked up and to the right. On the plant wall was a large yellow sign with THINK! printed on it in bold type. Joe turned back quickly to the radiator caps.

Fifty years earlier in another factory, in another state, Joe's grandfather, Nat Davis, had looked up and seen another sign:

A Clean Machine Runs Better.
Your Body Is a Machine.
KEEP IT CLEAN.

Though he tried and tried, Joe Davis' grandfather was never able to get the dirt out from under his nails. Neither could his great-grandfather, who couldn't read.

In 1952 Mary Bird left her family in Charleston to earn money as a maid in a Philadelphia suburb. She earned thirty-five dollars a week, plus room and board, in a dingy retreat of a ranch-style tract house.

Twenty-eight years later she sits on a bus, heading toward her small room in north Philly. Across from her, on an advertising poster, a sumptuous meal is displayed. Golden fried chicken, green beans glistening with butter and flecked by pimento, and a fluffy cloud of rice fill the greater part of a calico-patterned dinner plate. Next to the plate sits a steaming boat of gravy, and an icy drink in an amber tumbler. The plate is on a quilted blue placemat, flanked by a thick linen napkin and colonial silverware.

As Mary Bird's hungers are aroused, the wording on the placard instructs her: "*Come home to Carolina.*"

**Shopping List**

paper towels
milk
eggs
rice crispies
chicken
snacks for kids (twinkies, chips, etc.)
potatoes
coke, ginger ale, plain soda
cheer
brillo
peanut butter
bread
ragu (2 jars)
spaghetti
saran wrap
salad
get cleaning, bank, *must pay electric!!!*

On his way to Nina's house, Sidney passed an ad for Smirnoff vodka. A sultry beauty with wet hair and beads of moisture on her smooth, tanned face looked out at him. "*Try a Main Squeeze.*" For a teenage boy the invitation transcended the arena of drink; he felt a quick throb-pulse at the base of his belly and his step quickened.

In October of 1957, at the age of two and a half, Aaron Stone was watching television. Suddenly, from the black screen, there leaped a circus clown, selling children's vitamins, and yelling "Hi! boys and girls!" He ran, terrified, from the room, screaming.

For years after, Aaron watched television in perpetual fear that the vitamin clown would reappear. Slowly his family assured him that the television was just a mechanical box and couldn't really hurt him, that the vitamin clown was harmless.

Today, as an adult, Aaron Stone takes vitamins, is ambivalent about clowns, and watches television, although there are occasional moments of anxiety.

These are some of the facts of our lives; disparate moments, disconnected, dissociated. Meaningless moments. Random incidents. Memory traces. Each is an unplanned encounter, part of day-to-day existence. Viewed alone, each by itself, such spaces of our lives seem insignificant, trivial. They are the decisions and reveries of survival; the stuff of small talk; the chance preoccupations of our eyes and minds in a world of images—soon forgotten.

Viewed together, however, as an ensemble, an integrated panorama of social life, human activity, hope and despair, images and information, another tale unfolds from these vignettes. They reveal a pattern of life, the structures of perception.

As familiar moments in American life, all of these events bear the footprints of a history that weighs upon us, but is largely untold. We live and breathe an atmosphere where mass images are everywhere in evidence; mass produced, mass distributed. In the streets, in our homes, among a crowd, or alone, they speak to us, overwhelm our vision. Their presence, their messages are given; unavoidable. Though their history is still relatively short, their prehistory is, for the most part, forgotten, unimaginable.

The history that unites the seemingly random routines of daily life is one that embraces the rise of an industrial consumer society. It involves explosive interactions between modernity and old ways of life. It includes the proliferation, over days and decades, of a wide, repeatable vernacular of commercial images and ideas. This history spells new patterns of social, productive, and political life.

# WEASEL WORDS

## William Lutz

ONE PROBLEM ADVERTISERS HAVE when they try to convince you that the product they are pushing is really different from other, similar products is that their claims are subject to some laws. Not a lot of laws, but there are some designed to prevent fraudulent or untruthful claims in advertising. Even during the happy years of nonregulation under President Ronald Reagan, the FTC did crack down on the more blatant abuses in advertising claims. Generally speaking, advertisers have to be careful in what they say in their ads, in the claims they make for the products they advertise. Parity claims are safe because they are legal and supported by a number of court decisions. But beyond parity claims there are weasel words.

Advertisers use weasel words to appear to be making a claim for a product when in fact they are making no claim at all. Weasel words get their name from the way weasels eat the eggs they find in the nests of other animals. A weasel will make a small hole in the egg, suck out the insides, then place the egg back in the nest. Only when the egg is examined closely is it found to be hollow. That's the way it is with weasel words in advertising: Examine weasel words closely and you'll find that they're as hollow as any egg sucked by a weasel. Weasel words appear to say one thing when in fact they say the opposite, or nothing at all.

### *"Help"—The Number One Weasel Word*

The biggest weasel word used in advertising doublespeak is "help." Now "help" only means to aid or assist, nothing more. It does not mean to conquer, stop, eliminate, solve, heal, cure, or anything else. But once the ad says "help," it can say just about anything after that because "help" qualifies everything coming after it. The trick is that the claim that comes after the weasel word is usually so strong and so dramatic that you forget the word "help" and concentrate only on the dramatic claim. You read into the ad a message that the ad does not contain. More importantly, the advertiser is not responsible for the claim that you read into the ad, even though the advertiser wrote the ad so you would read that claim into it.

The next time you see an ad for a cold medicine that promises that it "helps relieve cold symptoms fast," don't rush out to buy it. Ask yourself what this claim is really saying. Remember, "helps" means only that the medicine will aid or assist. What will it aid or assist in doing? Why, "relieve" your cold "symptoms." "Relieve" only means to ease, alleviate, or mitigate, not to stop, end, or cure. Nor does the claim say how much relieving this medicine will do. Nowhere does this ad claim it will cure anything. In fact, the ad doesn't even claim it will *do* anything at all. The ad only claims that it will aid in relieving (not curing) your cold symptoms, which are probably a runny nose, watery eyes, and a headache. In other words, this medicine probably contains a standard decongestant and some aspirin. By the way, what does "fast" mean? Ten minutes, one hour, one day? What is fast to one person can be very slow to another. Fast is another weasel word.

Ad claims using "help" are among the most popular ads. One says, "Helps keep you young looking," but then a lot of things will help keep you young looking, including exercise, rest, good nutrition, and a facelift. More importantly, this ad doesn't say the product will keep you young, only "young *looking*." Someone may look young to one person and old to another.

A toothpaste ad says, "Helps prevent cavities," but it doesn't say it will actually prevent cavities. Brushing your teeth regularly, avoiding sugars in foods, and flossing daily will also help prevent cavities. A liquid cleaner ad says, "Helps keep your home germ free," but it doesn't say it actually kills germs, nor does it even specify which germs it might kill.

"Help" is such a useful weasel word that it is often combined with other action-verb weasel words such as "fight" and "control." Consider the claim, "Helps control dandruff symptoms with regular use." What does it really say? It will assist in controlling (not eliminating, stopping, ending, or curing) the *symptoms* of dandruff, not the cause of dandruff nor the dandruff itself. What are the symptoms of dandruff? The ad deliberately leaves that undefined, but assume that the symptoms referred to in the ad are the flaking and itching commonly associated with dandruff. But just shampooing with *any* shampoo will temporarily eliminate these symptoms, so this shampoo isn't any different from any other. Finally, in order to benefit from this product, you must use it regularly. What is "regular use"—daily, weekly, hourly? Using another shampoo "regularly" will have the same effect. Nowhere does this advertising claim say this particular shampoo stops, eliminates, or cures dandruff. In fact, this claim says nothing at all, thanks to all the weasel words.

Look at ads in magazines and newspapers, listen to ads on radio and television, and you'll find the word "help" in ads for all kinds of products. How often do you read or hear such phrases as "helps stop...," "helps overcome...," "helps eliminate...," "helps you feel...," or "helps you look ..."? If you start looking for this weasel word in advertising, you'll be amazed at how often it occurs. Analyze the claims in the ads using "help," and you will discover that these ads are really saying nothing.

There are plenty of other weasel words used in advertising. In fact, there are so many that to list them all would fill the rest of this book. But, in order to identify the doublespeak of advertising and understand the real meaning of an ad, you have to be aware of the most popular weasel words in advertising today.

### *Virtually Spotless*

One of the most powerful weasel word is "virtually," a word so innocent that most people don't pay any attention to it when it is used in an advertising claim. But watch out. "Virtually" is used in advertising claims that appear to make specific, definite promises when there is no promise. After all, what does "virtually" mean? It means "in essence of effect, although not in fact." Look at that definition again. "Virtually" means *not in fact*. It does *not* mean "almost" or "just about the same as," or anything else. And before you dismiss all this concern over such a small word, remember that small words can have big consequences.

In 1971 a federal court rendered its decision on a case brought by a woman who became pregnant while taking birth control pills. She sued the manufacturer, Eli Lilly and Company, for breach of warranty. The woman lost her case. Basing its ruling on a statement in the pamphlet accompanying the pills, which stated that, "When taken as directed, the tablets offer virtually 100 percent protection," the court ruled that there was no warranty, expressed or implied, that the pills were absolutely effective. In its ruling, the court pointed out that, according to the *Webster's Third New International Dictionary*, "virtually" means "almost entirely" and clearly does not mean "absolute" (*Whittington* v. *Eli Lilly and Company*, 333 F. Supp. 98). In other words, the Eli Lilly company was really saying that its birth control pill, even when taken as directed, *did not in fact* provide 100 percent protection against pregnancy. But Eli Lilly didn't want to put it that way because then many women might not have bought Lilly's birth control pills.

The next time you see the ad that says that this dishwasher detergent "leaves dishes virtually spotless," just remember how advertisers twist the meaning of the weasel word "virtually." You can have lots of spots on your dishes after using this detergent and the ad claim will still be true, because what this claim really means is that this detergent does not *in fact* leave your dishes spotless. Whenever you see or hear an ad claim that uses the word "virtually," just translate that claim into its real meaning. So the television set that is "virtually trouble free" becomes the television set that is not in fact trouble free, the "virtually foolproof operation" of any appliance becomes an operation that is in fact not foolproof, and the product that "virtually never needs service" becomes the product that is not in fact service free.

## *New and Improved*

If "new" is the most frequently used word on a product package, "improved" is the second most frequent. In fact, the two words are almost always used together. It seems just about everything sold these days is "new and improved." The next time you're in the supermarket, try counting the number of times you see these words on products. But you'd better do it while you're walking down just one aisle, otherwise you'll need a calculator to keep track of your counting.

Just what do these words mean? The use of the word "new" is restricted by regulations, so an advertiser can't just use the word on a product or in an ad without meeting certain requirements. For example, a product is considered new for about six months during a national advertising campaign. If the product is being advertised only in a limited test market area, the word can be used longer, and in some instances has been used for as long as two years.

What makes a product "new"? Some products have been around for a long time, yet every once in a while you discover that they are being advertised as "new." Well, an advertiser can call a product new if there has been "a material functional change" in the product. What is "a material functional change," you ask? Good question. In fact it's such a good question it's being asked all the time. It's up to the manufacturer to prove that the product has undergone such a change. And if the manufacturer isn't challenged on the claim, then there's no one to stop it. Moreover, the change does not have to be an improvement in the product. One manufacturer added an artificial lemon scent to a cleaning product and called it "new and improved," even though the product did not clean any better than without the lemon scent. The manufacturer defended the use of the word "new" on the grounds that the artificial scent changed the chemical formula of the product and therefore constituted "a material functional change."

Which brings up the word "improved." When used in advertising, "improved" does not mean "made better." It only means "changed" or "different from before." So, if the detergent maker puts a plastic pour spout on the box of detergent, the product has been "improved," and away we go with a whole new advertising campaign. Or, if the cereal maker adds more fruit or a different kind of fruit to the cereal, there's an improved product. Now you know why manufacturers are constantly making little changes in their products. Whole new advertising campaigns, designed to convince you that the product has been changed for the better, are based on small changes in superficial aspects of a product. The next time you see an ad for an "improved" product, ask yourself what was wrong with the old one. Ask yourself just how "improved" the product is. Finally, you might check to see whether the "improved" version costs more than the unimproved one. After all, someone has to pay for the millions of dollars spent advertising the improved product.

Of course, advertisers really like to run ads that claim a product is "new and improved." While what constitutes a "new" product may be subject to some regulation, "improved" is a subjective judgment. A manufacturer changes the shape of its stick deodorant, but the shape doesn't improve the function of the deodorant. That is, changing the shape doesn't affect the deodorizing ability of the deodorant, so the manufacturer calls it "improved." Another manufacturer adds ammonia to its liquid cleaner and calls it "new and improved." Since adding ammonia does affect the cleaning ability of the product, there has been a "material functional change" in the product, and the manufacturer can now call its cleaner "new," and "improved" as well. Now the weasel words "new and improved" are plastered all over the package and are the basis for a multimillion-dollar ad campaign. But after six months the word "new" will have to go, until someone can dream up another change in the product. Perhaps it will be adding color to the liquid, or changing the shape of the package, or maybe adding a new dripless pour spout, or perhaps a ____. The "improvements" are endless, and so are the new advertising claims and campaigns.

"New" is just too useful and powerful a word in advertising for advertisers to pass it up easily. So they use weasel words that say "new" without really saying it. One of their favorites is "introducing," as in, "Introducing improved Tide," or "Introducing the stain remover." The first is simply saying, here's our improved soap; the second, here's our new advertising campaign for our detergent. Another favorite is "now," as in, "Now there's Sinex," which simply means that Sinex is available. Then there are phrases like "Today's Chevrolet," "Presenting Dristan," and "A fresh way to start the day." The list is really endless because advertisers are always finding new ways to say "new" without really saying it. If there is a second edition of this book, I'll just call it the "new and improved" edition. Wouldn't you really rather have a "new and improved" edition of this book rather than a "second" edition?

## *Acts Fast*

"Acts" and "works" are two popular weasel words in advertising because they bring action to the product and to the advertising claim. When you see the ad for the cough syrup that "Acts on the cough control center," ask yourself what this cough syrup is claiming to do. Well, it's just claiming to "act," to do something, to perform an action. What is it that the cough syrup does? The ad doesn't say. It only claims to perform an action or do something on your "cough control center." By the way, what and where is your "cough control center"? I don't remember learning about that part of the body in human biology class.

Ads that use such phrases as "acts fast," "acts against," "acts to prevent," and the like are saying essentially nothing, because "act" is a word empty of any specific meaning. The ads are always careful not to specify exactly what "act" the product performs. Just because a brand of aspirin claims to "act fast" for headache relief doesn't mean this aspirin is any better than any other aspirin. What is the "act" that this aspirin performs? You're never told. Maybe it just dissolves quickly. Since aspirin is a parity product, all aspirin is the same and therefore functions the same.

## *Works Like Anything Else*

If you don't find the word "acts" in an ad, you will probably find the weasel word "works." In fact, the two words are almost interchangeable in advertising. Watch out for ads that say a product "works against," "works like," "works for," or "works longer." As with "acts," "works" is the same meaningless verb used to make you think that this product really does something, and maybe even something special or unique. But "works," like "acts," is basically a word empty of any specific meaning.

## *Like Magic*

Whenever advertisers want you to stop thinking about the product and to start thinking about something bigger, better, or more attractive than the product, they use that very popular weasel word, "like." The word "like" is the advertiser's equivalent of a magician's use of misdirection. "Like" gets you to ignore the product and concentrate on the claim the advertiser is making about it. "For skin like peaches and cream" claims the ad for a skin cream. What is this ad really claiming? It doesn't say this cream will give you peaches-and-cream skin. There is no verb in this claim, so it doesn't even mention using the product. How is skin ever like "peaches and cream"? Remember, ads must be read literally and exactly, according to the dictionary definition of words. (Remember "virtually" in the Eli Lilly case.) The ad is making absolutely no promise or claim whatsoever for this skin cream. If you think this cream will give you soft, smooth, youthful-looking skin, you are the one who has read that meaning into the ad.

The wine that claims "It's like taking a trip to France" wants you to think about a romantic evening in Paris as you walk along the boulevard after a wonderful meal in an intimate little bistro. Of course, you don't really believe that a wine can take you to France, but the goal of the ad is to get you to think pleasant, romantic thoughts about France and not about how the wine tastes or how expensive it may be. That little word "like" has taken you away from crushed grapes into a world of your own imaginative making. Who knows, maybe the next time you buy wine, you'll think those pleasant thoughts when you see this brand of wine, and you'll buy it. Or, maybe you weren't even thinking about buying wine at all, but now you just might pick up a bottle the next time you're shopping. Ah, the power of "like" in advertising.

How about the most famous "like" claim of all, "Winston tastes good like a cigarette should"? Ignoring the grammatical error here, you might want to know what this claim is saying. Whether a cigarette tastes good or bad is a subjective judgment because what tastes good to one person may well taste horrible to another. Not everyone likes fried snails, even if they are called escargot. (*De gustibus non est disputandum*, which was probably the Roman rule for advertising as well as for defending the games in the Colosseum.) There are many people who say all cigarettes taste terrible, other people who say only some cigarettes taste all right, and still others who say all cigarettes taste good. Who's right? Everyone, because taste is a matter of personal judgment.

Moreover, note the use of the conditional, "should." The complete claim is, "Winston tastes good like a cigarette should taste." But should cigarettes taste good? Again, this is a matter of personal judgment and probably depends most on one's experiences with smoking. So, the Winston ad is simply saying that Winston cigarettes are just like any other cigarette: Some people like them and some people don't. On that statement, R. J. Reynolds conducted a very successful multimillion-dollar advertising campaign that helped keep Winston the number-two-selling cigarette in the United States, close behind number one, Marlboro.

## *Can't It Be Up to the Claim?*

Analyzing ads for doublespeak requires that you pay attention to every word in the ad and determine what each word really means. Advertisers try to wrap their claims in language that sounds concrete, specific, and objective, when in fact the language of advertising is anything but. Your job is to read carefully and listen critically so that when the announcer says that "Crest can be of significant value . . . ," you know immediately that this claim says absolutely nothing. Where is the doublespeak in this ad? Start with the second word.

Once again, you have to look at what words really mean, not what you think they mean or what the advertiser wants you to think they mean. The ad for Crest only says that using Crest "can be" of "significant value." What really throws you off in this ad is the brilliant use of "significant." It draws your attention to the word "value" and makes you forget that the ad only claims that Crest "can be." The ad doesn't say that Crest *is* of value, only that it is "able" or "possible" to be of value, because that's all that "can" means.

It's so easy to miss the importance of those little words, "can be." Almost as easy as missing the importance of the words "up to" in an ad. These words are very popular in sales ads. You know, the ones that say, "Up to 50 percent Off!" Now, what does that claim mean? Not much, because the store or manufacturer has to reduce the price of only a few items by 50 percent. Everything else can be reduced a lot less, or not even reduced. Moreover, don't you want to know 50 percent off of what? Is it 50 percent off the "manufacturer's suggested list price," which is the highest possible price? Was the price artificially inflated and then reduced? In other ads, "up to" expresses an ideal situation. The medicine that works "up to ten times faster," the battery that lasts "up to twice as long," and the soap that gets you "up to twice as clean" all are based on ideal situations for using those products, situations in which you can be sure you will never find yourself.

### *Unfinished Words*

Unfinished words are a kind of "up to" claim in advertising. The claim that a battery lasts "up to twice as long" usually doesn't finish the comparison—twice as long as what? A birthday candle? A tank of gas? A cheap battery made in a country not noted for its technological achievements? The implication is that the battery lasts twice as long as batteries made by other battery makers, or twice as long as earlier model batteries made by the advertiser, but the ad doesn't really make these claims. You read these claims into the ad, aided by the visual images the advertiser so carefully provides.

Unfinished words depend on you to finish them, to provide the words the advertisers so thoughtfully left out of the ad. Pall Mall cigarettes were once advertised as "A longer finer and milder smoke." The question is, longer, finer, and milder than what? The aspirin that claims it contains "Twice as much of the pain reliever doctors recommend most" doesn't tell you what pain reliever it contains twice as much of. (By the way, it's aspirin. That's right; it just contains twice the amount of aspirin. And how much is twice the amount? Twice of what amount?) Panadol boasts that "nobody reduces fever faster," but, since Panadol is a parity product, this claim simply means that Panadol isn't any better than any other product in its parity class. "You can be sure if it's Westinghouse," you're told, but just exactly what it is you can be sure of is never mentioned. "Magnavox gives you more" doesn't tell you what you get more of. More value? More television? More than they gave you before? It sounds nice, but it means nothing, until you fill in the claim with your own words, the words the advertisers didn't use. Since each of us fills in the claim differently, the ad and the product can become all things to all people, and not promise a single thing.

Unfinished words abound in advertising because they appear to promise so much. More importantly, they can be joined with powerful visual images on television to appear to be making significant promises about a product's effectiveness without really making any promises. In a television ad, the aspirin product that claims fast relief can show a person with a headache taking the product and then, in what appears to be a matter of minutes, claiming complete relief. This visual image is far more powerful than any claim made in unfinished words. Indeed, the visual image completes the unfinished words for you, filling in with pictures what the words leave out. And you thought that ads didn't affect you. What brand of aspirin do you use?

Some years ago, Ford's advertisements proclaimed "Ford LTD—700 percent quieter." Now, what do you think Ford was claiming with these unfinished words? What was the Ford LTD quieter than? A Cadillac? A Mercedes Benz? A BMW? Well, when the FTC asked Ford to substantiate this unfinished claim, Ford replied that it meant that the inside of the LTD was 700 percent quieter than the outside. How did you finish those unfinished words when you first read them? Did you even come close to Ford's meaning?

### *Combining Weasel Words*

A lot of ads don't fall neatly into one category or another because they use a variety of different devices and words. Different weasel words are often combined to make an ad claim. The claim, "Coffee-Mate gives coffee more body, more flavor," uses Unfinished Words ("more" than what?) and also uses words that have no specific meaning ("body" and "flavor"). Along with "taste" (remember the Winston ad and its claim to taste good), "body" and "flavor" mean nothing because their meaning is entirely subjective. To you, "body" in coffee might mean thick, black, almost bitter coffee, while I might take it to mean a light brown, delicate coffee. Now, if you think you understood that last sentence, read it again, because it said nothing of objective value; it was filled with weasel words of no specific meaning: "thick," "black," "bitter," "light brown," and "delicate." Each of those words has no specific, objective meaning, because each of us can interpret them differently.

Try this slogan: "Looks, smells, tastes like ground-roast coffee." So, are you now going to buy Taster's Choice instant coffee because of this ad? "Looks," "smells," and "tastes" are all words with no specific meaning and depend on your interpretation of them for any meaning. Then there's that great weasel word "like," which simply suggests a comparison but does not make the actual connection between the product and the quality. Besides, do you know what "ground-roast" coffee is? I don't, but it sure sounds good. So, out of seven words in this ad, four are definite weasel words, two are quite meaningless, and only one has any clear meaning.

Remember the Anacin ad—"Twice as much of the pain reliever doctors recommend most"? There's a whole lot of weaseling going on in this ad. First, what's the pain reliever they're talking about in this ad? Aspirin, of course. In fact, any time you see or hear an ad using those words "pain reliever," you can automatically substitute the word "aspirin" for them. (Makers of acetaminophen and ibuprofen pain relievers are careful in their advertising to identify their products as nonaspirin products.) So, now we know that Anacin has aspirin in it. Moreover, we know that Anacin has twice as much aspirin in it, but we don't know twice as much as what. Does it have twice as much aspirin as an ordinary aspirin tablet? If so, what is an ordinary aspirin tablet, and how much aspirin does it contain? Twice as much as Excedrin or Bufferin? Twice as much as a chocolate chip cookie? Remember those Unfinished Words and how they lead you on without saying anything.

Finally, what about those doctors who are doing all that recommending? Who are they? How many of them are there? What kind of doctors are they? What are their qualifications? Who asked them about recommending pain relievers? What other pain relievers did they recommend? And there are a whole lot more questions about this "poll" of doctors to which I'd like to know the answers, but you get the point. Sometimes, when I call my doctor, she tells me to take two aspirin and call her office in the morning. Is that where Anacin got this ad?

## *Read the Label, or the Brochure*

Weasel words aren't just found on television, on the radio, or in newspaper and magazine ads. Just about any language associated with a product will contain the doublespeak of advertising. Remember the Eli Lilly case and the doublespeak on the information sheet that came with the birth control pills. Here's another example.

In 1983, the Estée Lauder cosmetics company announced a new product called "Night Repair." A small brochure distributed with the product stated that "Night Repair was scientifically formulated in Estée Lauder's U.S. laboratories as part of the Swiss Age-Controlling Skincare Program. Although only nature controls the aging process, this program helps control the signs of aging and encourages skin to look and feel younger." You might want to read these two sentences again, because they sound great but say nothing.

First, note that the product was "scientifically formulated" in the company's laboratories. What does that mean? What constitutes a scientific formulation? You wouldn't expect the company to say that the product was casually, mechanically, or carelessly formulated, or just thrown together one day when the people in the white coats didn't have anything better to do. But the word "scientifically" lends an air of precision and promise that just isn't there.

It is the second sentence, however, that's really weasely, both syntactically and semantically. The only factual part of this sentence is the introductory dependent clause—"only nature controls the aging process." Thus, the only fact in the ad is relegated to a dependent clause, a clause dependent on the main clause, which contains no factual or definite information at all and indeed purports to contradict the independent clause. The new "skincare program" (notice it's not a skin cream but a "program") does not claim to stop or even retard the aging process. What, then, does Night Repair, at a price of over $35 (in 1983 dollars) for a .87-ounce bottle do? According to this brochure, nothing. It only "helps," and the brochure does not say how much it helps. Moreover, it only "helps control," and then it only helps control the "*signs* of aging," not the aging itself. Also, it "encourages" skin not to *be* younger but only to "look and feel" younger. The brochure does not say younger than what. Of the sixteen words in the main clause of this second sentence, nine are weasel words. So, before you spend all that money for Night Repair, or any other cosmetic product, read the words carefully, and then decide if you're getting what you think you're paying for.

## *Other Tricks of the Trade*

Advertisers' use of doublespeak is endless. The best way advertisers can make something out of nothing is through words. Although there are a lot of visual images used on television and in magazines and newspapers, every advertiser wants to create that memorable line that will stick in the public consciousness. I am sure pure joy reigned in one advertising agency when a study found that children who were asked to spell the word "relief" promptly and proudly responded "r-o-l-a-i-d-s."

The variations, combinations, and permutations of doublespeak used in advertising go and on, running from the use of rhetorical questions ("Wouldn't you really rather have a Buick?" "If you can't trust Prestone, who can you trust?") to flattering you with compliments ("The lady has taste." "We think a cigar smoker is someone special." "You've come a long way baby."). You know, of course, how you're *supposed* to answer those questions, and you know that those compliments are just leading up to the sales pitches for the products. Before you dismiss such tricks of the trade as obvious, however, just remember that all of these statements and questions were part of very successful advertising campaigns.

A more subtle approach is the ad that proclaims a supposedly unique quality for a product, a quality that really isn't unique. "If it doesn't say Goodyear, it can't be polyglas." Sounds good, doesn't it? Polyglas is available only from Goodyear because Goodyear copyrighted that trade name. Any other tire manufacturer could make exactly the same tire but could not call it "polyglas," because that would be copyright infringement. "Polyglas" is simply Goodyear's name for its fiberglass-reinforced tire.

Since we like to think of ourselves as living in a technologically advanced country, science and technology have a great appeal in selling products. Advertisers are quick to use scientific doublespeak to push their products. There are all kinds of elixirs, additives, scientific potions, and mysterious mixtures added to all kinds of products. Gasoline contains "HTA," "F-130," "Platformate," and other chemical-sounding additives, but nowhere does an advertisement give any real information about the additive.

Shampoo, deodorant, mouthwash, cold medicine, sleeping pills, and any number of other products all seem to contain some special chemical ingredient that allows them to work wonders. "Certs contains a sparkling drop of Retsyn." So what? What's "Retsyn"? What's it do? What's so special about it? When they don't have a secret ingredient in their product, advertisers still find a way to claim scientific validity. There's "Sinarest. Created by a research scientist who actually gets sinus headaches." Sounds nice, but what kind of research does this scientist do? How do you know if she is any kind of expert on sinus medicine? Besides, this ad doesn't tell you a thing about the medicine itself and what it does.

## *Advertising Doublespeak Quick Quiz*

Now it's time to test your awareness of advertising doublespeak. (You didn't think I would just let you read this and forget it, did you?) The following is a list of statements from some recent ads. Your job is to figure out what each of these ads really says.

DOMINO'S PIZZA: "Because nobody delivers better."
SINUTAB: "It can stop the pain."
TUMS: "The stronger acid neutralizer."
MAXIMUM STRENGTH DRISTAN: "Strong medicine for tough sinus colds."
LISTERMINT: "Making your mouth a cleaner place."
CASCADE: "For virtually spotless dishes nothing beats Cascade."
NUPRIN: "Little. Yellow. Different. Better."
ANACIN: "Better relief."
SUDAFED: "Fast sinus relief that won't put you fast asleep."
ADVIL: "Better relief."
PONDS COLD CREAM: "Ponds cleans like no soap can."
MILLER LITE BEER: "Tastes great. Less filling."
PHILIPS MILK OF MAGNESIA: "Nobody treats you better than MOM (Philips Milk of Magnesia)."
BAYER: "The wonder drug that works wonders."
CRACKER BARREL: "Judged to be the best."
KNORR: "Where taste is everything."
ANUSOL: "Anusol is the word to remember for relief."

DIMETAPP: "It relieves kids as well as colds."
LIQUID DRĀNO: "The liquid strong enough to be called Drāno."
JOHNSON & JOHNSON BABY POWDER: "Like magic for your skin."
PURITAN: "Make it your oil for life."
PAM: "Pam, because how you cook is as important as what you cook."
IVORY SHAMPOO AND CONDITIONER: "Leave your hair feeling Ivory clean."
TYLENOL GEL-CAPS: "It's not a capsule. It's better."
ALKA-SELTZER PLUS: "Fast, effective relief for winter colds."

## *The World of Advertising*

In the world of advertising, people wear "dentures," not false teeth; they suffer from "occasional irregularity," not constipation; they need deodorants for their "nervous wetness," not for sweat; they use "bathroom tissue," not toilet paper; and they don't dye their hair, they "tint" or "rinse" it. Advertisements offer "real counterfeit diamonds" without the slightest hint of embarrassment, or boast of goods made out of "genuine imitation leather" or "virgin vinyl."

In the world of advertising, the girdle becomes a "body shaper," "form persuader," "control garment," "controller," "outerwear enhancer," "body garment," or "anti-gravity panties," and is sold with such trade names as "The Instead," "The Free Spirit," and "The Body Briefer."

A study some years ago found the following words to be among the most popular used in U.S. television advertisements: "new," "improved," "better," "extra," "fresh," "clean," "beautiful," "free," "good," "great," and "light." At the same time, the following words were found to be among the most frequent on British television: "new," "good-better-best," "free," "fresh," "delicious," "full," "sure," "clean," "wonderful," and "special." While these words may occur most frequently in ads, and while ads may be filled with weasel words, you have to watch out for all the words used in advertising, not just the words mentioned here.

Every word in an ad is there for a reason; no word is wasted. Your job is to figure out exactly what each word is doing in an ad—what each word really means, not what the advertiser wants you to think it means. Remember, the ad is trying to get you to buy a product, so it will put the product in the best possible light, using any device, trick, or means legally allowed. Your own defense against advertising (besides taking up permanent residence on the moon) is to develop and use a strong critical reading, listening, and looking ability. Always ask yourself what the ad is *really* saying. When you see ads on television, don't be misled by the pictures, the visual images. What does the ad say about the product? What does the ad *not* say? What information is missing from the ad? Only by becoming an active, critical consumer of the doublespeak of advertising will you ever be able to cut through the doublespeak and discover what the ad is really saying.

Professor Del Kehl of Arizona State University has updated the Twenty-third Psalm to reflect the power of advertising to meet our needs and solve our problems. It seems fitting that this chapter close with this new Psalm.

**The Adman's 23rd**

The Adman is my shepherd;
I shall ever want.
He maketh me to walk a mile for a Camel;
He leadeth me beside Crystal Waters
  In the High Country of Coors;
He restoreth my soul with Perrier.
He guideth me in Marlboro Country
For Mammon's sake.
Yea, though I walk through the Valley of the
  Jolly Green Giant,
In the shadow of B.O., halitosis, indigestion,
  headache pain, and hemorrhoidal tissue,
I will fear no evil,
For I am in Good Hands with Allstate;
Thy Arid, Scope, Tums, Tylenol, and Preparation H—
They comfort me.
Stouffer's preparest a table before the TV
In the presence of all my appetites;
Thou anointest my head with Brylcream;
My Decaffeinated Cup runneth over.
Surely surfeit and security shall follow me
All the days of Metropolitan Life,
And I shall dwell in a Continental Home
With a mortgage forever and ever.

*Amen.*

# SLANTING THE STORY

## Trudy Lieberman

"Our country must have a whole new generation of conservative journalists. . . . In the long run, our nation can't survive under a big media liberal monopoly. . . . The liberals' virtual media monopoly persists in most areas, largely due to a lack of qualified conservative alternatives."

—*Senator Trent Lott, fund-raising letter, March 1996*

"Liberal media bias is out of control. It's indecent."

—*Congressman J. C. Watts, Jr., fund-raising letter, November 1998*

ON NOVEMBER 25, 1994, a few weeks after the midterm elections propelled Newt Gingrich and his band of conservatives to the pinnacle of legislative power, conservative think tanks hit paydirt in the media. In news stories that day, The Heritage Foundation was mentioned fourteen times, the Cato Institute seven times, the American Enterprise Institute seven times, the Manhattan Institute twice, and the Competitive Enterprise Institute once. Newspapers, including big ones like the *New York Times* and the *Washington Post* and regionals like the *Palm Beach Post* and *Rocky Mountain News*, quoted think-tank officials on topics ranging from taxes and prisoners to welfare and the new Congress. The *Washington Post* quoted John J. Miller, an immigration expert with the Manhattan Institute, who said it was a disservice to call noncitizens in federal prisons "immigrants," since they were "drug smugglers, not people coming here to make a better life for themselves and their families."[1] A Cato Institute official observed in the *Rocky Mountain News* that American aid doesn't actually help people in the Third World.[2] *USA Today* quoted the ever-present Norman Ornstein, the American Enterprise Institute's congressional scholar, on the role of the Senate minority leader.[3]

That morning the *New York Times* editorial page published an op-ed piece on welfare written by Myron Magnet, editor of the Manhattan Institute's *City Journal*,[4] and a *Times* news story about Germany's baby bust quoted Nicholas Eberstadt of the American Enterprise Institute.[5]

In the evening, *The MacNeil/Lehrer NewsHour* presented a program on welfare reform. Guests included Linda Chavez, representing the Manhattan Institute, and Douglas Besharov, of the American Enterprise Institute, a representative from the Ford Foundation (a safe choice for the progressive viewpoint), and Theresa Funiciello, an author and former welfare recipient who did not contribute much balance against the conservative perspective and instead seemed to bolster the conservative view. Funiciello said that what people are opposed to is the "extraordinary growth in the welfare state, which is inclusive of an enormous range of social welfare professionals who make their living off poor people. Most of the money in the welfare system never gets anywhere near poor people." That night the *NewsHour* also featured commentary by Ornstein, who gave his thoughts on the future of conservatism.[6]

All in all, it was a very good showing for conservatives, who claim they are hard-pressed to get their views into the mainstream media. In their fund-raising letters, conservatives like Trent Lott and J. C. Watts continue to deplore the liberal hegemony over the media, but in reality, the right's viewpoint is pervasive and ubiquitous.

How the right wing has come to dominate public policy debates is one of the most significant political stories of the last two decades. The right-wing success stems largely from a variety of aggressive strategies used by well-financed think tanks and policy institutes to influence the media's coverage of political and economic issues. The effectiveness of groups such as the Manhattan Institute, the Capital Research Center, the National Taxpayers Union, The Heritage Foundation, the Cato Institute, the Competitive Enterprise Institute, Citizens for a Sound Economy, and the Washington Legal Foundation (whose activities are detailed in this book) has sometimes resulted in misleading and one-sided reporting that has given the electorate a distorted view of many important issues.

Those organizations have seized upon weaknesses and problems of government programs and agencies, have attacked other organizations that stand in their way, and have successfully persuaded the media to see the solutions they want to impose as the only reasonable and feasible ones to society's problems. The result has been little or no discussion of alternatives, such as raising revenues to adequately fund Medicare, increasing the age of eligibility for early Social Security benefits, or more adequately funding the FDA to speed up drug approvals. "The reason there's no liberal Rush Limbaugh or a liberal National Empowerment Television is that the American people don't want to buy liberal products," maintains Dan Mitchell, a senior fellow at The Heritage Foundation.[7] Is it that the public doesn't want to buy them or that none are offered for sale, leaving the public with little choice?

Backed by huge sums of money from a handful of ideologically grounded foundations, right-wing think tanks operating in the states and in the national political arena have become idea peddlers extraordinaire, every bit as skillful as the sellers of toothpaste and detergent. To further their agendas, they have marketed the flat tax, medical savings accounts, Medicare reform, privatization of Social Security, and school vouchers in much the same way Procter and Gamble sells Crest. "The sophisticated ability to relate ideology to constituencies is what counts," explained William J. Baroody, Jr., former president of the American Enterprise Institute. "We pay as much attention to dissemination of product as to the content."[8] Ideas once considered the crank notions of right-wing ideologues have become law—medical savings accounts and restrictions on lawsuits for securities fraud, to take just two examples. Indeed, says Jeanette Goodman, executive vice president of the National Center for Policy Analysis (the group that brought medical savings accounts from the germ of an idea to a viable insurance product), selling ideas is no different from marketing in a for-profit company. One hit cannot make a difference, she points out. The same clear, concise message must come from every direction.[9]

And it does. Through newsletters filled with tidbits for talk shows, weighty studies and surveys, luncheons where ideas are floated over plates of chicken and vegetables, and spokespersons given friendly hearings by reporters, these groups have spread their messages to opinion leaders and to men and women on the street.

While groups on the left sometimes use the same techniques, the right has used them more effectively, and increasingly reporters are relying on them. By embracing the right-wing spin, giving it independent credibility, and spreading its messages uncritically, the press has become a silent partner, and the public is none the wiser. Says one TV journalist who asked not to be named: "They [right-wing groups] understand the propaganda potential. Viewers are confused about what's hard news and out-and-out propaganda. They can't tell the difference between Paul Weyrich [president of the conservative Free Congress Foundation] and Dan Rather."

If viewers, readers, and listeners are so confused, that bodes poorly for the media as an essential ingredient of American democracy. Ben Bagdikian, the press critic and former dean of the Graduate School of Journalism at the University of California, Berkeley, put it this way: "What gets reported enters the public agenda. What is not reported may not be lost forever, but it may be lost at a time when it is most needed."[10]

Foundations controlled by Pittsburgh philanthropist Richard Mellon Scaife, and the Olin, Bradley, Smith Richardson, McKenna, Koch, Earhart, and Lambe foundations—as well as a handful of less well known but influential organizations—are shaping American thinking. A study by the National Committee for Responsive Philanthropy found that between 1992 and 1994, twelve conservative foundations with combined assets of more than $1 billion targeted $210 million to think tanks and advocacy groups to support conservative programs and objectives. Those groups in turn have sold their ideas to the media. Specifically, those foundations gave $9.3 million to state-based think tanks and advocacy groups, $10.5 million to conservative, pro-market law firms and legal projects, and $16.3 million to support media watchdog groups, alternative media outlets, and public television and radio for issue-oriented public affairs or news reporting.[11]

The sums available from some of these foundations are significant. Take, for instance, the Milwaukee-based Lynde and Harry Bradley Foundation, whose money was derived from the manufacturing of motor controls. In 1997, the Bradley foundation gave these organizations the following amounts just for public and government-affairs programs.[12]

- *American Enterprise Institute* $810,000 for fellowships, lecture series, and foreign and defense policy studies program
- *American Spectator Educational Foundation* $127,500 for operating support, special projects, and dinner discussion meetings
- *Cato Institute* $75,000 for economic, regulatory, and tax policy studies
- *Citizens for a Sound Economy* $25,000 for general operating support
- *Competitive Enterprise Institute* $40,000 for "death by regulation" project
- *Educational Broadcasting Corporation* $100,000 for Think Tank program with Ben Wattenberg
- *Ethics and Policy Center* $325,000 for general operating support and senior fellow
- *Free Congress Research and Education Foundation* $425,000 for programming for National Empowerment Television and general operating support

- *The Heritage Foundation* $825,000 for domestic policy studies, Bradley fellows, a state relations department and a senior fellow in Southeast Asian studies
- *Hudson Institute* $250,000 for a welfare policy center
- *Manhattan Institute* $150,000 for the Center for Civic Innovation and $18,875 for a project on congregational mobilization for community transformation
- *National Center for Policy Analysis* $100,000 for research on welfare reform
- *Reason Foundation* $75,000 for general operating support
- *US Term Limits Foundation* $25,000 for general operating support

Add these sums to similar amounts given by other foundations, wealthy individuals, and corporations, and it's not hard to see the vast resources the right-wing network has at its disposal. The National Committee for Responsive Philanthropy found that in 1996 the top twenty conservative think tanks spent $158 million, most of it provided by foundations and corporations. The committee estimates that by 2000, those think tanks will have spent about $1 billion to further their strategic goals for U.S. policy.[13]

Does the public know where the ideas come from and who pays to put them on the agenda? Ask anyone why health reform failed in 1994, and fingers invariably point to a public unwilling to support a government-run program. While the infamous "Harry and Louise" commercials sponsored by the insurance industry became the symbol, it was really behind-the-scenes work by right-wing think tanks that doomed efforts at reform. Talk-show hosts and direct-mail campaigns by conservative groups fueled the ultimate scare-story that turned the public against reform—the fostered threat that people would not be able to choose their own doctor. "Some say the talk-show hosts made the biggest difference," says Jeanette Goodman. "As we saw a new issue or a new idea, we immediately addressed it. It was the most important thing for talk shows because they got materials they could feed in at a time when people were interested in what it all meant."[14] Lisa McGiffert, an advocate in Consumers Union's regional office in Austin, Texas, recalled that during a radio tour in early 1994, radio hosts all seemed to ask the same questions about doctors going to jail.[15] They apparently had gotten the question from the same source. "Heritage was instrumental in stopping the Clinton plan," says Cheryl Rubin, director of public relations at Heritage.[16] The National Center and Heritage properly claim credit for their less-than-visible accomplishments, which are a true measure of their effectiveness. "If you're effective in your advocacy work, journalists or anyone else are not aware of it," says Michael Pertschuk, co-director of the Advocacy Institute.[17]

Right-wing think tanks have found a congenial home for their messages in today's simplified journalism. Perhaps because the news business has changed so radically, groups like Heritage, Cato, and Citizens for a Sound Economy can now help define the news, and influence and shape public opinion. During a radio show in 1994 that dissected how right-wing organizations like Floyd Brown's Citizens United fed the press tidbits about Clinton's Whitewater real estate deal, *Boston Globe* reporter John Aloysius Farrell made an astonishing comment. "Floyd Brown is the media now," he declared.[18]

Conservative groups have learned to boil down their messages to fit the new model of soundbite journalism, leaving the details for the weighty studies and policy analyses disseminated in more elite venues.

Media emphasis on soundbites, anecdotal journalism, and headline services opens the door to organizations with highly partisan motives and specific narrow agendas to get on the air or in print, especially if what they have to say is titillating or outrageous. Mark Weaver, a news reporter at WMAL-AM in Washington D.C., was blunt: "Our news director says, 'I don't care what story you put on the air, but it better be interesting.' It may be ridiculous, funny, anything that gets people's attention. That's what makes money."

Weaver amplified his station's thinking for attendees at a seminar on how to manage the media for grassroots community groups sponsored a few years ago by the Free Congress Foundation. "Radio-station news departments are designed to attract and hold more audience, which in turn generates more profit, not necessarily to impart 'important' information," Weaver told his listeners. "Radio news has become a headline service. We want as many as we can get. We want them bam, bam, bam. The more stories you have, the more you cram in, the more the perception that the audience is being informed."[19]

Newspapers, too, are making stories shorter, hoping they will be more palatable to readers. When the *Buffalo News* redesigned its front page to include only three stories running about 250 to 500 words apiece, it bought radio spots to promote the change: "You can get the facts without straining your brain."[20] Consultants for the *Winston-Salem Journal* suggested that front-page stories should be six inches or less, and that a reporter should use a press release and/or one or two "cooperative sources," take no more than 0.9 hours to do each story, and produce forty such stories in a week.[21] Right-wing groups stand ready as cooperative sources to fill the abbreviated news holes.

Shorter stories inevitably mean less context and less analysis to help readers or listeners understand what's really at stake. The new-model journalism is tailor-made for the simplistic, even alarmist, messages preached by the right wing. It's easy to headline the notion that Social Security is going bankrupt and won't be around thirty years from now. The left has yet to figure out how to communicate the message that it will be. Does it take more ink or time to tell a fuller story, or is it that the left has not learned to effectively bullet-point its ideas? Or is the left unsure of its message?

At the same time, the normal constraints of the old journalistic model make it difficult to promote a reasoned dialogue on political issues in this era of idea marketing and ideological drumbeating. Dane Smith, a political reporter for the *Minneapolis Star-Tribune*, explained the futility of trying to counter the constant repetition of the right wing's messages. "There's only so far you can go in the news columns in flat-out contradicting or confirming so-called spin," he said. "It's the nature of the beast. You can't run the same story every day. It's just not what we do."[22] At least that's not what the media does unless the topic involves glamour, sex, or scandal. Monica had more cachet as a daily news story than Medicare did.

When I first began this project some five years ago, I assumed that the mainstream media were relying on right-wing groups for "balance" quotes and spokespersons "for the other side." Instead, I found an influence penetrating far beyond the occasional quote for balance. Conservative organizations are designing the agenda, and other groups—liberal, progressive, and in-between—are called for the occasional balance quote.

This book demonstrates how, with help from the mainstream media, right-wing think tanks and organizations have discredited their opponents, moved their ideas to the front of the national agenda, dominated the debate, and engineered big changes in public policy. They have cleverly used the media, sometimes with far-reaching consequences.

I hope journalists will learn from those examples and begin to apply to interest groups (and the corporations and foundations that fund them) the same skepticism and suspicion they now heap on politicians and government officials. The media must begin to examine the "products" these groups are selling, scrutinizing both the sales claims and the consequences of "buying" them.

In 1981, the *Columbia Journalism Review* published an article detailing the many activities of Richard Mellon Scaife. That story concluded: "Scaife has helped to create an illusion of diversity where none exists. The result could be an increasing number of one-sided debates in which the challengers are far outnumbered, if indeed they are heard from at all."[23] At that time, Scaife was a new phenomenon and The Heritage Foundation, which he was funding, was a relative neophyte in the political landscape. In the past nineteen years, Scaife, Heritage, and similar organizations have come of age. Indeed, debate *has* become one-sided. The implications for the future of American democracy are profound.

## Notes

1. Pierre Thomas, "One Out of Four Federal Prisoners Not a U.S. Citizen; Drug Trade Major Factor in Rising Detention Rate," *Washington Post*, 25 November 1994, p. A1.
2. "Helms and a Real Issue," Denver *Rocky Mountain News*, editorial, 25 November 1994, p. 71A.
3. Richard Wolf, "Congressional Leaders Still Campaigning; House, Senate Members Vie for Party Posts," *USA Today*, 25 November 1994, p. 4A.

4. "The Welfare Gap—Problem No. 1: The Children," Myron Magnet, *New York Times*, 25 November 1994, p. 37.
5. "$650 a Baby: Germany to Pay to Stem Decline in Births," Stephen Kinzer, *New York Times*, 25 November 1994, p. 3.
6. "Helping the Needy; Political Wrap," The *MacNeil/Lehrer NewsHour* (Educational Broadcasting and GWETA: 25 November 1994).
7. Dan Mitchell, senior fellow, The Heritage Foundation, interview with author.
8. Sidney Blumenthal, *The Rise of the Counter Establishment* (New York: Harper & Row, 1988), pp. 37, 43.
9. Jeanette Goodman, vice president, National Center for Policy Analysis, interview with author.
10. Sally Covington, "Moving a Public Policy Agenda: The Strategic Philanthropy of Conservative Foundations" (Washington, D.C.: National Committee for Responsive Philanthropy, July 1997), p. 23.
11. Sally Covington, op. cit., p. 5.
12. The Foundation Grants Index, 27th Edition, The Foundation Center, 1999, p. 1526.
13. David Callahan, *$1 Billion for Ideas: Conservative Think Tanks in the 1990s* (Washington, D.C.: National Committee for Responsive Philanthropy, March 1999), p. 7.
14. Jeanette Goodman, op. cit.
15. Lisa McGiffert, Consumers Union, interview with author.
16. Cheryl Rubin, interview with author.
17. Michael Pertschuk, interview with author.
18. "On the Media," WNYC, May 1994.
19. Krieble Institute, Free Congress Foundation, Satellite Conference "How to Manage the Media II," Washington, D.C., 27 January 1996.
20. Howard Kurtz, "The Bad News Starts at Work in the Nation's Newsrooms," *Washington Post*, 30 October 1995, p. A8.
21. Jeremy Iggers, "Get Me Rewrite," *Utne Reader* (September–October 1997), p. 46f.
22. Dane Smith, statehouse reporter, *Minneapolis Star Tribune*, interview with author.
23. Karen Rothmyer, "Citizen Scaife," *Columbia Journalism Review* (July–August 1981), p. 50.

## THIS TEXT: READING

1. Do you agree with the title that says we are in "the shadow of the image"? Do you feel images from advertising somehow dominate your life? Do you recognize your own story in theirs?
2. What is the semiotic situation the Ewens are writing about?
3. Lutz gives a kind of semiotic reading of the language of advertising in his seminal essay. Be honest: How often have weasel words gotten you to buy something?
4. Do you see a difference between manipulation by news outlets and manipulation by advertisers? Is it the same thing or different? Why?
5. How does Lieberman's experience as a journalist bolster or undermine her authority on media manipulation? Did you find that you trusted her? Why? Why not?

## Your Text: Writing

1. Write a comparative essay examining the Lieberman and Lutz essays. How might the corporate media try to sell you the news? How do advertisers or companies try to pass off spin or public relations about a product as news?
2. Write a persuasive essay in which you argue that media manipulation is just fine, that as literate consumers, we should take responsibility for finding out "real information" ourselves.
3. Find a book or essay whose mission is to expose the "liberal media." Write a comparative paper in which you analyze that text and Lieberman's (or the Cohen/Solomon text). Which argument do you find the most convincing?
4. Write an essay in which you distinguish among "spin," "manipulation," "public relations," and "lie." How do you distinguish? Give an example of each.
5. Give a semiotic reading of the Manipulation Suite. Have we tried to manipulate you in this suite? If so, how? How might we have engaged in "manipulation by omission"?

---

# READING OUTSIDE THE LINES

## Classroom Activities

1. Find an event or occurrence—a Supreme Court decision, a major decision or action made by the President, a law passed or not passed by Congress—and find an article from a conservative newspaper or magazine, a liberal one, and one that seems to be moderate. Compare how they evaluate the decision or action. What are their criteria? Can you tell what they value based on how they argue their point?
2. Watch and tape an episode of the local news. Do some sign-reading first. What impressions do you get from the set itself? How do you know it's a news set? What are the anchors wearing? Why is that important? What about the symbols—both in the "field" and the graphics section? How might this differ from a newspaper's coverage?
3. Share your experiences with dealing with a reporter, either from a school newspaper, a television station, or local newspapers. What are some common elements of these perceptions? Do you find yourself wishing the reporters handled themselves differently? In what way?
4. As a class, come up with a code of ethics, a set of ideas that all media should live by. Now critique it. What practical restrictions would this place on media outlets? How would it change the interpretation of the

first amendment (freedom of speech)? How would it affect the way you receive news?

5. If you were a reporter, what type of reporter would you want to be? Why? What do you think the rewards of being a member of the media are?
6. Looking at some advertisements, either print or broadcast, what trends do you notice? Have these trends changed over time? What human characteristics do you think advertising appeals to? Do you think advertisers know you well enough to appeal to you? To the general public?
7. Notice the signs of advertisements. What elements do you see again and again?
8. Write a code of ethics for advertisers, advising them of the tactics they should or should not use when selling products to the public. If put into place, how would this change advertising as well know it?

## Essay Ideas

1. Read a week of editorial pages from a local newspaper. What are some things you notice? How do columnists use particular words? What do they stand for?
2. See the attached handout on a rhetorical analysis.
3. Examine some of the signs of an advertisement.
4. Put yourself in the shoes of an advertiser for a particular product. Write an ad campaign for that product taking into account target audience, signs, and the medium you would use to advertise it.
5. What issues on campus could be covered better (or at all) by the local media? Why do you think they are not covered now?

## Assignment: The Rhetorical Analysis

One of the easiest ways of analyzing an advertisement is by using Aristotle's three appeals; the appeals provide a natural organization of the paper.

### Aristotle's Three Appeals: Ethos, Pathos, Logos

#### Ethos—the Ethical Appeal

An advertisement or other visual text uses the trustworthiness and credibility of the author to make its appeal.

The ethos many times is the brand name itself—a brand we are familiar with itself may bring credibility. Or the advertiser may use someone famous or with expertise to present the advertisement. Politicians will often use endorsements to provide credibility.

Many times the ethical appeal is the weakest in an advertisement, however.

### Pathos—Appeal to Emotions

This appeal tries to get the reader to feel a particular emotion through the use of images or words, or both. An advertisement typically wants us to be motivated to purchase the particular item. The copywriters may do this by presenting images, colors, people, letters, or a combination of the above to evoke feelings of intrigue, happiness, or pleasure in some form. The images are often aimed at reminding us of other ideas or images.

The appeal to emotions is often the strongest in an advertisement.

### Logos—Appeal to Reason or Logic

Advertisements will often try to present a logical appeal, using facts of one sort or another. For example, an advertisement might use claims that it is the most popular brand or has won the most awards. It might claim the time to purchase the item is sooner rather than later because of the discounts its manufacturer is providing.

## The Target Audience

When talking about visual texts, you might also talk about who its target audience is—how old or young, how rich or poor, where they are from, and so on.

*A Typical Paper*

1. An introduction talking about advertising.
2. A thesis statement describing the argument you are making about the ad.
3. A paragraph providing an organized general description of the ad.
4. Three or more paragraphs about the strengths and weaknesses of the three appeals.
5. A paragraph that talks about the target audience.
6. A concluding paragraph that explains why one appeal is stronger than another.

# 9

# Reading Music

We can't escape music. Almost wherever we go music is playing—in the supermarket, at the Starbucks, in the car, and on television. Accordingly, music often serves as the soundtrack for our lives; we often attach memories to particular songs, and those song–memory attachments tend to be long lasting. As you read these words, music is probably playing in the background.

Music too is one medium we are at once reading actively (by listening to lyrics) and passively as we emotionally connect to the sounds and tones—we don't think so much about the mood a song evokes as much as how it makes us feel. Accordingly, we actively read music, if we read it at all, by focusing on its lyrics—after all, the content of what's sung in a song is the easiest element to interpret. In addition, we have the tools for interpreting words already: We know how to read and make sense of language or literature. And such tools can be useful in understanding music.

But we have any number of other considerations to decipher a song's intentional meanings, as well as some of its unintentional ones. Here are some to keep in mind when listening to and writing about music.

## Music is made up of genres.

Both professional and amateur listeners often classify a music's type in trying to understand or enjoy it. There are many types of music—classical, rhythm and blues, rock and roll, rap, country, jazz, and "pop," as well as numerous subgenres within these groups (alternative, trip-hop, fusion, etc.). Bands often combine genres, transcend genres, or even comment on them as they play within them. Sometimes, for example in the case of rap music, the commentary is part of the music itself. Genres are especially important for some when deciding to listen to particular music—they want ways to understand what experience is ahead of them, and whether, based on past experience, they will like a particular song or band.

Of the genres we've listed, the one hardest to qualify is pop music (which is why we place it in quotes). For many, the term has negative connotations—it stands for "popular," which in some circles means unsophisticated or that it panders to a popular sensibility instead of artistic integrity.

For the authors, pop music is an umbrella which often covers parts or wholes of entire genres at one time or another—classical music was the pop music of its day, as was early jazz or swing. Even much "classic rock" was once popular. Having said that, what is popular oftentimes is worth studying for the light it may shed on our contemporary world.

## Music is (or isn't) a reflection of the culture that surrounds it.

Music is often of a time and place and can offer clues to the society in which it's written. For example, much of Bob Dylan's work in the turbulent '60s directly reflects the world around it; his songs are often about protests or are themselves protests. Gangsta rap also seemingly helps tell the stories from disadvantaged areas with its focus on the dilemmas of living in such areas. These forms of music can bring a broader understanding of various social ailments to the "average" listener.

But making automatic leaps from music to culture and vice versa can be problematic. Songwriters sometimes have social aims that go along with their music, and sometimes they don't. Even if they do, there can be unintended messages that flow from their music; music may unintentionally reflect society as well. For example, some people believe that disco music with its programmed beats and the sexual innuendo in many of its lyrics reflected the so-called shallow values of the 1970s, though those writing the music probably did not intend their music to have this effect.

On a purely musical level, we can also listen to a song and place it in a particular era because of certain musical conventions of the period—particular instruments or sounds in general will often give this away. Can you think of some conventions used today? Some used in previous eras? Think not only of songs, but of commercials. Do you remember when rap beats became a big part of commercials? It wasn't always so. . . .

Finally, sometimes musicians write songs that seem not to be of a time and place. Gillian Welch's popular album *Revival* sounds as though it is a relic from early twentieth-century Appalachia, yet Welch, a Californian with classical music training, recorded the album in 1995. Smash Mouth could fool some into believing they were around in the early '60s. What qualities do these songs have? What do they avoid?

## The packaging of music reflects the aims of the bands, or the record companies, or both, and it has an effect on the way we view the music.

The packaging of music involves a variety of things. Consumers are presented bands not only with their music, but their record cover, their band name, the album or song name—components that sit outside of the actual music itself. As you know, how musicians present themselves can be crucial to how we perceive them and probably how we perceive their music. For example, how would we view the music of Britney Spears coming from Tupac Shukar, and vice versa? The persona of each of these artists contributes to the way we perceive them and their work.

Often we learn to perceive performers not only from the packaging of an album, but visually through photographs in rock magazines, reports on entertainment shows, live concerts, and videos. In particular, the music video is a way for the handlers of the musician or the musician himself or herself to provide another way of determining how potential consumers see the artist. Web sites do similar work but may offer different portrayals of the performer if the artist, a fanatical listener, or the record company sponsors the site.

Sometimes the packaging of an artist helps us understand what musicians think they are doing; other times the package is a wall that interferes with our experiencing music honestly or directly. The listener has to recognize that packaging comes as a part of listening to the music, and one can do with that information as he will. For example, many fans of musicians assume that these musicians "sell out" when they sign a record deal with a large corporation, often looking for evidence of such behavior in the music, as did the fans of the band R.E.M. in the 1990s. Others just listen to the music with little regard to packaging, marketing, or in some instances, lyrics.

Packaging also can reflect the times—if we see an image of a band from a different time, we may understand a more complex relationship between the band and its era. But in reading packaging of bands from different eras we have to take into account the same factors we do in evaluating packaging from our own era.

## While the music we like may reflect personal taste, it may also reflect cultural tastes.

How many of you have heard of Toni Price? Kathy McCarty? The Derailers? The Gourds? The Damnations? Dale Watson? Texan students may recognize these names, as all of these performers are hugely popular in the Austin, Texas area, selling out concerts and receiving considerable airtime on local radio stations. Yet, few people outside of Austin and even fewer outside of Texas know this music, despite the fact that Austin enjoys a reputation as a progressive musical city. Similarly, if you have grown up in a small town outside of Austin, rap, grunge, and trip-hop may never make it to local radio stations or to the record collections of your friends, and, therefore, by extension, it may never make its way into your life (although MTV's presence now makes that less likely). Even worse, if you are from the United States, you may never get exposure to British punk bands, fado music from Portugal or Bulgarian *a cappella* choruses. Record stores and video music channels have gotten much better at featuring international music in the past few years, but there remain vast quantities of music we will never hear, simply because those forms of music belong to other cultures and places.

Furthermore, for many people, what they encounter in popular media determines their musical tastes. If bands do not make videos or are not featured in popular magazines, we may never know they exist. Many forms of alternative music never make it onto the airwaves; thus, potential listeners never find music outside of the mainstream. American trends toward playing and replaying market-tested music like pop, rock, country, and rap tends to reinforce listening tastes and habits. In short, you may like the music you do simply because that's all you've been exposed to. Thus, our tastes may depend less on comparison shopping or eclectic listening than the demands of the marketplace.

## The music itself contains readable elements that contribute to the listener's experience.

Music creates moods as well as meaning. It's often hard to isolate the aspects of songs that make us feel a particular way. Often, performers intend the pace of a song, its intensity, or the sounds of the notes to affect listeners in specific ways. Hard-driving punk, smooth jazz, rap with samples and scratches, and string concertos with a lot of violins spark conscious and subconscious reactions. Sometimes, these reactions are strong and mysterious; other times, we know all too well why we feel what we do. Music functions much like poetry in that it evokes as much as it overtly states.

We can often tell by the pace of a song what the mood is—a fast song means something different than a slow song. The instruments in a song indicate/signify something (the presence of trumpets or violins). They are there to make the song sound better, but the way they sound better is often indicative of something else as well. Similarly, how the lyrics are sung may indicate how we are to read the song. For instance, Kurt Cobain's voice demands a kind of response that Celine Dion's does not; how we read Johnny Cash's voice will differ from how we read Aretha Franklin's.

### The listeners create the music.

What we as listeners make of this sound, the packaging, and lyrics is largely up to us. We can choose to ignore the packaging, the lyrics, or the music, or a combination of the above, and arrive at one kind of interpretation. We can read biographies of musicians, watch their videos, or read the lyric sheets in a CD to get at a more complete reading of a musician or band. We can choose to listen to music on an expensive system that enhances the effects of a CD, listen to them on a car stereo, or a Walkman, and have that transform our understanding of the song. Or we can put our car radios on scan and find the first song that we like. . . .

# Worksheet

## THIS TEXT

1. Notice how each writer approaches the song or artist differently. Why do you think that's the case?
2. Do you think all the writers are music critics? What might distinguish a critic from a writer?
3. Do you think the writers are fans of the music they are writing about? What about their writing makes you draw that conclusion? Do you think writers should be fans of the music they write about?
4. Notice whether you can get the criteria for each writer's idea of what a good song or album would be.
5. How much do these writers think about the social impact of the music they write about? Do you think they think about it enough, or too much?
6. How are things like race and gender a part of the analysis here?
7. How does the background of the authors influence their ideas about music?
8. While it will be impossible for you to know this fully, try to figure out the writing situation of each author. Who is the audience? What does the author have at stake?
9. What social, political, economic, and cultural forces affect the author's text? What is going on in the world as he or she is writing?
10. What are the main points of the essay? Can you find a thesis statement anywhere?
11. How does the author support her argument? What evidence does he use to back up any claims he might make?

12. Is the author's argument valid and/or reasonable?
13. Do you find yourself in agreement with the author? Why or why not?
14. Does the author help you read music better than you did before reading the essay? If so, why?
15. How is the reading process different if you are reading an essay, as opposed to a short story or poem?
16. What is the agenda of the author? Why does she or he want me to think a certain way?
17. Did I like this? Why or why not?

## BEYOND THIS TEXT

### Lyrics

**Theme:** What are some of the themes of the song (themes are generally what the author thinks of the subject)? Are there both intentional and unintentional themes?

**Plot:** Is there a plot to the song? Does the song tell a story or convey a narrative?

**Literary devices:** Do you notice any such devices such as the use of figurative language (metaphor, simile) or repetition or rhyme? Are there notable symbols? Are these devices effective? Do they add to your enjoyment? What about heavy symbolism?

**"Literariness":** Do you think the lyrics have literary quality? Would the lyrics stand alone as a poem? Why or why not?

### Music

**The instruments:** What instruments does the band use? Do they use them effectively? Does their use symbolize anything outside of normal use?

**Mood:** What is the mood of the song? How does the music reflect this—through the makeup of its instruments, its speed, its tone (minor or major), or a combination of factors?

**Technology:** Are there technological aspects in the song? What are they? What effects do they have on the song?

### The Whole Package

**Genre:** How would you classify this song by genre? Would you do so by the lyrics or music? Why? Are there ways that songs resist classification? If so, in what ways?

**Effectiveness:** Does this song "work"? Why or why not? Is there an element of the song that's stronger than the other?

**How and where it's played:** Unlike a poem, you can hear songs in the car, in a dance club, in the elevator, on a date, in the doctor's office, and at church. How does setting influence how you hear a song?

# MUSICAL CHEESE: THE APPROPRIATION OF SEVENTIES MUSIC IN NINETIES MOVIES

Kevin J.H. Dettmar and William Richey

In this piece (1999), Kevin Dettmar and William Richey use the term "cheese" to examine the idea of music in movies. In doing so, they acknowledge the power that directors have in shaping not only audience responses to the music but to the movies in which music appears.

RECENTLY, WROQ, A GREENVILLE, SOUTH CAROLINA, radio station with a "classic rock" format, had a seventies weekend, featuring all the music from the 1970s that the station's moguls are trying to smuggle in under the classic rock umbrella (primarily dreck like Boston, Kansas, Aerosmith, et al.). At one point late on Saturday afternoon, the DJ came on the air at the close of a song and pleaded, with a note of some real desperation in his voice, not to have to field any more requests for the Bee Gees or Barry Manilow.

In our local battle of the FM airwaves, the other new player is a station, called "The New Q," that fashions itself as a homey, corporate alternative-rock venue (playing bands such as Pearl Jam, R.E.M., Soundgarden, Collective Soul, and Nirvana). Every Friday morning, however, they have an all-request show that features extended dance-mix versions of disco songs you haven't heard or thought about in years (but remember instantly—with a groan—when they come on). Listeners sat by helplessly the other morning as the full, unedited, and unexpurgated "Disco Duck" came on, followed in short order by Donna Summer's witty and sublime "MacArthur Park." In the few months since its inception, this retro-disco show has been successful enough that a local nightclub has installed a lighted, shamrock-shaped dance floor on which eighteen and ups can shake their boo-tays all night long: they can boogie-oogie-oogie till they just can't boogie no more. As we write this, we've now learned that they've instituted a platform-shoe night on Tuesdays. Lawsuits just waiting to happen.

So what's going on here? Just when you thought it was safe to turn the radio back on, seventies' schlock is back, in spades (and in bell-bottoms).

And remember, this is South Carolina we're talking about, not L.A. or New York or Chicago. We're not a remarkably avant-garde group; this state has been sending Strom Thurmond to the U.S. Senate since before we were born.

What we would argue is that this new fondness for the disco decade is simply the South Carolina manifestation (or, to use a more regionally appropriate metaphor, infestation) of the national phenomenon that some commentators have called "cheese." Like "camp"—which Susan Sontag in the 1960s saw as so uniquely characteristic of the modern sensibility—cheese is a highly rhetorical embrace of those things that many would consider to be in bad taste. But, as a postmodern version of this mentality, cheese—we believe—differs from camp in two primary ways. First, it is somewhat more exclusive than camp, in that cheese is derived solely from the detritus of consumer culture. Thus, while Sontag can list both "The Brown Derby restaurant on Sunset Boulevard in LA" and "Bellini's operas" in her "canon of Camp," cheese is almost entirely a celebration of canceled TV shows, artless pop songs, and useless cultural artifacts like the lava lamp and the Chia Pet.[1] Second, we would argue that the attitudes encoded in cheese are even more indecipherable than those of camp. Despite camp's apparent delight in things usually considered excessive or overwrought, it never really loses sight of what good taste is. With cheese, however, the distinction between good and bad taste threatens to break down altogether, to the point that it becomes nearly impossible to tell when something is being celebrated and when it is being parodied.[2]

To explore the rather twisted metaphysics of cheese, we wish to examine how this current taste for third-rate music, to which WROQ's request line and The New Q's disco-on-demand program bear witness, has begun to assert itself in recent films, specifically how, over the past few years, movie soundtracks have started recycling some of the very worst of seventies' and eighties' pop/rock.[3] Our first example is Ben Stiller's *Reality Bites* (Universal Pictures, 1994), a film that at first glance appears to exemplify the concept of cheese perfectly. For the film's central quartet, the flotsam and jetsam of seventies' and eighties' popular culture assume an almost cultic status; they adorn their apartments with posters of Shawn Cassidy and disco-era Travolta, they pass their days watching reruns of seventies' sitcoms such as *Good Times* and *One Day at a Time*, and, of course, they delight in listening to the most mindless music from this thoroughly forgettable period in rock 'n' roll history. The most glaring instance of this adoration of cheese occurs when the Knack's "My Sharona" comes on the radio as the main characters are purchasing Pringles and diet Pepsis at an AM/PM mini-mart. After persuading the clerk to pump up the volume, the two women (Lalaina and Vicki) begin a manic but clearly choreographed dance routine to the song, much to the amazement of the forty-something clerk and the apparent distaste of their friend, Troy, the group's resident grunge philosopher.

Though the film's trailer would emphasize Lalaina and Vicki's giddy gyrations, the scene in its original context indicates that Troy's disdain is the appropriate response. Once the women have abandoned themselves to their dance, the camera cuts to a long shot in which we see them boogalooing wildly through the window of the convenience store. Seemingly, then, this moment of ironized fun soon gives way to some rather dour social commentary in which Stiller equates the music of the Knack with the disposable consumerism of contemporary society. This is junk music for a junk food culture, the film none too subtly says—or, to put it in Jamesonian terms, "post-modernism is the consumption of sheer commodification as a process."[4] The Knack, of course, provides perfect fodder for such a reading as they never pretended that they were anything more than a hit-making machine. In fact, as the *Meet the Beatles*–inspired cover of their first album suggests, the Knack's primary model was the Fab Four of the early sixties, the producers of catchy, easy-to-dance-to hits, not the Beatles' later incarnation as the prophets of universal peace and love. And "My Sharona" is essentially "I Want to Hold Your Hand" repackaged to cash in on the relaxed sexual mores of the seventies ("When you gonna give it to me, give it to me / It's just a matter of time, Sharona").[5]

A similarly ironic use of seventies' music immediately follows this scene. The film cuts directly from the convenience store back to Lalaina's apartment as she is getting ready for a date with Michael, a rising executive for a new music video network (it's "like MTV, but with an edge") whom Troy instantly deems a "yuppyhead cheeseball." Though somewhat sympathetically portrayed by Stiller himself, we soon realize that Michael is bad news, and again it is the soundtrack that provides the principal clue. As Michael and Lalaina sit in his BMW convertible drinking Big Gulps, Peter Frampton's "Baby I Love Your Way" plays in the background. When Lalaina naively asks, "Who's this again?" Michael replies incredulously, "I can't believe you don't remember *Frampton Comes Alive*. That album like totally changed my life." Frampton's music—though wildly popular in the late seventies—is no less gimmicky or vapid than the Knack's (e.g., "Ooh baby I love your way / Wanna tell you I love your way"); and so the film clearly indicates that the only fitting response to a man who claims his life was changed by such music is, "Get a life."[6] When Frampton serves as the accompaniment to Michael's seduction of Lalaina, it forcefully demonstrates how morally and aesthetically tainted she is becoming in this relationship: it's as if she's sleeping with her father's record collection. But, if Lalaina has temporarily lost her ironic distance from this seventies' dreck, Troy has not. Happening along just as Lalaina and Michael begin making love, he seems as disgusted by the Frampton as by Lalaina's taste in men. Once again, music acts as a kind of diacritical marker alerting us to the presence of irony. And the filmmakers assume that we can read the clues. While otherwise there might be some ambiguity to Michael's character, the music serves as a surefire sign that Michael is as slickly shallow as an Abba single.

Despite the film's gestures toward cheese, then, its irony ultimately takes a rather stable and traditional form: it enacts, in effect, a kind of a musical morality play. As her documentary about Gen Xer's "trying to find [their] own identity without having any real role models or heroes or anything" suggests, the character of Lalaina represents her generation's potential for optimism, and so her relationship with Michael poses the danger that her idealism might become corrupted. By contrast, Troy's problem is a deep-seated, almost crippling cynicism. During a club appearance with his band, Hey That's My Bike, he performs "I'm Nuthin'," a song that neatly sums up his sense of aimlessness and resentment. Here, he not only characterizes the nineties as a time of diminishing expectations ("I'm sick of people talkin' / About American dreams"), but he explicitly blames the previous generation, the baby boomers, for causing this situation.[7] By abandoning their youthful sixties' ideals for the greedy consumerism of the seventies and eighties, the boomers have at once destroyed their own moral credibility and sold the next generation down the river ("Before I was born / It was all gone"). In short, they pawned the future in exchange for big TVs, flashy garages, and designer drugs. The song's most potent irony, however, comes from its sly appropriation of the opening riff to the Stones' "Street Fighting Man." Whereas this sixties' rock anthem exhibits a similar sense of alienation ("'Cause in sleepy London town / There's no place for a Street Fighting Man"), the speaker's outrage seems on the verge of erupting into decisive action ("the time is right for a palace revolution").[8] For the despairing speaker of "I'm Nuthin'," this kind of action—thanks to the failed example of the boomers—has ceased to be a viable option. Sixties-style rebellion has become just another discredited cliché, a cultural myth that is no more believable than the American dream; the Beatles' "Revolution" is now just a Nike commercial. Thus, unlike the "street fighting man," who can define himself through his opposition to the status quo, this speaker has lost all sense of identity. He's "nuthin'," as alienated by the left as by the right, by the counterculture as much as by the establishment.

Ultimately, though, Troy's jaded perspective is no more valorized than Lalaina's naïveté because something like sixties' idealism consistently threatens to rear its long-haired head from beneath the film's ironic surface. Lalaina—as we have seen—hopes that her documentary will have some impact on her g-g-g-generation and makes a promise to herself not to "unintentionally commercialize it." And even Troy says that he would like his band to "travel the country like Woody Guthrie," harking back to a time before music had become a multimillion dollar industry. As a result, much of the soundtrack has a distinctly sixties' flavor. While several selections sound like warmed-over psychedelic rock (e.g., Dinosaur Jr.'s "Turnip Farm"), others have a retro-folk (Lisa Loeb's "Stay") or sixties-revival quality (the Posies' "Going, Going, Gone") that contrasts with the slickly produced hits of contemporary Top 40. But, predictably, the film's touchstone for sincerity and commitment comes from those poster boys of socially conscious rock, U2, whose ballad "All I Want Is You" accompanies the "Dover Beach"–like efforts of Lalaina and Troy to find love and security amid the chaos of nineties' America, to blend their respective idealism and skepticism into a harmonious and productive union. Clearly, then, the film's sensibility is a long way from the irony Jameson sees as characteristic of our postmodern moment, an attitude characterized by "a new kind of flatness or depthlessness, a new kind of superficiality."[9] This is not to say that Jameson misunderstands postmodernism but rather that *Reality Bites*—for all its hipper-than-thou attitude—is just faux po-mo. Troy talks bravely about "riding his own melt," and most of the characters, for most of the film, seem happy enough with Bono's injunction to "slide down the surface of things";[10] but when the going gets really tough—when Troy's dad dies, and Troy and Lalaina's relationship seems on the verge of breaking up—the film shows its true colors. It comes through with a big, orchestrally reinforced ballad to reassure us that everything'll be all right.

By now, we hope it's clear how much the value system that *Reality Bites* promotes grows out of, or is disseminated through, its soundtrack. The Knack and Frampton, we are led to believe, are "bad" because their vacuousness is symptomatic of the commercialism of the seventies and eighties; U2 and the other usually acoustic, sixties-tinged music on the soundtrack is "good" because it symbolizes the social commitment of that decade. Still, despite the simplicity of this allegory, the film's use of music is actually more sophisticated than that of most rock soundtracks. Rather than using a sixties' song simply to evoke the decade of the sixties as *The Big Chill* or *Forrest Gump* do, *Reality Bites* uses the music and musical styles of the sixties, seventies, and eighties to frame and comment on its Generation X narrative. Moreover, unlike most soundtracks, it is not simply our response to this music that is important but that of the characters as well. Throughout *Reality Bites*, we regularly see the central characters listening to, reacting to, and talking about the songs on the soundtrack, and it is principally these reactions that enable us to assess their states of mind and values. In Bret Easton Ellis's *American Psycho*,[11] we know not to trust Patrick Bateman in part because he can narrate entire chapters about Huey Lewis and the News and (post–Peter Gabriel) Genesis; in *Reality Bites*, we know that Troy and Lalaina are OK because Bono sings at their reunion.

A purer, less processed form of cheese appears in *Wayne's World*, the 1992 Mike Myers film that we would argue began this trend toward ironically recontextualizing baby boomer music in Gen X movies. Of course, *Wayne's World* takes nothing from the previous generation seriously. The movie opens with some poor middle-aged schmuck named Ron Paxton showcasing his new invention, the Suck Kut, on Wayne and Garth's public-access cable show. Bad idea, Ron. Wayne's first comment is that Ron's brain-child "certainly does suck," and while Ron's doing a demo trim on Garth's melon, Wayne surreptitiously calls in the "Get-A-Load-Of-This-Guy Cam." Poor Paxton's sent packing as the show ends, with Wayne remarking that the Suck Kut is "a totally amazing, excellent discovery. Not!" Later in the film, of course, the hapless, terminally unhip video arcade tycoon Noah

Van Der Hoff gets much the same treatment when Wayne uses his idiot cards as message boards with which to make an idiot of the founder of Noah's Arcades during his live interview on "Wayne's World," calling Van Der Hoff a "sphincter boy," suggesting that "this man has no penis," and insisting that "he blows goats. I have proof."

But like *Reality Bites, Wayne's World*'s most sublime irony, for our money, comes when Myers gets his hands on the boomers' music. The obvious place to start is with the film's use and abuse of Queen's "Bohemian Rhapsody." Wayne, cruising down the street in the passenger's seat of his buddy Garth's vintage AMC Pacer (a.k.a. the Mirthmobile), queries the passengers about car tunes: "I think we'll go with a little 'Bohemian Rhapsody,' gentlemen?" His pilot, Garth, answers in the affirmative ("Good call"), and Wayne pops his cassette into the tape deck (though we almost expect an 8-track player), while the whole carful—including a drunk guy in the back seat named Phil who's upright only because he's wedged between two others—sing along and begin to thrash their stringy hair (in fact, obviously cheap hairpieces, like Wayne's and Garth's) in synch with the music and one another. In the process, seventies' superstars Queen—and particularly one of their signature songs, "Bohemian Rhapsody"—get "spun" in *Wayne's World*. It seems clear to us that Myers is sending the band up; the overproduced and deadly self-important music of Queen and the torch singer role so eagerly adopted by Freddie Mercury make a great source of cheese, and Myers uses Wayne and Garth's devotion to them as a way to flesh out their characterization. But it's finally a judgment call, for there's no firm textual or contextual evidence that the boys in the Mirthmobile think the song is anything but "Excellent": Wayne maintains a steady accompaniment of air guitar and air drums throughout and has a beatific grin on his face (as does Garth) as the song fades out that looks strangely like afterglow. Indeed, the sing-along participation in the song in the tight space of Garth's Pacer represents, among other things, a socially sanctioned moment of male bonding in a youth culture that provides few such opportunities. How bad can a song be, finally, if it allows adolescent males to connect in the midst of a homophobic atmosphere that forbids absolutely any such engagement?

This is the kind of unstable, postmodern irony that Linda Hutcheon describes: suspicious of "transcendental certitudes of any kind, including the subject" (and, we might add, taste), "postmodern irony . . . denies the form of dialectic and refuses resolution of any kind in order to retain the doubleness that is its identity."[12] Try as you might, you'll find no way to establish an ironic reading of this scene. To judge it an ironic treatment of "Bohemian Rhapsody," as we are, one must assert a distance between Mike Myers as writer and Wayne Campbell as narrator. This is doubly difficult because part of the dynamic in *Wayne's World* is that Myers is himself a late boomer rather than a Generation Xer: his character, Wayne, however, is an Xer, a slacker, all dressed up in black T-shirt and blue jeans—as well as "an extensive collection of name tags and hair nets"—but no place to go. It thus seems to us that the irony of "Bohemian Rhapsody" in the Mirthmobile—Schlock Opera lip-synched in the 1970's version of the Edsel—cuts two ways. The music of Queen is shown up as cheesy through the comic stylings of Wayne, Garth, and crew; thus Myers points a condemning finger at the excesses and narcissism of the progressive seventies' art rock with which he must have grown up that contrasts so sharply with the self-consciously disposable pop of "My Sharona." At the same time, however, Wayne and Garth are indicted, for they've pulled "Bohemian Rhapsody" from the trash heap of contemporary history, dusted it off, and popped it into the tape deck; no saturation airplay has forced them to listen to, and hum along with, Queen against their will. They've brought this on themselves.

But wait: there's more. It gets weirder. After *Wayne's World*'s theatrical release, and the MTV video of the boys popping their heads to "Bohemian Rhapsody" in their Pacer got a lot of airplay, Queen actually enjoyed something of a renaissance, akin to the brief *Reality Bites*–inspired rebirth of the Knack—including a retrospective (and, in Freddie Mercury's case, posthumous) live album and live videos released and put in heavy rotation on MTV—which leads us to suspect that the irony that we think we see was missed by much of the audience. Freddie Mercury's death from AIDS in November 1991, only months before the film's release, doubtless had something to do with the revival of Queen's fortunes, and we don't wish to downplay this aspect. But an entire generation of music consumers was introduced to Queen, and "Bohemian Rhapsody," by *Wayne's World*, and they didn't see anything wrong with it: indeed, they thought it was "Excellent."

There are any number of other examples of this unstably ironic use of boomer tunes in the film. One thematic that we'd like to note briefly is the way that this avowedly cheesy music determines the structure of romantic and sexual desire in the Dynamic Duo. Garth's pure, chaste love of the Dreamwoman who works behind the counter at Stan Mikita's donut shop is figured in the soundtrack by Tchaikovsky's "Fantasy Overture" from *Romeo and Juliet*, surely a musical cliché of romantic love if ever there was one. But tellingly, when spurred on by Cassandra actually to break his silence and speak to her, Garth soundtracks his daydream/fantasy with Jimi Hendrix's "Foxy Lady." The choreography of this number is absolutely masterful; at one point in his waltz toward the counter, it appears as though Garth is being pulled toward his Dreamwoman by an invisible fishhook in the zipper of his trousers; as he gyrates toward her, he looks down in amazement at his seemingly possessed crotch. And as for the lyrics: well, most of us who listened to Hendrix before he was retro didn't listen for the lyrics, and when Garth makes little feral ears with his fingers while calling his Lady "Foxy," we're painfully reminded of *why* we ignored the lyrics. Ouch. As for Wayne and his lady, Cassandra, his theme song is—gulp—Gary Wright's eminently forgettable "Dream Weaver."

Aerosmith is the moral/aesthetic equivalent of Queen in *Wayne's World 2*. How many folks turned out to see *Wayne's World 2* simply because it contains live footage of Aerosmith? This makes for very complicated irony, of course, because Aerosmith, we think, takes itself pretty seriously even if Mike Myers doesn't. As with all interesting, postmodern irony, the use of Queen and Aerosmith in the *Wayne's World* films poses one particularly tricky question: *you* know that Mike Myers doesn't take Steve Tyler as seriously as Tyler takes himself, and *we* know it, but *how* do we know it? This irony is unstable because one can never prove with any certainty that it is even irony. Watching Aerosmith at Waynestock, the spectator is at some loss to discover precisely how s/he's to read Aerosmith's concert performance and Steve Tyler's adolescent mike humping. It's as if Wayne and Garth put Aerosmith up on the Waynestock stage and announce, "Hey, these guys are great! Not!!" But that "not" teasingly remains unvoiced.

In fact, the closest we get to a theory of irony in the *Wayne's World* films is at the end of the first movie, after the credits have been rolling for a time. Wayne and Garth are suddenly back up on the screen, to bid us adieu, and Wayne says into the camera: "Well, that's all the time we have for our movie. We hope you found it entertaining, whimsical, and yet relevant, with an underlying revisionist conceit that belied the film's emotional attachments to the subject matter." Wow! This is Wayne Campbell talking? Suddenly Wayne's become a native philosopher of postmodernism, positing in one economical sentence a theory of postmodern irony as compelling as anything written by Jameson or Hutcheon. But Wayne and Garth are a team; Wayne's brief disquisition is only half the story without Garth's rejoinder: "I just hope you didn't think it sucked." For postmodern irony can allow nothing to stand unscathed, not even Wayne's definition of postmodern irony itself.

In the soundtracks to the films of Quentin Tarantino, we also find something approaching an aesthetics of pure cheese. The director's fondness for bad pop music is unmistakable, for rather than simply mixing in an occasional rock song for period color, he constructs entire soundtracks out of successions of not-quite-forgotten pop singles. *Reservoir Dogs*, for example, uses nothing but K-Billy's "Super Sounds of the Seventies" for the film's musical score, a strategy that, according to Tarantino himself, provides "somewhat of an ironic counterpoint to what you are seeing on the screen."[13] This is, for the most part, an accurate assessment: these unrelentingly superficial songs generally do help to distance us from the blood and often gut-wrenching violence of the film. Plus the cheesiness of the soundtrack constantly reminds us of the fact that this is a story about cheap hoods. Unlike its precursors in the heist movie genre—*The Asphalt Jungle*, *Riffifi*, *The Killing*—*Reservoir Dogs* does not ask us to empathize with the characters or to find tragic dignity in their plight, something that would be far more likely to happen if it had used a more conventional Miklos Rozsa/Jerry Goldsmith score. At the same time, though, we have to take the "somewhat" in Tarantino's statement seriously. Often, his specific musical choices have an unexpected aptness as in the most famous and memorable scene from the film: the torture sequence performed to Stealers Wheel's "Stuck in the Middle with You."[14] At first, the bouncy, hand-clap–accented beat of this "Dylanesque, pop, bubble-gum favorite" seems thoroughly out of keeping with the uncompromising violence of the scene. But without this accompaniment, we would miss the glee that the torturer, Mr. Blonde, takes in his task, especially when he breaks into an impromptu dance in between his assaults on the young cop tied to the chair. Moreover, as the scene continues, the nasal drone of Gerry Rafferty's vocal becomes increasingly irritating, thereby intensifying the agony of this already agonizing scene. And, finally, if we can bring ourselves to concentrate on the lyrics to the song, we notice that Tarantino himself seems to be taking an almost sadistic glee in the grim ironies of the scene. While the opening line, "I'm so scared I guess I'll fall off my chair," clearly contrasts with the condition of this thoroughly bound and gagged cop, the words of the song's title become cruelly literalized. The cop is stuck in the middle of this warehouse where his torturer is sticking him in the gut with a razor.

In *Pulp Fiction*, Tarantino's use of music is even more creative and unorthodox. With its eclectic mix of various music genres from the sixties, seventies, eighties, and nineties, the soundtrack exhibits the kind of "depthlessness" that Frederic Jameson decries in his jeremiads against postmodern art, and so—in sharp contrast to most rock soundtracks—it provides no reliable contextual clues to ground the narrative or situate the viewer. The opening credits sequence exemplifies how this kind of aesthetic and temporal destabilization works. First, we hear Dick Dale's sixties' surf guitar instrumental, "Misirlou," and then, in what may be an ironic nod at the soundtrack of *Reservoir Dogs*, the channel is changed to a new station on which Kool and the Gang's R&B hit "Jungle Boogie" is playing. Tarantino's rationale for these choices is instructive. "Misirlou" he describes as sounding like "the beginning of like *The Good, the Bad, and the Ugly* with those trumpets, that almost Spanish sound. Having 'Misirlou' as your opening credits, it just says, 'You're watching an epic, you're watching this big old movie, just sit back.'" The sudden switch to Kool and the Gang, however, works both to startle the viewer and to signal the film's "other personality": its appropriation of "this black exploitation thing."[15]

In this way, Tarantino provides his viewer with quite a bit of information. There is no whiter music on the planet than surf music, while "Jungle Boogie" is obviously very black and urban. The only common denominator is their mutual cheesiness. With the coming of the British Invasion, psychedelia, and the Summer of Love, surf music was—until its recent Dick Dale–led renaissance—rendered terminally uncool, its clean-cut, All-American image being totally out of step with the increasingly radicalized atmosphere of the sixties. Similarly, Kool and the Gang are never going to be confused with Stevie Wonder or Marvin Gaye, and this song in particular seems designed to create as insulting a stereotype of African-American culture as possible. Nonetheless, Tarantino claims to be genuinely fond of both songs. He says that he "always really dug surf music," and while he admits "if I had to choose between Al Green or 'Jungle Boogie' I would probably choose Al Green," he maintains that "the early Kool and the Gang records were great." Here, then, the irony seems to be at least as unreadable as anything in *Wayne's World*. While in that film the distinction between Wayne and Mike Myers occasionally blurs, in *Pulp Fiction* such a distinction is impossible to find because Tarantino seemingly recognizes the ironic effect that such musical choices have but refuses to pass judgment on them or to acknowledge them as bad. This is a man who truly likes surf music and who can distinguish between the early, golden age of Kool and the Gang and their later decadence—who can distinguish for us among the good, the bad, and the ugly.

This suspension of judgment—this mixture of emotional involvement and ironic detachment—is, we believe, the principle on which Tarantino's brand of postmodernism depends. To construct his narrative, he creates a pastiche of B-movie allusions (*Kiss Me Deadly*, *The Killers*, *The Set-Up*) as well as several references to more mainstream fare (*Rocky*, *Deliverance*), but he puts them to unfamiliar, unexpected ends; he carefully creates atmosphere and attitude but divorces them from any clearly identifiable content or message. His use of pop music works similarly. These familiar or seemingly familiar songs set our toes tapping and heads bobbing involuntarily, even as our minds ask, "What *is* this shit?" They both draw us in and draw attention to themselves. During the episode in which the hit man, Vincent Vega, takes Mia Wallace, his boss's young wife, out on a date, we see two more examples of this strategy in action. When Vincent first comes to pick her up, she is playing Dusty Springfield's "Son of a Preacher Man" on the stereo. According to Tarantino, he wrote the scene with this song in mind: "That whole sequence, I've had in my head for six or seven years. And it was always scored to 'Son of a Preacher Man.' That was the key to the sequence. I can't even imagine it without 'Son of a Preacher Man'." But to most viewers—ourselves included—the immediate reaction would be simply, "Why?" What is it about this song that is so central to this scene? First of all, that Mia would be playing this song seems highly unlikely given the fact that it was released before she would have been born. Plus, when we consider the lyrics to the song, they seem to contradict the situation in the film flatly: this heroin-shooting hit man is unlikely to be taken for the son of a preacher man. And yet—as in Tarantino's earlier use of "Stuck in the Middle with You"—there is indeed something right about the way the song works in this scene. Much of the tension in the episode results from the fact that Mia, like the preacher's son, is off limits; it's not just that she's the wife of Vincent's boss but that her husband reportedly ordered another employee to be thrown out of a four-story building for giving Mia a foot massage. She's forbidden fruit—something that Mia herself underscores later in the episode when she says, "Besides it's more exciting when you don't have permission"—and it's this taboo aspect of the meeting that makes Mia and Vincent so desirable to one another.

Furthermore, this white man's—or in this case—white woman's soul music helps to establish the ersatz quality that will pervade the rest of the episode. Mia's choice of a restaurant is Jack Rabbit Slim's, a faux-fifties' diner, complete with Ed Sullivan, Marilyn Monroe, and Buddy Holly impersonators and tables inside Chrysler convertibles. Though this environment creates a superficial sense of wholesomeness (the soundtrack for much of this segment is by that most clean-cut of fifties' pop idols, Ricky Nelson), the seaminess of Tarantino's pulp fiction is never far beneath the surface. For example, when Mia excuses herself—in good fifties' fashion—to go "powder my nose," Tarantino perversely literalizes this seemingly decorous euphemism by showing her snorting coke in the bathroom. Once they return to Mia's house—euphoric over their victory in the Jack Rabbit Slim's dance contest—the sexual subtext becomes overt. Now, when Vincent goes off to "take a piss," Mia puts on some mood music—which, in one further knowing anachronism, she plays on a reel-to-reel tape recorder. This time her choice is somewhat more contemporary—Urge Overkill's cover version of Neil Diamond's "Girl, You'll Be a Woman Soon"—and here, again, Tarantino seems to be constructing a largely unreadable irony. On one level, this song serves as the flip side of "Son of Preacher Man." Just as Vincent is clearly no preacher's kid, Mia—with her Cleopatraesque hairdo, her vampish makeup, and sex-kitten manner—is clearly already a woman. Still, the irony does not work through simple inversion or kitsch. Tarantino doesn't appear to be ridiculing this silly love song, and, as we might expect by now, he claims even to like the original version: "Well, I love Neil Diamond, and I have always loved Neil Diamond's version of that song, but [Urge Overkill's] version is even better." Here, however, we think Tarantino is being somewhat disingenuous as there is no way that the scene would have worked if he had used the Neil Diamond version: the irony would be overdetermined, and we would laugh out loud as we do at "My Sharona" in *Reality Bites* or "Dream Weaver" in *Wayne's World*. On the other hand, by using this bass-heavy, flamenco version, Tarantino defamiliarizes Neil Diamond's cheesy ballad so that—in spite of its pedigree—the song succeeds in heightening the intensity of the scene. In this case, rock 'n' roll really does have "the beat of sexual intercourse"[16]—and so while we may be aware that this is a Neil Diamond song, we don't let that intrude on the mounting sexual tension until the scene yields a final grim irony. Mistaking Vincent's heroin for a bag of cocaine, Mia snorts it, with the result that it seems this girl will be a corpse soon.

Perhaps, though, the best way to demonstrate what makes Tarantino's use of music so distinctive is by viewing it in direct comparison with Ben Stiller's more conventional handling of his films' soundtracks. In a key scene from Stiller's recent directorial effort, *The Cable Guy*, Jim Carey's Chip Douglas, the title character, performs a thoroughly over-the-top karaoke version of Jefferson Airplane's "Somebody to Love." Gyrating in front of a TV screen swirling with psychedelic colors and patterns, he flaps the ridiculously long fringes of his sixties' leather jacket while grotesquely exaggerating the vibrato of Grace Slick's original vocal. Clearly, the song is being ironized as we are asked to participate in this knowing send-up of Bay Area psychedelia, but, at the same time, we are also intended to recognize how revealing this character's choice of songs is. After all, the entire narrative of the film revolves around the attempts of this TV-obsessed cable guy to achieve some real human contact by befriending a customer: he truly does want someone to love. Thus Stiller's basic strategy is to make fun of the song's surface features while using its lyrical content to further the plot and provide reliable insight into his character's psyche.[17] As his use of "Son of a Preacher Man" and "Girl, You'll Be a Woman Soon" indicates, Tarantino's modus operandi is the exact opposite. Unlike Stiller, he never openly parodies the music he selects, and—rather than using the soundtrack to underscore the film's narrative line—he often creates a highly unstable, even contradictory relationship between the song lyrics of the soundtrack and the action taking place on the screen.

A second example comes from what is for us a very fortuitous coincidence. At one point, Tarantino considered using "My Sharona" for the "sodomy rape sequence" during the later "Gold Watch" episode in *Pulp Fiction* because, as he explains, " 'My Sharona' has a really good sodomy beat to it." The plan eventually fell through because the Knack objected to this appropriation of their song and decided to let Stiller use it in *Reality Bites* instead. Thinking back on his original plan, Tarantino is now pleased that he had to use "Comanche," another surf music cut: "I like using stuff for comic effect, but I don't want it to be har, har, wink, wink, nudge, nudge, you know?"[18] Once again, this kind of irony is for Tarantino too broad and easily decipherable, and so he sets up a far more complex and demanding scenario for his viewers. He expects us to recognize the songs he selects and to acknowledge their cheesiness, but, by using them in unexpected and unfamiliar contexts, he alters our experience of them. As a result, we start to hear them in something like the way Tarantino himself does, a man who boasts of liking "certain music that nobody else on the planet has an appreciation for."

From this last comment, it seems to us, a whole new problematic arises because here Tarantino appears to take a perverse pride in his sense of taste, a stance that appears to conflict with his usual self-representation as an aesthetic man of the people. In a recent *New York Times* interview, for instance, he dismissed the idea that he is a "collector" of pop culture by saying, "I don't believe in elitism. I don't think the audience is this dumb person lower than me. I am the audience."[19] But, as in the above quotation, Tarantino does on occasion appear to congratulate himself for having a more highly evolved sensibility, an aesthetic sense so acute that he can find beauty in things that most people see as having no socially redeeming value. It may be something of a Bizarro standard of taste, but it's a standard of taste nonetheless. Such a statement, then, reveals how difficult it is to maintain the kind of instability and undecidability that we see as the hallmarks of cheese and how tenuous the distinction between camp and cheese really is. Cheese may be, finally, all about self-consciousness, but, paradoxically, cheese that betrays its self-consciousness, its aesthetic investments, quickly spoils and loses its ability to delight and instruct.

## Notes

1. Susan Sontag, "Notes on Camp," in *A Susan Sontag Reader* (New York: Vintage, 1983), p. 107.
2. Since cheese is of relatively recent vintage, there have been few academic or theoretical treatments of it. To our knowledge, the fullest discussion is in Michiko Kakutanti's August 7, 1992, *New York Times* article, "Having Fun by Poking Pun: A New Esthetic Called Cheese" (B1, B6). Here, Kakutani usefully compares cheese to camp, noting very accurately that cheese "willfully focuses on the vulgar, the meretricious, the bogus"; she goes on to argue that, unlike the "generous" spirit of camp, "cheese tends to be judgmental, cynical, and detached" (B6). This—as the following examples we hope will demonstrate—is a severe misrepresentation of how genuine cheese functions. No less than camp, cheese "relishes, rather than judges" (Sontag, "Notes," 119), but it takes this process one step further, effectively obliterating or at least ignoring the distinctions between good and bad art, high and popular culture that underlie most standards of aesthetic judgment.
3. For other analyses of rock music soundtracks, see Claudia Gorbham, *Unheard Music: Narrative Film Music* (London: BFI, 1987); R. Serge Denisoff, *Risky Business: Rock in Film* (New Brunswick, NJ: Transaction, 1991); Lawrence Grossberg, "The Media Economy of Rock Culture: Cinema, Post-Modernity, and Authenticity" in *Sound and Vision: The Music Video Reader*, ed. Simon Frith, Andrew Goodwin, and Lawrence Grossberg (London: Routledge, 1993), pp. 185–209.
4. Fredric Jameson, *Postmodernism: or, The Cultural Logic of Late Capitalism* (Durham, NC: Duke University Press, 1991), pp. x, 17.
5. The Knack, "My Sharona," *Reality Bites* (RCA 44364, 1994).
6. Peter Frampton, "Baby I Love Your Way," *Frampton Comes Alive* (A&M 540930, 1976; reissue, 1998).
7. Ethan Hawke, "I'm Nuthin'," *Reality Bites*.
8. The Rolling Stones, "Street Fighting Man," *Beggar's Banquet* (ABKCO 7539, 1968).
9. Jameson, *Postmodernism*, p. 9.
10. U2, "Even Better than the Real Thing," *Achtung Baby* (Island 314–510 347-2, 1991).
11. Bret Easton Ellis, *American Psycho* (New York: Vintage, 1991).
12. Linda Hutcheon, "The Power of Postmodern Irony," in *Genre, Trope, Gender: Critical Essays by Northrop Frye, Linda Hutcheon, and Shirley Neuman* (Ottawa: Carelton University Press, 1992), p. 35.
13. "Truth and Fiction," liner notes to *Pulp Fiction/Reservoir Dogs* (MCACD 11188, 1994), p. 7.
14. Stealer's Wheel's "Stuck in the Middle with You," *Reservoir Dogs* (MCA 10541, 1992).
15. "Truth and Fiction," pp. 5–7.
16. This infamous quotation is, of course, from Allan Bloom, *The Closing of the American Mind* (New York: Simon and Schuster, 1987), p. 73. Bloom continues with a

comment that sheds an interesting light on the flamenco feel of Urge Overkill's cover: "That is why Ravel's *Bolero* is the one piece of classical music that is commonly known and liked by them ["young people"]."

17. As in *Reality Bites*, Stiller's use of music may not be as enigmatic as Tarantino's, but it is by no means simplistic. This scene works on an additional level as well because Carey's performance is intercut with the foreplay of Steven—the Cable Guy's would-be friend—and a young woman whom we later learn is a prostitute hired by the Cable Guy. The song thus also applies to Steven—especially when we consider that he only subscribes to cable because he has just broken up with his girlfriend. This may only be a pay-per-screw version of the Summer of Love, but Steven, too, is seeking someone to love.
18. "Truth and Fiction," p. 16.
19. Lynn Hirschberg, "The Man Who Changed Everything," *New York Times Magazine*, 16 November 1997, p. 116.

---

### This Text: Reading

1. What value does Dettmar place on the intelligent use of music in movies? How do we know this? Do you have similar values?
2. Review Dettmar's definition of cheese. Is it a positive definition or a negative one? Name something else that is "cheesy."
3. How often do you pay attention to the music in movies? Or do you try to avoid paying attention?
4. Like other forms of expression, music necessarily reflects a variety of factors, some of them beyond the control of the musician. What do you think of Quentin Tarantino's ideas about using music in movies? Do you think they are consistent with the musician's intent?

### Your Text: Writing

1. Do your own examination of cheese in a popular text. What other popular culture form contains its share of cheese?
2. Music soundtracks are notorious for being manipulative. Watch—and listen to—a movie and document where the director uses music to indicate mood. Write a short paper examining this idea.
3. How does "seeing" a favorite song change your view of it? Write a short paper examining your response to a favorite song in a movie.

## IS TUPAC REALLY DEAD?

Fouzia Baber

---

Fouzia Baber was in a freshman honors composition course at Virginia Commonwealth University in 2001 when she wrote this piece, which required a reading of a cultural text combined with research.

EVEN THOUGH TUPAC AMARU SHAKUR was gunned down on the streets of Las Vegas in front of at least a hundred people, there are those who refuse to believe that he died from the wounds he suffered that hot September night. Is he "dead or alive?" Many people concerned with the 25-year-old rap artist and film star continue to raise this question. Although reported evidence of his death has been convincing to many Tupac fans, the role of the media and commercial industries have led some to believe that the gangster rap star is still alive today. New conspiracies claiming that Tupac faked his own death accumulate on the World Wide Web and in magazines, books, and television. Some people have chosen to believe that Tupac is still alive, with rumors that he is hiding somewhere in Cuba, and has been seen in Manhattan, Arizona, South America, and the Caribbean. The main question that came to my mind about Tupac's death was not whether he is "dead or alive," but how and why anyone would disavow his death. The answer is simple: money. More specifically, Death Row Records, the record label that Tupac was signed under, attracted media hype about Tupac's death in order to earn publicity and increase their sales. Facts about Tupac's life and work lead many to believe that he legitimately faked his death. The actual shooting and the autopsy, his supposed "rebirth," his lyrics and videos, and accusations on Death Row Records all distort truthful evidence of his death.

> I'm ready to die right here tonight
> And mother* they life
> That's what they screamin' as they drill me
> But I'm hard to kill, so open fire.
>
> *2Pac, "Ambitionz az a Ridah"*

Some people believe that Tupac is still living because of the seemingly unresolved nature of events following his death. To many, Tupac's death seemed more like a setup than an actual death. On the night of September 7, 1996, Tupac was leaving a Mike Tyson fight without his bulletproof vest (something very uncommon and unusual for Tupac to do), with Death Row Records owner, and close friend, Suge Knight, when an unknown assailant fired thirteen bullets at the BMW. Tupac was allegedly shot five times. He lived through the shooting and was taken to a nearby hospital in Las Vegas and was not pronounced dead until Friday, September 13. Much of the speculation dealing with the murder stems from the air of secretiveness surrounding the events after his death. One reason why his death could be questioned is because no one ever saw the body leave the hospital. Many people claim that no photographs were taken after the murder showing his injuries. The one autopsy photo that was taken does not show the tattoo on his neck with the word "Cleopatra" written on it, increasing doubt to the public of his actual death (Light 123). Lieutenant Brad Simpson, who oversaw Las Vegas Metro's criminalistics unit, which included the photo lab, said his office's photos of the Tupac Shakur investigation have been locked up. "There was interest from some of the tabloids in getting some of those photos," Simpson said. "The tabloids offered a lot of money, but they didn't get any photos" (Scott 171). Of all the photos taken, all were kept except one, which tabloids such as the *Globe* and the *National Enquirer* offered as much as $100,000 for (Scott 170). The press hoped readers might take to the theory that Tupac faked his own death. They pointed out the missing tattoo on his neck to the public, leading it to believe it was not Tupac after all. Another issue that Tupac-is-alive theorists cite is the fact that he was cremated instead of buried As shown in the quote from "Ambitionz az a Ridah," Tupac often rapped about his funeral and being buried, but instead Tupac was cremated one day after the autopsy in Los Angeles, where he had no family or close friends.

Mixed with the mystery conspiracies attached to Tupac's memory is grief from the fans. The night his death was confirmed, crowds began to disperse around the hospital, blaring "If I Die Tonight": "I'll live eternal / Who shall I fear/Don't shed a tear for me nigga / I ain't happy here. / I hope they bury me and send me to my rest / Headlines readin' murdered to death / My last breath. . . ." These lyrics suggest that Tupac wanted to be out of the limelight. Threatened by East–West Coast "gangsta rap," troubled with the law, and harassed by the public, it is no surprise that Tupac may not have been satisfied with his life. This assumption leads many people to believe that he wanted to "die" in the eyes of the world and live secretly, away from the glare of publicity, thus faking his death. Even actor Tim Roth told *Showbiz* magazine that "Tupac talked about dying a lot because he knew it would happen. He knew he wasn't going to live to ripe old age. He really wanted to get away from what was expected from him, from how people had pigeonholed him, and move away from all these different things" (Dyson 89). Confused and shocked by the apparent death of their rap idol, numerous fans turned to the inspiration of Tupac's poetry and lyrics to help them cope with his death, or even deny it altogether.

Another reason some believe that Tupac faked his own death comes from Tupac's obsession with the teachings of political philosopher Niccoló Machiavelli, who some believe inspired Tupac's desire to get out of the limelight. While in prison, Tupac studied his books in depth. Machiavelli was a sixteenth-century philosopher who advocated the staging of one's death in order to evade one's enemies and gain power. In one of Machiavelli's books, *Discourses Upon the First Ten Books of Titus Livy*, he says, "a prince who wishes to achieve great things must learn to deceive" (Book 2, Chapter 13) ("Tupac Fans—Machiavelli"). This is Machiavelli's main idea and is the connection between him and what many believe as Tupac's own deceitful death. Only six weeks following his passing, Death Row Records released Tupac's posthumous album, *The Don Killuminati: The 7 Day Theory* under the pseudonym "Makaveli." Another one of Machiavelli's recognized theories seen in his book, *The Prince*, is the "Seven Day Theory" which refers to faking one's death. The cover of Tupac's *7 Day Theory* album depicts Tupac nailed to a cross under a crown of thorns, with a map of the country's major gang areas superimposed on it ("Tupac Fans—Is He Alive?"). There is a great deal of evidence that leads many people to believe that Tupac followed Machiavelli's teachings and faked his own death. There was nothing in the new album that said "Tupac R.I.P. 1971–1996" or anything to pay respects to the dead artist. The only thing mentioned are the words "EXIT TUPAC, ENTER MAKAVELI," leading people to believe that Tupac has died and Makaveli is born. In an interview while in jail in 1994, Tupac states that when he returns from prison he will be reborn into a new man. Perhaps this means he will be reborn into Makaveli. He claims,

> When I ended up in jail, my spirit died. The addict in me knew if I went to jail, then it couldn't live. The addict, the old Tupac is dead. The excuse maker in Tupac is dead. The vengeful Tupac is dead. The Tupac that would stand by and let dishonorable things happen is dead. God let me live for me to do something more extraordinary than this (Light 46).

The title of the album by Makaveli, *The 7 Day Theory*, has many symbolic references to Tupac's death. For instance, Tupac was shot on September 7th, and died seven days later. Tupac officially died at 4:03 PM; 4 + 3 = 7. Also he died at age 25; 2 + 5 = 7. Tupac's album, *All Eyes on Me* was released on February 13, 1996, and Tupac died on September 13, exactly seven months later. These references of marketing hype by Death Row and the media have brought incredible amounts of attention to Tupac's death. Death Row could even have used the seven-day strategy to attract buyers. It makes perfect sense for Death Row to indirectly lead people to think that Tupac is still alive. The album sold over three million copies, which proves that Death Row was successful in marketing Tupac's music even after his death, perhaps even because of his death. Tupac's lyrics and music videos have also led many people to believe he staged his death and may still be alive today. There are various references that Tupac makes to his own death in his songs. For example, the video "I Ain't Mad at Cha" was released only a few days after his death. The video shows Tupac as an angel in heaven. In the video, Tupac was shot after leaving a theater with a friend, which is very similar to how he was shot in real life. In the video "Hail Mary," released under the name Makaveli, there is a gravestone that says Makaveli, but the gravestone is cracked and there is a hole right in the front of it, implying that Makaveli rose from the dead (Dyson 20). In rapper Richie Rich's album *Seasoned Veteran*, which was released on the same day as *The 7 Day Theory*, on the song "N*ggas Done Changed" which is a duet with Tupac, Tupac says the following: "I've been shot and murdered, can't tell you how it happened word for word / but best believe that n*ggas' gonna get what they deserve." This phrase implies that Tupac knows he will be dead when Richie Rich's album is released. In Tupac's song "Ambitionz az a Ridah" on the album *All Eyes On Me*, he says "Blast me but they didn't finish, didn't diminish my powers BUT I'M BACK REINCARNATED." This may imply that Tupac is reincarnated as Makaveli. In the song, "Hold Ya Head" on the Makaveli CD, before Tupac begins rapping, a voice says, "Can you see him?" and another voice replies, "I see him." Then Tupac softly says, "I'm alive." Clearly, Tupac's lyrics and videos showed numerous references to his murder.

Even if they didn't actively conspire against Tupac, music companies, especially Death Row Records, had and have monetary incentive to make Tupac's death seem like more of a conspiracy than an accident. One speculation is that the killing of Tupac (and to an extent, Biggie Smalls) was a by-product of top record-company executives as a way of boosting sales. The similarities in the lives and deaths of Tupac Shakur and rap artist Biggie Smalls are striking. Both rappers, who were controversially considered as enemies in the East–West Coast rivalry, were at the peak of their careers before their deaths, both were killed in drive-by shootings, and both of the murder cases remain unsolved today. While the murders of Tupac and Biggie spurred record sales, the long-term effects were not good for business. The big record companies and distributors questioned whether business should continue as usual or if they needed a new strategy. The CEO of Death Row Records Marion "Suge" Knight's state of affairs definitely took a turn for the worse after Tupac's death. Rumors were already swirling about trouble at Death Row, and now he'd lost his top moneymaker, Tupac Shakur. Some have gone as far as to say Death Row was on the brink of failure (Scott 107). Some speculation even goes as far as questioning whether Suge himself ordered Tupac's attack to sell more CDs and make a financial comeback for Death Row. Is Tupac worth more dead than alive? Kevin Powell, a writer for the *New York Times* and the music industry had this to say about Tupac's death:

> Here's my theory. At first these rap artists are small-time investments. They're lucky if they make one album. When they start getting up to four albums, they're big investments. Then they become a liability. And they remain a liability as long as they're alive. But if they're dead and they've already cut their albums, their record companies are just selling their albums and not giving money to them anymore (Scott 159–160).

Making money off of Tupac's albums after his death was not a problem at all since he had so many songs yet to be released. Within three days after his release from prison, he had recorded seven songs. The period after his release from prison marked the beginning of about 200 songs that Tupac would record between this time until his fatal shooting a year later (Dyson 84). The trail clearly leads to money. The record companies benefit from all of Tupac's albums. Makaveli's (Tupac's) posthumous *7 Day Theory* album, released six weeks after Tupac's death, sold 664,000 units in the first week and 3 million copies by April 1997 ("Tupac Fans—The #1 Resource for Tupac Shakur Fans"). Death Row records sold hats, T-shirts, and sweatshirts connected with Tupac's murder. Clearly the record labels were interested in making money off of Tupac, when he was alive and when he was dead.

No matter how many times we read about it, hear about it, and learn about it, so many of us still cannot grasp the idea of Tupac being dead. We could research and study and ask questions and speculate about every aspect of the murder, but it remains a conspiracy. Perhaps Tupac's death is legendary in the same way as those of John F. Kennedy or Martin Luther King, Jr.—who was responsible? Maybe we'll never know. It might be postmortem denial, along with several ironic coincidences that lead so many to believe that Tupac's death was a hoax. The only sure thing is that Death Row Records was well aware of the influence and impact that Tupac's life, work, and death had on his fans. Indeed, they played off of it very well, making money off of his work, dead, alive, or just faking dead. The bittersweet reality of the music world is that it does not really matter who owns the music. The real question is, who gets the money for releasing it or playing it? As for the fans, there are those who believe that Tupac's story is legendary, just as there are those who believe we will reunite with him and Elvis some day. However, it's not just about the special days of his death or of his birthday that we celebrate. For the real fans and the real believers, we celebrate Tupac every day, through his music, and through his words. They say that a person is never truly gone until he is forgotten. If that is the case then Tupac lives forever.

## Works Cited


Donno, Daniel. "Is Tupac Alive?" *Tupac Fans—The #1 Resource for Tupac Shakur Fans*. December 31 1999. <http://www.tupacfans.com>.

Dyson, Eric Michael. *Holler if You Hear Me: In Search of Tupac Shakur*. New York: Civitas Books Group, 2001.

Ledeen, Michael A. "Machiavelli." *Tupac Fans—The #1 Resource for Tupac Shakur Fans*. 4 November 1998. <http://www.tupacfans.com>.

Light, Alan. *Tupac Shakur*. New York: Three Rivers Press, 1998.

Scott, Cathy. *The Killing of Tupac Shakur*. Nevada: Huntington Press, 1997.

Shakur, Tupac. *The Rose That Grew From Concrete—Volume 1, An Interpretation of 2pac's Poetry*. Amaru/Interscope Records.


---

## This Text: Reading

1. What makes this paper appropriate for a music chapter?
2. In what ways did Baber's research enhance this work? Are there other sources she might have consulted?
3. Why is this subject an important one for many people?

## Your Text: Writing

1. Do your own investigation of a popular phenomenon in popular culture that people continue to disagree on (UFOs, other rock star deaths, etc.).
2. Do a short paper examining Tupac's legacy as a musician. How does his death play into his reputation?
3. Do a short paper examining celebrity deaths as a popular culture phenomenon. Are there patterns to how they are portrayed in American culture?

# RIGHT ON TARGET: REVISITING ELVIS COSTELLO'S *MY AIM IS TRUE*

Sarah Hawkins

Sarah Hawkins wrote this review/re-evaluation for an advanced composition class at the University of San Francisco in 2001. A persuasive piece of sorts, she tries to reintroduce an artist, with whom many of her professors are familiar, to a younger audience.

ELVIS COSTELLO IN A NUTSHELL: a frustrated, neurotic, nonconformist who just so happens to be endlessly talented. With a song-writing capability second only to John Lennon and an Ani Difranco-esque tenacity, Elvis Costello is a pop music figure that cannot be ignored. *My Aim Is True* blends the personal with the political, shapes music to emotion, and captures moods ranging from stark depression to danceable irony. Costello writes songs on edge, displaying the sensitivity and conceit of any true elitist. Ever feel a little at odds with society? Feel left out by the mainstream? Feel simultaneously rejected and superior? Well, Elvis Costello has and he is not going to take it lying down. Successfully, he throws all of these feelings in a bag with a dry sense of humor, adds more than a pinch of cynicism, and blends them with musical accuracy. The result? A musical masterpiece that deserves attention even twenty-four years after its release.

The underdog offbeat brilliance of *My Aim Is True* has aged like fine wine, creating a modern cult following much like that of actor John Cusack. Both speak a familiar language—that of the common man experiencing failure. Costello through his lyrics, Cusack through roles such as the downtrodden record store owner Rob in the movie *High Fidelity*, or the awkward teens he plays in both *Say Anything*, and *Better Off Dead*. Part of the attraction to figures such as Costello and Cusack is that people of an ordinary nature can relate to them. Everyone wants to see pop stars that are not perfect looking, perfectly graceful, or perfectly happy. And everyone likes to see the underdog represented in a way that is unique rather than stereotypical. Both Elvis Costello and John Cusack do this and do it well.

Take for example the opening song from Costello's *My Aim Is True*. He launches into the album singing, "Welcome to the Working Week," and reaching out to any unsatisfied employee. One of the album's simplest moments, this song places the chorus "Welcome to the working week, I know it don't thrill ya I hope it don't kill ya," against a fierce yet sing-along tune, automatically winning the hearts of all those disgruntled, tired and unsure. A manifesto of the working class, this song portrays the life of pre-fame Elvis. Just an average Joe working a passionless day job as a computer operator, straining his eyes day in and day out to the point where he needs those now infamous thick-rimmed glasses reminiscent of Buddy Holly and favored among members of his current cult following.

The glasses might have helped a man born Declan McManus to see, but they framed the style and stage presence of Elvis Costello, making Declan the computer operator look every bit Elvis's intellectual/outcast/critic of society. Yes, even the stage name, taken from "the King" of popular rock 'n roll, is an attack on the music industry. In the face of an emerging, dance-happy new wave, *My Aim Is True* threw a monkey wrench in the commercialized system. While pseudo-angry, underground, punk rock bands only managed to reinforce the traditional conventions of the music industry, Elvis Costello and his band the Attractions presented a vastly talented, deliriously fresh voice for stale angst. Only an album with such sophisticated musical influences—think British Rock classics: the Beatles, the Kinks, and the Who meet Motown—could possibly be taken seriously when fronted by such a funny-looking guy. No glam rock. No gimmick. No apologies. No love songs.

Well—no love songs in the traditional sense, anyway. There is "Allison," the fifth track, and the reflective breath amidst a furious storm, the bluesy phantom that promises in its opening lines not "to get too sentimental like those other sticky Valentines." The music strikes a sorrowful chord, one any regretful lover could appreciate. Proving more elusive, the lyrics refuse the position of the heartbroken crooning for lost love. Instead, Costello once again widens the scope by reaching out for his more comfortable position as a keen observer, obscuring this obviously personal experience—so personal, in fact, that he no longer performs the song live. While affectionate and regretful, the song is also edgy and controlled. Using the encounter with a past flame to cynically portray marriage, Costello huskily vocalizes his disapproval, "Well I see you've got a husband now / did he leave your pretty fingers lying in the wedding cake / you used to hold him right in your hand / I bet it took all that he could take."

As quickly and comfortably as Elvis slipped into the introspective shoes of Allison, he ditches them for the furious funk of "Sneaky Feelings." One would get the impression that Mr. Costello must indeed have a closet full of shoes he fills quite perfectly. In "I'm Not Angry"—yeah, right—he sports a good pair of trainers. The first five seconds of fast guitar, intense keyboard and oddly timed cymbals are enough to get anyone running. No, Elvis Costello is not angry, he's irate. While some might mistake this as a chip on his embittered shoulder, the truth is that Elvis Costello's songs extend far beyond self-depreciation and personal failures. Take "Less Than Zero" for example—a song written in response to a disturbing broadcast he saw on T.V., the BBC segment on the supposed reform of Oswald Moseley, one of the British leaders of the fascist regime. Capturing what he sees as the ultimate decline of an already unraveling society, Costello creates a narrative in which Moseley is the main character, representing not only himself but consumer society at large. "Mr. Oswald has an understanding with the law / he said he heard about a couple living in the USA / they traded in their baby for a Chevrolet / let's talk about the future / we'll put the past away." This song shows that if London is welcoming the likes of Moseley back with open arms, it is no place for Elvis Costello.

Similar bitter irony is reflected in the songs "Waiting for the End of the World," "Cheap Reward," "No Dancing," and "Pay it Back." Okay, so Mr. Costello may never get the award for most happy camper. He *admits* in an interview that most of his songs are inspired by "regret and guilt." He *does* sing about failure and misunderstanding and bitterness and all the things people never want to talk about but feel all the time. He *really* used to keep a list—a blacklist—of all the record executives and industry bigwigs he saw as the root of musical evil. BUT. He managed to break the system. He got the last laugh. He made it. Unleashing his fury in the form of *My Aim Is True,* he broke musical ground. He blended jazz, funk, rock and new age with impeccable perfection. He said something that mattered at a time when no one was saying anything. He mastered language and music, introduced them, made them shake hands, then fight, then dance together and laugh about it all.

Most importantly, he didn't stop there. He went on to build a musical legacy. Not only did he record an expansive body of work showcasing his varying talents, he became a producer, guiding other brilliant bands. As a producer, Costello worked with bands as diverse as his own influences. One of these bands, the Specials, embodies the soul of two-tone ska, a musical genre emphasizing the importance of racial diversity and social consciousness. Another band that he worked with—The Clash—has been an instrumental part of the punk rock scene. Echoes of Costello can be heard in much of today's experimental indie rock. Elliot Smith, indie rock darling, cites Costello as a major influence. One of the most impressive contemporary songwriters, Smith wrote songs that while of a mellower and more melodic musical variety, echo the underdog sentiments popularized by Costello.

Perhaps his contribution to indie sensibilities of attitude and style are equal if less tangible than those he made in music. To be indie is to have a love of irony and embrace—on multiple levels—social awkwardness. In fact, indie owes much of this attitude to Costello. This "anti-king" of pop was the first one to successfully bring these two elements into the spotlight. Traces of his fashion statement, namely the trademark glasses, can be seen among geek rock favorites like Weezer and on the faces of infinite "indie kids." And it all started twenty-four years ago. One little record untouchable in the eyes of major record labels. A record heralded by *Rolling Stone* as 1977's album of the year and remembered by VH1 as one of the best rock albums of all time. If the industry originally believed he had missed the mark, at least Elvis Costello knew he was right on target.

---

## Your Text: Reading

1. How would you describe the tone of this piece? Does it work for you? Why or why not? Is it appropriate for the type of writing she's doing?
2. How would you classify this piece? Is it a review? An essay? A paper? What makes you think so?
3. Why does the writer like Elvis Costello? How does she try to make others like him? Who does she think will like him? Look at specific places in the text where she does this work.
4. What other albums of a certain age deserve this type of revisiting? Name a few and talk about them in class.

## Your Text: Writing

1. Do an assignment similar to Hawkins: find an older album and reintroduce it to a younger crowd. What things might you have to consider about "youth" and "age" when doing this assignment?
2. Think about your criteria when choosing to listen to an album. How does that change when looking at an older album? Write a short paper about why you choose what you listen to.
3. If it's possible, go to the record collection of an older friend or relative and interview them about the experience with one of their favorite albums. Now go back and listen to it on your own and write a paper about your experience.

# Reading Music—The Song Suite

Our focus here is songs because we believe they are the basic element of music. Though we might think in albums, we feel in songs—their immediacy may engage our brain, but it more often targets the heart. Albums to an extent are the extended element of an artist's vision, but a song often captures a feeling or a moment.

Here we've chosen a diverse group of pop songs and diverse approaches to them. Most if not all of these songs are familiar to you. "Johnny B. Goode" is a "classic" song from the 1950s, a song truly revolutionary for its time. So are "I am the Walrus," "Like a Rolling Stone," and "Smells Like Teen Spirit." In a paper written in 2001, student Matt Compton gives a cultural review of "Smells Like Teen Spirit," arguing that the song is the "perfect articulation" of American youth in the early 1990s. "Cop Killer" shows the machinery at work when a controversial song enters public consciousness.

## "JOHNNY B. GOODE"

Dave Marsh

BURIED DEEP IN THE COLLECTIVE UNCONSCIOUS of rock and roll there's a simple figure drawn from real life: One man, one guitar, singing the blues. But he's not any man. He's black, Southern, poor, and (this is the part that's easiest to miss) dreaming. In many ways, his story is terrible and terrifying. We're speaking after all of someone like Robert Johnson, by all the evidence every bit as sensitive and perceptive as, say, F. Scott Fitzgerald, but rather than pursuing lissome Zeldas through Alabama mansions, enduring the pitiless reality of sharecropping segregation, the threat of lynching, and all but inescapable twentieth-century serfdom in Mississippi.

Chuck Berry's genius lay in his ability to shape those gruesome facts into a story about joy and freedom. Not that he didn't have to make concessions to the reality he was subverting. He says in his autobiography that he wanted to sing "There lived a colored boy named Johnny B. Goode," rather than the "country boy" we now have, but "I thought it would seem biased to white fans." Especially, no doubt, those white listeners who programmed the radio stations that would determine whether the record became a hit or was not heard at all.

Already a star, Chuck Berry was on intimate terms with the pop game and the limits it imposed on famous men with black skin. Standing at the edge of the rules, Berry shot himself right past one crucial dilemma of American culture into the center of another. By changing "colored" to "country," he found that, instead of speaking for himself alone, he'd created a character who also symbolized the likes of Elvis Presley, another kid whose momma promised that "someday your name will be in lights." Horrible as the source of the compromise may have been, its effect was to treble the song's force. For ultimately, if you could identify with either Presley or Berry, there was a chance you could identify with both. The result is history—and not just pop music history.

But that isn't all. "Chuck Berry's gotta be the greatest thing that came along / He made the guitar beats and wrote the all-time greatest songs," the Beach Boys once sang. They knew this better than most since Brian Wilson not only converted "Sweet Little Sixteen" into "Surfin' U.S.A.," a tale oft-told because it wound up in court, but modernized "Johnny B. Goode," right down to the guitar intro, into that much less ambiguous anthem, "Fun Fun Fun."

You can't copyright guitar licks and maybe that's good, because if you could, Chuck might have hoarded them as he does his Cadillacs. Without The Chuck Berry Riff, we'd lose not just the Beach Boys, but essential elements of the Beatles, the Rolling Stones, Bob Dylan, Bob Seger, and Bruce Springsteen—to mention only the most obvious examples. In a way, what was at the center of the first wave of the British Invasion could be described as a Chuck Berry revival.

In those days, you weren't a rock guitarist if you didn't know the riveting lick that kicks off "Johnny B. Goode." Cut without echo or reverb, a basic progression that still demanded a suppleness that immediately separated the worthy from the merely aspiring, this—more than any other—is what people mean when they talk about "The Chuck Berry Riff." Throughout the record, that machine-gun burst of notes never leaves center stage, even after Chuck sprays out those indelible opening lines, each multisyllabic phrase all one word, a voice in imitation of a guitar:

> DeepdowninLouisiana'crossfromNewOrleans,
> waybackupinthewoodsamongtheevergreens.

Rattled off in just six seconds, it's the most exciting way that Berry could have found to sing the song, and he slows down only long enough to set the scene. When he hits the chorus, the guitar returns, splitting each phrase, propelling Chuck Berry toward fame, ecstasy, any old place he chooses that's gotta be better than here and now.

In the bridge, the riff—which by now seems to have its own life, separate from the guitar and whoever plays it—collaborates with Johnny Johnson's chugging piano to form the kind of solo conceived by guys who had to think on their feet in barrooms night after night, already beat from their day jobs but *hoping*. It's that hope that "Johnny B. Goode" drives home just like a-ringin' a bell.

# "I AM THE WALRUS"

Ian MacDonald

WHEN THE BEATLES CEASED TOURING IN AUGUST 1966, Brian Epstein lost what he saw as his main function in life. While holding him in real affection and respectful of his business sense, the group had never taken his musical judgement seriously and, feeling superfluous to their new studio-bound career, he fell into a cycle of binge and depression, quickly becoming addicted to the prescription drugs with which he maintained a semblance of normality. A lonely and hypersensitive homosexual, he was easily hurt by his protégés' flippant gibes. However the sad truth is that his private life was a tormented mess beyond outside help. While witnesses differ over his mood in August 1967, he was long on the road to ruin, and his death from an apparently accidental overdose on the 27th had been imminent for at least a year.

The Beatles were nonetheless shattered by the news. Only four days earlier, Epstein had paid his final visit to one of their recording sessions (at Chappell, the second of the two for YOUR MOTHER SHOULD KNOW). The following evening, the group had attended a lecture by the Maharishi Mahesh Yogi at the London Hilton, and had been excited enough to cancel a further studio date on the 25th to pursue the guru to a weekend retreat in Wales. Learning of Epstein's death, they cut their stay short and reconvened at McCartney's house in St John's Wood on 1st September to decide what to do. McCartney realised that the psychological force holding them together would soon dissipate without some new creative focus, and argued that they must now get on with the *Magical Mystery Tour* project. The others glumly agreed, Lennon acquiescing despite seeing with his usual withering clarity that, without Epstein, The Beatles would soon fall apart. (Why they chose one of his songs to continue with is unknown. Possibly it was a smart move on McCartney's part, based on the calculation that his partner, if allowed to brood, might become intractable.)

Lennon's mood in August 1967, when he wrote I AM THE WALRUS, was, as usual, paradoxical. Passively introspective, he was interested mostly in his own LSD-enhanced impressions, though also fascinated by the spiritual issues these raised. (In this respect, he was closest to Harrison, whose regard for Hindu religion he shared and who, by way of returning the compliment, admired Lennon's recent 'message' songs of peace and tolerance.[1]

---

[1]During a visit to San Francisco on 8th August, Harrison strolled, minstrel-style, through the city's hippie enclave Haight-Ashbury, playing guitar and singing BABY, YOU'RE A RICH MAN.

At the same time, Lennon's astringent cynicism remained as a balancing factor and, during 1967's 'Summer of Love,' this found much to feed on. It was then that the British establishment, disconcerted by the explosion of the counterculture in the UK and aware of the unrest and civil disobedience associated with its parent movement in America, moved to stifle it at home by making examples of its leading representatives (notably the underground paper *International Times,* raided for 'subversive material' by the police in March). Though the MBE-inoculated Beatles were immune, their outrageous colleagues The Rolling Stones were fair game and within months Mick Jagger, Keith Richards, and Brian Jones had all been arrested on drugs charges.[2] With the trial of Jagger and Richards impending, Lennon and McCartney (who had recently publicly admitted to taking LSD) made a gesture of solidarity by singing backing vocals on the Stones' opportunistic protest single 'We Love You'.[3] Jailed, respectively, for three months and one year, Jagger and Richards were freed only after the editor of *The Times* took up their case, famously demanding to know, in the words of Alexander Pope, 'Who Breaks A Butterfly Upon A Wheel?' Soon after this, despite an outcry from the country's younger generation, Britain's hugely popular and perfectly harmless 'pirate' radio stations were officiously banned. The times they were a-changing.

At home in Weybridge around this time, Lennon was prodding about on his piano when he heard the droning two-note siren of a police-car in the distance. Whether or not as a symbol of mean-spirited authority, he instantly absorbed this pattern into an obsessive musical structure built round a perpetually ascending/descending M. C. Escher staircase of all the major chords without tonic sharps or flats—the most unorthodox sequence he ever devised. The words took longer to come, arriving over several acid-heightened weekends and passing through a number of phases. According to Lennon's friend Pete Shotton, the original inspiration was a letter from a boy at their old school, Quarry Bank, describing how his English class was analysing the Beatles' lyrics, a fact which Lennon found hilarious. (His teachers at Quarry Bank, particularly his English teachers, had always dismissed him as a talentless

---

[2]Further drug 'busts' among London's hippie community soon afterwards led to a pro-cannabis rally in Hyde Park and the founding of Release. Lennon remained inviolable only so long as he 'played the game' (i.e., remained a sort of eccentric national jester). As soon as he broke this compact by appearing nude with a Japanese girl on the sleeve of *Two Virgins* (publicised before its release), he was immediately busted—and 'planted', if Pete Shotton, who witnessed the raid, is to be believed (*John Lennon in My Life,* p. 185).

[3]This was accompanied by a promotional film featuring Jagger as Oscar Wilde, Marianne Faithfull as Lord Alfred Douglas, and Richards as the Marquess of Queensberry. The Who joined the protest by issuing a cover of an appropriate Jagger–Richards song, 'Under My Thumb'.

disrupter—a rejection which left deep scars.[4]) Reminiscing, he and Shotton recalled a typical playground nonsense chant: 'Yellow matter custard, green slop pie/All mixed together with a dead dog's eye.' Returning to the song, Lennon wrote 'Yellow matter custard dripping from a dead dog's eye', adding a string of the most meaningless images he could think of.[5] Yet as the lyric progressed, it grew more pointed, rising above the level of a schoolboy nose-thumb to embrace his festering resentment of the British establishment as a whole. Gradually turning into an angry sequel to the darkly melancholic STRAWBERRY FIELDS FOREVER, I AM THE WALRUS became its author's ultimate anti-institutional rant—a damn-you-England tirade that blasts education, art, culture, law, order, class, religion, and even sense itself. The hurt teenager's revenge on his 'expert textpert' schoolmasters ('I'm *crying*') broadens into a surreal onslaught on straight society in general—an anti-litany of smiling pigs in a sty, city policemen in a row, corporation vans, and the guardians of conventional morality beating up a fellow psychedelic rebel (the opium-addicted surrealist Edgar Allan Poe). A trace of the more peaceably philosophical Lennon remains in the song's opening line, but the rest is pure invective (including a swipe at the mechanical mantra-chanting of the Hare Krishna movement to which his friend Harrison was amiably disposed[6]).

Usually regarded as a cheerful exercise in anarchic nonsense, I AM THE WALRUS takes on a different cast when seen in context. This is not, however, to underestimate its element of pure linguistic mischief. Apart from attacking his old teachers and the establishment, Lennon was satirising the fashion for fanciful psychedelic lyrics cultivated by Dylan's then much-discussed output of 1965–6.[7] Yet here, too, he was ambivalent. If there was a model for I AM THE WALRUS it was Procol Harum's 'A Whiter Shade of Pale', his favourite record of summer 1967 and famous in the pop world for taking portentous meaninglessness to rococo lengths (a fact which did not prevent it entrancing the British public long enough to keep it at No. 1 for six weeks). While 'A Whiter

---

[4]Trying to judge Lennon's outlook from his own words is an exercise complicated by an emotional instability which could tip him into wild exaggerations. In the *Rolling Stone* interview (1970) this happens when Jann Wenner probes his childhood memories of being 'difficult' and misunderstood. Cursing uncontrollably, Lennon careers into a violent diatribe about the pain and resentment of being 'looked down on'. (Wenner, *Lennon Remembers.* New York: Warner Books, pp. 163–4.)

[5]One of these—policemen flying 'like Lucy in the sky'—alludes to the misinterpretation of LUCY IN THE SKY WITH DIAMONDS as a code for LSD (Pete Shotton and Nicholas Schaffner, *John Lennon in My Life.* Steint Day, 1983, p. 124).

[6]Lennon later claimed that the line sniped at Beat poet Allen Ginsberg, whose recitals around this time chiefly consisted of him playing a harmonium and chanting mantras. (On 4th October, Lennon and Harrison appeared together on an edition of ITV's *The Frost Programme* devoted to the subject of Transcendental Meditation, answering questions about it from an invited audience.)

[7]Recalling his mood at the time of writing I AM THE WALRUS, Lennon remarked: 'Dylan got away with murder. I thought, I can write this crap, too.' He later wrote a Dylan parody entitled 'Stuck Inside of Lexicon With the Roget's Thesaurus Blues Again'.

Shade of Pale' and I AM THE WALRUS are related mainly by mood and tempo, it is no secret that Lennon loved such nonsense for the sake of it—indeed, his favourite author, Lewis Carroll, provided the title of the song (a garbled reference to his poem *The Walrus and the Carpenter*[8]). The nonsense of I AM THE WALRUS is, though, anything but whimsical. A song of self-definition amounting to a manifesto, it is defensive to the point of desperation. Confronting his boyhood dilemma over whether he was mad or a genius, Lennon here concludes (after the style of contemporary radical psychologist R. D. Laing) that his madness is at least more real to him than the repressive *mores* of an insane world.[9] In short I AM THE WALRUS marks the start of a period in which its author allowed expressive integrity to override ordinary sense completely. (With an irony he must have relished, this satire on repressive inflexibility was banned by the BBC for its use of the revolutionary codeword 'knickers'.)

Lennon enjoyed himself recording it, but this song was close to home and the fact that work on it began only nine days after Epstein's death must have exacerbated its bitterness. (His vocal was snarled so harshly into the microphone that the mix barely masks the resulting peak-distortions.) Fired by Lennon's imagination, George Martin created his finest arrangement for any Beatles song, developing aspects of the lyric and backing-track just as he had with STRAWBERRY FIELDS FOREVER. Only the final mix, complete with a random radio scan that broke into a Third Programme broadcast of *King Lear*, leaves anything to be desired, its alterations of timbre and balance achieved at the cost of bass-response.

Representing Lennon's final high-tide of inspiration for The Beatles, I AM THE WALRUS is (apart, perhaps, from Dylan's surrealistic anti-nuclear nightmare 'A Hard Rain's A-Gonna Fall') the most idiosyncratic protest-song ever written. Though its author continued to write exceptional songs for the group, he never rose to this stunning level again.

---

[8]Lennon later regretted picking the Walrus after re-reading Carroll's poem and realising that he was 'the bad guy'.

[9]In the film of *Magical Mystery Tour,* Lennon mimed I AM THE WALRUS wearing an 18th-century madman's cap. The line that suggested this, 'I am the Eggman', was allegedly inspired by his friend Eric Burdon's predilection for cracking eggs on the bodies of the women he made love to. (Albert Goldman, *The Lives of John Lennon.* New York: Morrow, 1968, p. 286.)

# "LIKE A ROLLING STONE"

Robert Shelton

IN 1976, *NEW MUSICAL EXPRESS* CALLED IT "the top rock single of all time." It develops suspense right through its six minutes. At first, the narrator seems vindictive, as if he enjoys watching an overprotected person forced out into a cruel world. Dylan had little sympathy with those who hadn't fought easy comforts. Yet this and subsequent versions reveal a sad resignation that softens the tone of "I told you so." One night, I got Dylan to talk about this song:

"Why does everybody say of something like 'Like a Rolling Stone,' 'That Dylan . . . is that all he can do, put down people?' I've never put down anybody in a song, man. It's their idea. 'Like a Rolling Stone,' man, was very vomitific in its structure. . . . It seemed like twenty pages, but it was really six. I wrote it in six pages. You know how you get sometimes. And I did it on a piano. And when I made the record, I called the people who made the record with me, and I told them how to play on it, and if they didn't want to play it like that, well, they couldn't play with me. . . . When I wrote 'all you got to do is find a school and learn to get juiced in it,' I wasn't making this song about school. That's their idea. Their definition of school is much different than mine. My language is different than theirs. I mean REALLY TOTALLY DIFFERENT! The finest school, I mean, might just be out in the swamps. 'School' here can be anything. This song is definitely not about school."

He was probably using "school" as a symbol of a way of life. He sees horror enveloping anyone who suddenly makes a break after being closely attached to any form of life. For some, the experience is liberating; to others, it brings panic and helplessness. The "schoolgirl" he seems to be chastising here is probably anyone afraid to step out of his or her cocoon and into life's mainstream without guidance, parents, structure, or crutches. The words seem crueler on the page than they sound in performance. A song that seems to hail the dropout life for those who can take it segues into compassion for those who have dropped out of bourgeois surroundings. "Rolling Stone" is about the loss of innocence and the harshness of experience. Myths, props, and old beliefs fall away to reveal a very taxing reality.

Musically, the song jells beautifully; there is little feeling of prestudio rehearsal, just of a group that takes off on a splendid progression of chords. Dylan says the song was recorded in one take. The organ work—Al Kooper's strongly cohesive legato tones, the lighter filigree of runs and configurations—is brilliant. Thanks to Mike Bloomfield's guitar, even clichés are flavorful and skillfully timed. The drums swing brightly, while Dylan's voice urgently seems to anticipate the beat. The basic chord sequence is curiously familiar, suggesting "La Bamba," "Guantanamera," "Twist and Shout." Yet the massive, full sound moves away into a very complex structure. In *Backstage Passes*, Al Kooper tells how he improvised what is now a famous instrumental part to the delight of Dylan and all hands. Twenty years later, Dylan recalled recording it in a single day. Sara and he lived in a Woodstock cabin and he wrote it there. "It just came, you know," he said.

# "SMELLS LIKE TEEN SPIRIT"

Michael Azerrad

"IT WAS BASICALLY A SCAM," Kurt says of the song. "It was just an idea that I had. I felt a duty to describe what I felt about my surroundings and my generation and people my age."

One night, Kurt and Kathleen Hanna from Bikini Kill had gone out drinking and then went on a graffiti spree, spray painting Olympia with "revolutionary" and feminist slogans (including the ever-popular "GOD IS GAY"). When they got back to Kurt's apartment, they continued talking about teen revolution and writing graffitti on Kurt's walls. Hanna wrote the words "Kurt smells like Teen Spirit." "I took that as a compliment," says Kurt. "I thought that was a reaction to the conversation we were having but it really meant that I smelled like the deodorant. I didn't know that the deodorant spray existed until months after the single came out. I've never worn any cologne or underarm deodorant."

Virtually ever since he arrived, Kurt had been inundated with the Calvinists' discussions of "teen revolution" in Olympia coffee shops; after all, that's what bohemian people in their early twenties do—it's in the rule book. "I knew there was some kind of revolution," he says. "Whether it was a positive thing or not, I didn't really care or know."

The Calvinists would bridle at the comparison, but in many respects, teen revolution resembled the aims of the Woodstock Nation. It meant that young people were creating and controlling their own culture as well as their political situation, rescuing them from a cynical and corrupt older generation. The idea was to make youth culture honest, accessible, and fair in all respects—on the artistic side, on the business side, and even in the audience—making it the diametrical opposite of what corporate America had turned it into. After that, political change would be inevitable.

Kurt didn't doubt that the Calvinists were earnest and he liked their ideas, but he also was dubious about their prospects. He found their altruism naive—they didn't seem to realize it was all a pipe dream. "Everyone seems to be striving for Utopia in the underground scene but there are so many different factions and they're so segregated that it's impossible," Kurt says. "If you can't get a fucking underground movement to band together and to stop bickering about unnecessary little things, then how the fuck do you expect to have an effect on a mass level?"

Kurt even felt that pressure was being put on Nirvana to help with the revolutionary effort. "I just felt that my band was in a situation where it was expected to fight in a revolutionary sense toward the major corporate machine," says Kurt. "It was expected by a lot of people. A lot of people just flat out told me that 'You can really use this as a tool. You can use this as something that will really change the world.' I just thought, 'How dare you put that kind of fucking pressure on me. It's stupid. And I feel stupid and contagious.'"

So "Teen Spirit" is alternately a sarcastic reaction to the idea of actually having a revolution, yet it also embraces the idea. But the point that emerges isn't just the conflict of two opposing ideas, but the confusion and anger that that conflict produces in the narrator—he's angry that he's confused. "It's fun to lose and to pretend" acknowledges the thrill of altruism, even while implying that it's plainly futile. "The entire song is made up of contradictory ideas," Kurt says. "It's just making fun of the thought of having a revolution. But it's a nice thought."

Part of embracing the revolution is blasting the apathetic types who aren't part of it. Even Kurt admits that his generation is more blighted by apathy than most. "Oh, absolutely," he says. "Especially people in rock bands who aren't educated. That's also an attack on us. We were expected to shed a minimal amount of light on our ideals, where we come from, but we're not even capable of that, really. We've done a pretty good job of it, but that was never our goal in the first place. We wanted to be in a fucking band."

"Teen Spirit" sounds violent—the drums clearly take a vicious pounding, the guitars are a swarming mass of barely contained brutality, the vocals are more screamed than sung. "I don't think of the song like that," Kurt says. "It's really not that abrasive of a song at all, really. It only really screams at the end. It's so clean and it's such a perfect mixture of cleanliness and nice candy-ass production and there were soft spots in it and there was a hook that just drilled in your head throughout the entire song. It may be extreme to some people who aren't used to it, but I think it's kind of lame, myself."

Kurt's family turmoil may have had a lot to do with why Nirvana's music sounds so angry. "I'm sure it did," Kurt says, "but I have enough anger in me just toward society that I would definitely have looked for this kind of music anyhow."

Dave Grohl has a slightly different take on the song's message. "I don't think there was one, to tell you the truth," he says. "Most of it has to do with the title of the song, and that was just something that a friend had written on the wall. It was funny and clever. That, paired with the video of us at the pep rally from hell, I think that had a lot to do with it. Just seeing Kurt write the lyrics to a song five minutes before he first sings them, you just kind of find it a little bit hard to believe that the song has a lot to say about something. You need syllables to fill up this space or you need something that rhymes."

Impromptu scribblings aside, one remarkable aspect of "Teen Spirit" was that unlike many previous songs of its type, it didn't blame the older generation for anything—it laid the blame at the feet of its own audience. That implies a sense of responsibility that didn't quite fit the slacker stereotype.

Although "Teen Spirit" was a bold and provocative dare, Kurt feels he crossed the line into condemnation. "I got caught up in pointing the finger at this generation," says Kurt. "The results of that aren't very positive at all. All it does is alienate people and make them feel the same feeling you get from an evil stepdad. It's like, 'You'd better do it right' or 'You'd better be more effective or I'm not going to like you anymore.' I don't mean to do that because I know that throughout the eighties, my generation was fucking helpless. There was so much right wing power that there was almost nothing we could do."

"I know that I've probably conveyed this feeling of 'Kurt Cobain hates his audience because they're apathetic,' which isn't the case at all. Within the last two years, I've noticed a consciousness that's way more positive, way more intelligent in the younger generation and the proof is in stupid things like *Sassy* magazine and MTV in general. Whether you want to admit that or not, there is a positive consciousness and people are becoming more human. I've always been optimistic, but it's the little Johnny Rotten inside me that has to be a sarcastic asshole."

"Introducing that song, in the position that we were in, I couldn't possibly say that I was making fun or being sarcastic or being judgmental toward the youth-rock movement because I would have come across as instantly negative. I wanted to fool people at first. I wanted people to think that we were no different than Guns n' Roses. Because that way they would listen to the music first, accept us, and then maybe start listening to a few things that we had to say, after the fact, after we had the recognition. It was easier to operate that way."

## "SMELLS LIKE TEEN SPIRIT"

Matt Compton

IN 1991 A SONG BURST FORTH onto the music scene that articulated so perfectly the emotions of America's youth that the song's writer was later labeled the voice of a generation (Moon). That song was Nirvana's "Smells Like Teen Spirit," and the writer was Kurt Cobain; one of the most common complaints of the song's critics was that the lyrics were unintelligible (Rawlins). But while some considered the song to be unintelligible, to many youth in the early 90s, it was exactly what they needed to hear. Had the song been presented differently, then the raw emotions that it presented would have been tamed. If the lyrics had been perfectly articulated, then the feelings that the lyrics express would have been less articulate, because the feelings that he was getting across were not clear in themselves. One would know exactly what Kurt Cobain was saying, but not exactly what he was feeling. The perfect articulation of those raw emotions, shared by so many of America's youth, was conveyed with perfect inarticulation.

1991 was a year when the music scene had become a dilute, lukewarm concoction being spoon-fed to the masses by corporations (Cohen). The charts and the radio were being dominated by "hair bands" and pop ballads; popular music at the time was making a lot of noise without saying anything (Cohen). Behind the scenes "underground" music had been thriving since the early eighties. Much of this underground music was making a meaningful statement, but these musicians shied away from the public eye. The general public knew little about them, because they had adopted the ideology that going public was selling out (Dettmar). Nirvana was a part of this "underground" music scene.

In 1991 Nirvana broke the credo, signing with a major label, DGC, under which they released the chart-smashing *Nevermind*. "Smells Like Teen Spirit" was the first single from the record, and it became a huge hit quickly (Cohen). Nirvana stepped up and spoke for the twenty-something generation, which wasn't exactly sure what it wanted to say (Azerrad 223–233). A huge part of America's youth felt exactly what Cobain was able to convey through not just "Smells Like Teen Spirit" but all of his music. Nirvana shot into superstar status and paved the way for an entire "grunge" movement (Moon). No one complained that they could not hear Cobain, but many did complain that they could not understand what he was saying.

Kurt Cobain did not want his music to just be heard and appreciated; he wanted it to be "felt" (Moon). His music often showed a contrast of emotions; it would change from a soft lull, to a screaming rage suddenly. And few could scream with rage as could Cobain (Cohen). There is a Gaelic word, "yarrrrragh," which ". . . refers to that rare quality that some voices have, an edge, an ability to say something about the human condition that goes far beyond merely singing the right lyrics and hitting the right notes." This word was once used to describe Cobain's voice by Ralph J. Gleason, *Rolling Stone* critic (Azerrad 231). It was that voice, that uncanny ability to show emotions that Cobain demonstrated in "Smells Like Teen Spirit."

Cobain's raging performance spoke to young Americans in a way that no one had in a long while (Moon). Michael Azerrad wrote in his 1993 book, *Come as You Are: The Story of Nirvana*, "Ultimately it wasn't so much that Nirvana was saying anything new about growing up in America; it was the way they said it" (Azerrad 226). Cobain's music was conveying a feeling through the way that he performed. It was a feeling shared by many of America's youth, but it was also a feeling that could not have been articulated any way other than the way that Cobain did it (Cohen).

"Smells Like Teen Spirit" starts out with one of the most well-known guitar riffs of the 90s. The four chord progression was certainly nothing new, nothing uncommon. The chords are played with a single guitar with no distortion, and then suddenly the bass and drums come in. When the drums and bass come in the guitar is suddenly distorted, and the pace and sound of the song changes. The song's introduction, with its sudden change, forms a rhythmic "poppy" chord progression to a raging, thrashing of the band's instruments (Moon), sets the pace for the rest of the song.

The chaos from the introduction fades, and it leads in to the first verse, which gives the listener a confused feeling (Azerrad 213). In the first verse the tune of the song is carried by the drums and bass alone, and a seemingly lonely two-note guitar part that fades in and out of the song. The bass, drums and eerie guitar give the listener a "hazy" feeling. Here Cobain's lack of articulation aids in the confused feeling, because as he sings, one can catch articulate phrases here and there. The words that the listener can discern allow them to draw their own connections. Cobain's lyrics do in fact carry a confused message, "It's fun to lose, and to pretend" (Azerrad 213).

The pre-chorus offers up clear articulation of a single word, but this articulation is the perfect precursor to the coming chorus. As the first verse ends, the pre-chorus comes in; Cobain repeats the word "Hello" fifteen times. The repetition of the word Hello draws the confusion that he implicates in the first verse to a close, and in a way reflects on it. As the tone and inflection of his voice changes each time he quotes "Hello," one is not sure whether he is asking a question or making a statement, or both. It is like he is saying, "Hello? Is anybody at home?" while at the same time he exclaims, "Wake up and answer the door!"

The reflection that he implicates in the pre-chorus builds to the raw raging emotions that he expresses in the chorus, as the guitar suddenly becomes distorted, and he begins to scream (Azerrad 214, 226). In the chorus he screams, but somehow the words in the chorus are actually more articulate than those in the verse. As Cobain sings, "I feel stupid, and contagious," anyone who has ever felt like a social outcast understands exactly what Cobain is saying (Cohen), and they understand exactly why he must scream it.

I remember the first time that I heard that line and thinking about it; I was about thirteen, and I thought that there was no better word than "contagious" to describe the way it feels being in a social situation and not being accepted. Because no one wants to be around that person, they will look at the person with disgust, as if they have some highly *contagious* disease. There is certainly a lot of anger and confusion surrounding those feelings. People needed to hear Cobain scream; they knew how he felt, because they knew how they felt.

People who were experiencing what Cobain was expressing understood what he was saying, because they understood how he felt. In much the same way when someone hits their hand with a hammer that person does not lay down the hammer and calmly say, "Ouch, man that really hurt." They throw the hammer down, and simultaneously yell an obscenity, or make an inarticulate roar, and one knows that they are going to lose a fingernail. Anyone who has smashed their finger with a hammer understands why that person is yelling; in the same way anyone who has felt "contagious" or confused about society knows why Cobain is screaming about feeling "stupid and contagious." Cobain is not examining society. He is experiencing the same things as his audience (Moon); he is "going to lose a fingernail." As the chorus draws to a close, the music still rages, but it changes tempo and rhythm slightly.

The chorus is the most moving part of the song; it is a display of pure emotion. In the chorus Cobain demonstrates what it was that connected with so many; his lyrics said what he meant (Moon). But what he said had been said before, and whether he was articulate or not, people felt what he meant. It was the articulation of that feeling that gained the song such high praise (Moon).

The chorus ends with the phrase, "A mulatto, an albino, a mosquito, my libido"; this line is a reference to social conformity. Cobain is referring to things, or the ideas associated with them that are "outside" of social conformity, and then relating those things back to himself with the phrase "my libido" (Azerrad 210–215). This end to the chorus again goes back to reflect on the feelings expressed in the chorus, and ties them together with a return to the confusion expressed in the verses.

The articulation of the lyrics in the second verse gives the confusion more focus than in the first verse. He begins the second verse with the lyric, "I'm worse at what I do best, and for this gift I feel blessed." Although the lyrics are more articulate in the second verse, the feelings of confusion are still there, due to the tempo and rhythm of the music. After Cobain has sung the second verse he returns to the pre-chorus, the repetition of the word Hello. The cycle begins anew.

"Smells Like Teen Spirit" in its entirety gives the listener a complete feeling after listening to it, especially if that listener is feeling confused and frustrated. The song carries one through an entire cycle of emotions, from confusion, to reflection, to frustration. Tom Moon, a Knight-Ridder Newspaper writer, described Nirvana's music as having moments of "tension and release." Being carried through those emotions allows the listener to "vent" their own feelings of confusion and frustration, and at the same time know that someone else feels the same way (Azerrad 226–227). Despite the connection that Cobain made with many there were still many who did not "get" the song; these people often complained about the inarticulation of the lyrics (Azerrad 210).

Weird Al Yankovic utilized the common criticism of the song in his parody "Smells Like Nirvana"; Yankovic parodied "Smells Like Teen Spirit," based entirely on Cobain's obscure articulation. Yankovic is known for parodying popular music, and with lines such as, "And I'm yellin' and I'm screamin', but I don't know what I'm saying," Yankovic stated exactly what so many of the song's critiques had, though he did it with a genuine respect for the song, and its impact (Rawlins).

Weird Al Yankovic's version struck a note with many who liked Cobain's music but could not understand his lyrics (Rawlins). There were many people who did not understand the feelings of confusion, frustration, and apathy that Cobain was getting across. In 1991 when "Smells Like Teen

Spirit" first came out I was only 9, and I did not like that kind of music at all. I remember my brother, who is nine years older than me, and who listened to a lot of "heavy metal," bought Yankovic's *Off the Deep End*, with his parody "Smells Like Nirvana" on it. He thought it was funny because he did not like Nirvana. He never really connected with Cobain's message; even though he did not get what Cobain was saying, he could still enjoy the music. When I became older I did connect with Cobain's music, and Nirvana was one of my favorite bands. My brother never did understand, like many people who never did understand what it was that Cobain was saying (Azerrad 210).

Nirvana made the generation gap clear. It was Nirvana that spoke for a large part of that generation (Moon), where no one else had ever really addressed the confusion and frustration about growing up in America at that time, or at least no one had expressed it in the same way that Nirvana did. They were not the first to vocalize a problem with corporate America, but they were the first *popular* band to convey the feelings that many were feeling *because* of growing up in corporate America, in the way that they did. Cobain did not just show that he has experienced those feelings, but that he was still *experiencing* them, and many young people connected with that (Moon).

In 1992 singer-songwriter Tori Amos illustrated why Cobain's "Smells Like Teen Spirit" had connected with so many by making a cover of the song that was a clear contrast to the original. She rendered the song with a piano, and a clear articulate voice. Her cover of the song became fairly popular, because it was different, and because many people could now understand the lyrics that Cobain had already popularized (Rawlins). The cover was interesting, to say the least; however, it would have been impossible for her version ever to have had the same impact as Cobain's (Rawlins). The lyrics to the song have meaning, and depth, but the emotions that the song conveyed were in and of themselves abstract.

Amos's version of the song articulated each word clearly, her clear voice hit each note on key; her song was comparable to a ballad. Cobain's "Smells Like Teen Spirit" could be described as "sloppy," his guitar distorted through much of the song; he either screamed or mumbled most of the song (Azerrad 214). The two versions of the song illustrate a clear contrast: it is as if Cobain is "angry about being confused" (Azerrad 213), while Amos sings the song to lament Cobain's feelings.

Amos's version of the song became popular for the same reason that it could never have paved the way as Cobain's version did. It was like a ballad, and after everyone heard what Cobain was saying, about society, about America, about growing up, there is one clear emotion that follows the confusion and frustration: sadness. Her "ballad-like" cover of "Smells Like Teen Spirit" exemplified that sadness. But at the same time, people had written ballads about being confused or frustrated, and performed them as Amos performed "Smells Like Teen Spirit"; that was nothing new.

However, no one had yet *demonstrated* such clear and yet abstract confused, frustrated emotions as Cobain did, and at that moment in time that was exactly what America needed to hear (Azerrad 224–225).

Cobain had written and performed a song about his own confusion, and in the process he had connected with young people all over the United States (Moon). He had helped those people to understand their own confusion better. The problem with "Smells Like Teen Spirit" was not that Cobain was not articulate; he could not have articulated his point more clearly than he did. The problem was that not everyone knew what he was talking about, just like not everyone knows what it is like to strike their finger with a hammer. And in the same way, if someone doesn't know what it is like they might say something foolish like, "That couldn't hurt *that* bad," or "What's *his* problem?" when someone else hits their finger with a hammer, and they make an inarticulate roar. That roar expresses exactly what that person is feeling, but only those who know that feeling can really understand it. As Michael Azerrad, author of *Come as You Are: The Story of Nirvana* put it, "you either get it, or you don't" (Azerrad 227). Thus was the case with Cobain's music. "Smells Like Teen Spirit" was his inarticulate roar; it was articulate in that it expressed exactly what he was trying to point out; however, not everyone could grasp what that was.

### Works Cited

Azerrad, Michael. *Come as You Are*. New York: Doubleday, 1993.

Cohen, Howard and Leonard Pitts. "Kurt Cobain Made Rock for Everyone but Kurt Cobain." *Knight Ridder/Tribune* 8 April 1994: Infotrac.

Dettmar, Kevin. "Uneasy Listening, Uneasy Commerce." *The Chronicle of Higher Education*. 14 Sept. 2001: 18. Lexis-Nexis.

Moon, Tom. "Reluctant Spokesman for Generation Became the Rock Star He Abhorred." *Knight-Ridder/Tribune* 9 April 1994. Infotrac.

Nirvana. *Nevermind*. David Geffen Company, 1991.

Rawlins, Melissa. "From Bad to Verse." *Entertainment Weekly*. 5 June 1992: 57. Infotrac.

## COP OUT? THE MEDIA, "COP KILLER," AND THE DERACIALIZATION OF BLACK RAGE (CONSTRUCTING [MIS]REPRESENTATIONS)

Christopher Sieving

FOR ABOUT SEVEN WEEKS in the sizzling summer of 1992, the most contentious issue in American society was not about who deserved to be elected to the presidency in the upcoming election or what should be done to rebuild the nation's second largest city after it had suffered the worst civil disturbances in the United States in a century and a half. Instead, the most hotly debated concern involved a black, thirtyish rap artist named Tracy Marrow (better known as Ice-T) and the multimedia conglomerate (Time Warner) that represented him. Specifically, at issue was a song Ice-T recorded for Sire/Warner Bros. Records with his thrash-metal band, Body Count. The sentiments evoked in the lyrics to "Cop Killer," Ice-T's detractors cried, constituted an exhortation to kill police officers. For two months, the recording industry, public officials, police groups, and civil liberties advocates squared off over the right to express and circulate these ideas in public, culminating with Ice-T's "voluntary" withdrawal of the song on July 28.

The public debate over "Cop Killer" was unique in many respects, but perhaps one of its most striking characteristics was that only a tiny minority of Americans actually heard the song at all. "Cop Killer" was not played on the radio, it was not shown on MTV, and the album on which it appeared (*Body Count*) sold fewer than 500,000 copies before the song was permanently withdrawn from distribution. For this reason, the key issues for a cultural analysis of the "Cop Killer" controversy involve how the song was put into discourse and circulated in other forms of media. If "Cop Killer" was too "hot" for direct experience, the American press was more than willing to supply its own mediated versions. This is how L.A. County Supervisor Gloria Molina, one of the many elected officials who called on Time Warner to have "Cop Killer" withdrawn, initially encountered it: "I have not listened to this song, but I am convinced by what I've read in news accounts that this is a totally inappropriate rap (sic) song" (Goldberg 1992, M2).

The willingness with which interested parties accepted versions of Ice-T's words at least once removed from the context he had intended them to appear in should remind one of Foucault's ideas on the social dimensions of discourse, as modified by John Fiske. In an age marked by a promiscuity of image and sound representations, no person may dictate the ways in which they are represented. "The way that experience, and the events that constitute it, is put into discourse," Fiske (1996, 4) writes, "is never determined by the nature of experience itself, but always by the social power to give it one set of meanings rather than another." Ice-T's experience, his black knowledge (to use another of Foucault's terms) of the policing system in Los Angeles, entered into dramatic contestation with white power. To retain its status of truth, white power had to repress Ice-T's black knowledge by seizing control of it and making it mean in very different ways. To a large extent, it succeeded.

The explosive racial dimensions of the "Cop Killer" affair also dictate a close examination of the media's part in fanning the flames of controversy. The ways in which candidates Dan Quayle, Bill Clinton, and George Bush employed the press to attack "Cop Killer," Ice-T, and black culture in general have been duly noted and are consonant with the methods by which the presidential and vice presidential candidates used race as a wedge issue in 1992. Furthermore, some critics, including Robin D.G. Kelley (1996, 131), have also noted the media's substantive role in creating and putting into discourse the notion of a black, criminalized "underclass," that shadowy, nebulous body responsible for all of America's social ills.

While accusations of the white-controlled American media's complicity in the promulgation of '90s-style institutional racism are well founded, it is also true, as Tricia Rose (1994, 101) alludes to in her study of rap and black culture, *Black Noise*, that the current-day system of mass cultural production—"mass-mediated and mass-distributed"—grants oppressed groups far greater access to popular media than previously possible. "The media" are not a homogeneous blob, devouring all potential discourses that run counter to the ideology of capitalist enterprise. Rather, they are a site of struggle, analogous to Gramsci's notion of "common sense," as explained by Stuart Hall (1980, 20–21). The conservative Right's "family values" battled Ice-T's black consciousness in the media for a place within the common sense of the American public. The fact that Ice-T's black consciousness lost the battle—his words erased from the public record—does not mean that the war is unwinnable. Through a close analysis of the strategies and countertactics used by both sides in the "Cop Killer" dispute, I hope to clarify how Ice-T's case was weakened by the misguided attempts of his defenders to deracialize "Cop Killer." Their disarticulation of lower-class black struggle from the debate mirrored, and thus empowered, the strategies employed by their detractors. In analyzing how this was accomplished, I hope to provide suggestions on how to avoid similar tactical mistakes in the racial and cultural clashes of the future.

*Body Count* was released by Sire/Warner Bros. in March 1992. The first album recorded by Ice-T's rock band, it was his first group project for the label after four gold-selling solo albums. The album's tracks, all recorded between September and December 1991, were mostly versions of songs the group had performed on tour with the previous summer's Lollapalooza festival. *Body Count* closed with "Cop Killer," a staple of the band's live show. In a spoken-word lead-in, Ice-T "dedicated" this final track to "every cop that has ever taken advantage of somebody, beat 'em down or hurt 'em" out of blind prejudice or race hatred (*Body Count* 1992b). Ice-T's lyrics (the music was written by lead guitarist Ernie C.), printed in full in the accompanying CD booklet, forcefully dramatized the vengeful intent of the song's narrator. Switching between first- and second-person address, the would-be Cop Killer describes the ritual of preparing for an ambush ("I got my black gloves on / I got my ski mask on") before serving notice to his target: "I know your family's grieving, but tonight we get even." The narrator's motivation for settling the score is, at first, purely personal ("A pig stopped me for nuthin'!"); later, a call-and-response chorus suggests a larger, more broadly social revenge: "Fuck the police, for Rodney King / Fuck the police, for my dead homies" (*Body Count* 1992a).

Such sentiments raised few eyebrows prior to the late spring of 1992—the period of L.A.'s black and Latino uprisings in the wake of the acquittals in the Rodney King trial. In early June, however, "Cop Killer" was condemned publicly for the first time: a Dallas police captain, writing in his column for the Dallas Police Association newsletter, urged his readers to "boycott any and all Time Warner products and movies until such time as they have recalled this tape" (Duffy and Orr 1992). This suggestion was immediately taken up and amplified by the Combined Law Enforcement Association of Texas (CLEAT). CLEAT's press conference on June 11 at Six Flags amusement park in Arlington broke the story nationwide. In calling for a boycott of Time Warner entertainment (including Six Flags), CLEAT director Mark Clark specified who his organization was targeting (and previewed a major discursive strategy of the anti-"Cop Killer" forces): "Our quarrel is not with Ice-T, but with the beautiful people that run Time Warner who like to present themselves as being in the business of family entertainment . . . the people who made a decision to reap huge dividends by distributing music that advocates the murder of police officers" (Philips 1992a). Within a week, the New York State Sheriff's Association joined ranks with CLEAT, and Alabama Governor Guy Hunt called for a statewide ban on selling the *Body Count* album. This initial burst of protest culminated with Dan Quayle's attack on Time Warner for "making money off a record that is suggesting it's O.K. to kill cops" at a luncheon for the National Association of Radio Talk Show Hosts ("Vice President Calls Corporation Wrong" 1992).

Why "Cop Killer"? Why did this song prove to be such an attractive target for conservative forces? Why did the formation of a strong counter-discourse in opposition to Ice-T's ideas come to be seen by the nation's power brokers as a top national priority? The motives were many and varied. The justification most often given for opposing the distribution of "Cop Killer"—the fear that it would incite murder and mayhem—was undoubtedly a genuine one for some. But their concern does not explain why this particular work—one of countless mediated representations of violence—was singled out for special criticism.

Three major contextual factors brought about the targeting of "Cop Killer" at this time. One was the growing white hostility toward certain types of rap music. The increasingly confrontational style of several major rap artists put the genre on a collision course with white authorities by the late 1980s. The outcry over Professor Griff's (of Public Enemy) anti-Semitic remarks in a *Washington Times* interview, the NWA song "—tha Police" (which Ice-T cites in "Cop Killer"), and the 2 Live Crew album *As Nasty as They Wanna Be* influenced the increasingly negative coverage of rap in the mainstream press. As public hysteria broke out over the nation's perceived inability to contain its hyperviolent black population, rap music came to be seen as the original sin of the underclass. The equation of black crime with black culture was made explicit by pundits such as George Will (1990), who implied that the sexual violence depicted in 2 Live Crew's lyrics influenced the infamous Central Park "wilding" incident of April 1989. And Timothy White (1991), in a controversial *Billboard* editorial, condemned Ice Cube's 1991 album *Death Certificate* for advocating violence against Koreans and Jews. Although *Body Count* was not a rap group (and "Cop Killer" was not a rap song), it was drawn into this nexus by virtue of employing Ice-T (noted "gangsta" rapper, who had previously been singled out by Parents' Music Resource Center head Tipper Gore for the "vileness of his message") (Donnelly 1992, 66) as its lead singer.

The L.A. rebellion of late April and early May 1992 further helped to foreground in the minds of white Americans the link between rap artists and black insurrection. In the absence of "rational" (white) explanations for the destruction of South Central L.A., television, radio, and print coverage of the rebellion relied heavily on the contextualizing commentary of rappers, those whose music provided, in Alan Light's (1992a, 15) words, the only "source . . . available to communicate the attitudes of inner-city America to the white mainstream." Ice-T quickly emerged as one of the "hard-edged rappers" the *Washington Post* later designated as "[spokespersons] for the black lower class, delegates of America's angry youth" (Mills 1992, B1). Yet, for all the likeminded opinions expressed in the media on the premonitory power of L.A. hard-core, an equal number of dissenters felt that rap had incited, as opposed to predicted, the violence that followed the first Rodney King verdict. Ice Cube's (1991) rap "Black Korea," an attack on South Central's Korean store owners, was frequently cited by columnists for its couplet "Pay respect to the Black fist / Or we'll burn your store right down to a crisp." For some white Americans, residual hostility toward the rioters and "looters" surely fed the hostility toward those black cultural voices who claimed to represent them.

Finally, Bill Clinton's criticisms of rapper / activist Sister Souljah (Lisa Williamson), occurring just three days prior to Quayle's attack on "Cop Killer," helped to legitimate the vilification of rappers as an election year discursive strategy. Democratic candidate Clinton, following Jesse Jackson at a Rainbow Coalition convention, denounced remarks made by Souljah in a *Washington Post* interview ("I mean, if black people kill black people every day, why not have a week and kill white people?") (Mills 1992, B1). While it may have been the case (as was widely believed) that Clinton was more concerned about his appeal with conservative voters than about the impact of Souljah's words, the immediate result of his Rainbow Coalition address was to put rap on the political map. In the scramble for swing issues (à la Willie Horton) they could claim as their own, Republicans were only too receptive to the increasingly vocal cries of the upholders of law and order.

In the wake of Dan Quayle's condemnation on June 19, police organizations across the country pledged to support CLEAT's call for a Time Warner boycott; in addition, the 23,000-member National Sheriffs

Association spearheaded a movement to persuade sympathetic law enforcement organizations with Time Warner investments to divest ("Quayle, Congressmen" 1992, 83). State officials began calling on Time Warner to withdraw *Body Count* from the marketplace. In Los Angeles, councilwoman (and congressional candidate) Joan Milke Flores and the Los Angeles Police Protective League—echoed later by the Los Angeles Police Commission—motioned for just such a ban in a city council meeting (Philips 1992b). A Florida sheriff petitioned the state attorney general to investigate whether Time Warner's marketing of "Cop Killer" violated sedition laws, an action also advocated by Iran-Contra figure Oliver North ("Count Rises" 1992, 74). Perhaps most significantly (and ominously), sixty congressional representatives (including three Democrats and fifty-seven Republicans) sent a letter to Time Warner vice president Jeanette Lerman stating that the conglomerate's "decision to disseminate these despicable lyrics advocating the murder of police officers is unconscionable" ("Quayle, Congressmen" 1992, 83).

As the controversy was reaching fever pitch, Time Warner held its annual shareholders' meeting on July 16 at the Regent Beverly Wilshire Hotel in Beverly Hills. As had been anticipated for weeks, the meeting was infiltrated by angry police group representatives and conservative spokespersons such as 2 Live Crew prosecuting attorney Jack Thompson (who was roundly booed) and Charlton Heston, who recited the lyrics to "Cop Killer" and "KKK Bitch" (a second *Body Count* song) to the stunned stockholders. Time Warner president and co-CEO Gerald Levin fielded hostile inquiries indoors, while outside the hotel around thirty protesters (some of whom reportedly chanted "Ice-T should be put to death") (Trent 1992) picketed the corporation (Morris 1992b, 71).

The result of this highly visible, direct confrontation was perhaps surprising, at least for the protesters: Time Warner refused to budge. In public, Levin continued to uphold the right of his artist to express himself in accordance with his First Amendment rights. In response, his opposition turned up the heat even further. Following a July 21 appearance by Ice-T on *The Arsenio Hall Show*, Hall's office received a flood of threatening phone calls from angry viewers (Shaw 1992). On July 23, *The Today Show* fanned the flames of the controversy by broadcasting excerpts from a home video of Ice-T addressing a crowd of L.A. urban dwellers on the third day of the Los Angeles rebellion; in the video, Ice-T tells the crowd that "police ain't shit to me and never will be. . . . They're a Gestapo organization in Los Angeles and until you start taking them cops down out here in the street, then y'all still fucking pissing in the wind, you know what I'm sayin'?" (Morris 1992c, 83). Most seriously, as reported in *Entertainment Weekly*, Time Warner's headquarters had received at least one bomb threat, while "one exec received a phone death threat from an anonymous bigot who called him a 'nigger-loving Jew'" (Sandow 1992).

As he would later recount in his book *The Ice Opinion*, the various threats made to Time Warner executives and to his own fifteen-year-old daughter played a pivotal part in Ice-T's decision to voluntarily pull "Cop Killer" from the *Body Count* album (Ice-T and Siegmund 1994, 176). In his press conference of July 28, Ice-T announced that Time Warner would cease the distribution of *Body Count* in its original form. Subsequent editions of the album would not contain the "Cop Killer" track.

Jon Pareles (1992b, C13), writing in *The New York Times* the day following Ice-T's press conference, was one of many who appreciated the irony of the "Cop Killer" protest, acknowledging the protesters' "part in building the album's popularity." The notoriety bestowed on the *Body Count* album clearly boosted its sales; in the month prior to Ice-T's announcement, *Body Count* had sold about 100,000 copies, despite the fact that at least a half-dozen major music retailers refused to carry it. (Barry Layne [1992], writing one month earlier in *The Hollywood Reporter*, dryly noted that "the first fruits of [CLEAT's] action . . . was a tripling of '*Body Count*' album sales in the Lone Star state.") The demand for the album immediately intensified upon news of its withdrawal; by the beginning of August, *Body Count* surged from number seventy-three to number twenty-six on *Billboard*'s pop album chart, and runs on the original version were reported in several cities ("A Run on Ice-T's Album" 1992).

So what did these police organizations and public officials gain from publicizing an album and a song that might otherwise have barely registered on the cultural imaginary? Quite a bit, in fact, and a close reading of the discursive strategies these white-dominated groups employed during the "Cop Killer" controversy throws some of these suppressed motivations into sharp relief.

"Cop Killer" posed a problem for those who wished to demonize it. It was written and performed by a black group; thus, those who called for its censoring risked appearing overtly racist. The musician who wrote the lyrics was primarily associated with rap music, a form increasingly unpopular with "middle" America; however, the song was not, strictly speaking, a rap song. Furthermore, the sentiments of "Cop Killer" were protected by the First Amendment, and the song had the backing of a gigantic, American-owned conglomerate—a powerful symbol of free market enterprise.

How, then, could "Cop Killer" be fought? What strategies could be employed, and what sentiments could be exploited? Not surprisingly, the strategies the Right eventually settled on were, for the most part, profoundly deracializing. Even though racial difference had played an undeniable role in the creation, transmission, and reception (an *Entertainment Weekly* poll found that "nearly 60 percent of nonblacks said they were angry at [Ice-T], as opposed to 34 percent of blacks") (Sandow 1992) of "Cop Killer," its critics had to recode that difference as something "beyond" race. The discursive strategy summed up by the now-familiar tenet "race had nothing to do with it" that had been deployed, with some success, just weeks earlier in the official white reaction to the L.A. rebellion. *The Source* editor James Bernard (1992) noted how the news media's riot coverage had focused almost exclusively on the "mindless" destruction of black-owned businesses as "a particularly tragic example of Black-on-Black violence, that these people wouldn't even give their own hardworking middle class a chance" (p. 41). In doing so, reporters and newscasters implied (and, at times, explicitly stated) that the rebellion was not motivated by anger over racial injustice but by sheer lawlessness, or that it was, as *Billboard*'s Chris Morris (1992a) described it, simply "beyond rational explanation." It is no surprise, then, that this discourse of deracialization was applied in the attacks on Ice-T's black rage. What is surprising is how often the defenses against these attacks were equally deracializing.

## Reaccentualization

As the U.S. market economy and its institutions have become more integrated over the past several decades, the importance of language as a way to construct one's identity, to create one's own space—in sum, to serve as a tactic of resistance—has exploded. Perhaps the most helpful theoretical explication of the defiant social uses of language is found in Russian philosopher Volosinov's (1973) *Marxism and the Philosophy of Language*—particularly in his conception of accentuality. He argues that words do not have predetermined, fixed meanings; rather, the "meaning of a word is determined entirely by its context. . . . It is precisely a word's multiaccentuality that makes it a living thing" (pp. 79, 81). Volosinov's observation that "in the alternating lines of a dialogue, the same word may figure in two mutually clashing contexts" is certainly applicable to the debate over the meaning of the "Cop Killer"'s lyrics (p. 80). These words, spoken with a black accent by Ice-T, are spoken with a white accent by Charlton Heston and thus "mean" in vastly different ways. Heston's July 16 reaccenting of "Cop Killer" verifies Volosinov's idea that accent is where the social politics of the speaker enter the linguistic system. Heston's imposition of the voice of white authority so completely changed the original black meaning of the song that, for many of the shareholders in attendance, the song now seemed to contain its own rebuttal. An L.A. resident who heard Heston's recitation over KFI radio certified the objectives of this reaccenting in her letter to the *Los Angeles Times:* "It was rather startling to listen to such words coming from the magnificent voice of Moses, Andrew Jackson, John the Baptist, but I am grateful to him for expressing this aspect of the album" (Agreda 1992).

As a counterstrategy, Heston's reaccenting method is much subtler than the explicit race baiting found in a contemporaneous piece for the *National Review*, in which James Bowman (1992, 37) doubts "that Sister Souljah or Ice-T or even the Los Angeles ghetto dwellers for whom both of them have at various times purported to speak are actually oppressed; rather, they have inherited from their ancestors, who were, a form of speech and imagery characterized by a kind of fantastical moral chiaroscuro." In the end, Heston's is clearly the more effective strategy, as it was readily taken up by the mainstream; the attempt to account for racially differentiated modes of reception is relegated to the pages of a marginal right-wing periodical.

It seems apparent, then, that one way to counter the widespread deracialization of "Cop Killer" would have been to call attention to its black accent and to the ways in which meaning is struggled over by blacks and whites. Thomas Kochman's (1981) account of "fighting words" in his influential book *Black and White Styles in Conflict* illustrates the cultural framework that governs the codes used in urban black language. Kochman's research on the use of fighting words in both black and white communities demonstrates that

> angry verbal disputes [or woofing], even those involving insults and threats, can be maintained by blacks at the verbal level without violence necessarily resulting. . . . On the streets [woofing's] purpose is to gain, without actually having to become violent, the respect and fear from others that is often won through physical combat. (pp. 48, 49)

Ice-T himself says as much when he declares that "within my community, rap is verbal combat. We get around a lot of fights and aggression simply by talking" (Ice-T and Siegmund 1994, 103).

The failure of Ice-T's defenders to use a theoretical framework such as Kochman's to explain the verbal arrows slung throughout *Body Count* is perhaps attributable to the white community's inability to conceive of fighting words as anything but an invitation to physical aggression; according to Kochman (1981, 48), "whites tend to see the public expression of hostility as a point on a words–action continuum." The furor over "Cop Killer" illustrates the full extent of white ignorance, conscious or not, of what John Fiske (1996, 187) terms "sociocultural conventions that are clear to [their] native speakers." During the controversy, Ice-T repeatedly asserted that language is raced and expressed his frustration with having to explain his lyrics to whites. Before deciding to withdraw the *Body Count* album, Ice-T told *Time* that "[white America] shouldn't sweat us on what words we use with each other. I hate to say rap is a black thing, but sometimes it is" (Donnelly 1992, 66). Unfortunately, white America refused to listen to his admonitions.

## *Decontextualization*

The reaccenting of "Cop Killer" by white voices was mirrored by the selective excerpting of the song's lyrics by its opponents. By extracting certain lines (or "sound bites," to borrow a phrase) from the context of the song, the album, and Ice-T's body of work in their entirety, Ice-T's opponents more easily succeeded in making his statements fit their own discursive project, one that explained the song in terms of brutal lawlessness. Bill Clinton put the strategy of decontextualization to use in his attack on Sister Souljah; not only did Clinton ignore the meaning of Souljah's *Washington Post* comments within the larger context of the L.A. rebellion, but he ignored the whole of the quotation itself:

> I mean, if black people kill black people every day, why not have a week and kill white people? You understand what I'm saying? In other words, white people, this government and that mayor were well aware of the fact that black people were dying every day in Los Angeles under gang violence. So if you're a gang member and you would normally be killing somebody, why not kill a white person? Do you think that somebody thinks that white people are better, or above dying, when they would kill their own kind? (Mills 1992, B1)

*The Today Show* aided Clinton's efforts by broadcasting only one segment of Sister Souljah's music video, a segment in which a white police officer is shot and killed by a black woman (Leo 1992). The context for the character's action—the reimplementation of slavery in the United States—was excised from NBC's "sampling."

To my knowledge, the lyrics to "Cop Killer" were never reprinted in full in any mainstream or "general-interest" American magazine or newspaper (even though they were readily available to anyone who took a look at the album's sleeve). *The Los Angeles Times'* initial report on the boycott excerpted what would become perhaps the most reprinted verse of the song, "I got my 12 gauge sawed off / I got my headlights turned off / I'm 'bout to bust some shots off / I'm 'bout to dust some cops off" (Philips 1992a). Paul M. Walters (1992) repeated this excerpt in his *Times* op-ed piece of July 8, adding that "the verse and chorus that follow are far too vulgar to discuss." This sentiment was apparently shared by Mike Royko (1995, 175), who deleted the "obscenities" from the portion of the song he cited in his June 23 syndicated column, and by the National Rifle Association, whose full-page advertisements in the June *26 USA Today* and the June 28 *Washington Times* quoted the chorus to "Cop Killer" as "DIE PIG DIE! (expletive) the Police . . . don't be a (expletive). Have some (expletive) courage . . . I'm a (expletive) Cop Killer!" ("White Time Warner Counts Its Money" 1992).

The forced dislocation of the Cop Killer's murderous intentions from the rest of his narrative served to frame his imagined crimes as groundless. The intent of extracting, for example, only the words "'bout to dust some cops off" and "die, pigs (sic), die" from the song, as was the case in an Associated Press report of June 19, was to justify the application of just such a meaning ("Rapper Ice-T Defends Song" 1992). Thus, Michael Kinsley (1992), writing in both the *New Republic* ("Momma Dearest" 1992) and *Time*, can point to the call-and-response chorus and the line "I know your family's grievin'—f— 'em" as evidence that "Cop Killer"'s message is that "premeditated acts of revenge against random cops . . . is a justified response to police brutality" (Kinsley 1992). Few media pundits agreed with Ice-T's claim ("better you than me . . . if it's gonna be me, then better you") (Ice-T and

Siegmund 1994, 168) that the song's protagonist acts in self-defense; none, to my knowledge, excerpted the spoken-word track that prefaced the song on the *Body Count* CD.

Like the Rodney King and the Latasha Harlins videos, with which there are intriguing parallels, "Cop Killer" was almost never publicly "aired" in its entirety; the public knew little, even during the height of the furor, of what preceded the "fuck the police" chorus. Few of Ice-T's defenders, in fact, looked to the larger context of the album (the only way in which "Cop Killer" could be experienced, as it received no radio play and was not commercially available as a single); had they done so, they would have discovered a song titled "The Winner Loses," which puts forth an unequivocally anti-drug statement at odds with white America's conception of the narcoticized young black male. While it should be apparent why the anti-"Cop Killer" contingent felt it necessary to suppress Ice-T's larger critique of racially differentiated policing, it is less understandable why Ice-T's defenders failed to reintroduce this critique into the context of the debate.

## Articulation with Sexism and Racism

Volosinov's (1973) shifting of the social struggle paradigm from the traditional Marxists' class-versus-class model to a more heterogeneous subordinated model allows for the cultural analyst to admit that a step forward in racial politics may represent a step backward in gender politics. John Fiske's (1996, 66) notion of multiaxiality, informed by the realization that "because power is everywhere, it flows along all the axes of social difference," modifies Volosinov's and Foucault's ideas through observing that the knowledge flowing along a single axis of power often works by repressing other knowledge. Critics such as Robin D. G. Kelley (1996, 143) understand this when they qualify their endorsements of contemporary urban black culture, such as rap, with stinging critiques of the misogyny and homophobia of several leading black artists (including Ice-T). It is clear even to rap's defenders that rap's struggle over race cannot be won by repressing the gender struggle, as many male rappers have discovered.

Although "Cop Killer" makes no mention of gender issues, critics frequently articulated its message with the misogyny (alleged or otherwise) found elsewhere on *Body Count*, in Ice-T's rap music, and in mass culture in general. The editors of the *Los Angeles Times* placed "Cop Killer . . . in the dubious tradition of a long line of exploitative commercial work, along with heavy-metal songs that bash gays, women or minorities" ("Outrage and Ice-T" 1992); Sheila James Kuehl (1992) added that "like too much of rap, the cuts before and after 'Cop Killer' are an insistent demand, a veritable how-to, of mutilated women." Kuehl, a director at the California Women's Law Center, enriches the debate by bringing the question of woman-bashing to the table, but her more hyperbolic statements are not far removed from the outright distortions advanced by Charlton Heston (1992), who falsely asserted that "KKK Bitch" advocated the raping of women and the sodomizing of "little girls."

More problematic than accusations of sexism, however, is the articulation of black rap with racism against whites. David Samuels's (1991, 28) assertion (voiced in a notorious 1991 *New Republic* cover story on "the black music that isn't either") that rap reduces racism to "fashion" is typical of the rhetoric that asserts that contemporary racism is the product of inflammatory black people, with whites serving as the victims. "Cop Killer" was frequently articulated (and, by implication, equated) with anti-Semitic expression, despite the fact that several Time Warner executives—those who most consistently defended Ice-T's work—were Jewish. At the July 16 Time Warner shareholders meeting, Charlton Heston asked Gerald Levin, a Jew, "[if] that line were 'Die, die, die, Kike, die,' would Time Warner defend it then?" while CLEAT president Ron DeLord compared Time Warner executives to Joseph Goebbels (Morris 1992b, 71).

Another favorite strategy of critics of Ice-T and Sister Souljah—including Bill Clinton (Philips 1992c, Calendar 6), John Leo (1992), and Barbara Ehrenreich (1992)—was to link their black adversaries with ex-Klansman and defeated Louisiana gubernatorial candidate David Duke. *The New Republic* even linked "Cop Killer" to George Bush's infamous Willie Horton ad ("Momma Dearest" 1992). These types of strategies served to disarticulate white, illegal policing methods from public discussions of racism. The qualitative difference between the racist effects of, on one hand, lynchings and the Holocaust and, on the other hand, black resistance to racially motivated police brutality in Los Angeles was never explained.

## *Corporatization*

Perhaps the most common deracializing strategy used by Ice-T's opponents during the "Cop Killer" controversy was one of corporatization, or the transference of blame for "Cop Killer"'s potential ill effects from its author to the company that distributed it. The idea that the kinds of messages black rap acts choose to advance are dictated by their white employers is one that had gained significant credibility within the white media by the summer of 1992; David Samuels's (1991) *New Republic* article had perhaps the most success in popularizing this theory.

A strategy such as this might seem counter to the conservative agenda. However, if one adopts Gramscian notions of "hegemony" and "common sense," it becomes easier to understand how conservative capitalists could recast the issue as a referendum on corporate ethics. Stuart Hall (1980, 16) has remarked on how Gramsci's conceptualization of hegemony "implies that the actual social or political force which becomes decisive in a moment of organic crisis . . . will have a complex social composition. . . . Its basis of unity will have to be, not an automatic one, given by its position in the mode of economic production, but rather a 'system of alliances.'" Under late capitalism, there may be (and frequently are) splits within social groups lumped together by ideology theorists under the category of "ruling class"; the alliance between corporate America and the political Right forged along the economic axis is susceptible to breakdown along the cultural, moral, or legal axes.

The "Cop Killer" case is perhaps the clearest manifestation of this principle from this decade. In Foucauldian terms, Ice-T's black knowledge entered into contestation with white knowledge; to retain its status as "troth," white knowledge found it necessary to repress that of Ice-T. However, in order for white power to operate at maximum efficacy within a hegemonic order, it has to exercise its power "invisibly." The problem, then, for these white interests lay in the fact that the censoring of an artwork, especially one created by blacks, is bound to be very visible. By recoding the debate as an issue of ethics, Quayle, Heston, and their compatriots were allowed to talk about race through nonracial discourse.

From the very beginning, those opposed to "Cop Killer" couched their opposition in terms of corporate responsibility. When Ice-T addressed his audience at the New Music Seminar in New York on June 19 and stated "if the cops got a problem, let them come after me, not Time Warner," Mark Clark of CLEAT responded in *The New York Times* that the issue "is Time Warner making a corporate decision to make a profit off of a song that advocates the murder of police officers and they are the ones we are going to attempt to hold accountable" (Rule 1992, C16). In his speech of the same day, Dan Quayle implied that the inability of the U.S. government to revoke Ice-T's free speech rights dictates that Ice-T's sponsor be targeted in his stead ("Vice President Calls Corporation Wrong" 1992). As was the case in his Murphy Brown speech one month earlier (a speech primarily comprising his observations on the causes of the L.A. rebellion), Quayle avoided charges of election year race baiting by recoding race problems into the effects of the nation's poverty of values. George Bush echoed Quayle's strategy two weeks later at an appearance at a new Drug Enforcement Administration office in Manhattan. "I stand against those who use films or records or television or video games to glorify killing law enforcement officers," Bush proclaimed. "It is wrong for any company—I don't care how noble the name of the company—it is wrong for any company to issue records that approve of killing law enforcement officers" (Rosenthal 1992). The will with which police organizations avoided assigning responsibility to Ice-T reached its height after the artist decided to pull the song, when a representative of the Los Angeles Police Protective League lauded Ice-T for showing "more intestinal fortitude than Time Warner" (Cusolito 1992).

Stuart Hall (1986, 53) conceives of articulation as the formation of linkages, "the form of the connection that can make a unity of two different elements, under certain conditions." The fluid status of any one articulation necessitates the articulation of elements that, in that particular combination, expose the artificiality of the dominant articulation. In recoding "Cop

Killer" as the product of an unethical corporation, Quayle and his colleagues disarticulated what Ice-T's defenders needed, but barely attempted, to rearticulate: the links between black hostility toward police officers and the racist system of policing in the United States.

This is not to say that all of those who opposed the distribution of "Cop Killer" employed the strategies of deracialization to denigrate it before the eyes of middle America. Some critics, such as James Bowman (1992) in the *National Review*, risked accusations of racism by drawing articulations between the (presumed) black audience for *Body Count* and the white stereotype of the hyperviolent, narcoticized black criminal. Doug Elder, president of a Houston police organization, warned that "Cop Killer," when mixed "with the summer, the violence and a little drugs (sic) . . . [will] unleash a reign of terror on communities all across this country," while the head of the Fraternal Order of Police opined that "people who ride around all night and use crack cocaine and listen to rap music that talks about killing cops—it's bound to pump them up" (Donnelly 1992, 66; Philips 1992b). These articulations are relatively oblique compared with Rush Limbaugh's: On his syndicated radio show, Limbaugh labeled Ice-T's fans "savages and the people who beat up Reginald Denny" (Pollack 1992).

A more subtle form of racialization was performed by the countless number of reporters, officials, and spokespersons who referred to "Cop Killer" and *Body Count* as rap music rather than metal. Rose's (1994, 130) claim that, within white discourse, metal fans are "victims of its influence" whereas rap fans "victimize us" helps to clarify the purpose behind the shift in labeling. Ice-T is thus correct to assert that the word rap was used during the "Cop Killer" debate to "[conjure] up scary images of Black Ghetto" (Ice-T and Siegmund 1994, 170); even the widespread, less misleading use of the designation "rapper Ice-T" served a similar end.

And yet the tracks on *Body Count* are rap, in a certain sense; more specifically, *Body Count* is a "rock album with a rap mentality," as Ice-T himself has suggested (Light 1992b, 30). Sans sampling, the rap "mentality" manifests itself on *Body Count* not only in the gritty, urban scenarios carried over from Ice-T's solo projects but in Ice's clipped, decidedly nonmelodic vocal delivery. I wish to suggest that the considerable fuss raised by Ice-T and his comrades over the media's use of the term rap to categorize "Cop Killer" is misdirected and in fact serves to obscure the debate's more significant implications as explained throughout this article.

The fact that Ice-T's defenders repeatedly, if unknowingly, participated in obscuring these implications is perhaps the most revealing aspect of the media coverage of the controversy. A range of tactics was used to discredit the conservative attacks on "Cop Killer," yet for the most part these avoided assessing the efficacy of Ice-T's message as a strategy of resistance. Instead, many in the pro-Ice-T faction chided their opponents for believing a rock song could inspire its listeners to murder. "Entertainment is about fantasy and escapism," asserted ACLU chair Danny Goldberg (1992) in a

*Los Angeles Times* column: "literalism has nothing to do with entertainment" (p. M2). Goldberg's thesis is founded in the timeworn axiom "it's only a representation," a justification that rings somewhat hollow in an alleged age of Baudrillardian "hyperreality."

Another common tactic used by Ice-T's supporters was to articulate *Body Count* with "legitimate" (i.e., white) art. Writers, including David Hershey-Webb (1995) and Jon Pareles (1992b), decontextualized "Cop Killer"'s black American origins and specificity by placing the song within American culture's "long-established anti-authoritarian streak that often casts the police as symbols of oppression" (Pareles 1992b, C13). Likewise, Barbara Ehrenreich (1992) and Chuck Philips (1992c) invoke rock heroes Bob Dylan, the Beatles, the Rolling Stones "and the other '60s icons who stormed the gates of the Establishment" (Philips 1992c, Calendar 6). "Look, white artists wrote anti-Establishment songs, too," these pundits seem to argue, using a kind of logic easily adaptable for those who wished to associate "Cop Killer" with more commonly denigrated white forms of entertainment. Ehrenreich (1992), Andrew Rosenthal (1992), and Ice-T himself (Philips 1992d) duly noted that neither Dan Quayle nor George Bush saw fit to condemn the cop-killing character played by Bush supporter Arnold Schwarzenegger in *The Terminator* and *Terminator 2: Judgment Day,* while Pareles (1992a) blasted police associations for failing to call for a boycott of "any of the Warner film studio's so-called 'body count' movies." While Pareles's intent may have been to simply bring about a more level playing field, his articulation of "Cop Killer" and Schwarzenegger shoot-em-ups furthers the wrenching of Ice-T's words from their social context.

The most consistent tactic used to support Ice-T's right to express the sentiments of "Cop Killer" was the invocation of his rights under the First Amendment. Employed so frequently that it served as the discursive counterpart to the opposition's corporate ethics articulation, the freedom-of-speech defense was first established by Time Warner in its initial "official" response to the CLEAT boycott: "Time Warner is committed to the free expression of ideas for all our authors, journalists, recording artists, screenwriters, actors and directors. We believe this commitment is crucial to a democratic society, where the full range of opinion and thought—whether we agree with it or not—must be able to find an outlet" (Philips 1992a). The mainstream news media immediately took the bait Time Warner had set: Peter Jennings (1992) defined the "Cop Killer" furor as a "freedom of speech" story on the June 19 telecast of *World News Tonight*. The recording industry and civil liberties groups rallied around Time Warner on these grounds. The president of Capitol Records/EMI Music informed the *Los Angeles Times* that "when you realize that this giant multibillion-dollar corporation is taking a free-speech stand on a record that barely sold a few hundred thousand copies, there can be only one reason why they're holding their ground. It's a matter of principle" (Philips 1992c, 77). The call to ban "Cop Killer" became, to some extent, a free speech issue for Ice-T as well; in the altered version of the album sold by Time Warner starting in August, the First Amendment appears in place of the printed lyrics to "Cop Killer" in the *Body Count* cassette inset and CD booklet.

The freedom-of-speech defense for "Cop Killer" is deficient in many ways, not the least of which is how its use seemed to endorse the defense of the work only on these grounds. Editorials in both *Billboard* and the *Los Angeles Times* lamented that ink had to be spilled in defense of a song "repugnant . . . to most law-abiding citizens," an "artless and mediocre effort" ("Body Count: The Issue Is Censorship" 1992; "Outrage and Ice-T" 1992); the *Times* reminded Time Warner that "while Americans highly value their strong First Amendment rights, they weary of the Constitution being trotted out to justify any hate-filled, titillating venom that hits the airwaves or bookstores" ("Outrage and Ice-T" 1992). This kind of rhetoric—used to oppose a ban on "Cop Killer"—perhaps influenced Ice-T's later thoughts on the controversy:

> I didn't need anybody to come and say I had the fight to say it. I needed people with credibility to step up and say, "Ice-T not only has the fight to say it, but also fuck the police! . . . We're not apologizing to you cops for what YOU'VE been doing. It's time for people to get angry along with the guy who wrote "Cop Killer." (Ice-T and Siegmund 1994, 171)

Finally, the defenders of Ice-T must share responsibility with the voices of the Right for the evacuation of considerations of hybridity, or "genre crossing" in regard to *Body Count* and "Cop Killer." The interface of cultures represented by Ice-T's thrash-metal experiment was "the unmentionable" in the debate, as neither side wished to engage the implications of the mix of frequently segregated "black" and "white" cultures.

The discourse of gangsta rap is emblematic of our historical period, one in which the power bloc (to borrow Gramsci's term) is relatively insecure and in crisis. American society in the 1990s is characterized by heterogeneity and assimilation, brought about by economic and demographic shifts. Adding to white uncertainty is the effort by subordinated peoples to force the nation to face up to its racial divisions. The racially polarized, discursive fallout from the Rodney King beating, the L.A. rebellion, and the O. J. Simpson trial have encouraged some quarters of white America to locate the problems of American society outside the (figurative and literal) borders of "whiteness."

The significance of rap within this social climate is enormous. Rap is, in Rose's (1994, 100) paraphrasing of James Scott, "a hidden transcript . . . [using] cloaked speech and disguised cultural codes to comment on and challenge aspects of current power inequalities." White anxieties over these distinctly black recodings of hostility and resentment are given expression through the deracialized attacks on rap music and artists by pundits such as David Samuels (1991). Samuels's "exposé" of rap's young white audience instead exposes the white fear of black cultural infiltration, the targets of which are white children.

Blacks justifiably fear that white audiences and manufacturers may "steal" black culture through the increasing commodification of rap. Nevertheless, Ice-T's incursion into white rock and roll should be seen, rather than a concession to white interests, as the tactical theft of white culture. There is a crucial difference: whereas whites have long appropriated black cultural forms (including rhythm and blues, the site of rock and roll's origin) for the sake of profit, *Body Count*'s counterappropriation—though it also makes money—serves to break down the barriers that help segment American culture into white and black contingents. Ice-T was very much aware of the alarms his cultural miscegenation would set off; in his *Rolling Stone* interview, he noted how *Body Count* "got inside suburbia a little deeper than a normal rap record would. . . . I think by being rock it infiltrated the homes of a lot of parents not used to having their kids play records by rappers" (Light 1992b, 30). In the same article, Ice-T estimated that "ninety-nine percent of the *Body Count* fans are white"—a hyperbolic statement, perhaps, but one that matches in spirit the press accounts of the racial breakdown of *Body Count* album sales and the nearly all-white audiences at the band's live shows (Light 1992b, 31; Muller 1992; Cusolito 1992).

Through the use of the thrash-metal format, Ice-T designed the *Body Count* album to be heard by an audience whose racial composition he understood from his band's experience on the 1991 Lollapalooza tour. This complicates our understanding of the lyrics to "Cop Killer"; Kochman's (1981) work on fighting words does not readily apply to a case in which blacks, in their own accent, speak to whites. This point is absolutely essential for a deeper appreciation of what Ice-T attempted to pull off with his rock band. In disseminating "white" music with a black accent, *Body Count*—to a greater degree than Ice-T's rap material—teaches the suburban white teenager about social conditions far outside of his or her lived experience: a project of extreme importance in an increasingly multicultural, multidiscursive age.

In nearly all of the many interviews Ice-T granted in the year of "Cop Killer," the rapper expresses his insistence that white America learn to listen to its ghettoized black counterpart. For Ice, rap's popularity with suburban white teens is not a cause for concern but a cause for hope: "They're saying: 'Hold up, these rappers are talking to me, and it's making me understand. Why did John Wayne always win? Weren't we taking that land from the Indians? Haven't we been kind of fucked-up to people?' They're starting to figure it out" (Light 1992a, 17). In *The Ice Opinion*, Ice-T writes,

> We are entering a renaissance period, an educational revolution, where people are questioning the lies. . . . Our country can't run off lies for much longer. The key to keeping the lies alive for the racists was the elimination of communication. They kept saying, "Don't let them communicate. Don't let them talk to

each other. They'll never know how much they have in common." (Ice-T and Siegmund 1994, 137)

The upshot of David Samuels's (1991) argument in the *New Republic* is that white rap fans use their interaction with "hard" black culture as a substitute for "real," meaningful social interaction with blacks (and, presumably, assistance in the alleviation of black poverty). This conclusion is used as a club by Samuels to discredit all whites who enjoy hard-core black music: that is, white fandom does nothing to address the real problem; it only exempts you from it. Rose (1994, 4) provides a useful corrective to the Samuels position in *Black Noise:* "To suggest that rap is a black idiom that prioritizes black culture and that articulates the problems of black urban life does not deny the pleasure and participation of others." Whereas Samuels's view, ironically, ridicules white "cultural tourism" without suggesting a constructive alternative, Rose's view illuminates the possibility that the mixing of black and white culture may educate America, teaching us that social struggle in the late twentieth century must be a partnership. It is a lesson embedded in the hybridity of Ice-T's music and one we should not soon forget.

## References

Agreda, Ann Latham. 1992. An artist reflects society. *Los Angeles Times*, 10 August, F4.

Bernard, James. 1992. The L.A. rebellion: Message behind the madness. *The Source*, August, 38–48.

Body Count. 1992a. Cop killer. *On* Body Count. Sire/Warner Bros. Records.

———. 1992b. Out in the parking lot. *On* Body Count. Sire/Warner Bros. Records.

Body Count: The issue is censorship. 1992. *Billboard*, 18 July, 4.

Bowman, James. 1992. Plain brown rappers. *National Review*, 20 July, 36–38, 53.

Count rises on dealer Body Count ban. 1992. *Billboard*, 18 July, 3, 74.

Cusolito, Karen. 1992. Ice-T tells WB to kill "Cop." *The Hollywood Reporter*, 29 July.

Donnelly, Sally B. 1992. The fire around the Ice. *Time*, 22 June, 66–68.

Duffy, Thom, and Charlene Orr. 1992. Texas police protest Ice-T song. *Billboard*, 20 June, 98.

Ehrenreich, Barbara. 1992. . . . Or is it creative freedom? *Time*, 20 July, 89.

Fiske, John. 1996. *Media matters*. Minneapolis: University of Minnesota Press.

Goldberg, Danny. 1992. By taking today's pop culture literally, critics miss the point of entertainment. *Los Angeles Times*, 28 June, M2, M6.

Hall, Stuart. 1980. Gramsci's relevance for the study of race and ethnicity. *Journal of Communication Inquiry* 20 (2): 5–27.

———. 1986. On postmodernism and articulation: An interview with Stuart Hall. *Journal of Communication Inquiry* 10 (2): 45–60.

Hershey-Webb, David. 1995. Number one, with a bullet: Songs of violence are part of America's folk tradition. In *Rap on rap: Straight-up talk on hip-hop culture*, edited by Adam Sexton, 100–6. New York: Delta.

Heston, Charlton. 1992. Heston speaks for women. *Los Angeles Times*, 3 August, F4.

Ice Cube. 1991. Black Korea. *On* Death Certificate. Priority Records.

Ice-T, and Heidi Siegmund. 1994. *The Ice opinion: Who gives a fuck?* New York: St. Martin's.
Jennings, Peter, anchor. 1992. *World News Tonight with Peter Jennings*, ABC, 19 June.
Kelly, Robin D. G. 1996. Kickin' reality, kickin' ballistics: Gangsta rap and postindustrial Los Angeles. In *Droppin' science: Critical essays on rap music and hip hop culture*, edited by William Eric Perkins, 117–58. Philadelphia: Temple University Press.
Kinsley, Michael. 1992. Ice-T: Is the issue social responsibility . . . *Time*, 20 July, 88.
Kochman, Thomas. 1981. *Black and white styles in conflict*. Chicago: University of Chicago Press.
Kuehl, Sheila James. 1992. Ice-T critics miss the rapper's real target. *Los Angeles Times*, 27 July, F3.
Layne, Barry. 1992. Quayle, black cops blast "Killer." *The Hollywood Reporter*, 22 June.
Leo, John. 1992. Rap music's toxic fringe. *U.S. News & World Report*, 29 June, 19.
Light, Alan. 1992a. Rappers sounded warning. *Rolling Stone*, 9–23 July, 15–17.
———. 1992b. Ice-T: The Rolling Stone interview. *Rolling Stone*, 20 August, 28–32, 60.
Mills, David. 1992. Sister Souljah's call to arms. *Washington Post*, 13 May, B1, B4.
Momma dearest. 1992. *New Republic*, 10 August, 7.
Morris, Chris. 1992a. TV a platform for rappers' reactions to riot as Ice-T, Chuck D, MC Ren, others speak out. *Billboard*, 16 May, 65.
———. 1992b. The spotlight turns to freedom in the arts: Police, Time Warner face off over "Cop Killer." *Billboard*, 25 July, 1, 71.
———. 1992c. "Cop" removal satisfies foes, to a point. *Billboard*, 8 August, 1, 83.
Muller, Judy, correspondent. 1992. *World News Tonight with Peter Jennings*, ABC, 24 July.
Outrage and Ice-T: What is the responsibility of the artist? 1992. *Los Angeles Times*, 4 August, B6.
Pareles, Jon. 1992a. Dissing the rappers is fodder for the sound bite. *The New York Times*, 28 June, sec. 2, 20.
———. 1992b. The disappearance of Ice-T's "Cop Killer." *The New York Times*, 30 July, C13, C16.
Philips, Chuck. 1992a. Texas police calls for boycott of Time Warner. *Los Angeles Times*, 12 June, F7.
———. 1992b. Police groups urge halt of record's sale. *Los Angeles Times*, 16 June, F1.
———. 1992c. The uncivil war. *Los Angeles Times*, 19 July, Calendar 6, 76, 77.
———. 1992d. A q&a with Ice-T about rock, race and the "Cop Killer" furor. *Los Angeles Times*, 19 July, Calendar 7.
Pollack, Phyllis. 1992. Uninformed media serve Ice-T bashers' aims. *Billboard*, 11 July, 4.
Quayle, congressmen, L.A. polls join "Cop Killer" posse. 1992. *Billboard*, 4 July, 1, 83.
Rapper Ice-T defends song against spreading boycott. 1992. *The New York Times*, 19 June, C24.
Rose, Tricia. 1994. *Black noise: Rap music and black culture in contemporary America*. Hanover, NH: University Press of New England/Wesleyan University Press.
Rosenthal, Andrew. 1992. Bush denounces rap recording and gives D'Amato a hand. *The New York Times*, 30 June, A21.
Royko, Mike. 1995. A different story if it were "Exec Killer." In *Rap on rap: Straight-up talk on hip-hop culture*, edited by Adam Sexton, 173–76. New York: Delta.
Rule, Sheila. 1992. Rapping Time Warner's knuckles. *The New York Times*, 8 July, C15–C16.

Run on Ice-T's album. 1992. *The New York Times*, 30 July, C16.
Samuels, David. 1991. The rap on rap. *New Republic*, November, 24–29.
Sandow, Greg. 1992. Fire and Ice. *Entertainment Weekly*, 14 August, 30.
Shaw, Bella, anchor. 1992. Ice-T appears on "Arsenio" to discuss controversy. *CNN Showbiz Today*, 22 July.
Trent, Andrea D. 1992. Cops not constructive. *Billboard*, 8 August, 6.
Vice president calls corporation wrong for selling rap song. 1992. *The New York Times*, 20 June, 9.
Volosinov, V. N. 1973. *Marxism and the philosophy of language*. New York: Seminar Press.
Walters, Paul M. 1992. Ice-T's "Cop Killer" can't be justified. *Los Angeles Times* (Orange County ed.), 8 July, B11.
While Time Warner counts its money, America may count its murdered cops (advertisement). 1992. *USA Today*, 26 June, 9A.
White, Timothy. 1991. Editorial. *Billboard*, 23 November, 8.
Will, George F. 1990. America's slide into the sewer. *Newsweek*, 30 July, 64.

---

*Author's note:* I would like to extend my appreciation to my colleagues from Professor John Fiske's media events seminar at the University of Wisconsin–Madison, spring 1997, for their helpful comments and suggestions regarding the first draft of this article. In particular, I wish to thank Doug Battema, John Fiske, Jennifer Fuller, Elana Levine, and Jennifer Wang.

## Your Text: Reading

1. What criteria is Marsh using to qualify "Johnny B. Goode" as "great"? Do you share these criteria? If not, what are they?
2. How important is it to you that a song is "influential"? Does it enhance your enjoyment of a particular song to know the influences?
3. What role does race play in these pieces? In music generally?
4. How important is it that a group sings their own songs? In other words, what roles do composition of the song and performance play in your acceptance of a song?
5. What songs do you feel qualify as "poetry"? Does thinking about songs as poetry affect the way you experience the song?
6. What are some of the effects the Beatles use? What role do they play in shaping the mood of the song? What is the mood of the song? Do other songs have similar effects (think about today's music)?
7. Dylan is considered to be one of rock music's most important lyricists and performers. Do you get a sense of that in listening to this song?
8. In what ways does the music of "Smells Like Teen Spirit" reflect the lyrics?
9. What do you think of the approach of Kurt Cobain and Nirvana to songwriting? Do you get a sense of their considerations while writing? Does knowing this approach affect the way you understand the song?

10. How are the two approaches to the song different? Which piece is more analytical? More geared to getting the flavor of the song?
11. Some critics think songs like "Like a Rolling Stone" and "Smells Like Teen Spirit" are the "song of a generation"—do you agree? If so, who makes up these generations—who was Bob Dylan and Nirvana speaking to (and for)? Do you think these songwriters would think they were speaking for anyone?
12. What approach is the author taking in his examination of "Cop Killer"? Do you think it's effective—why or why not? Can you think of other songs for which this approach might be effective?

### YOUR TEXT: WRITING

1. Choose a song you think is poetic. Write about the poetic aspect of it. Now write about how music either enhances or detracts from the poetic intent.
2. Choose a song that you think symbolizes what some people in your generation (age group) believe. Examine how well this song addresses this idea.
3. Compare two songs like "Smells Like Teen Spirit" and "Like a Rolling Stone" that some critics have labeled as songs that represent a particular generation.
4. Look at a song that tells a movie story. "Hurricane" by Bob Dylan is one that comes to mind. How is the song effective at telling the story? What are the differences between the song and the movie?
5. Mirroring Matt Compton's approach, look at how the lyrics and sounds of the song work together.
6. Are there any albums you are familiar with that sound like a song with many parts? Instead of focusing on a song, look how songs work together on an album.

## READING OUTSIDE THE LINES

### Classroom Activities

1. Compare your experiences listening to songs and reading the lyrics. First listen to a song, then read its lyrics. For a different song, reverse the procedure. What differences in understanding the song does this make?

2. If possible, listen to a song, then watch a video. What differences in understanding the song does this make?
3. Before listening to its content, read its album/CD cover. What symbols and themes do the band use in designing the cover? What do they suggest about the album's content? About the nature of the band? Now listen to some of the music. How do your preconceived ideas about the music compare to those presented by the music itself?
4. Watch a section of a movie with a soundtrack. What emotions does the soundtrack try to convey? Now watch the same movie with the sound lowered. Do you get the same ideas without the music? Does the music enhance your understanding of the movie? Detract from it?
5. Come up with some sample band names. Name genres for which the band's name would be appropriate. What does this exercise say about the way we view a band's name?

## Essay Ideas

1. Pick a song. What is the mood of the music compared to its lyrics? Do they work well together? Why or why not? Are the lyrics more sophisticated than the music or vice versa? Write a paper that makes an argument about the compatibility of music and lyrics.
2. Find a CD you do not know well. Study its cover, making notes on what the cover is "saying" to a potential listener. Now listen to the songs (reading the lyrics if you wish). Does the message behind the cover reflect the music? Why or why not? You can also do similar work with the band's name.
3. Find a well-known song you like. How would you find out information about the song? What sources might be appropriate? How might you approach writing a paper if you had this information? As you think about this question, look for information on the song. When you have gathered enough information, think of arguments or ideas about the song about which you could write.
4. Take a band you like that has produced more than one album. Trace its critical history. What elements of the band's work do the critics pick up on on a consistent basis? What is their general opinion of the band? How do they classify its genre? Now sit and think about whether you agree or disagree with these critics—and why.
5. Find two songs that have similar subjects. Compare and contrast their approaches to the subject, through both their music and lyrics. What approach do you favor, and why?
6. Find a band or bands with an explicitly political approach. Do you know their politics through their music or outside of it? Does their outside behavior argee with their music? How do critics and other members of the

media approach their relationship between politics and music? What do their fans think?

7. Find a movie or television show with a prominent soundtrack—does the music work well with the movie or TV series? What are your criteria? Is there a specific moment in the movie or television show that embodies the success or failure of the director's use of music?

# 10

# READING TECHNOLOGY

What does it mean to read technology? Technology is not a traditional text like a poem, nor does it have the clearly defined elements that public space and architecture have. It's both the idea of technology—the often symbolic elements that we think of when we hear the word—and the concrete applications that are worth reading, that on examination yield insight into how the world works. Most of us use technology without actively considering it. We often think about technology as computers, when in reality, we use technology when we do any number of simple tasks from washing our faces to turning on a light, listening to music, to talking on the telephone, to running errands in our car. Even the places we live are built using technologies our ancestors could not have imagined.

While the selections here often focus on computers, we want you to consider the technological components that often play an important role in our daily lives, the impact they have, and the impact their absence might have. Here are some other ideas that may help you read and write about technology in more complex ways.

## Technology has artistic components.

While technology is generally concerned more with function (how it works) than form (how it looks), we know by experience that design plays an important function in whether consumers purchase and use technology such as cars, computers, and even faucets. How technological elements look may not be a factor in *how* something works, but they may indeed be a factor in *whether* someone uses it. Indeed, the word technology comes from the Greek word *technae*, which means "art." The most practical car may not be the most beautiful—which is why not everyone owns a Volvo—and the more attractive computer may not be the most practical—not everyone owns a Macintosh. Yet technology relies on many of the same characteristics that we look for in art, such as symmetry, flow, exchange, and utility. We tend to forget that people create, design, and to some degree make tools, radios, personal digital assistants, cell phones, CD burners, can openers, pens, and scissors. Elements of design go into the shape, weight, feel, and function of each of these items.

## Technology has both an intentional and an unintentional impact on people and environments.

When a person invents something in response to a perceived problem or void—those are technology's intentional aspects. But with almost every invention comes a consequence that its inventor may not have considered, whether it's to the environment, to society's work or play habits, or to our domestic habits. Cell phones, for example, have made it more convenient to contact people and be contacted, but perhaps with this convenience has come safety and etiquette implications. Driving behind someone who is talking on the phone can be as annoying as hearing a cell phone ring during a movie. Is the convenience of communication worth the inconvenience that accompanies it? The proliferation of the Internet and home computing has had similar, hard-to-measure effects. We get things done quicker, but we also have more to do. Cell phones, pagers, laptops, and email make it harder to get away from work. As Marshal McLuhan suggests, we are surrounded by technology—we have built it into our environment. The question persists: does increased technology mean increased freedom or more work—or both?

Technology also has a complicated relationship with the environment. Our history is littered with the negative effects technology has had on the environment, especially in its release of pollutants into the air and water, and the growing landfills that contain manmade elements that are not biodegradable. But often technology is marshaled against environmental problems as well—it was technology that helped fight technology's impact on our growing industrial world. We mention this only because it's important to recognize we often use technology against itself, whether it's solar power plants and windmills battling nuclear power plants, or ergonomic chairs battling carpal tunnel syndrome caused by overusing word processing equipment. In a sense, technology is always confronting itself—which, in a sense, means humans are doing the same.

## Technology has societal impacts, including race, gender, and class.

Especially in the era of the computer, technological advances tend to affect individuals directly, whether it's the invention of the cell phone, the proliferation of home computers, or PDAs. But the accumulation of individual effects forces societal impact as well, whether it is driving with cell phones (or having them ring during class, the authors note) or increased access to the World Wide Web. In turn, a more tuned-in populace forces employers to crack down on e-mail use, forces advertisers to respond to an increased use of the remote control, movie theaters to post notices about cell-phone use, etc. Then, there are the environmental effects—pollution and the filling of landfills, to name two—which of course affect society as well.

Individuals in various groups who do not have access to technological changes or are not prone to use technology are obviously affected by technological changes; they often make it harder to keep up with those who have increased access to such technology. Recent studies have shown the existence of a digital divide between rich and poor and between white Americans and members of various ethnic groups, particularly African Americans and Hispanics. Men and women often have a different and complicated relationship with technology, which may shed light on their traditional roles. On the other hand, technology can be liberating to those who find that it can level the playing field; the young and skilled, whatever their identity, often have the advantage over the old and experienced when it comes to utilizing technology.

## Technology has changed the way we work and play.

Whether it's easier constant access to others through cell phones or e-mail or the ability to do work from anywhere, technology has changed our lives in ways its inventors might not have been able to anticipate. Perhaps because of technology, the lines between work and play have blurred; emails are always waiting for us, and the cell phone can make us instantly available to both friends and colleagues. Many of us prefer this lifestyle, while others find it intrusive. Technological advances often make us think about these divisions, and accordingly, how we live our lives and why we do what we do, for better or worse.

Technology has also redefined work and play; the Internet is the most outstanding example. Many businesses block employees from surfing the web or employ web site trackers that monitor what sites workers visit. Similarly, the proliferation of videos, portable CD and DVD players, and video games has utterly changed our notions of play, relaxation, and entertainment. Contemporary Americans spend so much time intimately involved with technology, some critics have speculated about more direct connections between technology and the human body. Are we already cyborgs—beings that are part human and part machine?

# Worksheet

## THIS TEXT: READING

1. How does the background of the authors influence their ideas about technology?
2. Do the authors have different ideas about class, race, and gender and their place in technology? In what ways?
3. While it will be impossible for you to know this fully, try to figure out the writing situation of each author. Who is the audience? What does the author have at stake?
4. What is his or her agenda? *Why* is she or he writing this piece?
5. What social, political, economic, and cultural forces affect the author's text? What is going on in the world as he or she is writing? Has that world changed?
6. What are the main points of the essay? What is the thesis statement?
7. How does the author support her argument? What evidence does he use to back up any claims he might make?
8. Is the author's argument reasonable?
9. Do you find yourself in agreement with the author? Why or why not?
10. Does the author help you read technology better than you did before reading the essay? If so, why?
11. How is the reading process different if you are reading an essay, as opposed to a short story or poem?
12. Did you like this? Why or why not?
13. Do you think the author likes technology overall?

## BEYOND THIS TEXT: WRITING

**Use:** What is this piece of technology for? What does it do? What doesn't it do that it's supposed to do? That its designers imply it should do?

**Need:** What human needs does this technology attempt to meet? Does it meet those needs?

**Design:** What are the strengths of this piece of technology's design? Its weaknesses? What is artistic about the design?

**Unintended effects:** What are some of the unintended effects of this piece of technology? Could the designer have foreseen such effects? Can improvements to its design or function change these effects?

**Societal impact:** What impact has this piece of technology had on society? What impact will it have?

**Personal impact:** What impact has this piece of technology had on you? On those who you know? Can you see any future impact it may have?

# INFURIATING BY DESIGN: EVERYDAY THINGS NEED NOT WREAK HAVOC ON OUR LIVES

Donald A. Norman

Though he has a Ph.D. in mathematical psychology and a master's in engineering, Donald Norman, like the rest of us, still has trouble with technology and design. Taken from his book *The Psychology of Everyday Things* (1988), this piece examines the frustrating nature of poorly designed technology. Notice the mix of both the personal and research material in this work.

EVERDAY THINGS NEED NOT wreak havoc on our lives. "You would need an engineering degree from MIT to work this," someone once told me, shaking his head in puzzlement over his brand-new digital watch. Well, I have an engineering degree from MIT. Give me a few hours and I can figure out the watch. But why should it take hours? I've talked with many people who couldn't use all the features of their washing machines or cameras, who couldn't figure out how to work a sewing machine or a video-cassette recorder, who habitually turned on the wrong stove burner.

Why do we put up with the frustrations of everyday objects, with devices that we can't figure out how to use? After all, we already know how to design certain common items so that they may be used gracefully, the very first time, without explanation. But time and again we are stymied by products that promise to do everything but are constructed in such a way as to make it impossible to do anything.

I have gathered, from among the thousands of items with which we have daily contact, examples of good and bad design that illustrate why the interaction between people and things sometimes goes well but more often does not. With these, I offer some general principles of good design that can be used both by those who construct devices and by those who use and misuse them.

Take car door handles, for example. They come in an amazing variety of shapes and sizes. The outside door handles of most modern automobiles are excellent examples of design. They are often recessed into the door, immediately indicating what to do with them: The handles cannot be used except by inserting the fingers and pulling.

Strangely enough, the inside door handles of automobiles tell a vastly different story. Here the designers have faced another set of problems, and the appropriate solution has yet to be found. As a result, these handles are often difficult to find, hard to figure out and problematic to use.

Why should this be? After all, with doors, we need to know only two things: what to do and where to do it. But how do you best convey that to the user? One general principle is to ensure that the knowledge required for a task is available in the world or readily derivable from it. In the case of doors, physical placement of the hardware or the color and composition of the handle can offer strong signals. With car doors, a horizontal slit on the outside door readily guides the hand into a pulling position; no such clue is available for the inside door handle.

Before beginning actual construction of an everyday object, a designer needs to develop a conceptual model of it that is appropriate for those who use the object, that captures the important parts of its operation and that is readily understandable by those who use it.

Think of the standard room thermostat. How does it work? Here is a device that offers almost no evidence of its operation except in a highly roundabout manner. You enter a room and feel cold, so you set the thermostat higher. Eventually you feel warmer. But suppose you are in a hurry to get warm?

Many people reach for the thermostat dial and turn it all the way up, mistakenly believing that a maximum setting yields maximum heating. But the thermostat is actually only a simple on-off switch; it does not control the amount of heat. The heater remains on, at full power, until the temperature setting on the thermostat is reached. Setting it to maximum does not heat the room any more quickly, yet the design of the device gives people no information that would counter this belief.

Using everyday devices should be simple, requiring a minimal amount of planning or problem solving. When such tasks become unnecessarily complex, technology can be used to restructure them and simplify their operation.

However, applying technology can be tricky. A designer must avoid the temptation to add functions to a device that make it even more complicated. Telephones, for example, used to be marvelous examples of simple design. The telephone on my desk today, however, has 24 functions, some of which I have never learned how to use. This is not simply a matter of having too many functions; my car has about 110 functions, none of which puzzles me in the least. Why is the telephone so much more difficult to master?

The answer, in part, lies in the ratio of controls (knobs, dials or levers) to the number of functions. The telephone has only 15 buttons to control all 24 tasks. Each button may activate more than one function. On the other hand, the car, with rare exceptions, has only one control for each function. That is, each control is specialized. Generally, whenever the number of possible functions of a device exceeds the number of controls, as in my telephone, there is apt to be difficulty in using it.

Designers must also pay attention to the limits of memory and to the limit on how many active thoughts people may pursue at once. Long-distance telephone charge cards, for example, are notoriously difficult to use for just this reason. Each company insists upon providing a long code, with individual numbers for each account. In addition some provide codes that are so secret, they aren't even printed on the long-distance charge card. If I wish to dial a long-distance number using my credit card from a hotel, I often must dial nearly three dozen digits in a precisely regulated sequence—assuming that I am able to remember what I am dialing. No wonder my failure rate for dialing correctly the first time is so high.

Physical and motor skills also place limits on certain abilities. Tying a shoelace, for example, is one standard task that is actually quite difficult to learn. Adults may have forgotten how long it took them, but injury, age or disease may provide a quick reminder through the loss of agility in the fingers. The introduction of Velcro fasteners, however, has now made the task simpler, requiring a minimum of motor skills and, for children, a minimum of memory.

People who use everyday objects need to know what kinds of things they can do with them and how these actions should be completed. One way to accomplish this is to offer ample visual hints. These should be readily interpretable and should match most people's intentions and expectations. In other words, the possible outcome of any action should be immediately obvious to the user of a device.

When important sensory cues are missing, the result can be more than inconvenient. I once stayed in the guest apartment of a technological institute in the Netherlands. The building was newly completed and contained many interesting architectural features. All was fine until I took a shower. The bathroom seemed to have no ventilation at all, so everything became wet, and eventually cold and clammy.

I looked all over the bathroom but never did find anything that looked like a ventilation grate or opening. However, I was able to find a switch that I thought might be the control for an exhaust fan. When I pushed it, a light nearby went on. The light stayed on, but nothing seemed to happen. Further pushing seemed to have no effect. Each time I returned to the apartment, however, I noticed that the light had gone off.

Later, I learned that the button did indeed control the exhaust fan in the bathroom. It was on as long as the light remained on, and it turned itself off, automatically, after about five minutes. Too bad I never figured this out. In this case, the architect was too successful in concealing feedback from the ventilation system. A ventilation grate or a noise of some kind would have signaled that there really was a change in the air.

Not only should a device's controls be visible but the spatial relationship between a device and its controls should also be as direct as possible.

The controls should either be on the device itself or arranged to have an analogical relationship with it. Similarly, the movement of the controls should be analogous to the expected operation of the device.

The seat adjustment control in a Mercedes Benz automobile is an excellent example of what I call "natural mapping." The control is in the shape of the seat itself. To move the front edge of the seat higher, the driver lifts up on the front part of the button. To make the seat-back recline, the driver simply pushes the button backward. There are no directions—none are needed. This is important, since if labels are required, this is a signal that the design for the device may be faulty. Labels are often necessary, but the appropriate use of natural mapping can minimize the need for them.

The seat control succeeds because there is a natural relationship between the switch movements and the seat motion. If it isn't possible to make the choices in using a device as obvious as this, another solution is to limit the number of possible bad choices. In other words, a device should have constraints built in so that the user feels as if there is only one thing to do—the right thing.

Good designers can anticipate almost any conceivable error that a user of an everyday object might make. In fact, a good rule of design is to assume that any possible error will be made. One clever design incorporating this consideration is the package shelf found in some public rest rooms. It is placed on the wall just behind the cubicle door, folded into a vertical position. To make it into a shelf, you have to lower it to the horizontal position, where the weight of a package keeps it there. To get out of the cubicle, you have to remove whatever is on the shelf in order to raise it out of the way of the door. This forces you to remember your package.

Not all everyday objects are so well thought out. In fact, many people have died needlessly in building fires because architects did not anticipate all the errors people could make. When fires break out, people tend to flee in panic, down the stairs, past the ground floor and into the basement, where they become trapped. The solution—which has been reinforced by fire safety laws throughout the country—is to hinder simple passage from the ground floor of most large buildings to the basement.

This safety feature is mainly a nuisance in normal use. I have never yet been in a burning building, but it often happens that I must pass from a higher floor to the basement, encountering all kinds of obstacles along the way. Yet I believe that this minor problem is worth the bother, since it undoubtedly saves many lives.

Sometimes a designer cannot provide all of the necessary information to use an everyday object or cannot fully exploit natural mapping. Then there is generally only one viable choice: Standardize the actions, outcomes, layout and displays involved in its use. The nice thing about standardization is that no matter how arbitrary, it only has to be learned once.

A case in point is the layout of the modern typewriter keyboard, which has a long and peculiar history. In the end, the keyboard was designed by an evolutionary process, but the main driving forces were mechanical. Almost all typewriters and computers today make use of the "Qwerty" keyboard, named for the first six letters appearing at the upper left-hand side. Better designs exist (the so-called "Dvorak" keyboard can increase the top speed of expert typists by at least 10 percent), but that is not enough to merit a change. Millions of people would have to learn a new style of typing and millions of typewriters would have to be replaced.

Once a satisfactory product, such as a keyboard, has been standardized, further change may be counterproductive, especially if the product is successful. Standardization is not the ideal solution, but sometimes it is the only choice and, when followed consistently, it works well.

If I were placed in the cockpit of a jet airplane, my inability to perform gracefully would neither surprise nor bother me. But I shouldn't have trouble with doors, switches, water faucets and stoves. Moreover, I know that other people have the same unnecessary troubles. Instead of causing problems, design of everyday objects should eliminate them, without any need for words or symbols and certainly without any need for trial and error.

Remember, problems with design affect all of us. Recently, a computer scientist at my university proudly showed me his new compact disc player, complete with remote control. The remote unit had a little metal loop protruding from one end. My friend told me that when he first got the set, he assumed that the loop was an antenna, and he always tried to aim it at the player. Unfortunately, the remote control barely functioned this way. Later he discovered that the loop was only a loop, meant to be used to hang up the control when it wasn't in use. He had been aiming the unit at his own body for weeks, an unknowing victim in the battle against poor design.

---

## This Text: Reading

1. Can you think of examples of Norman's phenomenon in your own life?
2. Though this was written more than 10 years ago, does this seem dated? Why or why not?
3. Why aren't designers of technology more responsive to customer use (given the purpose of technology is to make something easier to do)?
4. In what ways is the use or misuse of technological design a culture problem? What cultures are clashing, according to Norman?

## Your Text: Writing

1. Write about a problematic relationship you have or had with a piece of technology.
2. Write about an invention or design you find especially useful or helpful. What sets apart this design from more problematic designs?
3. Write an open letter to designers suggesting changes in the way understand the consumer. Cite specific examples of poorly designed technology.

4. Read Katherine Benzel's piece on the perfect classroom in Chapter 3. Write a paper designing a friendlier classroom, avoiding some of the pitfalls you see in your own classrooms.

## THE GIRL-GAME JINX

Elizabeth Weil

In this piece of reporting (1997), Elizabeth Weil of *salon.com* finds a gender gap still exists when it comes to gaming. Although the work is mostly reporting, Weil clearly takes a position here about the place of women in gaming specifically and technology and science generally.

THE 1997 COMPUTER GAME DEVELOPERS CONFERENCE, held earlier this year in Santa Clara, Calif., featured five sessions on computer games for girls, all of which were packed past fire code. This was not like past Computer Game Developers Conferences. Previously, discussion of computer games for girls consisted of some punk with a $100 million company saying, "Girls don't like our games? Well, good!" This year, when a staffer pinned a "session full" sign outside the final panel on "What Do Female Game Players Really Want?" a riot nearly broke out.

The trouble started with a Microsoft man proclaiming, loudly, that he was being denied access to the only session that mattered—the only session geared at opening up a new market. Then the 30 or so shut-outs stormed the conference room.

Inside, decorum did not resume. The stragglers lined the windowless walls. They gaped as the '70s-feminist moderator (who was sure she knew what girls wanted) knocked heads with the frustrated industry vets (who clearly had no idea). The moderator wrote on the white board: "Female players want games that are social, games without gratuitous human violence, games that make them feel." The vets skewered her maxims as offensively neat.

A woman in the back corner raised her hand. "Excuse me, but I'm a woman and I'm antisocial."

Next a guy from Columbia Tristar Online suggested: "Couldn't we just rename this session 'How to Create Games for Somebody Other Than a 14-Year-Old Boy?'"

Finally, a designer with unruly brown hair slammed two fists on the table. "You want to know what female players would really like?" she said. "It's like this eighth-grade girl once told me: I would like it if it was good."

No one left with answers. No one left feeling good. Afterwards a few women stood cross-armed in the atrium, griping about the fact that few conference attendees seemed capable of making eye contact with a female, let alone capable of making an interactive experience to engage, wow or otherwise entice one.

But the issues surrounding the creation of computer games for girls are far more complicated than that. Over the past few years, two attitude-altering events have occurred. One, the gaming industry severely overextended itself in the adolescent boy niche, filling store shelves with look-alike products. Two, between October 1996 and March 1997, a game called "Barbie Fashion Designer" sold half a million units to supposedly technophobic little girls.

No one quite expects the girls' market to rival the $1.8 billion boys' market. Still, what we're seeing now is the adolescence of the gaming industry: The boys spent their formative years shunning female players, doing their best to make them squirm. But now they're having second thoughts. The cooties have subsided—they see the appeal of girls.

Postures are shifting on the female side as well. Several girl-oriented companies have emerged over the past three years. Some are led by women, like Girl Games Inc.'s Laura Groppe, who didn't notice until recently that the boys were into some serious and lucrative fun. Others are run by long-time gamers like Sheri Graner Ray of Her Interactive.

Meanwhile, at least one pioneer of the girl-game cause has recently given up on it. Heidi Dangelmaier publicly took on the boys two years before anybody else—but as she now sees it, the girl game is a doomed enterprise. The terms are all wrong. To label a product for girls implies that it's not for everyone who values intimacy, expression, depth of feeling—all the things girls want. And to label a product a game implies that it's derivative and lightweight—as if software that enables intimacy, expression and depth of feeling wouldn't be a revolution in and of itself.

Dangelmaier's Manhattan office floats on the top floor of a building on 32nd Street and Lexington Avenue. The loft has a shiny bronze floor and cool blue walls. The windows span 270 degrees. Visitors, upon walking in, often feel an ashramlike calm. Dangelmaier, however, feels no such peace. "Why isn't the product fresh?" she laments. "Why isn't the product elegant?" Her eyes seem to move closer together when she gets worked up. "I'm just so fucking tired of all this sterile righteous stereotypical girl stuff. I've had to dissociate myself from that."

Dangelmaier is 33, artsy, a scientist by training and unafraid of critique. In 1993 she published a groundbreaking article in the influential newsletter Digital Media. She demanded to know why, with half a billion girls aching for computer software, the industry had never made an intelligent effort to create products to meet their needs. The following year she leveled the charge again, this time in person at the Computer Game Developers' Conference. As she expected, the gaming community reacted with a firestorm of personal and professional attacks.

"What all these new girl products should have done was open up different ways the interactive medium can integrate into our free time and our social time, and instead what's being produced is just really cheesy and petty." Dangelmaier flings open a set of French doors and steps out onto the 18th-story deck. As she sees it, no one's thinking beyond electronic teen magazines and after-school specials. No one's cracked open a whole new form. "What needs to happen is for girls' games to get out of the realm of gender and into the realm of design."

Dangelmaier walks to the deck's railing, stares across at the Chrysler and Empire State buildings and proceeds to share her own design insights—most fundamentally, her belief that the history of the gaming industry is the history of how things evolve in an inbred male niche. When "Pong" booted up the market in 1974, videogames were not a boy thing or a girl thing. When "Ms. PacMan" hit the arcades in 1979, gender issues were no big deal. Nobody lost any quarters when, in the late '80s, the percentage of female videogame players started to decline. But in 1992, Dangelmaier decided to ditch her computer science Ph.D. program at Princeton to "lay my head into this sucker." She wanted to find out why girls were walking away from games, and why the game makers didn't seem to care.

Dangelmaier wangled herself a desk at Sega. She spent two years poking into play patterns, sex typing, software trends, and marketing, and what she concluded was stunningly simple: The gaming console itself was gender-neutral, but personal priorities—the priorities of the young male gamers working in the industry—dictated the products being made. "It's really basic," Dangelmaier says, downshifting her voice from passionate advocate to logical theorist, moving back from the edge to the deck's interior and sitting down on a wicker couch. "If you have to explain why something's fun it's not going to get funded. So I might come up with some game that's really exciting to me"—one that pushes female hot buttons—"but in order to get it produced, some boy of tech had to look at it and say, 'That's cool.'"

Thus boy bosses green-lighted boy-oriented projects because those were the ones they understood and liked. Myopic maybe, not nefarious. Still, the trend had consequences few thought to predict. Within a matter of years, gaming hardware started adapting to fit the titles boys preferred. Then, as now, more games were played on video consoles than on PCs. Then, as now, fighter titles—bleed-and-twitch, as they're called—were all the rage. Bleed-and-twitch games required quick response times and minimal storage. To hone the genre—to create really sublime diversions for boys—platform memory was sacrificed for speed. "Why don't game machines have memory?" asks Dangelmaier. "It's a choice. You don't need it for any response games."

All this leads up to Dangelmaier's point: Response games do not fulfill everyone's entertainment needs. They do not fulfill the needs of almost all girls. They do not fulfill the needs of most non-adolescent males, who along with most females, tend to prefer constructing things—relationships, block piles, Barbie fashions, whatever—as opposed to blowing shit up. "And guess what?" she says. "You need memory to run those other kinds of software." PC hardware, of course, has memory. The extension of the gaming industry onto the computer desktop has changed the technical landscape—but not the industry's boy orientation. So ends Dangelmaier's parable of the gaming industry and the narrow niche: A small group of hard-core male gamers indulged their sense of what was fun to do, and eventually that's what the hardware could do best.

* * *

Out in Albuquerque, Sheri Graner Ray, Her Interactive's director of product development, sits in a cramped office in a clunky two-story building playing "Bad Mojo," a CD-ROM game involving a cockroach. She's twirled her blinds shut to the glare. Shoved in the back corner, still in shrink-wrap, lies a single copy of "MacKenzie & Company," Her Interactive's first title, a game about finding a date for the prom.

"We're still sort of like the dancing dog," Graner Ray says of the girl games business, scuttling her roach about the on-screen kitchen. "One marvels less at how well the dog dances than that the dog dances at all." Here she nabs a fly, let's out a "yesss!" and offers some personal history: "Back when I was working at Origin Systems I asked this producer, 'Why don't you make games to include your female players?' And he looked at me and said, 'I have more left-handed players than I have female players and I don't make games for left-handed people. Why should I make games for you?'"

Graner Ray is 35, pale-skinned, a hard-core gamer with an unfussy manner from a first career training dogs. She came to the industry the old-fashioned way: through Dungeons & Dragons. As far back as 1989, she had a sign propped on her desk that read, "And what if the player were female?" But her male co-workers—who outnumbered her female co-workers 66–3—laughed. Then they got mad. And when Graner Ray kept pushing the issue, they quit telling her where to find team meetings. "Two years ago, there were 3,000 titles out there for boys, and if you were a 14-year-old girl, there wasn't anything out there for you," she says. Even the marketing channels, she notes, conspire against women. "You can't put a girls' game in Egghead and expect it to sell. Girls don't shop there. They aren't comfortable. Not any more comfortable than they'd be in a men's underwear department."

More than the other contenders in the emerging girls' market, Graner Ray has kept her eye focused on the word "games." As part of a women's studies degree she's completing at the University of New Mexico, she has forged a neatly packaged theory of male and female entertainment requirements. She cites three main areas of "actual, physiological" variance. One, males respond most to visual stimuli, females to emotion and touch. Two, males like to tackle conflicts head-to-head; females prefer compromise, diplomacy, negotiation and manipulation. Three, males tend to be satisfied with visual rewards, while females require emotional resolution.

In other words, you can't put "Doom" in a pink box and expect it to sell. "If you're going to make interactive games for women, you must give them mutually beneficial solutions to socially significant problems," Graner Ray summarizes. "By mutually beneficial, I mean the solution benefits both the player and the characters in the game. And socially significant? I don't mean solving world hunger. I mean any situation that involves other people, a social group."

For examples, Graner Ray notes that your basic screaming car chase will excite only men, but put a kidnapped child in the first car and a panicked mother in the second and you'll excite women, too. She cites "Myst," a game that requires solving a family's problems in order to rescue them off a deserted island—a game that, albeit unintentionally, drew a huge female audience, selling 3.5 million units, far more than any other computer game to date. From all this one might logically deduce that what girls want is better games. Unfortunately, though, that's not what's being produced under the "girls" banner.

One piercingly bright Tuesday morning I sit in as Graner Ray summons her crew—five men, three women, all gamers but not devoted players of girl games—around a fake-wood conference table, gripping 24-ounce coffee mugs, braced for an ad hoc team meeting. Today the task at hand is to drum up new plot twists and puzzles for Her Interactive's upcoming title, "Nancy Drew, The Case Files: Secrets Can Kill." A few minutes are spent rehashing last evening's highly charged tournament of the classic fighter game "Tekken Two." Then they settle in, loose but focused. Initially, at least, the team seems to be working in a productively irreverent way.

First, Her Interactive's webmaster suggests that Nancy engage in some low-grade hacking, cracking open a program called Ventana '97.

Next, the woman who designs the interiors spins an elaborate subplot involving Nancy breaking in to the teacher's lounge with glass cutters or, even more amusingly, *plastique*.

Nearing 11 a.m., Graner Ray herself chips in with a promising tangent about Nancy trapping the villain in the boiler room with the aid of an acetylene torch.

Yet somehow, by noon, all that's slipped away, and a more predictable scenario—Nancy finds a purse, complete with compact, lipstick and credit card—goes up on the board. "We're going to get hit with, 'It's so stereotypical. It's such a girl game,'" a graphic designer says under her breath. "But what are you going to do, you know? Girls like lipstick. I have lipstick in my purse."

It is tempting to assert that girl games fall flat because of their subject matter. But in fact most girl games today flounder because they're poorly executed, shallow and underrefined. The products can feel like artless preteen musings—and to a certain extent, they are.

"I've had so many girls' eyes on my stuff. I never took a step without having their feedback," says Girl Games Inc.'s Laura Groppe, the force behind "Let's Talk About Me!" a title that boasts such characters as Miss Hottie Bottie, who advises drinking six to eight glasses of water a day for clear skin, and Señora Obscura Sabidez, who counsels carrying tissues, chapstick and a wet suit if your boyfriend kisses like a dead fish. "To me it seems so obvious how to succeed in this market: You do your research. You know your customer. You know the corporations who know your customer. You come at it from the mind-set of a 12-year-old girl."

Groppe is charming, blond, an Academy Award-winning producer, a formidable self-promoter with a coy Texas drawl. In 1994 she left Hollywood for Austin and founded Girl Games Inc. She spent a couple of summers at Rice University studying "what girls really want from technology." Now she refers to 9-to-12-year-old females as "her girls." For fun—or so she claims—she reads Seventeen, watches "Sabrina" and hangs at the mall.

"My programmers are always telling me buttons have to be in these specific states and handing me books this big on interface design," she says, spreading her thumb and index finger, playing up her role as anti-technologist/girl-advocate. "But I don't give a shit. I tell my programmers what the girls are responding to and what they intuitively get. . . . Half the time the guys are looking at me and saying, that's fun? And I'm saying, yeah, that's fun. That's a barrel of monkeys."

In Silicon Valley, Purple Moon, an offshoot of Interval Research, has taken a similarly studied, if more rigorous, approach to creating games for girls—basing much of its work on research by digital-design legend Brenda Laurel. As Purple Moon president and CEO Nancy Deyo explains it, the company spent three years hanging around with anthropologists, sociologists, primates and actual human children, acquiring what Deyo refers to as "a deep knowledge of girls."

For starters, Purple Moon pried into gaming myths: Girls don't like violence (truth: Girls just are bored by die-and-start-over, beat-the-game challenges products); girls aren't competitive (truth: Girls compete, but often in subtle and indirect ways). Next they "co-created, if you will"—designing products "almost in unison with parents and with girls." And now, finally, with the aid of a strong-arm PR firm, they've launched "Rockett's New School," a "friendship adventure for girls."

Merchandising is central to Purple Moon's business plan: According to Deyo, for each of Rockett's characters, a posable 3-D doll and playing card will be available at extra cost. Girls will encounter these characters not just on CD-ROM but on the Internet, in books and on TV. "Eight-to-12-year-old girls just have an intense fascination with characters who span media forms," she says, betraying her background in brand management, coolly pitching her empire-to-be. "They love that ubiquitousness, that feeling of, oh my God, this character's everywhere! We want girls to hang out with Purple Moon wherever they go. And that pervasiveness, we believe, will help us deliver on a suite of experiences that is just really really relevant and meaningful to them."

In other words, Deyo wants a product like Barbie. Barbie has 99 percent market penetration. Ninety-nine percent of American girls between the ages of 3 and 10 own at least one Barbie doll, says Mattel, which claims the average number is nine. Barbie is ubiquitous and Barbie can haul in enough cash to make even Purple Moon's owner—Bill Gates' former partner Paul Allen—proud.

Inconveniently, though, Barbie on CD-ROM seems to require constant spin control. Critics have a way of demanding that software be good for girls. Thus, these days, Nancie Martin—creator of "Barbie Fashion Designer," former editor in chief of Tiger Beat, author of "Miss America Through the Looking Glass"—spends much of her energy dreaming up redemptive qualities for her work.

When I meet Martin for coffee, she's dressed in a pastel jacket and French cuffs. She explains that Barbie has to have the figure she does so she will look normal in the hang and nap of her clothes. She explains that girls aren't supposed to aspire to look like Barbie—Barbie is supposed to be a vehicle through which they can play out their aspirations and their dreams. In a sort of rope-a-dope, she concedes the existence of "a certain kind of feminist framework which doesn't allow for the presence of a Barbie-like object." But then she comes back with a reference to Carol Gilligan.

"Recently I've been rereading 'In a Different Voice,'" she says. "I really wanted to do something about that plummeting self-esteem. I've always felt like it's really important to give girls something they can feel good about, a sense of mastery. And if we can do that with 'Barbie Fashion Designer' when they're 6 or 7 or 8, and if that carries over to when they're 11 or 12 or 13, then we'll be ahead of the game."

The exercise in rationalization is ludicrous, as ludicrous as claiming that this year's hot-selling "Duke Nukem"—a title that packs massive guys, massive guns and erotic dancers who for five Duke dollars flash their low-res breasts—is actually good for boys. As enlightened insiders are fond of saying, everybody knows there's nothing redeeming about the gaming industry. And in fact, only outsiders seem to be doing anything good for girls—people like 28-year-old Theresa Duncan, a New York artist who spent her childhood dressing up in dime-store tiaras and shooting frogs with a BB gun and who names her goal as creating good art, not making millions or elevating psyches.

"What's the name of that movie where everybody's a zombie and you're the only real person?" Duncan asks from her office at Nicholson NY, her employer du jour. "I feel what I'm trying to do is just so alien to the rest of the market. It's like they take their inspiration from McDonald's and I take mine from Maurice Sendak."

Like alternative artists in both music and film, Duncan lacks a distributor but enjoys a cult following. She works when passion strikes her. She signs on actual artists—author David Sedaris, conceptual artist Jeremy Blake, Fugazi drummer Brendan Candy—to narrate, illustrate and compose music for her work. Thus far, she's released three titles: "Chop Suey," the sweet-yet-edgy story of Lily and June Bugg, who eat too much Chinese food and proceed to trip out, and "Mimi Smartypants," the kooky-arty small-town adventures of an overly brainy 9-year-old girl, and "Zero Zero," a Parisian fantasia. Once again, what Duncan's dishing out is not the careful deadness of market research but the subversive lyricism of modern storytelling, the folksy wit of cartoon art. "You know, I'm glad girls are finally getting some attention, but I'm worried that people are patronizing to them. I don't want to sound cocky," she says, "but I think I'll be here doing my thing long after some of those other, larger, producers are gone."

On the final day of the Computer Games Developers Conference, the big players in the girl games market all sat on the veranda of the Santa Clara Westin and ate salads for lunch. The mood was buoyant, edging toward sassy. Waiters flitted. Iced-tea tumblers clinked. A man slinked over and passed out his business card, letting the ladies know he wouldn't mind a job. The women spent a few minutes discussing how they would live up to their billing as "visionaries" for that afternoon's panel about how to succeed in the girl games market. But as Nancie Martin explained, this was really a victory party. "The guys said we couldn't do it and now we're doing it, so the girls are going nyah nyah nyah."

Shortly before 3, the women walked from the hotel to the conference center, taking their seats on the podium in front of the standing-room-only crowd. Groppe spoke first, claiming that the secret to the girl market is to collect prodigious amounts of market data and work backwards from there. Graner Ray talked next, spinning out her gender-based game theories, showing how to appease marginally more females by tweaking—really, blanching—standard bleed-and-twitch, find-the-treasure gaming modes. Finally, Martin chipped in, half-joking about Mattel's ability to trade on the nag factor, Freud's view of what women want and Barbie's kindly gesture of opening up the pink-software market for the rest of the group.

But in the end the audience learned precisely nothing. No one said computer games, while equal parts high tech and big business, eventually come down to handicraft. No one dared mention that market research is no substitute for inspiration, that transcendent products do not emerge from conference rooms. In the end, the secret to divining what female players really want is far simpler and more complex than anyone ever imagined. What it takes is the faith of vision, the courage of the blank screen, the quiet to hear the words of an eighth grader: *I would like it if it was good.*

---

## THIS TEXT: READING

1. Do you find in your own experience examples of the phenomenon Weil describes?
2. Do you think it's true that men like games better? Why do you think that is?

3. Does the scenario Weil describes have any impact beyond simple game playing?
4. This article was written more than five years ago. What, if anything, has changed since then?

### YOUR TEXT: WRITING

1. Think of another activity that seems to separate men and women. Write a paper examining why this might be true.
2. As Weil describes in her article, one of the most difficult things to do is design specifically for gender use without resorting to stereotyped behaviors. Write a short paper suggesting how designers address this problem.
3. Look at Daphne Spain's article "Spatial Segregation in the Workplace" in Chapter 3. Write a paper comparing Spain's and Weil's concerns.

## WHERE DO YOU WANT TO GO TODAY? CYBERNETIC TOURISM, THE INTERNET, AND TRANSNATIONALITY

Lisa Nakamura

Lisa Nakamura (2000) looks at the relationship between culture, technology, and advertising, taking as her thesis the idea that advertisers are using foreign culture as a way of selling technological innovation.

There is no race. There is no gender. There is no age. There are no infirmities. There are only minds. Utopia? No, Internet.

—*"Anthem," television commercial for MCI*

THE TELEVISION COMMERCIAL "Anthem" claims that on the Internet, there are no infirmities, no gender, no age, that there are only minds. This pure, democratic, cerebral form of communication is touted as a utopia, a pure no-place where human interaction can occur, as the voice-over says, "uninfluenced by the rest of it." Yet can the "rest of it" be written out as easily as the word *race* is crossed out on the chalkboard by the hand of an Indian girl in this commercial?

It is "the rest of it," the specter of racial and ethnic difference and its visual and textual representation in print and television advertisements that appeared in 1997 by Compaq, IBM, and Origin, that I will address in this chapter. The ads I will discuss all sell networking and communications technologies that depict racial difference, the "rest of it," as a visual marker. The spectacles of race in these advertising images are designed to stabilize contemporary anxieties that networking technology and access to cyberspace may break down ethnic and racial differences. These advertisements, which promote the glories of cyberspace, cast the viewer in the position of the tourist, and sketch out a future in which difference is either elided or put in its proper place.

The ironies in "Anthem" exist on several levels. For one, the advertisement positions MCI's commodity—"the largest Internet network in the world"—as a solution to social problems. The advertisement claims to produce a radical form of democracy that refers to and extends an "American" model of social equality and equal access. This patriotic anthem, however, is a paradoxical one: the visual images of diversity (old, young, black, white, deaf, etc.) are displayed and celebrated as spectacles of difference that the narrative simultaneously attempts to erase by claiming that MCI's product will reduce the different bodies that we see to "just minds."

The ad gestures towards a democracy founded upon disembodiment and uncontaminated by physical difference, but it must also showcase a dizzying parade of difference in order to make its point. Diversity is displayed as the sign of what the product will eradicate. Its erasure and elision can only be understood in terms of its presence; like the word "race" on the chalkboard, it can only be crossed out if it is written or displayed. This ad writes race and poses it as both a beautiful spectacle and a vexing question. Its narrative describes a "postethnic America," to use David Hollinger's phrase, where these categories will be made not to count. The supposedly liberal and progressive tone of the ad camouflages its depiction of race as something to be eliminated, or made "not to count," through technology. If computers and networks can help us to communicate without "the rest of it," that residue of difference with its power to disturb, disrupt, and challenge, then we can all exist in a world "without boundaries."

Another television commercial, this one by AT&T, that aired during the 1996 Olympics asks the viewer to "imagine a world without limits—AT&T believes communication can make it happen." Like "Anthem," this narrative posits a connection between networking and a democratic ethos in which differences will be elided. In addition, it resorts to a similar visual strategy—it depicts a black man in track shorts leaping over the Grand Canyon.

Like many of the ads by high tech and communications companies that aired during the Olympics, this one has an "international" or multicultural flavor that seems to celebrate national and ethnic identities. This world without limits is represented by vivid and often sublime images of displayed ethnic and racial difference in order to bracket them off as exotic and irremediably other. Images of this other as primitive, anachronistic, and picturesque decorate the landscape of these ads.

Microsoft's recent television and print media campaign markets access to personal computing and Internet connectivity by describing these activities as a form of travel. Travel and tourism, like networking technology, are commodities that define the privileged, industrialized first-world subject, and they situate him in the position of the one who looks, the one who has access, the one who communicates. Microsoft's omnipresent slogan "Where do you want to go today?" rhetorically places this consumer in the position of the user with unlimited choice; access to Microsoft's technology and networks promises the consumer a "world without limits" where he can possess an idealized mobility. Microsoft's promise to transport the user to new (cyber)spaces where desire can be fulfilled is enticing in its very vagueness, offering a seemingly open-ended invitation for travel and new experiences. A sort of technologically enabled transnationality is evoked here, but one that directly addresses the first-world user, whose position on the network will allow him to metaphorically go wherever he likes.

This dream or fantasy of ideal travel common to networking advertisements constructs a destination that can look like an African safari, a trip to the Amazonian rain forest, or a camel caravan in the Egyptian desert. The iconography of the travelogue or tourist attraction in these ads places the viewer in the position of the tourist who, in Dean MacCannell's words, "simply collects experiences of difference (different people, different places)" and "emerges as a miniature clone of the old Western philosophical subject, thinking itself unified, central, in control, etc., mastering Otherness and profiting from it" (xv). Networking ads that promise the viewer control and mastery over technology and communications discursively and visually link this power to a vision of the other which, in contrast to the mobile and networked tourist/user, isn't going anywhere. The continued presence of stable signifiers of otherness in telecommunications advertising guarantees the Western subject that his position, wherever he may choose to go today, remains privileged.

An ad from Compaq that appeared in the *Chronicle of Higher Education* reads "Introducing a world where the words 'you can't get there from here' are never heard." It depicts a "sandstone mesa" with the inset image of a monitor from which two schoolchildren gaze curiously at the sight. The ad is selling "Compaq networked multimedia. With it, the classroom is no longer a destination, it's a starting point." Like the Microsoft and AT&T slogans, it links networks with privileged forms of travel, and reinforces the metaphor by visually depicting sights that viewers associate with tourism. The networked classroom is envisioned as a glass window from which networked users can consume the sights of travel as if they were tourists.

Another ad from the Compaq series shows the same children admiring the networked rain forest from their places inside the networked classroom, signified by the frame of the monitor. The tiny box on the upper-right-hand side of the image evokes the distinctive menu bar of a Windows product, and frames the whole ad for its viewer as a window onto an "other" world.

The sublime beauty of the mesa and the lush pastoral images of the rain forest are nostalgically quoted here in order to assuage an anxiety about the environmental effects of cybertechnology. In a world where sandstone mesas and rain forests are becoming increasingly rare, partly as a result of industrialization, these ads position networking as a benign, "green" type of product that will preserve the beauty of nature, at least as an image on the screen. As John Macgregor Wise puts it, this is part of the modernist discourse that envisioned electricity as "transcendent, pure and clean," unlike mechanical technology. The same structures of metaphor that allow this ad to dub the experience of using networked communications "travel" also enables it to equate an image of a rain forest in Nature (with a capital *N*). The enraptured American schoolchildren, with their backpacks and French braids, are framed as user-travelers. With the assistance of Compaq, they have found their way to a world that seems to be without limits, one in which the images of nature are as good as or better than reality.

The virtually real rain forest and mesa participate in a postcyberspace paradox of representation—the locution "virtual reality" suggests that the line or "limit" between the authentic sight/site and its simulation has become blurred. This discourse has become familiar, and was anticipated by Jean Baudrillard pre-Internet. Familiar as it is, the Internet and its representations in media such as advertising have refigured the discourse in different contours. The ads that I discuss attempt to stabilize the slippery relationship between the virtual and the real by insisting upon the monolithic visual differences between first-and third-world landscapes and people.

This virtual field trip frames Nature as a tourist sight and figures Compaq as the educational tour guide. In this post-Internet culture of simulation in which we live, it is increasingly necessary for stable, iconic images of Nature and the Other to be evoked in the world of technology advertising. These images guarantee and gesture toward the unthreatened and unproblematic existence of a destination for travel, a place whose beauty and exoticism will somehow remain intact and attractive. If technology will indeed make everyone, everything, and every place the same, as "Anthem" claims in its ambivalent way, then where is there left to go? What is there left to see? What is the use of being asked where you want to go today if every place is just like here? Difference, in the form of exotic places or exotic people, must be demonstrated iconographically in order to shore up the Western user's identity as himself.

This idyllic image of an Arab on his camel, with the pyramids picturesquely squatting in the background, belongs in a coffee-table book. The timeless quality of this image of an exotic other untouched by modernity is disrupted by the cartoon dialogue text, which reads "What do you say we head back and download the results of the equestrian finals?" This dissonant use of contemporary vernacular American techoslang is supposed to be read comically; the man is meant to look unlike anyone who would speak these words.

The gap between the exotic Otherness of the image and the familiarity of its American rhetoric can be read as more than an attempt at humor, however. IBM, whose slogan "solutions for a small planet" is contained in an icon button in the lower left hand side of the image, is literally putting these incongruous words into the Other's mouth, thus demonstrating the hegemonic power of its "high speed information network" to make the planet smaller by causing everyone to speak the *same* language—computer-speak. His position as the exotic Other must be emphasized and foregrounded in order for this strategy to work, for the image's appeal rests upon its evocation of the exotic. The rider's classical antique "look and feel" atop his Old Testament camel guarantee that his access to a high speed network will not rob us, the tourist/viewer, of the spectacle of his difference. In the phantasmatic world of Internet advertising, he can download all the results he likes, so long as his visual appeal to us, the viewer, reassures us that we are still in the position of the tourist, the Western subject, whose privilege it is to enjoy him in all his anachronistic glory.

These ads claim a world without boundaries for us, their consumers and target audience, and by so doing they show us exactly where and what these boundaries really are. These boundaries are ethnic and racial ones. Rather than being effaced, these dividing lines are evoked over and over again. In addition, the ads sanitize and idealize their depictions of the Other and Otherness by deleting all references that might threaten their status as timeless icons. In the camel image, the sky is an untroubled blue, the pyramids have fresh, clean, sharp outlines, and there are no signs whatsoever of pollution, roadkill, litter, or fighter jets.

Including these "real life" images in the advertisement would disrupt the picture it presents us of an Other whose "unspoiled" qualities are so highly valued by tourists. Indeed, as Trinh Minh-Ha notes, even very sophisticated tourists are quick to reject experiences that challenge their received notions of authentic Otherness. Trinh writes, "the Third World representative the modern sophisticated public ideally seeks is the *unspoiled* African, Asian, or Native American, who remains more preoccupied with his/her image as the *real* native—the *truly different*—than with the issues of hegemony, feminism, and social change." Great pains are taken in this ad to make the camel rider appear real, truly different from us, and "authentic" in order to build an idealized Other whose unspoiled nature shores up the tourist's sense that he is indeed seeing the "real" thing. In the post-Internet world of simulation, "real" things are fixed and preserved in images such as these in order to anchor the Western viewing subject's sense of himself as a privileged and mobile viewer.

Since the conflicts in Mogadishu, Sarajevo, and Zaire (images of which are found elsewhere in the magazines from which these ads came), ethnic difference in the world of Internet advertising is visually "cleansed" of its divisive, problematic, tragic connotations. The ads function as corrective texts for readers deluged with images of racial conflicts and bloodshed both at home and abroad. These advertisements put the world right; their claims for better living (and better boundaries) through technology are graphically acted out in idealized images of Others who miraculously speak like "us" but still look like "them."

The Indian man (pictured in an IBM print advertisment that appeared in *Smithsonian*, January 1996) whose iconic Indian elephant gazes sidelong at the viewer as he affectionately curls his trunk around his owner's neck, has much in common with his Egyptian counterpart in the previous ad. (The ad's text tells us that his name is Sikander, making him somewhat less generic than his counterpart, but not much. Where is the last name?) The thematics of this series produced for IBM play upon the depiction of ethnic, racial, and linguistic differences, usually all at the same time, in order to highlight the hegemonic power of IBM's technology. IBM's television ads (there were several produced and aired in this same series in 1997) were memorable because they were all subtitled vignettes of Italian nuns, Japanese surgeons, and Norwegian skiers engaged in their quaint and distinctively ethnic pursuits, but united in their use of IBM networking machines. The sounds of foreign languages being spoken in television ads had their own ability to shock and attract attention, all to the same end—the one word that was spoken in English, albeit heavily accented English, was "IBM."

Thus, the transnational language, the one designed to end all barriers between speakers, the speech that everyone can pronounce and that cannot be translated or incorporated into another tongue, turns out not to be Esperanto but rather IBM-speak, the language of American corporate technology. The foreignness of the Other is exploited here to remind the viewer—who may fear that IBM-speak will make the world smaller in undesirable ways (for example, that they might compete for our jobs, move into our neighborhoods, go to our schools)—that the Other is still picturesque. This classically Orientalized Other, such as the camel rider and Sikander, is marked as sufficiently different from us, the projected viewers, in order to encourage us to retain our positions as privileged tourists and users.

Sikander's cartoon-bubble, emblazoned across his face and his elephant's, asks, "How come I keep trashing my hardware every 9 months?!" This question can be read as a rhetorical example of what postcolonial theorist and novelist Salman Rushdie has termed "globalizing Coca-Colonization." Again, the language of technology, with its hacker-dude vernacular, is figured here as the transnational tongue, miraculously emerging from every mouth. Possible fears that the exoticism and heterogeneity of the Other will be siphoned off or eradicated by his use of homogeneous technospeak are eased by the visual impact of the elephant, whose trunk frames Sikander's face. Elephants, rain forests, and unspoiled mesas are all endangered markers of cultural difference that represent specific stereotyped ways of being Other to Western eyes. If we did not know that Sikander was a "real" Indian (as opposed to Indian-American, Indian-Canadian, or Indo-Anglian) the presence of his elephant, as well as the text's reference to

"Nirvana," proves to us, through the power of familiar images, that he is. We are meant to assume that even after Sikander's hardware problems are solved by IBM's "consultants who consider where you are as well are where you're headed" he will still look as picturesque, as "Indian" as he did pre-IBM.

Two other ads, part of the same series produced by IBM, feature more ambiguously ethnic figures. The first one of these depicts a Latina girl who is asking her teacher, Mrs. Alvarez, how to telnet to a remote server. She wears a straw hat, which makes reference to the Southwest. Though she is only eight or ten years old, her speech has already acquired the distinctive sounds of technospeak—for example, she uses "telnet" as a verb. The man in the second advertisement, an antique-looking fellow with old fashioned glasses, a dark tunic, dark skin, and an untidy beard proclaims that "you're hosed when a virus sneaks into your hard drive." He, too, speaks the transnational vernacular—the diction of Wayne and Garth from *Wayne's World* has sneaked into *his* hard drive like a rhetorical virus. These images, like the preceding ones, enact a sort of cultural ventriloquism that demonstrates the hegemonic power of American technospeak. The identifiably ethnic faces, with their distinctive props and costumes, that utter these words, however, attest to the importance of Otherness as a marker of a difference that the ads strive to preserve.

This Origin ad appeared in *Wired* magazine, which, like *Time, Smithsonian*, the *New Yorker*, and *The Chronicle of Higher Education*, directs its advertising toward upper-middle-class, mainly white readers. In addition, *Wired* is read mainly by men, it has an unabashedly libertarian bias, and its stance toward technology is generally utopian. Unlike the other ads, this one directly and overtly poses ethnicity and cultural difference as part of a political and commercial dilemma that Origin networks can solve. The text reads, in part,

> [W]e believe that wiring machines is the job, but connecting people the art. Which means besides skills you also need wisdom and understanding. An understanding of how people think and communicate. And the wisdom to respect the knowledge and cultures of others. Because only then can you create systems and standards they can work with. And common goals which all involved are willing to achieve.

The image of an African boy, surrounded by his tribe, seemingly performing a *Star Trek* Vulcan mind meld with a red-haired and extremely pale boy, centrally situates the white child, whose arm is visible in an unbroken line, as the figure who is supposedly as willing to learn as he is to teach.

However, the text implies that the purpose of the white boy's encounter with an African boy and his tribe is for him to learn just enough about them to create the "systems and standards that THEY can work with." The producer of marketable knowledge, the setter of networking and software-language standards, is still defined here as the Western subject.

This image, which could have come out of *National Geographic* any time in the last hundred years, participates in the familiar iconography of colonialism and its contemporary cousin, tourism. And in keeping with this association, it depicts the African as unspoiled and authentic. Its appeal to travel across national and geographical borders as a means of understanding the Other, "the art of connecting people," is defined as a commodity which this ad and others produced by networking companies sell along *with* their fiber optics and consulting services.

The notion of the computer-enabled "global village" envisioned by Marshall McLuhan also participates in this rhetoric that links exotic travel and tourism with technology. The Origin image comments on the nature of the global village by making it quite clear to the viewer that despite technology's claims to radically and instantly level cultural and racial differences (or in a more extreme statement, such as that made by "Anthem," to literally cross them out) there will always be villages full of "real" Africans, looking just as they always have.

It is part of the business of advertising to depict utopias: ideal depictions of being that correctively reenvision the world and prescribe a solution to its ills in the form of a commodity of some sort. And like tourist pamphlets, they often propose that their products will produce, in Dean MacCannell's phrase, a "utopia of difference," such as has been pictured in many Benetton and Coca-Cola advertising campaigns.

Coca-Cola's slogan from the seventies and eighties, "I'd like to teach the world to sing," both predates and prefigures these ads by IBM, Compaq, Origin, and MCI. The Coca-Cola ads picture black, white, young, old, and so on holding hands and forming a veritable Rainbow Coalition of human diversity. These singers are united by their shared song and, most important, their consumption of bottles of Coke. The viewer, meant to infer that the beverage was the direct cause of these diverse Coke drinkers overcoming their ethnic and racial differences, was given the same message then that many Internet-related advertisements give us today. The message is that cybertechnology, like Coke, will magically strip users down to "just minds," all singing the same corporate anthem.

And what of the "rest of it," the raced and ethnic body that cyberspace's "Anthem" claims to leave behind? It seems that the fantasy terrain of advertising is loath to leave out this marked body because it represents the exotic Other which both attracts us with its beauty and picturesqueness and reassures us of our own identities as "*not* Other." The "rest of it" is visually quoted in these images and then pointedly marginalized and established *as Other*. The iconography of these advertising images demonstrates that the corporate image factory *needs* images of the Other in order to depict its product: a technological utopia of difference. It is not, however, a utopia *for* the Other or one that includes it in any meaningful or progressive way. Rather, it proposes an ideal world of virtual social and cultural reality based on specific methods of "Othering," a project that I would term "the globalizing Coca-Colonization of cyberspace and the media complex within which it is embedded."

### *Acknowledgments*

I would like to thank the members of the Sonoma State University Faculty Writing Group: Kathy Charmaz, Richard Senghas, Dorothy Freidel, Elaine McHugh, and Virginia Lea for their encouragement and suggestions for revision. I would also like to thank my research assistant and independent study advisee at Sonoma State, Dean Klotz, for his assistance with permissions, research, and all things cyber. And a very special thanks to Amelie Hastie and Martin Burns, who continue to provide support and advice during all stages of my work on this topic.

### References

Hollinger, David. *Postethnic America: Beyond Multiculturalism*. New York: Basic Books, 1995.

McCannell, Dean. *The Tourist: A New Theory of the Leisure Class*. New York: Schocken Books, 1989.

McLuhan, Marshall. *Understanding Media: The Extensions of Man*. Cambridge: MIT Press, 1994.

Rushdie, Salman, "Damme, This Is the Oriental Scene For You!" *New Yorker*, 23 and 30 June 1997, 50–61.

Trinh Minh-ha. *Woman, Native, Other: Writing Postcoloniality and Feminism*. Bloomington: University of Indiana Press, 1989.

Wise, John Macgregor. "The Virtual Community: Politics and Affect In Cyberspace." Paper delivered at the American Studies Association Conference, Washington D.C., 1997.

---

## This Text: Reading

1. What about the relationship between commerce and technology is Nakamura exposing?
2. What is the logic behind the ads Nakamura talks about? Why might people be inclined to purchase these products?
3. What assumptions about technological change are the ads implying? Do you think this is general trend among manufacturers? The media?

## Your Text: Writing

1. Nakamura looks at the world through the reflection of advertising. Write about an ad that does similar forms of advertising.
2. Is there a special need to be truthful when advertising for technology? Does Nakamura think so? Write a short piece that examines some of the ways computer makers and Internet merchants use technological advances as promises to the consumer.

3. In what ways does the United States pretend that it is similar to other countries when it comes to technology? What is the reality? Write a paper talking about the technological dominance of the United States, and why we have an ambivalent relationship with this idea.

# MAIL-ORDER BRIDES: THE CONTENT OF INTERNET COURTSHIP

Virginia Colwell

Virginia Colwell wrote this paper for "Introduction to Visual Cultures" as a student at Virginia Commonwealth University in 2001. Focusing on Internet mail-order brides, she examines the way the Internet has become a place where "reality, identity, and fantasy" meet.

WITHIN MAIL-ORDER BRIDE WEBSITES women are arranged on the monitor in yearbook-like configuration. A suitor can select a bride by clicking on her picture which leads to her personal page and gives details such as her occupation, height, religion, and eye color while also providing a brief personal statement and several photographs. Once a suitor has become interested in a bride he can purchase her email address to begin the relationship. While mail-order bride sites illustrate new arenas for communication and courtship on the Internet, they also illuminate the ways which this technology effects our traditional cultural conventions. Aided by the insight of A.R. Stone, author of *The War of Desire and Technology at the Close of the Mechanical Age*, I became "interested in prosthetic communication for what it shows of the 'real' world that might otherwise go unnoticed. I am interested because of the potential of cyberspace for the emergent behavior for new social forms that arise in a circumstance in which *body, meet, place*, and even *space* mean something quite different from our accustomed understanding."[1] Though often stereotyped and blurred by taboo, mail-order bride websites provide an ample basis for analyzing how people are pioneering new transitions between meeting and interacting in virtual reality with the intention of transferring this relationship into a real life affair. Challenging traditional ideas of dating and the importance of face to face contact for developing intimacy, mail-order bride websites exemplify a contemporary sense of reality, identity, and fantasy.

To begin my analysis I shall examine communication via the Internet and how it affects our perceptions of reality. As the Internet has become more widely accessible to the public, social constructions must adapt to the ambiguous nature of the Web and thus develop new behaviors to supercede the Internet's limitations. Secondly I shall examine how the hyperreality of the Internet affects how each individual constructs an identity. The translation of one's self from reality to virtual reality is an explicit example of portraying the self that is uniquely postmodern in its fabrication. And finally, as one generates themselves on the Web in pursuit of a relationship, a contemporary sense of seduction and fantasy become apparent. Romance takes on an especially fantastical context in the electronic format as one's imagination has an unparalleled freedom within cyberspace. Through this analysis of mail-order bride websites it is evident that they provide a perplexing insight into social behaviors that straddle reality and technology as brides look to make a clean transformation from virtual reality into the real world with an intimate relationship intact.

Central to our postmodern culture is the way in which we grapple with the distinction between reality and an increasingly prominent virtual sphere. Electronic formats permit both a concrete and simulated perspective of reality, often blurring the two. Interactive communication highlights this ambiguous area as words and text become disembodied from their authors and without any tangible referents. In a interview entitled "The Work of Art in the Electronic Age," Jean Baudrillard contends that the goals of communication can be surmounted by the medium when dealing with electronic formats: "It is often said that we are within communication and we are perhaps no longer exactly within exchange. At this time, what has changed is that the means of communication, the medium, is becoming a determinant element in exchange . . . and then the strategies which revolve around the medium . . . become more essential than the strategies which concern the contents."[2] The Internet can provide an amazing capacity for communication, yet it also involves a paradoxical connection and disconnection simultaneously. The important dialogue of gesture, touch, sound, and smell are deprived, thus editing a full range of communicative possibilities and bringing into question the reality and depth of correspondence via the Net. A complete sense of reality is further suspended because the viewer can have no personal experience in which to add a greater amount of information or verify that which is received. What results from this incomplete amount of information is a hyper-reality in which the "reality or unreality, the truth or falsity of something" can no longer be discerned.[3] These difficult aspects of hyper-reality are especially disconcerting when establishing sincere relationships via the Internet. One of the tricky aspects of the web is the ability of one to play with their identity. Truth is constantly called into question online, as the possibility for deception is a reality. However, in spite of this common fear, online courtship centers flourish as people attempt to find love within the hypertext.

Online match-making places are an interesting study in trusting another's identity. However, the acknowledgment that plays of identity do happen on the Internet makes it difficult to completely trust any source of personal information. Because mail-order bride sites look to develop real life intimate relationships in virtual reality, this can be problematic. Further complicating the problem is the structure for an individual bride's personal page which gives a synopsis version of her identity. Much like a driver license with some additional personal statements, the tendency of these mail-order bride sites is to present a vague notion of a bride's identity rather than solidifying a bride's personality through many images and lengthy personal information. While the visual information and personal statistics given are specific enough to judge one's own likes and dislikes against, for example someone might be too tall or too young, they can also lead to simplified conclusions. This curtailed information through images and personal statistics allows only a simplified judgment and conclusion based on vague and flexible details. This might not be so much of a concern—after all it is similar to the way dating columns or dating agencies work—however, considering that the relationship will have its primary basis online, one can continue to believe their idea of an individual purely through conclusions based upon text-based information and some photos without any palpable experience to demonstrate otherwise. On the web a persona is reduced to flexible words and images that not only carry with them a questionable truth but also are inherently a simulacrum of one's true self. Yet, before entirely discounting the presentation of one's identity through the Internet, I feel that the contemporary state of identity in the real world must be examined for a more precise understanding.

The creation of an identity on the Internet exemplifies a contemporary questioning of the self and how one begins to present the self to others. In her book, *Life on the Screen*, Sherry Turkle argues that, "Internet experiences help us to develop models . . . that are in a meaningful sense postmodern: They admit a multiplicity and flexibility. They acknowledge the constructed nature of reality, self, and other."[4] Contemporary scholars on postmodern identity have argued a range of vantage points on the postmodern self, yet most generally admit that the fast pace of our culture along with a globalized and media saturated landscape have fragmented and destabilized the notion of identity. Thus, there is no longer the one true self which modernity maintained with its essentialist ideas. Also unlike modernity, an identity crisis no longer has a distinct resolution but is a forever unresolvable riddle of what constitutes the self.[5] From these vantage points the Internet becomes a logical and luminous ground upon which to further continue the postmodern identity play. According to Kenneth Gergen, as the sense of an authentic self recedes into the past, what emerges in its place is the pastiche of personality. "The pastiche personality is a social chameleon, constantly borrowing bits and pieces of identity from whatever sources are available and constructing them as useful or desirable in a given situation."[6] The Internet, because it is restricted to text and images, forces users to creatively manipulate these two avenues to present a synopsis of character. On brides' personal pages they aim to show a variety of complex ideas regarding their character through only a few posed photographs. Take for example Natalia Dedyukhina, a bride who has a page on the Internet. We first encounter her close up, the largest of the pictures, in which we are invited to feel an intimacy, focusing on the features of her face and warm smile. In a smaller picture Natalia poses playfully wearing blue patent leather pants and a zebra striped blouse tied at her navel. In the third photograph Natalia is dressed in a tailored white blouse looking sophisticated and easy going. And in another, Natalia appears in an evening gown, striking a forties movie star pose to convey femininity and beauty. The result of this photo collage is the impression that Natalia is not simply one definable persona, but rather various personality types which are presented and easily understood through poses and clothing that emphasize traits that she wishes to demonstrate as her own. What is especially interesting about this is that Natalia is Russian and by using the Internet's global reach, is appealing to American men. Thus, Natalia and women like her are adopting internationally understandable images and meanings to more aptly portray a more detailed sense of self to the viewer despite the constraints of the Net.

However, despite the fact that the images and words can be manipulated to express a greater sense of character, maintained throughout the Internet medium is a suspended reality that can be difficult to overcome and especially precarious for transposing relations from virtual reality to real life. As discussed earlier, the Internet adds a strange distortion to its contents because they lack direct referents. The repercussions of this are not only a blurred distinction between reality and virtual reality but also what Jean Baudrillard contends is a powerful self fulfilling prophecy. Baudrillard argues that, "Miracles never result from a surplus of reality but, on the contrary, form a sudden break in reality and the giddiness of feeling oneself fall . . . Something emerges for want of something better."[7] In the format of the Internet what emerges is an imagined array of sensations which merely compensate for a lack of reality undermined by hyper-reality. Thus, because a multitude of concrete information cannot be derived from the images and personal descriptions giving by a prospective bride, the viewer projects their imagination of these sensations onto her, filling that void. Reconsidering Natalia the viewer can understand through her photographs that she can be fun, easygoing, or sexy but it is up to the viewer to extrapolate the varying degrees to which she is these things. For the mail-order bride, her ability to electronically seduce can be attributed to how clear yet provoking her personal presentation is. To go with a sweet face one might project a sweet voice (in clear unbroken English of course), or an even temperament, or imagine a graceful gait when constructing a fuller identity for a bride. Thus, the lack of a concrete personality, the adoption of cultural images as signifiers of identity, and the hyper-reality of the Internet format all create a masterful world for this seduction that, if orchestrated well, benefits the appeal of the mail-order bride. Furthermore, because a suitor's courtship of a bride mostly rests upon emails exchanged over time, it is conceivable that he can continue to enhance the seductive image without the context of experience to verify it.

But someday swooning lovers online want to continue their pursuit of marriage and thus must meet. Their meeting will determine whether online seduction can carry over into real life. Scholarly writers on online relationships are skeptical of the possibilities and often include several stories of cyber romance disappointment, highlighting the complaint that those involved developed inaccurate interpretations of the other. Yet, there are some redeeming relationships written about where couples are able to successfully cross that difficult divide between real life and virtual reality. Nonetheless, the desire and ability to forge online relationships raises the question of whether we can ever have accurate interpretations of Internet correspondence because of its leniency toward imagination and seduction. Romance, being one of the ultimate frontiers that plays to the imagination, has an amazing adaptability to the Internet despite the restraints of the electronic format. The suitors of mail-order brides have the possibility of conversing with these women via the Internet and constructing an intimate relationship while simultaneously floating within the vast array of possibilities generated by one's own fantasy. Ultimately these sites take on an area in which one can be forever intrinsically intertwined in fantasy through the seductive nature of Internet relationships, while also conceivably believing in the possible reality for a future fiancé. As flexible as one is imaginative, the initial allure of the mail-order bride is in the disjointed space of virtual reality which she occupies far removed from tangible reality. Though avant-garde in their approach to pursuing marriage, these sites provide a perplexing question to how the Internet affects our perception of reality, construction of identity, and seduces our imagination. The result of these electronic courtship havens is a creation of fantasy and romance that is fitting for our postmodern electronic age.

## Endnotes

1. A.R. Stone, *The War of Desire and Technology at the Close of the Mechanical Age* (Cambridge: MIT Press, 1995). 37.
2. Mike Gane ed., *Baudrillard Live* (London: Routledge, 1993). 145.
3. Gane, 146.
4. Sherry Turkle, *Life on Screen* (New York: Simon and Schuster, 1995). 263.
5. Douglas Kellner, "Popular Culture and the Construction of Postmodern Identities," in *Modernity and Identity*. Scott Lash and Jonathan Friedman, eds. (Oxford: Blackwell, 1992). 141–144.
6. Kenneth Gergen, *The Saturated Self* (New York: Basic Books, 1991). 150.
7. Jean Baudrillard, *Seduction* (New York: St. Martin's Press, 1990). 63.

## Works Cited

Baudrillard, Jean. *Seduction*. New York: St. Martin's Press, 1990.

Gane, Mike. ed. *Baudrillard Live*. London: Routledge, 1993.

Gergen, Kenneth. *The Saturated Self*. New York: Basic Books, 1991.

Kellner, Douglas. "Popular Culture and the Construction of Postmodern Identities." In *Modernity and Identity*. eds. Friedman, Jonathan and Lash, Scott. Oxford: Blackwell, 1992.

Stone, A.R. *The War of Desire and Technology at the Close of the Mechanical Age*. Cambridge: MIT Press, 1995.

Turkle, Sherry. *Life on the Screen*. New York: Simon and Schuster, 1995.

---

## This Text: Reading

1. In this piece, Colwell uses the mail-order bride as a window into several ideas about modern communication. What are those ideas and how does she use the Internet mail-order bride as a window into them?
2. How does Colwell use research in this work? What effect does it have on her argument?
3. This paper could have easily gone in Chapter 6, on reading gender. What are some ideas about gender that Colwell discusses?

## Your Text: Writing

1. Examine another Internet phenomenon that could be used as a window into modern ideas.
2. Write a paper which compares this phenomenon to Internet dating generally.

# The Internet and Identity Suite

Technological innovation necessarily has a significant impact on those who come in contact it. But few new technologies have changed our lives as quickly and directly as the growth of the Internet.

In these selections we focus on one particular element—identity. We think immediacy, scope, and potential anonymity have changed for many the way they consider themselves. In one piece, Frederick McKissack (1998) discusses the relationship many African Americans have to the Internet; the gap between black and white use of the Internet is often referred to as the digital divide. Glen Martin (1995) discusses the way some Native Americans are using cyberspace to provide connections between groups of people historically divided and the problems caused by such efforts. Brenda Danet (1996) takes a complicated view of the way people construct views of themselves through expression over the Internet; Andrew Sullivan (1999) talks about why that's a good thing.

## CYBERGHETTO: BLACKS ARE FALLING THROUGH THE NET

Frederick C. McKissack Jr.

I LEFT JOURNALISM LAST YEAR and started working for an Internet development firm because I was scared. While many of my crypto-Luddite friends ("I find e-mail so impersonal") have decided that the Web is the work of the devil and is being monitored by the NSA, CIA, FBI, and the IRS, I began to have horrible dreams that sixteen-year-old punks were going to take over publishing in the next century because they knew how to write good computer code. I'd have to answer to some kid with two earrings, who will make fun of me because I have one earring and didn't study computer science in my spare time.

You laugh, but one of the best web developers in the country is a teenager who has written a very sound book on web design and programming. He's still in his prime learning years, and he's got a staff.

What should worry me more is that I am one of the few African Americans in this country who has a computer at home, uses one at work, and can use a lot of different kinds of software on multiple platforms. According to those in the know, I'm going to remain part of that very small group for quite some time.

The journal *Science* published a study on April 17 which found that, in households with annual incomes below $40,000, whites were six times more likely than blacks to have used the World Wide Web in the last week.

Low-income white households were twice as likely to have a home computer as low-income black homes. Even as computers become more central to our society, minorities are falling through the Net.

The situation is actually considerably worse than the editors of *Science* made it seem. Some 18 percent of African American households don't even have phones, as Philip Bereano, a professor of technical communications at the University of Washington, pointed out in a letter to the *New York Times*. Since the researchers who published their study in *Science* relied on a telephone survey to gather their data, Bereano explains, the study was skewed—it only included people who had at least caught up to the Twentieth Century.

About 30 percent of American homes have computers, with the bulk of those users being predominantly white, upper-middle-class households. Minorities are much worse off: Only about 15 percent have a terminal at home.

The gulf between technological haves and have-nots is the difference between living the good life and surviving in what many technologists and social critics term a "cyberghetto." Professor Michio Kaku, a professor of theoretical physics at City University of New York, wrote in his book *Visions: How Science Will Revolutionize the Twenty-first Century*, of the emergence of "information ghettos."

"The fact is, each time society made an abrupt leap to a new level of production, there were losers and winners," Kaku wrote. "It may well be that the computer revolution will exacerbate the existing fault lines of society."

The term "cyberghetto" suggests that minorities have barely passable equipment to participate in tech culture. But most minorities aren't even doing that well.

Before everybody goes "duh," just think what this means down the line. Government officials are using the Web more often to disseminate information. Political parties are holding major online events. And companies are using the Web for making job announcements and collecting résumés. Classes, especially continuing-education classes, are being offered more and more on the Web. In politics, commerce, and education, the web is leaving minorities behind.

The disparity between the techno-rich and techno-poor comes to a head with this statistic: A person who is able to use a computer at work earns 15 percent more than someone in the same position who lacks computer skills.

"The equitable distribution of technology has always been the real moral issue about computers," Jon Katz, who writes the "Rants and Raves" column for *Wired* online, wrote in a recent e-mail. "The poor can't afford them. Thus they will be shut out of the booming hi-tech job market and forced to do the culture's menial jobs."

This technological gap, not Internet pornography, should be the public's main concern with the Web.

"Politicians and journalists have suggested frightening parents into limiting children's access to the Internet, but the fact is they have profoundly screwed the poor, who need access to this technology if they are to compete and prosper," Katz said. "I think the culture avoids the complex and expensive issues by focusing on the silly ones. In twenty-five years, when the underclass wakes up to discover it is doing all the muscle jobs while everybody else is in neat, clean offices with high-paying jobs, they'll go berserk. We don't want to spend the money to avoid this problem, so we worry about Johnny going to the *Playboy* web site. It's sick."

In his 1996 State of the Union address, President Clinton challenged Congress to hook up schools to the Internet.

"We are working with the telecommunications industry, educators, and parents to connect . . . every classroom and every library in the entire United States by the year 2000," Clinton said. "I ask Congress to support this educational technology initiative so that we can make sure the national partnership succeeds."

The national average is approximately ten students for every one computer in the public schools. According to a study by the consulting firm McKinsey & Co., the President's plan—a ratio of one computer to every five students—would cost approximately $11 billion per year over the next ten years.

Some government and business leaders, worried about a technologically illiterate work force in the twenty-first century, recognize the need for increased spending. "AT&T and the Commerce Department have suggested wiring up schools at a 4:1 ratio for $6 or $7 billion," says Katz.

But according to the U.S. Department of Education, only 1.3 percent of elementary and secondary education expenditures are allocated to technology. That figure would have to be increased to 3.9 percent. Given the tightness of urban school district budgets, a tripling of expenditures seems unlikely.

Then there's the question of whether computers in the schools are even desirable. Writer Todd Oppenheimer, in a July 1997 article for *Atlantic Monthly* entitled "The Computer Delusion," argued that there is no hard evidence that computers in the classroom enhance learning. In fact, he took the opposite tack: that computers are partially responsible for the decline of education.

Proponents of computers in the classroom struck back. "On the issue of whether or not technology can benefit education, the good news is that it is not—nor should be—an all-or-nothing proposition," writes Wendy Richard Bollentin, editor of *On The Internet* magazine, in an essay for *Educom Review*.

There is an unreal quality about this debate, though, since computer literacy is an indispensable part of the education process for many affluent, white schoolchildren.

Consumers are beginning to see a decline in prices for home computers. Several PC manufacturers have already introduced sub-$1,000 systems, and there is talk of $600 systems appearing on the market by the fall. Oracle has spent a great deal of money on Network Computers, cheap hardware where software and files are located on large networks. The price is in the sub-$300 range. And, of course, there is WebTV, which allows you to browse on a regular home television set with special hardware.

Despite the trend to more "affordable" computers, a Markle Foundation-Bellcore Labs study shows that this may not be enough to help minorities merge onto the Information Superhighway. There is "evidence of a digital divide," the study said, with "Internet users being generally wealthier and more highly educated, and blacks and Hispanics disproportionately unaware of the Internet."

So, what now?

"For every black family to become empowered, they need to have computers," journalist Tony Brown told the *Detroit News*. "There is no way the black community is going to catch up with white society under the current system. But with a computer, you can take any person from poverty to the middle class."

This is the general line for enlightened blacks and community leaders. But having a computer won't bridge the racial and economic divide. Even if there is a 1:1 ratio of students to computers in urban schools, will students' interest be piqued when they don't have access to computers at home? One out of every forty-nine computer-science professors in the United States is black. Will this inhibit black students from learning how to use them? And even if every black student had a computer at home and at school, would that obliterate all racial obstacles to success?

Empowerment is not just a question of being able to find your way around the Web. But depriving minorities of access to the technology won't help matters any. We need to make sure the glass ceiling isn't replaced by a silicon ceiling.

## INTERNET INDIAN WARS: NATIVE AMERICANS ARE FIGHTING TO CONNECT THE 550 NATIONS—IN CYBERSPACE

Glen Martin

BLUE SNAKE'S LODGE. To a certain kind of seeker, it was irresistible. You logged on to the America Online seminar, and the old ways swelled up around you, evoking sparkling rivers, virgin forests, and yawning plains teeming with game. You were in, well, North America. But before it was called North America. After all, North America is merely an Anglo rubric applied to a vast land once inhabited by myriad peoples living in harmony with the Earth.

Yes, in Blue Snake's Lodge, you were privy to the mysteries and ceremonies of the American Indian. Blue Snake was an online chief of the Eastern Shawnee, and in the photo provided with his AOL bio, you could see a stocky middle-aged man with abundant gray whiskers, accoutered in a blanket and holding a long pipe. He was devoted to inculcating non-Indians with the healing ways of Native American spirituality.

His introductory "teaching" ushered you onto the cybernetic equivalent of Native holy ground:

> Before you is a lodge, a large tepee. . . . The silhouettes of its inhabitants are cast upon the canvas sides by the fire in the center. You hear only night sounds, a stream chuckles in the distance as it hurls itself headlong through the forest, an owl challenges the darkness as she hunts for prey, a coyote voices his loneliness as he waits for his mate.
>
> Blue Snake is seated at the back of the lodge. At his feet, beside the fire, a pipe carved in the image of a rattlesnake rests on a cedar box. The pipe is a symbol of his authority. He bids you welcome. He raises the pipe then lowers it and points the stem at each of his guests. Six times he draws smoke . . . six times he exhales it, once to each of the four directions, once to the Everywhere Spirit above, once to Grandmother Earth below. . . . Blue Snake speaks, "Welcome to my lodge. May you always feel welcome here, as in your own lodge."

Wow. Or as Blue Snake would say, oneh (a Shawnee analog, Blue Snake reveals, of aloha, meaning everything from hello to I agree profoundly). No doubt about it, Blue Snake offered a moving spiritual message, particularly resonant in a world where the dollar is king and nature is becoming a vague memory.

There was, however, a problem: it was all a charade. Blue Snake was Don Rapp, a software consultant living in southern Ohio, who was about as Indian as Barbara Bush. Rapp created the Blue Snake persona and successfully pitched it to America Online, where he conducted seminars and hosted a chat room. Online Native wannabes flocked to Rapp, who made them honorary Indians by declaring them members of the "Evening Sky Clan" of the "Red Heart Tribe." He also bestowed names on his followers during elaborate online benedictions—Crystal Bear Woman, Stormcloud Dancer, and Darkness Runs From Her.

By early 1993, Blue Snake's teachings had worked their way around AOL and into the hearts and minds of thousands of cybersurfers who were convinced they had found the answer to their manifold spiritual dilemmas. But in March 1993, some real Indians logged onto the seminars—and Blue Snake's Lodge began to fall apart under its own spurious weight.

The easy use of alternative personae, of course, lies at the heart of cyber culture. People get online because it embodies freedom—not just freedom to be all they can be, but freedom to be everything they can't or won't be in the world of flesh, blood, and three dimensions. *Wired* Native Americans find this element of cyberspace appealing. But tradition-minded

Indians assert that there's an uncrossable line in both cyberspace and the real world, a line that separates tribal religious rites from the commerce of everyday life. Such rituals, these Natives maintain, are sacred, proprietary—and indeed, exclusionary.

Blue Snake's peddling of "Indian spirituality" was thus repugnant to the Native Americans who discovered his seminars, and they went on the offensive. "There's a difference between adopting online identities and perpetrating fraud," says Marc Towersap, a Shoshone-Bannock engineer from Idaho and one of the first Indians to query America Online about Blue Snake's tribal credentials. "Rapp was promoting himself as a genuine Native elder, and AOL was making money on the chat room because a lot of people logged on to it. They were making money on a bogus product. Is selling fake mutual funds over the telephone acceptable? This was the same thing, except we're talking about spirituality rather than stocks, and the Internet instead of the phone. It's fraud, not role-playing."

Tracy Miller, a salty, blunt-spoken Eastern Band Cherokee and Native activist who lives in southern New England, was likewise incensed when she stumbled onto Blue Snake's maunderings. "A Native friend e-mailed me and told me to check out this guy Blue Snake on AOL," recalls Miller. "I couldn't believe it. His seminars were a hodgepodge of the worst kind of bullshit stereotypes and gobbledygook possible. All the hippies and crystal gazers were just gobbling it up, of course, but I knew that there was no way in hell he could be a real Native."

Miller, a seasoned Net surfer, knows that information isn't the only thing that wants to be free; so does misinformation. And misinformation, she claims, strikes at the heart of Native sensibilities—and survival. Miller asserts that preserving Native culture is foremost a matter of keeping Natives and Native memory around. "But it isn't just about biological survival," says Miller. "It's also about spirituality and culture. There is a thread of rituals and beliefs that parallels our physical cohesiveness as tribal peoples, a thread that goes back thousands of years. It defines who we are as much as our DNA does."

Miller says that many Native religions and rituals are secret because they are sacrosanct, appropriate for tribal members alone. "Natives don't proselytize Native religions," observes Miller. "We're not looking for converts. It isn't about shunning people—it's about keeping what little we have left."

Such contentions are antithetical to the free and unfettered exchange of ideas and data in cyberspace. They also raise thorny questions: In the age of information, can any data be legitimately considered sacred? How do you upload holiness? "We know you can't police cyberspace," sighs Miller. "But like everything else, it's a matter of education and dialog."

To Miller's community, a particularly egregious example of Rapp's cultural rip-off was Blue Snake's "pipe ceremonies." Proprietary rituals involving pipes are sacred to many tribes. The pipe, its accouterments, ceremonies surrounding the pipe—indeed, even spoken or written allusions to the pipe—are thus freighted with great spiritual significance. "His mumbo jumbo surrounding the pipe was especially offensive," says Miller.

After monitoring Blue Snake for a while from the sidelines, Miller, Towersap, and a few of their pals began challenging the azure serpent and his starry-eyed gaggle of Red Hearted converts. They demanded that Rapp desist from conducting his seminars and fought his online doctrines, byte by byte, with their own. Eventually, they became so obstreperous they were tossed from the room by testy AOL guides. Miller, who has been permanently barred from AOL since 1994, still gets online by arranging payment through friends and employing a rich variety of pseudonyms. She admits her own duplicities constitute a rather sharp irony, given her ire with Blue Snake over his online misrepresentations, but she also argues that her actions are ethical and necessary. Miller insists there's a palpable world of truth out there—Native truth, tradition, and history—that must be protected from the vagaries of casual data-play.

Miller and her running mates ultimately enlisted the aid of the three recognized tribes of the Shawnee nation in their quest to hamstring Blue Snake: the Absentee-Shawnee Tribe of Oklahoma, the Loyal Shawnee Tribe of Oklahoma, and the Eastern Shawnee Tribe of Oklahoma. A joint resolution drafted by leaders of the three tribes was e-mailed to AOL and Blue Snake. In it, the leaders declared that Rapp was not a recognized member of any Shawnee tribe or band, adding: "It is said that imitation is the greatest form of flattery. However, the reports of Mr. Rapp's 'teachings' and Native American 'classes' would indicate that perhaps his intentions are less than honorable."

"The true Shawnee peoples are very traditional, and their ceremonies and rituals are not for public consumption. They practice their traditional beliefs and rites as a matter of religion—no public 'powwows' or 'gatherings' are conducted."

AOL apparently was chastened by the letter. It relieved Rapp of his host status, replacing Blue Snake's Lodge with a room dubbed Native American Chat. (Which still meets more or less regularly, usually on Tuesday evenings.) But again, complains Miller, the hosts were—and are—demonstrably non-Native. They couldn't or can't produce the federal enrollment credentials demanded by the genuine Indians who logged in to the room.

"There's a lot of controversy in the Native community about the significance of federal enrollment," observes Miller. "The irony of enrollment is that a system designed by the conquerors and oppressors of Natives is now the benchmark for determining who is and isn't Native. Not every Native is enrolled, and we recognize this. But enrollment does definitively establish tribal affiliation—something we think is critical for host status." A potential host shouldn't necessarily be rejected if an enrollment number can't be produced, Miller says, but in that case, a vetting process conducted by recognized and respected Native Americans would be in order. "Otherwise, it's like a Swedish national claiming he could conduct a course on black American culture from an insider's perspective," laughs Miller.

Rapp, for his part, is somewhat bemused by all the heat and bile generated by his online persona. "Basically, what we did was done in fun," he observes. "We certainly didn't intend any disrespect."

Rapp acknowledges freely that he has no Shawnee ancestry but says he was adopted into the tribe by John Reese, a chief of the Eastern Band Shawnee. "The honored status of adoptees is a tradition among the Shawnee, though I never claimed I had Shawnee blood," Rapp says.

Rapp says that he provided some of his attackers with documents from Reese establishing his tribal bona fides, but that they were rejected out of hand. And as far as vitiating sacred rites, says Rapp, he discussed only rituals that have long been documented in books such as Black Elk Speaks. "All that material was and is available through published texts," he asserts. "Can you take back what's already printed? I acknowledge that there is sacred and proprietary information and ceremonies in the Indian nations—I've witnessed some of them. And what I've witnessed that's truly sacred, I've never discussed."

For Rapp, the experience with Blue Snake's Lodge was distressing, but he nevertheless feels his seminars were a positive force both on the Net and in Indian Country. "At least I touched a nerve," he points out. "People loved me or hated me, but at least they were involved. I consider that an accomplishment."

At AOL, spokeswoman Margaret Ryan maintains the company was not obliged to ascertain Rapp's Native credentials because the seminars were conducted in a "member" room as opposed to a fully sanctioned chat room. "We monitor the member areas to ensure online standards of conduct are upheld," she says, repeating the corporate disclaimer, "but we cannot screen public communication to make sure the topics discussed are legitimate. We advise our members to be as careful in their evaluation of information and opinions on AOL as they are in everyday life."

Miller admits she and her online Native colleagues enjoyed chivying the devotees of the spurious Snake—a guilty pleasure that helped mitigate their anger. But anger, Miller emphasizes, was the dominant emotion—especially when their protests were repeatedly stonewalled by AOL. "I was e-mailing a Sioux friend about it, and we came to the conclusion that the company didn't want us disturbing the fantasy," said Miller. "It doesn't want real Indians—we're not 'Indian' enough. It wants the buckskin fringes and the feathers."

The problem had cropped up before—offline. For years, says Miller, fake or "renegade" Indians have offered non-Natives entree into the mystic realm of Native American spirituality, driving Native traditionalists nuts. "The worst was a guy named Sun Bear, a Cheyenne who died a few years ago," recalls Miller. "He conducted seminars all over the country, had followers who gave him money and gifts. He was prostituting the culture of his tribe—the Cheyennes loathed him."

Still, online Natives figured such poseur high jinx were small potatoes compared with the drivel flooding cyberspace. Misinformation spread by word of mouth during retreats and seminars multiplies more or less arithmetically. But the rate of spread is exponential online—an assault on Native sensibilities, claim activists, equivalent to the wars of extermination of the last century.

How could they deal with this cultural analog of the Wounded Knee massacre? The online compatriots were stumped—they could neither lick their foes nor join them. Confronting AOL directly got them tossed. And any attempt at compromise, they felt, would defeat their own purpose—this seemed to them a situation of right or wrong, black or white. So the idea dawned: If they couldn't work with existing online communities, they could build one of their own. They would create an alternative that would allow Native Americans from the Aleut villages of Alaska to the Apache reservations of Arizona free and advanced access to computer-based telecommunications. A simultaneous goal: to provide non-Natives accurate information on Native cultures by allowing access to legitimate Indian spokespersons rather than self-styled shamans.

At first, the idea was simply that—a vaporous notion that didn't seem likely to go beyond the gee-wouldn't-it-be-great stage. The obstacles, the friends well knew, were enormous. Indeed, the simple precedents of past attempts dampened spirits. Previous stabs at a Native American Net presence had met with less-than-stellar success. In 1992, George Baldwin, an instructor at Henderson State University in Arkansas who now directs the Institute for Community Networking in Monterey, California, formed IndianNet, an electronic bulletin board based in Rapid City, South Dakota, that provided information on grants and employment opportunities and allowed users to post messages. But the long-distance rates were prohibitively expensive from the places where most users lived—remote reservations in the West.

Another service now running is NativeNet, a mailing list and developing website. It deals primarily with Native policy issues and is used mostly by academics. Finally, a few tribes maintain bulletin boards of varying scope. But that's about it. Of the 550 federally recognized tribes and Native villages in the continental United States and Alaska, only four—the Oneida and Onondaga of New York, the Navajo of Arizona and New Mexico, and the Sioux of North and South Dakota—have any significant Net presence. At the beginning of 1995, only 3 of the 28 Native-controlled colleges offered Net connections.

Much of the problem stems from the lack of wiring in Indian Country. Simply put, there is little copper wire or fiber-optic cable in most of the lands controlled by North American Natives. No one knows how many Natives have phones, says Towersap, but the number is decidedly below the 94 percent figure cited for the American populace at large. "Many reservations don't even have electricity," observes Towersap. "And many Natives who do have phones have them only sporadically—they lose service when they can't pay their bill, which is commonplace." Such were the monumental real-world problems faced by Miller and her crew once they spurned the slippery cyberspace game of who's who; these conditions made it impossible for the great majority of their fellow Natives to even enter the contest.

Nevertheless, in late 1994, Miller, Towersap, and three compatriots—Disney executive Dawn Jackson (who is Saginaw Chippewa), attorney Tamera Crites Shanker (Arapaho), and advertising creative director Victoria Bracewell Short (Creek)—incorporated as the nonprofit Native American Communications Council, and began work on the project.

Though proficient with computers, the partners aren't monomaniacal technophiles. Rather, they see computers and wire as the best and brightest chance of reestablishing tribal bonds that were sundered with the massacre at Wounded Knee, an event remembered as ending all organized Indian resistance in North America. "When we get together, what we talk about is power (not computers)," says Short. "The Net is a tool that will allow us to forge bonds between the Indian nations. The only thing we have right now that facilitates intertribal communication is the powwow circuit (pantribal gatherings throughout the country, many open to the general public, that feature dances, food, handicrafts, and seminars). It's fine as far as it goes, but we need more."

Short observes that Natives have always been open to new technologies and disposed to elegant communications systems. "We've always esteemed useful tools and goods," says Short. "We've always maintained ties with one another. We know from artifacts that trade routes threaded the continent. Gulf Coast pearls have been found at sites in New Mexico. The plains tribes all spoke different languages but shared a sign language that was understood by all. Smoke signaling may seem quaint when you see it in the movies, but it was an effective means of communicating information over long distances. Natives in the interior knew of the whites long before the whites knew of them."

The council's goals are straightforward: to develop a Native-owned and operated telecommunications network that will provide Native Americans with easy access to information stored on the council's server while simultaneously offering most Internet functions, including gopher, ftp, telnet, as well as a website. The council's primary server will be linked to local servers on reservations, Alaskan Native villages, and urban Native service centers. Concomitantly, courses would be provided to local service centers to aid Natives in managing local nodes, navigating the Net, and creating Web home pages. "We also hope to launch an interactive service that will provide updated information on grant, job, and educational opportunities and legal and health issues," says Short.

Such ambitions are right in line with the plans of the Smithsonian's National Museum of the American Indian, says Marty Kreipe de Montaño, a Prairie Band Potawatomi who is creating interactive databases that will link images of the museum's one million objects with its reams of curators' comments and more than 250,000 explanatory documents. "The museum will eventually have four sites," observes de Montaño. "The first is the George Gustav Heye Center, which was founded in 1916 and conjoined with the Smithsonian in 1990. The second will be a state-of-the-art storage and research facility that we plan to build in Suitland, Maryland, by 1997. The third will be the Smithsonian Mall museum, which is scheduled for completion by 2001."

And the fourth site, says de Montaño, will be an "electronic museum without walls." This service will allow electronic access to the museum and provide information about real Natives in real time. "We consult with a number of tribal councils on everything we do," she notes, "and they consider the fourth museum the most important because it will help people living in Indian Country today. The council's project is similar. It's just what's needed."

Some elements of the council's system will be like Native religious rites, say the partners—for Natives alone. But how will this be possible, given the porous nature of the Net? "In the beginning, everybody will probably be able to tap into everything," acknowledges Towersap. "But there are some things we'll want to keep exclusive—that's one of our primary reasons for starting this project. There's groupware evolving that will make this possible—applications that require membership passwords and are pretty secure."

At the Smithsonian, de Montaño agrees with Towersap that many Native objects, images, and rites are sacred and not for public dissemination, but she is somewhat dubious about the prospect of adequately protecting such information. "It's the nature of the Net that it's difficult to control," she observes. "But we're always working with tribal elders to determine which objects and what information are appropriate only for tribal members, and we're always working on high-tech ways to protect them."

Connections to the museum would allow academicians and the merely curious access to the quotidian issues and concerns of American Indians without all the hype, hoopla, and out-and-out bullshit that has characterized most online interactions between Native and non-Native peoples. The museum will allow dissemination of accurate information on Natives and will facilitate direct, unfiltered, one-on-one communication between Indians and everybody else, says Shanker, who coordinates the council's legal affairs.

The main thing standing between the council and a *Wired* Native America, not surprisingly, is money. "We've applied for a grant from the Eagle Staff Fund (a corporate fund that supports a variety of Native projects) that we're reasonably optimistic about getting," said Shanker. "That would give us about US $35,000 and get us up and running for the pilot project. It's also especially critical money because several of the other grants we have pending are predicated on matching funds."

Shanker and her fellow council members are only too aware that a few thousand dollars won't fulfill the council's grand goal of linking up all 550 nations. By any measure, the job is huge. But council members are sanguine, even serene.

"The simple fact is that Natives need to be a significant presence on the Net, and we need to make that happen on our own terms," says Shanker, who acknowledges that the slippery nature of online data swapping makes any attempt to define and preserve fixed identities tricky in the extreme. "If we don't define who we are on the Net, other people will do it for us," says Shanker. "And when that happens, part of who we are disappears."

Blue Snake himself wishes Shanker the best in her endeavors. "If what happened on AOL contributes in some way to a viable Native telecommunications network, then I'm happy," observes Rapp. "It's what I've always wanted to see."

# TEXT AS MASK: GENDER AND IDENTITY ON THE INTERNET*

Brenda Danet

IT IS A REMARKABLE FACT that many people who have never before been particularly interested in "drag," or in "passing," or "cross-dressing" (Garber, 1993) as a member of the opposite gender are now experimenting extensively with gender identity in typed encounters on the Internet. Males are masquerading online as females, and females are masquerading as males (Van Gelder, 1990; Stone, 1991; Reid, 1991, 1995; Turkle, 1995). It is probably no exaggeration to say that some people are leading double if not multiple lives, not only with different identities, but with different gender identities. Others are trying out what it might mean to be gender-free—neither male nor female—not only in one's own behavior, but in the response elicited from one's interlocutors. With the advent of the digital era, science fiction is merging with reality—the new cultural domain of cyberspace, an abstract space which consists of live links between millions of computers around the globe, is making all this experimentation possible. (1)

## *The Tyranny of Gender*

So salient have gender and the perception of gender been to our consciousness until now that it may be no exaggeration to speak of the tyranny of gender. Only in science fiction was the idea of a possibly gender-free

---

**Note:* This is an online version of a printed essay.

existence even conceivable. Feminist science fiction writers have written of this possibility.

Thus, Ursula LeGuin's (1969) novel *The Left Hand of Darkness* is a "thought-experiment" about the possibility of genuine cultural, as well as biological androgyny. In his "field notes," an observer of this imaginary society who comes from Earth writes:

> Our entire pattern of socio-sexual interaction is non-existent here. The Gethenians do not see one another as men or women. This is almost impossible for our imaginations to accept. After all, what is the first question we ask about a newborn baby? Yet you cannot think of a Gethenian as an "it." They are not neuters. They are potentials . . . One is respected and judged only as human being. (Le Guin, 1969).

In this society people exist in a state of non-gender until they come into "kemmer" when they develop sexually for a brief period randomly as either males or females, and consequently the absence of sexuality is a "continuous social factor" for most of the time (Bassnett, 1991). It is not difficult to document the pervasiveness of gender stereotypes in contemporary life. In the famous, so-called "Baby X" study, adults interacted with a three-month-old in a yellow jumpsuit in one of three conditions, in which the infant was labeled "male," "female," or not labeled at all. Predictably, toys chosen for the infant were affected by the inducement of gender perceptions; when the infant was labeled a "girl," subjects were especially prone to choose a doll for it to play with, rather than a football or teething ring. A majority of those exposed to the non-labeled infant thought that the infant was male, and many explicitly asked whether the child was a boy or girl (Seavey, et al., 1975).

In human cultures there has always been pressure for individuals, from early childhood, to signal that they are clearly either "male" or "female," and to maintain an external appearance which is consistent with culturally constructed gender identity. In other words, they learn to perform "maleness" or "femaleness," "masculinity" or "femininity." (2) Not surprisingly, inculcation of gender stereotypes begins at a very young age. By the end of the first year of age, children shown pictures of adults of both sexes and asked "Where is Mummy?" and "Where is Daddy?" already choose a picture of the correct gender (Belotti, 1976:51).

Many prominent components of 20th-century fashion, e.g., jeans and other types of pants, T-shirts, hats, short hair cuts and either very light makeup or no makeup at all for women, and longer hairstyles and earrings for men, the preference for a slim, boyish body shape for women, and so on, have greatly contributed to the cultivation of an androgynous look. One has only to think of Michael Jackson as cultural hero: with his light skin color, makeup, long hair, and costumes, he is neither black nor white, neither male nor female.

At the same time, despite this fascination with androgyny, heterosexual individuals, if not homosexual ones, rarely wish to be perceived as truly neither male nor female, as unequivocally neuter. Fred Davis, a longstanding student of the sociology of fashion, confirms my hunch: Notwithstanding fashion's frequent encouragement to women to borrow items and modes of men's dress, the norms of Western society demand that gender identity be grounded finally in some irreducible claim that is clearly either male or female, not both or some indeterminate middling state. To forestall discrediting insinuations of "butch lesbianism" or "gay transvestism," Western dress codes operate to blunt any too blatant appropriation of the opposite gender's identity.

It is characteristic, therefore, for cross-gender clothing signals . . . to be accompanied by some symbolic qualification, contradiction, jibe, irony, exaggeration, etc., that in effect advises the viewer not to take the cross-gender representation at face value (Davis, 1992: 42). Women wearing men's clothes usually display their femininity in some aspect of their appearance, as is evident in a photograph of Marlene Dietrich wearing a man's suit, shirt, tie and beret; even apart from her familiar face, other features give her away as a woman: her makeup, hourglass figure and protruding breasts (Lurie, 1981: 244). In Davis's own example, a woman wearing otherwise "male" clothing softens her look with a scarf headband (Davis, 1992: 42); in yet another photograph, a woman is shown in the "Annie Hall look"; wearing men's clothing, but the clothes are oversize, thus communicating the woman's childlike vulnerability, and softening what might otherwise be perceived as a tough male look.

Women trying to "dress for success" in the business world are told to wear suits, but to add secondary details which mark them as "feminine" (Molloy, 1977; Davis, 1992). As Goffman (1976) showed, advertisements encode gender in a host of subtle ways, constantly reinforcing our internalization of these cultural categories. This may be changing in the postmodern period, as some advertisements, e.g., those of Calvin Klein, have been promoting a more fully ambiguous adrogynous look.

So powerful are the forces at work in the social construction of gender that when we encounter strangers whose gender cues are ambiguous, we struggle to classify them as one or the other. Film after film plays on this curiosity of ours. In *Victor/Victoria*, the central character is a woman who plays a man impersonating a woman; from the beginning, the audience knows of the impersonation (Garber, 1993), and is invited implicitly to ask, again and again, "Does she really look like a man?" In the play *M. Butterfly* a man impersonates a woman, "taking in" both the audience and the person's lover—the high point of the play is the astonishing revelation that the "man" is "really" a woman. There is a similar shock effect in *The Crying Game*. When male actors play women, as in *Some Like It Hot, Tootsie*, or *Mrs. Doubtfire* we scrutinize them over and over to see how well they carry off their role.

Similarly, individuals who are real-world (RL) transsexuals—who have undergone sex-change operations—are a source of endless fascination. Do former males "really" now look female, or do they still look male? Thus, the photographs in Kate Bornstein's part autobiographical, part analytic book on her transformation from a formerly married, biological male to a transsexual lesbian invite readers to compare her formerly male "look" with the now-female/lesbian one (Bornstein, 1994; frontispiece and p. 100). Can that dashing man in a marine officer's uniform really be the same person as the attractive woman with the long, luxuriant hair, plunging neckline and earrings in the frontispiece photograph?

## *Cyberspace: A New Cultural Domain for Gender Games*

Cyberspace is a strange new, frontier-like "space" without physicality; when we "enter" it, we leave our bodies behind (Gibson, 1984; Benedikt, 1991, Introduction; Stone, 1991; Biocca, 1992). The Internet is the largest of the many networks that make it up today. To date, most communication in cyberspace is text-based; individuals communicate by typing, and can't see one another.

Therefore, conventional signals of gender identity such as intonation and voice pitch, facial features, body image, non-verbal cues, dress and demeanor, all the cues I've been discussing till now, are absent. A humorous New Yorker cartoon brings this point home: its caption is "On the Internet no one knows you're a dog."

There are two main types of computer-mediated communication (CMC): (1) asynchronous communication, including ordinary private electronic mail, and many-to-many communication in listserv discussion groups, Usenet newsgroups, BBSs, etc.; and (2) synchronous chat modes, including Internet Relay Chat (IRC), and MUDs and MOOs (Figure 1). In this paper I will discuss developments in both of these modes.

IRC is the world's most popular chat mode, with about 25,000 individuals or so participating, as of this writing, and 10,000 and more logged on at any one time. MUDs are Multi-User Dungeons (an elaboration of the Dungeons and Dragons game)—text-based virtual realities in which participants collectively construct an ongoing fantasy world with many stable features over time. MUDs offer a fixed environment within which players must play within the rules of the game as constituted by the software. On MOOs, the software enables individuals to create a built environment, that is, to change the software, adding, for example, "rooms" to a "mansion," "furnishing" them, etc.

There are primarily game-oriented MUDs and MOOs, social or recreational ones, and professionally oriented ones, like MediaMOO, designed for media researchers (in practice even these professional ones are very playful; see Marvin, 1995). In this paper I am concerned with interaction on social MOOs. (3)

**Asynchronous**

One to one: Private e-mail

Many to many: Listserv discussion groups (like letters only faster)
BBSs
Usenet newsgroups

**Synchronous**

Two-person: "Talk" on Unix

Many to many: IRC (Internet Relay Chat) people adopt nicks, chat in channels, MUDS, MOOs:* people develop personas, engage in elaborate role playing

*MUDs: Multi-User Dungeons, Multi-User Domains; MOOs: Multi-User Domains, Object-Oriented.

**Figure 1** Types of Computer-Mediated Communication

Most of the participants on both IRC and MOOs are young people, typically students, and more often than not, male. Chatting on IRC and MOOs has become a new form of leisure for the young, educated, and computer-literate. Players play with language, the software, cultural content of all kinds, as well as with aspects of their identity (Danet, et al., in press; Ruedenberg, et al., 1995; Danet, 1995; Danet et al., 1995; Bechar-Israeli, 1995).

Even in private e-mail and postings to discussion groups and Usenet newsgroups, individuals are sometimes able to mask their RL identity., e.g., through use of a nickname in their "userid." Thus, the address of a person who wrote me to ask for a copy of a paper was "Technosmurf@xxxxxxx." However, there is no question that play with identity, including gender identity, flourishes primarily in chat modes, both in the nom de plume that players adopt and in their contributions.

The paradoxical combination of both anonymity and intimacy in this textual medium (one can type in one's pyjamas, in the middle of the night) releases people from their usual inhibitions, allowing them to pretend to be someone other than they are in RL. On both IRC and MOOs, the software enables individuals to cultivate stable virtual or online identities which may be radically different from their RL ones. Some individuals are already living part of their daily life in these chat modes, adopting either a gender-free identity, or playing a role as a member of the opposite gender.

### *Playing with Gender Identity on IRC*

On IRC many people are "regulars" in one or more channels, which function, in effect, as virtual pubs or cafes. There are 100s and even 1000s of channels. Some are professional or computer-related, as in #www for a channel to discuss aspects of the World Wide Web; most are social, some with a geographical base, e.g., #gb for Great Britain or #israel for Israel, and others without a clear geographical base, such as #friendly and #nicecafe, whose regulars are from all over the world.

Most people adopt a "nick," or nickname; all one has to do to create one is to type, e.g., /nick topsy, and one's nick is immediately registered for all to see as "topsy." Although it is possible to change one's nick at any moment, even again and again, players generally choose their nick carefully and then use it continuously over long periods of time. Players even respect each others' rights over their nicks (Bechar-Israeli, 1995). In the eternal "night" of textual cyberspace, their typed nick is their mask.

Like RL masks, nicks echo the two great principles in nature: the principle of camouflage, on the one hand, and the principle of conspicuous marking, on the other (Gombrich, 1984: 6). Nicks both hide players' RL identity and call attention to the players in virtual guise. (4) One can also make it difficult for others to find out who one really is by logging on from different servers around the world, and even by using different e-mail accounts. A famous case in point is that of an IRC personality called <Valerie>; for weeks if not months, players debated who s/he is and where s/he really is in the world.

Re-examining Haya Bechar-Israeli's corpus of 260 nicks gathered from four IRC channels, I find that less than one-fifth are identifiable with respect to gender. Thus, <Arafat>, <dutchman>, and <madman> are all obviously male, and <Sylvie>, <pcWoman>, and <Darkgirl> are female, but <Emigrant>, <meat>, and <surfer> are just a few of the many gender-neutral nicks. In how many of these cases does the ostensible gender match the RL one? There is no way to find out.

In another of our studies of IRC, an analysis of the log of a virtual party on IRC in which the participants simulated "smoking dope" with the meager resources of the computer keyboard, most of the nicks used by the participants were unidentifiable with respect to gender (Figure 2). One player used the nick <Kang>—those in the "know" would recognize this as

**Nick Userid and Address Additional Material**
Lucia soulr@vml.huji.ac.il
Thunder root@xxxxxxxxxxxxxxxxxx (-: Raam/Chundeung :-)
Kang GENGHISCON@xxxxxxxx ()
Rikitiki rpa3@xxxxxxxxxxxxxxxxx
BlueAdept dlahti@xxxxxxxxxxxxxxxx
Jah miksma3@xxxxxxxxxxxxxx (Baba)
Lizardo lizardo@xxxxxxxxxxxxxxxx (Doctor Lizardo)
Teevie ssac@xxxxxxxxxxxxxxxxxxx

**Figure 2** Nicks of the Players at a Virtual Party on IRC

the name of a male character in Star Trek. From extended interaction with the main player in this sequence, we knew that he was indeed male (Ruedenberg, et al., 1995; Danet, et al., in press). Although the other players were very likely male also, we do not know this for sure.

These findings suggest that many participants on IRC successfully camouflage their gender identity, even over long periods of time. At the same time, we should not exaggerate: many whose nicks are gender-ambiguous may either intentionally or unintentionally reveal their gender through their contributions. Thus, a person choosing a neutral nick such as <Meatloaf> might flirt outrageously with players having clearly female nicks, revealing or at least inviting the inference that this person is in fact male. Nevertheless, I would argue that the choice of a gender-neutral nickname does reflect some desire to experiment with release from gender, and that Bechar-Israeli's corpus invites the hypothesis that most players not only choose a nick rather than their real name, but also choose one which is gender-ambiguous. (5)

## *Playing with Gender Identity on MOOs*

Preliminary evidence suggests that play with gender identity is much more elaborate, and probably much more far-reaching in its consequences on MOOs than on IRC. To recapitulate, MOOs are role-playing text-based virtual realities.

IRC is a sort of vast cyberspace neighborhood containing hundreds of virtual pubs and cafes, where players may participate in more than one channel at a time. In contrast, MOOs are specific locations in cyberspace, within which different areas or "rooms" can contain different activities. It would be more accurate to characterize them as miniature societies without physical existence, rather than as virtual pubs or cafes.

The most famous MOO, LambdaMOO (Curtis, 1992), now has about 8,000 characters; it has become the virtual equivalent of a small town (Coe, 1995). LambdaMOO is purely recreational–social. Another MOO, MediaMOO, was created by Amy Bruckman, a doctoral student at M.I.T., for researchers of new media. Despite its professional goals, it is also very social, running, for example, a "Happy Hour" at the end of the work week. On LambdaMOO, the RL identity of the players behind the characters is not revealed, whereas on MediaMOO, in keeping with its partially professional nature, the RL names of players are known. (6)

When they join a MOO, individuals create an elaborate "persona" or "character," whose description is registered and available for reading by anyone logged on to them (Bruckman, 1992, 1993; Turkle, 1995). They then role-play in this guise for months if not years. Thus, a male college student might create "Samantha, a gorgeous blonde with a fabulous figure." In extended role-play over time, "Samantha" could conduct love affairs with males, have virtual sex, and even "get married"—all online in the MOO.

Players may even play different fantasy characters, of different genders, in different MOOs simultaneously, in separate windows on their computer screen (Turkle, 1995). The following account illustrates many aspects of the impersonation of females by males on MUDs and MOOs:

> Christian Sykes is no nerd: he's 23, married, a religious studies major at the University of Kansas. . . . He played on MUDs long enough to become bored with them, so as a "performance art piece," he decided to find out whether he could portray a woman convincingly. Many males who impersonate females on MUDs are easy to detect, for they behave not as real women do but rather as late-adolescent males wish they would, responding with enthusiasm to all sexual advances, sometimes in quite explicit terms; . . . he kept the description of his character simple and as consistent with his own appearance as possible. Women on the MUD spoke among themselves about boyfriends, menstruation, or even gynecological problems; he drew upon lore gleaned from his wife and female friends. . . .
>
> Sykes' major revelation . . . was the extent of sexual harassment of women. Though not one person suspected Sykes' prank, he abandoned it after four months because he could not write programs without being constantly interrupted by male advances. . . . Revealing the hoax didn't even end Sykes' problems, for one male player who apparently had a crush on Eris [his character's name] became so irate that he tried to get Sykes banished from the MUD (Leslie, 1993).

The software of MOOs has been programmed to offer an amazing variety of genders from which to choose. Figure 3 lists the genders available on MOOs, e.g., on MediaMOO, a MOO for media researchers created and run by Amy Bruckman at M.I.T., and LambdaMOO, the "mother of all MOOs" created by Pavel Curtis and others (Curtis, 1992). Besides "male" and "female" one can choose "neuter," "either," "Spivak," "splat," "plural," "egotistical," "royal" (as in the royal "we"), "2nd," and "person." As Figure 3 shows, each gender has its own set of pronouns. Some are familiar from ordinary usage—for "neuter," the pronouns are "it, its, itself." In the case of "either," the player will be consistently represented with "s/he, him/her, his/her, his/hers, (him/her)self, and so on. (7) To make the unfamiliar ones comprehensible, I have added all the permutations of the simple sentence "I read my book myself", in each of the genders. Thus, in the "royal we" choice, the sentence "We are reading our book" would appear on the screen.

MediaMOO recently added an additional gender choice not available on LambdaMOO: "person." This now allows players to say "Person reads pers book perself." Such seemingly bizarre sentences are more comprehensible when we take into account that much of the dialogue on MUDs and MOOs is, in fact, rendered in the third person: chatting on MOOs is more like writing collective fiction than like writing the dialogue of a drama (IRC dialogue, on the other hand is more traditionally dramatic in nature—players write primarily in the first person). (8)

>> @gender _male_
Gender set to male
Your pronouns: he, him, his, his, himself, He, Him, His, His, Himself
Example: he reads his book himself.

>> @gender _female_
Gender set to female
Your pronouns: she, her, her, hers, herself, She, Her, Her, Hers, Herself
Example: she reads her book herself.

>> @gender _neuter_
Gender set to neuter
Your pronouns: it, it, its, its, itself, It, It, Its, Its, Itself
Example: it reads its book itself.

>> @gender _either_
Gender set to either
Your pronouns: s/he, him/her, his/her, his/hers, (him/her)self, S/He, Him/Her, His/Her, His/Hers, (Him/Her)self
Example: s/he reads his/her book him/herself.

>> @gender _spivak_
Gender set to Spivak
Your pronouns: e, em, eir, eirs, eirself, E, Em, Eir, Eirs, Eirself
Example: e reads eir book eirself.

>> @gender _splat_
Gender set to splat
Your pronouns: *e, h*, h*, h*s, h*self, *E, H*, H*, H*s, H*self
Example: *e reads h*s book h*self.

>> @gender _plural_
Gender set to plural
Your pronouns: they, them, their, theirs, themselves, They, Them, Their, Theirs, Themselves
Example: they read their book themselves.

>> @gender _egotistical_
Gender set to egotistical
Your pronouns: I, me, my, mine, myself, I, Me, My, Mine, Myself
Example: I read my book myself.

**Figure 3** Available Genders on MediaMOO and LambdaMOO

>> @gender _royal_
Gender set to royal
Your pronouns: we, us, our, ours, ourselves, We, Us, Our, Ours, Ourselves
Example: We read our book ourselves.>>

@gender _2nd_
Gender set to 2nd
Your pronouns: you, you, your, yours, yourself, You, You, Your, Yours, Yourself
Example: you read your book yourself.

@gender _person_*
Gender set to person
Your pronouns: per, per, per, pers, perself, Per, Per, Per, Pers, Perself
Example: per reads pers book perself.

*MediaMOO only

**Figure 3** *(continued)*

I obtained data on the distribution of actual gender choices on LambdaMOO and MediaMOO. (9) Figure 4 demonstrates that substantial numbers of players on both MOOs are choosing unconventional genders for their characters. The relative proportions choosing each gender alternative are remarkably similar in the two MOOs (upper half of Figure 4). The single most common choice is "male," followed by "female," but the biggest surprise is the substantial proportion choosing a category other than these two. To sharpen the contrast between categories, I have collapsed them into just three, in the lower half of Figure 4. Thus we can now see clearly that on both MOOs, about half the players choose "male" gender, with the proportions choosing "female" and "unconventional" or "neuter" reversed on the two MOOs. On MediaMOO nearly a third chose an unconventional gender; on LambdaMOO it drops to about a fifth.

Figure 4 is actually only part of the story.

Besides the fixed gender options, players on these MOOs can also create their own idiosyncratic gender. Only 3–4% of persons with registered characters chose to tailor their own, on both of these MOOs. Thus, on LambdaMOO, in addition to the 7065 persons choosing one of the fixed gender categories, another 243 persons created their own. In addition to the 1015 choosing one of the fixed genders on MediaMOO, another 40 tailored their own.

Even though these proportions are tiny, the material is very interesting. We can learn a great deal from inspecting the name of each character and its tailored gender. First of all, choices jibe with the patterns already discussed. On both MOOs, the large majority of non-standard choices are clearly neutral,

| Gender | MediaMOO* | LambdaMOO** |
|---|---|---|
| male | 495 | 3651 |
| female | 197 | 2069 |
| neuter | 280 | 1162 |
| spivak | 10 | 74 |
| either | 9 | 15 |
| plural | 7 | 26 |
| royal | 6 | 30 |
| splat | 5 | 17 |
| egotistical | 2 | 16 |
| 2nd | 2 | 5 |
| person | 2 | — |
| Total | 1015 | 7065 |
| Percent male | 48.8% | 51.7% |
| Percent female | 19.4 | 29.2 |
| Percent unconventional | 31.8 | 19.1 |
| | 100.0% | 100.0% |
| | (1015) | (7065) |

*Breakdown as of January 17, 1996.

**Breakdown as of February 9, 1996.

**Figure 4** Conventional and Unconventional Genders Actually Chosen on MediaMOO and LambdaMOO

e.g., "Chaos," "salty," "neutral," "opus," or "none" on MediaMOO, or "lover," "me," "Ghost," "wood," and "married" on LambdaMOO. (10)

Thus, the proportions choosing neutral genders, including both standard and non-standard choices, is slightly higher than that shown in the lower half of Figure 4. But surely the significance of these data lies not only in percentages. The fact is that if we combine the numbers for MediaMOO and LambdaMOO, between 1500 and 2000 persons are playing a neutral character! (11) Also worth noting are choices like "whatever I feel at the time" ("Tanya") or "mood-dependent, usually neuter" ("The-Prisoner") "s-he" ("Natalia"), for three characters on LambdaMOO. Since the majority of players on MOOs and in cyberspace generally are known to be male, we can be quite sure that many males on both MOOs are choosing either "female" or some unconventional gender designation for their characters.

Unfortunately, data are not available as to the match or lack of match between RL and MOO gender identity, at least not for LambdaMOO. In the case of MediaMOO, since RL names are known, in principle one might be able to figure out the actual gender of players, except in cases where the RL person has a gender-ambiguous name such as "Lee."

As the account from the article by Jacques Leslie indicated above (Leslie, 1993), players who "cross-dress" textually sometimes get into trouble when their RL gender identity is revealed (Van Gelder, 1990; Stone, 1991). For instance, a New York Jewish male psychiatrist in his 50's played a female called "Talkin' Lady" on Compuserve; he created an elaborate persona of a woman who had been in a car accident in which her fiance had been killed; "she" had been hospitalized and was now in a wheelchair.

At first "depressed," "she" gradually became more outgoing. When virtual friends arranged to meet "her" for lunch, s/he peeked from afar. Eventually the subterfuge was discovered, much to the chagrin of those who had been taken in (Van Gelder, 1990). A particularly dramatic instance is that of a couple called "Mik" and "Sue" who met and fell in love on MUD1. For a very long stretch "Sue" was able to pass as a woman because she presented a coherent and consistent image (Jacobson and Dana, 1995; Goffman, 1959). One person who had interacted extensively with "Sue" reported:

> . . . it had occurred to me several times that Sue might have been male, but every "test" I set was passed with flying colours. We'd even get little unsolicited details, like when she didn't reply to a message immediately because she'd just snagged a nail. I remember once I printed some MUD sweatshirts which had the opening description printed on them, "You are standing on a narrow road between the Land and whence you came. To the north and south are the foothills of a pair of majestic mountains . . ."; Sue told me she liked hers (size small), but people kept looking at her funny as the words "pair of majestic mountains" were emblazoned right across her, well, her majestic mountains! It was little details like this which made her so convincing. (Reid, 1994, Appendix 3). (12)

## *Language, Writing and the Performance of Gender: Some Questions for Research*

At least on the face of it, virtual cross-dressing should be much easier than real-life (RL) cross-dressing. Although the gussied up creatures of drag comedy are not really trying to fool anyone, true RL transvestites and transsexuals must go to elaborate lengths in order to pass—learning to dress, use makeup, walk, speak like women, and so on (Garber, 1993; Bornstein, 1994). At the same time, textual passing may be more difficult than appears at first glance. . . . once [males] are online as female, they soon find that maintaining this fiction is difficult. To pass as a woman for any length of time requires understanding how gender inflects speech, manner, the interpretation of experience (Turkle, 1995: 212).

Elizabeth Reid's experience while doing online ethnography for her M.A. thesis on MUDs/MOOs confirms these difficulties:

> It is indeed a truly disorienting experience the first time one finds oneself being treated as a member of the opposite sex. My own forays into the realm

> of virtual masculinity were at first frightening experiences. Much as some of us may deplore what we see as the negative sides of our culture's sexual politics, we are brought up to align ourselves with gender-specific social navigation mechanisms. Once deprived of the social tools which I, as female, was used to deploying and relying on, I felt rudderless, unable to negotiate the most simple of social interactions. I did not know how to speak, whether to women or to "other" men, and I was thrown off balance by the ways in which other people spoke to me. It took much practice to learn to navigate these unfamiliar channels, an experience that gave me a greater understanding of the mechanics of sexual politics than any other I have ever had. (Reid, 1994, chap. 3).

I propose to problematize these linguistic and textual aspects of the performance of gender online. The descriptive data presented in this paper can serve as an orienting base from which to embark on a research program of intensive observation of the performance of gender online and in-depth interviews with persons playing gender games. Here are some questions for future research.

1. What are the textual equivalents of the RL phenomena discussed in the first half of this paper and documented in the photographs? How is gender performed when one has to do it by typing, in the dark "night" of cyberspace? What linguistic and substantive features actually characterize role-playing male or female gender online? For ideas on what to look for with respect to the linguistic aspects of typed "passing," one could analyze the scripts of films in which men play women (*Tootsie, Some Like It Hot,* etc.)
2. How do these choices relate to known differences between genders in the research literature in sociolinguistics and discourse analysis? In particular, what are the implications of the fact that the medium is writing, rather than speech?
3. What linguistic and other features characterize the attempt to be neuter?
4. What can the availability and use of gender-free pronouns on MOOs contribute to the debate about sexism in RL language (a different issue from that of gender differences in actual language use; see, e.g., Martyna, 1980; MacKay, 1983; Smith, 1985, chap. 3)? Can extended use of neutral pronouns change perceptions about gender—not only about others' gender but about one's own?
5. What differences are there between the communication styles of genuine males and pretend males? What differences are there between genuine females and pretend females? (To study this question one would of course have to solve the problem of how to identify the RL gender of these individuals; in the case of MediaMOO this is possible.)
6. Do "cross-dressed" males caricature textual femininity? Do they mobilize stereotypes about "female" speech, in a manner which echoes the

behavioral characterization of stereotypical female intonation or body movement? Is there evidence that RL males caricaturize "femaleness" more than RL female caricaturize "maleness"?

7. When does textual cross-dressing succeed, and when does it break down and why? The beginning of an answer lies, apparently, in Goffman's concepts of coherence and consistency (Goffman, 1974; Jacobson and Dana, 1995). Successful "passers" present a coherent, self-consistent image; but how is this constructed textually?
8. Is "passing" mainly a matter of supplying consistent, coherent substantive cues, as the examples from Leslie (1993) and Reid (1994), discussed above, suggest, or is it a matter of packaging one's contributions linguistically in stereotypically female ways?
9. How is gender experimentation different on IRC and on MOOs? What is the significance of the differences? Is there ethnographic evidence for the argument here that experimentation is far more extensive, and more profound in its consequences, among MOOers than among IRC players?
10. What is the cultural significance of experimentation with gender online? What are implications of these forms of role-playing for identity in the postmodern era? Is androgyny becoming a more viable cultural option? Can we actually entertain the vision of a future with some genuine release from the tyranny of gender?
11. How will the advent of video conferencing alter these experiments with gender identity? There is already much speculation as to whether video conferencing will replace textual communication in cyberspace. Some argue that text will continue to be the preferred medium, not only because it will remain the cheaper one, but also because its limited technical possibilities offer a creative challenge to users, and, most pertinent of all to this paper, because the anonymity of text will continue to have its charms. It is evident that video will make it harder to "pass" as a member of the opposite gender, or to pretend to be gender-free. On the other hand, video could offer new opportunities for dressing up!

## Notes

1. I am grateful to Efrat Tseelon of Leeds Metropolitan University for the opportunity to present this paper at the conference on "Masquerade and Gendered Identity." Special thanks to Lee-Ellen Marvin and Keith Wilson for material on gender on MediaMOO and LambdaMOO. Amia Lieblich led me to the "Baby X" study mentioned here.
2. It should be apparent that in this paper I am not concerned with psychological traits of masculinity, femininity or androgyny, but with the external performance of these cultural categories by the individual, and the perception of them by others.

3. Another example of a social MOO is "The Sprawl," named after the megalopolis from Boston to Atlanta on the East coast of the United States, which appears in William Gibson's quintessential cyberpunk novel *Neuromancer* (Gibson, 1984).
4. For a typology of nicks, e.g., those that play with language vs. those whose main interest is in the reference to some substantive area, such as science fiction or cinema, and the distribution of types of nicks actually used on the four channels, see Bechar-Israeli (1995).
5. It is interesting to compare these results with those of Susan Kalcik in a study of the "handles" chosen by female CB radio activists. In Kalcik's (1985) corpus, most women chose female-marked handles, such as "Sweet Sue," "Cinderella," or "Queen Bee." Some women whose husbands were also involved in CB chose a handle which reflected their relationship to him, e.g., "North Star's Lady," or "Comanche's Angel." By and large, women chose handles reflecting one of the two classic female sterotypes, the sex kitten (e.g., "Hot Pants," "Midnight Delight," "Bouncing Boobs"), and the sweet, gentle woman ("Sweet Pea," "Sugar Cookie," "Sweet Angel"). While some gender-neutral handles were chosen (e.g., "Bookworm," "Stargazer," "Cricket," "Carrot-top"), and there are even a few instances of male-sounding handles ("Lucky Louie," "Samurai") these women did not, by and large, play with gender in the ways discussed in this paper. Of course the populations involved in CB radio in the 1980's and in IRC and MOOs in the late 1990's are very different.
6. Personal electronic communication from Lee-Ellen Marvin.
7. Elizabeth Reid comments that some of these options were drawn from science fiction but does not cite specific novels or stories (Reid, 1994).
8. See Danet (1995), Introduction, for a more extended discussion of the differences between IRC and MOOs, and for the suggestion that MOO interaction is a kind of verbal puppetry.
9. These data were supplied to me by Lee-Ellen Marvin and Keith Weston, known on MOOs as "Luna" and "Lemper," respectively. The data are available directly from the MOO software at these sites.
10. Choices like "married" for the character "Inky_the_Worm_Bitch," or "Sandwich" for the character "Ham_on_Bri" on LambdaMOO show that in such cases, the gender slot was used to supply additional information about the character not related to gender designation at all.
11. A word of caution: some characters may be inactive, that is registered, though their creators do not participate much on the MOO; personal communication from Lee-Ellen Marvin.
12. The full text of this particularly dramatic case is presented in the Appendix. "Sue" turned out to be a man arrested for financial fraud in real life.

## References

Bassnett, Susan. (1991). Remarking the old world: Ursula Le Guin and the American tradition. In Lucie Armitt, ed., *Where no man has gone before: women and Science Fiction* (pp. 50–66). London: Routledge.

Basso, Keith H. (1974). The ethnography of writing. In Richard A. Bauman and Joel Sherzer, eds., *Explorations in the ethnography of speaking* (pp. 425–432). Cambridge University Press.

Beall, Anne E. (1993). A social constructionist view of gender. In Anne E. Beall and Robert J. Sternberg, eds. *The psychology of gender* (pp. 127–147). New York and London: Guilford Press.

Bechar-Israeli, Haya. (1995). From to: nicknames, play and identity on internet relay chat. *Journal of Computer-mediated Communication*, 1,2, special issue on "Play and Performance in Computer-Mediated Communication," Brenda Danet, guest editor. <http://shum.huji.ac.il/jcmc/vol1/issue2/vol1no2.html> or <http:www.ascusc.org/ jcmc/vol1/issue2/>

Belotti, Elena Gianini. (1976). *What are little girls made of? the roots of feminine stereotypes.* New York: Schocken.

Benedikt, Michael (Ed.) (1991). *Cyberspace: first steps.* Cambridge, MA: MIT Press.

Biocca, Frank (Ed.) (1992). Virtual reality: a communication perspective. Special issue, *Journal of Communication*, 42, 4.

Bornstein, Kate. (1994). *Gender outlaw: on men, women and the rest of us.* New York and London: Routledge.

Bruckman, Amy. (1992). Identity-workshop: emergent social and psychological phenomena in text-based virtual reality. Available from Bruckman at <asb@media-lab.media.mit.edu>.

______. (1993). "Gender Swapping on the Internet." *Proceedings of INET93.*

Butler, Judith P. (1990). *Gender trouble: feminism and the subversion of identity.* New York: Routledge.

Coates, J. (1986). *Women, men, and language.* New York: Longman.

Coe, Cati. (1995). Difference and utopia in an electronic community. Paper presented at the Annual Meeting, American Anthropological Association, November, 1995, Washington, D.C., session on "Cyberspace Neighborhoods."

Curtis, Pavel. (1992). Mudding: social phenomena in text-based virtual realities. *Proceedings of DIAC '92.* <ftp: parcftp.xerox.com/pub/MOO/papers/DIAC92>.

Danet, Brenda (Ed.) (1995). Play and performance in computer-mediated communication. Special issue, *Journal of Computer-mediated Communication*, 1,2. <http://shum.huji.ac.il/jcmc/vol1/issue2/vol1no2.html> or <http://www.ascusc.org/jcmc/vol1/issue2/>.

Danet, Brenda. The ethnography of writing. In *Encyclopedia of semiotics*, Paul Bouissac (Ed.), Oxford: Oxford University Press.

Danet, Brenda, Lucia Ruedenberg, and Yehudit Rosenbaum-Tamari. In press. "Hmmm . . . where's that smoke coming from?" writing, play and performance on internet relay chat. In Sheizaf Rafaeli, Fay Sudweeks, and Margaret McLaughlin (Eds.), *Network and netplay: virtual groups on the internet* (pp. 47–85). Cambridge, MA: AAAI/MIT.

Danet, Brenda, Tsameret Wachenhauser, Haya Bechar-Israeli, Amos Cividalli, and Yehudit Rosenbaum-Tamari. (1995). Curtain time 20:00 GMT: experiments in virtual theater on internet relay chat. *Journal of Computer-Mediated Communication*, special issue on "Play and Performance in Computer-mediated Communication," Brenda Danet (guest ed) 1,2. <http://shum.huji.ac.il/jcmc/vol1/issue2/vol1no2.html> or <http://www.ascusc.org/jcmc/vol1/issue2/>.

Davis, Fred. (1992). *Fashion, culture, and identity.* Chicago: University of Chicago Press.

Garber, Marjorie. (1993). *Vested interests: cross-dressing and cultural anxiety.* London: Penguin.

Gibson, William. (1984). *Neuromancer*. New York: Ace.

Goffman, Erving. (1959). *Presentation of self in everyday life*. Garden City, NY: Anchor Books.

______. (1976). *Gender advertisements*. London: Macmillan.

Gombrich, E.H. (1984). *The sense of order: a study of the psychology of decorative art*. London: Phaidon.

Graddol, D. and J. Swann. (1989). *Gender voices*. Oxford: Basil Blackwell.

Herring, Susan C. (1993). Gender and democracy in computer-mediated communication. *EJC: Electronic Journal of Communication*, 3, 2, <comserve@cios.llc.rpi.edu; message: send herring v3n293>.

Jacobson, David, and Adrianne Dana. (1995). Play and not-play in cyberspace: frames and cues in text-based virtual reality. Paper presented at the Annual Meeting, American Anthropological Association, Washington D.C., November, 1995, session on "Cyberspace Neighborhoods."

Kalcik, Susan. (1985). Women's handles and the performance of identity in the cb community. In Rosan Jordan and Susan Kalcik (Eds.), *Women's folklore, women's culture*. Philadelphia: University of Pennsylvania Press.

Lakoff, Robin. (1975). *Language and woman's place*. New York: Harper & Row.

Le Guin, Ursula K. (1969). *The left hand of darkness*. New York: Ace.

Leslie, Jacques. (1993). MUDS: the new agora. *Wired Magazine*. <http://www.hotwired.com.archives>.

Lurie, Alison. (1981). *The language of clothes*. New York: Vintage.

MacKay, Donald G. (1983). Prescriptive grammar and the pronoun problem. In Barrie Thorne, Cheris Kramarae, and Nancy Henley (Eds.), *Language, gender and society*. Rowley, MA: Newbury House.

Martyna, Wendy. (1980). The psychology of the generic masculine. In Sally McConnell-Ginet, Ruth Borker, and Nelly Furman (Eds.), *Women and language in literature and society* (p. 69). New York: Praeger.

Marvin, Lee-Ellen. (1995). Spoof, spam, lurk, and lag: aesthetics of text-based virtual realities. *Journal of Computer-mediated Communication*, 1, 2, special issue on "Play and Performance in Computer-mediated Communication," Brenda Danet (guest ed.), <http://shum.huji.ac.il/jcmc/vol1/issue2/vol1no2.html> or <http://www.ascusc.org/jcmc/vol1/issue2>.

Molloy, John. (1977). *The woman's dress for success book*. New York: Warner.

Philips, Susan U., S. Steele, and Christine Tanz (Ed.) (1987). *Language, gender and sex in comparative perspective*. Cambridge: Cambridge University Press.

Reid, Elizabeth. (1991). *Electropolis: communication and community on internet relay chat*. <emr@munagin.ee.mu.oz.au> or <ftp.eff.org;/pub/cud/papers/electropolis>.

______. (1994). *Cultural formations in text-based virtual realities*. Unpublished M.A. thesis, Dept. of English, University of Melbourne.

______. (1995). Virtual worlds: culture and imagination. In Steven Jones (Ed.), *Cybersociety: Computer-mediated Communication and Community* (pp. 164–183). Thousand Oaks, CA: Sage.

Ruedenberg, Lucia, Brenda Danet, and Yehudit Rosenbaum-Tamari. (1995). Virtual virtuosos: play and performance at the computer keyboard. *EJC: Electronic Journal of Communication*, 5,4. Available to subscribers at http://www.clos.org.

Seavey, Carol A., Phyllis A. Katz, and Sue R. Zalk. (1975). Baby X: the effects of gender labels on adult responses to infants. *Sex Roles 9*, 103–110.

Smith, Philip M. (1985). *Language, the sexes and society*. Oxford: Basil Blackwell.

Stone, Allucquere Rosanne. (1991). Will the real body please stand up? Boundary stories about virtual cultures. In Michael Benedikt (Ed.), *Cyberspace: first steps* (pp. 81–118). Cambridge, MA: MIT Press.

Tannen, Deborah. (1990). *You just don't understand: women and men in conversation.* New York: Ballantine.

Thorne, Barrie, and Nancy Henley (Eds). (1975). *Language and sex: difference and dominance.* Rowley, MA: Newbury House.

Turkle, Sherry. (1995). *Life on the screen: identity in the age of the internet.* New York: Simon & Schuster.

van Gelder, Lindsy. (1986). "The strange case of the electronic lover." In Gary Gumpert and Sandra L. Fish (Eds.), *Talking to strangers: mediated therapeutic communication* (pp. 128–142). Norwood, NJ: Ablex.

# THE INNERNET

## Andrew Sullivan

I SUPPOSE WE SHOULDN'T BE SURPRISED that the newest technological revolution was forged by money and sex. Much of civilization has been.

What was hard to foresee is how, in the World Wide Web, both money and sex have begun to disappear.

Money no longer exists for the most part in coins and bills but flickers around the planet as pixels on a screen. Sex has similarly come to thrive in a space where no physical body can eat or breathe or copulate. For men above all, the Web has become a place where sexual fantasy is finally real and always available, as long as you have a screen name and a chat room.

Technology has achieved a convergence of mind and body that for previous generations existed only in dreams.

Unhappy with your body? Don't bother with the gym. Attach some digital scans of an Abercrombie & Fitch model and pose as someone else altogether. Then talk with the woman of your dreams and turn on the switches in her cybermind in ways you have never been able to do in a bar. Cyrano now requires no disguise, no proxy, no hideaway in the new millennium. Just a modem.

Unhappy with your marriage? Commit interactive infidelity where only instant messages are exchanged. Of course, you've fantasized about these things before. But now it's possible to actually do them with someone else, in real time if not in real space, and with someone on whom you can equally project any visual fantasy you desire.

The old paradigm of hiding the *Playboy* between *Commentary* and *Popular Mechanics,* and scurrying away for the fulfillment of your predatory passions, has now been retired. It can all happen at once, with complete anonymity and perfect reciprocation.

This virtual sex is, of course, light-years away from the physical procreation of generations past. It can never substitute for reality. There will still be—for most women and some men at least—the tantalizing fantasy of actually meeting their cybermate someday. You've already seen this in such movies as *You've Got Mail.* But it isn't, strictly speaking, necessary. Even without a physical meeting, cybersex is still in some fundamental sense sex. Your partner can still surprise; she can still shock; she can still reply. She is no longer a mere centerfold on a page or a pause button on a remote. She is real . . . somewhere. She may not be in your bed, but she is still on your screen.

Unless, of course, she's a he. For if the meeting of mind and body in cybersex is forging new boundaries, then the virtuality of gender is even more adventurous. Here, convergence meets deviance at an even deeper level. How, after all, do you know the real gender of your virtual cyberpartner? Even Cyrano's voice gave something away. But with the instant message and the email, there is no voice, no timbre, no soprano or bass. What the deconstructionists long dreamed about, what the sex radicals endlessly pontificated about—the social construction of gender—is now within our reach. Just as mind and body have converged, so, too, have male and female.

If you want to know how it feels to be a woman being seduced by a man, there is no need for makeup anymore. You need only switch your screen name and enter a new reality. The plots of half of Shakespeare's comedies have suddenly become moot. Cross-dressing is no longer a prerequisite.

Even the mysterious origins of sexual orientation can be undone by the click of a mouse. If you want to explore your homosexual tendencies, log on. The old forbidden spaces of closetedness—the parks and library stacks, the public rest rooms and riverbanks of yesterday's furtive couplings—are no longer necessary. And the threats of exposure, of imprisonment, of arrest, of shame and discovery, are far more remote. The anonymity that every closeted gay man has ever craved is now available instantly in the privacy of his own password.

Even the closet itself is no longer an either–or proposition. If you've been out for years, a swift profile change and you can be back in again. Miss that shame and thrill of the forbidden? Get it back with a detour through America Online.

There are those who argue that cyberfantasy will liberate sexual practices more profoundly than the somewhat clumsy sexual innovations of the 1960s. The world of cyberspace, they point out, will give everyone a bite of the forbidden apple and make us all less able to return to the Victorian Eden. You can see their point. Thanks to the Internet, thousands of closeted, married men, for example, have been able for the first time to talk to a fullfledged homosexual. Thanks to the Web, thousands of frustrated housewives have been able to express their deepest desires without paying for a therapist. Thanks to chat rooms, thousands of teenagers have gotten off without getting someone pregnant. And all this, in its way, must chip away somewhere at our society's built-in emotional and sexual defenses.

But it's perfectly possible, I think, that the opposite may also be the case. Although mind and body and male and female and straight and gay may finally be converging in cyberspace, in real time and space, divergence might actually increase. It may be, paradoxically, that by allowing us this completely anonymous outlet, this safety valve of unreality, the new technology might actually release our natural sexual tension and help us sustain the fictions and duties of bourgeois morality in the rest of our lives.

Victorianism, after all, was not about suppressing vice. It was about separating it completely from virtue, relegating it to a forbidden sphere, and ensuring that the two worlds never met. It was about keeping up appearances, while allowing a suitable expression for unleashing subterranean desire.

What happened in the 20th century is that the structures that allowed this hypocrisy to survive—the power of men over women, of rich over poor, of straight over gay, of city over country—slowly crumbled. For a while, it became impossible to separate reality from fantasy without the two spying on each other, and the subsequent honesty and liberation undermined traditional values and appearances.

But as the century ends, it may be possible again to put those appearances back together without giving us all a nervous breakdown. We might be able to relegate our sexual ids to cyberspace and preen our familial superegos in the society at large. Because sexual anonymity is far more successfully assured than ever before, the separation between vice and virtue can be even more watertight than the Victorians ever hoped for.

When Edwardian husbands trolled bordellos for mistresses, when Depression-era homosexuals lingered on park benches for their trysts, when young writers in the 1950s took to distant brothels for their comings-of-age, there was, after all, the terrible risk of something going wrong: of a chance encounter with the official world, of imprisonment, of publicity, of incriminating disease. Now, with technology creating a sexual netherworld for all, there is merely the risk of a lost encryption, an undeleted file, an occasionally too-honest self-pic. There is greater security in hypocrisy, and less to lose by risking honesty. So the possibility of Victorianism beckons anew.

We human beings, after all, have a way of keeping our foibles one step ahead of our technology. For a while, science may have the better of us—but rarely for long. The present moment—with its tantalizing unity of what is and what could be, of what we are and what we want to be—may turn out to be only a fleeting phenomenon. Which, of course, is only one more reason to enjoy it while we can.

## This Text: Reading

1. What common threads tie these articles together?
2. What are some of the different ways the authors use the idea of identity both explicitly and implicitly? Why might technology affect someone's view of himself or herself?
3. What exactly is a cyber-ghetto? How does this compare to a real ghetto? What comment about public spaces is McKissack making with this term? What do the other authors think about the relationship between public space and cyberspace?
4. McKissack also engages assumptions about race, class, poverty, and technology. How do the other authors engage these issues? In what ways does Martin engage these ideas?
5. Sullivan and Danet show how the Internet can both "anonymize" and empower some people. What is the relationship between those two concepts? Why might being anonymous help someone discover who they are?

## Your Text: Writing

1. Do some "lurking" in chat rooms that purport to be devoted to a particular identity. What can or did you learn by being in these rooms that you might not otherwise?
2. Write a short piece about your own relationship to the Internet. Has the Internet changed you? Brought out different pieces of your personality? How have these changes manifested themselves?
3. No one has to tell you that e-mail has changed the way we communicate with each other (even if you don't use it very much). In what ways is that a positive thing? In what ways is it a negative thing? How has this manifested itself in your own life and in those of your friends and family?
4. Do you see yourself in particular in any of these articles? Which ones? What about these articles engages certain ideas about you?

---

# READING OUTSIDE THE LINES

## Classroom Activities

1. Take five minutes and find something in the immediate area that is designed poorly. Explain why—and talk about what could make it better.
2. What single technological advance do you think has been the most important in your lifetime? Why? In the last 50 years? In the last 200 years? Ever? Do you notice a trend in this development?

3. What technological advances do you think have been the most harmful in your lifetime? Do these advances have advantages too? How should we balance the strengths and weaknesses of technology: Through the free market? Government intervention?
4. Do you know people who resist new technology? What are their reasons for doing so? Do you find their logic convincing? Do you know people who embrace all new technology? Can you make any determinations of how they view the world from their ideas about technology?
5. How does the media portray technology—positively or negatively? Why?
6. How do movies and television portray technological advances? How about people who are fascinated with technology? Why?
7. Would you say that the United States embraces or resists technology? Why?

## Essay Ideas

### Trace Technology

Find a technological advancement, modern or otherwise, and read media accounts of its invention through the present time. According to the initial invention, has the promise of this invention been fulfilled? Why or why not? What mistakes in judgment did the inventors—and reporters—make when they first communicated about this technology? Do these mistakes represent a trend of any sort?

### Read a Piece of Technology

Sit down with a piece of technology such as a computer, household appliance, your automobile, anything. First, read the piece without thinking too much about its use. What messages does the technology give you in terms of design and function? Now think about its use. Do the messages coincide? If you were using this piece of technology for the first time, would you be disappointed with the execution of the technology compared to its promise? Is this important?

### Find a Technological Hole

Can you think of something that you would like to do that a technological advance would aid? Why do you think the technology has not been invented? What might some of the implications of this particular advance be?

### Read and Evaluate an Artistic Portrayal of Technology

Find a text such as *The Matrix* or another movie or television episode that has at its center technology as a subject. What do the writers think of technology generally? How do they show this stance in their portrayal? Do you agree with their assessment? If not, what might they not be taking into account?

# Appendix

## How Do I Cite This Car?: Guidelines for Citing Popular Culture Texts

As you probably know, it's very important to cite or acknowledge any kind of text (written or otherwise) that you use in an academic or professional essay. Most students think that citing work has mostly to do with avoiding plagiarism—and that's certainly an important part of it—but there are other reasons why citing work is important.

As a researcher, your job is often to make sense of a particular phenomenon and in doing so, make sense of the work done before you on the same subject. When you do that, you perform a valuable service for your reader, who now not only has your perspective on this phenomenon, but also has an entry into the subject through the sources you cite. For this very reason, professional researchers and academics often find the works cited pages and footnotes as interesting as the text itself.

As writers in the humanities, you will typically use MLA (Modern Language Association) formatting in your papers. There are two other major forms of citing—APA (American Psychological Association), often used in the social sciences and science, and "Chicago" or "Turabian," often used in history and political science.

All three ways of citing are part of a *system* of citation. How you cite (say where information comes from) is directly related to the bibliography or, in the case of MLA, the works cited page. You indicate in the text who wrote the article or book, and at the end of the paper, the sources are listed in alphabetical order, so the reader can see the whole work, but without the intrusion of listing that whole work within the text; seeing (Alvarez 99) is much easier than seeing (Alvarez, Julia. *How the Garcia Girls Lost Their Accents*. New York: Plume, 1992) in an essay.

## USING PARENTHETICAL REFERENCES

In MLA, you cite using parenthetical references within the body of your essay. The format for the parenthetical reference is easy. If you know the author's name, you include the author's last name and the page number(s) in parentheses *before* the punctuation mark. For instance, if you are quoting from LeAnne Howe's novel *Shell Shaker*, your parenthetical reference would look like this:

> The novel *Shell Shaker* does a great job of conveying Choctaw pride: "I decide that as a final gesture I will show the people my true self. After all, I am a descendent of two powerful ancestors, Grandmother of Birds and Tuscalusa" (Howe 15).

If the author's name has already been used in the text, then you simply need to provide the page number (15). If there are two or three authors, then list the authors' last names and the page number (Silverman and Rader 23). For more than three authors, use et al. (Baym et al. 234).

The same holds true for citing an article. Simply list the last name of the author of the article or story or poem, followed by the page number (Wright 7). You don't need to list the title of the book or magazine.

## BUILDING THE WORKS CITED PAGE

A works cited page consists of an alphabetized list of the texts that you cite in your paper. This list goes at the end of an essay in MLA format. This list tells your readers all of the pertinent publication information for each source. It is alphabetized by the last name of the author or, if there is no author, by the title or name of the text. Generally, works cited pages start on a new page and bear the heading "Works Cited." For books, you will use the following format, not indenting the first line but indenting the remaining lines.

Clements, Brian. *Essays Against Ruin.* Huntsville: Texas Review Press, 1997.

Notice the crucial aspects in this citation—the author's name, the title of the work, the date it was published, and who was responsible for publishing it. The general rule of citing work is to find all four of these elements in order to help a fellow researcher (or your teacher) find the source and to give appropriate credit to both those who wrote the book and who brought the book to the attention of the general public. Of course, citing a magazine requires a different format but with the same idea, as does citing a Web page or a song or a movie. We have provided examples of many different sources below.

## PLAGIARISM

Citing your work is critical. If you quote from a text in your paper, or if you use information in any way but do not cite this source, the use of this material is plagiarism. At most institutions, plagiarism is grounds for failing the assignment and even the class. Furthermore, at many universities and colleges, students can be dismissed from the institution entirely if plagiarism can be proven.

A student can commit plagiarism in several different ways. One is the deliberate misrepresentation of someone else's work as your own—if you buy a paper off the Internet, get a friend's paper and turn it is as your own, or pay someone to write the paper, you are committing the most serious form of plagiarism.

Then there is the above example of using someone's work in your text but without citing it, also a serious offense. Some students do this inadvertently—they forget where their ideas came from, or mean to find out where the information came from later but do not. Still others want their teacher to think they are intelligent and think that using someone else's work may help. The irony of the last way of thinking is that teachers will often be more impressed by the student who has taken the time to do research and thoughtfully incorporate those ideas into a paper—that's what real researchers do.

It is also possible to commit plagiarism without such intent. If you do not paraphrase a source's work completely—even if you cite the source—that is also plagiarism.

Besides the general ethical problem using someone else's work as your own, the more practical issue with plagiarizing is that you are likely to get caught. As teachers, we become so familiar with the student voice in writing, and a particular student's voice, that it is often not very difficult to catch a cheating student.

## WORKS CITED EXAMPLES

The examples below cover most citation contingencies; however, if you have trouble deciding how to cite a source, there are a number of options. The best option will be to consult the *MLA Handbook for Writers of Research Papers*, which your library will own, if you do not. Otherwise, you can find any number of World Wide Web pages that provide examples of MLA documentation. We recommend the Purdue Writing Center site (http://owl.english.purdue.edu/) and the award winning "Guide For Writing Research Papers" site at Capitol Community College (http://webster.commnet.edu/mla.htm).

## Citing Books

Book entries include the following information: Author's last name, Author's first name. *Title*. City of publication: Publisher, year of publication.

A Book by a Single Author

Clements, Brian. *Essays Against Ruin*. Huntsville: Texas Review Press, 1997.

**A Book by Two or Three Authors.** After the first author, list subsequent authors' names in published (*not* alphabetical) order.

Clements, Brian and Joe Ahearn, eds. *Best Texas Writing*. Dallas: Rancho Loco Press, 1997.

**Two or More Books by the Same Author.** Arrange entries alphabetically by title. After the first entry, use three hyphens instead of the author's name.

Garber, Frederick. *Thoreau's Fable of Inscribing*. Princeton: Princeton UP, 1991.
---. *Thoreau's Redemptive Imagination*. New York: NYU Press, 1977.

An Anthology or Compilation

Silverman, Jonathan and Dean Rader, eds. *The World Is a Text: Writing, Reading, and Thinking about Culture and Its Contexts*. New York: Prentice Hall, 2003.

A Book by a Corporate Author

Bay Area AIDS Foundation. *Report on Diversity: 2001*. San Francisco: City Lights Books, 2001.

A Book with No Author

*A History of Weatherford, Oklahoma*. Hinton: Southwest Publishers, 1998.

**A Government Publication.** If no author is known, begin with the government's name, and then add the department or agency and any subdivision. For the U.S. government, the Government Printing Office (GPO) is usually the publisher.

United States. Forest Service. Alaska Region. *Skipping Cow Timber Sale, Tongass National Forest: Final EIS Environmental Impact Statement and Record of Decision*. Wrangell: USDA Forest Service, 2000.

#### The Published Proceedings of a Conference

Ward, Scott, Tom Robertson, and Ray Brown, eds. *Commercial Television and European Children: an International Research Digest. Proceedings of the Research Conference, "International Perspectives on Television Advertising and Children: The Role of Research for Policy Issues in Europe," Held in Provence, France, July 1st–3rd 1984*. Brookfield: Gower, 1986.

#### An Edition Other Than the First

Gibaldi, Joseph. *MLA Handbook for Writers of Research Papers*. 5th ed. New York: Modern Language Association, 1999.

## Citing Articles

Articles use a similar format as books; however, you will need to include information for the article and the source of its publication. They follow the following format:

Author(s). "Title of Article." Title of source day month year: pages.

For newspapers and magazines, the month or the day and the month appear before the year, and no parentheses are used. When quoting from a scholarly journal, the year of publication is in parentheses. When citing articles from periodicals, the month (except May, June, and July) is abbreviated.

#### An Article from a Reference Book

Deignan, Hebert G. "Dodo." *Collier's Encyclopedia*. 1997 ed.
Voigt, David G. "America's Game: A Brief History of Baseball." *Encyclopedia of Baseball*. 9th ed. New York: MacMillan, 1993: 3–13.

#### An Article in a Scholarly Journal

Crawford, Rachel. "English Georgic and British Nationhood." *ELH* 65.1 (1998): 23–59.
Ingrassia, Catherine. "Writing the West: Iconic and Literal Truth in *Unforgiven*." *Literature–Film Quarterly* 26.1 (1998): 53–60.

**A Work in an Anthology.** Begin with the author of the poem, article, or story. That title will go in quotation marks. Then, cite the anthology as above. Include the page numbers of the text you use at the end of the citation.

Haven, Chris. "Assisted Living." *The World Is a Text: Writing, Reading, and Thinking about Culture and Its Contexts*. Eds. Jonathan Silverman and Dean Rader. New York: Prentice Hall, 2003. 89–99.

**An Article in a Monthly Magazine**

Sweany, Brian D. "Mark Cuban is Not Just a Rich Jerk." *Texas Monthly* March 2002: 74–77.

**An Article in a Weekly Magazine.** If the article does not continue on consecutive pages, denote this with a plus sign (+).

Gladwell, Malcolm. "The Coolhunt." *The New Yorker* 17 March 1997: 78+.

**An Article in a Newspaper**

Hax, Carolyn. "Tell Me About It." *The Washington Post* 29 March 2002: C8.

**An Article with No Author**

"Yankees Net Bosox." *The Richmond Times-Dispatch* 1 September 2001: D5.

**A Letter to the Editor**

McCrimmon, Miles. "Let Community Colleges Do Their Jobs." *The Richmond Times-Dispatch* 9 March 1999: F7.
Silverman, Melvin J. "We Must Restore Higher Tax on Top Incomes." *The New York Times* 8 March 1992: E14.

**A Review**

Smith, Mark C. Rev. of *America First! Its History, Culture, and Politics*, by Bill Kauffman. *Journal of Church and State* 39 (1997): 374–375.

**A Cartoon**

Jim. Cartoon. *I Went to College and It Was Okay*. Kansas City: Andrews and McNeel, 1991. N. pag.

## Electronic Sources

**A Book Published Online.** If known, the author's name goes first, followed by the title of the document or page in quotation marks. If the document/page is part of a larger work, like a book or a journal, then that title is underlined. Include the date of publication, the date of access if known, and the address or URL (uniform resource locator) in angle brackets.

Savage, Elizabeth. "Art Comes on Laundry Day." *Housekeeping—A Chapbook. The Pittsburgh Quarterly Online*. Ed. Michael Simms. December 1997. 20 March 2002 <http://trfn.clpgh.org/tpq/hkeep.html>.

**An Article from a Website**

Silverman, Jason. "*2001*: A Re-Release Odyssey." *Wired News* 13 October 2001. 20 March 2002 <http://www.wired.com/news/digiwood/0,1412,47432,00.html>.

**A Review**

Svalina, Mathias. Rev. of *I Won't Tell a Soul Except the World*, by Ran Away to Sea. *Lost at Sea* July 2001. 2 March 2002 <http://lostatsea.net/LAS/archives/reviews/records/ranawaytosea.htm>.

**A Mailing List, Newsgroup, or E-Mail Citation.** If known, the author's name goes first, followed by the subject line in quotations, the date of the posting, the name of the forum, the date of access and, in angle brackets, the online address of the list's Internet site. If no Internet site is known, provide the e-mail address of the list's moderator or supervisor.

**An E-Mail to You**

Brennan, Brian. "GLTCs." E-mail to the author. 21 Mar. 2002.

**An Electronic Encyclopedia**

"Alcatraz Island." *Encyclopedia Britannica*. 3 Apr. 2002 On-line. <http://www.eb.com>.

**An Article from a Periodically Published Database on InfoTrac**

Gordon, Meryl. "Seeds of Hope." *Ladies Home Journal* Sept. 1999. 2 Apr. 2002. *InfoTrac*.

## Other Sources

**A Television or Radio Program.** List the title of the episode or segment, followed by the title of the program italicized. Then identify the network, followed by the local station, city and the broadcast date.

"Stirred." *The West Wing*. NBC. WWBT, Richmond, VA. 3 Apr. 2002.

### A Published Interview

Schnappell, Elissa. "Toni Morrison." *Women Writers at Work*: The Paris Review *Interviews*. Ed. George Plimpton. New York: Modern Library, 1998: 338–375.

### A Personal Interview

Heinemann, Alan. Personal interview. 14 Feb. 2001.

### A Film

Byington, Bob, dir. *Olympia*. With Jason Andrews, Carmen Nogales, and Damien Young. King Pictures, 1998.

### A Sound Recording from a Compact Disc, Tape or Record

The Asylum Street Spankers. *Spanks for the Memories*. Spanks-a-Lot Records, 1996.

### A Performance

R.E.M. Walnut Creek Auditorium. Raleigh, N.C. 27 August 1999.

### A Work of Art in a Museum

Klee, Paul. *A Page from the Golden Book*. Kunstmuseum, Bern.

### A Photograph by You

United States Post Office. Bedford, NY. Personal photograph by author. 15 August 2001.

### An Advertisement

Absolut. Advertisement. *Time* 17 Dec. 2002: 12.

**Cars, Buildings, Outdoor Sculptures and Other Odd Texts.** While many of your teachers would not require you to cite a primary text like a car or a building, if you have to do so (or want to), we suggest you follow the guidelines for a text like a movie, which has a flexible citing format, but always includes the title and the date, and hopefully an author of some kind. For example, if you were going to cite something like a Frank Lloyd Wright building, you might do something like this:

Wright, Lloyd Frank, arch. *Robert P. Parker House*. Oak Park, IL: 1892. (Arch. stands for architect like dir. stands for director.)

If for some reason, you were to cite a car, you might do something like this:

Toyota Motor Company. *Camry*. 1992.

or

Toyota Motor Company. *Camry*. Georgetown, Ky.: 1992. (if you knew where the car was built.)

But if you knew the designer of the car, you could use her as an author, similar to the way you can use a screenwriter or a director or an actor for the "author" of a movie.

# Acknowledgments

## Text Credits

"How Do I Write a Text for College? Making the Transition from High School Writing" by Patti Strong. Reprinted by permission of the author.

"Blood-Burning Moon" from CANE by Jean Toomer, 1923.

"Goodtime Jesus" from RIVEN DOGGERIES by James Tate. Copyright © 1973, 1975, 1976, 1977, 1978, 1979 by James Tate. Reprinted by permission of HarperCollins Publishers, Inc.

"Ode to My Socks" reprinted from NERUDA AND VALLEJO: Selected Poems ed. by Robert Bly. Beacon Press, Boston, 1971, 1996. Copyright © 1971, 1996 by Robert Bly. Used with his permission.

"The Colonel" from THE COUNTRY BETWEEN US by Carolyn Forché. Copyright © 1981 by Carolyn Forché. Originally appeared in WOMEN'S INTERNATIONAL RESOURCE EXCHANGE. Reprinted by permission of HarperCollins Publishers, Inc.

"Young Goodman Brown" by Nathaniel Hawthorne.

"Sonnet 130" by William Shakespeare.

"My Life had stood–a Loaded Gun" by Emily Dickinson.

"Slapstick" from VIEW WITH A GRAIN OF SAND by Wislawa Szymborska, trans. by Stanislaw Baranczak and Clare Cavanaugh. Copyright © 1993 by Wislawa Szymborska. English translation copyright © 1995 by Harcourt, Inc. Reprinted by permission of the publisher.

"The Story of an Hour" by Kate Chopin.

"Harlem" from THE COLLECTED POEMS OF LANGSTON HUGHES by Langston Hughes. Copyright © 1994 by The Estate of Langston Hughes. Used by permission of Alfred A. Knopf, a division of Random House, Inc.

"Isla" from THE END OF FREE LOVE by Susan Steinberg. Copyright © 2003 by Susan Steinberg. Reprinted by permission of Fiction Collective Two, FSU.

"Dust World: For Sherman Alexie" from AMONG THE DOG EATERS by Adrian Louis. Copyright © 1992 by Adrian C. Louis. Reprinted by permission of Adrian Louis.

"My Papa's Waltz" from THE COLLECTED POEMS OF THEODORE ROETHKE by Theodore Roethke. Copyright 1942 by Hearst Magazines, Inc. Used by permission of Doubleday, a division of Random House, Inc.

"Citizens of the World: Turn on Your Television" by Sallie Tisdale, *www.Salon.com*, January 24, 2000. Copyright © 2000 by Sallie Tisdale. Reprinted by permission of the author.

"TV Can Be a Good Parent" by Ariel Gore, *www.Salon.com*, August 16, 1999. Copyright © 1999. Reprinted with the permission of Salon.com.

"Life According to TV" by Harry F. Waters, *Newsweek*, December 6, 1982. Copyright © 1982 by Newsweek, Inc. Reprinted by permission. All rights reserved.

"How Soaps Are Integrating America" by Michelle Cottle, *The New Republic*, August 27, 2001. Copyright © 2001 by The New Republic, Inc. Reprinted by permission of THE NEW REPUBLIC.

"'Not That There's Anything Wrong with That': Reading the Queer in Seinfeld" by Katherine Gantz from STRAIGHT WITH A TWIST: Queer Theory and the Subject of Heterosexuality ed. by Calvin Thomas. Copyright © 2000 by Board of Trustees of the University of Illinois. Used with permission of the University of Illinois Press.

"Society's Need for a *Queer* Solution: The Media's Reinforcement of Homophobia Through Traditional Gender Roles" by Archana Mehta. Reproduced by permission of the author.

"The Last Christian TV Family in America" by Les Sillars in *The Alberta Report*, October 21, 1996. Copyright © 1996. Reprinted by permission.

"Worst Episode Ever" by Jaime J. Weinman from *www.Salon.com*, January 24, 2000. Copyright © 2000 by Jaime J. Weinman. Reprinted by permission of the author.

"The Simpsons" from SHOULD YOU READ SHAKESPEARE? Literature, Popular Culture, and Morality by Anne Waldron Neumann. Copyright © 1999 by the author. Published by the University of New South Wales Press. This essay was originally published in *Quadrant*, December 1996. Reprinted by permission of the author.

"'Black Bart' Simpson: Appropriation and Revitalization in Commodity Culture" by Peter Parisi, *Journal of Popular Culture*, Summer 1993. Copyright © 1993. Reprinted by permission of Popular Press.

"Media Journal: *The Rosie O'Donnell Show*" by Hillary West. Reprinted by permission of the author.

"Spatial Segregation and Gender Stratification in the Workplace" in GENDERED SPACES by Daphne Spain. Copyright © 1992 by the University of North Carolina Press. Used by permission of the publisher.

"Caught Looking: Problems with Taking Pictures of People Taking Pictures at an Exhibition" by Robert Bednar. Reprinted by permission of the author.

From "Case Study: 'Room for Learning with Latest Technology'" from THE ROOM IN CONTEXT: Design Beyond Boundaries by Katherine F. Benzel. Copyright © 1988. Reprinted by permission of The McGraw-Hill Companies.

"How Suburban Design Is Failing Teen-Agers" by William L. Hamilton, *The New York Times*, May 6, 1999. Copyright © 1999 by the New York Times Co. Reprinted by permission.

"A White Migration from Miami" by William Booth, *The Washington Post*, November 9, 1998. Copyright © 1998 by The Washington Post Writers Group. Reprinted by permission of the publisher.

"A Remedy for the Rootlessness of Modern Suburban Life?" by Sarah Boxer, *The New York Times*, August 1, 1998. Copyright © 1998 by the New York Times Co. Reprinted by permission.

"New Urbanism Needs to Keep Racial Issues in Mind" by Whitney Gould, *Milwaukee Journal Sentinel*, June 14, 1999. Copyright © 1999 by Journal Sentinel, Inc. Reproduced with permission.

"Growing Up, Growing Apart" by Tamar Lewin, *The New York Times*, June 25, 2000. Copyright © 2000 by the New York Times Co. Reprinted by permission.

"Describing Race, Ethnicity, and Culture in Medical Research: Describing the Group Studied Is Better Than Trying to Find a Catchall Name" by Kwame McKenzie and N.S. Crowcroft, *British Medical Journal*, April 27, 1996, v312, #7038. Copyright © 1996 by BMJ Publishing Group. Reprinted by permission of the publisher.

"In Living Color: Race and American Culture" by Michael Omi in CULTURAL POLITICS IN CONTEMPORARY AMERICA ed. by Ian H. Angus & Sut Jhally. Copyright © 1989. Reprinted by permission of Routledge, Inc., part of The Taylor & Francis Group.

"How America Was Discovered" by Handsome Lake.

"Mother Tongue" by Amy Tan. Copyright © 1990 by Amy Tan. First appeared in THE THREEPENNY REVIEW. Reprinted by permission of the author and the Sandra Dijkstra Literary Agency.

"Why Are All The Black Kids Sitting Together in the Cafeteria?" by Beverly Daniel Tatum, *The Brown University Child and Adolescent Behavior Letter*, October 1977, v13, #10. Copyright © 1977 by Manisses Communications Group. Reprinted by permission of the publisher.

"The Sports Taboo" by Malcolm Gladwell, *The New Yorker*, May 19, 1997. Copyright © 1997 by The New Yorker. Reprinted by permission of the author.

"Race, Labels and Identity: Millions Live in An America Bent On—And At Odds About—Categorizing Them" by Jeffry Scott, *Atlanta Journal*, May 6, 1997. Copyright © 1997 by Atlanta Journal. Reproduced with permission of Atlanta Journal in the format Textbook via Copyright Clearance Center.

"Is There Room in This Sweet Land of Liberty for Such a Thing as a 'Cablinasian'?: Face It, Tiger: If They Say You're Black, Then You're Black" by Leonard Pitts, Jr., *The Miami Herald*, April 29, 1997. Copyright © 1997 by Miami Herald. Reproduced with permission of Miami Herald in the format Textbook via Copyright Clearance Center.

"Melding in America" by George F. Will, *The Washington Post*, May 4, 1997. Copyright © 1997, 1998, The Washington Post. Reprinted with permission.

"Census and the Complex Issue of Race" by Ellis Cose, *Society*, Vol. 34, No. 6, 1997. Copyright © 1997 by Transaction Publishers. Reprinted by permission of Transaction Publishers.

"Race Is a Four-Letter Word" from IN THE SHADOW OF RACE: Growing Up as a Multiethnic, Multicultural, and "Multiracial" American by Teja Arboleda. Copyright © 1998. Published by Lawrence Erlbaum Assoc. Reprinted by permission of Copyright Clearance Center.

"High-School Confidential" by David Denby, *The New Yorker*, May 31, 1999. Copyright © 1994 by David Denby. Reprinted by permission of the author.

"Class and Virtue" from MAKE-BELIEVE MEDIA by Michael Parenti. Copyright © 1992. Reprinted with permission of Wadsworth, an imprint of the Wadsworth Group, a division of Thomson Learning. Fax 800 730-2215.

"Mock Feminism: *Waiting to Exhale*" from REEL TO REEL: Race, Sex, and Class at the Movies by bell hooks. Copyright © 1996. Reprinted by permission of Routledge, Inc. part of The Taylor & Francis Group.

"Holy Homosexuality, Batman!: Camp and Corporate Capitalism in *Batman Forever*" by Freya Johnson, *Bad Subjects: Political Education for Everyday Life*, December 1995, Issue # 23. Copyright © 1995 by Freya Johnson. Reprinted by permission of the author.

Review of "Moulin Rouge" by Roger Ebert, June 1, 2001. Copyright © 2001 by Universal Press Syndicate. Reprinted by permission of Universal Press Syndicate.

"Stanley Kauffmann on Films: Seeing is Disbelieving," *The New Republic*, June 11, 2001. Copyright © 2001 by The New Republic, Inc. Reprinted by permission of THE NEW REPUBLIC.

"'Moulin Rouge': An Eyeful, an Earful, Anachronism" by Elvis Mitchell, *The New York Times Online*, May 18, 2001. Copyright © 2001 by the New York Times Co. Reprinted by permission.

"Ballroom Blitz" by Owen Gleiberman in *Entertainment Weekly*, May 25, 2001. Copyright © 2001 by Entertainment Weekly, Inc. Reprinted by permission of Entertainment Weekly, Inc.

"Film Bodies: Gender, Genre and Excess" by Linda Williams, *Film Quarterly*, Vol. 4, No. 4, 1991. Copyright © 1991 by The Regents of the University of California. Reprinted by permission of the publisher and the author.

"Dear John Wayne" from JACKLIGHT by Louise Erdrich. Copyright © 1984 by Louise Erdrich. Reprinted by permission of Henry Holt and Company, LLC.

"Texas Chainsaw Massacre" from OLD SHIRTS & NEW SKINS by Sherman Alexie. Copyright © 1993 by Sherman Alexie. Reprinted by permission of Sherman Alexie, author of THE TOUGHEST INDIAN IN THE WORLD, writer/director THE BUSINESS OF FANCYDANCING.

"Tough Talk on Entertainment" from *TIME*, June 12, 1995. Copyright © 1995 by Time, Inc. Reprinted by permission.

"Wears Jump Suit. Sensible Shoes. Uses Husband's Last Name" by Deborah Tannen. *The New York Times Magazine*, June 20, 1993. Copyright © 1993 by Deborah Tannen. Reprinted by permission. Originally titled "Marked Women, Unmarked Men" by the author.

"Gender Role Behaviors and Attitudes" from GENDER BLENDING: Confronting the Limits of Duality by Holly Devor. Copyright © 1989 by Holly Devor. Reprinted by permission of Indiana University Press.

"Being a Man" from SUNRISE WITH SEAMONSTERS by Paul Theroux. Copyright © 1985 by Cape Cod Scriveners Co. Reprinted by permission of Houghton Mifflin Company. All rights reserved.

"Tu Me Quieres Blanca (You Want Me White)" from SELECTED POEMS OF ALFONSINA STORNI translated by Corn, et al. Translation copyright © 1988 by White Pines Press. Reprinted by permission of White Pines Press.

"*The Woman Warrior:* The Problem of Using Culture to Liberate Identity" by Whitney Black. Reprinted by permission of the author.

"Construction of the Female Self: Feminist Readings of the Disney Heroine" by Henke, Umble, and Smith, *Women's Studies in Communication*, Summer 1996. Copyright © 1996 by Organization for Research on Women and Communication. Reproduced by permission of the publisher.

"American Cinderella" by Jane Yolen in *Children's Literature in Education*, Vol. 8, no. 1, 1977. Copyright © 1977 by Kluwer Academic/Plenum Publishers. Reprinted by permission of the publisher.

From THE WOMAN WARRIOR by Maxine Hong Kingston. Copyright © 1975, 1976 by Maxine Hong Kingston. Used by permission of Alfred A. Knopf, a division of Random House, Inc.

"Andy Warhol: The Most Controversial Artist of the 20th Century?" by Alan Pratt. Reprinted by permission of the author.

"America, Seen Through Photographs, Darkly" from ON PHOTOGRAPHY by Susan Sontag. Copyright © 1977 by Susan Sontag. Reprinted by permission of Farrar, Straus and Giroux, LLC.

"This will be fun" by Kimberly Davenport. Reprinted by permission of the author.

"Difficult and frustrating" by Erica E. Hirshler. Reprinted by permission of the author.

"A very humbling experience" by Suzanne Folds McCullagh. Reprinted by permission of the author.

"I could not resist" by Stephan F. F. Jost. Reprinted by permission of the author.

"Is the NAMES Quilt Art?" by Michael Crichton from CRITICAL ISSUES IN PUBLIC ART: Content, Context, and Controversy ed. by Harriet F. Senie and Sally Webster. Copyright © 1992 by Harriet F. Senie and Sally Webster. Used by permission of the publisher.

"(Re)Versing Vision: Reading Sculpture in Poetry and Prose" by Dean Rader. Reprinted by permission of the author.

"Reading Cindy Sherman and Gender" by Anne Darby. Reprinted by permission of the author.

"It Isn't Pretty... But is it Art?" by Dana Mack, *The Christian Science Monitor*, November 9, 1999. Copyright © 1999 by The Christian Science Publishing Society. Reprinted by permission of the author.

"Those Nasty Brits" by Peter Schjeldahl, *The New Yorker*, October 11, 1999. Copyright © 1999. Reprinted by permission of the author.

"Giuliani's Own Exhibit" by William F. Buckley Jr, *National Review*, November 8, 1999. Copyright © 1999 by National Review. Reprinted by permission of Universal Press Syndicate.

"'Modern Art is a Load of Bullshit': Why Can't the Art World Accept Social Satire from a Black Artist?" by Benjamin Ivry, *www.Salon.com*, February 10, 1999. Reprinted by permission of the author.

"Some Hated Commercials Inspire Violent Fantasies" by Dave Barry, February 2, 1997. Copyright © 1997 by Dave Barry. Reprinted by permission of Tribune Media Services.

"Annals of Style" by Malcolm Gladwell, *The New Yorker*, March 17, 1997. Copyright © 1997 by The New Yorker. Reprinted by permission of the author.

"Advertising and People of Color" from RACE, MULTICULTURALISM, AND THE MEDIA by Clint C. Wilson and Felix Gutierrez. Copyright © 1995 by Clint C. Wilson and Felix C. Gutierrez. Reprinted by permission of Sage Publications, Inc.

"Ad Report Card: Diet Coke's Underwear Strategy" by Rob Walker, SLATE, July 9, 2001. Copyright © 2001 by SLATE/Distributed by United Feature Syndicate, Inc.

"Hanes Her Way" by Brittany Gray. Reprinted by permission of the author.

"15 Questions About the 'Liberal Media'" from THROUGH THE MEDIA LOOKING GLASS: Decoding Bias and Blather in the News by Jeff Cohen and Norman Solomon. Copyright © 1995 by Jeff Cohen and Norman Solomon. Reprinted by permission of Common Courage Press.

"Mainsteam and Alternative Perspectives on HIV/AIDS" in QUESTIONING THE MEDIA by Kevin Williams and David Miller. Copyright © 1995 by Kevin Williams and David Miller. Reprinted by permission of Sage Publications, Inc.

"Introduction" from DERAILING DEMOCRACY by David McGowan. Copyright © 2000 by David McGowan. Reprinted by permission of Common Courage Press.

"In the Shadow of the Image" from CHANNELS OF DESIRE: Mass Images and The Shaping of American Consciousness by Stuart and Elizabeth Ewen. Copyright © 1982 by the authors. Originally published by The McGraw-Hill Company. Reprinted with permission of the authors.

Excerpt from DOUBLESPEAK: From Revenue Enhancement to Terminal Living by William Lutz. Copyright © 1989 by William Lutz. All rights reserved. Used by permission of the author.

"Introduction" from SLANTING THE STORY: The Forces That Shape the News by Trudy Lieberman. Copyright © 2000. Reprinted by permission of The New Press. (800)233-4830.

"Musical Cheese: The Appropriation of Seventies Music in Nineties Movies" in READING ROCK & ROLL by Kevin J. H. Dittmar and William Richey. Copyright © 1999. Reprinted by permission of Columbia University Press.

"Is Tupac Really Dead?" by Fouzia Babar. Reprinted by permission of the author.

"Right on Target: Revisiting Elvis Costello's 'My Aim is True'" by Sarah Hawkins. Reprinted by permission of the author.

"Johnny B. Goode" from THE HEART OF ROCK & SOUL: The 1001 Greatest Singles Ever Made by Dave Marsh. Copyright © 1989 by Duke and Duchess Ventures, Inc. Reprinted by permission of the author.

"I Am the Walrus" from REVOLUTION IN THE HEAD: Beatle's Recordings and the Sixties by Ian MacDonald. Copyright © 1998 by Ian MacDonald. Reprinted by permission of HarperCollins Publishers Ltd.

From NO DIRECTION HOME: The Life and Music of Bob Dylan by Robert Shelton. Copyright © 1986 by Robert Shelton. Reprinted by permission of HarperCollins Publishers, Inc.

From COME AS YOU ARE: The Story of Nirvana by Michael Azerrad. Copyright © 1993 by Michael Azerrad. Used by permission of Doubleday, a division of Random House, Inc.

"Smells Like Teen Spirit" by Matt Compton. Reprinted by permission of the author.

"Cop Out? The Media, 'Cop Killer', and the Deracialization of Black Rage" by Christopher Sieving, *Journal of Communication Inquiry*, October 1998, vol. 22, no. 4. Copyright © 1998 by the University of Iowa. Reprinted by permission of Sage Publications, Inc.

"The Psychopathy of Everyday Things" from THE PSYCHOLOGY OF EVERYDAY THINGS by Donald A. Norman. Copyright © 1988 by Donald A. Norman. Reprinted by permission of Basic Books, a member of Perseus Books, L.L.C.

"The Girl-Game Jinx" by Elizabeth Weil, *www.Salon.com*, December 10, 1997. Copyright © 1997. Reprinted with the permission of Salon.com.

"'Where Do You Want to Go Today?': Cybernetic Tourism, the Internet, and Transnationality" by Lisa Nakamura in RACE & CYBERSPACE, ed. by Beth

Kolko, Lisa Nakamura, Gilbert E. Rudman. Copyright © 2000 by Lisa Nakamura. Reprinted by permission of Routlege, Inc., part of The Taylor & Francis Group.

"Mail-Order Brides: The Content of Internet Courtship" by Virginia Colwell. Reprinted by permission of the author.

"Cyberghetto: Blacks are Falling Through the Net" by Frederick L. McKissack, Jr., *The Progressive*, June 1998. Copyright © 1998 by Frederick L. McKissack., Jr. Reprinted by permission of The Progressive, 409 E. Main St., Madison, WI 53703, *www.progressive.org*.

"Internet Indian Wars: Native Americans Are Fighting to Connect the 550 Nations—in Cyberspace" by Glen Martin, *Wired*, December 1995. Reprinted from Wired News, *www.wired.com*. Copyright © 1995 by Wired Digital Inc., a Lycos Network site. All rights reserved.

"Text as Mask: Gender and Identity on the Internet" by Brenda Danet. Reprinted by permission of the author.

"InnerNet" by Andrew Sullivan in *Forbes ASAP*, October 4, 1999. Copyright © 1999 by Forbes, Inc. Reprinted by permission of FORBES ASAP Magazine.

## Photo Credits

Wearing Black pride, Black Bart teeshirt, New York, NY. Photo: Beryl Goldberg

Monument Valley with telescope. Photo: Robert Bednar

"Scenic View"—Glen Canyon. Photo: Robert Bednar

View of Mount Rushmore. Photo: Robert Bednar

*Stupid Comics* ©1998 by Jim Mahfood. " true tales of amerikkkan history Part II: the true Thanksgiving . . ." Jim Mahfood

John Wayne in "The Telegraph Trail." Photofest

MTV Movie Awards 1999 Ceremony. The actor Jackie Chan with his award. Photo: Trapper Frank. Corbis/Sygma

Leonardo da Vinci (1452–1519). *Mona Lisa.* Oil on wood. Photo: R.G. Ojeda. Louvre, Paris, France. Art Resource, N.Y.

Britney Spears at the Super Bowl Party hosted by Britney Spears and Justin Timberlake to benefit their individual foundations. Planet Hollywood, New York, NY. AP/Wide World Photos

Exterior of the Parthenon and surrounding ruins, Athens, Greece. Photo: Bill Bachman. PhotoEdit

State Capitol Building designed in Greek architectural style with unfluted Ionic columns, Richmond, VA. Photo: Dennis MacDonald. PhotoEdit

Evelyn Street Laundry. Photo: Cheryl Aaron. *Laundry* © 1997 Cheryl Aaron.

Teddy bears hanging on clothesline. From *American Beauty* by David Graham

Mexican flag hangs on white block wall. Photo: Tony Freeman. PhotoEdit

American flag. Photo: Joseph Nettis. Photo Researchers, Inc.

Andy Warhol, *Marilyn Monroe,* 1962. Dwan Gallery

Andy Warhol, *One Hundred Cans,* 1962. Oil on canvas, 72 x 52in. © Copyright The Andy Warhol Foundation for the Visual Arts/ARS. Art Resource, N.Y.

Washington, DC: The AIDS memorial quilt is spread out near the White House, forming an ellipse. Photo: Agence France Presse. CORBIS

Volunteers and others walk on the 21,000 panel Names Project AIDS Memorial Quilt in Washington. Photo: Shayna Brennan. AP/Wide World Photos

AIDS quilt—overhead shot. Photo: Vanessa Vick. Photo Researchers, Inc.

T. Paul Hernandez, *In the Mist of Ireland and Louisiana.* Photo: T. Paul Hernandez, University of San Francisco, Department of English.

*Understanding Comics* by Scott McCloud © 1994 Harper Collins Publishers, Inc.

Chris Ofili, *The Holy Virgin Mary.* From *The New Yorker,* October 11, 1999, vol. 75, issue no. 30, p. 104. Photo: Diane Bondareff. AP/Wide World Photos

AT&T ad in Chinese. Advertisement developed for AT&T by Kang & Lee Advertising. Art reprinted by permission of AT&T and C. J. Yeh.

# Index

"#27: Reading Cindy Sherman and Gender," 530–33

## A

"Advertising and People of Color," 572–80
"AIDS News and News Cultures," 588–97
Alexie, Sherman, 386–88
"America's Cinderella," 452–60
"America Seen Through a Lens Darkly," 485–96
"The America the Media Don't Want You to See," 598–604
"Andy Warhol: The Most Controversial Artist of the Twentieth Century?," 480–85
Arboleda, Teja, 324–28
"Assisted Living," 89–99
Azerrad, Michael, 671–73

## B

Baber, Fouzia, 654–60
"Ballroom Blitz," 366–69
Barry, Dave, 555–57
Bednar, Robert, 224–29
"Being a Man," 429–33
Benzel, Katherine F., 229–32
Black, Whitney, 435–39
"'Black Bart' Simpson: Appropriation and Revitalization in Commodity Culture," 182–99
"Blood-Burning Moon," 52–59
Booth, William, 237–43

Boxer, Sarah, 243–47
Buckley, William F., Jr., 540–41

## C

"Caught Looking: Problems with Taking Pictures of People Taking Pictures at an Exhibition," 224–29
"Census and the Complex Issue of Race," 317–24
Chopin, Kate, 79–81
Chrichton, E.G., 503–11
"Citizens of the World, Turn on Your Televisions!," 112–15
"Class and Virtue," 343–46
Cohen, Jeff, 586–88
"The Colonel," 62–64
Colwell, Virginia, 727–32
Compton, Matt, 673–78
"Construction of the Female Self: Feminist Readings of the Disney Heroine," 440–52
"The Coolhunt," 557–72
"Cop Out? The Media, 'Cop Killer,' and the Deracialization of Black Rage (Constructing [Mis]Representations)," 678–97
Cose, Ellis, 317–24
Cottle, Michelle, 126–30
Crowcroft, N.S., 274–77
"Cyberghetto: Blacks Are Falling Through the Net," 733–36

## D

Danet, Brenda, 744–61
Darby, Anne, 530–33
"Dear John Wayne," 385–86
Denby, David, 337–43
"Describing Race, Ethnicity, and Culture in Medical Research: Describing the Groups Studied Is Better than Trying to Find a Catchall Name," 274–77
Dettmar, Kevin J.H., 641–54
Devor, Holly, 424–29
Dickinson, Emily, 75–77
"Diet Coke's Underwear Strategy," 581–82
"Dust World," 99–101

## E

Ebert, Roger, 359–61
Erdrich, Louise, 385–86

Ewen, Elizabeth, 606–11
Ewen, Stuart, 606–11

## F

"Film Bodies: Gender, Genre, and Excess," 370–85
Forché, Carolyn, 62–64

## G

Gantz, Katherine, 130–52
"Gender Role Behaviors and Attitudes," 424–29
"The Girl-Game Jinx," 710–18
Gladwell, Malcolm, 301–10, 557–72
Gleiberman, Owen, 366–69
"Goodtime Jesus," 59–60
Gore, Ariel, 115–19
Gould, Whitney, 247–50
Gray, Brittany, 582–85
"Growing Up, Growing Apart," 259–74
Gutierrez, Felix, 572–80

## H

Hamilton, William L., 233–37
Handsome Lake, 289–91
"Hanes Her Way," 582–85
"Harlem," 82–83
Haven, Chris, 89–99
Hawkins, Sarah, 660–63
Hawthorne, Nathaniel, 64–74
Henke, Jill Birnie, 440–52
"High-School Confidential: Notes on Teen Movies," 337–43
"Holy Homosexuality Batman!: Camp and Corporate Capitalism in *Batman Forever*," 353–59
hooks, bell, 346–52
"How America Was Discovered," 289–91
"How Soaps Are Integrating America: Color TV," 126–30
"How Suburban Design Is Failing Teen-Agers," 233–37
Hughes, Langston, 82–83

## I

"I Am the Walrus," 666–69
"Infuriating by Design: Everyday Things Need Not Wreak Havoc on Our Lives," 705–709

"In Living Color: Race and American Culture," 277–89
"The InnerNet," 761–63
"Internet Indian Wars: Native Americans Are Fighting to Connect the 550 Nations—in Cyberspace," 736–44
"In the Shadow of the Image," 606–11
"Isla," 83–89
"Is the NAMES Quilt Art?," 503–11
"Is There Room in This Sweet Land of Liberty for Such a Thing as a 'Cablinasian'? Face It, Tiger: If They Say You're Black, Then You're Black," 313–15
"Is Tupac Really Dead?," 654–60
"It Isn't Pretty … But Is It Art?," 534–36
Ivry, Benjamin, 542–44

## J

"Johnny B. Goode," 664–65
Johnson, Freya, 353–59

## K

Kauffmann, Stanley, 361–63
Kingston, Maxine Hong, 460–69

## L

"The Last Christian TV Family in America," 169–71
Lewin, Tamar, 259–74
Lieberman, Trudy, 624–31
"Life According to TV," 119–26
"Like a Rolling Stone," 669–70
Louis, Adrian, 99–101
Lutz, William, 611–24

## M

MacDonald, Ian, 666–69
Mack, Dana, 534–36
Mahfood, Jim, 296–98
"Mail-Order Brides: The Content of Internet Courtship," 727–32
"Marked Women, Unmarked Men," 419–24
Marsh, Dave, 664–65
Martin, Glen, 736–44
McCloud, Scott, 516–30
McGowan, David, 598–604
McKenzie, Kwame J., 274–77
McKissack, Frederick C., Jr., 733–36

"Media Journal: *The Rosie O'Donnell Show*," 202–205
Meeks, Kenneth, 218–24
Mehta, Archana, 152–68
"Melding in America," 315–17
Miller, David, 588–97
Mitchell, Elvis, 364–66
"Mock Feminism: *Waiting to Exhale*," 346–52
"'Modern Art Is a Load of Bullshit': Why Can't the Art World Accept Social Satire from a Black Artist?," 542–44
"Mother Tongue," 291–96
"*Moulin Rouge*," 359–61
"*Moulin Rouge*: An Eyeful, an Earful, Anachronism," 364–66
"Musical Cheese: The Appropriation of Seventies Music in Nineties Movies," 641–54
"My Life had stood–a Loaded Gun (Poem 759)," 75–77
"My Mistress' Eyes Are Nothing Like the Sun (Sonnet 130)," 74–75
"My Papa's Waltz," 101–102

## N

Nakamura, Lisa, 718–27
Neruda, Pablo, 60–62
Neumann, Anne Waldron, 175–82
"New Urbanism Needs to Keep Racial Issues in Mind," 247–50
"No Name Woman," 460–69
Norman, Donald A., 705–709
"'Not That There's Anything Wrong with That': Reading the Queer in *Seinfeld*," 130–52

## O

"Ode to My Socks," 60–62
Omi, Michael, 277–89

## P

Parenti, Michael, 343–46
Parisi, Peter, 182–99
Pitts, Leonard, Jr., 313–15
Pratt, Alan, 480–85

## Q

"15 Questions About the 'Liberal Media'," 586–88

## R

"Race, Labels and Identity; Millions Live in an America Bent on—and at Odds About—Categorizing Them," 311–13
"Race Is a Four-Letter Word," 324–28
Rader, Dean, 512–16
"A Remedy for the Rootlessness of Modern Suburban Life?," 243–47
"(Re)Versing Vision: Reading Sculpture in Poetry and Prose," 512–16
Richey, William, 641–54
"Right on Target: Revisiting Elvis Costello's *My Aim Is True*," 660–63
Roethke, Theodore, 101–102
"Room for Learning with Latest Technology," 229–32

## S

Sachs, Andrea, 388–95
Schjeldahl, Peter, 536–40
Scott, Jeffry, 311–13
"Seeing Is Disbelieving," 361–63
"Sequential Art: 'Closure' and 'Art'," 516–30
Shakespeare, William, 74–75
Shelton, Robert, 669–70
"Shopping in a Mall While Black: A Coach's Story," 218–24
Sieving, Christopher, 678–97
Sillars, Les, 169–71
"*The Simpsons*," 175–82
"Slanting the Story," 624–31
"Slapstick," 77–79
"Smells Like Teen Spirit" (1), 671–73
"Smells Like Teen Spirit" (2), 673–78
Smith, Nancy J., 440–52
"Society's Need for a *Queer* Solution: The Media's Reinforcement of Homophobia through Traditional Gender Roles," 152–68
Solomon, Norman, 586–88
"Some Hated Commercials Inspire Violent Fantasies," 555–57
Sontag, Susan, 485–96
Spain, Daphne, 211–18
"Spatial Segregation and Gender Stratification in the Workplace," 211–18
"The Sports Taboo," 301–10
Steinberg, Susan, 83–89
Storni, Alfonsina, 433–35
"The Story of an Hour," 79–81

Sullivan, Andrew, 761–63
Szymborska, Wislawa, 77–79

## T

Tan, Amy, 291–96
Tannen, Deborah, 419–24
Tate, James, 59–60
Tatum, Beverly Daniel, 298–301
"*Texas Chainsaw Massacre*," 386–88
"Text as Mask: Gender and Identity on the Internet," 744–61
Theroux, Paul, 429–33
"Those Nasty Brits: How Sensational Is *Sensation*?," 536–40
"*Time* Forum: Tough Talk on Entertainment," 388–95
Tisdale, Sallie, 112–15
Toomer, Jean, 52–59
"True Tales of Amerikkkan History Part II: The True Thanksgiving," 296–98
"TV Can Be a Good Parent," 115–19

## U

Umble, Diane Zimmerman, 440–52

## W

Walker, Rob, 581–82
Washburn, Susanne, 388–95
Waters, Harry F., 119–26
"Weasel Words," 611–24
Weil, Elizabeth, 710–18
Weinman, Jaime J., 171–75
West, Hillary, 202–205
"Where Do You Want to Go Today? Cybernetic Tourism, The Internet, and Transnationality," 718–27
"Which Art Will Top the Chartes?: Four Curators Share Their Top 10 Picks and Reasoning Behind the Most Influential Visual Artworks of the Past 1,000 Years," 496–503
"A White Migration North from Miami," 237–43
"Why Are All the Black Kids Sitting Together in the Cafeteria?," 298–301
Will, George F., 315–17
Williams, Kevin, 588–97
Williams, Linda, 370–85
Wilson, Clint C., 572–80

"*The Woman Warrior:* The Problem of Using Culture to Liberate Identity," 435–39
"Worst Episode Ever," 171–75

## Y

Yolen, Jane, 452–60
"Young Goodman Brown," 64–74
"You Would Have Me White," 433–35